THE ROYAL NAVY DAY BY DAY

This book is dedicated by the gracious permission of
Her Majesty Queen Elizabeth II
to
The Lord High Admiral of the United Kingdom

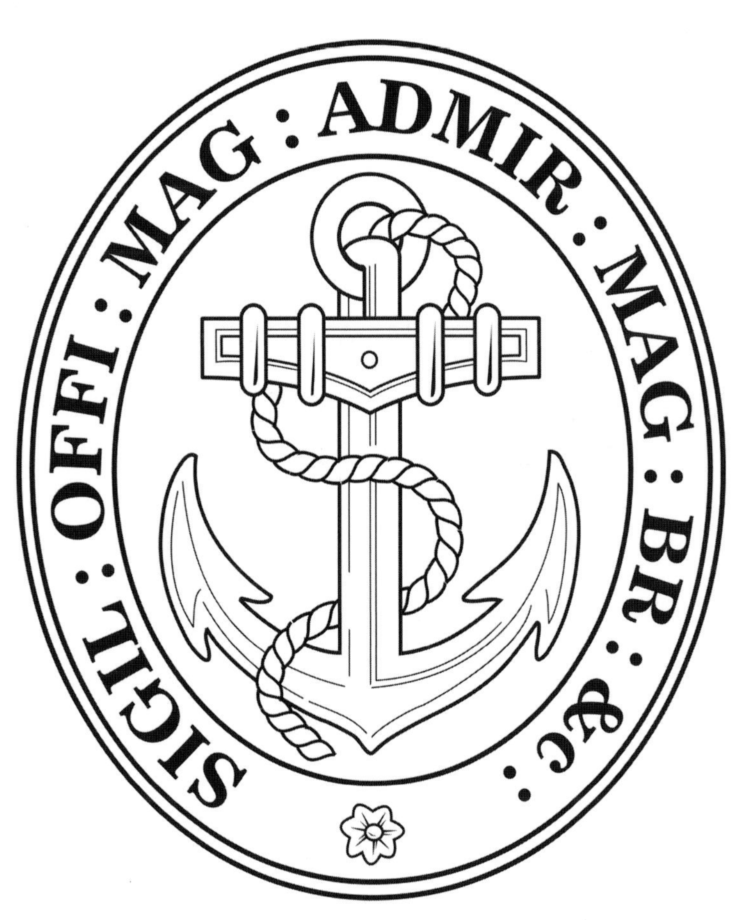

THE ROYAL NAVY DAY BY DAY

LIEUTENANT-COMMANDER LAWRIE PHILLIPS TD, RD, RNR
Lately Senior Vice-President, the Navy Records Society
Vice-President, the Society for Nautical Research

FOREWORD BY ADMIRAL SIR MARK STANHOPE GCB, OBE, ADC,
FIRST SEA LORD AND CHIEF OF NAVAL STAFF

'The Royal Navy Day by Day, *probably one of the most well-thumbed and valued books Captains of Her Majesty's Ships possess.*'

– Vice-Admiral Sir Jeremy Blackham, Editor, *The Naval Review*, August 2009

'So little care there hath been to this day to know or keep any history of the Navy.'

– Samuel Pepys, 16 January 1668

'Let us pause a while and ponder,
In the light of days gone by,
With their strange old ships and weapons,
What our fathers did, and why.'

– Captain Ronald Hopwood RN

First published 1979

This edition published in 2011
by Spellmount, an imprint of The History Press
The Mill, Brimscombe Port
Stroud, Gloucestershire, GL5 2QG
www.thehistorypress.co.uk

British Library Cataloguing in Publication Data.
A catalogue record for this book is available from the British Library.

ISBN 978 0 7524 6177 9

Typesetting and origination by The History Press
Printed in India

FOREWORD TO THE FIRST EDITION, 1979

By Admiral Sir Terence Lewin, GCB, MVO, DSC, ADC, *First Sea Lord*

Such is the richness of our Naval Heritage that every day is an anniversary not just of one, but of a whole series of events stretching back in time to the beginnings of our Nation. Some of these events changed the course of history, some may have involved just one or two men in a boat, but each has made its contribution to the tradition and reputation of the Royal Navy of today.

It is the nature of sea warfare that glory belongs to all, as much to the cook as to the coxswain; all are literally in the same boat. The battle is won as much in the preparation and training as in the heat of the action. Our Naval Heritage is an ever growing tapestry to which every man and woman now serving is adding his or her contribution. To serve the Royal Navy as a regular or a reservist or as a civilian is not just to have a profession or a job, but to be part of a Service which occupies a unique place in the history of our country and the world.

The idea for this book was born from the need to find inspiration for a particular speech, and a need to fill the gap left by the demise of the old Admiralty Desk Diary, which showed the major naval anniversaries. The initial research, undertaken by Lieutenant-Commander R.E.A. Shrubb, Royal Navy, produced enough material to fill six booklets which were published for a naval readership. This in turn attracted further interest and it was decided to expand it into a more comprehensive and illustrated book for a wider readership, and the task of continuing this work was generously undertaken by Captain A.B. Sainsbury, VRD, Royal Naval Reserve.

The book provides the bare outline of the picture on the tapestry canvas; the fuller stories of the great victories and of the myriad of minor actions provide the detail, and the light and shade which go to complete the masterpiece. *The Royal Navy Day by Day* deserves a place on the bookshelves not only of every naval ship and estblishment, but in the home of anyone who has the sea in his blood. In our country that must include most of us. If your interest is stimulated and you are encourged to delve deeper, I promise you will be well rewarded.

FOREWORD TO THE SECOND EDITION, 1992

By Admiral Sir Julian Oswald, GCB, ADC, *First Sea Lord*

Reference books are not necessarily great works of literature, or exciting to read, but the second edition of this most popular Royal Navy history book is an outstanding exception and I am honoured to be asked to write this Foreword. It is difficult to keep track of the many notable anniversaries that occur each day but this book has achieved the almost impossible task of collating our rich history with recent events and presenting the story in a stimulating and highly readable way.

The Royal Navy has strived to maintain the highest standard of professionalism, dedication and tradition while taking advantage of modern science and systems. But the nature of ships at sea means that the success of any unit depends on every member of the ship's company fulfilling his or her duties, often in difficult and challenging circumstances. There are many examples of this related here, but far more are not.

Many high honours have been awarded to sailors through the centuries, but countless brave and honest seamen have done their duty unrecognised by awards and medals. They are recognised by the Royal Navy as the greatest single factor, not only in the winning of wars at sea but also in our day-to-day operations. Without those who endure the rigours of life at sea, and those that support them at home with their unique and indomitable sense of humour and pride, the nation, and indeed the world, would be a very different place.

This book, with its evocative illustrations and detailed descriptions, brings together a wealth of maritime history that challenges and tempts you to delve further. The Royal Navy has every right to be proud of its history and tradition, and this record shows why.

FOREWORD TO THE THIRD EDITION, 2005

By Admiral Sir Alan West, GCB, DSC, ADC, *First Sea Lord*

The Royal Navy of the twenty-first century is modern, forward-looking and trained to meet the demands of the new millennium. In the final analysis it remains as it always has done the ultimate guarantee of our nation's independence in the face of external threat. The dependence of our nation upon the sea and the Royal Navy is something politicians, officials and the nation at large forget at our peril. It is not surprising that despite its modernity the Service is a product of its past. Its character has been shaped by wars and conflicts big and small, by countless engagements fought by generations of sailors, in great ships and modest ones, in home waters and distant seas. These ships have had names that ring like a bell down the years: *Dreadnought*, *Ark Royal*, *Invincible*, *Defiance*, *Britannia*, *Goliath*, *Thunderer* and, indeed, *Victory*. The Navy is not of course just an instrument of battle, but it is a living entity with its unique traditions, special customs, peculiar mannerisms and particular ways. This new edition of *The Royal Navy Day by Day* reflects all this and more. It is packed with fascinating information on how the Royal Navy was organised and trained, how its ships were designed and manned, how it deterred aggressors, supported friends and fought Britain's battles. Not only are the famous naval occasions recorded but the reader is taken down less familiar byways to find unexpected nuggets of naval history. The whole is a treasure trove of naval lore. The third edition of this now familiar and much-loved book, published in association with the Royal Naval Museum at Portsmouth and illustrated principally from the Museum's collections, is the joint work of Tony Sainsbury, former Staff Captain to the Admiral Commanding Reserves, and Lawrie Phillips, long-serving Head of Media Operations on the staff of the Commander-in-Chief Fleet and former Head of Publicity at the Ministry of Defence. They are both leading naval historians with a deep admiration for the Royal Navy and a profound understanding of its business. Those who serve at present in the Royal Navy can look back with confidence and see how previous generations faced and surmounted the challenges and dangers of their own days. Ships and weapons have changed but the spirit of the Service remains a constant. I have no doubt that this new edition of *The Royal Navy Day by Day*, published in the 200th anniversary year of the Battle of Trafalgar, one of the greatest naval endeavours, will be well received in the Fleet and that our people will draw fresh inspiration from it in the years to come. I commend this admirable book to all those interested in our maritime history.

FOREWORD TO THE FOURTH EDITION, 2011

By Admiral Sir Mark Stanhope, GCB, OBE, ADC, *First Sea Lord*

As I write the foreword for this fourth edition of *The Royal Navy Day by Day*, the Royal Navy that is emerging – in the wake of the recent Strategic Defence and Security Review – is, while a little smaller, essentially doing tomorrow what it did yesterday. Indeed, the review recognised that the Royal Navy is, and will continue to be, fundamental to the delivery of the United Kingdom's global responsibilities, economy and ambitions.

As this book attests, we have faced tough times before in our long history, but we have always endured and – because we are an island nation – we always will. This thorough account of our rich maritime heritage reminds us that, within an ever-changing security environment, the characteristics of the sea and the attributes of maritime forces are constants. Consequently, the drumbeat of maritime history is deliberate and measured. Counter-piracy and disaster relief operations, for example, are nothing new; the Royal Navy was protecting British trading interests in the Indian Ocean in the eighteenth century, and contributing to disaster relief operations around the world at the dawn of the twentieth century.

So while those serving in the Royal Navy rightly focus on the delivery of today's operations and the needs of the future, we must not lose sight of the pertinence of the past. This celebrated reference book, cataloguing the events and endeavours of our British naval heritage over some 500 years, is well-recognised for both its incisive historical authority and its ability to capture the enduring character and ethos of the Royal Navy. Extensively researched and refreshingly presented, this edition is a response to the demand for greater insights and a reflection of the pace of organisational change. While the spirit of the book remains unchanged, this edition in particular allows the reader to make tangible connections: between past and present, between the historic and the hilarious, and between the Royal Navy and navies around the world.

I am especially grateful to Lawrie Phillips for his six years of tireless labour on this much-expanded fourth edition of *The Royal Navy Day by Day*. The product is a fine record of our maritime heritage. A record and heritage of which we can be rightly very proud. As such, it is a legacy for past accomplishments and an incentive for future achievements. It serves as a source of inspiration and aspiration for us all.

Mark Stanhope

INTRODUCTION

Admiral Sir Mark Stanhope, the First Sea Lord, kindly refers in his Foreword to *The Royal Navy Day by Day* as 'this celebrated reference book'. It started life in 1977 as a set of six slim home-produced booklets intended for Service use and compiled by Lieutenant-Commander 'Bushey' Shrubb, then Assistant Secretary to Admiral Sir Terence Lewin, Commander-in-Chief Naval Home Command.

The work proved so popular both in and out of the Service that a bound edition, edited by Commander Shrubb and Captain Tony Sainsbury, was published in 1979. It soon became the Royal Navy's unofficial BR on British naval history. Captain Sainsbury published a second edition in 1992 and he and I edited a third in the Trafalgar bicentenary year of 2005. This is the fourth and much expanded edition and it is a solo production.

The book records British naval occasions across the many centuries, what the Royal Navy and Royal Marines did for the nation, and what was done to them by the enemy, the sea and the Admiralty. The anniversaries of triumphs and disasters, involving ships big and small, are presented chronologically by day and month. I am told that Executive Officers, hard-pressed to find something for Daily Orders to jolly up their ships' companies, have found the book a boon, as have countless guest speakers seeking inspiration before a mess dinner. Vice-Admiral Sir Jeremy Blackham has described *The Royal Navy Day by Day* as 'probably one of the most well-thumbed and valued books Captains of Her Majesty's Ships possess.' I hope this new edition will continue to be of use in the Fleet.

The work has to cover 500 years of naval endeavour and, although expanded by 222 pages, hard judgements have had to be made. The sheer wealth of material, from the Armada to Afghanistan, and the finite space between two covers, has posed almost endless challenges of selection and judgement. The business side of the Service, the battles and actions down the years, much of it sublime in achievement and self-sacrifice, provides the core of the book. Entries have had to be brief but long enough for their significance to be clear. That said, this is not an anthology, and to condense into twenty or thirty words a brilliant group action or splendid personal efforts – like the recent gallantry of Leading Seaman Kate Nesbitt MC and Lance-Corporal Matthew Croucher GC – has been a chastening task.

Moreover, this is not a naval encyclopaedia; not every ship and action can be mentioned. Nor yet is this a Guinness Book of Naval Records, although many of the firsts, lasts, oldest and biggest are also significant dates. A balance has had to be struck between the operational and the administrative, the old and the more recent, between materiel and personnel – the latter between the Royal Navy and Royal Marines – and in the last century or so between the WRNS, Fleet Air Arm, the Submarine Service and the Royal Fleet Auxiliary. Some key events in the histories of Commonwealth navies whose service in peace and war has been so closely bound up with our own have well merited inclusion.

Much of the material in the current edition has been revised, corrected where necessary, augmented and updated. Several of the panels on specific topics like the Corfu Incident and the Cod Wars have had to be sharpened up and new ones produced on such hitherto neglected operations as the Palestine Patrol. A brief mention is also made of some recent incidents, very few in number, where the Royal Navy did less than its best. To help the XO with those Daily Orders, and where there is a choice, I have deliberately mentioned the services of old vessels of war whose names are borne by ships today, those 'employed, and to be employed, in the Fleet'.

The late Richard Ollard reflected that 'By its very nature the Navy, perhaps more than any other profession, has lived its own life'. To capture the 'feel' of the Service and to leaven the mix, I have tried to bring out something of the funny, the quirky, the quaint, the odd, the sheer whimsy and also the sometimes ridiculous that is part of the Royal Navy's life, punctuated as it is with the odd own goal and the occasionally plain daft; in Admiral Stanhope's words the 'historic and the hilarious'.

'Another damned, thick, square book! Always scribble, scribble, scribble! Eh, Mr Gibbon?' cried King George III's brother, William, Duke of Gloucester, not one of the world's great readers, when Edward Gibbon presented him with a copy of the first volume of *Decline and Fall of the Roman Empire*. This new edition of *The Royal Navy Day by Day* is another 'damned, thick, square book' but it is not a story of decline and fall. Though we are not now that power which in old days moved earth and heaven, the Royal Navy and the Royal Marines are still very much in action across the seas doing the job they have done down the centuries and know so well.

The Royal Navy's history is not all broadsides and battleships. Recent humanitarian operations have continued a fine tradition. 'I never ever thought I would be so glad to see the Union Jack', a rescued American citizen told a television reporter as he came up the brow of HMS *Cumberland* at Benghazi in March 2011. Seventy-five years earlier, during the Spanish Civil War in 1936, the Royal Navy's humanitarian work prompted a leader in *The Times* which said of the British sailor: 'When he is arranging a nursery or turning his destroyer into a hostel for ladies, he is doing his proper job as much as when he is manning a gun or running his engines. In each case he is serving the peace and well-being of the world. And that is what he is there for.'

It has been a privilege to produce this book on and for the Royal Navy. It is a splendid story of the very finest of our nation. Fine tradition, however, has to be lived up to, not lived on. I hope that this latest edition of *The Royal Navy Day by Day* will serve to be, in Admiral Stanhope's words, 'a source of inspiration and aspiration for us all'.

Lawrie Phillips
Northwood
2011

The Naval Prayer

O Eternal Lord God, who alone spreadest out the heavens and rulest the raging of the sea; who hast compassed the waters with bounds until day and night come to an end: be pleased to receive into thy almighty and most gracious protection the persons of us thy servants and the fleet in which we serve. Preserve us from the dangers of the sea and of the air and from the violence of the enemy; that we may be a safeguard unto our most gracious Sovereign Lady, Queen Elizabeth, and her dominions, and a security for such as pass on the seas upon their lawful occasions; that the inhabitants of our Islands and Commonwealth may in peace and quietness serve thee our God; and that we may return in safety to enjoy the blessings of the land with the fruits of our labours and with a thankful remembrance of thy mercies to praise and glorify thy holy Name.

ACKNOWLEDGEMENTS

I am grateful for the goodwill and kindness of Dr Richard Sainsbury and Mr Mark Sainsbury, sons of my dear friend and colleague, the late Captain A.B. (Tony) Sainsbury MA, VRD, RNR, the godfather of *The Royal Navy Day by Day*, with whom I had the privilege of working on the 1992 edition and of co-editing with him the third edition in 2005. Tony died in August 2010, having suffered declining health for some years but he has been with me in spirit, cautioning, questioning and challenging – and perhaps giving the occasional nod of approval – as each new entry took shape. God rest his brave soul.

My principal obligation and gratitude is owed to my old and valued friend Admiral Sir Jonathon Band GCB, successively Commander-in-Chief Fleet and First Sea Lord, for his sustained friendship, support and encouragement. Vice-Admiral Sir Alan Massey KCB, CBE, lately Second Sea Lord and Commander-in-Chief Naval Home Command, has been generous with his time and advice since our first meeting to discuss the project when we were serving together at Northwood; Admiral Sir Mark Stanhope GCB, ADC, First Sea Lord, has been a keen supporter throughout and I am grateful to him for writing the foreword to this edition; Vice-Admiral Sir Jeremy Blackham KCB, Editor of *The Naval Review*, proved a staunch ally and a consistently friendly voice down the line. Admiral Sir Jock Slater GCB, LVO, DL, and Admiral The Lord Boyce KG, GCB, OBE, talked me through some key issues. Admiral Sir Trevor Soar KCB, ADC, Commander-in-Chief Fleet; Vice-Admiral George Zambellas DSC, Chief of Staff at the Permanent Joint Headquarters and later Deputy Commander-in-Chief Fleet, and Rear-Admiral Mark Anderson CB, lately Commander (Operations), have been most generous with their time. Commander David Hobbs MBE, RN; Admiral of the Fleet Sir Benjamin Bathurst GCB, DL; Mr Graham Mottram, Director, Fleet Air Arm Museum, RNAS Yeovilton, and Lieutenant-Commander Gavin Simmonite DFC, RN, gave expert guidance on naval aviation. Captain Andrew Welch RN and Commander Ninian Stewart RN, provided specialist guidance on the Icelandic Cod Wars and the Palestine Patrol respectively. Mr Alan Marshall read the draft text and offered very wise advice. Mr Stephen Prince, Dr Malcolm Llewellyn-Jones MBE, Lieutenant-Commander Jock Gardner RN, and Major Mark Bentinck RM of the Naval Historical Branch, Miss Jenny Wraight, Admiralty Librarian, and Mr Iain Mackenzie, gave patient and valuable assistance as did Mr Stephen Courtney and Mr George Malcolmson of the National Museum of the Royal Navy at Portsmouth and Gosport. Mr Alan Home Henderson, Mr Andrew Bodle, Mr Barry Murphey and Mrs Tracey Peters were of invaluable practical assistance.

Commander (now Captain) Steve Pearson RN of the Naval Public Relations Staff was an enthusiastic supporter. His promotion and departure for Norfolk, Virginia, when this book was on the home strait, was a great loss. The penalty was alleviated in part by Lieutenant-Commander Stuart Antrobus BEM, RN, parachuted-in at 2359, with his matchless photographic knowledge and technical skills. Mr Steve Saywell, the Fleet Picture Manager at HMS *Excellent*, responded with promptitude to every late request for images.

Colleagues in the Society for Nautical Research, the Navy Records Society, the Naval Dockyards Society and the Anchorites have readily answered my queries and generously shared their wide and deep knowledge of matters maritime.

In six years' work on this edition many busy people afloat and ashore have answered my importunities with patience and kindness. I am indebted to: Admiral Sir Peter Abbott GBE, KCB; Mrs Lyn Agar; John Ambler; Rear-Admiral Derek Anthony MBE; Lieutenant-Commander J. Graeme G. Arbuckle RCN; Lieutenant-Commander Faye Arend RN; Admiral of the Fleet Sir Edward Ashmore GCB, DSC; Lieutenant Paul Atkins RN; BAE Systems (Mr Neil Lauderdale, Ms Gillian Shepherd, Ms Linda Kuhl); Lieutenant-Colonel C.M.J. Barnett ALS; Captain Michael Barritt RN; Lieutenant (A) John Beattie RN; Captain Ian Beaumont RN; Commander Anthony Bosustow RN; Mr Johnny Bugeja, Gibraltar; Rear-Admiral Chris Bennett, SA Navy; Lieutenant-Commander R.A. Bernard RN; Commander Eric Berryman USNR; Hans Christian Bjerg, Historian, Royal Danish Navy; Admiral Sir Jeremy Black GBE, KCB, DSO; Captain Jeremy Blunden LVO, RN; Petty Officer (Photographer) Brad Bradbury; Mr Robin Brodhurst MA; Mrs Judith Burke; Lieutenant-Commander Charlotte Butterworth RN; Dr Ian Buxton; Captain Richard Campbell OBE, RN; Captain Andrew Cameron RN; Lieutenant-Commander Bryony Carpenter RN; Lieutenant-Commander Jonathan Carrigan RN; Colonel Brian Carter OBE, RM; Captain Richard Channon RN; Lieutenant Philip Chisholm RN; Ms Susie Churchman; Commander Alan Cole RN; First Officer Nicholas Colvill RFA; Vice-Admiral Robert Cooling CB; Lieutenant-Commander David Costigan RN; Commodore Christopher Craig CB, DSC, RN;

Commander C.W. Crichton OBE, RN; Commander Steve Dainton RN; Lieutenant Jim Dale RN; Lieutenant Tony Dalton RN; Lieutenant-Commander Andrew David RN; Petty Officer Michael Down; Major Alastair Donald RM; Mr Bob Downie; Commodore Peter Eberle CBE, RN; Lieutenant-Commander Mark Ellis RN; Commander Charles Evans RN; Major Martin Everett TD, RRW; Commander Tim Ferns RN; Petty Officer (Photographer) Colin Foord; Captain David Freeman LVO, RN; Commander David Frost RN; Lieutenant-General Sir Robert Fulton KBE; Lieutenant-Commander Carlos Garreta RN; Mr Robert Gieve; Rear-Admiral James Goldrick AM, CSC, RAN; Simon Goddard; Commander David Gordon RN; Professor Barry M. Gough; Lieutenant-Colonel Ian Grant RM; Captain W.F.G. Griffin RN; Dame Anne Griffiths DCVO; Professor Eric Grove; Vice-Admiral Sir Paul Haddacks KCB; Captain John Hall CBE, RN; Squadron Leader Bob Hall RAF; Professor Richard Harding; Dr John Harland; Commodore Tim Harris RN; Captain (N) Harry Harsch OMM, CD, RCN; Captain David Hart-Dyke CBE, LVO, RN; Lieutenant-Commander Polly Hatchard RN; Ms Frances Hathaway; Professor John Hattendorf; Mr Kevin Hayes; Marion Hebblethwaite; Ms Charlotte Henwood, Keeper of the MoD Art Collection; Commodore Paul Herington RN; Lieutenant-Commander M.J. Hill RN; Rear-Admiral Richard Hill; Rear-Admiral Paul Hoddinott CB, OBE; Rear-Admiral Robin Hogg CB; Lieutenant-Colonel Matt Holmes DSO, RM; the late Brigadier Richard Holmes CBE, TD; Captain Timothy Hosker RN; House of Lords Information Office; Rear-Admiral Peter Hudson CBE; Lieutenant-Commander David Hunkin RN; Brigadier Sir Miles Hunt-Davis KCVO, CBE; Commander Phillip Ingham RN; Commander Alasdair Ireland RN; Lieutenant Tom Jenkins RN; Major Nick Jepson RM; Vice-Admiral Sir Adrian Johns KCB, CBE; Commander Paul Jones RN; Mr Peter Keat; Professor Roger Knight; Dr C.S. Knighton; Commander Andrew Kye RN; Professor Derek Law; Vice-Admiral Sir John Lea KBE; the late Admiral of the Fleet Sir Henry Leach GCB, DL; Lieutenant-Commander M.D. Lewis RD, RNR; the late Vice-Admiral Sir Louis Le Bailly KBE, CB, DL; Mr Matthew Little; Commander Arnold Lustman RN; His Honour Judge Lyons CBE (Captain Shaun Lyons RN); Lieutenant Lee Madigan RN; Captain Fergus Maclaine RD, RNR; Captain P.A. McAlpine OBE RN; Vice-Admiral Sir Tim McClement KCB, OBE; Dr Alan McGowan; Vice-Admiral Sir Fabian Malbon KBE; Ms Annie Manson; Commodore Angus Menzies RN; Rear-Admiral Stephen Meyer; Commander Stig Meyer, Royal Danish Navy; Ms Kate Mole; Mr John Montgomery; Commander James Morley RN; Rear-Admiral Roger Morris CB; Commodore Anthony Morrow CVO, RN; Commodore James Morse RN; Captain Karen Mosley; Father Denis Mullier; First Officer Mark Munday RFA; Captain Steve Murdoch RN; Commander Paul Murnane RN and Ms Karen Kristiansen; Mr Trevor Muston; Rear-Admiral J.A.L. Myres CB; Lieutenant Paul Newall RN; Ms Margaret Newell; Mr Peter Nixon, Channel Dash Association; Lieutenant-Commander Peter Noblett RN; Captain Derek Oakley MBE, RM; Admiral Sir William O'Brien KCB, DSC; Lieutenant-Commander H.A. O'Grady MBE, RN; Commander Adrian Orchard OBE, RN; Dr Richard Osborne; Lieutenant-Commander Lucy Ottley RN; Rear-Admiral Christopher Parry CBE; Lieutenant-Commander C.J. Parry RNR; Mrs Glynne Parsons; Captain Hugh Peltor CBE, RN; Captain Jonathan Pentreath RN; Admiral Sir James Perowne KBE; Mr Trevor Piper; the late Mr Tom Pocock; Captain Ian Powe RN; Captain Richard Powell RN; Commander Jonathan Powis RN; Commander John Prichard RN; Rear-Admiral David Pulvertaft CB; Commander Martin Quinn RNR; Lieutenant-Colonel David Rainey; Surgeon Commander Martin Randle RN; Mr Justin Reay; Mr Bill Rice; Commander Ian Riches OBE, RN; Commander W.K. Ridley OBE, RN; Lieutenant Gart Rimay-Muranyi RNR; Lieutenant-Commander Ben Roberts RN; Professor Nicholas Rodger; Commander Paul Romney RN; Mr Richard Rose; Dr Susan Rose; Chief Petty Officer Writer Reg Rundle; Mrs Ann Ryder; Lieutenant-Commander Frank Scott RN; Lieutenant-Commander Peter Sellers RN; Captain Christopher Skidmore RN; Commander O.D. Somerville-Jones RN; Lieutenant-Colonel Ewen Southby-Tailyour OBE, RM; Mr Steve Spear; Captain Andrei Spence RN; Lieutenant-Commander Robert Stephens RN; Dr David Stevens; Mr Jeremy Stewart; Lieutenant-Commander James Stride RN; Captain Ian Sutherland RN; Lieutenant-Colonel Neil Sutherland MBE, RM; Captain David Swain RN; Colonel Krzysztof Szymanski; Commander Aidan Talbot RN; Commander Duncan Tilley RN; Mr Bob Todd; Commander Alison Towler RN; Dr Pieter van der Merwe; Lieutenant-Commander Richard Walters RNR; Lieutenant-Commander Ben Warlow RN; Mr Roger Welby-Everard; Admiral The Lord West of Spithead GCB, DSC; Mr Mark Wilby; Mr Adrian Williams; Mr John Williams; Commander Alastair Wilson RN; Major P.A. Wilson 9/12 Lancers; Warrant Officer 1 Kevin Winter; Commander Rob Wood RN; Captain Richard Woodman THS; Captain Nicholas Wright LVO, RN; Captain Peter Wykeham-Martin RN. There are many other kind people who have helped. They will, I trust, accept my gratitude.

Lieutenant-Commander Michael Forder RN, the indexer, deployed his expert knowledge of naval history. My editor, Siubhan Macdonald, and my publisher, Jo de Vries, proved models of calm professional competence in times of turmoil and looming deadlines. I record my admiration and thanks to them both.

Finally, my dear wife, Jennifer, has carried the heavy burden of centuries of naval history around our home for longer than is reasonable. No one will be more pleased than she to see this project brought to a conclusion. Both this writer and the Royal Navy owe her a very real debt of gratitude.

1 JANUARY

1586 Sir Francis Drake captured San Domingo (*Bonaventure*, *Tiger* and *Primrose*).

1653 Pay set at 24*s* per month for Able Seaman (unaltered until 8 May 1797).

1693 Appointment of first officers at Dock (now Devonport Dockyard).

1758 *Adventure* (32) captured the Dunkirk privateer *Machault* close off Dungeness.

1761 A British squadron blockading Pondicherry was hit by a hurricane. Rear-Admiral Charles Stevens in *Norfolk* (74), Capt Richard Kempenfelt, cut his cable and ordered other ships to follow. *Panther* (60), *America* (60), *Medway* (60), and *Falmouth* (50) were dismasted but rode out the storm. But *Newcastle* (50), *Queenborough* (20) and the *Protector* fireship were wrecked. The *Duc d'Aquitaine* (64), *Sunderland* (60), and the *Drake* storeship foundered with almost all hands. A total of 1,100 souls were lost. The Seven Years War.

See 15 January 1761.

1771 Capt Maurice Suckling entered his nephew, 'Horace' (Horatio) Nelson, as a midshipman in the Muster Book of *Raisonnable* (64) at The Nore.

See 24 April 1771.

1798 Court martial in the frigate *Circe* (28) in the Medway sentenced Capt John Williamson to be placed at the bottom of the Post Captains List and 'rendered incapable of ever serving on board any of his Majesty's ships or vessels in the Royal Navy' for his conduct when commanding *Agincourt* (64) at Camperdown.

See 11 October 1797.

1801 Present form of white and other ensigns established after Irish Union.

1801 Rear-Admiral Sir Horatio Nelson promoted vice-admiral of the blue.

See 23 April 1804.

1807 The Dutch colony of Curacoa (Curacao) captured by a Jamaica Station squadron commanded by Capt Charles Brisbane in

HMS *Formidable* in 1908. (*NMRN*)

Arethusa (38) with *Latona* (38), Capt James Athol Wood; *Anson* (44), and *Fisgard* (38). Brisbane and Wood knighted.
Battle Honour: Curacoa 1807.

1809 Brig Sloop *Onyx* captured the Dutch *Manly*, 60 miles N.W. by W. of the Texel.
Battle Honour: *Manly* 1809.

1849 Good Conduct Badge with pay introduced.

1859 *Britannia* became cadet training ship at Portland. Moved to Dartmouth September 1863.

1875 Admiral Superintendent of Naval Reserves first appointed, by Order in Council: Vice-Admiral Sir John W. Tarleton.
See 1 January 1977.

1890 RNB Devonport commissioned as HMS *Vivid*. Name changed to *Drake* 1934.
See 1 January 1934, 1 August 1974.

1892 Gambia River expedition. *Sparrow*, *Thrush* and *Widgeon*.

1906 *Dryad* commissioned in Naval Academy Buildings, Portsmouth.
See 27 September 1941.

1910 David Beatty promoted rear-admiral. At 38 (seventeen days short of 39) he was the youngest Captain advanced to the Flag List since Nelson in 1797.
See 30 June 1955.

1911 Royal Naval Detention Quarters (RNDQs) opened at Portsmouth.
See 4 September 1995.

1913 First RNAS station commissioned on Isle of Grain in Medway.

1914 All Army airships transferred to Naval Wing of RFC.

1915 *Formidable*, battleship, fourth of name, torpedoed and sunk by U-24, 21 miles E. of Start Point; 547 lost.

1915 Engineer Officers given military status with executive curl, but kept purple cloth.

1916 Winston Churchill, having resigned as First Lord of the Admiralty, appointed to command the 6th Royal Scots Fusiliers in France as a lieutenant-colonel.
See 24 October 1911.

1919 Armed yacht *Iolaire* ex-*Amalthea*, carrying naval personnel (mainly RNR) from Kyle of Lochalsh following war service foundered on Beasts of Holm outside Stornoway Harbour; 205 men lost, 181 of them from the Western Isles.

1920 New Zealand station established.
See 1 October 1941.

1934 RNB Devonport, commissioned on 1 January 1890 as HMS *Vivid*, renamed HMS *Drake*. New cap tallies issued Saturday 20 January 1934.
See 1 August 1974.

1937 Battleship *Prince of Wales* laid down at Cammell Lairds, Birkenhead and *King George V* at Vickers Armstrong on the Tyne.
See 4 May 1939, 19 January 1941, 10 December 1941.

1943 Light cruiser *Scylla* homed on to German blockade runner *Rhakotis* in Bay of Biscay by Coastal Command aircraft and sank her.

1943 First FAA Grumman Avenger squadron (832) took delivery of aircraft at Norfolk, Virginia.

1947 Half-lacing of cuffs, a wartime economy measure, abolished.

1948 'The Home Fleet, and other ships on the home station, are now on the telephone. A radio-telephone service between all subscribers and these ships is now in operation. The charge is 10*s* 6*d* for three minutes conversation' – *The Navy*, January 1948, p.26.
See 28 April 1972.

1952 RNR and RNVR stripes finally straightened, with R in curl.
See 31 March 1951, 1 July 2007.

1957 Seaman, Engineer, Electrical and Supply Officers combined on the General List with, initially, 'wet' and 'dry' lists for seamen. Branch Officers became Special Duties Officers. AFO 1/56.

1960 'The use of the terms "Morning Colours" and "Evening Colours" is to be avoided. "Colours" and "Sunset" should invariably be used in all signals, correspondence and documents within the Royal Navy.' – AFO 6/60.

1971 Computerisation of naval pay began with 500 accounts from *Sultan*.

1972 Abolition of Shipwright specialisation.

1975 Operations Branch formed.

1977 The last Admiral Commanding Reserves, Rear-Admiral Hubert 'Hugo' Hollins, hauled down his flag. CINCNAVHOME henceforth responsible for the Naval Reserves.
See 1 January 1875, 1 March 1976.

1977 Electronic Warfare training transferred from *Mercury* to *Dryad*. DCI(RN) 500/76.
See 18 December 1992.

1983 Married unaccompanied food charges introduced for accommodated personnel.

1984 RFA *Reliant* with NP 2200 and 846 NAS relieved *Fearless* off Lebanon and assisted in the evacuation of over 5,000 civilians in four weeks.
See 15 October 1958, 18 and 28 November 1983, 18 and 20 July 2006.

1985 Title of Port Admiral Gibraltar lapsed and FO Gibraltar became also Naval Base Commander. DCI(RN) 434/84. HM Dockyard Gibraltar became Gibraltar Ship Repair Ltd.
See 30 March 1959.

The end of the old Navy: slinging the hammock in the destroyer HMS *Caprice* in April 1974. (*Author*)

Lt Polly Hatchard RN at the South Pole, 2007. (*RN*)

1990 Admiral of the Fleet Sir John Fieldhouse created Baron Fieldhouse of Gosport – *London Gazette*.
See 7 March 1990, 17 February 1992.

1993 British Carrier Task Group deployed to the Adriatic to support UN Protection Force in former Yugoslavia.
See 20 December 1995.

1995 Navy Board granted permission for RM establishments to fly White Ensign. Union Flag no longer to be flown at masthead.

1997 Morse Code SOS discontinued; no longer taught to communications ratings.
See 4 May 1962.

2007 Lt Polly Hatchard RN, one of an all-female expedition to the South Pole, became the first servicewoman of any nationality to reach 90 degrees S. on foot.
See 17 May 2000, 22 May 2003, 27 December 2006.

2008 Judge Advocate of the Fleet post abolished. The 29th and last JAF was former Pusser, His Honour John Lionel Sessions (1995–2008) Functions of JAF, a civilian judge, including power to review courts martial finding and punishment, transferred to Judge Advocate General under the Armed Forces Act 2006.
See 15 January 2004, 8 November 2006, 31 October 2009.

2008 Royal Marines Police abolished as a separate statutary police force and incorporated into Royal Navy Police.

2009 Director of Service Prosecutions became the Prosecuting Authority for the Royal Navy.

2 JANUARY

1757 Capture of Calcutta by Vice-Admiral Charles Watson (*Kent*) and troops under Col Robert Clive. Ships: *Bridgewater, Kent, Kingfisher, Tiger.*

1779 Chapel of Greenwich Hospital destroyed by fire, the loft containing many instruments and memorabilia accumulated by the Board of Longitude. Rebuilt by 'Athenian' Stuart and reopened in 1789. Renovated and rededicated in the presence of HM Queen Elizabeth The Queen Mother, 1955.

See 21 June 1955.

1783 *Magicienne* (32) outsailed *Endymion* (44) and fought the French *Sibylle* and *Railleur* 500 miles E. of Grand Bahama Island.

1793 Brig sloop *Childers* (14), Cdr Robert Barlow, reconnoitering the French fleet in Brest, was fired on in the Iroise by shore batteries. One shot hit which effectively marked the start of the Revolutionary War although France did not declare war on Britain and the Dutch Republic until 1 February. Barlow landed at Fowey on 4 January and hastened to London to deliver both his report and the French shot to the Admiralty.

See 8 June 1755, 19 June 1793, 25 March 1802, 5 August 1914.

Admiral Sir Bertram Ramsay (1883–1945). (*NMRN*)

1807 Boats of *Cerberus* (32) cut out two French privateers from under a battery near the Pearl Rock, Martinique.

1815 Prince Regent increased the membership of the Order of the Bath, much to the wrath of St Vincent who had no desire to have a Grand Cross (though perhaps mischievously prone to wear it on unusual occasions). In view of the Hundred Days this was a confident if premature 'commemoration of the end of the long and arduous contest in which the Empire has lately been engaged'.

Withdrawal of the Naval Gold Medal. A few more were awarded but the order to return those held by new KCBs was withdrawn.

1858 Naval Brigade from wood screw frigate *Shannon* at the action at the Kali Nadi bridge. Indian Mutiny Medal.

1873 Vice-Admiral Sir Astley Cooper Key appointed the first Admiral President, RNC Greenwich.

See 1 February 1873, 20 June 1997.

1879 Major gun explosion in turret battleship *Thunderer* during gunnery exercises off Ismed in Sea of Marmara. The turret crew failed to notice that one of the twin, 12-in, muzzle-loading (MLR) guns had failed to fire. Both guns were hydraulically reloaded. The double-shotted gun exploded, wrecking the turret and killing eleven men. This led to a return to breech-loading guns in new ships. This unlucky ship (she had had a fatal boiler explosion in 1876) was commanded by Capt Alfred Chatfield, father of the future Admiral of the Fleet Lord Chatfield, Beatty's Flag Captain in the First World War, and later First Sea Lord.

See 12 July 1871, 25 March 1872, 26 July 1929.

Vice-Admiral Watson's squadron off Calcutta showing his flagship, HMS *Kent* (70), on the right, 1757. (*NMRN Ad Lib MSS 356*)

1915 Preliminary bombardment of Dar-es-Salaam by battleship *Goliath* and cruiser *Fox*.

1933 Fleet carrier *Courageous* recommissioned, with first (hydraulically controlled) arrester gear.

1941 Monitor *Terror*, with river gunboats *Aphis* and *Ladybird*, provided harassing fire in support of assault on Bardia.

1943 Minesweeper *Alarm* severely damaged by aircraft at Bone, and written off, her gun salvaged by the local Royal Artillery as an anti-aircraft weapon.

1944 Helicopters first used in sea warfare (Sikorsky R4 and MV *Daghestan* in convoy HX 274).

1945 Admiral Sir Bertram Ramsay, Allied Naval C-in-C of Operation Overlord, killed in air crash.

Ramsay retired on 10 October 1938 but was re-employed on the outbreak of war. As Vice-Admiral Dover in 1940 he had organised the Dunkirk evacuation and was reinstated as a vice-admiral on the Active List on 26 April 1944 and promoted admiral the following day. He was Allied Naval C-in-C in Operation Overlord that June. Eisenhower and Cunningham attended his funeral at Saint-Germain-en-Laye on 8 January. Memorial windows in Portsmouth Cathedral.

See 10 December 1941.

1947 *Royal Arthur* commissioned at Corsham: first petty officers' training establishment. Courses for POs were started in *Excalibur* in May 1944, transferred to *Raleigh* that October and to Corsham in 1947. *Royal Arthur* had been the Adult New Entry Training Establishment for all branches at Skegness, dealing with over a quarter of a million men during the Second World War. It moved to Corsham in 1950 after which training was dedicated to petty officers.

1959 'Their Lordships have reviewed the design of the officers' boat cloak and have decided that the naval officers' combined coat and cape . . . is outmoded. The boat cloak for all officers will in future be a lengthened version of the separate cape . . . lined with white for naval officers and crimson for RM officers. . .' – AFO 21/59.

1961 *Harrier*, RN School of Meteorology and Aircraft Direction, Kete, Dale, Pembrokeshire, paid off. Commissioned 1 February 1948. AFO 3334/60.

2000 Patrick O'Brian (Richard Patrick Russ), novelist of the Royal Navy in the Napoleonic and Revolutionary Wars, died in Dublin, aged 85. Creator of Capt Jack Aubrey and Dr Stephen Maturin.

3 JANUARY

1670 George Monck, Duke of Albemarle, died.

1695 *Nonsuch* taken by the French *Français* 200 miles W. of the Scilly Isles.

1707 *Fowey*, *Milford* and *Romney* destroyed the French *Content* in Almeria Bay, Spain.

1799 *Wolverine* (38) fought the French luggers *Furet* and *Ruse* 5 miles N.N.E. of Boulogne.

1801 Boats of *Melpomene* (38) in the Senegal River, West Africa, cut out the French *Sénégal* which was wrecked while being brought out.

1833 Capt J.J. Onslow in the brig sloop *Clio* reclaimed the Falkland Islands from the Argentine *Sarandi*.

1864 *Haughty*, wood screw gunboat, sank two pirate junks, one inside and one outside Pinghai Bay, China.

1900 New Royal Yacht *Victoria and Albert* heeled over in dry dock in Pembroke Dockyard while fitting out, leading to resignation of Sir William White, Director of Naval Construction.

See 9 May 1899, 6 December 1954.

1904 *Pallas*, second-class cruiser, arrived Puerto Plata, Dominican Republic and, with US cruiser *Detroit*, prevented rebel Dominican gunboat *Independencia* from bombarding the unfortified town. 'Identifiable as one of the final instances of Palmerstonian gunboat diplomacy.'

1919 Armoured cruiser *Kent* arrived at Vladivostok to join Allied warships supporting White Russians against growing Bolshevik threat. She arrived during a snowstorm, berthing between the Japanese battleship *Mikasa* and the US Navy cruiser *Brooklyn*. Despite the freezing temperatures, *Kent* paraded a guard and band on the quarterdeck to salute the foreign ships. Only the drums worked because the wind instruments

HMS *Talent* conducting Dive and Surface Drills in Kyle of Lochalsh on 15 December 2009. (*RN*)

The First Aircraft Carrier Squadron – HMS *Implacable*, *Indefatigable* and *Glory* at Melbourne in January 1946. (*Cdr David Hobbs RN*)

froze after a few notes. 'The results were not wasted on the American sense of humour and we learned a lesson.' – *Expedition to Siberia. The Great War – Eastern Front*, RM Museum.

See 6 April 1919.

1941 Battleships *Barham*, *Valiant* and *Warspite* bombarded Bardia, captured by British troops on 5 January.

1943 'Chariot' human torpedo sank the Italian light cruiser *Ulpio Traiano* in Palermo harbour. The first successful employment of these weapons by the RN in the Second World War.

1945 Assault on Akyab, Burma. Operation Lightning. Ships: *Napier* (RAN), *Nepal*, *Shoreham*. Bombardment force: *Newcastle*, *Nigeria*, *Phoebe*, *Pathfinder*, *Raider*, *Rapid*.

1952 Admiral Sir George Creasy hoisted his flag as C-in-C Home Fleet in the battleship *Vanguard*.

1978 Flag Officer Submarines moved from HMS *Dolphin*, Gosport, to HMS *Warrior*, Northwood, to be co-located with CINCFLEET. DCI(RN)S 31/76.

See 3 May 1905, 30 September 1998.

2001 Rear-Admiral John Clarke retired as the last two-star Hydrographer of the Navy. His historic title assumed by Captain(H) at Devonport, Capt Mike Barritt. The post of Chief Executive Hydrographic Agency assumed by Dr Wynford Williams who also became National Hydrographer.

See 11 September 1795, 1 April 1990.

2005 Frigate *Chatham* arrived off east coast of Sri Lanka, joined by RFA *Diligence* on 5 January, to provide humanitarian aid after the 26 December 2004 underwater earthquake and tsunami. Operation Garron. *Scott*, oceanographic surveying ship, conducted sea-bed survey of the earthquake epicentre and fracture zone, 24 January to 15 February.

See 13 October 1996.

4 JANUARY

1761 Fir-built frigate *Trent* (38) captured the French *Bien-Aimé* 30 miles S.S.E. of Cape Tiburon, Haiti.

1781 *Courageux* and *Valiant* (74s) captured the French *Minerve* (32) 30 miles W. of Ushant.

1866 John Dinnen, the first Inspector of Machinery Afloat and the first naval engineer to serve in Whitehall, died after being knocked down by a hansom cab when leaving the Admiralty.
See 1 July 1918.

1879 First casualty of Zulu war – a naval rating devoured by a crocodile.
See 23 June 1883.

1911 Capt R.F. Scott RN in *Terra Nova* reached Ross Island, Antarctica.

1915 Submarine C 31 lost off Belgian coast.

1916 Start of operations for the relief of Kut-al' Amara, Mesopotamia. River gunboats: *Gadfly, Butterfly, Cranefly, Dragonfly*; from 10 January *Flycatcher* (ex-Turkish patrol boat).

1940 Minesweeper *Borde* successfully detonated first magnetic mine by a magnetic field projected ahead.

1945 Airstrike on oil refineries at Pangkalan Brandan, Sumatra, by Rear-Admiral Sir Philip Vian (*Indomitable*). Operation Lentil. *Indefatigable, Indomitable, Victorious, Argonaut, Black Prince, Ceylon, Suffolk* and eight destroyers of 25th and 27th DF. FAA Sqns: Avenger: 849, 857; Corsair: 1834, 1836; Firefly: 1770; Hellcat: 888, 1839, 1844; Seafire: 887, 894.

1965 Frigate *Whirlwind* of the West Indies Station arrived in New Orleans on a five day visit to mark the 150th anniversary of the Battle of New Orleans, the last engagement in the War of 1812.
See 24 December 1814.

Below and Opposite: Sea King helicopters of 845 NAS deployed to the former Yugoslavia in support of the United Nations Protection Force, photographed by the author at Mostar in 1994. (*Author*)

A flight of FAA Avengers during an attack on Japanese-held oil refineries in Sumatra in January 1945. (*NMRN*)

1974 Lt HRH The Prince of Wales RN joined the frigate *Jupiter* in the Far East.
See 16 September 1971, 2 September 1974, 9 February 1976, 15 December 1976.

1983 Fraser Gunnery Range, Eastney, facility transferred to HMS *Cambridge*, Wembury, Plymouth. The end of naval gunnery training in the Portsmouth area. DCI(RN) 533/82.
See 30 June 1958, 30 March 2001.

1994 Royal approval given for UK personnel to wear the Russian government's Arctic Convoys Medal.

2001 Final two Sea King helicopters of 845 NAS, Lt-Cdr S.R. Gordon RN, returned to RNAS Yeovilton from their base in Split after eight years' continuous service during which 845 Squadron helicopters operated 13,500 flying hours in support of UN and NATO operations in former Yugoslavia.
See 15 March 1954.

5 JANUARY

1795 *Blanche* (32) captured the French *Pique* (38), after a five-hour fight, 3 miles W. of Marie Galante, West Indies.
Battle Honour: *Pique* 1795.

1798 *Pomone* (44), a French prize taken in 1744, captured the French privateer *Chéri* 280 miles S.W. of Ushant (44).

1807 *Nautilus* (18), ship sloop, wrecked on uncharted reef near Cerigotto (Antikythera) N.W. of Crete. Many of the 122 ship's company got ashore, but only sixty-four were alive when relief arrived six days later. One of the few authenticated cases of cannibalism in RN history.

The ship, commanded by Capt Edward Palmer, was carrying urgent dispatches from Rear-Admiral Sir Thomas Louis at the Dardanelles to Vice-Admiral Lord Collingwood. Court martial of senior surviving officer found that 'the loss of His Majesty's late sloop the *Nautilus* was occasioned by the Captain's Zeal to forward the public dispatches, which induced him to run in a dark, tempestuous night for the passage between the Islands of Cerigotto and Candia [Crete], but that the Sloop passed between Cerigotto and Pauri [Pori], and was lost on a Rock . . . which Rock does not appear to have been laid down in Heather's Chart, by which it is said the said Sloop was navigated, it being the only one of those seas on board. That no blame attaches to the Conduct of Lieut. Alex Nesbitt, or such of the surviving Officers and Ship's Company . . .' Many other HM ships and their people lost in the Battle of Crete in 1941 lie in the same waters.

1809 *Loire* (38), taken ten years before, took the *Hébé*, laden with provisions for San Domingo, in the Bay. Taken into the Service as *Ganymede*.

1814 *Blazer, Desiree, Hearty, Piercer, Redbreast, Shamrock* and gunboats at the capture of Glückstadt, Holstein.
Battle Honour: Glückstadt, 1814.

1814 The French-held fortress of Cattaro (Kotor) in the Adriatic surrendered to *Bacchante* (38),

The frigate *Blanche* captures *La Pique* after a five-hour battle in 1795. (*NMRN*)

The central arched carriageway entrance to the Admiralty in Whitehall, flanked by colonnades, designed by the Scottish architect, Robert Adams, and completed in 1760. (*Crown Copyright. MOD Art Collection*)

Capt William Hoste, and the brig-sloop *Saracen* (18), Capt John Harper, after a ten-day bombardment.
Battle Honour: Cattaro 1814.
See 13 March 1811.

On 28 January Ragusa (now Dubrovnik) surrendered to these two ships and to British and Austrian troops besieging the town. The island of Paxo (now Paxos) surrendered to *Apollo* (38), Capt Bridges Watkinson Taylor, on 13 February and by the end of that month, ships of the squadron, under Rear-Admiral Thomas Francis Fremantle (Captain of *Ganges* (74) at Copenhagen and of *Neptune* (90) at Trafalgar), aided by Austrian troops, had cleared the French from Dalmatia, Croatia, Istria and Frioul, and the offshore islands.

1847 *Dauntless*, the first British wood screw frigate, fitted with the new Penn trunk engines, launched at Portsmouth (the first launching there for eight years). An outbreak of yellow fever in the ship at Barbados in November 1852 killed fifteen officers and sixty-four men in three months (memorial in St Matthias Anglican church, Hastings, Barbados). During the Russian (Crimean) War she served in the Baltic in 1854 and the next year was at the bombardment of Sebastopol and the Kinburn forts in the Black Sea.
Battle Honours: Baltic 1854; Crimea 1854–5.
See 17 October 1855.

1942 Submarine *Upholder* sank the Italian S/M *Ammiraglio Saint Bon* off the Lipari Islands (38.22N, 15.22E).

1943 US Task Force, including *Achilles*, bombarded Munda and Kolombangara Island (Guadalcanal campaign). *Achilles* damaged by Japanese aircraft.
Battle Honour: Guadalcanal 1942–3.

1951 Evacuation of Inchon, Korea.

The Chinese offensive in Korea began on 31 December 1950, and military forces were pulled south in the face of heavy enemy action. In the Inchon area, the cruisers *Kenya* and *Ceylon* and Australian destroyers *Warramunga* and *Bataan* together with USS *Rochester* and *Evertsen* (Dutch) formed the Gun Fire Support Group, providing interdiction for the Army, who reported Inchon as completely evacuated by 5 January. A total of 68,913 personnel, 1,404 vehicles and 62,144 tons of cargo were lifted from Inchon to Taejon and Pusan. In December, 105,000 US and ROK military personnel and 91,000 civilian refugees had been lifted by sea from Hungnam.

6 JANUARY

1745 *Captain*, *Dreadnought*, *Hampton Court* and *Sunderland* fought the French *Fleuron* and *Neptune* 250 miles W. of Ushant. *Captain* recaptured the British privateer *Mars*, but there were parliamentary questions about the escape of the two Frenchmen.

1767 First publication of the *Nautical Almanack* by Nevil Maskelyne, fifth Astronomer Royal.

1801 Boats of *Mercury* captured fifteen sail of a French convoy between Sète and Marseilles.

1813 Boats of *Bacchante* and *Weazle* captured five French gunboats 15 miles S.E. of Cape Otranto, Calabria.

1814 *Niger* and *Tagus* captured the French *Cérés* 240 miles S. of Cape Verde Islands.

1900 *Powerful*'s Naval Brigade at the repulse of the Boers on Waggon Hill, Ladysmith. South Africa Medal: clasp 'Defence of Ladysmith'.
See 25 October 1899.

1915 The foundation stone of the RN Hospital, Mtarfa, Malta, laid by General Sir Leslie Rundle, Governor and C-in-C Malta. Originally known as the Royal Artillery and Naval Hospital, it was opened on 29 June 1920. Mtarfa took over all naval medical services when RNH Bighi closed in 1970. Mtarfa closed in 1978 and the building now houses the Sir Temi Zammit Secondary School.
See 23 March 1830.

1916 *King Edward VII*, battleship and name-ship of the class known as 'The Wobbly Eight', sunk by mine 25 miles off Cape Wrath. Ship's company taken off by destroyers *Fortune*, *Marne*, *Musketeer* and *Nessus* without loss of life. King Edward had directed at her launch that she should always be a flagship; she was lost on her first voyage as a private ship.

1916 Submarine E 17 wrecked off Texel. Conning tower salvaged 1986 and now in RN Submarine Museum.

1918 First aviation flag officer afloat. Rear-Admiral Richard Phillimore appointed Admiral Commanding Aircraft.
See 25 November 1912, 19 November 1917, 2 April 1931, 19 July 1938.

1944 Trawler *Wallasea* sunk by the German E-boat S-138 south of Mounts Bay, Cornwall. Convoy WP 457.

1945 Operations in Lingayen Gulf, Philippines, by US forces from the 5th to the 9th, when troops landed. Present: *Arunta*, *Australia*, *Gascoyne*, *Shropshire*, *Warramunga*, *Warrego* (all RAN).
Battle Honour: Lingayen Gulf 1945.

The return of HMS *Powerful* to Portsmouth in 1900 was marked by a civic reception, torchlight procession and banquet for the crew. (*NMRN*)

This figurehead from HMS *Queen Charlotte* (1810) is one of the finest in the possession of Royal Navy. The ship was Lord Exmouth's flagship at the bombardment of Algiers in 1816 and was re-named HMS *Excellent* in 1859 when she became the Portsmouth gunnery training ship. The figurehead is displayed in the open on Whale Island but needs to be moved under cover if it is to survive. (*Author*)

1945 Destroyer *Walpole* mined off Flushing: CTL.

1956 Admiralty Fleet Order 9/56:

1. The general Admiralty policy is not to allow more than one naval burial in any naval grave.

2. Investigation has, nevertheless, shown that naval graves vary considerably in depth according to locality. It has, therefore, been decided that a uniform practice is to be followed in future.

3. Accordingly, naval graves are to be dug to the following depths:

   a. In Naval Cemeteries: to a depth of six feet.

   b. In Civil Cemeteries (including Naval Reservations and Churchyards): to the minimum depth allowed by the responsible local authority for a single burial.

1958 'Flying over the National Maritime Museum yesterday was a flag which had not been flown for 125 years – the old Navy Board flag, three gold anchors on a red ground – established by Patent of 24 April 1545 and abolished in 1832' – *The Times*, 7 January 1958. The flag had been acquired as the Museum's flag but the Royal Navy later took it back.

See 31 March 1964.

1961 Ships' names are to be prefixed by HMS or by the definite article, except in signals. AFO 8/61.

1971 Admiral Sir David Luce, submariner, who resigned as First Sea Lord over the cancellation of the new carrier programme in 1966, died aged 64, at Bath. He was the first submariner on the Admiralty Board and the first C-in-C Far East. Memorial service in St Martin-in-the-Fields 20 January.

See 23 January 1906, 28 November 1962, 22 February 1966.

1977 Admiral Sir Douglas Eric (Deric) Holland-Martin died. As Flag Officer Flotillas Mediterranean he commanded over 100 British ships in landings at Port Said in November 1956, probably the last RN flag officer to command so many in operations. As Acting Vice-Admiral aged 51 in October 1957, the youngest and most junior officer to be appointed Second Sea Lord in the history of the post.

1987 Superintendent Anthea Savill became the first WRNS officer to attend the RCDS.

2000 First Flag promotion and appointment in (the generally accepted) twenty-first century: Rear-Admiral Nigel Guild, to be Executive Director 4 of Defence Procurement Agency and Controller of the Navy.

7 JANUARY

1730 Royal approval given for the first single volume, consolidating the 'Regulations for the Naval Service', predecessor of QR&AI.

1746 George Keith Elphinstone, the future Admiral Viscount Keith, born.

1778 'Battle of the Keys' – an attack by David Bushell with primitive mines on the British Fleet in the Delaware, foiled by ice.

1779 Court martial of Admiral Augustus Keppel began.
See 27 July 1778, 11 February 1779.

1794 *Moselle* taken by the French on entering Toulon which she failed to observe they had reoccupied.

1804 Cdre Samuel Hood (*Centaur*) seized the Diamond Rock, S.W. of Martinique. Fortified and commissioned by Lt Maurice.
See 2 June 1805.

1806 Boats of *Franchise* cut out the Spanish *Raposa* at Campeche, Mexico after a 15-mile pull into the Bay by moonlight.

1807 Cochrane in *Imperieuse* (38) stormed and burned Fort Roquette, Arcachon, spiking the guns without loss.

1841 Capture of the Chuen pi and Tai kok tau forts in the Boca Tigris, Canton River. Chuen pi – *Calliope, Hyacinth, Larne*, Bengal Marine steamers *Enterprise, Madagascar, Nemesis, Queen*. Tai kok tau – *Samarang, Druid, Modeste, Columbine*. Seamen and marines of *Blenheim, Melville* and *Wellesley*. Troops: Royal Artillery, 26th and 49th Regiments, 37th Madras Native Infantry, Bengal Volunteer Regiment. Medal: China, 1841–2.

The First Chinese War, 1841–2

Napoleon's description of Britain as a 'nation of shopkeepers' was not far from the truth, and it was the wealth she accrued from her trade which subsidised the coalitions which eventually led to his downfall. It is not surprising therefore that unimpeded trade should be one of the main considerations in Britain's foreign policy.

China's exports were very attractive to the West and when the Chinese began to interrupt the opium trade, as well as failing to discourage the piracy which was endemic in the Far East, relations with other trading powers began to deteriorate. Further ill-treatment of British residents and traders followed, and a punitive expedition was mounted. In a series of joint Army and Navy operations, the Chinese were defeated and agreed to British terms.

1841 *Nemesis* and boats of *Calliope, Hyacinth, Larne, Starling* and *Sulphur* destroyed thirteen war junks in Anson's Bay. Medal: China, 1841–2.

1862 Landing party from *Falcon* destroyed Robene, Sierra Leone.

1883 Andrew Browne Cunningham, the future Admiral of the Fleet, Viscount Cunningham of Hyndhope, born.
See 12 June 1963.

1900 Blockade of Laurenço Marques, Mozambique, by *Forte, Thetis, Magicienne*. First use of wireless to coordinate action.

1909 A pinnace landing men from the cruiser *Encounter* in Sydney harbour run down by MV *Dunsmore*. Fifteen men lost were buried in a communal grave at Rookwood Cemetery, Sydney. Their ship was transferred to the RAN in 1912 (permanently from December 1919). Scuttled off Sydney 14 September 1932.

1916 Officers allowed to wear soft collars at sea, and grey trousers with monkey jackets when landing for recreation.

1917 Sea Lions in A/S experiments in Gare Loch.

1918 SS *Braeneil* rammed and sank U-93 in S.W. Approaches.

1940 *Undine*, lead boat of the 69 U-class submarines, sunk by German auxiliary minesweepers M-1201, M-1204 and M-1207 in shallow water in Heligoland Bight. The first submarine lost to enemy action in the Second World War and the first of twenty-three large submarines lost in 1940. Crew all captured.

Admiral of the Fleet Sir Andrew Cunningham (1883–1963) inspects the Guard of Honour, RNB, Portsmouth, 1945. (*NMRN*)

1940 Submarine *Seahorse* sunk in Heligoland Bight (59.19N, 07.30E) by German 1st Minesweeping Flotilla, within hours of the loss of *Undine* (previous entry). Crew all lost.

1940 Ships on foreign stations to report to the Admiralty, in accordance with AFO 2109/39, on the suitability of earthenware butter dishes after six months of trials.

See 27 July 1939 panel.

1941 Corvette *Anemone* sank the Italian S/M *Nani* 500 miles W. of N. Ireland.

1944 Frigate *Tweed* sunk by U-305 600 miles W. of Cape Ortegal (44.18N, 21.19W). Operation Stonewall.

1945 Operations in the Kaladan River, Burma. Ships: *Jumna* and *Narbada* (both RIN); ML 381, 829.

1955 Temporary Acting Senior Commissioned Signal Boatswain F.C. Tarling MBE, MSM, RN (retd) appointed Section Minewatching Service Officer, Bristol Channel.

1966 'The Admiralty Board has decided that the term "escort" is no longer to be used as a generic title for destroyers and frigates . . . The reason for this decision is that the term "escort" fails to give a proper idea of the many functions which destroyers and frigates are capable of performing as individual ships.' The term 'escort' would continue to be used in the NATO context. – DCI(RN) 10/66.

2000 Type 22 frigate *Campbeltown*, Capt Tim Harris RN, sailed from Devonport to relieve frigate *Coventry* in STANAVFORLANT. The first RN warship deployment in the (popularly regarded) twenty-first century.

2011 Fleet Submarine *Ambush* launched at BAE Systems, Barrow.

See 22 October 2003, 16 December 2010.

8 JANUARY

1758 *Hussar* captured the French privateer *Vengeance* 60 miles W. of Lizard Head.

1761 *Unicorn* (28) captured the French *Vestale* (32) 30 miles S.W. of Belle Ile.
Battle Honour: *Vestale* 1761.

1780 Admiral Sir George Bridges Rodney (*Sandwich*), with eighteen sail of the line, captured a Spanish convoy and its escort (twenty-two sail) 300 miles W. of Cape Finisterre.
See 16 January 1780.

1798 *Kingfisher* captured the French privateer *Betzy* 150 miles W. of Burling Island, Portugal.

1806 Body of Vice-Admiral Lord Nelson taken upriver from Greenwich to the Admiralty by barge, where it rested overnight before his funeral in St Paul's Cathedral.

1862 Landing party from *Falcon* and a detachment of the 2nd West India Regiment destroyed Robaga, Sierra Leone.

1912 Naval War Staff established. Additional Civil Lord appointed to Board of Admiralty.

1916 Evacuation of Gallipoli Peninsula completed.

1918 *Cyclamen* sank UB-69 off Bizerta (37.30N, 10.38E).

1932 *Sturgeon* launched. Lead ship of first batch of twelve S-class submarines. The second group of fifty was led by *Safari*, launched on 18 November 1941.

1940 First aircraft detonation of a magnetic mine.

1942 River gunboat *Aphis* bombarded Halfaya Pass in support of the Army advance from Egypt.

Nelson's body being taken upstream from Greenwich in the royal barge of Charles II, built *c*.1670. The barge can be seen in the National Museum of the Royal Navy at Portsmouth. (*NMRN*)

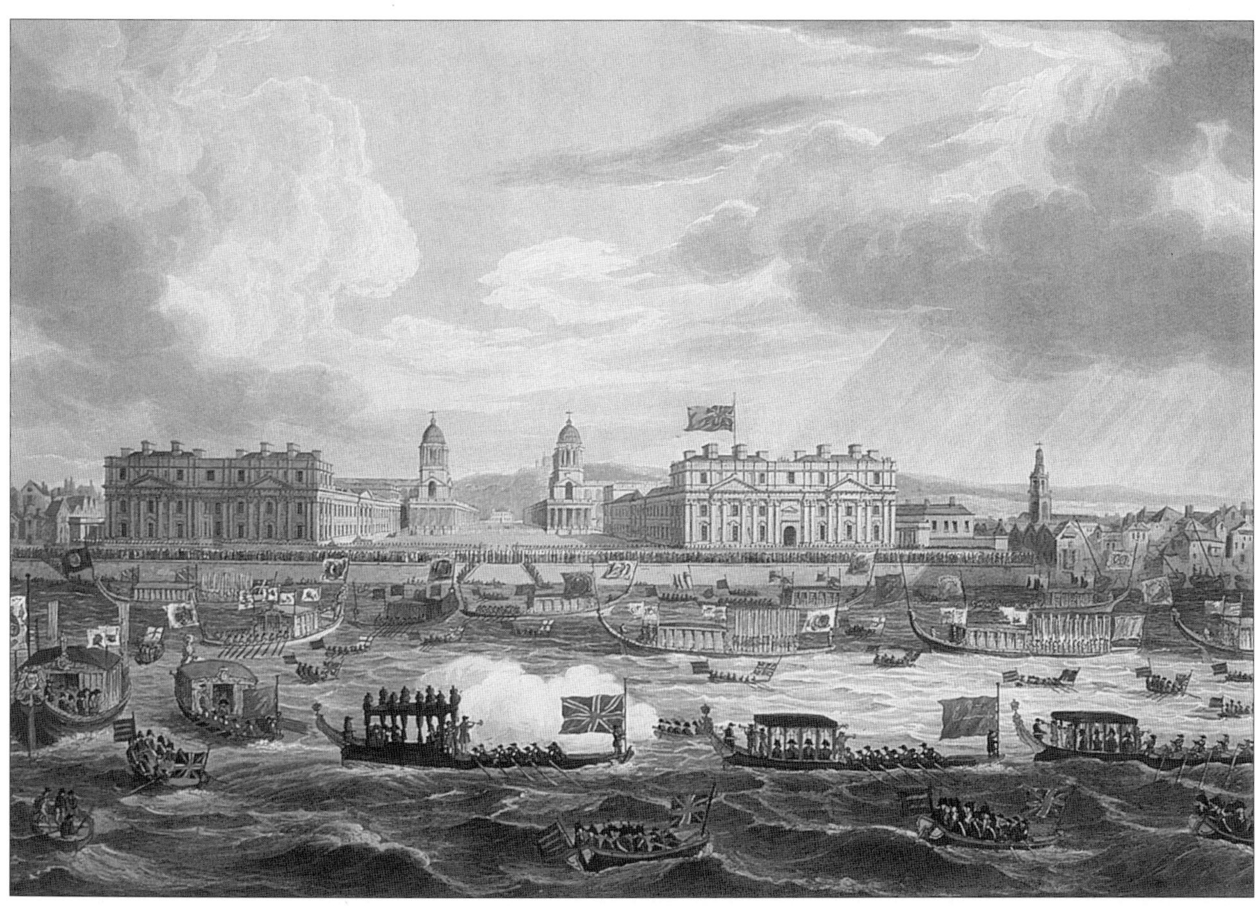

The frigate HMS *Richmond* landed a Guard for the commemoration service held at Suda Bay Commonwealth War Cemetery in May 2001 to mark the sixtieth anniversary of the battle of Crete. (*Author*)

1943 Submarine P 311 (*Tutankhamen*) believed to have been mined off Maddalena, Sardinia with several charioteers on board.

1944 Frigate *Bayntun* and corvette *Camrose* (RCN) sank U-757 in S.W. Approaches. Convoy OS 64/KMS 38.

1944 Sunderland U/10 (RAAF) sank U-426 in Bay of Biscay.

1960 The Chief Engineer of RFA *Fort Constantine*, Mr D.C. Leathley, appointed the first Commodore Chief Engineer, RFA, a rank approved in AFO 435/60.

See 7 October 1951.

2004 Capt Henry Lockhart St John Fancourt, DSO, believed to have been the last surviving British officer who fought at the Battle of Jutland, died, aged 103. Fancourt served in a 13.5-in turret in the battlecruiser *Princess Royal*. He qualified on No. 1 Naval Pilots' Course 1924 and made the first British deck-landing on a US carrier, USS *Wasp*, in Gloster Gladiator N2274.

9 January

1760 Board approved construction of windmill to lift fresh water at Gosport on the Weovil estate, site of Clarence Yard.

1781 *Fairy* taken by a French privateer 30 miles S.S.W. of the Scilly Isles.

1801 *Constitution*, cutter, taken by two French cutters off Portland. Recaptured by the Revenue cutter *Greyhound*.

1806 Funeral of Vice-Admiral Lord Nelson in St Paul's Cathedral.

See 23 May 1799.

1810 *Plover* recaptured the British brig *Pomona* – prize to the St Malo privateer *Saratu* – 70 miles W.S.W. of the Scilly Isles.

1811 *Princess Charlotte* captured the French privateer *Aimable Flore* 210 miles W.S.W. of Ushant.

1862 General Sir Arthur Stransham appointed Second Inspector-General, RM, for five years.

1867 Maj-Gen J. Travers appointed third and last Inspector-General, RM, for one year.

Admiral of the Fleet Lord Fisher of Kilverstone (1841–1920)

Jacky Fisher, the greatest naval administrator since St Vincent and 'the last Titan to direct the Royal Navy' (Lambert, *Admirals*, p.332), was born in Ceylon in 1841 and entered the Royal Navy in 1854 on the nomination of the last surviving of Nelson's captains. Fisher, First Sea Lord from 1904–10, directed his volcanic energy to reforming the comfortable Royal Navy and preparing it for war with Germany which he believed was inevitable. He came like a thunderclap upon both the Admiralty and the Navy and he rocked the Service to its foundations. 'But the Navy was not a pleasant place while this was going on' (Churchill).

Fisher introduced great reforms. He introduced the all-big-gun, turbine-propelled battleship, HMS *Dreadnought* in 1906 and the first battlecruiser, HMS *Invincible*, in 1908. Many obsolete gunboats, sloops and second and third-class cruisers that showed the flag around the Empire, an 'arrangement that pleased the Foreign Office and the consuls' daughters who needed tennis and waltzing partners', were brought home and scrapped. Fighting ships in reserve were to be manned with two fifths of their normal complement to allow their mobilisation at short notice. The growing realisation of the German threat led the Admiralty steadily to concentrate the cream of the fleet in home waters.

Fisher's reforms were anathema for the old guard and many modern-thinking officers were alienated by Fisher's intolerance of contrary views. Men who questioned his views were enemies to be crushed. Individual critics were 'damnable skunks' or 'pestilent pimps'. The Admiralty had never seen the like. The cost was deep dissention throughout the officer corps of the Royal Navy. Arthur Marder, who edited Fisher's correspondence in *Fear God and Dread Nought*, wrote in his preface that Fisher was 'regarded by the Royal Navy in his own lifetime either as a saint or a devil, as a genius who raised the efficiency of the Fleet to a peak never reached before, or as an evil old man who raised havoc with naval discipline and efficiency . . . there was no half-way house'. However, Winston Churchill, who recalled Fisher in 1914 for what proved a fatal experience for both men, judged Fisher as 'a man truly great despite his idiosyncrasies and truly good despite his violence'.

Churchill brought Fisher back as First Sea Lord in 1915 but the old man's megalomania alarmed both the Admiralty and the government. He resigned over the Dardanelles fiasco the next year. Fisher died on 10 July 1920 at 19 St James's Square, home of the Duchess of Hamilton (another admiral, another Hamilton). After a naval funeral in London he was buried at Kilverstone near Thetford, Norfolk. His headstone reads 'Seest thou a man diligent in his business? He shall stand before kings, he shall not stand before men' and 'Organiser of the Navy that won the Great War'. On his footstone 'Fear God and Dread Nought'.

HMS *Cornwallis*, a battleship of 1901, torpedo nets out, engages Turkish shore batteries in the Dardanelles, 1915. (*NMRN*)

1917 Battleship *Cornwallis*, Capt A.P. Davidson RN, torpedoed by U-32 62 miles S.E. of Malta; fifteen men killed. The first torpedo struck the starboard side after boiler room and counter flooding of the port side 6-in magazines, engine room and wings reduced the list and allowed the destroyer *Beagle* to take off all the remaining ship's company. The ship capsized after a second torpedo hit the starboard side over an hour after the first. Her sister ship *Russell* had been mined and sunk off Malta in 1916; they were the tenth and eleventh of thirteen British battleships lost in the First World War.

See 18 February 1915, 27 April 1916.

1918 Destroyer *Racoon* wrecked on N.W. coast of Ireland.

1940 Submarine *Starfish* scuttled after depth charge attack by the German minesweeper M-7 in the Heligoland Bight.

1942 Destroyer *Vimiera* sunk by mine in the Thames Estuary off East Spile Buoy (51.28N, 00.55E). Convoy FS 693. First of forty-six destroyers lost in 1942.

1987 Award for salvage services by *Anglesey* to FV *Milford Star* on 21 October 1984 announced in DCI(RN). Each share worth £11,996. Unlike that made to *Torquay*, this award seems not to have been amended.

See 5 December 1986, 16 January 1987.

HMS *Starfish* in May 1937. (*NMRN*)

10 JANUARY

1711 *Resolution* (70), Capt Richard Haddock, wrecked off Barcelona.

1749 Captains of over and under three years seniority distinguished by different-coloured facings on coats.

1761 Admiral Edward Boscawen, 'Old Dreadnought', died. When his wife lamented his absence from home during the harvest, he replied on 30 July 1756 from *Royal George* off Brest, 'I beg my dear will not be uneasy at my staying out so long. To be sure I lose the fruits of the earth, but then I am gathering the flowers of the sea.' Buried at Penkevel, Cornwall.

See 19 August 1711.

1761 *Seahorse* fought the French *Grand* 100 miles S.W. of Start Point.

1761 *Juno* and *Venus* captured the French *Brune* 170 miles W. of Ushant.

1797 *Phoebe* captured the French *Atalante* 60 miles N. of the Scilly Isles.

Admiral Edward Boscawen (1711–1761). (*NMM Neg. No. C7649*)

1806 Cape Town and its defences capitulated to the forces under Maj-Gen Sir David Baird and Cdre Sir Home Riggs Popham (*Diadem*). A Naval Brigade was landed.

Battle Honour: Cape of Good Hope 1806.

1810 Boats of *Armide* and *Christian VII* captured six French coasters in Basque Roads.

1810 *Plover* captured the St Malo privateer *Saratu* 20 miles S.S.W. of the Scilly Isles.

1854 *Illustrious* (74) became cadet training ship.

1912 Acting Cdr Charles Rumney Samson RN made the first flight from a British warship, taking off in a modified Short-Sommer S.27 pusher aircraft from a ramp built over the forecastle of the battleship *Africa* moored to a buoy at Sheerness.

See 18 November 1911, 2 May 1912, 2 August 1917.

1915 TB 10 (ex-*Greenfly*) sunk by mine in North Sea.

1920 Formal end of the war between Great Britain and Germany. The armistice had been signed on 11 November 1918. The Treaty of Versailles, signed on 28 June 1919, was ratified by most former belligerents on 10 January 1920. 'His Majesty, by and with the advice of His Privy Council, is pleased to order, and it is hereby ordered, that the said tenth day of January shall be treated as the date of the termination of war between His Majesty and Germany.' Order in Council L.3012.1920.

See 18 October 1921.

1924 Submarine L 24 sunk with all hands after collision with battleship *Resolution* on exercises off Portland. Memorial in St Ann's church, Portsmouth.

See 1 May 2008.

1940 Training camp for mobilised RN specialist reservists opened on a 200-acre site between Gosport and Fareham and was commissioned as *Collingwood* (one day after a similar camp

at Torpoint was commissioned as *Raleigh*). It became TE for radar and electrical ratings when the Electrical Branch formed on 1 April 1946 and the RN WE School when branch was renamed in 1960s.

1941 Destroyer *Gallant* severely damaged by mine 120 miles W. of Malta, where she was towed by *Mohawk*. Bombed 5 April 1942 and sunk as breakwater in September 1943. First of twenty-two destroyers lost in 1941.

1941 Portsmouth heavily bombed from 1930 until 0200. 'A first-class blitz', wrote Admiral Sir William James, C-in-C Portsmouth; in the Dockyard 'the blazing stores were a sight not to be forgotten. The big paint store became a veritable furnace and the paint pots were exploding like artillery fire'. Accommodation blocks in the RN barracks burned out. Fire raged down Queen Street and engulfed The Hard. King's Road, much of the historic High Street, Aggie Weston's in Queen Street, the town hall and the garrison church were destroyed. Portsmouth Cathedral was saved from fire by sailors living within it. All the *Vernon* artificers deployed to restore electrical power to the city.

See 12 and 24 August 1940, 23 December 1940, 10 March 1941, 17 April 1941, 8 June 1959.

1941 Destroyer *Hereward* sank the Italian TB *Vega* 6 miles S. of Pantelleria. (*Bonaventure*, *Jaguar* and *Southampton* also engaged.) Operation Excess.

At the start of 1941 convoys were being run to the Piraeus and Malta in Operation Excess, involving all naval forces in the Mediterranean. The carrier *Illustrious* formed part of the escort of a convoy from Alexandria to Malta. On 10 January the situation was dramatically challenged with the unexpected attack on her and the battleships *Warspite* and *Valiant* by the Luftwaffe. Thirty aircraft of Fliegerkorps X of the Luftwaffe attacked *Illustrious*, and ten engaged the other ships. The flying was brilliant, the aircraft diving from 12,000ft at angles of 65° to 80°, releasing bombs at 800ft and following with gun attacks on the carrier. There were six aircraft in the dive at any one time throughout the six-minute attack. *Illustrious* was badly damaged but limped into Malta. There, despite continuous Luftwaffe attacks, she was repaired sufficiently in thirteen days to sail for Alexandria. She had lost 30 per cent of her aircrew and was withdrawn from the Mediterranean for repairs, leaving the Luftwaffe in control of the central Mediterranean airspace.

1941 DSO: Henry Morgan Lloyd, RNVR, Chaplain of *Illustrious* 'for great courage and devotion to duty in the face of enemy air attack' off Pantelleria. The only DSO won by a naval chaplain in the Second World War.

1943 GC (ex-AM): AB E. Hawkins, for saving life on burning and sinking ship in North Atlantic, which also earned him Lloyd's War Medal – a rare award for a serviceman.

1943 First FAA Barracuda squadron formed at Stretton.

1964 Submarine *Tiptoe*, Lt-Cdr David Brazier RN, went aground in thick fog 40yds off Greenock Esplanade opposite the home of the Captain-in-Charge, Clyde. Court martial at Portsmouth 12 March 1964: Severe Reprimand.

See 13 July 1965, 22 October 2010.

1969 Submarine *Trump*, the last of the submarines loaned to the Royal Australian Navy for ASW training, sailed from Sydney for UK. Boat credited with the last torpedo attack by a British submarine on an enemy vessel in the Second World War.

See 25 July 1945, 3 August 1945.

1986 Squadron commanders to wear a squadron command pennant to replace the 'outward sign of authority' represented by the traditional black bands painted on the funnels of squadron leaders which were removed by CINCFLEET in 1984. The short, white, swallow-tailed pennant with red edges to be worn by all Captains (D) and (F) and by squadron commanders the First, Third and Tenth MCM Squadrons. DCI(RN) 3/86.

See 11 March 2002.

2002 Capt Charles Anthony Johnstone-Burt promoted first substantive RN commodore. Prior to this date commodore had been a temporary appointment for a captain, not a substantive rank.

See 27 June 1734, 7 October 1951, 26 September 1958, 29 October 1997, 4 February 2003, 22 June 2004.

11 JANUARY

1782 Capture of Trincomalee by Vice-Admiral Sir Edward Hughes (*Superb*) and the Hon. East India Company's troops. Ships: *Burford, Eagle, Exeter, Monarca, Superb, Worcester.* Frigates, etc.: *Combustion, Nymph, Seahorse.*
See 6 May 1816, 15 October 1957.

1783 Flag officers given a gold embroidered full dress coat similar to that worn by General officers of the Army – a change attributed to Keppel. He died in 1786 and the coat was abolished in 1787. They were also given an all-blue undress coat on which rank was denoted by the arrangement of buttons. Commodores and first captains were granted a rear-admiral's ring.

1783 *Cyclops* captured the French *Railleur* 80 miles E. of Cape Henry, Virginia.

1794 Capt Samuel Hood in the frigate *Juno* (32), having entered Toulon believing it was in allied hands, escaped after a midshipman saw that two port officers who had boarded *Juno* were wearing tricolour cockades.

1810 *Cherokee* captured the French privateer *Aimable Nelly* at Dieppe.

1829 Boat of *Alacrity* captured a Greek piratical mistico under Cape Palipuri, Gulf of Kassandra.

1846 Capture of Kawiti's pah at Ruapekapeka, New Zealand, by Naval Brigade and troops. Ships: *Calliope, Castor, Elphinstone, North Star, Racehorse.* Troops: Royal Artillery, Royal Sappers and Miners, 58th and 99th Regiments. Medal: New Zealand, 1845–7.

1904 Committee of Imperial Defence established. A naval and military council, comprising the parliamentary heads of the Navy and Army with their Service chiefs, presided over by the prime minister 'which would consider the great problems of defence lying outside the province of a single department and requiring the cooperation of both services in their solution' – Marder, *Anatomy of British Sea Power*, p.80.

1917 *Ben-my-Chree*, Wing Cdr C.R. Samson RN, seaplane carrier and former Isle of Man

HMS *Tally Ho* in 1947. (*NMRN*)

HMS *Prince Consort,* launched at Pembroke Dockyard in 1862, had been laid down as the 90-gun *Triumph* in 1860 but as a temporary measure to maintain Britain's strength in capital ships she and two other wooden ships were completed as timber-hulled ironclads. They were the backbone of the Mediterranean fleet in the 1860s. (*Author*)

ferry, sunk in action by Turkish batteries off Kastelorizo Asia Minor. Raised in 1920 and broken up.

1924 Cruiser *Capetown*, Capt K.G.B. Dewar RN, lightened ship and steamed 20 miles up the Coatzacoalcos River to safeguard a British oil refinery and staff at Minatitlan during a Mexican civil war. 'The news of our arrival at Minatitlan was not welcomed by the Commander-in-Chief [Vice-Admiral Sir Michael Culme-Seymour], who did not like a ship of 4,000 tons proceeding up an uncharted river' (Dewar). However, units of the NA&WI Station deployed in succession. Fighting around the refinery intensified during the presence of the cruiser *Constance* (16 February–10 March). Her CO, Capt A.C. Strutt RN, informed the combatants 'that he could not approve of the firing of the [warring] ships' guns in his vicinity' and suggested that the battle 'should take place elsewhere' – and it was.

1933 Admiral Sir Howard Kelly, C-in-C China Station, laid the foundation stone of the China Fleet Club in Wanchai. The Club was opened on 21 March 1934 by Cdre Frank Elliot, Commodore Hong Kong. The site was redeveloped and a new club was opened in May 1985 by Sir Edward Youde, Governor of Hong Kong. Finally closed 30 November 1992.

1941 First operational and unfruitful launch from RN Fighter Catapult ship (*Pegasus*). Like the CAM (Catapult Armed Merchant) ships, she and her three sisters carried expendable fighters, usually Sea Hurricanes. The pilots had to be prepared to ditch or parachute near a friendly ship unless land was near.

See 1 November 1941.

1941 Light cruiser *Southampton* (wearing the White Ensign worn by the light cruiser *Southampton* at Jutland in 1916) bombed by German aircraft 180 miles E. of Malta; eighty men lost. Fires were soon uncontrollable and ship was abandoned. Survivors taken off by light cruiser *Gloucester* and destroyer *Diamond* which latter torpedoed her (34.54N, 18.24E). First of seven cruisers lost in the Mediterranean in 1941. 'The first major modern warship destroyed by aircraft while operating at sea' – Stephen Prince, Operation Excess.

1944 *Tally Ho*, submarine, sank Japanese cruiser *Kuma* in Malacca Strait off Penang (05.28N, 99.55E).

1954 HMY *Britannia* accepted from John Brown's at sea by A/Capt J.S. Dalglish and White Ensign hoisted. FORY's flag was in Shaw Saville liner *Gothic* for Royal Commonwealth Tour 1953–4.

See 20 June 1982.

1972 Formation of Commando Logistics Regiment RM.

12 JANUARY

1742 *Tiger* lost on Tortuga. Crew salvaged sufficient to live on for two months until their boats took a sloop in which they reached Jamaica.

1797 *Spitfire* captured the French *Allerger* 90 miles W. of Ushant.

1798 *Gorgon* recaptured the *Ann* brig off Dartmouth and captured the French privateer *Henri* 170 miles S.W. of Ushant next day.

1810 *Scorpion* captured the French *Oreste* off Basse Terre, Guadeloupe.
Battle Honour: *Oreste* 1810.

1832 Graham Island sank off Sicily.
See 1 August 1831.

1857 Admiral of the Fleet Horatio, Viscount Hornblower, lately C-in-C The Nore, died aged 80 and was buried in Nettlestead churchyard. Minute guns fired at Chatham Dockyard.

1905 The Australian Commonwealth Naval Board constituted.

1915 Capture of Mafia Island, German East Africa.

1918 Destroyers *Narbrough* and *Opal* wrecked in a gale on Hesta Head, Pentland Skerries, E. of Ronaldsay outside Scapa Flow.

'My poor two destroyers had a terrible ending. They tried to make the anchorage in a blinding snowstorm which, of course, was wrong, and they paid the penalty, both running full tilt on to the rocks, where they were battered to pieces in a very short time. Only one survivor out of 180. . .' – Admiral Beatty to Lady Beatty, 17 January 1918. The event recorded as a short story by Bartimeus, 'The Survivor', in his book *Navy Eternal*.

1922 *Victory* moved into No. 2 Dock in Portsmouth Yard, the oldest dry dock in the world, following a national appeal launched by the Society for Nautical Research.

1934 Battleship *Nelson*, flagship of Admiral Sir William Boyle, C-in-C Home Fleet, leaving from Portsmouth for the Spring Cruise to the West Indies, went aground at high water on the Hamilton Bank outside the harbour entrance. Tugs assisted by the wash of seven destroyers steaming past at full speed and the ship's company fallen in aft jumping up and down failed to move her. A signal from the Submarine Base at Fort Blockhouse inviting the battleship's officers to consider themselves honorary members of the *Dolphin* Mess for the while did not help.

1939 The first aircraft to land on carrier *Ark Royal* – Swordfish of 820 NAS led by Lt-Cdr A.C.G. Ermen RN.

1942 Submarine *Unbeaten* sank U-374 off Cape Spartivento.

1945 Minesweeper *Regulus* sunk by mine off Corfu. Both propellers blown off.

1945 Assault on Myebon, Burma. Operation Pungent. Ships: *Napier* (RAN), *Jumna* and *Narbada* (RIN), HDML 1248, ML 854.

In January 1945 the Japanese were being driven from Burma, and 3rd Cdo Brigade, Royal Marines was sent by sea to secure Myebon. This was achieved with some opposition. They were then relieved by Army units and launched an attack by landing craft along 27 miles of river to Kangaw. They achieved surprise and captured the hills overlooking the beaches, cutting off the Japanese Army. On the 31st the Japanese attacked and kept up the attacks on Hill 170 for thirty-six hours with waves of Banzai charges.

At the end of the battle the ground was thick with Japanese dead, but the hill was still held by 41 and 42 Cdos. Special order of the day: 'The Battle of Kangaw has been the decisive battle of the whole Arakan campaign, and that it was won was largely due to your magnificent courage on Hill 170', by GOC XV Corps.

1949 New RN Hospital built 1,377ft up on The Peak, Hong Kong, to replace its war-damaged predecessor, received its first patients.
See 23 March 1830, 1 November 1959.

1950 *Truculent* sank after collision with MV *Divina* in Thames estuary. First submarine lost after the Second World War. AM: Lt F. Hindes and Chief E.R.A. Hines. Posthumous.

Admiral of the Fleet Sir John Tovey. (*RN*)

1952 Royal Naval Mine Watching Service instituted.

1964 A Marxist coup in newly independent Sultanate of Zanzibar. The frigate *Rhyl*, with soldiers of the Staffordshire Regt., the surveying ship *Owen* and the RFA *Hebe* remained at Zanzibar until 20 January to cover the evacuation of 130 British nationals to Mombasa. Situation remained tense for several months requiring frequent visits by Royal Navy ships.

See 20 January 1964.

1968 Submarine *Alliance*, returning from exercises, ran aground on the Bembridge Ledge on the Isle of Wight. Refloated after forty-eight hours. Captain dismissed his ship.

1971 Admiral of the Fleet John Cronyn Tovey, first Baron Tovey of Langton Matravers, died at Funchal, Madeira, aged 86. C-in-C Home Fleet 1940–3; with the battleships *King George V* (flag) and *Rodney* he sank the *Bismarck* in 1941. Buried at Swanage. Peerage became extinct.

See 7 March 1885.

1999 Frigate *Norfolk* with RM FSRT deployed to support government of Sierra Leone in operations against rebel forces. Relieved by frigate *Westminster* (Atlantic Patrol Ship South) 3 February until 18 March. Supported by RFAs *Oakleaf*, *Gold Rover*, *Grey Rover*. One destroyer/frigate and one RFA on station at a time. Operation Basilica.

13 January

1794 *Sphinx* captured the French *Trompeuse* 120 miles S.W. of Cape Clear.

1797 *Amazon* and *Indefatigable*, Capt E. Pellew, drove ashore and wrecked the French *Droits de l'Homme* in Audierne Bay, Brittany, returning from Hoche's Irish expedition. *Amazon* also wrecked.
Battle Honour: *Droits de l'Homme* 1797.

1855 *Bittern* and her boats destroyed two pirate junks off Flap (Flat) Island, near Foochow.

1873 Review of Fleet at Portsmouth by Shah Nasr-ed-din of Persia in whose honour the armoured frigate *Blonde*, ready for launching at Portsmouth Dockyard, was renamed *Shah*. The new name, hastily painted on the ship's stern, was rendered upside down. 'Somebody would have been shortened by a head if the Dockyard officers had been subjects of the potentate concerned' – Ballard.
See 29 May 1877.

1901 Operations in Gambia River by cruiser *Forte*, and gunboats *Dwarf* and *Thrush*, which all landed armed parties.

1915 Minesweeper *Roedean* mined and sunk at Longhope.

1928 The morning after the notorious ball on board *Royal Oak*, second flagship of the First Battle Squadron, Mediterranean Fleet, in Grand Harbour, Valletta, during which Rear-Admiral B. St G. Collard swore at Bandmaster

The Chaung beachhead at Kangaw established by RM Engineer Cdo to supply the Commando on Hill 170. See 12 January 1945. (*NMRN 7/19/8(20)*)

HMS *Shah* (1873), anchored in Portsmouth harbour. (*NMRN*)

Percy Barnacle (a godsend to music hall comedians) on the quarterdeck and set in motion a 'seismic disturbance' (Roskill) and naval cause célèbre.

Allegations against Collard by Capt Dewar and Cdr Daniel (Flag Captain and Commander respectively) led to Admiral Sir Roger Keyes, C-in-C Mediterranean Fleet, delaying the sailing of the Fleet on 10 March for combined exercises with the Atlantic Fleet and convening a Court of Inquiry. Collard was ordered to strike his flag and Dewar and Daniel were relieved. The Board decided to place Collard on the Retired List. Dewar and Daniel were court-martialled on board *Eagle* on 4 April 1928 while the combined fleets were at Gibraltar and in the glare of world press attention. Both officers were severely reprimanded and dismissed their ship. The episode was 'one of those, happily rare, occasions when the Royal Navy has made a public fool of itself' (Roskill, *Naval Policy between the Wars*, vol.1, p.47) and contributed to Keyes' being denied the post of first sea lord when Madden retired in July 1930. *The Times* expressed 'relief and thankfulness' that the affair was over, but remarked 'with regret and astonishment sharpened by impatience that the elaborate ceremonial and procedure of naval justice should have been engaged by things of so little moment'. 'For the Royal Navy, which instinctively shuns publicity, the whole episode had been an undeserved and intollerable humiliation, deeply and widely resented' – Aspinal-Oglander, *Roger Keyes*, p.198. Collard had gained earlier notoriety in 1906 when reprimanded for his part in the 'On the knee' incident at RN Barracks, Portsmouth.

See 4 November 1906, 5 April 2007.

1942 *Aphis*, river gunboat, bombarded Halfaya Pass in support of the Army.

1943 *Ville de Québec* (RCN), corvette, sank U-224 off Cape Tenez. Convoy TE 13.

1944 Wellington L/172 sank U-231 in N.W. Atlantic.

1968 NATO Standing Naval Force Atlantic (STANAVFORLANT) formed at Portland.

14 January

1676 Boats of Cdre Sir John Narbrough's squadron destroyed four Algerine men-of-war at Tripoli. Ships: *Harwich, Henrietta, Portsmouth*.

1694 *Conquest*, a merchantman with eight guns, fought a French 26-gun ship for six hours off the mouth of the Tagus, and rammed her. The survivors escaped to Lisbon.

1809 Capture of Cayenne in French Guiana by Capt James Lucas Yeo (*Confiance*) and Portuguese troops.
Battle Honour: Cayenne 1809.

1846 *Amphion* launched at Woolwich. The first screw frigate converted to steam while on the stocks.

1848 Boats of *Philomel* captured the slaver *Wandering Jew* off the Gallinas (Kife) River, Sierra Leone.

1917 *Penshurst* (Q 7) sank UB-37 20 miles off Cherbourg (50.07N, 01.47W).

1918 Submarine G 8 lost in North Sea.

1918 German destroyer raid on Yarmouth.

1919 Meritorious Service Medal instituted for ratings. Withdrawn in 1928.

1941 GC: Probationary Temporary/Sub-Lt John Bryan Peter Miller, RNVR, Probationary Temporary/Sub-Lt William Horace Taylor, RNVR, AB Stephen John Tuckwell. (*Gazette* date.) Bomb and mine disposal.

1942 *Triumph* reported lost. Presumed sunk by mine in the south Aegean. First of eighteen submarines lost in 1942.
See 16 February 1938.

1943 Destroyers *Hursley* and *Pakenham* and Beaufort aircraft sank the Italian S/M *Narvalo* S.E. of Malta. Convoy ME 15.

Washing clothes in the battleship HMS *Duncan*, 1901. (*NMRN*)

A Victorian Navy capital ship: HMS *Minotaur* photographed off Milford Haven in about 1883. With *Agincourt* and *Northumberland* she was one of the longest and largest single-screw fighting ships ever built or rigged with five masts.(*Author*)

1943 New Admiralty post of Chief of Naval Information established to plan and coordinate all forms of naval publicity. Admiral Sir William James, lately C-in-C Portsmouth, first in post. He was returned as MP for Portsmouth North the following month.

See 17 February 1943, 13 August 1965, 17 August 1973.

1969 Phantom Training Unit, 767 NAS, Lt-Cdr Peter Marshall RN, formed at RNAS Yeovilton to train aircrew for the first operational unit, 892 NAS, which commissioned in March 1969.

See 30 April 1968.

1991 The first Wrens to serve at sea as members of a ship's company sailed in the frigate *Brilliant*. Operation Granby.

See 8 October 1990, 24 January 1991.

1999 Frigate *London* arrived alongside the cruiser *Belfast* in the Pool of London on her last visit to the capital before transfer to Romania.

2008 The formidable Polish-born Rear-Admiral Jozef Czeslaw Bartosik, DSC, died aged 90. Jo Bartosik joined the Polish Navy in 1935 and served in Polish destroyers under RN command in the Second World War (DSC for Arctic Convoys). He transferred to the RN in 1948. Commanded destroyer *Comus* 1955–6, *Scarborough* and Fifth Frigate Squadron 1960–1, *Seahawk*, RNAS Culdrose 1962–3 and destroyer *London* 1964–5. Bartosik was promoted rear-admiral on 7 July 1966 and appointed to the new post of ACNS(Ops). Retired 1968.

See 19 April 1900, 6 November 2008.

Lt Jeremy Black was appointed Gunnery Officer of *Comus*, Cdr J.C Bartosik DSC, RN, which recommissioned in Singapore in 1955. It was not a happy commission. 'Commander Bartosik was extremely hard on his officers and made their life a misery . . . [they] came in for the thick end of his very demanding, bullying and uncaring style of conducting the business of running his ship. . . Had I been more senior at the time, say a First Lieutenant, I think I would have resigned my commission . . . Reluctantly, I have to say the *Comus* was an efficient ship, but though not lacking in efficiency under Bartosik's command, she was a ship devoid of kindness and mutual respect' – Admiral Sir Jeremy Black, *There and Back*, (2005).

15 January

1704 *Lyme* (32), escorting a convoy, fought off a French 46-gun ship 6 miles S.W. of Dodman Point.

1743 *Sapphire* sank two and severely damaged three Spanish privateers at Vigo.

1761 Following the loss of several ships in a New Year's Day hurricane, Rear-Admiral Charles Stevens resumed the siege of Pondicherry which, reduced by famine, surrendered on 15 January. 'Thus ended the French power on the coast of Coromandel' – Laird Clowes, *The Royal Navy*, vol.3, pp.224–5. The Seven Years War.
See 1 January 1761, 16 October 1778.

1815 Emma, Lady Hamilton, died at Calais.
See 6 May 1831.

1815 The big American frigate *President* (44), Capt Stephen Decatur, surrendered to British warships blockading New York.
See 24 December 1814.

Decatur slipped out of New York in a snowstorm on 14 January in a vain attempt to elude the British blockade but was seen and chased. A running engagement with *Endymion* (40) led to a brisk action 70 miles S.E. by S. of Long Island in which both ships sustained damage and heavy casualties. *Endymion* could not continue the chase but the *President* was overhauled by two Royal Navy 38-gun frigates. After a few token broadsides *President* struck to *Pomone* and was boarded by *Tenedos*. This capture in the last months of the War of 1812 was a PR coup for the Royal Navy. This was the last Gold Medal action and the only one for the action in American waters.

1822 Establishment of HM Coastguard by Treasury minute, putting under the Board of Customs the Preventive Water Guard, the Riding Officers and the Revenue Cruisers.

1915 Air attack on U-boat at Zeebrugge Mole.

1922 Reconstitution of HM Coastguard.

1941 880 Squadron FAA became first operational users of Sea Hurricane.

1942 Destroyer *Hesperus* sank U-93 off Cape St Vincent.

1942 GC: Lt George Herbert Goodman MBE, RNVR, for dismantling Italian self-destroying torpedo.

The Sea Hurricane, the first British single-seat monoplane fighter operated from Royal Navy aircraft carriers. It was also deployed in catapult aircraft merchantmen in the Battle of the Atlantic. (*FAAM*)

A RN Polaris missile, launched from a submerged submarine. (*NMRN*)

1942 Swordfish of 815 Squadron FAA sank U-577 N.W. of Mersa Matruh (32.40N, 25.48E).

1945 Escort carrier *Thane* torpedoed by U-482 off the Clyde lightvessel. Towed in by *Loring*, but found to be damaged beyond repair.

1953 HRH The Duke of Edinburgh appointed an Admiral of the Fleet. He made his first public appearance in the uniform on 16 March 1953 when welcoming Marshal Tito of Yugoslvia to London.

See 16 July 1950, 30 June 1952.

1957 RNVR Air Branch to be disbanded. Cost to RN was eleven squadrons and 100 aircraft, 401 pilots and observers, 300 other officers and 426 ratings. No more national servicemen to be trained as aircrew.

See 18 February 1957.

1969 The first Type 42 destroyer, *Sheffield*, laid down at Vickers, Barrow.

See 4 May 1982.

1986 HMY *Britannia*, with *Newcastle*, *Jupiter* and *Hydra* and French and Soviet ships evacuated refugees from S. Yemen.

2004 Chief Naval Judge Advocate post abolished and replaced by Director of Naval Legal services. After this date the Royal Navy had no uniformed Judge Advocates following a judgement by the European Court of Human Rights.

See 16 December 2003, 1 January 2008.

16 JANUARY

1636 *Sovereign of the Seas* laid down.

1668 Samuel Pepys wrote in his *Diary* 'So little care there hath been to this day to know or keep any history of the Navy.' – *Diary*, IX, p.26.

1780 Admiral Sir George Bridges Rodney (*Sandwich*) defeated eleven Spanish sail of the line under Admiral Don Juan de Langara (*Fénix*) 12 miles S. of Cape St Vincent.
Battle Honour: St Vincent 1780.
Captured: *Diligente, Fénix, Monarca, Princesa.* Captured but wrecked: *San Eugenio, San Julian.* Blew up: *Santo Domingo.* Ships: *Ajax, Alcide, Alfred, Bedford, Bienfaisant, Culloden, Cumberland, Defence, Edgar, Invincible, Marlborough, Monarch, Montagu, Prince George, Resolution, Royal George, Sandwich, Terrible.* Frigates: *Andromeda, Apollo, Hyena, Pegasus, Triton.*

The Moonlight Battle 1780

The Royal Navy entered a more offensive phase during the War of American Independence when Admiral Rodney was sent with a strong squadron to escort a convoy to relieve Gibraltar and Minorca, and then to reinforce the West Indies station. Off Cape Finisterre he encountered a Spanish convoy of seventeen merchant and five warships, which he captured on 8 January. Eight days later he sighted a squadron of eleven Spanish warships, off Cape St Vincent. The Spanish steered for Cadiz and were chased 'as they came up, and from leeward': one blew up and six were taken. The first fleet action to be fought at night. The outcome was a British victory which resulted in an easing of the pressure on Gibraltar. From the Mediterranean, Rodney sailed for the West Indies, where two years later he was to transform the Royal Navy's battle tactics at the Battle of the Saintes.

1798 Boats of *Babet* captured the French schooner *Désirée* between Dominica and Martinique.

1799 *Flora* recaptured the British merchant brig *Nymph* 120 miles N.N.E. of Cape Ortegal, N.W. Spain.

1808 *Linnet* captured the French privateer *Courrier* 30 miles E. of Cape Barfleur.

1809 *Melampus* captured the French *Colibri* 160 miles N.E. of Barbuda, West Indies.

1809 Death of Sir John Moore at Corunna, covering the embarkation of the Army.

1814 *Venerable* (74) *Cyane* (22) and *Jason* (32) captured French frigate *Alemene* 200 miles S.S.W. of Madeira. *Cyane* pursued second French frigate *Iphigenie* (40).
See 20 January 1814.

1849 Admiralty Circular No. 46 promulgated award of GCBs for ratings after five, ten and fifteen years, with extra pay of 1*d*, 2*d* and 3*d* respectively. Pay but not badge forfeited on advancement to PO until 1857.

1855 The paddle yacht *Victoria and Albert* launched. This second royal yacht of the name built at Pembroke Dockyard served Queen Victoria for the rest of the monarch's life.
See 26 April 1843, 9 May 1899.

1873 RN College, Greenwich established by Order in Council.

1894 *Havock*, first torpedo boat destroyer, accepted into service.

1901 *Sybille*, second-class cruiser, wrecked in Lambert's Bay, South Africa, day after landing a Naval Brigade. One man lost.

1911 Super Dreadnought *King George V* laid down at Portsmouth and her sister ship *Centurion* laid down at Devonport. The *Centurion* was finally scuttled off Normandy on D-Day in 1944 to form a breakwater for landing craft.

1914 Submarine A 7 lost, diving into mud in Whitesand Bay.

1917 The greatest naval intelligence coup ever. Germany planned to declare unrestricted submarine warfare on 1 February and hoped to keep the US neutral. The famous Zimmerman telegram from Berlin to the German ambassador in Mexico offering the return of the former Mexican territories of Texas, New Mexico and Arizona if Mexico entered the war on the German side, was intercepted by Room 40, the Intelligence Division at the Admiralty.

Admiral Lord Rodney (1718–1792)

George Bridges Rodney entered the Royal Navy in 1732 and was made post in 1743 aged 25. His victories over the Spanish in the Moonlight Battle (16 January 1780) and over the French at The Saintes (12 April 1782) raised him to high rank and the peerage but he was never popular in the Navy. Rodney seemed unable to work harmoniously with subordinate flag officers and captains. However, he cooperated splendidly with the Army; few admirals could have landed 14,000 troops in twenty-four hours as Rodney did at Martinique. David Syrett, who edited Rodney's private papers for the Navy Records Society, describes him as 'overbearing, avaricious, difficult and uncongenial'. He treated his peers with hauteur and 'attributed to others just those qualities of avarice and malice which independent observers thought characteristic of him' (Nicholas Rodger). He had an 'extraordinary talent for self-destruction'. Rodney was an uncontrolled spender and his later life was plagued with debts and moneylenders. Contemporaries were disgusted by what they saw as 'his degrading obsession with money'. He was even accused of hazarding Caribbean naval operations in quest of prize money. 'As a man of action and a fighter he is universally accepted', writes his biographer David Spinney, but 'there was an aura of dissipation about him . . . and more than a whiff of corruption' (see 14 October 1780). For all that, Rodney's career spanned the Wars of the Austrian Succession, the Seven Years War and the War of American Independence through all of which he proved a resolute sea officer, a fine tactician and took great care of his men. He was one of the great British naval commanders of the eighteenth century. He died on 24 May 1792.

See 3 July 1759, 16 February 1762.

The publication of the telegram on 1 March outraged the American public and the US declared war on 6 April. 'No other single cryptanalysis has had such enormous consequences . . . Never before or since has so much turned upon the solution of a secret message' – David Kahn, *The Codebreakers*.

1943 Fortress G/206 sank U-337 in N. Atlantic. Convoys ONS 160 and ON 161. By now Coastal Command was operating ninety-six four-engined A/S bombers, twenty-four of them USAAF, a significant increase in its striking power. USN aircraft were also under command.

1945 *Amethyst*, *Hart*, *Loch Craggie*, *Peacock* and *Starling* sank U-482, 6 miles off Machrihanish.

1945 Russian *Deiatelnyi* (ex-*Churchill*) sunk by U-997 with homing torpedo 60 miles E. of Kola Inlet.

1962 Fleet carrier *Ark Royal*, Capt D.C.E.F. Gibson RN, returning from the Mediterranean, grounded in Plymouth Sound on her way up the deep water channel to Devonport Dockyard. Survey by *Shackleton* on 18 January found two buoys marking the channel were out of position. Courts martial of CO and NO at Plymouth 23, 24, 27 and 28 February. Reprimands. Findings quashed on review. Civil Lord of the Admiralty in Parliamentary Written Answer on 20 July said 'the evidence did not support the findings'.

See 9 October 1970.

1968 Prime Minister Harold Wilson announced that British forces would be withdrawn from the Far East and Persian Gulf within three years although there would be frequent visits by the Royal Navy East of Suez thereafter.

1986 Last pay parade, in *Raleigh*. Cash no longer put onto cap or into hand, but credited to ratings' accounts.

1987 Hard luck for ships' companies of frigate *Torquay* and RMAS *Sheepdog*. Amended DCI(RN) corrected unit value of salvage shares: For £1,831 read £1.831, and for £1,381 read £1.381.

See 5 December 1986, 9 January 1987.

17 JANUARY

1682 *Adventure* and *James Galley* drove ashore and burned the Algerine *Flower Pot* near Mazagran, Algeria.

1773 Capt James Cook made first crossing of the Antarctic Circle.

1794 *Pigot* East Indiaman beat off the French privateers *Vengeur* and *Résolue* at Benkulen, Sumatra, after two brisk hours.

1799 *Flora* recaptured the American merchant ship *Six Sisters* 80 miles N.N.E. of Cape Ortegal, N.W. Spain.

1813 *Narcissus* (32) took the USS *Viper* (18) off Havana.

1862 Boats of *Falcon* and a detachment of the 2nd West India Regiment destroyed Mafengbi and Majohn up the Kate (Ribbi) River, Sierra Leone.

1871 David Beatty, the future Admiral of the Fleet, Earl Beatty, born.

1885 Battle of Abu Klea, Sudan. Naval Brigade from *Helicon*, *Iris* and *Monarch*, under Lord Charles Beresford in attempt to relieve General Gordon. Egyptian Medal: clasp 'Abu Klea'.

1895 The Navy League founded in London 'to urge upon government and the electorate the paramount importance of an adequate navy as the best guarantee of peace'.

1904 Admiral of the Fleet Sir Harry Keppel, Queen Alexandra's 'beloved little Admiral', died.
See 14 June 1809, 26 June 1902.

1912 Capt R.F. Scott reached the South Pole.

Robert Falcon Scott was born in Devonport and entered the Navy in 1882. In 1900–4 he led the National Antarctic Expedition and in 1911 a second expedition in an attempt to reach the South Pole. Beset by many misfortunes, defective equipment and ill health, he made the final assault on foot in the company of 'Birdie' Bowers, 'Titus' Oates, Edgar Evans and 'Doc' Wilson. Enduring tremendous hardship in sub-zero temperatures they pressed on towards the Pole. On 17 January 1912 as they approached their goal they saw a flag fluttering in the cold wind – Amundsen the Norwegian explorer had got there first. Bitterly disappointed, the party set off back in appalling conditions and despite self-sacrifice and bravery, they perished only 11 miles from a depot. When Scott's diaries were found the whole tragic story was told and it elevated Scott and his men to a high place in British heroism. His widow was treated as if he had been knighted. Their son Peter served with distinction in Coastal Forces as Lieutenant-Commander RNVR.

1942 *Gurkha*, destroyer, fourth of the name and second in the Second World War, sunk by U-133 off Mersa Matruh (31.50N, 26.14E). Convoy MW 8B.
See 9 April 1940.

The decorative stern of HMS *Pitt* (ex-*Trafalgar* 1820) when used as a coal hulk in the 1880s. (*NMRN*)

The Type 42 destroyer HMS *Nottingham* in heavy weather in the Atlantic during high seas firing of her Sea Dart missile system in September 2004. (*RN*)

1942 Destroyer *Matabele* sunk by U-454 off Murmansk. Convoy PQ 8.

1942 Destroyer *Jupiter* sank the Japanese S/M I-16 in Sunda Strait, between Sumatra and Java. *Jupiter* sunk 28 February 1942.

1943 Submarine *United* sank the Italian destroyer *Bombardiere* N.W. of Marettimo, western Sicily (38.15N, 11.43E).

1944 Frigate *Glenarm* and destroyer *Wanderer* sank U-305 in Atlantic (49.39N, 20.10W).

1968 Following a major earthquake in Sicily the 7th MCM Squadron, *Walkerton* (Cdr Ian Powe RN), *Ashton*, *Stubbington*, *Crofton* and RFA *Sea Salvor*, arrived at Trapani on N.W. coast of the island from Malta with disaster relief stores, tents, food, blankets and medical supplies. A medical team of fifteen led by Surg-Cdr M. Boyle RN, had flown in ahead of the ships. The grateful community of Monte Vago in the mountains behind Trapani renamed their main street 'Via Commandante Powe' when it was re-built after being destroyed in the earthquake. Cdr Powe recalled 'renewed understanding and admiration for the manner in which Jolly Jack will take on any task he thinks worthwhile'.

See 12 August 1953, 14 September 1953.

1986 Diving Branch of the RNR to be established for Ships' Divers, Port Divers and Clearance Divers. DCI(RN) 9/86.

18 JANUARY

1691 Elias Waffe appointed the first Master shipwright of Plymouth Dock.

1695 *Adventure* and *Falmouth* captured the French *Trident* 30 miles N.W. of Pantelleria. *Plymouth* (Capt James Killigrew) also engaged. Killigrew, who was in command of the squadron, was killed while engaging the other French ship *Content*.

1695 *Carlisle* captured the French *Content* 70 miles W.N.W. of Marettimo, Sicily.

1801 *Garland*, assisted by boats of *Cyane*, *Daphne* and *Hornet*, captured the French *Eclair* in Trois Rivières Bay, Guadeloupe.

1806 The Dutch Settlement at the Cape of Good Hope, with all its Dependencies, surrendered.
See 10 January 1806.

1816 Boats of *Bann* captured the slaver *Rosa* off the mouth of the Gallinas (Kife) River, Sierra Leone.

1915 Submarine E 10 lost in North Sea.

1916 Submarine H 6, Lt. R.N. Stopford, sailed from Harwich to support an operation against Zeppelin sheds at Hoyer on the Schleswig coast but early next morning she ran aground at Schiermonnikoog off Ameland in the West Frisian Islands. The destroyers *Firedrake*, with Capt A.K. Waistell, Captain S8, embarked, and *Medea* came to her assistance. The boat's position so close to German bases on the Ems made salvage inpractical and a boat from *Medea* took off the CBs and two officers and key senior rates, leaving Stopford to arrange his boat's internment in neutral Netherlands. The boat was refloated in February 1916 by the Dutch who bought her from the British government and commissioned her into the Royal Netherlands Navy as 0-8. The submarine was scuttled at Willemsoord/Den Helder in May 1940 ahead of the German advance. The Germans salvaged her and in turn commissioned her into the Kriegsmarine as UD-1. She was scuttled at Kiel on 3 May 1945. The submarine had been built in 1915 by Canadian Vickers at Montreal.

1918 *Campanula*, sloop, sank UB-66 off Sicily (35.35N, 14.39E).

HMS *Wilton* (1972). (*NMRN W&L 3080*)

Cap badge of the RNXS showing landing mine. (*NMRN*)

1919 The Admiralty announced a scheme for junior naval officers, whose education had been interrupted by the war, to spend two terms at Cambridge University. Kipling wrote in *The Scholars*: 'Hallowed river, most gracious trees, Chapel beyond compare, Here be gentlemen tired of the seas – take them into your care, Far have they come, much have they braved, give them their hour of play'.

See 24 April 1915.

The first 400 officers, who wore uniform, went up at Easter Term 1919 with one Private, Royal Marines, per ten officers, to look after them. These numbers proved too great to be absorbed and were reduced to about 140 a term. The Admiralty made it clear that, as they were subject to KR&AI, they could not also be disciplined by the university. Trinity, Selwyn and Corpus objected, pointing out that their constitutions long pre-dated the foundation of the Royal Navy. The issue was squared away by the First Lord in consultation with the three Masters concerned and the scheme settled down under the command of Capt (later Admiral Sir Eric) E.J.A. Fullerton RN based at the Royal Navy Office, 22 Silver Street. The last of 1,200 officers went down after Lent Term 1923. 'It was a happy idea sending us to Cambridge. I think it civilised us a bit after four years of war and in some queer way made us normal again . . . Cambridge took us in her stride and taught us a lot' – Capt Eric Bush RN, *The Flowers of the Sea*, p.253.

1942 HM Trawlers *Erin* and *Honjo* sunk and *Imperialist* damaged in Gibraltar, not by frogman as first thought but by a bomb placed in a depth charge in *Erin* by a dockyard worker, who was executed.

1954 Admiral The Earl Mountbatten received the Freedom of the City of Edinburgh. He mentioned that the First Sea Lord, Admiral of the Fleet Sir Rhoderick McGrigor, was a Scot as were his three predecessors. Sir John Lang, Permanent Secretary of the Admiralty, was another. 'What is more, you have chosen, as High Commissioner of the General Assembly of the Church of Scotland, our most distinguished admiral of the fleet, Lord Cunningham, whose banner hangs in the Thistle Chapel here. So it is beginning to look like a closed shop.'

See 27 September 1945.

1963 Change of title of the RN Minewatching Service (RNMWS) to RN Auxiliary Service (RNXS). AFO 99/62.

See 6 December 1952.

1972 Mine Countermeasures Vessel *Wilton*, the world's first warship built from glass reinforced plastic (GRP) launched by Vosper Thornycroft at Woolston, Southampton. Similar to the Ton-class, she cost £2.25 million although fitted with reconditioned machinery and equipment taken from the scrapped *Derrington*. She entered service with MCM2 at Vernon and in 1991 became the Dartmouth Training Ship. She paid off at Portsmouth 27 July 1994 and was sold in August 2001. She is now moored at Leigh on Sea and employed as the headquarters ship of the Essex Yacht Club.

19 January

1759 *Ripon* engaged the St Pierre forts, Martinique, and had to be towed off after a three-hour struggle.

1762 Harrison's fourth chronometer passed first Board of Longitude test (*Deptford*) at Jamaica.

1826 Capture of Melloon (Minhla) by the Irrawaddy flotilla and troops. Flotilla: *Diana* steamer, boats of *Alligator* and others and Hon. East India Company's gunboats. Troops: 13th, 38th, 41st, 47th, 87th and 89th Regiments, Bengal and Madras Artillery, Bengal Engineers, Madras Pioneers, 18th, 28th and 43rd Madras Native Infantry.
Battle Honour: Burma 1824–26.

During the operations connected with this First Burmese War which began in 1824, *Diana* became the first steam vessel to be employed in military operations. Ships: *Alligator, Arachne, Boadicea, Champion, Larne, Liffey, Sophia, Stanley, Tamar, Tees.*

See 9 February 1825.

1839 Aden seized by the government of Bombay; the first accession of territory in Queen Victoria's reign. Crown Colony from 1937.
Battle Honour: Aden 1839.

See 21, 26 and 29 November 1967.

1875 *Nassau* and *Rifleman* captured Fort Mozambique, Mombasa.

1917 Submarine E 36 lost in North Sea, possibly in collision with E 43.

1918 UB-22 sunk by mine off Heligoland.

1918 Submarine H 10 lost in North Sea.

1940 Destroyer *Grenville* sunk by mine 23 miles off the Kentish Knock, Thames estuary (51.39N, 02.17E). First of thirty-four RN destroyers lost in 1940.

1941 *Greyhound*, destroyer, sank the Italian S/M *Neghelli* off Phalconera.

1941 Battleship *Prince of Wales* commissioned at Birkenhead on a Sunday. It was to be the shortest commission of any British battleship.

See 4 May 1939, 1 January 1937, 10 December 1941.

1943 *Antelope* and *Port Arthur* (RCN) sank the Italian S/M *Tritone* off Bougie. Convoy MKS 6.

1944 *Violet*, corvette, sank U-641 in North Atlantic (50.15N, 18.49W). Convoys OS 65/KMS 39.

1945 *Porpoise* sunk, probably by aircraft, Malacca Strait. Last of seventy-four large RN submarines lost in action in the Second World War. Altogether, 341 officers and 2,801 ratings were lost in action in submarines in the Second World War; 50 officers and 310 ratings were made POW.

See 6 March 1945.

The chronometer 'H4' made by John Harrison (*c.* 1693–1776), which lost only five seconds on its 81-day test voyage. (*NMM*)

The escort carrier HMS *Hunter* ahead of the light cruiser HMS *Royalist* about to enter Keppel Harbour, Singapore, at the end of hostilities in 1945. (*Cdr David Hobbs RN*)

1960 Britain's first converted commando carrier, *Bulwark*, Capt R.D. Franks RN, commissioned at Portsmouth. After work-up she deployed to the Far East service with 42 Cdo and 848 NAS (Whirlwinds) embarked.

1998 An important day for British naval aviation. In the run up to the Strategic Defence Review, Admiral Sir Jock Slater, First Sea Lord, and Air Chief Marshal Sir Richard Johns, Chief of the Air Staff, signed a paper entitled 'Joint Force 2000' which agreed the continuing need for long range precision air attack, the importance of expeditionary operations and, of historic significance in that it was signed by CAS, the need for carrier-borne air power; a major step towards the new fleet carriers.

See 30 July 1963.

2000 Rank of Second Sea Lord and CINCNAVHOME reduced from four-star to three-star. Admiral Sir John Brigstocke was succeeded by Vice-Admiral Peter Spencer, lately Controller of the Navy, on promotion; the first engineer to hold the appointment and perhaps the first engineer officer to be a C-in-C.

See 22 October 1963, 21 April 1970, 2 April 1979, 26 August 1989.

2001 Vice-Admiral Sir Roderick Macdonald, in 1959 the first Commander Sea Training at Portland under Peter Gretton, died aged 79. Roddy Macdonald was Flag Lieutenant to his father-in-law, Admiral of the Fleet Sir Algernon Willis, C-in-C Portsmouth, and in 1965 was Commander Naval Forces Borneo during the Indonesian Confrontation. He commanded the new frigate *Falmouth*, the Londonderry Squadron in *Galatea*, and the Type 82 destroyer *Bristol*.

See 21 February 1921.

As Captain of the Fleet at Northwood in 1971 he republished, with some of his own thoughts, the slim booklet 'Your Ship', distilled advice to new warship captains, first produced by Admiral Willis when Second Sea Lord in 1944: 'as a commanding officer you are an autocrat, and you are subject to the same temptations as an autocrat . . . You are treated with deference and ceremony. You may even find that your small jokes appear more successful than they have been in the past. This has the effect of accentuating your weaknesses, unless you watch yourself most carefully.' Admiral Macdonald's gifts as an artist flowered in his retirement on the Isle of Skye.

20 JANUARY

1615 Nicholas Downton (*New Year's Gift*), with three other East Indiamen, repulsed a Portuguese armada off Surat.

1735 John Jervis born, the future Admiral of the Fleet, the Earl of St Vincent.

1801 *Mercury* took fifteen merchantmen in convoy, bound to relieve the French Army in Egypt and then captured the French *Sans-Pareille* 20 miles N.W. of Minorca.

1814 *Venerable* (74) captured the French *Iphigenie* (40) 300 miles W.S.W. of Palma Island, Canary Islands. No casualties on either side. *Cyane* (22) was also awarded the medal, having chased the enemy since the engagement four days earlier.

See 16 January 1814.

1815 Earl St Vincent attained 'the 80th year of his age on Friday, the 20th of January, on which occasion his Lordship gave an elegant entertainment at Rochets-hall, in Essex, at which the Noble Admiral presided in perfect health and spirits' – *The Naval Chronicle*, vol.33, p.112.

1918 Monitors *Raglan* and M 28 sunk by *Sultan Selim* (ex-*Goeben*) off Imbros, outside the Dardanelles. *Medilli* (ex-*Breslau*) mined. *Lizard* and *Tigress* engaged.

1921 The large steam-driven submarine K5, Lt-Cdr J.A. Gaimes RN, lost with all fifty-seven hands 125 miles S.W. of the Scilly Isles 48.53N, 08.52W., while exercising with the Atlantic Fleet on its Spring Cruise to the Mediterranean. Cause unknown but the boat probably went into an uncontrollable dive and was crushed. The Atlantic Fleet – 6 battleships, 2 battlecruisers, 6 light cruisers, 17 destroyers and the carrier *Argus* – returning from the Mediterranean, hove-to on 20 March at the location of the submarine's loss, ships half-masted colours and the *Revenge*, flag of Vice-Admiral Sir Stanley Fremantle, held a memorial service. A volley was fired and officers and men marched off the quarterdeck to 'Land of Hope and Glory' – *The Times*.

1925 Embarrassingly unsuccessful attack trials on battleship *Marlborough* by aircraft, cruisers and battleships.

1936 Accession of King Edward VIII.

See 12 December 1936, 28 May 1972.

1941 The RNZN training establishment, HMNZS *Tamaki*, commissioned on Motuihe Island, Hauraki Gulf, which trained 6,000 New Zealand naval personnel in the Second World War.

See 4 February 1965.

A First World War postcard promoting the Royal Navy. The armoured cruiser HMS *Warrior* was lost at Jutland in 1916. (*Author*)

John Jervis: Admiral of the Fleet the Earl of St Vincent (1735–1823)

Admiral of the Fleet, the Earl St Vincent (1735–1823). (*NMRN 1971/12(39)*)

Jervis joined the Navy at the age of 14, was a Lieutenant at 20 and by 1795 was Admiral in command of the Mediterranean fleet blockading Cadiz. He had been made KB in 1782 for his spirited capture of the *Pégase* (74). In 1797 he defeated twenty-seven Spanish ships with fifteen of his own off St Vincent. For this he was created an earl. He was known as a firm disciplinarian, particularly in handling mutineers in the fleet during 1797 and 1798. In 1801 he was appointed First Lord of the Admiralty and during the Peace of Amiens concentrated his efforts on reforming the dockyards. His actions aroused much enmity, but succeeded in exposing the corruption that was rife, although the pruning almost killed the plant. Inevitably there were political repercussions and he was obliged to resign from the Admiralty in 1804. By 1806, after a change of government, St Vincent returned to become acting admiral of the fleet, but finally retired because of ill health in 1807. At the coronation of King George IV in 1821 he was promoted admiral of the fleet.

1942 *Deloraine*, *Katoomba*, *Lithgow* (all RAN) and the USS *Edsall* sank the Japanese S/M I-124 in the Timor Sea off Port Darwin.

1943 MTB 260 sank the Italian S/M *Santorre Santarosa* off Tripoli, Libya.

1946 Completion of operation to scuttle 110 surrendered U-boats in deep water 30 miles N. of Malin Head. Operation Deadlight.

1963 President Achmad Sukarno of Indonesia announced a policy of 'confrontation' with the new Malaysian Federation of Malaya, Singapore, British North Borneo and Sarawak. The start of the RN's last major operation in the Far East.

See 12 December 1962, p.706 panel.

1964 The overthrow of the government of Zanzibar was the forerunner of army mutinies in Tanganyika and later in Uganda and Kenya. Intervention by carriers *Albion*, *Victorious* and *Centaur*, destroyers *Cambrian* and *Diana*, frigates *Eskimo*, *Rhyl* and *Salisbury*, RFA *Tiderange*, 41 Cdo, 45 Cdo and army units. British Commander of Tanganyika Rifles conferred on board *Centaur* and decision made to storm mutineers' barracks at Colito outside Dar-es-Salaam. Destroyer *Cambrian* laid down diversionary fire with her 4.5-in guns and the Commandos went ashore in the carrier's Wessex A/S helicopters. One group of mutineers was rounded-up by a Wessex pilot waving a pistol from the cockpit window of his hovering aircraft. A battalion at Tabora, 340 miles up-country surrendered after Sea Vixens from *Centaur* made low-level passes over their barracks. In Dar-es-Salaam armed sailors helped the Commandos restore order. Deployment lasted until 19 March.

See 12 January 1964, 24 January 1968.

2007 The last Flag Officer Medway, Rear-Admiral William Alleyne 'Bill' Higgins, died. Son of Cdr Henry Gray Higgins, First World War submariner (DSO 1917). He entered the RN College on 1 September 1945 just in time to qualify for a war gratuity. Secretary to Capt Michael Le Fanu at *Ganges* and to Admiral Sir Terence Lewin when First Sea Lord; DGNPS, then Secretary of the D Notice Committee.

21 JANUARY

1782 *Hannibal* (50) surrendered to the French *Heros* off Sumatra.

1807 Boats of *Galatea* captured the French *Lynx* 10 miles E. of La Guaira, Venezuela, after a 15-mile chase by six of her boats.

1810 Boats of *Freija* cut out three French vessels and destroyed two batteries in Mahault Bay, Guadeloupe.

1810 *Amazon* captured the St Malo privateer *Général Perignon* 25 miles S. by E. of Belle Ile.

1833 All line-of-battle ships to replace as many casks as possible with new 4 cubic ft modular tanks. Originally for water, later for biscuit and meat.

1843 Tenders invited for RN's first 'iron war steamer' *Trident*. The Hon. East India Company already had one: *Nemesis*.

1857 Boxer's Metal Time Fuse adopted for RN.

1866 Parachute light balls design approved (fore-runner of starshell).

1887 Naval Intelligence Department started.

The Foreign Intelligence Committee, which had been set up in December 1882, became the Naval Intelligence Department, though 'to start a new department in the Admiralty was no easy task'. Beresford, a captain but Junior Lord of the Admiralty, played a considerable part in this development, resigning over the question of DNI's involvements. It is hard to exaggerate the importance of the creation of NID: it was the embryo of the Naval Staff; from it emerged the Trade Division, and its thinking was responsible for the War Course and the Staff Course. Until 1901 its name was always at the bottom of the Departmental List, but in the *Navy List* of April 1903 it appears as second only to the Secretary and the Hydrographer, and DNI became directly responsible to the First Sea Lord – a fact which probably impressed his peers more than the work he did.

1914 Flight of Lt J.W. Seddon from Medway to Plymouth in five and a half hours to help in salvage of A 7.

1918 Cdr Andrew Cunningham paid off the destroyer *Scorpion* of which he had taken command at Harwich on 11 January 1911. He joined her as a lieutenant and left her as commander (D).

'I left her with deep regret after seven years and three weeks. I am not unduly sentimental. Ships are expendable; but the *Scorpion* was a staunch little vessel. I knew all her particular idiosyncrasies, all her dents and patches, almost every bolt and rivet. Even now I think I could find my way blindfold along her upper deck.' – Admiral of the Fleet Viscount Cunningham of Hyndhope, *A Sailor's Odyssey*, p.87.

1920 *Topaze*, second-class cruiser, and sloops *Espiegle*, *Clio* and *Odin*, initially with *Ark Royal*, started a three-week classic combined operation by all three Services against the 'Mad Mullah' of Somaliland, a Naval Brigade storming his fort at Galbaribur.

1930 *St Genny*, rescue tug, foundered in the W. Approaches. Twenty-three lost. Five saved by her sister ship, *St Cyrus*, lost on a mine in the Humber eleven years later to the day.

HMS *Marlborough*, a Type 23 frigate, launched at Swan Hunter's shipyard on the Tyne on 21 January 1989. (*NMRN W&L 4733*)

WRNR degaussing specialists training in HMS *President*, London Division, RNR, in April 1973. Jennifer Phillips (centre) married another naval reservist and their daughter, Victoria Phillips, followed them into naval uniform. See 2 February. (*Author*)

1940 Cruiser *Liverpool* intercepted the Japanese mail steamer *Asama Maru* 35 miles off Tokyo and removed twenty-one German passengers. Japanese thereafter agreed to refuse passage in Japanese ships to German reservists trying to get back to Germany.

1940 Destroyer *Exmouth* sunk by U-22 off Tarbat Ness, in Moray Firth. Lost with all hands (58.18N, 02.25W).

1941 Monitor *Terror* and river gunboats *Gnat* and *Ladybird* bombarded Tobruk.

1943 Submarine P 212 (later *Sahib*) sank U-301 W. of Corsica.

1943 Andrew Browne Cunningham promoted admiral of the fleet: 'my Union Flag was hoisted in the *Maidstone* [at Algiers] at 8am on that date.'

1945 *Icarus*, destroyer, and *Mignonette*, corvette, sank U-1199 off the Wolf Rock. Convoy TBC 43.

1945 Assault on Ramree Island, Burma. Operation Matador. Ships: *Ameer, Flamingo, Kistna* (RIN), *Llanstephan Castle, Napier, Pathfinder, Phoebe, Queen Elizabeth, Rapid, Redpole, Spey*.

1955 The First Sea Lord, Admiral of the Fleet Sir Rhoderick McGrigor, installed as Rector of Aberdeen University. Following tradition, the Rector was carried shoulder-high by students to a public house to drink his health. The local constabulary had other ideas and barred the way. Snowballs and policemen's helmets were thrown. Police batons were drawn as the First Sea Lord and the Deputy Chief Constable faced one another across the heads of their respective troops over whom neither appeared to exercise effective command.

2008 Carrier *Illustrious* sailed from Portsmouth to lead the Orion 08 task group to the Far East but had to return two days later for repairs to main refrigeration plant. Nothing as serious as the Global 86 calamity of 2 April 1986.

22 JANUARY

1617 *Dolphin* armed merchantman beat off five Barbary corsairs in succession off Sardinia.

1783 *Hussar* (28) captured the French *Sibylle* (36) 120 miles S.E. by E. of Cape Henry, Virginia.

1794 *Britannia* and *Nonsuch* East Indiamen captured the French privateers *Vengeur* and *Résolu* N. of Thwartway Island, Sunda Strait.

1809 *Cleopatra* and *Jason* captured the French *Topaze* close off Pointe Noire, Guadeloupe.

1849 The Indus flotilla at the siege and capture of Multan. An IN Naval Brigade served in the siege batteries as a complete unit.

1865 Henry Francis Oliver born at Kelso, Roxburghshire. Entered the Service in *Britannia* 1878. Midshipman 21 January 1881; Admiral of the Fleet forty-seven years later to the day, 21 January 1928.

See 15 October 1965.

1879 Col Charles Pearson's column, including a Naval Brigade landed from the iron screw corvette *Active* on 19 November 1878, defeated a major Zulu force on the Inyezane River in the Anglo-Zulu War. First operational use of the Gatling gun by RN. In the action with another Zulu force at Isandlwana on the same day Signalman 2nd Class William Aynsley from *Active*, batman to Lt Berkeley Milne, the only naval casualty among the 1,300 British troops killed, 'was last seen backed against a wagon wheel defending himself with his cutlass'.

See 27 February 1881.

1901 Accession of King Edward VII.

1913 Launch at Armstrong Whitworth's Elswick yard of the battleship *Rio de Janeiro* for Brazil. In 1914 with the ship almost complete, Brazil 'repented of their bargain' and the ship was bought by Turkey with funds raised 'by enthusiastic public subscription' and renamed *Sultan Osman 1*. The Admiralty seized the ship

The Silver Jubilee of the carrier HMS *Ark Royal*. The guard paraded for the visit of The Queen to the ship at Portsmouth on 5 November 2010. (*RN*)

HMS *Agincourt* (1913). (*NMRN*)

on the outbreak of war and renamed her HMS *Agincourt*. The ship thus had three nationalities within one year. *Agincourt* carried her fourteen 12-in guns in seven turrets named after days of the week and was the last British battleship to carry 12-in guns although the Lord Clive-class monitors carried the same armament through the First World War.

1920 RN Dental Branch established by Order in Council.
See 19 October 1939.

1925 Lindsay Sutherland Bryson, future Controller of the Navy, born on a Glasgow council estate; he left school aged 14.
See 24 March 2005.

1944 Anzio Landing. Operation Shingle. Ships: *Albacore, Barmond, Barndale, Beaufort, Boxer, Bruiser, Bude, Bulolo, Cadmus, Cava, Circe, Crete, Delhi, Dido, Espiegle, Faulknor, Fly, Glengyle, Grenville, Hornpipe, Inglefield,* Janus,* Jervis, Kempenfelt, Laforey, Loyal, Mauritius, Orion, Palomares, Penelope, Prinses Beatrix, Rinaldo, Rothesay, Royal Ulsterman, Sheppey, Spartan,* St Kilda, Tetcott, Thruster, Twostep, Ulster Queen, Ultor, Uproar, Urchin, Waterwitch*. MLs: 121, 134, 295, 307, 338, 443, 554, 558, 565, 567, 569, 575, 581.
*Sunk.
Battle Honour: Anzio 1944.

1945 Assault on Kangaw, Burma. Ships: *Jumna* and *Narbada* (RIN), MLs: 416, 843, 854, 885, 892. 3rd Cdo Brigade: 42 and 44 RM Cdos, 1 and 5 Army Cdos.
See 31 January 1945, Memorable Date.

1960 Lord Carrington, newly appointed First Lord of the Admiralty and then little-known in the Fleet, left Portsmouth after a three-day acquaint visit. He and his private secretary, Mr P.D. Nairne, had worn the traditional Admiralty uniform of blue serge suit with naval buttons and peaked cap with the red badge, which caused some confusion about who was who. Mr Nairne was piped on board the coastal minesweeper *Shoulton* and shown round by the Captain, Lt-Cdr G.H. King RN, piped ashore again when the ship came back alongside and shown to his car by Rear-Admiral J.H. Unwin, Admiral Superintendent, with Lord Carrington trailing behind. Press coverage of Mr Nairne's visit caused red faces in Portsmouth Dockyard.

1965 'The Admiralty Board have approved the privilege of wearing plain clothes is to be extended to Leading Rates and below landing from HM Ships in Naval dockyard ports in the United Kingdom and in main Naval bases and refitting ports abroad.' – DCI(RN) 154/65.

1968 Frigates *Euryalus* and *Zest*, on passage from Beira to Gan, diverted to Mauritius following civil disorder in the capital.
See 24 January 1968.

2011 Officers and Ship's Company of *Ark Royal* marched through Portsmouth to the Guildhall to mark the close affiliation between the ship and her home port before she paid off.

23 JANUARY

A Memorable Date observed by 45 Cdo Royal Marines – Montforterbeek

1759 Bombardment of Basse Terre, Guadeloupe, by Cdre John Moore (*Cambridge*). Ships: *Berwick, Burford, Cambridge, Lion, Norfolk, Panther, Ripon, St George*. 50s and smaller: *Amazon, Bonetta, Bristol, Ludlow Castle, Renown, Roebuck, Spy, Winchester, Woolwich*. Bombs: *Falcon, Granado, Infernal, Kingfisher*.

1761 *Minerva* (36) captured the French *Warwick* (34) 90 miles N. by W. of Cape Penas, north coast of Spain.

1774 Lieutenants, having complained about the plainness of their uniform, were given white lapels and cuffs.

1798 *Melampus* captured the French *Volage* 100 miles W. of the Scilly Isles.

1801 *N.S. De Los Dolores*, ex-Spanish felucca (one gun) captured the Spanish guardacosta *Santa Maria* (six) near Cape Rosario, South America.

1805 Uniform regulations for surgeons made by Order in Council.

1814 *Astraea* and *Creole* fought the French *Étoile* and *Sultane* close off English Road, Mayo Island, Cape Verde Islands.

1833 Admiral Edward Pellew, Viscount Exmouth, died.

1861 A gun's crew of *Pelorus* at the defence of No. 3 Redoubt in front of Huirangi, New Zealand. Medal: New Zealand, 1860–1.

1906 David Luce, first submariner to sit on the Admiralty Board, first C-in-C Far East and First Sea Lord, born at Halcombe St Mary, Malmesbury, Wiltshire, son of Admiral John Luce who commanded the light cruiser *Glasgow* at Coronel and the Falklands in 1914.

See 1 November 1914, 17 June 1934, 22 February 1966, 6 January 1971.

1910 Admiral Lord Charles Beresford hauled down his flag and came on shore.

See 6 September 1919.

1917 Harwich Force fought the German 6th Destroyer Flotilla off the Schouwen lightvessel. *Simoom*, torpedoed by the German S 50, sunk by *Matchless*.

Ships: *Aurora, Centaur, Conquest, Cleopatra, Grenville, Manly, Mansfield, Matchless, Melpomene, Meteor, Milne, Moorsom, Morris, Nimrod, Penelope, Phoebe, Radstock, Rigorous, Rob Roy, Simoom, Sorceress, Starfish, Surprise, Undaunted.*

1935 Battlecruisers *Hood*, Capt F.T.B. Tower RN, flag of Rear-Admiral S.R. Bailey, damaged starboard side aft in collision with *Renown*, Capt H.R. Sawbridge RN, off Arosa Bay, N.W. Spain. Another example of an admiral's intentions being unclear. Courts martial in Great Cabin of *Victory* 26, 27 and 28 February; Admiral and Flag Captain 'Not Guilty' to hazarding charges; but the Admiralty unable 'to absolve them of all blame'. Capt Sawbridge dismissed his ship but Admiralty reduced to Severe Reprimand. There was bad feeling between the ships before and after collision.

See 22 June 1893.

1936 New light cruiser *Newcastle* named by the Duchess of Northumberland at Vickers

Admiral of the Fleet Lord Lewin of Greenwich (1920–1999). (*NMM Neg. No. D6958*)

HMS *Dauntless* taking part in sea trials during July 2009. (*BAE*)

Armstrongs, Walker-on-Tyne, but launched without ceremony. Invitations to guests had been cancelled due to national mourning for King George V who died three days earlier.

1942 Four Swordfish aircraft of 830 Sqn, Malta, under Lt F.H.E. Hopkins, in bad weather, torpedoed an escorted Italian storeship making for Tripoli, Libya.

1943 Bombardment of Zuara, Libya. Ships: *Cleopatra, Euryalus, Javelin, Jervis, Kelvin, Nubian.*

1944 Destroyer *Janus* sunk with heavy loss of life by German torpedo aircraft off Anzio. Operation Shingle.

1945 45 Cdo RM in action, Montforterbeek.

In January 1945 Allied forces were advancing north-east against the Germans in Holland. 1 Cdo Brigade was given the task of clearing the area of the left flank of the 7th Armoured Division between the Division and the River Maas. The Montforterbeek was a small stream running across the front, taking its name from the village of Montfort. A fine action was fought in this area by 45 Cdo. VC (posthumous) L/Cpl H.E. Harden, RAMC.

1999 Admiral of the Fleet Lord Lewin of Greenwich died, the outstanding naval officer of his generation; First Sea Lord, Chief of the Defence Staff and a Knight of the Garter. 'What I would most like to be remembered for is a real improvement in attitudes and mutual respect between officers and ratings, and the effect that this had on the well-being and efficiency of the Navy.' – TTL to ABS.

Si monumentum requiris, circumspice.

See 19 November 1920.

2007 *Dauntless*, second of the Type 45 air defence destroyers, launched at Govan by Lady Burnell-Nugent, wife of Admiral Sir James Burnell-Nugent, C-in-C Fleet.

See 19 May 1807, 1 February 2006, 27 November 2007, 2 December 2009.

24 January

1709 Admiral of the Fleet Sir George Rooke died. 'I do not leave much but what I leave was honestly gotten: it never cost a sailor a tear or the nation a farthing.'

1761 *Granado, Hound* and *Richmond* destroyed the French *Félicité* 3 miles N.E. of the Hook of Holland. Action on the 24th, when she ran ashore. Found abandoned on the 25th, and burned on the 26th.

1794 Cdr James Cook, eldest son of Capt James Cook RN, drowned off Portsmouth while returning in an open boat in heavy weather to his ship, the sloop *Spitfire*. His brother, Midshipman Nathaniel Cook, was lost in *Thunderer* (74) in the Caribbean 5 October 1780.

See 14 February 1779, 5 October 1780, 13 May 1835.

1915 The Battle of Dogger Bank. Vice-Admiral Sir David Beatty with the battlecruisers *Lion* (flag), *Tiger, Princess Royal, New Zealand* and *Indomitable*, and supporting forces, fought a running action with a German squadron commanded by Rear-Admiral Franz von Hipper (*Seydlitz*, flag) off the Dogger Bank. The German armoured cruiser *Blücher* was sunk and the two flagships severely damaged but the Germans were alerted to the vulnerability of capital ship magazines to flash from shellfire which they remedied before Jutland.
Battle Honour: Dogger Bank 1915.

1939 Cruisers *Exeter* and *Ajax* provided humanitarian aid after the earthquake at Concepción. Chilean government awarded forty-one medals in gold, silver and bronze to landing parties.

1940 *Gladiolus*, first Second World War Flower-class corvette, launched at Middlesbrough.

See 1 July 1940.

1941 Battleship *King George V* arrived in American waters with Viscount Hallifax, new British ambassador, on board; the first official intimation that the ship was in service.

1945 Clasp to Long Service and Good Conduct Medal introduced.

1945 Carrier-based air strikes on Japanese-held oil refineries at Palembang and Pladjoe, southern Sumatra, by aircraft from *Indomitable* (flag of Rear-Admiral Sir Philip Vian), *Indefatigable, Illustrious* and *Victorious*. 820, 849, 854, 857, 887, 888, 894, 1770, 1830, 1833, 1834, 1836, 1839 and 1844 NAS. Operation Meridian 1. Strikes repeated on 29 January.
Battle Honour: Palembang 1945.

HMS *Lion* (1910), Beatty's flagship at the action off the Dogger Bank. (*NMRN*)

Vice-Admiral Sir Frank Twiss (1910–1994). (*NMRN*)
See 26 January 1994.

1965 Winston Churchill died; First Lord of the Admiralty in two world wars.
See 18 December 1964.

To Lady Churchill: 'The Admiralty Board, the Royal Navy and the Royal Marines have learned with deepest regret of the death of Sir Winston Churchill and with grateful memories of his inspiring leadership offer their heartfelt sympathy to you and the members of your family. Truly can it be said of him that he forced every sea and land to be the highway of his daring. His unique contribution to Naval policy and the admiration and affection he inspired throughout the Fleet will always endure in the annals of the Navy.' – DCI(RN) 216/65.

1968 Destroyer *Cambrian* landed two armed platoons of sailors on Rodriguez Island, a dependency of Mauritius, to restore order following civil unrest after a cyclone. Fourteen ringleaders were taken to Mauritius in the RFA tanker *Tidereach*.
See 20 January 1964, 22 January 1968.

1972 Destroyer *Devonshire* made a 24-knot passage from Portsmouth to Copenhagen for the funeral of His late Majesty, King Frederik of Denmark, senior honorary admiral in the RN. Her men escorted His Majesty's body through the streets in sub-zero temperatures and bitter wind. *Devonshire* half-masted her colours and fired an 81-gun salute. The ancient title of King of the Goths and Vends ended; Queen Margrethe II was known only as Queen of Denmark after her coronation in July 1972.
See 17 September 1948.

1986 Last surviving naval VC of First World War, Rear-Admiral Sir Victor Crutchley (Ostend 9/10 May 1918), died aged 92 at Mappercombe near Bridport. Buried St Mary's church, Powerstock.

1991 Iraqi Mirage/Exocet and MiG-23 attack on Allied forward ships. Operation Granby. Attackers destroyed by Saudi F-15s, and no further Iraqi attacks on HM ships except by missiles.

1991 Board agreed to employment of WRNS as aircrew, originally in A/S helicopters.
See 14 January 1991.

1998 Iraq Crisis. *Invincible* and RFA *Fort Victoria* sent from Mediterranean to the Gulf and passed through Straits of Hormuz on 24 January. Operation Bolton. Two destroyers/frigates and one RFA oiler of Armilla Patrol joined the force and the MCM Group arrived in the Gulf on 13 February. The *Illustrious* group relieved the *Invincible* group on 8 March. Air sorties flown from carriers over southern Iraq 'no fly' zone. Operation Southern Watch/Jural. Carrier Group sailed from Gulf 16/17 April after RAF Tornadoes ashore increased in strength. MCM Group departed early May. Armilla Patrol remained. Ships: *Bridport, Coventry, Herald, Inverness, Invincible, Illustrious, Nottingham, Sandown, Somerset*. RFAs: *Bayleaf, Brambleleaf, Diligence. Fort Victoria, Fort George*, FAA Sqns: Sea Harrier: 800, 801; Sea King: 814, 820, 849 B Flight. RAF: Harrier GR7s embarked in carrier.

2006 Ice patrol vessel *Endurance*, Capt Nicholas Lambert RN, visited the Argentine port of Ushuaia in Tierra del Fuego, the first RN ship visit there since her namesake, the previous *Endurance*, Capt Nicholas Barker RN, called in January 1982. A joint commemoration was held in honour of the dead in the Falklands campaign of 1982.

25 JANUARY

1747 *Grand Turk* captured the St Malo privateer *Tavignon* 10 miles S. of Lizard Head.

1782 Rear-Admiral Sir Samuel Hood (*Barfleur*), who had seized his enemy's anchorage at Basse Terre, St Kitts, thrice repulsed an attack by Vice-Admiral Comte de Grasse (*Ville-de-Paris*) with twenty-nine sail of the line. Ships: *Ajax, Alcide, Alfred, America, Barfleur, Bedford, Belliqueux, Canada, Centaur, Intrepid, Invincible, Monarch, Montagu, Prince George, Prince William, Princessa, Prudent, Russell, Resolution, Shrewsbury, St Albans, Torbay*. Frigates, etc.: *Champion, Eurydice, Expedition, Gros Islet, Nymphe, Sibyl, Solebay*. Regiments: 13th, 28th, 69th. The Captain of *Resolution*, Robert Manners, regarded this as 'the most masterly manoeuvre he ever saw'.
Battle Honour: St Kitts 1782.

1783 *Fox* captured the Spanish *Santa Catalina* off Havana.

1788 Founding of Australia. Marines hoisted flag at Sydney Cove, New South Wales.

1798 *Mercury* captured the French privateer *Constance* 80 miles N.W. of Burling Island, Portugal.

Vice-Admiral Sir John 'Jacky' Fisher (1841–1920). (*NMRN*)

1841 John Arbuthnot Fisher, the future Admiral of the Fleet, Lord Fisher of Kilverstone, born at Rambodde, Ceylon. He hauled down his flag as First Sea Lord on 25 January 1910, his 69th birthday.

See 22 November 1880, 10 July 1920.

1841 Capt Sir Edward Belcher, HMS *Sulphur*, landed on Hong Kong Island 'at 15 minutes past 8 a.m. and being the *bona fide* first possessors, Her Majesty's health was drank [sic] with three cheers on Possession Point'.

1910 Admiral of the Fleet Sir Arthur Wilson VC, who had hauled down his flag as C-in-C Channel Fleet in March 1907, recalled to succeed Admiral of the Fleet Lord Fisher as First Sea Lord. The appointment had been gazetted on 2 December 1909 and was 'received with profound satisfaction by the Navy and the public'. But Wilson proved a dead hand at the Admiralty and 'the Sea Lords resented his obstinacy, high-handedness and secretiveness' – Marder, *From the Dreadnought to Scapa Flow*, vol.1, pp.211, 213. His incompetence during the Agadir crisis in 1911 stunned the government, and Churchill, who took over as First Lord

The fleet carrier HMS *Victorious* in dry dock in Singapore in 1964. (*Cdr David Hobbs RN*)

of the Admiralty in October 1911, sent Wilson back to Norfolk within the month.

See 4 March 1842, 4 March 1907, 23 August 1911, 25 May 1921.

1915 Battlecruisers *Repulse* and *Renown* laid down – an appropriate date, it being their progenitor's seventy-fourth birthday.

See 25 January 1841.

1917 German destroyer raid on Southwold and Wangford, Suffolk.

1917 AMC *Laurentic*, former White Star liner, mined and sunk 2 miles 070° from Fanad Point, Lough Swilly. The next *Laurentic* also taken as an AMC and sunk in N.W. Approaches 3 November 1940.

1942 *Bruno Heinemann* sunk by mine laid by *Plover* W. of Ostend.

1943 *Corncrake* foundered in N. Atlantic.

1963 AFO 150/63: Medical Treatment of Snake-Bite. 'For many years conflicting recommendations have been made for the first-aid treatment of snake-bite . . . Early in 1961 the Board of the British Red Cross Society asked the Royal Society of Tropical Medicine and Hygiene for advice . . . The following recommendations were made: 1. Kill the snake . . .'

1964 45 RM Cdo landed at Dar-es-Salaam to suppress mutiny in Tanganyika Rifles. Relieved by 41 Cdo.

2006 Fleet submarine *Spartan*, Cdr Paul Halton RN, departed Clyde Naval Base at the end of twenty-eight years of service for laying up at Devonport. Admiral Sir Raymond Lygo, whose late wife launched the boat in 1978, was guest of honour at the paying-off ceremony on 20 January. *Spartan* spent seventy-four days dived during Operation Corporate in 1982.

2006 Maritime Reserves Command established. In a ceremony on the quarterdeck of *Victory*, Rear-Admiral Nicholas Harris, FOSNNI, became in addition Flag Officer Reserves (flag in *Neptune*) and Cdre Nelson James Elliott Reynolds RNR became the first Commander Maritime Reserves.

26 JANUARY

1782 Hood again repulsed de Grasse.
See 25 January 1782.

1800 *Penelope* captured the Spanish privateer *Carmen* 30 miles W. of Alboran Island, western Mediterranean.

1804 *Cerberus* captured the French *Chameau* and drove another gunboat ashore close to Cap de la Hogue.

1826 *Sulphur* launched at Chatham. Last bomb vessel in RN.

1841 Hong Kong formally occupied by Cdre Sir James Gordon Bremer (*Wellesley*). 'The marines were landed, the union [sic] hoisted on our post, and formal possession taken of the island by Cdre J.J.G. Bremer, accompanied by the other officers of the squadron, under a feu-de-joie from the marines and a royal salute from the ships of war.' – Capt Belcher.

One hundred and forty-six years later, shortly before the hand-over of Hong Kong in June 1997, the last British naval commander in the colony, Cdre Peter Melson, revisited Possession Point with the last Royal Marine in Hong Kong, Maj John Herring.
See 25 January 1841, 30 June 1997.

1918 Destroyer *Leven* sank UB-35 off Calais, and U-109 mined (51.03N, 01.46E).

1918 Patrol Craft P.62 rammed and sank U-84 in S.W. Approaches.

1932 Submarine M 2 (ex-K 19) sank on exercises off Portland, with loss of all hands including two RAF aircrew for the Parnall Peto Seaplane.

1940 Admiralty Fleet Order required that officers given temporary commissions for the period of hostilities would in future, with certain exceptions, have had to serve at least three months on the lower deck.

Hong Kong harbour with the depot ship *Tamar* (left), *c.*1900. (*NMRN*)

HMS *Brave Borderer*, launched by Vosper at Porchester on 7 January 1958 and accepted on 26 January 1960. With *Brave Swordsman*, they were the last operational fast attack craft built for the Royal Navy. In the MTB mode they carried four 21-in torpedoes and one 40mm Bofors gun; as MGBs two Bofors and two torpedoes. (*Author*)

1943 General Sir Thomas Hunton, RM, appointed last Adjutant-General RM, a post established in 1914, before which the senior active RM officer had been designated Deputy Adjutant-General since 1 July 1867. General Hunton went on to become the first and only GOC, RM, and retired as their first Commandant-General.

1945 Assault on Cheduba Island, Burma. Operation Sankey. Ships: *Ameer*, *Kenya*, *Newcastle*, *Nigeria*, *Norman*, *Paladin*, *Phoebe*, *Raider*, *Rapid*, *Spey*, *Teviot*.

1959 Two inshore minesweepers, *Cardingham* and *Etchingham*, intended for the Hong Kong RNVR, were loaded onto the deck of the Ben Line heavy lift ship *Benarty* at Chatham for passage to the Far East.

1960 First of Brave-class FPBs, *Brave Borderer*, accepted from Vospers at HMS *Dolphin*.

1966 The RN's second Buccaneer Mk 2 Squadron, 809 NAS, Lt-Cdr Linley Middleton RN, commissioned at RNAS Lossiemouth on the 25th anniversary of the commissioning of the first 809 Squadron which was equipped with Fairey Fulmars. Capt Middleton commanded the carrier *Hermes* during the Falklands War in 1982.

1972 Carrier *Eagle* arrived at Devonport after exercises in the Far East, to pay off for disposal. (Paying-off ball at the London Hilton Saturday 29 April: double ticket £13.50.) DCI(RN) T.53/72.

See 6 August 1975, 4 December 1978.

1994 Admiral Sir Frank Twiss died. Commander Far East Fleet 1965–7, Second Sea Lord 1967–70, Black Rod 1970–8. Gunnery Officer of *Exeter*, sunk 1942. POW of Japanese until 1945. When asked what it had been like replied, 'Oh, not so bad I suppose, if you had been to Dartmouth'.

See 7 July 1910.

2007 First steel cut for the Type 45 destroyer *Duncan* at BAE Systems, Glasgow.

See 11 October 2010.

2011 Frigate *Chatham*, Cdr Simon Huntingdon RN, entered Devonport Naval Base for the last time. Paid off 8 February.

See 19 October 2010, 10 February 2011.

27 JANUARY

1626 'A proclamation for the better furnishing of the Navy. . . Every ordinary Sailor to receive 14 shillings a month besides an allowance out of it of 4d to a Preacher, 2d to a Barber and 6d to the Chest as proposed by the Lord High Admiral and approved by the Privy Council.' The Lord High Admiral was the Duke of Buckingham; the Chest was the Chatham Chest.

See 23 August 1628, 8 March 1689.

1799 *Flora* captured the French privateer *Intrépide*, and *Caroline* recaptured the British letter of marque (privateer) *Jane* 170 miles N. by W. of Cape Ortegal, N.W. Spain.

1805 *Amazon* captured the Spanish *Gravina* 140 miles W. of Cape St Vincent.

1807 *Jason* (32) captured the French *Favorite* (16), a former RN sloop taken on 6 January 1806, 30 miles off the coast of Dutch Guiana.

1807 *Caroline* captured the Spanish register-ship *San Rafael* (alias *Palas*) in Albay Gulf, Philippines.

1813 The Royal Navy's first *Daring*, a gun brig of 12 guns, Lt William Pascoe, chased off Sierra Leone by two new and powerful French frigates out of Nantes, *Arethuse* (40) and *Rubis* (40), ran his ship ashore on one of the Islas de los Idolos, off present-day Konakry in French Guinea, and burnt her to avoid falling into enemy hands.

See 7 February 1813.

1814 William Hoste, fresh from taking Cattaro (Kotor) in the Adriatic, landed two mortars and two 18-pdrs to menace Ragusa (now Dubrovnik) after a 6-mile march via a drained aqueduct. French capitulated at British ranging shots. Some 151 enemy guns and 360 troops victualled for six weeks surrendered for loss of one seaman. Hoste created baronet and received Austrian knighthood.

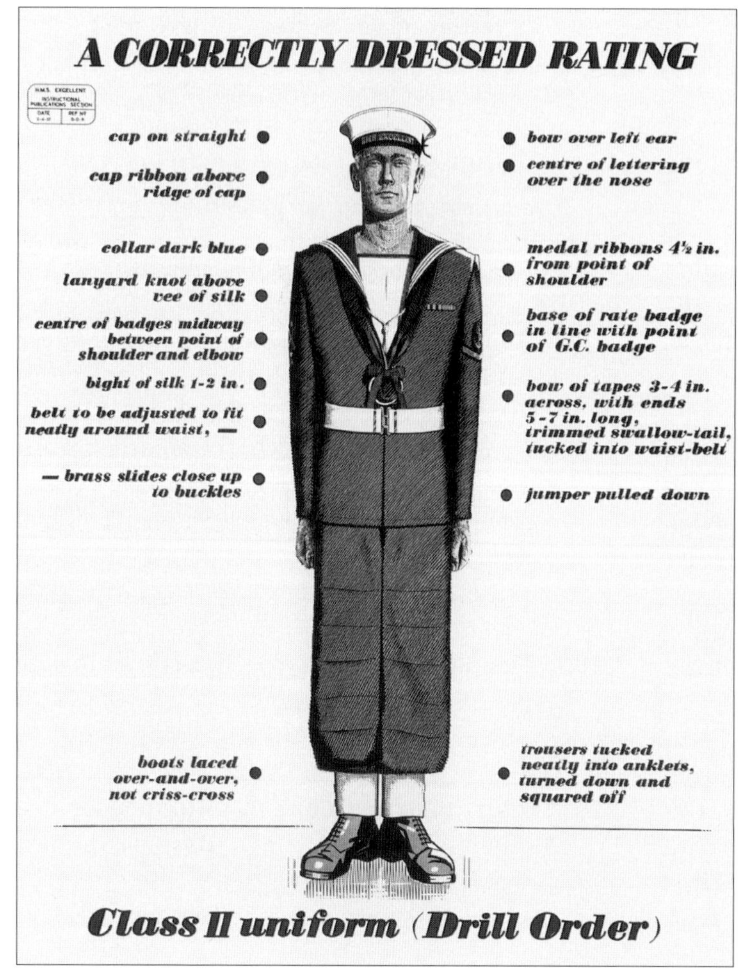

Correctly dressed rating, 1957. (*NMRN*)

1816 Admiral Samuel, Viscount Hood died.

1866 Electric firing cartridges introduced.

1918 Arab forces seized the Turkish Dead Sea Flotilla at El Mezraa.

1942 *Thanet* and *Vampire* (RAN) fought a Japanese cruiser and three destroyers off Endau, east coast of Malaya. *Thanet* sunk.

1944 Cruiser *Mauritius* and destroyer *Kempenfelt* bombarded the coast road and town of Formia, Italy.

1945 Captain-class frigates *Bligh*, *Tyler* and *Keats* of the 5th Support Group sank U-1172 in St George's Channel, W. of Cahore Point, W.N.W. of Holyhead 52.24N. 05.42W. The day before U-1172 had torpedoed the frigate *Manners* (stern blown off by a homing torpedo) 21 miles W. of Anglesey; thirty-six men lost. The ship was towed to Barrow but CTL.

The biggest warship ever to dry dock in Gibraltar. The battleship HMS *Vanguard* enters No.1 Dock on 27 January 1953 with 8ft clearance either side. (*Cdr David Hobbs RN*)

1953 Battleship *Vanguard*, 44,500 tons standard, went into No. 1 Dock at Gibraltar for a short refit, the biggest warship ever to be dry-docked at Gibraltar. *Vanguard* 814.5ft long, 108.5ft beam; dock 871ft by 125ft.

1956 A Guided Weapons Group formally opened at HMS *Excellent* by Admiral of the Fleet Sir George Creasy, C-in-C Portsmouth, in advance of the introduction of guided weapons into Fleet service.

See 24 July 1956, 10 June 1960.

1976 RN Regulating School opened in old Armourer's School on Whale Island.

1989 The end of Blue Liners, RN duty-free cigarettes and tobacco, heralded in DCI(RN) 11/89. 'Given its responsibility to promote the health and physical fitness of RN personnel, the Board have come to the conclusion that the medical evidence for discouraging smoking is so strong that it would be inappropriate for the concession to continue.' Prices were to be increased over two years to parity with those of commercial tobacco.

See 1 June 1951.

1994 Frigate *Norfolk*, Capt J.F. Perowne RN, with RFA *Grey Rover*, arrived at Cape Town; the first RN ship visit to South Africa since October 1974 when TG 317.2, led FOF1, Vice-Admiral Henry Leach, arrived off Cape Town and *Blake* fired the 21-gun salute which so upset the new Labour government in Britain.

See 12 June 1967, 14 October 1974.

1995 Frigate *Marlborough* stood by off Sierra Leone until 8 February to evacuate British nationals following rebellion.

1995 Cook and Catering sub-branches amalgamated. DCI(RN) 4/95.

28 January

1596 Death of Sir Francis Drake from yellow fever off Porto Bello, West Indies.

1744 *Fly* captured the Spanish privateer *N.S. Del Rosario* 80 miles W. of Ushant.

1796 Admiralty telegraph, based on Murray's shutter system, began working to Portsmouth and to Chatham. Extended to Plymouth in 1806 and to Yarmouth in 1808. Popham's semaphore was introduced as a possible replacement on an experimental line to Chatham in 1816, to Portsmouth in 1822 and, though uncompleted, to Plymouth in 1829.
See 16 July 1795.

1801 *Oiseau* and *Sirius* captured the French *Dedaigneuse* 2 miles off Cape Belem (Veo), N.W. Spain.

1802 *Black Joke* caught fire and sank in Sutton Pool, Plymouth.

1806 *Growler* captured the French privateer *Voltigeur* 40 miles N.N.E. of Ushant.

1806 *Attack* captured the French privateer *Sorcier* 40 miles N.N.W. of Ushant.

1881 Reverse at Laing's Nek, Transvaal. Naval Brigade from *Boadicea* and *Flora*. Troops: RA, KDG, 21st, 58th and 60th Regiments, Naval Military Police.

1915 Cabinet decided to make a naval attack on the Dardanelles.

1918 Old torpedo gunboat *Hazard* lost in collision in Channel.

1918 VC: Lt-Cdr Geoffrey Saxton White (E 14). Posthumous.
E 14 destroyed by Turkish depth charges and gunfire near Nagara Pt., Dardanelles in pursuit of *Sultan Selim* (ex-*Goeben*).

1927 Destroyer *Sylph*, sold in December 1926, stranded at Aberavon and broken up there.

1936 Funeral of His late Majesty King George V. A naval gun's crew from Chatham hauled the gun carriage – ninety-eight manning the drag ropes ahead and forty abaft – from Westminster Hall to Paddington Station. At Windsor the gun carriage, which had been used at the funerals of Queen Victoria and King Edward VII, was drawn by men from HMS *Excellent*, Portsmouth, commanded by

Sir Francis Drake (*c.*1540–1596)

'It matters not, man! God hath many things in store for us.' Sir Francis Drake died of fever off Porto Bello on the Caribbean coast and was buried at sea from his ship the *Defiance*. Born near Tavistock, he was the first English Admiral to achieve international fame. He claimed Nova Albion (San Francisco) for The Queen in 1579, and on this three-year voyage the dividend paid to investors was £47 for every £1 invested – probably the most successful voyage in history. With a group of English seamen, he was likely one of the founders of the Chatham Chest for the relief of wounded seamen. He was Mayor of Plymouth, its MP and arranged the supply of water to the town from Dartmoor. Buckland Abbey, which was his, and also Sir Richard Grenville's home, is now open to the public.

Sir Francis Drake (*c.*1540–1596). *(NMRN 1985/187)*

Capt A.J. Power RN, Captain of Whale Island. 'A sailor king he was appropriately borne home by bluejackets' – *The Times*.

See 2 February 1901, 28 January 1960, 30 January 1965.

1937 Sloop *Sheldrake* launched by Miss James, daughter of Vice-Admiral Sir William James, DCNS, at Thornycroft, Woolston, and destroyer *Ilex* launched by wife of Paymaster Capt R.C. Jerram, Secretary to the First Sea Lord, at John Brown's, Clydebank.

1943 Under direction from Prime Minister Winston Churchill, the Admiralty 'decided' to 'abandon the system under which submarines were numbered and to revert to the arrangement under which names were assigned' – CAFO 146/43. Initially, thirty-two boats were given names.

See 3 July 1902, 24 September 1926, 5 November 1942, 19 December 1942, 27 December 1942.

The names allocated were: P.31 *Ullswater*; P.34 *Ultimatum*, P.35 *Umbra*, P.37 *Unbending*, P.42 *Unbroken*, P.43 *Unison*, P.44 *United*, P.45 *Unrivalled*, P.46 *Unruffled*, P.49 *Unruly*, P.51 *Unseen*, P.53 *Ultor*, P.54 *Unshaken*, P.55 *Unsparing*, P.56 *Usurper*, P.211 *Safari*, P.212 *Sahib*, P.214 *Satyr*, P.216 *Seadog*, P.217 *Sibyl*, P.219 *Seraph*, P.221 *Shakespeare*, P.223 *Seanymph*, P.224 *Sickle*, P.225 *Simoom*, P.228 *Splendid*, P.229 *Sportsman*, P.247 *Saracen*, P.312 *Trespasser*, P.314 *Tactician*, P.315 *Truculent*, P.339 *Taurus*.

'Action should be taken for the names to be brought into use forthwith.' Admiral Beatty, First Sea Lord, directed in 1925 that submarines should have names as 'there can be little loyalty to a number'. The first post-war boat was launched at Chatham in 1926 as *Oberon*. The system was again changed early in the Second World War when, to conceal the number of submarines being built, reversion was made to numbers.

1944 Sunderland D/461 (RAAF) sank U-571 off Blacksod Bay, Ireland. Convoys ON 221 and SC 151.

1957 The second volume of Capt Stephen Roskill's *The War at Sea*, the official Cabinet Office history of maritime operations in the Second World War, was published. This book, subtitled *The Period of Balance*, covers January 1942 to May 1943.

See 10 May 1954, 21 October 1960, 4 November 1982.

Cdr Edward Young DSO, DSC and bar. (*NMRN*)

1960 Admiral of the Fleet Sir Arthur Power died at Gosport aged 70. He was first Captain of the carrier *Ark Royal* in 1938, C-in-C East Indies 1944–5, Second Sea Lord, C-in-C Mediterranean Fleet, C-in-C Portsmouth and the first NATO Allied C-in-C Channel. As Captain of *Excellent* he commanded the naval party which drew the gun carriage at Windsor at the funeral of His Majesty King George V, exactly twenty-four years earlier. 'Arthur John' was promoted admiral of the fleet in 1952.

See 28 January 1936, 3 September 1945.

2003 Cdr Edward Young DSO, DSC and bar, died aged 89; first RNVR officer in the Second World War to command a submarine (*Storm*). Author of *One of our Submarines* (1952), republished as the 1,000th Penguin book in 1954.

See 8 November 1995.

2009 The first Type 45 destroyer, *Daring*, Capt Paul Bennett, entered Portsmouth for the first time. PAAMS named *Sea Viper*.

See 1 February 2006, 23 July 2009, 2 December 2009, 22 September 2010.

29 JANUARY

1673 Navy Board offices near the Tower of London, which had survived the Great Fire of London in 1666, were burned down. Some naval records and Pepys' papers destroyed. New Wren-designed offices on the same site were completed in 1684. Here the Navy Board remained until it moved to the new Somerset House in 1786.

1696 The Royal Navy's most prestigious ship, the three-decker *Royal Sovereign* (100), built by Peter and Phineas Pett at Woolwich and launched as the *Sovereign of the Seas* in 1637 (renamed 1660), was destroyed by fire in the Medway off Chatham while preparing for a major rebuild. Seaman Thomas Crouch who had left an unattended candle received thirty lashes and life imprisonment.

1780 *Surprise* captured the French privateer *Duguay-Trouin* 40 miles S. by W. of Dodman Point.

1801 *Bourdelais* captured the French *Curieuse* 20 miles E. of Barbados. Sank while prisoners were being shifted.

1801 *Incendiary* taken in the Mediterranean by Rear-Admiral Ganteaume, and scuttled.

1810 Boats of *Jalouse* and *Phoenix* captured the French privateer *Charles* 270 miles W. by S. of Ushant.

1856 Victoria Cross instituted by Royal Warrant, to be worn on a blue ribbon by naval recipients.

1876 Admiralty decision to found Engineering College.

1892 Battleship *Victoria* ran aground at Snipe Point, Plataea, Greece, and after being lightened by 1,253 tons, was pulled off by the battleships *Edinburgh* and *Dreadnought* on 4 February, 'during which period the ship's hammocks were never got down' – Parkes. The ship was refitted in Malta, the first ship to enter the newly completed Hamilton Dock at the head of French Creek. The *Victoria* was lost the following year.

See 9 April 1887, 22 June 1893.

The first presentation of the Victoria Cross in Hyde Park, 26 June 1857. A reporter noted that the blue jackets' 'free and easy rollicking walk contrasted with the measured symmetrical tread of the Guards.' (*NMRN*)

The *Royal Sovereign* (ex-*Sovereign of the Seas (1637)*), first of eight ships of the name. (*NMRN 1986/228*)

1915 Walney Island airship shed (Barrow-in-Furness) shelled by U-21. First operation by a German submarine in the Irish Sea.

1917 Steam-powered submarine K 13, Lt-Cdr Godfrey Herbert RN, foundered during builder's acceptance trials in Gare Loch. Four 3ft diameter air intakes into the boiler room had not been secured. A sea rider, Cdr Francis Goodhart, CO of K 14, also building at Fairfields on the Clyde, was drowned in a gallant attempt to escape from the conning tower to brief rescuers; posthumous AM (*London Gazette*, 23 April 1918); thirty-two lost, forty-eight survived. K 13 salvaged and commissioned as K 22. No subsequent submarine has been numbered 13.
See 23 October 1915.

1925 Sloop *Elphinstone* (RIN) (ex-*Ceanothus*), wrecked on Nicobar Island.

1941 GC (ex-AM): D.G.M. Hay, Cadet RNR, SS *Eurylochus*, for saving life in shark-infested sea after ship sank.

1943 Corvettes HMNZS *Kiwi* and *Moa* sank Japanese submarine I-1 off Cape Esperance, Guadalcanal. Significant capture of enemy cipher material.

1944 *Spartan*, cruiser, sunk by German Hs 293A glider bomb off Anzio. Operation Shingle.

1945 Air-strike on oil refineries at Palembang, Sumatra. Operation Meridian II.
See 24 January 1945.

1965 The flag of Rear Admiral J.H. Walwyn hauled down and post of Flag Officer Flotillas Mediterranean ended.

1979 Destroyer *Southampton* launched at midnight by Vosper Thornycroft management at Woolston to catch the high tide after boilermakers in dispute had refused to launch the ship as planned after her midday naming by Lady Cameron, wife of Marshal of the Royal Air Force Sir Neil Cameron, CDS. The ship had been laid down on Trafalgar Day 1976.
See 3 September 1988.

1988 Eyesight requirements for Seamen officers (over 22-years-old) slightly relaxed because tasks and design of ships allowed requirements to be less stringent. DCI(RN) 33/88.

1991 *Brazen*, *Gloucester*, *Cardiff* and *Manchester*, their Lynx helicopters firing Sea Skua missiles, attacked the Iraqi Navy, sinking ten vessels before 15 February. In the Battle of Bubiyat Channel next day, the ships neutralised 25 per cent of the Iraqi Navy.

2004 *Guernsey* and *Lindisfarne*, the last of seven Island-class fishery protection vessels in RN service, paid off and transferred to the Bangladesh Navy at Portsmouth. Renamed BNS *Turag* and BNS *Sangu* respectively.
See 16 July 2003.

2004 Cdre A.J. Rix (COMUKTG) became the first British officer to command the coalition TF 150 deployed to the north-west Indian Ocean in support of global counter-terrorism.

30 January

1649 Power of the Crown seized by the Commonwealth. Public execution in Whitehall of Charles I, observed by a youthful Pepys.

1655 Launch of *Naseby* (80), renamed *Royal Charles* at the Restoration in 1660, and taken by the Dutch in the Medway 12 June 1667.

1761 *Amazon* and *Solebay* captured the French privateer *Chevrette*, which had run ashore a few miles W. of Calais.

1797 *Andromache* captured an Algerine frigate 15 miles S.S.W. of Cape de Santa Maria, Portugal.

1814 *Fylla* (ex-Danish) captured the French privateer *Inconnu* 30 miles S.E. by S. of Guernsey.

1855 Royal Marines designated a Light Corps and became Royal Marine Artillery (Blue Marines) and Royal Marines Light Infantry (Red Marines).

1857 Uniform introduced for POs, seamen and boys, and badges for chiefs, POs and leading seamen.

See 1 October 1907.

1867 *Captain* laid down. Full-rigged turret-ship.

See 7 September 1870.

1903 Torpedo Boat Destroyer *Orwell*, Lt-Cdr P.A. Robarts RN, collided with third-class cruiser *Pioneer*, Cdr G.P.W. Hope RN, off Cape Varlam, Corfu. *Orwell* cut in two; fore part sank, after part towed to Corfu. Fifteen men (eight named William) lost. Memorial erected in the Upper Barraca Gardens at Malta and in British Cemetery, Corfu Town.

1918 *Wellholme* ketch (*Danton*) (Q-ship) sunk by U-55 in the English Channel.

1940 Sloop *Fowey*, destroyer *Whitshed* and Sunderland Y/288 sank U-55 off Ushant. The first U-boat sinking involving a Coastal Command aircraft. Convoy OA 80G. A coincidental anniversary.

See 30 January 1918.

1942 *Thorn*, submarine, sank the Italian S/M *Medusa* south of Brioni Island in the Adriatic.

1943 *Samphire*, corvette, sunk by U-596 N.E. of Bougie (37.07N, 05.32E). Convoy TE 14.

1944 Destroyers *Meteor* and *Whitehall* sank U-314 off North Cape. Destroyer *Hardy*, second of the name in the Second World War, torpedoed by U-278 and sunk by own forces off Bear Island. Convoy JW 56B.

1944 Wellington K/172 sank U-364 in Bay of Biscay.

1945 Admiral Sir William Goodenough died. Captain BRNC Dartmouth 1905–7, cruiser Commander in the First World War, C-in-C Africa Station 1920–2, C-in-C The Nore 1927–9. His father, Cdre James Goodenough, Commodore on the Australia Station, died in August 1875 after being attacked in the British Solomon Islands by natives using poisoned arrows. '"Barge" Goodenough, though more talkative than most of his kind, was a very attractive character, full of enthusiasm, and with a salty air about him. He had one clearly marked ace: a great gift of leadership. He also possessed the firmest of grips on the essentials of his business as a cruiser admiral' – Marder, *From the Dreadnought to Scapa Flow*, vol.2, p.13.

See 2 June 1867, 20 August 1875, 25 August 1907.

1945 Diesel submarine *Astute*, first British warship of the name, launched at Vickers Armstrong, Barrow. Yard No. 904. One of sixteen 'A'-class boats completed (thirty cancelled) which had been intended for Far East operations.

See 8 June 2007.

1946 Eleven Fairmile D-class MTBs, stripped of guns and engines, lost in sudden storm in eastern Mediterranean under tow from Malta to Alexandria.

1951 The annual £5,000 pension granted by Parliament on 22 July 1806 (Royal Assent) under the Trafalgar Estates Act of 1806 to Horatio Nelson's grasping brother, the Revd

The memorial in the Upper Barraca Gardens in Valetta to the fifteen men from the TBD HMS *Orwell* lost in the collision with the cruiser HMS *Pioneer* in 1903 off Corfu. (*Author, 2000*)

William Nelson, and his successors, ended with the death this day of Horatio Nelson's great-great nephew, the Rt Honourable Edward Agar Horatio Nelson, 5th Earl Nelson of Trafalgar and Merton, Viscount Merton of Trafalgar and of Merton in the County of Surrey, and Baron Nelson of the Nile and of Burnham Thorpe, Norfolk, following legislation passed by the Attlee government in 1948 to 'terminate without compensation' the commitment. Parliament also removed restrictions on the sale of the Trafalgar Estates bestowed on the first Earl and his successors; Trafalgar House and 3,415 acres near Salisbury were sold privately in May 1948 to the Duke of Leeds. All of the relics at the house were bought by the National Maritime Museum for £25,000.

1952 First NATO Supreme Allied Commander Atlantic appointed.

1965 State funeral of Sir Winston Churchill in St Paul's Cathedral.

Although Sir Winston Churchill's service career was spent in the Army, he was twice First Lord of the Admiralty. His coffin was hauled on a gun carriage by a party of sailors, ninety-eight men ahead and forty astern, a practice normally carried out only at royal funerals since 2 February 1901 when the Royal Horse Artillery horses at Queen Victoria's funeral became unmanageable.

See 2 February 1901, 28 January 1936.

1999 Carrier task group deployed to Gulf. Maritime interdiction operations and air surveillance operations over Iraqi southern 'no fly' zone. Operation Bolton II. *Invincible*, destroyer *Newcastle* and RFA *Fort Austin* entered area 30 January and joined by Armilla Patrol units. Sailed for Adriatic (Operation Magellan) 1 April. Ships: *Invincible*, *Boxer*, *Newcastle*, *Cumberland*. RFA: *Brambleleaf*, *Fort Austin*. FAA Sqns: 800, 814, 849 B Flight.

2005 Admiral Sir Horace Law died aged 93. Distinguished gunnery officer in Second World War, Captain BRNC Dartmouth, FOST, FOSM, Controller of the Navy 1965–70 during the battle for naval fixed-wing aviation and the cancellation of the new fleet carriers and finally CINCNAVHOME. A committed Christian.

Service of Thanksgiving at Portsmouth Cathedral 10 May 2005. HM The Queen and HRH The Duke of Edinburgh represented by Admiral Sir Peter Abbott, the Prince of Wales by Admiral Sir James Eberle.

See 23 June 1911.

31 JANUARY

A Memorable Date observed by 42 Cdo RM – Kangaw

1748 *Nottingham* (60) and *Portland* (50) captured the French *Magnanime* (74) 250 miles W.S.W. of Ushant. 'A remarkably fine ship.'
Battle Honour: *Magnanime* 1748.

1779 *Apollo* captured the French *Oiseau* in the Baie de St Brieuc, Brittany.

1824 *Cameleon* and *Naiad* captured the Algerine *Tripoli* in Algiers Bay.

1831 Maj-Gen Sir James Cockburn, Bt, appointed first Inspector-General of Royal Marines for five years. Thereafter the post in abeyance until 9 January 1862.

1874 Defeat of the Ashantis at Amoaful. Naval Brigade from *Active, Amethyst, Argus, Beacon, Bittern, Coquette, Decoy, Druid, Encounter, Merlin, Tamar, Victor Emmanuel.*
Battle Honour: Ashantee 1873–4.

1880 Training frigate *Atalanta* (ex-*Juno*, launched in 1844), sailed from Bermuda and foundered in N. Atlantic with loss of 113 ship's company and 170 trainees. Memorial in St Ann's church, Portsmouth.

1918 Submarine E 50 mined and lost in North Sea. K 4 and K 17 lost in Fleet exercise off May Island, K 4 rammed by K 6 and K 17 rammed and sunk by *Fearless*. K 14 rammed by K 22, and the latter by *Inflexible*: both severely damaged. K 22 had been K 13; lost on trials, she was recovered and re-numbered. One hundred and three lives lost. It was said that the K-boats as a class came to grief because 'they had the speed of a destroyer, but the turning circle of a battleship and bridge facilities of a motor-boat'.
See 25 June 1921.

1938 Four hundred Birmingham citizens, led by the Lord Mayor, travelled by special train to Portsmouth to present drums and silver bugles to the new light cruiser *Birmingham*, Capt E.J.P. Brind RN, before her departure the following day for the China Station. One of her midshipmen was Edward Beckwith Ashmore, the future First Sea Lord and CDS.
See 1 September 1936, 4 October 1963.

1940 Sir James Lithgow, shipbuilder and industrialist, appointed Controller of Mercantile Shipbuilding and Repairs with a seat on the Board of Admiralty. He had been Director of Merchant Shipbuilding in 1917.

1941 *Huntley* sunk by Italian torpedo aircraft off Sidi Barrani, Libya (31.25N, 26.48E).

1942 *Belmont* sunk by U-82 S.E. of Nova Scotia (42.02N, 57.18W). Convoy NA 2.

HM Submarine K 2, one of the ill-fated K-class steam-driven boats seen here in the 1920s. (*NMRN*)

HMS *Talent* departs the Clyde on her way to her home port of Devonport, 6 February 2009. (*RN*)

1942 *Culver* sunk by U-105 S.W. of Ireland (48.43N, 20.14W). Convoy SL 98.

1943 GC (ex-AM): Lt-Cdr W.H.D. McCarthy for trying to save life off Benghazi.

1944 Sloops *Magpie*, *Starling* and *Wild Goose* sank U-592 in W. Approaches.

1945 MTB 715 (Norwegian) sank M-382 N. of Molde (63.06N, 07.32E).

1945 The Battle of Kangaw in Burma. After two days of hand-to-hand fighting 42 Cdo RM captured Hill 170 and over several days held the position against Japanese counter attack.

1949 Home Fleet under command of Admiral Sir Rhoderick McGrigor, flag in the battleship *Duke of York*, with the carrier *Theseus*, flag of Rear-Admiral M.J. Mansergh, *Superb*, flag of Vice-Admiral Hon. Guy Russell, three other cruisers, ships of the 4th and 5th Destroyer Flotillas, submarines and auxiliaries sailed from Portland on the annual Spring Cruise to Gibraltar and for combined exercises with the Mediterranean Fleet. 'Coming so soon after the successful Autumn Cruise to the West Indies and South Africa this activity is another indication of the return of the Royal Navy to its pre-war standard of training' – *The Navy*, February 1949.

See 17 July 1947, 23 September 1948.

1992 Four RNR units paid off. *Essex* (Shoeburyness), *Hallam* (Sheffield), *Palatine* (Preston) and *Paragon* (Stockton, Middlesbrough). DCI(RN) 6/1992.

2001 Submarine *Astute*, first of class, laid down at Barrow, one hundred years to the day after the keel was laid at Barrow of Holland 1, the Royal Navy's first submarine.

See 30 January 1945, 22 October 2003, 8 June 2007, 11 March 2005, 24 March 2009, 27 August 2010.

1 FEBRUARY

1793 France declared war on Britain and Holland. Start of French Revolutionary War.
See 2 January 1793.

1806 Naval Academy at Portsmouth renamed Royal Naval College at request of King George III.

1807 *Lark* captured a Spanish gunboat in Puerto Cispata, Colombia.

1829 *Black Joke* captured the Spanish slaver *Almirante* 200 miles S.E. by S. of Lagos, Nigeria.

1855 Black Sea ports blockaded.

1858 *Teazer* and boats of *Ardent*, *Childers*, *Pluto*, *Spitfire* and *Vesuvius* destroyed nine towns up the Great Scarcies River, Sierra Leone.

1873 The RN College, Greenwich, established by Order in Council on 16 January, opened 'for the instruction of the Gunnery Lieutenants and Sub-Lieutenants who are to form a large part of its inmates, and life and animation will again pervade the old Hospital which is inseparably entwined with the memories of the Royal Navy' – *The Times*.
See 2 January 1873, 20 June 1997.

1897 Fleet Canteen in Malta, built on Corradino Heights with £7,000 granted by the Admiralty, opened by the C-in-C Mediterranean Fleet, Admiral Sir John Hopkins. Situated above the Parlatorio and Canteen Wharves, the club's single tower and dome were prominent marks for ships berthing alongside. Before the Second World War it had thirty-six snooker tables. Later renamed the RN Fleet Club, it closed in 1968.
See 31 May 1968.

1911 *Thunderer*, Orion-class super-Dreadnought, launched at Thames Iron Works at Blackwall, from the same slip as the *Warrior* in 1860. The last major warship built on the Thames. The contract bankrupted the company and the Works closed on 21 December 1912. Gunboats and smaller craft were built up-river as far as Chiswick until the end of the First World War.

1917 German 'unrestricted' submarine warfare began.

1926 RN Shore Wireless Service instituted by Order in Council.

1937 GC (ex-EGM): C.G. Duffin, Senior Shipwright Diver, HM Dockyard, Portsmouth. (*Gazette* date.)

1940 *Gannet* and *Falcon* damaged by Japanese aircraft and laid up at Chungking. Half crews sent home on a six-day drive wearing uniform concealed by odd garments but keeping ship's time and watches and enjoying entitlement of up spirits.

1942 Fourth wheel added to U-boat Enigma. Vital U-boat key Triton lost to Bletchley Park until December after addition of a fifth wheel to the German Enigma machine.
See 30 October 1942.

1942 Eaton Hall, Chester, to where cadet training had been transferred from Dartmouth, commissioned as *Britannia*.

1943 Minelayer *Welshman*, the first and only ship of the name, torpedoed and sunk by U-617, 45 miles E. of Tobruk (32.12N, 24.52E). Mine deck flooded; ship capsized and sank within three minutes. One hundred and fifty-two men lost.
See 25 October 1941.

1943 845 NAS formed at NAS Quonset Point, Rhode Island, as a TBR unit equipped with Grumman Avenger Mk 1 aircraft. Served in *Illustrious* and *Ameer* in the Indian Ocean and Far East. Disbanded at Gourock 7 October 1945.
See 15 March 1954, 4 January 2001.

1949 WRNS became a permanent and integral part of the Naval Service though not subject to Naval Discipline Act.

1952 WRNVR established.

1953 Submarine *Sirdar*, in dry dock in Sheerness with plating removed, and frigate *Berkeley Castle* in

HMS *Daring*, the first of the Royal Navy's next generation of destroyers, was launched from the BAE Systems, Scotstoun on 1 February 2006 by the Countess of Wessex. (*RN*)

Reserve Fleet, foundered when sea defences on Sheppey were breached. Both CTL.
See 15 December 1954.

1960 The Royal Navy's second Sea Vixen all-weather fighter squadron, 890 NAS, commissioned at Yeovilton and embarked in *Hermes* in July.
See 2 July 1959.

1963 'Their Lordships consider the time appropriate for the Royal Navy to discontinue the use of the traditional but now unsuitable term "Asdic" (Allied Submarine Detection Investigation Committee) and to adopt the term "Sonar" (Sound Navigation and Ranging). Sonar is the official NATO term and is used by most other countries. In the interests of economy, existing publications and drawings are not to be amended and existing tally plates on equipment and compartments are not to be changed.' – AFO 152/62.
See 5 June 1917, 6 July 1918.

1967 First Captain S/M 10 appointed. 'It was not by accident that when the RN was entrusted with the responsibility of deploying the national nuclear deterrent, the new Squadron formed by the Polaris submarines was entitled the Tenth' – Lord Fieldhouse. This was a tribute to the 10th S/M Flotilla in the Mediterranean in the Second World War.
See 21 September 1944, 30 November 1959.

1968 Royal Canadian Navy became the Canadian Forces Maritime Command (MARCOM) on the unification of the three Canadian armed services. (Date of Royal assent to the Canadian Forces Reorganisation Act C-90). Prefix HMCS threatened but survived. An unpopular common green uniform and common military rank structure introduced. In 1985 the Services reverted to their own distinctive uniforms, the Navy with Beatty-type six brass buttons instead of eight, but rank insignia remained.
See 4 May 1910, 29 August 1911, 15 February 1965, 11 June 2010.

1988 London Division of RNR moved to shore HQ in St Katharine's Dock. DCI(RN) 5/88.
See 30 June 1988.

1995 Destroyer *Exeter* joined 23-ship, six-nation force to cover withdrawal of UN ground forces from Somalia. Operation Triad.

1999 The Naval and Military Club, which had occupied Cambridge House on Piccadilly – the famous 'In and Out' – since 1866, moved to 4 St James's Square where the clubhouse was opened by Viscount Astor. Built in 1679, the house was requisitioned from the Astor family in 1942 for use as the London HQ of Free French Forces.

2004 Supply Branch renamed Logistics Branch. SO became LO. Admirals' Secretaries became Executive Assistants.
See 13 October 1922, 26 October 1944, 1 April 2003.

2006 *Daring*, first of the Type 45 air defence destroyers designed to replace the veteran Type 42s, launched by HRH The Countess of Wessex at BAE Systems Yard, Scotstoun. Armed with PAAMS (Principal Anti-Air Missiles System), Daring was the most powerful destroyer ever built for the Royal Navy and the biggest warship built at Scotstoun. The eighth of the name but with no battle honours.
See 10 August 1949, 23 January 2007, 27 November 2007, 17 November 2008, 28 January 2009, 23 July 2009, 21 October 2009, 11 October 2010.

2011 RFA *Fort George*, Capt Jamie Murchie, entered Plymouth for the last time to pay off. She entered service in 1994.

2 FEBRUARY

1652 Appointment of 'one Advocate to attend the Fleet' at 8*s* per day.
See 19 July 1985.

1747 *Edinburgh* and *Nottingham* captured the French privateer *Bellone* 100 miles N.W. by W. of Ushant. *Eagle* also in company.

1780 *Defiance* wrecked in operations at Charleston.
See 11 May 1780.

1785 First meeting of the Navy Club.
See 4 February 1765.

1811 *Theban* engaged a French lugger privateer, and her boats recaptured the latter's prize from under the batteries near Dieppe. *Skylark* covered the latter operation.

1813 Boats of *Kingfisher* captured one trabaccolo and destroyed five others near Cape Agia Katerina, Corfu.

1842 'The rating of "Leading Stoker", having been added to the establishments of her Majesty's steam-vessels, by Order in Council of the 2nd of February, 1842; the commanding officers off all such vessels are hereby acquainted, that the object of this rating is to improve the practice of "stoking", to which too little importance has hitherto been attached . . . By Command of their Lordships.'

1859 *Pearl*'s Naval Brigade returned on board from operations in the Gorakhpur District.
See 12 September 1857.

1867 Writer rating introduced.

1901 Lt the Hon. Algernon Boyle, commanding the RN guard of honour from *Excellent* at Windsor GWR station, awaiting the arrival of the coffin of Queen Victoria, assisted by Sub-Lt Percy Noble, took charge of the gun carriage from the Royal Horse Artillery when their horses became restive. The sailors grounded arms and, using 'some of the trappings from the horses, the communication cord from the Royal Train and sundry bits of rope' (letter from Admiral Sir Percy Noble to Admiral Earl Mountbatten in 1960), towed the gun carriage to St George's Chapel. Thus are traditions established.

At King Edward VII's funeral in 1910 the gun carriage was drawn by 150 seamen from *Excellent*. King George V presented the gun carriage to *Excellent* on 6 June 1910.

See 30 January 1965, 28 January 1936, 15 February 1952.

1941 *Ark Royal* aircraft attacked power plant (Tirso Dam), Sardinia. Operation Picket. FAA Sqns: 800 (Skua), 810 (Swordfish).

1941 *Formidable* aircraft attacked Mogadishu, Italian Somaliland. Operation Breach. FAA Sqns: 826, 829 (Albacore).

Sailors drawing the gun carriage at the funeral of Sir Winston Churchill, January 1965. (*NMRN*)

University Royal Naval Units

The University Royal Naval Units (URNUs) were established to attract high-calibre undergraduates into the Service and to educate future opinion formers about the role and essential need for the Royal Navy. Their origin was a presentation at HMS *Excellent* in September 1964 at which the views of university careers officers were sought on how to improve RN officer recruiting. Aberdeen University later submitted that RN formal interviews, however well-crafted, could not compete with the attraction and insight provided by three years in the Army Officer Training Corps (OTC) or the University Air Squadrons (UAS). Although expensive, these three years gave the student time to consider whether he or she would fit into service life and for the Service to decide if he or she was wanted. Aberdeen proposed a scheme to provide sea experience in the way that the UAS gave flying training and exposure to an enthusiastic officer in mid-career. The UNRU idea was born. A pilot scheme was launched at Aberdeen in 1966 under Lt-Cdr Neil Murray, then in command of HMS *Exmouth*. Twelve keen students and the inshore minesweeper HMS *Thornham* formed the trial unit which proved highly successful. There are now fourteen flourishing URNUs each with a 20-metre Archer-class P2000 which constitute the 1st Patrol Boat Squadron.

Honorary Midshipman Victoria Phillips of Cambridge University Royal Naval Unit training with HMS *Raider* at Gloucester. Her great-grandfather, Walter Lewis, served as a Boy in HMS *Northampton*, then a training ship, a century earlier. See 18 November 1876. (*Author*)

1942 *Westcott* sank U-581 S.W. of the Azores.

1943 Revival of 'frigate' to designate new class of twin-screw escort vessels.

1944 *Orion* and *Soemba* (Neth.) bombarded the Formia area, N.W. of Naples.

1953 Appointment of Flag Officer Royal Yachts established and flag of Vice-Admiral Conolly Abel Smith hoisted in HMY *Victoria and Albert*.

AFO of 20 March 1953 called for volunteers for Royal Yacht Service, which had been disbanded when the flag of Vice-Admiral Sir Dudley North, Vice-Admiral Commanding Royal Yachts, was struck on 18 September 1939.

1966 Separation Allowance announced, effective from 1 April, for married servicemen separated from their families for an aggregate of at least twelve months overseas to get 4*s* a day during further periods of separation.

1971 Imperial Defence College renamed Royal College of Defence Studies and began its first course. Opening speaker was the Prime Minister, Mr Edward Heath.

3 FEBRUARY

1781 Admiral Sir George Bridges Rodney (*Sandwich*), with twelve sail of the line, captured St Eustatius, West Indies, six Dutch men-of-war and 180 merchantmen. The islands of Saba and St Martin were seized at the same time. The Dutch were practically defenceless and surrendered on being summoned.

1807 Capture of Montevideo by Brig-Gen Sir Samuel Auchmuty and Rear-Admiral Charles Stirling (*Diadem*). Ships: *Ardent, Charwell, Daphne, Diadem, Encounter, Howe* (storeship), *Lancaster, Leda, Medusa, Pheasant, Raisonnable, Staunch, Unicorn*. A Naval Brigade was landed.

1809 *Aimable* (32) (captured French prize) captured the French *Iris* 10 miles E. by S. of Aberdeen.

1810 *Valiant* captured the French armed merchantman *Confiance* 30 miles S. by W. of Belle Ile.

1812 *Southampton* captured the Haitian *Améthyste* (also called *Heureuse Réunion*) 3 miles S. of Rochelois Bank, Haiti.

1814 *Majestic* (74) gave up pursuit of the American *Wasp* to capture the French *Terpsichore* 300 miles N.N.W. of Madeira. Second French prize of the name.

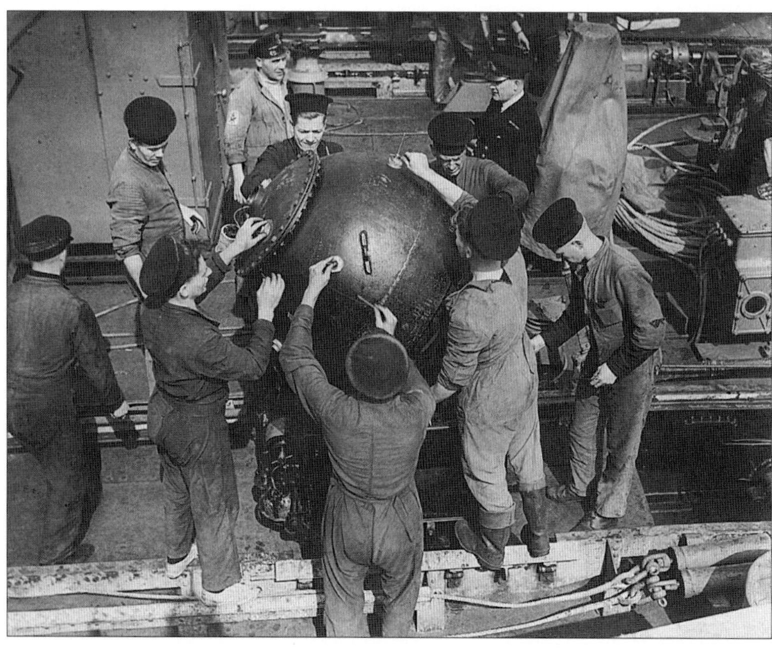

Seamen preparing mines for laying during the Second World War. (*NMRN*)

1834 Pusser's waste allowance reduced from one-eighth to one-tenth.

1839 Capture of Karachi by *Algerine* and *Wellesley*, *Constance* (Indian Navy), the 40th Regiment and 2nd Bombay Native Infantry.

1847 Wood paddle sloop *Thunderbolt*, Cdr Alexander Boyle RN, grounded on Cape Recife when entering Algoa Bay, South Africa. Run ashore at mouth of Baken's River and ship's company lived in tents ashore. Salvage abandoned on 21 May. Court martial found that the Captain and Master 'did negligently trust to their eye, and did disregard the charts and instructions furnished for their guidance'. Reef now named Thunderbolt Reef and remains of ship are beneath reclaimed land.

1885 Capt Lord Charles Beresford (*Safieh*) rescued Col Sir Charles Wilson's party on River Nile. Unsuccessful in attempt to relieve General Gordon at Khartoum.

1900 'Grant's guns' – four 4.7-in and four 12-pdrs from *Doris* and *Barrosa* joined the Simon's Town Naval Brigade at the Modder River.

See 2 October 1900.

1915 Repulse of the Turkish attack on the Suez Canal. Ships: *Swiftsure, Ocean, Clio, Minerva, Proserpine, Himalaya*, TB 043 Royal Indian Marine, *Dufferin, Hardinge*. Armed Tugs: *Fanny, Lubeck, Mainstay, Mansoura, Prompt, Virginia*. French: *D'Entrecasteaux, Requin, Robuste, Sylphe*. British War Medal: clasp 'Suez Canal' approved but not issued.
Battle Honour: Suez Canal 1915.

1931 *Dunedin* and *Diomede*, light cruisers, and sloops *Laburnum* and *Veronica* of the New Zealand Station, assisted in the aftermath of severe earthquake at Hawkes Bay, North Island. *Veronica* went briefly aground

The helicopter carrier HMS *Ocean* and the destroyer HMS *Liverpool* pass in the Gulf during Operation Telic, Britain's biggest amphibious operation for nearly fifty years, 2003. (*RN*)

when the shock raised the level of the seabed at Napier (a unique defence had a court martial been convened).

1940 Minesweeper *Sphinx* bombed by German aircraft 15 miles N. of Kinnaird Head, Aberdeen. Foundered next day (57.57N, 02.00W). The first RN ship lost to air attack.

1942 GC: Lt-Cdr William Ewart Hiscock DSC, for torpedo disposal at Malta. (*Gazette* date.)

1943 Fortress N/220 sank U-265 in Atlantic.

1945 *Bayntun*, *Braithwaite* and *Loch Eck* sank U-1279 in Shetland/Faroes gap.

1945 Trawler *Arley* damaged by mine off Sheringham buoy, Norfolk. Sank in tow.

1960 Rear-Admiral Sir Murray Sueter, pioneer of RN aviation, and MP for Hertford 1921–45, died at Watlington, Oxfordshire aged 87. 'His enthusiasm for aircraft sometimes tended to overrun his discretion and judgement.' – *The Times*, 5 February 1960.

See 25 November 1912.

2009 Trident submarine *Vanguard* and French SSBN *Le Triomphant*, 'while on separate routine patrols', collided under the Atlantic. No casualties. Boats returned to their respective bases at Faslane and Brest.

See 1 September 1875.

4 February

1303 King Edward I said to have granted to one Gervase Alard the first commission to an English admiral.

1695 *Dartmouth* taken by two French ships in the English Channel after six hours, during which her Captain was killed.

1762 Fort Royal, Martinique, surrendered after a well-coordinated joint amphibious operation mounted by Maj-Gen the Hon. Robert Monckton and the Leeward Islands squadron under Rear-Admiral George Rodney. A thousand sailors were landed to haul guns over rough ground: 'the service they did us, both on shore and on the water, is incredible.' Monckton, who had been Wolfe's deputy at Quebec in 1759, referred to 'the harmony that subsists between the Fleet and the Navy, and the cordial assistance we have received from Admiral Rodney'. The Seven Years War.
Battle Honour: Martinique 1762 (ships included *Dragon*, *Echo*, *Nottingham* and *Vanguard*).
See 16 February 1762, 22 March 1794.

1765 Founders' Day of the Royal Navy Club of 1765 and 1785 (United 1889). The club was formed by the amalgamation in 1889 of The Royal Naval Club of 1765 and The Navy Club of 1785. Members are all officers of commander rank and above, who are, or were, eligible to be appointed to command one of HM ships of war at sea. Cdr Vanessa Spiller RN became a member on 30 June 2005, the first woman to do so.

'At a meeting at Captain Keith's on Monday the 4th of February 1765, it was resolved by the undermentioned gentlemen to set on foot a society of their brother officers at the St Alban's Tavern on this day sevenight: Captn George [Anthony] Tonyn, Captn Sir John Strachan, Captn John Carter Allen, Captn [Sir] Basil Keith, Captn Mich[ae]l Clements, Captn John Luttrell [Lord Newark], Captn [later Admiral Sir] R[ichar]d Onslow, Captn [later Admiral Sir] Hyde Parker Jnr.' These eight captains founded the Navy Society which was to include Nelson (elected 1784), Collingwood, Howe, Hood, Kempenfelt and St Vincent among its members. It was renamed the Royal Naval Club of 1765 in 1829.

The Navy Club of 1785 first met at the Star and Garter tavern in the City on 2 February 1785. Prince William Henry, later King William IV, was a member as were Nelson and Jervis. In 1800 meetings were moved to the Thatched House Tavern and continued there until 1862. The Club became known as the 'Thatched House Club'. From 1862 until 1889 both clubs held their meetings at Willis' Rooms. By 1888 the purposes and membership of the two Clubs were overlapping and they shared the same secretary, Mr Henry J. Kelly, Paymaster RN. On 1 January 1889 they amalgamated to form the Royal Navy Club of 1765 and 1785 (United 1889).

1781 *Monarch*, *Panther* and *Sibyl* captured the Dutch *Mars* and a convoy of twenty-four sail 30 miles W. by N. of St Martin, West Indies. Dutch admiral killed in action.

1786 A new church dedicated to St Ann, replacing an earlier building consecrated in 1704, opened in Portsmouth Dockyard. The Revd Mr Brown preached the inaugural sermon, taking his text from the 'Book of Job', 'which may be summarised as "I wish I had never been born"'.
See 21 August 1704, 18 February 1907, 21 June 1934, 11 November 1993.

1793 Capt Nelson, on half-pay since December 1787, left Burnham Thorpe for the last time, to join *Agamemnon*.

1804 Four boats of *Centaur* carrying seventy-two men cut out the French *Curieux* in Fort Royal harbour, Martinique after a 20-mile pull.
Battle Honour: *Curieux* 1804.

1805 *Acheron* and *Arrow* (in defence of a convoy of thirty-two sail, of which only three were captured) taken by the French *Hortense* and *Incorruptible* 30 miles N. of Cape Tenez, Algeria.
Battle Honour: Cape Tenez 1805.

1853 Repulse by the Burmese of a combined British force near Donabew (Danubyu) and capture of Prome. Landing party from *Fox*, *Sphinx* and *Winchester*, *Phlegethon* (Bengal Marine) and 67th Bengal Native Infantry.

1858 *Pelorus*' Naval Brigade, Capt F.P.B. Seymour left the ship at Rangoon to garrison the fort at Medway (Myede), Burma.
See 14 April 1858.

Members of HMS *Invincible* ship's company honour guard during the ship's visit to Gibraltar in January 2005. (*RN*)

1874 Ordahsu carried and Coomassie (Kumasi) taken.
Battle Honour: Ashantee 1873–4.
See 31 January 1874.

1874 The Royal Navy's third *Daring*, a barque rigged composite screw sloop (iron frame, teak shell), launched at Wigram's Yard at Blackwall on the Thames and armed and masted at Sheerness. She commissioned for the Pacific in 1875 under Cdr John J.G. Hanmer and in 1877 surveyed the entrance to the Skeena River on the Canadian N.W. coast where Daring Point on Kennedy Island and Hanmer Point, Hegan Point and Veitch Point commemorate the ship and her officers. *Daring* came home in 1879 for refit and then went out to the China Station for six years. She was sold in 1889.
See 12 August 1953.

1915 Drifter *Tarlair* fitted with prototype A/S hydrophones.

1918 *Zubian* (½ *Nubian* ½ *Zulu*) sank UC-50 off Essex coast (50.47N, 00.59E). *Zulu* had been mined off Dunkirk 8 November 1916, and *Nubian* torpedoed 27 October 1916. Both reached home and the undamaged halves were combined at Chatham in a composite hull named *Zubian*.
See 7 June 1917, 9 December 1942, 30 June 1966.

1918 First WRNS Regulations promulgated.
AFO 414/1918.

1919 *Penarth* mined off Yorkshire coast.

1937 Battleship *Royal Oak* bombed by Spanish aircraft off Europa Point, Gibraltar, during Spanish Civil War.

1943 *Beverley* and *Vimy* sank U-187 in N. Atlantic. Convoy SC 118.

1945 *Loch Scavaig*, *Loch Shin*, *Nyasaland* and *Papua* sank U-1014 in N.W. Approaches.

1949 *Royal Sovereign* returned by USSR after five years' service as *Archangelsk*.

1958 Aircraft carrier *Victorious* left Portsmouth Dockyard for sea trials after seven years' reconstruction.
See 1 May 1952.

1965 The first entry of officer trainees at HMNZS *Tamaki* on Motuihe Island in the Hauraki Gulf.
See 20 January 1941.

1997 Able Seaman Jack Gearing, the then oldest surviving naval rating and the last survivor of naval operations in the 1915 Gallipoli campaign (cruiser *Theseus*), died aged 102. Left the Service in 1919. Trained as a lighterman in the family sailing barge *Mayflower* on the Thames, Gearing was turned down by the RN in 1939 due to age but accepted by the Royal Engineers. Sgt Gearing, aged nearly 50, towed a crane to Normandy in 1944 with the orders 'follow that destroyer'.
See 24 July 1997, 31 May 2006.

2003 Capt Angus Menzies RN became the first Supply Officer promoted to the substantive rank of Commodore (and appointed Naval Assistant to the Naval Secretary).
See 10 January 2002.

5 FEBRUARY

1722 *Swallow* captured the pirate *Ranger* (James Skyrm) 30 miles N. by W. of Cape Lopez, French Equatorial Africa.

1800 *Fairy* and *Harpy*, joined by *Danae*, *Loire* and *Railleur* captured the French *Pallas* close off Les Sept Iles, Brittany. *Pallas* commissioned as *Pique*.

1804 *Eclair* fought the French *Grand Décide* 200 miles N. of Tortola, West Indies.

1810 Capture of Guadeloupe by Lt-Gen Sir George Beckwith with Vice-Admiral the Hon. Sir Alexander Cochrane (*Pompee*). A continuation of their conjoint campaign which had begun at Martinique the previous year.
Battle Honour: Guadeloupe 1810.

Ships and vessels: *Abercrombie, Achates, Alcmene, Alfred, Amaranthe, Asp, Attentive, Aurora, Bacchus, Ballahou, Bellette, Blonde, Castor, Cherub, Cygnet, Elizabeth, Fawn, Forester, Freija, Frolic, Gloire, Grenada, Guadeloupe, Hazard, Laura, Loire, Melampus, Morne Fortunee, Netley, Observateur, Orpheus, Pelorus, Perlen, Plumper, Pompee, Pultusk, Ringdove, Rosamond, Savage, Sceptre, Scorpion, Snap, Star, Statira, Superieure, Surinam, Thetis, Vimiera, Wanderer.*

1836 *Pike*, schooner, wrecked on the Pelican reef off Jamaica through the negligence of the Commanding Officer. But her Mate was also dismissed the Service for having torn a page from her log, which earned him three months in the Marshalsea.

HMS *Dolphin* (1882), a composite screw sloop, served as a submarine depot ship between 1912 and 1925, and was finally scrapped in 1977. (*NMRN*)

The Gulf campaign medal awarded for service on Operation Granby, the campaign to liberate Kuwait in 1990–91. Eligibility was set out in DCI(Gen) 185/91. (*Author*)

1888 Bruce Fraser, the future Admiral of the Fleet, Lord Fraser of North Cape, born.
See 26 December 1943, 12 February 1981.

1902 First dive by RN's first submarine.

1918 Royal Air Force established by Order in Council, formed on 1 April 1918 by amalgamation of Royal Naval Air Service and Royal Flying Corps.

1940 Destroyer *Antelope* sank U-41 in S.W. Approaches (49.21N, 10.04W). Convoy OA 84.

1942 Corvette *Arbutus* sunk by U-136 S. of Iceland (55.05N, 19.43W). Convoy ON 63.

1943 Admiral of the Fleet Sir Andrew Cunningham appointed C-in-C Mediterranean for the second time. "I have to confess I had considerable personal gratification" – *A Sailor's Odyssey* p.521. Only one earlier precedent, Vice-Admiral Sir Pulteney Malcolm 1828–1830, and again in 1833.

1978 Admiral of the Fleet Sir Peter Hill-Norton enobled as Baron Hill-Norton of South Nutfield in the County of Surrey.
See 13 March 1971, 16 May 2004.

1990 Decision announced in the House of Commons 'to extend the employment of members of the WRNS to include service at sea in surface ships of the Royal Navy'.

2004 A memorial to the former RN Engineering Colleges, Keyham and Manadon, was unveiled by Vice-Admiral Sir Robert Hill on the Manadon Park housing estate at Plymouth: 'On these 100 acres stood the Royal Naval Engineering College, Manadon, commissioned as HMS *Thunderer* 1946–1995 to replace the first RNEC at Keyham 1880–1958 for training Engineer Officers of the Royal Navy . . .'
See 9 May 1958, 15 September 1995.

2007 Reclaim Building on Horsea Island, Portsmouth, RN Diving HQ, renamed Bridge Building in honour of Second World War diving and bomb disposal officer, Lt-Cdr John Bridge GC, GM and bar, RNVR, on what would have been his 92nd birthday.
See 20 June 1944, 1 June 1948, 25 October 1979.

6 FEBRUARY

1799 *Argo*, in company with *Leviathan*, Cdre J.T. Duckworth, captured the Spanish *Santa Teresa* 30 miles N. of Minorca.

1806 Battle of San Domingo. Vice-Admiral Sir John Duckworth (*Superb*) beat the French squadron of five sail of the line under Rear-Admiral Leissequès (*Impérial*) in San Domingo Bay. Captured: *Alexandre, Brave, Jupiter.* Destroyed: *Diomède, Impérial*; three frigates escaped. Ships: *Agamemnon, Atlas, Canopus, Donegal, Northumberland, Spencer, Superb.* Frigates, etc: *Acasta, Epervier, Kingfisher, Magicienne.* Foundered on passage to England.

The last fleet engagement for which the large Gold Medal was awarded. Three hundred and ninety-six survivors qualified for the Naval General Service medal introduced on 1 June 1847.

Battle Honour: San Domingo 1806.

1842 *Charybdis* (6) and crew of fifty-five under Lt de Courcy took the Cartagenan corvette *Coretta*, sank a brig, and put two schooners to flight, the Cartagenans having seized two British ships and refused any compensation or to release the crews. Deservedly promoted, de Courcy eventually reached the Flag List.

Battle of San Domingo, 1806

Although Trafalgar had marked the end of Franco-Spanish hopes of gaining command of the seas, the French resolved upon a *guerre de course* to prevent the flow of trade which gave Britain the wealth to continue to oppose Napoleon on the continent. One squadron was sent on this mission to the West Indies. A squadron under Sir John Duckworth destroyed the main French squadron, and only the frigates escaped. The French had driven two ships ashore in an endeavour to escape, but they were destroyed by boats of the British squadron.

1845 *Terrible* (sixth of the name), wood paddle frigate, launched at Deptford. First four-funnelled ship in RN.

1865 Iron screw ship *Hector* fitted with first armour-piercing steel shot.

Vice-Admiral Sir John Duckworth's action off San Domingo, 1806. (*NMRN 1969/5(1)*)

The Devonport-built sloop HMS *Wellington*, a familiar sight on the Thames in central London, was commissioned in 1935 and served initially on the New Zealand Station, watching over British possessions in the western Pacific. After six years' wartime convoy escort duties – she escorted 103 Atlantic and Arctic convoys – she was laid up in the Reserve Fleet in Milford Haven. On 6 February 1947 the *Wellington* was sold to the Honourable Company of Master Mariners (HCMM) and was fitted out at Chatham for her new role as the company's livery hall. She arrived at her Temple Stairs berth on the Victoria Embankment in December 1948; curiously, the ship's bows are moored in the City of Westminster and stern moorings in the City of London. In 2005 she was handed over to the Wellington Trust to manage her conservation and charitable functions. (*HCMM*)

1912 Submarine A 3 lost in collision with *Hazard* off Bembridge, IoW.

1915 Destroyer *Erne* wrecked off Rattray Head, Aberdeen.

1942 *Rochester* and *Tamarisk* sank U-82 in N. Atlantic. Convoy OS 18.

1943 *Louisburg* (RCN) sunk by German aircraft 60 miles N.E. of Oran. Convoy KMS 8. First Canadian warship to be sunk by aircraft or in the Mediterranean.

1947 Sloop *Wellington* became HQ ship of the Honourable Company of Master Mariners.

1952 Accession of HM Queen Elizabeth II.
See 15 February 1952.

Happier days in Hong Kong, 1977. Cdr Bruce Richardson, Captain of HMS *Amazon*, Lt-Cdr Bill Hutchinson, First Lieutenant, and the frigate's Buffer, PO (Sonar) Monty Stockham, with Jenny 'Side Party' and her girls on board her sampan in the Basin at HMS *Tamar*. Jenny painted the sides of visiting warships for over fifty years. Her first award was the LS&GC, presented to her by the cruiser *Dorsetshire* before the war, which she hid in the heel of her shoe during the Japanese Occupation; she received the BEM from the Governor, Sir Murray Maclehose, on 27 October 1980. Jenny was held in enduring regard and affection by the Royal Navy. (*Author*) See 19 February 2009.

7 FEBRUARY

1602 Capture of Puerto Bello by *Pearl* and *Prudence* privateers, under William Parker.

1793 Nelson commissioned *Agamemnon* (64) at Chatham.
See 16 June 1809.

1794 East Indiaman *Pigot* taken by the French *Prudente*, *Cybèle*, *Duguay-Trouin* and *Ile-de-France* at Benkulen, Sumatra.

1811 *Hawke* captured the French privateer *Furet* 20 miles S.W. by W. of Beachy Head.

1813 Frigate *Amelia* (38), Capt Hon. Frederick Irby, and the French *Arethuse* (40), Cdre Pierre Bouvet, fought a furious broadside gunnery action at night off the island of Tamara near present-day Konakry, French Guinea, one of the last frigate actions of the Napoleonic War. Most of the British officers were killed or mortally wounded, including Lt William Pascoe, late Captain of the gun brig *Daring* (see 27 January 1813) and command finally devolved upon the Master, Mr Anthony de Mayne. Having fought to a standstill in 'so slaughterous a contest' (*The Naval Chronicle*) the exhausted ships parted company at daylight.
See 13 June 1796.

1859 Rev. Dr James Inman, Professor of the Royal Naval College, Portsmouth, and the School of Naval Architecture, died aged 83. Memorial in St Ann's church, Portsmouth.
See 15 April 1821.

1863 *Orpheus*, wood screw corvette, and flagship of Cdre W. Farquarson Burnett on the Australian Station, wrecked on bar outside Manukau on west coast of North Island, New Zealand. Commodore and 166 men lost. Memorial 'erected as a token of the discipline and heroism displayed by all on board' is in the chapel of the Old RN College, Greenwich.

1878 *Active*'s Naval Brigade at Battle of Guintana.

1910 The *Dreadnought* Hoax. Civilian impostors from the Bloomsbury group – including Horace de Vere Cole, Duncan Grant and Virginia Woolf's brother, Adrian Stephen – purporting to be the Emperor of Abyssinia and his suite, were received by the C-in-C Home Fleet, Admiral Sir William May, in *Dreadnought* at Weymouth. At each new feature of the flagship the bearded and burnoused visitors exclaimed 'Bunga! Bunga!' There was uproar when the story broke in the press. When it appeared that Admiral May might be reprimanded, Stephen and Grant called on Mr McKenna, First Lord of the Admiralty, to apologise. McKenna bundled them out of his office but cries of 'Bunga! Bunga!' pursued the Admiralty and the Royal Navy for months.

1919 Paddle minesweeper *Erin's Isle* mined off The Nore.

1941 W. Approaches command shifted from Plymouth to Liverpool.

1943 Fortress J/220 sank U-624 in N. Atlantic (55.42N, 26.17W). Convoy SC 118.

1944 Midget submarine X 22 sunk in collision with *Syrtis* in Pentland Firth. During towing exercise, OOW in *Syrtis* washed overboard and while turning in rescue effort *Syrtis* sank X 22 with loss of CO and three crew. *Syrtis* lost, probably mined, off Bodø, Norway, 23 March 1944.

1963 The Hawker P.1127 VSTOL aircraft, prototype of the Harrier, piloted by Hawker Chief Test Pilot Bill Bedford, made its first carrier landing in *Ark Royal*.
See 24 November 2010.

1967 Naval author, 'Bartimeus', Capt(S) Sir Lewis Ritchie RN, died aged 80. He served on Jellicoe's staff in *Iron Duke* and in the Royal Yacht *Victoria and Albert* until 1939. Name changed from Ricci by Deed Poll 1941. Press secretary to King George VI from 1944–7. His first of many naval books written over thirty years, *Naval Occasions*, appeared in 1914; 'In this and in later volumes his sketches of naval life were at once uncommonly veracious and quietly stirring' – *The Times*, 9 February 1967.

The Fleet submarine HMS *Swiftsure* (1971). (*NMRN*)

1967 Submarines *Tabard* and *Trump* sailed from New Zealand to provide shore working parties after major bush fires in S. of Tasmania.

1980 Refit and refuelling began on *Swiftsure*, the first nuclear submarine to enter the new Submarine Refit Complex in Devonport Dockyard.

1983 Flag Officer Admiralty Interview Board retitled Commodore Admiralty Interview Board.
See 31 March 1995.

1995 Conspicuous Gallantry Cross (CGC) instituted by Royal Warrant to remove distinctions of rank in awards for bravery. Replaces DSO for gallantry, the Conspicuous Gallantry Medal and the Distinguished Conduct Medal.

2005 Ellen MacArthur met by fishery patrol vessel *Severn* off Ushant at the end of her record-breaking, solo, non-stop circumnavigation in trimaran *B&Q*. Time: 71 days 14 hours 18 minutes 33 seconds. Made DBE and Hon. Lt-Cdr RNR. The First Sea Lord signalled 'All of us in the Royal Navy have watched with fascination and huge admiration as you have taken on this daunting challenge . . . HMS *Severn* will escort you home . . . her presence marks the Royal Navy's deep admiration for you'. The following HM ships spoke: 6 December (Day 9), frigate *Iron Duke* off West Africa; 13 January (Day 47), destroyer *Gloucester* off Falklands; 20 January (Day 54), Antarctic patrol ship *Endurance* off Brazil and 6 February (Day 69), destroyer *Liverpool* in North Atlantic.
See 4 April 1581, 7 July 1967, 22 April 1969.

8 FEBRUARY

1794 *Fortitude* and *Juno* bombarded Mortella Tower, Gulf of St Florent, Corsica.

1805 *Curieux* captured the French privateer *Dame Ernouf* 60 miles E. of Barbados, in a sharp engagement.

1813 Boats of *Belvidera*, *Junon*, *Maidstone* and *Statira* captured the American *Lottery* in Lynnhaven Bay, off Chesapeake Bay.

1916 British government requested naval assistance from Japan, leading to deployment in April of two Japanese destroyer flotillas in the Mediterranean.

1917 Destroyer *Liberty* rammed and sank UC-46 in Dover Strait (51.70N, 01.39E).

1917 Destroyer *Thrasher* sank UC-39 4½ miles S. of Flamborough Head (54.03N, 00.02E).
See 29 September 1897.

1917 Destroyer *Ghurka* sunk by mine 4 miles S.W. of Dungeness; seventy-five men lost.
See 1 May 2008.

1918 UB-38 sunk by mine off Dover. A modest dividend from so great a barrage.

1918 Destroyer *Boxer* sunk in collision with SS *St Patrick* in English Channel.

1919 All cruisers on East Indies station to be painted white.

1942 *Alysse* (Free French) torpedoed by U-654 off Newfoundland, having left convoy ONS 61. Taken in tow but foundered two days later.

The cruiser HMS *Manchester* (1937), in white and buff livery for tropical service. (*NMRN*)

An A-class submarine passing HMS *Lincoln* (1959). (*NMRN*)

1943 Corvette, *Regina* (RCN) sank the Italian S/M *Avorio* off Philippeville, Algeria. Convoy KMS 8.

1943 A/S trawler *Bredon* sunk by U-521 off the Canary Islands. Convoy Gibraltar II.

1944 *Woodpecker* and *Wild Goose* sank U-762 in S.W. Approaches. Convoys SL 147/MKS 38.

1963 First experimental touch-and-go by VTOL P.1127 on *Ark Royal* off Portland.

1984 846 NAS began operations off Beirut from RFA *Reliant*.

9 FEBRUARY

1746 *Portland* (50) captured the French *Auguste* 80 miles S. by E. of the Scilly Isles and towed her into Plymouth with 144 dead.
Battle Honour: *Auguste* 1746.

1799 *Daedalus* (32) captured the French *Prudente* (36) 120 miles S. of Cape Natal, S.E. Africa.

1808 Boats of *Meleager* cut out the French privateer *Renard* at Santiago de Cuba.

1825 First operational use of steam vessel: *Diana*, built at Kidderpore Dockyard, 1823, and bought into the Service on advice of Capt F. Marryat in 1824, engaged a 36-gun stockade with her rockets, receiving 160 shots. First Burmese War.

See 19 January 1826.

1916 *Mimi* and *Toutou* sank the German *Hedwig von Wissman* on Lake Tanganyika, thereby securing command of the lake. 'A nice example of sea power.'

1937 First flight of Blackburn Skua, FAA's first monoplane, a cross between a fighter and a dive-bomber.

See 10 April 1940.

1939 Heavy cruiser *Devonshire*, Capt G.C. Muirhead-Gould RN, carried the Nationalist Civil Governor of Majorca to Minorca to negotiate the peaceful surrender of the island to the Nationalists. She evacuated 450 Spanish Republicans 'whose lives or liberty would almost certainly have been forfeit' (*The Times*) and took them to Marseilles. Spanish Civil War.

1941 Bombardment of Genoa by Force H, under Vice-Admiral Sir James Somerville (*Renown*). Operation Result. Ships: *Malaya*, *Renown*, *Sheffield*. Screen: *Duncan*, *Encounter*, *Fearless*, *Firedrake*, *Foresight*, *Foxhound*, *Fury*, *Isis*, *Jersey*, *Jupiter*. Simultaneous attack by FAA from *Ark Royal* on Spezia, Pisa and Leghorn. FAA Sqns: 800, 808, 810, 818, 820 (Skua, Fulmar, Swordfish).

1942 *Herald*, ex-surveying ship, ex-sloop *Merry Hampton*, scuttled at Seletar. Raised by Japanese and employed as *Heiyo*.

See 14 November 1944.

1943 Corvette *Erica* sunk by British mine between Benghazi and Derna.

1943 *Dolfijn* (Dutch) sank Italian S/M *Malachite* S. of Sardinia.

1944 Sloops *Kite*, *Magpie* and *Starling* sank U-238, and *Starling* and *Wild Goose* sank U-734 in S.W. Approaches. Convoys SL 147/MKS 38. This was a furious and prolonged encounter: 150 depth charges were used in three hours, one counter-mining a torpedo from the U-boat only a few yards off *Starling*'s quarterdeck.

Lt HRH The Prince of Wales receives HM The Queen and HRH The Duke of Edinburgh aboard HMS *Bronington* under his command, November 1976. (*NMRN*)

Lance Corporal Matthew Croucher, aged 24, a Royal Marine Reservist who dived on a live grenade to save his comrades in Afghanistan, 2008. (*RN*)

1945 *Venturer*, submarine, while submerged off Bergen, sank U-864 en route to the Far East with depth charge parts for Japan; her second success against U-boats. The first sinking of one submerged submarine by another (60.46N, 4.35E).

See 11 November 1944.

1950 Light cruiser *Kenya*, escorted by the Indian Navy frigate *Tir*, arrived at Rangoon from Colombo carrying sacred Buddha relics on loan to Burma from the Temple of the Sacred Tooth at Kandy in Ceylon. On board were fifty dancers and a guard of 100 monks who held a service every three hours in the admiral's quarters as the ship crossed the Indian Ocean.

1976 Lt HRH The Prince of Wales took command of *Bronington* MCMV.

See 16 September 1971, 4 January 1974, 2 September 1974, 15 December 1976.

1977 Admiral Sir Edward Beckwith Ashmore, First Sea Lord 1974–7, promoted admiral of the fleet on taking over as CDS. Son of Vice-Admiral L.H. Ashmore and brother of Vice-Admiral Sir Peter Ashmore. C-in-C Western Fleet and first CINCFLEET 1971–3.

See 30 June 1955, 1 November 1971.

2001 Fast fleet tanker RFA *Wave Ruler*, 35,000 tons, launched at BAE Systems, Scotstoun, on the Clyde after christening by Elaine Dumelow, wife of Defence Secretary Geoff Hoon. *Wave Ruler* and her sister ship *Wave Knight* replaced the ageing tankers *Olwen* and *Olna*.

See 29 September 2000.

2008 GC: Lance Corporal Matthew Croucher, RMR, 40 Cdo RM. L/Cpl Croucher, serving in 40 Cdo Group's Cdo Recce Force in Helmand Province, Afghanistan, tripped a wire-connected grenade booby trap during a night-time reconnaissance of a suspected Taliban IED-making compound. He shouted a warning to the men in his section and threw himself on top of the grenade, pinning it between his day sack and the ground. The grenade exploded, ripping the sack from his back and pitting his body armour and helmet with grenade fragments. Miraculously, Croucher survived. 'His magnificent displays of selflessness and gallantry are truly humbling and are the embodiment of the finest traditions of the Service' – *London Gazette*, 23 July 2008.

See 16 February 1942.

10 FEBRUARY

1586 Sir Francis Drake captured Cartagena.

1715 First diving equipment demonstrated in Thames and accepted into service (Andrew Becker, first naval assistant to the Hydrographer's Department).

1720 Edward Hawke, destined to be one of the greatest fighting admirals in Royal Navy history, joined his first ship, the sloop *Seahorse* (20), fitting out in a wet dock at Deptford, as a volunteer aged 15; the future victor of Quiberon Bay in 1759, First Lord of the Admiralty and Admiral of the Fleet.

See 20 November 1759, 17 October 1781.

1722 *Swallow* captured the pirate *Royal Fortune* (Bartholomew Roberts) 30 miles W. of Cape Lopez, French Equatorial Africa.

1809 French frigate *Junon* (36), which escaped on 7 February from the blockaded harbour of the Saintes in the West Indies, taken by *Horatio* (38), Capt George Scott, *Latona* (38), Capt Hugh Pigot, and other British ships off that island. The French flag was struck 'after a most creditable and skilful resistance to greatly superior force' in which she lost 130 of her 323 ship's company. Commissioned at Halifax under Capt John Shortland. Re-taken from Shortland by the French before the end of the year.

See 13 December 1809.

1810 *Thistle* captured the Dutch *Havik* 480 miles S.E. by S. of Bermuda.
Battle Honour: *Havik* 1810.

1816 Sixth-rate frigates *Ariadne* and *Valorous*, the first ships built at Pembroke Dockyard, launched from the same slip. *Ariadne* was Capt Frederick Marryat's last command from 10 November 1828. His second novel, *The King's Own*, completed on board.

1846 Lord Charles Beresford, the future Admiral Lord Beresford, born.

See 8 November 1907, 6 September 1919.

1906 *Dreadnought* launched by King Edward VII, having been built in a year and a day. First major vessel driven by turbines.

1913 A search party found the bodies of Capt R.F. Scott, Dr Wilson and Lt Henry Bowers in their tent in Antarctica.

See 30 March 1912.

The launch of HMS *Dreadnought*, the first of her kind, 1906. (*NMRN*)

The Fairey Swordfish. which wrote its own page in British naval history: 'The name of the Swordfish will remain imperishable in the annals of the Fleet Air Arm. Few aeroplanes, with the exception of the Spitfire, ever received and deserved such universal acclaim. It was known to everybody as the "Stringbag"; its achievements became a legend, and it earned the affection and respect of generations of Fleet Air Arm pilots during its decade of service in the Royal Navy' – Owen Thetford, *British Naval Aircraft since 1918*, p.139. (*NMRN*)

1916 German government informed US government that all defensively armed merchant ships would be treated as belligerents from 1 March onwards.

1916 Sloop *Arabis* sunk by three German TBDs off the Dogger Bank.

1922 The infamous 'Geddes Axe' fell. Sir Eric Geddes, former First Lord of the Admiralty and chairman of the Committee on National Expenditure, proposed savage naval cuts – 35,000 officers and men including one third of the Captains' List – 'and earned for himself lasting obloquy' – Roskill. Countless careers were destroyed. 'The Geddes Axe was one of the greatest injustices, and incidentally the worst advertisement, the Royal Navy ever suffered.' – Cunningham. A similar disaster in 1939–45 was largely avoided by meeting wartime expansion with temporary RNVR commissions.

See 20 July 1917, 24 December 1917, 22 June 1937, 19 October 2010.

1938 The sloop *Milford*, Capt R.L.B. Cunliffe RN, sailed from Portland to join the South Atlantic Station having spent a week embarking stores for Tristan da Cunha. 'The only incident that caused any excitement was when a bundle of clogs, the gift of the Dutch government, fell into the sea by the side of the coaling pier' – *The Times*, 10 February 1938.

1940 *Salvo* and *Servitor* swept first magnetic mine with LL sweep off Sunk lightvessel.

1943 Commemorative standard candlesticks, commissioned by the Dean and Chapter of Westminster Abbey in memory of the 862 men lost in the battleship *Barham*, were dedicated after Evensong in the presence of Vice-Admiral Sir Henry Pridham-Wippell whose flag she had been wearing when torpedoed on 25 November 1941. 'Since the candles in these holders are lit at every service held in the nave, *Barham*'s men will be honoured daily for as long as the Abbey stands' – Dr C.S. Knighton in *The Westminster Abbey Chorister* 41 Winter 2005/6.

See 21 March 1955.

1944 Wellington 0/612 damaged U-545 in N.W. Approaches. Submarine scuttled by own crew.

1944 Swordfish A/842 (*Fencer*) sank U-666 in W. Approaches.

1947 Battleship *Vanguard*, carrying the King, Queen and two Princesses to South Africa, crossed the line. 'The King had begun the proceedings by halting between two ends of a massive 28-in hawser on the foredeck which Capt W.G. Agnew told him was the main-brace. "Well, it's in a sorry state. You had better splice it", said the King, and all hands cheered when the bo'sun, obeying the royal orders, piped "Splice the main-brace", meaning a double issue of rum for all on board as a celebration tonight' – *The Times*.

See 11 July 1935.

2011 Destroyer *Manchester*, Cdr Rex Cox RN, entered Portsmouth for the last time.

See 19 October 2010, 26 January 2011.

11 FEBRUARY

1744 Admiral Thomas Mathews (*Namur* (90)) and Rear-Admiral Lestock fought the Franco-Spanish fleet of twenty-eight ships of the line under Vice-Admiral de Court (*Terrible*) and Rear-Admiral Don Juan Jose Navarro (*Real Felipe*) off Toulon, 20 miles S.S.W. of Cape Sicie. The Spanish *Poder* was captured (by Edward Hawke in *Berwick* leaving the line) then retaken; abandoned later and burned by the British on the following night.

Ships: *Anne* galley fire-ship, *Barfleur*, *Bedford*, *Berwick*, *Boyne*, *Buckingham*, *Cambridge*, *Chichester*, *Dorsetshire*, *Dragon*, *Dunkirk*, *Elizabeth*, *Essex*, *Kingston*, *Marlborough*, *Namur*, *Nassau*, *Neptune*, *Norfolk*, *Princessa*, *Princess Caroline*, *Revenge*, *Royal Oak*, *Rupert*, *Russell*, *Somerset*, *Stirling Castle*, *Torbay*, and *Warwick*.

The attack was made with the English line ill-formed. Lestock was out of station and though court-martialled was acquitted, while Mathews was dismissed. 'It taught those who were minded to learn that gallantry was less important than formal adherence to the line of battle, and that cowards with political friends had nothing to fear' – N.A.M. Rodger, *Command of the Sea. A Naval History of Britain, 1649–1815*, p.245.

1747 *Enterprise* captured the French *Vestale* 24 miles W. of Cape Tiburon, Haiti.

1779 Admiral Keppel's honourable acquittal of 'malicious and ill-founded charges' after Admiral Palliser's battle off Ushant led to court martial of the latter, who received a 'censorious acquittal'.

See 27 July 1778.

1797 Cdre Horatio Nelson (*Minerve*) hove to and lowered a boat to pick up a man, when closely pursued by two Spanish ships of the line in Gibraltar Bay. 'By God I'll not lose Hardy: back the mizzen topsail.' This disconcerted the enemy who were taken aback.

1841 Order in Council authorised a £50 pay rise to the Surgeon of Pembroke Dockyard to 'enable him to keep a horse for the purpose of visiting his distant patients . . . in consequence of many of the men being obliged to reside at a considerable distance from the yard'.

1916 Light cruiser *Arethusa* mined off the North Cutler buoy, Harwich. Broke her back on a shoal and sank.

1917 GC (ex-AM): Lt D.P.T. Stembridge for saving pilot from burning aircraft.

The Tribal-class destroyer HMS *Maori* during the Spanish Civil War, with Neutrality Patrol markings on B gun turret. The ship was sunk in a German air attack on Malta on 12 February 1942. She was raised and scuttled off Malta on 5 July 1945. (*Cdr David Hobbs RN*)

The monitor HMS *Erebus* (1916), armed with two 15-in guns, in August 1939. (*NMRN*)

1918 *Westphalia* (*Cullist*) (Q-ship) sunk by U-97 in the Irish Sea.

1938 Singapore Naval Base, with its 1,006ft-long King George VI graving dock, inaugurated by the Civil Lord of the Admiralty, Col J.J. Llewellin MP, and the Governor of the Straits Settlements, Sir Shenton Thomas.
See 16 February 1888.

1941 Monitor *Erebus* bombarded Ostend.

1941 *Snapper* sunk S. of Ushant by fifty-six depth charges from three German minesweepers, M-2, M-13 and M-25. First of twelve large submarines lost in 1941.

1942 *Spikenard* (lent to RCN) sunk by U-136 S. of Iceland (56.10N, 21.07W). Convoy SC 67.

1944 Wellington D/407 (RCAF) sank U-283 in N.W. Approaches.

1944 Sloops *Wild Goose* and *Woodpecker* sank U-424 in W. Approaches.
See 20 February 1944.

1944 *Launceston* and *Ipswich* (RAN) and *Jumna* (RIN) sank the Japanese S/M RO-110 in Bay of Bengal.

1945 *Pathfinder* (second of the name) damaged by Japanese aircraft S. of Akyab, Burma. Towed to Chittagong but CTL.

1964 GC: CPO Jonathan Rogers DSM, RAN, posthumously, for gallantry in the sinking of the Daring-class destroyer HMAS *Voyager* in collision with the carrier HMAS *Melbourne*, 11 February 1964. He helped fifty to sixty men escape from the ship's sinking forward section and stayed below leading trapped men in prayer. CPO Rogers, an ex-RN PO, won his DSM when Coxswain of MTB 698 in action in May 1944. He joined the RAN in 1950.
See 1 May 1942, 2 August 1962.

1979 The White Ensign flew over Westminster Abbey during a service to commemorate the life and achievements of Capt James Cook, RN, killed on duty 14 February 1779.

1998 Frigate *Monmouth* (West Africa Deployment Ship) dispatched to Sierra Leone to provide humanitarian aid and to assist British High Commissioner during civil war. Operation Resilient.

12 FEBRUARY

1756 Rear-Admiral Charles Watson (*Kent*), and Rear-Admiral Pocock, with some East India Company ships and troops under Col Robert Clive, destroyed the pirate stronghold of Tulagi Angria at Geriah (Vijaydurg), W. coast of India. Ships and vessels: *Bridgewater, Cumberland, Kent, Kingfisher, Salisbury, Tiger*. Hon. East India Co.: *Bombay, Drake, Guardian, Protector, Revenge, Triumph, Viper, Warren*.

1811 Boats of *Active* and *Cerberus* cut out eleven Venetian vessels and burned two military storehouses at Ortona, E. coast of Italy.

1844 Boats of *Harlequin* and *Wanderer* burned the villages on the Merdoo (Morodu) River, Sumatra.

1848 Boats of *Alarm* and *Vixen*, with a detachment of the 38th Regiment, destroyed a fort at Serapaqui, River San Juan de Nicaragua.

1918 Armoured cruiser *Roxburgh* rammed and sank U-89 off north Donegal (55.33N, 07.32W).

1928 John David Elliott Fieldhouse born at Bramley, Leeds; C-in-C Fleet during the Falklands War 1982.

See 17 February 1992.

1931 Admiralty Librarian, William Gordon Perrin, died. Buried at Haywards Heath 16 February and, at the Admiralty's request, the coffin was covered with the Union Flag.

1938 *Walrus*, destroyer, ran ashore in Filey Bay, Yorkshire. Refloated a month later but CTL.

1940 Surveying ship/minesweeper *Gleaner* sank U-33 laying mines in the Firth of Clyde. First capture of Enigma wheels.

1940 Light cruiser *Glasgow* captured the German trawler *Herrlichkeit* off Tromsø (69.56N, 16.49E).

1940 *Hasty* captured the German SS *Morea* in Atlantic (41.42N, 15.03W). Operation V.O.

The Channel Dash, 1942

The German battlecruisers *Scharnhorst* and *Gneisenau* and the cruiser *Prinz Eugen* were under regular air-attack at their base at Brest, and Hitler wanted them back in the relative safety of German home ports.

They slipped out on the night of 11 February to make a dash up-Channel, with a strong aircraft umbrella and E-boat escorts.

At 1055 Lt-Cdr Esmonde with 825 Squadron of Swordfish torpedo bombers learned of the German move. In spite of heavy snow the squadron was airborne at 1230 to attack the Germans 23 miles away. Only ten Spitfires arrived to cover the attack and these had to weave to fly slowly enough to remain in touch with the 'stringbag' biplanes.

The Spitfire cover was hopelessly inadequate and by the time Esmonde started his run-in, he had half a wing shot away. Still he kept on until an FW 190 shot him down. All the other aircraft were shot down and not one hit on the enemy was recorded.

Esmonde was posthumously awarded the VC on the recommendation of the RAF, and 4 DSOs and one CGM were awarded. Of the aircrew taking part in the attack there were only five survivors, four of whom were wounded.

'There can, in the history of forlorn hopes, be few more moving stories than that of the last flight of No. 825 Squadron. Its leader – the same officer who had led the Swordfish from the *Victorious* to attack the *Bismarck* in May 1941 – typified all that was finest in the newest branch of the naval service and the junior members of her squadron followed him faithfully to the end.' – S.W. Roskill.

1942 Destroyer *Maori* sunk by aircraft in Grand Harbour, Malta. Caught fire, blew up and damaged destroyer *Decoy*.

1942 Unsuccessful attack on the German *Gneisenau, Scharnhorst* and *Prinz Eugen* during their escape up-Channel. Ships: *Campbell* (D 21), *Vivacious, Worcester, Mackay* (D 16), *Whitshed*. MGB: 41, 43. MTB: 32, 44, 45, 48, 71, 219, 221. FAA: 825 Sqn – Swordfish V4523, W5907, W5978, W5983, W5984, W5985 (all lost). RAF: Twenty-eight Beaufort aircraft of 42, 86 and 217 Squadrons, one of which, from 42 Squadron, dropped a torpedo which missed *Campbell*, standing by *Worcester*, which had been damaged.

'The Channel Dash' – Operation Fuller. Painting by Reg Mitchell who, then aged 19, was serving in MTB 48 depicted in the bottom right hand corner of the picture. (*The Channel Dash Association*)

VC: Lt-Cdr (A) Eugene Esmonde (W5984/825). Posthumous. 'A mothball attack by a handful of ancient planes, piloted by men whose bravery surpassed any other action by either side that day' – a tribute from the German Foreign Office.

'If ever a failure can be glorious, then this must have been the most glorious failure in all British naval history.'

See 6 April 1941, 12 February 2010.

1942 *Luciana*, an Italian tanker which had been guaranteed safe conduct, inadvertently sunk by submarine *Una* while leaving Taranto for the Atlantic.

1943 Hudson F/48 sank U-442 in Atlantic (37.32N, 11.56W).

1944 *Khedive Ismail*, in convoy of five troop transports en route from Mombasa to Colombo and escorted by cruiser *Hawkins* and destroyers *Petard* and *Paladin*, torpedoed and sunk by Japanese submarine I-27 off Maldives (01.25N, 72.22E); 1,297 lives lost, including twenty Wrens. I-27 sunk in counter-attack by torpedo because Colombo had issued the destroyers with AA shells, the only 4-in ammunition available. A hat-trick for *Petard* which had sunk U-559 on 30 October 1942 and a pair of Italian submarines on 15 December 1942 and 4 May 1943 – the only RN ship to sink enemy submarines of all three nationalities.

1944 Indian Ocean sinking due to Ultra intelligence. Following the defeat of the Atlantic U-boat campaign in May 1943 German submarines were deployed to the Indian Ocean and supplied by tankers at remote rendezvous. Enigma decrypts gave C-in-C Eastern Fleet warning that four U-boats were scheduled to refuel from the tanker *Charlotte Schliemann* on the night of 11/12 February south of Mauritius. In an operation carefully engineered to avoid compromising the special intelligence element, the tanker was located by a Catalina flying boat on 11 February. She was intercepted by the destroyer *Relentless* at 0040 and scuttled herself.

See 12 March 1944.

1945 Submarine *Venturer* sank German M-381 off northern Norway.

1945 Light cruiser *Delhi* damaged by explosive motorboat in Split harbour, Adriatic: CTL.

See 26 March 1941.

1960 Chatham Port Trophy Store transferred to Portsmouth and Commodore RNB to be responsible from 1 April 1960. AFO 432/60

1970 Explosion in forward accommodation space in submarine *Auriga*, Lt-Cdr C.J. Mayer RN, east of Gibraltar during battery charging.

See 30 August 1966, 29 September 1971, 21 March 2007.

1981 Admiral of the Fleet Lord Fraser of North Cape died.

See 26 December 1943, 5 February 1888.

2007 MOD announced that the assault ship *Intrepid*, laid up in Portsmouth harbour since 1999, was to be 'recycled at a British facility'.

See 25 June 1964, 17 February 2008.

2010 Memorial to the thirteen men of 825 NAS who died in the Swordfish attack led by Lt-Cdr Eugene Esmonde VC on the German battlecruisers *Scharnhorst* and *Gneisenau* on 12 February 1942 during their daytime passage from Brest to Germany – the Channel Dash – unveiled by Admiral Lord Boyce at Ramsgate Harbour. The names of the fallen read by Rear-Admiral Simon Charlier, Rear-Admiral Fleet Air Arm.

2010 The end of an ERA. The last Marine Engineering Artificers Qualifying Course passed out from HMS *Sultan* at Gosport. Engine Room Artificers (ERAs) first entered the Royal Navy in 1868 and Artificer Apprentices or 'Boy Artificers' in 1903. Henceforth RN engineering specialists were rated Engineering Technicians (ME), (WE) or (AE).

13 FEBRUARY

1718 George Bridges Rodney born.
See p.34.

1810 Boats of *Armide*, *Christian VII* and *Caledonia* captured a French gunboat and burned three chasse-marées in Basque Roads.

1812 *Apollo* captured the French *Merinos* off Corsica.

1814 *Boyne* and *Caledonia* fought the French *Adrienne* and *Romulus* close off Cape Brun, outside Toulon.

February 1830

Disease remained by far the greatest killer of seamen until the First World War. Throughout the nineteenth century, surgeons struggled to overcome the most common killers. How heroically they struggled is illustrated by the story of Dr McKinnel of *Sybille* off Lagos.

The ship's company had contracted yellow fever from *Eden*, and 101 men had died out of a complement of 160. Morale was so low that McKinnel believed many were dying of sheer fatalism when they perceived a symptom. He therefore took a pint of black vomit from a patient who was dying of disease, publicly drank it down and walked around the deck until it was clear to all that it was no trick. The improvement in morale had a dramatic effect on the death rate.

1878 Vice-Admiral Sir Geoffrey Phipps Hornby, C-in-C Mediterranean Fleet, flag in *Alexandra*, took his fleet through the Dardanelles, and four ships on to Constantinople, to make a diplomatic presence during tension between Britain and Russia. A task conducted more felicitously than Sir John Duckworth's similar mission in 1807. Phipps Hornby anchored short of the city limits and a Russian army stopped at the city gates.

1892 Admiral of the Fleet Sir Provo Wallis died aged 101 after a career on the Active List of (officially) almost ninety-seven years. Wallis was the sole surviving naval officer who had fought in the French Revolutionary War, having been a midshipman in the *Cleopatra* (32) eighteen months before the Peace of Amiens on 25 March 1802, and the sole surviving flag officer on the Active List who had fought in the Napoleonic Wars and the American War of 1812–15.
See 13 April 1885, 15 April 1887, 11 July 1929, 2 March 1940, 14 September 1947, 19 April 1967.

The future Admirals of the Fleet Lord Chatfield and the Earl of Cork and Orrery had joined *Britannia* in 1886 and 1887 when Wallis was still alive and still on the Active List. Wallis had served in the Navy with Admiral of the Fleet Sir Peter Parker, born in 1721, who entered the Service in 1735 and who died in 1811. Thus, when Chatfield and Cork died in 1967, these three generations had served on the Active List of the Royal Navy without a gap for about 240 years. (Michael Lewis, *A Social History of the Navy*, pp.184–85.)

Provo William Parry Wallis was born at Halifax, Nova Scotia, on 12 April 1791 and entered on the ship's books of *Oiseau* fifth rate as an able seaman on 1 May 1795 aged 4 years 18 days but did not go to sea until 1800. He was promoted admiral 2 March 1863. Compulsory age-related retirement regulations introduced in 1870 exempted officers who had commanded a rated ship during the late French wars. Such officers remained on the Active List to be promoted by seniority as vacancies arose. Wallis, Second Lieutenant of HMS *Shannon* had commanded her in the later stages of victorious action with the USS *Chesapeake* after her Captain was wounded and the First Lieutenant was killed and so he qualified. He became an admiral of the fleet on 11 December 1877 and died at Funtington, near Chichester and was buried in nearby St Mary's church.

1913 First cadet midshipmen entered RAN College, Osborne House, Geelong, later moving to the new RAN College at Jervis Bay.

1940 The Admiralty appealed for the services of 10,000 fishermen for minesweeping.
See 21 February 1940.

1941 Heavy cruiser *Shropshire* bombarded Mogadishu, Italian Somaliland.

1941 Albacore aircraft of 826 and 829 Sqn (*Formidable*) attack Massawa, Eritrea. Operation Composition.

HMS *Alexandra* (1875), at Malta. A central battery ironclad, she served as a flagship for twenty-three years. (*NMRN*)

1942 *Scorpion*, river gunboat, sunk by Japanese ships off Sumatra.

1942 Submarine *Tempest* depth-charged by the Italian TB *Circe* in the Gulf of Taranto near scene of sinking of *Lucania* the previous day. Sank later in tow. *Circe* sank three, if not four, Allied submarines.

1943 Auxiliary AA ship *Pozarica* capsized after damage by aircraft off Bougie, Algeria, on 29 January.

1945 Corvette *Denbigh Castle*, escort of Convoy JW 64, torpedoed by U-992 off Kola Inlet. Beached in Bolshaya Volokovaya Bay but capsized later. This was the first JW convoy to get through intact.

1952 The Secretary of the Admiralty announced that the following message to the Royal Navy has been received from The Queen: 'On my accession to the Throne, I wish to send a message of gratitude to the Royal Navy and all my other naval forces for the distinguished services which they rendered during the reign of my beloved father. He received his early training in the Royal Navy and maintained throughout his life a close personal interest in the ships and men of the naval services. As the wife of a serving officer, I too have a specially intimate link with the Royal Navy. I have seen both at home and overseas how its great traditions, tested and proved in two world wars, are constantly maintained by all who serve under the White Ensign. I shall endeavour to keep in touch with the activities and welfare of all ranks and ratings of my naval forces throughout the Commonwealth. Grateful for their services in the past, proud of their present efficiency, and confident that they will uphold their high standards, I send to them all this expression of the trust which I and my peoples throughout the Commonwealth repose in them.'

See 6 and 15 February 1952.

1959 Admiral Sir Guy Grantham, C-in-C Mediterranean Fleet during the Suez Crisis of 1956 and later passed over for First Sea Lord, appointed Governor and C-in-C of Malta; the first naval officer to hold this appointment since Rear-Admiral Sir Alexander Ball, who had commanded the *Alexander* at the Battle of the Nile in 1798.

See 5 September 1800.

1970 'Blue berets, as at present provided for wear by aircrew with working dress . . . may in future be worn with working uniforms at sea.' – DCI(RN) 202/70.

14 FEBRUARY

1779 Capt James Cook (*Resolution*) murdered by natives of Hawaii during his third voyage of exploration.

See 21 February 1779, 11 February 1979.

1797 'A victory is very essential to England at this moment' – Jervis. Battle of Cape St Vincent. Twenty-four miles W. by S. of Cape St Vincent. Admiral Sir John Jervis (*Victory*) defeated twenty-seven Spanish sail of the line under Vice-Admiral Don José de Córdoba (*Santissima Trinidad*). Four captured: *Salvador Del Mundo*, *San Josef*, *San Nicolas*, *San Ysidro*. Ships: *Barfleur*, *Blenheim*, *Britannia*, *Captain*, *Colossus*, *Culloden*, *Diadem*, *Egmont*, *Excellent*, *Goliath*, *Irresistible*, *Namur*, *Orion*, *Prince George*, *Victory*. Frigates, etc.: *Bonne Citoyenne*, *Fox*, *Lively*, *Minerve*, *Niger*, *Raven*, *Southampton*. Regiments: 2/1st 11th, 18th, 50th, 51st, 69th, 90th. The 69th, now the Royal Welsh, have the Naval Battle Honour: 'St Vincent, 1797'.

See 12 April 1782.

Battle of Cape St Vincent, 1797

Sir John Jervis leading a fleet of fifteen ships of the line encountered a Spanish fleet (twenty-seven of the line) which was sailing from Cartagena to Cadiz as a first step towards combination with the French. Jervis led his close-hauled line through the scattered formations of the enemy, intending to reverse course and attack the main body which was to leeward. Soon after the leading ship (*Culloden*) had turned, Nelson in the *Captain* (third from the rear) realised the enemy might escape. He therefore wore ship and headed straight for the enemy, supported by Collingwood and others. As a result of this bold but risky manoeuvre the Spanish fleet was thrown into confusion. Warned of the danger of colliding with two enemy ships, Troubridge in the *Culloden* made the matter-of-fact but memorable reply to his First Lieutenant, 'Can't help it, Griffiths: let the weakest fend off.'

'Nelson was probably the first British flag officer to lead a boarding party in person since Sir Edward Howard in 1513' Rodger, *Command of the Ocean. A Naval History of Britain 1649–1815*, p.439.

1805 *San Fiorenzo* (36) took the French *Psyche* (32) 4 miles E.S.E. of Ganjam, Bay of Bengal in the early hours. *Psyche* subsequently commissioned into the Fleet under her own name. Battle Honour: *Psyche* 1805.

1807 *Bacchante* captured the French *Dauphin* 80 miles N. by E. of Cape Rafael, San Domingo.

The eleven ships of the Royal Navy's Taurus 09 task group in the Mediterranean in March 2009. (*RN*)

The Battle of Cape St Vincent, 1797. (*NMRN 1977/206*)

1808 Boats of *Confiance* cut out the French *Canonnier* in the mouth of the Tagus.

1813 Boats of *Bacchante* captured the French *Alcinous* and a convoy of eight vessels 20 miles E.N.E. of Otranto.

1858 Naval Brigade, landed from wood screw corvette *Pelorus*, arrived at Meaday, Burma.

1913 Appointment of first SNO of New Zealand Division, Capt H.J.T. Marshall.

1942 VC: T/Lt Thomas Wilkinson, RNR (*Li Wo*). Posthumous. Action with an escorted Japanese convoy off Singapore.

The *Li Wo*, a small auxiliary patrol vessel armed with one old 4-in gun, met the advance force of the Japanese invasion fleet south of Singapore. She turned and engaged despite the odds, and finally rammed a transport before being sunk. Ten of her crew and passengers survived, and her Captain, Lt T.S. Wilkinson, RNR, was posthumously awarded the VC.

1942 River gunboats *Dragonfly* and *Grasshopper* sunk by Japanese aircraft off Sumatra.

1942 First RM Commando formed; now 40 Cdo RM.

1943 Catalina J/202 sank U-620 off Portugal. Convoy KMS 9.

1944 Submarine *Tally Ho* sank the German U-It.23 (ex-Italian S/M *Reginaldo Guiliani*) off Penang, Malaya.

1945 Frigates *Bayntun*, *Braithwaite*, *Loch Dunvegan* and *Loch Eck* sank U-989 N. of Shetlands.

1945 RCN's 29th Flotilla lost five boats in an explosion (heard in England) in Ostend Harbour which destroyed twelve MTBs; seventy-three killed.

1956 Admiral Sir Walter Cowan died. He won his first DSO in 1898 and his second in 1943 at the age of 73. 'The only officer in the Grand Fleet who was sorry the war was over' – Geoffrey Bennett, *Cowan's War*.

See 11 June 1871, 18 April 1998.

1969 Capt Michael Reece, the first RM officer to command a FAA helicopter squadron, took over 848 NAS in the commando carrier *Albion* at Singapore.

See 29 March 2001.

1979 *Ark Royal*, fourth of the name, paid off at Plymouth, twenty-four years to the day after her first ship's company embarked at Cammell Laird, Birkenhead.

1985 Admiral Sir Peter Stanford succeeded Admiral Sir Desmond Cassidi as C-in-C Naval Home Command. Admiral Cassidi was the last CINCNAVHOME to have served in the Second World War.

2003 Lt-Cdr Frederick 'Ben' Rice, DSM, died. The first rating-pilot to land on an aircraft carrier (*Courageous*, February 1939).

See 13 April 1940.

15 FEBRUARY

1760 A squadron under Admiral Edward Boscawen, flag in *Royal William* (100), sailing to command the fleet in Quiberon Bay during the Seven Years War, was caught in strong gale in the S.W. Approaches which increased to hurricane force and was driven back up-channel. *Ramillies* (90), Capt Wittewrong Taylor, detached from the rest of the squadron, mistook Burgh Island well into Bigbury Bay for Looe Island. The Master thus continued east looking for Rame Head but found Bolt Tail; unable to weather it and both bower cables having parted, she went ashore in Ramillies Cove near Salcombe, and broke up. One midshipman and twenty-five men survived and 700 lost.

See 19 February 1758.

1783 *Magnificent* captured the French *Concorde* 30 miles S.W. of Nevis, West Indies.

1797 *Lapwing* captured the Spanish privateer *San Cristobal* 30 miles S.W. of St Kitts.

1804 Nathaniel Dance (*Earl Camden* Hon. East India Company), in charge of an unescorted merchant convoy of twenty-seven ships, beat off an attack by five French warships under Rear-Admiral Durand Linois (*Marengo*) at the southern entrance to Malacca Strait and saved his convoy. Ships: *Earl Camden, Royal George, Ganges* (brig). Dance's confident tactics so affected the imagination of the French that Linois declined to attack him, which produced the acid remark from Napoleon that his admirals 'have discovered, I know not how, that war can be made without running risks'.

1807 'Our force has lately experienced a diminution from an event which I now with grief relate to you': The third-rate *Ajax* (74), part of Vice-Admiral Sir John Duckworth's squadron at anchor off the Dardanelles, caught fire at 2100 on 14 February. Dense smoke prevented the fire from being fought and, when flames burst up the main hatchway, the ship was abandoned. Capt Hon. Henry Blackwood, who had commanded the frigate *Euryalus* at Trafalgar, 'leaped' from the spritsail yard and was rescued by a boat from *Canopus*; of 650 ship's company, 383 were saved and 267 lost. The *Ajax* burned all night and drifted onto the island of Tenedos where she exploded at 0500 on 15 February. Blackwood was exonerated at a board of enquiry held in *Canopus* and honourably acquitted at his later court martial. He served in subsequent operations as a volunteer in Duckworth's flagship *Royal George* (100). The cause of the fire, which began in the after cockpit, was never determined.

See 17 March 1800.

1809 *Belle Poule* captured the French *Var* from under the batteries at Valona, Albania.

1857 *Auckland* (IN) and *Eaglet* destroyed five mandarin junks and captured a 30-gun battery in Tung Chung Bay, near Hong Kong. A detachment of Bombay Artillery was serving in *Auckland* as marines.

1897 Royal Marines landed at Chania, Crete.

1909 Institution of Reserve Decoration (RD) and Volunteer Reserve Decoration (VRD).

1913 Rank of Mate resurrected as a lower-deck promotion; thirteen made.

1918 German destroyer raid in Dover Strait, on the Folkestone–Griz Nez Barrage.

1930 GC (ex-EGM): AB George Willet Harrison (*Hood*) for gallantry in rescuing a trapped shipwright.

1940 Germany announced that in future all British merchant ships would be treated as warships.

1940 Heavy cruiser *Exeter* reached Plymouth from Falkland Islands after the Battle of the River Plate. First Lord first on board.

1942 Singapore capitulated to Japanese land forces.

1943 Liberator S/120 sank U-225 700 miles S.W. of Iceland. Convoy SC 119.

1952 The RN and RM participation in the funeral of HM King George VI was acknowledged in a message to the First Lord of the Admiralty: 'Her Majesty the Queen has commanded me to express her satisfaction that it was possible for

Royal Navy counter piracy operations in the Indian Ocean. On 15 February 2011 the frigate HMS *Cornwall*, Cdr David Wilkinson RN, sighted a dhow acting suspiciously near a South Korean merchant vessel. A Royal Marines and Royal Navy boarding party found powerful outboard motors, AK47s, RPGs and ammunition on board the dhow. The threat to those 'who pass on the seas upon their lawful occasions' was removed. (*RN*)

the Royal Navy and Royal Marines to be so fully represented at the funeral of her beloved father. Her Majesty noted with pride the fine bearing of all those who were on duty on this solemn occasion. Her Majesty feels that it was especially fitting that the gun-carriage on the last journey from Westminster Hall to St George's Chapel, Windsor, was drawn by men of the service in which her father spent the early years of his life and which he loved so well'.

See 2 February 1901, 13 February 1952, 30 January 1965.

1953 Sloop *Snipe* landed a British magistrate accompanied by two policemen and fifteen Royal Marines on Deception Island in Antarctica to arrest and expel a party landed in January by Argentine naval vessels and who 'were becoming a nuisance'.

1965 The White Ensign hauled down in ships of the Royal Canadian Navy at 1200 and replaced by the Maple Leaf national flag.

See 1 February 1968.

1967 Submarines *Opportune*, departing from HMS *Dolphin*, and *Orpheus* entering Portsmouth Harbour, collided in darkness and heavy weather just outside the harbour entrance. Portsmouth court martial on 13 April found Lt-Cdr Charles Baker RN of *Opportune* not guilty of hazarding his vessel.

1968 First British Polaris missile fired, by *Resolution*, Port Crew, Cdr M.C. Henry RN, at 1115 EST submerged 30 miles off Cape Kennedy. The second firing made by Starboard Crew, Cdr F. Frewer RN, on 4 March 1968.

See 6 November 2008.

1970 First RN hovercraft (BHN7) to evaluation trials at Lee-on-Solent.

1971 Cash accounts and all other monetary data decimalised.

1972 Icelandic Parliament passed a bill extending the national fishing limits to 50 miles. The Second Cod War started six months later.

See 31 August 1958.

1991 RN element of UN MCMV force – *Herald*, *Dulverton*, *Atherstone*, *Cattistock*, *Ledbury* and *Hurworth* – began mine clearance operations in northern Gulf, allowing US battleships to take up NGS positions.

16 FEBRUARY

1762 The French island of Martinique finally taken after a well-planned amphibious operation led by Maj-Gen the Hon. Robert Monkton, who had been Wolfe's second-in-command at Quebec in 1759, and the Leeward Islands squadron commanded by Rear-Admiral George Rodney. The Seven Years War.
Battle Honour: Martinique 1762.
See 4 February 1762, 22 March 1794.

Ships: *Foudroyant* (84, flag), *Dublin* (74, flag Cdre Sir J. Douglas), *Dragon* (74), *Temeraire* (74), *Culloden* (74), *Temple* (70), *Vanguard* (70), *Marlborough* (68), *Alcide* (64), *Devonshire* (64), *Modeste* (64), *Raisonnable* (64), *Stirling Castle* (64), *Nottingham* (60), *Norwich* (50), *Falkland* (50), *Rochester* (50), *Sutherland* (50), *Woolwich* (44), *Penzance* (40), *Dover* (40), *Stag* (32), *Repulse* (32), *Crescent* (28), *Lizard* (28), *Levant* (28), *Echo* (24), *Greyhound* (20), *Nightingale* (20), *Rose* (20), *Barbados* (14), *Virgin* (12), *Antigua* (12), *Zephyr*, *Amazon*, *Basilisk*, *Thunder*, *Granado* (bombs), *Crown* (storeship).

1782 Vice-Admiral Sir Edward Hughes (*Superb*) and squadron captured six sail of a French convoy 10 miles S.E. of Madras.
See 17 February 1782.

1783 *Argo* taken by the French *Amphitrite* and *Nymphe* off Sombrero, West Indies.

1798 *Alfred* (74)captured the French privateer *Scipion* at Basse Terre, Guadeloupe.

1854 Wood paddle sloop *Barracouta* and two boats of *Winchester* captured seven pirate junks off the Lema Islands, near Hong Kong.

1858 Boats of iron paddle vessel *Bloodhound* captured a 6-gun battery in the Benin River.

1888 Opening of the Calliope Dry Dock at Auckland, then the largest dry dock south of the Equator. Named after the frigate *Calliope* in which Capt Owen Stanley had surveyed Auckland harbour in 1845. The screw corvettes *Calliope* and *Diamond* were docked that day.
See 11 February 1938.

1909 *Pelorus*, third-class cruiser, 2,135 tons, 'came to with starboard bower in 9 fathoms at Iquitos; veered to 4 shackles'. On her way home from South Africa she had been ordered to South America and sailed on 19 January from Belém (Pará) in Brazil 2,200 miles up the Amazon to Iquitos in Peru whence she returned on 9 March after eight days in Peru.

Lt Roberts, VC (1917–1979) (left) and PO Gould, VC (1914–2001). (*NMRN*)

1915 *Cadmus*, sloop, landed armed party to contain Indian Army mutiny at Singapore; one RN casualty.

1916 War Office took over the anti-aircraft defence of United Kingdom from the Admiralty.

1937 Three destroyers of the 3rd DF, Mediterranean Fleet, *Active*, *Worcester* and *Antelope* collided during exercises in heavy weather off the Hurd Bank, E.N.E. of Valletta (35.55N. 14.49E). No casualties.

See 23 December 1943.

1938 Three submarines launched at Vickers-Armstrong, Barrow: *Triumph* by wife of Vice-Admiral J.F. Somerville, C-in-C East Indies; *Unity* by wife of Rear-Admiral J.H.D. Cunningham, ACNS(Air); and *Ursula*, by wife of Mr J. Callander, General Manager of the builders.

See 29 April 1940, 14 January 1942.

1940 Destroyer *Cossack* released British prisoners from the German *Altmark* in Jossing Fjord. Operation D.T.

See 18 August 1759, 5 September 1926.

The cruiser *Arethusa* and the 4th Destroyer Flotilla (Capt Vian) were searching the Norwegian coast for enemy shipping, including the *Altmark*, one of *Graf Spee*'s supply ships and believed to be carrying British merchant seamen captured by the raider. *Arethusa* sighted the *Altmark*, but two Norwegian torpedo boats, *Trygg* and *Kjell*, frustrated attempts of parties from *Intrepid* and *Ivanhoe* to board her. *Altmark* then entered Jossing Fjord, followed by *Cossack*. Again, a Norwegian torpedo boat prevented boarding, claiming *Altmark* was in neutral waters, was unarmed and carried no prisoners of war. That evening *Cossack* re-entered the fjord, went alongside and released 299 prisoners to the cry of 'The Navy's here', a cry that 'rang throughout the length and breadth of the nation' – Roskill.

1942 VC: Lt Peter Scawen Watkinson Roberts, PO Thomas William Gould, for removing two bombs from the casing of submarine *Thrasher*.

See 6 December 2001, 9 February 2008.

When the submarine *Thrasher* attacked a ship off Suda Bay in Crete, she was counter-attacked heavily. She surfaced two hours after dark to find two unexploded bombs in the casing. Although the submarine would have to dive immediately if detected by enemy forces in the area, which would inevitably drown the men in the casing, Lt P.S.W. Roberts and PO T.W. Gould volunteered to go out and dispose of the bombs. Both were awarded the Victoria Cross. 'The VCs were awarded on the recommendation of the C-in-C Mediterranean, Admiral Sir Andrew Cunningham, but were opposed by the Honours and Awards Committee in London, which argued that the acts of bravery had not been performed in the presence of the enemy, as VC warrant stipulated, and that the George Cross would be more appropriate. Cunningham, however, retorted that two large enemy bombs, in a submarine off an enemy coastline, constituted quite enough enemy presence' – Gould's obituary in the *Daily Telegraph* (7 December 2001).

1944 Light cruiser *Mauritius* bombarded the Formia area.

1945 Frigate *St John* (RCN) sank U-309 off Shetland.

1945 Assault on Ruywa, Burma. Ships: *Flamingo* and *Narbada* (RIN).

1953 Carrier *Hermes* (ex-*Elephant*, renamed 5 November 1945) launched at Vickers, Barrow, by Mrs Winston Churchill. Sold to India in November 1986 and commissioned as *Viraat*.

See 20 March 1987.

1953 His Majesty King Paul of the Hellenes appointed an honorary admiral in Her Majesty's Fleet.

See 2 August 1889, 17 September 1948, 1 May 1951, 2 July 1958, 4 August 2001.

1962 Admiralty approved the establishment of a W/T station on Ascension Island; NP 1984 to be borne on books of HMS *President* for accounting and HMS *Mercury* for administration. AFO 302/62.

See 15 October 1957, 28 February 1962, 30 March 1976.

2001 Admiral Sir Michael Boyce, First Sea Lord, was appointed Chief of the Defence Staff.

17 FEBRUARY

1782 First battle between Vice-Admiral Sir Edward Hughes (*Superb*) and twelve ships under Cdre Chevalier de Suffren (*Héros*) 9 miles S.E. of Sadras.

Ships: *Burford, Hero, Isis, Eagle, Exeter. Monarca, Monmouth, Superb, Worcester.* Frigate: *Seahorse*. Fireship: *Combustion*. Detachments of the 98th Regiment served as marines. *Exeter* badly damaged. On being asked by the Master what was to be done, Capt King replied, 'There is nothing to be done but to fight her till she sinks.'
Battle Honour: Sadras 1782.

1794 Capture of the Convention Redoubt, San Fiorenzo (St Florent), Corsica, by Lt-Gen David Dundas and Cdre Robert Linzee (*Alcide*). Ships: *Alcide, Egmont, Fortitude.* Frigates: *Juno, Lowestoffe*. Seamen from the squadron were landed.

See 19 February 1794.

1805 *Cleopatra* (32) attacked but was taken by the French *Ville-de-Milan* 240 miles S.E. of Bermuda.

See 23 February 1805.

1810 Capture of Amboina, Moluccas, South China by Capt Tucker in *Cornwallis* with *Dover, Samarang* and a detachment of the Madras European Regiment.
Battle Honour: Amboina 1810.

1855 *Curacoa*, wood screw frigate, *Furious* and *Valorous*, paddle frigates, and *Viper*, screw gun-vessel, assisted in repelling a Russian attack on the Turkish entrenchments at Eupatoria, Crimea. Crimean Medal.

1858 *Pearl*'s Naval Brigade, with detachments of the 1st Bengal Military Police Battalion and Gurkha allies, destroyed the fort at Chandipur, Gogra River. Indian Mutiny Medal.

1886 Ranks of Fleet and Staff Paymasters and Engineers created.

1912 PO Edgar Evans died, returning from the South Pole with Capt Scott.

1917 VC: Cdr Gordon Campbell, decoy ship HMS Q.5 (ex-*Loderer* ex-*Farnborough*), for destruction

HMS *Pearl* (1855), a wood screw corvette of 2,187 tons. Her crew provided a Naval Brigade that fought in many actions throughout India, 1858. (*NMRN*)

Admiral of the Fleet Sir John Fieldhouse (1928–1992), submariner, and one of the great officers of the Royal Navy in the later twentieth century. John Fieldhouse was successively C-in-C Fleet, First Sea Lord and Chief of the Defence Staff. (*Author*)

of U-83 off S.W. Ireland (51.34N, 11.23W) in exceptional circumstances, an action which also gained two DSOs, three DSCs, ten DSMs and twenty-four mentions in Despatches.

See 22 March 1916, 7 June 1917, 8 August 1917.

Cdr Campbell, patrolling off S.W. Ireland in HMS Q.5, a 3,200-ton former collier, saw an approaching torpedo but deliberately manoeuvred to be hit aft rather than avoid the attack. The pre-planned panic party abandoned ship but the U-boat Commander, Kapitanleutnant Bruno Hoppe, still very cautious, made a submerged assessment, passing 10yds down the side of Q.5. U-83 surfaced 300yds away on the port beam and Hoppe, climbing onto his bridge, saw the White Ensign broken out in Q.5 and he was killed in the storm of gunfire which riddled his submarine. Q.5, with boiler and engine rooms flooded and awash aft, signalled Queenstown 'Q.5 slowly sinking respectfully wishes you goodbye' but she was brought into Berehaven and beached. The C-in-C at Queenstown, Admiral Sir Lewis Bayly, made 'Splendidly done; your magnificent perseverance and ability are well rewarded'. Cambell's *Gazette* entry gave little away, referring to his 'conspicuous gallantry, consummate coolness and skill in command of one of H.M. ships'.

1943 Destroyer *Paladin* and Bisley W/15 (SAAF) sank U-205 off Derna (32.56N, 22.01E).

1943 Destroyer *Fame* sank U-69 and destroyer *Viscount* sank U-201 480 miles E. of Newfoundland. Convoy ONS 165, which lost only two ships.

1943 Destroyers *Easton* and *Wheatland* sank the Italian submarine *Asteria* off Bougie. Convoy TX-1. Enigma machine salvaged.

1943 Admiral Sir William James, lately C-in-C Portsmouth and newly appointed as the first Chief of Naval Information at the Admiralty, returned as MP for Portsmouth North in a by-election caused by the incumbent, Admiral of the Fleet Sir Roger Keyes, having been raised to the peerage. Chief Petty Officer Walter Foster, a gunner's mate, had announced his intention of standing for the seat 'if he can obtain the Admiralty's permission' but did not do so.

See 19 February 1934, 7 September 1939, 14 January 1943, 17 August 1973.

1945 Frigates *Bayntun* and *Loch Eck* sank U-1278 N.N.W. off Shetland.

1945 Corvette *Bluebell* sunk in less than thirty seconds by U-711, and *Alnwick Castle* and *Lark* sank U-425, off Kola Inlet. Convoy RA 64. *Lark* torpedoed by U-968 and beached at Murmansk. Salvaged by Russians and taken into service as *Neptune*.

1992 Admiral of the Fleet Lord Fieldhouse of Gosport died at Southampton. His ashes were scattered at sea on 28 February. The first five-star submariner.

See 12 February 1928, 2 August 1985.

2008 Amphibious assault ship *Fearless* left Portsmouth under tow for the breakers at Ghent, Belgium.

See 12 February 2007, 12 September 2008.

18 FEBRUARY

1653 First day of battle between the Joint Admirals Robert Blake and Richard Deane (*Triumph*) with about eighty-five ships, and Admiral Marten Tromp with a large convoy, off Portland. Five Dutch ships destroyed and one captured, with forty of the convoy.

The first Dutch war. By 1650, the Dutch were outstripping the English in the race for maritime power. Their merchant and fishing fleets were far more numerous than the English. However, the main artery of their trade was the English Channel. The English claimed a salute at sea whenever they met a foreign warship in the Channel. In 1652, Tromp refused to salute Blake off Dover. In this last battle Tromp won, having lashed a broom to his masthead to show that he swept the English off the seas. The sea battles of the Kentish Knock, Dungeness and Portland (the Three Days Battle) ensued. The next sea battle of the first war was the Battle of the Gabbard, when the English fleet under Monck and Deane won a definite victory. The last battle was Scheveningen in which Tromp was killed.

1797 Trinidad captured from the Spanish by Rear-Admiral Henry Harvey in *Prince of Wales* (98) with three 74s, a 64 and seven smaller ships, with troops under Lt-Gen Sir Ralph Abercromby. They anchored within long gunshot range of a Spanish squadron anchored at Chaguaramas near Port of Spain (where RN frigates underwent AMPs until recent years). The Spanish set fire to their ships and on 18th Trinidad capitulated. This was a quick and efficient operation that St Vincent hoped, in vain, that Nelson would repeat at Tenerife.

Ships: *Prince of Wales* (98), *Bellona* (74), *Vengeance* (74), *Invincible* (74), *Scipio* (64), *Arethusa* (38), *Alarm* (32), *Favourite* (16), *Zebra* (16), *Acorn* (16), *Victorieuse* (12), *Terror* bomb.

See 24 July 1797.

1800 Nelson in *Foudroyant*, with *Alexander*, *Northumberland* and *Success* captured the French *Généreux* 10 miles W.S.W. of Cape Scalambri, Sicily seeking to relieve Malta. She had taken *Leander* after the Nile. The French *Ville de Marseilles* had been captured earlier in the day by *Alexander*.

See 17 August 1798.

1807 *Bacchante*, *Dauphin* and *Mediator* captured a fort, two French schooners and their prizes in Samana Bay, San Domingo.

1827 Frigate *Diamond* (46), 'lately returned from South America under the command of Lord Napier', burned to the waterline while lying in ordinary at Portsmouth under the care of her standing warrant officers. Sister ship of *Trincomalee* preserved at Hartlepool.

1852 Boats of *Cleopatra*, *Semiramis* (Indian Navy) and *Pluto* (Bengal Marine) destroyed a pirate stronghold in the Tungku River, Borneo.

1861 Landing parties from *Arrogant* and *Torch*, with detachments of the 1st and 2nd West India Regiments, burned two towns up the Gambia River.

1897 Capture of Benin, Nigeria. Naval Brigade of 1,200 ratings and Royal Marines under Rear-Admiral Sir Harry Rawson from *Alecto*, *Barrosa*, *Forte*, *Magpie*, *Philomel*, *Phoebe*, *St George*, *Theseus*, *Widgeon*. Three future admirals involved: Bacon (DSO), Cowan and Stephenson. East and West Africa General Service Medal: clasp 'Benin 1897'. The medal and clasp were also awarded to two RN officers and three RN nursing sisters who were serving in the hospital ship *Malacca*. First occasion of women in the naval service serving afloat, and their first award of campaign medals. Battle Honour: Benin 1897.

1907 St Nicholas' church, RN Barracks Devonport, dedicated by the Rt Revd Archibald Robertson, Bishop of Exeter.

See 21 August 1704, 4 February 1786, 16 March 1905, 21 June 1934, 11 November 1993.

1915 German submarine blockade of Great Britain began.

1915 Battleship *Cornwallis* fired the first shell in the naval bombardment of the Turkish Gallipoli forts. In December she covered the Suvla evacuation and was the last British capital ship to leave the Dardanelles theatre of operations. Battle Honour: Dardanelles 1915.

See 9 January 1917.

HMS *Bulwark* leaves Devonport on 8 February 2009 for a six-month deployment to the Far East. (*RN*)

1916 Allied forces completed the conquest of the Cameroons. Ships: *Cumberland* and *Challenger*. Battle Honour: Cameroons 1914.

1940 Destroyer *Daring*, Cdr S.A. Cooper RN, escorting Convoy HN12, torpedoed and sunk by U-23, Kapitanleutnant Otto Kretschmer, 40 miles E. of Duncansby Head, S.E. of the Shetlands (58.38N, 0.40E). Captain, eight officers and ten men lost. The first British destroyer lost to submarine attack in the Second World War.

See 7 April 1932, 13 November 1939, 14 December 1944.

1944 Light cruiser *Penelope* torpedoed and sunk by U-410 35 miles off Anzio (40.55N, 13.25E). Capt G.D. Belben RN lost. Operation Shingle. Nicknamed 'Pepperpot' because so perforated by bomb damage at Malta, she was the heroine of C.S. Forester's *The Ship*. The last RN-manned cruiser lost in action in the Second World War.

See 16 September 1918.

1944 Frigate *Spey* sank U-406 in Atlantic (48.32N, 23.36W) and captured some German operational researchers interested in radar countermeasures. Convoy ONS 29.

1944 *Mauritius*, light cruiser, and *Laforey*, destroyer, bombarded the Formia area.

1952 Frigate *Veryan Bay* and RM reinforcements sent to the Falkland Islands.

1957 RNVR (Air) Branch finally disbanded. Established in February 1939 and disbanded after the war. Re-formed in 1947.

See 15 January 1957.

1980 The destroyer *Nottingham* launched at Vosper Thornycroft, Woolston, by Lady Leach, wife of Admiral Sir Henry Leach, First Sea Lord.

See 8 April 1983, 7 July 2002.

1982 South African frigate *President Kruger* (British Rothesay-class) sunk in collision with replenishment ship *Tafelberg* 80 miles S.W. of Cape of Good Hope; thirteen lost.

2009 *Bulwark*, wearing broad pennant of Cdre Peter Hudson RN, COMATG, sailed from Devonport leading the Taurus 09 deployment to the Middle East and SE Asia: Ocean, frigates *Argyll* and *Somerset*, surveying ship *Echo*, SSNs *Trafalgar* and *Talent*, RFAs *Lyme Bay*, *Mounts Bay*, *Fort Austin* and *Wave Ruler*, US destroyer *Mitscher* and French destroyer *Dupleix*. 40 Cdo RM embarked. Returned August 2009. The largest Far East deployment since Rear-Admiral Alan West's Ocean Wave group which covered the departure from Hong Kong in 1997.

2010 Submarine *Astute*, Cdr Andrew Coles RN, dived for the first time in the Scottish Exercise Areas, with the frigate *Montrose* in support.

See 22 October 2010.

19 February

1653 Second day of the battle between Blake and Tromp off the Isle of Wight.

1667 *Pearl* fought a Dutch 50-gun ship in the North Sea.

1694 Major disaster off Gibraltar. *Sussex* (80), flag of Rear-Admiral Sir Francis Wheler, with *Cambridge* (70), *Lumley Castle* (56), the *Serpent* bomb vessel and two ketches, attempting to enter the Mediterranean with a trade convoy in foul weather, mistook the Bay of Gibraltar for the Straits and were embayed. All the warships were wrecked with great loss of life. *Sussex* was carrying gold coin for the Duke of Savoy, an ally in Britain's war with France. Her wreck has been discovered lying at 2,500 feet and believed to contain bullion worth £2.5 billion.

1743 Unsuccessful attack on La Guaira, Venezuela.

1758 *Invincible* (74), Capt John Bentley, part of an expedition under Admiral Edward Boscawen sailing to capture the French fortress of Louisbourg, Nova Scotia, stranded herself on Horse Tail Bank, Dean Sands, in the Eastern Solent after her rudder jammed and she became a total wreck. *Invincible*, first ship of the name in the Royal Navy and her first 74-gun ship, was a three-year-old French prize taken by Anson off Cape Finisterre in 1747. The wreck was discovered in 1979 and has provided a rich haul of naval artefacts.

See 3 May 1747, 15 February 1760, 16 March 1801.

1783 Second *Invincible* recaptured *Argo* 55 miles N. of Puerto Rico.

1794 Occupation of San Fiorenzo (St Florent), Corsica and capture of French *Minerve*.

See 17 February 1794.

1801 *Phoebe* (36) captured the French *Africaine* (40) off Ceuta, North Africa. Capt Barlow knighted. Battle Honour: *Africaine* 1801.

1801 Admiral the Earl of St Vincent appointed First Lord of the Admiralty in Henry Addington's administration. He was succeeded as C-in-C Channel Fleet by Admiral Sir William Cornwallis.

1807 Vice-Admiral Sir John Duckworth (*Royal George*) forced the passage of the Dardanelles and moored 8 miles off Constantinople. Eleven sail of the Turkish squadron destroyed and remaining two taken by the division under Rear-Admiral Sir Sidney Smith (*Pompée*). Ships: *Canopus, Pompée, Repulse, Royal George, Standard, Thunderer, Windsor Castle* and volunteers from *Ajax*. Frigates: *Active, Endymion.* Bombs: *Lucifer, Meteor.*

Vice-Admiral Sir John Duckworth's fleet forcing the Dardanelles, 1807. (*NMM Neg. No. A1057*)

One of the great characters of the Royal Navy in Hong Kong. Mrs Ng Muk Kah BEM – Jenny of Jenny's Side Party – who died in 2009. Her folder of recommendations from generations of RN captains was extensive. That from Capt David Williams of HMS *Devonshire* dated 9 September 1965 reads: 'Jenny and her cheerful girls have been absolutely invaluable in preparing the ship's side for a Royal visit in Tokyo and in helping the ship on deck and below decks. I have absolutely no hesitation in recommending her and her side party to any ships that visit Hong Kong – and in applauding their efficient and cheerful service and their loyalty and charm.' See 6 February 1977. (*Author*)

1888 Tom Spencer Vaughan Phillips, the last British admiral killed in action, born at Pendennis Castle, Falmouth.
See 10 December 1941.

1915 British and French ships began bombardment of the other forts of the Dardanelles. The start of Gallipoli fiasco and a botched attempt to emulate Duckworth on this day in 1807. Ships: *Agamemnon, Cornwallis, Inflexible, Triumpth, Vengeance*; French: *Bouvet, Gaulois* and *Suffren*. Battle Honour: Dardanelles.

1915 *Goldfinch*, destroyer, wrecked in fog on Sandoy Island, Orkney.

1917 *Lady Olive* (Q 18) sank UC-18 12 miles W. of Jersey (49.15N, 02.34W), but was also sunk.

1919 Disbandment of WRNS announced.

1934 Admiral of the Fleet Sir Roger Keyes, former C-in-C Portsmouth and future head of combined operations, elected MP for Portsmouth North.
See 23 May 1757, 23 April 1918, 17 February 1943.

1943 Destroyers *Hursley* and *Isis* and Wellington aircraft of 38 Sqn sank U-562 off Benghazi. Convoy XT 3.

1944 Wellington B/172 sank U-268 off Ushant.

1944 Sloops *Starling* and *Woodpecker* sank U-264 in N. Atlantic. Convoy ON 224.

1944 *Spey*, River-class frigate, sank U-386 in N. Atlantic. Convoy ONS 29. Admiral Horton, C-in-C W. Approaches, a man more noted for his criticism than his praise, wrote on her Captain's ROP 'This is how it should be done'.

1960 The Admiralty signalled all ships at 1632: 'Birth of a son, Prince Andrew, to Her Majesty Queen Elizabeth announced. Splice the Main Brace.'
See 11 July 1935, 15 November 1948.

1976 Iceland, a NATO ally, broke off diplomatic relations with the United Kingdom over the disputed 200-mile fishing limit. Third Cod War.
See 31 August 1958.

1979 First appointment of a WRNS officer as First Lieutenant of an RN establishment – First Officer R.N. Ball, *Mercury*.
See 20 September 1988.

2009 Mrs Ng Muk Kah BEM, Jenny of Jenny's Side Party, who served the Royal Navy in Hong Kong from 1928 to 1997, died aged 92. Jenny and her girls 'washed and ironed, cleaned ship, chipped rust and painted, attended as buoy jumpers, and, dressed in their best, waited with grace and charm upon guests at cocktail parties'. Her obituary in the *Daily Telegraph* was headed just 'Jenny' – *Daily Telegraph* obituary 25 March 2009.
See p.76.

2010 HRH the Duke of York promoted honorary rear admiral on his fiftieth birthday.

2010 Landing Ship Dock RFA *Largs Bay*, Capt Ian Johnson, arrived at Port au Prince, Haiti, with disaster relief supplies following an earthquake. Food was also landed from the ship by mexeflote at Gonaives and Anse a Veau. Operation Panlake.
See 11 October 1954.

20 FEBRUARY

1653 Third day of the battle between Blake and Tromp, in the waters between Beachy Head and Calais.

1807 *Carrier* captured the French privateer *Ragotin* 60 miles N. of Goeree, Netherlands.

1815 *Cyane* (22) and *Levant* (20) 'with much gallantry but less judgement' tried conclusions with and were taken by the American *Constitution* (44) 180 miles W.S.W. of Madeira.

1851 Boys to enter the Service at age 13 instead of at 14.

1858 *Pearl*'s Naval Brigade, with a detachment of the 1st Bengal Military Police Battalion and Gurkha allies, defeated the Indian rebels at Phulphur. Indian Mutiny Medal.

1900 General Cronje, the Boer Commander, confined on board cruiser *Doris* for expatriation to St Helena.

See 7 August 1815.

The Navy's here! The landing ship RFA *Largs Bay* arrived off Port au Prince, Haiti, on 19 February 2010 with emergency relief supplies and trained personnel following the earthquakes which devastated the island. Capt Ian Johnson RFA and a US Navy Officer discuss a coordinated plan to distribute humanitarian supplies. (*RN*)

The funeral of Admiral of the Fleet Lord Fraser of North Cape at St Barbara's church, HMS *Excellent*, 1981. Fraser took his title from the action off the North Cape of Norway on Boxing Day 1943 in which a squadron from the Home Fleet, led by his flagship *Duke of York*, sank the German battleship *Scharnhorst*. As C-in-C British Pacific Fleet he signed the Japanese surrender document on behalf of Britain and the British Empire on board the USS *Missouri* in Tokyo Bay in 1945. Lord Fraser died on 12 February and his ashes were committed to the sea from the destroyer *Sheffield* on 25 February. (*Author*)

1907 Opening of Prince of Wales Basin.

The Prince of Wales Basin in Devonport Dockyard was opened by the Prince of Wales, future King George V, who came up harbour for the ceremony in the Admiralty Yacht *Vivid*. The size of the ten years' work on the basin and the Keyham extension to the dockyard, can be estimated by the materials used: 2½ million cu ft of granite (1½ million from Cornwall, 1 million from Norway), 170,000 cu ft of limestone, 220,000 tons of cement from the Thames. An area of 114 acres was turned into a fitting-out yard with docks, basins, etc. The cost was £6 million. The giant cantilever crane was one of the items completed in 1909.

1941 Trawler *Ouse* sunk by mine at Tobruk.

1944 Destroyer *Warwick* sunk by U-413 20 miles off Trevose Head, Cornwall.

1944 *Woodpecker*, sloop, torpedoed by U-256 S. of Ireland (48.49N, 22.11W). Homing torpedo blew off her stern and she sank in tow on the 27th off the Scilly Isles in a gale (49.39N, 06.08W).

See 11 February 1944.

1945 *Vervain*, corvette, sunk by U-1208 20 miles S. of Waterford, Ireland. Last of twenty-eight corvettes lost in the Second World War. *Amethyst*, 2nd Escort Group, sank U-1208 in S.W. Approaches, S. of Wolf Rock, 27 February 1945.

1953 St Edward's Crown adopted for all epaulettes, badges and buttons.

1963 The first operational Buccaneer squadron, 801 NAS, embarked in *Ark Royal*.

See 30 April 1958.

1967 Greenland supply ship MV *Anita Dan* bought from the J. Lauritzen Line of Copenhagen to replace the former netlayer *Protector* as the Falkland Islands Dependencies guardship. Converted at Harland and Wolff. Renamed *Endurance* 27 July 1967 and deployed south for the 1968 season.

See 10 May 1955.

1998 *Ocean* named by HM The Queen at yard of prime contractors, Vickers, Barrow. The first purpose-built helicopter carrier in RN.

See 11 October 1995, 30 September 1998.

21 FEBRUARY

1729 Order in Council established the Naval Academy and abolished King's Letter Boys.
See 7 May 1661, 1 February 1806.

1759 Capt Samuel Hood in *Vestal* (22), captured the French *Bellone* (32) 600 miles S.W. of Lizard Head and took her into Plymouth, where she was commissioned as *Repulse* (second of the name).
Battle Honour: *Bellone* 1759.

1779 Remains of Capt Cook buried at sea from *Resolution* off Kealakekua, Hawaii.
See 14 February 1779.

1783 *Cerberus* wrecked leaving Bermuda in pursuit of a privateer.

1790 *Guardian*, Lt Edward Riou, arrived at Table Bay, having sustained very severe hull injuries by striking an iceberg on 24 December 1789 en route to Australia.

1810 *Horatio* captured the French *Nécessité* 400 miles S. by E. of Flores, Azores.

1861 Naval Brigade from *Arrogant*, *Falcon* and *Torch* with the 1st and 2nd West India Regiments, destroyed the stockades at Saba, Gambia River.

1916 German government informed US government that defensively armed merchant ships would henceforth be regarded as cruisers.

1921 Roderick Douglas Macdonald, future Captain of the Fleet and distinguished marine artist, born in Batavia (Jakarta).
See 19 January 2001.

1939 *King George V* launched at Vickers Armstrong. With *Anson* (Swan Hunter 1940), *Duke of York* (Clydebank 1940), *Howe* (Fairfield 1940) and *Prince of Wales* (Cammell Laird 1939) – the last class of British battleships ever built, the first

Capt James Cook (1728–1779) by William Hodges. (*NMM*)

Captain James Cook, RN (1728–1779)

Cook began his life at sea as an apprentice to ship-owners at Whitby. He volunteered for the King's Service in 1755 and by 1759 was a master in HMS *Mercury* employed in surveying the St Lawrence River and in piloting ships of the Fleet. He published four highly accurate volumes of sailing directions (1766–8) after surveying operations off the coasts of Newfoundland and Labrador. In 1768, he was commissioned lieutenant in command of HMS *Endeavour*, and carried out astronomical observations with other scientists for the Royal Society in the Pacific; here he also sailed round, examined and charted the coast of New Zealand and explored the west coast of Australia. He returned in 1771. He sailed again as Commander of HMS *Resolution* in July 1772, accompanied by HMS *Adventure*, heading for the Pacific. He sailed close to the ice, passing the Antarctic Circle for the first time in January 1773. He reached Easter Island by January 1774 after exploring several of the South Pacific islands and not having seen land for 104 days. He returned to England in July 1775. In 1776 the Royal Society honoured him with the Copley Gold Medal for his paper on ship's hygiene. During his long voyage, only one man died and his crew were remarkably free from scurvy and had no fever. He was promoted captain in August 1775 and appointed to Greenwich Hospital. He sailed again in July 1776 for the North Pacific, to discover a passage round North America. He again visited New Zealand and discovered the Sandwich Islands (Hawaii) on his way to the west coast of America in March 1778. He conducted a running survey of the west coast north until turning back and west at the end of August to the Sandwich Islands for the winter months. On 14 February 1779 he was tragically killed by natives on Hawaii.

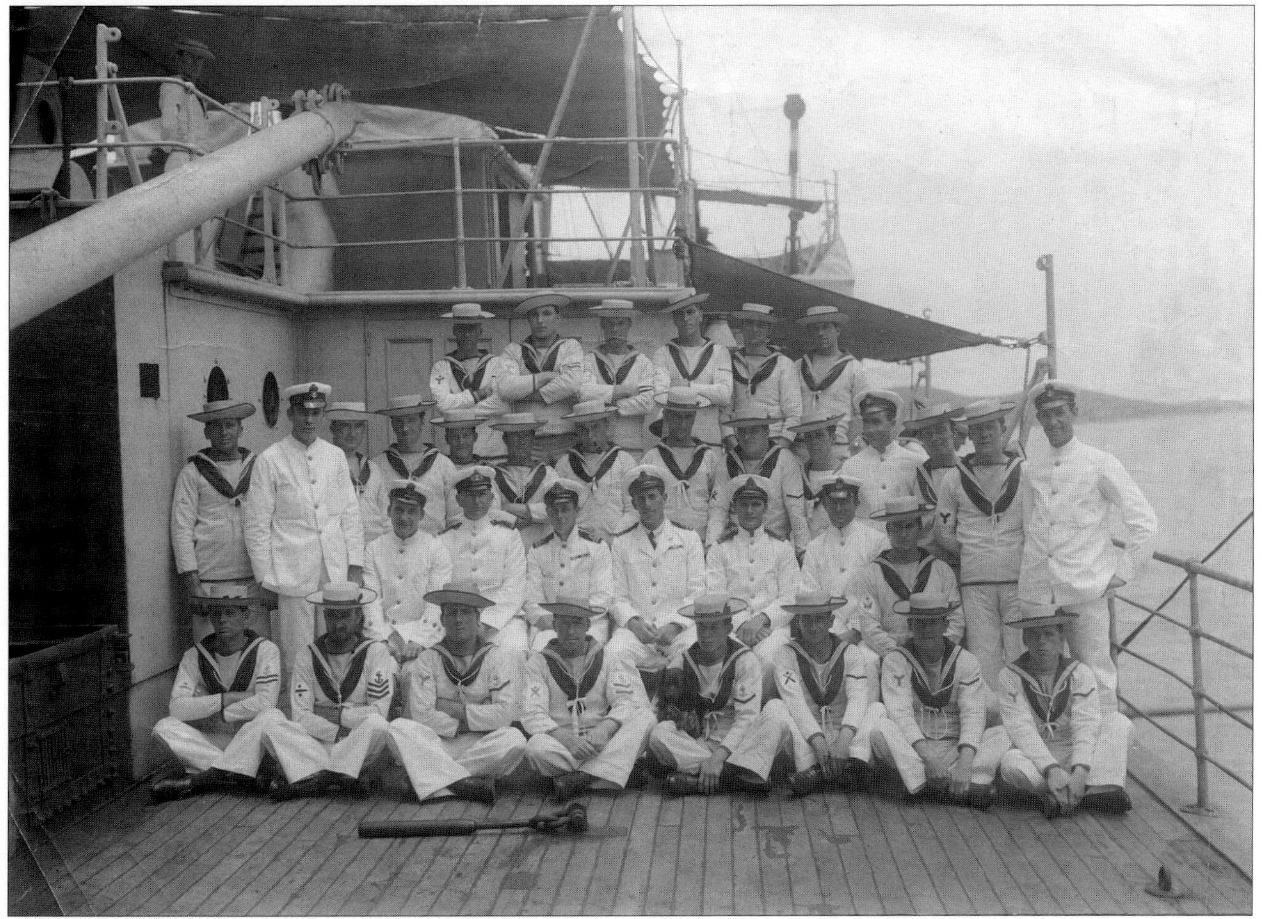

The crew of a British submarine in tropical whites on board their depot ship in about 1920. Straw Sennet hats were withdrawn in 1921. See 16 March 1921. (*Cdr David Hobbs RN*)

designed to carry aircraft and the only British battleships to mount main armament in quadruple mountings.

1940 Light cruiser *Manchester* and destroyer *Kimberley* (Northern Patrol) captured the German SS *Wahehe* in N. Atlantic. Operation W.R.

1940 The Admiralty declined the services of conscientious objectors in minesweepers.
See 13 February 1940.

1941 Albacore aircraft of 826, 829 Sqn (*Formidable*) attacked Massawa.

1943 Liberator T/120 sank U-623 in N. Atlantic. Convoy ON 166.

1945 First flight of Hawker Sea Fury, the last piston-engined aircraft in frontline service in FAA.

1952 Admiral Sir Arthur Power appointed first NATO C-in-C Channel.
See 2 June 1994, 31 December 2003.

2003 Frigate *Iron Duke* and RFA *Black Rover* deployed to Sierra Leone until 31 March. Operation Keeling.

2004 Destroyer *Glasgow*, Cdr M.J. Wainhouse RN, on her (APT(South)) deployment, rendezvoused with *Endurance* in the Weddell Sea and 'recorded the southernmost latitude for a RN warship since 1911'.

22 February

1692 Capt Wrenn (*Norwich*), with *Antelope*, *Diamond*, *Mary* (62) and *Mordaunt* escorting the trade from Barbados to Jamaica, repulsed a superior French force under Capt Comte de Blenac when off Desirade, West Indies, and saved his convoy after a five-hour fight.

1773 Capt Tobias Furneaux of the *Adventure* on Capt Cook's second voyage 'served half allowance of liquor extra to the ship's company' at the end of a testing day in the Southern Ocean, (52.48S, 83.35E). Her Second Lieutenant, James Burney, ended his day's journal 'Spliced the Main Brace', the earliest recorded use of this term as a reward for 'arduous exertion'.
See 19 May 1797.

1797 French force landed in Fishguard Bay. Surrendered on the morning of the 24th.

1799 *Espoir* captured the Spanish *Africa* 9 miles S.S.E. of Marbella, south coast of Spain.

1806 Earl of St Vincent returned to sea, aged 71. The Cabinet 'deemed that on the appearance afloat of a once First Lord . . . the Union Jack at the main, as now the Admiral of the Fleet, was the becoming flag for his Lordship to hoist'.
See 13 March 1823.

1812 *Victorious* and *Weazle* captured the French *Rivoli*, and destroyed *Mercure* 14 miles N.W. by W. of Cape Salvore, in the Gulf of Trieste. Battle Honour: *Rivoli* 1812.

1862 First officers commissioned in RNR.

1894 Gambia expeditionary force landed by *Raleigh*, iron screw frigate. East and West Africa Service Medal: clasp 'Gambia 1894'.

1895 Destruction of Nimbi, Brass River, by Naval Brigade from *Barrosa*, *St George*, *Thrush*, *Widgeon* and Niger Coast Protectorate Forces. East and West Africa G.S. Medal: clasp 'Brass River 1895'.

During the action of 22 February 1812 the 74-gun ship *Rivoli* was raked; over 400 of her men were killed or wounded. (*NMRN 1976/250–1*)

HMS *Raleigh* (1873), an iron-hulled unarmoured frigate of 5,200 tons. At the time of the Gambia expedition, 1894, she carried a mixed armament of both muzzle- and breech-loading guns. (*NMRN*)

1937 *Sterlet*, last of the first batch of S-class submarines, launched. She was sunk in Skagerrak 18 April 1940 by German A/S trawler.

1940 RM Depot at Lympstone opened. Now Commando Training Centre, Royal Marines.

1941 *Shropshire* bombarded Brava, Italian Somaliland.

1943 *Burza* (Pol) and USS *Campbell* sank U-606 in N. Atlantic.

1943 Corvette *Weyburn* (RCN) sunk by mine off Cape Spartel (35.46N, 06.02W). Convoy MKS 8.

1945 Corvette *Trentonian* (RCN) sunk by U-1004 off Dodman Pt. Convoy BTC 76.

1945 *Pincher, Recruit* and *Evadne* sank U-300 off Portugal. Convoy Appian Flight F.

1965 Minister of Defence (Royal Navy), Christopher Mayhew, announced disbandment of the Royal Naval Volunteer (Supplementary) Reserve. Some RNV(S)R officers transferred to Active List of RNR; remainder placed on Retired List of RNVR. Disbandment marked by a dinner at RN College, Greenwich, 16 December 1965. DCI(RN) 1637/65.

See 11 November 1936, 10 December 1936.

1966 First Sea Lord, Admiral Sir David Luce, resigned in protest at the cancellation of CVA-01 (HMS *Queen Elizabeth*) and the new generation of Royal Navy aircraft carriers. Navy minister, Christopher Mayhew, had resigned five days earlier.

See 23 January 1906, 17 June 1934, 30 July 1963, 6 January 1971, 13 July 1995.

'Sir David's action, even more than that of Mr Mayhew, emphasizes the profound disquiet felt in naval circles at the abandonment of the carrier programme . . . That there were other members of the Admiralty Board who shared Admiral Luce's views has been made clear by Mr Healey [Secretary of State for Defence]. He said that at a press conference that they had agreed to remain at their posts "for the good of the Navy" . . . Mr Healey also said "This is not in any sense the end of the Royal Navy"' – *The Times*, 23 February 1966. A naval general message to the Fleet from VCNS, Vice-Admiral Sir John Bush, said 'the Admiralty Board have had to accept the cancellation of the CVA-01 which, it recognizes, will be a great loss to the Navy'. The new First Sea Lord was Admiral Sir Varyl Begg, C-in-C Portsmouth.

2007 The last holder of the office of First Lord of the Admiralty died. George Patrick John Rushworth Jellicoe, the Second Earl Jellicoe, KBE, DSO, MC, was the son of Admiral of the Fleet Earl Jellicoe of Scapa, C-in-C Grand Fleet 1914–1916 (including Jutland) and First Sea Lord 1916–1917.

See 20 November 1935, 26 and 31 March 1964.

23 FEBRUARY

1633 Samuel Pepys born.

1674 *Tiger* captured the Dutch *Schakerloo* in Cadiz Bay.

1694 Small 5th Rate *Pembroke* (32), Capt Roger Bellwood, seriously damaged in action with the French privateer *Ville de St Malo* on 22 February in the Soundings W. of the English Channel, suffered further when engaged next day by another French privateer, the *Louis of Bordeaux*, to which she struck. The *Pembroke* was too damaged to save and, the ship's company having been taken off, it was intended to burn her. Instead she was run ashore 3 miles W. of the Lizard (49.59.30N 05.15.15W) and broke up. The court martial in *Britannia* at Spithead on 1 May 1694 acquitted the Captain and officers.

1695 *Centurion* engaged four Dunkirk privateers, capturing one, 15 miles E.N.E. of the North Foreland.

1746 Navy Club resolved to send three officers to wait upon their Lordships and ask for a uniform for officers.

1805 *Leander* (50) captured the French *Ville-de-Milan* (32) and recaptured *Cleopatra* (40) 300 miles S.E. by S. of Bermuda.

See 17 February 1805.

1810 *Royalist* captured the Boulogne privateer *Prince Eugène* off Dungeness.

1854 Admiral Napier appointed to command the North Sea Fleet in the Russian war, and Rear-Admiral Dundas the Mediterranean.

Samuel Pepys (1633–1703)

Pepys was the epitome of a man for all seasons. 'His qualities were an outstanding combination of judgement, orderly business habits and methods, great energy and administrative ability' – Sir John Lang at the Pepys commemoration service at St Olave's, London, 2 June 1955. His life spanned England's only excursion from monarchy: it began when Charles I was on his throne, and he was 9 when the Civil War started. His career began during the Protectorate, blossomed with the Restoration of Charles II and soared through the Dutch Wars, the Plague and the Great Fire of London. Religion nearly cost him his life; ironically the Glorious Revolution cost him his career.

Even so, it was a memorable one, and his Diary ensures his imperishable reputation, not only as a man with a perpetually enquiring mind, who became a Fellow and President of the Royal Society, Master of the Clothworkers' Company, an Elder Brother and twice Master of Trinity House and a Governor of Christ's Hospital as well as the first Secretary of the Board of Admiralty, but also as an avaricious but adorable, ambitious but endearing man about town and citizen of the world.

Samuel Pepys (1633–1703). (*NMM Neg. No. 22*)

Admiral Sir Charles Napier (1786–1860), who took command of the North Sea Fleet at the age of 68. (*NMRN 1991/442*)

1858 *Algerine*, wood screw gunvessel, and two boats of *Calcutta* destroyed four pirate junks in Long Harbour, Mirs Bay, Hong Kong.

1915 Royal Marines occupied Lemnos.

1917 UC-32 blew up on her own mines off Sunderland.

1927 Cruiser *Colombo* sent to Corinto to protected British subjects in Nicaragua.

1940 Destroyer *Gurkha* sank U-53 S. of the Faroes.

1940 Ships' companies of the cruisers *Exeter* and *Ajax*, home from the Battle of the River Plate, were received at the Guildhall by the Lord Mayor of London. The men marched from Waterloo Station via Horse Guards where they were inspected by the King who held an investiture. On the same day men of the light cruiser, HMNZS *Achilles*, marched through Auckland to a similar civic reception.

See 13 December 1939.

The monitor HMS *Terror*, at Benghazi in 1941. (*NMRN*)

1942 Submarine *Trident* torpedoed the German cruiser *Prinz Eugen* off Norway, destroying 30ft of her stern.

1942 Submarine P 38 sunk by the Italian TBs *Circe* and *Usodimare* off Tripoli; *Circe*'s second success in ten days.

1943 *Bicester*, with *Lamerton* and *Wheatland*, Hunt-class destroyers, sank U-443 off Algiers (36.55N, 02.23E). A three-day hunt demonstrating 'the value of persistent effort' – *Naval Staff History*.

1943 Cutter *Totland* sank U-522 in Atlantic. Convoy UC 1.

1945 *La Combattante* (Free French) (ex-*Haldon*) sunk by mine off East Dudgeon Light.

1979 Former commando carrier *Bulwark* recommissioned at Portsmouth. She had been brought out of reserve and converted into an anti-submarine warfare carrier to fill the gap between paying-off of *Ark Royal* and completion of the Invincible-class carriers. A gallant old ship but her electrics were not up to it.

See 22 June 1948, 15 March 1980, 9 November 1980.

24 February

1809 Capture of Martinique by Lt-Gen George Beckwith and Rear-Admiral the Hon. Sir Alexander Cochrane (*Neptune*). Ships and vessels: *Acasta, Aeolus, Amaranthe, Bacchus, Belleisle, Bellette, Captain, Cherub, Circe, Cleopatra, Cuttle, Demerera, Dominica, Eclair, Ethalion, Eurydice, Express, Fawn, Forester, Frolic, Gloire, Goree, Haughty, Hazard, Intrepid, Liberty, Mosambique, Neptune, Pelorus, Penelope, Pompee, Port d'Espagne, Pultusk, Recruit, Ringdove, St Pierre, Snap, Star, Stork, Subtle, Superieure, Surinam, Swinger, Ulysses, Wolverine, York*. The Military General Service Medal was bestowed on the Army, and the French eagles sent home were the first seen in England.
Battle Honour: Martinique 1809.

1809 *Defiance, Caesar, Donegal* and *Amelia* drove ashore the French *Calypso, Cybèle* and *Italienne* at Sables d'Olonne, west coast of France. *Cybèle* became a total wreck.

1813 *Peacock* (18) taken by the American *Hornet* (20) off the mouth of the Demerera River, British Guiana, despite the weather gauge and her immaculate appearance which earned her the nickname 'The Yacht'.

1841 Repulse of boats of *Termagant* by a Spanish brig 15 miles W.N.W. of Cape Mount, Sierra Leone.

1855 *Leopard* and the French *Fulton* destroyed ten guns and other Russian government property at the estuary of the Kuban River, Black Sea.

1857 First awards of the Victoria Cross announced in the *London Gazette*; twenty-seven RN and RM names out of eighty-five listed.
See 26 June 1857.

1917 Reoccupation of Kut-al' Amara. River gunboats: *Butterfly, Mantis*. Supports: *Gadfly, Moth, Snakefly, Tarantula*.

The Navy's here! Leading Seaman Mamie Battersby (left) and Leading Seaman Michelle King (opposite) carry children ashore at Malta, two souls among the 207 rescued by their ship, the frigate HMS *Cumberland*, at Benghazi, from the dangers of insurrection in Libya on her first evacuation mission. (*RN*)

1940 Battleship *Anson*, ex-*Jellicoe*, launched at Swan Hunter by Lady Pound, wife of Admiral of the Fleet Sir Dudley Pound, First Sea Lord.

1941 *Dainty*, destroyer, sunk by German aircraft off Tobruk.

1941 The twin 15-in gun monitor *Terror*, Cdr J.H. Haynes RN, capsized and sank at 0420, 25 miles N.W. of Derna, Libya (32.40N, 22.30E), after two days of air attack. The only British monitor lost in the Second World War.
See 19 July 1965.

Terror had been bombed on 22 February by Italian aircraft at Benghazi. The three ships sailed for Tobruk at dusk that day but *Terror* was further damaged by acoustic mines. She was again dive-bombed by German aircraft at 231830, 90 miles from Tobruk. Near misses broke her back between the bridge and the turret, the boiler room was flooded, and she began to settle by the bows. The C-in-C ordered the cruisers *Perth* and *Ajax*, with two destroyers, to raise steam at Alexandria to go to her assistance. Just before midnight, with 4ft of freeboard forward and her quarterdeck awash, she was abandoned, with her seacocks opened and depth charges exploded to hasten her end. Her crew rescued by the corvette *Salvia* and minesweeper *Fareham*.

1943 The new submarine *Vandal*, Lt J.S. Bridger RN, commissioned four days earlier, failed to surface after deep diving trials in Upper Inchmarnock, Holy Loch. A Board of Enquiry held on board *Forth* on 27 February failed to find cause but criticised Third Submarine Flotilla for delay in initiating submarine overdue procedures. Her hull was located by the minehunter *Hurworth* on 12 June 1994 N.W. of Lochranza, Isle of Arran, lying in 95m. Wreck declared a war grave.
See 12 June 1994, 3 May 1997.

1944 *Waskesiu* (RCN), frigate, sank U-257 in N. Atlantic. Convoy SC 153.

1944 First U-boat detected by MAD (Magnetic Anomaly Detection); two USN Catalinas detected U-761 off Gibraltar (35.05N, 05.45W). Catalinas attacked with retro-bombs, destroyers *Anthony* and *Wishart* with depth charges and with further contributions from a RAF 202 Sqn Catalina and a USN Ventura. Submarine's Captain and forty-seven crew rescued by the destroyers.

1945 Frigates *Duckworth* and *Rowley* sank U-480 and Warwick K/179 sank U-927 in S.W. Approaches. Convoy BTC 78.

1970 824 NAS formed at Culdrose, first operational deployment of Westland Sea King helicopters.
See 2 July 1969, 19 August 1969.

1983 Minehunter *Brocklesby* collided with coastal minesweeper *Nurton* in fog off Portland and holed *Nurton*'s port side amidships. Most of ship's company of *Nurton* abandoned ship onto bows of *Brocklesby*.

1991 UN ground offensive against Iraq began. Operation Desert Sabre. RN MCMV continued to sweep battleship fire support areas for battleships USS *Missouri* and *Wisconsin*. Operation Granby.

2011 Frigate *Cumberland*, Capt Steve Dainton RN, returning from the Gulf to pay off for disposal, diverted to Gulf of Sirte; on several runs into Benghazi she extracted 454 people (129 of them British) fleeing insurrection in Libya and landed them in Malta.
See 19 October 2010.

25 FEBRUARY

1744 *Solebay* captured the Spanish *Concordia* 30 miles W. of Cadiz.

1744 William Cornwallis, C-in-C Channel Fleet, 1801–2, 1803–6, born.
See 17 June 1795.

1781 *Cerberus* captured the Spanish *Grana* 60 miles W. of Cape Finisterre in fifteen minutes.

1814 *Eurotas* engaged the French *Clorinde* 180 miles W.S.W. of Ushant and would have taken her had she not surrendered to *Dryad* and *Achates*, who towed her into Portsmouth where she was commissioned as *Aurora*.
Battle Honour: *Clorinde* 1814.

1915 Bombardment of Dardanelles forts resumed. Outer forts partially destroyed by the 26th. Battleship *Queen Elizabeth* in action for the first time.

1917 German destroyer raid on Margate and Westgate.

1917 AMC *Laconia* sunk by U-50 124 miles W. of Valentia Island, Ireland.

1936 GC (ex-EGM): Edwin Crossley, HM Dockyard, Chatham. (*Gazette* date.)

1940 Destroyers *Escort*, *Imogen*, *Escapade* and *Inglefield* escorting convoy HN 14, S.E. of the Shetlands, alerted by submarine *Narwhal*, destroyed U-63. CO of *Imogen*, Cdr (later Vice-Admiral Sir) Alastair Ewing, had a mantra:

Good, better, best
Never let us rest
Until our good is better
And our better, best.

HMS *Canopus* (1897), a pre-Dreadnought battleship, bombarding Turkish positions with her 12-in guns, Gallipoli 1915. (*NMRN*)

HMS *Renown* launched at Birkenhead, 1967. (*NMRN*)

1941 Destroyer *Exmoor* sunk by the German E-boat S-30 off Lowestoft (52.29N, 01.50E). Convoy FN 417.

1941 *Upright*, submarine, sank the Italian cruiser *Armando Diaz* in six minutes off Kerkenah Bank, 60 miles E. of Sfax, Tunisia. The submarine developed the technique of dealing with Italian acoustic mines by firing machine guns into the sea ahead of the boat.

1944 Destroyer *Mahratta* sunk by U-990 with a homing torpedo, 280 miles W. of North Cape. Catalina M 210 sank U-601. Convoy JW 57.

1944 Destroyer *Inglefield* sunk by glider bomb off Anzio. Operation Shingle.

1944 Frigates *Affleck*, *Gore* and *Gould* sank U-91 in N. Atlantic.

1955 *Ark Royal* (fourth of the name) commissioned. First RN carrier built with angled deck.

1960 The Countess Mountbatten of Burma, who died on a tour of Borneo on 20/21 February, was buried at sea 4 miles off the Nab from the frigate *Wakeful*, escorted by the Indian Navy frigate *Trishul*. 'She was piped aboard; an honour which I have never before known to be accorded to any woman other than a reigning sovereign' – Mountbatten to Nehru.

See 5 September 1979.

1966 MCD Branch sub-specialisation for Seamen Officers formed. DCI (RN) 278/66.

See 7 March 1952.

The Minewarfare and Clearance Diver Branch was formed in response to the increasing complexity of minewarfare, which makes minesweeping in the old sense impractical. Clearance divers are highly qualified and often work at the limits of modern technology. Their tasks include all the more complex underwater operations as well as mine countermeasures and training teams of ships' divers for the less complex diving tasks.

1967 *Renown*, third Royal Navy Polaris submarine, launched at Cammell Laird, Birkenhead, by Mrs Healey, wife of the Secretary of State for Defence. The Bishop of Chester, Dr Ellison, who conducted the religious service, said 'there was a long and valued tradition that prayers should be said at the launching of a ship of the Royal Navy' but it did not mean that they condoned the prosecution of war. The prayers he offered were for 'all that shall serve in this ship, that she may be used for the preservation of peace among men' – *The Times*, 27 February 1967. He offered no prayer for the boat herself but Mrs Healey did.

See 15 March 1968, 15 November 1968.

1970 Concept of the Military Salary approved in Parliament.

1991 Destroyer *Gloucester* destroyed Iraqi Silkworm missile with her Sea Dart just short of USS *Missouri*. Operation Granby.

1994 HMY *Britannia* completed 1 million nautical miles.

26 FEBRUARY

1801 Admiral the Hon. William Cornwallis hoisted his flag in the *Ville de Paris* (110) in Torbay, succeeding Admiral the Earl of St Vincent as C-in-C Channel Fleet.

1813 *Furieuse* and *Thames* with the 2nd Bn, 10th Regiment, captured Ponza Island, west coast of Italy.

1814 *Dryad* (36) received the surrender of the French *Clorinde*. *Eurotas* was fast coming up under jury rig, having been dismasted in the action on the previous day.

1841 Capture of the Wantong and Anung Hoi forts in the Boca Tigris, Canton River. Ships: *Alligator, Blenheim, Calliope, Druid, Herald, Melville, Modeste, Samarang, Wellesley*. Bengal Marine Steamers: *Madagascar, Nemesis, Queen*. Troops: Royal Artillery, 26th and 49th Regiments, Madras Artillery, 37th Madras Native Infantry, Bengal Volunteer Regiment. Medal: China, 1841–2.

1852 Troopship *Birkenhead*, carrying troops mainly from the 73rd Regiment, to Algoa Bay, South Africa, struck a reef off Danger Point, Simon's Bay, broke up and sank; 438 men lost and 193 survived, including all the women and children. The order 'women and children first' became known as the Birkenhead Order. The discipline displayed by the soldiers under Col Alexander Seton was remarkable and has been widely recorded; the King of Prussia had the account read to every man in the Prussian Army. A token court martial was held in *Victory* at Portsmouth on 8 May 1852.

A marble memorial plaque in St Mary's church, Bury St Edmunds, to the fifty-five soldiers of the (12th) Suffolk Regiment, who were among the 438 men lost in the wreck of HMS *Birkenhead* in Simon's Bay, South Africa, 1852. (*John Williams*)

1891 Queen Victoria christened two new warships in Portsmouth Dockyard: the battleship *Royal Sovereign* (undocked) and the first class cruiser *Royal Arthur* (launched).

1915 VC: Lt-Cdr Eric Gascoigne Robinson (*Vengeance*) at Gallipoli for charging two 4-in guns in turn under heavy fire.

1916 Completion of evacuation of Serbian Army by RN and Italian force.

1917 Operations following the reoccupation of Kut-al' Amara. Recaptured: *Firefly, Sumana*.

1935 First British seaborne radar tested.

1948 GC (ex-AM): CPO J. Lynch (*Nigeria*) for saving life of rating lost overboard in gale at Port Stanley, Falkland Islands.

The great naval administrator Sir John Barrow, Second Secretary of the Admiralty (Permanent Secretary in modern terms) almost without break from 1804 to 1845, served eleven First Lords of the Admiralty and played a major role in the developmet of the nineteenth-century Royal Navy. 'Mr Barrow of the Admiralty' was a powerful supporter of Arctic exploration by the Royal Navy, particularly in search of a north-west passage. His is perpetuated on Polar charts with Barrow Strait, Barrow Point and Cape Barrow, names allocated by aspiring naval officers with a weather eye open on their futures. Barrow was a founder of the Royal Geographical Society. Oil painting by John Lucas. (*Crown Copyright: MOD Art Collection*)

1953 First Lord of the Admiralty presented the 1953–4 Navy Estimates to Parliament.

Manpower: 151,000; Strength of fleet: one battleship, five aircraft carriers, eleven cruisers, 31 destroyers, 31 frigates, 37 submarines, 48 minesweepers; Ships on training or experimental duties: four aircraft carriers, two cruisers, nine destroyers, 17 frigates, 14 minesweepers; Reserve Fleet: four battleships, two aircraft carriers, 13 cruisers, 67 destroyers, 113 frigates, 16 submarines, 114 minesweepers, two monitors, one fast minelayer; Under construction: 13 frigates, 95 minesweepers.

1955 Carrier *Ark Royal* accepted from Cammell Laird, Birkenhead, and commissioned at Devonport.

See 3 May 1950, 22 September 1980.

1964 Keel of *Resolution*, the first RN SSBN, laid by Sir Alfred Sims, DG Ships.

See 15 September 1966, 2 October 1967, 15 June 1968.

1966 Vice-Admiral Richard Bell Davies VC, DSO, AFC, one of the original squadron commanders of the RNAS when formed in July 1914, died at Haslar aged 79. He was the original RNAS pilot to remain in the Royal Navy after the formation of the Royal Air Force.

See 19 November 1915, 24 May 1939.

27 FEBRUARY

1806 *Hydra* captured the French *Furet* 30 miles S.E. by S. of Cape de Santa Maria, Portugal.

1841 Capture of the Whampoa forts, Canton River. Ships: *Alligator, Calliope, Herald, Modeste, Sulphur.* Bengal Marine Steamers: *Madagascar, Nemesis.* Medal: China, 1841–2.

1847 Senior Engineers became commissioned officers by Order in Council; still 'civil' officers and non-combatants.

1847 The new steam frigate *Dauntless*, manned by dockyard riggers and men from *Victory*, was towed out of Portsmouth harbour to the Nab where she set sail down-Channel for Tobermory with 'a large quantity of meal for the relief of the destitute in the north of Scotland' thence to Napiers on the Clyde for installation of her engines.

See 5 January 1847.

1859 No. 4 Detachment, Indian Navy, with the 1st Assam Light Infantry and Assam Local Artillery, stormed and captured Romkong (Rengging) and Passi, Assam.

1869 Ironclad battleship *Audacious* launched in a gale at Napiers Govan Yard on the Clyde. Name ship of class (*Invincible, Iron Duke, Vanguard*). At 6,010 tons displacement she was smaller than the SSN *Audacious*, 7,800 tons submerged. The first armoured capital ship afloat in the world with twin screws. Flagship on the China Station for most of her career and one of the steadiest gun platforms in the Fleet.

1881 Cdr Francis Romilly RN of the iron screw corvette *Boadicea*, commanding a naval brigade landed from *Boadicea* and *Dido* at Durban on 6 January to support Maj-Gen Sir George Pomeroy Colley in countering a Boer uprising against British interference in the Transvaal, mortally wounded by an explosive bullet during the Boer attack on Majuba Hill near Laing's Nek, Transvaal. He died on 2 March from 'mortification of the intestines' (peritonitis). Naval Brigade lost 20 men killed, including Lt C.J. Trower RN and Gunners George Hammond and Samuel Witheridge, and thirteen wounded out of sixty-four in the action.

See 22 January 1879.

1899 Eight men returning to the destroyer *Bruizer* in Samos Bay, Kefalonia, drowned when their collapsible Berthon boat was overwhelmed in a squall. Four men buried at Sami.

1900 Capture of Cronje's final laager at Paardeberg. Naval Brigade of sixty-four men, more than half of whom were killed, from *Barrosa* and *Doris* with Grant's guns. South Africa Medal: clasp 'Paardeberg'.

1941 Light cruiser *Leander* (New Zealand) sank the Italian disguised raider *Ramb I* in Indian Ocean.

1942 Destroyer *Electra* sunk by *Asagumo* in the Java Sea. Also sunk: Dutch: *De Ruyter* (Rear-Admiral K. Doorman) by *Haguro, Java* by *Nachi, Kortenaer* and *Evertsen* (beached, destroyed on the 28th). Damaged: light cruiser *Exeter* and the USS *Houston*. Destroyer *Jupiter* sank early on the 28th, on a Dutch mine off Surabaja (06.45S, 112.06E).

See 1 March 1942.

1943 Submarine *Tigris* presumed lost to depth charges of UJ-2210, S.E. of Capri (40.26N, 14.16E).

1945 Frigate *Loch Fada*, Lt-Cdr B.A. Rogers, part of the 2nd Escort Group escorting coastal convoy BTC 81 in S.W. Approaches, in a counter-attack following the sinking of the Norwegian freighter *Corvus*, sank U-1018 with Squid off the Lizard (49.56N, 05.20W); two survivors.

See 28 February 1945, 21 August 1967.

1945 A memorial tablet to Robert Blake, naval commander in the seventeenth-century Dutch Wars and 'the copy of naval courage' (Clarendon), was unveiled in Westminster Abbey by his kinsman Vice-Admiral Sir Geoffrey Blake, Gentleman Usher of the Black Rod.

See 7 August 1657, 9 September 1661, 15 December 1948.

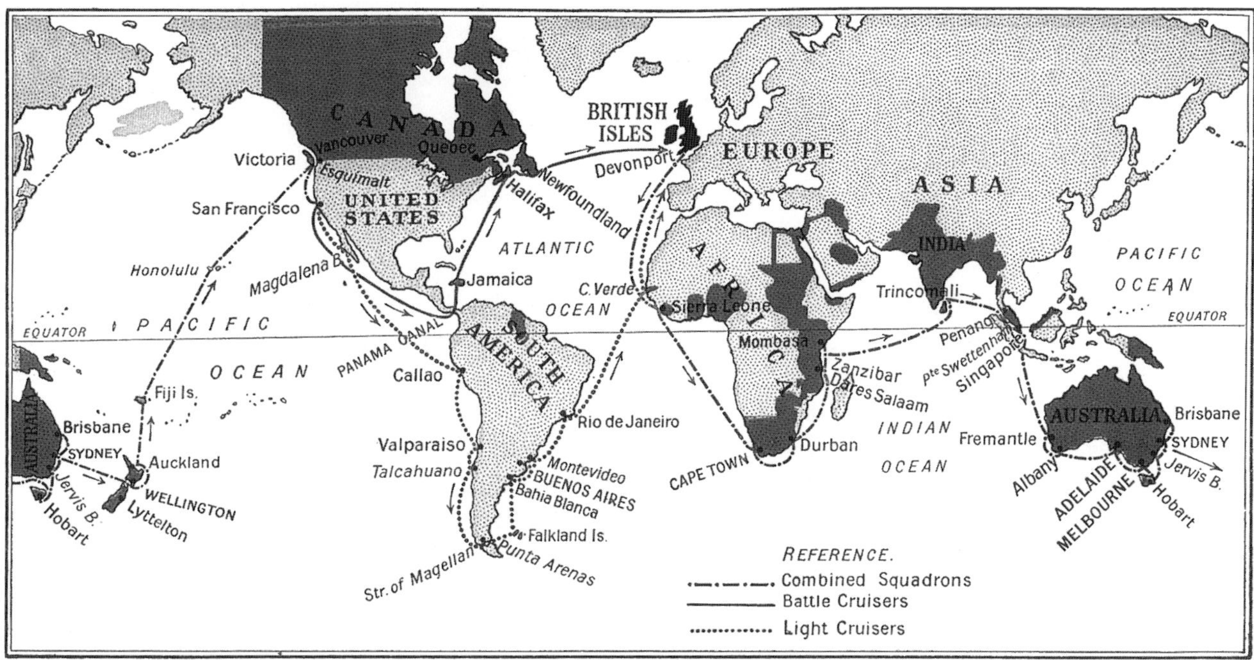

A map showing the course of the 'Special Service Squadron' on the world cruise 1923–4. (*NMRN*)

1953 The old colours of the Plymouth Division Royal Marines were laid up in the King's Chapel, Gibraltar, in presence of C-in-C Home Fleet, Admiral Sir George Creasy, and CGRM, Lt-Gen J.C. Westall. The colours, which had been presented to the RMLI by the Duke of Saxe-Coburg and Gotha in July 1896, were badly damaged when the RM Officers' Mess at Plymouth was bombed in 1940. They were marched from the airfield to the chapel by RM detachments from battleship *Vanguard*, light cruiser *Swiftsure* and carriers *Theseus* and *Implacable*.

1959 Riot by workforce in Malta Dockyard.

'Dockyard Riot in Malta. 6,000 dismissed workers. Two-hour battle with police. Admiral stoned. Rioting broke out in the dockyard here today after the Admiralty had informed more than 6,000 workers that it could no longer employ them after March 29. The information was on a slip of paper included in their pay packets at noon . . . stones were thrown, windows broken, and an office wrecked . . . a mobile workshop was thrown into the sea . . . Inhabitants of the "three cities" surrounding the docks shouted encouragement from the bastions . . . Rear-Admiral J. Lee-Barber, Admiral Superintendent, and the Captain of the Dockyard, who tried to intervene, were stoned and then assaulted, receiving minor injuries' – *The Times*, 28 February 1959, p.6 col. A.

See 15 April 1942, 30 March 1959.

1966 Frigate *Lowestoft* first ship on Beira Patrol off Mozambique, establishing oil embargo on Rhodesia after UDI.

See 19 December 1967, 25 June 1975, 10 April 1966, 10 May 1966.

1970 Michael Lewis, naval historian and author, died. Taught at Osborne and Dartmouth and succeeded Sir Geoffrey Callender as Professor of History and English at Greenwich.

1970 Admiral Sir William O'Brien (seniority 4 April 1970) succeeded Admiral Sir John Bush as C-in-C Western Fleet. He was to be the only officer to command the Western Fleet throughout his appointment.

See 6 June 1967, 1 October 1967, 1 November 1971, 15 October 1971.

2004 Tigerfish, the Mk 24 Mod 2 heavyweight torpedo, withdrawn after thirty-seven years' service. Submarine *Triumph* was the last boat to carry this weapon.

2006 Single role minehunter *Grimsby*, Lt-Cdr N.P. May RN, ran aground on a submerged rock in a fjord 90 miles N. of Bergen during an exercise. Transported to Rosyth on the chartered German heavy lift vessel *Condock 1*, arriving on Easter Monday, 17 April.

See 7 July 2002, 16 December 2008, 8 April 2009.

28 FEBRUARY

1579 Francis Drake (*Golden Hind*) captured the Spanish *Cacafuego* off Cape San Francisco, Ecuador.

1748 John Thomas (later Admiral Sir John) Duckworth born at Leatherhead.

1758 *Monmouth* (64) captured the French *Foudroyant* (80), the largest ship afloat at the time. *Revenge* (64) and *Berwick* (64) captured the French *Orphée* (64) 20 miles S. of Cartagena. *Monarch* (74) and *Montagu* (60) drove *Oriflamme* (50) ashore at Monte Cope. Battle Honour: *Foudroyant* 1758.

See 16 June 1897.

1760 *Aeolus, Brilliant* and *Pallas* captured the French privateers *Blonde, Maréchal de Belleîle* and *Terpsichore* 6 miles S. of the Mull of Galloway. The French had taken Carrickfergus Castle on the 21st and sailed for home on the 27th but the Lord-Lieutenant sent 'expresses' to Capt Elliot at Kinsale, and he took his three frigates to sea at once. Three French ships parted company, the other three were taken.

1810 Sea Fencibles disbanded: 61 captains, 245 lieutenants and 23,455 men.

1842 HM Queen Victoria paid her first visit to Portsmouth and stayed at Admiralty House.

Dinner guests included the Duke of Wellington (who stayed at the George in the High Street). Despite the rain and wind 'The Star and Garter Hotel, at The Point, was lit up with variegated lamps outside, and with wax candles along the whole range of the windows inside. . . This house has been the resort of naval officers for upwards of a century'. Fireworks from Semaphore Tower. The Prince Consort visited the block mills in the dockyard and gunnery training ship *Excellent* and the Queen boarded the *St Vincent*, flagship of Admiral Sir Edward Codrington. The Queen tasted grog on board the *Queen* ex-*Royal Frederick*, the first three-decker launched since her accession.

1866 Grapeshot declared obsolete in RN.

1921 Royal Navy ships evacuated British nationals from Batum on the E. shore of the Black Sea about to fall to Bolshevik forces. Operation lasted until 19 March.

1945 Frigate *Loch Fada*, with frigate *Labuan* and sloop *Wild Goose*, escorting Convoy ONA 287, following a sighting by Liberator H/112 (USN), sank U-327 off the Scillies (49.46N, 05.47W). No survivors. The second success for *Loch Fada* in two days.

See 21 August 1967.

1947 Lt Prince Philip of Greece and Denmark RN, 'a serving officer in His Majesty's forces', took the Oath of Allegiance to the King and became a naturalised British subject as Philip Mountbatten – *London Gazette*, 18 March 1947.

1948 Cruisers *Sheffield* and *Devonshire* ordered to Belize to deter any military move by Guatemala to claim to British Honduras. *Sheffield*, flagship of Vice-Admiral Sir William Tennant, sailed from Cargtagena, Colombia, and landed her Royal Marines. *Devonshire* deployed from Jamaica with the 2nd Bn Gloucestershire Regiment.

1959 RN Armament Depot, Durban, closed. AFO 76/59.

1962 RN Wireless Station at Mauritius took over operationally from Ceylon West WT at Wellisara (HMS *Highflyer*) at 0001Z. C-in-C South Atlantic and South America commissioned the station on 19 March 1962 as HMS *Mauritius*. AFOs 567/62 and 334/62.

See 16 February 1962, 30 March 1976.

1976 Frigate *Arrow* commissioned. Therafter, Founder's Day at Harrow School each year was jollied-up with a congratulatory signal from HMS 'arrow'.

1983 The last Type 15 post-war full conversion frigate, *Grenville*, arrived at Rochester for breaking up.

See 1 October 1951, 6 July 1971.

At the opening of the Cold War the Royal Navy's most modern anti-submarine frigates, the Loch-, Bay-, River- and Castle-class, were markedly slower than

HMS *Soberton*. (*RN*)

the submerged speed of new Soviet Whisky-class submarines, based on the German Type XXI U-boats. As an interim, twenty-three wartime destroyers were rebuilt as full conversions to specialist anti-submarine ships with forecastle decks extended well aft and equipped with Squid or Limbo mortars and twin 4-in guns abaft the mainmast. The conversions were highly successful and, with a top speed of 31 knots, the Type 15s proved the best anti-submarine vessels in the world. The first ships in service were *Relentless* and *Rocket*; the last, *Grenville*, served as a trials ship for ASWE before paying off at Easter 1974.

1990 Abolition of rum issue in RNZN.

1991 Ceasefire against Iraqi forces in Operation Granby. A total of 2,821 RN and RM personnel had been deployed afloat and 565 ashore, including 1,771 Reservists. Cdre Paul Haddacks, SNO Middle East, relieved 3 December 1990 by Cdre Christopher Craig who became also CTG 321.1. Some 200 replenishments at sea had been made and eighteen hits secured from twenty-six Sea Skua missiles fired. Ships: *Atherston, Battleaxe, Bicester, Brave, Brazen, Brecon, Brilliant, Brocklesby, Cardiff, Cattistock, Dulverton, Exeter, Gloucester, Hecla, Herald, Hurworth, Jupiter, Ledbury, London, Manchester, Opossum, Otus, York*. RFAs: *Argus, Bayleaf, Diligence, Fort Grange, Olna, Orangeleaf, Resource, Sir Bedivere, Sir Galahad, Sir Percivale, Sir Tristam*. FAA Sqns: 815, 826, 829, 845, 846, 848. Mine clearance and embargo enforcement continued. The Armilla patrol re-established.

See 1 and 9 August 1990.

1992 Fishery protection vessel HMS *Soberton* paid off at Rosyth after thirty-five years' continuous service. *Soberton* was built by Fleetlands Shipyards, Gosport, and commissioned on 17 September 1957. Designed as a minesweeper, she served throughout her career in the Fishery Protection Squadron, and sailed on her last patrol on 7 February 1992. She sailed up the Thames on 20 February for a farewell visit to London with Admiral Sir Jock Slater, C-in-C Fleet and a former CO, embarked.

See 5 October 1993.

1996 Service at St Paul's Cathedral in the presence of Her Majesty The Queen to dedicate a memorial to the forty-seven British servicemen who died in the Gulf War August 1990 to July 1991.

See 4 May 1991, 23 October 2005, 14 June 2007.

2006 The last embarkation of a Fleet Air Arm fixed wing aircraft. Two SHAR FA2 of 801 NAS landed on *Illustrious* as part of the ship's predeployment work-up.

See 13 November 1978, 28 March 2006.

29 FEBRUARY

1812 Boats of *Menelaus* cut out the French *St Joseph* a little E. of d'Agay Roads, near the Gulf of Fréjus, S. of France.

1812 *Semiramis* captured the St Malo privateer *Grand Jean Bart* 80 miles S. by W. of the Scilly Isles.

1884 VC: Capt Arthur Knyvet Wilson (*Hecla*) for fighting off a fierce attack on gun single-handed and carrying on although wounded. Naval Brigade at the (second) Battle of El Teb, Sudan. Ships: *Euryalus, Carysfort, Hecla, Briton, Dryad, Sphinx*. Egyptian Medal: clasp 'El Teb'.

See 4 March 1842, 4 March 1907, 25 January 1910.

1916 *Alcantara* (AMC) fought the German raider *Greif* 70 miles N.E. of Shetland. *Alcantara* torpedoed and sunk. *Greif* abandoned, and sunk by *Andes*.

1940 Cruiser *Despatch* intercepted the German SS *Troja* which was scuttled off Aruba.

1940 A white ensign, 'torn and tattered', which the heavy cruiser *Exeter* wore as a battle ensign at the Battle of the River Plate, was presented to the City of Exeter by Capt F.S. Bell RN.

See 1 March 1948.

1996 Rear-Admiral John Grant died. Flag Officer Commanding Reserve Fleet 1959–60, and the last British admiral to fly his flag in a battleship afloat (*Vanguard*).

See 7 June 1960.

Admiral of the Fleet Sir Arthur K. Wilson, Bt, VC, GCB, OM, GCVO (1842–1921)

Capt Arthur Wilson commanded HMS *Hecla* during the Egyptian and Sudanese Wars of 1882 and 1884–5. On 29 February 1884, he marched out to the Battle of El Teb with an infantry square, purely as a spectator – but the square broke under enemy attack. Springing into the gap, he beat off the Dervishes single-handed and, when his sword broke, fought on using his bare fists although he had been wounded in the head. His action saved the day and he was recommended for the Victoria Cross though he remained unmoved by what he had done. Returning to his ship he wrote home: 'I have just returned from a very pretty little fight . . . .' A typical entry in his diary reads, 'Docked ship. Awarded VC'. He went on to become a successful and much admired admiral who, by rigorous training and realistic battle-practice, did more than any other sea-going officer to prepare the Navy for war before 1914. He was recalled from retirement to be First Sea Lord in 1910.

Capt A.K. Wilson, *c.*1885 when commanding HMS *Raleigh*. (*NMRN*)

Blue Jackets Hauling the Guns in the Sudan, 1884

Seamen were often employed as expert gunners during the Victorian Colonial wars because they were usually excellently trained and because their guns usually had a greater range than the lighter Army pieces. The classic use of naval artillery was at Ladysmith in 1899 (second Boer War) when the British were completely outgunned by the Boers' fine 6-in 'Long Toms'. It is likely that the town would have fallen had not a Naval Brigade from HMS *Powerful* arrived just in time with two naval 4.7-in guns on improvised carriages. Exploits such as these so captured the public imagination that they were re-enacted in England at various naval displays. From these re-enactments developed the competitions that were a popular feature of every Royal Tournament. Between the accession and the death of Queen Victoria there were at least thirty-eight occasions when Naval Brigades were landed, in countries as distant as South America and the Sudan, New Zealand and West Africa, the Baltic and the Black Sea. Based on the 'landing party' in the ships' Watch and Quarter Bills, and on the number of ships deployed, they varied from platoons to battalions, often operating far from their ships in time and in distance. The hardiness ashore that won the thanks of the Army in the eighteenth and nineteenth centuries has been demonstrated ever since.

Blue jackets hauling the guns in the Sudan, 1884. (*NMRN*)

A medallion, showing a two-decker on the slips at Pembroke Dockyard on launching day, was issued to mark the opening of the Pembroke Dock National School in 1844. (*Author*)

1 MARCH

1799 *Sybille* captured the French *Forte* in Balasore Road, Bay of Bengal.
Battle Honour: *Forte* 1799.

1807 *Blenheim* (74), flagship of Rear-Admiral Sir Thomas Troubridge, sailing from Madras to the Cape with *Java* (32) and *Harrier* sloop, was lost with all hands in a hurricane off Rodriguez Island, E. of Mauritius (20.21S, 64.11E). *Java* also lost. Troubridge in *Culloden* had led the British Fleet into action at the Battle of St Vincent (14 February 1797) and commanded her at the Nile (1 August 1798) where she ran aground at the entrance to Aboukir Bay and took no part in the fighting. 'Thus perished one of the most outstanding officers of his generation' – N.A.M. Rodger.
See 4 May 1810, 2 July 1853.

1814 *San Domingo* captured the American letter of marque *Argus* 370 miles S.W. of Bermuda.

1859 End of Indian Mutiny. Naval Brigade from *Pearl*, wood screw corvette, rejoined ship at Calcutta after seventeen months ashore and having engaged in twenty-six actions.

1864 RNR officers' uniform instituted, each stripe composed of two thin interwoven waves.
See 31 March 1951, 1 January 1952, 1 July 2007.

1878 The Russian War Scare. RN acquired four armoured warships then building in British yards, three for Turkey and one for Brazil. The Brazilian *Independencia* became *Neptune* and the three Turkish ships, *Hamidieh*, *Pakyi-Shereef* and *Boordyi-Zaffir*, which could not be delivered because of neutrality requirements during the Russo-Turkish War, became *Superb*, *Belleisle* and *Orion*.
See 10 September 1874, 23 October 1903.

1881 RN Medical School, Haslar, opened.

1904 The Australian Defence Act 1903 came into force transferring warships owned by individual states to the Commonwealth of Australia.
See 25 November 1910, 10 July 1911.

1907 Cap ribbons and bedding issued in lieu of a gratuity, and ready-made uniforms instead of material to be made up. Loan clothing introduced.

1911 Admiral Hon. Sir Assheton Curzon-Howe, C-in-C Portsmouth, and great grandson of Richard, Earl Howe, died at Admiralty House. He 'was one of the most polite men who ever served in the Navy' – Admiral Sir Reginald Bacon. Memorial in St Ann's church, Portsmouth.
See 27 October 1890.

1913 Rear-Admiral David Beatty, appointed to command the 1st Battlecruiser Squadron, hoisted his flag for the first time in *Lion* at Devonport, in which ship it flew almost continuously until 27 November 1916, when he succeeded Admiral Sir John Jellicoe as C-in-C Grand Fleet.

1916 German extended submarine campaign began.

1916 Sloop *Primula* torpedoed by U-35 in E. Mediterranean.

1917 *Pheasant*, destroyer, sunk by mine 1 mile W. of the Old Man of Hoy. All hands lost except one midshipman who died ashore.

1918 AMC *Calgarian*, 9th CS, escorting convoy off N. Ireland, sunk by U-29 off Rathlin Island.

1919 All surveying ships to be painted white.
See 1 June 1998.

1928 *Courageous* recommissioned. First carrier with transverse arrester wires.

1935 Battleship *Royal Sovereign*, flagship of Admiral Sir William Fisher, C-in-C Mediterranean Fleet, arrived at Phaleron Bay to protect British interests following the Greek monarchist revolt.

1941 Albacore aircraft of 826 Sqn (*Formidable*) attacked Massawa, Eritrea.

1942 Cruisers *Perth* (RAN) and USS *Houston* sunk by *Mogami* and *Mikuma* and destroyers in the Java Sea (05.45S, 106.13E).

HMAS *Perth* and USS *Houston* left Batavia at 2100 on 28 February to slip through the Sunda Strait. At 2300 they encountered a Japanese invasion force. They engaged the enemy at once, and fought until their magazines were empty and even the practice rounds had been fired. They were finally overwhelmed and sunk soon after midnight.

1942 Heavy cruiser *Exeter* sunk by Japanese cruisers *Haguro* and *Nachi*, and destroyer *Encounter* sunk by *Myoko* and *Ashigara* in Java Sea. The wrecks of *Exeter* and *Encounter* were located in 2008, 200ft down, 90 miles N. of Bawean Island, 60 miles from the position reported by Capt Oliver Gordon of *Exeter*. *Exeter* was first of eight cruisers and *Encounter* the ninth of forty-six destroyers lost in 1942.
Battle Honour: Sunda Strait.

Exeter lived up nobly to the example set by her predecessor on 17 February 1782. 'The diminished ABDA [American, British, Dutch, Australian] squadron was destroyed by an enemy superior in every department except courage' – Roskill, *The War at Sea*, vol.2, p.17.

Over 800 survivors from the two British ships were made POW. In 1945 the senior surviving officers submitted their reports to the Admiralty. 'One cannot help but marvel at the clearness and accuracy of these accounts, written as they were three and a half years after the events which they described, and from such tenuous records as the officers had managed to secrete from the persistent searches of their captors. In all the annals of sea fights there can exist few more moving documents' – Roskill, *The War at Sea*, vol.2, p.17.

1944 Frigate *Gould* torpedoed 480 miles N.N.E. of Azores by U-358 after a fourteen-hour hunt. U-358 surfaced to sink her and was sunk by frigate *Affleck* (45.46N, 23.10W).

The longest continuous U-boat hunt, 1944

The First Escort Group of Captain-class frigates was on patrol in the W. Approaches and detected and sank U-91 on 25 February 1944. Early on the 29th *Garlies* gained an Asdic contact with U-358 and the group attacked with Hedgehog and depth charges. All through the night and next day contact was maintained and a total of 104 depth charges expended. *Gore* and *Garlies* returned to Gibraltar, while *Affleck* and *Gould* maintained Asdic contact. At 1920, *Gould* was hit by an acoustic homing torpedo, and the submarine surfaced.

Affleck opened fire at 1,500yds, and then attacked with depth charges. One survivor was picked up from U-358.

1948 A memorial window to the officers and men of the heavy cruiser *Exeter* killed in action dedicated in Exeter Cathedral by the Bishop of Exeter on the sixth anniversary of her loss off Java.
See 29 February 1940, 1 March 1942.

1956 Submarine *Thorough*, Lt-Cdr R.C.H. Mason RN, bombarded a terrorist position in the Malayan jungle, with her 4-in gun.
See 22 September 1951, 23 August 1956.

1967 Chatham to be developed as the second dockyard for refitting nuclear submarines.
See 20 March 1970.

1967 RN NBCD School at Tipner reverted to its traditional name of HMS *Phoenix*, remaining a tender to *Excellent*. DCI(RN) 176/67.

1967 The Royal Australian Navy hauled down the White Ensign for the last time and hoisted the new Australian White Ensign. DCI(RN) 234/67.
See 9 December 1950, 23 December 1966, 20 June 1968.

1974 Admiral Sir Michael Pollock promoted Admiral of the Fleet at the end of his appointment as First Sea Lord.
See 27 September 2006.

1975 Instructor Branch officers rank prefix 'Instructor' abolished. DCI(RN)S 32/75
See 18 November 1918, 6 April 1962.

1976 CINCNAVHOME assumed full command of the RNR. Post of ACR lapsed 1 January 1977. DCI(RN)S 31/76; DCI(RN) 565/76.
See 1 January 1977.

1983 First male admitted to QARNNS.

1991 RFA *Fort George*, fleet replenishment ship, launched at Swan Hunters, Wallsend-on-Tyne.
See 12 June 1990.

2004 *Ranger*, 49-ton Archer-class patrol vessel, returned to Portsmouth after thirteen years' unbroken service with the Gibraltar Squadron.
See 11 April 1866.

2 March

1709 *Assistance, Assurance* (Capt Tollett, who was very ill and conducted the battle from a deck-chair), and *Hampshire*, with a convoy, fought a French squadron of five ships under Capt René Duguay-Trouin (*Achille*) 24 miles S.S.W. of Lizard Head. Five of the convoy were taken.

1783 *Resistance* captured the French *Coquette* 8 miles N.W. of Grand Turk Island, West Indies.

1795 *Lively* captured the French *Espion* 40 miles N.W. of Ushant.

1800 *Nereide* captured the French privateer *Vengeance* 180 miles W. of Rochefort.

1808 *Sappho* (18) captured the Danish *Admiral Jawl* (28) 20 miles N.E. of Flamborough Head.

1808 Capture of Marie Galante Island, West Indies, by *Cerberus*, *Circe* and *Camilla*.

1858 *Pearl*'s Naval Brigade made an unsuccessful attack on the fort at Belwa, India.

1911 First four officers, chosen from over 200 applicants, reported to the Royal Aero Club's aerodrome at Eastchurch on the Isle of Sheppey for pilot training in private aircraft provided free of charge: Lt C.R. Samson, scout cruiser *Foresight*; Lt R. Gregory, armoured cruiser *Antrim*; Lt A.M. Longmore, HMTB 24 and Lt E.L. Gerrard RMLI, cruiser *Hermione*.

See 25 April 1911.

1914 Submarines AE 1 and AE 2 left Portsmouth for Australia, manned by loan crews from Devonport. AE 1 was lost without trace off the Bismarck Archipelago 14 September 1914 and AE 2 was scuttled 30 April 1915 in the Sea of Marmara after damage by Turkish shore batteries.

See 14 September 1914.

The light cruiser HMS *Dunedin* (1918). (*NMRN*)

HMS *Thunderer* (1872), one of the first mastless seagoing turret ships with four 12-in muzzle-loading guns in fore and aft turrets. (*NMRN*)

1926 First naval engineer officer to be ADC to the King; Engineer Capt E.P. St J. Benn, commanding the RN Engineering College, Keyham. 'His decorations include one presented by the Emperor of China in recognition of service as an instructor at the Chinese Imperial Naval College at Nanking in 1911' – *The Times*.

1940 Cruiser *Berwick* intercepted the German SS *Wolfsburg* in Denmark Strait. *Wolfsburg* was scuttled.

1940 Light cruiser *Dunedin* intercepted the German M.V. *Heidelberg* 60 miles W.S.W. of the Mona Passage, S. of San Domingo, West Indies: *Heidelberg* scuttled.

See 8 March 1940.

1940 The Admiralty announced that in future all admirals of the fleet would remain on the Active List for life.

1945 A raiding force of 500 men, supported by destroyer *Liddesdale*, captured Piskopi, N.W. of Rhodes.

1953 Hawker Sea Hawk jet fighter entered service, with 806 NAS at RNAS Brawdy.

Agadir, 1960

When two earth tremors struck Agadir on the night of 1/2 March 1960, *Tyne* was dispatched from a visit in Spain to assist. She arrived six days after the tremors had struck, with many extra supplies she had embarked at Gibraltar, and with some sixty wooden huts prefabricated onboard during the passage by the shipwrights. She was allowed to land this equipment, but not to land personnel. The bay in which she anchored was unsafe as the earth tremor, believed to have been centred out to sea, had raised the sea bed, and the harbour was out of action. The temperature was 105 in the shade and flies abounded. The final death toll was reported at 12,000, and over 20,000 were left homeless – but exact figures will never be known.

1992 Admiral Sir Julian Oswald promoted Admiral of the Fleet at the end of his appointment as First Sea Lord. Born 11 August 1933, son of Capt George Oswald RN. Entered BRNCD May 1947; Captain destroyer *Newcastle* 1977–9 and of BRNCD 1980–2; ACDS (Programmes) and ACDS (Policy and Nuclear) 1982–5; FOF3 1985–7 and CINCFLEET 1987–9; appointed First Sea Lord May 1989. Admiral Oswald was President of FRINTON (Former Russian Interpreters of the Navy).

2004 The First Sea Lord approved the retrospective Battle Honour East Indies 1940–5. *Illustrious*, *Raider*, the future *Queen Elizabeth*, some FAA squadrons and several RAN, RNIN and former RIN units qualify.

2009 Sir Donald Gosling promoted honorary rear-admiral, RNR.

See 1 November 1958, 1 June 2004, 1 August 2010.

3 MARCH

1795 *Illustrious* (74) (first of the name) abandoned and set on fire, having grounded while trying to anchor in Valence Bay, between Spezia and Leghorn.

1799 *Leander* (first of the name) returned by Russia and Turkey after capitulation of Corfu. Taken by the *Généreux* after the Battle of the Nile, she had been taken there and efforts were made to suborn her crew. These were vigorously resisted by her maintopmen!

A commemorative medal by Mills in silver for Admiral Sir John Duckworth (1748–1817). (*A.B. Sainsbury*)

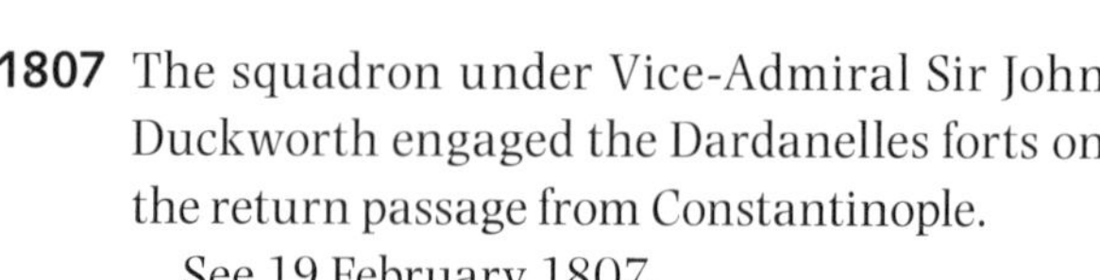

1807 The squadron under Vice-Admiral Sir John Duckworth engaged the Dardanelles forts on the return passage from Constantinople.
See 19 February 1807.

1811 *Nymphen* captured the French privateer *Vigilante* 40 miles E. of Yarmouth.

1812 Board contracted with Portsea Island Water Works Co. to supply fresh water through

The guided missile destroyer HMS *Glamorgan* leaving Singapore naval base on 31 October 1971 for passage home. (*Author*)

Ditching British Pacific Fleet aircraft from the maintenance carrier HMS *Pioneer* off Australia in late 1945. American Lend-Lease aircraft had to be paid for in dollars or destroyed. Many British-built aircraft were also ditched to save the cost of returning them to the United Kingdom. (*Cdr David Hobbs RN*)

elm-wood pipes at 6*d*, under supervision of 'a trusted person from the Yard' at cask filling point near Victory gate.

1940 Heavy cruiser *York* intercepted the German SS *Arucas* off Iceland (63.30N, 15.13W). *Arucas* was scuttled.

1945 Destroyers *Rapid*, *Rocket*, *Roebuck* and *Rotherham* (Force 68) bombarded Port Blair, Andaman Islands.

1971 Britain's first nuclear submarine, *Dreadnought*, reached North Pole.

See 19 April 2004.

The nuclear submarine HMS *Sovereign* (1973) in the Arctic ice. (*NMRN*)

4 March

1653 *Leopard*, Capt Appleton, and three hired merchantmen, *Levant Merchant*, *Peregrine* and *Samson*, taken by the Dutch squadron under Capt Johan van Galen off Leghorn. *Samson* was burned by a fireship. A fourth hired ship, *Bonaventure*, blew up, and a fifth, *Mary*, escaped.

1709 *Portland* fought the French *Coventry* and *Mignon* 40 miles N. by W. of Puerto Bastimentos, Colombia. A detachment of Brig-Gen Thomas Handasyd's regiment was present.

See 6 March 1709.

1806 *Diadem* captured the French *Volontaire* in Table Bay, South Africa, which had surrendered in January.

1807 Boats of *Glatton* (56) cut out a Turkish treasure-ship in Port Sigri, Lesbos.

1842 Arthur Knyvet Wilson, future VC, First Sea Lord and Admiral of the Fleet, born at Swaffham, Norfolk, third son of Cdr George Knyvet Wilson who had been Second Lieutenant of the frigate *Talbot* at Navarino.

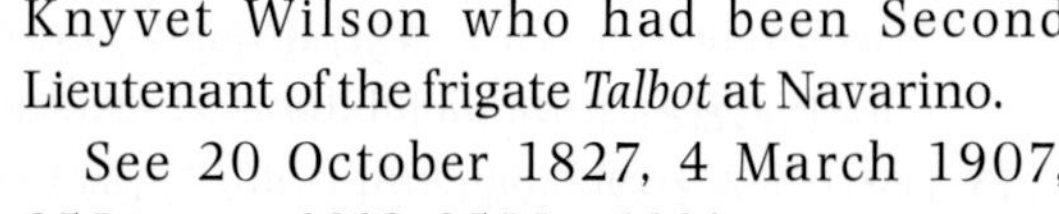

See 20 October 1827, 4 March 1907, 25 January 1910, 25 May 1921.

1844 Order in Council re-established Deptford as a building yard.

1850 *Medea*, with a party from *Hastings*, captured thirteen pirate junks in Mirs Bay, Hong Kong.

1872 First warship model test (*Greyhound*) at Admiralty Experimental Works, Torquay.

1907 Admiral of the Fleet Sir Arthur Knyvet Wilson VC, C-in-C Channel Fleet and 'Old 'ard 'art' to the lower deck, hauled down his flag in the battleship *Exmouth* at Weymouth on his 65th birthday and 'went on shore without ceremony of any kind' – Bradford, p.221. But see 25 January 1910.

See 29 February 1884.

1915 Destroyers *Ghurka* and *Maori*, destroyed U-8 near the Varne lightvessel (50.56N, 01.15E) by modified sweep. First success with indicator nets.

1941 Transportation of Imperial troops from Egypt to Greece. Ended on 24 April, when the evacuation began. Operation Lustre.

1941 Successful Anglo-Norwegian raid on the Lofoten Islands, Norway. Operation Claymore. Ships: *Bedouin, Eskimo, Legion, Prinses Beatrix, Queen Emma, Somali* (D 6), *Sunfish, Tartar.* Close support: *Edinburgh, Nigeria.*

On 1 March a force of five destroyers under Capt C. Caslon in *Somali* and two cross-Channel steamers, carrying 500 men of 3 and 4 Cdos, 50 Royal Engineers and some Norwegian troops sailed from Scapa Flow on Operation Claymore. The objective was to destroy the Norwegian oil factories on the Lofoten Islands, which were valuable to the Germans. A submarine was used as a navigational beacon, and the force achieved complete surprise with

In the stokehold of HMS *Majestic* (1895). (*NMRN*)

The light carrier *Centaur* leaving dry dock at Gibraltar in September 1962. (*Author*)

a first landing at 0500 on 4 March. All the objectives including a fish factory ship were destroyed. By 1300 the troops had re-embarked with 200 German prisoners, and the force returned on 6 March. This was a good example of the exploitation of sea power as a flexible aid to military force, where a small force can strike where and when required, and keep large numbers of enemy troops employed guarding many places. Most important was the acquisition from the trawler *Krebs* of a set of Enigma rotors; this may have been a matter of luck but it led to the capture of *Munchen* on 7 May.

1942 Destroyer *Stronghold* and sloop *Yarra* (RAN), with MMS 51 sunk by Japanese surface forces 300 miles S. of Java, 220 miles S. of Sunda Strait (11.30S, 109.03E).

1943 Destroyer *St Croix* and corvette *Shediac* (both RCN) sank U-87 in N. Atlantic. Convoy KMS 10.

1943 Hudson V/500 sank U-83 E. by S. of Cartagena (37.10N, 00.05E).

1944 Destroyer *Onslaught* and Swordfish B/816 (*Chaser*) sank U-472 off North Cape (73.05N, 26.40E). Convoy RA 57.
See 5 March 1944.

1944 Heavy cruiser *Shropshire* bombarded Hauwei Island, Admiralty Islands, ahead of US attack.

1960 Light cruiser *Gambia* arrived at Port Louis, Mauritius, with emergency supplies following an Indian Ocean cyclone. Landing parties repaired power supplies and telephone links, gave typhoid inoculations and built emergency accommodation.

1961 Light fleet carrier *Hercules*, laid up almost complete at Faslane from 1946 to 1957, commissioned into the Indian Navy as INS *Vikrant* after a major refit at Harland & Wolff, Belfast.
See 5 July 1948, 28 October 1955, 29 August 1957, 20 March 1987.

1965 Vice-Admiral J.M.D. Gray appointed the last C-in-C South Atlantic and South America station. Flag in *Afrikander*. Flag hauled down April 1967 after 170 years of station's existence. Gray was born 13 June 1913; died 3 February 1998 aged 84.
See 11 April 1967.

1983 *Dreadnought*, the RN's first nuclear-powered warship, paid off at Chatham. DCI(RN) 136/83.
See 21 October 1960.

1992 *Vanguard*, tenth of the name and first of the RN Trident submarines launched at Barrow-in-Furness.

5 March

1800 *Phoebe* captured the French privateer *Heureux* 200 miles W.S.W. of Cape Clear.

1804 Boats of *Blenheim* repulsed in an attempt to cut out the French *Curieux* at St Pierre, Martinique.

1804 Boat of *Eclair* cut out the French privateer *Rose* at Deshayes, Guadeloupe.

1858 *Pearl*'s Naval Brigade, with the Bengal Yeomanry, a detachment of the 1st Bengal Military Police Battalion and Gurkha allies, Baruk and Gorakhnath Regiments, totalling 1,261 men, completely defeated the 14,000 Indian rebels at Amorha, thereby preventing a second extensive rising in the Trans-Gogra district. Indian Mutiny Medal: clasp 'Amorha 1858'. One captured gun turned on rebels by three RN officers and an AB.
Battle Honour: Amorha 1858.

1915 Bombardment of the Smyrna forts began; continued for five days. Ships: *Euryalus*, *Swiftsure*, *Triumph*, *Anne Rickmers* (seaplane carrier). Minesweepers: *Okino* and four others. Sunk: M/S *Okino*.

1942 VC: Cdr Anthony Cecil Capel Miers (*Torbay*). Attack on shipping in Corfu Roads. Gazetted 7 July 1942. Invested at Buckingham Palace 28 July 1942 at which other *Torbay* personnel decorated. DSO: Lt (E) Hugh Kidd, DSC; bars to DSC: Lts Paul Chapman, DSC and D.S. Verschoyle-Campbell, DSC; and twenty-four ratings received DSMs or bars to DSM.

1944 Swordfish F/816 (*Chaser*) sank U-366 off northern Norway. Convoy RA 57.
See 4 March 1944.

1946 The start of the Cold War. Winston Churchill, speaking at Fulton, Missouri, said: 'From Stettin in the Baltic to Trieste in the Adriatic, an iron curtain has descended across the continent.'
See 25 December 1991.

1954 *Explorer*, the first of two experimental, unarmed submarines, designed to try a new diesel and electric power plant incorporating High Test Hydrogen Peroxide (HTP), launched at Vickers, Barrow. She and her sister-ship *Excalibur*, which followed her down the ways on 25 February 1955, were inevitably known as the 'blonde boats'.
See 25 September 1945, 16 June 1955, 12 August 2000.

These 780 ton submarines were a development of the Walther engine that had powered U-1407, captured in 1945 and commissioned into the RN as HMS *Meteorite*. They achieved underwater speeds of 25 knots and, incidentally, provided fast underwater exercise targets for surface

The submarine *Valiant*, Cdr Peter Herbert RN, arriving alongside the depot ship *Forth* in Singapore on 5 March 1967 after a mainly submerged passage from Britain. (*Author*)

A Westland Sea King Mark 6 helicopter refuels while hovering over a flight-deck. (*NMRN*)

forces. Hydrogen Peroxide used with diesel oil offered an attractive closed-cycle submarine propulsion system but it proved a prohibitively volatile and dangerous fuel, instanced by the explosion of a HTP-powered torpedo which sank *Sidon* in 1955 and, more disastrously, the Russian SSGN *Kursk* in 2000. (*Explorer* was nicknamed 'Exploder'). The development of a nuclear reactor small enough to fit in a submarine ended further experiments and both boats were discarded in the 1960s.

1967 Submarine *Valiant* arrived in Singapore after a mainly submerged passage from Britain (the boat had spent four days in Mauritius). Cdr Peter Herbert, her CO, was 'greeted and congratulated' on board the depot ship *Forth* by Vice-Admiral Sir Frank Twiss, COMFEF. Herbert told reporters 'there had been no signs of ill-effects among the crew after their endurance test' – *The Times*.

1996 Flag of FOSNNI shifted from Pitreavie, Rosyth, to *Neptune*, Clyde Submarine Base.

See 1 April 1994.

6 March

1709 *Portland* captured the French *Coventry* 40 miles N. by W. of Puerto Bastimentos.
See 4 March 1709.

1741 Vice-Admiral Edward Vernon (*Strafford*) bombarded Puerto Cartagena, Colombia – ineffectively.

1797 *Phaeton* (38) captured the French privateer *Actif* 120 miles S. of Ushant.

1811 Landing parties from Rear-Admiral Sir Richard Keats' squadron destroyed French batteries between Rota and Puerto de Santa Maria on Spanish coast. Ships: *Milford, Implacable, Warrior.* Bombs: *Hound, Thunder.*

1838 *Pincher*, schooner (5), capsized with all hands off The Owers.

1890 First promotion to new warrant rank of Signal Bosun: M.H.W. Evans, the top of the list, also became the first Chief Signal Bosun and, in 1903, the first Signal Warrant Officer.

1902 Queen Alexandra's Royal Naval Nursing Service constituted by Order in Council, replacing the naval nursing sisters.
See 1 April 1983.

1913 Direct public school entry to RN College Dartmouth announced.

1918 GC (ex-AM): Flt Lt V.A. Watson for saving life in blazing naval airship. (*Gazette* date.)

1918 Submarine H 5 sunk in collision with SS *Rutherglen*, not as some thought a Q-ship, but a merchant vessel whose ramming a friendly submarine was not denounced by the Admiralty, in order to encourage others. First USN submarine casualty on active service – Ensign E.F. Childs, USN, appointed H 5 for experience.

Nurses from Queen Alexandra's Royal Naval Nursing Service at camp, early twentieth century. (*NMRN*)

1920 Light cruiser *Calcutta* dealt with serious fire in the American *Balabac* at Port of Spain, Trinidad. Admiralty approved acceptance of rare award of the Presidential Life Saving Medal, made without reference to Congress, by President Wilson.

1921 China Station light cruiser *Carlisle* and sloop *Foxglove* stood by passenger steamer SS *Hong Moh* ashore and broken-backed on the Lamock Rocks, 40 miles E. of Swatow; 226 saved from 1,100 souls on board, mainly by drifting Carley floats downwind. A British sailor twice went overboard from the cruiser in heavy seas with a line but was neither named nor recommended by Capt E.R.G.R. Evans RN of the *Carlisle* in his ROP. A direct order from the Commodore, Hong Kong, revealed the man was Evans himself; the first ever Lloyd's Gold Medal for Saving Life at Sea.

See 21 April 1917.

1938 The Spanish nationalist cruiser *Baleares* torpedoed with heavy loss of life by a Spanish Republican destroyer off Cape Palos, E. of Cartagena during Spanish Civil War. Capt Rhoderick McGrigor RN, Captain (D) Fourth Destroyer Flotilla, in *Kempenfelt*, with *Boreas* in company, found the ship, bows down and on fire; 'the men still alive were mustered, in perfect discipline, on the slanting quarterdeck by their few remaining officers'. McGrigor put his bows under the cruiser's stern between her two screws and rescued 470 men while being bombed by Republican aircraft.

After the Civil War the Spanish government wished to give him the Cross of Naval Merit and other decorations to his men. They could not accept but 'the action of Captain McGrigor and his destroyers will long be held in honoured memory by the Spanish Navy' – Capt Alan Hillgarth RN in *The Times*, 29 December 1959.

See 22 July 1936, 23 July 1938, 3 December 1959.

1941 'We must assume that the Battle of the Atlantic has begun' – Winston Churchill. Five years later it was defined by the Admiralty as 'the most protracted and bitterly fought campaign in which the British Empire and her allies have ever been engaged'.

1944 Swordfish X/816 (*Chaser*) sank U-973 off northern Norway. Convoy RA 57. Second *Chaser* success in two days.

1944 Destroyer *Icarus* and corvette *Kenilworth Castle*, with *Chaudiere*, *Chilliwack*, *Fennel*, *Gatineau* and *St Catherines* (all RCN), sank U-744 in N. Atlantic (52.01N, 22.37W). Convoy HX 280.

1945 Midget submarine XE 11 collided with boom defence vessel *Norina* in Loch Striven and sank. CO and two men lost. Last RN submarine loss of the Second World War.

See 19 January 1945.

1987 Cross-Channel ferry *Herald of Free Enterprise* capsized off Zeebrugge. RN clearance divers assisted in rescue operations and returned on 10 April to help recover bodies.

1993 Retirement of CPO W. Price, last of the 'promised men' who joined the RN in 1948 and in 1970 were guaranteed employment until age 65. He served for twenty-two years at the RN Detention Quarters, Portsmouth.

7 March

1665 *London* blown up by accident at The Nore.

1762 *Milford* captured the French letter of marque *Gloire* 400 miles S.W. by S. of Cape Finisterre.

1778 *Yarmouth* sank the American *Randolph* (blew up) 150 miles E. of Barbados.

1795 *Berwick*, under jury rig, taken by the French *Alceste*, *Vestale* and *Minerve* in San Fiorenzo Bay.

1797 *Alcmene* captured the French privateer *Surveillant* and her prize 30 miles S.W. of Mizen Head.

1804 Boats of *Inconstant* cut out a French vessel at Goree, which surrendered on the 9th.

1810 Vice-Admiral Cuthbert, Lord Collingwood, died on board his flagship, the *Ville de Paris* (110), one day out from Port Mahon, Minorca, having finally received permission to come home on sick leave; 'then I may yet meet the French once more'. He had assumed command of the Mediterranean Fleet after Vice-Admiral Lord Nelson was killed in action at Trafalgar. Collingwood had always hoped for a Trafalgar of his own.

Sir John Knox Laughton dismissed Collingwood in his DNB entry as 'an admirable second-in-command, but without the genius fitting him to rise to the first rank as commander-in-chief' – damning him with faint praise for not being Nelson. Collingwood deserves better than this; he was a dedicated officer who, like others, wore himself out in the service of his country. A better epitaph is a phrase from one of his own letters: 'The patient courage which waits for the opportunity it cannot make' – Lloyd, *Captain Marryat and the Old Navy*, p.126.

See 26 September 1748, 11 May 1810, 19 March 1949.

Vice-Admiral Lord Collingwood (1748–1810). (*NMRN 1984/486*)

1814 Provisions of uniform regulations of 19 September 1810 extended to the Governors of the RN Hospital and Asylum, and the Lieutenant-Governors of Greenwich Hospital and of the RN College, Portsmouth.

1864 *Zealous* launched at Pembroke Dockyard. The first armoured ship to cross the Equator and, in 1866, the first to enter the Pacific Ocean.

1885 John Cronyn Tovey, C-in-C Home Fleet in the Second World War, born.

See 12 January 1971.

1889 The Two Power Standard of British naval strength, 'that it should at least be equal to the naval strength of any two other countries', was announced by Lord George Hamilton, First Lord of the Admiralty. In the following four years seventy new ships, including ten battleships and forty-two cruisers, would be built under the Naval Defence Act 1889.

1899 Grog money of 4*d* per week sanctioned by Order in Council in lieu of savings.

1902 King Edward VII laid foundation stone of Britannia Royal Naval College, Dartmouth.

See 2 July 2005.

HMS *Echo* (2002), surveying ship. (*RN*)

1915 *Winifred* and *Kavirondo* drove the German *Mwanza* ashore at south end of Lake Victoria, thus establishing local naval supremacy.

1916 Destroyer *Coquette* mined off east coast of England.

1916 Submarine E 5 lost in North Sea.

1916 Second attempt to relieve Kut-al' Amara. River gunboats: *Dragonfly, Gadfly, Mantis, Mayfly, Sawfly.*

1916 E 24, the first British minelaying submarine, began operational submarine minelaying in mouth of River Elbe. She was mined and lost on second minelaying patrol.

1918 King George V designated the King's Squad and instituted King's Badge for Royal Marines under training.

1918 Start of naval operations against Murmansk and Archangel. Ships: *Glory, Cochrane, Attentive* and *Nairana.*

1941 Corvettes *Arbutus* and *Camellia* sank U-70 (after ramming by MV *Mijdrecht*) in N.W. Approaches. Convoy OB 293.

1941 U-47 (*Prien*) sunk on her tenth patrol, probably by destroyer *Wolverine*, escorting convoy OB 293 (60.47N, 19.13W).
See 17 March 1941.

1943 Fortress J/220 sank U-633 in N. Atlantic.

1945 Frigates *La Hulloise, Strathadam* and *Thetford Mines* (all RCN), sank U-1302 in Irish Sea.

1952 Clearance Diving branch (later MCD) formed. AFO 857/52.
See 25 February 1966.

1986 'As a result of a cost-cutting exercise CS(Rep S) is unable to continue printing Form S1828 (wine chit). While the future printing of this form is under discussion ships and establishments who have exhausted their stock of Form S1828 should comply with BR18 Annex 3J – 2 Para 9 and use locally produced alternatives' – DCI(RN) 65/86.

1990 Admiral of the Fleet Lord Fieldhouse introduced into the House of Lords. His supporters were Admiral of the Fleet Lord Lewin and Field Marshal Lord Bramall. He made his maiden speech on 12 June 1991.
See 1 January 1990, 17 February 1992.

2003 *Echo*, first of class of two new multi-role (hydrographic/oceanographic) surveying ships commissioned at Devonport. She and sister ship *Enterprise* built at Appledore. *Echo* launched 27 April 2002. *Enterprise* launched 2 March 2002. Similar manning scheme to *Scott*; ships' companies each seventy-two with forty-nine embarked at any time, permitting over 300 operational days a year.
See 13 October 1996.

8 March

1297 First recorded use of the word 'admiral' in English.

1689 Office of Lord High Admiral of England effectively removed from the Monarch (James II) by the appointment of Lords Commissioner for executing the office, a procedure first used on the death of the Duke of Buckingham in 1628 and reversed in 1964.

See 27 January 1626, 23 August 1628, 19, 26 and 31 March 1964.

1748 Capture of Port Louis (St Louis), Hispaniola (Haiti), by Rear-Admiral Sir Charles Knowles (*Canterbury*). Ships: *Canterbury, Cornwall, Elizabeth, Oxford, Plymouth, Strafford, Warwick, Worcester.* Sloops: *Merlin, Weazle.*

1796 Capture of Neira Island, Banda group of the Moluccas, by Rear-Admiral Peter Rainier (*Suffolk*). Ships and vessels: *Amboyna, Centurion, Orpheus, Resistance, Suffolk, Swift.* A captain's prize share was £15,000.

1801 Vice-Admiral Lord Keith, C-in-C Mediterranean Fleet, landed 16,000 men in boats of the Fleet in Aboukir Bay commanded by Capt Sir Sidney Smith. Smith disparagingly referred to by Nelson (Duke of Bronte in Sicily) as 'the Swedish Knight' because of his foreign title.

1806 Boats of *Egyptienne* cut out the French privateer *Alcide* at Muros, N.W. Spain.

1808 *St Fiorenzo* (38) captured the French *Piedmontaise* (40) S. of Cape Comorin, India. Battle Honour: *Piedmontoise* 1808.

1855 *Viper* destroyed a Russian Martello tower at Djimiteia near Anapa, Black Sea.

1856 The screw gunboats *Drake* and *Janus* launched from the same slip at Pembroke Dockyard. *Drake* went first but as the *Janus* went down the ways she carried away the staging holding the ships' sponsor, Mrs Mathias of Lamphey Court, her daughters and dockyard officials; all 'were hurled with frightful violence' onto the slipway. Mrs Mathias broke her collarbone and was brought out delirious.

'This lady being deeply sensible of the kindness which some of the men present evinced in promptly assisting her . . . expressed her gratitude to them by rewarding each of them with the sum of ten shillings' – *Haverfordwest and Milford Haven Telegraph*, 12 March and 19 March 1856.

1872 The wood screw frigate *Ariadne*, sailing to Gibraltar, hove to when a seaman fell overboard from the main topmast crosstrees 130 miles off the Portuguese coast (40.15N, 12.10W) In an unsuccessful rescue attempt both ship's cutters were swamped and two officers, Sub-Lts Jukes and Talbot, and eight men were drowned.

1916 John Frederick Thomas Jane, founder of *Jane's Fighting Ships*, died at 26 Clarence Parade, Southsea, aged 50.

See 6 August 1865.

1937 A four-power naval patrol established by UK, France, Germany and Italy to prevent outside intervention in the Spanish Civil War. It proved less than effective.

HMS *Cowslip* (1941), a Flower-class corvette. One of the numerous escort ships that fought in the Battle of the Atlantic. (*NMRN*)

HM Ships *Albion*, *Bulwark* and *Cornwall*, and RFA *Mounts Bay*, on exercises off Norway on 8 March 2008, sail past the location of the destroyer HMS *Hunter*, lost in the Norwegian Campaign on 10 April 1940. (*RN*)

1940 *Dunedin*, light cruiser, and destroyer HMCS *Assiniboine*, took the German MV *Hannover* in the Mona Passage, between San Domingo and Puerto Rico, West Indies. Prize rebuilt at Bootle then Blyth as the first escort carrier and commissioned as *Empire Audacity* 20 June 1941; renamed *Audacity* 31 July 1941.

See 2 March 1940, 17 December 1941.

1944 Destroyers *Tenacious* and *Troubridge* bombarded Pupnat and Blato, Korcula Island, off Yugoslavia.

2008 Service of commemoration held in Narvik fjord near Ofotfjorden over the hull of the destroyer *Hunter* lost on 10 April 1940 during the Battle of Narvik and found in 305 metres by HNoMS *Tyr* during NATO naval exercise 'Armatura Borealis'. Ceremonies held in *Albion* (flying Capt Warburton-Lee's last signal 'Continue engaging the enemy'), *Bulwark*, *Cornwall* and RFA *Mounts Bay*.

See 13 May 1937, 10 April 1940.

Battle of the Atlantic, 1941

U-47, commanded by Gunther Prien, who sank *Royal Oak*, sighted outward bound convoy OB 293 and called other U-boats to the area. After dark, the U-boats closed and attacked in the normal way. However, the escorts were gaining new skills and UA (Eckermann) was damaged by a depth charge attack and had to return to base. U-70 was forced to the surface by two corvettes and sunk. U-99 (Otto Kretschmer) was forced to withdraw with half his torpedoes remaining. Only two merchant ships were sunk. U-47 shadowed the convoy and was caught coming out of a rain squall by the veteran destroyer *Wolverine*, and after several attacks by depth charges and cunning shadowing, *Wolverine* sank her.

A few days later U-110 (Lemp, who sank the liner *Athenia* on the first day of the war) homed U-boats on to a homeward-bound convoy south of Iceland. U-99 came, together with U-100 (Schepke, who was rivalling Kretschmer for first place in tonnage sinkings). A strong escort of five destroyers and two corvettes kept the U-boats at long range on the first night and only one merchant ship was sunk. More U-boats attacked the next night, and five ships were sunk. But the convoy system worked, as it lured the U-boats to the escort, and the escort held on. U-100 was detected on the surface by the destroyer *Walker*, which brought the destroyer *Vanoc* in to ram and sink the submarine. U-99, out of torpedoes, was going round the stern of the convoy to return to base. Her CO left a junior officer on the bridge who sighted the *Vanoc* recovering survivors from U-100 and dived. But *Walker*, covering *Vanoc*, attacked and forced U-99 to the surface before sinking her. The first sinking of a U-boat directly attributable to radar – Howse. (See 17 March 1941).

Four U-boats had been sunk in one fortnight, with three of Germany's most successful captains.

9 March

1686 Pepys signed contract for purchase of rum in lieu of brandy for HM ships at Jamaica.

1741 Partial reduction of the batteries at Puerto Cartagena, Colombia, by Vice-Admiral Edward Vernon (*Princess Caroline*). Ships: *Boyne, Burford, Chichester, Defiance, Deptford, Dunkirk, Falmouth, Hampton Court, Jersey, Lichfield, Lion, Montagu, Norfolk, Orford, Prince Frederick, Princess Amelia, Princess Caroline, Princess Louisa, Ripon, Russell, Shrewsbury, Strafford, Suffolk, Tilbury, Torbay, Windsor, Worcester, Weymouth, York.* Frigates, etc.: *Alderney, Astraea, Cumberland, Eleanor, Etna, Experiment, Firebrand, Goodley, Phaeton, Pompey, Seahorse, Sheerness, Shoreham, Squirrel, Strombolo, Success, Terrible, Vesuvius, Virgin Queen, Vulcan, Wolf.*

1778 *Ariadne* and *Ceres* captured the American *Alfreda* 200 miles N. of Barbados.

HMS *Ashanti* (1959), Type 81 Tribal-class frigate. (*NMRN*)

1797 *St Fiorenzo* (38) and *Nymphe* (36) captured the French *Résistance* (44) and *Constance* (22) 10 miles S.W. of Brest. *Resistance* taken into the Service as *Fisgard*, as she had landed a French force there.
Battle Honour: *Résistance* 1797.
See 22 February 1797.

1860 *Niger*'s landing party in defence of New Plymouth. Start of second New Zealand war.

1914 Lieutenants of eight years' seniority became lieutenant-commanders.

1940 *Kelly* rammed *Gurkha* and made the signal: 'Have been hit by mine or torpedo: am uncertain which', to which the latter responded 'That was not mine but me'.

1941 Destroyers *Southdown* and *Worcester* repulsed an attack by German S-boats on convoy FS 429A in North Sea.

The amphibious assault ship HMS *Albion* launched by HRH The Princess Royal at Barrow-in-Furness, 2001. (*RN*)

1942 Albacore aircraft of 817 and 832 Sqn (*Victorious*) made an unsuccessful attack on the German battleship *Tirpitz* off Norway.

1944 *Asphodel*, corvette, sunk by U-575 in S.W. Approaches (45.24N, 18.09W). Convoys SL 150/MKS 41.

1959 *Ashanti*, first frigate designed and built with gas turbines incorporated in her main propulsion (COSAG), launched at Yarrow, Scotstoun, first of seven Type 81 Tribal-class frigates. Commissioned 23 November 1961.

The Tribals were the first and only two-funnel frigates (one required for gas turbine vent); the first warship with guided missiles (Seacat close-range air defence) and to incorporate a helicopter (Wasp) into ship's systems; the first frigates with cafeteria messing, full air conditioning and bunk sleeping accommodation; and the last destroyers or frigates with scuttles in hull.

See 5 June 1962, 20 July 1968, 26 April 1971.

1966 General Sir Lewis Halliday, the oldest surviving VC, died at Dorking aged 95. A RMLI officer, he won his VC defending the British Legation in Peking during the Boxer rebellion in 1900 and, although shot through the lung, he recovered and went on to become Adjutant General Royal Marines. Joint memorial service for Halliday and Lt Finch VC held at St Andrew's church, RMB Eastney 3 May 1966.

See 24 June 1900, 15 March 1966.

1976 Sir Michael Cary died, last Secretary of the Board of Admiralty and first RNVR officer to be named in letters patent constituting a Board.

1978 Duke of Edinburgh instituted award of 'the Prince's Badge' to celebrate the twenty-fifth anniversary of his appointment as Captain-General of the Royal Marines. To be awarded to the best all-rounder in each year's intake.

2001 The amphibious assault ship *Albion*, ninth of the name, was launched at BAE Systems, Barrow-in-Furness, by HRH The Princess Royal. The event was more successful than the launch of the battleship *Albion* on 21 June 1898.

See 16 May 1763, 21 June 1898, 6 May 1947, 19 June 2003.

10 MARCH

1650 Robert Blake, commanding an English fleet, arrived off the Tagus in pursuit of Prince Rupert. The Portuguese, friendly to the Stuart cause, would not allow the Republican forces to attack the Royalists in Lisbon. Blake blockaded the Tagus throughout the summer. Rupert made unsuccessful attempts to escape on 16 July and 7 September. At the end of October, while Blake was refitting his ships at Cadiz, Rupert escaped into the Mediterranean. Blake caught up with him in November off Cartagena and captured or drove ashore most of the Royalist ships.

See 20 April 1657, 7 August 1657.

1705 Leake's second relief of Gibraltar. Allied Fleet under Vice-Admiral Sir John Leake (*Hampton Court*) captured or destroyed the French squadron under Cdre Baron de Pointis (*Magnanime*) 9 miles S.W. of Marbella, southern Spain. Ships: *Antelope, Bedford, Canterbury, Expedition, Greenwich, Hampton Court, Larke, Leopard, Newcastle, Nottingham, Pembroke, Revenge, Swallow, Tiger, Warspite* and nine others, with four Dutch and eight Portuguese. Captured: *Ardent*,* *Arrogant*, *Marquis*.* Destroyed: *Magnanime*, *Lys*.

*Captured by Dutch ships.

Battle Honour: Marbella 1705.

1761 *Ripon* (60) fought the French *Achille* (64) 60 miles W. of Ushant.

1777 James Aitken, known as Jack the Painter, executed at the gate of Portsmouth Dockyard for setting fire to the Rope House on 7 December 1776. The 67ft-high gibbet was made from the mizzen mast of *Arethusa*. His body was afterwards hung in chains on Block House Point at the mouth of the harbour.

See 7 December 1776.

1796 *Phaeton* captured the French *Bonne-Citoyenne* 120 miles W.S.W. of Cape Finisterre.

The Naval Academy building, Portsmouth, in the 1880s. (*NMRN*)

1800 *Repulse* (fourth of the name) struck a rock off Ushant and, though refloated, became CTL at Quimper.

1810 *Owen Glendower* captured the French privateer *Camille* 10 miles N. of Cape Barfleur.

1823 Admiral George, Viscount Keith, C-in-C Channel Fleet, 1812–15, died.

1842 Repulse of the Chinese attacks on Ningpo and Chinhai. Ships: *Blonde, Columbine, Hyacinth, Modeste*. Steamers: *Sesostris* (IN), *Phlegethon, Queen* (Ben. Mar.). Regiments: 18th, 26th, 49th and 55th, Madras Artillery. Medal: China, 1841–2.

1915 *Ariel*, with *Attack* and *Acheron*, sank U-12 off Fife Ness, N. of the Forth.

1917 Submarine G 13 torpedoed and sank UC-43 off Shetland at 2,300yd (60.57N, 01.11W).

1917 VC: Lt Archibald Bisset Smith, RNR (cargo steamer *Otaki*). Posthumous. Gallantry in *Otaki*'s action with the German disguised raider *Möwe* (37.50N, 18.00W).

1941 A seven-hour air raid on Portsmouth by an estimated 300 German aircraft. Destroyer *Witherington* seriously damaged, 'about' twenty-five men killed in an air raid shelter in HMS *Vernon*, RNDQs partly demolished, RN Barracks church destroyed, the Old Naval Academy ruined (Navigation School housed there moved to Southwick House – AFO 4109/41), and a bomb in No. 1 Dock blew a hole 8ft by 15ft in the port bow of HMS *Victory*. Three bombs hit Admiralty House but did not explode. 'It's going to be a long job digging them out but we are not going to put off a cocktail party arranged for tomorrow . . . we will warn our guests . . .' – Admiral Sir William James, C-in-C Portsmouth.

See 12 August 1940, 24 August 1940, 5 December 1940, 23 December 1940, 10 January 1941, 17 April 1941, 3 April 1944.

1944 Destroyers *Blankney, Blencathra, Brecon* and *Exmoor* sank U-450 off Anzio. Operation Shingle.

1944 *Mull*, trawler, sank U-343 N. of Bizerta.

1944 *Forester* and *Owen Sound, St Laurent* and *Swansea* (RCN) sank U-845 in N. Atlantic (48.20N, 20.33W). Convoy SC 154.

1944 Sunderland U/422 (RCAF) sank U-625 in Atlantic (52.35N, 20-19W).

1956 World air speed record of 1,132 mph (1,823 kph) set by Lt-Cdr Peter Twiss, OBE, DSC and bar, RNVR, flying from Boscombe Down in a Fairey Delta 2 between Chichester and RNAS Ford, Sussex. The first person to fly at over 1,000 mph.

See 25 September 1953.

2004 The last RN court martial at which swords were worn. A sailor from *Albion* pleaded guilty at Portsmouth to two counts of being AWOL and one of behaving with contempt to a superior officer. Dismissed Her Majesty's Service, deprived of one GCB and to suffer consequential penalties.

See 15 March 2004.

11 MARCH

1708 The Cruisers and Convoys Acts allocated prize money to captors at the Crown's expense; a great incentive to captains and crews.

Prize Money (Cruisers and Convoys) Acts, 1708

The interdiction of enemy trade in the eighteenth and nineteenth centuries was an essential part of maritime war. The Prize Money Acts ensured that much of the value of any enemy merchant vessels and their cargoes captured was paid to the ships' companies of the captor ship. This prize money was a major inducement to service in the Royal Navy, at a time when basic pay was very low compared with the Merchant Navy. However, prize money became so sought after that particularly in small ships the main business of attacking and sinking enemy warships sometimes took second place.

'Head Money' was therefore introduced, which amounted initially to £10 per gun in every enemy ship sunk. This rate became too low (£740 for a 74-gun ship). The amount was therefore increased to £5 per head of the enemy crew (£3,000 for a 74-gun ship). Both prize money and head money were shared according to laid-down proportions among the whole ship's company.

1727 *Royal Oak* captured the Spanish *N.S. del Rosario* 60 miles N.W. of Cape Spartel, Morocco. *Royal Oak* was launched at Deptford in 1674, rebuilt at Chatham in 1690, at Woolwich in 1713 and – eventually – at Plymouth in 1741, where she was broken up in 1764. A varied ninety years.

1756 *Warwick* (60) taken by the French *Atalante* (34) and *Prudente* (74) off Martinique, 'so crank that she could not use her lower deck guns' – Capt Shuldam.

1757 James Saumarez, C-in-C in the Baltic, 1808–13, born.

1787 Capt Horatio Nelson of *Boreas* (28) and Mrs Frances Nisbet married at Montpelier House, Nevis. Prince William, future King William IV, was best man.

1804 'The great thing in all Military Service is health; and you will agree with me, that it is easier for an Officer to keep men healthy, than for a Physician to cure them' – Nelson from HMS *Victory* to Dr Moseley, Chelsea Hospital.

1810 *Echo* captured the French privateer *Capricieux* 5 miles N.W. of Dieppe.

1812 *Phipps* captured the French privateer *Cerf* in Dover Strait.

1815 *Acasta*, *Leander* and *Newcastle* recaptured *Levant* at Porto da Praia, Cape Verde Islands. Escape of the American *Constitution* and her other prize, *Cyane*.

1845 *Hazard* and a detachment of the 96th Regiment at the defence of Port Russell, New Zealand, which was abandoned to Heke and the Maoris. Medal: New Zealand, 1845–7.

1854 First RN steam fleet sailed for operations. Fifteen ships left Spithead for the Baltic under Admiral Napier.

1873 Iron screw frigate *Raleigh* launched at Chatham. She served three successive commissions as flagship on the Cape of Good Hope and West African Station. When Rear-Admiral Sir Frederick Bedford hauled down his flag in 1895 *Raleigh* was the last square-rigged flagship in RN history.

1900 *Terrible*'s Naval Brigade left Natal for China.

1915 AMC *Bayano* sunk by U-27 off Corsewall Point, Stranraer.

1917 British forces captured Baghdad, Mesopotamia. River gunboats: *Butterfly*, *Firefly*, *Gadfly*, *Mantis*, *Moth*, *Snakefly*, *Tarantula*.
Battle Honour: Mesopotamia 1915–17.

1918 *Retriever* with *Sturgeon* and *Thrush* sank UB-54 in North Sea (53.07N, 02.43E).

1927 AFO 626/27 recognised 'Heart of Oak' and 'A Life on the Ocean Wave' as the marches of the RN and RM, 'Nancy Lee' for the advance in review order and 'Iolanthe' as a Flag Officer's salute. 'Heart of Oak' first performed in David Garrick's pantomine *Harlequin's Invasion* in 1759, the 'Glorious Year' of the march.

'Equity or a Sailor's Prayer before Battle.' (*NMRN 1984/485*)

1936 Admiral of the Fleet Earl Beatty, Viscount Borodale of Wexford and Baron Beatty of the North Sea, died.
See 16 March 1936.

1942 Light cruiser *Naiad* sunk by U-565 N. of Mersa Matruh (32.00N, 26.19E).

1943 Convoy HX 228 in N.W. Atlantic attacked by U-boat pack. *Harvester* rammed, and later with *Aconit* (Free French), sank U-444 (51.14N, 29.18W). *Harvester* sunk by U-432 (51.23N, 28.30W), where *Aconit* sank U-432.

1944 Catalina D/279 and P/262 (SAAF) sank the German U-It 22 (ex-Italian S/M *Alpino Bagnolini*) off Cape of Good Hope (41.28S, 17.40E). This episode is associated with the sinking of the U-boat supply tanker *Brake* next day. Thirty-two Italian submarines were deployed from the Mediterranean into the Atlantic; sixteen did not return.

1957 C-in-C South Atlantic, Vice-Admiral Sir Geoffrey Robson, left Admiralty House, Simons Town, and moved to the new headquarters at Youngsfield, near Wynberg. The house had been the residence of the British naval commander for 143 years.
See 2 April 1957.

1961 End of the First Cod War when HMG accepted the Icelandic 12-mile limit.
See 31 August 1958.

1966 Naval Radiological Protection Service to be formed 'in view of the wide and increasing use of radioactive materials and other sources of ionising radiation within the Naval Service.' – DCI(RN) 329/66.

1982 Secretary of State for Defence, Mr John Nott, announced HMG's decision to buy Trident II D5, instead of Trident I C4 missiles.
See 13 July 1980.

2002 The traditional squadron organisation in the Fleet replaced by the Fleet Waterfront Organisations (FWOs) at Portsmouth, Plymouth and Faslane. The Portsmouth and Devonport flotillas headed by commodores – COMPORFLOT and COMDEVFLOT – and at Faslane by a captain – CAPFASFLOT. The seven submarine, destroyer and frigate squadrons disbanded at the end of March. DCI(RN) 31/02.
See 10 January 1986.

2005 The First Sea Lord, Admiral Sir Alan West, laid the keel of *Artful*, the third of the Astute-class SSNs, Yard No. 1124, at BAE Systems, Barrow.
See 31 January 2001, 22 October 2003, 24 March 2009.

2011 Capt Jeremy Kyd RN, and 150 remaining ship's company, paid off *Ark Royal* at Portsmouth.
See 1 November 1985.

2011 Jetstream aircraft of 750 NAS, Lt-Cdr Nick Armstrong RN, made final flight from RNAS Culdrose.

12 March

1672 Capt Sir Robert Holmes (*St Michael*) fought the Dutch Smyrna fleet (fifty convoy and six escort) off the Isle of Wight. Ships: *Cambridge, Diamond,* Fairfax, Gloucester,* Resolution, St Michael, Success,* York*.
*Joined on the 14th.

1704 Rear-Admiral Thomas Dilkes (*Kent*) captured the Spanish *Porta Coeli, Santa Teresa* and the armed merchantman *San Nicolas* 20 miles W. by S. of Cape Spartel, Morocco. Ships: *Antelope, Bedford, Kent, Panther, Suffolk*.

1821 Capt William Broughton RN, explorer of the Pacific and discoverer of Chatham Island, died in Florence and was buried in the English cemetery in Livorno.
See 29 November 1971, 17 May 1797.

1909 Australia and New Zealand offered to provide a battlecruiser each to the RN.

1917 US government announced the arming of all merchant vessels in the war zone.

1917 Submarine E 49 sunk off Shetland by a mine laid by U-76 in company with UC-43.

1917 *Privet* (Q 19) sank U-85 24 miles S. by E. of Start Point. *Privet* sank next day in Plymouth Sound. Salvaged.

1943 Submarine *Turbulent* presumed mined off Corsica.
See 25 May 1943.

Royal Naval ratings working on a depth-charge thrower. (*NMRN*)

Able Seaman Kate Nesbitt with her Military Cross at Buckingham Palace on 27 November 2009. (*RN*)

2009 The first woman in RN to win the MC. Able Seaman Kate Louise Nesbitt (21), a medical assistant attached to 3 Cdo Brigade, for 'exemplary gallantry' during a Taliban ambush in Helmand Province, Afghanistan. Kate, all 5ft tall, ran under enemy fire and saved the life of L/Cpl John List of 1 RIFLES who had been hit in the neck. Her MC was awarded by HRH Prince Charles at Buckingham Palace on 27 November 2009. Operation Herrick.

Citation: 'Nesbitt's actions throughout a series of offensive operations were exemplary; under fire and under pressure her commitment and courage were inspirational and made the difference between life and death. She performed in the highest traditions of her service.'

1943 Destroyer *Lightning* sunk by German E-Boat S-55 off Bizerta (37.53N, 09.50E). *Legion* rescued 170 men.

1944 The German U-boat replenishment tanker *Charlotte Schliemann* scuttled herself off Mauritius on 12 February 1944 after interception by destroyer *Relentless*, an encounter based on Ultra intelligence. The movements of a replacement tanker, *Brake*, were also known through Ultra but concerns about imperilling security of Ultra by rousing German suspicions delayed an attack for several days. *Brake* finally sunk by destroyer *Roebuck* on 12 March.

See 12 February 1944.

1945 Frigates *Loch Ruthven* and *Wild Goose* sank U-683 in S.W. Approaches.

See 24 November 1957.

Anti-submarine Weapons

The depth charge, a canister of explosive designed to explode at a variable depth and destroy a submarine, was an effective weapon against all but the fastest submarines in both world wars.

Its great disadvantage during the Second World War lay in the fact that a ship had to steam over a submarine in order to drop it usefully, and the place where Asdics are least effective is dead astern, where propeller noise and water disturbance make sound-wave detection impossible.

Two weapons were invented to solve the problem – both ahead-firers. The Hedgehog fired a large number of small bombs ahead of the ship as indicated by Asdic echoes. They exploded only on contact and so had limited deterrent power. The Squid fired three large depth bombs ahead of the ship, set at a depth predicted by the Asdic and these proved highly effective.

13 March

1672 Continuation of Holmes' action. Capture of the Dutch *Klein Hollandia* and five merchantmen. All this happened before war had been declared, and may have been intended to provoke it.
See 12 March 1672.

1708 *Leopard* recaptured the French *Salisbury* (ex-RN) in the Firth of Forth, on an abortive Jacobite expedition to Scotland.
See 10 April 1703.

1761 *Vengeance* captured the French *Entreprenant* 200 miles S. of Ushant.

1762 RNH Stonehouse, Plymouth, opened.
See 31 March 1995.

1780 *Courageux* captured the French privateer *Monsieur* 140 miles S.W. by S. of the Scilly Isles.

1793 *Scourge* took the *Sans Culotte* off the Scilly Isles. The first engagement with the French at sea in the original Great War.

1795 *Lively* captured the French *Tourterelle* 40 miles N. of Ushant.

1795 Action off Genoa between Vice-Admiral William Hotham and a French fleet under Rear-Admiral Pierre Martin. *Agamemnon* and *Inconstant* fought the French *Ça-Ira*.
See 14 March 1795.

1801 'I hate your pen and ink men; a fleet of British ships of war are the best negotiators in Europe' – Nelson to Lady Hamilton, on his way to Copenhagen.

1804 *Fort Diamond*, with a party from *Emerald*, captured the French privateer *Mosambique* in Ceron Cove, Martinique.

1806 *London* (98) captured the French *Marengo* (74) and *Amazon* (38) captured *Belle-Poule* (40) 640 miles W. by S. of the Canary Islands.
Battle Honour: *Marengo* 1806.

1808 *Emerald* destroyed the French *Apropos* in Ria de Vivero, north coast of Spain.

1811 Capt William Hoste's frigate action, close off the north point of Lissa (Vis) in the Adriatic. Capture of the Franco-Venetian *Bellona* and *Corona* and destruction of *Favorite*. Ships: *Active, Amphion, Cerberus, Volage*.
Battle Honour: Lissa 1811.
Hoste made only one signal beyond the minimum executive orders – 'Remember Nelson.'
See 5 January 1814.

1823 Admiral of the Fleet the Earl of St Vincent died. 'We expect too much of men; we do not make sufficient allowances, and perhaps we are too apt to over rate the services we render them' – Brenton, *Life*, vol.2, p.356.
See 22 February 1806.

1841 Capture of the Macao Passage fort, Canton River. Ships: *Modeste, Starling*. Steamer (Bengal Marine): *Madagascar*. Boats of *Alligator, Blonde, Calliope, Conway, Cruizer, Herald, Hyacinth, Nimrod, Pylades*.

1841 *Nemesis* (Bengal Marine), with boats of *Atalanta* (Indian Navy) and *Samarang*, destroyed Mo To fort and several other forts and junks during a three-day passage up the Broadway estuary and through various inland waterways to the Canton River.

1855 Bombardment of Soujak Kale, Novorossisk Bay, Black Sea. Ships: *Highflyer, Leopard, Swallow, Viper*, and the French *Fulton*. Crimean Medal.

1858 VC: AB Edward Robinson (*Shannon*) at the siege of Lucknow. Gravely injured when exposing himself to heavy fire at 50yd to put out a fire.

1859 *Clown, Janus* and boats of *Niger* destroyed a village, twenty pirate junks, eleven fast boats and a 36-gun stockade in the neighbourhood of the Broadway estuary. Operations lasted for three days.

1869 *Druid*, wood screw corvette, the 'last ship ever to leave the slips from the very ancient and historic dockyard of Deptford' – Ballard.

Morning prayers in the battleship HMS *Magnificent*, 1895. (*NMRN*)

1884 Battle of Tamaai, Sudan. Naval Brigade from *Briton*, *Carysfort*, *Dryad*, *Euryalus*, *Hecla* and *Sphinx*. Egyptian Medal: clasp 'Tamaai'.

1908 Submarine C 17 launched at Chatham. Vickers had built her forty-five predecessors. The C class were the last petrol-driven boats. Thirty-eight were built, of which eleven were lost.

1917 *Warner* (Q 27) sunk by U-61 in S.W. Approaches.

1940 AMC *Maloja*, ex-P&O liner, intercepted the German SS *La Coruña*, which was scuttled in the Iceland–Faroes Channel.

1941 Sloop *Scarborough* intercepted *Star XIX* and *Star XXIV*, captured Norwegian whale catchers, off Cape Finisterre, which were scuttled.

1943 *Prescott*, corvette, (RCN) sank U-163 with nine depth charges W. of Cape Finisterre, on her third patrol (45.05N, 15.00W).

1944 Frigate *Prince Rupert* (RCN), USS *Haverfield* and USS *Hobson* and Allied aircraft sank U-575 in Atlantic.

1945 Amphibious assault on Letpan (E. of Ramree Island, Burma). Operation Turret. Covering force: *Eskimo* and *Roebuck* with *Cauvery* and *Jumna* (both RIN).

1971 Admiral Sir Peter Hill-Norton promoted admiral of the fleet at the end of his appointment as First Sea Lord.

See 16 May 2004.

14 March

1757 Admiral Byng executed on board *Monarch* after being court-martialled for dereliction of duty. 'At 12 Mr Byng was shot dead by six marines and put into his coffin' – Master's Log, HMS *Monarch*.

'On Monday, March 14th, 1757, all the men-of-war at Spithead were ordered to send their boats with the captains and all the officers of each ship, accompanied with a party of marines under arms, to attend the execution of Mr. Byng. Accordingly they rowed from Spithead, and made the harbour a little after 11 o'clock, with the utmost difficulty and danger, it blowing prodigiously hard at N.W. by N., and the tide of ebb against them. It was still more difficult to get up so high as the *Monarch* lay, on board which ship the admiral suffered. Notwithstanding it blew so hard and the sea ran very high, there was a prodigious number of other boats round the ship, on the outside of the ship's boats, which last kept all others off. Not a soul was suffered to be aboard the *Monarch*, except those belonging to the ship. Mr. Byng, accompanied by a clergyman who attended him during his confinement, and two gentlemen of his relations, about 12 came on the quarterdeck, when he threw his hat on the deck, kneeled on a cushion, tied a handkerchief over his eyes, and dropping another which he held in his hand as a signal, a volley from six marines was fired, five of whose bullets went through him, and he was no more. He died with great resolution and composure, not showing the least sign of timidity in the awful moment.'

'It was a sad sight, and a shaming example of what fear of political disfavour could do to the unity of a fleet.' – David Erskine.

1779 *Rattlesnake* captured the French privateer *Frelon de Dunkerque* 12 miles N.W. of Le Havre.

1795 Vice-Admiral William Hotham (*Britannia*) fought an inconclusive action with a French fleet of fifteen sail under Rear-Admiral Pierre Martin (*Sans Culotte*) 20 miles S.W. of Genoa. Capture of the French *Ça-Ira* and *Censeur*.

Ships: *Agamemnon*, *Bedford*, *Britannia*, *Captain*, *Courageux*, *Diadem*, *Egmont*, *Fortitude*, *Illustrious*, *Neapolitan*, *Princess Royal*, *St George*, *Tancredi*, *Terrible*, *Windsor Castle*. Frigates, etc.: *Fox*, *Inconstant*, *Lowestoffe*, *Meleager*, *Minerva*, *Moselle*, *Palade*, *Poulette*, *Romulus*, *Tarleton*. Regiments: 11th, 25th, 30th, 50th, 69th. On such an anniversary, it may be wondered why Hotham did not engage the enemy more closely.
Battle Honour: Genoa 1795.

HMS *Sultan* sunk off Malta in 1889. See p.640. (*NMRN*)

1795 *Illustrious* (74), third rate, first of name, wrecked at Avenza, off Livorno, after Hotham's action.

1808 *Childers* fought the Danish *Lougen* off Lindesness, Norway.

1842 Admiralty Compass Department set up.

1889 The battleship *Sultan* grounded on an uncharted rock in the South Comino Channel off Malta. Attempts by *Temeraire* to tow her off failed and during a gale on 14 March she slipped off and sank. An Italian firm raised her and, after repairs in Malta Dockyard, the ship returned to Portsmouth in December under her own steam. In a major and unjustified refit between 1893 and 1896, *Sultan* was stripped of her sailing rig and re-engined, rejoining the Fleet in a transformed aspect. She served as an artificers' training ship as *Fisgard IV* from 1906 to 1931, reverted to *Sultan* as a mechanical repair ship in the 1930s and was depot ship for Portsmouth-based minesweepers in the Second World War.

1915 *Kent*, *Glasgow* and *Orama* found the German light cruiser *Dresden*, the last survivor of the German East Asiatic squadron, at Juan Fernandez. She was scuttled after a token resistance.

1921 New Zealand Naval Board instituted by Order in Council. RNZN founded 1 October 1941.

See 20 June 1921, 1 October 1941.

1940 A 250lb bomb being returned to the magazines of the fleet carrier *Eagle* in the Indian Ocean exploded, killing thirteen men, and the flash destroyed several Swordfish in the hangar. Many injured men in the bomb room were rescued by Sub-Lt Alexander (Sandy) Hodge, RNVR, who was awarded the EGM, immediately translated into the George Cross (*Gazette*, 2 August 1940). Capt Hodge was CO Forth Division RNVR 1953–7 and died 4 January 1997, aged 80.

1942 Submarine P 34, later *Ultimatum*, sank the Italian S/M *Ammiraglio Millo* in Ionian Sea.

1943 *Moravia* sunk by mine off Orfordness.

1943 Submarine *Thunderbolt* (ex-*Thetis*) sunk by the Italian corvette *Cicogna* off Cape St Vito.

See 1 June 1939, 15 December 1940.

1943 U-1021 mined and sunk (50.40N, 05.07W).

1943 Corvette *Hadleigh Castle* fitted with first Squid A/S weapon.

See 12 March, Anti-submarine Weapons.

1944 MTB 353 sank German M-10 3 miles off Dunkirk.

1945 U-714 damaged by frigate *Natal* (SANF) and sunk with all hands by *Wivern* off the Farnes.

See 1 May 2008.

1956 Archbishop Makarios III, Primate of the Greek Orthodox Church of Cyprus, arrived at Mahe in the Seychelles from Mombasa in the frigate *Loch Fada*, having been exiled by the British for suspected involvement in the guerrilla organisation Eoka. In 1960 Makarios became the first President of the new Republic of Cyprus.

See 25 October 1931, 21 August 1967.

1958 Final parade at *Ceres*, RN Supply School at Wetherby, before paying off on 31 March and moving to Chatham.

See 22 March 1950, 14 April 1958.

1959 A book of remembrance containing the names of 329 WRNS personnel who died while serving since 1917 was dedicated in the Chapel of the RN College, Greenwich, by the Venerable Darrell Bunt, Chaplain of the Fleet.

1997 Destroyer *Birmingham* (later relieved by destroyer *Exeter*) stood by off Durres, Albania, to evacuate British nationals during internal unrest. Operation Helvin (ended 8 April).

2005 Lt-Col Richard van der Horst RM, aged 38, CO of the SBS, died after a diving accident with a submersible swimmer delivery vehicle during an amphibious exercise in Norway.

15 MARCH

1360 Winchelsea burned by the French. Cinque Port ships captured thirteen enemy ships and killed 400 men. The churchyard had to be enlarged to accommodate them and is still called 'Deadmen's Lane'.

1793 Three gunboats, manned from *Syren*, at the defence of Willemstadt, Netherlands.

1798 *Kingfisher* captured the French privateer *Lynx* 120 miles N.W. by W. of Oporto.

1842 Defeat of the Chinese on the heights of Segaon, near Mingpo. Steamers: *Sesostris* (IN), *Nemesis*, *Phlegethon*, *Queen* (Bengal Marine). Boats of: *Blonde*, *Cornwallis*. Naval Brigade from: *Blonde*, *Columbine*, *Cornwallis*, *Hyacinth*, *Modeste*. Regiments: 18th, 26th and 49th, Madras Artillery, Madras Sappers and Miners, 36th Madras Native Infantry. Medal: China, 1841–2.

1865 Armoured corvette *Pallas* launched at Woolwich Dockyard. First ship designed primarily as a ram and the first warship to have compound engines.

1915 Light cruiser *Blonde* attacked by German aircraft. First merchant ship to be so attacked.

1917 Destroyer *Foyle* sunk by mine in Straits of Dover.

1918 Destroyers *Michael* and *Moresby* sank U-110 in N.W. Approaches (55.49N, 08.06W).

1918 *Furious* recommissioned. First carrier with aircraft lifts.

1918 Submarine D3 accidentally sunk by French airship in English Channel.

1929 Hulk of the ironclad *Warrior* (launched in 1860) arrived at Pembroke Dock in tow of naval tugs *St Clears* and *St Mellons* for employment as a berth for RFA tankers. She had been surplus to requirements since *Vernon* moved ashore in 1923. Admiralty Memorandum of 2 April 1925 had offered the hulk for sale but there were no takers.

1942 Destroyer *Vortigern* sunk by the German S-104 off Cromer (55.06N, 01.22E). Convoy FS 749.

1942 Light cruisers *Dido* and *Euryalus*, with six destroyers, bombarded Rhodes. Operation M.F.8.

1942 X 3, first RN midget submarine, launched in Hamble River.

1944 Sloops *Starling* and *Wild Goose*, and Swordfish A/825 (*Vindex*), sank U-653 in Atlantic.

1946 Admiral Sir Harold Burrough, British Naval C-in-C Germany, handed over to Vice-Admiral

HMS *Pallas* (1865), wooden central battery ironclad corvette. (*NMRN*)

X-Craft, midget submarine XE7 in 1946. (*NMRN W&L 836A1*)

Sir Harold 'Hooky' Walker (he had lost a hand in the Zeebrugge raid in 1918) who was redesignated Vice-Admiral Commanding British Naval Forces Germany.
See 25 December 1916, 13 July 1945.

1954 The RN's first frontline A/S warfare helicopter squadron. 845 NAS, which had disbanded in 1945 after Far East service, reformed at Gosport with Whirlwind HAS 22 aircraft from 706 NAS. Disbanded at Lee-on-Solent October 1958.
See 1 February 1943, 4 January 2001.

1957 RN Barracks and RNAS Lee-on-Solent amalgamated as a single establishment under a Captain RN, to be known as HMS *Daedalus*. The post of Commodore RNB Lee-on-Solent lapsed.
See 29 March 1996.

1963 'The operation of helicopters from small ships is a major undertaking embracing a difficult art. It throws great responsibility upon young and relatively inexperienced aviators. The approach to this new problem must be made with great care, and no necessary time spared to ensure success in a field almost wholly unexplored.' – AFO 460/63.

1966 Lt Norman Augustus Finch, the last surviving RM holder of the VC, died aged 74. Sgt Finch RMA won his award whilst second-in-command of the Lewis guns in the foretop of the cruiser *Vindictive* in the Zeebrugge raid on 23 April 1918. All in the top were killed except Finch who, though severely wounded, kept his gun in action. Two VCs were allocated to the Royal Marines and Finch was selected by ballot. Joint memorial service for Finch and General Halliday VC held at St Andrew's church, RMB Eastney 3 May 1966.
See 9 March 1966.

1968 *Revenge*, the fourth Royal Navy Polaris submarine, launched at Cammell Laird, Birkenhead, by Lady Law, wife of Vice-Admiral Sir Horace Law, Controller of the Navy. The religious service was conducted by the Revd M.B. Dewey, Dean of Pembroke College, Cambridge, and a former chaplain of the battleship *Revenge*. His prayers, which included both the men and the 'the ship in which they sail', were more embracing than those offered at the launch of *Renown* the previous year.
See 25 February 1967, 25 May 1992.

1980 Fire in A1 boiler room in the commando carrier *Bulwark* during a visit to Philadelphia. Damage considered too costly to repair.
See 23 February 1979, 9 November 1980, 27 March 1981.

1992 Lt-Cdr Peter Kemp RN, submariner, wartime naval intelligence officer in the OIC and, from 1951–68, Admiralty librarian and head of the Naval Historical Branch (succeeding David Bonner Smith), died aged 88. A distinguished naval historian and mentor of many aspiring maritime historians who included the American Arthur Marder, Kemp had retired from the Service in 1928 after losing a leg in a gallant attempt to prevent a fatal accident to a liberty boat.

2004 The first naval court martial to be held without swords being worn convened at *Drake*, Devonport. 'My Lords, the Royal Navy has determined . . . that there is no longer a requirement for the escort accompanying a defendant in a naval court martial to carry a drawn sword, or for members of the court martial to wear sheathed swords' – Lord Bach, Parliamentary Under-Secretary of State, MOD, in House of Lords 22 March 2004.
See 10 March 2004.

16 March

1712 *Dragon* (38), Capt George Martin, sailing from Guernsey to England, wrecked on the Casquet Rocks off Alderney.

1757 *Greenwich* taken by the French *Brune*, *Diadème* and *Eveille* 30 miles off Cape Cabron, San Domingo. She fought in Forrest's action on 21 October but sank, returning to France.

1781 Vice-Admiral Arbuthnot (*Royal Oak*) beat the French squadron under Capt Sochet des Touches (*Duc-de-Bourgogne*) 40 miles N.E. by E. of Cape Henry, Virginia, thus regaining control of Chesapeake Bay. Ships: *Adamant*, *America*, *Bedford*, *Europe*, *London*, *Prudent*, *Robust*, *Royal Oak*. Frigates: *Guadeloupe*, *Iris*, *Pearl*.
Battle Honour: Chesapeake 1781.

1782 *Success* and *Vernon* captured the Spanish *Santa Catalina* 50 miles W.S.W. of Cape Spartel.

1801 *Invincible* (74), second of the name and second to be wrecked, lost off Happisburgh on the Norfolk Coast.
See 19 February 1758.

1858 *Shannon*'s Naval Brigade at the capture of Lucknow by the forces under General Sir Colin Campbell. Naval Brigade manned all the breaching artillery on one side of the Gumti River. Indian Mutiny Medal: clasp 'Lucknow'.
Battle Honour: Lucknow 1857–8.

1889 The screw corvette *Calliope*, Capt H.C. Kane RN, of the Australian Station, sent to Samoa where a tense international situation involved German and United States warships, escaped from Apia in Samoa by 'skilful seamanship' in a hurricane which sank or stranded all six German and United States warships present.
See 29 August 1914.

'Captain Kane showed, in their Lordships' opinion, both nerve and decision in determining to steam to sea in the teeth of a hurricane which destroyed all the vessels which remained at the anchorage he left; and, in conveying to him the thanks of the Admiralty, my Lords' desire to express their thorough approval of his skilful seamanship, and of the measures taken by him throughout to secure the safety of his ship . . . The conduct of all concerned was highly commendable, and my Lords are of opinion that great credit is due to the officer commanding for the example he set and the confidence he instilled into those under his orders.'

These included Horace Hood who was killed in the battlecruiser *Invincible* at Jutland. Admiral Sir Henry Kane died in 1917. His gallant ship in 1907 became the first drill-ship of Tyne Division RNVR and wore the flag of Flag Officer, Tyne, in the Second World War. She was sold in October 1951 and was broken up at Blyth.

1905 Foundation stone of St Nicholas' church, Devonport, laid by Admiral of the Fleet Sir Edward Seymour, in his last public duty as C-in-C Plymouth. An 'oaken chest' containing *The Times* and the Plymouth newspapers was placed beneath the foundation stone.
See 18 February 1907.

RN Ratings wearing Sennet hats, worn up to 1921. (*NMRN*)

The launch of HMS *Antelope*, 16 March 1972. (*Author*)

1915 Royal Assent given to amend the Naval Discipline Act 1866 to permit naval courts martial to be held on shore (Section 59).
See 5 August 1915

1917 The German raider *Leopard*, formerly the British steamer *Yarrowdale*, attempting to break out into the Atlantic, intercepted 240 miles N. of the Shetlands by the armoured cruiser *Achilles*, Capt F.M. Leake RN, and the armed boarding steamer *Dundee*, Cdr S.M. Day RNR.
Battle Honour: *Leopard* 1917.

While a boarding party from the *Dundee* led by Lt F.H. Lawson RNR was inspecting the ship, which carried the name *Rena* and Norwegian colours, Cdr Day became convinced of her false identity and opened fire, raking the *Leopard* with 4-in gunfire, to which the enemy replied with torpedoes; additional gunfire from *Achilles* set the *Leopard* ablaze. The Germans fought their ship with great courage. Lt Lawson and his men went down with the entire German crew.

1917 Trawler *Cambria* achieved first operational cutting of a mine's mooring cable with the paravane.

1921 Sennet hats, the Royal Navy wide-brimmed sailors' straw hats worn in summer in home waters by petty officers, men and boys dressed as seamen, abolished. Replaced in home waters by white uniform cap and on foreign stations by sun helmets; ratings dressed as seamen to wear helmets with ships' cap ribbons around them; all other ratings negative cap ribbons or pugarees. 'Stocks on board H.M. ships on the South America Station . . . should be sold locally on the best terms available.' – AFO 664/21.

1936 Admiral of the Fleet Earl Beatty, C-in-C Grand Fleet 1916–19 and First Sea Lord 1919–27, buried in St Paul's Cathedral. The last interment in the cathedral.

1940 Old battleship *Iron Duke* and heavy cruiser *Norfolk* damaged in German air raid on Scapa Flow.

1941 Combined operation to recapture Berbera, British Somaliland, 140 miles S. of Aden, from Italians. Bombardment followed by landing of mainly Punjabi troops from cruisers *Glasgow* and *Caledon*, destroyers *Kandahar* and *Kingston*, and *Chakadina*, *Natravali*, *Chantala* and *Patravali* (RIN). DSO: Capt Harold Hickling, *Glasgow*, Force Commander.
See 27 June 1794.

'"Everybody aft, Sir". The Commander saluted and I climbed on top of the after capstan . . . "As you know His Majesty the King has been pleased to decorate me with the Distinguished Service Order. Let me make this quite clear, it was not on me really that this honour was bestowed, but on our ship and every officer and man who sails in her. You all have a share in it. You can write home to your wives and sweethearts and tell them that you have earned . . ." I stopped and turned to Boutwood: "Paymaster Commander, how many men were victualled today?"

"Seven hundred and thirty one, Sir."

". . . that you have won one seven-hundred-and thirty-oneth part of a DSO."

The honour was in due course Gazetted: "For skill and enterprise", the citation ran, "in the re-capture of" – here the printer's mind must have wandered to his girl friend – Barbara. All my friends wrote to me asking what my girl friend was like.' – Vice-Admiral Harold Hickling, *Sailor at Sea* (London, 1965).

1944 Frigate *Affleck*, destroyer *Vanoc* and three US Catalina aircraft sank U-392 in Straits of Gibraltar.

2002 Deployment of 42 Cdo RM to Northern Ireland. Fortieth deployment to Northern Ireland since 1969.

17 MARCH

1794 Boats of Vice-Admiral Sir John Jervis's fleet captured the French *Bienvenue* in Fort Royal harbour, Martinique, but had to abandon her briefly.
Battle Honour: Martinique 1794.
See 20 March 1794.

Ships: *Asia, Assurance, Avenger, Beaulieu,* Blonde, Boyne, Dromedary, Experiment, Irresistible, Nautilus, Quebec, Rattlesnake, Roebuck,* Rose, Santa Margarita, Seaflower,* Spiteful, Tormentor, Ulysses,* Vengeance, Venom, Vesuvius, Winchelsea, Woolwich, Zebra.*
*Awarded the medal, though not present on this day.

1796 Capt Sir Sidney Smith, 'the Swedish Knight' in *Diamond*, with *Aristocrat* and *Liberty*, destroyed the French *Etourdie* and seven other vessels in Port Erqui, Brittany, also spiking the guns of its fort and coming off with the French colours.

1800 *Queen Charlotte* (100) blew up at Leghorn. Lord Keith's flagship; 673 lost out of 829.
See 15 February 1807.

1800 Mutineers handed over *Danae* (20) to the French, having taken her into Brest on the 14th. The French promptly arrested them, and returned Capt Proby and his officers on parole.
See 8 August 1898.

1804 *Loire* captured the French privateer *Brave* to the south-west of Cape Clear.

1814 *Ajax* captured the French *Alcyon* 90 miles S. of the Scilly Isles.

1858 Boats of *Calcutta* and *Starling* captured or destroyed five pirate junks in Deep Bay, Hong Kong, and recaptured *Heather Bell* yacht.

1869 RM Fourth (The Court) Division at Woolwich disbanded by Order in Council.

1912 Capt Lawrence Oates, 5th Inniskilling Dragoons, died in Antarctica by walking out into a blizzard in a vain attempt to improve the chances of survival for Capt Scott's party: 'I am just going outside and may be some time.' It was his 32nd birthday.

1916 *Crescent*, depot ship and former first-class cruiser, the first ship to enter the Basin at Rosyth Dockyard.
See 28 March 1916.

1917 German destroyer raid in Dover Strait. Ships: *Laertes, Laforey, Llewellyn, Paragon. Llewellyn* torpedoed and *Paragon* sunk by the German S-49 and G-86.

1917 *Mignonette*, convoy escort sloop based at Queenstown, mined and sunk 1½ miles off Galley Head, south-west Ireland. Her sister ship *Alyssum* mined and sunk the following day in same location.

The end of the Type 15 frigate HMS *Rapid* seen through the periscope of HMS *Onyx*, which torpedoed her in the Western Approaches on 3 September 1981. The first torpedo blew off her bows and the second struck her amidships, breaking her back. (*Author*)

HMS *Volage* (1943) flying paying off pennant in peacetime. (*NMRN W&L 1189A*)

1917 Admiralty Compass Department moved to Slough.

1941 The first sinking of a U-boat due to radar. The old destroyer *Vanoc*, Cdr J.G.W. Deneys RN, fitted with Type 286M radar and part of the 5th Escort Group escorting homeward-bound convoy HX.112 S. of Iceland, detected at night the surfacing U-100, which she rammed and sank; (61.04N, 11.30W). While she was hove-to rescuing survivors, the Group Leader, Cdr Donald Macintyre RN, in the destroyer *Walker*, depth charged an Asdic contact astern of *Vanoc* and brought U-99 to the surface; scuttled (61.00N, 11.30W). The respective submarine captains, Joachim Schepke and Otto Kretschmer were leading U-boat commanders; another, Prien, had been lost in U-47 ten days earlier.

See 7 March 1941.

1942 Submarine *Unbeaten* sank the Italian submarine *Guglielmotti* off Sicily.

1945 Destroyers *Rapid*, *Saumarez* (D 26) and *Volage* bombarded Sigli, Sumatra.

1945 Minesweeper *Guysborough* (RCN) sunk by U-878 in Bay of Biscay (46.43N, 09.20W).

1948 Brussels Treaty signed (Belgium, France, Luxembourg, Netherlands, and United Kingdom).

After the Second World War the USSR moulded its 'area of influence' into a virtual empire. The Brussels Treaty was an attempt to restore the balance of power, but the democracies of Western Europe were so weakened by the war that the balance could only be restored by forming the wider, North Atlantic Alliance. This secured the North Atlantic Area (including Europe) by the declaration that an attack on one of the partners would be regarded as an attack upon them all.

1967 Fleet Dental Surgeon to C-in-C Home Fleet established. 'The appointment is to be held by the Command Dental Surgeon to C-in-C Portsmouth.' – DCI(RN) 308/67.

2008 Wreck of the light cruiser HMAS *Sydney*, sunk with all hands in action with the German raider *Kormoran* off Western Australia on 19 November 1941, found by sonar 250km S.W. of Carnarvon (26.14.37S, 111.13.03E), at a depth of 2,470m. The *Kormoran* located 12nm away a week earlier.

18 March

1784 Nelson appointed to command frigate *Boreas* (28).

See 24 March 1784, 30 November 1787.

1799 Capt Sir Sidney Smith in *Tigre* captured six French gunvessels and a siege train and recaptured *Torride* off Cape Carmet, Syria, thus preventing any disturbance of the siege of Acre. Battle Honour: Acre 1799.

1799 *Telegraph* captured the French *Hirondelle* 30 miles N.W. of Ile de Bas, Brittany.

1813 Boats of *Undaunted* cut out a French tartan and stormed a battery at Carry, near Marseilles.

1841 Destruction of the last forts in the approaches to Canton. Ships and vessels: *Algerine, Herald, Hyacinth, Louisa, Modeste, Starling, Young Hebe*. Bengal Marine Steamers: *Madagascar, Nemesis*. Boats of *Blonde, Conway*. Medal: China, 1841–2.

1882 Launch of fourth *Edinburgh* at Pembroke Dockyard. First RN battleship to carry a main armament of breech-loading guns and to have compound instead of iron armour. Last of the Victorian citadel ships.

1904 Submarine A 1 run down by SS *Berwick Castle* at Spithead with loss of all her crew. Subsequently salvaged. First sinking of a RN submarine.

See 3 July 1902.

1912 Mr W.S. Churchill presented his first naval estimates since being made First Lord on 24 October 1911.

1915 Allied attack on the Narrows in the Dardanelles. Battleships *Ocean* and *Irresistible* mined and sunk. First instance in British naval history of two battleships, of wood or steel, being lost in action on the same day.

Securing a submarine scout airship on the deck of HMS *Furious* (1918). (*NMRN*)

Two capital ships, the battleship *Prince of Wales* and the battlecruiser *Repulse*, were sunk on 10 December 1941. Three battlecruisers were lost at Jutland. Five battleships were lost in the Gallipoli Operation, March–May 1915, which also has no parallel in a single RN operation.
See 5 July 1898, 13, 25 and 27 May 1915.

1915 Maiden flight of non-rigid naval airship SS (Submarine Scout) No. 1 at Kingsnorth on Medway.

1915 Battleship *Dreadnought* rammed and sank U-29 in Moray Firth (58.21N, 01.12E).

1917 German destroyer raid on Ramsgate and Broadstairs. Vessels: TB 4, *Redwald* and five other drifters.

1917 *Alyssum*, sloop, sunk by mine 3 miles S. 31°E. of Galley Head, south-west of Ireland.
See 17 March 1917.

1917 *Duchess of Montrose*, paddle minesweeper, mined off Dunkirk.

1919 Vice-Admiral Sir Roger Keyes presented to the Mayor of Dunkirk the Distinguished Service Cross which the King had conferred on the town 'for its great services to the British Navy' in the First World War.

1941 *Andromeda* (Italian) sunk by A/C of 815 Squadron, FAA in Valona Bay, Albania.

1942 Submarine *Upholder* sank the Italian S/M *Tricheco* off Brindisi. The third Italian loss in a week.

1945 Destroyers *Lookout* and *Meteor* sank the German TA-29 (ex-Italian *Eridano*) (43.46N, 09.18E), and TA-24 (ex-Italian *Arturo*) (43.49N, 09.24E), off Spezia. A third enemy escaped.

1959 Cruiser *Tiger* commissioned By Capt R.E. Washbourn RN, over seventeen years after she was laid down at John Brown's on the Clyde. Work was suspended on *Tiger, Blake* and *Lion* in July 1946 and resumed in 1954.
See 10 August 1966, 28 September 1986.

1961 *Blake* completed at Fairfields, the last cruiser finished for the Royal Navy.
See 28 September 1986.

1977 '*Achilles*, Bridge, Engage': minehunter *Maxton* fired four live 40mm Bofors rounds into the frigate *Achilles* near the Mull of Kintyre.
See 10 August 1966.

1981 HRH The Crown Prince Harald of Norway appointed an honorary colonel Royal Marines.
See 7 June 1940, 21 September 1957, 2 July 1958.

1983 The Cross of Nails, a crucifix made from medieval iron nails salvaged from the ruins of Coventry Cathedral and presented to the destroyer *Coventry* on commissioning in 1978, was returned to the cathedral by Capt David Hart Dyke RN. The cross had been recovered by naval divers from the wreck of the ship bombed and sunk in Falklands waters in May 1982. It was placed in the cathedral's 'Navy Room' in the crypt which houses memorials to the Type 42 destroyer and to the anti-aircraft cruiser *Coventry* sunk in 1942. The cross was inherited by the next *Coventry*, the Type 22 frigate, and returned again to the cathedral in 2002.
See 14 September 1942, 25 May 1982.

2002 Submarine *Trafalgar* entered Devonport following operational firing of TLAMs against al-Qaeda positions in Afghanistan.
See 18 November 1998, 24 March 1999, 22 September 2001, 7 October 2001.

2002 *Fearless*, last RN steam-powered surface warship, entered Portsmouth for the last time on return from the Indian Ocean.
See 10 September 1971, 23 November 1979, 24 September 2000, 2 August 2002.

2010 Surveying ship, *Roebuck*, Lt-Cdr Richard Bird RN, entered Devonport to pay off having steamed 431,000 miles in her after twenty-four years of service.

19 MARCH

1726 Richard Howe, victor of the Glorious First of June, born.

1759 *Aeolus* and *Isis* fought the French *Blonde*. *Aeolus* captured the French *Mignonne* off Yeu Island, France.

1779 *Arethusa* wrecked on Ile Molène, near Ushant, after engaging the French *Aigrette*.

1813 Boats of *Apollo* and *Cerberus* destroyed four vessels, a battery and a tower 3 miles N.W. of Porto di Monopoli.

1847 Admiralty order that Wednesday 24 March be observed as a Day of Public Fasting and Humiliation, Divine Service to be specially performed in recognition of Irish Famine. Reaction of ship's companies and their pursers not recorded.

1857 Boats and landing party of *Hornet* destroyed seventeen pirate junks at St John Island, S.W. of Macao.

1863 Ironclad *Ocean* launched at Devonport Dockyard. She had been laid down 23 August 1860 as a wooden second rate and converted while in frame to an ironclad with a 21ft section of hull inserted. Commissioned for the Channel Fleet but transferred to the Mediterranean. On 18 June 1867 *Ocean* left Gibraltar for Hong Kong and arrived at Batavia after 133 days mainly under sail; she was the only armoured ship ever to double the Cape under canvas. She served on the China Station from 1867–72 without docking and returned home under steam at 4.5 knots, arriving at Plymouth 164 days after leaving Singapore. 'From the day she hoisted her pennant until the end of her sea career she never anchored in British waters' – Oscar Parkes, *British Battleships*, p.58.

See 5 July 1898, 8 July 1944, 11 October 1995.

1872 Collective responsibility restored to Board of Admiralty by Order in Council.

The Admiralty Act of 1832, passed to amend the laws relating to the civil departments of the Admiralty, had vested in the Board the whole powers of the Navy Board. H.C. Childers, when First Lord in 1869, had procured an Order in Council which specified and restricted the duties of each Lord, thus destroying their collective responsibility.

1943 Destroyer *Derwent* torpedoed in Tripoli harbour by air-dropped circling torpedo. Beached, salvaged and towed to Plymouth but never repaired.

1945 Destroyers *Rapid*, *Saumarez* (D 26) and *Volage* bombarded Port Blair, Andaman Islands.

1946 Carrier *Eagle* launched at Harland & Wolff, Belfast.

See 3 May 1950, 26 January 1972, 6 August 1975.

1949 Admiral of the Fleet Sir James Somerville died. 'It was not his good fortune to be identified with a successful, classic sea battle, unlike other admirals of the fleet – Andrew Cunningham and Matapan, Tovey and the *Bismarck*, Fraser and the *Scharnhorst* – but he was responsible for handing *Bismarck* to Tovey almost on a plate, he was as important as Cunningham in maintaining Britain's Mediterranean position and in the Eastern Fleet he trained many of the ships and men who went on with Fraser to the final round in the Pacific. . . [he] recognised . . . the multi-faceted nature of sea power and practised the arts of Admiralty both ashore and afloat with a consummate professionalism worthy to be remembered with the great admirals of the past' – Michael Simpson, *The Somerville Papers*, Navy Records Society 1995, pp.597–8.

See 7 March 1810, 17 July 1882, 2 December 1940, 28 March 1942.

1964 The Commissioners for executing the Office of Lord High Admiral held a farewell dinner in the Painted Hall at Greenwich, attended by HRH The Duke of Edinburgh. The following message was received: 'I much regret that I cannot be with you at Greenwich this evening. I have twice had the high honour of serving as First Lord, and with many memories of my tenure I send you all my greetings tonight as the Board of Admiralty commemorates and celebrates the

The ironclad ram HMS *Hotspur* (1870), with her anti-torpedo nets deployed. (*NMRN*)

many centuries of its duties to Sovereign and Nation. Although the Lords Commissioners may disappear administratively in twelve days time, I know that the spirit of their great service, though under a different title, will continue to inspire the Navy in its proud and patriotic traditions' – Winston Churchill.

The following reply was sent by the First Lord on behalf of the Board of Admiralty: 'The Commissioners for executing the Office of Lord High Admiral, assembled with their guests at Greenwich, are proud to receive this warm message of faith and encouragement from the Former Naval Person and thank him for the inspiration that he has given them and which will always be part of the Navy's heritage. They wish him many more years to enjoy the harvest of his great endeavours and assure him that they share his confidence in the continuing ability of the Royal Navy to serve their Sovereign and the Nation' – Jellicoe. AFO 644/64.

See 8 May 1731, 31 March 1964.

1969 The frigate *Minerva* landed her twenty Royal Marines and the frigate *Rothesay* men of 2 Para on the island of Anguilla to restore order following its breakaway from the federation with St Kitts-Nevis. They were greeted by bemused islanders and Operation Sheepskin was ridiculed in the international press for its perceived overkill. The troops were soon relieved by British policemen.

1974 Ordinary Seaman Walter Talbot (73), who deserted the light cruiser *Calcutta* at Montreal in 1920, walked up the brow of the frigate *Jupiter* visiting San Diego and surrendered himself to the Officer of the Day. A swift signal to CINCFLEET from Cdr John Gunning secured Talbot's even swifter discharge.

1982 Illegal Argentine landing and hoisting of national flag on South Georgia. *Endurance* sent from Falkland Islands to remove it.

1998 First female commanding officers of HM ships appointed. Lt Melanie Robinson, *Express* (Cardiff URNU), and Lt Suzanne Moore, *Dasher* (Bristol URNU).

See 9 December 2003.

2011 SSN *Triumph* fired Tomahawk missiles against military targets in Libya following the UK response to UNSCR 1975. Frigates *Westminster* and *Cumberland* in theatre. Operation Ellamy.

See 18 November 1998.

20 March

A Memorable Date observed by 40 Cdo RM and UK Landing Force Command Group – Al Faw

1707 *Resolution* attacked by six French ships and run ashore near Genoa. Burned by her own people on the following day to avoid capture.

1734 Edward Hawke made post on appointment to the frigate *Flamborough* (24).

1780 *Lion*, Capt the Hon. William Cornwallis, *Bristol*, *Janus*, *Kingston* and *Gayton* privateers fought the French *Annibal*, Cdre La Motte-Picquet, three others of the line and a frigate 25 miles N. of Monte Cristi, Haiti.

1794 Landing party from *Zebra* captured Fort Louis, Martinique. *Bienvenue* retaken. Cdr Faulkner, who had taken the prize, was made post on the quarterdeck of *Boyne* and appointed to command the *Bienvenue*, which Jervis renamed: 'Like yourself, sir – *Undaunted*.'

See 17 March 1794.

1796 *Pomone*, *Anson*, *Artois* and *Galatea* captured the French *Etoile* and four vessels of a convoy off Pointe du Raz, Brittany.

1805 *Renard* destroyed the French privateer *Général Ernouf* 100 miles N.E. of Cape Haitien. Enemy blew up. Her Captain had asked Capt Coughlan if he would strike, to which he replied 'Yes, and damned hard too', which he did, defeating his enemy in thirty-five minutes.

1832 Navigating, Medical and other non-executive officers adopted the uniform jacket of the Executive branch, distinguished by the pattern of their button.

1852 Pursers designated Paymasters of the Navy by Order in Council.

1858 Introduction of experimental cork beds, in place of coir or hair. An unsuccessful experiment.

1918 Destroyer *Loyal* depth-charged UC-48 which surrendered for internment in Ferrol.

Royal Marines from 42 Cdo prepare to land from HMS *Albion* on 21 January 2010. (*RN*)

1922 The Admiralty ordered that first rate *Victory* should be preserved in No. 2 Dock, Portsmouth Dockyard.

See 16 December 1921.

1941 Battleship *Malaya* torpedoed by U-106 in mid-Atlantic. Convoy SL 68.

1941 *Helvellyn*, auxiliary AA ship, sunk by German aircraft in Thames.

1942 Destroyer *Heythrop* sunk by sister ship *Eridge*, having been torpedoed by U-652 E. of Tobruk.

1943 Fortress B/206 sank U-384 in N. Atlantic (54.18N, 26.15W). Convoys HX 229 and SC 122.

1944 Submarine *Graph* (ex-U-570) wrecked on the west coast of Islay. Salvaged but scrapped 1947.

See 27 August 1941.

1944 Submarine *Stonehenge*, Lt D.S.McN. Verschoyle-Campbell DSO, DSC and bar, RN, operating from Trincomalee, reported lost to unknown cause with all hands on patrol off N. coast of Sumatra; the first of three RN submarines lost in the war against Japan. Her CO was the youngest officer to command a submarine (*Sealion*) in 1943.

1945 Sloop *Lapwing* torpedoed and sunk by U-968 in Kola Inlet (69.26N, 33.43E). Last of eleven sloops lost in the Second World War.

1945 Frigate *New Glasgow* (RCN) rammed and sank U-1003 in N.W. Approaches.

1945 Liberator B/86 sank U-905 N. of Scotland.

1953 First naval helicopter lift of troops into combat (RN Sikorskys in Malaya).

1954 First RN squadron equipped with Sea Venom all-weather fighter aircraft – 890 NAS – formed at Yeovilton.

1970 Post of Admiral Superintendent Devonport combined with that of Flag Officer Plymouth. DCI(RN) 185/70.

See 1 July 1969, 15 September 1971.

1970 Fleet submarine HMS *Valiant*, the first nuclear submarine to visit Chatham, arrived for refit and refuelling.

See 1 March 1967.

1987 Light fleet carrier *Hermes*, flagship of the British Falklands task force in 1982, commissioned into the Indian Navy as INS *Viraat* after a major refit at Devonport Dockyard.

See 5 July 1948, 16 February 1953, 28 October 1955, 29 August 1957, 4 March 1961.

2003 British military action launched against the Saddam Hussein regime in Iraq. Operation Telic/Iraqi Freedom. The largest deployment of British armed forces since the Gulf War of 1990 and the biggest allied amphibious operation since Suez in 1956. On 20 March, RN SSNs fired Tomahawk cruise missiles against targets in Iraq; 40 Cdo RM carried out helicopter assault on Al Faw from *Ark Royal*, *Ocean* and Kuwait. Conspicuous Gallantry Cross: L/Cpl Justin Thomas, 40 Cdo.

Ships: *Ark Royal*, *Bangor*, *Blyth*, *Brocklesby*, *Chatham*, *Edinburgh*, *Grimsby*, *Ledbury*, *Liverpool*, *Ocean*, *Marlborough*, *Ramsey*, *Richmond*, *Roebuck*, *Sandown*, *Shoreham*, *Splendid*, *York*, *Turbulent*. FAA Sqns: 814, 815, 820, 845, 847, 849. RFA: *Argus*, *Bayleaf*, *Bedivere*, *Brambleleaf*, *Diligence*, *Fort Austin*, *Fort Rosalie*, *Fort Victoria*, *Grey Rover*, *Sea Crusader*, *Sir Galahad*, *Sir Orangeleaf*, *Sir Percivale*, *Sir Tristram*. RNR: personnel from *Cambria*, *Calliope*, *Caroline*, *Dalriada*, *Eaglet*, *Flying Fox*, *Forward*, *King Alfred*, *President*, *Scotia*, *Sherwood*, *Vivid* and the RNR branch at *Heron*. RM and Commando Forces: HQ 3 Cdo Bde, 40 Cdo, 42 Cdo, UK Landing Force Command Support Gp, 29 Cdo Regt RA, 539 Assault Sqn RM, 4 and 9 Assault Sqns RM, 59 Ind Cdo Sqn RE, 131 Ind Cdo Sqn RE(V); elements of 45 Cdo, HQ Commander UK Amphibious Forces, UK Amphibious Forces, 20 Cdo Bty RA, Fleet Protection Gp RM, Fleet Diving Units 2 and 3, Fleet Support Units 1 and 2, RM Band Service. RMR: City of London, Scotland, Bristol, Merseyside, Tyne. Attachments: C Sqn The Queen's Dragoon Guards, C Sqn The Royal Scots Dragoon Guards, 18 Sqn RAF.

21 March

1793 John Western, Third Lieutenant of *Syren* (32), fifth rate, killed in boat action against the French on the Dutch coast; first naval officer killed in action in French Revolutionary War.

1799 'My dear Lord – The promotion to the Flag [14 February 1799] has happily removed a number of officers from the command of ships of the line who at no period of their lives were capable of commanding them; and I am sorry to have occasion to observe that the present state of the upper part of the list of captains is not much better than it stood before' – Admiral the Earl of St Vincent to Earl Spencer, First Lord of the Admiralty.

1800 *Peterel* (16), commanded by Jane Austen's brother Francis, captured the French *Ligurienne* (16) and two vessels of her convoy close off Cape Couronne, near Marseilles. Battle Honour: *Ligurienne* 1800.

1807 Capture of Aboukir Castle and then of Alexandria, Egypt by forces under General Frazer. Ships under Capt Sir Sidney Smith: *Tigre, Apollo, Wizard.*

1813 Boats of *Brevdrageren* and *Blazer* cut out the Danish *Liebe* and *Jonge Troutman* in the Elbe River.

1846 Crossed sword and baton introduced to epaulettes of Flag Officers. Lieutenants to wear two plain epaulettes and mates one. Crown added to cap badge.

1855 *Bittern* destroyed eight pirate junks at Brig Island, near Swatow.

1862 The Royal Marines divided into two separate corps, Royal Marine Artillery (RMA) and Royal Marines Light Infantry (RMLI), until 1923: the Blue and the Red Marines.

See 22 June 1923, 1 June 1927.

The ship's company of HMS *Duncan* (1901). (*NMRN*)

The patrol vessel HMS *Wolverton* of the Hong Kong Squadron leaving Tamar Basin in 1978. (*Author*)

1890 Formation of RM Depot Band.

1901 *Duncan* launched at Thames Iron Works. Name-ship of the last class of battleships to be painted black, white and buff.

1918 Destroyer action between Allied ships and eighteen German destroyers off Dunkirk. Ships: *Botha, Matchless, Morris, Myngs, North Star, Swift, CMB 20A; General Craufurd, M 25, Terror.* French: *Bouclier, Capitaine-Mehl, Magon, Oriflamme.* Germans sunk: A-7 and A-19.

1944 Revd H.C.W. Mauger, RNVR, of 42 RM Cdo, killed in action in Arakan. Sixteenth and last chaplain to be killed on active service in the Second World War.

1955 A memorial to Admiral Sir Tom Phillips and the 764 officers and men lost in *Prince of Wales* and *Repulse* in the form of a silver high altar cross and two candlesticks, intended for St Andrew's Cathedral, Singapore, were handed to the High Commissioner of Malaya by Sir Shenton Thomas, lately Governor of the Straits Settlements, at Malaya House, London.
See 10 February 1943.

1968 Post of Captain-in-Charge Clyde lapsed and that of RNO Greenock established. DCI(RN) 509/68.

1980 *Brecon*, first of Hunt-class MCMVs, commissioned.

1983 The last class of direct entry artificers entered *Fisgard*, Torpoint. DCI(RN) 214/83.
See 21 December 1983

2003 DCI(RN) 37/03 restored the entitlement, withdrawn in 1991, of RN officers who had completed the All Arms Commando Course to wear the gold on blue commando dagger badge. To be worn above the curl on the right sleeve of No. 1 uniform jackets and mess jackets.
See 3 November 2006.

2007 Explosion of a self-contained oxygen generator (SCOG) in submarine *Tireless* while submerged under the Arctic ice killed two crew members.
See 30 August 1966, 12 February 1970, 29 September 1971.

22 March

1794 Capture of Fort Bourbon and the whole of Martinique by General Sir Charles Grey and Vice-Admiral Sir John Jervis (*Boyne*). The Naval Brigade manned several of the breaching batteries on shore.
Battle Honour: Martinique 1794.
See 4 and 16 February 1762, 17 March 1794.

1797 Boats of *Hermione* cut out three French privateers and their twelve prizes from a bay at the west end of Puerto Rico.

1808 *Nassau* and *Stately* captured the Danish *Prinds Christian Frederik* after two hours. She went ashore immediately afterwards on Sjaellands Odde, Kattegat, and was burned next day.

1813 *Captain* (74), which had been Lord Nelson's ship when he took the *San Josef* and which had recently been hulked at Plymouth, caught fire and was totally destroyed. The *San Josef*, which was lying alongside, was preserved with difficulty.
See 14 February 1797.

1885 Action at Tofrek (McNeill's zareba), Sudan. Naval Brigade from *Carysfort*, *Condor*, *Coquette*, *Dolphin* and *Sphinx*. Egyptian Medal: clasp 'Tofrek'.

A zareba was an improvised but major entrenchment, fortified by thorn bushes. General Sir John McNeill, VC, constructed one as an intermediate supply post in the desert outside Suakin. The work was unfinished, and the troops were eating a meal when they were suddenly attacked by 5,000 tribesmen. The British squares were at first overrun by stampeding animals and tribesmen, but in twenty minutes had re-formed and killed 1,000 tribesmen and 900 camels.

1899 Miniatures replaced medals for officers in ball dress.

1903 Caspar John born at 18 Fitzroy Street, London; future admiral of the fleet and first naval aviator to become First Sea Lord (1960–3). Son of Augustus John, painter.
See 23 May 1960, 11 July 1984.

1911 Royal Fleet Auxiliary established by Order in Council, but RFA celebrated its centenary on 3 August 2005.
See 3 August 1905.

1916 Decoy ship Q-5 *Farnborough*, Lt-Cdr Gordon Campbell, sank U-68 off west coast of Ireland.
See 17 February 1917, 7 June 1917, 8 August 1917.

Campbell commissioned the 3,200-ton collier SS *Loderer* at Devonport on Trafalgar Day 1916 and, after a name change to *Farnborough* to cover her tracks, sailed for Queenstown from where she operated under Admiral Sir Lewis Bayly. On 22 March 1916 she sighted a trimmed-down submarine and Campbell took no action to avoid a torpedo which passed close ahead. The U-boat surfaced astern, came up the port side, and fired a shot across her bows. The standard panic party set about abandoning ship during which the submarine closed to 800 yards when Campbell hoisted the White Ensign and opened fire with his 12-pdrs, hitting the U-boat several times before she submerged. *Farnborough* ran in over the scene and dropped depth charges. U-68 (Kapitanleutnant Ludwig Guntzel), on her first war patrol, was lost with all hands.

Campbell DSO and promoted commander; two DSCs, three DSMs.

1918 Sloop *Gaillardia* sunk while escorting minelayers in Northern Barrage, off Orkney.

1942 Second Battle of Sirte (34.10N, 18.10E). Rear-Admiral Philip Vian (*Cleopatra*) repulsed an attack by a superior Italian force on convoy MW 10. 'One of the most brilliant actions of the war' – Admiral Sir Andrew Cunningham. Ships: *Breconshire*, *Carlisle*, *Cleopatra*, *Dido*, *Euryalus*, *Legion*, *Penelope*. 5th DF: *Avon Vale*, *Beaufort*, *Dulverton*, *Eridge*, *Hurworth*, *Southwold*. 14th DF: *Jervis*, *Kelvin*, *Kingston*, *Kipling*. 22nd DF: *Hasty*, *Havock*, *Hero*, *Lively*, *Sikh*, *Zulu*. It was *Euryalus* (fifth of the name) who made 'Enemy in sight', as her predecessor had done before Trafalgar, 137 years before.
Battle Honour: Sirte 1942.

A convoy sailed for Malta from Alexandria, with a heavy escort of four cruisers and ten destroyers, which was joined later by another cruiser and seven destroyers. Italian naval forces sailed from Taranto and Messina to intercept the

HMS *Cleopatra* laying a smokescreen at the second Battle of Sirte, seen from HMS *Euryalus*, 1942. (*NMRN*)

convoy, which was also subject to heavy air attacks. On 22 March at 1427 part of the enemy force was sighted. The four British light cruisers, together with the fleet destroyers, turned towards the enemy, leaving the convoy, which was under air attack in the keeping of an AA cruiser and the smaller destroyers. The British force were to windward and used smoke to cover the convoy and their approach to the Italian force, which included heavy cruisers. The enemy were driven off, but returned at 1640 having been reinforced by more ships, including a battleship. Once again, the light cruisers and fleet destroyers closed, and attacked with torpedoes and gunfire, using smoke and the weather gauge to close to effective range. Three British destroyers (*Havock*, *Kingston* and *Lively*) were hit by 15-in shells but the enemy were held at bay and finally driven off. This was a brilliant victory by Admiral Vian, in command of the 15th Cruiser Squadron, which was marred only by the loss of half the convoy to air attack the next day as they neared Malta. Vian and his ships returned to Alexandria on 25 March. Cunningham signalled 'Well done 15th Cruiser Squadron'. 'From one who carried the cult of the Silent Service to the edge of paranoia it was a Pindaric Ode' – Ollard.

1942 GC: Lt Dennis Arthur Copperwheat, *Penelope*, for ammunition disposal in Valetta Harbour.

1943 River gunboat *Aphis* bombarded Gabes in support of the 8th Army.

1945 Liberator M/120 sank U-296 in N.W. Approaches.

1946 Corvette *Dawson* (RCN) foundered off Hamilton, Ontario.

1950 Hansard, Column 1973 No. 148: 'The Royal Marine establishment being closed down at Chatham will be replaced by a naval establishment, HMS *Serious*, the training establishment of the Supply and Secretariat Branch . . .'

See 14 March 1958, 14 April 1958.

1993 *Bristol*, Type 82 destroyer, relieved *Kent*, County-class destroyer, at Portsmouth as the RN Cadet Forces Accommodation and Training Ship. DCI(RN) 64/93.

See 30 June 1969.

2003 Two Sea King Mk VII of 849 Sqn A Flight, flying from *Ark Royal* on vital ground surveillance missions to support Royal Marines ashore on the Al Faw peninsula, collided over the northern Arabian Gulf. Two pilots and five observers killed. Posthumous MiD to observer, Lt Tony King. Operation Telic.

2007 Carrier *Ark Royal*, Capt M.P. Mansergh RN, recommissioned at Portsmouth after a two-year refit at Rosyth.

See 3 December 2010.

23 March

1742 Victualling yard on Tower Hill transferred to Deptford by Order in Council.

1757 Capture of Chandernagore by Vice-Admiral Charles Watson (*Kent*) and Col Robert Clive. Ships: *Kent, Tiger, Salisbury, Bridgewater.*

1791 *Pandora* arrived at Tahiti in search of *Bounty* mutineers.

1804 *Osprey* fought the Bordeaux privateer *Egyptienne* 200 miles E. of Barbados.

1805 Boats of *Stork* cut out the Dutch privateer *Antilope* under Cape Roxo, Puerto Rico.

1806 Boats of *Colpoys* cut out three Spanish luggers at Aviles, north coast of Spain.

1812 The admiral of the fleet distinguished from other admirals for the first time, by the addition of a fourth stripe on his full dress, and a distinctive undress uniform. All captains and commanders to wear two epaulettes, but the two grades of captain to be distinguished by having a crown and anchor, as opposed to an anchor. Lieutenants to wear one plain epaulette on right shoulder.

Boy John Travers Cornwell at his gun in the light cruiser HMS *Chester* at Jutland in 1916. (*RN*)

1815 *Penguin* (18) taken by the American *Hornet* (20) off Tristan da Cunha.

1830 The foundation stone of the RN Hospital, Bighi, Kalkara, Malta, laid by Vice-Admiral Sir Pulteney Malcolm, 'Commander-in-Chief of the Naval Forces and Commissioner of the Navy in the Mediterranean' (foundation stone) as the ship's band of HMS *Asia* played the National Anthem. It was completed on 24 September 1832 and closed on 17 September 1970 when services were transferred to Mtarfa in the N. of the island. The last RN Medical Officer in Charge was Surg-Capt C.T.L. McClintock.

See 6 January 1915.

1859 Boats of *Heron, Spitfire, Trident* and *Vesuvius*, a Colonial gunboat, and the 1st West India Regiment captured Kambia, Great Scarcies River, Sierra Leone.

1875 Steam corvette *Challenger*, Capt George Nares RN, engaged on her famous scientific expedition 1872–6, sounded a then world record ocean depth of 4,475 fathoms, 26,850ft, in the Mariana Trench in the Pacific (11.24N, 143.16E). The Challenger Deep was visited again in 1951 by the surveying ship *Challenger* when a depth of 5,960 fathoms, 35,760ft, was recorded.

See 21 December 1872, 24 May 1876, 27 September 1952.

1917 Destroyer *Laforey* sunk by mine in English Channel.

1917 The painting of Boy John Travers Cornwell VC at his 6-in gun in the light cruiser *Chester* at Jutland, commissioned by the Lord Mayor and Corporation of London and painted by Frank Salisbury, presented to the First Lord of the Admiralty, Sir Edward Carson, at the Mansion

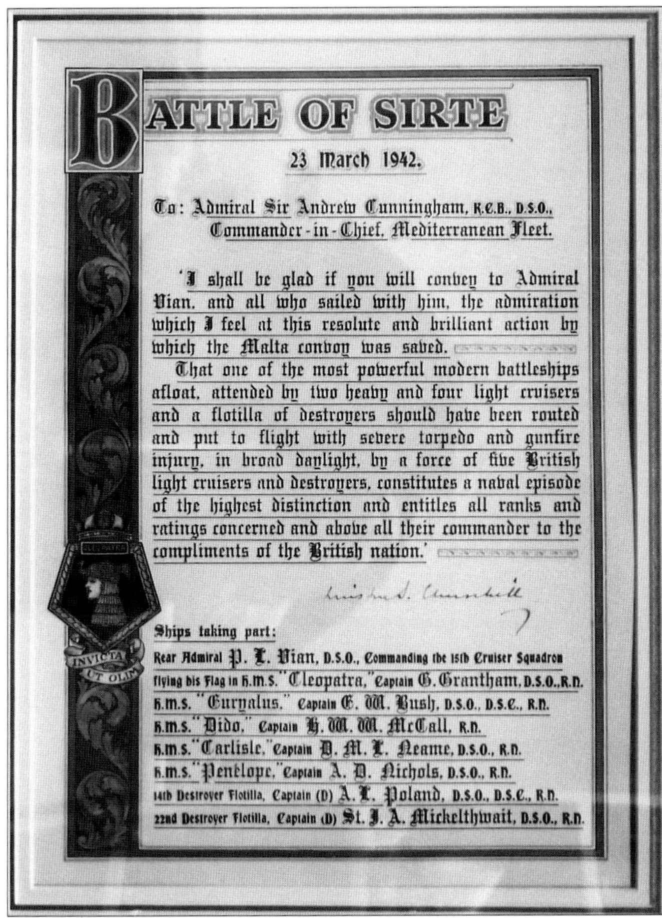

BATTLE OF SIRTE

23 March 1942.

To: Admiral Sir Andrew Cunningham, K.C.B., D.S.O.,
Commander-in-Chief, Mediterranean Fleet.

'I shall be glad if you will convey to Admiral Vian, and all who sailed with him, the admiration which I feel at this resolute and brilliant action by which the Malta convoy was saved.

That one of the most powerful modern battleships afloat, attended by two heavy and four light cruisers and a flotilla of destroyers should have been routed and put to flight with severe torpedo and gunfire injury, in broad daylight, by a force of five British light cruisers and destroyers, constitutes a naval episode of the highest distinction and entitles all ranks and ratings concerned and above all their commander to the compliments of the British nation.'

Ships taking part:

Rear Admiral P. L. Vian, D.S.O., Commanding the 15th Cruiser Squadron
flying his Flag in H.M.S. "Cleopatra," Captain G. Grantham, D.S.O., R.N.
H.M.S. "Euryalus," Captain E. W. Bush, D.S.O., D.S.C., R.N.
H.M.S. "Dido," Captain H. W. W. McCall, R.N.
H.M.S. "Carlisle," Captain D. M. L. Neame, D.S.O., R.N.
H.M.S. "Penelope," Captain A. D. Nichols, D.S.O., R.N.
14th Destroyer Flotilla, Captain (D) A. L. Poland, D.S.O., D.S.C., R.N.
22nd Destroyer Flotilla, Captain (D) St. J. A. Micklethwait, D.S.O., R.N.

RN Trophy No. 7,894. A tribute to 15th Cruiser Squadron and the 14th and 22nd Destroyer Flotillas following their gallant action in the Battle of Sirte in March 1942 sent by Prime Minister Winston Churchill to Admiral Sir Andrew Cunningham, C-in-C Mediterranean Fleet. (*Lt-Cdr David Costigan RN and* Navy News)

House. The restored painting hangs in St Paul's church, HMS *Raleigh*, Torpoint, and was rededicated on 20 March 2009.

See 31 May 1916.

1918 Destroyer *Arno* lost in collision with destroyer *Hope* off Dardanelles.

1922 Submarine H42, Lt D.C. Sealy RN, sunk with all twenty-six hands in collision with the destroyer *Versatile*, Cdr V.L.A Campbell RN, during 3rd Submarine Flotilla tactical exercises with the Atlantic Fleet off Europa Point, Gibraltar. The submarine surfaced 40yds ahead of the destroyer which was steaming at 20 knots.

1941 *Visenda*, A/S trawler, sank U-551 in N.E. Atlantic.

1941 Sloop *Shoreham* intercepted the German SS *Oder* near Perim, Red Sea. *Oder* scuttled.

1944 Light fleet carrier *Albion* laid down at Swan Hunters, Wallsend-on-Tyne.

See 6 May 1947, 26 May 1954.

1960 Sheerness Main Signal Office closed down at 1700. AFO 696/60.

See 30 and 31 March 1960.

1990 A single naval aviation authority to be known as Flag Officer Naval Aviation (FONA) established, which assumed the previous responsibilities of Flag Officer Naval Air Command (FONAC), the Fleet Aviation responsibilities of Flag Officer Flotilla Three (FOF3), and the responsibilities of the Assistant Chief of Staff (Aviation) to CINCFLEET. DCI(Gen) 8/90.

See 1 April 2000.

2002 Commandant-General Royal Marines, Maj-Gen Rob Fry, as COMUKAMPHIBFOR assumed role of UK Maritime Component Commander in Operation Enduring Freedom in Afghanistan/Gulf Area. The first time a RM officer exercised command of RN and coalition maritime forces on operations.

24 March

1387 The tenth Earl of Arundel captured nearly the whole of a Franco-Burgundian merchant fleet.

1740 Bombardment and capture of Chagres by Vice-Admiral Edward Vernon (*Strafford*). Ships: *Alderney, Falmouth, Norwich, Princess Louisa, Strafford, Goodley* and *Pompey* tenders (*Greenwich* and *Windsor*). Bombs: *Cumberland, Terrible*. Fireships: *Eleanor, Success*.

1784 Nelson took command of the frigate *Boreas* (28) in Long Reach on the Thames.
See 30 November 1787.

1804 *Wolverine* taken by the French privateer *Blonde* 600 miles N. by E. of the Azores. Of the *Wolverine*'s convoy, two were taken and six escaped.

1811 *Berwick* chased *Amazone* into bay near Barfleur light, where she was burned by her captor.

1878 *Eurydice* (training frigate) lost in storm off Ventnor. Three hundred and thirty trainees lost; two survivors.

1910 'Their Lordships have approved the issue of a second typewriter to Battleships and First Class Cruisers.' AWO 178/1910.

1916 Submarine E 24 mined in Heligoland Bight.

1927 British and US warships bombarded Nanking to cover the evacuation of foreign nationals after attacks on consulates by Chinese troops.

1940 The First Lord, Winston Churchill, minuted the Fourth Sea Lord: 'Backgammon would be a good game for wardroom, gunroom, and warrant officers' mess, and I have no doubt it would amuse the sailors . . . Backgammon is a better game than cards for the circumstances of war-time afloat, because it whiles away twenty minutes or a quarter of an hour, whereas cards are a much longer business.'
See 29 October 1939, 27 November 1939.

1942 Destroyer *Southwold* sunk by mine off Zanter Point, Malta.

1942 Minesweeper *Sharpshooter* sank U-655 off N. Cape (73.00N, 21.00E). Convoy QP 9.

1948 Royal Marine Act authorised formation of Royal Marine Forces Volunteer Reserve.
See 1 November 1958, 1 October 1966.

1959 Admiralty announced Lt-Cdr B.F.P Samborne RN to be CO of Britain's first SSN, *Dreadnought*, and Lt-Cdr P.G. Hammersley RN to be MEO.
See 28 September 2002.

1960 *Yarmouth*, first of nine Rothesay-class anti-submarine frigates, commissioned at John Brown's, Clydebank, by Capt H.R. Hewlett RN, shortly to be Captain (F) Sixth Frigate Squadron. The first ship to be equipped with the new Seacat missile.

1961 Closure of The Nore Command on 31 March marked by parade of 2,000 serving and retired personnel through Chatham, marching past Admiral Sir Robin Durnford-Slater, C-in-C The Nore. Queen's Colour of The Nore Command laid up in St George's church, RN Barracks, Chatham. Royal Netherlands Navy sent destroyer *Limburg*, flying the flag of Rear-Admiral Baron der vos van Steenwijk, C-in-C Netherlands Home Squadron in commemoration of the Dutch attack on the medway in 1667.
See 10 June 1667.

The raising of the wreck of HMS *Eurydice*, 1878. (*NMRN 1954/43*)

Admiral Edward Vernon (1684–1757)

Having joined the Navy in 1701 Vernon received a special award of 200 guineas from the Queen in 1704 for conspicuous gallantry at Gibraltar. He became a Member of Parliament and an opponent of Walpole. He had a fiery temper and was tempted by Walpole to make a statement that he could take Porto Bello in Panama with six ships of the line. This unfortunate challenge was taken up by the government and he was given his six ships, although hopelessly ill-equipped and ill-manned. By brilliant planning he capured Porto Bello losing only seven men doing it. The government reinforced him and sent him to attack Spanish strongholds in the West Indies. These expeditions were not a success. Vernon's nickname was 'Old Grogram' because of the material of which his boat cloak was made. He insisted on the rum ration being diluted and henceforth watered-down rum was known as 'grog'. (See 21 August, 1740.)

Admiral Edward Vernon (1684–1757). (*NMRN 1976/192*)

1964 Royal Warrant transferred responsibility for the Victoria Cross from the Secretary of State for War to the Secretary of State for Defence.

1999 UK maritime forces deployed to Adriatic to join NATO operations to deter Serbian ethnic cleansing in Kosovo. Mainly an air bombing campaign which started 24 March and ended 10 June. Operation Allied Force (UK Operation Kingower). *Splendid* fired Britain's first operational Tomahawk missile against Serb targets in Kosovo 24 March. Aircraft from *Invincible* joined Allied air operations. Frigate *Somerset*, relieved by frigate *Grafton* 23 April, operated with French *Foch* CAG under French operational control (French Operation Trident). *Invincible* Group arrived from the Gulf ex-Operation Bolton 12 April and left 21 May. Ships: *Invincible, Newcastle, Iron Duke, Somerset, Norfolk, Grafton, Coventry, Splendid, Turbulent*. RFA: *Fort Austin, Bayleaf, Argus*. FAA Sqns: 800, 814, 849 A Flight.

See 18 November 1998, 18 March 2002.

2005 Admiral Sir Lindsay Bryson, who entered the Royal Navy as an electrical mechanic 1945 and was the first engineer officer to be Controller of the Navy (1981–4), died aged 80. He headed the Royal Navy's guided weapons programmes between 1973 and 1981. The first naval officer to be president of the Institution of Electrical Engineers (1985–6).

See 22 January 1925.

'The design of the present Duke-class of general purpose frigates was finalised and contracts placed during his time. The story goes that Admiral Sir John Fieldhouse, First Sea Lord, came to Bryson's office to view the contractor's model. "But it doesn't have a gun!" exclaimed Fieldhouse, fresh from his experience as C-in-C during the Falklands crisis. "That's the considered staff line, sir – the all-missile age," said Bryson.

"Nonsense, give it a gun."

It fell to Bryson to make the painful phone call to the prime contractor.' – *The Times*, 29 March 2005.

2009 Submarine *Audacious*, fourth boat of SSN Astute-class, laid down at Barrow by Defence Secretary John Hutton. First submarine of the name.

See 26 June 1867, 31 January 2001, 22 October 2003, 11 March 2005.

2011 Carrier *Invincible* towed from Portsmouth Dockyard to shipbreakers at Izmir, Turkey.

25 March

1675 *Mary*, first Royal Yacht, wrecked off Skerries.

1797 *Suffisante* captured the French privateer *Bonaparte* 30 miles S.S.W. of Start Point.

1800 *Cruizer* captured the French privateer *Flibustier* to the eastward of Smith's Knoll, North Sea.

1802 Peace of Amiens ended Revolutionary War with France. Hostilities resumed when Britain declared war on France 18 May 1803 and continued until 30 June 1814 and ended with the Treaty of Paris. The Hundred Days War followed.

See 2 January 1793, 18 May 1803.

1804 *Penguin* destroyed the French privateer *Renommée* at Senegal. Driven ashore on the 17th.

1804 Two-decker *Magnificent*, Capt William Jervis, on blockade duty off Brest, struck the Boufoloc reef on an ebb tide when standing out to sea at night in worsening weather. Ship broke up but all her people were saved. 'Thus has perished one of the finest 74s in the Service' – *The Naval Chronicle*.

1806 *Reindeer* fought the French *Phaeton* and *Voltigeur* S.E. of San Domingo.

1855 Boats of *Hornet*, *Spartan*, *Sybille* and *Winchester* destroyed nine pirate junks in Port Shelter, near Hong Kong.

1872 Battleship *Thunderer* launched at Pembroke Dockyard. She and her Portsmouth-built sister ship *Devastation* were the first seagoing mastless turret-ships. A boiler explosion during trials in Stoke's Bay in 1876 killed forty-five men and a gun explosion off Ismed in the Sea of Marmara in 1879 killed eleven turret crew. Despite her troubles *Thunderer* proved a good seaboat and a good gun platform. Admiral Colomb called her 'that steady old rock which nothing disturbs'.

See 12 July 1871, 14 July 1876, 2 January 1879.

The fleet carrier HMS *Indomitable* after her major refit and modernisation at Portsmouth 1947–50. The de Havilland Sea Hornet (one is on her flight deck) was the first twin-engined single-seat fighter in Royal Navy Service. (*NMRN*)

'A Jig Around the Statue of Peace', October 1801. Caricature published following the signing of the Preliminaries which led to the Treaty of Amiens. (*NMRN 1973/275(2)*)

1915 The Dutch *Medea* sunk by U-28 after visit and search. First neutral ship to be so sunk.

1916 Light cruiser *Cleopatra* rammed and sank the German G-194, 5 miles W. of Horns Reef light-vessel.

1916 Destroyer *Medusa* foundered after collision with destroyer *Laverock* off Danish Coast.

1941 First sea trials of Type 271 10-cm radar began on board the corvette *Orchis* in the Clyde; rough weather trials on passage from Lough Foyle to the Clyde on 1 April. The first equipment able to detect a periscope.

1943 Fortress L/206 sank U-469 south of Iceland. Convoy RU 67.

1944 'Tsetse' Mosquito aircraft L/248 and I/248 sank U-976 off Bordeaux with 6pdr cannon.

1945 World's first deck landing of a high-performance twin-engined aircraft; a de Havilland Mosquito Mk 6 from RAE Farnborough on *Indefatigable* off Ailsa Craig and Arran piloted by Lt-Cdr Eric 'Winkle' Brown RNVR.

See 3 December 1945, 19 June 1950.

1959 RNAS Bramcote, HMS *Gamecock*, paid off and transferred to the Army. AFO 925/59.

26 March

1806 Frigate *Pique* (36), on passage from San Domingo to Curaçao, captured the French *Phaeton* (16) and *Voltigeur* (16). They had been attacked two days earlier by brig-sloop *Reindeer* (18). Both prizes commissioned into RN, *Phaeton* as *Mignonne*, later *Musette*, and *Voltigeur* as *Pelican*.

1814 *Hannibal* captured the French *Sultane* 30 miles S.S.E. of Lizard Head.

1857 Capture of Khorramshahr, Persia. Ships and vessels: *Ajdaha, Assaye, Berenice, Clive, Comet, Falkland, Ferooz, Semiramis, Victoria* (all Indian Navy). With the exception of a few Bombay Artillery, 'the gentlemen in blue had it all to themselves, and left us naught to do' – Brig-Gen Henry Havelock in private letter.

1875 William Wordsworth Fisher, C-in-C Mediterranean 1933–6, born.
See 24 June 1937.

1898 Capture of Shendi, River Nile. Gunboats: *Fateh, Nasr, Zafir.*

1913 First proposal for Defensively Equipped Merchant Ships (DEMS) made by Winston Churchill as First Lord of the Admiralty.

1917 Destroyer *Myrmidon* lost in collision with SS *Hamborn* in English Channel.

1918 PC 51 sank U-61 in Bristol Channel (51.48N, 02.52W).

1941 Heavy cruiser *York* hit by Italian explosive motor boats in Suda Bay, Crete. Beached by destroyer *Hasty* and then bombed by German

The Last Meeting of The Lords Commissioners of the Admiralty – 26 March 1964

The First Lord recorded in the minutes:

'We are now about to hold the last meeting of this Board in this room. It will be the last meeting of the Lords Commissioners for executing the Office of Lord High Admiral, a body which has been in being, with some interruptions, since 1628 and which has formed, and forms, part of our naval, indeed of our national, tradition.

This Board Room is a very lovely room. It was even more lovely in the days before the Admiralty was enlarged. Then there was a view from these windows right down the Mall. But it is not only a beautiful room. It is also an historic one since it is from here that naval operations have been directed during three major wars, spread over a century and a half. From this chair, former naval persons like Admiral Lord St Vincent and Sir Winston Churchill have directed the sea affair. (The first news of Trafalgar was delivered to this room, at about one in the morning, when the Board had just finished their day's work). But nowadays naval operations cannot be conducted in a room equipped only with a windvane; wireless, teleprinters and computers are also needed.

The next time we meet we shall be the Admiralty Board, not the Board of Admiralty. Whether the nature of our discussions will be changed or not is a thing that time will show. But in one way there will be no change. The shop will remain open and the purpose of the shop will remain the service of the Royal Navy, and through the Royal Navy, the nation.'

The crimson and gold anchor flag of the Lord High Admiral was hauled down at sunset on 31 March when Her Majesty the Queen resumed the title of Lord High Admiral and the Commissioners for executing that office became the Admiralty Board of the Defence Council.

The heavy cruiser HMS *York* (1928). (*NMRN*)

aircraft on 24 April. Officially paid off 22 May 1941.

'While the Italians on the whole displayed little enterprise and initiative at sea, it always amazed me how good they were at these sorts of individual attacks. They certainly had men capable of the most gallant exploits.' – Cunningham.

See 12 February 1945.

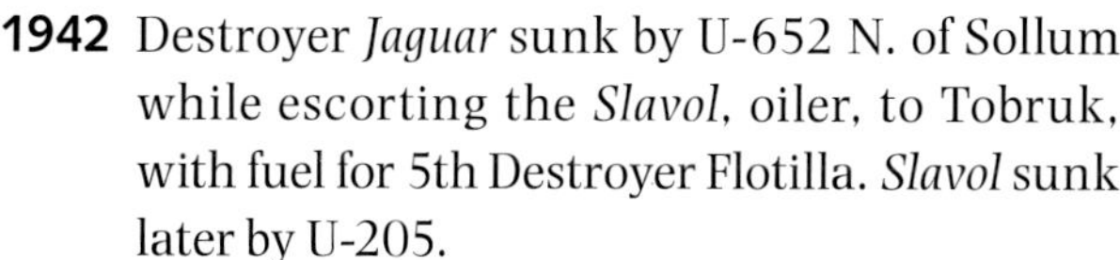

1942 Destroyer *Jaguar* sunk by U-652 N. of Sollum while escorting the *Slavol*, oiler, to Tobruk, with fuel for 5th Destroyer Flotilla. *Slavol* sunk later by U-205.

1942 Destroyer *Legion* and submarine P 39 sunk by German aircraft at Malta. Light cruiser *Penelope* damaged.

1945 Frigate *Duckworth* sank U-399 off Land's End (49.56N, 05.22W).

1945 *Puffin*, patrol vessel, damaged by ramming a midget submarine and detonating its warhead off the Scheldt.

1945 Aircraft of Task Force 57, under Vice-Admiral Sir Bernard Rawlings (*King George V*), attacked the airfields on Myako and Ishigaki Islands (Sakishima group). Operation Iceberg. Carriers: *Illustrious, Indefatigable, Indomitable, Victorious*. Ships: *Howe, King George V, Argonaut, Black Prince, Euryalus, Gambia, Swiftsure*. FAA Sqns: Avenger 820, 849, 854, 857. Corsair 1830, 1833, 1834, 1836. Firefly 1770. Hellcat 1839, 1844. Seafire 887, 894. Battle Honour: Okinawa 1945.

Operation Iceberg – British Pacific Fleet, 1945

In March 1945 the British Pacific Fleet was employed on attacks on Sakishima Gunto, an operation which did much to restore the position of the Royal Navy in the Pacific. The carrier force flew 5,335 sorties, dropping almost 1,000 tons of bombs and firing 1,000 rockets. Half a million rounds of ammunition were fired and fifty-seven enemy aircraft were destroyed in combat. The same number were destroyed on the ground.

1955 A 2cwt solid-silver ship's bell, bought from the ship's fund of the carrier *Ark Royal* (III), sunk in November 1941, handed over to the Captain of the new *Ark Royal* (IV) at Portsmouth by Mr W.F.H. Vatcher who was a chief cook in the carrier lost in the Mediterranean. The bell went to *Ark Royal* (V). The Canteen Committee of the third *Ark Royal* decided specifically to commission a new bell for the next ship of the name. It was cast during the war and held in the custody of the RN Barracks, Lee-on-Solent. AFO 376/55.

1964 The last meeting of the Board of Admiralty, chaired by the Earl Jellicoe, the last holder of the office of First Lord of the Admiralty, was held in the historic Board Room.

See 30 September 1725, 19 and 31 March 1964, 6 April 1964.

2004 *Mersey*, offshore patrol vessel, commissioned in Canada Dock, Liverpool.

See 14 June 2003.

2005 Lt Leonard James Callaghan RNVR, later the Rt Hon. Baron Callaghan of Cardiff KG, PC, died at Ringmer, E. Sussex, one day short of his 93rd birthday. Born Portsmouth 27 March 1912, son of a CPO RN serving in the Royal Yacht; educated Portsmouth North Grammar School; entered RN as Ordinary Seaman 1942, served in East Indies Fleet and commissioned in RNVR in 1944. Returned as MP for Cardiff South 1945; Prime Minister 1976–9. 'While in the Navy he was tattooed, a fact which embarrassed him in later life. He refused to wear short sleeves' – *Daily Telegraph*, 28 March 2005.

27 March

1680 *Adventure* engaged the Algerine *Citron Tree*, wrecked later off Arzila, Morocco.

1759 *Windsor* engaged four French East Indiamen, capturing *Duc de Chartres* 200 miles W.N.W. of Cape Finisterre.

1759 *Southampton* and *Melampe* captured the French *Danae* off Westkapelle. *Harmonie* engaged, but escaped.

1804 *Hippomenes*, taken from the Dutch the previous year, captured the Bordeaux privateer *Egyptienne* 180 miles E. of Barbados.

1811 Royal Marines at Anholt beat off a Danish attack on the island, which was commissioned as one of HM ships. Ships: *Tartar*, *Sheldrake*, *Anholt*. Only *Sheldrake* was awarded the medal.

1812 *Rosario* and *Griffon* defeated twelve French brigs of the 14th Division of the Boulogne Flotilla off Dieppe, capturing two and driving two others on shore.

1814 *Hebrus* captured the French *Etoile* off the Nez de Jobourg after a 24-hour chase. *Hannibal* took the *Sultane* which had parted company from *Etoile*. Last action against the French for which the gold medal was awarded.
Battle Honour: *Etoile* 1814.

1854 Britain and France declared war on Russia. The start of the Russian 'Crimean' War.

1865 Capt Geoffrey Hornby, future admiral of the fleet, took the Channel Fleet flagship *Edgar* (91), screw two-decker, out of Portsmouth Harbour under sail, the last time a battleship left the port without using steam.
See 30 March 1856.

1912 Leonard James Callaghan, later Lt RNVR and Prime Minister, born at Portsmouth.
See 26 March 2005.

1918 Destroyer *Kale* sunk by mine in North Sea.

1942 Destroyers *Aldenham*, *Grove*, *Leamington* and *Volunteer* sank U-587 S.W. of Ireland (47.21N, 21.39W). Convoy WS 17.

1943 Escort carrier *Dasher* destroyed by a massive aviation fuel explosion and fire at anchor 5 miles off Little Cumbrae Island in the Firth of Clyde (55.40N, 04.57W). The ship sank in eight minutes with the loss of 379 men; the Captain and 148 men survived. The Admiralty concluded that the explosion was caused by inadequate protection of AVGAS tanks in the American-built mercantile hull. Later Lend-Lease ships were modified. After the loss of life in the battleship *Royal Oak* in October 1939, this was the second biggest naval catastrophe at anchor in home waters in the Second World War.
See 17 September 1939, 14 October 1939.

1943 Fortress L/206 sank U-169 in N. Atlantic (60.54N, 15.25W). Her second success in two days.

1943 *Laforey* and *Blyskawica* (Polish) carried out a feint landing and bombardment near Cape Serrat.

1945 Frigate *Conn* sank U-722 off Hebrides (58.34N, 05.46W).

1967 Frigate *Dundas* and minesweeper *Highburton*, with FNS *Le Breton*, present in St Nazaire for the 25th anniversary of the wartime raid.

1976 Third Cod War. Four collisions between Icelandic Coastguard vessel *Baldur* and frigate *Diomede* which was seriously damaged. The 'Avoid damage to frigates' policy was promulgated that evening (lifted 6 May 1976).
See p.496 panel.

1981 Carrier *Bulwark*, which had suffered two major fires in 1980, entered Portsmouth for the last time. She left under tow on 10 April 1981 for the breakers at Cairnryan.
See 29 October 1954, 15 March 1980, 9 November 1980.

HMS *Albion* at sea in company with HMS *Ocean*, RFAs *Oakleaf* and *Fort Rosalie*, HMS *Sutherland* and HMS *Marlborough* during Exercise Aurora 2004. (*RN*)

1942 Russian Convoy PQ 13

A gale scattered this convoy as it was bound for Russia. By 27 March not one merchant ship was in sight of the escort. Enemy aircraft sighted and on 28th sank two merchant ships. Three German destroyers sailed from Kirkenes to attack and early on 29th they caught a Panamanian freighter. From her crew they learned where the rest of the convoy might be, and altered their sweep. Just before 0900 they came across the cruiser *Trinidad* and the destroyers *Fury* and *Eclipse*. There was a sharp action in low visibility, snow and freezing spray. One German destroyer was sunk, but *Trinidad* was hit by a torpedo. After she had reached the Kola Inlet on 30th, it was found that it was one of her own torpedoes that had circled back at her. *Eclipse* was also badly hit, but *Fury* managed to sink U-585. This was the first Russian convoy to suffer large casualties (five out of nineteen merchantmen).

The *Trinidad* sailed for UK on 13 May, and suffered heavy air attack. Late on 14th she was hit by a bomb and was flooded by near misses blowing off repair patches. Despite a 14° list she continued at 20 knots and manoeuvred to avoid torpedoes. At 0120 the next morning she was abandoned, and sunk by *Matchless* (73.37N, 23.27E)

2000 RFA *Fort George*, oiler/replenishment ship, arrived at Mozambique to provide relief to flood victims, using ship's boats and Sea King helicopters of 820 NAS.

2004 Hull of frigate *Scylla*, the last warship built in a Royal Dockyard, scuttled in Whitsand Bay, west of Plymouth, to form an artificial reef for recreational diving.

See 8 August 1968.

28 March

1696 Act for the increase and encouragement of seamen passed.

1760 *Penguin* taken by the French *Malicieuse* and *Opale* near the Isles Cies, at the entrance to Vigo Bay.

1779 *Kite* fought a French frigate off Portland.

1795 *Cerberus* and *Santa Margarita* captured the French *Jean-Bart* off Brest.

1806 *Niobe* captured the French *Nearque* off Lorient.

1814 *Phoebe* and *Cherub* captured the American *Essex* and *Essex Junior* off Valparaiso.
Battle Honour: *Essex* 1814

1860 VC: LS William Odgers (*Niger*). First to enter the pah and haul down enemy's colours at Omata, New Zealand. This engagement was the start of the second, six-year operation against the Maoris. Medal: New Zealand, 1860–6.
Battle Honour: New Zealand 1860–61.

1868 ERAs established.
See 21 March 1983, 21 December 1983.

1903 Engineers given military rank, but not status.

1916 Battleship *Zealandia*, first ship to pass through the Lock and to dry dock at Rosyth.
See 17 March 1916.

1933 Lt-Cdr Roland Leeds RN of the light cruiser *Durban*, flagship of Cdre R.H.O. Lane-Poole RN, commanding the South American Division of the America and West Indies Squadron, died ashore in Valparaiso. In accordance with his last wish, he was buried at sea; this was done with full naval honours by the Chilean Navy from the destroyer leader *Almirante Uriba* ex-HMS *Broke*. In September 1955 a trawler brought up the lead coffin in her nets and landed it at Valparaiso. The Chilean Navy later took Cdr Leeds back to sea and committed his body to the deep.
See 21 April 1917.

1940 *Transylvania* (AMC) intercepted *Mimi Horn* in Denmark Strait. *Mimi Horn* later scuttled. She was the fifth and final German blockade runner destroyed in March, trying to return home.

1941 Battle of Cape Matapan (35.25N, 21E). Admiral Sir Andrew Cunningham (*Warspite*) defeated the Italian Fleet under Admiral Angelo Iachino (*Vittoria Veneto*). 'Never was a naval victory more desperately needed or more thirstily received' – Ollard. Ships: *Ajax, Barham, Formidable, Gloucester, Orion, Perth* (RAN), *Valiant, Warspite*. 2nd DF: *Hasty, Hereward, Ilex, Vendetta* (RAN). 10th DF: *Greyhound, Griffin, Havock, Hotspur, Stuart* (RAN), *Defender*. 14th DF: *Janus, Jervis, Mohawk, Nubian, Jaguar, Juno*. FAA Sqns: Shipborne Swordfish and Walrus: 700. Carrier-borne Fulmar, Albacore and Swordfish: 803, 806, 826, 829. Swordfish from Maleme, Crete: 815. RAF Sqns: 84, 113, 211 and 201 Group (flying-boats). Sunk: *Fiume, Pola, Zara* (cruisers); *Vittorio Alfieri, Giosue Carducci* (destroyers). On the fleet returning to Alexandria, Cunningham ordered services of thanksgiving to be held.
Battle Honour: Matapan 1941.
See 1 August 1798, 21 November 1918, 29 March 1951, p.179 panel.

1942 VC: Cdr Rupert Edward Dudley Ryder (MGB 314), Lt-Cdr Stephen Halden Beattie (*Campbeltown*), AB William Alfred Savage (MGB 314), Lt-Col Augustus Charles Newman (Essex Regiment), Sgt Thomas Frank Durrant, RE (ML 306). Savage and Durrant awarded posthumously. Attack on St Nazaire by light forces under Cdr R.E.D. Ryder (MGB 314) and Commandos under Lt-Col A.C. Newman. Destruction of lock gates of the Normandie dock. Operation Chariot. Ships: *Atherstone, Campbeltown, Tynedale*, MGB 314, MTB 74, ML: 156, 160, 177, 192, 262, 267, 268, 270, 298, 306, 307, 341, 443, 446, 447, 457. RAF: Aircraft from No. 19 Group.
Battle Honour: St Nazaire 1942.
See p.180.

1942 Admiral Sir James Somerville, still on the Retired List, hoisted his flag in battleship *Warspite* at Colombo as C-in-C Eastern Fleet.
See 28 June 1940, 5 and 9 April 1942, 3 August 1944, 19 March 1949.

Lt-Cdr David Howard RN, CO of 736 NAS, and his Observer, Lt Peter Matthews RN, met by Capt A.B.B. Clark RN, CO of RNAS Brawdy, on their return to the station on 28 March 1967 after bombing the tanker *Torrey Canyon* stranded on the Seven Sisters reef off Land's End. (*Author*)

1943 Hudsons L/48, V/48 and L/233 attacked U-77 in W. Mediterranean (37.42N, 00.10E). She sank on the 29th.

1943 Royal Dockyard Schools, established by Order in Council in 1843, celebrated their centenary. First Lord of the Admiralty, Mr A.V. Alexander, presented the annual prizes at Portsmouth. In founding the dockyard schools, and making attendance obligatory, the Admiralty anticipated by twenty-seven years the adoption of state education.

1944 Submarine *Syrtis* sunk by mine off Bodø, Norway.

1952 Two MTBs exercising with the RNlN collided 30 miles off the Hook of Holland. MTB 1030 foundered; MTB 1032 towed into Rotterdam.

1967 Fleet Air Arm Buccaneer aircraft from 736 NAS and 800 NAS operating from RNAS Brawdy bombed and set on fire the stranded 61,000-ton tanker *Torrey Canyon* aground for ten days on the Seven Stones reef between Land's End and the Scillies (Channel Pilot: 50.02N, 06.07W). Destroyers *Barrosa* and *Delight* patrolled a 7-mile exclusion zone. Seven Stones lightship towed into Mounts Bay.

1996 Bell-bottoms with seven horizontal creases, applied with the trousers turned inside out, disappeared. Flared trousers were introduced with up-and-down creases and were retained after uniform review.

2003 RFA *Sir Galahad*, landing ship, entered the newly captured port of Umm Qasr carrying the first shipload of humanitarian aid into Iraq following US and UK action. Operation Telic.

2003 Production of *Daring*, the first of the Type 45 air-defence destroyers, formally begun 'first steel cut' by Lord Bach, Defence Procurement Minister, at BAE Systems, Glasgow.

See 10 December 2008, 28 January 2009.

2006 The last Sea Harrier FA2 squadron, 801 NAS, paid off at RNAS Yeovilton, having completed operational flying on 9 March.

See 27 November 1978, 28 February 2006, 24 November 2010.

29 March

1681 *Adventure* and *Calabash* engaged the Algerine *Golden Horse* 25 miles S.W. of Cape de Gata, S. coast of Spain: she surrendered to *Nonsuch*. Battle Honour: *Golden Horse* 1681.

1745 *Anglesea* taken by the French *Apollon* off Kinsale, having piped the hands to dinner, assuming *Apollon* to be her consort *Augusta*. Her Captain was killed in the action and the surviving Second Lieutenant, who surrendered, was court-martialled and shot.

1779 *Kite* fought a French 20-gun privateer 30 miles S.W. of Needles Point.

1797 *Kingfisher* captured the French privateer *Général* 40 miles W.S.W. of Oporto.

1798 Rear-Admiral Sir Horatio Nelson hoisted his flag in *Vanguard*.

See 21 May 1998.

1843 Two boats of *Nimrod* with *Assyria* (Hon. East India Company steamer), in the Indus River during the conquest of Sind.

1883 Completion of *Agamemnon* (third of the name) and, next day, of the fifth *Ajax*, last battleships to be armed with rifled, muzzle-loading guns and first to have a specific secondary armament.

1920 Battlecruiser *Hood* commissioned at Rosyth with a high proportion of officers and men from the battlecruiser *Lion* which had paid off. She sailed south from Rosyth on 15 May, hoisted the flag of Rear-Admiral Sir Roger Keyes in Cawsand Bay and entered Plymouth Sound, her home port for the first ten years. The heaviest RN warship at the time, still the longest ever built and the Navy's 16th and last battlecruiser.

See 24 May 1941.

1942 German attack on convoy PQ 13. *Trinidad* and *Eclipse* sank the German Z-26 off Murmansk (72.15N, 34.22E). *Trinidad* torpedoed herself but reached Murmansk.

1943 Submarine *Unrivalled* sank the German Uj-2201 and Uj-2204 at Palermo.

Battle of Matapan – 28 March 1941

British convoys were being run to support fighting in Greece. The C-in-C received warning of sorties by the Italian Fleet against them. He cleared the area of convoys, and sent four cruisers and three destroyers to be off Gavdo Island by first light 28 March. At noon on 27th, an RAF reconnaissance aircraft sighted three enemy cruisers 320 miles W. of Crete. That evening the British main force of three battleships, an aircraft carrier and nine destroyers sailed. The original force of cruisers and destroyers under Vice-Admiral Light Forces (VALF) was ordered to join them. At dawn on 28th, air searches revealed the enemy force near VALF's force. Shortly afterwards, VALF sighted them, as well as another enemy force, which included a battleship, to the north. At 1230 the two British forces joined in pursuit of the enemy, whose forces were all proceeding westward at speed. Air strikes were unsuccessful until 1530 when a torpedo hit slowed the enemy battleship (*Vittorio Veneto*). A further strike brought the cruiser *Pola* to a standstill. There were a total of nine air strikes from RAF and FAA aircraft (shore and sea-based) and these two hits were the only successes.

At 1830 the Italian admiral detached the cruisers *Zara* and *Fiume* with destroyers to escort the *Pola*, believing the British to be further east. VALF had been detached to chase the main force and passed the *Pola* at 2100, leaving her to the slower battle fleet. It was a dark and cloudy night, with visibility 2½ miles. At 2200 *Valiant* detected *Pola* on radar, and the battle fleet closed. At 2220 the battle fleet detected the returning Italian force, and opened fire at 3,000yd range, sinking the *Zara* and *Fiume*. The destroyers *Stuart*, *Greyhound*, *Griffin* and *Havock* sank two Italian destroyers and the *Jervis* and *Nubian* sank the *Pola* after taking off many of the ship's company.

Contact with the enemy's main force was not regained, and the convoys were restarted. The Italians lost three cruisers and two destroyers, with one battleship damaged; the British lost one aircraft. The action took place 100 miles S.W. of Cape Matapan.

Capt Philip Kelly, first RM fixed-wing pilot to qualify for forty years, 2001. (*RN*)

1944 Sloop *Starling* sank U-961 E.S.E. of Faroes (64.31N, 03.19W). Convoy JW 58.

1945 Liberator O/224 sank U-1106 off Shetland (61.46N, 02.16W).

1945 RCN frigate *Teme*, torpedoed by U-246 6 miles N.W. of Land's End. Towed to Falmouth but, with her stern blown off, she was a CTL. The submarine had a short time to savour its success. Within hours she was located and destroyed by the frigate *Duckworth* (49.58N, 05.25W).

1951 Admiral of the Fleet Viscount Cunningham's memoirs, *A Sailor's Odyssey*, published at a Foyle's literary luncheon presided over by Lord Hall, First Lord of the Admiralty; the tenth anniversary of Matapan.

1968 The beginning of the end of the fathom. The first of the new metric Admiralty charts, No. 3105 of Chiba Ko in Tokyo Bay, published, with depths and heights shown in metres and decimeters. This was followed on 5 April by Chart 2247 of ports in the Black Sea, and on 12 April by Chart 438 of Boulogne.

See 25 May 1801, 15 November 1919.

1996 RM School of Music, Deal, closed and band training moved to old RNDQs in Portsmouth Dockyard. RM at Deal since 1861.

See 8 May 1861.

1996 *Daedalus*, RNAS Lee-on-Solent, paid off. First opened as a seaplane school in 1917.

See 15 March 1957.

2001 Capt Philip Michael Kelly RM qualified as a Sea Harrier pilot, the first RM fixed-wing pilot to qualify for forty years.

See 14 February 1969.

St Nazaire – 28 March 1942

St Nazaire had the only dock on the Atlantic seaboard in German hands where the battleship *Tirpitz* could be docked. It was 1,148ft by 164ft and had been built for the liner *Normandie*. A surprise attack was mounted to damage this dock in case the Germans should decide to use *Tirpitz* on commerce raiding as they had with the *Bismarck*. An ex-USN destroyer, the *Campbeltown*, was modified to cross shallow sandbanks and to ram the dock caisson. She was escorted by an MGB, an MTB (in case the *Campbeltown* failed to make the caisson) and sixteen MLs with commandos. A U-boat was attacked on passage, and the force temporarily altered course to the south-west. The U-boat reported the force, and torpedo boats were sent to investigate; this reduced the opposition met when the force reached St Nazaire that night. The RAF raid to divert the enemy's attention had only alerted them, and low cloud made their bombing inaccurate. The force, however, crossed 400 miles of open sea, and was 3 miles up the estuary before the alarm was given, and a false identity signal allowed them more time for their last 2 miles before the enemy opened fire. *Campbeltown* rammed the lock gate at 0134 and the commandos were landed. At 0250 the force withdrew to seaward and were met by the returning German torpedo boats. Only four MLs reached home safely. The explosives in the *Campbeltown* went up late, just as a large party of German officers had boarded her. In contrast to Zeebrugge in the First World War, the objectives at St Nazaire were achieved. A working model of the raid can be seen at the Imperial War Museum, London.

30 March

1798 *Cambrian* captured the French privateer *Pont-de-Lodi* 400 miles S.W. of the Scilly Isles.

1800 *Foudroyant*, *Lion*, *Penelope* and *Vincejo* captured the french *Guillaume Tell*. Action began by *Penelope* and *Vincejo* just outside Valetta harbour, Malta, and ended 20 miles S.W. of Cape Passero, Sicily. Only *Penelope* and *Vincejo* were awarded the medal.
Battle Honour: *Guillaume Tell* 1800.

1811 *Arrow* engaged the battery at St Nicholas, to the northward of Ile de Ré, and captured the French chassemarées *Frederick* and *Paix Desirée*.

1837 Original Royal Navy College, Portsmouth, closed.

1856 Treaty of Paris signed: end of the Russian 'Crimean' War.

See 27 March 1854, 23 April 1856.

1912 Capt Robert Falcon Scott RN and the remainder of his party died in the Antarctic. 'It seems a pity but I do not think I can write more.' 'For God's sake, look after our people.'

See 6 June 1868, 17 February 1912, 17 March 1912, 10 February 1913.

1943 Light cruiser *Glasgow* intercepted the German blockade runner *Regensburg*, from Rangoon. German vessel scuttled in N. Atlantic.

1944 Destroyer *Laforey* torpedoed and sunk by U-223 at the end of a five-hour hunt off Palermo. Last RN vessel to be sunk by S/M in Mediterranean. *Tumult*, *Blencathra* and *Hambledon* sank U-223 (38.45N, 14.18E).

1945 Frigates *Conn*, *Rupert* and *Deane* sank U-965 off Point of Stoer, Hebrides (58.19N, 05.31W).

1959 HM Dockyard, Malta, transferred to Bailey (Malta) Ltd. on a £30,000 per annum lease expiring on 29 March 2058. Post of Admiral Superintendent Malta (Rear-Admiral J. Lee-Barber) lapsed and authority for all naval purposes passed to Flag Officer Malta.

In ceremony previous day in the Red State Room of the Palace in Valletta, Rear-Admiral Nicholas Copeman, Fourth Sea Lord, accompanied by Sir John Lang, Secretary of the Admiralty, presented a 1ft-long brass key in the shape of a foul anchor, made by Maltese craftsmen, to the Governor, Sir Robert Laycock, who passed it

The *Guillaume Tell* (80) engaged by the *Penelope* (36) under command of Henry Blackwood (1770–1832), 1800. (*NMRN 1987/222*)

The Type 23 frigate HMS *Westminster*, Cdr Tim Green RN, was paying an official visit to London in 2011 when she was sailed in short order to the Mediterranean to support the British response to UNSCR 1973 following the insurrection in Libya. The ship is shown alongside in Grand Harbour, Valletta. (*RN*)

to Group Captain G.B. Bailey, Chairman of Bailey (Malta) Ltd.

See 27 February 1959, 30 March 1979, 1 January 1985.

1960 Boom and Salvage Depot, Sheerness, closed, 'after which date any correspondence or signals concerning Boom and Salvage matters should be addressed to the Commander-in-Chief The Nore'. AFO 696/60.

See 23 and 31 March 1960.

1971 The first 383 Fleet Chief Petty Officers announced to take effect from 30 September 1971.

See 24 May 1971.

Youngest were Chief Radio Electrical Mechanician (Air) R. Parsons (32), HMS *Heron*, who entered in 1955, and Chief Control Electrical Artificer B. Baxter (34), HMS *Eastbourne*. Among the oldest chiefs promoted were Chief Electrical Artificer (Air) R. Temple (55), serving in Singapore, and Regulating Chief Marine Engineering Artificer L. Watson (54) of the depot ship HMS *Tyne*. The most senior to be promoted was Chief Electrician (Air) W. Lamb, staff of FONAC, who had been a Chief since 1946. The first Chief Wren promoted was Beatrice Willis of the Cash Clothing Store at HMS *Neptune*, who joined the WRNS in 1947 and was promoted chief wren in 1955.

1976 HMS *Mauritius* on Mauritius paid off, having ceased to operate as a Main Communications Centre in the Defence Communications Network on 30 November 1975. DCI(RN)T2.

See 15 October 1957, 16 and 28 February 1962.

2001 HMS *Cambridge*, RN Gunnery Range at Wembury, near Plymouth, paid off by Capt Andrew Welch RN. Rear-Admiral John Chadwick, FOTR, took the salute at ceremonial divisions. Range commissioned 9 August 1956, a century to the day after the *Cambridge*, third rate, was first employed as a gunnery training ship at Devonport. Gunnery training transferred to the MWS at *Collingwood* and naval military training to *Raleigh*. *Cambridge* site sold to the National Trust.

See 30 June 1958, 4 January 1983.

2006 800 NAS re-commissioned at RAF Cottesmore as part of the re-brigaded RN/RAF Joint Force Harrier. Initially equipped with Harrier GR7/7A to be followed by Harrier GR9/9A.

See 28 March 2006, 24 November 2010.

31 March

1804 *Apollo* (38), with convoy of forty, went ashore in gale off Cape Mondago, Portugal with most of her charges.

1804 Boats of *Beaver* and *Scorpion* cut out the Dutch *Athalante* in Vlie Road, Netherlands.
Battle Honour: *Athalante* 1804.

1813 Boats of *Redwing*, *Undaunted* and *Volontaire* captured eleven and destroyed three sail of a French convoy at Morgiou, between Marseilles and Toulon, and also destroyed two batteries.

1823 Boats of *Thracian* and *Tyne* cut out the pirate *Zaragozana* in Puerto de Mata, Cuba.

1885 Following trials started in *Medway* in 1880, the RN had acquired 565 Nordenfelt guns, firing 1-in shot, plus 350 Gardner and 142 Gatling guns, developed mainly for rapid fire against small and fast-moving targets such as the evolving torpedo boats.

1941 Light cruiser *Bonaventure* sunk by the Italian S/M *Ambra* 90 miles S. of Crete. Convoy GA 8.

1941 Submarine *Rorqual* sank the Italian submarine *Capponi* 90 miles S. of Stromboli (33.20N, 26.35E).

1942 Allied shipping losses in March reached ½ million tons, mostly from U-boat attack.

1943 Royal Naval College Dartmouth vacated by RN for use by US Navy for Operation Overlord planning from 1 January 1944.
See 16 April 1953.

1951 Bermuda Dockyard closed and became a 'fleet anchorage'. HMS *Malabar* paid off in a ceremony at noon attended by seven officers and twenty ratings. Bermuda to remain HQ of America and West Indies Station.
See 1 June 1965, 31 March 1995.

1951 Distinctive rank lace for officers of the RNR (intertwined) and RNVR (wavy) discontinued and replaced by RN straight stripes with R in the curl; RNVR Air Branch to wear A in curl. Former RNVR wavy lace to be worn only by SCC and CCF officers. RNR and RNVR distinguishing buttons, withdrawn in 1922, reintroduced, but briefly.
See 1 January 1952, 1 July 2007.

1956 HMS *Siskin*, RNAS Gosport, paid off and following day commissioned as HMS *Sultan* as a TE for ratings of the Mechanical Engineering Branch. The new establishment was named after the old ironclad *Sultan* which served until 1943 as the RN mechanical training ship in Portsmouth Harbour.

1957 Ships launched in the year ended 31 March 1957:

Submarines *Porpoise* and *Rorqual*; frigates *Blackpool* and *Palliser*; coastal minesweepers *Ashton*, *Dartington*, *Maxton*, *Nurton*, *Puncheston*, *Soberton*, *Stubbington*, *Thankerton*, *Wolverton*, *Walkerton*, *Wilkieston* and *Wotton*; inshore minesweepers *Hovingham*,

Gatling-gun drill in the 1880s. (*NMRN*)

Georgeham, Fordham, Nettleham, Puttenham, Rackham, Thornham; seaward defence boat *Tilford*; fast patrol boats *Dark Killer, Dark Gladiator, Dark Hero* and *Dark Hunter*; and tugs *Dexterous* and *Director*.

Ships accepted into Service in year ended 31 March 1957:

Experimental submarine *Explorer*; frigates *Keppel, Lynx, Murray, Pellew, Russell, Salisbury, Torquay* and *Whitby*; coastal minesweepers *Aldington, Blaxton, Bossington, Carhampton, Jackton, Lullington, Maddiston, Maxton, Monkton, Picton, Sheraton, Singleton, Somerleyton, Upton*; inshore minesweepers *Fordham, Hovingham, Odiham, Rackham, Saxlingham, Shrivenham* and *Warmingham*; fast patrol boats *Dark Avenger, Dark Hunter, Dark Killer* and *Dark Rover*; tugs *Confident* and *Director*.

1958 The submarine depot ship *Maidstone* arrived at Portsmouth after taking part in the Home Fleet Spring Cruise and paid off after twenty years' continuous service in a single commission embracing the war in the Mediterranean and Pacific and peace-time duty with the Home Fleet.

1958 Humber Division RNVR paid off. AFO 1157/58.

1960 HM Dockyard, Sheerness, closed and post of Captain-in-Charge and Captain Superintendent Sheerness terminated. Sheerness telephone exchange closed at 2359. Last Captain-in-Charge and Captain Superintendent, Capt P.M.B. Chavasse DSC, RN (appointed 15 October 1957). 'To Sheerness, where we walked up and down, laying out the ground to be taken in [hand] for a yard, to lay provisions for cleaning and repairing of ships; and a most proper place it is for the purpose' – Pepys, 18 August 1665. AFO 696/60.

See 23 and 30 March 1960.

1961 The Nore Command closed. The 83rd C-in-C The Nore, Admiral Sir Robin Durnford-Slater ('Commander-in-Chief of Her Majesty's Ships and Naval Vessels in the rivers Thames and Medway and at the buoy at The Nore') hauled down his flag. Command established in 1752.

See 9 July 1958, 24 March 1961, 30 September 1983, 28 June 1984.

1961 Sir Clifford Jarrett succeeded Sir John Lang as Secretary of the Admiralty.

1964 The Lords Commissioners of the Admiralty hauled down their crimson flag with the horizontal gold fouled-anchor which had flown continuously over the Admiralty building (half-masted only on the death of the Sovereign) and the Monarch resumed the title of Lord High Admiral of the United Kingdom. Their Lordships were present as a naval guard presented arms on Horse Guards Parade and a Royal Marine band played 'Auld Lang Syne'. The Board of Admiralty continued as the Admiralty Board of the Defence Council.

See 9 June 1832, 19 and 26 March 1964.

1969 First operational Phantom squadron, 892 NAS, commanded by Lt-Cdr Brian Davies, commissioned at Yeovilton.

See 14 June 1970.

1969 HM Boom Defence Depot, Loyang, Singapore, closed and task transferred to Command Salvage and Mooring Officer, Captain of the Yard's Department, Singapore Dockyard. DCI(RN) 1221/68 and 382/69

1969 The last RN ships based on Malta, the Sixth MCM Squadron, sailed from Manoel Island.

1976 The last Hong Kong guardship, the aircraft direction frigate *Chichester*, Cdr R.P. Warwick RN, left the colony for home. In her three years' service there, forty-nine children had been born to families of the ship's company.

1977 HM Oil Fuel Depot, Lyness, Orkney, closed. The last RN establishment at Scapa Flow. DCI(RN) 138/77.

See 30 July 1976, 31 March 1978, 12 November 1982, 31 December 1983.

1978 The Admiralty oil fuel storage sites at Llanion and Llanreath, two of the three sites comprising HM Oil Fuel Depot, Pembroke Dock, closed. DCI(RN) 55/78.

See 31 December 1983.

1979 The flag of Rear-Admiral O.N.A. Cecil, the last Flag Officer Malta, hauled down at midnight at *St Angelo* by Radio Operator David Gilchrist.

HMS *Vigilant* (1900), a destroyer of 400 tons. (*NMRN*)

Admiral Cecil had been asked to wear plain clothes and Gilchrist was the only member of the British party in uniform. Mr Dom Mintoff, Prime Minister of Malta, and Col Gaddafi, President of Libya, were present. Admiral Cecil sailed from Grand Harbour in the destroyer *London*. The Queen's Colour of the Mediterranean Fleet, laid up in the Chapel of HMS *St Angelo* in 1967, was transferred to the Chapel of the RN College, Greenwich, where it now lies.

See 30 October 1956, 7 September 1958 (C-in-C East Indies), 31 March 1961 (C-in-C The Nore), 31 March 1964 (Admiralty), 11 April 1967 (C-in-C S Atlantic), 5 June 1967 (C-in-C Mediterranean), 26 May 1969 (C-in-C Plymouth), 25 July 1967, 7 July 1975, 19 June 1979, 30 September 1983 (FO Medway), 29 May 2005.

1980 First Sea Harrier squadron – NAS 800 – commissioned at RNAS Yeovilton. DCI(RN) 146/80.

1984 Chatham Dockyard closed, ending 437 years of Royal Navy presence in Chatham. Chatham Historic Dockyard Trust assumed responsibility for 80 acres of the Georgian dockyard on 1 April and opened to the public in April 1985.

1986 *Vernon* paid off. Became *Nelson* (Vernon Site) then *Nelson* (Gunwharf) in 1987. RN retained use of site until 31 March 1991.

See 26 April 1876, 1 October 1923.

1991 The RN Armaments Depot, Newton Noyes, Milford Haven, closed after fifty-two years, the explosive storage and mining tasks having been transferred to RNAD Trecwn in N. Pembrokeshire. DCI(RN) 2/91.

1992 Kit Upkeep Allowance (KUA) abolished, after seventy-five years.

1992 'Surplice' to requirements. The RNR Chaplains' Branch disbanded after nearly ninety years' service; Branch re-formed 1 January 2003.

1994 The RNR's 10th MCM Squadron disbanded. With the end of the operational requirement for deep armed team sweeping, the focus of the seagoing RNR changed from manning their own ships to augmenting the crews of RN ships. *Arun*, *Spey* and *Itchen* transferred to the Northern Ireland Squadron; *Orwell* replaced *Wilton* as the Dartmouth Navigation Training Ship; *Carron*, *Dovey*, *Helford*, *Humber* and *Waveney* transferred to Defence Sales on 12 November 1993. DCI(RN) 5/94.

1994 *Centurion*, Naval Drafting HQ at Gosport, paid off. Became Centurion Building, tender to *Sultan*.
See 5 April 1957, 16 October 1970.

1995 The end of the title Flag Officer Royal Yachts. Rear-Admiral R.N. Woodard, FORY, succeeded by Cdre A.J.C. Morrow who was the only officer to hold the title Commodore Royal Yachts (CORY) before HMY *Britannia* paid off. DCI(RN) 83/95.
See 7 February 1983, 11 December 1997.

1995 HMS *Malabar*, HM Naval Base on Ireland Island, Bermuda, paid off for the second time.
See 31 March 1951, 1 June 1965, 1 April 1976.

1995 Portland Naval Base closed.

1995 The RN Hospital, Plymouth, closed on 31 March 1995 after 233 years' continuous service. DCI(RN) 243/94.
See 14 June 1758, 13 March 1762, 29 June 1962.

1996 *Cochrane* at Rosyth paid off.

1996 The last admiral commanding inside the old dockyard walls at Portsmouth, Flag Officer Portsmouth and Naval Base Commander Portsmouth, Rear-Admiral Neil Rankin, hauled down his flag and was succeeded by Cdre Iain Henderson RN in the single post of Naval Base Commander, Portsmouth.
See 1 October 1984.

1999 *Warrior*, shore headquarters successively of the C-in-C Home Fleet, C-in-C Western Fleet and C-in-C Fleet at Northwood since 1963, paid off and continued as Joint Services Unit Northwood. Remained under CINCFLEET command until 1 April 2002 when, most Fleet HQ divisions having transferred to Whale Island, command was transferred to the Chief of Joint Operations at Permanent Joint Headquarters, Northwood.
See 31 December 1959, 30 April 1963, 1 April 1996.

1999 *Osprey*, Portland, which closed to flying on 12 February 1999, paid off and became a tender to *Heron*. FOST had moved to *Drake*, Devonport, on 21 July 1995.
See 24 April 1959.

1999 SD Officers List abolished. All officers, ex-lower deck and direct entry, entered on common list.

2006 Alan Pearsall, ISO, naval historian, gentle scholar and stalwart of the National Maritime Museum, died at Woolwich.

2006 The Second Sea Lord and C-in-C Naval Home Command, Vice-Admiral Adrian Johns, moved his HQ from Victory Building, Portsmouth Naval Base, and into Leach Building, Whale Island, on 1 April. The only remaining admiral within the old dockyard was Rear-Admiral K.J. Borley, FOTR.

2006 The last Sea Harrier withdrawn from service.

2008 RMAS disbanded and all marine services for the RN contracted out. RMAS ensign hauled down in low-key ceremony at RMAS HQ, Pembroke Dock, and in the salvage vessel *Moorhen* and at South Railway Jetty, where the Last Post was sounded by RM buglers. Ensign to be preserved in Semaphore Tower.
See 1 September 1970, 1 October 1976.

2011 *Caroline*, former light cruiser and the last RN ship to serve at Jutland, paid off for disposal. Lately HQ ship of Ulster Division RNR.

1 April

1694 *Paramour Pink* launched at Deptford: first naval surveying ship designed and built as such. Intended for Halley.

1761 *Isis* (50) captured the French *Oriflamme* (40) off Cape Tres Forcas.

1791 George Vancouver sailed from Falmouth in the sloop *Discovery*, with *Chatham*, in command of an expedition to survey the north-west coast of North America. Vancouver, who had sailed in Cook's second and third voyages, sighted Californian coast 18 April 1792. Determined the insularity of Vancouver Island. Returned to the Thames in October 1795.

See 29 November 1791.

1853 Introduction of Continuous Service for ratings.

1853 First provision for lower-deck pensions, after twenty-two years' service.

1855 Paymasters recognised as accountant officers for public money and made responsible for it to the Accountant-General and no longer solely responsible to the Controller of Victualling.

1857 Boats of *Auckland* (IN) captured a mandarin junk and stormed a battery in Tung Chung Bay, near Hong Kong.

1857 Occupation of Ahwaz, Persia, by an Indian Navy flotilla and detachments of the 64th Regiment and 78th Highlanders. Vessels (IN): *Assyria, Comet, Planet*. Gunboats Nos 5, 6 and 9, and boats of *Assaye, Falkland* and *Ferooz*.

1859 Capt Mansfield Cumming, RN, born, founder and first director in 1909 of the Secret Service Bureau, later MI6 and the Secret Intelligence Service. His code name C and use of green ink adopted by all later Directors of the Secret Intelligence Service.

1883 Naval Nursing Service formed. Became QARNNS in 1902.

See 6 March 1902.

1892 RN Artillery Volunteers disbanded: sixty-nine officers and 1,849 men.

1916 East coast of England attacked by German airships. L-15, first Zeppelin brought down by shore gunfire, landed in the Thames estuary and surrendered to *Olivine*.

1918 Destroyer *Falcon* lost in collision with trawler *John Fitzgerald* in North Sea.

1918 Transfer of 2,500 aircraft and 55,000 personnel from RN Air Service on its amalgamation with the Royal Flying Corps to form the Royal Air Force. The RAF controlled naval aviation for the next twenty-one years.

1921 RNVR reconstituted.

1923 Naval responsibility for HM Coastguard, accepted in 1856, transferred to Board of Trade.

1924 Former light cruiser *Caroline* became drill-ship of Ulster Division, RNVR. Now the last survivor of Jutland.

1924 Shipborne element of RAF recognised as Fleet Air Arm.

1931 *Glorious*, aircraft carrier, collided in fog with the French liner *Florida* off Gibraltar. The *Florida*, which lost twenty-four passengers and crew, was towed stern-first to Malaga by the destroyers *Verity* and *Wryneck*, escorted by *Glorious* which had taken off survivors.

See 8 June 1940.

1935 Salaries of the naval members of the Board of Admiralty were regularised by Order in Council. Commissioners had hitherto received the half pay of their ranks and also a commissioner's salary which was correspondingly low. In 1934 the First Sea Lord received £2,852 salary and £1,091 half pay. His consolidated salary from 1935 was £4,299. The Second Sea Lord's figures were £1,582 and £923, consolidated into £3,183. The amounts of the new salaries for these and the other Sea Lords were determined by the officer's relative position on the board and not by rank.

Royal Naval Artillery Volunteer. (*NMRN*)

1941 Swordfish of 824 Sqn disembarked from *Eagle*, wrecked the Italian destroyer *Leone* off Massawa.

1941 The Admiralty announced that His Highness the Nizam of Hyderabad had presented the Royal Indian Navy with the price of a corvette to be named *Hyderabad*. The Flower-class corvette *Nettle*, then building, was renamed on 23 April 1941, launched on 23 September, and went on to gain six battle honours.

1942 Submarines *Pandora* and P 36 sunk by German aircraft at Malta. *Pandora* was beached in Kalkara Creek and her wreck was sold in 1957. That June shipbreakers found the remains of two of her men. The submarine's former CO, Capt R.L. Alexander (by then Captain(D) 1st Destroyer Flotilla, Mediterranean Fleet), was present when their remains were committed to the sea 4 miles off Grand Harbour from the submarine *Tudor* on 1 July. P 36 was raised in 1958 and sunk in deep water.

1942 Submarine *Urge* sank the Italian cruiser *Giovanni delle Bande Nere* in the Mediterranean, 11 miles S.E. of Stromboli.The last of four sister ships sunk by RN.

See 19 July 1940, 13 December 1941.

1944 Destroyer *Beagle* and Avenger H/846 (*Tracker*) sank U-355 off N. Norway. Convoy JW 58.

1945 Aircraft carrier *Indefatigable* (Task Force 57) damaged by Japanese kamikaze air strikes on Myako and Ishigaki Islands. Operations continued on the 2nd and 6th.

1952 Male regular strength of the Royal Navy 135,500. (Army 214,800; RAF 171,500).

Source: *Brassey's Annual*, 1954, p.380.

1953 Male regular strength of the Royal Navy 133,700. (Army 211,300; RAF 188,900).

1956 After more than three centuries the rating of 'Boy' disappeared from ships' books and was replaced by Junior Rating. This method of entry, previously limited to the Seaman Branch, extended to the Engineering and Electrical Branches and FAA. AFO 963/56.

See 1 April 1999.

1958 *Ceres*, RN Supply and Secretariat School, Wetherby, Yorkshire, moved to *Pembroke*, RN Barracks, Chatham.

See 14 March 1958, 14 April 1958.

1958 RN Hospital, Great Yarmouth, transferred to Ministry of Health and to be known as St Nicholas Hospital. AFO 1205/58.

1961 Rear-Admiral Isaac William Trant Beloe appointed first Flag Officer Medway and Admiral Superintendent of Chatham Dockyard the day after the demise of The Nore Command.

1963 The Royal Navy took over BMH Gibraltar; henceforth RNH Gibraltar. AFO 773/63.

See 3 May 2008.

1964 Stores Accountant rating introduced and Catering Branch reorganised.

1964 Unified Ministry of Defence established. Defence (Transfer of Functions) Act 1964.

1964 Lovat uniforms with bronze buttons introduced for Royal Marines to replace khaki battledress.

1966 Director of Victualling assumed tri-service responsibility for procurement, storage and distribution of foodstuffs.

1968 Cooks (O) and (S) amalgamated into one category.

1968 Coxswain and Regulating Branches amalgamated.
See 15 September 1967.

1970 Badge pay abolished.

1971 *Goldcrest*, RNAS Brawdy, Pembrokeshire, paid off. Transferred to RAF. White Ensign hauled down, 31 May 1971. DCI (RN) 316/71.

1974 Aircrewman Branch of Fleet Air Arm formed at RNAS Portland.

1976 Cdre B.J. Straker RN, hauled down his broad pennant as SNOWI at HMS *Malabar*, Ireland Island, Bermuda, and was succeeded by Cdr D.I. Aldrich RN as Senior British Officer Bermuda, CO HMS *Malabar*, RNO Bermuda and Deputy Island Commander Bermuda. The SOO and Flag Lt to SNOWI was Cdr P.C. Abbott RN (CINCFLEET 1995).
See 31 March 1951, 1 June 1965, 31 March 1995.

Admiral The Lord Boyce, installed as Lord Warden and Admiral of the Cinque Ports and Constable of Dover Castle in 2005, the first sea officer since Robert Blake to hold this appointment. See 12 April 2005 (2 Inf. Bde). (*RN*)

1989 Admiralty Board decided that WRNS personnel should in future be trained to carry personal weapons for defensive purposes. To become effective for all new entrants to the WRNS from 1 April 1989. DCI(RN) 369/88, 352/89.

1990 Hydrographic Office became a Defence Support Agency within the MOD. The Hydrographer of the Navy became the Chief Executive of the Hydrographic Agency. DCI(RN) 89/90.
See 3 January 2001.

1992 Communications Centre Whitehall (CCW) commissioned as *St Vincent*; OC CCW became CO *St Vincent*. Paid off 31 March 1998.
Name transferred from Furze House, Queen's Gate Terrace, London, bought in 1954 as WRNS accommodation, commissioned as *St Vincent* on 15 September 1983 and paid off 31 March 1992. DCI(RN) 105/92.

1992 WRNS officers and ratings adopted gold lace and gold and red badges respectively.

1994 Whale Island recommissioned as *Excellent*. Commissioning ceremony held on 18 March 1994. DCI(RN) 21/94.

1994 Closure of HQ Commando Forces RM and HQ Training and Reserve Forces RM. Department of CGRM in London moved to *Nelson* (Gunwharf) in Portsmouth, formerly *Vernon*.

1994 RNXS disbanded.
See 6 December 1952, 18 January 1963, 17 June 1993.

1994 FOSNI became FOSNNI (Flag Officer Scotland, Northern England and Northern Ireland).
See 5 March 1996.

1994 The posts of Second Sea Lord and C-in-C Naval Home Command amalgamated to create a single Principal Personnel Officer for the Royal Navy. When Admiral Sir John Kerr,

CINCNAVHOME, hauled down his flag in *Victory* on 31 March 1993, Vice-Admiral Sir Michael Layard, Second Sea Lord, assumed the additional title of CINCNAVHOME. Admiral Sir Michael Boyce succeeded to the combined appointment in May 1995.

1996 Permanent Joint Headquarters (PJHQ) established at *Warrior*, Northwood, under a three-star Chief of Joint Operations, to plan and mount joint, and potentially joint, overseas military operations.
See 31 March 1999.

1997 Reserve Forces Act defined employers' responsibilities to employees mobilised for service.

1998 The Revd Dr Charles Edward Stewart, Church of Scotland minister, appointed the first non-Anglican Chaplain of the Fleet.
See 23 October 1876, 11 August 1902, 17 November 1943.

Dr Stewart was appointed Director General Naval Chaplaincy Service on 18 March 1997. However, he could not become Chaplain of the Fleet until The Queen had given permission through an Order in Council. The Order (the Naval Chaplaincy Order 1997), signed on 17 December 1997, stated, 'The powers of the Defence Council to appoint, with the approval of Her Majesty, a person to hold the position of Chaplain of the Fleet shall include a power to appoint a Minister or Priest of a religious body not in conformity with the Church of England'. Dr Stewart was consequently appointed Chaplain of the Fleet in April 1998. The Order also approved, in continuance, that the Principal Anglican Chaplain (Naval) shall be granted the ecclesiastical dignity of archdeacon under the Archbishop of Canterbury, whether or not he also holds the position of Chaplain of the Fleet.

1999 Reserve Decoration (RD) replaced by the Queen's Volunteer Reserve Medal (QVRM) and the Volunteer Reserves Service Medal (VRSM), both open to all ranks and ratings. QVRM by citation and with post-nominals; VRSM after ten years' service without post-nominals.

1999 The ranks of Junior Rating, Ordinary Rating and Able Rating merged to form one generic rank of Able Rating. Ranks of Junior, Marine 2nd Class and Marine 1st Class replaced by a single rank of Marine.
See 1 April 1956.

2000 Joint appointment of Air Officer Commanding 3 Group RAF and Flag Officer Maritime Aviation established at RAF High Wycombe. Rear-Admiral Iain Henderson first and penultimate incumbent. Flag Officer Naval Aviation abolished. RN Sea Harriers, FA2, RAF Nimrod MPA and RAF SAR helicopters joined RAF GR7 aircraft to form Joint Force Harrier (JFH). Three squadrons based at Yeovilton.
See 2 April 1931, 23 March 1990.

2000 QARNNS integrated into RN.

2002 CGRM, FOMA, FOSM, COMRFA and FOSF became part of new Fleet HQ in Portsmouth under Fleet First programme. CGRM became COMUKAMPHIBFOR, retaining CGRM title and responsibilities. DCI (Gen.) 117/02.

2003 RN Supply School (RNSS) renamed RN Logistics and Supply School (RNLSS) 'in order to provide consistency with the title of the seagoing Logistics and Supply Officer and to better reflect acknowledgment that the primary function of the Supply Branch is logistic support'. – DCI(RN) 53/03.
See 1 February 2004.

2004 RN Warrant Officers to be termed WO1. Made necessary by introduction of substantive rate of WO2 for RN artificers and technicians which replaced the existing non-substantive rate of Charge Chief Petty Officer (CCPO). Change from CCPO to WO2 'recognises and addresses long-standing concerns about the status, recognition and rewards associated with the CCPO rate'. – DCI(RN) 146/03.

2004 *Dryad* at Southwick paid off and SMOPS task transferred to *Collingwood*. *Dryad* commissioned 27 September 1941. Tactical School opened 2 June 1970.
See 23 May 1972, 14 May 2004.

2007 Four new RN regional headquarters to coordinate recruiting, publicity, advertising, presentations, ship visits, RNR, RMR, cadets and Aid to Civil Power established at London, Liverpool, Bristol and Rosyth with one-star Naval Regional commanders under FOSNNI.

2 APRIL

A Memorable Date observed by Fleet-Protection Group, Royal Marines – Comacchio

1797 At 4pm 'Commodore Nelson hoisted his flag on board the *Captain* [off Cadiz] on his Promotion to the Rank of Rear-Admiral of the Blue, and saluted with 13 guns, returned 11 guns'. Nelson's promotion was dated 20 February 1797.

1801 First Battle of Copenhagen. Vice-Admiral Lord Nelson's attack on the Danish hulks and batteries. Battle Honour: Copenhagen 1801.

Ships and vessels: *Agamemnon, Alcmene, Amazon, Ardent, Arrow, Bellona, Blanche, Dart, Discovery, Defiance, Desiree, Cruizer, Edgar, Elephant, Explosion, Ganges, Glatton, Harpy, Hecla, Isis, Jamaica, Monarch, Otter, Polyphemus, Russell, Sulphur, Terror, Volcano, Zebra, Zephyr*. Ships in support: *Defence, London, Raisonnable, Ramillies, St George, Saturn, Veteran, Warrior*. Troops: Royal Artillery (bomb vessels). The 49th Foot, the Hertfordshire Regiment, later the Duke of Edinburgh's Royal Regiment, and one company of the Corps of Riflemen later the Royal Greenjackets were awarded a naval crown, superscribed '2nd April 1801, Copenhagen' on their accoutrements; this tradition discontinued when RGJ became The Rifles in 2007.

1825 Capture of Donaby, Burma by Brig-Gen Sir Archibald Cameron and the Irrawaddy Flotilla under Capt Thomas Alexander (*Alligator*).
See 25 April 1825.

1844 The Royal Navy's second *Daring*, a 12-gun brig, 130 men, undocked at Portsmouth Dockyard. She served two commissions on the North America and West Indies Station. *Daring* was in a squadron which protected British interests in the Gulf of Mexico during the American-Mexico War 1846–8. While in those waters on 10 December 1846 she saved lives from the US brig *Somers* which had capsized in a squall off the blockaded Mexican harbour of Vera Cruz for which the US government five years later awarded medals to eleven of her officers and men. Her visit in 1855 to the Turks and Caicos Islands was recorded on a 20c postage stamp issued in 1973. The ship's figurehead, depicting a typical Victorian Jack Tar, is in the National Maritime Museum.
See 27 January 1813, 22 April 1847.

1879 Maj-Gen Lord Chelmsford's column defeated the Zulus at Gingindlovu inevitably referred to as 'gin, gin, I love you'. Naval Brigade from *Boadicea, Shah* and *Tenedos*.

1889 Cordite patented for British service.

1908 *Tiger*, destroyer, built by Thomson's of Glasgow as a private venture and bought into RN, sunk in collision with cruiser *Berwick* off St Catherine's Point, Isle of Wight.

1931 Rear-Admiral R.G.H. Henderson, 'one of the most brilliant officers of his generation' (Roskill), appointed Rear Admiral Aircraft Carriers (RAA) to be responsible 'for the tactical operations of the carriers and of the carrier-borne aircraft in that [the Atlantic] Fleet' and 'the recognised Naval Adviser to other fleets on all matters connected with the Fleet Air Arm' (AM 1634 dated 20 March 1931, Office Acquaint No. 99 dated 24 August 1931). Appointment approved 12 March 1931. He later served under Chatfield as Third Sea Lord and was directly responsible for armoured flight decks. He was not the first aviation flag officer; see 19 November 1917.
See 25 November 1912, 19 November 1917, 6 January 1918, 20 July 1918, 19 July 1938, 14 July 1959.

1943 Frigate *Black Swan* and corvette *Stonecrop* sank U-124 off Oporto (41.02N, 15.39W). Convoy OS 45.

1944 Destroyer *Keppel* sank U-360 in north Norwegian Sea (73.28N, 13.04E). Convoy JW 58.

1945 VC: Cpl Thomas Peck Hunter, 43 Cdo, RM. Battle of Comacchio, Italy. 43 Cdo was advancing northwards up the coast road north of Ravenna between Lake Comacchio and the sea, heading towards Porto Garibaldi. Hunter, in charge of a bren-gun section, charged across open ground, firing a bren from the hip, and cleared a German position, allowing his troop to advance. He was killed soon afterwards. His award was gazetted 12 June 1945 and his VC presented to his parents at Holyrood Palace, Edinburgh, 26 September 1945. The only RM VC of the Second World War.
See 1 June 1975, 1 May 1980, 1 October 2000.

1957 First Lord of the Admiralty, the Earl of Selkirk, handed over Simon's Town Dockyard to the South African Navy 143 years after its opening. The RN was to have use of the facilities in war and peace.

See 11 March 1957.

1966 C.S. Forester died; creator of Horatio Hornblower.

1967 Memorial bust of Admiral of the Fleet Viscount Cunningham of Hyndhope unveiled by HRH The Duke of Edinburgh in Trafalgar Square.

The design disappointed some: 'It was the bust of an amiable old gentleman,' said Admiral Sir Charles Madden who had been Commander of the battleship *Warspite* in the Mediterranean and ABC's Naval Secretary at the Admiralty, 'ABC was *not* an amiable old gentleman. He was fierce and dangerous looking . . .' Guard of Honour from HMS *Excellent*. Address by Admiral of the Fleet Sir Algernon Willis, Cunningham's former Chief of Staff. The date chosen was the Sunday nearest to the anniversary of Matapan, 28 March 1941. That afternoon a memorial plaque was dedicated in the Nelson Chamber at St Paul's Cathedral.

See 28 April 1967.

1969 The White Ensign hauled down at HMS *St Vincent*, the Boys' TE at Gosport. Training ceased end of autumn term 1968 and closing ceremony held 8 December. All NE training from 4 January 1969 concentrated at HMS *Raleigh*, Torpoint. DCI(RN) 185/69.

See 1 June 1927, 8 December 1968.

1979 Vice-Admiral William Thomas Pillar appointed Chief of Fleet Support. In 1982 he was the first engineer officer to be Commandant of the RCDS and in retirement the first engineer officer to be Lieutenant-Governor and C-in-C Jersey. *Sultan* commissioned a portrait of Admiral Pillar in 1998 and invited contributions to the cost (DCI(RN)174/98). He was described in the DCI as 'undoubtedly the most successful ME Officer of the modern era' and 'the only one to date to reach the rank of Admiral'. Admiral Pillar would have readily acknowledged Admiral Turner's earlier claim.

See 21 April 1970, 19 January 2000.

1982 Argentine invasion of the Falkland Islands. NP 8901 RM at Port Stanley surrendered on orders of the Governor. Operation Corporate began under CINCFLEET, Admiral Sir John Fieldhouse.

The most famous British fighting admiral of the Second World War. The bust of Admiral of the Fleet Viscount Cunningham of Hyndhope, C-in-C Mediterranean Fleet, unveiled by HRH The Duke of Edinburgh in Trafalgar Square on 2 April 1967, the nearest Sunday to the anniversary of Cunningham's victory at the Battle of Matapan in 1941. Photographed by the author in 2009. (*Author*)

1986 Explosion and fire in starboard forward gear room in *Illustrious*, Capt Alan Grose RN, wearing the flag of Rear-Admiral Robin Hogg, Flag Officer First Flotilla, as she left Portsmouth at the start of the planned eight-month Global 86 deployment westabout to the Far East. Air Group disembarked. Repairs cost £4 million and ship delayed until 21 July. *Illustrious* then went eastabout through the Suez Canal to pick up her programme at Singapore. Other ships, frigates *Beaver* (Captain F9) and *Amazon*, destroyer *Manchester*, and RFAs *Fort Grange*, *Olmeda* and *Bayleaf*. The first RN circumnavigation for a decade.

See 2 May 2000.

2001 Destroyer *Cardiff*, Capt T.P. Fraser RN, which arrived in the Danish capital on 28 March wearing the flag of Vice-Admiral Sir Fabian Malbon, Deputy C-in-C Fleet, took part in a bicentenary service of remembrance for those killed in the Battle of Copenhagen on 2 April 1801.

See 31 May 1966, 21 October 2005, 31 May 2006, 1 September 2007.

2002 Flag Officer Submarines/Chief of Staff (Operations) to CINCFLEET, FOSM/COS(OPS), became Commander Operations and Rear-Admiral Submarines, COM(OPS)/RASM. Rear-Admiral Niall Kilgour, appointed last FOSM 18 September 2001, became first holder of new appointment.

3 April

1762 *Hussar* captured two French privateers and destroyed two others under Fort Tiburon, Haiti.

1801 Boats of *Trent* cut out two French vessels off Brehat, in Gulf of St Malo.

1813 Boats of *St Domingo, Marlborough, Maidstone, Statira, Fantome* and *Mohawk* cut out four American privateers in the Rappahannock River, Virginia.

1845 The famous *Rattler–Alecto* Trial. In a series of trials to measure the relative merits of screw and paddle propulsion the frigates *Rattler* (screw) and *Alecto* (paddle), of similar size and power, were secured stern-to-stern off St Abb's Head. The conclusions were far from conclusive but in one serial *Rattler* towed *Alecto* astern at 2.7 knots. This was seized upon as proof of the overall superiority of screw propulsion.

See 20 June 1849, 13 November 1912.

1847 A combined force, under Maj-Gen George Charles D'Aguilar and Capt John McDougall (*Vulture*), spiked the guns of the forts in the Canton River and appeared before Canton to enforce British terms. Ships: *Vulture, Espiegle, Pluto* (Bengal Marine), *Corsair* (hired). Troops: Royal Artillery, Royal Sappers and Miners, 18th Regiment, 42nd Madras Native Infantry.

1862 A party from *Centaur* (in *Vivid* lorcha) destroyed a pirate lorcha off Friendly Island near Ningpo.

1875 Relief of Elcowe and of *Active*'s Naval Brigade by force from *Boadicea, Shah* and *Tenedos*.

1915 Dover Strait mine barrage completed.

1917 VC: Maj Frederick William Lumsden DSO, RMA – shore service with the Army in Flanders. Killed in action 3 June 1918; CB, DSO and three bars, Croix de Guerre.

See 9 July 1944.

1918 Seven British submarines destroyed at Helsingfors to avoid capture: E 1, E 9 and E 19; E 8, C 26, C 27 and C 35 some days later.

1919 Admiral Sir John Jellicoe and Admiral Sir David Beatty, consecutively C-in-C Grand Fleet in the First World War, both promoted admiral of the fleet.

See 1 January 1910.

1941 AMC *Worcestershire* torpedoed by U-74 in Atlantic (58.16N, 27.22W) but managed to reach Liverpool. Convoy SC 26.

1941 Swordfish aircraft, disembarked from *Eagle* at Port Sudan, attacked Italian destroyers on a final sortie into the Gulf of Suez as British troops advanced on Massawa, Eritrea, the main Italian naval base in E. Africa. Midshipman Eric Sergeant of 824 NAS attacked the *Nazario Sauro* W. of Jeddah (20.00N, 30.00E.W) and she sank within a minute. Sub-Lt S.H. Suthers of 813 NAS bombed the *Daniele Manin* which capsized and sank 100 miles N.E. of Port Sudan (20.20N, 30.10E). DSCs. *Cesare Battisti* bombed into scuttling by RN aircraft the same day off Scio Aiba on the Arabian coast. *Pantera* and *Tigre*, scuttled off Someina, on the Arabian coast after one had been torpedoed by destroyer *Kingston*.

1944 Aircraft from *Tracker* (Avenger G/846, Wildcat Y/846) and *Activity* (Swordfish C/819) sank U-288 in the Barents Sea (73.44N, 27.12E). Convoy JW 58.

HMS *Caprice*, the RN's last conventional destroyer, alongside at Swansea in April 1973 shortly before paying off at Devonport after thirty years afloat. (*Author*)

1944 FAA attacked the German battleship *Tirpitz* in Altenfjord. Operation Tungsten. Carriers: *Emperor, Fencer, Furious, Pursuer, Searcher, Victorious*. FAA Sqns: 800, 801, 804, 827, 829, 830, 831, 842, 880, 881, 882, 896, 898. 1834, 1836. Ships: *Anson, Belfast, Jamaica, Meteor, Milne, Onslaught, Royalist, Sheffield, Undaunted, Ursa, Verulam, Vigilant, Virago, Wakeful* and *Algonquin* and *Sioux* (RCN).

Fleet Air Arm Attack on the *Tirpitz*

The Admiralty had assessed that damage to the *Tirpitz* caused by the X-craft attack in September 1943 had probably been repaired. It was therefore planned to use two strikes each of twenty-one Barracudas protected by forty fighters to attack the *Tirpitz*, which was a threat to the northern convoys. A force led by the battleship *Anson*, comprising the carriers *Victorious, Furious, Emperor, Searcher, Pursuer* and *Fencer* with a screen of four cruisers and fourteen destroyers sailed. A part of the Home Fleet covered this force and convoy JW 58. Because the convoy escort seemed to be coping with enemy attacks, and the weather was good, the C-in-C decided to advance the operation by twenty-four hours. This proved fortunate as, when the first attack took place at 0529 on 3rd, the *Tirpitz* was weighing anchor for sea trials. The enemy was caught unawares, and AA fire did not start until the first attack had begun. The second attack took place an hour later, and the enemy were alert and had started a smokescreen. Each attack lost only one bomber, and one fighter was lost. Four hits were obtained with 1,600lb bombs and ten with 500lb bombs, causing 438 casualties and putting *Tirpitz* out of action for another three months. Unfortunately the FAA attacks were pressed home with such determination that the bombs were dropped too low to pierce the enemy's armour and inflict greater damage.

1944 Navigation School moved from Southwick to Seamen's Hospital at Greenwich. Southwick House became HQ for Operation Overlord.
See 10 March 1941.

1945 Liberator U/224 sank U-1276 off Shetland Islands (61.42N, 00.24W).

1959 The following names for RNR Headquarters Units approved:

RNR Northwood	HMS *Northwood*
RNR Portsmouth	HMS *Southwick*
RNR Plymouth	HMS *Vivid*
RNR Rosyth	HMS *Scotia*

AFO 823/59.
See 20 May 2000, 2 October 1964.

The figurehead of the brig HMS *Daring*, launched at Portsmouth 2 April 1844. (*RN*)

1973 *Caprice*, pennant number D01, the Royal Navy's last conventional destroyer, commanded by Lt-Cdr John C.E. Lloyd RN, paid off at Devonport after her last port visit to Swansea.

1974 Ice patrol ship *Endurance*, positioned off Cape Horn to keep an eye on entries in the first Whitbread Round-the-World Yacht Race rounding the Cape on the Sydney-Rio leg, fired a 9-gun salute to the RN's own entry, the Nicholson -55 *Adventure*, skippered by Capt George Vallings. The *Adventure*, passing close to *Endurance*, lifted to a particularly high wave as *Endurance* fired her last round and a large hole appeared in the yacht's headsail which Skipper Vallings and his ten shipmates spent the rest of the day sewing up.
See 25 December 2007.

1982 South Georgia garrison of twenty-one Royal Marines surrendered, having shot down one Argentine helicopter and damaged the frigate *Guerrico* with platoon weapons.

1982 Rear-Admiral J.F. Woodward sailed from Gibraltar, flag in *Glamorgan*, with *Antrim, Arrow, Brilliant, Coventry, Glasgow, Plymouth* and *Sheffield* with *Appleleaf* and *Tidespring*.

2001 Lt-Cdr Vanessa Spiller joined frigate *Kent*, the first female XO of a major warship.
See 7 November 1997, 30 June 2005.

4 April

1581 Francis Drake knighted by Queen Elizabeth I on board *Golden Hind* at Deptford.
See 30 June 1913, 15 May 1954, 7 July 1967.

1655 Admiral Robert Blake (*George*) destroyed the forts and nine Algerine warships at Porto Farina, Tunisia, having failed to obtain any satisfaction from the Dey of Algiers for the depredations of Algerine pirates. Ships: *Amity, Andrew, Bridgewater, Foresight, George, Kent, Merlin, Mermaid, Newcastle, Pearl, Princess Maria, Plymouth, Success Unicorn, Worcester.*
Battle Honour: Porto Faria 1655.

1680 *Adventure* drove ashore and wrecked the Algerine *Orange Tree* near Cape Spartel, Morocco.

1759 *Achilles* captured the French privateer *Comte de St Florentine* 180 miles W. of Cape Finisterre.

1760 *Bideford* and *Flamborough* fought the French *Malicieuse* and *Opale* 100 miles N.N.W. of Cape Roxent (da Roca), Portugal.

1794 Sir John Jervis (*Boyne*) and troops took St Lucia.

1798 *Pallas* (32), fifth rate, dragged her anchors in a gale in Cawsand Bay, Plymouth, and was wrecked on the Mount Batten Reef.

1806 *Renommée* captured the Spanish *Vigilante* under Fort Corralete, close to Cape de Gata, south coast of Spain.

1808 *Alceste, Grasshopper* and *Mercury* defeated twenty Spanish gunboats and captured seven of their convoy off Rota, near Cadiz.

1812 Boats of *Maidstone* captured the French privateer *Martinet* 30 miles S. by E. of Cape de Gata.

1854 Landing parties of *Encounter, Grecian* and the USS *Plymouth* defeated Chinese Imperial troops at Shanghai.

1905 Admiralty sold twenty-nine redundant warships by auction at Chatham.

1918 Destroyer *Bittern* lost in collision with SS *Kenilworth* off Portland Bill.

HMS *Argyll* firing a Harpoon GWS60 missile during a High Seas Firings in August 2004. (*RN*)

Lamport & Holt's passenger and cargo liner SS *Voltaire* was taken over by the Admiralty in 1939 and converted into an armed merchant cruiser. (*S. Courtney*)

1918 First successful launch of a two-seat reconnaissance aircraft from a ship. A Sopwith 1½-strutter, from platform over forward turret and guns of HMAS *Australia*, battlecruiser. Turret rotated into wind to avoid need for ship to alter course.

1928 Court martial of Capt K.G.B. Dewar and Cdr H.M. Daniel, battleship *Royal Oak*.

1941 AMC *Voltaire* sunk by the German merchant raider *Thor* (Schiff 10) in Atlantic.

1949 North Atlantic Treaty signed and NATO set up by Belgium, Canada, Denmark, France, Iceland, Italy, Luxembourg, the Netherlands, Norway, Portugal, the United Kingdom and the United States of America, all subscribers then to the doctrine that an attack on one member was an attack on all.

1966 RN Armaments Depot, Coulport, opened to support the Polaris squadron at Faslane.

1982 RMAS salvage tug *Typhoon*, Capt J.N. Morris, sailed from Portland for the South Atlantic, the first surface ship to deploy from Britain for Operation Corporate and one of the last to return.

See 24 September 1982.

The interwar years in the Mediterranean Fleet: the light cruiser HMS *Ceres*, Third Light Cruiser Squadron. The winners of the heavy gun shooting shield with Capt. John im Thurl RN, in February 1923. (*Cdr David Hobbs RN*)

5 April

1387 Sir Hugh Spencer defeated by the Flemish Jean de Bucq off Cadzand, Netherlands.

1654 Treaty of Westminster required ships of the United Provinces to salute the British flag.

1755 Fifty independent companies of Marines raised, and divided into three Grand Divisions at Chatham, Portsmouth and Plymouth.

1758 Admiral Sir Edward Hawke (*Ramillies*) prevented the sailing to America of a French convoy from Ile d'Aix. Ships: *Alcide, Chichester, Intrepid, Medway, Newark, Ramillies, Union.* Frigates: *Coventry, Hussar, Southampton.*

1769 Thomas Masterman Hardy born at Kingston Russell, Dorset. Flag Captain in *Victory* at Trafalgar.

1797 Boats of *Magicienne* and *Regulus* destroyed thirteen privateers and two batteries at Cape Roxo (Rojo), Puerto Rico.

1800 *Leviathan* and *Emerald* captured the Spanish *Carmen* and *Florentina* with cargoes of quicksilver and an archbishop, 80 miles W.S.W. of Cape Spartel, Morocco.

1804 *Swift* taken by the French privateer *Espérance* 10 miles E. of Palamos, S.E. of Spain.

1809 *Amethyst* (36) captured the French *Niemen* (40) 12 miles N. of Cape Machichaco, north coast of Spain. *Arethusa* came up, having 'steered to the sound of the guns'.
Battle Honour: *Niemen* 1809.

1852 Capture of Martaban, Burma by *Hermes, Rattler, Salamander* and the Bengal Marine steamer *Proserpine.*

1852 *Fox, Serpent*, the Bengal Marine steamers *Phlegethon* and *Tenasserim* and the 18th Regiment destroyed the Danot and da Silva stockades below Rangoon.

1852 Fixed rates of pay for pursers, now paymasters. Remuneration by emolument plus perquisites abolished.

1916 Third and final failure to relieve Kut-al' Amara. River gunboats: *Dragonfly, Gadfly, Mantis, Mayfly, Sawfly*; later – *Greenfly, Waterfly.*

1916 Le Havre Drifter Flotilla and the French *Le Trombe* forced UB-26 to surrender. She sank

Admiral of the Fleet Lord Hawke (1705–1781)

Edward Hawke, 'a man who may be fairly regarded as the first great professional officer of his naval service' (Mackay) was born in 1705 and became a captain at the age of 29. Off Toulon in 1744 (22 February) he bestowed some glory on an otherwise drawn battle by breaking out of the Line of Battle (still a grave offence) to seize the *Poder*. He was almost dismissed for this. However, he was promoted rear-admiral in 1747 and served with distinction. His most famous battle was the annihilation of the French Fleet at Quiberon Bay in 1759. When the pilot protested as he sailed in a November gale in the shoals, Hawke showed his mettle by replying: 'You have done your duty in pointing out the risk. Now lay me alongside the French Admiral.' Hawke became admiral of the fleet in 1768 and died in 1781.

Admiral Lord Hawke (1705–1781). (*NMRN 1976/181*)

later off Cape de la Heve. Drifters: *Comrades, Endurance, Pleasance, Pleiades, Stately, Welcome Star.*

1917 Submarine C 7 sank UC-68 in North Sea.

1918 British and Japanese marines landed at Vladivostok.

1921 The rank of brigadier-general, Royal Marines, established by Order in Council of 14 October 1913, abolished by another Order of this date, effective from 1 January 1921.

1939 Fleet carrier *Illustrious*, Yard No. 732, launched by Lady Henderson, wife of the late Third Sea Lord and Controller of the Navy, at Vickers Armstrong, the first carrier and the biggest ship built at Barrow. She worked up at Bermuda and was the biggest warship to visit the island. *Illustrious* became the first carrier to be fitted with radar.

1941 Sloop *Scarborough* and destroyer *Wolverine* sank U-76 in Atlantic (58.35N, 20.20W). Convoy SC 26.

1942 Minesweeper *Abingdon* sunk and destroyer *Lance* badly damaged in dry dock by Italian aircraft at Malta.

1942 Easter Sunday. Japanese dive bombers from the carriers *Akagi, Soryu* and *Hiryu*, following an attack on Colombo in which the AMC *Hector* and destroyer *Tenedos* were lost, went on to sink the heavy cruisers *Dorsetshire* and *Cornwall* off the Maldives (01.54N, 77.45E). *Cornwall* lost 190 men and *Dorsetshire* lost 234 men – 1,122 survivors. 'Had a word with Agar [Capt A.W.S. Agar VC, RN] who was Captain of *Dorsetshire*. The Japs hit with their first bombs and it was all over in less than fifteen minutes. The men behaved magnificently though they were in the water or on rafts for 30 hours before being picked up. Agar did very well and kept the men together and their spirits up.' – Admiral Sir James Somerville, C-in-C Eastern Fleet. The Japanese attacked Trincomalee four days later.

See 17 June 1919, 9 April 1942.

1943 Coastal Command Hudsons L/233 and W/233 attacked U-167 off Canary Islands (27.47N, 15.00W). Submarine scuttled. Salvaged 1951 and broken up.

Admiral Sir Thomas Masterman Hardy (1769–1839). *(NMRN 1971/12(30))*

1943 Liberator N/120 sank U-635 attacking convoy HX 231 (58.20N, 31.52W).

1949 Warrant Officers became Branch Officers.

1951 HRH Princess Elizabeth presented the new King's Colour to the Mediterranean Fleet at Malta; 2,500 men on parade.

1957 *Centurion* commissioned at Haslemere as Central Drafting authority. (Matthew 8:9)

See 16 October 1970.

1958 Gold badges, suspended during the Second World War, 'will again be worn' by RN ratings and RM Other Ranks, on their best uniforms.

1982 Carriers *Hermes* and *Invincible* sailed from Portsmouth for the South Atlantic, joined by frigates *Alacrity* and *Antelope* from Plymouth. Operation Corporate.

2007 Fifteen sailors and Royal Marines from the frigate *Cornwall*, detained by Iranian forces while engaged on boarding duties in the NAG twelve days earlier, were released. Review of ROE, training, boarding practices and much else followed.

See 13 January 1928.

6 APRIL

1776 *Glasgow* (20) fought off five American ships under Cdre Esek Hopkins (*Alfred*) 24 miles S.E. of Block Island.

1806 Cochrane in *Pallas* drove ashore the French *Garonne*, *Gloire* and *Malicieuse* at the mouth of the Gironde while most of his men were in her boats cutting out *Tapageuse* 20 miles upstream.

1811 *Persian* captured the French privateer *Embuscade* off Cape d'Antifer.

1909 Destroyer *Blackwater* sunk in collision with SS *Hero* off Dungeness.

1915 False bow-waves to be painted on all ships to confuse submarine attack.

1917 The USA declared war on Germany.

1919 Armoured cruiser *Kent* landed guns' crew at Vladivostok to support White Russians 4,500 miles W. on the Kama River in S. Urals.
See 3 January 1919.

1941 AMC *Comorin* destroyed by accidental fire in Atlantic (54.34N, 21.20W). Sunk by *Broke* which with *Lincoln* and MV *Glenartney* rescued 405 of 425 in gale.

1941 VC: FO K. Campbell, RAFVR, of 22 Sqn, for torpedoing *Gneisenau* in Brest. Posthumous.
See 12 February 1942.

1942 Destroyer *Havock* ran aground at 30 knots off Kelibia light, Tunis. Blown up by own forces.

1942 *Indus* (RIN) sunk by Japanese aircraft off Fakin Point, Akyab (20.07N, 92.45E).

1943 Liberator R/86 sank U-632 (58.02N, 28.42W). Convoy HX 231. Six merchant ships lost but fifty-five and all the escorts arrived safely.

1944 Frigate *Swale* sank U-302 in Atlantic (45–05N, 35–11W). Convoy SC 156.

1945 Destroyer *Watchman* sank U-1195 in English Channel (50–33N, 00–55W). Convoy VWP 16.

Operation Demon
The Royal Navy's evacuation of the Army from Greece, 1941

The Germans attacked Greece on 6 April and that night in an air attack on Piraeus, the *Clan Fraser* ammunition ship blew up, sinking ten other vessels and devastating the best-equipped supply port for the Army. British and Imperial forces so recently taken there (Operation Lustre) were forced to retreat. The evacuation from small ports and over open beaches began on night of 24/25 April and continued for five nights; 50,732 soldiers were rescued, about 80 per cent of the 58,000 taken to Greece without loss only weeks before in Operation Lustre. It was a re-run of Operation Dynamo at Dunkirk the previous year – the rescue of the Army, long sea passages under air attack and losses of fine ships (destroyers *Diamond* and *Wryneck*). 'I feel that the episode is one to which the Royal Navy and the Merchant Navy can look back with pride', wrote Admiral Cunningham, C-in-C Mediterranean Fleet; 'The conduct of the naval forces involved, including the special landing craft, was, with few exceptions, beyond praise. Officers and men went for many days almost without rest under conditions of great discomfort with their ships crowded with troops under constant air attack. . . A notable feature of the operation was the gallant and enterprising performance of the merchant seamen in the troopships. . .' Rear-Admiral H.T. Baillie-Grohman, SNO ashore in Greece, with Maj-Gen Bernard Freyberg, commanding the New Zealand forces, left in the light cruiser *Ajax* at 290300. 'The British campaign on the mainland of Greece was from start to finish a withdrawal' – Official History of the War in the Mediterranean. Battle Honour: Greece 1941.

Ships: *Ajax, Auckland, Calcutta, Carlisle, Coventry, Decoy, Defender, Diamond, Flamingo, Glenearn, Glengyle, Griffin, Grimsby, Hasty, Havock, Hereward, Hero, Hotspur, Hyacinth, Isis, Kandahar, Kimberley, Kingston, Muroto, Nubian, Orion*, HMAS *Perth, Phoebe, Salvia*, HMAS *Stuart, Ulster Prince*, HMAS *Vampire*, HMAS *Vendetta*, HMAS *Voyager*, HMAS *Waterhen, Wryneck*. See 27 April 1941.

HMS *Suffolk* and USS *Brooklyn* at Vladivostock in 1918. (*NMRN*)

1952 Prefix HMSAS (Her Majesty's South African Ship) replaced by SAS (South African Ship).

1958 Light cruiser *Bermuda* arrived in Bermuda on her first visit to the colony.

1959 C-in-C South Atlantic and South America, Vice-Admiral Sir Robert Watson, landed on Tristan da Cunha by helicopter from ice patrol ship *Protector*. The ship took off twelve people including the Chaplain, the Revd Philip Bell, his wife and four children, and Mr Godfrey Harris, the Administrator. 'He is relieved by Mr. P.A. Day, a former District Officer in Tanganyika.'

1962 AFO 2056/61 'reaffirmed that a vigorous Instructor Branch is, and will continue to be, essential to the Royal Navy . . . will remain as a separate Branch of the Royal Navy and its title will be unchanged . . .'

See 18 November 1918, 1 March 1975, 6 July 1996.

1964 First meeting of the new Defence Council in the newly constituted Ministry of Defence. 'There are those who believe that the whole idea has an unfortunate flavour of a supreme headquarters on the pattern of the German Oberkommando der Wehrmacht' – *The Times*.

See 31 December 1959, 26 March 1964.

1971 Cdr C. Coxon RN retired after thirty-two years' service as a naval pilot; the last FAA pilot still in flying practice who flew the Swordfish operationally during the Second World War.

1982 *Fearless*, broad pennant of Cdre M.C. Clapp (COMAW), sailed from Portsmouth, en route for Ascension. Operation Corporate.

1993 Type 23 frigate *Richmond* launched by Lady Hill-Norton, wife of Admiral of the Fleet Lord Hill-Norton, at Swan Hunter Shipbuilders, Wallsend. The last warship built at the yard.

See 7 November 1994, 16 May 2004.

7 April

1694 *Ruby* captured the French privateer *Entreprenant* 80 miles W. of the Scilly Isles.

1799 Sortie from Acre to destroy a mine under the walls of that town, led by Maj John Douglas, Marines, and A/Lt John Wesley Wright (*Tigre*). The operation was covered by *Theseus*.

1875 Launch of *Alexandra*. The first ironclad to be launched by a member of the Royal Family, the first with a religious launch ceremony conducted by the Archbishop of Canterbury, the last to carry a central battery and the only one to serve as a flagship throughout her entire active service.

1917 CMBs 4, 5, 6 and 9 attacked four German destroyers off Zeebrugge, CMB 9 sinking G-88. First RN success with coastal craft.

1919 Sir David Beatty, four days an admiral of the fleet, hauled down his flag in *Queen Elizabeth* and the Grand Fleet ceased to exist, being replaced by Home, Atlantic and Mediterranean Fleets. The first occasion on which an admiral of the fleet, apart from royalty, commanded the British battle fleet since Earl St Vincent in 1806.

Admiral of the Fleet Sir Edward Seymour commanded a squadron of one battlecruiser and four cruisers in 1910 for a visit to New York. It was the first time an admiral of the fleet had flown his flag at sea since the Duke of Clarence did so at a fleet review in 1814. Admiral Sir Charles Forbes, C-in-C Home Fleet, was promoted admiral of the fleet on 8 May 1940 and flew a Union Flag (sometime in *Rodney*) from May to October 1940 when he was relieved by Admiral Sir John Tovey, and by the Earl of Cork and Orrery during the Norwegian operation in 1940.

See 22 February 1806, 10 June 1900, 26 June 1902, 19 April 1967.

1932 Destroyers *Defender* and *Diamond* both named by Lady Eyres-Monsell, wife of the First Lord of the Admiralty, at Vickers Armstrong, Barrow. *Defender* launched that day but *Diamond* delayed by bad weather for twenty-four hours. *Daring* launched at Thornycroft, Woolston, on 7 April. The D-class destroyers of 1932 had a sad history: five units of the eight ship flotilla were lost in the first thirteen months of the Second World War (*Daring* was the first RN destroyer lost); *Defender* was sunk in July 1941, leaving only *Decoy* and *Diana*.

See 8 November 1932, 8 June 1937, 12 December 1939, 18 February 1940, 29 July 1940, 22 October 1940, 27 April 1941, 11 July 1941.

1943 Submarine *Tuna* sank U-644 off Jan Mayen Island (69.38N, 05.40W).

1943 HMNZS *Moa*, corvette, sunk in Japanese carrier air attack while operating with US ships off Tulagi, Guadalcanal in the Solomons.

1961 The title of the Fourth Sea Lord and Vice-Controller extended 'to indicate more clearly his full responsibilities'. New title: The Fourth Sea Lord (Chief of Supplies and Vice-Controller). AFO 782/61.

A 4.7-in gun lashed between two boats at the gunnery training school HMS *Excellent*, *c*.1903. (*NMRN*)

RN Philatelic Society commemorative cover to mark the centenary of the RN Submarine Service, 2001. (*NMRN*)

1967 The last naval air squadron to be based in Malta, 728 NAS, Lt-Cdr P.J. Wreford RN, joined by Buccaneer, Sea Vixen and Gannet aircraft from the carrier *Hermes*, Capt T.T. Lewin RN, made a farewell flight around the island from RAF Hal Far.

See 15 April 1945.

1972 Admiral Sir Michael Denny, Gunnery officer, C-in-C Home Fleet and CINCEASTLANT 1954–6, died at Gloucester aged 75. He was COS at Dover during the Dunkirk evacuation and commanded the light cruiser *Kenya* on Arctic and Mediterranean convoys and the carrier *Victorious* against *Tirpitz* and the Japanese in the East Indies. As Controller 1949–53 he introduced the Daring-class ships and the Ton-class minesweepers. 'He was shy and reserved . . . and unnecessarily feared for his knowledge and efficiency' – Horace Law. He was a son of the vicarage but was not religious: 'his only hobby was to form a collection of dolls.'

1997 Capt Nicholas John Barker, Captain of *Endurance* during the Falklands War of 1982, died. Nick Barker's memoirs of Operation Corporate, *Beyond Endurance*, were published a week before his death. His father, Lt-Cdr John Barker, commanding the destroyer *Ardent*, was killed in action in June 1940 defending the carrier *Glorious* from attack by the German *Scharnhorst* and *Gneisenau*.

See 8 June 1940.

2011 3 Cdo Bde deployed to Afghanistan on Operation Herrick 14. Brig E.G.M. Davis took over command of Task Force Helmand from Brig James Chiswell, Commander 16 Air Assault Bde at Lashkar Gah on 9 April.

See p.717 panel.

8 April

1740 *Kent*, *Lenox* and *Orford* captured the Spanish *Princesa* 120 miles N.W. of Cape Ortegal, north-west Spain after a gallant resistance of seven hours.

1814 Boats of *Boxer*, *Endymion*, *Hogue* and *Maidstone* destroyed twenty-seven American vessels and a quantity of naval stores at Pettipague Point (Essex), in the Connecticut River.

1835 *Skipjack* captured the slaver *Marie* 40 miles S.W. of Little Cayman, S. of Cuba.

1898 Battle of the Atbara, Sudan. Gunboats not engaged, but landed a rocket party under Lt David Beatty.

1904 Entente Cordiale agreement between United Kingdom and France signed in London. This ended long series of Colonial disputes in Egypt, Morocco, Siam, Madagascar, New Hebrides, Newfoundland and East and West Africa, and led to a period of rapprochement and alliance, driven principally by the shared concern at German naval expansion.

1927 Destroyer *Veteran*, steaming up Yangtze, fired on by Nationalist Chinese at Kweishang forts, 15 miles below Chinkiang, returned fire with her 4.7-in main armament. C-in-C made 'I strongly approve of your action'.

See 20 April 1949.

1930 Explosion of a depth charge gun cotton primer in the destroyer *Sepoy*, Lt-Cdr H.E. Reid RCN, during exercises off Hong Kong with the Eighth Destroyer Flotilla, caused minor damage to the ship but killed six men. The King sent word of his distress and 'heartfelt sympathy' to the First Lord of the Admiralty.

1940 VC: Lt-Cdr Gerard Broadmead Roope (*Glowworm*). Posthumous. *Glowworm* sank after ramming the German cruiser *Admiral Hipper* off the coast of Norway. First naval VC won in Second World War but not first gazetted.

Battle Honour: Norway 1940.

See 10 April 1940.

An accidental encounter at 64.27N, 06.28E., which marked the start of combined operations (which lasted until 8 June) in Norway under Admiral of the Fleet the Earl of Cork and Orrery and General Sir Claude Auchinleck. Ships: *Acasta, Acheron, Afridi, Amazon, Arab, Ardent, Arethusa, Ark Royal, Arrow, Ashanti, Aston Villa, Auckland, Aurora, Basilisk, Beagle, Bedouin, Berwick, Birmingham, Bittern, Black Swan, Bradman, Brazen, Cairo,*

HMS *Glowworm* ramming the *Admiral Hipper*, 1940. (*NMM Neg No. G5674*)

Irish politician and author John Wilson Croker was Secretary of the Admiralty (Civil Lord in later terms, a minister not an official) from 1808 to 1830. He was a competent naval administrator but not in the league of Pepys or Barham who, in fairness to Croker, had wars in which to gain distinction. He introduced gas lighting into the Admiralty – the first in a public building in London. Oil painting by Thomas Lawrence. (*Crown Copyright: MOD Art Collection*)

Calcutta, Campbell, Cape Chelyuskin, Cape Passaro, Cape Siretoko, Carlisle, Clyde, Codrington, Cossack, Coventry, Curacoa, Curlew, Delight, Devonshire, Diana, Echo, Eclipse, Effingham, Electra, Ellesmere, Encounter, Enterprise, Escapade, Esk, Eskimo, Fame, Faulknor, Fearless, Firedrake, Flamingo, Fleetwood, Forester, Foxhound, Furious, Galatea, Gaul, Glasgow, Glorious, Glowworm, Grenade, Greyhound, Griffin, Gurkha, Hammond, Hardy, Hasty, Havelock, Havock, Hero, Hesperus, Highlander, Hostile, Hotspur, Hunter, Icarus, Imperial, Impulsive, Inglefield, Ivanhoe, Jackal, Janus, Jardine, Javelin, Juniper, Kelly, Kimberley, Kipling, Larwood, Loch Shin, Manchester, Maori, Margaret, Mashona, Matabele, Melbourne, Mohawk, Northern Gem, Nubian, Pelican, Penelope, Porpoise, Protector, Punjabi, Ranen, Renown, Repulse, Resolution, Rhine, Rodney, Rutlandshire, St Goran, St Magnus, St Sunniva, Seal, Sealion, Severn, Sheffield, Sikh, Snapper, Somali, Southampton, Spearfish, Sterlet, Stork, Suffolk, Sunfish, Tarpon, Tartar, Thirlmere, Thistle, Triad, Trident, Triton, Truant, Ursula, Valiant, Vandyck, Vanoc, Vansittart, Veteran, Vindictive, Walker, Wanderer, Warspite, Warwickshire, Westcott, Whirlwind, Wistaria, Witch, Witherington, Wolverine, Wren, York, Zulu. Polish: *Blyskawica, Burza, Grom, Orzel.* Royal Marine and seaman detachments: *Barham, Hood, Nelson.* FAA Sqns: Skua: 800, 801, 803. Swordfish: 804, 810, 816, 818, 820, 823. Walrus: 701. GLadiator: 802. Swordfish and Walrus: 700 ships' flight.

1941 Cruiser *Capetown* torpedoed by the Italian MAS-213 off Mersa Kuba. Towed by *Parramatta* (RAN) to Port Sudan.

1944 Sloop *Crane* and destroyer *Cygnet* sank U-962 in N. Atlantic (45.43N, 19.57W).

1945 *Byron* and *Fitzroy* sank U-1001 (49.19N, 10.23W) and frigates *Bentinck* and *Calder* sank U-774 in S.W. Approaches (49.58N, 11.51W).

1983 Two Ro-Ro stores carriers, MV *Grey Master* (Norway) and MV *Lakespan Ontario* (Canada), taken into RFA service to augment freighting capacity following loss of RFA *Sir Galahad* and *Sir Tristram* in Operation Corporate. Ships renamed RFA *Sir Caradoc* and *Sir Lamorak*. DCI(RN) 142/83.

1983 Destroyer *Nottingham* commissioned by Cdr N.R. Essenhigh RN. Paid off 11 February 2010.

See 18 February 1980, 7 July 2002.

1994 The paying-off of eight RNR units announced: *Dragon* 30 June; *Camperdown, Mercia* and *Pellew* 29 July; *Ceres* and *Claverhouse* 31 July; *Salford* 12 August and *Wildfire* 2 September. DCI(RN) 74/94.

See 31 January 1992.

2008 40 Cdo RM began returning from a six-month deployment to Helmand Province, Afghanistan. Three men killed in action. One GC (L/Cpl Croucher RMR), one DSO (Lt-Col Stuart Birrell), one MBE, three MCs and three MIDs. Operation Herrick 7.

See 11 April 2007, 8 October 2007, 9 February 2008.

2009 Antarctic patrol ship *Endurance* arrived at Spithead on the Dutch heavy lift ship *Target* after flooding of the hull in the Magellan Strait on 16 December 2008.

See 3 September 1988, 27 February 2006.

9 April

1777 Horatio Nelson passed his examination for lieutenant.

1782 Rear-Admiral Sir Samuel Hood (*Barfleur*) fought the division under Cdre the Marquis de Vaudreuil (*Triomphant*) off Dominica.
See 12 April 1782.

1810 *Drake* captured the French privateer *Tilsit* 60 miles W. of the Texel.

1826 Boats from *Alacrity* (10) began a two-day operation against Greek pirate positions on Psara and Andros Islands in Grecian Peninsula.

1847 Hon. John Rodney, eldest son of Admiral Lord Rodney, died aged 82 at Boulogne, having held the rank of Captain RN for sixty-six years.
See 14 October 1780.

1853 Launch of *Malacca* at Moulmein, Burma. First warship fitted with high-pressure steam engine (60 psi).

1855 Second bombardment of Sevastopol by the Allied siege batteries, including those of the Naval Brigade.

1887 *Victoria* launched at Elswick, the first battleship built by Armstrong. With sister ship *Sans Pareil*, launched at Thames Iron Works on 9 May 1887, the first battleships powered by triple-expansion engines.
See 29 January 1892, 22 June 1893.

HMS *Victoria* (1887). (*NMRN*)

1936 P&O liner *Ranpura* departed Tilbury for Shanghai with Chinese treasures which had been exhibited at the Royal Academy in Burlington House. The collection had been brought to Britain in 1935 in the heavy cruiser *Suffolk*. The value of the treasures required a naval escort throughout the return voyage to China; the final stage from Colombo to the Woosung River, where she arrived on 17 May, was covered by the light cruiser *Dauntless*.
See 26 July 1935.

1940 *Renown* fought the German battlecruisers *Gneisenau* and *Scharnhorst* 50 miles W. of the Lofoten Islands. The first naval big gun action since Jutland in 1916.

1940 Destroyer *Gurkha*, Cdr Anthony Buzzard RN, bombed by German aircraft W. of Bergen (59.13N, 04.00E) which blew a 40ft hole in starboard side. Sank at 1900. DSO. Cruiser *Aurora* rescued 190 of her 207 men and landed them at Thurso where they spent two days in the town hall. First of twelve British-built Tribal-class destroyers lost in the Second World War and the first RN destroyer lost to air attack. Every man in the Brigade of Gurkhas contributed one day's pay towards the cost of a new ship; the destroyer *Larne* then building was launched as *Gurkha* 8 July 1940.
See 17 January 1942.

1940 Submarine *Truant* torpedoed the German cruiser *Karlsruhe* in the Skagerrak, 10 miles S. of Kristiansand. Sunk by own forces.

1942 Admiral Sir Andrew Cunningham, having handed over command of the Mediterranean Fleet *pro tem* to Vice-Admiral Pridham-Wippell, arrived in London and was met by the Board of Admiralty at Paddington Station. Cunningham was en route to Washington to relieve Admiral Sir Charles Little as Head of the British Admiralty Delegation. Churchill pressed him to take command instead of the Home Fleet and so replace Admiral Sir John Tovey. 'If Tovey drops dead on his bridge.'

The battlecruiser HMS *Renown* (1916) reconstructed and in Second World War camouflage. (*NMRN*)

responded Cunningham, 'I will certainly relieve him. Otherwise not.' – Simpson, *Cunningham Papers*, p.127.

See 10 October 1940, 4 October 1943.

1942 Destroyer *Lance* further damaged by German aircraft at Malta. Towed to Chatham in 1943. Scrapped.

1942 Carrier *Hermes* and destroyer *Vampire* (RAN) sunk by Japanese naval aircraft from carriers *Akagi*, *Hiryu*, *Shokaku* and *Zuikaku* off Batticaloa, S. of Trincomalee, Ceylon (07.35N, 82.05E). 'Forty bomb hits in ten minutes' – Roskill. The first sinking of a carrier by carrier-borne aircraft. Hospital ship *Vita* in company was not attacked by Japanese and she saved over 600 men; 307 lost in *Hermes*, eight in *Vampire*. Corvette *Hollyhock* sunk by aircraft from carrier *Soryu* 30 miles S.S.E. of Batticaloa (07.21N, 81.57E); fifty-three men lost. These losses followed four days after the sinking of the heavy cruisers *Dorsetshire* and *Cornwall* in the Indian Ocean: 'We are having a hell of a time and no mistake' – Admiral Sir James Somerville, C-in-C Eastern Fleet.

See 11 September 1919, 1 May 1923, 5 April 1942.

1945 Aircraft Handler Branch of FAA formed, known colloquially as 'Chockheads'.

1958 Submarine *Turpin*, with main engines OPDEF in the Caribbean, arrived at Devonport in tow of the tug *Samsonia*, after a thirty-day, 5,200-mile voyage from Kingston, Jamaica.

1965 'By Hand of Officer' marking for the conveyance of classified or sensitive service papers, discontinued. DCI(RN) 572/65.

1982 P&O liner *Canberra*, taken up from trade, sailed from Southampton for the South Atlantic, with most of 3 Cdo Bde embarked. Operation Corporate.

2004 RFA *Mounts Bay*, second of class of Landing Ship Dock Auxiliary (LSDA) launched on Good Friday at BAE Systems, Govan, by Lady Band, wife of Admiral Sir Jonathon Band, C-in-C Fleet. 'Named' 14 October 2005. Commissioned Falmouth 15 September 2006.

See 26 July 2003, 1 August 2003, 9 April 2005, 17 July 2006.

2005 Landing Ship Dock Auxiliary, RFA *Cardigan Bay*, third of class, launched at BAE Systems, Govan, a day after being named by Lady Stanhope, wife of Admiral Sir Mark Stanhope and a year to the day after her sister ship RFA *Mounts Bay*.

See 24 September 1926, 26 July 2003, 1 August 2003, 9 April 2004, 17 July 2006.

10 April

1703 *Salisbury* and the hired armed ship *Muscovia Merchant* together with four of their convoy, taken by a superior French squadron 50 miles W. of Goeree, Netherlands. *Salisbury* was recaptured in 1708.

See 13 March 1708.

1746 *Alexander* privateer captured the French (ex-RN) *Solebay* close off St Martin, Ile de Ré. An early gold-medal action.

1781 Nelson's 'favourite ship', third Rate *Agamemnon* (64), launched by Henry Adams at Buckler's Hard.

See 16 June 1809.

1786 Vice-Admiral the Hon. John Byron died: 'Foul-weather Jack.'

1795 *Astraea* (32) captured the French *Gloire* (42) 150 miles W. by S. of the Scilly Isles.
Battle Honour: *Gloire* 1795.

1855 Boatswain's Mate John Sullivan of *Rodney* (92) won the Victoria Cross at the siege of Sebastopol. He went ahead of his battery under fire to place a flag before a concealed Russian battery as an aiming point. His award was gazetted among the first recipients of the VC on 24 February 1857. Saw out his thirty-seven years' service as boatswain of Portsmouth Dockyard; he retired in 1884 to his native Co. Cork where he killed himself after two months. His VC is in the Wardroom, HMS *Nelson*, given by the government of Nova Scotia in exchange for that of William Hall, the first Canadian VC.

See 16 November 1857, 21 October 1989.

1918 Light cruiser *Dauntless* launched at Palmers Yard on the Tyne. Served in the Baltic in 1919, in the Particular Service Squadron on the Empire cruise in 1923–4, in the Mediterranean and on the America and West Indies Station; wartime service on the China and East Indies Stations. Sold 1946.
Battle Honour: Atlantic 1939.

See 2 July 1928, 15 June 1941, 23 January 2007.

1938 Carrier *Courageous* launched successful exercise strike against battlecruiser *Hood* despite the latter's fighter screen.

1940 VC: Capt Bernard Armitage Warburton Warburton-Lee (*Hardy*). Posthumous. First Battle of Narvik. Second DF sank two German destroyers (*Anton Schmidt* and *Wilhelm Heidkamp*) Ships: *Hardy*, *Havock*, *Hostile*, *Hotspur*, *Hunter*. Losses: *Hardy* beached, *Hunter* sunk after collision with *Hotspur*. Paymaster Lt Geoffrey H. Stanning, Captain's Secretary, *Hardy*, assumed command and decided to run the sinking *Hardy* ashore, after obeying the dying Capt Warburton-Lee's injunction to

The destroyer HMS *Hardy* (1936), later sunk at the first Battle of Narvik. (*NMRN*)

Launch of the *Agamemnon* at Buckler's Hard in the New Forest, 10 April 1781. (*NMRN 1964/19*)

'keep on engaging the enemy'. Stanning was appointed DSO, the only officer of his branch to be so honoured in the Second World War and the only paymaster officer to have taken command of a warship in action. Warburton-Lee's was the first naval VC gazetted in the war. Battle Honour: Norway 1940.

See 21 April 1917, 8 April 1940, 16 May 1945, 8 March 2008.

British Naval Losses in the Norwegian Campaign 1940

Glorious	Aircraft Carrier	Gunfire	8 June
Effingham	Cruiser	Wrecked	18 May
Curlew	AA Cruiser	Air attack	26 May
Glowworm	Destroyer	Gunfire	8 April
Gurkha	Destroyer	Air attack	9 April
Hardy	Destroyer	Gunfire	10 April
Hunter	Destroyer	Collision	10 April
Afridi	Destroyer	Air attack	3 May
Acasta	Destroyer	Gunfire	8 June
Ardent	Destroyer	Gunfire	8 June
Bittern	Sloop	Air attack	30 April
Thistle	Submarine	U-boat	10 April
Tarpon	Submarine	Surface attack	14 April
Sterlet	Submarine	Surface attack	18 April
Seal	Submarine	Surrendered	5 May
Oleander	RFA oiler	Air attack	8 June

First Battle of Narvik, 1940

In early April 1940, the Germans were invading Norway, and action was fast moving, with intelligence having to be gained on the spot. Capt Warburton-Lee, with four destroyers, was ordered to prevent the enemy taking Narvik. While on passage he learned that the enemy had landed there in some force, but decided to enter the fjord and attack the enemy shipping. He was joined by another destroyer just before arrival, and then made a dawn attack. The element of surprise allowed him to sink two large German destroyers and damage three others, but five other German destroyers joined in the action, and the *Hardy* and *Hunter* were sunk, and *Hotspur* damaged. However, two more German destroyers were severely damaged, and seven merchant ships sunk including an ammunition ship, before the British force withdrew.

1940 *Königsberg*, German light cruiser, sunk at Bergen by Blackburn Skua aircraft of 800 and 803 Naval Air Squadrons from RNAS Hatston, Orkney. First sinking of a major war vessel by air attack in wartime.

See 11 July 1915, 26 September 1939.

1940 Destroyer *Hero* sank U-50 N.N.E. of Shetland.

1940 Submarine *Thistle* sunk by U-4 off Skudenaes, N.W. of Stavanger, first of four submarine losses in a month.

1943 Wellington C/172 sank U-376 in the Bay of Biscay.

1943 *Adventure*, minelayer cruiser (completed with a transom stern which had to be hurriedly redesigned), intercepted German blockade-runner *Irene*, ex-Norwegian *Silvaplana*, from Saigon off Finisterre (43.18N, 14.26W). Merchant ship scuttled. In first quarter of 1943 the Axis sailed ten blockade-runners to Europe from the Far East and four made the return voyage. Three of the fourteen reached their destinations.

1945 Corvette *Tintagel Castle* and destroyer *Vanquisher* sank U-878 in S.W. Approaches. Convoy ON 295.

1966 Frigate *Berwick* boarded the Greek tanker *Manuela* off Portuguese Mozambique, the first action in the newly established Beira Patrol. UNSCR No. 221 authorised the British government 'to prevent, by the use of force if necessary, the arrival at Beira of vessels reasonably believed to be carrying oil destined for Rhodesia'. The Beira Patrol was maintained by the RN for nine years until Mozambique independence in 1975.

See 27 February 1966, 10 May 1966, 19 December 1967, 25 June 1975.

2001 Commemorative postage stamps, depicting submarines *Holland*, *Unity*, *Swiftsure* and *Vanguard*, issued by Royal Mail to mark the centenary of the RN Submarine Service.

See p.202 panel.

11 April

1680 *Hampshire* and *Adventure* enjoyed a ten-hour action with Algerian pirates off Tangier, driving two ashore and taking the *Calabash*. *Golden Horse* escaped but was taken later.

1746 Admiral Edward Vernon, victor at Porto Bello in 1739, removed by the King from the Flag List, dismissed the Service for publishing grievances in pamphlets 'calculated to mislead and deceive rather than inform' which were critical of the Admiralty and contained official correspondence, authorship of which Vernon would neither confirm nor deny.

See 22 November 1739.

1793 *Bedford* (74) inadvertently engaged *Leopard* (50) in the Channel, fortunately without success.

1794 Nelson began siege of Bastia, taken 21 May.

1795 *Hannibal* captured the French *Gentille* to the W.S.W. of the Scilly Isles, a continuation of yesterday's action.

1796 *Ça Ira* (80) burned out by accident at San Fiorenzo.

1804 *Wilhelmina* fought the French *Psyche* 100 miles E. of Trincomalee.

1809 Capt Lord Cochrane's fireship attack on the French fleet in Basque Roads, under the general direction of Admiral Lord Gambier (*Caledonia* (120)). Four French ships burned.

An inconclusive action, after which Gambier applied for a court martial and Cochrane, as an MP, opposed a parliamentary vote of thanks to his Admiral. Cochrane had joined the Flag on 3 April and on 4 and 5 April did what Gambier should have done long since, i.e. reconnoitre the defences at close range. Rear-Admiral Sir Eliab Harvey also exploded at Gambier's inactivity, which led to his own court martial. Battle Honour: Basque Roads 1809.

See 26 July 1809, 4 August 1809.

1856 Comprehensive uniform alteration for officers. Rank to be shown by stripes for all commissioned ranks. Cap of new pattern with crown and anchor within a laurel wreath for all officers, i.e. including cadets, midshipmen and warrant officers. For commanders and above the peak to be graced with gold. Executive and Civil branches to wear straight stripes but the former to have a curl on the top one and to have gold-edged epaulettes with silver devices, while the latter had gold devices and silver edges, and kept single-breasted coats with distinguishing arrangements of buttons.

1866 *Bellerophon* completed. Served a record fourteen years as flagship on the West Indies station.

See 1 March 2004.

1913 Paymaster Branch introduced into RNR.

1929 A replica of Drake's Drum presented to the heavy cruiser *Devonshire* by the people of Devon. Bad luck followed. In the Mediterranean three months later an explosion in an 8-in gun turret killed seventeen men, fifteen of them from the Plymouth Division RM. In a later commission a ship's whaler was fired on by Turks off Samos killing an officer. The Master-at-Arms represented to Capt Gerald Muirhead-Gould that the ship's company blamed the drum for the run of bad luck and, although two Royal Marines refused to handle it, the drum was landed and taken to St Nicholas' church in Devonport Dockyard. 'From that moment *Devonshire* never looked back. We had a most successful and happy commission' – Capt Eric Bush.

See 29 July 1969.

1939 Mrs (later Dame) Vera Laughton Mathews appointed Director WRNS, which was reconstituted next day. Daughter of naval historian Professor Sir John Knox Laughton.

See 23 November 1917.

1940 Submarine *Spearfish* torpedoed the German pocket battleship *Lützow* (ex-*Deutschland*) north of the Skaw.

1940 First coordinated attack by aircraft of more than one squadron – 816 and 818 FAA from *Furious* at Trondheim.

Dame Elvira (Vera) Laughton Mathews (1888–1959). (*NMRN*)

1941 River gunboats *Aphis* and *Gnat* bombarded the coast road near Bomba, Libya.

1941 Church bells rang in Malta for first time ever on a Good Friday – to sound All Clear after a German air raid.

1942 Destroyer *Kingston* destroyed in dock at Malta by German aircraft. Hull used as blockship.

1942 Women's Royal New Zealand Naval Service established.

See 29 July 1977.

1943 Destroyer *Beverley* torpedoed and sunk by U-188 S.W. of Iceland (52.19N, 40.28W) after collision with SS *Cairnvalona* on the 9th, which damaged her ASDIC. Convoy ON 176.

1945 Force 63, under Vice-Admiral H.T.C. Walker (*Queen Elizabeth*), bombarded Sabang and Oleheh, Sumatra. Operation Sunfish. Sabang: *Queen Elizabeth, London, Richelieu* (Fr). Oleheh: 26th DF *Saumarez, Venus, Verulam, Vigilant, Virago*, with *Cumberland, Emperor, Khedive*. FAA Sqn: 808 (Hellcat).

1946 White cap covers reintroduced.

See 18 April 1940, 30 April 1956, 1 May 1956.

1961 Patrol submarine *Finwhale*, Lt-Cdr John Wadman RN, berthed alongside *Adamant* at Faslane after 28-days' under-ice trials in the Arctic. She had been accompanied to the ice edge by *Amphion* which provided a communications relay link to FOSM.

1967 Vice-Admiral J.M.D. Gray, the last C-in-C South Atlantic and South America, struck his flag at 2359 at HMS *Afrikander*, Youngsfield, Wynberg, Cape, whence the HQ had moved after Simon's Town Naval Base was handed over the SAN in 1957. The final closure came on 28 April when the Queen's Colour of the Station and two ex-King's Colours were marched in slow time through Simon's Town Dockyard and embarked in the frigate *Lynx*. This marked the end of 170 years of permanent British naval presence at the Cape. The SA and SA naval command area was divided between C-in-C Home Fleet and COMFEF at longitude 33E. Post of SBNOSA established, a commodore with his broad pennant in HMS *Afrikander*, to be naval attaché and representative in South Africa of C-in-C Home Fleet. DCI(RN) 334/67

See 4 March 1965, 30 October 1956 (C-in-C NA&WI), 7 September 1958 (C-in-C East Indies), 31 March 1961 (C-in-C The Nore), 31 March 1964 (Admiralty), 5 June 1967 (C-in-C Mediterranean), 26 May 1969 (C-in-C Plymouth), 31 March 1979 (FO Malta), 19 June 1979; 30 September 1983 (FO Medway), 25 July 1967, 31 March 1979.

1969 RN Medical School at Alverstoke became the Institute of Naval Medicine.

1975 Admiralty Board decided, on economy grounds, to stop the publication of spring, summer and autumn editions of *The Navy List* and to publish one annual edition. To take effect from the spring 1975 edition. DCI(RN) T.240/75.

1997 White Ensign hauled down at *Tamar*, Stonecutters' Island, 100 years to the day after the troopship *Tamar* arrived in Hong Kong waters as Receiving Ship. *Tamar* was Britain's last naval base east of Suez.

2007 3 Cdo Bde returned from six months on operations in S. Afghanistan, having lost twelve men killed and fifty-five wounded. The brigade received two DSOs (Brigade Commander and Lt-Col Matt Holmes, CO 42 Cdo), two MBE, one CGC and eleven MC (seven to 42 Cdo) in the Honours and Awards List 29 July 2007. Operation Herrick 5.

See 7 October 2006.

12 April

1779 Court martial at his own request of Admiral Sir Hugh Palliser on his conduct at Ushant in 1778. Verdict was that he was not 'chargeable with misconduct or misbehaviour'.

1782 Second battle between Vice-Admiral Sir Edward Hughes (*Superb*) and twelve ships under Cdre Chevalier de Suffren (*Héros*) 12 miles N.E. by E. of Providien Rock (Elephant Rock, Clarke Point), Ceylon.

Ships: *Burford, Exeter, Eagle, Hero, Isis, Magnanime, Monarca, Monmouth, Sultan, Superb, Worcester*. Fireships: *Combustion, Seahorse*. Troops: 98th Regiment.
Battle Honour: Providien 1782.

See 17 February 1782, 6 July 1782, 3 September 1782.

1782 Battle of the Saintes. Twenty miles off the north end of Dominica. Admiral Sir George Bridges Rodney (*Formidable*) and Rear-Admiral Hood (*Barfleur*) defeated the French fleet of thirty sail of the line under Vice-Admiral Comte de Grasse (*Ville de Paris*). Captured: *Ardent, César, Glorieux, Hector, Ville de Paris*.
Battle Honour: The Saintes 1782.

* See 14 February 1797.

Ships: *Marlborough, Arrogant, Alcide, Nonsuch, Conqueror, Princessa, Prince George, Torbay, Anson, Fame, Russell, America, Hercules, Prothee, Resolution, Agamemnon, Duke, Formidable, Namur, St Albans, Canada, Repulse, Ajax, Bedford, Prince William, Magnificent, Centaur, Belliqueux, Warrior, Monarch, Barfleur, Valiant, Yarmouth, Montagu, Alfred, Royal Oak*. Frigates, etc.: *Alarm, Alecto, Alert, Andromache, Champion, Endymion, Eurydice, Flora, Triton, Zebra*. Troops: 69th Regiment, now the Royal Welsh, awarded the battle honour of a naval crown, superscribed '12 April 1782' on its colours*, and the 87th Regiment. *Ville de Paris* was the only French three-decker ever taken in action.

'The sun had not quite set upon the exhausted squadrons of Suffren and Hughes, anchoring after their fiercest battle off Ceylon, when his early rays shone upon the opening strife between Rodney and de Grasse' – Mahan.

The Peter Scott painting in the Naval Club, Mayfair of Lt Cdr Robert Hichens RNVR, killed on this date in 1943. (*Naval Club*)

The Battle of the Saintes ('Saints'), 1782

In the Seven Years War the Fighting Instructions had been substantially the same as those written during the Dutch wars 100 years earlier. Battles were fought by fleets sailing in line ahead on parallel courses, and were generally indecisive. Rear-Admiral Sir Samuel Hood, second in command on the station, was keen to break the deadlock, but no opportunity offered until 12 April 1782, when a British fleet under Rodney and a French fleet under de Grasse met off a group of islets called Les Saintes. At the onset of the battle the wind did not favour the British fleet and the French gained the weather gauge. However, as the British van drew clear of the French rear the wind shifted, enabling Rodney and Hood to pass through gaps in the French line and force many of the French ships to close action. Nelson wrote of this battle, 'the greatest victory, if it had been followed up, that our country ever saw'. Yet, to Hood's fury, no signal for general chase was hoisted by Rodney, who said 'we have done very handsomely as it is' and it was only some days later that Hood managed to follow up the victory.

1796 *Revolutionnaire*, herself captured from the French, captured the French *Unité* 60 miles S. by W. of Belle Ile.

See 19 April 1782.

1843 *Rattler*, wood screw sloop, the world's first screw-propelled warship, launched at Sheerness. Fitted with 220hp engines for the final screw trial with *Alecto* in 1845.

See 3 April 1845.

Women's Royal Naval Service

The Women's Royal Naval Service was formed in 1917 to replace men required for active service. In the two years before it was disbanded it grew to almost 7,000, its members having shown their ability to carry out not only domestic and clerical duties, but also such work as boat's crew and wireless telegraphist.

In April 1939 the Service was re-formed and by September there were 1,000 Wrens employed as communicators, writers, drivers, cooks and stewards, and a small number of WRNS officers. The number of personnel and their duties expanded considerably to include skilled work concerned with maintenance of aircraft, weapons and small craft, until by 1944 there was a total force of 74,635.

At the end of the war the WRNS rapidly reduced in number but many officers and ratings were still needed to meet the requirements of an extended service. On 1 February 1949 the Service, first created to meet the Navy's need in wartime, became an integral and permanent part of the Royal Navy and on 1 July 1977 the Women's Royal Naval Service became subject to the Naval Discipline Act for the first time, thereby accepting commitment with equal opportunity. WRNS disbanded on formal integration into RN on 1 November 1993.

1918 GC (ex-AM): Lt A.G. Bagot, DSC, RNVR (ML 356) for saving life after fire at sea.

1918 Grand Fleet base moved from Scapa Flow to Rosyth.

1918 CMB 33A destroyed by German shore battery at Ostend during the cancelled battleship operation at that port.

1918 Women's Royal Naval Service. General Order issued by Vice-Admiral Stuart Nicholson, Vice-Admiral East Coast of England, 12 April 1918:

'Officers and men of other RN services will salute officers of the WRNS who by their badges of rank are their seniors when they meet to pass them in a similar manner to officers of the RN. Officers of the WRNS will acknowledge such salute by bowing . . .'

1924 Battlecruiser HMAS *Australia*, which served under Beatty in the North Sea throughout the First World War, was scuttled off Sydney under the terms of the Washington Treaty.

See 23 and 30 June 1913, 4 October 1913, 29 August 1914.

1939 WRNS re-formed.

1941 Landing party from destroyer *Mansfield* destroyed the fish oil factory at Oyfjord, near Hammerfest.

1943 Lt-Cdr Robert Hichens, DSO and bar, DSC and two bars, RNVR, peacetime Cornish solicitor, killed in action in MGB 112 off the Dutch coast; the most highly decorated RNVR officer of the Second World War. His portrait by Lt-Cdr Peter Scott hangs in the Naval Club, Hill Street.

See 21 September 1989, 8 November 1995.

1945 Submarine *Tapir*, Lt J.C.Y. Roxburgh (a future FOSM), torpedoed and sank U-486 inbound to Bergen (60.44N, 04.39E). The last sinking by a British submarine in home waters.

U-486, Oberleutnant Gerhard Meyer, on her first patrol, had sunk the British troopship *Leopoldville* off Cherbourg with the loss of over 800 US soldiers, on Christmas Eve 1944. Two days later she torpedoed and sank the frigate *Capel* and torpedoed and seriously damaged the frigate *Affleck* (CTL).

See 13 April 2004.

1945 Frigate *Loch Glendhu* captured U-1024 off Isle of Man. The U-boat sank in tow off Holyhead on the 13th. Convoy BB 80.

1945 Task Force 57 including carrier *Indefatigable* attacked the airfield at Shinchiku and harbour at Kiirun, Formosa. Operation Iceberg Oolong. FAA Sqns: Avenger: 820; Firefly: 1770; Seafire: 887.

1982 Maritime Exclusion Zone of 200 miles declared around Falkland Islands, enforced by submarines, to deter re-supply of Argentinian forces by sea. Operation Corporate.

See 28 April 1982.

2001 *Herald*, ocean survey ship, returned to Devonport for the last time after a seven month deployment. Paid off 31 May 2001.

2005 Admiral the Lord Boyce installed as Lord Warden and Admiral of The Cinque Ports and Constable of Dover Castle in the room of Her late Majesty Queen Elizabeth The Queen Mother; the only admiral except Robert Blake (1656) to hold this appointment since its creation in the twelfth century. A 19-gun salute was fired by *Albion* in Dover Harbour followed by a Sea Harrier flypast.

See 20 July 1966, 1 April (p.189), 23 April 2011.

13 April

1665 *Mermaid* captured a Dutch 6-gun pirate ship in the North Sea.

1665 *Diamond* and *Yarmouth* captured the Flushing Directory Ships *Eendragt* and *Jonge Leeuw* in the North Sea.

1733 Edward Hawke appointed Master and Commander into the sloop *Wolf* (10) and joined next day at Port Royal, Jamaica.
See 10 February 1720, 20 November 1759, 17 October 1781.

1748 Uniform for executive officers and midshipmen introduced by Admiralty Order. Said to have been inspired by Diana, Duchess of Bedford and wife of the First Lord, being seen in an elegant blue and white riding habit by King George II in Hyde Park, and designed by Philip Saumarez with the approval of Anson.

1749 Admiral Boscawen's fleet anchored off Fort St David, Madras, hit by a cyclone. Flagship *Namur* (74), Capt Samuel Marshall, cut her cables in attempt to make open sea but foundered and broke up. Admiral and Flag Captain were ashore; two midshipmen and twenty-four men saved from ship's company of 500. The cables of *Pembroke* (60) parted and she drove ashore near Point Colderoon; Capt Thomas Fincher and 318 men lost. *Apollo*, storeship, wrecked.

1758 *Prince George* (90), on passage from England to the Mediterranean, destroyed by fire 180 miles W. of Ushant with loss of 485 lives.

1783 *Sceptre* captured the French *Naiade* 70 miles N.E. by E. of Cuddalore.

1797 *Viper* captured the Spanish privateer *Piteous Virgin Maria* 20 miles N.N.W. of Alboran Island, W. Mediterranean.

1800 Boat of *Calypso* cut out the French privateer *Diligente* off Cape Tiburon, Haiti.

1868 Naval Brigade at the capture of Magdala, Abyssinia, by Lt-Gen Sir Robert Napier. Ships: *Argus, Daphne, Dryad, Nymphe, Octavia, Satellite, Spiteful, Star, Vigilant*. Medal: Abyssinia, 1867–8.
Battle Honour: Abyssinia 1868.

1885 White helmet replaced cap in tropical rig.

1885 The last surviving Royal Navy officer who fought at Trafalgar nearly eighty years earlier died at Lymington, Hampshire. Admiral of the Fleet Sir George Sartorius, born in 1790, had entered the Service in June 1801 and was a midshipman in the 3rd rate *Tonnant* in the battle. Two of his three army sons won the VC.
See 2 July 1853, 15 April 1887, 13 February 1892.

1885 John Henry Dacres Cunningham born at Demerara, British Guyana; entered the Royal Navy in 1900, served in both world wars and succeeded his namesake as First Sea Lord in 1946.
See 7 June 1947, 13 December 1962.

1899 Landing party from torpedo cruiser *Porpoise* and screw corvette *Royalist* under Lt Guy Gaunt (*Porpoise*) repulsed a Maatafan attack at Samoa.

1912 Royal Flying Corps, of Naval and Military Wings, constituted by Royal Warrant.

1940 Second Battle of Narvik. Vice-Admiral W.J. Whitworth (*Warspite*) sank eight German destroyers at Narvik. U-64 bombed in Herjangsfjord by Swordfish floatplane from *Warspite*, piloted by PO(Airman) F.C. 'Ben' Rice. The first German submarine destroyed by the Fleet Air Arm in the Second World War. Ships: *Bedouin, Cossack, Eskimo, Forester, Foxhound, Furious, Hero, Icarus, Kimberley, Punjabi, Warspite*. Sunk: *Bernd von Arnim, Diether von Roeder, Erich Giese, Erich Koellner, Georg Thiele, Hans Lüdemann, Hermann Künne, Wolfgang Zenker*.
Battle Honour: Narvik 1940.
See 14 February 2003.

Following the action on 10 April, it was decided to clear the fjord of enemy shipping. The battleship *Warspite* and nine destroyers entered on 13 April, using *Warspite*'s

HMS *Warspite* and destroyers. second Battle of Narvik, 1940. (*NMRN*)

aircraft to detect enemy positions. The aircraft sank U-64 and warned of destroyers hidden in creeks. Eight large enemy destroyers were sunk by 15-in gunfire from the *Warspite* and in action with British destroyers. Two British destroyers – *Eskimo* and *Cossack* – were seriously damaged. Advantage of this action could not be taken by the British as no military forces were available.

1940 Force Sandall – 200 Royal Marines – landed by heavy cruiser *Suffolk* to occupy Faeroe Islands. See 10 May 1940.

1940 Cruiser *Effingham* landed French Foreign Legionnaires to outflank Narvik.

1941 AMC *Rajputana*, escorting convoy HX 117 in N. Atlantic, torpedoed by U-108 W. of Reykjavik (64.50N, 27.25W); 283 survivors rescued by destroyer *Legion* and landed in Reykjavik.

1945 MTBs 670 and 697 sank the German TA-45 (ex-Italian TB *Spica*) in the Gulf of Fiume.

1945 Task Force 57 including *Indefatigable* attacked the airfields at Matsuyama and Shinchiku, Formosa. Operation Iceberg Oolong. FAA Sqns: Avenger: 820; Seafire: 887; Firefly: 1770.

1951 Pre-1921 uniform buttons to be worn to distinguish RNR from RNVR. Wardmasters gave up purple for pink, and Electrical and Special Branch Officers showed a paler green.

1956 In conformity with the elimination of 'Boy' from the titles of naval ratings, the RM titles 'Boy Bugler' and 'Boy Musician' will be changed to 'Junior Bugler' and 'Junior Musician'. AFO 963/56.

1965 The first ex-RNVR officer to be FOST, Cdre P.G. Sharp RN, (Rear-Admiral 7 July) hoisted his flag (as Acting Rear-Admiral) at Portland. His successor as COMBRAX Portsmouth, Capt G.A. Henderson RN, was the first (S) specialist to be Commodore of a naval barracks.

2004 Admiral Sir John Roxburgh, wartime submarine commander and former FOST, FO Plymouth and FOSM (1969–72), died aged 84. See 12 April 1945.

14 April

1293 Sir Robert Tiptoft defeated Charles, Count of Valois, in mid-Channel, at a battle caused by a watering quarrel as a result of which the French hanged some English seamen with some dogs.

1781 *Roebuck* and *Orpheus* captured the American *Confederacy* 170 miles S. by E. of Sandy Hook.

1842 Repulse of attack by fire rafts at Tinghai, S. of Shanghai. Boats of: *Bentinck, Cornwallis, Hyacinth, Starling, Nemesis, Phlegethon* (Ben. Mar.), *Jupiter* transport.

1852 Capture of Rangoon in second Burma War by Rear-Admiral Charles John Austen (*Rattler*) and Maj-Gen Jeremy Godwin. Ships: *Fox, Hermes, Rattler, Salamander, Serpent*. Indian Navy: *Berenice, Ferooz, Medusa, Moozuffer, Sesostris, Zenobia*. Bengal Marine: *Enterprize, Fire Queen, Mahanuddy, Phlegethon, Pluto, Proserpine, Tenasserim*. Troops: 18th, 51st and 80th Regiments, Bengal Artillery, Madras Sappers and Miners, 40th Bengal Native Infantry, 9th and 35th Madras Native Infantry. Battle Honour: Burma 1852–3.

See 11 May 1824.

1857 *Raleigh* (50) (fourth of the name) wrecked on Raleigh Rock, off Macao, but Keppel fired salute to passing French warship while sinking.

See 17 January 1904, 8 August 1922, 18 May 1940, 26 May 2008.

1858 Naval Brigade from *Pelorus* returned on board.

See 4 February 1858.

1861 Boat of wood screw sloop *Lyra* captured a slave dhow in Chake Chake Bay, Zanzibar.

1915 Cruiser *Hyacinth* destroyed German *Kronburg* off East Africa, preventing her from supplying light cruiser *Königsberg*.

1916 RNAS aircraft from Mudros bombed Constantinople. Both pilots made DSO.

TS *Conway* (ex-HMS *Nile* (1839)), aground in the Menai Strait. Her wheel can be seen in the National Museum of the Royal Navy, Portsmouth. (*NMRN*)

1940 Naval force landed from 18th CS at Namsos. Operation Henry.

1940 Submarine *Sterlet* sank German minelayer *Brummer* in Kattegat. *Sterlet* was sunk on 18 April in Skaggerak.

1940 Submarine *Tarpon* sunk by depth charges from German *Schiff 40* (56.43N, 06.33E).

1941 River gunboat *Gnat* and destroyers *Griffin* and *Stuart* (RAN) bombarded enemy positions at Sollum.

1942 Sloop *Stork* and corvette *Vetch* sank U-252 in N. Atlantic. Convoy OG 82.

1942 Submarine *Upholder*, Lt-Cdr David Wanklyn VC, DSO, RN, sunk by the Italian torpedo boat *Pegaso* off Tripoli. The Admiralty announced her loss on 22 August 1942.

The communiqué made an extraordinary tribute: 'It is seldom proper for Their Lordships to draw distinction between different services rendered in the course of naval duty but they take this opportunity of singling out those of HMS *Upholder*, under the command of Lieutenant Commander Wanklyn for special attention. She was long employed against enemy communications in the Central Mediterranean, and she became noted for the uniformly high quality of her services in that arduous and dangerous duty. Such was the standard of skill and cool intrepidity set by Lieutenant-Commander Wanklyn and the officers and men under him that they and their ship became an inspiration not only to their own Flotilla, but to the fleet of which it was part and Malta, where for so long she was based. The ship and her company are gone, but the example and the inspiration remain.'

See 18 December 1941.

1943 Destroyer *Eskdale* (Nor) sunk by the German S-65, S-90 and S-112, E.N.E. of the Lizard Head. Convoy PW 323.

1944 Sloop *Pelican* and frigate *Swansea* (RCN) sank U-448 in N. Atlantic.

1944 Midget submarine X 24 laid two charges under the floating dock at Bergen. Dock undamaged, but the German SS *Bahrenfels* lying alongside was sunk.

1944 Cdr C.J. Cork, who had thirteen enemy aircraft to his credit, died in flying accident at China Bay, Ceylon.

1953 *Conway*, formerly *Nile* (92), second rate, cadet training ship since 1876, went ashore in Menai Strait off Plas Newydd en route to dry dock at Birkenhead for refit, and broke her back. Wreck burned 31 October 1956.

1958 RN Supply School, which had moved from *Ceres* at Wetherby, opened at *Pembroke*, RN Barracks, Chatham.

See 22 March 1950, 14 March 1958.

1977 Sailors from the frigate *Danae*, visiting Rio de Janeiro from 14–18 April as part of a task force commanded by Rear-Admiral Martin Wemyss, invited on board the escaped 'Great Train robber' Ronald Biggs, on the run from a thirty-year prison sentence in Britain. A political controversy ensued.

Questioned in the House of Commons, Mr Patrick Duffy, Under Secretary of Defence for the Royal Navy, said that 'ships' companies are encouraged to meet the local community – (loud laughter) – but are expected to show discretion – (more laughter) – in offering hospitality'. Rear-Admiral Morgan-Giles asked why, as a HM ship is British territory, Biggs had not been 'clapped in irons' (shout of 'Make him walk the plank'). The Minister replied that the ship had no power of arrest. A correspondent to *The Times* later pointed out that a British man of war is by legal fiction deemed to be within the parish of Stepney and that Biggs was therefore liable for arrest.

15 April

1759 *Favourite* captured the French *Valeur* 30 miles E. of Cape de Santa Maria, Portugal.

1795 *Artois* captured the French *Jean-Bart* 15 miles W. of Ile de Ré.

1795 Reduction of Trinidad.

1797 Mutiny began at Spithead in Bridport's flagship, *Queen Charlotte*. Ended 17 May.
See 12 May 1797.

1821 Professor James Inman DD of the Royal Naval College, Portsmouth, published his 'Treatise on Navigation and Nautical Astronomy for Seamen', including his celebrated tables.
See 7 February 1859.

1887 The last British officer survivor of Trafalgar, Lt-Col James Fynmore RM (first class volunteer in HMS *Africa* in which his father, also James, was Captain of Royal Marines), died at Peckham aged 93. He outlived the last RN officer survivor, Admiral of the Fleet Sir George Sartorius (midshipman in the *Tonnant*), by two years and two days.
See 13 April 1885.

1915 The RN's first two big-gun monitors launched; *M1* at Harland & Wolff, Belfast, and *M4* at Swan Hunter, Wallsend. Sister ships *M2* and *M3* were launched on 29 April by Harlands, Belfast, and Harlands, Govan, respectively. The ships were armed with US-built 14-in guns and in tribute the Admiralty renamed the ships *Admiral Farragut* (*M1*), *General Grant* (*M2*), *Robert E. Lee* (*M3*) and *Stonewall Jackson* (*M4*). This embarrassed the neutral US and, after hasty chopping and changing of names, the ships entered RN service as *Abercrombie*, *Havelock*, *Raglan* and *Roberts*.
See 20 January 1918.

1918 Raid by British light forces in the Kattegat.

Ships: Force A: *Cardiff, Cassandra, Ceres, Vanoc, Vega, Vehement, Vimiera, Violent*. Force B: *Calypso, Caradoc, Vendetta, Verulam, Wakeful, Winchelsea*. Force C: *Angora, Princess Margaret, Urchin, Venetia, Vesper, Viceroy*. Force D: *Caledon, Champion, Courageous, Gabriel, Galatea, Inconstant, Lion, Nerissa, Oriana, Penn, Phaeton, Royalist, Renown, Repulse, Tiger, Tower, Tristram, Ulster, Ursa, Ursula*. Cover: 5th BS: *Barham, Malaya, Valiant* and destroyers.

1940 Destroyers *Fearless* and *Brazen* sank U-49 in Vaagsfiord, N. Norway and made a very useful intelligence haul of documents.

1941 RAF Coastal Command came under operational control of Admiralty.

The merchant ships *Rochester* and *Melbourne Star* entering Valletta harbour, Malta, in August 1942. (*NMRN*)

1941 River gunboat *Ladybird* bombarded Gazala airfield, Cyrenaica. Sunk 12 May 1941 off Tobruk.

1942 GC: The Island of Malta. The only award of the GC that was not gazetted, and the first awarded to a body corporate rather than to an individual.

By 1942 Malta was encircled by Axis forces, but still proving a major thorn in the side of the Axis in North Africa, and it was essential to maintain the British presence there. In mid-June two convoys attempted to resupply the island, one from Gibraltar and the other from Alexandria (Operations Harpoon and Vigorous). These convoys nearly failed. Axis airpower covered the approaches to Malta, and Italian submarine and surface ship bases were close to the sea lane. In spite of very severe rationing (10½oz of bread per day, 3½oz lard or margarine and 1¾oz cheese) a careful estimate by the Governor revealed that the island would be obliged to surrender in mid-September. Fuel supplies were almost exhausted and three Sea Gladiator aircraft (assembled by AOC and his staff from parts left by *Glorious* and affectionately called 'Faith', 'Hope' and 'Charity') had gone long since. King George VI sent the following message to the Governor: 'To honour her brave people I award the George Cross to the island fortress of Malta to bear witness to a heroism and devotion that will long be famous in history.'

1942 On or about this date Rear-Admiral E.J. Spooner, DSO, Flag Officer Malaya, died from the effects of privations on the island of Tjedia off Sumatra, having been wrecked there during his escape from Singapore. He was placed on the Retired List to date 22 October 1943 with the rank of vice-admiral (*Navy List* December 1943, Pt 2) and this rank stands on his gravestone in Kranji Cemetery, Singapore; 'Steel true and blade straight'.

Admiral Spooner, late Captain of the battlecruiser *Repulse*, with Air Vice-Marshal C.W. Pulford, AOC Far East and an ex-RNAS pilot, had been ordered to leave Singapore on 13 February, two nights before it fell to the Japanese, with the hope of reaching Dutch forces in Batavia (Jakarta). Their craft, ML 310 (Lt J. Bull, RNZNVR), was attacked by the Japanese and was wrecked on Tjedia Island, one of the Tuju or Seven Islands Group off the E. coast of Sumatra, 30 miles N. of Banka Island. Nineteen of the party of forty-four, including both senior officers, died of hunger and/or malaria on the island. Most of the remainder were made POW. Admiral Spooner and AVM Pulford were reburied at Kranji after the war.

See 11 June 1847, 2 January 1945.

1945 Frigates *Grindall* and *Keats* sank U-285 in S.W. Approaches, and *Loch Killin* sank U-1063 off Land's End.

1945 RAF airfield at Hal Far, Malta GC, commissioned as HMS *Falcon*. Paid off 31 August 1965 and returned to RAF.

See 7 April 1967.

1960 'Their Lordships have decided to extend to Petty Officers under the age of 21 . . . the privilege of wearing plain clothes when proceeding on liberty from HM Ships, under the same conditions as is granted to Chief Petty Officers and Petty Officers over the age of 21.' – AFO 1069/60.

1965 Prime Minister Harold Wilson presented the ship's bell of HMS *Resolute* to President Lyndon Johnson in Washington.

See 17 December 1856.

1982 Rear-Admiral John 'Sandy' Woodward, FOF1, appointed Falklands Task Force Commander, transferred his flag from the DLG *Glamorgan* to the carrier *Hermes* N. of Ascension. The ships were 200 miles apart and the Admiral joined by Sea King Mk 4. Operation Corporate.

1988 Approval given for WRNS and WRNR senior rates to have the option to wear a uniform mess dress at mess functions. Design to be the same as WRNS officers (with appropriate rate badges), full length A-line skirt with bolero jacket. DCI(RN) 117/88.

16 APRIL

1695 Carelessness by the Officer of the Watch in *Hope* allowed her, *Anglesey* and *Roebuck* to leave their convoy and its other escorts, and they found themselves menaced by Duguay-Trouin with five French ships 150 miles W.N.W. of Ushant. *Anglesey* (48) engaged a 56 and escaped. *Hope* (70) was dismasted after seven hours and, with 7ft of water in her hold, surrendered off the Lizard by her surviving Lieutenant. His Captain being ashore sick, he was promoted for his efforts but the offender in *Hope*, though not shot, was paraded in ignominy at Chatham and dismissed the Service.

1703 Capt Richard Kirby, late of *Defiance* (64) and Capt Cooper Wade, late of *Greenwich* (54), were 'shot to death' on board *Bristol* (48) at Plymouth for cowardice in Benbow's action off Santa Marta, in August 1702. The French Commander, Du Casse, supposedly wrote to Benbow after the action 'Sir, I had little hopes on Monday last but to have supped in your cabin; but it pleased God to order it otherwise. I am thankful for it. As for those cowardly captains who deserted you, hang them up; for, by God, they deserve it!'

See 19 August 1702, 8 October 1702, 4 November 1702, 14 March 1757, 15 May 1797, 23 November 1812.

1781 Cdre George Johnstone (*Romney*), escorting a large convoy of East Indiamen and transports, repulsed the French squadron under Capt Chevalier de Suffren (*Héros*) at Porto da Prai, Cape Verde Islands. Johnstone fumbled the affair and de Suffren reached the Cape of Good Hope before him.

HMS *Turbulent* returning after the longest-ever deployment of a nuclear submarine, 2003. (*NMRN*)

1797 *Boston* captured the French privateer *Enfant-de-la-Patrie* 50 miles W. of Cape Ortegal, north-west Spain.

1810 Capture of Santa Maura (Levkas), Ionian groups, by Brig-Gen John Oswald and Capt George Eyre (*Magnificent*).

1917 Submarine C 16 and destroyer *Melampus* collided off Harwich. Submarine sank in 45ft of water with all hands.

1918 Submarine H 1 inadvertently sank Italian submarine H 5 in southern Adriatic.

1921 Allowance for milk for the Admiralty cat increased from 1*s* to 1*s* 6*d* a week.

See minutes opposite.

1941 14th DF (Capt Mack) destroyed an Axis convoy of five ships and its Italian destroyer escort off Sfax, Tunis. Ships: *Janus, Jervis, Mohawk, Nubian* (*Mohawk* sunk by *Janus* after being torpedoed). Enemy sunk: *Baleno, Luca Tarigo* and four of the convoy. *Lampo* driven ashore and left burning. Salvaged, recommissioned and sunk by aircraft on 30 April 1943.

1941 Light cruiser *Gloucester* bombarded the Fort Capuzzo–Bardia area.

1942 Royal Marines from the 11th Battalion landed by *Kelvin* and *Kipling* on Kuphonisi, Crete, to destroy the W/T station. Operation Lighter.

1943 Destroyers *Pakenham* and *Paladin* engaged Italian TB *Cassiopea* and destroyer escort *Cigno* at night S. of Marettimo (37.45N, 12.13E), sinking the latter and damaging the former. *Pakenham* damaged and taken in tow, but was bombed at daylight. Sunk by *Paladin*.

1945 Minesweeper *Esquimalt* (RCN) sunk by U-190 off Halifax, Nova Scotia.

1945 Destroyer *Viceroy* sank U-1274 off the Farnes. Convoy FS 1784.

1945 Air strike on Emmahaven, Padang, Sumatra, by Force 63, under Vice-Admiral H.T.C.

The Admiralty Cat

Admiralty Minutes. From the Binder (Mr H.E. Scotten) to the Office Keeper (Mr J.W. Stancer), 16 April 1921:

> Is it possible to allow a little extra for the cat? 13s a quarter does not go very far now, in fact it does not pay for the milk she has. I get 2d each day, this only equals 1d on what we used to get, and it is not too much; so if it can be slightly increased I should be obliged.

Accountant General (Sir Charles Walker) to Parliamentary and Financial Secretary (Leopold Amery), 13 May 1921:

> For many years past the Binder has been allowed the sum of 1s per week in respect of his feeding the office cat. The original papers on which the allowance was approved cannot now be traced, but records are available showing that the payment has been made at the rate of 1s a week since 1902. He now asks that the allowance may be increased, and in view of the fact that the cost of milk and cat's meat is still greatly in excess of pre-war prices, it is submitted that the present allowance of 1s a week be increased to 1/6d per week from 1 April last.

Parliamentary and Financial Secretary (Leopold Amery) to First Lord of the Admiralty (Mr A.H. Lee), 17 May 1921:

> I concur, but I feel that a paper of this importance should go to you . . . I understand that the Admiralty contains other cats which, however, are not on the establishment.

First Lord of the Admiralty (Mr A.H. Lee), 20 May 1921:

> I hesitate to commit the Treasury to this increased charge without being assured of the support of those of my colleagues on the Board. . . All that I insist on is that whatever decision is come to, it must not involve a supplementary estimate, or any discussion in Parliament. In these times, when it is incumbent on all good citizens to practice frugality and to share any necessary privations, it would be detrimental to the Admiralty and repugnant to its feelings to confer a bonus on its own cat . . .

Walker (*Queen Elizabeth*). Ships: *Cumberland, London, Queen Elizabeth, Richelieu* (Fr), *Saumarez* (D 26), *Venus, Verulam, Vigilant, Virago*. Carriers: *Emperor, Khedive*. FAA Sqn: Hellcat: 808. Operation Sunfish.

1945 Frigate *Ekins* mined twice, 13 miles N.W. of Ostend. Steamed home but CTL.

1953 HMY *Britannia* launched by HM The Queen at John Brown's, Clydebank.

RN College, Dartmouth, which had reverted to HMS *Britannia* in 1922 following loss of battleship of that name in First World War, became HMS *Dartmouth* in 1953. Maintained the historic link with the old ship by keeping the title Britannia Royal Naval College, Dartmouth.

1982 Fast fleet tanker RFA *Tidepool*, at Arica for handover to the Chilean Navy, ordered to return to join the Falklands Task Force. She transited the Panama Canal, loaded fuel at Curacao, embarked stores at Ascension and steamed south at best speed to join the Amphibious Group 1,000 miles S. of the island on 11 May. *Tidepool* was paid off again on 13 August 1982 and returned to Chile.

1992 *Unicorn* launched at Birkenhead, the last diesel submarine built for RN and last warship built by Cammell Laird. One of four Upholder-class boats transferred to Canada; renamed HMS *Windsor*.

See 16 October 1994.

1999 *Bangor*, Sandown-class single-role minehunter, launched at Vosper Thornycroft, Woolston, by Lady Spencer, wife of Vice-Admiral Sir Peter Spencer, Controller of the Navy. Commissioned 15 December 1999, *Bangor* was the last HM ship accepted into the Service in the (popularly regarded) twentieth century.

See 18 April 1988, 27 November 1999, 15 December 1999, 8 June 2000.

2003 *Turbulent* returned to Devonport after ten months and having steamed 50,000 miles. Longest-ever deployment of a RN nuclear submarine. Fired Tomahawk missiles against targets in Iraq. Operation Telic.

17 April

1746 *Defiance*, *Ruby* and *Salisbury* captured the French *Embuscade* 170 miles S. of the Scilly Isles.

1780 Admiral Sir George Bridges Rodney (*Sandwich*) fought Vice-Admiral Comte de Guichen (*Couronne*), with twenty-three ships of the line, 30 miles W.S.W. of the north end of Martinique. A disappointing engagement.

1796 Capt Sir Sidney Smith (*Diamond* (38), having taken the privateer *Vengeur* by boarding, was swept up the River Seine and taken prisoner with Midshipman Wright. Escaped 1798.

1806 *Sirius* captured the French *Bergère* off the mouth of the Tiber.

1809 *Recruit* (18) delayed the French *D'Hautpoult* (74) 30 miles S.W. by S. of Cape Roxo (Rojo), Puerto Rico until she could be taken by *Pompee* (80) and *Castor* (32). Capt C. Napier of *Recruit* promoted to command the prize.

1813 *Mutine* captured the French privateer *Invincible* 700 miles W. by S. of Cape Finisterre.

1858 Naval Brigade from *Pearl*, wood screw corvette, at Thamowlee (Jamauria), with the 13th Light Infantry, Bengal Yeomanry, 1st Bengal Military Police Battalion and Gurkha allies.

1862 British and French forces captured Tserpoo. Naval Brigade from *Pearl*, *Vulcan*, *Imperieuse*, *Flamer*, *Coromandel*. Troops: RA, 99th Regiment, 5th Bombay Native Light Infantry, 22nd Bengal Native Infantry, Ward's Chinese troops.

1915 Submarine E 15 grounded near Kephez Pt, Dardanelles. Damaged by Turkish gunfire and later blown up by picket boats of battleships *Triumph* and *Majestic*.

1917 Two Japanese destroyer flotillas joined the Allied forces in the Mediterranean.

1918 Drifters *Pilot Me* and *Young Fred* sank UB-82 in N.W. Approaches (55.13N, 05.15W).

1934 First flight of Fairey Swordfish, the famous 'Stringbag', TSR biplane.

1936 Civil disorder throughout Palestine triggered by a general strike by Arabs on this date required a strong RN involvement afloat and ashore in support of the civil authorities throughout the summer. Sea patrols started 26 June to interdict arms smuggling and landing parties reinforced the Customs and fought fires. Sabotage to railway lines and bridges (a skill taught to the Arabs twenty years earlier by Col T.E. Lawrence) was a major problem.

Two armoured trains were built to carry out night time patrols; one manned by two officers and 31 men drawn from the cruisers *Arethusa*, *Delhi* and *Durban*, patrolled the broad gauge line between Jaffa, Lydda and Jerusalem and comprised three 12-ton goods wagons protected by armour plate and armed with two 2-pdr pompoms dismounted from the Fleet, two Vickers machine guns, eight Lewis guns, a 10-in searchlight and its own generator. The other, manned by the cruiser *Shropshire*, patrolled the narrow gauge line between Haifa and Semakh at the southern end of the Sea of Galilee. The RN also introduced armoured lorries for road convoy escort, painted Mediterranean warship grey and armed with a naval 2-pdr pompom, crewed by one officer and five ratings and with the badge of their particular ship 'tastefully picked out on each side of the cab'. On return to London on 4 September after visiting the ships at Haifa, the First Lord of the Admiralty, Sir Samuel Hoare, said 'Once again the Navy has readily met an unexpected emergency. If I wanted an example of its adaptability, what better could I have than the armoured train fitted out and manned by naval personnel?' Before this emergency ended the Fleet was committed to another operation at the other end of the Mediterranean.

See 22 July 1936.

1940 Naval force including 700 seamen and Royal Marines from *Hood*, *Nelson* and *Barham* landed at Andalsnes, Norway. Operation Primrose. *Suffolk* damaged by German aircraft after bombarding Stavanger airfield. Operation Duck.

1941 GC: Lt Ernest Oliver Gidden, GM, RNVR, for RMS on Hungerford Bridge, London.

1941 Portsmouth Dockyard bombed. 'We had a real blitz . . . a very big fellow . . . knocked poor old

Admiral Sir Varyl Begg. (*RN*)

Admiralty House to pieces' recorded the C-in-C Portsmouth, Admiral Sir William James, who moved his office into Hardy's cabin in HMS *Victory*. Tactical School in the Old Naval Academy damaged. In a further raid on 3 May three bombs fell close to Admiralty House 'and blew to smithereens all the good work the dockyard had put in since the first direct hit'. The C-in-C's staff had already moved to Fort Wallington on Portsdown Hill, the Signal School to Leydene House near Petersfield, and the Navigation School to Southwick. The Torpedo School, *Vernon*, moved from the Gun Wharf to Roedean School ('If you want a mistress, ring the bell').

See 12 and 24 August 1940, 23 December 1940, 10 January 1941, 10 March 1941.

1941 Admiralty Board Room seriously damaged by two German bombs; gold and white tracery ceiling brought down, panelling destroyed and famous table damaged.

See 8 May 1945, 8 December 1955.

1951 HM MMS 1558 caught fire and sank.

1951 *Affray*, last British submarine lost at sea, sank in Channel off Alderney. Seventy-five men lost including Sub-Lt Anthony Frew, one of five survivors from *Truculent*, which sank off The Nore on 12 January 1950, and William Linton, son of Cdr J.W. Linton, lost as CO of *Turbulent*.

See 25 May 1943.

1968 *Dreadnought*, Britain's first nuclear-powered warship, commissioned.

1969 Admiral of the Fleet Sir Varyl Begg, Gunnery Officer of the Mediterranean Fleet flagship *Warspite* at Matapan in 1941 (DSO) and First Sea Lord 1966–8, sworn in as the first naval Governor and C-in-C Gibraltar.

See 5 December 1995, 27 September 2006, 26 October 2009.

1999 USS *Winston Churchill*, an *Arleigh Burke*-class guided missile destroyer, launched at Bath Yard, USA. Name changed to add the middle initial 'S' on 19 July 1999. Reciprocal exchange of officers established between this ship and HMS *Marlborough*. The Navigating Officer of USS *Winston S. Churchill* is routinely a Royal Navy officer. The first incumbent was Lt Angus Essenhigh RN.

2002 750 NAS became the first RN squadron to achieve fifty years of continuous commission. Originally formed 24 May 1939, disbanded 10 October 1945, re-formed 17 April 1952 at RNAS St Merryn, north Cornwall, as the Barracuda element of 796 NAS.

2009 Lt-Gen Sir Martin Garrod, CGRM 1987–90 and EU Administrator in Mostar 1993–8, died aged 73. His great-grandfather, Lt-Col W.G. Suther, commanded the Royal Marines at the capture of Shimonoseki, Japan, in 1864.

See 5 September 1864, 29 May 1935.

18 April

1667 *Princess*, on her way from Berwick-upon-Tweed to Gothenburg, fell in with some two dozen of the Dutch Rotterdam Fleet and fought her way through them from dawn to dusk, defeating three attempts to board her.

1782 *Aeolus* captured the French privateer *Aglae* 30 miles N. of Cape Cornwall.

1797 Boats of *Dido* and *Terpsichore* cut out the Spanish *Principe Fernando* at Santa Cruz, Tenerife.

See 29 May 1797.

1797 Spithead mutineers petitioned the Board of Admiralty.

Extract from petition by the Spithead mutineers to Admiral of the Fleet Earl Howe:

'It is now upwards of two years since your petitioners observed with pleasure the augmentations which had been made to pay of the army and militia, and the provision that took place with the respect of their wives and families, of such soldiers as were serving on board, naturally expecting that they should in their turn experience the same munificence, but alas no notice has been taken on them, nor the smallest provision made for their wives and families except what they themselves sent out of their pay to prevent them being burdensome to the parish.

That your petitioners humbly presumed that their loyalty to their sovereign is as conspicuous and their courage as unquestionable as any other description of men in His Majesty's Service as their enemies can testify, and as your Lordship can witness who so often led them to victory and glory and by whose manly exertions the British flag rides triumphant in every quarter of the globe.

And your petitioners humbly conceive that at the time when their wages were settled in the reign of Charles II it was intended as a comfortable support both for themselves and families, but at present by the considerable rise in the necessaries of life, which is now almost double, and an advance of 30% on slops, your Lordship will plainly see that the intentions of the legislature is counteracted by the before-mentioned causes and therefore most humbly pray for relief . . .'

1803 Second and expanded edition of Popham's signal book. Consolidated and reprinted in 1805 it enabled Nelson to make his penultimate and most famous signal, but requiring one word to be spelled out – Duty.

1813 *Unicorn* and *Stag* captured the American letter of marque *Hebe* 100 miles S.W. of Ushant.

1814 Capture of Genoa. Ships: *America*, *Aboukir*, *Caledonia*, *Boyne*, *Iphigenia*, *Furieuse*, *Cephalus*, *Edinburgh*, *Berwick*, *Curacoa*, *Pembroke*, *Prince of Wales*, *Rainbow*, *Pylades*, *Swallow*, *Union* and a Sicilian flotilla.

1905 Launch of A 13, first RN submarine with diesel engine.

HM Submarine *Affray* in May 1950. (*NMRN W&L 933e*)

1940 White cap covers optional for duration.
See 11 April 1946, 30 April 1956, 1 May 1956.

1940 *Sterlet*, submarine, sunk with all hands by German convoy escorts T-190 and M-75 in the Skagerrak (58.57N, 10.36E).

1941 *Fiona*, armed boarding vessel, sunk by aircraft off Sollum.

1941 Light cruiser *Gloucester* bombarded the Bardia area.

1943 Submarine P 615, ex-Turkish *Uluc Ali Reis*, sunk by U-123 120 miles S. of Freetown (06.42N, 12.56W).

1943 Submarine *Regent* believed sunk by mine off Monopoli, in the southern Adriatic.

1947 Royal Navy detonated 7,000 tons of unstable explosives – including 4,000 torpedo heads, 9,000 depth charges and 51,000 grenades – beneath Heligoland to demolish fortifications. 'The greatest non-atomic explosion in history' (*The Times*) but barely heard in Cuxhaven. Lt-Cdr Francis Mildred RN fired the charges from the naval cable ship *Lasso* 9 miles offshore on the fourth pip of the BBC time signal at 1300. Smaller charges were fired beforehand to scare away migratory birds.
See 11 May 1945.

1955 Admiral the Earl Mountbatten of Burma succeeded Admiral Sir Rhoderick McGrigor as First Sea Lord, an appointment his father, Admiral HSH Prince Louis of Battenberg, had taken up on 2 December 1912.

1969 The Admiralty Board noted 'with grave concern' the giving of 'Sippers' and drew attention to QRRN Article 1839(3) which prohibited all 'loan, transfer, gift or barter' of spirits or other intoxicating drink. DCI(RN) 466/69.

1988 *Sandown*, third of the name and first of class of single-role minehunters, launched by HRH The Duchess of Gloucester at Vosper Thornycroft, Woolston. Together with *Bridport* and *Inverness*, she was sold to Estonia on 14 September 2006. *Sandown* handed over at Rosyth 26 April 2007 and renamed *Admiral Cowan* in honour of Rear-Admiral Sir Walter Cowan whose First Light Cruiser Squadron held the ring in the Baltic in 1919 against the Bolsheviks and secured the independence of Finland, Estonia, Lithuania and Latvia. A classic example of the influence of sea power.
See 14 February 1956, 16 April 1999.

The ship's company of HMS *Cornwall* at the military funeral at the Al-Chatby War Cemetery in 2005 for five men killed at the Battle of the Nile in 1798. (*RN*)

2005 Bodies of five British sailors, marines and soldiers, found by archaeologists on Nelson Island, Aboukir Bay, near Alexandria, were reburied with military honours in Al-Chatby Commonwealth War Cemetery by a party from the frigate *Chatham*, Capt S.J. Chick RN, in the presence of the British Ambassador to Egypt, Sir Derek Plumbly. The five Britons, including Cdr James Russell (the only one to be identified), died at the Battle of the Nile in 1798.
See 1 August 1798, 25 April 2005.

1587 'Singeing of the King of Spain's beard' by Sir Francis Drake (*Elizabeth Bonaventure*) at Cadiz. Ships: *Dreadnought, Elizabeth Bonaventure, Rainbow* and about thirty merchantmen. He wrote a memorable letter to Sir Francis Walsingham, too long to reprint but well worth looking up.

1757 Edward Pellew, the future Admiral Viscount Exmouth, born.

1770 Capt James Cook started to survey eastern Australia.

1781 *Resource* captured the French *Unicorne* 20 miles S.W. by W. of Cape Blaise (San Blas), Gulf of Mexico. Detachment of the loyal American Rangers and of Artillery were present.

1782 Rear-Admiral Sir Samuel Hood (*Barfleur*) captured four French ships in the Mona Passage, between Puerto Rico and San Domingo. Ships: *Alfred, Barfleur, Belliqueux, Magnificent, Monarch, Montagu, Prince William, Valiant, Warrior, Yarmouth.* Frigates: *Alecto, Champion.*

1900 New first-class cruiser *Argonaut*, Capt George Henry Cherry RN, commissioned at Chatham for the China Station. The Captain was a rigid disciplinarian, 'as smart as paint and as taut as an iron bar', who consistently awarded the maximum punishments set-out in KR&AI. She was ordered home on 9 May 1903 and, on being paid off, the famous Cherry Medal was struck as a memento of the commission by the five surviving officers, the rest all having been court-martialled or otherwise removed.

See 14 January 2008.

1917 Peak of Merchant Ship sinkings by U-boats.

See 10 May 1917.

First World War: The Convoy System

By the beginning of 1917 Germany had about 100 U-boats operating, and with their numbers increasing rapidly there was a dramatic increase in the damage they inflicted. Losses to shipping were:

Month	Ships Sunk	Tonnage
January	181	298,000
February	259	468,000
March	325	500,000
April	423	849,000

On one day alone (19 April) eleven British merchant ships and eight fishing vessels were sunk by submarines and mines. These losses could not have been sustained for more than about five months without totally crippling Britain. The convoy system was introduced in May and losses dropped dramatically.

1917 Submarines E 50 and UC-62 collided, both submerged off N. Hinder lightvessel.

1920 Cdr Bruce Fraser, lately XO of the battleship *Resolution* in the Mediterranean Fleet, left Constantinople with a naval party to assist White Russian naval operations based at Enzeli (Bandar-e-Pahlavi) on the Caspian Sea. The party, five officers and twenty-six men, entrained at Batum on the Black Sea for the Azerbaijan capital Baku where they were arrested by Bolshevik forces and imprisoned for five months. They were released on 5 November and finally got back to Batum to embark in the battleship *Centurion*.

See 15 October 1943, 26 December 1943, 12 February 1981.

1941 *Glengyle* landed a raiding party of 460 men to attack Bardia, Libya.

1944 *Ula* (Nor) sank U-974 off Stavanger.

1944 Allied naval force from Trincomalee under command of the British C-in-C Eastern Fleet, Admiral Sir James Somerville, attacked Sabang on the N.E. tip of Sumatra where a Japanese naval base commanded the N. entrance to the Malacca Straits.

Battle Honour: Sabang 1944.

See 25 July 1944.

With his flag in the battleship *Queen Elizabeth*, Somerville had the carrier *Illustrious* (flag of Rear-Admiral C. Moody), the battleship *Valiant*, battlecruiser *Renown* (flag of Vice-Admiral Sir Arthur Power), four cruisers (flag of Rear-Admiral A.D. Reed, 4th CS, in *Newcastle*), and seven destroyers of the Royal Navy, the carrier USS *Saratoga* and three destroyers of the US Navy, the French battleship *Richelieu*, the cruiser *Tromp* and a destroyer of the Royal Netherlands Navy, the New Zealand cruiser *Gambia* and four destroyers of the Royal Australian Navy. The *Illustrious* launched seventeen Barracuda and thirteen Corsair fighters and *Saratoga* launched eleven Avengers, eighteen Dauntless dive-bombers and twenty-four Hellcat fighters. Surprise was complete. Most of the oil tanks and twenty-four aircraft on the ground were destroyed and the harbour damaged. *Saratoga* lost one fighter whose pilot was rescued by the submarine *Tactician* lying offshore. Operation Cockpit. 1944.

Ships: *Ceylon, Illustrious, London, Newcastle, Nigeria, Queen Elizabeth, Penn, Petard, Quadrant, Queenborough, Quilliam* (D4), *Racehorse, Renown, Rotherham* (D11), *Valiant* and *Tactician*; HMNZS *Gambia*; HMAS *Napier, Nizam* and *Quiberon*; USS *Saratoga, Cummings, Dunlap* and *Fanning*; FNS *Richelieu*, HNlMS *Tromp* and *Van Galen*; NAS 810, 847 (Barraccuda), 1830, 1833 (Corsair).

1945 First flight of de Havilland Sea Hornet, Navy's first twin-engined, single-seat fighter.

1956 Cdr (Special Branch) Lionel Kenneth Philip 'Buster' Crabb, OBE, GM, RNVR, clearance diver, disappeared at Portsmouth during the visit of Soviet leaders Kruschev and Bulganin in the Sverdlov-class cruiser *Ordzhonikidze*. Prime Minister Sir Anthony Eden told the House of Commons that it would 'not be in the public interest' to disclose the circumstances of Cdr Crabb's death.

See 12 October 1955.

1963 Admiralty Fleet Order 762/63: 'To Commanders-in-Chief, Flag Officers, Senior Naval Officers, Captains and Commanding Officers of HM Ships and Vessels, Superintendents or Officers in Charge of HM Naval Establishments and Admiralty Overseers concerned. The attached Orders having been approved by My Lords Commissioners of the Admiralty are hereby promulgated. Issue of Rubber Gloves. Rubber gloves may be issued to those cleaners engaged on lavatory cleaning duties. These gloves are to be worn only for the specific purpose of dealing with lavatories. Supplies should be demanded from Post Office Supplies Department. Prior Admiralty approval is not required.'

See p.427 panel.

1967 Admiral of the Fleet The Earl of Cork and Orrery, 'Ginger' Boyle to the Service, died aged 93. Captain of cruiser *Fox* in Red Sea and Indian Ocean 1915–17 and had much contact with Lawrence of Arabia who mentions Boyle in *Seven Pillars of Wisdom*. C-in-C Home Fleet with flag in *Nelson* 1933–5. C-in-C Portsmouth in August 1937 and promoted admiral of the fleet 21 January 1938. Hauled down flag June 1939. Although senior to the C-in-C Home Fleet, Boyle was appointed Flag Officer Narvik in 1940 following the German invasion of Norway and flew his Union Flag afloat in the cruisers *Aurora, Effingham, Cairo* and finally *Southampton* in which he returned home on 8 June aged 67.

See 30 November 1873, 13 February 1892, 7–8 April 1940.

2004 Nuclear submarines *Tireless*, Trafalgar-class, and USS *Hampton*, Los Angeles-class, surfaced together at the North Pole following combined operational exercises beneath the polar ice cap.

See 3 March 1971.

Annual assembly of the Home and Mediterranean Fleets in Gibraltar in March 1935. Three thousand men marched past the Governor of Gibraltar, General Sir Charles Harington and their respective Cs-in-C, Admiral the Earl of Cork and Orrery (*right*) and Admiral Sir William Fisher (*left*). Over eighty ships had gathered including nine capital ships, eleven cruisers and three aircraft carriers. (*NMRN*)

20 April

1657 Admiral Robert Blake (*George*) destroyed sixteen Spanish ships at Santa Cruz, Tenerife. Nelson's Band of Brothers' phrase is wonderfully anticipated in almost biblical language in Blake's dispatch written before the attack: 'We are all together and behold one another's face with comfort.'
Battle Honour: Santa Cruz 1657.
See 10 March 1650, 24 July 1797.

Ships: *Bridgewater, Bristol, Centurion, Colchester, Convert, Fairfax, Foresight, George, Hampshire, Jersey, Langport, Lyme, Maidstone, Nantwich, Newbury, Newcastle, Plymouth, Ruby, Speaker, Swiftsure, Unicorn, Winsby, Worcester.*

This was a great risk taken, and a great reward. 'The whole action was so miraculous that all men who knew the place wondered why any man, with what courage so ever endowed would have undertaken it, and they could hardly persuade themselves to believe what they had done, while the Spaniards comforted themselves with the belief that they were devils and not men who had destroyed them in such a manner.' Blake died on 7 August, just off Plymouth.

1667 *Princess* fought seventeen Dutch men-of-war off the Dogger Bank.
Battle Honour: North Sea 1667.

1807 Boats of *Richmond* cut out the Spanish privateer *Galliard* 18 miles N. of Peniche, Portugal.

1810 *Firm, Sharpshooter* and *Surly* captured the French privateer *Alcide* at Pirou, Granville Bay, north coast of France.

1814 *Orpheus* and *Shelburne* captured the American *Frolic* 15 miles N.N.W. of Puerto Matanzas, Cuba.

1837 Capt Robert Contart McCrea, with boats from brig sloop *Zebra*, captured the ex-Rajah of Kedah at Bruas, Perak.

1906 'The Navy is a very conservative service, tenacious of tradition, deeply and rightly imbued with the sentiment of its glorious past, and very suspicious of any innovations which seem to ignore that tradition' – *The Times*.

1917 Paddle minesweeper *Nepaulin* mined near Dyke lightvessel off Dunkirk.

HMS *Auckland* (1938), an Egret-class sloop. (*NMRN*)

Robert Blake (1599–1657)

Although Blake is not so well known as Drake or Nelson, he merits the same acclaim. He was the son of a merchant, noticed by Cromwell as a competent soldier and an able MP. He was an ardent Parliamentarian but in 1649 at the age of 50 became one of the three 'generals at sea'. Not only did he achieve eventual victory over the Dutch and place Britain in a leading position of maritime power, but his 'Fighting Instructions' formed the basis of fleet tactics at sea for the next century. He was also responsible for drafting the 'Laws and Ordinances of the Sea', the basis for the first Articles of War, which are the foundations of Naval discipline. 'He was the first that gave example of that kind of naval courage and bold and resoloute achievements' – Clarendon. With Samuel Pepys he was one of the founding fathers of the the modern Navy.

See 7 August 1667.

Robert Blake (1599–1657). (*NMRN 1971/12(46)*)

1940 Trawler *Rutlandshire* bombed and driven ashore, and *Auckland* damaged, at Namsos, by German aircraft.

1940 *Pansy*, Flower-class corvette, launched at Harland and Wolff. Promptly renamed *Heartsease*.

1949 *Amethyst*, frigate, fired on by Communist PLA batteries in Yangtze River east of Nanking. Opening of the Yangtze Incident.

See 8 April 1927, 30 July 1949.

1962 'Full dress sword belts are available to hire to Officers of Flag Rank (other than Admirals of the Fleet). The belts are provided in four sizes . . . Vocab 41023, Size 4, 44 inches . . . Apply to the Superintending Victualling Store Officer, HM Naval Victualling Depot, Crescent Road, Bolton.' – AFO 736/62.

1991 UK/Netherlands Landing Force, commanded by Maj-Gen R.J. Ross, MGRM, Joint Force Commander, deployed to Turkey–Iraq frontier areas on humanitarian mission to assist Kurdish refugees following Gulf War. Operation Haven. RFA *Argus*, RFA *Resource*, HQ 3 Cdo Bde, 40 Cdo, 45 Cdo, Cdo Logistic Regt, 3 Cdo Bde Air Squadron, Sea Kings from 845 NAS and 846 NAS.

HMS *Amethyst* at Hong Kong after the Yangtze Incident, showing damage from Chinese shore batteries, 1949. (*NMRN*)

21 April

1702 Overseer and Inspector of naval chaplains first appointed, by Order in Council.

1782 *Foudroyant* (80) took the French *Pégase* 30 miles N.N.W. of Ushant. Capt J. Jervis made KB and given a winged horse in his grant of arms.
Battle Honour: *Pégase* 1782.

1796 *Indefatigable* (38) captured the French *Virginie* (44) 80 miles W.S.W. of the Scilly Isles.
Battle Honour: *Virginie* 1796.

1798 New French two-decker *l'Hercule* (74) struck to the *Mars* (74) after a furious broadside to broadside engagement at anchor in the Passage du Raz (Raz de Sein) off Brest. Capt Alexander Hood of the *Mars* was mortally wounded by a musket ball but lived long enough to receive the sword of the equally gallant Capt Louis l'Heritier. The prize was commissioned into the Royal Navy as HMS *Hercule*.
Battle Honour: *Hercule* 1798.

1904 Capture of Illig, Somaliland. Ships: *Fox*, *Hyacinth*, *Mohawk* and the Italian *Volturno*. 1st Bn The Hampshire Regt Africa General Service Medal: clasp 'Somaliland 1902–4'.

1911 'A case having arisen in which a ship's compass was deflected from 3 degrees to 7 degrees by the proximity of a person wearing a truss which had become highly magnetised, it has been decided that no man who has to wear a truss is to take the duty of helmsman of quartermaster.' AWO 117/11.

1916 Unidentified U-boat sunk in nets of the smack *I'll Try It*.

1917 Destroyer leaders *Swift*, Cdr A.M. Peck RN, and *Broke*, Cdr E.R.G.R. Evans RN, augmenting the standard night-time Dover patrol, intercepted six German destroyers returning home at full speed after bombarding Dover and Calais. In a furious and confused action, *Swift* torpedoed G.85 and *Broke* rammed G.42 amidships. With her bows locked into G.42, *Broke* fired several rounds from her 4-in gun into the enemy at point blank range, officers on the bridge engaged with their revolvers and Midshipman D.A. Gyles RNR led a party on her forecastle repelling boarders with rifles and cutlasses 'in a hand-to-hand action reminiscent of an earlier age' – Halpern. The badly shot-up *Broke* had twenty-one men killed and was towed back to Dover with 140 German prisoners 'to whom, when I later visited the mess-deck, I found our men giving a fried egg and bacon breakfast' – Evans. The action thrilled the nation and raised the Royal Navy's stock; 'Evans of the *Broke*' became a household name. Awards included one CGM, nine DSCs, twenty-four DSMs and thirty-four Mentions in Despatches. Both Engineer Lt-Cdrs were promoted; Peck and Evans were both appointed DSO and promoted. A fine destroyer action to match that of Capt Warburton-Lee at Narvik in 1940 and the 26th DF off Singapore in 1945.
Battle Honour: Dover 1917.

See 28 October 1880, 6 March 1921, 22 October 1936, 10 April 1940, 16 May 1945, 20 November 1957.

1918 ML 413 sank UB-71 W. of Gibraltar (35.58N, 05.18W).

Make and Mend in the battleship HMS *Hindustan* (1903). (*NMRN*)

1941 Bombardment of Tripoli by Admiral Sir Andrew Cunningham (*Warspite*). Ships: *Barham, Gloucester, Hasty, Havock, Hereward, Hero, Hotspur, Jaguar, Janus, Jervis, Juno, Valiant, Warspite*. Mark ship: *Truant*. Albacores of 826 and 829 NAS and Fulmars of 803 and 806 NAS (*Formidable*).

1941 German air raid seriously damaged Devonport naval base, including St Nicholas' church.

1943 Submarine *Splendid* scuttled after depth-charge attack by the German-manned destroyer *Hermes* (ZG-3).* Finally sunk by gunfire 2 miles S.S.E. of Capri. *Ex-Hellenic *Vasilefs Georgios I*.

See 17 December 1942.

1945 *Bazely, Bentinck* and *Drury*, Captain-class frigates, sank U-636 in N.W. Approaches.

1945 Frigate *Retalick* engaged several German explosive motor boats 210° Ostende 28 miles, sinking four.

1958 Vice-Admiral Sir Stephen Carlill made an honorary vice-admiral in the Indian Navy, 'the first British officer in modern times to hold an honorary rank in any navy outside the Royal Navy' – Mountbatten. Admiral Carlill had been Chief of Naval Staff of the Indian Navy from 22 July 1955 to 21 April 1958, the last British officer in executive command of any Indian military forces. Indian Defence Minister Krishna Menon said it was a spontaneous expression of appreciation by the government and people of India for the great service Admiral Carlill had done for their navy.

1970 Vice-Admiral Sir Arthur Francis 'Attie' Turner, Chief of Fleet Support, promoted to admiral. The first marine Engineering Officer and the first of a non-executive branch to reach four-star rank in the Royal Navy following the introduction of the General List in 1956 which opened many posts to officers of any specialisation.

'. . . a little mention [of the promotion's significance] in Hickey [column, *Daily Express*] or Peterborough [column, *Daily Telegraph*] would fall as music on the ears of all that boot-faced purple crew who [seek?] to make my life a misery' – manuscript memo from Admiral Sir Michael Le Fanu, First Sea Lord, to DPR(N) dated 19 January 1970.

See 22 October 1963, 28 June 1976, 2 April 1979, 26 October 1991, 19 January 2000.

1989 *Quorn*, last of eleven Hunt-class MCMVs, commissioned.

2006 The frigate *Kent*, at anchor in the Hamoaze, fired a 21-gun salute to mark the 80th birthday of HM The Queen. The ship's company of the carrier *Illustrious*, on passage south through the Red Sea, fell in on the flight deck to spell out 'Happy 80th'.

The Bombardment of Odessa from a drawing by Lt O'Reilly of HMS *Retribution*, 1854. (*NMRN 1977/381*)

22 April

1793 All captains became entitled to half-pay when not actively employed.

1813 *Weazle* destroyed four French gunboats and eight vessels of a convoy in Boscaline (Marina) Bay, Adriatic.
Battle Honour: Boscaline Bay 1813.

1847 Detachment of North American and West Indies squadron – *Alarm*, *Daring*, *Hermes*, *Vesuvius* and *Persian* – protected British interests in Gulf of Mexico during American–Mexico War.

1848 *Erebus* and *Terror*, on Franklin's ill-fated expedition in search of the North West Passage, abandoned in the Arctic having been ice-bound since 12 September 1846. Sir John Franklin died on 11 June 1847.

1854 Bombardment of Odessa for twelve hours. British ships: *Arethusa*, *Furious*, *Retribution*, *Sampson*, *Terrible*, *Tiger*. French: *Caton*, *Descartes*, *Mogador*, *Vauban*. Rocket boats of *Agamemnon*, *Britannia*, *Highflyer*, *Sans Pareil*, *Trafalgar*. *Arethusa*, the only purely sailing ship in the squadron, operated separately. This was the last occasion when a sailing ship in action was manoeuvred under sail. Her consorts were all paddle steamers.

1861 Metropolitan Police of the 1st Division took over security duties at Woolwich Dockyard. Establishment: 1 superintendent, 10 inspectors, 30 sergeants and 149 PCs.

1916 Battlecruisers *Australia* and *New Zealand* collided. Former missed Jutland and never fired a shot in anger.

1918 Destroyers *Jackal* and *Hornet* drove off Austrian attack on Otranto defences.

1918 UB-55 sunk by mine north of Varne lightvessel.

1930 London Naval Treaty signed at St James's Palace.

1933 Vice-Admiral Sir William Rooke Creswell died aged 80. Former Lieutenant RN and cattle drover, and later the founder of the Royal Australian Navy.

Creswell was born at Gibraltar on 20 July 1852 (hence the name Rooke) and entered the RN in 1865 aged 13. He resigned in 1878 and migrated to Australia where he spent many years cattle droving in Northern Territory. An old shipmate, then Commandant of the South Australian Naval Forces, offered him an XO appointment in the Colony's only warship, *Protector*, which he accepted. Creswell later commanded the ship in Chinese waters during the Boxer Rebellion in 1900. Creswell was to become an articulate advocate of an Australian naval force which development gained power with the creation of the Commonwealth in 1901. In 1911 Creswell was made First Naval Member of the new Naval Board and de facto C-in-C of the newly constituted Royal Australian Navy. He retired in 1919 and was promoted vice-admiral in 1922. Plaque erected in Naval Chapel, Garden Island, Sydney, 1937. His name is perpetuated in HMAS *Creswell* at Jervis Bay.

1940 Sloop *Pelican* damaged by German aircraft off Norway (62.49N, 04.20E).

Battle of the Atlantic, March to May 1943

Nine hundred and twelve ships sailed in North Atlantic convoys during this period. March 1943, eastbound convoy HX 228 was escorted by an experienced mixed British, Free French and Polish escort group. The destroyer *Harvester* detected a U-boat on the surface by radar and rammed it. *Harvester* and the U-boat were damaged. The French corvette *Aconit* sank the submarine. *Harvester* then came to a standstill as a result of action damage and was torpedoed and sunk as *Aconit* returned to assist. *Aconit* sank the U-boat by depth-charging and ramming. U-121 also attacked the convoy, was hit by debris from an exploding ship and blinded, and just escaped being sunk by the escorts in a counter-attack. Five merchant ships were lost.

HX 229, which followed, had a weak escort and was set upon by thirty-eight U-boats in all. There was no air cover or rescue ship, and thirteen merchant ships were sunk. SC 122 was slightly ahead of HX 229, but slower. When the two convoys joined, the U-boats attacked and SC 122's regular escort was overwhelmed. Eight more ships were lost. One U-boat was sunk, and the battle ended when aircraft from Iceland were able to assist the escorts. Although on the face of it a German victory, German records revealed that two U-boats were severely damaged and nearly all other U-boats received bomb or depth-charge attacks.

In April HX 231 lost only three ships with two U-boats sunk. HX 233 lost one ship, with one U-boat sunk.

The turning point came with convoy ONS 5, escorted by Cdr Gretton's escort group. Forty ships sailed on 22 April with six escorts. After five days of gales one merchant ship had detached to Iceland for repairs, and one fallen behind. At one time eight were showing 'Not Under Command' lights. U-boats converged on 28th, and the escorts followed HFDF bearings to keep the 'homing' U-boats down. That night the escorts forced U-boats down six times, using radar to detect them in a rising gale.

The next day one merchant ship was sunk, but most U-boats went ahead to join another group and lie in wait. Five days of bad weather followed and the convoy was scattered by gales, and low visibility. On 5 and 6 May the U-boats struck: eleven ships were sunk. One U-boat was sunk by RCAF aircraft, another by a corvette escorting a group of eleven stragglers. Fog on the 6th gave the escort the chance to use their radar to advantage, and twenty-four attacks were detected and beaten off: U-638 sunk by *Sunflower* and U-125 by *Oribi*; U-531 was rammed by *Vidette* and U-438 sunk by depth charges from *Pelican* (just joining with the 1st Escort Group). A total of sixty U-boats attacked. Six were sunk and twelve merchantmen lost. Two other U-boats collided and were lost. Others were badly damaged. In all, twenty-seven U-boats were sunk during this period. U-boat command morale fell, and there was a reluctance to attack future convoys.

Poster issued by the Admiralty, 1941. (*NMRN 1996/26(3)*)

On 24 May 1943, U-boats were withdrawn from the North Atlantic routes, and the Battle of the Atlantic had been largely won.

1944 Frigates *Swansea* and *Matane* (RCN) sank U-311.

1966 HM The Queen extended to chief and petty officers the privilege of drinking the Sovereign's health seated 'when they are dining formally in their messes both ashore and afloat' – DCI(RN) 571/66.

1969 Lt Robin Knox-Johnston, RNR, arrived back at Falmouth in his 32ft yacht *Suhaili* after 312 days alone at sea and having achieved the first solo, non-stop circumnavigation of the world.

Sir Robin Knox-Johnston, Master Mariner, was knighted in 1995 having won the Jules Verne Trophy for the fastest-ever circumnavigation of the world under sail in 74 days 22 hours 18 minutes and 22 seconds.

See 4 April 1581, 7 July 1967, 7 February 2005.

1982 Wessex helicopter from destroyer *Antrim* retrieved SAS and FAA personnel from Fortuna Glacier, South Georgia in unusually bad weather. Operation Corporate.

1983 Admiral of the Fleet Lord Lewin of Greenwich appointed third naval KG since Admiral Lord Howe in 1797. Installed 13 June 1983. Other recipients were Queen Victoria's second son, the Duke of Edinburgh, and the Earl Mountbatten of Burma.

See 19 November 1982, 23 January 1999.

23 April

A Memorable Date observed by the Corps of Royal Marines – Zeebrugge

1349 Foundation of the Order of the Garter, originally that of St George, by King Edward III.

1697 George Anson, circumnavigator and First Lord of the Admiralty, born at Shugborough Hall, Colwich, Staffordshire.

1786 A Flag Captain 'is never his own master' – Capt Nelson, HMS *Boreas*, Carlisle Bay, Barbados, to his future wife, Frances Nisbet, at Nevis.

1794 *Arethusa, Concorde, Flora* and *Melampus* captured the French *Babet, Engageante* and *Pomone* 25 miles S.W. of Guernsey.

1797 *Magicienne* and *Regulus* repulsed a French attack on Fort Irois, Haiti.

1804 Viscount Nelson, Vice-Admiral of the Blue, C-in-C Mediterranean Fleet, gazetted Vice-Admiral of the White, the highest rank he attained in the Royal Navy.
See 1 January 1801.

1809 Boats of *Amphion, Mercury* and *Spartan* captured thirteen vessels at Porto Pesaro, E. coast of Italy.

1853 *James Watt* (80), screw second rate, 4,950 tons, one of the last wooden two-deckers built for the Royal Navy, launched at Pembroke Dockyard. The only ship of the name in the Service.

1856 Queen Victoria reviewed Fleet at Spithead; 240 ships, many having just returned from Baltic and Black Sea.

1895 *Vernon* shifted to Porchester Creek.
See 26 April 1876, 1 October 1923, 31 March 1986.

1915 Burial of Sub-Lt Rupert Brooke, RNVR, on Scyros, off Troy.
See 17 May 1961.

1916 Sloop *Bluebell* intercepted German *Aud* in effort to support Irish rebellion. Latter scuttled off Queenstown (Cork).

1918 St George's Day attack on Zeebrugge to block the German U-boat exit to the sea. VC: A/Capt Alfred Francis Blakeney Carpenter (*Vindictive*), Lt-Cdr George Nicholson Bradford* (*Iris*), Lt-Cdr Arthur Leyland Harrison* (*Vindictive*), Lt Richard Douglas Sandford (C 3), Lt Percy Thompson Dean, RNVR (ML 282), Capt Edward Bamford, DSO, RMLI, Sgt Norman Augustus Finch, RMA (4th RM Battalion), AB Albert Edward MacKenzie (*Vindictive*). *Posthumous. Blockship operations at Zeebrugge and Ostend. Battle Honour: Zeebrugge 1918.

Ships: *Afridi, Attentive,*† *Brilliant, Daffodil, Erebus, Faulknor,*† *General Craufurd,*† *Intrepid, Iphigenia, Iris, Lightfoot,*† *Lingfield, Lord Clive,*† *Manly, Mansfield, Marshal Soult,*† *Mastiff,*† *Matchless,*† *Melpomene, Mentor,*† *Moorsom, Morris, Myngs, North Star, Phoebe, Prince Eugene,*† *Scott, Sirius,*† *Stork, Swift,*† *Teazer, Tempest,*† *Termagant, Terror, Tetrarch,*† *Thetis, Trident, Truculent, Ulleswater, Velox, Vindictive, Warwick, Whirlwind, Zubian.*† Monitors: M 21,

HMS *Iris* and *Daffodil* at Dover after the Zeebrugge raid, April 1918. (*NMM Neg. No. N18123*)

Admiral Lord Anson (1697–1762). (*NMRN 1986/702*)

M 24, M 26. Submarines: C 1, C 3. CMB: 2, 4, 5, 7, 10, 12, 15A, 16A, 17A, 19A, 20A, 21B, 22B, 23B, 24A, 25BD, 26B, 27A, 28A, 29A, 30B, 32A, 34A, 35A. ML: 11, 16, 17, 22, 23, 30, 60, 79, 105, 110, 121, 128, 223, 239, 241, 252, 254, 258, 262, 272, 274, 276, 279, 280, 282, 283, 308, 314, 345, 397, 416, 420, 422, 424, 429, 512, 513, 525, 526, 532, 533, 549, 551, 552, 555, 556, 557, 558, 560, 561, 562. 4th Battalion RM. *Intrepid*, *Iphigenia* and *Thetis* sunk as blockships; C 3 expended; *Iris* and *Daffodil*, Mersey ferries, renamed *Royal Iris* and *Royal Daffodil* by command of King George V.

†Took part in the unsuccessful Ostend operation.

DSO: Revd Charles John Eyre Peshall, Chaplain of *Vindictive*. Under heavy enemy fire 'his cheerful encouragement and assistance to the wounded, calm demeanour during the din of battle, strength of character and splendid comradeship were most conspicuous to all with whom he came into contact. . . He showed great physical strength and did almost superhuman work in carrying wounded from the Mole over the brow of *Vindictive*.' Chaplain of the Fleet in 1933. He was a commanding presence at Greenwich in 'his archdeacon's black garb and gaiters, but his boxer's countenance and his row of medal ribbons alone gave any hint of his martial history' – Revd Gordon Taylor, *The Sea Chaplains*, p.343. Retired 1935. Rejoined RN 1940.

Zeebrugge and Ostend, 1918

In the First World War these ports were used by the Germans as submarine bases with easy access to the British sea lanes. Admiral Sir Roger Keyes planned the raids intended to block them which were launched on 23 April 1918. They were scarcely successful.

The Zeebrugge attack was carried through with great heroism under heavy enemy fire. Three old minelayers, *Intrepid*, *Iphigenia* and *Thetis*, filled with concrete, were sunk in the canal. The old cruiser *Vindictive* landed an assault party of seamen and marines on the Long Mole, held in position by two Mersey ferries, *Iris* and *Daffodil*. The obsolete submarine C 3 was driven in under the shoreward end of the Mole and blown up, cutting the Mole's defenders off from reinforcements. Motor launches were used in the attack and to take off blockship crews.

The battle on the Mole was ferocious and the crews of *Vindictive* and *Iris*, as well as the assault parties, carried out the attack with remarkable resolution, although their ships were shot full of holes and their casualties were terrible. There are dozens of tales of heroism and of the eight VCs awarded, some were allocated by ballot under Rule 13 of the Royal Warrant since it would have been impossible to choose between them. Fifty per cent of the Royal Marines were casualties, and as a special honour no other RM battalion has ever again been numbered the 4th. But the port was operational within two days.

The Ostend operation did not succeed since the blockships were sunk before reaching their target. *Vindictive* sailed again, this time as a blockship. Her bows are now a War Memorial in the port of Ostend.

1940 Troops and naval base staff landed at Mole, Norway.

1943 *Hesperus* sank U-191 in N. Atlantic (56.45N, 34.25W). Convoy ONS 4. First success by Hedgehog.

1947 Battleship *Warspite* ran ashore in Prussia Cove, Cornwall on her way to breakers. Broken up there instead.

1955 The First Lord of the Admiralty, Rt Hon. J.P.L. Thomas, took the salute when the Regimental Colour of Royal Marines Eastney was trooped to mark the Corps day of reunion and to commemorate the 200th anniversary of the Marines being established. The Colour trooped had been presented to Portsmouth Division Royal Marines by HRH The Duke of Kent on 3 December 1931.

See 7 May 1955.

1956 New Colours presented to RMB Eastney by HRH The Duke of Edinburgh, Captain General Royal Marines.

2011 Admiral the Lord Boyce, former First Sea Lord and CDS, became only the fourth naval officer since Admiral Howe in 1797 to be made KG. The third was Admiral of the Fleet Lord Lewin in 1983.

See 12 April 2005.

24 April

1546 Navy Board appointed by letters patent to assist the Lord High Admiral.

1590 Ten English merchantmen beat off an attack by twelve Spanish galleys near Gibraltar. Ships: *Ascension, Centurion, Crescent, Elizabeth, Margaret and John, Minion, Richard Duffield, Samuel, Solomon, Violet*.

1626 Seamen to be paid 14*s* per month, less 2*d* for the barber (i.e. surgeon), 4*d* for preacher and 6*d* to the Chatham Chest.

1709 *Bristol* taken by the French *Achille* and *Gloire* 330 miles S.W. by S. of Lizard Head. *Chester* captured *Gloire* and recaptured *Bristol*.

1771 Horatio Nelson ('Horace Nelson, Midshipman') joined his first ship, the *Raisonnable* (64), commanded by his uncle, Capt Maurice Suckling RN, at The Nore.

See 1 January 1771.

1778 *Drake* taken by John Paul Jones in the American *Ranger* off Carrickfergus, N. Ireland.

1808 *Grasshopper* and *Rapid* captured two Spanish vessels and two gunboats, and wrecked two more gunboats off Faro, Portugal.

1915 DSC: Mid Eric Wheler Bush, aged 15, the youngest-ever recipient. Commanded picket boat from cruiser *Bacchante* landing troops at Anzac Bay, Gallipoli. Captain of the cruiser *Euryalus* and three DSOs. In combat from the Battle of Heiligoland Bight in 1914 to operations against the Japanese on the Burmese coast in 1945. Captain of *Ganges* 1946–8 in Second World War.

1916 VC: Lt Humphrey Osbaldeston Brooke Firman RN and Lt-Cdr Charles Henry Cowley. In a desperate attempt to fight supplies through to General Townshend's besieged 10,000-strong British garrison at Kut-al' Amara on the Tigris in Mesopotamia, Brooke, with Cowley as his 2 i/c and an all-volunteer crew, set off up-river from Fallahiya at dusk in the 750-ton steamer SS *Julnar*. They came under intense Turkish shell and rifle fire and finally ran into a chain boom over the river below Magasis Fort, 5 miles short of Kut. Firman was killed on the bridge. Cowley, Baghdad-born and well known on the Tigris and Euphrates, was forced to surrender and was executed by the Turks. A war crimes investigation was inconclusive. Every man in the *Julna* was decorated. Both names are on the Basra war memorial. The awards were gazetted 2 February 1917. Townshend surrendered to the Turks on 29 April – with Singapore in 1941 perhaps the greatest ever humiliation in British military history.

See 28 September 1915.

1916 UB-3 destroyed off Zeebrugge by *Gleaner of the Sea*.

1916 Submarine E 22 conducted 'float-off' trials of two Sopwith Schneider seaplanes (Nos 3730, 3743). The purpose of this first submarine/aircraft trial was to achieve an up-threat interdiction of Zeppelins over the North Sea.

1918 The last wartime deployment into the North Sea by the Grand Fleet 'in full fighting array'. Admiral Sir David Beatty sailed with 193 ships including thirty-one battleships, four battlecruisers, twenty-four light cruisers and eighty-five destroyers to counter a reported sortie by the German High Seas Fleet.

1940 Light cruiser *Curacoa* damaged by German aircraft at Andalsnes.

1941 Operation Demon, the evacuation of Imperial troops from Greece, began on night of 24/25 April. 'And so it again fell to the Royal Navy to save what it could of a British Army at the end of a foredoomed campaign' – Correlli Barnett. All available Mediterranean Fleet ships, seven cruisers, nineteen destroyers, two sloops and two corvettes together with transports were involved under the command of Vice-Admiral H.D. Pridham-Wippell, flag in light cruiser *Orion* at Suda Bay in Crete.

See 29 April 1941, p.199 panel.

The Navy's steam-pickets towing boats ashore, April 1915. Of these operations at Gallipoli, the commander of the military force Sir Ian Hamilton's (1853–1947) dispatch read, 'throughout the events . . . the Royal Navy has been father and mother to the Army'. (*NMRN 1977/382*)

1943 Fortress D/206 sank U-710 south of Iceland (61.25N, 19.48W). Convoy ONS 5.

1943 Submarine *Sahib* sunk by depth-charge attack by the Italian corvettes *Gabbiano* and *Euterpe* and TB *Climene* north of Cape Milazzo (38.25N, 15.20E). The third submarine to be lost within one week, and the seventh in four months.

1944 Sunderland A/423 (RCAF) sank U-311 in W. Approaches (50.36N, 18.36W).

1959 RN Helicopter Station, Portland, the first Service helicopter station in the UK, opened by the C-in-C Portsmouth, Vice-Admiral Sir Manley Power. First FAA squadron based at Portland was 815 NAS with Whirlwinds.

1988 Frigate *Cornwall* commissioned at Falmouth. Attended by HRH The Princess of Wales, Duchess of Cornwall.

1991 RM and QARNNS deployed to S.E. Turkey and thence into N. Iraq, to provide security and humanitarian aid for Kurdish refugees after Operation Granby. Operation Haven.

25 April

Anzac Day

1513 Sir Edward Howard, the Lord High Admiral, killed in action with Chevalier Pregent de Bidoux off Brest: 'When he saw that he could not be saved he threw his silver whistle of office into the sea, that a British admiral's insignia should not fall into enemy hands, and so was drowned.'
See 2 August 1511.

1725 Augustus Keppel, the future Admiral Viscount Keppel, born.

1796 Boats of *Agamemnon*, *Diadem*, *Meleager* and *Peterel* captured four French storeships at Loana, Italian Riviera.

1825 Capture of Prome, Burma.
See 2 April 1825.

1831 *Black Joke* captured the slaver *Marinerito* 18 miles E.S.E. of Cape Horacio, Fernando Po.

1858 *Pearl*'s Naval Brigade at Amorcha, with the 13th Light Infantry, Bengal Yeomanry, 1st Bengal Military Police Battalion and Gurkha allies.

1868 Launch of the eighth *Repulse*. Last wooden capital ship, and last major ship launched at Woolwich. Completed at Sheerness.

1908 Cruiser *Gladiator* sunk in collision with the American SS *St Paul* in Solent with loss of twenty-seven men.

1911 First naval pilots completed initial flying training at Eastchurch and qualified for the Aviator's Certificate of the Royal Aero Club: Lts R. Gregory, A.M. Longmore and C.R. Samson, and Lt E.L. Gerrard, RMLI.
See 2 March 1911.

1915 VC: Cdr Edward Unwin (*Hussar*); Sub-Lt Arthur Walderne St Clair Tisdall, RNVR; Mid Wilfred St Aubyn Malleson (*Cornwallis*); Mid George Leslie Drewry, RNR (*Hussar*); William Charles Williams, Able Seaman RFR; George McKenzie Samson, Seaman RNR (*Hussar*). Landing at Gallipoli – V Beach (*River Clyde*). AB Williams RFR was the first posthumous naval VC and Drewry the first RNR VC. All were serving in the *River Clyde* at the time.

1916 German battlecruiser bombardment of Lowestoft and Yarmouth.

1916 Submarine E 22 torpedoed and sunk by UB-18 off Yarmouth after what in RAF parlance was a dogfight.

1918 Sloop *Jessamine* sank U-104 in south Irish Sea (51.59N, 06.26W).

1918 Minesweeper *St Seiriol* mined off Shipwash lightvessel.

1918 Sloop *Cowslip* torpedoed by UB-105 and sunk off Cape Spartel.

1918 *Willow Branch* (*Bombala*) (Q-ship) sunk by U-153 and U-154 east of the Cape Verde Islands (20.50N, 17.20W).

1925 RN Division Memorial, designed by Sir Edward Lutyens, dedicated on Horse Guards Parade, the tenth anniversary of the Gallipoli landings. Address by Mr Winston Churchill who, as First Lord of the Admiralty, had formed the RND.
See 26 May 1951, 31 May 1981, 13 November 2003.

The *River Clyde* at V Beach, Gallipoli, 1915. (*NMRN*)

A destroyer laden with troops, her bridge protected by splinter mats, Gallipoli 1915. (*NMRN*)

1940 Three Cricketer-class hired A/S trawlers, *Bradman*, *Hammond* and *Larwood*, sunk by German aircraft at Andalsnes, S. of Kristiansund. All three salvaged and entered service with Kriegsmarine.

1941 *Ulster Prince*, supply ship, destroyed by aircraft at Nauplia after grounding on the 24th. Operation Demon.

1941 Destroyer *Defender* embarked 250 soldiers and the Yugoslav crown jewels at Kalamata in the evacuation from Greece. Operation Demon.
See 11 July 1941.

1943 Destroyer *Pathfinder* and aircraft of 811 Sqn (*Biter*) sank U-203 in N.W. Atlantic (55.05N, 42.25W). Convoy ONS 4.

1945 *Venturer* recalled from last S/M patrol in home waters in Second World War.

1953 The extension of the Portsmouth naval war memorial commemorating officers and men from Portsmouth-manned ships and ratings of the Portsmouth port division lost in the Second World War unveiled by HM Queen Elizabeth The Queen Mother.

1956 *Porpoise*, the first operational submarine designed since the Second World War and incorporating lessons learned from the German Type XXI U-boats, launched at Vickers, Barrow, by Mrs J.D. Luce, wife of the Naval Secretary. Commissioned at Barrow by Lt-Cdr B.C.G. Hutchings RN, 17 April 1958; service conducted by Revd D. Welsh RN, Chaplain to *Adamant*, depot ship of the Third Submarine Flotilla.

1967 *Valiant*, Cdr Peter Herbert RN, the second of the RN's SSNs and the first of all-British design, arrived in the Clyde after a submerged passage from Singapore which she left on 28 March.

1982 Helicopters from *Antrim*, *Brilliant*, *Endurance* and *Plymouth* crippled Argentine S/M *Santa Fe* off South Georgia, *Endurance* helicopter claimed to have fired first missile used by RN, endorsed by C-in-C Fleet. Operation Paraquet.

2005 Frigate *Chatham*, Capt S.J. Chick RN, represented the Royal Navy at the 90th anniversary commemorations in Turkey of the First World War Gallipoli landings. The previous ship of the name, the light cruiser *Chatham*, took part in the Allied landings in 1915 and won the battle honour 'Dardanelles 1915–16'.
See 18 April 2006.

26 April

1780 *Fortune* (14), sloop, taken by two French frigates in West Indies.

1796 *Niger* destroyed the French *Ecureuil* under Penmarc'h Point, Brittany.

1797 *Emerald* and *Irresistible* captured the Spanish *Elena* and *Ninfa* in Conil Bay, near Cadiz.

1809 *Thrasher* fought forty French gunboats off Boulogne.

1810 *Sylvia* captured the Dutch *Echo* and two small transports 10 miles N. of Batavia.
Battle Honour: *Echo* 1810.

1810 First appointment to Milford dockyard, Pembrokeshire.

1810 The body of Vice-Admiral Lord Collingwood lay in state at Greenwich until his funeral in St Paul's Cathedral on 11 May 1810.
See 7 March 1810.

1843 The paddle yacht *Victoria and Albert*, 1,034 tons, launched. The first of three royal yachts of the name built at Pembroke Dockyard.
See 16 January 1855, 9 May 1899.

1861 *Brune* and *Fidelity*, with boats of *Alecto*, *Arrogant*, *Espoir* and *Ranger*, destroyed Porto Novo, Dahomey.

1865 *Bellerophon*, broadside ironclad, floated out of dry dock at Chatham. The first battleship to have a balanced rudder. 'Built at Chatham in the historical dry dock which was the cradle of iron ship construction in the Royal Dockyards, and was herself only the second government-built iron-hulled vessel.' – Ballard, *The Black Battlefleet*, p.67.
See 23 December 1863.

1876 *Vernon*, established in 1872 as torpedo instruction ship in Fountain Lake, and as tender to *Excellent*, became an independent command under Capt William Arthur RN with Cdr A.K. Wilson as Commander.
See 23 April 1895, 1 October 1923, 31 March 1986.

1881 Composite screw sloop *Doterel*, Cdr Richard Evans RN, newly built at Chatham, on her way to her first commission on the Pacific Station, sank off Punta Arenas in the Magellan Straits from an explosion in her fore magazine. Divers from composite screw corvette HMS *Garnet* found the ship in two parts lying in 11 fathoms with widely dispersed wreckage. Admiralty concluded on 3 September that the explosion caused by gasses from a particular paint and ordered all stocks in the Fleet to be destroyed. Memorial in Chapel of RN College, Greenwich, to 143 officers and men lost.
See 16 December 2008.

1916 *Helga*, an armed patrol vessel, bombarded Irish rebels in Dublin. Sold, ironically, to Irish government in 1922.

1922 Launch of oiler RFA *Oleander*, last ship built at Pembroke Dockyard. Sunk Harstad Bay 8 June 1940 during Norwegian campaign.

1928 First Admiralty production order for multiple pom-pom AA guns.

HMY *Victoria and Albert* entering Plymouth Sound, 1843. (*NMRN 1980/291*)

HMS *Bellerophon* (1865) leaving Hobbs Point, Pembroke Dock, where she was port guardship. (*Author*)

1940 Destroyer *Arrow* rammed by German mine-laying trawler (under Dutch colours) off Kristiansund (63.15N, 06.10E). Light cruiser *Birmingham* later sank the trawler.

1940 Destroyer *Griffin* captured the German Schiff 26 (ex-*Julius Pickenpack*), U-boat supply and depot ship, in Norwegian Sea (62.37N, 04.00E).

1940 German patrol boat VP-2623 boarded en route to Narvik. An intelligence haul spoilt by looting but still of great value. First break into the German naval Enigma.

1943 HM Landing Craft Gun (L) 15 and 16, together with a rescue boat launched from the sloop *Rosemary*, foundered in a storm off Freshwater West, Pembrokeshire; seventy-nine RN and RM personnel lost.

1944 Air strikes on German convoy off Bodø and on shipping there. Operation Ridge (Able). Carriers: *Furious, Victorious, Emperor, Pursuer, Searcher, Striker.* Ships: *Anson* (Vice-Admiral Sir Henry Moore), *Jamaica, Royalist* and fourteen destroyers. FAA Sqns: Hellcat: 804. Barracuda: 827. Seafire: 880. Corsair: 1834, 1836.

1944 Light cruiser *Black Prince* and destroyer *Ashanti*, with Canadian destroyers *Athabaskan, Haida* and *Huron* engaged three German destroyers off Ile de Batz. Operation Tunnel. *Haida* sank T-29, 7 miles W. of Les Heaux.

1944 Admiral Sir Bertram Ramsay moved into Southwick House followed by the Supreme Commander Allied Expeditionary Force, General Dwight D. Eisenhower, and Commander 21st Army Group, General Sir Bernard Montgomery, who had mobile HQs in Southwick Park. Ramsay vacated the house on 8 September and moved his HQ to France.

1963 Fast minelayer *Manxman*, Capt the Hon. T.V. Stopford RN, went aground outside Douglas Harbour in thick fog on visit to her 'adopted' Isle of Man. Screw damaged and dry docked at Devonport. CO and NO found guilty at Devonport courts martial 8 and 9 May of hazarding ship and causing ship to be stranded by negligence: Reprimand. Admiralty later quashed the hazarding charge.

1971 Launch of *Amazon* at Vosper, Woolston, by HRH Princess Anne. First of eight Type 21 frigates, the first major warships of the RN designed with all-gas-turbine main propulsion. Commissioned 11 May 1974. Last of class was *Avenger*, launched by Yarrow, Glasgow, 20 November 1975, commissioned 15 April 1978.

See 9 March 1959, 20 July 1968, 6 November 1969.

1982 *Antrim, Brilliant, Endurance* and *Plymouth* with *Tidespring*, elements of M Coy 42 RM Cdo and SAS retook Leith, thereby recapturing South Georgia, having retaken Grytviken the previous day. Operation Paraquet.

See 24 December 2009.

1991 Capt Paul Haddacks RN appointed Captain of the Fleet, the last Officer to hold this historic and distinguished post, known formerly as 'First Captain'. In the post-war years the Captain of the Fleet was the C-in-C's principal personnel officer with special responsibility for mentoring and advising commanding officers. Following the 1992 Fleet reorganisation which introduced, among other changes, a Flag Officer Surface Flotilla, the post of Captain of the Fleet was disestablished in 1993.

See 10 August 1966, 17 October 2005.

2011 Admiral of the Fleet Sir Henry Leach, First Sea Lord 1979–1982, died.

2011 The frigate *Cornwall*, Cdr David Wilkinson RN, returned to Devonport for the last time after an anti-piracy deployment in the Indian Ocean; the last of four Type 22 frigates to be paid off under the SDSR.

27 April

1297 All vessels of 40 tons or more and all vessels in Cinque Ports mobilised by royal writ to take an expeditionary force to France.

1770 Edward Codrington born; future Trafalgar captain and C-in-C at the Battle of Navarino in 1827.
See 20 October 1827, 28 April 1851.

1799 *Black Joke* captured the French *Rebecca* 18 miles W.S.W. of Ushant, the latter carrying papers intended for capture to distract Bridport at the start of Brieux's campaign.

1813 *Surveillance* and *Lyra* captured the American letter of marque *Tom* 85 miles N.N.W. of Cape Ortegal.

1858 Capt Sir William Peel, VC, commanding the Naval Brigade from *Shannon*, died of smallpox at Cawnpore. Memorial raised in Eden Gardens, Calcutta.
See 18 August 1857.

1876 Battleship *Inflexible* launched at Portsmouth Dockyard. She carried thicker armour than any warship before or since (24-in citadel), carried compound armour for the first time and had a higher metacentric height than any British warship to that date. She was 'one of the milestones in the history of British naval architecture' – Oscar Parkes, *British Battleships*, p.252.

HMS *Defence*, 1907. (*NMRN*)

1907 The last armoured cruiser built for the Royal Navy, *Defence*, launched at Pembroke Dockyard. Flagship of 1st CS, Rear-Admiral Sir Robert Arbuthnot, at Jutland and sunk with all hands by fire from the German battleship *Friedrich der Grosse*.

1908 Destroyer *Gala* sunk in collision with scout cruiser *Attentive* off Harwich, the latter's second collision within a year.

1915 VC: Lt-Cdr Edward Courtney Boyle (E 14) and Lt-Cdr Martin Eric Nasmith (E 11) for work in the Sea of Marmora, Dardanelles.
See 29 June 1965, 15 December 1967.

1916 Battleship *Russell*, flag of Rear-Admiral Sydney Fremantle, returning from the Dardanelles, was mined and sunk in a minefield laid by U-73 in the approaches to Grand Harbour, Malta; twenty-seven officers and ninety-eight men lost. Among the survivors was John Cunningham, future First Sea Lord. The sloop *Nasturtium* was lost in the same minefield on the same day. The battleship's wreck was located by the surveying ship *Herald* in 1999. Fremantle lost a family heirloom, a telescope given by Nelson – 'his best spying-glass' – to Capt Thomas Fremantle, who had commanded the *Ganges* (74) at Copenhagen and the *Neptune* (98) at Trafalgar.
See 8 August 1848, 9 January 1917, 29 April 1958.

1916 Destroyer *Firedrake* captured the German UC-5, which had grounded on the Shipwash shoal (52.05N, 01.46E), and took her into Harwich.

1917 German destroyer raid on Ramsgate. Ships: *Marshal Ney*, TB 4.

1937 The National Maritime Museum at Greenwich was opened by HM King George VI. His Majesty, with HM The Queen and

Lt-Cdr Boyle, VC and the crew of HM Submarine E 14, 1915. (*NMRN*)

HRH Princess Elizabeth, and the First Lord of the Admiralty, embarked at Westminster Pier in the launch of the C-in-C The Nore and, escorted by the destroyer *Wishart* and MTBs 3, 4, 5 and 6, went downriver and disembarked at the RN College, Greenwich. At the Museum 'the male staffs were all in morning dress, the hire of which they paid for themselves, the warders in their recently provided uniforms'. The Museum opened to the public on 29 April.

1941 Destroyers *Diamond*, Lt-Cdr P.A. Cartwright RN, and *Wryneck*, Cdr R.H.D. Dean RN, dive bombed and sunk at 1315 S. of Nauplia (36.30N, 23.34E), by nine German JU-88 aircraft, during evacuation of Greece. *Diamond* had on board troops saved from the Dutch transport *Slamat* sunk at 0715 on her way to Suda Bay with the loss of 500 soldiers. Destroyer *Griffin* found a few survivors on a raft at 0230 next day. A whaler from *Wryneck* reached Suda Bay with one officer, forty-one ratings and eight soldiers, the only survivors, none from *Diamond*. Ten destroyers were lost in the Mediterranean in April and May 1941.

See 7 April 1932, 8 November 1932, 29 April 1941, p.199 panel.

1941 *Patia*, fighter catapult ship, sunk by German aircraft off the Tyne.

1942 Minesweeper *Fitzroy* sunk on British mine 40 miles E.N.E. of Yarmouth.

1944 Submarine *Untiring* sank the German UJ-6075 off Toulon.

1945 Frigate *Redmill* torpedoed by U-1105 25 miles N.N.W. of Blacksod Bay (54.23N, 10.36W). Towed into Londonderry by *Jaunty*, rescue tug, but CTL.

1951 Ammunition ship RFA *Bedenham*, unloading depth charges into a lighter at Gun Wharf in Gibraltar, caught fire and exploded killing thirteen men and causing extensive damage ashore. The ship had been abandoned except for her Master and the Naval Armament Supply Officer who were blown into the water. Fatalities included Gibraltar Chief Fire Officer Andrew Indoe, Fire Service Sub-Officer George Henderson (posthumous GC), nine dockyard staff, two traders and a taxi driver. Awards included nine GMs.

See 14 July 1950.

2001 John Winton (Lt-Cdr John Pratt) died, aged 69. Naval engineering officer, submariner, historian, biographer and novelist. Creator of 'The Bodger' (*We Joined the Navy*), 'Benbow' in *The Naval Review*. Retired 1964. Born 3 May 1931.

2002 *Enterprise*, multi-role surveying ship, launched at Appledore. Sister ship *Echo* launched at same yard 2 March 2002.

28 April

A Memorable Date observed by the Corps of Royal Marines – Gallipoli

1789 Mutiny in HM Armed Transport *Bounty*, Lt William Bligh, at 0430, 30 miles from Tofua in Friendly Islands. Bligh and nineteen men, cast adrift in a 23ft open boat, began their epic voyage to Timor.

See 9 September 1754, 23 December 1787, 14 June 1789, 7 December 1817.

1799 *Martin* captured the French *Vengeur* off the Skaw, Denmark.

1813 Boats of *Orpheus* destroyed the American letter of marque *Wampo* 3 miles up the West River, Narragansett Bay.

1814 Napoleon surrendered to Capt Thomas Ussher, *Undaunted*, at Fréjus and sailed for exile in Elba, landing at Porto Ferrajo on 4 May.

1851 Admiral Sir Edward Codrington died at Eaton Square, London, on the day after his 81st birthday. Codrington served as a lieutenant in Howe's flagship, the *Queen Charlotte*, at the Glorious First of June in 1794 and took the despatches home for which he was promoted commander.

He was Captain of the *Orion* (74) at Trafalgar, C-in-C of the Allied Fleet at the Battle of Navarino in 1827 and C-in-C at Plymouth 1839–42. He was buried in the crypt of St Peter's church, Eaton Square, but his coffin was moved on a winter's night in 1952–3, with 400 others, for reburial in Brookwood Cemetery, Surrey. A memorial tablet was lost in a fire at St Peter's in 1987.

See 27 April 1770, 20 October 1827.

1864 Last major operation of the New Zealand wars. Naval Brigade landed from screw frigate *Curacoa*, corvettes *Esk* and *Miranda*, and sloops *Harrier* and *Falcon*, to attack a Maori fortification at Gate Pah, near Tauranga in the Bay of Plenty in New Zealand's North Island. VC won by Samuel Mitchell, Captain of the Foretop and Captain's Coxswain in *Harrier*, for rescuing mortally wounded Cdr Edward Hay who led the initial assault. Capt Fane Charles Hamilton of *Esk* also killed; city of Hamilton named after him.

1871 Royal Marines' wives at RM Barracks Forton and Eastney offered out-work, producing shirts and towels for the Fleet.

1896 *Hannibal*, Majestic-class battleship, 14,900 tons, launched, the last and biggest battleship built at Pembroke Dockyard.

Hannibal (1896), Majestic-class battleship, 14,900 tons, the last and biggest battleship launched at Pembroke Dockyard, completing at the dockyard's only alongside fitting out berth, a miracle of improvisation. (*Author*)

1915 3rd Royal Marine Battalion landed at Gallipoli.

1940 *Black Swan* damaged and *Cape Siretoko* sunk by German aircraft off Andalsnes.

1940 VC: Lt Richard Been Stannard, RNR, of the A/S trawler *Arab* at Namsos, Norway, between 28 April and 2 May. Citation: 'This continuous gallantry in the presence of the enemy was magnificent'. Invested at Buckingham Palace on first anniversary of outbreak of war, 3 September 1940.

1941 Destroyer *Douglas* sank U-65 in N. Atlantic (59.51N, 15.30W). Convoy HX 121.

1941 Submarine *Usk* presumed lost, within a year of her launch, on patrol in central Mediterranean, perhaps depth-charged by *Antonio Pigafetta.*

1943 Submarine *Unshaken* sank the Italian TB *Climene* in three minutes off Punta Libeccio, W. of Marettimo (37.45N, 11.33E).

1944 Wellington W/612 sank U-193 in Bay of Biscay (45.38N, 09.43W).

1954 Flag of FORY, Vice-Admiral Conolly Abel Smith, hoisted in HM Yacht *Britannia* at Malta for first time. A/Capt J.S. Dalglish, who had commissioned the ship, removed fourth stripe and became her Commander.

1967 Lady Cunningham, widow of Admiral of the Fleet Viscount Cunningham of Hyndhope, unveiled a plaque erected in her late husband's memory in St Paul's Anglican Cathedral, Valletta. It was dedicated by the Bishop of Gibraltar. Lesson by Rear-Admiral R.M. Dick, Cunningham's COS in the Mediterranean 1942 and 1943.

See 2 April 1967, 17 November 1974.

1971 Rear-Admiral J.A.R. Troup appointed Commander Far East Fleet with flag ashore at *Terror* in Singapore. The last COMFEF before the Western and Far East fleets amalgamated.

See 1 May 1971, 1 November 1971.

1972 Patrol vessels *Wasperton, Wolverton* and *Monkton* arrived at HMS *Tamar* to join the Sixth Patrol Craft Squadron in Hong Kong after a 16,461-mile voyage, having sailed from Britain on 12 January. They joined *Yarnton* and *Beachampton* which had arrived the previous September from service with the Ninth MCM Squadron in Bahrain.

See 16 September 1971, 1 June 1973.

1972 Radiotelephone calls to HM Ships. 'Calls will be connected through the Post Office Radio Station at Portishead. No charge is made for the connection to Portishead. The caller should ask the local exchange for "Ships' Telephone Service, Portishead Radio." When connected to Portishead, the caller should ask for a ships' [sic] radiotelephone call giving the name of the HM ship and name (or designation) of the person required. Portishead Radio will advise COMMCEN Whitehall of the booking. The Whitehall Duty Officer will obtain approval from the Ministry of Defence (Navy) (Duty Commander). . . a caller may be kept waiting for some hours before the call is connected . . .' – DCI(RN) S.115/72

See 1 January 1948.

1980 First WRNS Officer on RN Supply charge course.

1982 Total Exclusion Zone of 200 miles declared around Falkland Islands, from 30 April.

See 12 April 1982.

2005 Assault ship *Bulwark* commissioned by Capt J.H. Stanford RN.

See 29 October 1954, 15 November 2001, 12 July 2004.

29 April

1744 *Dreadnought* and *Grampus* captured the French *Medée* 140 miles S. of Ushant, earning Boscawen one of his nicknames, 'Old Dreadnought'.

1758 Vice-Admiral George Pocock (*Yarmouth*) fought Cdre Comte d'Ache (*Zodiaque*), with nine ships, 12 miles S.E. of Sadras. Ships: *Cumberland, Elizabeth, Newcastle, Salisbury, Tiger, Weymouth, Yarmouth*. Frigates, etc.: *Queenborough, Protector*. First of three inconclusive actions (3 August and 10 September) because of too strict an adherence to the Fighting Instructions. Battle Honour: Sadras 1758.

1780 Capture of Castillo Viejo, San Juan de Nicaragua. Capt Horatio Nelson (*Hinchinbrook*) had gone in command of the naval force but had been invalided before this date.

1781 Rear-Admiral Sir Samuel Hood (*Barfleur*) fought Vice-Admiral Comte de Grasse (*Ville-de-Paris*), with twenty ships of the line, W. of Martinique. Ships: *Shrewsbury, Intrepid, Torbay, Prince William, Russell, Centaur, Gibraltar, Montagu, Resolution, Ajax, Princessa, Terrible, Barfleur, Monarch, Invincible, Alcide, Belliqueux, Alfred*. Frigates, etc.: *Amazon, Lizard, Pacahunta*. The action was indecisive and the French convoy reached Port Royal.

1802 Marines styled 'Royal Marines' by George III 'for meritious service'. This was on the recommendation of St Vincent, who reflected in 1823 that he had never known 'an appeal made to them for honour, courage or loyalty that they did not more than realise my highest expectations. If ever the hour of real danger comes to England they will be found the Country's Sheet Anchor.'

1812 Admiralty committee of eight admirals and captains unanimously recommended adoption of Home Popham's new Telegraph Signals and Marine Vocabulary as 'of the greatest utility to the service'.

1812 *Goshawk, Hyacinth, Resolute* and Gunboat No. sixteen captured the French privateers *Brave* and *Napoleon* at Malaga.

1813 Boats of squadron, under the personal command of Rear-Admiral George Cockburn, destroyed American shipping and stores at Frenchtown, Elk River, Virginia. Ships and vessels: *Dolphin, Dragon, Fantome, Highflyer, Maidstone, Marlborough, Mohawk, Racer, Statira*.

1814 *Epervier* (18) taken by the American *Peacock* (22) 12 miles off Florida.

1849 *Inflexible*, wood paddle sloop, captured six pirate junks off Tamkan, near Hong Kong.

1858 *Pearl*'s Naval Brigade took Nugger, with the 13th Light Infantry, Bengal Yeomanry, 1st Bengal Military Police Battalion and Gurkha allies.

1859 Admiralty invited tenders for ironclad frigates *Warrior* and *Black Prince*.

1862 *Prince Albert* (first RN turret-ship) laid down at Samuda, Poplar.

1867 Canned meat added to ships' victualling stores.

See 24 August 1867.

1903 *Cadmus*, sloop, the last warship launched at Sheerness Dockyard and the last British warship to have been built with a figurehead. The figurehead was mounted in Hong Kong Dockyard after the ship was sold there on 1 September 1921.

See 8 December 1900, 7 September 1923.

1910 'Officers and men selected for the submarine service are to be of good physique and capable of sustaining a considerable amount of bodily strain . . . and . . . not addicted to alcohol in excess.' AWO 139/10.

1916 Surrender from starvation of Kut-al' Amara by Maj-Gen Townshend to the Turkish forces under Maj-Gen Khalil Pasha.

See 3 June 1915, 24 April 1916.

1921 Mutiny by RNR battalion at Newport (miners' strike).

1934 Cdr Lord Louis Mountbatten took command of the new destroyer *Daring* in the 1st Destroyer

Admiral Sir George Pocock, (1706–1792). (*NMRN 1986/482*)

Flotilla, Mediterranean Fleet, at Malta; his first command.

See 7 April 1932, 18 February 1940.

1940 GC (ex-EGM): Lt John Niven Angus Low and AB Henry James Miller, for gallantry when submarine *Unity* sank in collision with the Norwegian SS *Atle Jarl* off Blyth (55.13N, 01.19W). Both posthumous.

See 16 February 1938.

1940 Light cruiser *Glasgow*, with destroyers *Jackal* and *Javelin*, embarked His Norwegian Majesty King Haakon, the Crown Prince, Norwegian ministers and 23 tons of gold at Molde, on Romsdalfjord, S. of Kristiansund, ahead of invading German forces and landed them further north at Tromso. Six weeks later they were all taken off by the heavy cruiser *Devonshire* and taken to Britain. Destroyer *Glasgow* visited Molde on 29 April 2004, the anniversary of the rescue.

See 12 May 1940, 7 June 1940, 5 June 1945.

1941 River gunboat *Aphis* bombarded enemy positions in the Sollum area.

1941 Operation Demon, the evacuation of Imperial troops from Greece, completed. The operation was commanded by Vice-Admiral H.D. Pridham-Wippell (flag in the cruiser *Orion*). Battle Honour: Greece 1941.

See 24 and 27 April 1941, 24 April 1942, p.199 panel.

1942 Submarine *Urge* presumed sunk by mine leaving Malta for Alexandria, the 10th S/M flotilla moving there only two weeks after loss of *Upholder*.

1943 Rear-Admiral Philip Mack, lately Captain (D) 14th Destroyer Flotilla Mediterranean Fleet and later Flag Captain to Admiral Sir John Tovey, C-in-C Home Fleet, in the battleship *King George V*, killed in an air crash, one of three serving flag officers who died in similar circumstances in the Second World War. 'Few men have inspired in me such admiration and personal affection. In all respects he was a grand man and a fine officer, a fighting seaman of the very first quality with the supreme knack of making himself loved, respected and trusted' – Admiral Cunningham.

See 6 November 1943, 2 January 1945.

1944 Destroyers *Haida* and *Athabaskan* (both RCN) covering a minelaying operation (Operation Hostile 26) engaged two German destroyers 11 miles N.E. of Ushant, driving T-27 ashore and setting her on fire. *Athabaskan* torpedoed and sunk (48.29N, 04.09W). Second success in seventy-two hours for *Haida*.

1945 The last convoy battle of the Second World War fought off Kola Inlet around twenty-four merchant ships in convoy RA 66 returning to UK. U-286 sunk (69.29N, 33.37E), and U-307 sunk (69.24N, 33.37E), by frigates of 19th Escort Group *Anguilla*, *Cotton*, *Loch Shin* and *Loch Insh*. Frigate *Goodall* torpedoed by U-968 (69.25N, 33.38E); a magazine explosion destroyed her forward section. Sunk by own forces. Convoy continued without further attack and arrived at the Tail o' the Bank on VE Day, 8 May. *Goodall*, the last major British warship lost to U-boat attack and last of ten frigates lost in the war.

See 2 May 1945, 26 July 1945.

1958 Admiral Sir Sydney Fremantle died. He was referred to by his father, Admiral the Hon. Sir Edmund Fremantle, as 'my boy Syd' even when Fremantle junior was C-in-C Portsmouth 1923–6.

See 27 April 1916.

1967 The Naval Officers' Pavilion in Gibraltar, built in 1897, held its final event before demolition. The NOP was re-built as the United Services Officers' Club.

30 April

1697 *Medway* captured the French privateer *Pontchartrain* 60 miles S. of Kinsale.

1704 End of siege of Gibraltar.

1748 The Treaty of Aix-la-Chapelle ended the War of Jenkins' Ear which broke out in 1739 between Britain and Spain and was subsumed into the wider European War of the Austrian Succession in which France, Spain and Britain were the main combatants at sea. The treaty was more of a truce; hostilities resumed in 1756 – the Seven Years War.
See 19 October 1739.

1815 *Rivoli* captured the French *Melpomène* 4 miles N. of Ischia, west coast of Italy.

1851 *Valorous*, the last paddle frigate built for the RN, launched at Pembroke Dockyard. Remained in service until 1891.

1861 Instructor officers first appointed by commission.
See 22 December 1836, 6 April 1962, 6 July 1996.

1903 New RN Barracks at Chatham commissioned as *Pembroke*. Occupied by 5,000 officers and men who had marched from the hulks in No. 2 Basin led by the Depot Band.
See 26 July 1905.

1915 Submarine AE 2 (RAN) sunk by the Turkish TB *Sultan Hissar* near the Island of Marmara. She was the first Allied submarine to transit the Dardanelles and to enter the Sea of Marmara.

1917 VC: A/Lt William Edward Sanders, RNR (*First Prize-Q 21*) in action with U-93 120 miles S.W. of the Fastnet.

1917 Sloop *Tulip* operating as decoy ship *Q 12* sank in tow of sloop *Daffodil* having been torpedoed by U-62 150 miles W. of N. Valentia Island (51.10N, 05.27W).

1917 Prime Minister David Lloyd George's 'celebrated descent' on the Admiralty to 'take peremptory action on the question of convoys'.

Faced with rising merchant shipping losses to U-boats the Admiralty had no effective countermeasures and was dithering over the introduction of convoy. The PM did not, as Beaverbrook claimed, seat himself in the First Lord's chair and take over the Admiralty for the day, but 'the menace implied in this procedure was unmistakable. No greater shock could be administered . . . The naval authorities realised that it was a case of "act or go"' – Churchill. Sir John Jellicoe, the First Sea Lord, had already approved a trial convoy on 27 April; seventeen ships sailed from Gibraltar on 10 May and arrived twelve days later without loss.

1918 Sloop *Coreopsis* sank the German UB-85 off Isle of Man (54.47N, 15.27W).

1940 Sloop *Bittern* damaged by German aircraft off Namsos (64.28N, 11.30E). Sunk by light cruiser *Carlisle*.

1940 First Type C German parachute mine discovered at Clacton and rendered safe next day.

1940 Minesweeper *Dunoon* sunk by mine off Great Yarmouth (52.45N, 02.23E).

1941 *Parvati* (RIN) sunk by mine near Mocha, Red Sea.

1942 Light cruiser *Edinburgh* torpedoed by the German U-456 in Barents Sea (73.08N, 33.00E). Convoy QP 11 – cover. *Edinburgh* was carrying 465 gold bars, each weighing 23lb. In 1981, 431 were salvaged from 780ft.
See 2 May 1942.

1943 The Man Who Never Was. Operation Mincemeat. A corpse given identity of Captain, Acting Major, William Martin, RM, put into the sea from the submarine *Seraph* off Huelva, Spain. He carried secret papers intended to deceive the enemy, through German agents in Spain, that Allies intended to invade Sardinia and not Sicily. The story was told by the intelligence officer who planned the operation, Lt-Cdr Ewen Montagu, RNVR, in his book *The Man Who Never Was*, and by former First Lord, Duff Cooper, in his novel *Operation Heartbreak*.
See 19 July 1985.

1943 Italian destroyer *Leone Pancaldo* finally sunk, by Allied air attack, 2 miles N. of Cape Bon.
See 10 July 1940.

1945 Destroyers *Hesperus* and *Havelock* sank U-325 (53.42N, 04.53W) and, with Sunderland H/201, U-242 in the Irish Sea.

1945 Bombardment and air strike on Car Nicobar airfields and bombardment of Port Blair, Andaman Islands, by Force 63. Operation Bishop. Carriers: *Empress, Shah*. FAA Sqns: Hellcat: 804 and Avenger: 851. Ships: *Queen Elizabeth* (Vice-Admiral H.T.C. Walker), *Richelieu* (Fr), *Cumberland* (Rear-Admiral W.R. Patterson – CS 5), *Ceylon, Suffolk, Tromp* (Neth), *Rotherham* (D 11), *Tartar* (D 10), *Nubian, Penn, Verulam*.

1945 Destroyers *Roebuck* (Cdre D), *Racehorse* and *Redoubt* (Force 62) destroyed a Japanese troop convoy of ten vessels proceeding from Rangoon to Moulmein. Operation Gable.

1946 GC: Lt George Gosse, RANVR, for oyster mine detection and disposal.

1954 HM The Queen embarked in *Britannia* for first time, at Tobruk, Libya.

1956 Blue caps worn for last time.
See 18 April 1940, 11 April 1946, 1 May 1956.

1958 The prototype Blackburn NA39 – the Buccaneer – made its maiden flight at RAE Bedford piloted by Lt-Cdr Derek Whitehead.
See 20 February 1963.

1963 RN Detached Unit, Northwood, comprising the staffs of C-in-C Home Fleet and NATO C-in-C Eastern Atlantic Area, commissioned as HMS *Warrior* (a tender to President for pay and accounting). AFO 814/63; C-in-C Home Fleet HF463/8. Admiral Sir Charles Madden, who became C-in-C Home Fleet exactly fifty years after his father was C-in-C Atlantic Fleet, tried unsuccessfully to have his HQ named HMS *Iron Duke* after his father's old ship in the First World War.
See 31 December 1959, 1 April 1996, 31 March 1999.

1964 45 Cdo RM began operations in the Radfan, Aden.

1968 Phantom trials squadron, 700P, commissioned at Yeovilton with three aircraft that had arrived from the USA the day before.
See 14 January 1969.

1986 Order placed with Vickers Shipbuilding for *Vanguard*, the Royal Navy's first Trident submarine.
See 14 September 1993, and next entry.

1992 *Vanguard*, first RN Trident submarine, 'officially named' at Barrow by HRH The Princess of Wales.

1992 NATO Standing Naval Force Mediterranean, STANAVFORMED, activated to replace the Naval On-Call Force Mediterranean (NAVOCFORMED).

1992 The Leander-class frigate *Ariadne* became 'non-operational' at Portsmouth; the Mk 10 mortar, already obsolescent, was withdrawn from service. DCI(RN) 73/92 and 298/92.

2002 Flag of CINCFLEET shifted from Northwood to Whale Island.

2003 MC: Mne Liam Armstrong, 23, 45 Cdo, for 'outstanding bravery, initiative and leadership well beyond his rank and service experience' in Afghanistan, April to July 2002, Operation Jacana. He was then the youngest-ever non-commissioned serviceman to receive the MC.

2009 British land forces combat mission in Iraq formally ended, but maritime operations continued until 22 May 2011. Op Telic. Iraq campaign medal awarded to 6,403 RN and 3871 RM personnel. The medal with clasp for engagement in the initial action from 20 March 2003 (OP Telic 1) awarded to an additional 4305 RN and 533 RM personnel. HM The Queen and HRH The Duke of Edinburgh attended a service in St Paul's Cathedral on 9 October to 'mark the end of combat operations in Iraq'.
See 9 June 2005.

Marine Liam Armstrong. (*MOD*)

1 May

1689 Battle of Bantry Bay. Admiral Arthur Herbert (*Elizabeth*) fought the French fleet of twenty-four ships of the line under Vice-Admiral Comte de Chateaurenault (*Ardent*) who sought to support King James II. Herbert failed in his tactics, but he was nevertheless created Lord Torrington.

1707 *Grafton* (70) and *Hampton Court* (70), with twenty-two out of a convoy of forty-five sail, taken by nine sail of the line under Cdre Comte de Forbin (*Mars*) 20 miles off Beachy Head. *Royal Oak* (70) escaped.

1759 Capture of Guadaloupe: Cdre John Moore and Maj-Gen the Hon. John Barrington.

1790 The Kymin, a naval temple much admired by Nelson, built above Monmouth. Extended after the Battle of the Nile 1798 and dedicated by Boscawen's daughter, the Duchess of Beaufort.

1795 Second-rate *Boyne* (98), Capt Hon. George Grey, flagship of Vice-Admiral Sir John Jervis, caught fire aft in the forenoon while at anchor at Spithead, possibly caused by Marines exercising musketry on the windward side of the poop. The fire was quickly out of control and shot from the loaded guns killed two men in the *Queen Charlotte*. The anchor cable burned through at 1330 and the ship went aground on Horse Sand Spit opposite Southsea Castle where she blew up at about 1700. Eleven men lost.

1797 First Spithead Mutiny ended with issue of Admiralty orders against abuses.

1808 Capt Thomas Hurd RN succeeded Alexander Dalrymple as Hydrographer of the Navy, the first naval officer to hold the appointment. 'Hurd is truly Father of the Surveying Service' – Rear-Admiral Steve Ritchie.

See 12 August 1795, 11 September 1795, 15 November 1819.

1810 Boats of *Nereide* (36) captured the French *Estafette* and stormed batteries at Jacotet, Mauritius.

The *Boyne* on fire. She eventually grounded on the Horse Shoal near Southsea Castle. (*NMRN 1973/385*)

HMS *Hermes* pictured in 1930. (*RN*)

1811 *Pomone*, *Scout* and *Unite* destroyed the French *Girafe*, *Nourrice* and an armed merchantman in Sagone Bay, Corsica.

1813 First edition of Robert Southey's *Life of Nelson* published by John Murray. 'I am such a sad lubber that I feel half ashamed of myself for being persuaded ever even to review the *Life of Nelson* much more to write one . . . I walk among sea terms as a cat does in a china pantry, in bodily fear of doing mischief, and betraying myself.' His book has gone through over a hundred editions since, and has seldom been out of print. 'John Murray probably expected that sales would be brisk, but he can hardly have anticipated that [he] . . . was to endow the world with a classic' – Sir Geoffrey Callender in the Dent (1922) edition of Southey.

1814 First official quarterly *Navy List* published. The first few editions had been monthly, and their predecessors were private ventures.

1815 *Penelope*, 5th Rate, employed as a troopship and bound for Quebec, ran aground in the St Lawrence River in sub-zero temperatures. Discipline broke down and ship broke up; 216 men drowned or froze to death.

1825 Boats of the Irrawaddy flotilla captured eight Burmese war boats above Prome.

1838 John Charles Ready Colomb born in Isle of Man. RMA officer and imperial naval strategist.

See 27 May 1909.

1862 Capture of Kalding near Shanghai by Brig-Gen Charles Staveley, with British and Indian troops, and British and French Naval Brigades. Naval Brigade of *Imperieuse*, *Pearl*, *Vulcan*, *Flamer* and *Coromandel*.

See 17 April 1862.

1891 Gunnery School on Whale Island commissioned as *Excellent*.

1912 Fleet Reorganisation Scheme: first continuous commissioning of ships, and institution of an Immediate Reserve of 5,000 men.

1915 Submarine E 14 sank the Turkish *Nur-ul-Bahir* in Sea of Marmara.

1915 VC: L/Cpl Walter Richard Parker, RMLI, for gallantry as stretcher-bearer at landing on Gallipoli.

1915 Destroyers *Laforey*, *Leonidas*, *Lawford* and *Lark* sank the German A-2 and A-6 off the North Hinder lightvessel.

1915 Destroyer *Recruit* sunk by UB-6 off the Galloper lightvessel.

1915 The American *Gulflight* torpedoed without warning by U-30 off the Scilly Isles. First US merchant ship to be so attacked.

1917 Submarine E 54 sank U-81 in S.W. Approaches.

1918 Minesweeper *Blackmorevale* mined and sunk off Montrose.

1922 Admiralty Weekly Orders became Admiralty Fleet Orders – AFOs – until 1964.

1923 *Hermes* commissioned: 'the first ship in the world to be designed, ordered and built as an aircraft carrier' – Cdr David Hobbs RN. Completed for operational service 18 February 1924. Sunk by Japanese aircraft in the Indian Ocean 1942.

See 8 June 1918, 11 September 1919, 9 April 1942.

1932 John Forster 'Sandy' Woodward born. Entered RN in 1946 aged 13. Submariner; commanded *Warspite* 1969. Rear-Admiral 1981

A Wessex Mk 5 of 845 Naval Air Squadron operating from HMS *Hermes* (*RN*)

and appointed FOF1. Commanded Falklands Task Force 1982 and knighted. FOSM 1983. Vice-Admiral 1984. DCDS 1985. Admiral and CINCNAVHOME. Retired 1989.

See 5 November 1940.

1939 Painted Hall Greenwich opened as Mess of the Royal Naval College.

See 11 July 1939.

1942 Destroyer *Punjabi*, Cdr the Hon. J.M. Waldegrave RN, sunk in collision with the Home Fleet flagship *King George V* in fog 300 miles E. of Iceland, 66.00N, 08.00W. The Home Fleet, covering the Russian convoy PQ15, ran into fog and the flagship suspended the zigzag routine. *Punjabi* did not receive the signal in time and ran under the bows of *King George V* and was cut in two. The stern part sank quickly and her fused depth charges exploded, killing many men and seriously damaging the battleship's bows. The forward section remained afloat for forty minutes allowing 206 men to escape. The tragedy was compounded the next day when the Polish submarine *Jastrzab* was sunk in a blue on blue attack by the convoy escort.

See 12 December 1939, 2 October 1942, 2 August 1962, 11 February 1964.

1942 Hudson M/233 damaged U-573 in W. Mediterranean (37.00N, 01.00E). U-boat reached Cartagena and was interned, before being sold later to Spain.

1944 Swordfish C/842 (*Fencer*) sank U-277 off N. Norway. Convoy RA 59.

1945 Destroyers *Catterick* and *Kimberley* provided NGS for Commando raids on Rhodes and Alimnia.

1946 RNAS Wingfield handed over to South African Civil Aviation and became Cape Town Airport.

See 18 May 1942.

1951 His Majesty King Gustavus VI Adolf of Sweden, of the Goths and the Vends, appointed an honorary admiral in His Majesty's Fleet.

See 25 June 1975.

1952 'Reconstruction of the [carrier] *Victorious* is being seriously delayed due to lack of particular craftsmen and shipwrights. There is obviously a surfeit of "maties", and visitors to Portsmouth Dockyard are not impressed by the number of loafers who represent "Full employment" in the town' – *The Navy*, May 1952.

See 4 February 1958.

1955 Upper Yardmen TE, HMS *Temeraire*, commissioned at Port Edgar from the Hawke Division at BRNC Dartmouth. Paid-off 19 August 1960 and training reverted to Dartmouth as the Temeraire Division starting Christmas Term 1960. AFO 1191/60.

1956 White cap covers put on for last time, i.e. not removed on 30 September as usual in home waters but worn all the year round in future.
See 18 April 1940, 11 April 1946, 30 April 1956.

1957 Last midshipman on General List 'ceased to serve in the Fleet at sea' but midshipmen later reappeared afloat.

1957 Light cruiser *Gambia*, Capt W.J. Munn RN, commissioned at Rosyth for service as the last flagship on the East Indies Station before it closed in 1958. She was the first major RN warship to commission at Rosyth.
See 28 May 1958, 7 September 1958.

1962 RN-manned boom defence vessels in home waters formed into two Boom Defence Squadrons, one based on each coast of Scotland. 1st Boom Defence Squadron (based on the Forth): *Laymoor, Barbican, Barnstone*; attached vessel: BDV *Barfield*. 2nd Boom Defence Squadron (based on the Clyde): *Barrage, Barrington, Barnard*; attached vessels: BDV *Moorsman*, BDV *Barnehurst*. AFO 1135/62.

1970 Revival of continuous commissioning of HM ships.

1970 The Admiralty Reactor Test Establishment at Dounreay commissioned as HMS *Vulcan* and with functional title of Royal Naval Propulsion Test and Training Establishment.
See 22 May 1981.

1971 C-in-C Western Fleet, Admiral Sir William O'Brien, assumed full operational and administrative command of the Far East Fleet. COMFEF, Rear-Admiral J.A.R. Troup, delegated operational command of the ships in his area until he hauled down his flag in HMS *Terror*, Singapore, on 1 November 1971.
See 28 April 1971, 1 November 1971.

1980 Comacchio Group RM formed.
See 2 April 1945, 1 June 1975, 1 October 2000.

1982 Carrier Battle Group entered Total Exclusion Zone. First bombing of Port Stanley airfield by FAA Sea Harriers and an RAF Vulcan. First Harrier air-to-air victories and first NGS and A/S operations in Operation Corporate.

2000 *Illustrious*, with frigates *Argyll* and *Chatham* and RFA *Fort George* deployed to Sierra Leone in support of UN operations. RM Cdos landed on beaches by Sea Kings. Amphibious Ready Group, *Ocean*, RFAs *Sir Tristram* and *Sir Bedivere* stood offshore. HMS *Chatham* dispatched up uncharted Sierra Leone River overnight 18/19 May in attempt to bring 4.5-in gun within range of land operations: DSC Capt George Zambellas RN, HMS *Chatham*. Operation Palliser.
See 24 May 2000.

2008 Ten military shipwrecks added to the forty-eight already designated by MOD under the Protection of Military Remains Act 1986 to protect them from unauthorised interference by divers. The ships were:

HMS *Delight* off Portland. 29 July 1940
HMS *Gurkha* off Dungeness. 8 February 1917
HM Submarine *L24* off Portland. 10 January 1924
HMS *Loyalty* off The Nab Light. 22 August 1944
HMS *Penylan* in English Channel. 3 December 1942
SS *Storaa* off Hastings. 3 November 1943
German *U-714* near Firth of Forth. 14 March 1945
HMS *Amphion* in North Sea. 6 August 1914
HMS *Curacoa* in N.W. Approaches. 2 October 1942
MV *Atlantic Conveyor* off the Falkland Islands. 25 May 1982

2 May

1694 *Adventure, Dragon* and *Monck* captured the French privateer *Diligente* 4 miles outside St Mary's Sound, Scilly Isles.

1781 *Canada* captured the Spanish *Santa Leocadia* 450 miles W. of Cape Finisterre.

1809 Boats of *Mercury* and *Spartan* captured twelve vessels and blew up a tower at Porto Cesenatico, east coast of Italy.

1813 Royal Marines of *Redwing, Repulse, Undaunted* and *Volontaire* destroyed the batteries at Morgiou, near Marseilles.

1814 Admiral Alexander Hood, Viscount Bridport, died.

1818 Rear-Admiral Sir George Hope, a Lord Commissioner of the Admiralty, died in the Admiralty. Born 6 July 1767. Commanded *Defence* (74) at Trafalgar. Buried in Westminster Abbey.

See 4 May 1810, 5 August 1834, 20 September 1839.

1912 First launch of an aircraft from any ship under way. Acting Cdr Charles R. Samson took off in a Short-Sommer S.38 pusher biplane from a wooden deck on the forecastle of the battleship *Hibernia* steaming at 5 knots off Portland Harbour breakwater. He landed at Lodmoor Marsh near Weymouth. He repeated the performance at the Royal Review in Weymouth Bay on 9 May.

See 18 November 1911, 10 January 1912, 2 August 1917.

1917 Destroyer *Derwent* sunk by mine 2 cables N. of the Whistle buoy, Le Havre.

1918 UB-31 mined and UC-78 sunk by drifters in Strait of Dover.

1932 Publication of BR.224. *The Gunnery Pocket Book*. 'Having been approved by My Lords Commissioners of the Admiralty is hereby promulgated . . . By Command of Their Lordships . . .'

Chapter XXVI. Bugle Calls.
VII. Bathers to enter the water, or Stations for anchoring.
VIII. Bathers to come out of the water, or Light guns' crews take cover.
XXIV. Man ship, or Lull in the action, collect wounded.
XXV. Close aft for prayers, everybody aft, or Action about to commence.
XXVII. Repel aircraft

1941 Destroyer *Jersey* sunk by mine in entrance to Grand Harbour, Malta.

Short S.38 biplane taking off from HMS *Hibernia*, 1912. (*NMRN*)

HMS *Conqueror* returning from the Falklands, 1982. (*NMRN*)

1942 Destroyers *Wishart*, *Wrestler* and Catalina C/202 sank U-74 in W. Mediterranean.

1942 Submarine *Jastrzab* (Pol) (ex-P 551) (ex-USN S 25) sunk in blue on blue attack by destroyer *St Albans* and minesweeper *Seagull* off northern Norway.

1942 Light cruiser *Edinburgh* (fifth of the name) torpedoed on 30 April, sunk by destroyer *Foresight* (71.51N, 35.10E) having been torpedoed by German Z-24.

Foresight and *Forester* damaged the *Hermann Schoemann* which was scuttled by Z-24.

1943 Sunderland M/461 (RAAF) sank U-465 in Bay of Biscay (44.48N, 08.58W).

1944 Light cruiser *Ajax* bombarded Rhodes.

1944 Swordfish B/842 (*Fencer*) sank U-674 and U-959 off northern Norway. Convoy RA 59. A notable double.

1945 Minesweeper (trawler) *Ebor Wyke* sunk by U-979 7 miles N. of Skagi, Iceland. Last British warship sunk by U-boat in Second World War.

See 29 April 1945, 7 May 1945, 26 July 1945.

1945 Mosquito aircraft of 143, 235 and 248 Sqns, 404 Sqn (RCAF) and 33 Sqn (Nor) sank U-2359 in Kattegat.

1945 First wave of amphibious assault by 26th Indian Division on Rangoon. Operation Dracula. LSH: *Largs* (Rear-Admiral B.C.S. Martin – Force W), *Nith*, *Waveney*. LSI: *Glenroy*, *Persimmon*, *Prins Albert*, *Silvio*. Depot ship: *Barpeta*. Support squadron: *Phoebe*, *Royalist*, *Emperor*, *Hunter*, *Khedive*, *Stalker*, *Saumarez* (D 26), *Venus*, *Vigilant*, *Virago*. FAA Sqns: Hellcat: 800, 808. 807, 809. 1700.

1976 Fire in SSN *Warspite* caused £5,914,000 damage: a failure of a coupling released lubricating oil in the DG compartment. DCI(RN) 737/78.

1982 *Conqueror* torpedoed and sank the Argentine heavy cruiser *General Belgrano* off the Burdwood Bank, Falkland Islands (55.27S, 61.25W). Operation Corporate. DSO: Cdr Christopher Wreford-Brown. The first sinking by a British submarine for thirty-seven years and the first torpedo attack by a SSN. The Mk 8 Mod IV torpedoes used were in their fiftieth year of service. Boat returned to Faslane flying Jolly Roger.

See 13 September 1914.

2000 First RN circumnavigation for fourteen years. NTG 2000 Deployment (TG 349.01) sailed eastabout: frigates *Cornwall*, Capt T.P. McClement RN, flag of COMUKTG, Rear-Admiral S.R.Meyer, and *Sutherland*, Cdr M.R.B. Wallace RN; destroyer *Newcastle*, Cdr S.J. Ancona RN, tbrb Cdr S.J. Pearson RN; FNS *Aconit*, Cdr Benoit Silve FN; submarines *Tireless*, Cdr M.J. Hawthorne RN, and *Triumph*, Cdr P.J.A. Buckley RN; and RFAs *Fort Victoria*, Capt A. Roach, tbrb Capt P. Taylor, RFA *Diligence*, Capt P. Farmer, and *Bayleaf*, Capt B. Waters. First RN group visit to Hong Kong (5–11 August) since the 1997 handover. Returned UK 25 November.

See 2 April 1986.

3 May

1746 Battle in Loch nan Uamh between three British and two French ships. First of six attempts to rescue the Young Pretender. This, not Culloden, was the last battle of the '45.

1747 The first decisive naval success of the War of the Austrian Succession. Vice-Admiral George Anson in *Prince George* (90), and Rear-Admiral Peter Warren in *Devonshire* (66), with fourteen ships of the line, intercepted two major French convoys, outbound from Rochefort and temporarily combined, one bound for Canada and one for India, 25 miles N.W. of Cape Ortegal on the N.W. Spanish coast.
Battle Honour: Finisterre 1747.

See 19 October 1739, 14 October 1747, 19 February 1758.

The Marquis de La Jonquiere, the French convoy escort commander, in *Serieux* (64), although facing a greatly superior force, displayed courage and skill in forming a line with his six battle ships and three Indiamen, heading N.W.. He stood his ground allowing most of the convoy to escape to the S.W., and then broke his line and also bore away to the S.W.. Anson ordered General Chase (the first time this had been ordered by flag signal) and all of the French warships and six merchantmen were overtaken and captured: *Diamant, Gloire, Invincible* (which became the first of the name in the Royal Navy), *Jason, Rubis, Serieux, Apollon, Dartmouth* (ex-British privateer), *Modeste, Philibert, Thetis* and *Vigilant*. 'They all behaved very well and lost their ships with honour and reputation' reported Anson to the Duke of Newcastle on 11 May. Capt Thomas Grenville of the *Defiance* was killed in action. Anson arrived at St Helen's with his prizes on 16 May. Prize money totalled £300,000. Anson received a peerage and Warren was made a KB.

Ships: *Bristol, Centurion, Defiance, Devonshire, Falkland, Monmouth, Namur, Nottingham, Pembroke, Prince Frederick, Prince George, Princess Louisa, Windsor, Yarmouth.* Frigates etc: *Ambuscade, Falcon, Vulcan.*

This major naval victory vindicated the formation in 1745 of a Western Squadron to patrol the W. Approaches to the English Channel and to cruise between Ushant and Finisterre, to windward of all the French Atlantic ports, a deployment further endorsed by Hawke four months later off Ushant.

HMS *James Watt*, one of the last wooden two-deckers built for the RN, was launched at Pembroke Dockyard on St George's Day, 1853. (*Author*)

1808 Imperial Russian sloop *Diana*, on a scientific voyage round the world and unaware of war between Britain and Russia, boarded by frigate *Nereide* in Simon's Town but escaped 28 May.

1810 *Spartan* engaged the Franco-Neapolitan *Achilles*, *Cérés*, *Fame*, *Sparvier* and eight gunboats in Naples Bay. *Sparvier* captured. Capt (later Vice-Admiral Sir) Jaheel Brenton severely wounded but created a baronet and KB. Like his relative, Capt Edward Pelham Brenton, he turned to naval history.

1813 Boats of *Undaunted* captured a French ship from under the batteries at Marseilles.

1813 Boats of squadron, under the personal command of Rear-Admiral George Cockburn, destroyed American shipping, military storehouses and a cannon foundry in the Susquehanna River and at Havre de Grace, Virginia. Ships: *Dolphin*, *Dragon*, *Fantome*, *Highflyer*, *Maidstone*, *Marlborough*, *Mohawk*, *Racer*, *Statira*.

1840 Admiralty trials of *Archimedes*, an early screw ship.

1905 Fort Blockhouse taken over from Royal Engineers and commissioned as *Dolphin*.
See 30 September 1998.

1940 *Bison* (French) badly damaged in air attack at Namsos and scuttled by destroyer *Afridi* (65.42N, 07.17E). *Afridi* bombed and sunk two hours later with heavy loss of life including most French survivors.
See 8 June 1937.

1940 Battleship *Resolution* and cruisers *Aurora* and *Effingham* bombarded Beisfjord, Narvik.

1941 Admiralty House, Portsmouth, damaged in air raids on 17 April and 3 May. C-in-C Portsmouth moved his war HQ to Fort Wallington on Portsdown Hill.

1944 Wellingtons E and T/621 drove ashore U-852 at Bandar Bela, Italian Somaliland. Submarine blown up by own crew. First attacked on the 2nd.

1945 Allied troops entered Rangoon. Operation Dracula.

1945 Beaufighters of 236 and 254 Squadrons RAF sank U-2524 in the Kattegat. Rocket-firing Typhoons of 184 Sqn sank U-2521 off Schleswig-Holstein.

1950 Carrier *Ark Royal* launched at Cammell Laird, Birkenhead, seven years to the day after being laid down.
See 26 February 1955, 3 May 1977, 22 September 1980.

1968 Ice patrol ship HMS *Protector* arrived at Portsmouth at the end of her final commission in the Antarctic. MOD(N) signalled: 'Welcome home after your 13th and last season in the Antarctic. For an old lady of 33 *Protector*'s achievements have shown remarkable agility and she will be remembered with affection in the Service and in the South Americas. All who have served in her can take pride in her distinguished and long service and in her contribution to British scientific endeavour.' The former fast netlayer was succeeded by HMS *Endurance* (ex-*Anita Dan*) then completing conversion at Harland and Wolff, Belfast.

1977 *Invincible*, first of class, launched at Vickers, Barrow, by HM The Queen, twenty-seven years to the day after *Ark Royal* above.
See 11 July 1980, 3 August 2005.

1988 Submarines *Turbulent* and *Superb* surfaced at North Pole.
See 3 March 1971, 19 April 2004.

1997 A memorial cairn to the submarine *Vandal* lost on trials on 24 February 1943, and located by the minehunter *Hurworth* N.W. of Lochranza, Isle of Arran, on 12 June 1994, was unveiled by the Flag Officer Submarines, Rear-Admiral James Perowne, near the ferry terminal at Lochranza overlooking the submarine's position.
See 24 February 1943.

2008 The RN Hospital Gibraltar paid off. The gates were closed by the youngest member of staff, MA Kirsty Taylor, watched by the last CO, Surg-Cdr Martin Randle RN. Task transferred to the Princess Royal Medical Centre at Devil's Tower Camp.
See 1 April 1963.

4 May

1786 'Duty is the great business of a Sea-officer. All private considerations must give way to it, however painful it is.' Nelson to Frances Nisbet.

1796 *Spencer* captured the French *Volcan* 360 miles N.E. of the Bahama Islands.

1806 Boats of *Nautilus* and *Renommée* cut out the Spanish *Giganta* at Torrevieja, S.E. Spain.

1809 *Parthian* captured the French privateer *Nouvelle Gironde* 150 miles N. of Cape Ortegal.

1810 Boats of *Armide*, *Cadmus*, *Daring* and *Monkey* destroyed thirteen vessels at Port de Loix, Ile de Ré.

1810 Capt John Conn, who had commanded the *Dreadnought* (98) at Trafalgar, was drowned when he fell overboard from *Swiftsure* (74) off Bermuda.

See 1 March 1807, 2 May 1818, 28 May 1831, 5 August 1834, 20 September 1839, 2 July 1853.

1811 Landing party from *Alceste* and *Belle Poule* destroyed a French 14-gun brig at Porto di Parenzo, Istria. She was taking supplies to survivors of Lissa.

1812 Boats of *Bermuda*, *Castilian*, *Phipps* and *Rinaldo* recaptured *Apelles* which had run ashore 3 miles E. of Etaples, N. France. *Skylark* had also grounded in the vicinity and was burned by her own crew who got away in the boats.

1910 The Canadian Parliament passed the Naval Service Act, (Canadian Act 9-10 Edw. VII, c.43) establishing the Naval Service of Canada, precursor of the Royal Canadian Navy. In October 1910 King George V authorised the addition of the prefix 'Royal' to the title of the Naval College of Canada. Royal Canadian Navy dates from 29 August 1911.

See 29 August 1911, 1 February 1968.

1916 Light cruisers *Galatea* and *Phaeton* brought down Zeppelin L-7 10 miles S. of Horns Reef lightvessel. E 31 completed her destruction and rescued seven survivors.

1917 First division of US destroyers arrived at Queenstown, under RN operational command.

1936 The Emperor of Abyssinia, Haile Selassie, following the Italian invasion of his country in October 1935, embarked with his family in the light cruiser *Enterprise* at the French Somaliland port of Jibouti and sailed with a RN escort of two cruisers and four destroyers, to Haifa, 'taking with him into exile the sympathy of the civilised world' – *The Times*. The cruiser *Capetown* later brought him to Britain.

1939 Battleship *Prince of Wales* launched at Cammell Laird, Birkenhead, by the Princess Royal.

See 1 January 1937, 19 January 1941, 10 December 1941.

1941 Minesweeper *Fermoy* destroyed in dry dock at Malta by German aircraft.

1941 First successful trial of Leigh Light when the inventor himself with prototype in Wellington P 2521 from Limavady succeeded in illuminating H 31.

1942 Battle of the Coral Sea.

See 7 May 1942.

1943 Liberator of 86 Squadron RAF on bay transit patrol sank U-109 W.N.W. of Cape Finisterre (47.22N, 22.40W).

1943 Destroyers *Nubian*, *Paladin* and *Petard* sank the Italian TB *Perseo* 7 miles E. of Kelibia, Tunisia.

1944 Minesweeper *Elgin* damaged by mine off Portland.

1944 *Blankney*, USS *Joseph E. Campbell*, and *Sénégalais* (Fr) sank U-371 in Mediterranean (39.49N, 05.39E). Convoy GUS 38.

1944 Wellington M/407 (RCAF) sank U-846 in Bay of Biscay.

1945 Beaufighters of 236 and 254 Squadrons RAF sank U-236, U-393, U-2338 and U-2503 near Omö, Great Belt.

The flight deck of HMS *Formidable* after being hit by a Japanese kamikaze aircraft, 1945. (*NMRN*)

1945 U-boats ordered to cease hostilities.

1945 The last big war operation by the Home Fleet. Vice-Admiral R.R. McGrigor sailed from Scapa Flow on May Day with cruisers *Diadem* and *Norfolk*, escort carriers *Queen*, *Searcher* and *Trumpeter*, and destroyers *Carysfort*, *Opportune*, *Savage*, *Scourge* and *Zambesi*, and RFA *Blue Ranger*, joined by destroyers *Obedient* and *Orwell* returning from Murmansk, to attack the German Arctic U-Boat base in Kilbotn near Narvik. Avengers and Wildcats of 846, 853 and 882 NAS sank the depot ship *Black Watch* and destroyed U-711. Operation Judgement. 'One feels that the pilots and observers of the *Ark Royal*, *Glorious* and *Furious*, who had taken on such heavy odds in the early days, and so few of whom survived, would have been proud of the feats of their successors' – Roskill, *The War at Sea*, vol.3 pt. 2, pp.262–3.

See 3 December 1959.

1945 *Formidable*, fifth of the name, operating off Sakishima, hit by kamikaze aircraft and demonstrated the superiority of the armoured flight deck over the wooden flight deck in USN fleet carriers.

1960 Naval Services raised £1,923 for a wedding present for Princess Margaret: an eighteenth-century two-drawer cabinet presented at Clarence House. AFO 2035/60.

1962 'The use of semaphore in the Fleet is decreasing and Officers and Ratings of the Seaman Branch nowadays are rarely ever required to signal by this method. Their Lordships have therefore decided that semaphore should no longer be taught to Cadets and Midshipmen at Britannia Royal Naval College Dartmouth nor to Seamen generally.' – AFO 830/62.

See 1 January 1997.

1973 NATO Standing Naval Force Channel inaugurated at Ostend.

1982 Destroyer *Sheffield* hit by Exocet missile from Argentine air force Super Etendard, 163° Pembroke Light 72 miles. Abandoned, proved an unsuccessful lure and sank under tow by *Yarmouth* on 10 May (52.11S, 53.50W). The first RN ship lost in action since 1945. Operation Corporate.

See 15 October 1940.

1991 The Gulf War Service of Remembrance and Thanksgiving held in St Mungo's Cathedral, Glasgow, in the presence of Her Majesty The Queen, HRH Prince Philip, the Prime Minister and Chiefs of Staff.

See 28 February 1996, 23 October 2005, 14 June 2007.

5 May

1794 *Orpheus* captured the French *Duguay-Trouin* 3 miles off the north-east corner of Mauritius.

1794 *Swiftsure* began to chase *Atalante* off Cork.

1801 Vice-Admiral Lord Nelson appointed C-in-C in the Baltic.

1804 Capture of Surinam by Cdre Samuel Hood (*Centaur*) and troops under Brig-Gen Sir Charles Green. Ships: *Alligator, Centaur, Drake, Emerald, Hippomenes, Pandour, Serapis, Unique*, and boats of *Guachapin*. Troops: Royal Artillery, Sappers and Miners, 16th, 2/60th, 64th and 6th West India Regiments.

1855 Squadron of Sir Edmund Lyons forced the Straits of Yenikale, Sea of Azov.

1861 *Cockchafer, Firm* and *Haughty*, with boats of *Pearl*, destroyed the pirate town of Tsingchow near Swatow, S.E. China.

1911 Coronation of King George V. 'Officers on the Active List witnessing the Royal Procession on 22, 23 and 29 June 1911, or witnessing the Naval Review on board His Majesty's Ships of War, or attending the Gala Performance at the Royal Opera or His Majesty's Theatre, are to appear in full dress uniform.' AWO 132/11.

See 9 July 1976.

1917 Sloop *Lavender* sunk by UC-75 22 miles S.W. of Waterford harbour.

1918 Sloop *Rhododendron* torpedoed and sunk by U-70 in North Sea.

1919 Minesweeper *Cupar* mined and sunk off Tyne.

1940 *Grom* (Polish) sunk by German aircraft in Ofotfjord, Narvik.

1940 Minelaying submarine *Seal* surrendered after prolonged attack in Kattegat. Commissioned into Kriegsmarine 30 November 1940 as UB. Scuttled at Kiel 3 May 1945. Lt-Cdr R.P. Lonsdale honourably acquitted at Portsmouth court martial 11 April 1946.

1942 Attack on Diego Suarez, Madagascar. Sunk: Vichy-French – *Bévéziers, Bougainville* by aircraft.

See 7 May 1942.

HMS *Cockchafer*, a composite screw gunboat of 1881. (*NMRN*)

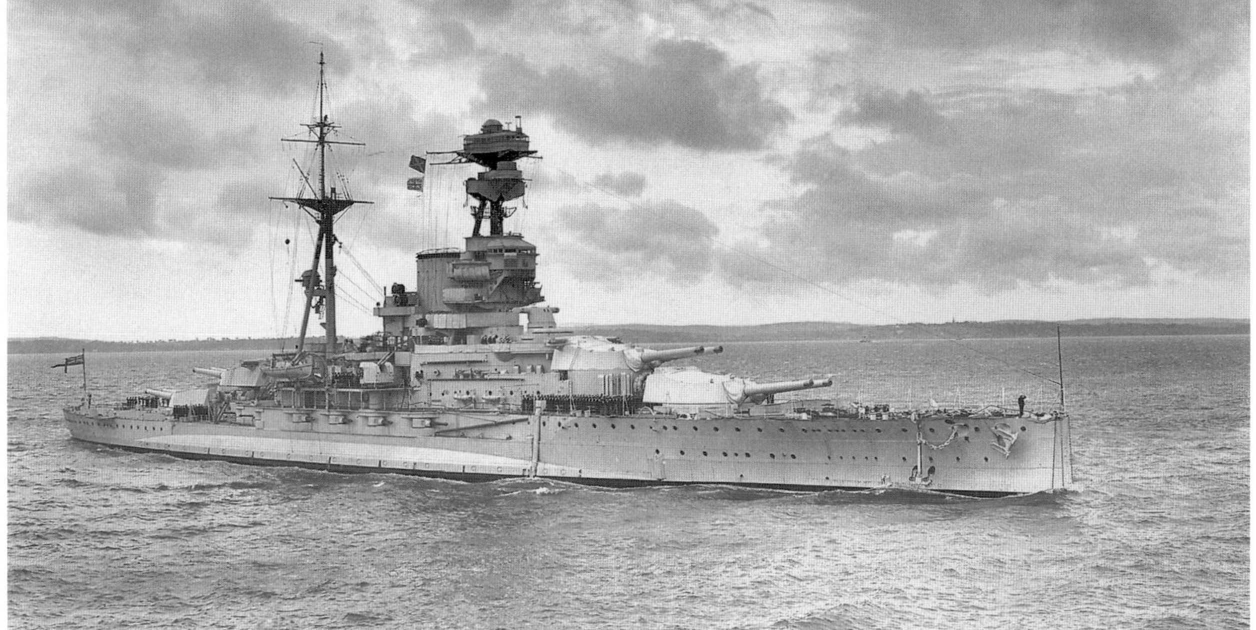

HMS *Ramillies* entering Portsmouth harbour in 1939. (*NMRN W&L 453A*)

Operation Ironclad – Capture of Diego Suarez, 1942

On 18 March 1942 it was decided to capture Madagascar, which was under Vichy-French control and an excellent base for the Japanese to threaten shipping in the Indian Ocean and Middle East. Forces sailed from UK and assembled at Durban. Slow and Fast convoys sailed from Durban on 25 and 28 April respectively, and met 35 miles off Cape Amber on 4 May. Minesweepers swept the way to the first anchorage and then to the assault position, which was reached at 0330 next day. The enemy were caught unawares as they had regarded the unlit and treacherous channels as impassable at night. Aircraft from *Illustrious* and *Indomitable* attacked the harbour and airfield, the cruiser *Hermione* created a diversion off the east coast with pyrotechnics, while the *Devonshire* and four destroyers covered the landings from seventeen ships on the west coast. By the evening most troops were ashore, but fresh resistance was met from new defences. The next evening the destroyer *Anthony* took fifty Royal Marines from *Ramillies* in under the eastern coastal defences, and landed them at the naval base in a heavy sea by coming stern to the jetty. Their impact was so successful that they were embarrassed by the number of prisoners they took, and by 0300 on the 7th the town and its defences were taken. At 1040 the *Ramillies* started a bombardment of the eastern coastal defences, which surrendered after ten minutes. In sixty hours from the first landing the operation was completed for the loss of the corvette on a mine. There had been good inter-Service cooperation and the ability to take troops over thousands of miles of ocean and land them with carrier-borne air cover was well demonstrated.

1944 Sloops *Starling*, *Wild Goose* and *Wren* attacked U-473, which was sunk on the 6th in Atlantic (49.29N, 21.22W).

1944 MTB 708 accidentally destroyed by friendly aircraft.

1945 Bombardment and air strikes (begun on the 4th) on Sakishima Gunto area by Task Force 57.

1945 Four Liberator aircraft destroyed four U-boats making for Norway, U-3503, U-534, U-2365 and U-2521, in the Kattegat. U-534 raised and now preserved at Birkenhead.

1955 West Germany joined NATO.

1962 Submarine *Ocelot* launched, the last RN warship built at Chatham. Now preserved in Chatham Historic Dockyard.

1970 The RN Tactical School moved from Woolwich to Southwick. 'As the Royal Naval Tactical School moves to its new home in Southwick Park the Admiralty Board expresses its warm appreciation to the Army Board for the hospitality and happy association the Royal Navy has enjoyed during its twenty-three years in the precinct of the old Royal Military Academy, Woolwich.' DCIs(RN) 432/70; 618/70.

See 2 June 1970.

1997 Destroyer *York*, working with HM Customs and Excise, boarded MV *Simon de Dancer* off Portugal and seized cannabis with a street value of £10 million. Crew of eight arrested and landed at Devonport. Arrested ship escorted to UK by destroyer *Nottingham*.

2011 Chief Petty Officer Claude Stanley 'Charlie' Choules ex-RN and ex-RAN, died in Perth, Western Australia, aged 110; the last surviving combat veteran of the First World War.

6 May

1673 St Helena recaptured from the Dutch, together with three Dutch East Indiamen. Ships and vessels: *Assistance, Castle, Mary & Martha, William & Thomas*, convoying an East India Company fleet.

1674 Half-pay, awarded to Flag Officers after the second Dutch war, extended after the third to captains who had commanded first or second rates or who had served as flag captains – another move towards fostering a corps of professional officers, neither courtiers nor tarpaulins.

1682 *Gloucester* (54), Capt Sir John Berry, wrecked on the Lemon and Ower Shoal off Yarmouth carrying the Duke of York to Leith; 130 men lost including 'several noblemen and gentlemen of the Duke's suite'. Capt James Aire, responsible for navigation, was dismissed the Service.

See 16 August 1742, 22 May 1941.

1770 Cook discovered Port Jackson (Sydney).

1801 *Speedy* captured the Spanish *Gamo* 15 miles S.W. of Barcelona.

1806 *Adamant* captured the Spanish *N.S. de los Dolores* 360 miles N.W. by N. of Tristan da Cunha.

1814 Capture and destruction of the fort at Oswego, Lake Ontario, by ships of the Lake Squadron and troops under Lt-Gen Gordon Drummond. Ships: *Charwell, Magnet, Montreal, Niagara, Prince Regent, Princess Charlotte, Star.* Troops: Royal Artillery, Royal Sappers and Miners, De Watteville's Regiment, Glengarry Fencible Light Infantry.

Admiral Thomas, Lord Cochrane (1775–1860)

Cochrane was a brilliant sloop and frigate commander in the Napoleonic Wars. His red head matched his temperament and he was said to be 'always holding out his toes to be trodden on and he possessed 10 of them'. In 1800, in command of the sloop *Speedy* he gained a great reputation for seizing Spanish prizes. A 32-gun ship, the *Gamo*, was specially commissioned to fight him and in May 1801 the two ships met. The *Speedy* defeated its much larger opponent. Cochrane was appointed to *Pallas* (32) and thence to *Imperieuse* (38). In 1809 he was in command of the fireship raid in the Basque Roads for which he was created KB. However, as a Member of Parliament he was constantly attacking the government, opposed a vote of thanks to his C-in-C, and he was placed on half-pay until 1813. He was fined and sent to prison as a result of stock exchange deals, and from 1817 he commanded the Chilean, Brazilian and Greek navies in turn. He achieved remarkable success with these forces, though again not without constantly upsetting his superiors. In 1832 he received a free pardon at home and served from 1848 to 1851 as C-in-C North America and West Indies station. Promoted GCB in 1847. Buried in Westminster Abbey.

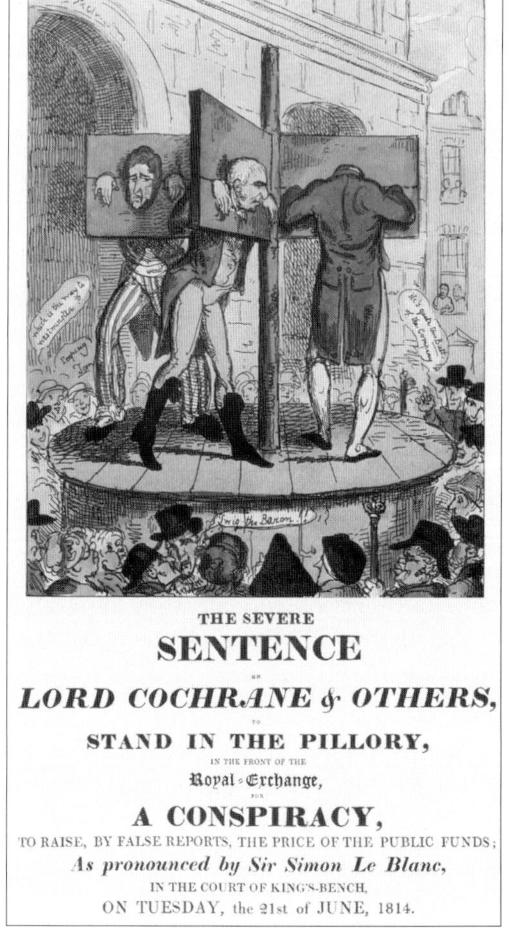

Part of Cochrane's questionable sentence for fraud in 1814 was to stand in the public pillory for an hour. Caricaturists could not resist picturing the scene – he is here on the left in the striped trousers of a seaman – but in fact, fearing a riot, the authorities remitted this part of the sentence. *(NMRN 2000/76(3))*

1816 Order in Council authorised naval establishment and dockyard at Trincomalee 'to serve as the principal refitting station for His Majesty's ships and vessels in the East Indies'.
See 11 January 1782, 15 October 1957.

1831 'Frances Herbert, Viscountess Nelson, Duchess of Bronte, departed this life, aged 73 years; buried at Littleham, near Exmouth with her son Josiah, stepson of Lord Nelson and a Captain RN, died 14 July 1830.'
See 15 January 1815.

1910 Accession of King George V.

1941 *Camito*, hired escort ship, sunk by U-97 in Atlantic (50.40N, 21.30W).

1942 Swordfish aircraft of 829 Sqn (*Illustrious*) sank the Vichy-French S/M *Héros* off Madagascar. Operation Ironclad.

1943 Destroyer *Oribi* rammed U-125, and corvette *Snowflake* hit her with gunfire before she was scuttled (52.30N, 45.20W). Corvette *Loosestrife* sank U-192 on her first Atlantic patrol, S. of Cape Farewell (53.06N, 45.02W). Corvette *Pelican* sank U-438 (52.00N, 45.10W). Sloop *Sunflower* sank U-638 with ten depth charges (54.12N, 45.05W). Destroyer *Vidette* hedgehogged and sank first U-630 (52.30N, 44.50W) and then U-531, her second of the day (52.48N, 45.18W). The battle of convoy ONS 5 lasted for ten days. Twelve merchantmen totalling 56,000 tons were sunk; so were six U-boats – three Type VII and three Type IX – and two more which sank one another in collision.

1944 Frigates *Aylmer, Bickerton, Bligh* and Swordfish A/825 and X/825 (*Vindex*) sank U-765 in Atlantic (52.30N, 25.28W).

1945 Liberator G/86 sank U-3523 in the Skagerrak – her second kill in two days – and K/86 sank U-2534 in the Kattegat.

1945 Continuation of Operation Bishop. Air-strikes by aircraft from *Emperor, Hunter, Khedive* and *Stalker*, supported by *Royalist*, on area between Mergui and Victoria Point, Burma. FAA Sqns: 800, 808, 807, 809.
See 30 April 1945.

1947 Light fleet carrier *Albion* launched at Swan Hunters, Wallsend-on-Tyne.
See 23 March 1944, 26 May 1954, 9 March 2001.

1957 'Off caps' at payment replaced by hand salute. Hitherto cash was placed in sailor's inverted cap.

1976 Third Cod War – 'Riding Off' policy resumed. Collision between Icelandic Coastguard vessel *Baldur* and frigate *Mermaid*. Frigate returned to the UK with potentially serious damage.
See p.496 panel.

2000 *St Albans*, last of Type 23 Duke-class frigates, launched at Yarrow, Glasgow.
See 10 July 1987.

2005 *Norfolk*, Type 23 frigate, paid off at Devonport after fifteen years' service. First of class and first to go for disposal. Commissioned in June 1990 by Capt Jonathon Band RN who attended the paying off as CINCFLEET.
See 29 October 1984, 1 June 1990.

2005 Naval Historical Branch officially opened in No. 24 Store, HM Naval Base, Portsmouth, by Admiral Sir Alan West, First Sea Lord, Capt C.L.W. Page RN, Head of Naval Historical Branch and Miss Jenny Wraight, Admiralty Librarian. The NHB had been accommodated in Great Scotland Yard, Whitehall, since 1989 after moving from Empress State Building. The Admiralty Library is an integral part of the Branch. Its historic collection, together with the Archive, forms the basis of the corporate memory of the Royal Navy.

2011 *Diamond*, Cdr Ian Clarke RN, commissioned at Portsmouth. The commissioning cake was cut by Mrs Joanne Clarke and Engineering Technician Ross Hindmarch.

7 May

1661 Institution of the 'King's Letter Boys'. 'His Royal Highness (being desirous to give encouragement to such young gentlemen as are willing to apply themselves to the learning of navigation, and fitting themselves for the service of the sea) has determined that one volunteer shall be entered on any ship now going forth, and, for his encouragement, that he shall have the pay of a midshipman, and one midshipman less to be borne on the ship' – William Coventry, Secretary to the Lord High Admiral of England, to Rear-Admiral Sir Richard Stayner.
See 21 February 1729.

1765 *Victory* 'floated' out of the Old Single Dock at Chatham. Designed by Sir Thomas Slade whose plans were finished in 1759, the *annus mirabilis* in which her keel was laid on 23 July. Her name was determined on 28 October 1760. It had been intended to launch her on St George's Day.

1794 *Swiftsure* captured the French *Atalante* 400 miles W. of Cape Finisterre, after a two-day chase.

1797 Outbreak of second mutiny at Spithead.

1798 British naval garrison from *Badger* and *Sandfly* repulsed a French attack on the Iles de St Marcouf, north coast of France. Troops: Royal Artillery, Invalids.

HMS *Victory*, shown in 1778. (*NMRN 1956/90*)

1808 *Redwing* captured or destroyed a Spanish convoy and its escort off Cape Trafalgar. Only two of the seven escorts and one of the twelve enemy escaped.

1879 New and illustrated uniform regulations published. Engineers and assistant paymasters of eight years' seniority to wear a half ($^3/_{16}$-in) stripe above their single ½-in straight – an innovation discontinued in 1903. Frock coat introduced as morning dress.

1901 *Viper* commissioned: first turbine-driven TBD.

1909 No. 1 Rigid Naval Airship, unofficially known as *Mayfly*, ordered from Vickers Sons and Maxim for £35,000 under the 1909–10 Navy Estimates. She took exactly two years to build but never flew; she was wrecked being removed in high winds from her shed on 24 September 1911 after modifications but this marked the start of British naval aviation.

1913 *Hermes* (sixth of the name), a second-class cruiser launched in April 1898, recommissioned having been converted to be first ship to deploy seaplanes.

1915 Destroyer *Maori* sunk by mine off the Wielingen lightvessel, near Zeebrugge.

1936 Remains of destroyer leader HMAS *Anzac* ceremonially scuttled.

1940 RNEC opened at Manadon.
See 15 September 1995, 5 September 2004.

1941 Minesweeper *Stoke* sunk by aircraft at Tobruk.

1941 *München*, German weather ship, 'pinched' off Iceland. Operation EB. A capture of great significance to Ultra intelligence since it gave the keys for June.

1942 Capture of Diego Suarez by a combined force under Rear-Admiral E.N. Syfret (*Ramillies*) and Maj-Gen R.G. Sturges, RM. Operation Ironclad. Ships: *Active, Anthony, Auricula,* Bachaquero, Cromarty, Cromer, Cyclamen, Devonshire, Duncan, Freesia, Fritillary, Genista, Hermione, Illustrious, Inconstant, Indomitable, Jasmine, Javelin, Karanja, Keren, Laforey, Lightning, Lookout, Nigella, Pakenham, Paladin, Panther, Poole, Ramillies, Romney, Royal Ulsterman, Thyme, Winchester Castle.* FAA Sqns: Swordfish: 810, 829, 881, 882, 800, 806, 827, 831, 880. Battle Honour: Diego Suarez 1942.

*Mined on the 5th and sank on the 6th.

See 5 May 1942.

1942 Battle of the Coral Sea (4–8 May) south of the Solomon Islands. US Task Force 17, under Rear-Admiral F.J. Fletcher, USN, defeated a Japanese force and thus removed the threat of invasion of northern Australia. The first major action in which only aircraft carriers were engaged; the heavy surface escorts never sighted one another. RAN ships: *Australia, Hobart*. Battle Honour: Coral Sea 1942.

1943 Destroyers *Jervis, Nubian* and *Paladin* bombarded Kelibia, Tunisia.

1943 Hudsons X and I/233 sank U-447 S.W. of Cape St Vincent (35.30N, 11.55W).

1943 Sunderland W/10 (RAAF) on transit patrol sank U-663 in Bay of Biscay (47.06N, 10.58W).

1943 U-209 foundered after depth-charge attack on the 4th (56.38N, 42.32W).

1944 Frigate *Valleyfield* (RCN) sunk by U-548 off Cape Race. Escort Group C 1.

1945 Last British merchantman and last U-boat to be sunk in Second World War: *Avondale Park*, torpedoed by U-2336, 7 miles S.E. of May Island, and U-320 by Catalina X/210 off Shetland (61.32N, 01.53E).

See 3 and 14 September 1939, 2 May 1945.

1947 705 NAS formed at Gosport, the Royal Navy's first full helicopter squadron, initially tasked as Fleet Helicopter Requirements Unit.

1955 The Royal Marines received the Honorary Freedom of the City of Plymouth in a ceremony on Plymouth Hoe. The Freedom accepted by the Commandant General, General Sir John Westall, on the 200th anniversary of the formation of the Plymouth Division.

See 23 April 1955, 14 May 1959.

1956 Frigate *Redpole*, Lt-Cdr M.R. Collins RN, sailing from Copenhagen, collided with the anchored Danish royal yacht *Dannebrog* 'through a gust of wind suddenly moving the royal yacht' (*The Times*), carried away her bowsprit, severed her moorings and set her adrift. *Redpole* arrived at Portsmouth on 18 May on one shaft. The yacht was able to bring Their Danish Majesties King Frederik and Queen Ingrid to London in July that year.

See 9 May 1945, 4 September 1964, 24 January 1972.

1965 Portsmouth Command of the Royal Navy received the Freedom of the City of Portsmouth 'and thereby the right, privilege, honour and distinction of marching through the City to the beat of drums, with bayonets fixed and colours flying'. The honour was conferred on 10 November 1964.

See 7 May 1955.

1971 New TORs for the Captain HMS *Royal Arthur*. Primary Purpose: To train personnel to lead men. DCI(RN) 505/71.

1982 Further exertion of seapower in South Atlantic – any Argentine vessel or aircraft found more than 12 miles from their coast would be regarded as hostile.

2001 *Tireless*, SSN, sailed from Gibraltar after repairs to her reactor coolant system which took almost a year.

See 19 May 2000.

2009 Centenary of British naval aviation linked to Admiralty order for His Majesty's Rigid Naval Airship No. 1, the *Mayfly*. Fly past over *Illustrious* at Greenwich.

8 May

1576 Martin Frobisher (*Gabriel* and *Michael*) sailed for Baffin Island (in search of the North–West passage to Cathay (China)). Knighted 1588.

1671 Vice-Admiral Sir Edward Spragge (*Revenge*) destroyed seven Algerine men-of-war and their three prizes having forced the boom with a fireship at Bougie, North Africa. Ships: *Advice, Dragon, Garland, Mary, Revenge, Portsmouth*. Fireship: *Little Victory* (expended).
Battle Honour: Bugia 1671.

1731 Board of Admiralty first dined in Painted Hall, Greenwich.
See 19 March 1964.

1744 *Northumberland* taken by the French *Content, Mars* and *Venus* off Ushant. Her Captain had ignored his recall and it seems hard that her Master should have been sentenced to life imprisonment in the Marshalsea.

1797 Sailors' Bill passed to improve Service conditions.

1799 *Fortune* taken and *Dame de Grace* sunk by the French *Salamine* off Jaffa.

1804 Brig sloop *Vincejo* (18) (taken from the Spanish on 19 March 1799) becalmed in Quiberon Bay and captured. Cdr John Wesley Wright taken to Paris and died in the Temple prison 28 October 1805 'in circumstances which strongly suggested foul play' – Laird Clowes.

1807 Boats of *Comus* cut out the Spanish packet *San Pedro* at Las Palmas, Canary Islands.

1811 *Scylla* captured the French *Canonnière* between the Plateau des Triagoz and the Pongaro ledge, off N. Brittany.

1861 Board of Admiralty approved Controller's submission that all ships building or to be built should be armoured: end of 'wooden walls'.

1861 Royal Marines Depot opened at Deal.
See 29 March 1996.

1863 *Flamer*, wood screw gunboat, destroyed ten pirate junks to the N. of Shihpu, S. of Ningpo.

1895 *Renown* launched at Pembroke Dockyard. The first British battleship with all-steel armour plating.

1918 *Basilisk* and *Lydonia* sank UB-70 off Majorca (38.08N, 03.02E).

1918 Sloop *Wallflower* sank U-32 between Malta and Sicily (36.07N, 13.28E).

1940 Second Type C German parachute mine located on Maplin Sands and dealt with next tide.

1940 Admiral Sir Charles Forbes, C-in-C Home Fleet, promoted admiral of the fleet on the day Lord Chatfield completed five years in that rank. Only three admirals of the fleet were permitted to be of less than five years seniority in the rank. To be qualified for such promotion an admiral must have been First Sea Lord, commanded the Home or Mediterranean Fleets or 'have distinguished war service to his credit'.
See 2 December 1940, 24 August 1943.

1941 Light cruiser *Ajax* and destroyers *Havock, Hotspur* and *Imperial* bombarded Benghazi.

1941 First Type G German parachute bomb-mine discovered at Dumbarton. A significant development in this part of the war: it weighed 2,200lb and had not only an advanced fusing system and an anti-sea-surfacing device, but also a photoelectric anti-stripping device. Second dropped in Belfast and dealt with on 11 May.

1941 Heavy cruiser *Cornwall* sank the German disguised raider *Pinguin* (Schiff 33) in Indian Ocean (03.27N, 56.38E).

The tanker *British Emperor* was sunk by the German raider *Pinguin* (six 5.9-in guns) north of the Seychelles. She managed to make a distress signal which was received in *Cornwall*, 500 miles to the south. *Cornwall* immediately turned and closed at high speed, and used her aircraft to search ahead. Early on 8 May, the raider sighted the *Cornwall* and turned away, but one of the cruiser's aircraft detected her. The raider identified herself as the Norwegian ship *Tamerlane*. The cruiser closed and ordered her to stop, and fired warning shots. The raider then revealed herself and opened fire and hit the cruiser, damaging her steering gear. However, the German vessel was heavily hit and blew up at 0526. Twenty-two British prisoners and sixty German survivors were rescued.

1942 Destroyers *Active* and *Panther* sank the Vichy-French S/M *Monge* off Madagascar. Operation Ironclad.

See 7 May 1942.

1942 Submarine *Olympus* sunk by mine 6 miles off Malta, with heavy loss of life.

1943 Admiral Cunningham made 'sink, burn and destroy – let nothing pass' to naval forces closing Axis escape route from N. Africa – his own abbreviation of Vernon's exhortation.

See 23 June 1652, 1 August 1739, 18 September 1740, 21 May 1798.

1945 VE Day. The end of the Second World War in Europe. By the King's command, the Royal Navy spliced the main-brace. A full meeting of the Board of Admiralty met in the bomb-damaged old Boardroom; 'the principal business', recalled Admiral of the Fleet Viscount Cunningham, First Sea Lord, 'being the drinking of a bottle of Waterloo brandy produced by the First Lord, Mr A.V. Alexander'. The following day came a signalled bleat from Admiral Sir James Somerville, head of the British Admiralty Delegation in Washington:

> Poor B.A.D. can splice no brace,
> because of rum there is no trace.

But see next entry.

See 15 August 1945.

1945 Sir James Somerville promoted admiral of the fleet. He had been invalided out of the RN with tuberculosis in 1939 but returned to the Active List and commanded Force H and the East Indies station.

1956 Destroyer *Corunna*, Cdr T.T. Lewin RN, visited La Corunna in Spain, with the Governor and C-in-C Gibraltar, HE Lt-Gen Sir Harold Redman, embarked. Guard paraded at the grave of Sir John Moore and wreaths laid by RN and British regiments which fought under Moore at the Battle of Corunna on 16 January 1809.

See 7 October 1969.

1964 DCNS dropped the additional title of Fifth Sea Lord with the creation of the unified MOD on 1 April 1964. 'The DCNS will . . . continue to be the chief focus through which the interests of the Fleet Air Arm will be represented on the Admiralty Board. This Instruction is to be brought to the notice of all Fleet Air Arm personnel.' – DCI(RN) 185/64.

See 22 December 1916, 23 October 1917.

1965 Admiralty Board to Lord Chatfield: 'On the occasion of the 30th anniversary of your promotion to Admiral of the Fleet, the Admiralty Board of the Defence Council sends you their congratulations on behalf of the Officers and Men of the Royal Navy. The Board recall that your promotion in 1935 was during your busy years as First Sea Lord, when on your shoulders rested the responsibility for the preparation for war and the expansion of the Royal Navy. I and all the Board wish you many more years of happy retirement. David Luce.' – DCI(RN) 714/65.

See 27 September 1873, 15 November 1967.

9 May

1795 Boats of *Melampus* (Sir Richard Strachan), *Diamond*, *Hebe*, *Niger* and *Syren* captured ten vessels of a French convoy and two of the escort, which had been driven ashore 4 miles N. of Cape Carteret, Normandy.

1810 *Favourite* and *Orestes* captured the French privateer *Dorade* 10 miles W.S.W. of Land's End.

1876 *Temeraire* launched at Chatham. Became *Indus II* in 1904 and *Akbar* in 1915 though generally referred to affectionately as 'the Great Brig'. Carried longest lower yards ever (115ft), had a foresail which was the largest unit of canvas ever stitched in an Admiralty sail loft and was the last armoured ship to enter harbour under sail alone. Six of her ten 11-in guns were mounted in a main-deck central battery, and two on Moncrieff disappearing mountings.

See 3 October 1890.

1899 The twin-screw royal yacht *Victoria and Albert* launched at Pembroke Dockyard.

See 3 January 1900, 6 December 1954.

1917 Destroyer *Milne* rammed and sank UC-26 in Dover Strait (51.03N, 01.40E).

1918 *Queen Alexandra* transport, taken up in two wars, rammed and sank UB-78 in the Channel (49.50N, 01.40W).

1926 Submarine H 29, Lt F.H.E. Skyrme RN, completing a refit at Devonport Dockyard, sank in No. 2 Basin while the boat's trim was being adjusted. When No. 3 main ballast tank aft was flooded, the stern sank and water entered the hull through the open engine room hatch fouled by a ventilation hose. One Chief ERA and five dockyard workers lost. First Lt dismissed HMS *Maidstone* and severely reprimanded. Submarine scrapped at Pembroke Dock.

1940 German minesweeper M-134 sunk in Bergen Roads by 254 Sqn RAF: the first RAF sinking in Second World War. Ship salvaged and re-entered service as escort vessel *Jungingen*.

See 27 September 1943.

1941 GC (ex-AM): OS A. Howarth for saving life at sea, though injured.

1941 Boarding party from destroyer *Bulldog* captured secret Enigma signal-cyphering equipment from U-110 in N. Atlantic (60.31N, 33.10W), the greatest intelligence coup in British, or any other country's, naval history.

Bulldog (Cdr A.J. Baker-Cresswell), *Broadway* and the corvette *Aubrietia* were part of the escort of convoy OB 318. U-110 surfaced and abandoned ship after a depth-charge attack by *Aubrietia*. A boarding party from *Bulldog* led by Sub-Lt David Balme spent several hours on board the submarine, unknown to the German survivors who had been hastened below decks in *Bulldog*. Dönitz therefore remained ignorant of this extraordinary compromise of U-boat cyphers and refused to accept the fact into the 1980s. Cdr Baker-Cresswell appointed DSO and Sub-Lt Balme received DSC from King George VI, who remarked that this was perhaps the most important single event of the whole war at sea. The Captain of U-110, Kapitanleutnant Fritz-Julius Lemp, who died with his boat, had sunk the Donaldson liner *Athenia* on the first day of the war, when in command of U-30. 'History is written in terms

A German, four-rotor Enigma machine. Originally recovered from Norway Harbour Police and presented by HMS *Mercury* to the Royal Naval Museum. (*NMRN 1983/793*)

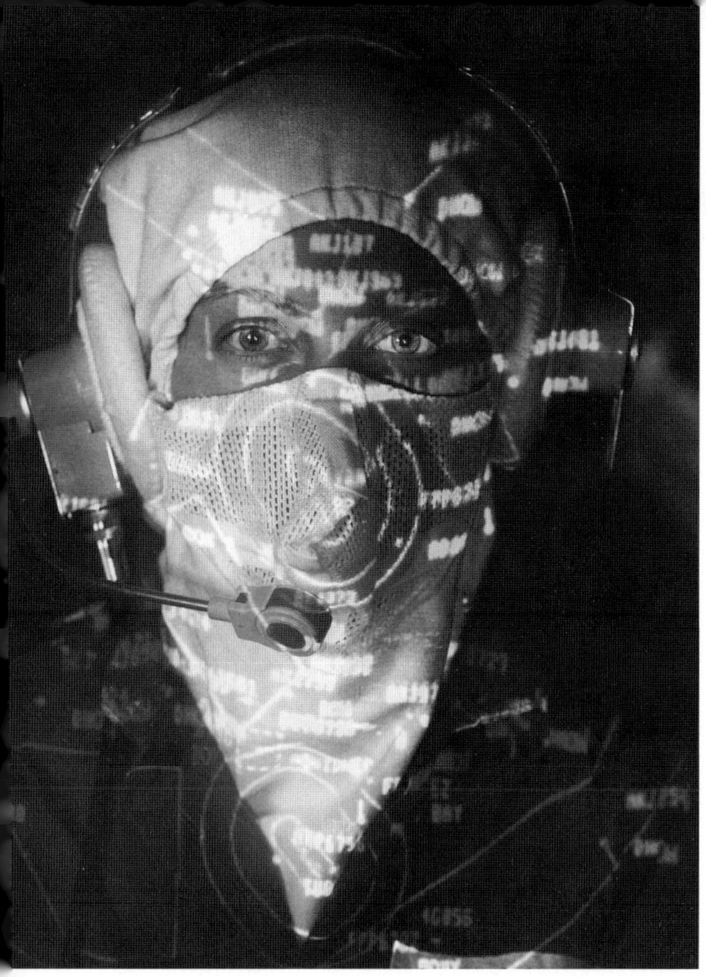

An Operations Room rating on duty onboard HMS *Somerset* in the Gulf in August 2004. (*RN*)

of Trafalgars and Jutlands, but by any standard the seizure of U-110 should rate as a major victory at sea' – Lewin, *Ultra Goes to War*, p.207.

See 11 and 20 August 1914, 30 November 1914, 9 May 1945.

1943 Destroyers *Jervis*, *Nubian* and *Paladin* bombarded Kelibia, Tunisia.

1945 Surrender of German forces in the Channel Islands signed on board the destroyer *Bulldog* (in company with *Beagle*) in St Peter Port, Guernsey, 'thus restoring the only part of the British Isles which the enemy had occupied' – Roskill, *The War at Sea*, vol.3, pt 2, p.307. Operation Nestegg.

See 9 May 1941.

1945 Liberation of Copenhagen. The light cruisers *Birmingham*, Capt H.W. Williams RN, wearing three very large White Ensigns, and *Dido*, Capt R.F. Elkins RN, with destroyers *Zephyr*, *Zest*, *Zealous* and *Zodiac*, entered Copenhagen, passing the German cruisers *Prinz Eugen* and *Nürnberg*. 'The Danes greeted the British warships rapturously' – Roskill, *The War at Sea*, vol.3 pt.2 p.263. Operation Cleaver. The ships had sailed from Rosyth on 6 May with minesweepers in company to clear a passage through the Skagerrak and had been given A/S and CAP cover on passage by the escort carriers *Queen*, *Trumpeter* and *Searcher*.

See 13 May 1945, 7 May 1956.

1958 RN Engineer Officers annual dinner, presided over by the Engineer-in-Chief, Vice-Admiral N.E. Dalton, marked the closure of the RN Engineering College, Keyham, the oldest naval mess, and move to Manadon.

See 1 July 1880, 28 June 1888, 5 February 2004.

1975 *Ardent*, Type 21 frigate, launched at Yarrow. Lost to Argentine air attack 21 May 1982. DSC: Cdr A.W.J. West, RN. Operation Corporate. The third successive *Ardent* sunk in action.

See 31 May 1916, 8 June 1940.

1981 Aircraft carrier *Hermes* (eighth of the name) recommissioned after being fitted with ski-jump to assist aircraft launches.

1982 Argentine trawler *Narwal* bombed by Sea Harriers and boarded by SAS and a RM party from *Invincible*. A moderate intelligence haul, and confirmation that the trawler and two others were under the command of a naval officer, who had failed to destroy his orders. Operation Corporate.

2006 Lt-Cdr John Walter George Wellham DSC, the last surviving pilot of the Fleet Air Arm attack on Taranto in 1940, died aged 87. Born on the Isle of Bute 2 January 1919, the son of a retired Petty Officer.

See 11 November 1940, 31 August 2005.

10 May

1694 *Monmouth*, *Resolution* and *Roebuck* destroyed the French *Jersey* and twenty-five sail of a convoy in Blancs Sablons Bay, Brittany.

1794 *Castor*, escorting a Newfoundland convoy, taken by the French *Patriote* to the south-west of Cape Clear. Most of the convoy were also taken by other ships of Rear-Admiral Joseph Neilly's squadron.

1804 *Ethalion* captured the Dutch privateer *Union* 50 miles W.S.W. of Bergen.

1806 Capt Cochrane launched aerial propaganda attack on France (kites from *Pallas*).

1812 Boats of *America*, *Eclair* and *Leviathan* cut out eighteen vessels of a French convoy at Laigueglia, Italian Riviera.

1862 Capture of Ningpo by *Encounter*, *Hardy*, *Kestrel*, *Ringdove*, and the French *Confucius* and *Etoile*.

1865 *Haughty* destroyed four pirate junks 40 miles S.W. of Macao.

1870 Reginald Yorke Tyrwhitt born. Commanded Harwich Force, 1914–18, and C-in-C China, 1927–9.

1917 Sloop *Cyclamen* sank the Italian S/M *Alberto Guglielmotti*, believing her to be German.

1917 Experimental convoy sailed from Gibraltar to the United Kingdom with *Mavis* and *Rule* (Q 26 and Q 35) as escort.

See p.225 panel.

1918 VC: Lt Victor Alexander Charles Crutchley (*Vindictive*), Lt Roland Richard Louis Bourke, RNVR (ML 276) and Lt Geoffrey Heneage Drummond, RNVR (ML 254).

Blockship operation at Ostend. *Vindictive* sunk in the harbour. Ships: *Faulknor*, *Prince Eugene*, *Trident*, *Velox*, *Vindictive*, *Warwick*, *Whirlwind*; CMB: 22B, 23B, 24A, 25BD, 26B, 30B. ML: 254, 276. Battle Honour: Ostend 1918.

1918 Submarine E 34 sank UB-16 in North Sea (52.06N, 02.01E).

1938 Anson K8758 from RAF Martlesham Heath detected Swordfish and Nimrod aircraft taking off from and landing on *Courageous* at 8 miles with first side-scan ASV radar.

1940 Naval demolition parties landed at Antwerp, Flushing, Hook of Holland and Ijmuiden. Operation X.D.

The destroyer *Brilliant* sailed from Dover with a demolition party embarked and reached Antwerp on 10 May. Their task was the sailing of twenty-six Allied ships and fifty tugs, which left on 12th. By noon on 14th some 600 barges, dredgers and floating cranes had been sailed, and by the evening of 17th, 150,000 tons of oil had been made unusable and the entrances to the docks and basins blocked to hinder the advance of the German forces.

1940 Britain occupied Iceland to prevent its capture by the Germans following the invasion of Denmark and Norway. In an unopposed landing, 815 men of the 2nd Royal Marines Battalion, including RN crews for two 3.7-in howitzers, commanded by Col R.G. Sturges, were put ashore unopposed at Reykjavik from the heavy cruiser *Berwick*, the light cruiser *Glasgow* and the destroyer *Fearless*. The force was relieved by 147 Infantry Brigade on 17–19 May. MNBDO later established a naval base at Hvalfiord, N. of Reykjavik. On 23 May the transport *Ulster Prince* landed troops at Thorshavn (where the Royal Marines had landed on 13 April) to secure the Danish Faeroe Islands.

See 14 August 1816, 3 April 1940, 7 July 1941.

1940 Winston Churchill became Prime Minster and was succeeded as First Lord of the Admiralty by A.V. Alexander.

1945 First U-boat surrendered – U-1009. Some 156 were received in all, of which 110 were sunk; 221 had been scuttled to avoid surrender. Operation Pledge.

1945 Light fleet carrier *Bulwark* laid down at Harland and Wolff, Belfast.

See 22 June 1948.

The surrendered German U-Boat U-776 being brought up the River Thames for public display, 1945. (*NMRN*)

1954 The first volume of *The War at Sea*, the official history of maritime operations in the Second World War, by Capt S.W. Roskill RN, published. The first two years were ones of endurance for the RN. The greatest naval achievements were the saving of the British armies from Norway, France, Greece and Crete, and the defeats inflicted on the German and Italian surface fleets. It ends with the entry of Japan into the war and the loss of the *Prince of Wales* and *Repulse*.

See 28 January 1957, 21 October 1960, 4 November 1982.

1955 Netlayer *Protector*, completed in 1936, converted into an Antarctic patrol ship for service in the Falkland Islands Dependencies. She served for eleven years before being replaced by *Endurance* and was sold on 10 February 1970 after thirty-four years' service.

See 20 February 1967.

1966 Fleet carrier *Eagle*, Capt J.C.Y. Roxburgh RN, returned to Singapore after seventy-one days at sea, a peacetime record for a British carrier. She had been engaged on the Beira Patrol maintaining the UN embargo on oil supplies reaching Southern Rhodesia.

Her Buccaneer, Sea Vixen, Scimitar and Gannet aircraft had carried out over 1,000 sorties, flown 600,000 miles in 2,000 flying hours searching for oil tankers. RFA *Tidepool* arrived at Singapore after eighty days at sea, and having conducted seventy-eight fuel replenishments off Beira. 'This operation, which is under the overall direction of C-in-C Middle East, Admiral Sir Michael Le Fanu, once again illustrates the Royal Navy's ability to maintain a military presence in an area a long way from its base in support of the policy of HM government' – *The Naval Review*.

See 27 February 1966, 10 April 1966, 25 June 1975.

1968 HM Queen Elizabeth The Queen Mother opened the Clyde Submarine Base.

1988 *Abdiel*, last minelayer to be designed as such, paid off.

2005 Vice-Admiral Sir John Parker, wartime signals officer, died. He had the distinction of having survived the sinking in the Arctic of two cruisers in twelve days: the light cruiser *Edinburgh*, escorting Convoy QP-11 from Murmansk, torpedoed in the Barents Sea on 30 April 1942 and scuttled by destroyer *Foresight* on 2 May; he and other survivors including Rear-Admiral S.S. Bonham-Carter, were transferred to the light cruiser *Trinidad*, then under repair at Murmansk, which was attacked on her way home by German JU-88 bombers N. of Murmansk on 14 May 1942 and sunk by the destroyer *Matchless* in the early hours of the next day. Final appointment was Flag Officer Medway 1966–9.

11 MAY

1780 Capitulation of Charlestown, South Carolina, to Vice-Admiral Arbuthnot (*Roebuck*) and troops under General Sir Henry Clinton. Ships: *Blonde, Camilla, Defiance, Europe, Fowey, Perseus, Raisonnable,* Raleigh, Renown, Richmond, Roebuck, Romulus, Virginia.*

1808 *Bacchante* captured the French *Griffon* close off Cape San Antonio, Cuba.

1810 Vice-Admiral Lord Collingwood buried in St Paul's Cathedral.
See 7 March 1810.

1813 *Lyra, Royalist* and *Sparrow* at the defence of Castro Urdiales, north coast of Spain.

1824 Rangoon captured by naval forces under Cdre Charles Grant in First Burmese War. *Liffey* (50), *Larne* (20) (Capt Frederick Marryat), *Slaney* (20), *Sophie* (18), the paddle vessel *Diana* (the first steam warship used in action by RN) and four Hon. East India Company cruisers. First battle honour awarded for a campaign as distinct from an action: Burma 1824–6.
See 14 April 1852.

1853 *Rattler* captured six pirate junks and a lorcha in Nam Kwan harbour, near Foochow.

1860 Garibaldi and his Thousand landed at Marsala, Sicily, in a campaign which led to the unification of Italy. The presence at Marsala of the wood screw gunvessel HMS *Intrepid* and the wood paddle sloop HMS *Argus* deterred the Bourbon Neapolitan defenders from effectively intervening and the Royal Navy thus played a role in the birth of Italy.

1918 Submarine E 35 sank U-154, a cruiser-type submarine off Madeira (36.45N, 12.00W).

1940 Fortress Unit RM landed at Narvik to mount naval guns.

1941 Destroyers *Jackal, Kashmir, Kelly* (D 5), *Kelvin* and *Kipling* bombarded Benghazi. *Ladybird* bombarded Gazala north landing ground.

1942 Destroyers *Lively, Kipling* and *Jackal* attacked by German aircraft in E. Mediterranean during Operation M.G.2. *Lively* sank immediately (33.24N, 25.38E) and *Kipling* (32.38N, 26.20E). *Jackal* damaged and taken in tow by *Jervis* but had to be sunk early on the 12th (32.33N, 26.25E).

1943 Sloop *Fleetwood* and Halifax D/58 sank U-528 in S.W. Approaches. Convoy OS 47.

1944 Destroyer *Bicester* bombarded targets in the Ardea area, south of Rome.

1945 Surrender of Heligoland taken by Rear-Admiral Muirhead Gould, British Naval Commander N.W. Germany, having arrived in a German-manned R-boat accompanied by a company of Scots Guards embarked in five German minesweepers.
See 18 April 1947.

1955 Vice-Admiral A. de Booy, C-in-C Royal Netherlands Navy, in a ceremony in the Wardroom RNB Portsmouth, presented a marine painting by the Dutch artist Ludolph Backhuysen to Admiral of the Fleet Sir George Creasy, C-in-C Portsmouth, as a token of gratitude for British hospitality to Dutch seamen during the war. Capt Creasy, Captain (D) 1st Destroyer Flotilla in *Codrington*, had brought Princess (later Queen Juliana) to safety in Britain in 1940.
See 12 May 1940.

1961 Frigate *Plymouth*, Capt J.C. Cartwright DSC, RN, commissioned at Plymouth.

1964 HMS *Mediator*, the last fleet tug serving under the White Ensign, returned to Devonport from Malta to pay off for disposal.

1969 RN Phantoms in *Daily Mail* Transatlantic Air Race, staged to commemorate fiftieth anniversary of first transatlantic flight by Alcock and Brown. Aircrew, using helicopters and bicycles at both ends, with Phantoms in the middle, completed flight from Empire State Building, New York, to Post Office Tower, London, in 5 hours 11 minutes 22 seconds. Air-to-air

HMS *Diana* (the paddle steamer shown on the right) leading the attack on stockades at Pagoda Point on the Rangoon River, 1824. (*NMRN 1976/130*)

refuelling six times by RAF Victor tanker controlled by *Nubian*. Phantom XT 858, flown by Lt-Cdr Brian Davies, CO of 892 NAS, established the fastest overall west-to-east time with a new record crossing-time of 4 hours 46 minutes 57 seconds, averaging a true airspeed of 1,100mph.

1982 Rear-Admiral John 'Sandy' Woodward, who had no MCMVs under command, ordered the frigate *Alacrity*, Cdr Christopher Craig RN, to transit N. up Falkland Sound to locate and disrupt any enemy resupply or mining activity, in effect to act as a minesweeper (San Carlos was the intended amphibious landing area). 'I shall remember him [Chris Craig] as one of the bravest men I ever met. This was Victoria Cross material but, strangely, only if it went wrong' – Admiral Woodward. The night-time transit, with the ship's company dispersed in small groups around the ship, found the passage clear. En route, *Alacrity* detected and destroyed by gunfire the Argentinian naval transport *Isla de los Estados*, loaded with 325,000 litres of aviation fuel. This was the only surface action between British and Argentinian ships during the Falklands War. Operation Corporate.

See 21 May 1982.

1991 Capt Hugh Anthony Kidd, RN, died aged 74. The only submarine engineer officer to be appointed DSO, for service in *Torbay* in the Mediterranean 1941–2. He received his DSO from King George VI in July 1942 at same investiture as Cdr Miers received the VC. *Torbay*'s First Lieutenant and Navigating Officer received bars to their DSCs and twenty-four ship's company (including eight of Kidd's engine-room department) received DSMs or bars to their DSMs.

One of the RN Phantoms flown in the *Daily Mail* Transatlantic Air Race, 1969. (*FAAM*)

12 May

1652 *President* (42), second of the name, which became *Bonaventure* at the Restoration, *Nightingale* (30) and *Recovery* (26) fell in with a Dutch convoy of seven off Start Point, escorted by three men-of-war, each carrying a flag officer. Their admiral surrendered but his subordinates had to be persuaded, the vice-admiral telling Capt Young that he had been threatened with execution should he strike.

1689 The French *Railleuse* and *Serpente* taken off the Casquets by the *Nonsuch*, commanded by the Bosun, Mr Sincoch, on the death of Capt Coyle whom he was promoted to succeed.

1694 Capt Warren in *Monck* (60) captured Duguay-Trouin in *Diligente* (36) and took him to Plymouth whence he escaped.

1796 *Phoenix* captured the Dutch *Argo* and recaptured *Duke of York* 30 miles N. of the Texel. *Sylph* captured the Dutch *Mercury* off Terschelling. *Pegasus* drove ashore two Dutch brigs, *Echo* and *De Gier*, on Terschelling.

1797 Mutinies in the Home Ports. Mutiny broke out in Bridport's flagship *Queen Charlotte* at Spithead and lasted until 15 May. It had spread to The Nore in *Sandwich* on 12 May and lasted until 13 June. There was a minor eruption from 16 to 23 May at Plymouth. The country had been virtually defenceless for two months and in greater danger than at any other time in the long wars with France and Spain.

1846 *Fantome* and her boats repulsed Moorish pirates while salving the remains of the wreck of the British *Ruth* 6 miles W. of Cape Tres Forcas, Morocco.

1854 *Tiger* (16) ran ashore in a fog, under Russian batteries 5 miles S. of Odessa. Crew forced to burn her rather than surrender.

1862 British and French forces captured Tsingpu. Naval Brigade from *Imperieuse*, *Pearl*, *Vulcan*, *Flamer*, *Coromandel*. French gunboat: No. 12. Troops: Royal Artillery, Royal Engineers, 31st

Plaque at Clyde Submarine Base marking the end of the last Polaris deterrent patrol, 1996. (*Author*)

and 67th Regiments, 5th Bombay Native Light Infantry, 22nd Bengal Native Infantry.

1865 Two boats of *Wasp*, wood screw sloop, captured an Arab slave dhow off Zanzibar.

1898 Cruiser *Fox* made punitive raid up Bompol River, Sierra Leone.

1918 Submarine D 6 sank UB-72 off Portland (50.08N, 02.41W) after first German effort at wolf-pack tactics.

1918 AMC *Olympic*, carrying 9,000 US soldiers to France and in a new camouflage of yellow, red and blue by war artist Norman Wilkinson, rammed and sank U-103 off the Lizard (49.16N, 04.51W).

1940 Destroyers *Venomous* and *Verity* landed 200 Royal Marines at the Hook of Holland. Operation Harpoon.

1940 Destroyer *Codrington*, Capt George Creasy, Captain D1, embarked Dutch Crown Princess (future Queen Juliana of the Netherlands) and her family at Ijmuiden and brought them to Britain two days after the German invasion. Previous day cruiser *Arethusa* and two destroyers escorted two merchantmen carrying Dutch gold reserves from Ijmuiden to Britain.

See 7 June 1940, 11 May 1955, 31 October 1972.

1940 A.V. Alexander (later Viscount Alexander of Hillsborough) succeeded Winston Churchill as First Lord of the Admiralty and served until 25 May 1945.

1941 *Ladybird*, river gunboat, sunk by aircraft off Libyan coast.

1943 Destroyer *Hesperus* sank U-186 in Atlantic (41.54N, 31.49W). Convoy SC 129.

1943 U-456 sunk west of Ireland by Liberator B/86 with three depth charges and one Mk 24 mine – in fact a homing torpedo, scoring its first operational success.

1943 Destroyer *Broadway* and frigate *Lagan* and Swordfish B/811 (*Biter*) sank U-89 in N. Atlantic. Convoy HX 237.

1946 Britain's last battleship, *Vanguard*, Capt W.G. Agnew RN, commissioned at Greenock on a Sunday. Princess Elizabeth, who had launched the ship in November 1944, attended 'after an all-night train journey from London'.

See 2 October 1941, 30 November 1944.

1976 *Broadsword*, Type 22 frigate, first of class, launched at Yarrow. Commissioned 3 May 1979, the first British warship with an all-missile main armament (Exocet and Sea Wolf).

1982 *Brilliant*, Type 22 frigate, destroyed three Argentine Skyhawk aircraft in the first operational use of Sea Wolf. Her Lynx helicopter was the first to fire Sea Skua in action. *Glasgow*, Type 42 destroyer, damaged by bomb which failed to explode. Operation Corporate.

1996 End of last deterrent patrol by *Repulse*, the 229th mounted by the four Polaris SSBNs in twenty-eight years' service. FOSM signalled BZ to boat at 1200.

See 15 June 1968, 28 August 1996.

2007 Gieves, the naval tailors and outfitters, which traded throughout the twentieth century at 22 The Hard, closed their shop in the Gunwharf (lately HMS *Vernon*) and so ended a presence in Portsmouth dating back 222 years. The almost legendary position of Gieves in the Royal Navy is commemorated in stained glass windows in the Lady Chapel of Portsmouth Cathedral in the High Street of Old Portsmouth where, at No. 73, the company opened for business as Meredith's in 1785.

13 May

1660 Pepys watched a crown and CR being substituted for the State's arms in a new standard for a new king, who also insisted on the removal of the harp.

1731 Halley presented his quadrant to the Royal Society.

1757 *Antelope* drove ashore and wrecked the French *Aquilon* in Audierne Bay, Brittany.
Battle Honour: *Aquilon* 1757.

1764 Harrison's fourth chronometer tested successfully in *Tartar*.

1768 James Cook passed for lieutenant.

1779 *Cabot*, *Experiment*, *Fortune*, *Pallas* and *Unicorn* captured the French *Danae* and destroyed the rest of the escort to a flotilla of French troops en route from St Malo to attack Jersey.

1787 First convict convoy eventually sailed from Spithead for Botany Bay, arriving 19 January 1788. *Sirius* (Capt Arthur Phillip, who experienced some difficulty over a commodore's pennant, and who shifted to *Supply*), six transport and three store ships.

1793 *Iris* fought the French *Citoyenne-Française* 200 miles W.S.W. of Cape Finisterre. An indecisive action but the first afloat in the French wars.

1835 Elizabeth Cook, widow of Capt James Cook for fifty-six years, died aged 94. She was buried with her two sons in Great St Andrew church, Cambridge.
See 14 February 1779, 5 October 1780, 24 January 1794.

1854 Screw first rate *Royal Albert* (121) launched by HM Queen Victoria at Woolwich. The first warship named by a British monarch.

1859 Senior chaplain of Greenwich Hospital recognised as 'Head of the Naval Chaplains' and 'Chaplain to the Fleet'.
See 30 May 1859, 23 October 1876.

1889 Officers' tunic replaced by monkey jacket.

1915 Battleship *Goliath* sunk by the German-manned Turkish destroyer *Muavanet-i-Miliet* off Gallipoli.

1916 Monitor M 30 sunk by Turkish batteries in Gulf of Smyrna.
See 18 March 1915, 25 and 27 May 1915.

1916 Drifters *Dulcie Doris* and *Evening Star II* sank the Austrian S/M U-6 12 miles E.N.E. of Cape Otranto.

1926 Submarines L 11, L 21 and M 3 supplied electric power to Millwall and Royal Docks in London during the General Strike.

1937 Destroyer *Hunter*, Lt-Cdr B.G. Scurfield RN, mined 5 miles off Almeria when on non-intervention patrol during the Spanish Civil War; eight killed, four injured. AM: Cdr Scurfield; EGM: Lt-Cdr P.N. Humphreys and PO J. Smail; MBE for Meritorious Service ABs J.F. Collings, E. Thomas and H. Abrahams. Ship towed stern-first to Gibraltar by light cruiser *Arethusa* escorted by destroyer *Hardy*. Dead buried in Almeria and Gibraltar. A British compensation

HMS *Hunter* receiving a towing wire after being mined in 1937. (*NMRN*)

German U-Boat Losses in the Second World War

Number of U-boats built		1,162
Number of U-boats lost		782
Causes for loss:	Surface ship attack	249
	Air attack	289
	Joint air/surface	47
	Submarines	21
	Mines	26
	Other	87
	Bombing raids	63

(Of these 521 were sunk by British forces, 166 by US forces, 12 shared.)

claim for £127,054 was never paid. Cdr Scurfield commanded the destroyer *Bedouin* sunk on the Operation Harpoon convoy to Malta in 1942 and he met a sad end in captivity.

See 10 April 1940, 15 June 1942, 22 October 1946, 8 March 2008.

1941 AMC *Salopian* sunk by U-98 in N. Atlantic (56.43N, 38.57W).

1941 Submarine *Undaunted* lost in Mediterranean.

1942 Light coastal forces attacked the escorts to a large German ship off Ambleteuse. MTB 220 missing. Sunk: TB *Iltis* and *Seeadler* (50.47N, 33.00E).

1943 Corvette *Drumheller* (RCN), frigate *Lagan* and Sunderland G/423 (RCAF) sank U-753 in Atlantic (48.37N, 22.39W). Convoy HX 237.

1943 Surrender of Axis forces in N. Africa.

1945 Heavy cruiser *Devonshire*, with fast minelayers *Apollo* and *Ariadne*, escorted by destroyers *Savage*, *Campbell*, HMCS *Iroquois* and HNoMS *Arendal*, arrived in Oslo carrying Crown Prince Olav, Rear-Admiral Elias Corneliussen, C-in-C Royal Norwegian Navy, General Sir Andrew Thorne, GOC Scotland, and Rear-Admiral James Stuart Ritchie, FO Norway designate. Operation Kingdom.

Merchant Ship Losses in the Second World War

Total of Allied Merchant Shipping lost		6,439 ships
		24,390,000 tons
of this total Britain lost		3,194 ships
		12,251,000 tons

(54 per cent of total British merchant shipping tonnage at opening of hostilities.)

Causes for loss:	Submarines	2,775 ships
	Air attack	753 ships
	Surface attack	237 ships
	E-boat attack	99 ships
	Other	411 ships
	Mines	521 ships
	Marine causes	1,643 ships

FO Norway's HQ established 14 May. Following the German surrender on 8 May, 350,000 German troops remained in Norway and on 10 May the 1st Airborne Division secured Norwegian airfields. Most of the Kriegsmarine (570 warships) was in Norwegian ports and the securing of these posed an urgent operational task for the Royal Navy. *Devonshire* sailed on to Copenhagen where she relieved *Birmingham*. On 24 May, *Devonshire* and the light cruiser *Dido*, escorted the German cruisers *Prinz Eugen* and *Nürnberg* to Wilhelmshaven.

See 7 June 1940, 9 and 17 May 1945, 5 June 1945.

1970 Sea King fitted with extra fuel tanks and piloted by Lt-Cdr Victor Sirett RN, CO of 700S NAS, made a record 602.95-mile flight from Land's End to John o' Groats in 4 hours 19 minutes 21 seconds.

1994 *Westminster*, Type 23 frigate, commissioned in the Pool of London. Commissioning ceremony held in the Tower of London. Cdr Richard Clapp, RN, CO, presented the Constable of the Tower with a keg of wine, the traditional Constable's Dues. Service of Blessing held in Westminster Abbey.

14 May

1741 The *Wager* (24), Capt David Cheap, an ex-East Indiaman employed as store ship of Anson's squadron deploying to the Pacific, parted company with the Commodore in a gale off Cape Horn on 23 April and was engulfed in the Golfo de Penas in S. Chile and wrecked on what is now Wager Island (47.40.43S, 75.02.57W). on this date. Mutiny and complete breakdown of naval discipline among the survivors was as bad as any in RN history, a sad business relieved only by the crew's extraordinary endurance.

The court martial on 14 April 1746 enquired only into the loss of the ship; a trial for mutiny would have raised too many difficult issues for the Admiralty. The mutineers could claim that as their pay stopped with the loss of the ship, so did the authority of the officers. This semi-legal loophole was closed by an Act of 1747 which continued the pay of personnel shipwrecked and/or captured.

See 18 September 1740, 11 September 1994.

1781 *Nonsuch* fought the French *Actif* 50 miles N.W. by W. of Ushant.

1798 Sea Fencibles established by Order in Council.

1806 *Pallas* (32) fought the French *Minerve* (40) and three brigs off Ile d'Aix, Basque Roads.

1829 Admiral Francis Beaufort appointed Hydrographer.

1847 *Driver*, wood paddle sloop, arrived at Spithead from the Pacific, the first steam vessel to circumnavigate the world.

The Royal Navy and the Palestine Patrol

During the First World War the British government favoured a national home for Jews in the area known in the West as Palestine. The war ended with much of the Ottoman Empire in British hands and in 1922 the League of Nations gave Britain a mandate to govern Palestine and bring the land to self-rule. With incompatible demands from Jews and Arabs, the aim of a composite state proved impossible to achieve; it was a task, in Naomi Shepherd's phrase, 'like ploughing sand'. Jewish immigration led to unrest among the far larger Arab population and in 1936 the Arabs revolted. For over two years ships of the Mediterranean Fleet were stationed at Haifa, undertaking various tasks ashore, including running the railway. In early 1939 the Royal Navy was called on to arrest vessels bringing in illegal Jewish immigrants until the Marine Police could cope. The start of the Second World War ended the requirement.

'In the aftermath of the Second World War, no task that fell to the Royal Navy was more demanding than the interception of sea-borne illegal immigrants into Palestine' wrote Admiral Sir Nigel Essenhigh in the *Naval Staff History*. Small craft started landing survivors of the Holocaust in disregard of the quota for legal immigrants. The Palestine government requested assistance. Coastal patrols by destroyers, sloops, frigates and minesweepers began. RAF aircraft undertook reconnaissance further out. The post of Commodore Palestine was established at Haifa. The early arrests were peaceable but attempts to free immigrants held ashore resulted in new arrivals being held in Cyprus. This in turn led to arrests being fiercely resisted. Vessels carrying illegal immigrants manoeuvred violently and boarding parties met fierce resistance. Ships engaged in the illegal trade increased in size and the Navy's tasks expanded to cover the whole Mediterranean.

By 1947, the British government could see no way of reconciling Arabs and Jews, so invited the UN to resolve the problem; the outcome was unacceptable to both sides. 'The world at large watched the sordid drama without gratitude, blaming the British both for creating the problem and for failing to solve it . . . Nagged by the United Nations, pestered by the Americans, bewildered by the Zionists, insulted by the Arabs, excoriated by world opinion, exhausted by the strain of it, impoverished by the cost, disillusioned, embittered, in December 1947 the British government announced that . . . they would have no more of it' – James Morris, *Farewell the Trumpets* 1978 pp.431–4. The British withdrew from Palestine in 1948. Fighting between Arabs and Jews necessitated three Royal Marine Cdos being present to cover various stages of the withdrawal.

See 14 May 1948, 30 June 1948.

Rear-Admiral Francis Beaufort (1774–1857) as a midshipman. (*NMRN 1976/467(2)*)

She left Portsmouth on 12 March 1842 and went eastabout via Simon's Town to join the East Indies and China station. On her return she had been in commission longer than any ship, other than surveying vessels, since the end of the French wars and had sailed and steamed 75,696 miles.

1917 Posts of First Sea Lord and Chief of Naval Staff combined.

1918 Destroyer *Phoenix* torpedoed and sunk in Adriatic by Austrian submarine U-XXVII.

1940 Royal Marines and demolition parties evacuated in destroyer *Malcolm* from the Hook of Holland.

1941 *Puriri*, trawler (RNZN), sunk by mine in Hauraki Gulf, off Auckland, New Zealand.

1944 Generalmajor Heinrich Kreipe, captured in a raid mounted by Maj Patrick Leigh Fermor and Maj Stanley Moss of SOE on 26 April near Heraklion, taken off in darkness from Rodakino on coast of Crete by ML 842 and taken to Mersa Matruh in Egypt.

1945 Capture of Wewak peninsula and airfield, New Guinea, by 6th Australian Division. Ships: *Newfoundland* and *Arunta*, *Colac*, *Dubbo*, *Hobart*, *Swan*, *Warramunga*, *Warrego* (all RAN).

1948 The British mandate in Palestine formally ended at midnight. The broad pennant of COMPAL (Commodore Palestine), Cdre A.T.G.C. Peachey RN, was struck and the British High Commissioner, General Sir Alan Cunningham, (brother of ABC), departed from Haifa in the light cruiser *Euryalus*, Capt C.C. Harvey RN, at 2315. She was escorted from Palestine waters by the aircraft carrier *Ocean*, Capt E.M.C. Abel-Smith RN, wearing the flag of Vice-Admiral Sir Thomas Troubridge, Flag Officer (Air) and Second-in-Command Mediterranean Fleet, together with HM ships *Chevron*, *Childers*, *Volage*, *Pelican* and *Widemouth Bay*.

See 30 June 1948, 21 and 29 November 1967.

1955 Warsaw Pact created.

1955 The first jet squadron of the RNVR formed at HMS *Black Cap*, RNAS Stretton; No. 1831 NAS exchanged Sea Fury piston-engined aircraft for Supermarine Attackers.

See 17 August 1951.

1959 The Duke of Edinburgh, as Captain General Royal Marines, received the Freedom of the City of Portsmouth on behalf of the Corps.

See 7 May 1955, 7 May 1965.

1982 SAS landed by Sea Kings from *Hermes* to destroy eleven enemy aircraft on Pebble Island. *Glasgow* provided NGS. Active service declared for all units between 7° and 60°S, initially for three months. Everyone in the Task Force became subject to the Naval Discipline Act, with several interesting consequences, many fortunately putative. NAAFI personnel serving in HM ships though not elsewhere might enlist in the RN and enjoy all the benefits. Thus a canteen manager in *Ardent* remustered as a PO on 15 May and was awarded DSM for gallantry in manning a gun on the 21st. Everyone was also protected by the Geneva Convention 'and if the worst happened was assured that his estate would be free of death duties'.

2004 The 137th and last PWO course passed out at *Dryad* (already paid off). PWO training continued at *Collingwood*.

See 23 May 1972.

15 May

1293 Ships of Cinque Ports defeated French fleet off Cape St Matthieu, Normandy. Sacking of Poitou led to war.

1780 Admiral Sir George Bridges Rodney (*Sandwich*) fought Vice-Admiral Comte de Guichen (*Couronne*), with twenty-three ships of the line, 20 miles E. of Martinique. Ships: *Ajax, Albion, Boyne, Centurion, Conqueror, Cornwall, Elizabeth, Grafton, Intrepid, Magnificent, Medway, Montagu, Preston, Princess Royal, Sandwich, Stirling Castle, Suffolk, Terrible, Trident, Triumph, Vigilant, Vengeance, Yarmouth*. Frigates, etc.: *Andromeda, Deal Castle, Greyhound, Venus*. Troops: 5th and 87th Regiments. Another formal and inconclusive encounter in which a shift in the wind cost Rodney the weather gauge.

1794 *Hebe* captured the French *Maire-Guiton* and recaptured eleven of a recently taken British convoy 130 miles N.N.E. of Cape Villano, N.W. Spain.

1797 End of second Spithead mutiny.

1797 Capt Henry Allen of the sloop *Rattler* hanged at the starboard foreyard arm of the frigate *Adventure* 'for the detestable sin of sodomy'.

See 16 April 1703, 23 November 1812.

1801 The *London Gazette* announced the raising of Vice-Admiral Lord Nelson to be Viscount Nelson following the Battle of Copenhagen.

See 2 April 1801.

1813 *Bacchante* captured Carlobago (Karlovac), Adriatic.

1829 Experimental manually propelled paddle steamer launched at Portsmouth. One hundred and ninety men produced 3 knots.

1839 Launch at Portsmouth of Symonds' *Queen* (110): 'the zenith of construction of sailing men o' war'.

1915 Admiral of the Fleet Lord Fisher of Kilverstone, First Sea Lord, then aged 74, following a final disagreement with Winston Churchill, First Lord, resigned and walked out of the Admiralty. He was later found in the Charing Cross Hotel: Prime Minister Asquith wrote 'In the King's name, I order you at once to return to your post'. Fisher enjoyed the support of the Board but lost that two days later, when, with the German High Seas Fleet being reported putting to sea, he did not return to the Admiralty.

See 30 October 1914, 28 May 1915, 10 July 1920.

During the following week Fisher's megalomania alarmed and alienated even his closest supporters. On the 19th he made preposterous terms and conditions to the government, including demands for an entire new Board of Admiralty and for absolute personal power, which no government could accept. Asquith told the King that Fisher's demands 'indicated signs of mental aberration'. Fisher left for Scotland on 22 May. A telegram from the Prime Minister reached him at Crewe: 'I am commanded by the King to accept your tendered resignation as First Sea Lord of the Admiralty.' Jacky Fisher's great career was over. King George V said at Balmoral in August 1921, a year after Fisher's death, 'If I had been in London when Fisher was found I should have told him that he should have been hanged at the yardarm for desertion of his post in the face of the enemy. It really was a most scandalous thing which ought to be punished with dismissal from the service with degradation' – Mackay, p.503.

1917 VC: Skipper Joseph Watt, RNR (*Gowan Lea*) for engaging an Austrian cruiser at 100yds' range with his only gun, refusing to surrender and subsequently rescuing the crew of another drifter.

Austrian naval raid in Otranto Strait by three light cruisers. Fourteen British drifters sunk out of forty-seven, putting up what Austrians called 'a united mad resistance'. *Admirable, Avondale, Coral Haven, Craignoon, Felicitas, Girl Gracie, Girl Rose, Helenora, Quarry Knowe, Selby, Serene, Taits, Transit, Young Linnett*. *Bristol* and *Dartmouth* pursued the three raiders. *Dartmouth* was torpedoed.

1918 German submarine raid on St Kilda.

HMS *Queen*, first rate of 110 guns launched in 1839, seen here later after being converted to steam. (*NMRN*)

1940 Destroyer *Valentine* bombed by German aircraft and beached off Walcheren, providing AA fire (51.20N, 03.49E).

1942 Light cruiser *Trinidad* sunk by destroyer *Matchless* off North Cape (73.37N, 23.27E) after being set on fire by German bombers late on the 14th, and having torpedoed herself on 29 March.

1943 Halifax M/58 sank the supply U-boat U-463 in Bay of Biscay (45.28N, 10.20W).

1943 Submarine *Sickle* sank the German Uj-2213 off the French Riviera.

1943 HM ships and 423 Squadron RCAF sank U-456 (48.37N, 22.39W).

1944 Light cruiser *Dido* bombarded targets in the Gulf of Gaeta, W. coast of Italy, in support of Army attack.

1944 Trawler *Blackfly*, sloop *Kilmarnock* and Catalinas P.1 and P.12 of VP/63 (US) sank U-731 off Gibraltar (35.55N, 05.45W).

1954 HM Yacht *Britannia*, with HM The Queen embarked, entered Pool of London for first time at end of Commonwealth Tour. First FORY, Vice-Admiral Conolly Abel Smith invested KCVO on board with own sword.

See 4 April 1581, 30 June 1913.

1957 Britain's first hydrogen bomb successfully detonated over the coral island of Malden, 400 miles S. of Christmas Island. HM Ships: carrier *Warrior*, broad pennant of Cdre R.B.N. Hicks RN, was Operational Control Ship; frigate *Alert*, surveying ship *Cook*, tank landing ships *Messina* and *Narvik*, ocean salvage vessel *Salvictor*, frigates HMNZS *Pukaki* and *Rotoiti*, RFA *Fort Beauharnois*, *Fort Rosalie*, *Gold Ranger*, *Wave Prince*, *Wave Ruler* and *Wave Victor*. Further tests on 15, 31 May and 19 June. *Warrior* aircraft employed on collecting air samples, SAR, weather reporting and radar tracking. On conclusion three Grumman Avengers catapulted off the flight deck and deliberately ditched between Pitcairn and Callao on 31 July. Operation Grapple.

See 3 October 1952, 16 May 1956, 24 December 1957.

2007 Naval Training Command, headed by a two-star officer known as Flag Officer Sea Training, to be responsible for all sea and shore training, and including JMOTS at Northwood, established by the amalgamation of FOST and FOTR. First incumbent, Rear-Admiral Richard Ibbotson, lately Naval Secretary.

16 May

1760 Siege of Quebec raised. *Diana*, *Lowestoffe* and *Vanguard* destroyed the French *Atalante*, *Pomone* and other vessels of the besieging force at Pointe aux Trembles.

1763 *Albion*, third rate, 74 guns, first of name, launched Deptford.
See 21 June 1898, 9 March 2001.

1804 Cdre Sir Sidney Smith (*Antelope*) defeated a division of the Franco-Batavian invasion flotilla off Ostend. Ships: *Aimable*, *Antelope*, *Cruizer*, *Favourite*, *Penelope*, *Rattler*, *Stag*.

1811 *Little Belt* taken by the American *President* 50 miles N.E. of Cape Henry in less than fifteen minutes. War had not been declared and Capt Bingham maintained that he had been attacked first and that he never surrendered.

1813 Boats of *Berwick* and *Euryalus* captured the French *Fortune* and fifteen of a convoy in Cavalaire Roads.

1813 *Shannon* (38) and *Tenedos* (38) captured the American privateer *Invincible* near Cape Ann town, Massachusetts.

1824 Boats of *Liffey* and the grenadier company of the 38th Regiment captured and destroyed three Burmese stockades near Killyumdine.

1863 Mates RN, a rank introduced by Earl St Vincent in 1802, became sub-lieutenants RN; their distinction lace of one ½-in ring caused lieutenants, commanders and captains, until then distinguished by one, two and three rings respectively, to each ship one extra ring. Mates reappeared from 1912 to 1931.
See 5 December 1804, 19 July 1912, 20 May 1931.

1908 D 1, first British diesel submarine, launched at Barrow. (A 13 carried experimental diesel engine and, though launched in April 1905, was not completed until 22 June 1908.)

1930 RN and RM sports control board established.

1940 Warships of the Royal Netherlands Navy arrived in British waters to cooperate with the Royal Navy.
See 22 May 1940.

1944 Sunderland V/330 (Nor) sank U-240 off Norway (63.05N, 03.10E).

1945 Destroyers *Saumarez* (D 26), *Venus*, *Verulam*, *Vigilant*, *Virago* and escort carrier *Emperor* (Avengers of 851 NAS from *Shah*) sank the Japanese cruiser *Haguro* and damaged the destroyer *Kamikaze*, 45 miles S.W. of Penang.
See 21 April 1917, 10 April 1940, 13 December 1941, 27 February 1942, 1 March 1942.

Operation Dukedom, 1945

The Japanese 8-in-gun cruiser *Haguro* was attempting to evacuate the garrison in the Andaman Islands. Having failed at a second attempt, she was returning down the Malacca Straits at high speed with a destroyer when she was sighted by an aircraft. The 26th Destroyer Flotilla, comprising the *Saumarez* (Leader) and four V-class destroyers, was off Sumatra and was diverted to engage the enemy. At about 2300 on 15th the *Venus* detected her at 34 miles on radar.

HMS *Queen Elizabeth* commissioned in 1915. (*NMRN*)

The cruiser turned towards the destroyers as they spread out for a torpedo attack, and the *Saumarez* was hit by enemy gunfire as she gained visual contact just after midnight. She managed to fire her torpedoes as the other destroyers also attacked, and it is thought that eight hits were achieved. The *Haguro* sank at 0147, and the Japanese destroyer *Kamikaze* was slightly damaged. *Saumarez* lost two killed and three wounded. Later in the day *Virago* lost four killed in a bomb near-miss. This was the only air attack (other than suicide attacks) to inflict damage on the East Indies Fleet.

1948 Battleship *Queen Elizabeth* ceremonially paid off at Portsmouth near the slip from which she had been launched in October 1913; on the quarterdeck were Admiral Lord Fraser of North Cape, C-in-C Portsmouth, and Vice-Admiral Sir Rhoderick McGrigor, C-in-C Home Fleet.

See 22 December 1914, 24 November 1950.

1956 *Diana*, Daring-class destroyer, steamed through nuclear fallout following the second atomic test explosion at Monte Bello Islands in the Pacific. Serial repeated after second explosion on 19 June 1956. 'The Chiefs of Staff wanted to know how the ship and men would stand up to such an ordeal' – Capt J.R. Gower DSC, RN, HMS *Diana*.

See 3 October 1952, 15 May 1957.

1966 Devonport Dockyard base passenger train service ceased.

1969 HM The Queen reviewed sixty-three ships from STANAVFORLANT and twelve NATO countries at Spithead to mark the twentieth anniversary of NATO; her first Spithead review in *Britannia*: HMY *Britannia*, Royal Standard and flag of Rear-Admiral P.J. Morgan, FORY; *Glamorgan*, flag of Admiral Sir John Bush, CINCHAN; *Blake*, flag of Rear-Admiral M.F. Fell, FOCAS (largest RN ship present); *Phoebe*; *Eastbourne*; *Puma*; *Tenby*; *Torquay*; *Tiptoe*; *Olympus*; *Shoulton*; *Wakeful*; *Alcide*; *Letterston*; RFA *Olmeda*; THV *Patricia*. The previous day CINCHAN, COMSTANAVFORLANT and senior officers called on C-in-C Portsmouth, Admiral Sir John Frewen, First and Principal Naval ADC to HM The Queen, in *Victory*.

1973 *Mermaid*, diesel frigate, commissioned into RN. She had been ordered from Yarrow, Scotstoun, by Ghana as presidential yacht but launched without ceremony on 29 December 1966. Last British ship to carry Mk XIX dual-purpose twin 4-in 45-cal. guns. Collision with *Fittleton* 20 September 1976. Sold to Malaysia. Commissioned 22 July 1977 as *Hang Tuah*, retaining her F76 pennant number.

HMS *Queen Elizabeth* pictured in 1915. (*NMRN*)

1975 Ships' dogs and cats effectively banned following rabies-control legislation. 'UK-based ships with ships' dogs, cats or other animals on board are advised to land them before sailing for foreign ports.' The list of doubtful creatures included vampire bats, jackals, mongooses, cheetahs, armadillos, kangaroos, great apes and spiny rats. DCI(RN) T300/75.

See 9 September 1977.

2004 Admiral of the Fleet Lord Hill-Norton died aged 89. He entered Dartmouth in 1928 aged 13. Gunnery Officer 1939. CO *Ark Royal* 1959. FOF2 Far East Fleet 1964–7. COMFEF 1969. Succeeded Admiral Sir Michael Le Fanu as First Sea Lord 1970 but after eight months became CDS. Chairman of the NATO Military Committee 1974. Ennobled as Lord Hill-Norton of South Nutfield, Surrey, 1979. An officer who operated on a very short fuse. 'Although Hill-Norton was feared, hated and respected in equal measure, he led from the front. His harsh manner and foul language belied a man who could, on rare occasions, demonstrate an otherwise well-concealed humanity' – *Daily Telegraph*, 19 May 2004.

See 5 February 1979, 6 April 1993.

17 May

1655 Capture of Jamaica by Admiral William Penn (*Swiftsure*) and troops under General Robert Venables.

1667 *Princess* (52) attacked by two Danish 40-gun men-of-war, off Norway, between the Sean and Malshond. Capt Dawes was killed after an hour, saying 'For God's sake don't surrender the ship to those fellows'; then the Lieutenant and then the Gunner. The guns crews got her to The Nore by the 23rd.

1795 *Hussar* and *Thetis* engaged four French ships, capturing *Prévoyante* and *La Raison*, 60 miles E. by N. of Cape Henry, Virginia.

1797 Sloop *Providence*, Capt William Broughton, surveying the N.W. Pacific in the wake of George Vancouver, wrecked on a reef N. of Miyako Shima island in the Japanese Sakishima Gunto group E. of Taiwan, which now bears the name of its victim. Survivors taken via Okinawa to Macao in accompanying schooner tender *Prince William Henry* which Broughton commissioned as a new *Providence* and in which he completed the four year survey. The *Providence* had been commanded by William Bligh on the second of his voyages (the first in *Bounty* having ended in mutiny) to collect breadfruit trees from Tahiti for transplant in Jamaica.

See 29 November 1791, 18 May 1945.

1805 Surgeons and Physicians given dress and undress uniforms of their own instead of that worn by warrant officers.

1807 Rear-Admiral Sir Thomas Louis, senior officer of the British Fleet in the Eastern Mediterranean, died aged 48 on board his flagship *Canopus* (80) – a Nile prize – at Alexandria. He had commanded *Minotaur* (74) under Nelson at the Nile and, although he chased Villeneuve to the West Indies, he missed Trafalgar having been sent into Gibraltar for supplies. He later served under Duckworth at San Domingo in 1806 and in the Dardanelles operation. Louis was buried on 8 June on Manoel Island in Marsamxett, Sliema Creek, Malta where the chief mourner was the British Governor of Malta, Rear-Admiral Sir Alexander Ball, who had commanded *Alexander* (74) at the Nile.

1862 Capture of Najaor by Brig-Gen Charles Staveley, with British and Indian troops, and British and French Naval Brigades. Naval Brigades repulsed a rebel Chinese attack near Tsiolin (or Cholin). Naval Brigade of *Imperieuse*, *Pearl*, *Vulcan*, *Flamer* and *Coromandel*. Troops: Royal Artillery, Royal Engineers, 31st, 67th and 99th Regiments, 5th Bombay Native Light Infantry, 22nd Bengal Native Infantry.

1917 Admiralty convoy committee set up.

1917 Second division of US destroyers arrived at Queenstown to work with the Royal Navy.

1917 Second experimental use of Sea Lions for detecting submarines.

Presentation of the Sovereign's Colour for the Royal Navy, given to the RNR, 2003. (*MOD*)

1917 Destroyer *Setter* lost in collision with sister ship *Sylph* off Harwich.

1917 *Glen*, auxiliary schooner (decoy ship), sank UB-39 off Cherbourg (50.05N, 01.25W).

1941 *Gnat*, river gunboat, bombarded Gazala airfield.

1943 Frigate *Swale* sank U-657 S.E. of Cape Farewell (58.54N, 42.33W) with hedgehog and depth charges. Convoy ONS 7.

1943 Hudson J/269 sank U-646 off Iceland (62.10N, 14.30W).

1943 Italian submarine *Enrico Tazzoli* sunk by air attack N.N.W. of Cape Ortegal.

1944 Wellingtons A/36, H/36 and X/36 and US ships sank U-616 in W. Mediterranean (36.46N, 00.52E). First attacked on the 14th.

1944 Allied air attack on Japanese naval base at Sourabaya. Operation Transom. Force 66: Carriers: *Illustrious* (Rear-Admiral C. Moody) and *Saratoga* (US), with twenty-seven Avengers, eighteen Dauntless, twenty-four Hellcats and sixteen Corsairs. Ships: *Renown* (Vice-Admiral Sir Arthur Power), *Kenya* (Rear-Admiral A.D. Read – CS4), *London*, *Suffolk* and *Tromp* (Neth), *Napier* (Cdre D), *Quadrant*, *Quality*, *Quiberon*; *Cummings*, *Dunlap* and *Fanning* (US); *Van Galen* (Neth). Force 65: *Queen Elizabeth* (Admiral Sir James Somerville), *Valiant*, *Richelieu* (Fr), *Ceylon*, *Gambia* (RNZN), *Nepal*, *Queenborough* (RAN), *Quickmatch* (RAN), *Quilliam*, *Racehorse*, *Rotherham*. FAA Sqns: Avenger: 832, 851; Corsair: 1830, 1833.

1945 Vice-Admiral Sir Rhoderick McGrigor, with the First Cruiser Squadron, Home Fleet, arrived in Bergen to secure the port following the German surrender.

See 13 May 1945.

1946 The light cruisers *Orion* and *Superb*, steaming through the Corfu Channel, were fired on by Albanian shore batteries. An Albanian demand for future warning of Royal Navy movements through the channel was rejected by Britain which regarded the channel as international waters. A serious sequel occurred in October.

See 22 October 1946, 24 October panel.

1961 Destroyer *Saintes*, Cdr M.J. Porter RN, landed a party on the Greek island of Skyros to find and restore the grave of poet Sub-Lt Rupert Brooke RNVR of the RN Division who died on board a French hospital ship in Tris Boukes Bay, S.W. Skyros, on 23 April 1915 and was buried ashore in an olive grove that night. 'The burial site will be officially charted so that any British warship visiting this region from time to time may clean and repair the grave.' – *The Times*.

1968 MOD(N) announced that the Scheme of Complement for Polaris submarines would in future 'provide for a Supply Officer with the rank of Lieutenant of the Supply and Secretariat specialisation of the General List'. DCIs(N) 611/68; 298/69.

1981 The last Navy Minister, Keith Speed, dismissed by Prime Minister Thatcher for his outspoken opposition to proposed cuts to RN.

See 25 June 1981.

1993 White Ensign hauled down at *Tamar*, Hong Kong Central, and RN base moved to Stonecutters' Island.

2000 Cpl Alan Chambers RM and Mne Charlie Patton completed the first unsupported journey to the North Pole.

See 22 May 2003, 27 December 2006, 1 January 2007.

2003 The Sovereign's Colour for the Royal Navy presented to the Royal Naval Reserve by the Prince of Wales on Horse Guards Parade. The centenary of the establishment of the Royal Naval Volunteer Reserve in 1903.

See 17 July 1959.

18 MAY

1709 *Falmouth*, escorting a convoy, fought a French 60-gun ship 70 miles W. of the Scilly Isles. The French cut away her shrouds and chased the convoy but Capt Riddell made such rapid repairs that he was able to retrieve the situation and bring his convoy safely home.

1759 *Thames* and *Venus* captured the French *Arethuse* in Audierne Bay.

1803 Britain declared war on France marking the end of the Peace of Amiens and the start of the Napoleonic War. Vice-Admiral Viscount Nelson appointed C-in-C Mediterranean 16 May and hoisted his flag in *Victory* 19 May. Admiralty ordered Nelson to establish a position off Toulon that would 'be most proper for enabling you to take, sink, burn, or otherwise destroy, any Ships or Vessels belonging to France'.

See 1 August 1739, 21 May 1798, 25 March 1802.

1809 Occupation of Anholt, Kattegat. Ships: *Avenger*, *Owen Glendower*, *Ranger*, *Rose Standard* and *Snipe* and 120 Royal Marines under Lt Nicholls.

1842 Capture of Chapu by Vice-Admiral Sir William Parker (*Cornwallis*) and Lt-Gen Sir Hugh Gough. Ships and vessels: *Algerine*, *Bentinck*, *Blonde*, *Columbine*, *Cornwallis*, *Jupiter Transport*, *Nemesis*, *Modeste*, *Phlegethon*, *Queen* (Bengal Marine), *Sesostris* (Indian Navy), *Starling*. Troops: Royal Artillery, 18th, 26th, 49th and 55th Regiments, Madras Artillery, Madras Sappers and Miners, 36th Madras Native Infantry.

1940 *Princess Victoria*, hired minelayer, sunk by mine off the Humber.

1940 Cruiser *Effingham*, carrying 2nd Bn South Wales Borderers from Ankenes to Bodø in Norway, stranded on a pinnacle 12 miles off Harstad. Sunk by gunfire 21 May (67.17N, 13.58E). 'Caused by a soft pencil and precise navigation – the line drawn on the chart to show HMS *Effingham*'s course obscured an isolated, shallow pinnacle and the ship was exactly on track' – David Brown, Head of the Naval Historical Branch. First of twenty-three cruisers lost in Second World War. Sister ship *Raleigh* also wrecked, off Labrador, 8 August 1922.

See 14 April 1857, 30 May 1906, 21 August 1910, 14 November 1918, 8 June 1921, 8 August 1922, 7 July 2002, 26 May 2008.

1941 VC: PO Alfred Edward Sephton (*Coventry*) for gallantry in an air attack on cruiser *Coventry* south of Crete by German aircraft which had been attacking the hospital ship *Aba*. The medal was stolen on 25 September 1990 while on display in Coventry Cathedral; never recovered.

1942 Fleet Air Arm occupied Wingfield near Cape Town as RNAS Wingfield.

See 1 May 1946.

1944 Catalina S/210 sank U-241 off S.W. Norway (63.36N, 01.42E).

1945 Fleet carrier *Formidable*, part of British Pacific Fleet, lost thirty aircraft in a hangar fire during a RAS. The ship was engaged in air strikes on Sakishima Gunto and Formosa in support of US landings on Formosa. Operation Iceberg.

See 17 May 1797.

HMS *Effingham* at Portsmouth in 1938. (*NMRN W&L 39G1*)

HMS *Speedy*, a torpedo gunboat, being launched at Chiswick, River Thames on 18 May 1893 (see 3 September 1914). (*NMM Neg. No G12579*)

1962 The broad pennant of the Commodore Cyprus struck and CBF Cyprus established. AFO 1020/62.

1972 Anti-terrorist quartet including two Royal Marines parachuted into Atlantic alongside RMS *Queen Elizabeth 2* to search for a reported bomb.

The Battle of Crete May–June 1941

The Battle of Crete involved the Royal Navy in the fiercest and most sustained fighting for 275 years – since the Four Days Battle of the Dutch Wars in 1666. The Navy had escorted the Army to Greece in March (Operation Lustre) and evacuated them to Crete in April (Operation Demon). It was intended to hold the island. Destroyers and a fast mine-layer – the only ships that could make the round trip in darkness from Alexandria – fought in reinforcements and supplies over several weeks. On 20 May the Germans attacked Crete with airborne forces which suffered heavy losses. The Royal Navy prevented invasion attempts by sea but the enemy had complete air superiority and the island could not be held. On 27 May orders were given to evacuate. Over the next four nights about 17,000 men out of 32,000 were rescued (18,600 Roskill, 16,500 Cunningham), initially from Heraklion and then over open beaches at Sfakia on the south of the island.

An unidentified soldier wrote: 'Having reached the sea. . . With a torch we flashed an SOS and, to our tremendous relief, we received an answer. It was the Navy on the job; the Navy for which we had been hoping and praying all along the route.' Despite the losses Cunningham insisted on continuing the operation. Exhausted ships' companies went in again and again to save the Army: 'It takes three years to build a ship', Cunningham told his staff, 'it would take three hundred years to rebuild a tradition'. The losses were heavy: during the short Battle of Crete the Mediterranean Fleet lost the cruisers *Gloucester*, *Fiji* and *Calcutta*, the destroyers *Juno*, *Greyhound*, *Kashmir*, *Kelly*, *Hereward* and *Imperial*. The battleships *Warspite* and *Barham*, the fleet carrier *Formidable*, cruisers *Dido* and *Orion*, and destroyers *Kelvin* and *Nubian* were damaged beyond repair in theatre. Many other ships suffered. 'Of the grand men of the fleet who had shared our triumphs and adversities for so long over 2,000 were dead' – Admiral Sir Andrew Cunningham, C-in-C Mediterranean Fleet. On 2 June a message from General Sir Archibald Wavell was promulgated to the fleet: 'I send to you and all under your command the deepest admiration and gratitude of the Army in the Middle East for the magnificent work of the Royal Navy in bringing back the troops from Crete. The skill and self-sacrifice with which the difficult and dangerous operation was carried out will never be forgotten, and will form another strong link between our two services. Our thanks to you all and our sympathy for your losses'. (See 23 May 1940). Air Marshal Tedder, AOC-in-C RAF Middle East: 'May I express on behalf of myself and the Royal Air Force, Middle East, our deep admiration of the way in which the Royal Navy has once again succeeded in doing what seemed almost impossible.'

'So ended the Battle of Crete and a disastrous period in our naval history' – Cunningham. But what a brilliant one.
Ships: *Abdiel, Ajax, Auckland, Barham, Calcutta, Carlisle, Coventry, Decoy, Defender, Dido, Fiji, Flamingo, Formidable, Glengyle, Glenroy, Gloucester, Greyhound, Griffin, Grimsby, Hasty, Havock, Hereward, Hero, Hotspur, Ilex, Imperial, Isis, Jackal, Jaguar, Janus, Jervis, Juno, Kandahar, Kashmir, Kelly, Kelvin, Kimberley, Kingston, Kipling, Kos 21, Kos 22, Kos 23, Lanner, Naiad, Napier, Nizam, Nubian, Orion, Perth, Phoebe, Queen Elizabeth, Rorqual, Salvia, Stuart, Syvern, Valiant, Vampire, Vendetta, Voyager, Warspite, Waterhen, Widnes*; MLs 1011,1030, 1032; MTBs 67, 213, 216, 217, 314; 805 NAS.

19 May

1652 First battle of the Dutch Wars started when Blake demanded that Tromp salute the British flag. Admiral Robert Blake (*James*) fought Admiral Maerten Tromp (*Brederode*), with forty-two ships, off Dover. Ships and vessels: *Adventure, Andrew, Assurance, Centurion, Happy Entrance, Fairfax, Garland, Greyhound, James, Martin, Mermaid, Portsmouth, Reuben, Ruby, Sapphire, Seven Brothers, Speaker, Star, Triumph, Victory, Worcester.*
Battle Honour: Dover 1652.

1692 Battle of Barfleur, Admiral Edward Russell (*Britannia*) with the Anglo-Dutch fleet of William III (ninety-nine ships) defeated the French fleet of forty-four sail under Vice-Admiral Comte de Tourville (*Soleil Royal*).
Battle Honour: Barfleur 1692.

Ships: Red Sqn: *Britannia, Chester, Eagle, Elizabeth, Grafton, Greenwich, London, Restoration, Rupert, St Andrew, Mary Galley, Portsmouth.* Fireships: *Bonaventure, Burford, Captain, Centurion, Dragon, Falcon, Flame, Greyhound, Lenox, Roebuck, Royal Katherine, Spy, Vulture* (Russell), *Sovereign, St Michael.* Fireships: *Cambridge, Extravagant, Hampton Court, Hound, Kent, Oxford, Royal William, Ruby, St Albans, Sandwich, Swiftsure, Vulcan, Wolf* (Delaval). Fireships: *Fox, Hopewell, Phaeton, Strombolo* (Shovell).

Blue Sqn: *Adventure, Berwick, Defiance, Duchess, Edgar, Monmouth, Montagu, Vanguard, Victory, Warspite.* Fireships: *Aetna, Blaze, Griffin, Speedwell* (Ashby), *Advice, Albemarle, Expedition, Lion, Monck, Neptune, Northumberland, Resolution, Windsor Castle.* Fireships: *Cadiz Merchant, Charles Galley, Crown, Deptford, Dreadnought, Duke, Essex, Half-Moon, Hope, Lightning, Ossory, Owner's Love* (Rooke), *Stirling Castle, Suffolk, Tiger, Woolwich.* Fireships: *Hawke, Hunter, Thomas and Elizabeth, Vesuvius* (Carter).

White Sqn: Admiral van Almonde with thirty-nine Dutch of the line and nine fireships.

In 1692 James II, aided by Louis XIV of France, assembled a large army at La Hogue, and a French fleet in the Channel under the command of the Comte de Tourville. The English fleet drove de Tourville's ships into La Hogue. On 23 May 200 boats from the English fleet attacked the ships at anchor. When they left, La Hogue was on fire and six French three-deckers had been destroyed. Six other French ships, anchored under the Fort of St Vast, were attacked on the 24th. In spite of assistance from French cavalry, the French ships were boarded and the ships and the fort destroyed. The horsemen, sent into shallow water to aid their compatriots, were unhorsed by seamen with boathooks.

1724 Augustus John Hervey, the Royal Navy's 'Cassanova' and future vice-admiral of the blue, born into the 'wild and wicked' family headed by the Earl of Bristol.
See 22 December 1779.

1745 *Mermaid* and *Superb* captured the French *Vigilant* off Louisburg, Cape Breton Island.

1765 Gosport victualling yard established.

1777 *Beaver* captured the American privateer *Oliver Cromwell* 2 miles S.W. of the Sugar Loaf (Gros Piton), St Lucia.

1780 Second inconclusive action between Rodney and de Guichen, 120 miles E. of Martinique.
See 15 May 1780.

1794 Cdre John Ford (*Europa*) and Brig-Gen John Whyte captured Port au Prince, Haiti. Ships: *Belliqueux, Europa, Fly, Hermione, Iphigenia, Irresistible, Marie Antoinette, Penelope, Sceptre, Swan.* Troops: Royal Artillery, 22nd, 23rd, 41st Regts and Colonial.

1797 A Court of Inquiry held to investigate complaints from the ship's company of HMS *Cumberland* that their Captain had stopped their wine allowance, was told by Capt Bartholomew Samuel Rowley that 'the Wine so stopped was applied to the general good of the People, as far as it was expended, by splicing the Main Brace in bad weather, or by giving it to the People generally after much fatigue . . .' One of the earliest uses of the term but see 22 February 1773.

1803 Vice-Admiral Viscount Nelson hoisted his flag for the first time in the 38-year-old first-rate *Victory* at Portsmouth.
See 14 September 1805.

1807 The Royal Navy's first *Dauntless*, an 18-gun ship sloop, Cdr Christopher Strachey, sailing up the Vistula River with 600 barrels of

The Battle of Barfleur, 1692. (*NMM Neg. No. 3599*)

gunpowder for the besieged Hanseatic city of Danzig (Gdansk in present-day Poland), ran aground on The Holm, an islet (now called Ostrow) and beneath French batteries and 'after a plucky defence was obliged to strike' – Laird Clowes.

See 2 July 1928, 23 January 2007.

1808 *Virginie* captured the Dutch *Guelderland* 240 miles N.W. of Cape Finisterre.

1813 *Rattler* captured the American privateer *Alexander* which had run ashore on Wells Beach 5 miles S. of Kennebunkport, Maine. *Bream*, which was in company, helped to refloat the prize.

1821 Boats of *Revolutionnaire* captured two Greek pirate gunboats off Chiarenza Point (Cape Glarentza), west coast of Greece.

1845 Franklin sailed in *Erebus* with *Terror* in search of a North–West Passage.

1847 Gunboat tender of *Calliope*, with a detachment of the 58th Regiment, repulsed a Maori attack on Wanganui. Last naval commitment in first New Zealand war.
Battle Honour: New Zealand 1845–7.

1852 Capture of Bassein by Maj-Gen Henry Godwin and Cdre George Lambert (*Fox*). Ships: *Moozuffer* and *Sesostris* (Indian Navy); *Pluto* and *Tenasserim* (Bengal Marine); Royal Marines and a field gun's crew of *Fox*. Troops: 51st Regiment, Bengal Artillery, Madras Sappers and Miners, 9th Madras Native Infantry.

1930 'Mr E.C. Ockenden, of the Mission House, Wei-Hai-Wei, has been appointed officiating minister to Wesleyans serving in the Royal Navy at Wei-Hai-Wei (island). Mr E.N. Hill will continue to act as officiating minister to Wesleyans on the mainland.'

1940 Destroyer *Whitley* beached off Nieuport, after attack by German aircraft, and destroyed by *Keith*.

1943 Frigate *Jed* and *Sennen* (ex-USCG *Culler*) sank U-954 in N. Atlantic (54.54N, 34.19W), destroyer *Duncan* and corvette *Snowflake* sank U-381 (54.41N, 34.45W), Hudson M/269 sank U-273 (59.25N, 24.33W). Convoy SC 130.

1944 Wellingtons M/36 and U/36, Ventura V/500, *Ludlow* and USS *Niblack* sank U-960 in W. Mediterranean (37.35N, 01.39E).

1945 Submarine *Terrapin* reduced to CTL by depth-charging in Pacific.

1973 Second Cod War. RN units deployed inside Iceland's unilaterally imposed 50-mile fishing limit exclusion zone after the Icelandic Coastguard had fired on British trawlers. Frigates *Plymouth* (OTC) and *Cleopatra*, supported by RFA *Wave Chief* and the tugs *Irishman*, *Englishman* and *Statesman*.

See 31 August.

2000 *Tireless*, SSN, arrived at Gibraltar with reactor coolant defects. Repairs took almost a year.

See 7 May 2001.

20 May

1212 King John ordered Portsmouth Dock, built in 1194, to be strengthened.

1514 Henry VIII granted charter to the 'Guild of the Holy and Undivided Trinity and St Clement Deptford Strand for the Reformation of the Navy much decayed by the admission of young men without experience, and of Scots, Flemings and Frenchmen as landsmen [pilots]'.
See 8 September 1541.

1625 The Worshipful Company of Barbers & Surgeons fitted out Surgeons' chests and took control of Naval Surgeons.

1665 An English convoy of nine sail and their escort, a 34-gun ship, taken by Admiral Jacob van Wassenaer, Heer van Opdam, on the Dogger Bank.

1747 'On the 20th of May 1747, I took twelve patients in the scurvy, on board the *Salisbury* at sea' – Dr James Lind in his *A Treatise on Scurvy*, published in 1753, the first clinical trial of any kind. Dr Lind gave six pairs of men in the *Salisbury* (50) different additions to their normal diet. Those given citrus fruit made a remarkable recovery. The *Treatise*, dedicated to Lord Anson, First Lord of the Admiralty, probably led to Lind's appointment as Physician to the Naval Hospital at Haslar in 1758. Forty years passed, however, before the Admiralty ordered the regular issue of lemon juice, after which scurvy virtually disappeared from ships and naval hospitals.
See p.526 panel.

1756 Admiral the Hon. John Byng (*Ramillies*) fought a French fleet of equal force under Admiral the Marquis de La Galissonnière (*Foudroyant*) 30 miles S.S.E. of Port Mahon, Minorca. Ships: *Buckingham, Captain, Culloden, Defiance, Deptford, Kingston, Intrepid, Lancaster, Portland, Princess Louisa, Ramillies, Revenge, Trident*. Frigates, etc.: *Chesterfield, Dolphin, Experiment, Fortune, Phoenix*.
See 14 March 1757.

1776 Admiral Sir Edward Hawke, having been forced to resign as First Lord of the Admiralty because of renal calculi ('the gravel'), was raised to peerage as Baron Hawke of Towton in Yorkshire, where his wife's ancestors had been lords of the manor. King George III regretted 'the loss of so able and gallant an officer'.

1794 'I always was of opinion, have ever acted up to it, and never have had any reason to repent it, that one Englishman was equal to three Frenchmen' – Nelson to his wife from Corsica.

1799 Siege of Acre on the Levant coast raised, after a brilliant defence by Capt Sir Sidney Smith (*Tigre*), with *Theseus* and *Alliance*.
Battle Honour: Acre 1799.

1811 *Astraea, Galatea, Phoebe* and *Racehorse* engaged the French *Clorinde, Néréide* and *Renommée*, capturing the *Renommée* off Tamatave, Madagascar.
Battle Honour: Tamatave 1811.

1854 *Arrogant* and *Hecla* engaged the Russian batteries at Ekenas, Finland.

1855 Cdre Elliot (*Sybille*) with *Bittern* and *Hornet* discovered the Russian *Dvina* and *Aurora* in Castries Bay. An inconclusive pursuit, ending Crimean War operations in Far East.

1858 Anglo-French squadron under Rear-Admirals Sir Michael Seymour (*Calcutta*) and Rigault de Genouilly (*Nemesis*) captured the Taku forts. Ships: *Calcutta, Furious, Fury, Pique, Coromandel* (tender), *Hesper* (storeship). Gunboats: *Bustard, Cormorant, Firm, Leven, Nimrod, Opossum, Slaney* (flag for attack), *Staunch, Surprise*. French ship: *Nemesis*. French gunboats: *Avalanche, Dragoone, Fusée, Mitraille, Phlegeton*.

1862 British and French forces took Tsiolin (Cholin).
See 17 May 1862.

1903 Formation of RN Band Service.

1905 *Africa*, the last battleship launched at Chatham, the first ship built on No. 8 Slip and the heaviest ship built at that dockyard; 15,630 tons.

1916 The first steam-driven K-class submarine, K-3, launched at Vickers, Barrow. 'The classic story of the K-boat class was the tale of the Captain who telephoned to his First Lieutenant in the bows: "I say, No.1, my end is diving, what the hell is your end doing?"' – Cdr Stephen King-Hall, *My Naval Life 1906–29*, p.154.

1917 *Lady Patricia* (*Paxton*, Q 25) sunk by U-46 S.W. of Ireland.

1917 Flying-boat 8663 sank UC-36 in North Sea – first submarine sunk by RNAS.

1921 RN College Osborne closed. Two future kings of the United Kingdom, a royal duke and four future admirals of the fleet were among the 3,967 cadets who passed through, mostly going on to Dartmouth, since it was opened in 1903.

1931 Rank of Mate discontinued; all men promoted from lower deck to be appointed sub-lieutenants.
See 16 May 1863, 19 July 1912.

1937 HM King George VI reviewed Fleet at Spithead. The first time a fleet review had been illuminated at night and the BBC commentator, who had clearly been well entertained, describing the scene as the lights were switched on simultaneously, told the nation 'The Fleet's all lit up – we're all lit up.' The recording is occasionally replayed, to the BBC's credit. C-in-C Home Fleet, Admiral Sir Roger Backhouse, in *Nelson*; C-in-C Mediterranean Fleet, Admiral Sir Dudley Pound, in *Queen Elizabeth*; 145 British and Empire ships present, with eighteen foreign vessels including *Admiral Graf Spee*.

1941 Minesweeper *Widnes* (ex-*Withernsea*) sunk by German aircraft in Suda Bay. Salvaged and commissioned as Uj-2109. Sunk 17 October 1943 in Kalymnos harbour by gunfire of destroyers *Jervis* and *Penn*.
See 17 October 1943.

1942 Acting Admiral Sir Henry Harwood, victor of the Battle of the River Plate in 1939, hoisted his flag as C-in-C Mediterranean Fleet in the battleship *Queen Elizabeth*, in succession to Admiral Sir Andrew Cunningham. 'I should feel happier if someone more experienced . . . was to relieve me', wrote Cunningham to Pound, the First Sea Lord, on 15 March 1942. It was a big jump for the gallant Harwood, who had hitherto commanded only a small cruiser squadron, to take over the Navy's principal battle fleet. 'It was rather as if the owner of a corner shop had suddenly been put in charge of Harrods' – Correlli Barnett, *Engage the Enemy more Closely*, p.509. C-in-C Levant February 1943. His health broke down and, 'undermined by unsubstantiated charges of lethargy by Montgomery' (Simpson, *Cunningham Papers*, vol.1 p.169), he was invalided home March 1943 and became FOIC Orkney and Shetland. 'I am very sorry for Harwood but with a blood pressure of 255 . . . It is not surprising that he was not up to the mark' – Pound to Cunningham, 23 April 1943 (Simpson, *Cunningham Papers*, vol.2 p.74).
See 13 December 1939.

1943 Liberator P/120 sank U-258 in Atlantic (55.18N, 27.49W). Convoy SC 130.

1953 The reintroduction by Admiralty of the term 'Fleet Air Arm' after a lapse of seven years 'during which the air forces of the Royal Navy have been known officially as naval aviation' (*The Times*), announced in a written answer in the House of Commons. 'In deciding to reintroduce the title Fleet Air Arm the Admiralty had been greatly influenced by the strong appeal of its glorious wartime associations. This decision will be generally welcomed throughout the Fleet. The nebulous term naval aviation has never been popular . . .' – *The Times*, 21 May 1953. On the same day the Fleet Air Arm memorial at Lee-on-Solent was unveiled by HRH The Duchess of Kent commemorating the 1,931 officers and men 'who died in the service of their country in the Second World War and have no grave but the sea'.
See 24 May 1939, 1 June 2000, 11 September 2009.

1954 HRH Princess Margaret unveiled a memorial on The Hoe to 15,600 souls lost at sea in the Second World War and have no grave but the sea.

1966 Freedom of Gosport conferred on the Fleet Air Arm, and received by Vice-Admiral D.C.E.F. Gibson, FONAC, in a ceremony at St George's Barracks. Board of Admiralty represented by Mr J.P. Mallalieu, Navy Minister and contingents on parade from all RN air stations.

2000 *Wildfire*, RNR unit at Northwood, commissioned.
See 3 April 1959, 2 October 1964.

21 May

A Memorable Date observed by 3 Cdo Brigade Royal Marines and by RM Operational Landing Craft Squadrons – San Carlos

1692 Continuation of the chase after the Battle of Barfleur.

See 19 May 1692.

1794 Capture of Bastia, Corsica, after a siege of thirty-seven days, by troops under Lt-Col William Villettes (69th Regiment) and seamen under Capt Horatio Nelson (*Agamemnon*). Ships: *Agamemnon, Fortitude, Princess Royal, St George, Victory, Windsor Castle*. Frigates, etc.: *Imperieuse, Mulette, Proselyte*. Troops: Royal Artillery, Royal Sappers and Miners, 11th, 25th, 30th, 69th Foot.

1798 Rear-Admiral Sir Horatio Nelson, detached by Admiral Earl St Vincent with a small force to 'proceed in quest of the Armament preparing by the enemy at Toulon and Genoa . . . On falling in with the same Armament . . . to use your utmost endeavours to take, sink, burn or destroy them'. Nelson failed to intercept Napoleon's great expedition to Egypt by a few hours after his flagship, *Vanguard*, was dismasted in a gale.

See 23 June 1652, 1 August 1739, 18 September 1740, 18 May 1803, 8 May 1943.

If Napoleon had been captured by the Royal Navy that day Europe would have been saved a further seventeen years of civil war and European history would have taken a very different course. 'It was a momentous night, a real crux in history which might have had very different results if the flagship had only taken the same seamanlike precautions as the other ships in company' – N.A.M. Rodger, 'Nelson and the British Navy' in David Cannadine ed. *Admiral Lord Nelson. Context and Legacy* (Basingstoke, 2005) p.15. Two months passed before Nelson found and destroyed the French fleet at Aboukir; a great victory but the dazzling prize had escaped.

1800 Boats of blockading squadron under Vice-Admiral Lord Keith (*Minotaur*) cut out the Genoese *Prima* galley at Genoa.

1858 Admiral Sir Michael Seymour (*Coromandel*) occupied Tientsin.

1941 Destroyer *Juno*, Lt-Cdr St J. R.J. Tyrwhitt, sunk in less than two minutes by German and Italian aircraft (34.55N, 26.34E) during the Battle of Crete. Tyrwhitt was Second Sea Lord 1959–61.

1941 Destroyers *Ilex, Jervis* (D 14) and *Nizam* bombarded Scarpanto airfield.

The modified Dido-class light cruiser HMS *Royalist* anchored in the Clyde on 9 September 1943 having been completed that month by Scotts of Greenock. She served in the Royal New Zealand Navy from 1956 to 1966. (*Cdr David Hobbs RN*)

The British Aerospace Sea Harrier FRS1. (*NMRN*)

1941 'Rarely can the flexibility of maritime power have been more convincingly demonstrated than by *Ark Royal*'s accomplishment in flying Hurricanes to Malta from a position well inside the Mediterranean on 21 May and crippling the *Bismarck* with her torpedo bombers 500 miles to the west of Brest six days later' – Roskill, *The Navy at War*, p.162.
See 24 August 1940, 14 November 1997, 21 May 1998.

1943 Submarine *Sickle* sank U-303 while the German boat was on trials off Toulon (42.50N, 06.00E).

1944 Destroyers *Liddesdale*, *Tenacious* and *Termagant* sank U-453 off Cape Spartivento (38.13N, 16.38E). (First attacked on the 19th.)

1945 Last Swordfish squadron in the Royal Navy, 836 NAS, disbanded.
See 28 June 1945.

1982 The Battle of Falkland Sound. 3 Cdo Bde began the landings at San Carlos Bay. Men of 40 and 45 Cdos RM and 2 and 3 Para were put ashore by landing craft from *Fearless* and *Intrepid*. The logistic and transport shipping within San Carlos Water was protected by the thin grey line of escort vessels in adjoining Falkland Sound: destroyer *Antrim*; frigates *Argonaut*, *Broad sword*, *Brilliant*, *Plymouth*, *Yarmouth* and *Ardent*, supported by FAA Sea Harriers of 800 NAS and 801 NAS. Sustained fighter-bomber attacks by over forty enemy aircraft brought a day of intense naval warfare. Ten aircraft destroyed by Sea Harriers and by Sea Wolf and Seacat SAMs and many more damaged. *Ardent* hit by several bombs and fought to a standstill. Her blazing wreck was finally abandoned and she sank early on 22 May. *Argonaut*, seriously damaged, remained at anchor for the next eight days as a static AA platform. A UXB in flooded magazine was defused and removed by an officer of exceptional gallantry, Lt-Cdr Brian Dutton DSO, QGM, RN. First DSC to a fleet chief petty officer, FCPO M.G. Fellowes, for defusing UXB in *Antrim*. Most other warships damaged and all their captains decorated. By nightfall, 42 Cdo and supporting artillery and logistics were ashore without loss to themselves and a secure bridgehead established. This was the aim of the operation; a splendid achievement.

1998 Destroyer *York*, with RM FSRT embarked, detached from Operation Bolton in Gulf area to stand by for possible Australian-led national evacuation operation in Indonesia. Released 20 July. Operation Garrick. Another instance of the flexibility of sea power.
See 21 May 1941, 14 November 1997.

2007 Destroyer *Exeter*, the last major Falklands veteran still in commission, visited London on a 'round Britain' programme to commemorate the 25th anniversary of the San Carlos landings.

2007 The fourth Astute-class SSN, *Audacious*, ordered. The previous ship of the name was the battleship of 1912 mined in 1914.
See 27 October 1914, 8 June 2007.

22 May

A Memorable Date observed by the Cdo Logistic Regiment, Royal Marines – Ajax Bay

1660 Pepys recorded that *Naseby* had been renamed *Royal Charles*.

1681 *Kingfisher* fought seven Algerine men-of-war off Sardinia, and was twice on fire.

1692 Vice-Admiral Sir Ralph Delaval (*St Albans*), with *Ruby* and two fireships, burned the French *Admirable*, *Conquerant*, *Soleil-Royal* and *Triomphant* at Cherbourg.

See 19 May 1692.

1803 *Doris* captured the French *Affronteur* 20 miles S.W. by W. of Ushant.

1809 Rear-Admiral Eliab Harvey, who had commanded *Temeraire* at Trafalgar, court-martialled for imputing disrespect to Admiral Lord Gambier, his C-in-C; dismissed the Service but reinstated next year, promoted and knighted.

1812 *Northumberland* and *Growler* destroyed the French *Andromaque*, *Ariane* and *Mameluk* inshore of Ile de Groix.

1841 Boats of advanced squadron destroyed many junks and fire rafts in the approaches to Canton. Ships: *Algerine*, *Alligator*, *Calliope*, *Columbine*, *Conway*, *Cruizer*, *Herald*, *Hyacinth*, *Louisa*, *Modeste*, *Nimrod*, *Pylades*, *Sulphur*. Steamers: *Atalanta* (IN), *Nemesis* (Ben. Mar.). Boats of *Blenheim*.

1915 Submarine E 11 sank Turkish *Pelenk-i-Deria* off Seraglio Point, Constantinople.

1917 Mediterranean convoys began as local experiment.

1940 Fifty Dutch coasting vessels – schuytes – lying in the Pool of London and at Poole, Dorset, commissioned under the White Ensign by Cs-in-C The Nore and Portsmouth for the Dunkirk evacuation. At 1944 the Admiralty signalled '. . . the operation for which these ships are being prepared will be known as Dynamo'.

See 16 May 1940.

1941 Sunk this day by German aircraft during the Battle of Crete:

Fiji	34.35N, 23.10E
Gloucester	35.50N, 23.00E
Greyhound	36.00N, 23.10E
York	blown up in Suda Bay

1941 AM: Revd Christopher Champain Tanner, RNVR, Chaplain, light cruiser *Fiji*. Posthumous. 'Mr Tanner was one of the last officers to leave *Fiji* when she was attacked and sunk by air attack during the evacuation from Crete. Tanner, a rugby international, remained in the water helping injured survivors into life rafts, making thirty round trips. The effort exhausted him and he collapsed and died soon after he was taken from the sea.' – *London Gazette*, 24 April 1942.

The grave at Suda Bay Commonwealth War Cemetery in Crete of Commissioned Schoolmaster Charles Frederick Williamson RN, one of the 45 officers and 648 men lost in the light cruiser HMS *Gloucester*, sunk by air attack off Crete in May 1941. Husband of Ivy Grace Williamson of Ipswich. (*Author*)

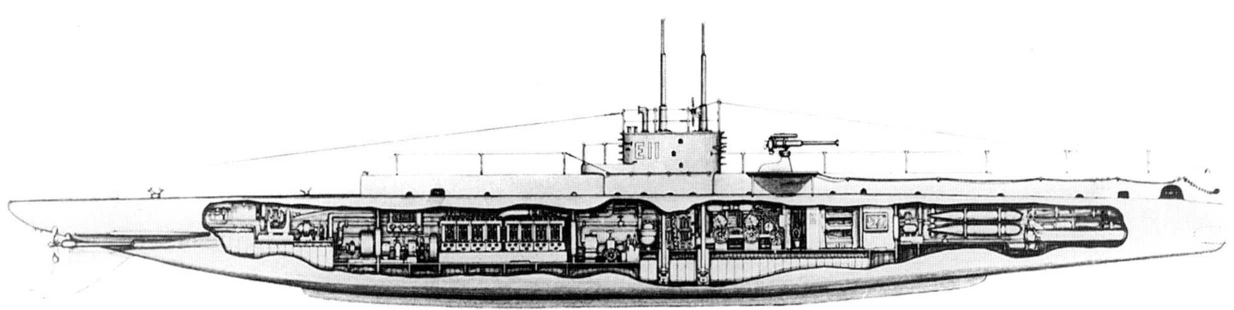

(Above) HM Submarine E 11 (1914). (*RMM*)
(Below) Cutaway diagram of HM Submarine E 11 (1914). (*Author*)

Destroyer *Kandahar* picked up crew of destroyer *Greyhound* including her CO Cdr, W.R. Marshall A'Deane RN. Later, while *Kandahar* was rescuing men from the cruiser *Fiji*, Capt A'Deane dived overboard in darkness to save a man in the water distant from the ship. He was never seen again.

1941 King George of the Hellenes rescued ('fetched off' – Roskill) from Agiaroumeli on the south coast of Crete by the destroyers *Decoy* and *Hero* on the night of 22/23 May and taken to Egypt. He had been appointed DSO the previous month for courage under enemy fire.
See 3 December 1922.

1947 Diesel submarine *Artful*, first British warship of the name, launched at Scotts, Greenock.

1969 The Churchill Estate at Faslane, comprising 730 houses built for men of the Polaris force and the Clyde Submarine Base, handed over to the RN – *The Naval Review*, vol.47, No. 4, October 1969, p.359.

1981 Training of naval nuclear propulsion plant operators, based since 1965 at HMS *Vulcan*, Dounreay, transferred to HMS *Sultan* in December 1980. *Vulcan* paid off. DCI(RN) 303/81.
See 1 May 1970.

1982 Landings at Ajax Bay, Falkland Islands. Cdo Logistic Regt RM landed and provided support for the three-week-long campaign. Argentine patrol boat *Rio Iguazu* beached after attack from Sea Harriers in Choiseul Sound. Operation Corporate.

2003 WO2 Dave Pearce, RM, a member of a joint RN/RM expedition, became the first member of the Naval Service to climb Mount Everest.
See 17 May 2000, 27 December 2006, 1 January 2007.

2010 Admiral Sir Peter White, the first supply officer to sit on the Admiralty Board (Chief of Fleet Support 1974–7) and the first to reach four-star rank in 1976, died aged 91.
See 28 June 1976.

23 May

1692 Vice-Admiral George Rooke (*Eagle*) with fire-ships and boats of fleet, burned the French *Ambitieux*, *Galliard*, *Glorieux*, *Magnifique*, *Marveilleux* and *St Phillippe* at La Hogue.

1757 Capt Richard Howe of *Dunkirk* (60) elected MP for Dartmouth at age 31. Seven Years War.
See 1 June 1794, 19 February 1934.

1794 Occupation of Bastia. Calvi besieged by General Stuart with squadron under Capt Nelson. Taken 10 August.

1799 Capt Ben Hallowell, *Swiftsure*, to Horatio Nelson: 'I have taken the liberty of presenting you a coffin made from the mainmast of *L'Orient*, that when you have finished your military career in this world you may be buried in one of your own trophies. But that that period may be far distant, is the earnest wish of your sincere friend, Ben Hallowell.' Nelson 'placed it upright against the bulkhead of his cabin, behind his chair, where he sat at dinner' – Southey, *Life of Nelson*. Dent 1922 edn, p.180. Nelson was buried in it on 9 January 1806.
See 1 August 1798.

1809 *Melpomene* beat off twenty Danish gunboats at Omö Island, Great Belt and was favoured by a wind getting up, without which she would have been taken.

1811 *Sir Francis Drake* and her boats captured fourteen French gunboats and two merchant prahus 10 miles N.E. of Rembang, Java. A few of the 14th Regiment were in the boats.

1822 *Comet*, the first paddle steamer built for the Royal Navy, launched at Deptford.

1918 Submarine H 4 sank the German UB-52 in Adriatic (41.46N, 18.35E).

1918 AMC *Moldavia* torpedoed and sunk by UB-67 off Brighton.

1928 GC (ex-AM): Lt R.W. Armytage and LS R. Oliver (*Warspite*) for rescuing a trapped stoker.

1934 First performance of Green's setting of 'Sunset', an evening hymn, by RM band at Malta.

1940 Naval demolition parties landed at Calais and Dunkirk, and with Royal Marines at Boulogne.
See 28 May 1941, 1 June 1941.

On the evening of 23 May, five V&W-class destroyers met off Boulogne to evacuate the troops trapped onshore by the advancing German forces. The *Whitshed* and *Vimiera* went alongside first, and took off detachments of the Welsh and Irish Guards and Royal Marines. Each ship then withdrew while *Wild Swan*, *Venomous* and *Venetia* entered harbour. During the embarkation, the shore batteries engaged the ships – the French had not had time to spike them – and tanks were firing along the streets at the destroyers, while they replied over open sights at 100yd range. A total of 4,360 men were saved by this action. Ships: *Wild Swan*, *Whitshed*, *Vimiera*, *Verity*, *Venomous* took troops over. Evacuation by them, negative *Verity*, but reinforced by *Keith*, *Vimy*, *Venetia* and *Windsor*. *Vimiera* made three runs, lifting 1,400 men in all. On one run, she carried 555 men and could not accept more than 5° of wheel.

Admiral Sir Bertram Ramsay, FO Commanding Dover, on 8 June promulgated to the commanding officers of all his destroyers a letter he had received from Lt-Col J.C. Haydon, the Colonel, 2nd Bn Irish Guards, which had been extracted from Boulogne: 'I am writing to you on behalf of the Battalion to thank you and your destroyers for all you did for us at Boulogne. As well you know, the situation was really far more difficult and critical than it had been at the Hook and we are all of us agreed that those who saw the actions fought by the destroyers while we were waiting to embark, and while we were actually embarking at Boulogne, are very unlikely ever to see anything more inspiring, gallant or magnificent. We all felt that the destroyers would have been completely justified in leaving the harbour and returning for us after dark. Had they done so, we should not have had the very smallest complaint, for we should have well understood and appreciated the position they were in. However, never for one second did there appear to be a thought of such a move, and the ships continued to embark the wounded and unwounded and to continue their fight with the shore batteries as if the whole affair was perfectly normal and hum-drum. I cannot tell you the depth of the impression which has been made upon us all, but I can assure you that there is no doubt of it and that the whole of the Battalion is filled with an

HMS *Kelly* (1938) at speed. Her after torpedo tubes have been replaced by a 4-in QF Mk V anti-aircraft gun. (*NMRN*)

affection and admiration for the sailors who have on two occasions done so much for them. I wish so very much you could sense the feeling that exists here. I believe it would make you more proud than ever of the men and the ships that you command. Would it be possible to let the Captains and crews know how clearly we realise the dangers they ran for us and how clearly we realise too that it is due to their courage and conduct that we are here now.'

1941 Destroyers *Kashmir* and *Kelly* sunk by German aircraft 13 miles S. of Gavdo (34.41N, 24.15E), during the Battle of Crete.

1943 Destroyer *Active* and frigate *Ness* sank the Italian S/M *Leonardo Da Vinci* N.E. of the Azores (42.18N, 15.53W). Convoys WS 30/KMF 15.

1943 Swordfish B/819 (*Archer*) sank U-752 in N. Atlantic (51.40N, 29.49W). Convoy HX 239. First operational success of air-to-sea rocket projectiles.

1955 Frigate *Leopard*, third of the Type 41 anti-aircraft frigates and name ship of the class, named by HRH Princess Marie Louise and launched from the only remaining building slip in Portsmouth Dockyard. The first major warship built at Portsmouth since 1942.

See 13 and 15 October 1961, 28 July 1963, 7 September 2006.

1960 Admiral Sir Caspar John, lately VCNS, and C-in-C Home Fleet designate, succeeded Admiral Sir Charles Lambe who had resigned as First Sea Lord following a heart attack; the first naval aviator to head the Service.

Admiral John departed the Admiralty on 6 August 1963 after six years in Whitehall having 'emphatically refused' to be CDS and having declined a peerage from Prime Minister Alec Douglas-Home (Rebecca John biography, p.207). He was succeeded by Admiral Sir David Luce, lately CINC Far East.

See 22 March 1903, 11 July 1984.

1972 First PWO course began at *Dryad*.

See 14 May 2004.

1980 Submarine Refit Complex at Devonport Dockyard opened by HRH The Prince of Wales.

1982 Frigate *Antelope* damaged in San Carlos Water by Argentine aircraft which left two unexploded bombs. Exploded next day while efforts were made to render them safe.

24 May

1692 Vice-Admiral George Rooke (*Eagle*) with fire-ships and boats of fleet, burned the French *Bourbon*, *Fier*, *Fort*, *St Louis*, *Terrible* and *Tonnant* at La Hogue.
See 23 May 1692.

1743 Admiral Sir Charles Wager died.

1756 The Hon. John Byng, Admiral of the Blue, held his fateful, and for him fatal, council of war on board *Ramillies* (74) at sea that resolved that 'we are unanimously of opinion that the fleet should immediately proceed for Gibraltar'.
See 14 March 1757.

1792 Admiral Lord Rodney, victor of the Battle of the Saintes, died, in Hanover Square, London.
See 12 April 1782, p.34 panel.

1795 *Mosquito* captured the French privateer *National Razor* off Cape Maze (Maysi), Cuba.

1796 Capture of St Lucia by Lt-Gen Sir Ralph Abercromby and Rear-Admiral Sir Hugh Cloberry Christian (*Thunderer*) after an attack begun on 27 April. A Naval Brigade was landed. Ships: *Alfred*, *Ganges*, *Madras*, *Thunderer*, *Vengeance*. Frigates, etc.: *Arethusa*, *Astraea*, *Beaulieu*, *Bulldog*, *Fury*, *Hebe*, *Pelican*, *Victorieuse*, *Woolwich*. Battle Honour: St Lucia 1796.

1814 Boats of *Elizabeth* cut out the French *L'Aigle* from under the guns of Vido Island, Corfu.

1841 Capture of the British Factory and the remaining river forts and batteries in the eastern approaches to Canton. Operations ended on the 26th. Ships: *Algerine*, *Columbine*, *Cruizer*, *Hyacinth*, *Modeste*, *Nimrod*, *Pylades*. Steamer: *Atalanta* (Indian Navy).

1855 Allied troops landed in Kamish-Burunski Bay, and the fleet obtained possession of the Kerch–Yenikale Strait, at the entrance to the Sea of Azov. *Snake* engaged the batteries and several Russian war vessels, sinking two of them. British fleet of thirty-three ships under Rear-Admiral Sir Edmund Lyons (*Royal Albert*). French under Vice-Admiral Bruat (*Montebello*).

1876 *Challenger*, steam corvette, returned to Spithead after a 3½-year oceanographic voyage, having sailed 68,890 miles and crossed the Equator eight times. One of the great voyages of British naval hydrography.
See 21 December 1872.

1898 Occupation of Wei-Hai-Wei.

1916 E 18 sunk by German submarine-trap (Q-ship) 'K' off Bornholm in Baltic.

1917 Experimental convoy sailed from Newport News to the United Kingdom, under escort of armoured cruiser *Roxburgh*.

1917 Third division of American destroyers arrived at Queenstown, making a total of eighteen within eight weeks of the United States entering the First World War.

1939 The Admiralty recovered control of the Fleet Air Arm from the RAF and renamed it the Air Branch of the Royal Navy. Rear-Admiral

HMS *Hood* and HMS *Prince of Wales* in action with *Bismarck* and *Prinz Eugen*. (*NMRN 1982/440*)

Royal Marine Cdos from *Ocean* landing on the beaches at Sierra Leone in support of UN operations ashore, 2000. (*RN*)

R. Bell-Davies VC, who had become a lieutenant-colonel RAF in April 1918 and reverted to the RN in May 1919, appointed rear-admiral naval air stations which comprised Lee-on-Solent, Ford (Sussex), Worthy Down (Winchester), Donibristle (Fife) and Bermuda. The stations were commissioned the same day as HMS *Daedalus*, *Peregrine*, *Kestrel*, *Merlin* and *Malabar*. Dual RAF commissions held by RN officers terminated.

See 19 November 1915, 30 July 1937, 20 May 1953.

1941 *Hood* sunk and *Prince of Wales* damaged by the German battleship *Bismarck* in Denmark Strait. Swordfish aircraft (*Victorious*) torpedoed *Bismarck*. FAA Sqn: 825.

1941 VC: Lt-Cdr Malcolm David Wanklyn for services in command of submarine *Upholder*.

1941 First investiture of the George Cross at Buckingham Palace; first naval direct recipient Lt-Cdr Robert Selby Armitage RNVR, awarded for bomb disposal work – *London Gazette*, 27 December 1940. GM 15 February 1944, presented 21 November 1944; *London Gazette*.

See 24 September 1940.

1966 Freedom of Greenwich conferred on the president, officers and staff of the RN College, Greenwich, and received by the Admiral President, Rear-Admiral P.U. Bailey in a ceremony held in the Painted Hall attended by HRH Prince Philip. The frigate *Tenby*, Cdr J.M. Hait RN, was moored off the college.

1967 Leander-class frigate *Andromeda* launched, last ship built in Portsmouth Dockyard in the twentieth century.

See 7 September 2006.

1967 Whitehall Fleet Weather Centre transferred from MOD(N) to C-in-C Home Fleet at Northwood at 240900ZMAY67. DCI(RN) 605/67.

1981 The last Navy Days at Chatham. Ships present included *Achilles*, *Berwick*, *Coventry*, *Diomede*, *Endurance*, *Falmouth*, *Rhyl* and *Torquay*.

1982 Landing ships *Sir Galahad* and *Sir Lancelot* hit in San Carlos Water by bombs that failed to explode and were removed by Fleet Clearance Diving Teams.

1988 Lt Charles Esme Thornton 'Jim' Warren RNVR, one of the first RN human torpedo charioteers, died. Joined RN as a stoker in 1931 and commissioned into RNVR 1944. With James Benson wrote wartime history of the 12th Submarine Flotilla in *Above us the Waves* (1953). In 1942 he was 'probably the only Stoker Petty Officer ever to be married in St George's, Hanover Square' – *Daily Telegraph*.

1990 *Lancaster*, Type 23 frigate, launched by HM The Queen, and the Duke of Lancaster, at Yarrows on the Clyde. Commissioned by Her Majesty on 1 May 1992. Original pennant number F232 changed to F229: Form 232 is the RN report form for groundings and collisions.

2000 Royal Marines of 42 Cdo landed in Sierra Leone from *Ocean* to relieve 2 Para in supporting government forces and evacuating UK nationals. QGM: Maj Phil Ashby RM, UN Military Observer. Operation Palliser.

See 1 May 2000, 10 September 2000.

25 May

1496 First dry dock in England completed at Portsmouth at a cost of £193 0s 6¼d. First used by *Sovereign*. Dock infilled in 1623.

1660 Charles II landed at Dover: restoration of the monarchy.

1696 *Assistance*, escorting a convoy, twice repulsed eight French privateers 40 miles S.E. by E. of Southwold.

1794 Admiral Earl Howe's fleet burned the French *Inconnu* and *Républicaine* W. of Ushant.

1795 *Thorn* captured the French privateer *Courrier National* 80 miles N.W. of St Thomas, West Indies.

1801 Boats of *Mercury* cut out the French *Bulldog* at Ancona, east coast of Italy, but had to abandon her.

1801 Publication of first dated Admiralty charts of Alexandria and the Egyptian coast. The first charts, of Quiberon Bay, had appeared, vexingly undated, in 1800.
See 15 November 1819.

1841 Capture of the forts immediately guarding Canton. (Operations concluded on the 30th.) Ships: *Algerine, Alligator, Blenheim, Blonde, Calliope, Columbine, Conway, Cruizer, Herald, Hyacinth, Modeste, Nimrod, Pylades, Starling, Sulphur*, and seamen and Royal Marines of *Wellesley* (from Wantong). Steamers: *Atalanta* (IN), *Nemesis* (Ben. Mar.). A Naval Brigade was landed. Troops: Royal Artillery, 18th, 26th and 49th Regiments, Madras Artillery, Madras Sappers and Miners, 37th Madras Native Infantry, Bengal Volunteer Regiment.

1841 Boats of *Wellesley* frustrated a fire-raft attack in the Boca Tigris.

1857 Gunboats and boats of squadron destroyed twenty-seven snake boats in Escape Creek, Canton River. Gunboats and tenders: *Bustard, Hong Kong, Sir Charles Forbes, Starling, Staunch*. Boats of: *Fury, Hornet, Inflexible, Sybille, Tribune*.

1859 *Warrior* laid down by Thames Iron Works at Blackwall, engined by Penn of Deptford.

1893 HMY *Britannia* won her first race.

1915 Battleship *Triumph* sunk by U-21 outside the Dardanelles (off Gaba Tepe).
See 18 March 1915, 13 and 27 May 1915.

1917 AMC *Hilary* sunk by U-88 60 miles W. of the Shetland Islands.

1921 Admiral of the Fleet Sir Arthur Wilson, VC, died. His father had fought at Navarino.
See 4 March 1842, 29 February 1884.

1940 *Illustrious* (fourth of the name) commissioned. First heavily armoured aircraft carrier.

1940 Destroyer *Wessex* sunk by air attack off Calais.

1941 Sloop *Grimsby* sunk by German aircraft 40 miles N. of Tobruk.

The Loss of HMS *Hood*

The German battleship *Bismarck* (42,500 tons) and cruiser *Prinz Eugen* sailed for commerce raiding in the Atlantic, in May 1941. The Admiralty was aware that German heavy units were at sea, and sailed the Home Fleet from Scapa Flow. The cruiser *Suffolk* sighted the *Bismarck*, and shadowed her in the mist using radar until the battlecruiser *Hood* and the newly completed battleship *Prince of Wales* were able to close. The British capital ships sighted the German force at 0535 on 24 May, and engaged at 13 miles at 0553. The German ships concentrated their fire on the *Hood*, while the British ships could use only their forward turrets because of the angle of their approach. *Bismarck*'s second and third salvoes hit *Hood*, and at 0600, she blew up, leaving three survivors from her complement of 95 officers and 1,324 men. The Germans shifted their fire to the *Prince of Wales*, which was hit within minutes by four 15-in and three 8-in shells. She broke off the engagement. *Bismarck*, however, had been hit by two of her 14-in shells, one of which caused an oil leak. As a result *Bismarck* decided to head for St Nazaire.
See 27 May 1941.

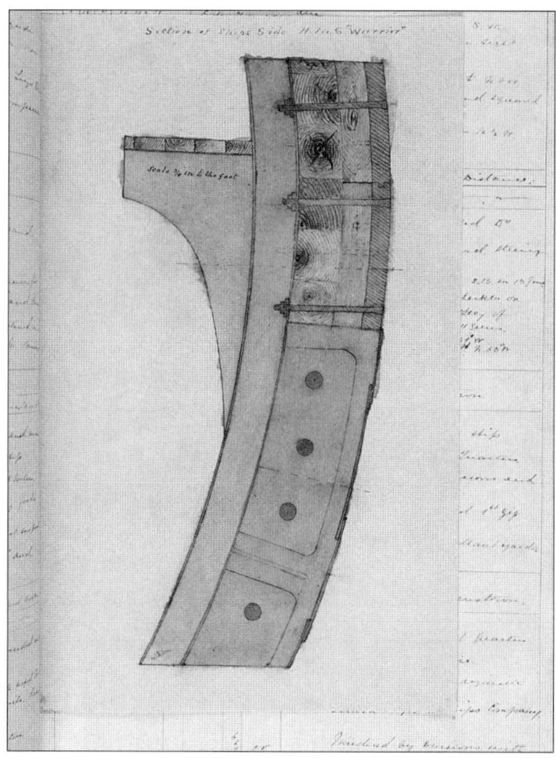

Section of the hull of *Warrior* showing the 4½in wrought-iron armour backed by 18in of teak outside the wrought-iron hull. (*NMRN 1981/149*)

1943 Liberator S/59 sank U-990 off S.W. Norway (65.05N, 07.28E).

1943 Lt A.H. Massey of HM Submarine *Umbra* invested with DSC by King George VI at Buckingham Palace. He later became the first South African to command one of HM submarines.

1943 VC: Cdr John Wallace 'Tubby' Linton RN, *Turbulent*. Posthumous. Boat posted missing in Mediterranean. His son, William, was lost eight years later in *Affray*.

See 12 March 1943, 17 April 1951.

1943 Dönitz ordered German U-boats to withdraw from N. Atlantic convoy routes after twenty-four submarines had been lost so far that month.

May 1943 was the turning point in the Battle of the Atlantic. The last straw for Admiral Dönitz came with the eastward passage of convoy SC 130 from Halifax which did not lose a single ship, although five U-boats were sunk attacking it. In May only fifty merchantmen were sunk for the loss of forty-one U-boats, thirty-eight of them in the Atlantic. The fitting of centimetric radar in ships and aircraft obliged U-boats to dive during battery-charging surface runs and made surface attack dangerous. In spite of the development of the schnorkel, which enabled submarines to charge batteries under the surface, the U-boat menace never again reached the proportions of 1942, when nearly 8 million tons of merchant shipping had been sunk, over 70 per cent by U-boats.

'The retreat of the Atlantic U-boats . . . was a smashing victory for the Allies, as important a strategic victory as Midway in the west and Stalingrad in the east' – Winton, *Convoy*, p.282. 'The victory here recounted marked one of the decisive stages of the war; for the enemy then made his greatest effort against our Atlantic life-line -- and he failed. After forty-five months of unceasing battle, of a more exacting and arduous nature than posterity may easily realise, our convoy escorts and aircraft had won the triumph that they so richly deserved' – Roskill, *War at Sea*, vol.2, p.377.

1982 Destroyer *Coventry* sunk and frigate *Broadsword* damaged N. of Falkland Sound by air attacks. *Atlantic Conveyor*, carrying important helicopter reinforcements, damaged by two air-launched Exocets while in company with carrier battle group 85 miles N.E. of Cape Pembroke, and sank later. Capt Ian North DSC one of twelve men lost. This was Argentina's national day but there was no sign of the eponymous carrier (*25 De Mayo*, originally HMS *Venerable* and then the Dutch *Karel Doorman*). Operation Corporate.

See 1 May 2008.

1989 Admiral Sir William Doveton Minet Staveley promoted admiral of the fleet at the end of his appointment as First Sea Lord. Dartmouth 1942. 1952–4 Flag Lt to Admiral Sir George Creasy, C-in-C Home Fleet; SO 104th (later 6th) Minesweeping Flotilla in Far East. Last Captain of *Albion* 1972–3; DN Plans and DN Future Policies; rear-admiral January 1977; FOF2, FOCAS, COS C-in-C Fleet. 1980–2 VCNS then C-in-C Fleet. He was the grandson of Vice-Admiral Sir Doveton Sturdee who defeated the German Vice-Admiral Graf Spee at the Battle of the Falklands in 1914. Admiral Staveley died on 13 October 1997.

1992 *Revenge*, the last of the four Polaris submarines to be commissioned and the first to pay off, sailed from Faslane for Rosyth at the end of fifty-six patrols to begin extended decommissioning.

See 15 March 1968.

26 May

1585 *Primrose* merchantman repulsed a Spanish attack at Bilbao.

1660 George Monck invested as KG at Canterbury by King Charles II whose restoration he had helped bring about, who also made him Duke of Albemarle and whom he served as an admiral, though he had been a Cromwellian General at Sea.

See 27 May 1660.

1703 Death of Samuel Pepys, first Secretary of the Admiralty.

1758 *Dolphin* and *Solebay* fought the French privateer *Maréchal de Belle Ile* off Montrose.

1811 *Astraea*, *Phoebe* and *Racehorse* captured the French *Neréide* and also recaptured *Tamatave*. Battle Honour: *Neréide* 1811.

1840 Admiral Sir William Sidney Smith died, one of the most extraordinary maverick officers in British naval history.

See 21 June 1764.

1845 Boats of brig *Pantaloon* captured the pirate *Borboleta* 100 miles S.S.W. of Lagos, west coast of Africa.

1855 Boats of Allied light squadron destroyed the Russian shipping at Berdyansk, Sea of Azov. Ships: *Arrow*, *Beagle*, *Curlew*, *Lynx*, *Medina*, *Miranda*, *Recruit*, *Snake*, *Stromboli*, *Swallow*, *Vesuvius*, *Viper*, *Wrangler*. French: *Brandon*, *Fulton*, *Lucifer*, *Megère*.

1918 *Lorna*, auxiliary patrol yacht, a venerable vessel built in 1904 and taken up in both world wars, sank UB-74 in Lyme Bay (50.32N, 02.32W).

1940 Evacuation of the BEF from Dunkirk. Operation Dynamo – lasted until 4 June. Battle Honour: Dunkirk 1940.

AA cruiser: *Calcutta*. Destroyers: *Anthony*,† *Basilisk*,† *Codrington*, *Esk*, *Express*,† *Gallant*,† *Grafton*† (sunk by U-62), *Grenade*,* *Greyhound*,† *Harvester*,† *Havant*,† *Icarus*,† *Impulsive*,† *Intrepid*,† *Ivanhoe*,† *Jaguar*,† *Javelin*, *Keith*,* *Mackay*, *Malcolm*,† *Montrose*,† *Sabre*,† *Saladin*,† *Scimitar*,† *Shikari*, *Vanquisher*, *Venomous*,† *Verity*, *Vimy*,† *Vivacious*,† *Wakeful*,* *Whitehall*,† *Whitshed*, *Wild Swan*, *Winchelsea*, *Windsor*,† *Wolfhound*,† *Wolsey*,† *Worcester*.†

Admiral Sir William Sidney Smith (1764–1840)

Smith entered the Navy in 1777 and he demonstrated brilliant abilities during the War of American Independence, especially at St Vincent (1780) and Dominica (1782), and was made a post captain at age 18. 'Possessing in the highest degree the essential military qualities of courage and resourcefulness and imagination', wrote Admiral Sir Herbert Richmond (*The Private Papers of George, second Earl Spencer, First Lord of the Admiralty, 1794–1801*, Navy Records Society, London 1924, p.28), 'he combined with them presumption, vanity and exaggerated self will'. Smith was naval adviser to King Gustavus of Sweden in the war with Russia and was made a Knight of the Sword. Nelson, his contemporary, referred dismissively to 'The Swedish Knight' but Nelson showed no reluctance when later he himself was made a Sicilian duke. 'But where Nelson won confidence and affection, Smith had a habit of creating suspicion and resentment' (Graham and Humphreys, *The Navy and South America*, Navy Records Society, London 1962, p.2). Routine fleet duties held no attraction for Smith and he ran a succession of special operations away from the Fleet, being more *of* the Royal Navy than *in* it. 'His restlessness and flamboyance and invincible self confidence' frequently antagonised superiors and colleagues. Smith became a national hero for his gallant and resourceful defence of St Jean d'Acre on the Levant coast against French attack led personally by Napoleon who ruefully commented, 'That man made me miss my destiny'. Smith often disobeyed his orders and paid scant regard to the established command structure of the Service. The Admiralty never managed to control him: 'There seems to me such a want of judgement in our friend Sir Sidney', remarked Lord Barham, First Lord of the Admiralty in 1805–6, 'that it is much safer to employ him *under* command than *in* command' (J.K. Laughton, *The Letters and Papers of Charles, Lord Barham, 1758–1813*, vol.3 (Navy Records Society, London 1911, p.162). Sidney Smith died in France in 1840 and is buried in the Cemetery of Père Lachaise.

Sloop: *Bideford.*† Corvettes: *Guillemot, Kingfisher.*† Minesweepers: *Albury, Brighton Belle,* Brighton Queen, Devonia,* Duchess of Fife, Dundalk, Emperor of India, Fitzroy, Glen Avon, Glen Gower, Gossamer, Gracie Fields,* Halcyon, Hebe,† Kellett,† Leda, Lydd, Marmion, Medway Queen, Niger, Oriole, Pangbourne,† Plinlimmon, Princess Elizabeth, Queen of Thanet, Ross, Salamander, Saltash, Sandown, Sharpshooter, Skipjack,* Snaefell, Speedwell, Sutton, Waverley,* Westward Ho.*† Gunboats: *Locust, Mosquito.** Trawlers: *Argyllshire,* Arley, Brock, Blackburn Rovers,* Calvi,* Cayton Wyke, Chico, Comfort,* Conidaw, Fyldea, Grimsby Town, Gulzar, Inverforth, John Cattling, Kingston Alalite,† Kingston Andalusite, Kingston Olivine, Lady Philomena, Lord Inchcape, Nautilus,* Olvina, Our Bairns, Polly Johnson,* Saon, Sargasso, Spurs,† Stella Dorado,* Thomas Bartlett,* Thuringia,* Westella,* Wolves.* Drifters: *Boy Roy,* Eileen Emma, Fidget, Fisher Boy, Forecast, Gervais Rentoul, Girl Gladys, Girl Pamela,* Golden Gift, Golden Sunbeam, Jacketa, Lord Cavan,* Lord Howard, Lord Howe, Midas, Netsukis, Paxton,* Shipmates, Silver Dawn, The Boys, Torbay II, Ut Prosim, Yorkshire Lass, Young Mun.* Armed Boarding Vessels: *King Orry,* Llanthony, Mona's Isle.*† Special service vessels: *Amulree,* Crested Eagle,* Golden Eagle, Grive,* Massey Shaw, Royal Eagle.* Personnel ships (Red Ensign): *Archangel, Autocarrier, Ben-my-Chree,† Biarritz,† Canterbury,† Fenella,* Killarney, King George V, Lady of Mann, Loch Garry, Lorina,* Maid of Orleans,† Malines, Manxman, Mona's Queen,* Normania,* Prague,† Princess Maud,† Queen of the Channel,* Royal Daffodil, Royal Sovereign, St Helier, St Seiriol,† Scotia,* Tynwald.* Hospital carriers: *Dinard, Isle of Guernsey,† Isle of Thanet,† Paris,* St Andrew, St David,† St Julian,† Worthing.*† FAA Sqns: 806, 810, 825, 826 (all disembarked, Skua, Swordfish, Albacore). MA/SB: 6, 7, 10. MTBs: 16, 67, 68, 100, 102, 107.

Allied Ships: Neth: Yacht: *Demog I* (under French orders). French: *Epervier, Leopard, Bouclier, Bourrasque,* Branlebas, Cyclone,† Flore, Foudroyant,* Incomprise, Mistral,† Sirocco.** Avisos: *Amiens, Amiral Mouchez, Arras, Belfort.* Trawlers: *Duperre,* Emile Deschamps.** Mail Packets: *Cote d'Argent, Cote d'Azure,* Newhaven, Rouen.* Drifter: *Pierre Marie.** Polish: *Blyskawica* (under British orders). And many, many anonymous little ships.

*Sunk. †Damaged.

1940 Cruiser *Curlew* sunk by German aircraft off Skudesnes, N. Norway (67.32N, 16.37E.)

1941 Fleet carrier *Formidable* (Rear-Admiral D.W. Boyd) attacked Scarpanto airfield, Karpathos Island. *Formidable* and destroyer *Nubian* damaged by German aircraft (32.55N, 26.25E). FAA Sqns: 803, 806 (Albacore, Fulmar) 826, 829.

1941 Swordfish aircraft (*Ark Royal*) torpedoed *Bismarck*. FAA Sqns: 810, 818, 820.

1943 Corvette *Hyderabad* and frigate *Test* sank U-436 in N. Atlantic (43.49N, 15.56W). Convoy KX 10.

1951 Rededication of Royal Naval Division memorial at Royal Naval College, Greenwich.

See 25 April 1925, 31 May 1981, 13 November 2003.

1954 Light fleet carrier *Albion* completed at Swan Hunters, Walsend-on-Tyne.

See 23 March 1944, 6 May 1947.

1957 Sea Venom of 893 NAS piloted by Lt John Herringshaw RN, with Lt Hugh McLennan RN as Observer, made the 10,000th deck landing in the second commission of the carrier *Ark Royal* off Cyprus.

1969 Vice-Admiral Sir Charles Mills, the last C-in-C Plymouth, hauled down his flag at Mount Wise; that of Rear-Admiral J.C.Y. Roxburgh, appointed the first Flag Officer Plymouth, was hoisted.

See 30 October 1956 (C-in-C NA&WI); 7 September 1958 (C-in-C East Indies); 31 March 1961 (C-in-C The Nore); 30 September 1983 (FO Medway); 31 March 1964 (Admiralty); 11 April 1967 (C-in-C S. Atlantic); 5 June 1967 (C-in-C Mediterranean); 25 July 1967; 1 July 1969; 31 March 1979 (FO Malta).

2008 Fleet submarine *Superb* on submerged passage through the Red Sea for the Gulf, collided with a charted pinnacle rock, damaging bows and sonar. Boat arrived at Suda Bay on 10 June for essential repairs before returning to UK where she was paid off. Portsmouth courts martial 15 March 2010: CO and NO Reprimand; OOW Severe Reprimand. A curious parallel with the loss of cruiser *Effingham* in 1940 where the line on the chart passed directly over a pinnacle.

See 18 May 1940, 6 November 2002.

27 May

1660 Edward Montagu invested as KG by King Charles II, who had returned to his kingdom in the former's flagship.
See 26 May 1660.

1672 De Ruyter surprised the Anglo-French fleet at anchor in Sole Bay. Start of third Dutch war, and death of Sandwich. Duke of York's Regiment of Foot first mentioned as Marines – a letter from Capt Taylor reported that 'those marines, of whom I have soe often wrote to you behaved themselves stoutly'.

1793 *Venus* fought the French *Sémillante* 370 miles N.W. by W. of Cape Finisterre.

1796 *Suffisante* captured the French privateer *Revanche* at the entrance to the Chenal du Four, near Ushant.

1811 Boats of *Sabine* cut out three French privateers at Chipiona, near Cadiz. *Papillon* and *Sabine* sank a French privateer.

1847 The first Naval General Service medal belatedly approved for all surviving personnel who served in the Royal Navy 'in the battles of the great war', 1793–1815, later extended to 1840.

Mrs McKenzie gave birth to a son in HMS *Tremendous* (74) at the Glorious First of June in 1794 and fifty-four years later Daniel Tremendous McKenzie successfully applied for his medal and clasp '1 June 1794'.

1852 *Agamemnon* launched at Woolwich. First screw battleship to be designed as such.

1855 Landing parties from Allied light squadron destroyed Russian stores and the rest of the shipping at Berdyansk, Sea of Azov.
See 26 May 1855.

1857 Boats of *Fury*, *Inflexible*, *Sybille* and *Tribune* destroyed thirteen war junks at Tungkun, Canton River.

1865 *Lord Warden*, ironclad battleship, launched at Chatham. With sister ship *Lord Clyde*, the last true broadside ironclads.

1903 Publication of Erskine Childers' novel *The Riddle of the Sands* in which two amateur yachtsmen discovered among the Frisian Islands covert German preparations to invade England while the Channel Fleet was decoyed away. Although wholly fictional it chimed with British fears and alerted the British public to the growing threat of the German Navy.

1909 Death of Capt Sir John Colomb, naval strategist who 'produced the first rational explanation of the naval place in national or even imperial defence thinking in the new era of iron ships and steam propulsion' – Schurman.
See 13 October 1899.

1911 Submarine D 4 launched, the first British submarine to carry a deck gun.
See 31 December 1974.

1915 Hired minelayer *Princess Irene* destroyed while priming mines at Sheerness.

1915 Battleship *Majestic* sank in seven minutes, torpedoed by U-21 outside the Dardanelles, off Cape Helles.
See 18 March 1915, 13 and 25 May 1915.

1916 UC-3 sunk by British mine off Zeebrugge (52.42N, 02.24E).

1916 Trawlers *Kimberley*, *Oku*, *Rodino* and *Searanger* sank U-74 in North Sea (57.10N, 01.20E).

1940 Animals in the Whale Island menagerie, mainly gifts to the Royal Family on overseas visits, were shot 'in preparation for German air raids'.

1941 Forces under Admiral Sir John Tovey (*King George V*) sank the German battleship *Bismarck* in the Atlantic (48.09N, 16.07W), after a chase lasting four days.

Ships: *Ark Royal*,† *Aurora*, *Dorsetshire*, *Edinburgh*, *Galatea*, *Hermione*, *Hood*,* *Kenya*, *King George V*, *Neptune*, *Norfolk*, *Prince of Wales*, *Renown*,† *Repulse*, *Rodney*, *Sheffield*,† *Suffolk*, *Victorious*. Destroyers: *Achates*, *Active*, *Antelope*, *Anthony*, *Cossack*, *Echo*, *Electra*, *Icarus*, *Inglefield*, *Intrepid*, *Maori*, *Mashona*,* *Nestor*, *Punjabi*, *Sikh*, *Somali*, *Tartar*, *Zulu*. Polish: *Piorun*. FAA Sqns:

Cdr Gilbert Stephenson RN. (*RN*)

Sinking of the *Bismarck*, 1941

The Home Fleet was joined by other units in the search for the German battleship *Bismarck*, heading for St Nazaire after being damaged by *Prince of Wales*. A 209 Sqn Catalina aircraft sighted her on 26 May, when she was within twenty-four hours' steaming of German air cover. The Home Fleet was 130 miles away. Aircraft from the *Ark Royal*, part of Force H diverted from Gibraltar as a 'long stop', took off in atrocious weather, as her flight deck was rising and falling through 56ft, only to attack the cruiser *Sheffield* by mistake. From this, however, it was discovered that the torpedoes were ineffective, and different firing pistols were fitted for the next attack, in which two hits were made on *Bismarck*, one of which damaged her steering. Soon afterwards Capt Vian arrived on the scene with five destroyers and kept *Bismarck* busy through the night until the main fleet arrived. *King George V* and *Rodney* engaged at 8 miles and within fifteen minutes *Bismarck* was heavily hit, and within one and a half hours reduced to a burning shambles. The cruiser *Dorsetshire* put three torpedoes into her, and *Bismarck* sank at 1036, her flag still flying, leaving 110 survivors.

Fulmar: 800Z (*Victorious*), 808 (*Ark Royal*). Swordfish: 810, 818, 820, 825 (*Ark Royal*, *Victorious*). RAF Sqns: 10, 201, 206, 209, 210, 221, 240, 269.
Battle Honour: *Bismarck* 1941
*Sunk. †Force H.

1942 Minesweeper *Fitzroy* sunk by mine off Great Yarmouth.

1944 Liberator S/59 sank U-292 off S.W. Norway (62.37N, 00.57E).
See 25 May 1943 for an anniversary just missed.

1945 General Officer Commanding Royal Marines (GOCRM) became their Commandant-General (CGRM).

1960 Frigate *Leopard* arrived at Portsmouth from the South Atlantic having steamed 1,144 miles up the Amazon, the furthest any HM ship had been up the river since HMS *Pelorus* in 1909.
See 9 July 1959.

1968 Admiral of the Fleet Sir Philip Vian died – twenty-seven years after the *Bismarck* action, at which he had been present as Captain(D) in *Cossack*.
See 15 June 1894, 16 February 1940.

1972 Cdre (Vice-Admiral, retired) Sir Gilbert Stephenson, who returned to active service in 1939 aged 62 to command the anti-submarine training base, HMS *Western Isles*, at Tobermory, died at Saffron Walden aged 94. 'Monkey' Stephenson ran a taut ship and was known as 'The Terror of Tobermory'.
See 12 July 1940.

1976 Post of QHM Scapa Flow abolished.

1982 RMS *Queen Elizabeth 2* arrived off Grytviken with 5 Infantry Brigade, cross-decked next day to *Canberra* and *Norland* who sailed for the Falklands on the 29th.

1993 Royal Fleet Review in a Force 9 gale off Moelfre, Anglesey to mark the fiftieth anniversary of the Battle of the Atlantic. HM King Harald of Norway and HRH The Duke of Edinburgh embarked in HMY *Britannia*. THV *Mermaid* followed rather than preceded the royal yacht. *Cornwall*, flag of Rear-Admiral Michael Boyce, FOSF.
See 28 and 29 July 1969.

2009 Destroyer *Exeter*, Cdr P.A.E. Brown RN, the last operational British warship with a Falklands 1982 battle honour, paid off at Portsmouth.

28 May

1672 Battle of Sole Bay. The first battle of the third Dutch war. Anglo-French fleet of ninety ships under the Duke of York (*Prince*) and Vice-Admiral Comte d'Estrées (*St Philippe*) fought Admiral de Ruyter (*Zeven Provincien*) with seventy-five ships.
Battle Honour: Sole Bay 1672.

Ships: *Bristol, Dartmouth, Diamond, Dunkirk, London, Monck, Old James, Resolution, Sweepstakes, Adventure, Cambridge, Dreadnought, Fairfax, Monmouth, Phoenix, Prince, Royal Katherine, St Michael, Victory, Yarmouth, Advice, Anne, Charles, Dover, Forester, Greenwich, Rainbow, York.*

Antelope, Bonaventure, Crown, Edgar, Henry, French Ruby, Gloucester, Leopard, Mary, Mary Rose, Montagu, Plymouth, Princess, Royal James (flag of Sandwich), *Ruby, Rupert, St Andrew, St George, Sovereign, Success, Tiger, Triumph, Unicorn, Warspite.*

1673 First action off Schooneveld and second battle of the third Dutch war. Seventy-nine ships of Prince Rupert (*Royal Charles*) and Vice-Admiral Comte d'Estrées (*Reine*) fought Admiral de Ruyter (*Zeven Provincien*) with fifty-two ships.
Battle Honour: Schooneveld 1673.

Anne, Constant Warwick, French Ruby, Happy Return, London, Resolution, Stavoreen, Triumph, Warspite, Crown, Edgar, Gloucester, Henry, Lion, Old James, Princess, Royal Charles, Royal Katherine, Rupert, Assurance, Charles, Mary Rose, Newcastle, Revenge, Victory, Yarmouth.

Advice, Bonaventure, Cambridge, Diamond, Dreadnought, Dunkirk, Falcon, Foresight, Greenwich, Hampshire, Henrietta, Mary, Monck, Prince, Rainbow, Ruby, Sovereign, St Andrew, St George, St Michael, Sweepstakes, Unicorn, York.

Tromp told his sister that he had quite enjoyed the day: 'We went into the dance and God be praised we are sound and have enjoyed ourselves like Kings' – a curious sentiment for a republican. Rupert was poorly supported by the French, and de Ruyter made brilliant tactical use of inferior force.

1708 Rear-Admiral Charles Wager (*Expedition*) fought twelve Spanish treasure-ships off Puerto Cartagena. Ships: *Expedition, Kingston, Portland*. Detachment of Brig-Gen Thomas Handasyd's Regiment was present. Spanish *Gobierno* captured; *San Jose* blew up. Wreck located 1986.

1781 *Atalanta* and *Trepassey* taken by the American *Alliance* about 120 miles S.E. of Halifax. All three captains killed and *Atalanta* retaken.

1794 Admiral Earl Howe's first action with Rear-Admiral Villaret-Joyeuse, 400 miles W. by S. of Ushant. Classic confusion. Howe was searching for Montagu, who was seeking Nielly.
See 1 June 1794.

1798 First Sick Bay introduced by Lord St Vincent in the Mediterranean Fleet.

1803 *Albion* captured the French *Franchise* 70 miles W. by S. of Ushant.

1803 *Victory* captured the French *Embuscade* 140 miles N.E. by N. of Cape Ortegal.

1831 The third-in-command at Trafalgar, William Carnegie, Earl of Northesk, Admiral of the Red, died in Albemarle Street, London. Born 10 April 1756. Flag in *Britannia* (100) in Collingwood's line at Trafalgar. C-in-C Plymouth 1827–30. Buried with Nelson and Collingwood in St Paul's Cathedral.
See 4 May 1810, 2 July 1853.

1855 Anglo-French squadron bombarded Arabat, Sea of Azov. British ships: *Ardent, Arrow, Beagle, Lynx, Medina, Miranda, Recruit, Snake, Stromboli, Vesuvius, Viper*. French ships: *Brandon, Fulton, Lucifer, Mégère.*

1855 *Swallow* and *Wrangler* captured or destroyed several Russian vessels off Genitchi (Genichesk), Sea of Azov.

1891 *Hearty* sailed from Kinsale for her first fishery protection patrol. First RN ship dedicated to fishery protection work. Her blue and yellow pennant had been authorised for signatories to the 1883 North Europe Maritime Powers Sea Fisheries convention.

1915 Admiral Sir Henry Jackson succeeded Admiral of the Fleet Lord Fisher as First Sea Lord, following Fisher's resignation over the Dardanelles debacle.
See 30 October 1914, 17 May 1915.

The light cruiser HMS *Ceylon* during the Korean War. (*NMRN W&L 1213F*)

1919 Dr John Holland Rose appointed the first Vere Harmsworth Professor of Naval History at Cambridge. The Chair was endowed by Lord Rothermere in memory of his son, Lt the Hon. Vere Sidney Tudor Harmsworth RNVR, of Hawke Division, RN Division, killed in action at the Battle of Ancre, the final act of the Battle of the Somme, 13 November 1916. Rose was succeeded in 1934 as Professor of Imperial and Naval History by Admiral Sir Herbert Richmond. The chair 'has long been lost to colonial historians' – Paul Kennedy.

See 28 September 1999.

1941 Destroyer *Mashona* sunk by German aircraft in S.W. Approaches (52.58N, 11.36W), returning from *Bismarck* action.

1941 Landing party from submarine *Upright* blew up the railway S.W. of Punto Stilo light, S. Italy.

1942 Destroyers *Eridge*, *Hero* and *Hurworth* sank U-568 off Sollum (32.42N, 24.53E).

1943 Liberator E/120 sank U-304 in N. Atlantic (54.50N, 37.20W). Convoy HX 240.

1943 Hudson M/608 sank U-755 N.E. of Valencia (39.58N, 01.41E). First sinking of a U-boat by the RAF with rockets.

1944 MTB 732 inadvertently sunk by *La Combattante* (Free French) off Selsey Bill.

1962 The First Boom Defence Squadron of the Scotland Command, HM ships *Laymoor*, *Barnstone* and *Barbican*, Cdr J.H. Groom RN, Commander B.D., sailed from Rosyth for a seven-day courtesy visit to Leirvik in Norway.

See 15 July 1960, 23 November 1979.

1964 Fiftieth anniversary of the foundation of the Royal Naval Air Service and the (roughly) 25th anniversary of the Admiralty regaining control of naval aviation celebrated in a royal review by HRH Prince Philip at RNAS Yeovilton. Prince Philip, accompanied by Vice-Admiral Sir Richard Smeeton, FONAC, opened the Fleet Air Arm Museum.

A flypast was led by a Swordfish piloted by Rear-Admiral P.D. Gick, FONFT, who flew in the *Bismarck* action and in the Western Desert; in the rear cockpit was Rear-Admiral H.R.B. Janvrin, FOAC, who had been a Swordfish observer at Taranto, and Lt-Cdr C. Topliss of HMS *Hermes* who flew in a Barracuda as a CPO TAG against the *Tirpitz*, was standing at the salute.

1972 Admiral of the Fleet HRH The Duke of Windsor died.

See 20 January 1936, 12 December 1936.

29 May

1758 Seven Years War. French two-decker *Raisonnable* (64), en route to Louisbourg, sighted off Ushant by a squadron under Capt Edward Pratten in *Intrepid*. He detached two ships to engage; *Dorsetshire* (70), Capt Peter Denis, caught and defeated the enemy before *Achilles* (60), Capt Hon. Samuel Barrington, caught up and settled the matter. *Raisonnable* 'being a fine ship, was bought into the Royal Navy' – Laird Clowes. Battle Honour: *Raisonnable* 1758, complemented on another May day 183 years later by *Bismarck* 1941 being gained by the heavy cruiser *Dorsetshire*.

See 27 May 1941.

1794 Admiral Earl Howe's second action with the French fleet under Rear-Admiral Villaret-Joyeuse, 400 miles W. by S. of Ushant. *Castor*, taken 10 May, retaken by *Carysfort*.

See 1 June 1794.

1797 Boats of *Lively* and *Minerve* cut out the French *Mutine* at Santa Cruz, Tenerife. A few of the 11th Regiment were in the boats.
Battle Honour: *Mutine* 1797.

See 18 April 1797.

1822 Half-module iron water tanks introduced for gunboats and small vessels.

1831 Philip Colomb, future vice-admiral and naval thinker, born.

See 13 October 1899, 27 May 1909.

1855 VC: Lt Cecil William Buckley (*Miranda*), Lt Hugh Talbot Burgoyne (*Swallow*), Gunner John Robarts (*Ardent*). Destruction of seventy-three Russian vessels and food stores at Genitchi (Genichesk), Sea of Azov. Ships: *Ardent, Arrow, Beagle, Lynx, Medina, Miranda, Recruit, Snake, Stromboli, Swallow, Vesuvius, Viper, Wrangler.*

1873 Starshell for rifled guns introduced.

1877 *Shah* and *Amethyst* (Rear-Admiral de Horsey) fought the Peruvian rebel *Huascar* off Ho, Peru. *Shah* fired first British torpedo used in action. Also demonstrated poor shooting with her 9-in gun, and inadequacy of its ammunition.

1917 First air/sea rescue (by flying boat).

1922 The light cruiser *Raleigh*, flagship of the NA&WI Station, arrived in Washington, the first ship of her size to fly the White Ensign within sight of the Capitol for more than a century. Admiral Sir William Pakenham, the C-in-C, was received by President Warren Harding. Ten weeks later the ship was lost.

See 8 August 1922.

1935 John Martin Carruthers Garrod, future CGRM, born at Darjeeling.

See 17 April 2009.

1940 Destroyer *Wakeful*, Cdr R.L. Fisher RN, torpedoed by German E-boat S-30 close to the Kwint Whistle Buoy off the Belgian coast after lifting hundreds of men of the British Expeditionary Force from Bray Dunes outside Dunkirk. The ship broke in two and sank quickly in 57ft

The tread-plate and badge of the destroyer HMS *Wakeful*. Sunk by an E-boat attack when carrying troops from Dunkirk, but recovered in 2004 and presented to the Royal Naval Museum. (*NMRN 2004/18*)

HMS *Shah* and HMS *Amethyst* in action with the rebel Peruvian ironclad *Huascar* in 1877. (*NMRN*)

of water with the loss of 690 men. Destroyer *Grafton* sunk by U-62 nearby. Destroyer *Grenade* and AA ship *Crested Eagle* sunk by German aircraft at Dunkirk. Operation Dynamo.

The *Wakeful* wreck, a designated war grave, lay undisturbed for sixty years. However, with the increasing draught of merchant ships using Antwerp, Zeebrugge and Ostend, the wreck of *Wakeful* posed an increasing hazard to shipping. The proposal to move the two parts of the hull of the V&W destroyer to a specially dredged deep trench were later amended to removing 10ft of her upper superstructure to allow clearance for shipping.

1941 *Hereward* sunk by German aircraft 5 miles S. of Crete (35.20N, 25.30E) and *Imperial* sunk by *Hotspur* (35.25N, 25.20E), after breakdown of steering gear. *Decoy, Dido, Ajax* and *Orion* damaged during the same operations, withdrawing troops from Heraklion. *Orion* reached Alexandria with 10 tons of fuel oil and two rounds of 6-in ammunition.

1942 Submarine *Turbulent* sank the Italian destroyer *Emanuele Pessagno* 78 miles N.W. of Benghazi, in less than a minute.

1982 3 Cdo Bde (2 Para) recaptured Darwin and, reinforced by a company of 42 Cdo, took Goose Green the next day.

VC: Lt-Col H. Jones, 2 Para. Posthumous.

1992 Malta Siege Bell Memorial dedicated in the presence of HM The Queen at Valetta, to the memory of the 7,000 who died, 10 June 1940 to 13 May 1943.

See p.696.

2005 Admiral Sir Gordon Tait died aged 83. Born 30 October 1921 at Timaru, South Island, New Zealand. He passed his 'Perisher' in 1946 and in the next ten years commanded a record number of submarines, *Teredo, Solent, Ambush, Onyx* and *Sanguine*. Naval secretary 1971–4. 'Tait was always at ease with himself and with the world. Although self-effacing, he was an excellent leader: quiet, intelligent and cool under pressure. He was also a superb shiphandler.' – *The Daily Telegraph*, 6 June 2005. As Second Sea Lord from 1977 he was the highest-ranking New Zealand-born officer in the Royal Navy. He retired to New Zealand, 'like an old salmon; I always knew I would come back'.

2005 Rear-Admiral Sir Nigel Cecil, the last Flag Officer Malta, presented to the Malta Maritime Museum the flags he had hauled down at *St Angelo* on 31 March 1979.

See 7 July 1975, 31 March 1979.

30 May

1757 *Eagle* and *Medway* captured the French privateer *Duc d'Aquitaine* 100 miles S.W. of Ushant.

1781 *Flora* (34) captured the Dutch *Castor* (36). *Crescent* struck to the *Briel* but was not taken. Both actions 100 miles W. of Cape Spartel, Morocco.

1798 *Hydra* drove ashore the French *Confiante* near Beuzeville, Normandy. *Confiante* abandoned and burned by *Hydra*'s boats next day. *Vesuvius* and *Trial* drove ashore the French *Vésuve* near the mouth of the Dives River. The French vessel was refloated and escaped.

1841 Boats of *Dolphin* captured the Brazilian slaver *Firme* off Whydah, Dahomey.

1859 Chaplain to the Fleet became Chaplain of the Fleet, to rank as a rear-admiral.

See 13 May 1859, 23 October 1876.

1862 Landing party of *Centaur* at the defence of Sungkiang, near Shanghai.

1887 Two boats of *Turquoise* captured a slave dhow off Pemba, East Africa.

1900 Royal Marines moved in to defend the Legations at Peking.

See 10 and 24 June 1900, 5 September 1900.

1906 The modern battleship *Montagu*, Capt T.B.S. Adair RN, ran aground on Shutter Point at the S.W. end of Lundy at 0212 in thick fog and was wrecked.

See 21 August 1910, 14 November 1918, 8 August 1922, 18 May 1940.

The 13,505-ton Duncan-class ship, commissioned at Devonport in July 1903, had been engaged in early WT trials in the Bristol Channel. Both screws were lost and efforts to haul her off failed. A major salvage operation mounted over several months by the Liverpool Salvage Association recovered her 12-in and 6-in guns but the ship was a CTL. Her wreck was sold for £4,250. Capt Adair and his Navigating Officer, Lt J.H. Dathan RN, were courts-martialled in *Victory* at Portsmouth from 16–21 August 1906 on charges that they did negligently and by default hazard, strand and lose his Majesty's ship *Montagu* and did 'suffer' the ship to be hazarded, stranded and lost. Both were found guilty and were severely reprimanded and dismissed their ship, Lt Dathan also losing two years' seniority.

The battleship HMS *Montagu* on the rocks at Lundy Island, 1906. (*NMRN*)

HMS *Agamemnon* (1852). (*NMRN*)

1915 Dummy *Tiger* sunk by UB-8 off Strati Island in Aegean.

1919 'Whereas we consider it necessary to employ a qualified Private RMLI to supervise the work of re-footing woollen socks at the Depot, Royal Marines, Deal . . . We beg leave humbly to recommend that Your Majesty may be graciously pleased, by Your Order in Council, to sanction the payment of an allowance of 1*s* a day to the Royal Marine appointed to supervise the work of re-footing socks at the Depot, Royal Marines, Deal, with effect from the 20th March, 1919. The Lords Commissioners of Your Majesty's Treasury have signified their concurrence in this proposal.' Admiralty Order in Council N.19515.1919.

See 10 August 1922.

1942 Battleship *Ramillies* damaged and *British Loyalty* (tanker) sunk by Japanese midget submarine at Diego Suarez.

1943 Submarine *Untamed* sunk by accident (flooded through log tube) in the Campbeltown Exercise Area. Salvaged 5 July and renamed *Vitality*.

1944 Destroyer *Milne* sank U-289 off Norway (73.32N, 00.28E).

1951 Admiral of the Fleet Sir Reginald Tyrwhitt died. Commanded Harwich forces in the First World War. C-in-C China Station, 1927–9; C-in-C The Nore, 1930–3.

See 21 May 1941.

1982 Maj-Gen J.J. Moore, RM, arrived at San Carlos in *Fearless* as Commander Land Forces. Operation Corporate.

1997 Hydrographic (H) and Meteorology and Oceanography (METOC) specialisations amalgamated to form a new X (HM) specialisation, reflecting the need to present unified environmental advice to the Command, embracing the atmosphere of the seabed. DCI(RN) 81/97.

31 May

1520 Henry VIII embarked in *Henry Grace à Dieu* en route for the Field of the Cloth of Gold.

1762 *Active* and *Favourite* captured the Spanish treasure-ship *Hermiona* 20 miles S.S.E. of Cape de Santa Maria, Portugal.

1796 *Agamemnon, Meleager, Peterel, Speedy* and boats of *Blanche* and *Diadem* captured six French vessels at Porto d'Oneglia, Italian Riviera.

1809 Boats of *Topaze* cut out nine vessels in Demata Bay, near Santa Maura (Levkas), Ionian group.

1900 Boxer Rebellion in China began. Called after the 'Righteous Harmony Fists'. Naval Brigade formed from *Centurion* (flag), *Barfleur, Endymion, Aurora, Orlando* and *Terrible*, and landed initially to reinforce RMLI at the Legations.

1910 Reserve Decoration, RD, instituted.

1915 Maiden flight of C1 – first coastal patrol non-rigid airship.

1916 Battle of Jutland. Admiral Sir John Jellicoe (*Iron Duke*) engaged the German High Seas Fleet under Vice-Admiral Scheer (*Friedrich der Grosse*).
Battle Honour: Jutland 1916.

Ships: Grand Fleet 1st BS: *Marlborough, Revenge, Hercules, Agincourt, Colossus, Collingwood, Neptune, St Vincent.* 4th BS: *Iron Duke, Royal Oak, Superb, Canada, Benbow, Bellerophon, Temeraire, Vanguard.* 2nd BS: *King George V, Ajax, Centurion, Erin, Orion, Monarch, Conqueror, Thunderer.* 3rd BCS: *Invincible,* Inflexible, Indomitable.*

1st CS: *Defence,* Warrior,† Duke of Edinburgh, Black Prince.** 2nd CS: *Minotaur, Hampshire, Cochrane, Shannon.* 4th LCS: *Calliope, Caroline, Constance, Comus, Royalist, Canterbury.* Attached: *Bellona, Blanche, Boadicea, Active, Oak, Abdiel.* 4th DF: *Tipperary,* Broke, Achates, Porpoise, Spitfire, Unity, Garland, Ambuscade, Ardent,* Fortune,* Sparrowhawk,* Contest, Shark,* Acasta, Ophelia, Christopher, Owl, Hardy, Midge.* 11th DF: *Castor* (LC), *Kempenfelt, Ossory, Mystic, Moon, Morning Star, Magic, Mounsey, Mandate, Marne, Minion, Manners, Michael, Mons, Martial, Milbrook.* 12th DF: *Faulknor, Marksman, Obedient, Maenad, Opal, Mary Rose, Marvel, Menace, Nessus, Narwhal, Mindful, Onslaught, Munster, Nonsuch, Noble, Mischief.*

Battlecruiser Fleet (Vice-Admiral Sir David Beatty): 1st BCS: *Lion, Princess Royal, Queen Mary,* Tiger.* 2nd BCS: *New Zealand, Indefatigable.** 5th BS: *Barham, Valiant, Warspite, Malaya.*

1st LCS: *Galatea, Phaeton, Inconstant, Cordelia.* 2nd LCS: *Southampton, Birmingham, Nottingham, Dublin.* 3rd LCS: *Falmouth, Yarmouth, Birkenhead, Gloucester, Chester.* Seaplane carrier: *Engadine.* 1st DF: *Fearless* (LC), *Acheron, Ariel, Attack, Hydra, Badger, Goshawk, Defender, Lizard, Lapwing.* 9th and 10th DF: *Lydiard, Liberty, Landrail, Laurel, Moorsom, Morris, Turbulent,* Termagant.* 13th DF: *Champion* (LC), *Nestor,* Nomad,* Narbrough, Obdurate, Petard, Pelican, Nerissa, Onslow, Moresby, Nicator.*

*Sunk. †Foundered next day.

German ships sunk: *Elbing, Lützow, Frauenlob, Pommern, Rostock, Wiesbaden,* S-35, V-4, V-27, V-29, V-48.

VC. Cdr the Hon. Edward Barry Stewart Bingham (*Nestor*). Cdr Loftus William Jones (*Shark*) (see 24 June 1916) for heroism during close action with enemy cruiser and destroyers. Posthumous. Although wounded twice (including loss of leg) he kept fighting and then went down with his ship.

Maj Francis John William Harvey, RMLI (*Lion*) 'whilst mortally wounded and virtually the only survivor after the explosion of an enemy shell in Q gun house, with great presence of mind and devotion to duty he ordered the magazine to be flooded, thereby saving the ship. He died shortly afterwards.' John Travers Cornwell, Boy 1st Class (*Chester*) for devotion to duty.

Jutland Losses, 1916

	British		German	
	Engaged	**Sunk**	**Engaged**	**Sunk**
Battleships	28	–	22	1
Battlecruisers	9	3	5	1
Armoured Cruisers	8	3	–	–
Light Cruisers	26	–	11	4
Destroyers	75	8	61	5
Casualties	**6,748 men**		**3,058 men**	

1918 Destroyer *Fairy* rammed and sank UC-75 in North Sea (53.57N, 00.09E).

1918 Royal Marine field force landed at Murmansk; based at *Glory III*.

1926 Pembroke Dockyard closed until 1941.

1940 Sloop *Weston* sank U-13 off Lowestoft. Convoy FN 184.

1940 General Viscount Gort VC, C-in-C British Expeditionary Force, taken off the beaches at La Panne near Dunkirk at dusk under heavy air attack by the minesweeper *Hebe*. 'Thank you for looking after me so nicely' said the general when he transferred at midnight to an MTB for passage to Dover.

1943 Light cruiser *Orion* bombarded Pantelleria.

1945 First class of Leading Patrolmen completed course at Beechwood Camp, Plymouth.

1966 Fiftieth anniversary of the Battle of Jutland commemorated in a service at St Martin-in-the-Fields attended by 500 veterans. Wreaths laid in Trafalgar Square at the busts of Admirals Jellicoe and Beatty by the Second Sea Lord, the West German Naval Attaché and by a representative of Admiral of the Fleet Lord Chatfield, the senior surviving officer. The destroyers *Defender* and *Dainty* rendezvoused with the Federal German Navy ships *Karlsruhe* and *Braunschweig* off Jutland where wreaths were put onto the waters.

See 2 April 2001, 21 October 2005, 31 May 2006.

1966 The Admiralty Chart and Chronometer Depot, Aden, closed. DCI(RN) 703/66.

1967 Naval War Memorial to RN men, especially men of the Malta Port Division, lost in the Mediterranean in the Second World War, unveiled in the Chapel of St Anne in HMS *St Angelo*, Malta. DCI(RN) 571/67.

1968 The RN Fleet Club Malta, formerly the Fleet Canteen, closed after seventy-one years' service.

See 1 February 1897.

1976 Dover Mooring and Salvage Depot closed.

1981 Last parade of RN Division Old Comrades Association at Greenwich.

See 25 April 1925, 26 May 1951, 13 November 2003.

2001 *Herald* paid off after twenty-seven years' Hydrographic service. Last of class of four, sister ships being *Hecate*, *Hecla*, *Hydra*.

2006 The destroyer *Edinburgh*, Cdr Scott Verney RN, and the German frigate *Hessen* held a combined service of commemoration at sea off the Jutland Bank for the men of both nations who were lost on 31 May and 1 June 1916, the 90th anniversary of the battle.

See 31 May 1966, 2 April 2001, 17 and 21 October 2005.

The Battle of Jutland, 1916

During the First World War both the German and British Fleets laid plans to catch the other at a disadvantage in order to obtain supremacy at sea. On 31 May 1916, the German Fleet made a sortie, and the British Fleet sailed in the hope of catching the German battlecruiser force. At about 1400 both fleets were at sea, and escorts of each closed to investigate a Danish steamer, and so sighted each other.

The British battlecruisers, with the modern Queen Elizabeth-class battleships in company, raced to attack, and sighted the enemy battlecruisers at about 1530. Fire was opened at 1549 at 15,000yds, and just after 1600, the *Indefatigable* blew up and sank. She was the first capital ship sunk in action since the Dutch wars. At 1626, the *Queen Mary* also blew up and sank. 'Beatty turned to me and said "There seems to be something wrong with our bloody ships today", a remark which needed neither comment nor answer.' – Chatfield, Beatty's Flag Captain in *Lion*. By now the German ships were being hard hit, and turned away to lead the British towards the main German Fleet.

At 1638, the *Southampton* sighted the main German Fleet. Admiral Beatty in *Lion* realised the trap, and turned to lead the Germans towards Admiral Jellicoe. At 1817, the Grand Fleet opened fire on the Germans. The battlecruiser *Invincible* blew up just after 1830, but four German battlecruisers were badly damaged. The main action was over by 2100.

During the night the German Fleet crossed astern of the British Fleet and reached safety, although they had to sink the battlecruiser *Lützow*. British destroyers sank the battleship *Pommern* with torpedoes.

Although the British lost twice as many men as the Germans, and also more ships, the Germans suffered more damage. While inconclusive in itself, the engagement was a strategic victory for the British Fleet.

1 June

1360 Establishment of Court of Admiralty.
See 1 June 1960.

1666 The first day of the 'Four Days' Battle', perhaps the longest and most intensive sea fight in the age of sail. The Duke of Albemarle (*Royal Charles*) fought the Dutch fleet of eighty-five sail under Admiral de Ruyter about 30 miles E.N.E. of the North Foreland. Having divided his fleet, Monck was badly outnumbered and severely handled.
Battle Honour: Four Days Battle 1666.

Ships: *Amity, Antelope, Assurance, Black Bull, Black Spread Eagle, Bonaventure, Breda, Bristol, Clove Tree, Convertine, Diamond, Dragon, Dreadnought, Essex, Expedition, Gloucester, Greyhound, Happy Entrance, Henrietta, Henry, Hound, House of Swyte (of Sweeds), Leopard, Lilly, Little Katherine, Little Unicorn, Loyal George, Mary Rose, Plymouth, Portland, Portsmouth, Princess, Rainbow, Reserve, Revenge, Richard, Royal Charles, Royal James, Royal Katherine, Royal Prince, St George, St Paul, Sevenoaks, Spread Eagle, Swallow, Swiftsure, Triumph, Vanguard, Victory, Young Prince.*

1705 First Pensioners arrived at Royal Hospital, Greenwich. The remains of many, buried opposite the hospital, were reburied in the Pleasaunce away to the east, in a mass grave under a single plaque which reads 'They served their country in the wars which established the naval supremacy of England, and died the honoured recipients of her gratitude.'

1794 'The Glorious First of June'. Admiral Earl Howe (*Queen Charlotte*) defeated Rear-Admiral Villaret-Joyeuse (*Montagne*) W. of Ushant.
Battle Honour: First of June 1794.

Institution of Naval Gold Medal, large for flag officers, small for captains, and award of gold chains on which to hang them for Howe, five of his six flag officers and his First Captain in *Queen Charlotte*. Ships: *Alfred, Barfleur, Bellerophon, Brunswick, Caesar, Culloden, Defence, Gibraltar, Glory, Impregnable, Invincible, Leviathan, Majestic, Marlborough, Montagu, Orion, Queen, Queen Charlotte, Ramillies, Royal George, Royal Russell, Sovereign, Thunderer, Tremendous, Valiant*; *Audacious* on 28 May only. Frigates, etc.: *Aquilon, Charon, Comet, Incendiary, Latona, Niger, Pegasus, Phaeton, Ranger, Rattler, Southampton, Venus*, Captured: *Achille, America, Impetueux, Juste, Northumberland, Sans-Pareil*. Sunk: *Vengeur-du-Peuple*. Regiments: 2nd, 25th, 29th, 69th.

The 2nd Foot, now the Princess of Wales's Royal Regiment (see 27 May 1847) and the 29th, now the Mercian Regiment, have as a battle honour a Naval Crown, superscribed '1 June, 1794'.

See 17 December 1857.

Admiral Howe's instructions were to safeguard British trade, to prevent a convoy of grain from America from reaching France, and to defeat the enemy fleet. His tactics were to close the enemy fleet, to break through the line at all points and to engage from the leeward position. He captured six ships and sank one, but the grain convoy reached France. Nelson referred disparagingly to less than decisive operations as 'Lord Howe victories'.

1795 Flag officers, captains and commanders given new dress uniform and epaulettes. An admiral's rank was denoted by stars on the latter. For captains they were plain, and a captain of less than three years' seniority wore a single epaulette on his right shoulder. A commander wore one on his left.

1795 Capt Horatio Nelson made a Colonel of Marines by Lord Spencer, First Lord of the Admiralty. This sinecure was given to the three senior serving post-captains and was given up on reaching flag rank.

1808 *Redwing* captured two Spanish vessels and destroyed another and a battery at Bolonia, S.W. Spain.

1813 Frigate *Shannon* (38) captured the American *Chesapeake* 20 miles off Boston, Massachusetts in less than fifteen minutes.
Battle Honour: *Chesapeake* 1813.

1847 Board of Selection gazetted, to decide who was entitled to the newly instituted Naval General Service Medal: Admirals Sir Thomas Byam Martin and Sir Thomas Bladen Capel, and Rear-Admiral Sir James Alexander Gordon. Their terms of reference were extended in 1848 and again in 1849. 'It cannot be pretended that the

Selection was well made . . . Honour was however tardily done to hundreds of gallant and deserving men.'

1848 *Scout* captured two pirate junks a few miles off Chimmo Bay.

1857 Destruction of over seventy war junks at Fat Shan Creek by gunboats, tenders and boats of squadron: *Bustard, Coromandel, Forester, Haughty, Hong Kong, Opossum, Plover, Sir Charles Forbes, Starling, Staunch.*

1901 Distinguished Service Cross, originally known as Conspicuous Service Cross, instituted for gallantry in the presence of the enemy for warrant and subordinate officers of the RN not eligible by rank for the DSO. Renamed October 1914 and opened to all naval officers below rank of Lt-Cdr. In 1931 eligibility extended to MN officers. In 1940 eligibility again extended to Army and RAF officers serving on board HM ships. Following the 1993 review of gallantry awards, DSM discontinued and the DSC was opened to all serving personnel for gallantry in action against the enemy at sea. Equivalent of the MC and DFC.

See 14 October 1914.

1909 Capt R.F. Scott's second expedition to the Antarctic left East India Docks, London, in *Terra Nova.*

1923 Official inauguration of the restoration of *Victory* in Portsmouth Dockyard. With the RM band of the battleship *Malaya* playing 'Rule, Britannia', Lady Fremantle, wife of Admiral Sir Sydney Fremantle, C-in-C Portsmouth, ceremonially lowered the supporting cherubs from the figurehead to allow work to start on restoring the bows to their Trafalgar aspect.

See 16 December 1921.

1927 *St Vincent*, Boys' Training Establishment commissioned at Forton Barracks, Gosport, by Capt P.L.H. Noble, RN, later Admiral Sir Percy Noble, C-in-C W. Approaches.

See 22 June 1923, 8 December 1968, 2 April 1969.

1933 Five naval officers serving on the China Station, having secured special leave, sailed from Hong Kong in the 24 ton 54ft ketch *Taimoshan* (built at their own expense) for the UK via Panama. Lt-Cdr M.B. Sherwood of the carrier *Hermes*, Surg-Lt C. Ommaney-Davis of the sloop *Bridgewater* and three submariners, Lt G.S. Salt, R.E.D. Ryder and P.S. Francis of *Oswald, Olympus* and *Otus*, arrived at Dartmouth on 31 May 1934.

See 1 August 1923, 15 October 1940, 28 March 1942.

1939 Submarine *Thetis* foundered in Liverpool Bay on acceptance trials. Submarine sank as a result of a torpedo tube rear door being opened after the vent, blocked by paint, gave a false indication of the tube being dry. Only four men escaped despite the stern being clear of the water and rescue forces being on the scene. The dead included senior shipyard workers. As a result a reamer was fitted to test vents and a clamp, known as the Thetis Clamp, was fitted to all subsequent boats. This clamp would allow the tube to be re-sealed if opened wrongly. Submarine salvaged and commissioned as *Thunderbolt*.

See 15 December 1940, 14 March 1943.

Fleet Air Arm Memorial outside the Ministry of Defence, Main Building, London. (*RN*)

Sea King Helicopters and equipment onboard RFA *Argus* when en route to the Adriatic. (*RN*)

1940 Destroyers *Basilisk*, *Havant*, *Keith* and minesweeper *Skipjack* sunk by German aircraft off Dunkirk. Operation Dynamo.

1941 Cruiser *Calcutta* torpedoed and sunk by German aircraft 100 miles N.W. of Alexandria (31.55N, 28.05E).

1941 The evacuation of the Army from Crete, which saw the fiercest fighting the Royal Navy had engaged in since the Four Days Battle (between 1 and 4 June 1666) in the Dutch Wars, ended.
Battle Honour: Crete 1941.
See p.306.

1942 Attack on Sydney harbour by four Japanese midget submarines: all sunk, including *Kuttabul*, an accommodation ship.

1943 Sloop *Starling* sank U-202 in N. Atlantic (56.12N, 39.52W).

1943 Beaufighter B/236 sank U-418 in E. Atlantic (47.05N, 08.55W).

1943 Light cruiser *Penelope* and destroyers *Paladin* and *Petard* bombarded Pantelleria in central Mediterranean.

1943 First FAA Corsair squadron (1830) formed.

1947 First of re-formed RNVR air squadrons formed; 1831 NAS (fighters) at RNAS Stretton near Warrington. Joined on 18 August 1952 by 1841 NAS (anti-submarine).
See 15 January 1957, 18 February 1957.

1948 *Reclaim* commissioned: RN's first deep-water diving tender.
See 25 October 1979, 5 February 2007.

1948 *Renown*, the last battlecruiser, paid off after thirty-one years' service.

1951 Coupons introduced to ration duty-free tobacco.
See 27 January 1989.

1954 First publication of (*Portsmouth*) *Navy News*, funded with £350 from the RN Barracks pig swill fund. Lead story was the commissioning of the carrier *Albion*.
See 19 June 2003.

1960 The 600th anniversary of the Court of Admiralty in England marked by a service of thanksgiving at St Paul's Cathedral attended by HRH The Duke of Edinburgh. AFO 1403/60.
See 8 June 1960.

1961 Royal Victoria Yard, Deptford, which had victualled warships since reign of George II, closed.

1963 HMS *Dunkirk*, Cdr C.R.A. O'Brien RN, paid off at Devonport after a 22-month commission, the last unconverted Battle-class destroyer in the Royal Navy.

1965 HMS *Malabar* recommissioned at Moresby House, Ireland Island, Bermuda.
See 31 March 1951, 31 March 1976, 31 March 1995.

1969 Installation of pay computer at Gosport in new *Centurion*.

1970 The fleet tanker RFA *Ennerdale*, 47,000 tons, struck a reef off the Seychelles and sank in 100ft of water. 'Probably the biggest ship under naval ownership [i.e. auxiliary] to be lost in peace or war' – Desmond Wettern, *The Decline of British Sea Power*, pp.368–9.
See 17 November 1962.

It was decided on immediate action to release her 42,000 tons of fuel while the S.E. monsoon would carry it clear of the islands. The swell prevented the placing of explosives alongside the hull using boats and divers. Lt-Cdr Brian H.L. Braidwood RN, Far East Clearance Diving Officer, working with Lt Max Kenworthy RN, Senior Pilot detached from 847 NAS, devised a method of lowering three mortar bombs on a pallet from a Wessex HU Mk 5 and of igniting the cortex fuse inside the aircraft. This breached the port tanks and released about 12,000 tons of oil. To breach the starboard tanks, divers secured a 45ft wire pennant to the top of the wreck and, using a Gemini, joined it to a similar wire lowered from the Wessex. The Gemini raced clear, the Wessex crew lit the cortex fuse and released the bomb tray which, on its 90ft pennant, sank along side the vents of the lower tanks. Later in the operation the submarine *Cachalot* was unable to torpedo the wreckage and the torpedo warheads were removed, positioned and detonated in the same way. Some warheads failed to explode and pre-cut delay fuses were added which Braidwood ignited on the surface while suspended from the helicopter's winch wire. Braidwood: QCBC; Kenworthy and Air Mechanician First Class Michael McSorley: QCVSA. DCI(RN) 118/71.

1973 Sixth Patrol Craft Squadron based at HMS *Tamar* renamed the Hong Kong Squadron with funnel badges of the Hong Kong lion. *Yarnton* (Leader), *Beachampton*, *Wasperton*, *Wolverton* and *Monkton*. First SOHKS Cdr W.M. Kelly RN.
See 16 September 1971, 28 April 1972.

1973 Wearing of CPOs' cuff buttons discontinued for FCPOs and Fleet Chief Wrens. DCI(RN) S.93/73.

1975 RM detachment of thirty-five men formed at Faslane to guard Clyde Submarine Base. Later expanded to become Comacchio Group, later Fleet Protection Group Royal Marines. Principal role to protect national nuclear deterrent.
See 2 April 1945, 1 May 1980, 1 October 2000.

1976 End of the third, and last, Cod War. HMG accepted the Icelandic 200-mile limit and soon followed suit.
See 31 August 1958.

1982 5 Infantry Brigade (Brig M.J.A. Wilson) disembarked from *Canberra* and *Norland* at San Carlos.

1990 *Norfolk*, Type 23 frigate and first of class, commissioned by Capt Jonathon Band RN.
See 29 October 1984, 10 July 1987, 6 May 2005, 22 November 2006.

1998 Lt Katherine Babbington, first woman to win the Queen's Sword at Dartmouth, presented with the sword by Her Majesty at Buckingham Palace. Lt Babbington was serving in *Sandown* in the Gulf when Divisions were held.

1998 Hydrographic ships changed their Pennant Number Designator (PND) from 'A' (Auxiliary) to 'H' (Hydrographic). The emphasis of the Hydrographic Surveying Squadron (HSS) had changed over the previous decade, with priority given to Combat Survey Operations and Rapid Environmental Assessment. The allocation of a new PND reflected concern that the use of 'A' on a White Ensign hull caused confusion over the legal and operational status of these warships. *Endurance* alone retains her 'A' pennant number. HM Surveying Ships completed a change of livery from white and buff to grey during summer 1997. DCI(RN) 88/98.
See 1 March 1919.

2000 Fleet Air Arm Memorial, a bronze, winged figure of Daedalus beside the Thames near the Ministry of Defence, commemorating more than 6,000 men and women who died while serving in the RNAS and FAA, unveiled by HRH The Prince of Wales. Guard of Honour from RNAS Yeovilton and flypast by Sea Kings of 810, 849 and 771 NAS. Memorial dedicated by the Chaplain of the Fleet. Attended by HRH The Duke of York, Admiral Sir Michael Boyce, First Sea Lord, Admiral of the Fleet Sir Benjamin Bathurst, President of the Memorial Appeal, and Rear-Admiral Colin Cooke-Priest, Appeal Chairman.
See 20 May 1953, 11 September 2009.

2004 HRH Prince Michael of Kent promoted honorary rear-admiral, RNR.
See 1 November 1958, 2 March 2009, 1 August 2010.

2005 The First Sea Lord, Admiral Sir Alan West, launched the third edition of *The Royal Navy Day by Day* at a reception in Admiralty House, Whitehall.

2 JUNE

1653 Joint Admirals George Monck and Richard Deane (*Resolution*), with 105 ships, fought Admiral Maerten Tromp (*Brederode*), with ninety-eight ships and six fireships, off the Gabbard. The Dutch were reinforced but Monck again attacked.
Battle Honour: Gabbard 1653.

Red Sqn: *Adventure, Advice, Ann and Joyce, Bear, Diamond, Fair Sisters, Falmouth, Golden Falcon, Guinea, Hamburgh Merchant, Hannibal, Heart's Ease, Hound, Laurel, London, Loyalty, Malaga Merchant, Marmaduke, Martin, Mary, Mermaid, Pelican, Phoenix, Providence, Resolution, Sapphire, Society, Sophia, Speaker, Sussex, Thomas and William, Tiger, Triumph, Worcester, Violet.* Fireships: *Fortune, Fox, Renown.*

White Sqn: *Andrew, Anne Piercy, Assistance, Assurance, Centurion, Crown, Duchess, Exchange, Exchange, Expedition, Foresight, Gilly Flower, Globe, Industry, James, Lion, Lisbon Merchant, Merlin, Middleboro, Pearl, Peter, Portsmouth, Princess Maria, Prudent Mary, Raven, Reformation, Richard and Martha, Ruby, Sarah, Thomas and Lucy, Victory, Waterhound.* Fireships: *Falcion (Falcon).*

Blue Sqn: *Adventure, Amity, Arms of Holland, Benjamin, Blossom, Brazil, Convert, Convertine, Crescent, Dolphin, Dragon, Dragoneare, Eastland Merchant, Entrance (Happy Entrance), George, Gift, Great President (President), Jonathan, Kentish, King Ferdinando, Nicodemus, Nonsuch, Oak, Paul, Roebuck, Samuel Talbot, Samaritan, Success, Rainbow, Tulip, Vanguard, Welcome, William and John.* Fireship: *Hunter.* (The names *Adventure, Exchange* and *Phoenix* were each borne by two ships in the battle.)

Flags:

	van	*Triumph*	Vice-Adm James Peacock
Red	centre	*Resolution*	Joint Adms Monck and Deane
	rear	*Speaker*	Rear-Adm Samuel Howett
	van	*Victory*	Vice-Adm Lionel Lane
White	centre	*James*	Adm William Penn
	rear	*Andrew*	Rear-Adm Thomas Graves
	van	*Vanguard*	Vice-Adm Joseph Jordan
Blue	centre	*George*	Adm John Lawson
	rear	*Rainbow*	Rear-Adm William Goodson

1666 The second day of the 'Four Days' Battle'. English – forty-four ships; Dutch – eighty ships. Captured: *Black Spread-Eagle, Convertine, Essex, Swiftsure.*

1779 *Ruby* captured the French *Prudente* off Ile de la Gonave, West Indies.

1779 Frigate *Glasgow* (20), Capt Thomas Lloyd, carrying a cargo of gunpowder for Jamaica, caught fire in Montego Bay after the purser's steward, Richard Brace, set fire to the spirit room while stealing rum. The ship was soon alight and Capt Lloyd and his First Lieutenant, Richard Oakley, valiantly and efficiently supervised the jettisoning of the gunpowder, assisted by Cdr Horatio Nelson of the brig *Badger*. The *Glasgow* could not be saved and, the ship's company having been embarked in *Badger*, the wreck was towed out to sea where she exploded and sank. The Master of the *Glasgow*, Mr James Cobby, died of burns the following day. Capt Lloyd was honourably discharged by a court martial held in *Bristol* at Port Royal the following month. Brace was punished, leniently perhaps, with 100 lashes.

1805 Boats of *Loire* (38) cut out the Spanish privateer *Esperanza* in Camarinas Bay, N.W. Spain.
See 4 June 1805.

1805 *Diamond Rock*, Cdr James Maurice, surrendered to a strong French squadron under Capt Cosmao-Kerjulien (*Pluton*), after three days' bombardment.
See 7 January 1804.

1854 Parliament passed an Act 'to empower the Commissioners of the Admiralty to construct a tunnel between H.M. Dockyard at Devonport and H.M. Steam Yard at Keyham'.

1867 William Edmund Goodenough born. Noted cruiser commander in the First World War and C-in-C The Nore. Son of Cdre James Goodenough, Commodore of the Australia Station, killed by natives firing poisoned arrows in the Solomon Islands in 1875.
See 20 August 1875, 30 January 1945.

1904 The Woolston, Southampton, shipbuilding yard of John I. Thornycroft opened.

1915 Sloop *Odin* sank the Turkish *Marmoris* on River Tigris.

Rear-Admiral Sir Philip Broke BT, KCB (1776–1841)

Broke joined the Royal Naval Academy, Portsmouth in 1792. From 1793 to 1795 he served in the Mediterranean and fought in the battle of Cape St Vincent as a lieutenant. He was promoted captain in 1805 and appointed to the *Shannon* (38) in 1806. During the period after Trafalgar when there was little sea warfare to be had he fitted the guns of the ship with sights and trained her gunners. This was a new departure, since Nelson's philosophy had always been to close the range and batter the enemy. At a time when several British frigates were taken in unequal fights with large American frigates, the *Shannon* encountered the frigate *Chesapeake* on 1 June 1813. *Chesapeake* had a new and untrained crew and *Shannon* invited the Captain of the *Chesapeake* to take a month's training before taking on the *Shannon*. *Chesapeake*, however, sailed to fight the *Shannon* and was defeated after eleven minutes. Her Captain died of his wounds and was buried with full military honours, with the American flag, six captains RN as pall-bearers and six captains of the 64th Foot as escort. Broke was severely injured, and retired having been made KB. He died in 1841 after suffering constant pain from his wounds. He declined a request by his First Lieutenant to hoist additional battle ensigns, remarking that 'we have always been an unassuming ship'.

Rear-Admiral Sir Philip Broke (1776–1841). (*NMRN 1973/291*)

1941 Corvette *Periwinkle* and destroyer *Wanderer* sank U-147 in N.W. Approaches (56.38N, 10.24W). Convoy OB 329.

1942 Blenheim aircraft of 203 Sqn and Swordfish of 815 Sqn crippled U-652 off Sollum (31.55N, 21.13E). Sunk by U-81.

1943 Destroyer *Jervis* and *Vasilissa Olga* (Greek) sank the Italian TB *Castore* and the two ships she was escorting 1 mile off Cape Spartivento.

1953 Coronation Day. Royal Salutes fired by HM ships worldwide, including the light cruiser HMS *Newcastle* 'lying within sight and sound of the enemy' in Korea – Brassey, 1954, pp.18, 399. HRH The Duke of Edinburgh appointed Captain-General Royal Marines.

1970 The new home of the RN Tactical School in the Woolwich Block at HMS *Dryad*, Southwick, opened by CINCNAVHOME, Admiral Sir Horace Law. The school was founded in 1925 and was located in the old Royal Military Academy, Woolwich from 1947 to May 1970.

See 5 May 1970.

1981 *Ark Royal*, fifth warship and fourth aircraft carrier of the name, launched by HM Queen Elizabeth The Queen Mother at Swan Hunter, Wallsend.

1994 The last British Major NATO Commander (MNC). Admiral Sir Hugo White, national C-in-C Fleet, hauled down his flag as Allied C-in-C Channel at Northwood on the abolition of the post.

See 21 February 1952, 31 December 2003.

2000 The first RN unit to receive the new Merlin HM Mk 1 helicopters, 824 NAS, Cdr Philip Shaw RN, commissioned at RNAS Culdrose; 824 NAS was the first RN operational squadron to be equipped with the Sea King HAS 1 A/S aircraft, embarked in *Ark Royal* in 1970.

2008 HRH Prince William joined BRNC Dartmouth as Sub-Lt Wales for two months' attachment to the Royal Navy.

3 June

1653 Continuation of the action off the Gabbard, ending in the defeat of the Dutch. Additional ships: *Culpepper, Eagle, Employment, Essex* (Admiral Robert Blake), *Hampshire, Hopewell, Luke, John and Abigail, Phoenix, Prosperous, Stork, Swan, Tenth Whelp* (*Whelp*), *William* and five others. Dutch lost: eleven captured, six sunk, and three blown up.

1665 Battle of Lowestoft. James, Duke of York, Lord High Admiral (*Royal Charles*) with Prince Rupert and 109 ships, defeated the Dutch fleet of 103 under Admiral Jacob van Wassenaer, Heer van Obdam (*Eendragt*), 40 miles S.E. of Lowestoft. 'The first British prince to command a fleet in battle since the Platagenets' – J.D. Davies. Batttle Honour: Lowestoft 1665.

Red Sqn: *Bristol, Coast Frigate, Diamond, Dover, Gloucester, Guinea, Martin, Norwich, Royal Exchange, Royal Oak, St George, Antelope, Blackamore, Coventry, Fountain, Happy Return, Loyal George, Mary, Mermaid, Norwich, Old James, Plymouth, Royal Charles, Yarmouth, Amity, Bonaventure, Eagle, Fairfax, George, Leopard, Little Mary, Portsmouth, Sapphire, Satisfaction, Success, Swiftsure.* Fireship: *Drake.*

White Sqn: *Colchester, Expedition, Hector, John and Abigail, Katherine, Lion, Monk, Newcastle, Paradox, Return, Ruby, Triumph, Assurance, Bendish, Exchange, Garland, Henrietta, Mary Rose, Merlin, Portland, Rainbow, Reserve, Revenge, Royal James, Advice, Anne, Bear, Constant Katherine, East India Merchant, Kent, Milford, Resolution, St Andrew, Speedwell, Truelove.*

Blue Sqn: *Assistance, Castle Frigate, Guernsey, Hambro' Merchant, Hampshire, Henry, Jersey, Lizard, Providence, Unicorn, York, Blackamore* (*Merchant*), *Breda, Centurion, Dragon, Dunkirk, Good Hope, John and Thomas, Maryland* (*Merchant*), *Montagu, Oxford Ketch, Pembroke, Royal Prince, Swallow, Adventure, Dreadnought, Essex, Forester, Golden Phoenix, Marmaduke, Paul, Princess, Royal Katherine, Society.*

Other ships possibly present: *Charity,* Clove Tree, Convertine, Golden Lion, Horseman, John and Katherine, King Ferdinando, London, Loyal Merchant, Maderas, Nightingale, Prudent Mary, Tiger, Vanguard, Young Lion.* Fireships: *Briar, Dolphin,† Fame,† Hound.*

*Captured. †Expended in action.

Dutch lost: thirty-two ships, but only nine prizes were brought in.

1666 The third day of the 'Four Days' Battle' against the Dutch. Monck withdrew towards the Thames to rendezvous with Prince Rupert. The *Royal Prince* (aka *Prince Royal*) (64), flagship of Sir George Ayscue, Admiral of the White, captured and later burned. *St Paul* also burned and *Sevenoaks* taken. 'Ayscue was (and still is) the most senior English sea officer ever to have been taken prisoner in action' – Rodger, *Naval History of Britain*, vol.2, p.75.'Sir George Ascue [sic] is carried up and down the Hague for people to see' – *Pepys' Diary*, 16 June 1666.

1711 *Newcastle* fought a French flotilla off St Pierre, Martinique.

1747 Captains who were not to be employed again were automatically promoted to flag rank and became 'Superannuated Rear-Admirals'. Nicknamed the Yellow Squadron.

1780 Frigate *Minerva* launched at Woolwich. The first 38-gun ship built for the RN and one of the first two frigates built for 18-pdr guns.
See 6 November 1778.

1832 Schooner *Speedwell* captured the slaver *Aquila* off the coast of Cuba.

1855 VC: Boatswain Henry Cooper (*Miranda*).

Ships and boats of Allied light squadron and launches from the Fleet destroyed Russian food stores at Taganrog, Sea of Azov. Ships and tenders: *Ardent, Beagle, Curlew, Danube, Medina, Miranda, Recruit, Snake, Stromboli, Salina, Vesuvius, Viper, Wrangler.* French: *Brandon, Fulton, Lucifer, Mégère, Mouette.* Two launches each from: *Agamemnon, Algiers, Hannibal, Princess Royal, Royal Albert, St Jean d'Acre* and eight French launches.

1896 Frederick John Walker, one of the outstanding commanders of the Battle of the Atlantic, born.
See 9 July 1944, 16 October 1998.

1915 British forces captured Kut-al' Amara, Mesopotamia. Ships and vessels: *Clio, Espiegle, Lawrence* (RIN), *Odin, Bahrein, Comet, Lewis Pelly, Miner, Muzaffri, Shaitan, Shushan, Sumana.*
See 29 April 1916.

HMS *Dauntless* – the second of six new Type 45 destroyers accepted by the Royal Navy. (*RN*)

1932 *Implacable* (ex-*Duguay-Trouin*) arrived Portsmouth and exchanged salutes with *Victory*, her Trafalgar adversary. Joined in July 1932 by *Foudroyant* (ex-*Trincomalee*).
See 4 November 1805, 2 December 1949.

1941 *Belchen*, first of *Bismarck*'s tankers, sunk by *Aurora* and *Kenya* in N. Atlantic.

1942 *Cocker* (ex-*Kos XIX*) sunk by U-331 between Tobruk and Bardia (32.06N, 24.14E).

1943 *Orion*, light cruiser, and destroyers *Ilex*, *Isis*, *Paladin* and *Troubridge* bombarded Pantelleria.
See 5 and 8 June 1943.

1944 Canso T/162 (RCAF) sank U-477 off Shetland (63.59N, 01.37E).

1957 Vice-Admiral Sir Benjamin Martin died, aged 65, in Natal, South Africa. Went to sea as a Boy First Class 1907. Warrant officer (gunner) in battleship *Malaya* at Jutland May 1916 and, in May 1941, exactly twenty-five years later, was Captain of the heavy cruiser *Dorsetshire* in the final attack on the *Bismarck*. First officer from the lower deck to become a rear-admiral on the Active List for eighty-seven years and the first boy from RN Hospital School, Greenwich, to reach flag rank.

1980 RN's first hydrofoil accepted. Commissioned 14 June as *Speedy* – a similar name to that of the Minister of State for the Navy. Sales list 12 February 1982.

1996 The first Anglican woman priest in the Royal Navy, Revd Sally Theakston appointed Assistant Chaplain at *Sultan*.
See 10 September 1990.

2010 *Dauntless*, Capt Richard Powell RN, commissioned at Portsmouth. The commissioning cake was cut by Mrs Carolyn Powell and Engineering Technician Robert Clough (17).
See 23 July 2009, 2 December 2009.

4 JUNE

1666 The last day of the 'Four Days Battle' against the Dutch, the greatest naval battle in the age of sail, and the fiercest and most intense fighting by the Royal Navy until operations in the eastern Mediterranean in summer 1941. The battle, fought 30 miles E.N.E. of the North Foreland, became a melee and ended with Albemarle's defeat by de Ruyter. Both fleets were exhausted. British lost about 4,250 men killed, wounded or captured, one fifth of their total strength. Ten British ships were lost including two flagships. Vice-Admirals Sir William Berkeley and Sir Christopher Myngs and ten captains killed. 'Mings is shot through the face and into the shoulder, where the bullet is lodged' – Pepys, 8 June. Berkeley was taken to The Hague: 'he lies dead in a Sugar Chest for everybody to see, with his Flagg standing up by him' – Pepys, 16 June. The Dutch, in fact, treated his body with respect and it lay in the Grote Kerk before being repatriated and buried in Westminster Abbey in August. Second Dutch War. *Diamond* and *Dragon* carry the Battle Honour: Four Days' Battle 1666.

White Sqn: *Assurance, Breda, Dragon, Leopard, Mary Rose, Plymouth, Royal James.*

Red Sqn: *Diamond, Essex, Henrietta, Portsmouth, Princess, Revenge, Victory.*

Blue Sqn: *Amity, Bonaventure, Dreadnought, Expedition, Reserve, Swallow.* Fireship: *Happy Entrance.* Captured: *Clove Tree.* Retaken: *Black Bull.*

British troops disembarking at Dover after evacuation from Dunkirk during Operation Dynamo, 1940. (*NMRN*)

1673 Second action off Schooneveld. Prince Rupert (*Sovereign*) and Vice-Admiral Comte d'Estrées (*Reine*) fought the Dutch fleet under Admiral de Ruyter (*Zeven Provincien*).
Battle Honour: Schooneveld 1673.

See 28 May 1673.

Red Sqn: *Anne, Constant Warwick, French Ruby, Happy Return, London, Stavoreen, Triumph, Warspite, Crown, Edgar, Gloucester, Henry, Lion, Old James, Princess, Royal Katherine, Rupert, Sovereign, Assurance, Charles, Mary Rose, Newcastle, Revenge, Victory, Yarmouth.*

Blue Sqn: *Foresight, Greenwich, Hampshire, Rainbow, St Michael, Sweepstakes, York, Advice, Dreadnought, Dunkirk, Henrietta, Prince, Royal Charles, St George, Swiftsure, Bonaventure, Diamond, Falcon, Mary, Monck, Ruby, St Andrew, Unicorn.*

White Sqn: Twenty-six French ships, less *Conquérant.* Fireships: *Trulove, Welcome.*

1742 *Rose* captured a Spanish snow (and her three prizes on the following day) in Exuma Sound, Bahama Islands.

1800 *Cynthia* and *Thames* destroyed the forts at the south-west end of Quiberon. Several small vessels were brought off and some were scuttled.

1802 New uniform for newly established Royal Marines first worn on King's Birthday Parade.

1805 *Loire* (38) captured the French privateers *Confiance* and *Belier*, together with a fort and a battery, in Muros Bay, N.W. Spain.

1844 Boats of *Samarang* destroyed twenty-seven pirate prahus in Patientie Strait, Jailolo Passage.

1846 Anglo-French squadron engaged the San Lorenzo batteries while escorting a large convoy down the Parana River, Argentina. British: *Alecto, Dolphin, Fanny, Firebrand, Gorgon, Harpy, Lizard.* French: *Coquette, Fulton.*

1852 Capture of Pegu by Maj-Gen Henry Godwin and Cdre John Tarleton (*Fox*). Boats of: *Fox*; *Moozuffer* (IN) and *Phlegethon* (Ben. Mar.). Troops: Madras Sappers and Miners, one company each of the 80th Regiment and the 67th Bengal Native Infantry.

1889 RN Barracks, Devonport, the first British naval shore barracks, first occupied when 500 men marched in from the depot ship *Royal Adelaide*. Commissioned 1 January 1890 as HMS *Vivid*; renamed *Drake* 1 January 1934.
See 30 September 1903, 1 August 1974.

1914 Wardroom to stand for National Anthem but to sit for Loyal Toast.

1940 Evacuation of the BEF from Dunkirk completed. Operation Dynamo.

The planning for Operation Dynamo was set in hand on 22 May as German troops were driving the Allied armies into the sea. The aim was to evacuate 45,000 men in two days. Dunkirk itself and its harbour had been totally destroyed, and only two breakwaters had enough water alongside them to berth small ships. However, by remarkable effort from ports across southern England a swarm of small craft gathered and in the face of constant heavy bombing, E-boat attacks and mines, they continued evacuating troops until 4 June. A total of 308,388 men were evacuated in British ships and craft, 29,388 in Allied vessels – including 26,175 French troops. Six British and three French destroyers had been sunk, together with eight passenger ships. Nineteen destroyers were severely damaged.

1941 Four more of *Bismarck*'s supply ships sunk.
See 3 June 1941.

1941 Kaiser Wilhelm II, 'Kaiser Bill', grandson of Queen Victoria, died aged 82 at Doorn in the Netherlands. Honorary admiral of the fleet until August 1914.

1941 First aircraft launch from a CAM ship; Sub-Lt M.A. Birren.
See 1 November 1941.

1943 Submarine *Truculent* sank U-308 off Faroes (64.28N, 03.09W).

1943 Hudson F/48 sank U-594 off Cape St Vincent (35.55N, 09.25W).

1963 Wasp helicopter Initial Flying Trials Unit, 700W NAS, formed at RNAS Culdrose. Next day 829 NAS commissioned as the HQ Squadron for all Small Ships Flights and moved to Portland December 1964. The RN received ninety-six Wasp aircraft; the last was withdrawn from service in March 1988.
See 28 October 1958.

1993 HM The Queen approved that the Saudi 'Liberation of Kuwait' medal and the Kuwaiti 'Liberation' Medal 'may be accepted as a keepsake, not to be worn'. – DCI(RN) 19/93 and 116/93.

2007 Universal right to elect trial by court martial. Any officer or rating whose offence was capable of being tried summarily could henceforth elect for court martial instead. RN Regulating Branch re-mustered as RN Police. Regulating ranks and rates unchanged. New slides and boards for officers and ratings with RN Police added to standard designs first shipped on 17 December 2008.
See 1 January 2008.

5 June

1805 *Helena* captured the Spanish privateer *Santa Leocadia* off Cork.

1806 *Vestal* captured the French privateer *Prospero* in Dover Strait.

1807 Boats of *Pomone* captured thirteen vessels of a convoy of twenty-seven sail and one of the escorting brigs off Sables d'Olonne and St Gilles-sur-Vie. Three more of the convoy were driven ashore.

1812 Boats of *Medusa* cut out the French *Dorade* from Arcachon Basin.

1829 *Pickle* captured the slaver *Boladora* off Puerto Naranjo.

1855 Massacre of several of a boat's crew of *Cossack*, flying a flag of truce, at Hangö (Hanko), Finland.

1855 Boats of Allied light squadron destroyed Russian stores at Marianpol, Sea of Azov. Battle Honour: Crimea 1854–5.

1900 Bearcroft's guns at occupation of Pretoria.

1902 Official trial of the new Bermuda floating dock. The old battleship *Sans Pareil*, 11,000 tons, with all her armour, guns and stores, 'was lifted bodily out of the water' in the Medway.

1914 Admiral Sir Percy Scott, prophet of naval gunnery, caused uproar with a famous letter to *The Times* in which he declared the battleship redundant: 'Submarines and aeroplanes have entirely revolutionized naval warfare; no fleet can hide itself from the aeroplane eye, and the submarine can deliver a deadly attack even in broad daylight . . . As the motor-vehicle had driven the horse from the road, so has the submarine driven the battleship from the sea.'

See 8 November 1907.

1915 U-14 sunk off Peterhead by armed trawlers *Oceanic II* and *Hawk*.

1916 Armoured cruiser *Hampshire*, on passage to north Russia, sunk by mine off Marwick Head, Orkney. Field Marshal Lord Kitchener, Secretary of State for War, his staff and 643 men lost.

1917 First experiments with Asdic devices at Harwich.

See 6 July 1918, 1 February 1963.

The principle of Asdic is simple. A sound wave is transmitted through the water. If it hits an object, such as a submarine, an echo is heard. The direction from which the echo comes and the time it takes to return indicate the bearing and range of that object. Refinements have been introduced to make the sound beam more directional, and to go further, but the essential principle is that of today's sonar: Sound Navigation And Ranging.

1917 Sheerness and naval establishments in the Medway raided by German aircraft.

1917 Light cruiser *Centaur* sank the German S-20 off Ostend.

1939 Admiral Sir Andrew Cunningham arrived at Alexandria in cruiser *Penelope* and took over next day from Admiral Sir Dudley Pound as C-in-C Mediterranean.

1941 Destroyer *Brilliant* forced *Egerland*, a U-boat supply tanker, to scuttle herself off St Paul's Rock, N.W. of Ascension.

1943 Light cruiser *Newfoundland* and destroyers *Paladin* and *Troubridge* bombarded Pantelleria.

See 3 and 8 June 1943.

1945 HM King Haakon of Norway embarked in cruiser *Norfolk* at Rosyth and, escorted by cruiser *Devonshire* (in which he had sailed to Britain after the German invasion in 1940) and four destroyers including HNoMS *Stord* sailed for Oslo, arriving with *Norfolk* wearing His Norwegian Majesty's standard. 'So ended the five years of trial and tragedy to which that gallant people had been subjected' – Roskill, *The War at Sea*, vol.3, pt.2, p.246.

See 7 June 1940, 7 June 1947, 21 September 1957.

HMS *Hampshire*, an armoured cruiser of 1903. (*NMRN*)

1962 Frigate *Ashanti*, Cdr David Hepworth RN, entered the Pool of London following the custom of the first of class paying an official visit to the capital. She was the first warship to come up the Thames on gas turbine engines and prudently came through Tower Bridge stern first to avoid having to turn with a single screw in the Pool on departure.

See 9 March 1959, 13 June 1984.

1967 The flag of the last C-in-C Mediterranean Fleet was hauled down at HMS *St Angelo* in Malta. Admiral Sir John Hamilton was the last of ninety British Cs-in-C in the Mediterranean since 1711.

From 060001 OPCON of HM ships in the Mediterranean chopped to C-in-C Home Fleet which became Western Fleet on the same day. Admiral Hamilton's successor, Rear-Admiral Dudley Leslie Davenport, hoisted his flag as the first Flag Officer Malta. The Queen's Colour of the Mediterranean Fleet was laid up in the Chapel at *St Angelo* until it was transferred to the Chapel of the RN College, Greenwich, on 19 June 1979. DCI(RN) 613/67.

See 31 March 1979 (FO Malta), 7 September 1958 (C-in-C East Indies), 31 March 1961 (C-in-C The Nore), 31 March 1964 (Admiralty), 11 April 1967 (C-in-C South Atlantic), 7 July 1975, 19 June 1979, 30 September 1983 (FO Medway).

6 June

A Memorable Date observed by the Corps of Royal Marines and RM Operational Landing Craft Squadrons – Normandy

1758 Destruction of the shipping and storehouses at St Malo by Cdre the Hon. Richard Howe (*Essex*) and troops under the Duke of Marlborough.

Ships: *Essex, Deptford, Jason, Portland, Rochester*. Frigates: *Active, Brilliant, Flamborough, Maidstone, Pallas, Richmond, Rose, Success, Tartar*. Sloops: *Diligence, Saltash, Speedwell, Swallow, Swan*. Fireships: *Pluto, Salamander*. Bombs: *Furnace, Grenado, Infernal*. Bomb tenders: *Neptune, Nancy, Endeavour*.

1762 Admiral of the Fleet Lord Anson died at Moor Park near Northwood HQ. Anson joined the Navy in 1712 and was made post-Captain in 1734. In 1737 he was appointed to the *Centurion* (60), and in 1740 placed in command of six small warships, two supply ships and 1,500 men and ordered to attack Spanish colonies in the Pacific. Although the force sounds quite strong, 500 of the soldiers were Chelsea pensioners and 300 untrained recruits. The ships were in poor condition and his crews in general were of low quality. The expedition suffered fearful losses. Although only four were lost in action, 1,300 men were lost through disease. All the ships except *Centurion* had to be abandoned. In 1743 off the Philippines he captured the Spanish treasure ship *Nuestra Senora de Covadonga*. When he returned to England in 1744 he brought huge treasure with him. The success of the expedition was almost entirely due to Anson's personal ability. He became so disillusioned at the treatment he received that he refused to serve further until the government had changed. He eventually became First Lord in 1751 and was made admiral of the fleet in 1761.

See 20 June 1743.

1800 Boats of *Impetueux, Thames, Amethyst, Amelia, Cynthia* and 300 of the 2nd Foot burned the French *Insolente* and several smaller vessels. Also captured five brigs, two sloops and two gunvessels in the Morbihan, France.

1829 The established Yacht Club at Cowes became the Royal Yacht Club when HRH The Prince Regent joined, and in 1833 the Royal Yacht Squadron. Its original flag was white with a Union in the hoist, recognised by French Customs as declaration of clearance for Customs. In 1829 the Admiralty issued a warrant that members might fly the White Ensign, a privilege to this day despite the abolition of the squadron's colours in 1864.

See 9 July 1864.

1846 Board approved flag-shift of C-in-C Portsmouth from *Excellent* to *Victory*.

1855 Third bombardment of Sevastopol. (Continued until the 10th.) Naval Brigade and Royal Artillery.

1868 Robert Falcon Scott born.

See 30 March 1912.

1944 Normandy Landing. Operation Neptune.
Battle Honour: Normandy 1944.

Ships: *Abelia, Adventure, Affleck, Ajax, Albatross, Alberni,* Albrighton, Albury, Algonquin,† Apollo, Ardrossan, Arethusa, Argonaut, Aristocrat, Armeria, Ashanti, Aylmer, Azalea, Bachaquero, Baddeck,† Balfour, Bangor, Beagle, Beaumaris, Belfast, Bellona, Bentley, Bickerton, Black Prince, Blackpool, Blackwood,* Blairmore,† Blankney, Bleasdale, Blencathra, Bligh, Bluebell, Boadicea, Bootle, Borage, Boston, Braithwaite, Bridlington, Bridport, Brigadier, Brissenden, Britomart,* Bulolo, Burdock, Buttercup, Calgary,† Cam, Camellia, Campanula, Campbell, Camrose,† Cape Breton,† Capel, Capetown, Caraquet, Catherine, Cato,* Cattistock, Celandine, Centurion, Ceres, Charlock, Chaudiere,† Chelmer, Clarkia, Clematis, Clover, Cockatrice, Cooke, Cotswold, Cottesmore, Cowichan,† Crane, Dacres, Dahlia, Dakins, Danae, Despatch, Deveron, Diadem, Dianella, Dianthus, Domett, Dominica, Dornoch, Douwe Aukes, Drumheller,† Duckworth, Duff, Duke of Wellington, Dunbar, Eastbourne, Eglinton, Elgin, Emerald, Emperor, Enterprise, Erebus, Eskimo, Essington, Fame, Fancy, Faulknor, Fernie, Forester, Fort William,† Fort York, Fraserburgh, Friendship, Frobisher, Fury,* Garlies, Garth, Gatineau,† Gazelle, Gentian, Geranium, Glasgow, Gleaner, Glenearn, Glenroy, Goatfell, Goathland, Godetia, Golden Eagle, Goodson, Gore, Gorgon, Gozo, Grecian, Grenville, Grey Fox, Grey Goose, Grey Owl, Grey Seal, Grey Shark, Grey Wolf, Grou,† Guysborough,† Haida,† Halcyon, Halsted, Hambledon, Hargood, Harrier, Hart, Havelock, Hawkins, Heather, Hilary, Hind, Holmes,*

Honeysuckle, Hotham, Hotspur, Hound, Huron,† *Hussar,** *Hydra, Icarus, Ilfracombe, Impulsive, Inconstant, Inglis, Invicta, Isis,** *Jason, Javelin, Jervis, Keats, Kellett, Kelvin, Kempenfelt, Kenora, Keppel, Kingcup, Kingsmill, Kitchener,*† *Kite, Kootenay,*† *Lapwing, Largs, Lark, Larne, Lavender, Lawford,** *Lawson, Lennox, Lightfoot, Lindsey,*† *Llandudno, Loch Fada, Loch Killin, Lochy, Locust, Londonderry, Loosestrife, Louisburg,*† *Loyalty,** *Lunenburg,*† *Lydd, Lyme Regis, Mackay, Magpie, Malpeque,*† *Matane,*† *Mauritius, Mayflower, Melbreak, Melita, Mendip, Meon, Meynell, Middleton, Mignonette, Milltown,*† *Mimico,*† *Minas, Misoa,*† *Montrose, Moorsom, Moosejaw,*† *Mounsey, Mourne,** *Narbrough, Narcissus, Nasturtium, Nelson, Nith, Northway, Obedient, Offa, Onslaught, Onslow, Onyx, Opportune, Orchis, Orestes, Oribi, Orion, Orwell, Ottawa,*† *Outremont,*† *Oxlip, Pangbourne, Parrsboro, Pelican, Pelorus, Pennywort, Persian, Petunia, Pickle, Pincher, Pink, Pique, Plover, Plucky, Poole, Poppy, Port Arthur,*† *Port Colborne,*† *Postillion, Potentilla, Prescott,*† *Primrose, Prince Baudouin,*†† *Prince Charles, Prince David,*† *Prince Leopold,*†† *Prins Albert,*†† *Prinses Astridd,*†† *Prinses Josephine Charlotte,*†† *Pursuer, Pytchley, Q'Appelle,*† *Qualicum, Queen Emma, Quorn,** *Ramillies, Rattlesnake, Ready, Recruit, Redpole, Regina,**† *Restigouche,*† *Retalick, Rhododendron, Rifleman, Rimouski,*† *Riou, Roberts, Rochester, Rodney, Romney, Ross, Rowley, Royal Ulsterman, Rupert, Ryde, Rye, St Helier, St John,*† *St Laurent,*† *Salamander, Saltash, Sandown, Saskatchewan,*† *Saumarez, Savage, Scarborough, Scawfell, Scorpion, Scourge, Scylla, Seagull, Seaham, Selkirk, Serapis, Seymour, Shark,** *Shippigan, Sidmouth, Sioux,*† *Sirius, Skeena,*† *Southdown, Southern Prince, Speedwell, Spragge, Starling, Starwort, Statice, Stayner, Steadfast, Stevenstone, Stockham, Stork, Stormont,*† *Strule, Summerside, Sunflower, Sutton, Svenner,** *Swansea,*† *Sweetbriar, Swift,** *Tadoussac,*† *Talybont, Tanatside, Tartar, Tasajera, Tavy, Teme, Tenby, Thames Queen, Thornbrough, Torrington, Tracker, Trentonian,*† *Trollope, Tyler, Ulster, Ulster Monarch, Ulysses, Undaunted, Undine, Urania, Urchin, Ursa, Vanquisher, Vegreville,*† *Venus, Versatile, Verulam, Vervain, Vesper, Vestal, Vidette, Vigilant, Vimy, Virago, Vivacious, Volunteer, Waldegrave, Walker, Wallflower, Walpole, Wanderer, Warspite, Waskesiu,*† *Wassaga,*† *Watchman, Waveney, Wedgeport, Wensleydale, Westcott, Whimbrel, Whippingham, Whitaker, Whitehall, Whitehaven, Whitshed, Wild Goose, Windsor, Woodstock,*† *Worthing, Wren, Wrestler,** X 20, X 23.

Stord and *Svenner** (Nor). Surveying: *Astral, Franklin, Gulnare, Scott.* Sixty-two A/S trawlers. Fifteen LL trawlers. Forty-two Danlayers. Ninety-five Mulberries. Blockships: *Centurion, Durban, Alynbank.* FAA Sqns: Swordfish: 819; Avenger: 849, 850, 852, 855, 858; Seafires: 808, 885, 886, 897. MGB flotilla: 1st (6). MTB flotillas: 1st (8), 5th (7), 13th (8), 14th (12), 21st (7), 22nd (7), 29th (8), 35th (10), 51st (7), 52nd (9), 53rd (7), 55th (12), 59th (8), 63rd (8), 64th (7), 65th (9). ML flotillas: 1st (8), 2nd (9), 4th (4), 5th (12), 7th (14), 10th (10), 11th (13), 13th (8), 14th (13), 15th (6), 19th (4), 20th (14), 21st (9), 23rd (8), 33rd (7), 50th (5), 51st (3), 103rd (8), 150th (9), 151st (9). Unattached (2). MMS flotillas: 101st (10), 102nd (10), 104th (10), 115th (1), 132nd (10), 143rd (10), 205th (11). BYMS flotillas: 150th (10), 159th (10), 165th (10), 167th (10). SGB flotilla: 1st (6).

*Sunk. †RCN. ††Belgian.

D-Day, 1944

Ships taking part in the Operation:

Warships	1,212
Landing Ships and Craft	4,026
Ancillaries	731
Merchant Vessels	864
Total	6,833

of which 78 per cent were British (including Canadian), 17 per cent were American, 5 per cent were French, Norwegian, Dutch, Polish and Greek. Over 10,000 Royal Marines took part, including 5 RM Cdos, an Armoured Support Group, an RM Engineering Cdo, Landing Craft Obstruction Units, signallers, drivers etc. Marines manned two-thirds of the assault landing craft.

1946 Admiral Sir John Cunningham succeeded Admiral of the Fleet Viscount Cunningham of Hyndhope as First Sea Lord. Sir John was the first navigation specialist to become Head of the Service.

1964 The first full production S2 (Spey-engined) Buccaneer aircraft (XN 974) made its maiden flight; eighty-four built for the Royal Navy.
See 4 and 14 October 1965.

1967 Home Fleet renamed Western Fleet.
See 6 July 1965, 1 October 1967.

1997 Vice-Admiral Malcolm Rutherford died, aged 56. Chief Naval Engineering Officer, mountaineer, sportsman, DCDS(Systems) 1994–5 and the first non-seaman officer to be Naval Secretary.

7 June

A Memorable Date observed by the Corps of the Royal Marines – Belle Isle

1673 *Crown* and *Nightingale* fought three Dutch men-of-war off the Galloper.

1761 The French island of Belle Isle, south of the Quiberon Peninsula on the Brittany coast, surrendered to a joint British Army and Marines force of 10,000 men under Maj-Gen Studholm Hodgson (Col James Mackenzie of the Marines) and Cdre Hon. Augustus Keppel after an amphibious assault on 22 April.
Battle Honour: Belle Isle 1761.

A forty-day siege of the Vauban-designed fortress of Palais on the north coast ended on 7 June when the French defenders were allowed to march out with all the honours of war after their stout defence. The island was held until the end of the Seven Years War in 1763. There had been excellent joint service co-operation and Keppel passed on Hodgson's request that: 'His Majesty may be informed of the goodness and spirited behaviour of that corps.' The Admiralty wrote to Keppel: 'The behaviour of the Marines has given Their Lordships great satisfaction and they may expect all the encouragement in Their Lordships' power.' It is traditionally believed that the laurel wreath on the Royal Marines cap badge was granted in recognition of Belle Isle. On the 200th anniversary of the action in 1961 Royal Marines buglers across the world sounded a fanfare.

Ships: *Achilles, Buckingham, Burford, Chichester, Dragon, Essex, Hampton Court, Hero, Monmouth, Prince of Orange, Sandwich, Swiftsure, Temeraire, Torbay, Valiant; frigates etc. Actaeon, Adventure, Aldborough, Druid, Escort, Flamborough, Fly, Launceston, Lynn, Melampe, Southampton*; Bombs: *Blast, Firedrake, Furnace, Infernal;* Fireships: *Aetna, Vesuvious.* Troops: Royal Artillery, 16th Light Dragoons, two Bns of Marines, 3rd, 9th, 19th, 21st, 30th, 36th, 67th, 69th, 75th, 76th, 85th, 90th, 97th and 98th Foot.

1777 *Fox* taken by the American *Hancock* and *Boston* off the Banks of Newfoundland.

1780 *Iris* fought the French *Hermione* 90 miles E. of Sandy Hook.

1854 Boats of *Vulture* and *Odin* repulsed in an attack on Gambia Karleby, now Kokkola, Gulf of Bothnia.

1855 VC: Thomas Wilkinson, Bdr, RMA, at siege of Sevastopol.

1915 VC: Flt Sub-Lt Reginald Alexander John Warneford, RNAS, for destroying Zeppelin LZ-37 near Ghent. First RNAS VC.

1915 RNAS aircraft destroyed Zeppelin LZ-38 in her shed at Evere, Belgium.

1917 Decoy ship *Pargust*, a 3,000 ton former tramp steamer, Cdr Gordon Campbell, VC, DSO, sank minelaying submarine UC-29, Kapitanleutnant Ernst Rosenow, 55 miles W. of Valentia Island, S.W. Ireland (51.50N, 11.50W), his third U-boat success.
See 22 March 1916, 17 February 1917, 8 August 1917.

Pargust had been torpedoed by UC-29, blowing a 40ft hole in the hull and, after a 'panic party' had taken to the boats, Campbell lured the then surfaced submarine into range and sank her by gunfire. The King awarded two VCs, the first ever elected VCs awarded to a ship, which were allocated by ballot (under Clause 13 of the Statutes of the VC) to Lt Ronald Neil Stuart DSO, RNR, and Seaman William Williams DSM, RNR. The action also gained one DSO, two DSCs, eight DSMs and eleven Mentions in Despatches. Cdr Campbell awarded a bar to his DSO and promoted captain. Crew awarded £1,000 by Admiralty and every man had his part in the VC ballot entered in his Service papers.

1917 Construction of composite destroyer *Zubian* completed.
See 4 February 1918, 30 June 1966.

1940 AMC *Carinthia* sunk by U-46 W. of Ireland (53.13N, 10.40W).

1940 HM King Haakon of Norway, the Crown Prince and 461 politicians, diplomats, British and Norwegian military personnel sailed from Tromso in cruiser *Devonshire* (flag of Vice-Admiral John Cunningham) for the Clyde. En route she took in the distress call from carrier *Glorious* but Cunningham did not break radio silence.
See 29 April 1940, 12 May 1940, 5 June 1945, 7 June 1947, 21 September 1957.

1942 Sunderland M/202 sank the Italian S/M *Veniero* off Minorca (37.52N, 04.05E).

1944 Sunderlands S/201 and R/228 sank U-955 and U-970 respectively in the Bay of Biscay.

D-Day and after, 1944

From D-Day to the fall of Le Havre in September 1944, there were 750 bombardments by cruisers and bigger ships. Destroyers and smaller warships also carried out many bombardments in support of the land forces. Ammunition expended by destroyers and larger warships was:

16in and 15in	3,371 rounds
7.5in and 5.25in	31,250 rounds
4.7in and 4in	24,000 rounds
Total	58,621 rounds

During this period 609 mines were swept, twenty-eight surface actions took place and there were landed: 1,410,600 tons of stores, 152,000 vehicles, 352,570 men. It was estimated during the Second World War that beachhead supplies for 250,000 men for one month would amount to 327,000 tons (tons were measured as approximately 40cu ft). To move these supplies thirty to thirty-five merchant ships and fifteen tankers would be needed. The supplies would consist of: 36,000 tons of food, 100,000 tons of petrol, oil and lubricants, 13,000 tons of other stores, 80,000 tons of building materials for bridges, roads and airfields and demolition work, 50,000 tons of air force parts and replacements, 33,000 tons of weapons and ammunition, 8,000 tons of fighting vehicles, 2,000 tons of medical supplies, 1,000 tons of transport equipment such as steel rails, cranes and locomotives, 1,000 tons of signalling equipment and 3,000 tons of miscellaneous supplies.

1944 Capture of Port-en-Bessin by 47 Cdo, Royal Marines.

1947 HM King Haakon of Norway invested the First Sea Lord, Admiral Sir John Cunningham, with the Grand Cross of the Order of St Olav on board the carrier *Vengeance* at Oslo. The Admiral's Secretary, Capt (S) G.P. Miller RN, was made Commander of the same Order and Admiral Cunningham's Maltese steward, CPO Francis Chetcutti, received the King Haakon Freedom Medal. This was the seventh anniversary of the embarkation of His Norwegian Majesty and members of his family in the heavy cruiser *Devonshire*, wearing flag of Vice-Admiral J.H.D. Cunningham (and with the same secretary and steward) at Tromso following the German invasion in 1940.

See 5 June 1945, 21 September 1957.

1960 The White Ensign hauled down at sunset for the last time in *Vanguard*, flagship of the Reserve Fleet, and Britain's last battleship, at Portsmouth. Rear-Admiral J. Grant's flag remained flying until transferred to the light cruiser *Sheffield* the next day.

See 2 October 1941, 30 November 1944, 9 August 1960, 29 February 1996.

1961 'Their Lordships are concerned at the heavy toll of Collisions, Groundings and Berthing accidents, which continue at an alarmingly high rate year by year. Not only does this seriously affect the operational availability of our ships, but also results in a heavy drain on the Navy votes. During 1960 there were 110 separate cases in which HM ships or Admiralty-owned vessels and craft, sustained appreciable damage' – twenty-five groundings, seventeen collisions between ships under way and sixty-eight berthing accidents. AFO 1439/61.

1973 Second Cod War. First collision between frigate *Scylla* and the Icelandic Coastguard vessel *Aegir*. Eleven further collisions were to follow.

See 31 August 1958.

1976 Training ceased at *Ganges*, Shotley Point, Ipswich, 'arguably the most feudal of all the Navy's institutions' (Richard Baker), which had first commissioned in 1905 and re-opened as a boys' TE in July 1945. Last mast-manning 6 June. White Ensign finally lowered 28 October 1976. Figurehead of Indian prince passed to Royal Hospital School, Holbrook. Training transferred to *Raleigh*, Torpoint.

See 4 October 1905, 8 December 1968.

1985 Women's Royal Australian Naval Service (WRANS) and Royal Australian Naval Nursing Service (RANNS) amalgamated into RAN on repeal of the Australian Naval Forces (Women's Services) Regulation.

1999 Surg Capt Rick Jolly, OBE, RN, Senior Medical Officer of 3 Cdo Bde in Operation Corporate, was given by HM The Queen 'unrestricted permission' to wear the insignia of the *Orden de Mayo (Oficial)* which he had conferred on him by the President of the Argentine Republic in Buenos Aires in March 1999. He was thus decorated by both sides for his services in the Falklands War of 1982.

8 June

1550 First recorded use of Medway as base for HM ships.

1755 First shots of the Seven Years War. *Dunkirk* (60), Capt Richard Howe, part of Vice-Admiral Hon. Edward Boscawen's squadron, deployed off the mouth of the St Lawrence to prevent French reinforcements reaching Quebec, engaged the flying *Alcide* (64), Capt de Hocquart, which struck when the *Torbay* (74), Boscawen's flagship, came up. This was the third time Boscawen had captured de Hocquart. The *Lys* (64), armed *en flute*, was taken by *Defiance* (64) and *Fougueux* (64). The Admiralty did not order French ships to be engaged on the high seas until 27 August 1755 and war was not declared until 18 May 1756 when news of the French invasion of Minorca reached London.
See 2 January 1793, 5 August 1914.

1794 *Crescent, Druid, Eurydice, Valiant* and three others fought the French *Brutus, Scevola* and four others off Guernsey.

1796 Two frigates, *Unicorn* (32), Capt Thomas Williams, and *Santa Margarita* (36), Capt Thomas Byam Martin, respectively took the French 36-gun frigates *Tribune*, Cdre Jean Moulston (American-born), and *Tamise*, after a day-long running fight W. of the Scillies. The corvette *Legere* (18) escaped. Capt Williams, who was knighted, reported to Vice-Admiral Kingsmill, C-in-C of HM Ships and Vessels on the coast of Ireland: 'I will not attempt to find words to convey to you, Sir, the sense I feel of the conduct of the officers and ship's company under my command.' The *Tamise*, captured by the French on 24 October 1793, was reinstated as HMS *Thames*; *Tribune* entered the Royal Navy under her own name. Two single-ship battle honours. *Unicorn*: *Tribune* 1796; *Santa Margarita*: *Tamise* 1796.

1801 French brig *La Prudente* of two guns and thirty-six men, bound from Toulon to Alexandria with ammunition, artificers' tools and comedians, taken by *Pigmy*, cutter, Lt W. Shepherd.

1915 King George V opened Rosyth Dockyard.

1918 *Eagle*, fleet carrier, launched at Armstrong's on the Tyne. She was laid down as the Chilean battleship *Almirante Cochrane*. Construction suspended in 1914 and converted on the slips. Completed at Portsmouth Dockyard. Her sister ship *Almirante Latorre* was completed as a battleship and commissioned into the Royal Navy as HMS *Canada*. *Eagle* introduced the round down on the after end of the flight deck and was the first British carrier to go to sea with a starboard island. She was torpedoed escorting a Malta convoy in 1942.
See 1 May 1923, 11 August 1942.

1921 Cruiser *Effingham* launched at Portsmouth Dockyard. The last warship completed for the RN carrying 7.5-in guns.
See 18 May 1940.

1937 First two Tribal-class destroyers launched at Vickers Armstrong, Walker-on-Tyne. *Afridi* named by Lady Foster, wife of Gen Sir Richard Foster, late CGRM, and *Cossack* named by Mrs Goodall, wife of Mr Stanley Goodall, DNC. The ships had brief but distinguished careers; *Afridi* was sunk off Namsos on 3 May 1940 and *Cossack* sank W. of Gibraltar on 27 October 1941. In contrast, the minelayer *Plover*, launched the same day at Denny, Dumbarton, remained in commission without a break until 4 December 1967.
See 7 April 1932, 16 February 1940, 23 and 27 October 1941, 4 December 1967.

1940 Aircraft carrier *Glorious* and destroyers *Acasta* and *Ardent* sunk by the German battlecruisers *Gneisenau* and *Scharnhorst* off Norway (68.45N, 04.30E). *Acasta* torpedoed *Scharnhorst*.
Battle Honour: *Scharnhorst* 1940.

The aircraft carrier *Glorious* was returning from Norway, escorted by the destroyers *Ardent* (Lt-Cdr J.F. Barker) and *Acasta* (Cdr C.E. Glasfurd), when she was caught unawares by the battlecruisers *Scharnhorst* and *Gneisenau*. The Germans opened accurate fire at 14 miles, and sank the carrier. The destroyers started to cover her by means of a smokescreen, and attacked with torpedoes. *Acasta* was the last to be sunk, ninety-eight minutes after the action started, but she had fired her torpedoes and one hit *Scharnhorst* abreast the after turret, damaging her severely. There were only forty-six survivors from HM ships.

1940 *Juniper* and *Orama* (transport) sunk by the German cruiser *Admiral Hipper* (67.20N, 04.10E) and (67.45N, 04.00E), and *Oil Pioneer* sunk by the *Gneisenau* off Norway (67.20N, 04.10E). RFA *Oleander* lost to air attack in Harstad Bay, Norway.

1940 Destroyers *Vesper* and *Wanderer* bombarded the main road between Abbeville and Tréport, N. France.

1941 Allied forces advanced into Syria, supported by naval force under Vice-Admiral E.L.S. King (*Phoebe* – 15th CS).

1943 Further bombardment of Pantelleria. Ships: *Aurora, Euryalus, Newfoundland* (Rear-Admiral C.H.J. Harcourt, 15th CS), *Orion, Penelope, Jervis, Laforey, Lookout, Loyal, Nubian, Tartar, Troubridge, Whaddon*; MTBs 73, 77, 84.
See 3 and 5 June 1943.

1944 Liberator G/224 sank U-373 (48.10N, 05.31W) and U-629 (48.27N, 05.47W) off Ushant, within half an hour.

1944 Frigate *Lawford* sunk by German aircraft in the Juno area, Seine Bay. Operation Neptune.

1945 Submarine *Trenchant* sank Japanese heavy cruiser *Ashigara* in Banka Strait (01.59S, 104.57E).

The submarine *Trenchant* (Cdr A.R. Hezlet) was on patrol off the entrance to Banka Strait (off Palembang, Sumatra), with the submarine *Stygian* further out to sea. The *Trenchant* was lying inside an Allied minefield. A Japanese destroyer was sighted approaching. *Trenchant* was detected, but fired a torpedo and escaped in the darkness. The *Stygian* sighted the destroyer at 1015, attacked it unsuccessfully, and was counter-attacked. At that time, *Trenchant* sighted a Nachi-class cruiser (12,700 tons) approaching, and fired a spread of eight torpedoes, of which five hit and blew off the enemy's bow, set her on fire and made her list to starboard. The cruiser, the *Ashigara*, sank at 1239 in a welter of smoke and foam which removed the only serviceable Japanese heavy cruiser from the area on the eve of the Australian landings in north Borneo. Cdr Hezlet was awarded the DSO and the US Legion of Merit.

1948 A Meteor piloted by Lt-Cdr Eric Brown landed on board *Implacable*, the first twin-engined jet aircraft to land on a British carrier.

1959 HM The Queen presented her Colour to Submarine Command at HMS *Dolphin*, Gosport. Royal Guard of 100 men drawn from submarines serving in home, Mediterranean, Canadian and Australian waters. Eight submarine VCs, some from the First World War, were present, together with Mrs Wanklyn, widow of Lt-Cdr David Wanklyn VC, and Mrs Linton, widow of Cdr J.W. Linton VC. The Queen also opened the re-built Portsmouth Guildhall which had been bombed on 10 January 1941.

1960 Frigate *Wakeful*, with MCMVs *Thames, Venturer, St David* and *Bossington*, arrived at island of Oléron off La Rochelle, carrying a copy of the Laws of Oléron, extracted from the *Black Book of Admiralty*.
See 1 June 1960.

The book had been handed to the Chaplain of the Fleet by the President of the Court of Admiralty at a service in St Paul's Cathedral on 1 June 1960 to mark the 600th anniversary of the Court of Admiralty in England. Oléron was celebrating the promulgation, about the year 1160, of the Laws of Oléron by Eleanor of Aquitaine, wife of King Henry II of England.

1982 Landing ships *Sir Galahad* and *Sir Tristram* abandoned after air attack off Fitzroy Cove, the former sunk by own forces and the latter salvaged. *Sir Galahad* sunk 52. 16.5S, 56. 45.35W. by HMS *Onyx*, 25 June 1982. DCI(RN) 83/88. Operation Corporate.
See 27 November 1987.

2000 *Kent*, Type 23 frigate, commissioned at Portsmouth. First RN ship commissioned in the popularly accepted, if strictly premature, twenty-first century.
See 16 April 1999, 27 November 1999, 15 December 1999.

2007 Attack submarine *Astute*, Yard No. 1122, launched at BAE Systems, Barrow, by HRH The Duchess of Cornwall. Laid down 31 January 2001 and over six years on the stocks. First CO, Cdr M.J.D. Walliker RN. Boat incorporates and reinstates covert insertion capability. Followed by *Ambush* (launched 7 January 2011) and *Artful* (laid down 11 March 2005), names revived from the 1945 A-class submarines. Remaining three boats to be given battleship names: *Audacious, Agamemnon* and *Anson*.
See 30 January 1945, 31 January 2001, 10 June 2007 (photograph).

9 June

1587 Drake took the *San Felipe*.

1796 *Southampton* (32) captured the French *Utilé* (24) in Hyères Road, Sir John Jervis having pointed her out as an eyesore to Capt Macnamara.

1799 Boats of *Success* cut out the Spanish *Belle Aurora* from Port Selva.

1801 *Kangaroo* and *Speedy* engaged the shore defences at Oropesa, sank four of the escort to a Spanish convoy and captured three vessels of the convoy.

1832 The Navy Board and Victualling Board abolished by the Admiralty Act 1832 (2 and 3 Will IV, c.40) introduced in Parliament by Sir James Graham, First Lord of the Admiralty. Sweeping changes brought all naval administration under the Board of Admiralty. Civil commissioners at the dockyards replaced by sea officers as naval superintendents. The new organisation was amended by Orders in Council 14 January 1869 and 19 March 1872 but then remained largely unchanged until 1964.

See 31 March 1964.

1836 Royal Marines of *Castor* at the defence of the 'ship' *Redoubt* (Carlist War).

1858 *Pearl*'s Naval Brigade and troops dispersed a rebel force at Amorha (second action).

1860 An initial commission to an officer with subsequent appointments replaced practice of issuing separate commissions for each appointment.

1919 Submarine L 55, Lt Charles Chapman RN, in attempting to torpedo the Russian battleship *Petropavlovsk* off Kronstadt, broke surface and was sunk by shellfire and lost with all hands.

See 22 November 1918, 20 July 2003.

The submarine was salvaged in 1928 and the Admiralty requested the return of the remains. The Russians refused entry of a warship and the coffins were embarked in the Ellerman-Wilson liner *Truro* from a lighter off Kronstadt on 30 August in the presence of a Russian naval guard of honour. All Russian ships in harbour flew half-masted colours and manned ship and each saluted the *Truro* as she passed out to sea. The bodies were transferred into the light cruiser *Champion* alongside at Reval (Tallinn) and she sailed on 1 September and arrived at Portsmouth on 5 September. Two days later the men of L 55 were buried in a single grave at Haslar. The names of the four officers and thirty-eight men are inscribed on memorials in the Church of the Holy Spirit in Tallinn and in Portsmouth Cathedral.

1931 Submarine *Poseidon* lost in collision with SS *Yuta* 21 miles N. of Wei-Hai-Wei on the N. China coast. First operational use of DSEA (Davis Submerged Escape Apparatus) and origin of SUBSUNK signal. Submarine sank in 130ft with twenty-four men. Of the eight men in the forward compartment six escaped and survived using DSEA. Albert Medal to PO P.W. Willis, Torpedo Gunner's Mate, and three promotions. The boat may have been raised by the Chinese in 1970.

1942 *Mimosa* (FF) sunk by U-124 in N. Atlantic (52.15N, 32.37W). Convoy ONS 100.

1942 Italian S/M *Zaffiro* sunk by aircraft S.S.E. of Majorca (38.21N, 03.21E). Operation Style.

1944 Liberator F/120 sank U-740 in W. Approaches (49.09N, 08.37W).

1944 Action off Ile de Bas (48.59N, 04.44W) between *Ashanti*, *Eskimo*, *Haida* (RCN), *Huron* (RCN), *Javelin* and *Tartar*, with the Polish *Blyskawica* and *Piorun* (10th DF), and four German destroyers. German Z-32 and ZH-1 (ex-Neth *Gerard Callenburgh*) destroyed and Z-24 badly damaged.

1947 Admiral Sir Reginald Bacon, torpedo specialist and 'a brilliant officer of the materiel school' (Kemp) died. Benin Expedition of 1897 (DSO). As Inspecting Captain of Submarines 1900–4 he was responsible for building Britain's first five submarines. First captain of the battleship *Dreadnought*. Succeeded Jellicoe as Director of Naval Ordnance in 1907 and would have followed Jellicoe again as Third Sea Lord and Controller in 1909 but he retired to be managing director of

The bow section of HMS *Dauntless* moving out of Vosper Thornycroft's Shipbuilding Hall in No.3 Basin Portsmouth Dockyard on 26 July 2006 to be loaded onto a barge for carriage to BAE Systems yard on the Clyde. (*RN*)

the Coventry Ordnance Works. He designed a new 15-in howitzer and went to France in January 1915 as a Colonel RM in the RM Siege Brigade to oversee its operational introduction, but Churchill, the First Lord of the Admiralty, recalled him in April 1915 to command the Dover Patrol. Like Jellicoe, Bacon was sacked by Geddes in December 1917. Retired 1919 and became biographer of his patrons, Fisher and Jellicoe. 'One of the best brains of his time' – Marder.

See 18 February 1897, 20 August 1901.

1964 Guided missile destroyer *Glamorgan* launched at Vickers Armstrong, Newcastle-upon-Tyne. She was the last warship fitted with steam turbines built by Parsons Marine at the Turbinia Works, Wallsend.

1966 HM ships *Nurton*, *Wolverton* and *Upton* arrived at Scheveningen near The Hague to join the Royal Netherlands Navy in commemorating the Four Days Battle between the two countries between 1 and 4 June 1666 during the Second Dutch War (1665–7).

1990 *Upholder*, the first Type 2400 diesel-electric SSKs, commissioned. Leased to Canada and renamed HMCS *Chicoutimi*.

See 2 December 1986, 5 October 2004.

2005 Battle Honour: Al Faw 2003, awarded to units involved in the major combat phase of Operation Telic in Iraq: *Ark Royal*, *Bangor*, *Blyth*, *Brocklesby*, *Ocean*, *Ledbury*, *Roebuck*, *Sandown*, 845 and 847 NAS.

See 30 April 2009.

The Honours relate to operations between 19 March and 30 April 2003. The main RN effort during Operation Telic was directed at the Al Faw peninsula and surrounding waters encompassing a major amphibious assault, port entry and subsequent sea lines of communications.

845 and 847 NAS both met the criteria for 'successful war service' and those laid down for 'combined operations' against significant enemy resistance. 845 NAS provided tactical mobility and combat support for every unit of 3 Cdo Bde in the AOA; Lynx and Gazelle aircraft of 847 NAS provided armed aviation patrols to the brigade, flying 160 combat missions against enemy positions. They came under frequent enemy fire. After the amphibious assault, the squadron moved forward to support the assault by 40 Cdo on Abu Al Khasib.

Ark Royal and *Ocean* merited the award for launching 845 and 847 NAS as part of the amphibious assault. It is usual in amphibious operations for involved aircraft carriers to receive battle honours but if the actual operation is distant from the carriers the escorting ships will not be eligible for the award.

2005 The bow section of *Daring*, the first Type 45 destroyer, built by Vosper Thornycroft in Portsmouth Dockyard, left Portsmouth on a barge for the Clyde where it was united with the ship's main hull at BAE Systems yard at Scotstoun.

See 1 February 2006.

Trafalgar Bicentenary Year: Capt Steve Bramley RN and Lord Nelson (actor Alex Naylor) watch the bow section of HMS *Daring*, the first Type 45 destroyer, built by Vosper Thornycroft at Portsmouth, leaving on a barge for Scotstoun on the Clyde to be joined to the ship's main hull. (*RN*)

10 JUNE

1665 *Loyal London* (96) presented by the City to replace the *London* (64) which had blown up on 7 March. *Loyal London* damaged by fire in 1667 and rebuilt three times.

1667 De Ruyter attacked Britain's principal fleet anchorage in the Medway in a Taranto-style operation that 'must be accounted one of the most brilliant, audacious, and completely successful strokes in the annals of naval warfare' – Marcus. Following the Plague in 1665 and the Fire of London in 1666 this was the latest in 'an apocalypse of misfortunes' – Rodger. Charles II was bankrupt and the main fleet was laid-up, unmanned and unprepared. Sheerness was captured by an advance squadron under Admiral van Ghent. It was 'probably the blackest day in English naval history' – Padfield. Worse was to follow.

See 12, 13 and 14 June 1667, 24 March 1961.

THE NAVY & ARMY ILLUSTRATED.

VOL. VIII.—No. 114.] SATURDAY, APRIL 8th, 1899.

Photo. W. M. Crockett. Copyright

THE "CABINET" OF THE "AURORA."

CAPTAIN E. H. BAYLY COMMANDER H. J. L. CLARKE, AND LIEUTENANT T. W. KEMP.

(See next page.)

Capt E.H. Bayley and officers of HMS *Aurora* before their departure for China, 1899. (*NMRN*)

1694 *Portsmouth* captured a French 30-gun privateer about 120 miles S. of Ushant. *Canterbury* came up just before the end of the action.

1795 First storekeeper appointed to base at Cape of Good Hope.

1804 *Hunter* captured the French privateer *Liberté* to the north-east of Jamaica.

1900 Boxer rebellion threatened Peking, and Admiral Sir Edward Seymour, C-in-C, left Tientsin with an expeditionary force of 2,129 drawn from eight nations. Capt E.H. 'Chawbags' Bayly, 'a heavy, burly thoroughbred seaman of the old school', in command of Naval Brigade left at Tientsin.

See 26 June 1902, 7 April 1919.

1940 AMC *Vandyck* sunk by German aircraft off Ankenes, Norway.

1940 Italy declared her entry into the Second World War with effect from the next day.

See 13 June 1940, 9 July 1940, 8 September 1943.

1941 Patrol vessel *Pintail* sunk by mine off the Humber (53.30N, 00.32E).

1944 Liberator K/206 and Mosquito W/248 sank U-821 off Ushant (48.31N, 05.11W).

1944 Submarine *Untiring* sank German UJ-6078 off La Ciotat, W. of Toulon.

Submarine losses of the Second World War

RN	76 lost of 216	35%
USN	52 lost of 288	18%
German	782 lost of 1,162	67%
Japan	130 lost of 181	72%
Italy	85 lost of 144	59%

Admiral Sir Jonathon Band at the launch of HMS *Astute*. See 8 June 2007. (*RN*)

1960 'A case has occurred in which items of officers' clothing have been damaged whilst stored in their cabin wardrobes. The damage was attributed to intermittent rubbing of the clothes against fittings which projected inside the wardrobes, resulting in excessive wear of clothes in direct contact with such items . . . Commanding Officers of HM Ships are to arrange for all officers' wardrobes to be examined . . .' – AFO 1549/60.

1964 Prompted by Admiral of the Fleet Earl Mountbatten, the Royal Marines adopted the 'Preobrajenky March' as their regimental slow march in place of 'The Globe and Laurel', based on 'Early one Morning'. The new march was the ceremonial slow march of the Preobrajenky Guards commanded by the Grand Duke Sergius of Russia, Mountbatten's uncle and Prince Philip's great-uncle. The first public performance was on Horse Guards Parade this day. AFO 143/64.

1960 *Devonshire*, the first of eight County-class guided missile destroyers, launched by HRH Princess Alexandra at Cammell Laird, Birkenhead. The entire Board of Admiralty was present including the First Lord, Lord Carrington, and the First Sea Lord, Admiral Sir Caspar John. 'Her Seaslug guided weapons system mounted on her quarterdeck will sound the death knell of the gun as the principal weapon in the Navy's armament' – *Navy* magazine, July 1960.

See 27 January 1956, 24 July 1956.

1971 First Type 42 destroyer, *Sheffield*, launched by HM The Queen at Vickers, Barrow. Her sister ship, *Hercules*, being built for the Argentine Navy, was laid down on the same slip 'within minutes' of the launching. *Sheffield* had been damaged by an explosion two months earlier and, to prevent delay in her launching, the Argentine Navy agreed to materials intended for *Hercules* being used to repair the British ship. Tributes were paid to them at the ceremony. *Sheffield* commissioned 16 February 1975. Lost in action with Argentine forces in the Falklands War 10 May 1982.

11 JUNE

A Memorable Date observed by 42 and 45 Cdos RM – Mount Harriet and Two Sisters 11/12 June 1982.

1730 First dinner in Painted Hall at Greenwich Hospital.

1779 Horatio Nelson 'made' – promoted post-captain – by appointment to *Hinchinbrook* (28) in command, three months before his 21st birthday.
See 30 June 1955.

'Interest': Naval Promotion in the Eighteenth Century.
Once an officer was 'made post' (appointed to a captain's command) he took his place at the bottom of a list which was headed by the admiral of the fleet. Provided the officer remained alive and was not court-martialled, he could be sure of promotion, whether employed or not. It is clear from this that the key to promotion was to be 'made post' at the earliest possible moment. To achieve seniority a boy with naval aspirations would be sent to sea at the earliest possible age, and his relatives would go to extraordinary lengths to get him first promoted to lieutenant and then captain. Nelson was well placed as nephew of the Comptroller of the Navy and was 'made post' aged 20, but, like Collingwood, was only a vice-admiral when he died.

1808 Boats of *Euryalus* and *Cruizer* cut out a Danish gunboat and destroyed two troopships in Nakskov Fjord.

1843 Boats of *Dido* destroyed the stronghold of the Saribas Dyaks at Paddi, in the Batang Saribas.

1847 Sir John Franklin, naval officer and Arctic explorer, died on his ill-fated expedition in *Erebus* and *Terror* to find the North–West Passage. While his fate was still uncertain he was promoted to rear-admiral of the blue 26 October 1852. When it was ascertained that he had died earlier, the Admiralty annulled the promotion and removed his name.
See 22 April 1848, 15 April 1942.

1871 Walter Cowan born at Crickhowell, Breconshire.
See 14 February 1956.

Capt Sir John Franklin (1786–1847). (*NMRN 1971/12(24)*)

1899 David Beatty, Commander of the battleship *Barfleur*, Capt Stanley Colville RN, and flagship of Rear-Admiral James Bruce, second-in-command on the China Station, landed with 150 men to defend Tientsin, the Treaty port on the Pei-ho River, during the Boxer uprising. For this service he was promoted captain on 9 November 1900 aged 29 and with less than two years' seniority as a commander.
See 15 November 1898, 1 January 1910.

1907 TB 99 foundered off Berry Head.

1917 *Zylpha* (*Q 6*) torpedoed by U-82 W.S.W. of Ireland (51.57N, 15.25W). Sank on the 15th.

1930 Three submarines launched by Vickers Armstrong, Barrow: *Regulus*, lost in Taranto Strait 1940; *Regent*, lost in Taranto Strait 1 6 April 1943 and *Rover*.

1934 Classic salvage of sloop *Hastings*, grounded in Red Sea – an accident indirectly attributable to the wardroom cat. Refloated 6 September 1935.

Lady Dorothy Macmillan, wife of the former prime minister, assisted by Capt. J.A. Templeton-Cothill RN, Captain (D), 23rd Escort Squadron, cutting the commissioning cake of the frigate HMS *Rhyl* at the start of the third commission on 3 June 1965. Lady Dorothy launched the ship at Portsmouth in 1959. (*Author*)

1940 Siege of Malta began with Italian air attack. Siege continued until 20 July 1943 when 3,340th air-raid alert was sounded.

1941 Capture of Assab by British and Indian troops. Ships: *Dido* and *Chakdina* with *Clive* and *Indus* (RIN).

1943 Surrender of Pantelleria after landing of troops and twenty-five minutes' bombardment. Ships: *Aphis*, *Aurora*, *Newfoundland*, *Orion*, *Penelope* and destroyers as on the 8th. Operation Workshop.

1943 Minesweeper *Wallaroo* (RAN) sunk in collision with SS *Gilbert Costin* off Fremantle.

1943 Fortress R/206 sank U-417 in Iceland/ Faroes Gap (63.20N, 10.30W) but crashed and was lost.

1944 Canso B/162 (RCAF) sank U-980 off Norway (63.07N, 00.26E).

1944 Attack on Le Hamel by 46 Cdo, Royal Marines.

1951 The chelengk, the diamond plume given to Nelson by the Sultan of Turkey after the Battle of the Nile, was stolen from the National Maritime Museum. The central star in this 'garish ornament' (Oliver Warner, *The Battle of the Nile*, p.145) revolved by clockwork and, although Nelson wore it on his hat with the King's permission, brother officers regarded it as 'an alien eccentricity and not part of naval uniform' (Walker, *Nelson Portraits*, p.281). The chelengk was never recovered but forty years later the thief confessed in a television programme and his exploit later earned for him an obituary in the national press.

1968 HM Queen Elizabeth The Queen Mother presented the battle ensign worn by the battleship *Collingwood* at Jutland to HMS *Collingwood* at Fareham. Her late husband, King George VI, served in the ship in the battle.

2010 Executive curl on Canadian naval officers' uniforms, removed on 1 February 1968, now restored.

12 June

1652 Capt Sir George Ayscue (*Rainbow*) with a squadron of four men-of-war and seven hired merchantmen, captured six ships of the Dutch outward-bound Portuguese trade off Lizard Head.

1667 The surprise Dutch attack on the fleet in the Medway continued. Admiral van Ghent broke the boom protecting Chatham and advanced into Gillingham Reach where the principal ships were at anchor. They burned the *Matthias* and *Monmouth*, and captured the British flagship *Royal Charles* without opposition. 'All hearts do now ake; for the news is true, that the Dutch have broke the Chain and burned our ships' – Pepys.

In December 1941, the Dutch corvette *Van Brakel* (named after the very man who broke the chain boom and towed away the *Royal Charles* nearly 300 years earlier) brought a convoy into the Medway and accidentally rammed the boom. Her signal to Chatham Dockyard for a diver to inspect her propellers for possible damage brought the reply 'What, again?'

See 13 and 14 June 1667, 24 March 1961.

1685 Boats of *Lark*, *Greyhound* and *Bonaventure* destroyed two Sali rovers at Mamora.

1745 *Fowey* destroyed the French privateer *Griffon* near Fécamp.

1797 End of the mutiny at The Nore. There were 412 men brought to trial, fifty-nine condemned to death (twenty-nine actually executed), nine flogged, twenty-nine imprisoned and remainder pardoned after the Battle of Camperdown.

1813 Boats of *Narcissus* cut out the American *Surveyor* up the York River, Chesapeake Bay.

1813 *Bacchante* cut out ten Neapolitan gunboats and captured a convoy of fourteen sail at Guilla Nova, near Abruzzi.

1869 Completion of *Monarch*. First RN sea-going turret-ship and first to carry 12-in guns.

1917 Trawler *Sea King* sank UC-66 off the Lizard.

1917 Naval party occupied Saliff, on Arabian coast.

1940 Light cruiser *Calypso* sunk by the Italian S/M *Alpino Bagnolini* off Crete (33.45N, 24.32E), on second day of war with Italy. The first RN loss in the Mediterranean campaign.

See 14 June 1940.

1941 *Bismarck*'s sixth tanker sunk by cruiser *Sheffield* much to the displeasure of First Sea Lord who had ordered that she should be spared to avoid compromising Ultra.

See 3 and 4 June 1941.

1942 *Grove* sunk by U-77 in the Gulf of Sollum (32.05N, 25.30E).

1943 Light cruisers *Aurora*, *Newfoundland*, *Orion*, *Penelope* and six destroyers bombarded Lampedusa, which surrendered.

Admiral Sir Andrew Cunningham (1883–1963)

Cunningham was a resolute and inspiring naval commander in the Second World War. As C-in-C of the Mediterranean Fleet, he was faced with overwhelming enemy forces when France surrendered to the Germans and Italy entered the war. He succeeded in persuading the French at Alexandria to immobilise their ships. He then won decisive victories over numerically superior Italian forces, and by his offensive use of seapower he kept Malta supplied and available as a base against Axis sea lanes to North Africa. He made the short sea passage from Greece and Italy to North Africa impassable to Axis merchant shipping, and thereby prevented Rommel from receiving the supplies he needed to complete his North African victories. In September 1943 he received the surrender of the Italian Fleet at Malta. When the First Sea Lord, Admiral of the Fleet Sir Dudley Pound died in October 1943, Cunningham succeeded him for the remainder of the war. He was invested with the Thistle rather than the Garter because of his Scottish ancestry.

Nelson wounded at Calvi, 1794, as depicted by William Bromley. (*NMRN 1978/265(7)*)

1954 HM The Queen reviewed the RNVR on Horse Guards Parade to mark the fiftieth anniversary of its foundation. The heavy rain caused 'running pipeclay from the hats of WRNVR members to make long, white marks down their backs'. Flypast by RNVR air divisions cancelled. HRH The Duke of Edinburgh attended jubilee dinner in the Painted Hall. The jubilee date was 30 June 1953 but this was soon after the Coronation and the parade was postponed.

1959 First sections of *Dreadnought*, first British nuclear submarine, laid by HRH The Duke of Edinburgh.

See 21 October 1960.

1963 Admiral of the Fleet Viscount Cunningham of Hyndhope died, aged 80, in a taxi to St Thomas's Hospital after attending the House of Lords. ABC's body lay in the Chapel of the RN Barracks, Portsmouth, guarded by four lieutenants keeping four-hour watches, before being embarked in the guided missile destroyer *Hampshire* at South Railway Jetty on Friday 18 June for burial at sea off the Isle of Wight in wet weather and a rising gale. The pall bearers were Admiral Sir Caspar John, First Sea Lord; Admiral Sir Wilfrid Woods, C-in-C Portsmouth; Admiral of the Fleet Sir George Creasy and most of the Board of Admiralty. Also present was ABC's great-nephew, Lt J.C.K. Slater RN, a future First Sea Lord. One of the wreaths carried a cap tally from the battleship *Warspite*, Cunningham's flagship in the Mediterranean. On return from The Nab it was too rough for the ship to enter harbour and guests were transferred down a very steep brow to a tug at Spithead. 'It was a scene which everyone felt ABC would have savoured' – Capt S.W.C. Pack. At his memorial service in St Paul's Cathedral on 12 July, the Bishop of Norwich, who had been chaplain of the battleship *Queen Elizabeth* and an old shipmate, thanked God for 'giving our people and nation such a man at such a time'.

See 21 October 1965, 7 January 1983.

1967 Destroyer *Kent*, frigates *Arethusa* and *Lynx* and RFA tanker *Olynthus* arrived at Capetown until 17 June. Major objections voiced by over fifty MPs. Mr Dennis Healey, Defence Secretary, said 'that to have cancelled the visit would have been taken as implying a ban on all future visits and would have called into question the continuance of the Simonstown Agreement of June 1955 which was essential to UK defence interests . . . to continue the naval visit but to cancel shore leave "would be to get the worst of both worlds".' Reuters reported from Capetown that the sailors said 'that they were given one instruction before they went ashore – that there should be no fraternisation with non-white girls'. 'In spite of all the fuss made in the Press and Parliament about coloured sailors in the RN ships visiting Capetown . . . the visit passed off without incident' – *Navy* magazine, July 1967.

See 14 October 1974, 27 January 1994.

1982 42 and 45 Cdos RM and 3 Para took Mount Harriet, Two Sisters and Mount Longdon respectively in night attacks supported by NGS from *Glamorgan*, *Avenger*, *Arrow* and *Yarmouth*. *Glamorgan* damaged by shore-based Exocet after bombarding Port Stanley. Operation Corporate.

1990 RFA *Fort Victoria*, fleet replenishment ship, launched at Harland and Wolff, Belfast. Completed by Cammell Laird, Birkenhead.

See 1 March 1991.

1994 Minehunter *Hurworth* found the hull of the submarine *Vandal*, lost on trials off the Isle of Arran in 1943.

See 24 February 1943, 3 May 1997.

13 JUNE

1514 Henry VIII launched *Henry Grace à Dieu* at Woolwich and paid the Chaplain who blessed her 6*s* 8*d*.

1667 The Dutch Admiral van Ghent's advance squadron of de Ruyter's fleet continued their operations in the Medway, burning the *Royal Oak*, *Loyal London* and *Royal James*. 'The destruction of these three stately and glorious ships of ours was the most dismall spectacle my eyes ever beheld', wrote Edward Gregory, clerk of the cheque at Chatham, 'and itt certainly made the heart of every true Englishman bleede to see such three Argos lost'.

See 10, 12 and 14 June 1667, 24 March 1961.

1673 Order-in-Council required 'that the Lord High Admiral be ready at all times to give his Majesty a perfect account of the state of his Navy relating to the condition both of his ships and yards, with the stores remaining, persons employed and services to be performed therin'.

1761 *Centaur* captured the French *Ste Anne* off Dona Maria Bay, Haiti.

1796 Frigate *Dryad* (36), Capt Lord Amelius Beauclerk, engaged the French frigate *Proserpine* (40) S. of Cape Clear. The enemy struck after forty-five minutes. The prize was commissioned into the Royal Navy as HMS *Amelia* after George III's daughter (and perhaps as a compliment to Capt Beauclerk).

See 7 February 1813.

1805 Boats of *Cambrian* captured the Spanish privateer *Maria* 240 miles to the S.E. of Bermuda.

1814 Boats of *Superb* and *Nimrod* destroyed seventeen sail of American shipping at Wareham, Mass.

1893 Navy Records Society founded. Regarded by some as the, de facto, unofficial historical department of the Naval Intelligence Division, then the war-planning staff of the Admiralty. The 'publication of rare or unedited works relating to the Navy' helped to inform

HM Submarine *Odin* (1928). (*NMRN*)

current debates on many aspects of naval policy. The NRS, which publishes annual volumes, remains central to historical study of the Royal Navy in the twenty-first century.

See 14 June 1910.

1901 Professor John Beaglehole, OM, New Zealand historian, biographer of Capt James Cook, RN, and editor of his journals, born at Wellington, where he died on 10 October 1971.

1918 AMC *Patia* torpedoed and sunk by UC-49 in Bristol Channel.

Operation Corporate. Falklands 1982

List of ships engaged:

Active, Alacrity, Ambuscade, Andromeda, Antelope, Antrim,† Ardent,* Argonaut,† Arrow, Avenger, Brilliant,† Bristol, Broadsword,† Cardiff, Coventry,* Endurance, Exeter, Hermes, Fearless, Glasgow,† Intrepid, Invincible, Glamorgan,† Minerva, Penelope, Plymouth,† Sheffield,* Yarmouth.* S/Ms: *Conqueror, Courageous, Onyx, Spartan, Splendid, Valiant.*

Minesweeping trawlers: *Cordella, Farnella, Junella, Northella, Pict.* Casualty ferries: *Dumbarton Castle, Hecla, Herald, Hydra, Leeds Castle.* RFAs: *Appleleaf, Bayleaf, Blue Rover, Brambleleaf, Engadine, Fort Austin, Fort Grange, Olmeda, Olna, Pearleaf, Plumleaf, Regent, Resource, Sir Bedivere, Sir Galahad** (CTL), *Sir Geraint, Sir Lancelot, Sir Percivale, Sir Tristram,† Stromness, Tidepool, Tidespring.* RMAS: *Goosander, Typhoon.* Merchant ships taken up from trade: *Alvega, Anco Charger, Astronomer, Atlantic Causeway, Atlantic Conveyor,* Avelona Star, Balder London, Baltic Ferry, British Avon, British Dart, British Enterprise III, British Esk, British Tamar, British Tay, British Test, British Trent, British Wye, Canberra, Contender Bezant, Eburna, Elk, Europic Ferry, Fort Toronto, Geestport, Iris, Irishman, Laertes, Lycaon, Nordic Ferry, Norland, Queen Elizabeth 2, Salvageman, Saxonia, Scottish Eagle, St Edmund, St Helena, St Edmund, Stena Seaspread, Stena Inspector, Tor Caledonia, Uganda, Wimpey Seahorse, Yorkshireman.*

*Sunk. †Damaged.

See p.342.

1940 AMC *Scotstoun* sunk by U-25 in N.W. Approaches (57.00N, 09.57W).

1940 Fifteen Skua aircraft (*Ark Royal*) attacked the *Scharnhorst* at Trondheim. Only one bomb hit, and that did not explode. Eight Skuas lost. FAA Sqns: 800, 803.

1943 Destroyer *Nubian* received the surrender of the Italian island of Linosa, W. of Malta.

1943 Submarine *Ultor* bombarded the D/F station on Salina, Lipari Islands.

1944 Destroyer *Boadicea* sunk by German torpedo aircraft S.W. of Portland Bill (50.26N, 02.34W). Convoy EBC 8.

1944 Canso T/162 (RCAF) sank U-715 off Shetland (62.45N, 02.59W).

1954 Memorial plaque honouring the 6,200 RNVR personnel who died in the Second World War unveiled at the Naval Club, Mayfair, by Admiral of the Fleet Viscount Cunningham of Hyndhope.

See 22 November 2000.

1984 Frigate *Jupiter* collided with London Bridge after slipping from the cruiser *Belfast* in the Pool of London under her own power and having declined assistance of tugs. Court martial at Portsmouth 4, 5, 6 and 7 December; Severe Reprimand.

See 5 June 1962.

14 JUNE

A Memorable Date observed by the Corps of Royal Marines – recapture of the Falkland Islands

1667 The Dutch fleet withdrew from the Medway after five days of barely opposed depredations taking with them the captured British flagship *Royal Charles* (whose stern carvings are still displayed in the Rijksmuseum in Amsterdam). Chatham dockyard survived but the Royal Navy had lost one first-rate, three second-rates and three third-rates taken, burned, sunk or scuttled as blockships. 'A combination of bankruptcy, complacency and incompetence had exposed the fleet to catastrophe' – Rodger. The operation put the Dutch in a position of strength at the Peace of Breda, signed on 21 July, which ended this Second Dutch War. 'In wisdom, courage, force, knowledge of our own streams, and success, the Dutch do end the war with victory on their side' – Pepys, 29 July 1667.

See 10, 12 and 13 June 1667, 24 March 1961.

1758 The commissioners of the Navy bought five fields near Stonehouse Creek on which the RN Hospital, Stonehouse, was built. It opened in 1762; the transfer of patients from the hospital ship *Canterbury* began on 20 November 1762.

See 15 September 1744, 29 June 1962, 31 March 1995.

1789 Capt William Bligh arrived at Kupang, Timor, after his 3,618-mile voyage in an open boat following the mutiny in *Bounty*.

See 9 September 1754, 23 December 1787, 28 April 1789, 7 December 1817.

1809 Boats of *Scout* cut out seven French storeships and stormed a battery near Cape Croisette.

1809 Harry Keppel, future admiral of the fleet, born.

See 14 April 1857 and next entry; 26 June 1902, 17 January 1904.

1843 Boats of *Dido* destroyed the Saribas town of Pakoo, Borneo.

1853 Chief Petty Officers. Admiralty Circular No. 121: 'My Lords consider that it would improve the discipline of her Majesty's ships, and be in other respects advantageous to the Service, to establish a class of chief petty officers, and they therefore direct that the following be established accordingly:

Chief petty officers – Masters-at-Arms, Chief Gunner's Mate, Chief Boatswain's Mate, Admiral's Coxswain, Chief Captain of Forecastle, Chief Quarter-Master, Chief Carpenter's Mate, Seamen's Schoolmaster, Ship's Steward, Ship's Cook.

As an inducement to render themselves proficient in all branches of their duty . . . My Lords are pleased to direct that a higher class of able seamen be established under the denomination "leading seamen" . . . to be exempted from corporal punishment, except by sentence of a court martial, or for mutiny.'

1910 The Society for Nautical Research established; 'A useful, if humble, ally to the Navy Records Society' – *The Times*, 25 March 1910.

See 13 June 1893, 21 October 1922, 17 July 1928.

1917 Admiralty eventually approved scheme for convoy of merchant ships.

1917 AMC *Avenger* sunk by U-69 80 miles W. of the Shetland Islands.

1917 Curtis H.12 flying boat 8677 destroyed Zeppelin L-43 off Vlieland.

1940 Submarine *Odin*, Lt-Cdr K.M. Woods, sunk by the Italian destroyer *Strale* in the Gulf of Taranto. First of three large submarines lost in three days, leaving only three of their size.

See 12 June 1940.

1940 First underwater RMS by AB R. Tawn of a German magnetic mine, in seven fathoms at Poole, a motor car horn his tool.

1943 Frigate *Jed* and sloop *Pelican* sank U-334 in N. Atlantic (58.16N, 28.20W). Convoy ONS 10.

1944 Destroyers *Ashanti* and *Piorun* (Polish) sank M-83 off Cap de la Hague and then M-343 south of Jersey.

1950 Destroyer *Diamond*, like her nominal successor the third of class and also built on the Clyde, launched at John Brown's by Mrs Denny, wife of Vice Admiral Michael Denny, Third Sea Lord and Controller. Admiral Denny referred to the Daring-class 'as the most comprehensive and capable ships which human ingenuity could devise' – *Navy* magazine.

See 27 November 2007.

1951 *Indomitable*, flag of Admiral Sir Philip Vian, C-in-C Home Fleet, arrived in Stockholm, the first British aircraft carrier visit to the Swedish capital.

1957 Submarine *Sidon*, which sank after an explosion at Portland on 16 June 1955, towed out to sea and scuttled in 20 fathoms for use as a seabed target.

1970 *Ark Royal* embarked first Phantoms, twelve aircraft of 892 NAS.

See 27 November 1978.

1982 Final assault on Port Stanley by 3 Cdo Brigade and 5 Infantry Brigade with NGS from *Active*, *Ambuscade*, *Avenger* and *Yarmouth*. 2 Para took Windy Ridge, the Scots Guards Mount Tumbledown. The Gurkhas took Mount William: 'We saw them. They saw us. They knew who we were. They ran away.'

Argentine forces surrendered to Maj-Gen J.J. Moore RM. 'Large numbers of the enemy abandoned their positions, threw away their weapons and stood about disconsolately.' South Atlantic medal awarded, its ribbon reminiscent of the 1939–45 Atlantic Star with a rosette for those who saw action south of 7 degrees South. Battle Honour: Falkland Islands 1982. Ships listed on p.340.

CLF: Maj-Gen J.J. Moore RM. 3 Cdo Brigade (enhanced) – 40, 42 and 45 Cdo RM with 2 Para and 3 Para. 5 Inf Brigade, 1 Welsh Guards, 2 Scots Guards, 1/7 Gurkhas. FAA Sqns: Sea Harrier: 800, 801, 809; Sea King: 820, 824, 825, 826, 846; Wessex: 845, 847, 848; Lynx: 815; Wasp: 829. RAF Sqns: Harrier: 1 (embarked in *Hermes*); Chinook: 18 (in *Atlantic Conveyor* with one ashore); Vulcan: 44, 50 and 101, who bombed Port Stanley airfield; Victor: 55 and 57 who refuelled them; Nimrod: 42, 51, 120, 201 and 206; and Hercules: 24, 30, 47 and 70, who covered the South Atlantic.

This campaign, in which 255 Task Force lives were lost, was characterised by 'a mixture of well-practised procedures and hectic improvisation . . . that were in the light of history nothing new to the Royal Navy' – *The Naval Review*. It epitomised, over 100 years later, the confidence of a sailor appealed to by his military colleagues in another part of the world on 28 December (1857). A correspondent in *The Times* noted, with apologies to Belloc, that 'Whatever happens, they have got The Exocet and we have Nott'. (Mr J. Nott, as he then was, was Secretary of State for Defence.)

2003 *Mersey*, offshore patrol vessel, launched at Vosper Thornycroft. The last ship built at Vosper's Woolston Yard on the River Itchen at Southampton – where John I. Thornycroft moved from Chiswick in 1904 – before Vosper's moved their work to Portsmouth Naval Base.

See 25 June 1907, 26 March 2004.

2006 *Clyde*, offshore patrol vessel (helicopter), 'loaded out' from the Vosper Thornycroft assembly hall in Portsmouth Naval Base. She was the first complete warship built at Portsmouth for thirty-nine years. The frigate *Andromeda*, launched 24 May 1967, was the last warship built in Portsmouth Dockyard. *Clyde*, a replacement for the Castle-class vessels employed in the Falkland Islands, is owned by the builders and leased by the MOD.

See 7 September 2006.

2007 Service of thanksgiving, attended by HM The Queen, HRH The Duke of Edinburgh, Prime Minister and Service chiefs, at the Falklands Memorial Chapel, Pangbourne, on the twenty-fifth anniversary of the surrender of Argentine forces in the Falkland Islands.

See 4 May 1991, 28 February 1996, 23 October 2005, 17 June 2007.

J Company, 42 Cdo, Royal Marines approaching Stanley at the end of their epic yomp, June 1982. (*RMM 7/10/18(442)*)

15 JUNE

1744 Cdre George Anson anchored at St Helens in *Centurion*, the sole survivor of the squadron which had sailed under his command from St Helens on 18 September 1740. He had circumnavigated the world in one of the great voyages of British history.

See 18 September 1740, 20 June 1743, 4 July 1744.

1779 Prince William Henry, third son of King George III and future King William IV and Lord High Admiral, joined *Prince George* (98), flagship of Rear-Admiral Robert Digby, at Spithead, as a midshipman. A Spanish admiral observed that 'Well does Great Britain deserve the sovereignty of the seas when princes of the blood royal are content to learn their duties in a humble station in her navy'.

1780 *Apollo* fought the French privateer *Stanislaus* off Ostend.

1812 *Sandwich* captured the French privateer *Courageux* off Guernsey.

1845 Landing parties from *Conway* and the French *Berceau* and *Zelée* repulsed in an attack on the forts at Tamatave, Madagascar.

1870 *Swiftsure* launched at Palmers, Jarrow. In 1893 the last rigged battleship to hoist sail during fleet operations at sea.

1881 *Polyphemus*, torpedo ram, launched at Chatham. The only RN ship designed and built for that purpose. Her engine room complement larger than upper-deck establishment. She was painted light grey and although never in action, she broke the wooden boom at Berehaven, Ireland on exercises in 1887.

1885 Battleship *Benbow*, the first ship to carry Elswick's 110-ton, 16.5-in BL gun, launched at Thames Ironworks. Her huge main armament gave *Benbow* high public status but the guns were unwieldy to operate and had a very short barrel-life, and the weight caused the muzzles to droop.

1894 Philip Louis Vian born.

See 16 February 1940, 27 May 1968.

1941 *Bismarck*'s seventh and last supply ship sunk by *Dunedin*. These successes alarmed those concerned to protect Ultra intelligence.

See 3, 4 and 12 June 1941.

1941 'On this day came three citizens of the United States of America, the first of their

The battleship *Benbow*, the first British ship to carry the Elswick 110-ton 16.5-in BL gun, lying at anchor off Pembroke Dock in about 1889. (*Author*)

countrymen to become Sea-Officers of the Royal Navy. In memory of those Americans who, between 1939 and 1941, when the fate of Great Britain and the cause of freedom hung in the balance, volunteered to serve in the Royal Navy' – Memorial in the Painted Hall, RN College, Greenwich.

See 18 October 1941, 3 October 2001, 22 June 2004.

1941 Light cruiser *Dauntless*, steaming up the Malacca Strait from Singapore at night, ran into the port side of the light cruiser *Emerald* en route to Singapore from the Gulf. *Emerald* lost sixteen men and *Dauntless* lost her paint store and 10ft of her bows that were removed from the port side of *Emerald* in dry dock in Singapore. This was her second major bump.

See 2 July 1928, 23 January 2007.

1942 Destroyer *Bedouin*, Cdr B.G. Scurfield RN, sunk by Italian torpedo aircraft off Tunisia (36.12N, 11.38E) after being disabled in a gallant attack on Italian cruisers threatening what remained of the Operation Harpoon convoy to Malta. The pilot of one aircraft was decorated forty-seven years later on the evidence of the ship's First Lieutenant. Cdr Scurfield was taken prisoner and after the Italian surrender he fell into German hands. He was killed in 1945 in an Allied air attack as advancing friendly forces were approaching his prison camp in N. Italy. He had won the AM for gallantry when his earlier command, the destroyer *Hunter*, was mined in 1937 off Almeria.

See 13 May 1937, 8 April 1940, 8 June 1940.

Cdr Scurfield's 'spirit was . . . typical of the British destroyer service throughout the war. Again and again did their Captains and ships' companies unhesitatingly sacrifice themselves to defend their charges against hopeless odds . . . the *Bedouin*'s name and her Captain should be remembered with those of *Glowworm*, *Acasta*, *Ardent* and the many, many destroyers lost in the Arctic, at Dunkirk, off Crete and in a hundred other fights' – Capt Stephen Roskill RN, *The War at Sea*, vol.2, p.67.

1942 Destroyer *Hasty* torpedoed by the German S-55 (34.10N, 22.00E) S.E. of Crete, sunk by *Hotspur*. *Airedale* bombed S. of Crete (33.50N, 24.00E); sunk by own forces. *Nestor* (RAN) bombed (33.36N, 24.30E) and taken in tow by *Javelin*, but had to be sunk on the 16th. Operation Vigorous.

1942 Submarine P 35 (later *Umbra*) sank the Italian cruiser *Trento* in central Mediterranean (35.10N, 18.40E).

1942 *Kingston Ceylonite*, on loan to USN, sunk in Chesapeake Bay by mine laid by U-701.

1944 Frigate *Mourne* sunk by U-767 with homing torpedo 40 miles S.S.W. of the Lizard (49.25N, 05.30W). Frigate *Blackwood* torpedoed by U-764 23 miles S.E. of Portland (50.07N, 02.15W). Sank in tow on 16th. Operation Neptune.

1944 Submarine *Satyr* sank U-987 off Norway (68.01N, 05.08E).

1944 *Sickle* sunk by mine in Aegean. The forty-fifth and last submarine lost in the Mediterranean.

1945 Air strike on, and bombardment of, Truk, Carolines, by Rear-Admiral E.J.P. Brind (*Implacable*). Operation Inmate. T.G.111.2. Ships: *Achilles*, *Implacable*, *Newfoundland*, *Ruler*, *Swiftsure*, *Teazer*, *Tenacious*, *Termagant*, *Terpsichore*, *Troubridge*, *Uganda*. Aircraft (*Implacable*): Seafire: 801, 880; Avenger: 828; Firefly: 1771.

1953 Coronation Review of the Fleet at Spithead. *Britannia* still building, hence *Surprise*, dispatch vessel of C-in-C Mediterranean Fleet, used as royal yacht. Only one battleship, *Vanguard*, flagship of Admiral Sir George Creasy, C-in-C Home Fleet, was present with 156 naval ships from sixteen nations. Fleet Air Arm flypast by 300 aircraft from thirty-eight squadrons. Only one RN ship present, the diving support ship *Reclaim*, was still in commission twenty-five years later.

1960 RN Hospital Mauritius taken over from the Army. Closed 13 February 1976.

1968 Polaris era in Royal Navy began with *Resolution* sailing on her first patrol.

See 12 May 1996, 28 August 1996.

16 June

1745 Capture of Louisburg and the whole of Cape Breton Island by Cdre Peter Warren (*Superb*) and Mr William Pepperell, commanding the Colonial troops. Ships: *Canterbury, Chester, Eltham, Hector, Lark, Launceston, Mermaid, Princess Mary, Sunderland, Superb.*
See 26 July 1758.

1797 *Boston* captured the Spanish privateer *St Bernardo* (alias *Conquestador*) 75 miles N.E. by N. of Cape Ortegal.

1809 Nelson's 'favourite' ship, *Agamemnon* (64), which he had commanded from 1793 to 1796, ran aground on an unmarked shoal off Maldonado in the Plate Estuary and broke up. Capt Jonas Rose, who was acquitted at a court-martial on board HMS *Bedford* at Rio de Janeiro 22 July, had been navigating by a Spanish chart and attributed the rapid flooding of his ship to her rotten timbers. The wreck is being excavated by nautical archaeologists. Nelson's old flagship *Foudroyant* was wrecked on the same day in 1897.
See 10 April 1781.

1812 *Swallow* fought the French *Renard* and *Goeland* off Ile Ste Marguerita, Gulf of Fréjus.

1842 Capture of Woosung and Paoshan. Ships: *Algerine, Blonde, Clio, Columbine, Cornwallis, Modeste, North Star, Jupiter.* Steamers (towing): *Medusa, Sesostris* (IN), *Nemesis, Phlegethon, Pluto, Tenasserim* (Ben. Mar.).

1855 Bombardment of Sevastopol. Ships: *Arrow, Highflyer, Miranda, Niger, Snake, Terrible, Tribune, Viper, Weser* and French steamers, *Danube* and launches of *Royal Albert.*

Operations Vigorous and Harpoon, 1942

These operations, aimed at supplying Malta, used two convoys, one from the east (*Vigorous*), and the other from the west (*Harpoon*), with ships arriving at Malta on successive days. The six ships in the *Harpoon* convoy passed through the Straits of Gibraltar on the night 11/12 June, escorted by the carriers *Eagle* and *Argus*, battleship *Malaya*, cruisers *Kenya*, *Liverpool* and *Charybdis* and eight destroyers. On the 14th, in calm weather – which made it difficult for the carriers to operate – the convoy was attacked by high-level, dive- and torpedo-bombers. One merchant ship was sunk, and the cruiser *Liverpool* badly hit. She had to be towed back to Gibraltar by the destroyer *Antelope*, and arrived there safely despite further air attacks. A U-boat also attacked the convoy, but did no damage.

At 2100 that day the convoy reached 'the Narrows', and the main escort detached, leaving the cruiser *Cairo* and nine destroyers to escort the convoy and some ten minesweepers bound for Malta. At 0630 on the 15th an enemy force of two cruisers and four destroyers closed the convoy. The fleet destroyers of the escort attacked at once, while the *Cairo* (an AA cruiser) and smaller escorts made smoke. *Bedouin* and *Partridge* were disabled, but one enemy destroyer was hit and the enemy turned away. Meanwhile, the convoy was attacked by dive-bombers, and the escort had to fight them off while the enemy surface force returned to harass the convoy. Three merchant ships were lost. The escort were reinforced by the fast minelayer *Welshman* that afternoon. She had gone ahead to deliver stores to Malta independently. As the convoy passed through the minefields in the approaches to Malta in the evening of the 15th, one of the two merchant ships hit a mine, but was brought to harbour. One destroyer was also lost in the minefield and three other escorts were damaged. The *Partridge* took the *Bedouin* in tow, but the enemy surface force returned, and while *Partridge* was defending her, the *Bedouin* was sunk by a torpedo bomber.

The *Vigorous* convoy of eleven ships sailed from Port Said on 11 June, with a covering force of eight cruisers and twenty-six destroyers, corvettes and minesweepers. On the 14th it suffered air and E-boat attacks, and three merchant ships were hit – two were sunk. On the 15th, Italian heavy units sailed from Taranto, and that day the convoy changed course several times to avoid enemy surface forces. By 1930 that day, the escort had only one-third of its ammunition left, and the convoy had been subject to 'all known forms of attack'. Two cruisers had been damaged and the destroyers *Hasty* and *Airedale* sunk. The convoy was recalled, and on the return passage the cruiser *Hermione* and destroyer *Nestor* were lost.

In summary, two merchant ships reached Malta out of seventeen that set out, and one cruiser and five destroyers were lost.

Sevastopol seen from HMS *Sidon*, 1855. (*NMRN 1977/380*)

1871 Iron screw frigate *Megaera* put ashore on St Paul's Island, Indian Ocean, her hull having rusted through.

1897 Two-decker *Foudroyant*, Nelson's brand new flagship in the Mediterranean 8 June 1799 to June 1800 and since 1890 employed as a boys' training ship, wrecked on Blackpool Sands during a fund-raising cruise round Britain. During the campaign to recapture Naples the revolutionary Francesco Caracciolo was sentenced to death on board and, suggests Colin White, Nelson's daughter Horatia was conceived.

See 28 February 1758, 30 June 1799, 16 June 1809.

1919 Minesweeper *Kinross* mined in Aegean.

1920 Battleships *Revenge* and *Ramillies*, seaplane carrier *Ark Royal* and destroyers in action against Turks at Istria (until 21st)

1923 Submarine X 1 launched at Chatham: the only post-First World War construction to have been scrapped before Second World War.

1924 The first RN officers 'appointed for services in the Air arm of the Fleet', thirty lieutenants, five sub-lieutenants and six RM officers, reported to RAF No. 1 Flying Training School, Netheravon, to begin six months' pilot training. They would be attached to the RAF for four years, granted RAF rank but retaining their RN or RM rank and uniform, and wear Fleet Air Arm distinguishing badges.

1940 Submarines *Grampus* sunk by the Italian TBs *Circe* and *Clio* off Syracuse, Sicily and *Orpheus* by Italian destroyer *Turbine* off Tobruk.

1940 AMC *Andania* torpedoed and sunk 200 miles S.E. of Iceland (62.36N, 15.09W) by U-A, originally a Turkish minelaying S/M taken up and converted by Germany, the mine tubes replaced by oil tanks.

1941 Swordfish of 815 Sqn, from Nicosia, torpedoed and sank the French destroyer *Chevalier Paul* off Turkish coast (35.18N, 35.18E).

1941 Light cruiser *Hermione* sunk by U-205 S of Crete (33.20N, 26.00E). Operation Vigorous.

1942 *Kujawiak* (Pol) sunk by mine E. of Grand Harbour, Malta (35.53N, 14.35E). Operation Harpoon.

1943 Hudson T/459 (RAAF) sank U-97 off Cyprus (33.00N, 34.00E).

1955 Submarine *Sidon* sank in Portland harbour after explosion of an experimental torpedo. AM: Surg-Lt C.E. Rhodes. Posthumous.

See 5 March 1954, 14 June 1957, 12 August 2000.

1969 *Repulse* sailed on her first Polaris patrol.

See 15 June 1968, 12 May 1996.

1969 New ensign first worn by RFA vessels. The plain upright yellow anchor dates from the late seventeenth-century badge of the Commissioners of Transport, many of the functions of which devolved upon the Fuel, Movements and Transport Department of the RNSTS. DCI(RN) 684/69.

1977 Frigate *Penelope*, trials ship for the Seawolf missile before its installation in *Broadsword*, first of the Type 22 frigates, engaged and destroyed a 4.5-in shell moving at Mach 2.

1987 *Warrior* (1860) arrived at Portsmouth. Ex-Hulk C77, removed from the *Navy List* as *Vernon III* in 1904, ex-*Warrior*, second of the name.

See 29 December 1860.

17 June

A Memorable Date observed by the Corps of Royal Marines – Bunker Hill

1693 Vice-Admiral Sir George Rooke (*Royal Oak*) and Rear-Admiral Philips van der Goes (*Admiral General*), with the famous Smyrna convoy, fought a French fleet of eighty sail under Admiral Comte de Tourville off Lagos. Dutch ships captured: *Wapen van Medemblik*, *Zeeland*. Convoy was scattered, with ninety-two vessels being taken or destroyed.

1694 *Weymouth* captured the French *Invincible* 140 miles W. of Cape Clear. *Dunkirk* was in company, but did little.

1755 James Cook, future Pacific explorer, entered the Navy.

1775 *Glasgow* and *Lively* cannonaded the enemy at the Battle of Bunker Hill. Two battalions of Marines engaged ashore: 'break and let the Marines pass through you.' Never was the reputation of the Marines more nobly sustained.

1778 *Arethusa* (28), taken in 1759, fought the French *Belle-Poule* (32). *Alert* captured the French *Coureur*. Both actions took place near Plouescat, Brittany.

1794 *Romney* captured the French *Sibylle* in Mykoni harbour.
Battle Honour: *Sibylle* 1794.

Admiral Lord Barham (1726–1813). *(NMRN 1971/12(29))*

1795 Cornwallis' Retreat. Vice-Admiral the Hon. William Cornwallis (*Royal Sovereign*) with five ships and two frigates fought Vice-Admiral Villaret-Joyeuse (*Peuple*), with thirteen of the line, fourteen frigates, two brigs and a cutter, off Penmarc'h Point, Brittany. Ships: *Bellerophon, Brunswick, Mars, Royal Sovereign, Triumph*. Frigates: *Pallas, Phaeton*. Regiments: 86th, 118th.
Battle Honour: Cornwallis' Retreat 1795.

1813 Admiral Charles Middleton, Lord Barham, First Lord of the Admiralty in 1805, died.
See 14 October 1726.

1815 *Pilot* fought the French *Egerie* off Cape Corse, Corsica.

1842 Capture of two Chinese batteries 6 miles above Woosung. Ships: *Clio, Columbine, Modeste*. Steamers (towing): *Phlegethon, Pluto* (Ben. Mar.), *Nemesis*.

1843 Boats of corvette *Dido* destroyed the Saribas town of Rembas, Borneo.

1855 Fourth bombardment of Sevastopol, Crimea. Naval Brigade and Royal Artillery. Sea bombardment by *Princess Royal, Highflyer, Miranda, Sidon, Snake, Viper*, launches of *Royal Albert*, and French steamers.
Battle Honour: Crimea 1854–5.

1900 Bombardment and capture of the Taku forts, China. Ships engaged: *Algerine, Fame* and *Whiting*; *Lion* (Fr), *Iltis* (Ger), *Bobr, Giliak, Koreytz* (Ru). *Fame* and *Whiting* captured four Chinese torpedo boats in the Peiho, below Tongku, China.

1904 Destroyer *Sparrowhawk* (third of the name) wrecked on uncharted rock at mouth of the Yangtze River.

1916 Zeppelin L-48 was shot down and yielded German naval signal book.

1918 *Lychnis*, the only First World War Q-ship to serve in Second World War, sank U-64 off southern Sardinia (38.07N, 10.27E).

Serving personnel, veterans and their families attend a parade at Horse Guards on 17 June 2007 to mark the 25th anniversary of the end of the Falklands War. (*RN*)

1919 VC: Lt Augustus Willington Shelton Agar RN. Agar in CMB4 attacked and sank the Russian cruiser *Oleg* with a single 18-in torpedo off the main Russian Baltic Fleet base of Kronstadt on Kotlin Island. He was officially operating under Foreign Office direction from a covert base at Terrioki on the Finnish coast inserting secret agents into Petrograd which necessitated a vague VC citation. A DSO followed in August.

See 22 November 1918, 18 August 1919, 5 April 1942, 20 July 2003.

1934 Two British submariners, Lt J.D. Luce of HMS *Osiris* (a future First Sea Lord), and Lt P.L. Field of *Oswald*, among twenty passengers kidnapped by Chinese pirates who took over and looted the steamer *Shuntien* E. of Tientsin off the mouth of the Yellow River (Huang He) in N. China before escaping with their hostages in pre-positioned junks. Japanese, United States and British warships, including the carrier *Eagle* and two destroyers from Wei-Hai-Wei, steamed to the area. On 20 June the Admiralty announced that, 'as a result of naval action', Luce, Field and two of the ship's officers were safe on board the destroyer *Whitshed*.

See 24 December 1941, 6 January 1971.

1940 *La Curieuse* (Fr) sank the Italian S/M *Provana* in the W. Mediterranean, 80 miles off Oran.

1940 Evacuation of BEF from north-west France (Brest and St Nazaire) began. Operation Ariel.

1942 Destroyer *Wild Swan* damaged by German aircraft off Bantry Bay (49.52N, 10.44W) and sank after colliding with Spanish fishing boat.

1944 Mosquito D/333 (Nor) sank U-423 off south-west Norway (63.06N, 02.05E).

1944 Allied landings to recapture Elba. On 16 June the 19th Minesweeping Flotilla swept a channel to the main landing beach at Campo Bay on the south coast of Elba, cutting forty-two mine moorings. A mainly French Commando force landed from thirty-eight RN landing craft under supporting fire from river gunboats *Aphis*, *Cockchafer* and *Scarab*. Operations Brassard and Cut Out. The CO of LCI(L) 184 reported that in the middle of the landings, which were not going well, 'a cheery soul from the shore hailed me with what sounded like "Can you make some coffee?" This seemed a little odd,' continued the report, 'but it transpired that he was a press representative asking "Can you take some copy?"' – Roskill, *The War at Sea*, vol.3, pt.2, p.80.

1958 A Scimitar naval strike aircraft, piloted by Lt-Cdr Derek Robbins RN, set-up a new flight time record from London to Valletta, Malta, of 2 hours 12 minutes 27.2 seconds. The 1,298 miles completed at an average speed of 588 mph.

See 19 July 1949, 27 November 1951.

1993 Disbandment of RNXS and drastic reductions in RNR announced in House of Commons.

See 5 November 1962, 18 January 1963, 1 April 1994.

2007 Falklands twenty-fifth anniversary parade on Horse Guards Parade.

See 14 June 2007.

18 JUNE

1794 Capt Nelson of *Agamemnon* (64) began landing troops and guns at the small inlet of Porto Agro, S.W. of Calvi, Corsica, to begin the siege of the French-held Calvi citadel.

See 12 July 1794, 10 August 1794, 16 June 1809.

1799 *Centaur, Bellona, Captain, Emerald* and *Santa Teresa* captured the French *Junon, Alceste, Courageuse, Salamine* and *Alerte* 60 miles S. of Cape Sicie, southern France.

1806 Haulbowline naval establishment set up by Order in Council at Queenstown.

1809 *Latona* (38) captured the French *Félicité* (*en flute*) 280 miles N. by W. of Puerto Rico.

1812 *Hind* captured the French privateer *Incomparable* 6 miles E.S.E. of Dodman Point.

1812 The United States declared war on Great Britain.

See 17 November 1810, 24 December 1814.

1826 *Sybille* (44) destroyed two Greek pirate misticoes off Kalo Limniones.

1855 British attack on the Great Redan; French attack on the Malakoff. Siege of Sevastopol, Crimea. Both attacks repulsed.

VC: Capt William Peel (*Leander*). When a live shell landed in the magazine, he picked it up and threw it away. He was wounded placing the first ladder for the assault on the Redan. Mid Edward St John Daniel was also awarded the VC for the above actions, though it was forfeited later. Lt Henry James Raby (*Wasp*), AB John Taylor and Boatswain's mate Henry Curtis awarded VC for a 70-yd dash under heavy and close fire to rescue a wounded soldier. Lt Raby (Cdr September 1855) was the first man to wear the VC, having been the senior officer of the Senior Service at the first VC investiture in Hyde Park, 26 June 1857. Also nominated, unsuccessfully, for VC was Mid Evelyn Wood, Queen, for what his recommendation quaintly reported as 'the most beautiful courage and conduct, and manners that were exemplary'. Wood left RN in 1855, joined the Army and three years later as Lt (later Field Marshal) Wood, 17th Lancers, won his VC during the Indian Mutiny.

1858 Naval Brigade from wood screw corvette *Pearl* and a company of the 13th Light Infantry defeated the rebel forces at Haraiya (north of Gogon Rise, India).

1864 American Civil War. CSS *Alabama* sunk by USS *Kearsarge* off Cherbourg. Last naval action in home waters in war in which UK not involved.

1916 Destroyer *Eden*, Lt A.C.N. Farquhar RN, escorting the transport SS *France* over the Channel, lost in collision during the middle watch when her charge's steering gear failed. Forward section sank; after section towed to Le Havre. Farquhar and thirty-eight officers and men lost.

Capt William Peel (1824–1858), VC. Following his service in the Crimea, he led the Shannon's Naval Brigade in the Indian Mutiny and was severely wounded at the relief of Lucknow (see 16 March 1858). He died of smallpox before his return home. (*NMRN 1984/439*)

Sea Harrier FRS1 (XZ451). (*FAAM*)

1924 The first purpose-designed and built minelayer, *Adventure*, launched at Devonport by Lady Chelmsford, wife of the First Lord of the Admiralty. Designated a cruiser minelayer, the ship carried a weak main armament of four 4.7-in guns on a displacement of 6,740 tons, the guns being sacrificed to carry a load of 280 mines. This hybrid ship had steam and diesel main propulsion (the diesel exhaust abaft the after funnel marred her appearance) and she proved too big and too slow for operational minelaying in enemy waters.

1925 Light cruiser *Delhi* persuaded HM King Hussein of Jordan, who had abdicated in favour of his son but presented a destabilising influence, to take passage from Aqaba to Cyprus, salvaging the Greek *Ekaterina Inglisi* on the way.

1940 RNAS Yeovilton (HMS *Heron*) commissioned. 'The new fighter training station . . . was nothing but three runways in an ocean of mud.' – Capt Eric Brown, *Wings on my Sleeve*, p.12.

1941 Destroyers *Faulknor, Fearless, Foresight, Forester* and *Foxhound* sank U-138 off Cadiz (36.04N, 07.29W).

1944 Destroyers *Fame, Havelock* and *Inconstant* sank U-767 off Brittany with first Hedgehog pattern (49.03N, 03.13W).

1944 Wellington A/304 (Pol) sank U-441 off Ushant (49.03N, 04.48W).

1944 Destroyer *Quail* foundered in tow (40.05N, 17.52E), after being mined at the entrance to Bari on 15 November 1943.

1944 MTBs 727 and 748 torpedoed M-133 S.W. of Jersey: towed to St Malo but scuttled on 6 August.

1979 First fully operational Sea Harrier FRS1 (XZ451) delivered to the Fleet Air Arm at Yeovilton.

1982 M Company 42 Cdo RM recaptured South Thule – Operation Corporate.

19 June

1594 *Dainty* fought six Spaniards (including *San Andres*) for three days off San Mateo Bay, Ecuador, and then had to surrender.

1793 Frigate *Nymphe* (36) captured the French *Cléopatre* 20 miles W. by S. of Start Point. First decisive action in French wars. The Pellew brothers in action, Edward as Captain of *Nymphe* (knighted ten days later) and Isaac as a volunteer. Prize brought into Portsmouth 21 June. Battle Honour: *Cléopatre* 1793.

1803 Admiralty alerted Home Ports to the risk of a Fulton attack.

1808 *Seagull* taken by the Danish *Lougen* 20 miles E.S.E. of Lindesnes, southern Norway.

1842 Occupation of Shanghai by a brigade under Lt-Col Patrick Montgomerie, Madras Artillery. Ships: *Clio, Columbine, Modeste, North Star.* Steamers (towing): *Nemesis, Pluto, Phlegethon* (Ben. Mar.), *Medusa* (IN), *Tenasserim.*

Naval Gunnery

The first, very primitive naval cannon were used at the Battle of L'Espagnols in 1350 (29 August), but cannon did not become the main weapon at sea until well into the sixteenth century. The basic design of the guns – muzzle-loading smooth-bores firing a solid shot – remained constant throughout the seventeenth and eighteenth centuries, and the only important changes were in methods of casting which enabled safer and heavier guns to be manufactured. Although they had an extreme range of over a mile, such guns were most effective when fired with a flat trajectory at close range, and since over such a short distance hitting was assured for both sides, speed of loading rather than accuracy became the crucial factor that won battles.

Throughout the nineteenth century, guns increased in size and the introduction of explosive shells led to the development of armour plating. This in turn led to bigger guns with greater powers of penetration, and above all with greater ranges so that projectiles could be made to plunge onto the target from a great height and therefore with greater energy. Other refinements, such as rifling, breech-loading and high explosives also date from this period. Unfortunately, the implications were not widely realised so that naval tactics did not keep pace with such developments. Naval manoeuvres still tended to take the form of close-quarter actions on the Nelsonian model, and target practice was conducted at ranges that were measured in hundreds rather than thousands of yards.

Eventually, by the turn of the twentieth century, a new generation of senior officers was emerging led by 'Jacky' Fisher, Arthur Wilson and Percy Scott, who insisted on a more scientific approach to gunnery. Practice shoots were conducted at realistic long ranges and human error minimised by the introduction of accurate range-finding instruments together with remote control of the guns from a director placed high above the smoke and noise of the battle. These developments, when linked with the specialised training provided at *Excellent*, the gunnery school on Whale Island, revolutionised naval gunnery and led to a tradition of ingenuity and innovation which served the Royal Navy well in two world wars.

9-in muzzle-loading rifle stern gun in the broadside ironclad battleship HMS *Achilles* of 1863. (*NMRN*)

The RNZN's frigate *Canterbury* at Portsmouth in June 1977. (*NMRN W&L 2500C5*)

1854 *Eurydice, Miranda* and *Brisk*, with two belated French ships, formed White Sea squadron against Russia. Main deployments were in Baltic and in Black Sea.

1917 CMB 1 sunk by German destroyers off Ostend.

1940 Armed trawler *Moonstone* captured the Italian S/M *Galileo Galilei* off Aden (12.48N, 45.12E). Latter became X 2, then P 711; hence numbering British X craft began with X 3.

The armed trawler *Moonstone*, operating from Aden, detected a submarine by Asdic. She attacked with depth charges, but lost contact. An hour later she gained a new contact, and attacked again. The Italian submarine *Galileo Galilei* surfaced, and the trawler hit the conning tower with a 4-in shell. The submarine surrendered, the destroyer *Kandahar* towed her to Aden, and documents captured led to the sinking of three other Italian submarines shortly afterwards.

1940 First sea trials of Type 286 radar in destroyer *Verity* at Spithead.

1950 First deck landing by a turboprop-powered aircraft; Lt-Cdr G.R. Callingham in a Fairey Gannet prototype on board *Illustrious*.

See 25 March 1945, 3 December 1945.

1979 The Queen's Colour of the Mediterranean Fleet, laid up in the Chapel of HMS *St Angelo* at Malta in 1967 when Admiral Sir John Hamilton, the last C-in-C Mediterranean Fleet, hauled down his flag, was transferred to the chapel of the RN College, Greenwich in a ceremony attended by Admiral Hamilton.

See 5 June 1967.

2003 *Albion*, Capt Peter Hudson RN, commissioned at Devonport in the presence of her sponsor, HRH The Princess Royal and Admiral of the Fleet Sir Henry Leach, Captain of the previous *Albion*.

See 21 June 1898, 1 June 1954, 9 March 2001.

20 JUNE

1581 Sir Francis Drake granted his coat of arms by the College of Heralds.

1743 Cdre George Anson (*Centurion*) captured the Spanish *Nuestra Senora de Covadonga* off Cape Espiritu Santo, Philippines, a prize of great worth. Battle Honour: *N.S. de Covadonga* 1743.
See 4 July 1744, 6 June 1762.

1747 *Kent, Hampton Court, Eagle, Lion, Chester, Hector, Pluto* and *Dolphin* captured forty-eight sail out of 170 of a French West Indies convoy 400 miles N.W. of Cape Ortegal.

1774 John Day lost in first submarine experiment in Plymouth harbour.

1779 Horatio Nelson, having been promoted post-captain into *Hinchinbrook* (28) on 11 June, was succeeded in command of the brig *Badger* by Cuthbert Collingwood.
See 8 December 1778.

1783 Fifth and final battle between Vice-Admiral Sir Edward Hughes (*Superb*) and Cdre Chevalier de Suffren (*Cleopatre*), with fifteen of the line and three frigates, off Cuddalore. Ships: *Africa, Bristol, Burford, Chaser, Cumberland, Defence, Eagle, Exeter, Hero, Inflexible, Isis, Gibraltar, Magnanime, Monarch, Monmouth, Sultan, Superb, Sceptre, Worcester.* Frigates, etc.: *Active, Combustion, Harriott, Juno, Lizard, Medea, Minerva, Naiade, Pondicherry, San Carlos, Seahorse.* A French victory: Hughes retired to Madras having failed in his attack on Cuddalore while de Suffren, with an inferior force, remained there.
See 17 February 1782, 12 April 1782, 6 July 1782, 3 September 1782.

1809 Boats of *Bellerophon* cut out three vessels and stormed a Russian battery at Hango (Hanko), Finland.

1837 Accession of Queen Victoria.

1842 *Medusa* (IN) and *Phlegethon* (Ben. Mar.), with a boat each from *Columbine* and *Cornwallis*, captured eight war junks and destroyed two batteries in the Yangtze 30 miles above Shanghai.

1849 Boat of *Pilot* captured a pirate junk off Ocksеu Island.

Royal New Zealand Navy White Ensign

The New Zealand Navy Board made to the Admiralty:

It has been decided that an Ensign which displays their National identity is now appropriate for HMNZ ships but the New Zealand Navy Board wishes to retain the traditional Union Flag and white background which are part of our National and Naval history. The New Zealand White Ensign therefore displays the four red stars of the Southern Cross in the fly replacing the St George's cross now worn in the White Ensign and is at the same time of the same design as the blue New Zealand Ensign.

The date for the change is in itself a mark of the special relationship which the Royal Navy has in its position of parent service with the Royal New Zealand Navy as it is the 47th anniversary of the Order in Council which created the New Zealand Division of the Royal Navy. The New Zealand Navy Board wishes to convey on this occasion its recognition of this relationship which is widely appreciated by the New Zealand Officers and Ratings who have undergone training or served in Royal Navy ships.

We are proud to have been the last Commonwealth Navy to fly the White Ensign.

The Admiralty Board replied:

The Admiralty Board sends congratulations and good wishes to the New Zealand Navy Board and the Royal New Zealand Navy on the occasion of the announcement of the introduction of the new New Zealand White Ensign.

We warmly welcome the new Ensign and its introduction on date a which symbolises the long and friendly partnership between the Royal Navy and the Royal New Zealand Navy. We hope that the bonds of friendship and collaboration between the two Navies will long continue. DCI(RN) 642/68.

1849 *Niger*, screw sloop, towed *Basilisk*, wood paddle sloop, stern-first at 1.46 knots. Although the famous *Rattler–Alecto* trial had been held four years earlier, the issue was clearly still unresolved.

See 3 April 1845.

1917 *Vernon*'s wireless section became Experimental Department of the Signal School at Portsmouth.

1917 *Salvia* (*Q 15*) sunk by U-94 in E. Atlantic (52.25N, 16.20W).

1921 Seagoing elements of NZ naval forces became the New Zealand Division of the RN, by Order in Council.

See 14 March 1921, 1 October 1941, 20 June 1968.

1940 Destroyer *Beagle* landed a demolition party at Bordeaux.

1940 Submarine *Parthian* sank the Italian S/M *Diamante* off Libya (32.42N, 23.49E).

1943 Submarine *United* sank Italian AMC *Olbia* off Cape Spartivento.

1943 His Majesty King George VI, accompanied by Admiral of the Fleet Sir Andrew Cunningham, sailed into Grand Harbour, Valletta, from Algiers in the light cruiser *Aurora*, Cdre W.G. Agnew RN, escorted by the destroyers *Eskimo*, *Jervis*, *Nubian* and *Lookout*. King George was the first Sovereign to land in Malta since 1911.

'The Baraccas and all other vantage points were thick with cheering people as the *Aurora* . . . passed through the breakwater at 8am [on that Sunday morning] and moored to her buoys. I have witnessed many memorable spectacles; but this was the most impressive of them all. The dense throngs of loyal Maltese, men, women and children, were wild with enthusiasm. I have never heard such cheering, and all the bells in the many churches started ringing as he landed.' – Admiral Cunningham.

1944 First German 'oyster' mine dealt with at Fluc-sur-Mer.

1944 Lt John Bridge GM and bar, RNVR, lately physics master at Firth Park Grammar School, Sheffield, and wartime bomb disposal officer, gazetted for the George Cross 'for the most conspicuous and prolonged bravery and contempt of death' during a ten-day operation in August 1943 to clear booby-trapped depth charges from Messina Harbour, Sicily, ahead of the invasion of Italy on 3 September. Lt-Cdr Bridge was invested by King George VI on 16 March 1945 and after the war he returned to his school. He died aged 91 on 14 December 2006.

See 5 February 2007.

1944 Capt Frederick John Walker awarded third bar to his DSO. His HSD (Higher Submarine Detector) PO W.H. 'Darby' Kelly was awarded an equally exceptional third bar to his DSM.

1947 GC (ex-AM): LS P.R.S. May (*St Margarets*) for rescuing seven men in fume-filled tank at Malta.

1968 Royal New Zealand Navy White Ensign introduced.

See 14 March 1921, 20 June 1921, 1 October 1941, 1 March 1967.

1982 *Illustrious* commissioned. The first RN warship to be commissioned at sea.

See 11 January 1954.

1983 First OASIS fit ashore accepted, at *Dolphin*. Onboard Automatic data processing Support in Ships and Submarines.

1997 The appointment of Admiral President, RN College, Greenwich, ended when Rear-Admiral Jeremy Blackham hauled down his flag. The last full-time Admiral President was Rear-Admiral John Carlill, appointed in July 1980. The post was then combined with that of 2SL and in November 1982 Vice-Admiral Sir Simon Cassels became Second Sea Lord and Admiral President. Vice-Admiral Sir Brian Brown assumed the presidency on becoming 2SL in September 1988 but the post was transferred to, and combined with that of ACNS during his appointment. Rear-Admiral John Brigstocke was the first ACNS to occupy the Admiral President's quarters in the college and his successor, Rear-Admiral Jeremy Blackham, the last.

See 2 January 1873, 28 October 1982.

21 June

1596 Capture of Cadiz by the Earl of Essex (*Repulse*) and Lord Charles Howard of Effingham (*Ark Royal*), and a Dutch force under Jonkheer van Duyvenvoorde, Admiral of Holland.
Battle Honour: Cadiz 1596.

Ships: *Ark Royal, Charles, Crane, Dreadnought, Lion, Lion's Whelp, Mary Rose, Mere Honour, Moon, Nonpareil, Quittance, Rainbow, Repulse, Swiftsure, Tramontana, Truelove, Vanguard, Warspite, Witness, Alcedo, Amulo, Archangel, Bark Rowe, Blue Pigeon, Brave, Brown Fish, Centurion, Chameleon, Cherubim, Corbett of Ipswich, Darling, Delight, Desire, Elizabeth of Hampton, Elizabeth of London, Experience, George, Gift of God, Grace of God, Great Katherine, Golden Dragon, Green Dragon, Hercules of Rye, Howard, Hoy of Sandwich, Hunter of Enkhuysen, Hunter of Schiedam, Jacob of Enkhuysen, Jacob of Rotterdam, John and Francis, Jonas, Jonathan, Joshua of Hamburg, Lioness, Mary Ann, Mary Margaret, Marygold, Mermaid, Mermaid of Dartmouth, Minion, Peter of London, Phoenix of Amsterdam, Pleasure of Bristol, Popinjay, Posthorse, Primrose, Prudence, Prudence of Plymouth, Roebuck, Roger and Katherine, Ruben (or Ruby), St Jacob of Akersloot, St Peter of Enkhuysen, Swan, Unicorn of Bristol, Vineyard, Violet of London, Yager of Schiedam.*

1764 William Sidney Smith born.
See 7 April 1799, 26 May 1840.

1782 *Squirrel* captured the French privateer *Aimable Manon* 15 miles N. by W. of Ushant.

1806 *Warren Hastings* (Indiaman) taken by the French *Piémontaise* 330 miles S.S.E. of Réunion, after a spirited defence of four hours.

1849 *Pilot*, brig sloop, captured a pirate junk off Lam Yit, China.

1854 VC: A/Mate Charles Davis Lucas (*Hecla*) for throwing a live shell overboard while its fuse was burning. *Hecla*, *Odin* and *Valorous* ineffectually bombarded Bomarsund. The first gallant act to win a VC.

1894 Admiralty confirmed the right of Trinity House vessels to wear the White Ensign at the foremasthead when dressed overall.

'On 21 May 1894, there occurred one of those incidents for which the 19th century has acquired a certain notoriety. The Trinity steamer *Satellite*, proceeding upon her lawful occasions, was ordered to stop by the officer commanding HMS *Mersey*. *Satellite* was dressed for some ceremonial occasion (possibly the birthday of the then Master of the Corporation) and at her masthead flew the white ensign. No protestation on the part of the *Satellite*'s master that the Corporation's vessels had long flown the ensign as a masthead flag would satisfy the zealous naval officer . . .' – Woodman, *Keepers of the Sea, A History of the Yachts and Tenders of Trinity House*, Lavenham, 1983, p.86.

'As a consequence of this incident all Trinity House vessels were issued with a letter from the Admiralty granting formal permission to fly the White Ensign at the foremasthead when dressed overall or wearing masthead flags. It was always one of the documents in my safe that had to be produced on demand on inspections and which I was supposed to wave at any other zealous Naval Officers challenging my right to fly the White Ensign at my foremasthead. The date of the letter was 21 June 1894.'

1898 *Albion*, battleship, launched by the Duchess of York at Thames Ironworks, Blackwall. Because of the narrowness of the River Thames near Canning Town the

The battleship HMS *Albion*, *c.*1908. (*NMRN*)

ship was launched broadside-on. The consequent wave engulfed a temporary viewing platform and forty onlookers perished.

See 5 July 1898, 1 June 1954, 9 March 2001, 19 June 2003.

1919 German High Seas Fleet scuttled at Scapa Flow. Eleven battleships, 5 battlecruisers, 5 cruisers and 22 destroyers sunk: 3 cruisers and 18 destroyers beached.

1934 Church of St Barbara at HMS *Excellent* on Whale Island dedicated by the first Lord Bishop of Portsmouth, Dr Neville Lovett.

See 21 August 1704, 4 February 1786, 18 February 1907, 11 November 1993.

1940 *Cape Howe*, a decoy ship operating as *Prunella*, sunk by U-28 in the W. Approaches (49.45N, 08.47W). Second World War equivalent of Q-ships of First World War. Eight were commissioned and referred to as 'freighters'. None ever sighted a U-boat, and two were torpedoed and sunk in June 1940. Such security surrounded them that they were in great danger of being sunk by friendly fire, and the six survivors were withdrawn by the end of September.

1940 Bombardment of Bardia by Vice-Admiral J.C. Tovey, *Orion* (Flag). Ships: *Neptune*, *Sydney* (RAN), *Lorraine* (Fr), *Dainty*, *Decoy*, *Hasty*, *Stuart* (RAN).

1942 *Parktown* sunk by the German S-54, S-56 and S-58 during the withdrawal from Tobruk (32.10N, 25.05E).

1942 Submarine P 514 (ex-USS R 19) sunk in collision with minesweeper *Georgian* (RCN), escort to convoy CL 43, off Cape Race (46.33N, 53.39W).

1944 Destroyer *Fury* damaged by mine in Sword area, Seine Bay. Broke away from tow and ran aground, scrapped. Operation Neptune.

1944 Air strike on Port Blair and Andaman Islands by Force 60 under Vice-Admiral Sir Arthur Power (*Renown*). Operation Pedal. Ships: *Illustrious*, *Renown*, *Richelieu* (Fr), *Ceylon*, *Kenya*, *Nigeria*, *Phoebe* and eight destroyers. FAA Sqns: Barracuda: 810, 847; Corsair: 1830, 1833, 1837.

1944 Submarine *Unsparing* sank the German Uj-2106 in the Aegean.

1944 MTBs sank the German TA-25 (ex-Italian *Intrepido*) off Spezia.

1955 Rededication of the restored chapel of the RN College, Greenwich, to St Peter and St Paul, in presence of HM Queen Elizabeth The Queen Mother. AFO 1529/55.

See 2 January 1779.

1963 'It is against the law of the Irish Republic for any member of a non-Irish force, without special authority, to land in the Republic wearing Service uniform, or to wear his Service uniform in public there. No officer or man is to travel to the Irish Republic, either on duty or on leave, in uniform.' – AFO 1168/63.

1983 *Hermione*, Leander-class frigate, the last warship refitted at Chatham, left the dockyard, escorted down the river by FO Medway. She fired a 13-gun salute to Rear-Admiral Bill Higgins.

1997 Cdr Charles Eckersley-Maslin, naval aviator, died aged 96 in Tasmania. In 1918, lying about his age, he enlisted in the Argyll and Sutherland Highlanders and was wounded in France. Found to be still only 16, he was returned to Bedford School 'where he was treated with some awe'. Served five years in RAF; resigned his reserve commission in February 1939 and joined the Royal Navy as a lieutenant-commander. Wartime service in carriers in Far East and Mediterranean and commanded HMS *Simbang*, the RNAS in Singapore, during Korean War. Father of Rear-Admiral David Eckersley-Maslin.

22 June

1372 Battle of La Rochelle, in which the Earl of Pembroke was defeated by a Castilian fleet under Ambrosio Bocanegra, Admiral of Castille.

1757 George Vancouver, protégé of Cook and naval surveyor of the north-west coast of North America, born at King's Lynn, Norfolk, fifteen months before Horatio Nelson at nearby Burnham Thorpe.

1796 *Apollo* and *Doris* captured the French *Légère* 50 miles W. of Ushant.

1798 *Princess Royal* packet, carrying mails to New York, beat off the French privateer *Aventurier*.

1813 Boats of *Castor* cut out the French privateer *Fortune* at Mongat, near Barcelona.

1815 Napoleon abdicated as French Emperor, four days after Waterloo.

See 15 July 1815.

1841 *Trafalgar*, first rate, launched at Woolwich in the presence of HM Queen Victoria and HRH Prince Albert by Nelson's niece, Lady Bridport, using a bottle of wine which had been in *Victory* at Trafalgar. The figurehead is in the RN Museum, Portsmouth.

1893 Mediterranean Fleet Flagship *Victoria* (Vice-Admiral Sir George Tyron) rammed and sunk by *Camperdown* (Rear-Admiral A.H. Markham) off Tripoli, Syria. The wreck was found in Lebanese territorial waters, 8 miles off the coast, in 2004. The hull was bows down and upright on the seabed. 1st Div. (Stbd): *Victoria, Nile, Dreadnought, Inflexible, Collingwood, Phaeton*. 2nd Div. (Port): *Camperdown, Edinburgh, Sans Pareil, Edgar, Amphion*.

See 9 April 1887, 29 January 1892, 11 November 1931, 23 January 1935.

The Price of Blind Obedience, 1893

Signal hoisted in Flagship *Victoria*: 'First division alter course in succession 16 points [180 degrees] to port preserving the order of the division.

'Second division alter course in succession 16 points to starboard preserving the order of the division.'

By semaphore *Camperdown* signalled to *Victoria*. 'Do you wish the evolution to be performed as indicated by signal?' but before it could be sent, *Victoria* signalled to *Camperdown*, 'What are you waiting for?'

Board of Inquiry

'Markham: It then flashed across my mind that there was only one interpretation of the signal and that was that I was to put my helm down and turn 16 points to starboard and the *Victoria* would ease her helm and circle round outside my division. I was all the more led to believe this as the signal to the second division was hoisted superior to that of the first division. I conferred hurriedly with the flag captain and Captain Johnstone. They were both on my way of thinking, and seeing that was the only safe way of performing the evolution I hoisted the signal . . .

The Court: With the columns at six cables apart, supposing the ships to turn towards each other with their full helm, did the absolute certainty of a collision occur to you?

Markham: Most certainly.'

1900 Capture of the Hsiku Arsenal, China. Naval Brigade from *Aurora, Centurion, Endymion*.

1917 Observer officers to wear RNAS uniform with wings instead of eagles on their sleeves.

1923 Amalgamation of RMA (Blue Marines) and RMLI (Red Marines) to reform the Royal Marines, by Admiralty Fleet Order. Confirmed by Order in Council 11 October.

On 1 August 1923 the RMLI's Forton barracks at Gosport were closed (later to become HMS *St Vincent*, which closed as a naval establishment in December 1968) and Eastney barracks became the home of Portsmouth Division, Royal Marines until 1991. The ranks of Gunner and Private were replaced by Marine.

See 21 March 1862, 1 June 1927.

1937 RN Photographic Branch instituted.

1937 *Ajax*, light cruiser, from Nassau to Trinidad in support of the civil power.

1937 Sir Eric Geddes, reforming First Lord of the Admiralty towards the end of the First World War, died at Albourne Place, Hassocks, Sussex.

Auxiliary Patrol Service Armed Motor Yacht *Campeador V*

'The gallant little *Campeador*' was commissioned for patrol service by Cdr C.H. Davey RN, aged 60, master of the Dartmoor Foxhounds, who had entered the *Britannia* in 1893 and was a midshipman in the cruiser *Grafton* on the China Station in 1896. He retired in 1911 but re-joined in 1914. His three RNVR sub-lieutenants were the owner, Mr Vernon W. McAndrew (59), Mr C.E. Turner (58), a docks superintendent and retired Surg Vice-Admiral John Reid Muir (67), Cook's biographer and author of *Messing about in Boats*. 'I am told Muir's age was really 71 but he gave it as 67 as he thought he might not be accepted at 71!' – Admiral Sir William James, C-in-C Portsmouth. They were sketched by the war artist, Sir Muirhead Bone. Davey had sent in recommendations for promotion for all three of his officers. 'I was so astonished at what I read', wrote Admiral James, 'that I sent copies to Churchill, who I knew would like to know about these gallant men. He wrote across the forms "Promote them. Age will be served"'. A tribute from 'A Naval Officer' in *The Times* of 23 July 1940 read: 'As they would have wished, they died together in the service of their country, but their example will for long remain an inspiration to the younger generation, and the little *Campeador* will be remembered and talked about, long after the war is over, by those who served in the same waters.'

When war broke out in 1914 Geddes was the General Manager of the North Eastern Railway; he was a born organiser. Prime Minister Lloyd George made him civilian Controller of the Navy in May 1917 to oversee the national shipbuilding programme (honorary temporary vice-admiral) and four months later he was appointed First Lord of the Admiralty in which post he sacked Admiral Sir John Jellicoe on Christmas Eve 1917. As chairman of the Committee on National Expenditure in 1922, he drastically reduced the officer strength of the Royal Navy – the 'Geddes Axe'.

See 26 September 1875, 20 July 1917, 24 December 1917, 10 February 1922.

1940 Armistice signed by France and Germany. Use of French Biscay ports greatly increased U-boat threat in Atlantic.

1940 The armed motor yacht *Campeador V* of the Auxiliary Patrol Service – 'the gallant little *Campeador*' (Churchill) – manned by elderly officers, mined and sunk off Portsmouth.

1944 *Bolzano*, an Italian heavy cruiser out of commission but prepared by Germany for use as a blockship, sunk by chariots at Spezia.

Cdre Carolyn Stait, the first woman to hold this substantive rank in the Royal Navy, 2004. (*RN*)

1948 Light fleet carrier *Bulwark* launched at Harland and Wolff, Belfast. Named by Countess Granville, wife of the Governor of Northern Ireland, sister of HM Queen Elizabeth The late Queen Mother. The tenth carrier built at the yard since 1935.

See 18 October 1899, 10 May 1945, 15 November 2001.

2004 Capt Carolyn Stait promoted commodore, the first woman to hold this substantive rank in the RN. Appointed Naval Base Commander (Clyde) 23 June.

See 27 June 1734, 26 September 1958, 29 October 1997, 10 January 2002.

2004 The loss of the destroyer *Veteran* with all hands on 26 September 1942 was commemorated in a service at RN College, Greenwich. The name of Surg-Lt Francis Mason Hayes RNVR of New York, a United States citizen who volunteered for service in the British Navy in 1941, and was lost in the *Veteran*, was added to the plaques, unveiled on 3 October 2001, listing the names of twenty-one fellow countrymen who volunteered for the RNVR before Pearl Harbor. Also remembered were three men of the Royal Canadian Navy who died with their ship: Lt Joseph C. Dwyer RCN, Supply Petty Officer Francis Owen Corrigan and Able Seaman Pearce B. Kelloway.

See 15 June 1941, 18 October 1941, 26 September 1942, 3 October 2001.

23 JUNE

1372 Earl of Pembroke's attempt to relieve La Rochelle failed: Castillian fleet destroyed his squadron.

1652 From Robert Blake in Dover road to Capt William Penn, Vice-Admiral of the Fleet and Captain of the *James*: 'These are to authorise you to do your utmost endeavour for the seizing of all Dutch ships and vessels, as well as men-of-war . . . To do your utmost for the sinking, burning, or otherwise destroying of them . . .' First Dutch War.

See 1 August 1739, 18 September 1740, 21 May 1798, 8 May 1943.

1745 *Bridgewater*, *Sheerness* and *Ursula* captured two Dunkirk privateers and their seven prizes off Ostend.

1795 Admiral Lord Bridport (*Royal George*) fought Rear-Admiral Villaret-Joyeuse (*Peuple*), with only twelve ships, off Ile de Groix, Brittany.

Ships: *Royal George*, *Queen Charlotte*, *Queen*, *London*, *Prince of Wales*, *Prince*, *Barfleur*, *Prince George*, *Sans Pareil*, *Valiant*, *Orion*, *Irresistible*, *Russell* and *Colossus*, with *Robust*, *Standard* and *Thunderer* from Capt Sir John Warren's squadron (Quiberon Bay expedition), which did not join up until the action was over. Frigates: *Revolutionnaire*, *Thalia*, *Nymphe*, *Aquilon*, *Astraea*, *Babet*. Sloop: *Megaera*. Hospital ship: *Charon*. Fireship: *Incendiary*. Cutter: *Dolly*. Luggers: *Argus*, *Galatea*. Regiments: 86th, 2/90th, 97th and 118th. French ships captured: *Alexandre*, *Formidable*, *Tigre*. 'Though a victory, not a very great one.'
Battle Honour: Groix Island 1795.

1800 Boats of *Renown*, *Defence* and *Fisgard* destroyed three batteries at Quimper.

1804 *Fort Diamond* taken by two boats of a French privateer in Roseau Bay, St Lucia.

1812 *Belvidera* fought the American *President* 100 miles S. of Nantucket.

1822 *Drake*, brig sloop, wrecked off Newfoundland.

1849 *Sharpshooter*, iron screw gunvessel, captured the slaver *Polka* at Macahe, Brazil.

1883 Lt Henry Leeke RN, aged 27, of the composite screw gunboat *Stork*, drowned in the Mayumba River, E. Africa, after his boat was attacked and stove in by a hippopotamus.

See 4 January 1879.

1906 *Agamemnon* launched at Beardmore. With *Lord Nelson* (Palmers, 4 September 1906), the last British battleships powered by reciprocating engines.

1911 Horace Rochfort Law born, descended from Lord Nelson's brother William (hence the Horace).

See 30 January 2005.

1913 The flag of Rear-Admiral George Patey, the first flag officer commanding Australian Fleet, hoisted in the new battlecruiser HMAS *Australia* at Portsmouth.

See 30 June 1913.

1915 First successful action of a RN decoy ship in anti-submarine operations. Disguised trawler *Taranaki*, Lt H.D. Edwards, towing submerged submarine C 24, Lt F.H. Taylor, intercepted by U-40, Kapitanleutnant Gerhardt Furbringer, off Aberdeen. U-boat put a shell across her bows and the trawler's crew simulated panic. Telephone link to C 24 failed and she could not slip her end of the tow. *Taranaki* therefore cast off her end and with 100 fathoms of 3.5-in wire hawser, 100 fathoms of coir hawser and 200 fathoms of telephone cable trailing from her bows C 24 torpedoed U-40 (57.00N, 01.50W). C 24 surfaced but had twenty turns of the telephone cable wrapped around her propeller shaft.

See 20 July 1915.

1918 British Expeditionary Force in destroyer *Syren* and light cruiser *Penelope* landed at Murmansk, N. Russia.

1925 River gunboat *Tarantula* landed an armed party to protect the British concession from rioting students at Shamseen, China. GC (ex-EGM): PO Robert Mills Chalmers.

Admiral Alexander Hood, Viscount Bridport (1727–1814)

Admiral Alexander Hood, Viscount Bridport (1727–1814). *(NMRN 1971/12(25))*

Younger brother of Samuel, Viscount Hood (see 12 December 1724). The Hoods are very confusing: the two viscounts had a pair of younger cousins, brothers with the same Christian names, though in their case, Alexander (1758–1798) who died on active service as a captain was the elder and Sam (1762–1814), who died as a vice-admiral and the 1st Baronet, the younger.

Son of the rector of Butleigh in Somerset, the elder Alexander was taken to sea in gratitude for the ecclesiastical hospitality enjoyed by a benighted post-captain to Plymouth on his way to join his ship in 1741. Promoted lieutenant in 1746, he was 'made post' in 1756 and distinguished himself as an aggressive captain in single-ship actions. Promoted to the Flag List in 1780, he assisted in the relief of Gibraltar in 1782 and two years later was second-in-command to Howe (see 1 June) for which he received an Irish peerage. Temporarily in command in 1795, he routed a stronger squadron off L'Orient and was raised to the English peerage. Succeeded Howe in 1797 but was relieved in 1800 by St Vincent as a result of a change of government, a political manoeuvre for which he was consoled by a Viscountcy and the appointments of Vice-Admiral of England and General of Marines. His monument instructs its student:

For his bravery, for his abilities,
For his advancement in his profession,
For his attachment to his King and Country,
Consult the annals of the British Navy
in which they are written in indelible characters.

1940 *Pathan* (RIN) sunk by unknown cause off Bombay (16.56N, 72.45E).

1940 Italian S/M *Galvani* sunk by sloop *Falmouth* in Gulf of Oman (25.55N, 56.55E).

1940 Destroyers *Kandahar* and *Kingston* and sloop *Shoreham* sank the Italian S/M *Torricelli* off Perim, Red Sea (12.34N, 43.16E). Destroyer *Khartoum* was damaged by unrelated explosion of torpedo airvessel, caught fire and was beached on Perim Island (12.38N, 43.42E).

1944 *Scylla*, light cruiser, mined off Normandy: CTL.

1986 Cdr David Tall took command of *Turbulent*. His brother, Jeff, had commanded *Churchill* since November 1984. They became the first brothers to command nuclear-powered submarines concurrently. Both later commanded Polaris submarines: Jeff, *Repulse* and David, *Resolution*. David Tall's crew hold the record for the longest continuously dived submarine patrol in RN history (108 days).

24 June

1340 Battle of Sluys, Edward III (*Thomas*) captured or destroyed the whole of the French fleet of about 200 vessels in the Zwyn, thus pre-empting a French descent on England, and recaptured the *Christopher*. His letter of 28 June to the Black Prince may count as the first naval dispatch.

1497 John Cabot (*Matthew*) discovered Newfoundland.

1795 *Dido* (28) and *Lowestoffe* (32) captured the French *Minerve* (38) 150 miles N. of Minorca. *Artemis* (36) escaped.
Battle Honour: *Minerve* 1795.

1801 *Swiftsure* (74) taken by the French *Indivisible*, *Dix-Aout*, *Jean-Bart* and *Constitution* 20 miles off Libyan coast. Recaptured at Trafalgar.

1840 Repulse of landing party of *Favourite* when attacking a stockade at Tongatabu, Friendly Islands.

1869 Wearing of beards and moustaches sanctioned but not one without the other. A reversal of the first edition of QR&AI.
See 6 August 1861.

Admiralty Circular Letter No. 36: Representations having been made to their Lordships that it would conduce to the health and comfort of men, under many circumstances of service, were they to be permitted to discontinue the use of the Razor on board Her Majesty's ships, they have been pleased to issue the following Regulations:

> 1. Clause 43, Chapter 44, of the Regulations is repealed, and Officers and Men on board Her Majesty's Ships, including the Royal Marines when embarked, will in future be permitted to wear Beards and Moustaches.
> 2. In all cases, when the permission granted in Clause 1 is taken advantage of, the use of the Razor must be entirely discontinued. Moustaches are not to be worn without the Beards, nor is the Beard to be worn without Moustaches.

Admiral Sir William Fisher (1875–1937)

William Wordsworth Fisher, a large man of imposing appearance, was known throughout the Service as 'The Great Agrippa'. He commanded the battleship *St Vincent* in the First Battle Squadron at Jutland and, with Chatfield, Beatty's flag captain, represented the cream of the Grand Fleet captains (his brother, Charles, a lieutenant, RNVR, had been lost in the battlecruiser *Invincible* at Jutland). He and Chatfield were the outstanding admirals in the inter-war period.

'He was a man of personal charm, exuberant vitality, mental and physical, of keen intellect and fine character, with a taste for the classics and the arts, particularly music, and an interest in social questions and in people . . . But for his death when C-in-C Portsmouth, he would probably have succeeded Chatfield and become, no doubt, one of the great First Sea Lords in British naval history' – Marder, *From the Dreadnought to Scapa Flow*, vol.2, p.16.

Fisher came from commanding the Mediterranean Fleet and had hoisted his flag in *Victory* on 7 July 1936. Preparations for the Coronation Review had, however, 'overburdened' him. Fisher's death was the first of a series of disasters that brought ruin to the flag plot in the two years before the outbreak of war. Admiral Sir Geoffrey Blake retired in December 1937; Rear-Admiral Bertram Ramsay, who had resigned as Backhouse's chief of staff in December 1935, was retired in October 1936; in 1939 Admiral Sir Reginald Henderson, Third Sea Lord and Controller, took ill in February and died that May; Admiral of the Fleet Sir Roger Backhouse, then First Sea Lord, died in post in July and Vice-Admiral Sir James Somerville, C-in-C East Indies, was retired on medical grounds the same month. 'This set of events revealed a dearth of flag officers of proven merit' – Michael Simpson, *Cunningham*, p.41. War was only two months away. Admiral Sir Dudley Pound, C-in-C Mediterranean Fleet, was brought back to succeed Backhouse as First Sea Lord and was relieved by Admiral Sir Andrew Cunningham. Admirals Ramsay and Somerville returned to active service and proved outstanding commanders, the latter remaining on the Retired List for most of the war although serving as a C-in-C. Memorials in St Ann's church, Portsmouth, and in St Paul's Cathedral, Malta.

The permission was not to be considered permanent: 'If neatness and cleanliness are not observed this order will be revoked.' Royal Marines on shore were to follow Army regulations. In the First World War reservists who had grown moustaches in private life were allowed to retain them.

1900 VC: Capt Lewis Stratford Tollemache Halliday RMLI in the defence of the British Legation in Peking during the Boxer Rebellion. Halliday, part of the force landed from the cruiser *Orlando*, led six men to eject Boxers from outbuildings of the legation. He shot four attackers but received a serious wound of the left shoulder and lung. VC presented by King Edward VII at St James's Palace on 25 July 1901. Halliday recovered and was Adjutant General Royal Marines from 1927–30 and Honorary Colonel Commandant from 1930–40. He retired at his own request in 1931 after forty-one years' service and died at Dorking in 1966 aged 95.

See 9 March 1966.

1911 King George V's Coronation Review of the Fleet at Spithead. One hundred and sixty-seven RN ships commanded by Admiral Sir Francis Bridgeman, and eighteen foreign vessels.

1916 Body of Cdr Loftus William Jones, killed in command of the destroyer *Shark* at Jutland, 31 May 1916, recovered off Swedish coast and buried in village churchyard, Fiskebakskil. Awarded posthumous VC 6 March 1917, when facts of action established. Memorial in St Peter's church, Petersfield.

1917 *Redcar* and *Kempton*, paddle minesweepers, mined off Spindle Bay, N. of Gravelines.

1919 Minesweeper *Sword Dance* mined in Dvina River, N. Russia.

1920 Start of operation against Turks on south coast of Sea of Marmara. *Iron Duke, Marlborough, Benbow, Stuart, Montrose, Shark, Sportive* and *Speedy*.

1937 Admiral Sir William Fisher, C-in-C Portsmouth, died aged 62 having collapsed from fatigue while taking the salute at a King's birthday parade on Southsea Common. Of the Royal Navy, he had written 'The Archangel Gabriel is only just good enough for such a Service. For the rest of us, it is only a question of the degree in which we fail to live up to the Navy' – cited in Admiral Sir Wm James, *Admiral Sir William Fisher*, p.158. Admiral Fisher was buried at sea off The Nab. The funeral was organised by Lt-Cdr Sir Charles Madden, First Lieutenant of *Excellent*. 'The officer who arranged the funeral of the previous C-in-C did not get promoted because the coffin was too light and when they committed it to the deep it didn't sink, and they had to fire at it for half an hour with a 12-pdr gun, while the sorrowing relatives were solaced with tea and buns on the disengaged side.' Madden weighted Fisher's coffin with two 6-in shells and all was well.

See 26 March 1875, 4 November 1936, 15 November 1967.

1941 Sloop *Auckland* sunk by German dive-bombers 20 miles E. of Tobruk (32.15N, 24.30E). One hundred and sixty-two survivors rescued by sloop *Parramatta* (RAN).

1942 Minesweeper *Gossamer* sunk by German aircraft in Kola Inlet, N. Russia (68.59N, 33.03E).

1943 Liberator H/120 sank U-194 in N. Atlantic (58.15N, 25.25W). Convoy ONS 11.

1943 *Starling*, sloop, sank U-119 and sloops *Wild Goose, Woodpecker, Wren* and *Kite* sank U-449 in Bay of Biscay (45.00N, 11.59W).

1944 MGBs 659 and 662 and MTB 670 sank Croatian TB T-7 in N. Atlantic.

1944 *Swift*, destroyer, sunk by mine in Sword area, 5 miles N. of Ouistreham, Seine Bay. Operation Neptune.

1944 Destroyers *Eskimo* and *Haida* (RCN) and Liberator O/311 (Czech) sank U-971 off Ushant (49.01N, 05.35W).

1944 VC: Flt Lt David Ernest Hornell, RCAF, in Canso P/162 (RCAF) sank U-1225 off Norway (63.00N, 00.50W). Posthumous.

1958 Dr Oscar Parkes, medical doctor, editor of *Jane's Fighting Ships 1918–1935*, author of *British Battleships* and warship authority extraordinary, died at Craigavad, Co. Down.

25 JUNE

1746 Cdre Edward Peyton (*Medway*) fought nine French ships under Mahe de La Bourdonnais (*Achille*) 27 miles off Negapatam, Madras. Ships: *Harwich, Lively, Medway, Medway's Prize, Preston, Winchester.* Not a very creditable action, which led to the recall of the Commodore.

1756 The Marine Society founded at the start of the Seven Years War by Jonas Hanway to encourage men and boys 'of good character' to join the Royal Navy. By the end of that war 5,451 men and 5,174 boys had been recruited. Britain's oldest public maritime charity.

1776 Capt James Cook sailed from Sheerness in *Resolution* for Plymouth at the start of his third and last voyage to the Pacific.

See 30 July 1768, 12 July 1776.

1859 Unsuccessful attempt by Rear-Admiral James Hope (*Chesapeake*) to force a passage up the Peiho. Attack on the Taku forts repulsed. Ships: *Chesapeake, Cruizer, Fury, Highflyer, Magicienne*; *Assistance, Hesper* (storeships). Gunboats: *Banterer, Cormorant*,*† *Forester, Haughty, Janus, Kestrel*,‡ *Lee*,† *Nimrod, Opossum, Plover*,*† *Starling*. French ships: *Duchayla, Norzagaray*. US ships: *Powhatan, Toey-Wan.*

*Flag for attack. †Sunk. ‡Sunk; raised later.

'Blood is thicker than water' – Admiral Josiah Tattnall, USN, explaining to his Secretary of the Navy why he had taken his flagship to help in the Peiho River.

1900 HSH Prince Louis Francis Albert Victor Nicholas of Battenberg, the future Admiral of the Fleet Earl Mountbatten of Burma, born at Frogmore House, Windsor.

See 27 August 1979, 5 September 1979.

1907 *Tartar*, Tribal-class destroyer, first warship launched by John I. Thornycroft at Woolston, Southampton, following the firm's move from Chiswick.

See 14 June 2003.

1908 *Indomitable* commissioned. First battlecruiser and first of the name.

1909 Royal Red Cross awarded to Sister Florence Porter of QARNNS for work in *Minerva* at Messina.

1920 Battleships *Revenge, Royal Sovereign, Marlborough* and destroyers with *Kilkis* (Greek) and four transports landed 8,000 Greek troops to occupy Panderma, Turkey. Two RN casualties.

1921 Steam-powered submarine K 15 sank in Portsmouth harbour as a result of oil in hydraulic system having expanded and overflowed in hot weather, allowing air to escape through vents. Raised and scrapped in 1923.

The K-class submarines were designed to work with the surface fleet, although they lacked appropriate communication facilities. Steam driven and fast on the surface, they inevitably took some time to dive and were unwieldy when submerged. They did not see active service until 1917 and did not justify their development.

See 31 January 1918.

1940 Destroyer *Fraser* (RCN) sunk in collision with light cruiser *Calcutta* in the Gironde (45.44N, 01.31W). (Evacuation from Bordeaux area.)

1941 Submarine *Parthian* sank the French submarine *Souffleur* off Beirut (33.49N, 35.26E).

1944 Frigates *Affleck* and *Balfour* sank U-1191 (50.03N, 02.59W) and frigate *Bickerton* sank U-269 off Lyme Bay (50.01N, 02.59W).

1950 The start of the Korean War. North Korean troops crossed the 38th parallel and went on to capture the South Korean capital, Seoul, and much of South Korea.

See 2 July 1950, 27 July 1953.

1953 The first diesel-powered major warship for the Royal Navy, the Type 61 aircraft direction frigate *Salisbury*, launched at Devonport. She was one of eight ships – four Salisbury-class and four Leopard-class AA frigates – built in the 1950s on an all-welded prefabricated common hull, prerequisites for ships to be quickly built in a home base partly destroyed in a nuclear attack. Diesel engines could be built and installed more

Royal Navy anti-narcotics patrol in the Caribbean. HMS *Iron Duke* intercepted the MV *Yalta* found to be carrying 3.7 tons of cocaine destined for Europe, 2003. (*RN*)

speedily, enabled a ship to get under way more quickly and afforded greater range, as displayed in the German *Graf Spee*, *Deutschland* and *Admiral Scheer* pocket battleships. When she was withdrawn from service in 1978 *Salisbury* was the last RN warship carrying Squid AS mortars.

See 25 June 1964, 25 June 1975.

1964 Destroyer *Diamond*, Capt J.D. Cartwright RN, in collision with frigate *Salisbury*, Capt W. Fitzherbert RN, off the Isle of Wight when the 23rd Escort Group was returning to Portsmouth after Staff College Sea Days. Courts martial at Portsmouth 18 and 19 August: Fitzherbert not guilty, Cartwright guilty of causing his ship to be hazarded by negligence.

See 25 June 1953, 29 September 1953, 27 November 2007.

1964 Assault ship *Intrepid* launched on the Clyde, the last warship built at John Brown's shipyard. Laid down 19 December 1962 (*Fearless* launched at Harland & Wolff, Belfast, on same date in 1963); commissioned 11 March 1967; paid off 31 August 1999 and left Portsmouth for the breakers at Liverpool on 12 September 2008 after thirty-two years' service.

See 19 December 1963, 25 June 1981, 21 May 1982, 12 February 2007.

1975 Frigate *Salisbury* completed the last Beira Patrol.

See 27 February 1966, 10 April 1966, 10 May 1966, 19 December 1967.

The purpose of the patrol, initiated by UN Security Council Resolution 221 in 1966, was to enforce an oil embargo on Rhodesia, which had unilaterally declared independence from Britain. The oil importation port of Beira in Portuguese Mozambique was blockaded by the Royal Navy for nine years. The blockade was not very effective because Rhodesia received oil through South Africa. The patrol was not only a major drain on naval resources but it was uneventful and boring for the ships' companies. To relieve the tedium, an inter-ship sports competition was launched in late 1968, probably by the destroyer *Dainty*, the trophy for which was the Beira Bucket. This was full of holes to emphasize the open-ended nature of the commitment. The need for the patrol ended with the independence of Mozambique in June 1975. The Beira Bucket is preserved in the National Museum of the Royal Navy, Portsmouth.

1975 His Majesty King Karl XVI Gustav of Sweden appointed an honorary admiral in Her Majesty's Fleet.

See 2 August 1889, 17 September 1948, 1 May 1951, 16 February 1953, 2 July 1958, 4 August 2001.

1981 John Nott, who succeeded Francis Pym as Secretary of State for Defence in January 1981, introduced 1981–2 Defence Estimates in 'The Way Ahead' White Paper. Drastic proposals to cut ships and personnel and reduce dockyard facilities dismayed the nation and the Navy. Number of destroyers and frigates to be cut to about fifty, including eight in reserve; only two of new carriers (*Invincible* and *Illustrious*) to be retained (*Ark Royal* still building); *Fearless* to go in 1984, *Intrepid* in 1982; manpower to be cut by 8,000–10,000 by 1986; Chatham Dockyard to be closed and Portsmouth much run down by March 1984. Most significantly, the carrier *Hermes* was to be sold to India and the ice patrol ship *Endurance* to be withdrawn from the South Atlantic. Both these decisions are generally acknowledged to have influenced the Argentine Junta's decision to proceed with *Operación Rosario*, the invasion of the Falkland Islands in the following April.

See 10 February 1933, 25 June 1981, 21 July 2004, 19 October 2010.

2003 Frigate *Iron Duke* intercepted the Panamanian-registered MV *Yalta* in the Caribbean, carrying 3.7 tons of cocaine worth £2.5 million destined for Europe. The arrest was made by the US Coastguard, put on board by *Iron Duke*.

26 JUNE

1690 First recorded use of the phrase 'a fleet in being', by the Earl of Torrington.

1795 Nine ships commanded by Cdre Sir John Borlase Warren in *Pomona* (44) covered landing of French royalists in fifty transports in Quiberon Bay, an eventual fiasco.

1806 Boats of *Port Mahon* cut out the Spanish letter of marque *San Jose* from Puerto Banes, Cuba.

1809 *Cyane* and *L'Espoir*, with twelve British and Sicilian gunboats, captured or destroyed twenty-two Neapolitan gunboats at Ischia in Bay of Naples.

1814 Boats of *Maidstone* and *Sylph* destroyed an American turtle (torpedo) boat on Long Island.

1830 Accession of King William IV.

1842 *Southampton* (60), *Conch* and detachments of the 25th and 27th Regiments quelled the Boer insurrection at Port Natal.

1854 *Prometheus*, wood paddle sloop, recaptured the British brig *Cuthbert Young*, taken by Riff pirates, in Zera Bay, 10 miles S.W. of Cape Tres Forcas, Morocco.

1855 *Racehorse*, sloop, recaptured the British lorcha *Typhoon* at Lam Yit. Her boats captured three pirate junks in Pinghai Bay and the vicinity.

1857 Queen Victoria held the first VC investiture in Hyde Park, decorating sixty-two of the eighty-five men gazetted. Thirteen of the twenty-seven RN and RM recipients had been attached to Naval Brigades.

See 24 February 1857.

1867 Title of Master abolished by Order in Council. Masters became Navigating Lieutenants, Second Masters became Navigating Sub-Lieutenants and Masters' Assistants became Navigating Midshipmen. Senior Masters had already assumed the title of Staff Captain and Staff Commander in 1863.

1867 Ironclad battleship *Audacious* laid down at Napiers, Govan.

See 27 February 1869, 24 March 2009.

1897 The Diamond Jubilee Review of the Fleet at Spithead by the Prince of Wales. The high point of the British Empire. The Fleet, under the command of Admiral Sir Nowell Salmon, VC, C-in-C Portsmouth, with his flag in *Renown*, included 21 battleships, 44 cruisers and 70 torpedo boats – 165 ships and 38,577 personnel.

The event was ambushed by the dramatic intervention of Charles Parsons' steam-turbine-powered yacht *Turbinia*, which raced down the ordered lines of international warships at over 30 knots, demonstrating to the world the future of marine engineering. It was a publicity triumph in which the British naval staff was undoubtedly complicit. Within the year the Admiralty had ordered the first RN turbine-powered warships from Parsons: *Viper*, experimental TBD, which was launched on 6 September 1899, and *Cobra*, also engined by Parsons.

See 28 June 1977.

1902 Admirals of the Fleet the Hon. Sir Henry Keppel and the Rt Hon. Sir Edward Hobart Seymour were the first two naval officers appointed to the new Order of Merit created by King Edward VII in Letters Patent of 23 June before his Coronation.

See 14 June 1809, 10 June 1900, 17 January 1904, 7 April 1919.

Subsequent appointments (stand fast Prince Philip and Prince Charles) were Lord Fisher (30 June 1905), Sir Arthur Wilson (8 March 1912), Lord Jellicoe (31 May 1916), Lord Beatty (3 June 1919), Sir Charles Madden (1 January 1931), Lord Chatfield (2 January 1939), Sir Dudley Pound (3 September 1943), Lord Cunningham (13 June 1946), and Lord Mountbatten (15 July 1965). Admiral Marquis Heichachiro Togo of the Imperial Japanese Navy was appointed to the OM on 21 February 1906, soon after the Battle of Tsushima.

1944 Destroyer *Bulldog* sank U-719 in N.W. Approaches (55.33N, 11.02W).

1944 Liberator N/86 sank U-317 off S.W. Norway (62.03N, 01.45E).

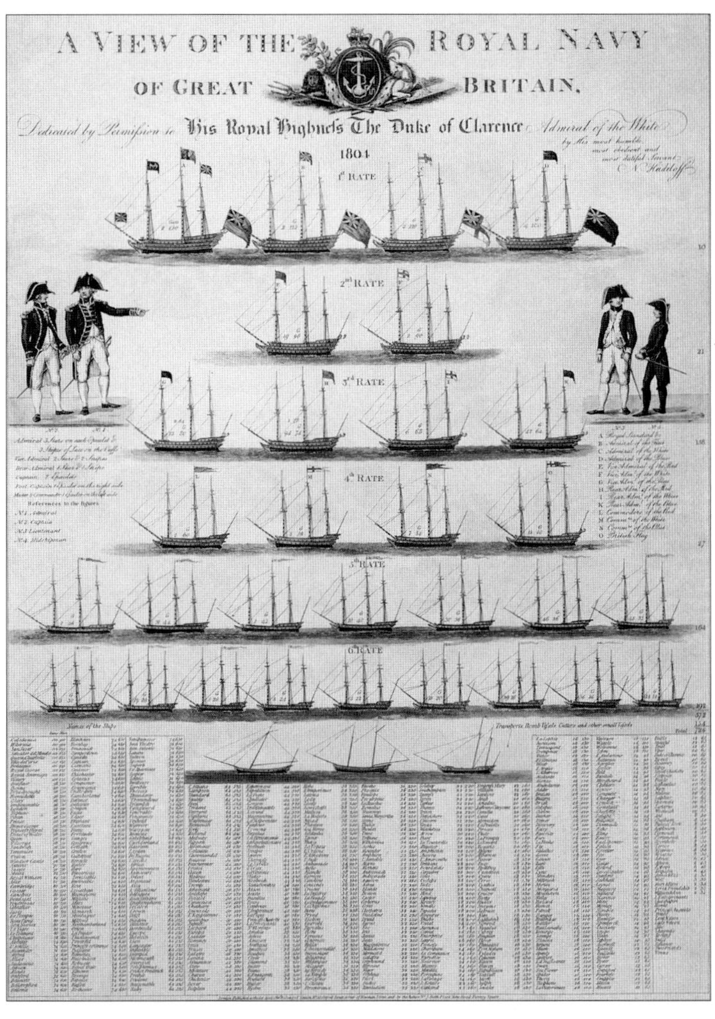

The ships of the RN, shown in 1804. The numbers of ships and men continued to expand during the Napoleonic Wars, and at a peak in 1813 over 147,000 men were borne on the ships' books. (*NMRN 1976/274*)

1944 Italian *Gorizia*, like *Bolzano* on the 22nd, sunk, but by an Anglo-Italian manned chariot.

1951 Cruiser *Mauritius*, Capt E.O.F. Price RN, dispatched to Abadan to protect British subjects of the Anglo-Iranian Oil Company's large refinery during a dispute with Iran. 'Her presence will give confidence to the company's 2,800 employees and is an insurance against their being made the victims of thwarted Persian passions' – *The Times*. Later joined by sloop *Flamingo*, Capt R.H. Courage RN. *Mauritius* relieved on 21 July by cruiser *Euryalus*, Capt P.L. Collard RN, when she sailed for Trincomalee and 'her normal duties on the East Indies Station'. In July the First DF, *Chequers*, *Chevron*, *Chivalrous* and *Chieftain* arrived from Malta to relieve *Euryalus* and they in turn handed over to four Battle-class destroyers *Armada*, *Saintes*, *Vigo* and *Gravelines*. On 4 October *Euryalus* returned and evacuated the remaining staff at the refinery.

1958 Light cruiser *Birmingham*, Capt T.D. Ross RN, arrived in Quebec for the 350th anniversary of the founding of the city.

1959 HMY *Britannia*, with The Queen and The Duke of Edinburgh embarked, sailed up the St Lawrence River, led by the frigate *Ulster*, for the formal opening of the St Lawrence Seaway. The frigates *Salisbury* and *Tenby* visited Cleveland, Ohio, the first British warship on Lake Erie since the battle of Lake Erie, 10 September 1813.

See 9 July 1959.

1997 RN elements serving at various NATO headquarters in S. Italy commissioned as *Agrippa* at a ceremony on Nisida Island off Naples. First new RN ship name in Mediterranean for a generation.

Junior rates wore *Centurion* cap tallies until the Gosport establishment paid off 31 March 1994. Pay accounts were thenceforth held locally. *Agrippa*, the first in the RN, recalls Roman sea general Marcus Vipsanius Agrippa who defeated Mark Antony and Cleopatra at Actium and held sway over the Mediterranean with a Roman galley fleet based at Miseno near Nisida Island.

27 JUNE

1734 First official recognition of the title Commodore as a temporary rank made by King George II. 'Our Will and Pleasure therefore is . . . That Commodores with Broad Pendants have the same Respects as Brigadiers General, which is, to have one Ruffle.'

1756 Surrender of Minorca. Restored in 1763, retaken 1798 and ceded 1802.

1794 King George reviewed Lord Howe's fleet, returned to Portsmouth after its victory over the French at the Glorious First of June. On board the flagship *Queen Charlotte* the King presented 'a most magnificent sword set with diamonds' to Admiral Howe who had it shown to every man in every ship.

See 16 March 1941.

1798 *Seahorse* captured the French *Sensible* 36 miles E.S.E. of Pantelleria in eight minutes.

1806 Capture of Buenos Aires by Cdre Sir Home Riggs Popham (*Diadem*) and Maj-Gen William Carr Beresford. Ships and vessels: *Diadem, Raisonnable, Diomede, Narcissus, Encounter.* Troops: R.A., 71st Regiment, 20th Light Dragoons, St Helena Artillery, St Helena Regiment. A Naval Brigade was landed.

1809 Frigate *Cyane* (22), Capt Thomas Staines, in a squadron commanded by Rear-Admiral George Martin in *Canopus* (80), attacking the islands of Ischia and Procida, fought the Franco-Neapolitan frigate *Ceres* (*Cerere* in Laird-Clowes) in the Bay of Naples until her ammunition ran out. The badly damaged ship returned to Britain for repairs and Staines was knighted on 6 December. Sir Thomas lost his left arm in the action and the other arm had been damaged in a duel 'so that he never after could bring his right hand within a foot of his mouth . . . [he] had his glass and tumbler with a long stem, and a long-handled knife and fork in one, and with these he managed well. . . He was often irritable, particularly when his face was itching . . .' – Captain John Harvey Boteler RN, *Recollections of my Sea Life 1808 to 1830* (Navy Records Society 1942) p.182.

1812 Royal Marines of *Leviathan, Imperieuse, Curacoa* and *Eclair* captured two batteries at Alassio and Laigueglia, Italy. The ships destroyed a convoy of eighteen sail.

1829 *Monkey* captured the Spanish slaver *Midas* S.W. of Little Stirrup Cay, Great Bahama Bank.

1860 Repulse of a British attack on the Maori pah at Puketakauere, New Zealand. Naval Brigade of wood screw corvette *Pelorus*, with the flank companies of the 40th Regiment and detachments of Royal Artillery and Royal Engineers.

1900 Capture of the Chinese Arsenal, Tientsin Naval Brigade from cruisers *Endymion* and *Orlando*.

Armed naval party being landed in China, 1900. (*NMRN*)

Naval Brigades

Naval Brigade from HMS *Shah* at Gingindlovu, 1879. (*NMRN*)

Naval Brigades were a familiar feature of the Victorian Colonial wars. Britain's possessions were too numerous and too scattered for her to maintain garrisons in each and so, at the first sign of rebellion, Royal Navy ships were diverted to the troublespots. The mere presence of the White Ensign was often sufficient to stop the fighting but usually parties of seamen and Royal Marines were landed to deal with the trouble or to keep it in check until a proper expedition could be organised. Some Victorian bluejackets saw more action ashore in the brigades than at sea in their ships.

The seamen seemed to be capable of almost any task which was required of them. Eyewitnesses constantly paid tribute to their willingness and adaptability and these qualities soon became legendary. Jack could dig trenches, march across Indian deserts or through African swamps, manhandle guns over very difficult terrain, man rocket batteries, 'board' an enemy fort, ferry a full-scale expedition up the cataracts of the Nile and even run an armoured train in Egypt. To the Victorians, he was known simply as 'the Handyman'.

However, the sailors' most constant contribution to the wars was their effect on morale. Their cheerfulness was infectious and they amused successive generations of soldiers by their refusal to abandon their nautical habits. In the Crimea, they raised the spirits of the besieging army during the terrible winter of 1854; in Abyssinia, in 1867–8, they organised dances with the Sikhs of the Punjab Volunteers, with whom they were great friends; and in the Punjab in 1848, a Brigadier reported that the sailors '. . . looked upon their batteries as ships, their 18 pounders as so many sweethearts and the embrasures as portholes . . .'

The days of Colonial wars have gone, but this gift for amphibious warfare remains as strong a part of the tradition and operational commitment of the Royal Navy as ever.

1939 Capt Lord Louis Mountbatten appointed to command the destroyer *Kelly*.
See 23 August 1939.

1940 Destroyers *Dainty*, *Defender* and *Ilex* sank the Italian submarine *Console General Liuzzi* S. of Crete (33.46N, 27.27E).

1941 Submarine *Triumph* sank the Italian S/M *Glauco* in Atlantic (35.06N, 12.41W).

1941 Corvettes *Celandine*, *Gladiolus* and *Nasturtium* sank U-56 in Atlantic (60.24N, 29.00W). Convoy HX 133.

1941 GC: Lt Geoffrey Gledhill Turner GM, RNVR, Sub-Lt Francis Haffey Brooke-Smith RNVR. (*Gazette* date.) Bomb and mine disposal.

1942 Convoy PQ 17 sailed for Russia. Eleven of thirty-six merchant ships arrived.

1944 *Pink*, corvette, torpedoed by U-988 E.N.E. of Barfleur. Towed to Portsmouth, but CTL.

2005 HRH The Duke of York promoted honorary captain, RN.

28 June

1550 Appointment of Edward Baeshe as first Surveyor of Victuals by letters patent at a fee of £50. Resigned in debt in May 1586.

1745 Cdre Warren took Louisburg.

1762 *Defiance* and *Glasgow* captured the Spanish *Venganza* and *Marte* off Mariel, Cuba.

1776 Bombardment of Fort Moultrie, Charleston. Ships: *Bristol, Experiment, Active, Solebay, Actaeon,* Syren, Sphinx, Friendship, Ranger, Thunder, St Lawrence.*

*Grounded and had to be burned by her own crew.

1803 Boats of *Loire* cut out the French *Venteux* at Ile de Bas, France.

1810 Boats of *Amphion, Active* and *Cerberus* cut out twenty-five gunboats at Porto Grado, Trieste.

1814 *Reindeer* (18) taken by the American *Wasp* (22) 240 miles W. of Ushant.

1859 Wood screw gunvessel *Cormorant* sunk by the Peiho Forts, having gone to the aid of *Plover* on the 25th.

See 1 July 1850.

1870 William Reginald Hall born in The Close, Salisbury, and entered the *Britannia* as a naval cadet in 1884. The outstanding director of Naval Intelligence in the First World War.

See 4 September 1913, 16 January 1917, 22 October 1943.

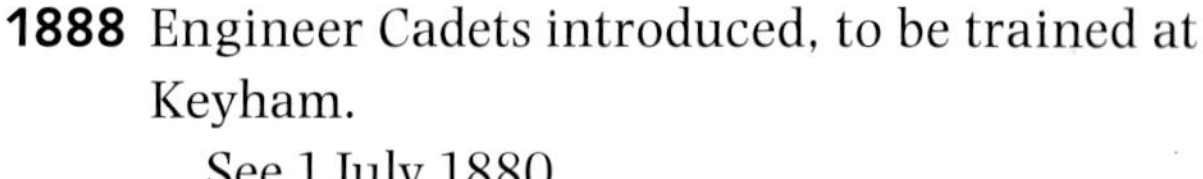

1888 Engineer Cadets introduced, to be trained at Keyham.

See 1 July 1880.

1918 Submarine D 6 sunk by UB-73 N. of Inishtrahull Island, west of Ireland.

1919 Treaty of Versailles signed which formally ended the First World War.

1934 Three destroyers launched: *Fame* by Lady Pound, wife of Vice-Admiral Sir Dudley Pound, Second Sea Lord, and *Firedrake* by Mrs Blake, wife of Rear-Admiral Geoffrey Blake, Fourth Sea Lord, both at Vickers-Armstrong, Barrow. *Forester* was launched at J. Samuel White, Cowes.

See 17 December 1942.

1940 Force H, assembled in short order to replace French maritime power in the W. Mediterranean, formed at Gibraltar: *Hood* (flag of Vice-Admiral Sir James Somerville hoisted 30 June), *Ark Royal, Valiant, Resolution, Hood, Arethusa* and seven destroyers. Somerville reported directly to the Admiralty and his ships had the ambiguous status of a 'detached squadron' to avoid chain-of-command difficulties with either C-in-C Mediterranean or with Admiral Sir Dudley North, Flag Officer North Atlantic, who flew his flag ashore at Gibraltar. The wiring diagram failed spectacularly.

See 21 October 1941, 11 September 1940.

1940 7th CS, under Vice-Admiral J.C. Tovey (*Orion*), chased three Italian destroyers, sinking *Espero* in central Mediterranean (35.18N, 20.12E). Ships: *Gloucester, Liverpool, Neptune, Orion,* and *Sydney* (RAN).

1941 *Perth* (RAN), *Carlisle* and five destroyers bombarded the Damur area, Syria.

Ships taking part in the International Fleet Review in 2005. (*RN*)

Her Majesty The Queen, His Royal Highness The Duke of Edinburgh and Admiral Sir Alan West on the bridge of HMS *Endurance* during the International Fleet Review in 2005. (*RN*)

1941 Cruiser *Nigeria* and destroyers *Bedouin* and *Tartar* boarded, rummaged and sank the German weather ship *Lauenberg* to the great benefit of Naval Intelligence Division.

1945 Fleet Air Arm's last operational flight of a Royal Navy biplane; a Swordfish from MAC ship *Empire Mackay*.
See 21 May 1945, 15 October 1945.

1961 Launch of *Leander*, name-ship and first of class of twenty-six frigates, at Harland and Wolff, Belfast. Commissioned 27 March 1963.
See 10 September 1971.

1965 Submarine *Totem* handed over to Israeli Navy at Portsmouth and renamed *Dakar*. Lost on passage to Israel.

1976 First Supply Officer promotion to admiral – Sir Peter White, CFS, already the first Pusser to sit on the Board.
See 21 April 1970, 22 May 2010.

1977 Silver Jubilee Review of the Fleet at Spithead by HM The Queen, Lord High Admiral. Largest RN ship *Ark Royal*. Capt E.R. Anson RN, flag of Admiral Sir Henry Leach, CINCFLEET. First Spithead fleet review to include nuclear-powered vessels but the first without battleships present.
See 26 June 1897.

1984 Admiral Sir Robin Durnford-Slater, last C-in-C The Nore, died.
See 9 July 1958, 31 March 1961.

1991 The MOD announced details of Gulf campaign medals. The reverse based on Second World War Combined Operations badge; ribbon based on that of Africa Star, with the colours of the three Services at either side, separated by a strip of pale buff representing the desert.

2005 HM The Queen reviewed an international fleet at Spithead from the Antarctic patrol ship *Endurance* led by the THV *Patricia*.
HM Ships present:

Albion, Archer, Bangor, Blazer, Bulwark, Cattistock, Cardiff, Chatham, Cumberland, Endurance, Enterprise, Example, Exeter, Explorer, Gloucester, Gleaner, Grafton, Grimsby, Invincible, Illustrious, Iron Duke, Lancaster, Ledbury, Marlborough, Middleton, Montrose, Nottingham, Ocean, Pembroke, Puncher, Raider, Ramsey, Ranger, Roebuck, Scott, Shoreham, Sovereign, Southampton, St Albans, Tracker, Trafalgar, Trumpeter, Turbulent, Tyne, Walney, Westminster. RFAs *Argus, Fort George, Fort Victoria, Hurst Point, Orangeleaf, Sir Bedivere, Sir Galahad, Sir Tristram, Wave Ruler*, HMAS *Anzac*, HMCS *Montreal*.

From Admiral Sir Alan West, First Sea Lord:

> 'I am commanded by the Lord High Admiral, Her Majesty The Queen, to pass the following message to the Royal Navy and to the Flag and Commanding Officers of Commonwealth ships assembled at Spithead today for the International Fleet Review:
>
> It gave me great pleasure to review the International Fleet assembled today at Spithead to commemorate the 200th anniversary of the death of Lord Nelson and to witness the maritime flypast. I was most impressed with the array of vessels and aircraft from the United Kingdom, the Commonwealth and the many nations which took part. This review reflects the true spirit of cooperation which exists between maritime nations and is a fitting symbol of the enduring legacy of the spirit of Nelson. To those of you who have participated in this memorable event, and to all who continue to contribute to and support the many demanding operations around the world, the Duke of Edinburgh and I send our best wishes and thanks. Splice the Mainbrace. Elizabeth R.'

29 June

1417 The Earl of Huntingdon's squadron took four Genoese carracks in the Channel.

1757 James Cook passed for Master.

1798 *Jason* (38) and *Pique* (36) captured the French *Seine* (38) to the northward of Ile de Ré. *Mermaid* (32) was in company.

1800 *Anson*, escorting a convoy, captured the Spanish *Gibraltar* and *Salvador* in Gibraltar Strait.

1807 Uniform regulations for masters and pursers made by Order in Council.

1940 Destroyers *Dainty* and *Ilex* sank the Italian submarine *Uebi Scebeli* in central Mediterranean. A valuable intelligence haul.

1940 Sunderland L/230 sank the *Rubino* in Ionian Sea (39.10N, 18.49E) and another Sunderland of the same squadron the *Argonauta* (34.24N, 19.00E). First RAF success on A/S patrol.

1940 Light cruiser *Enterprise* took bulk of bullion from Bank of England to Canada though the Captain did not qualify for Plate Money. Operation Fish. *Enterprise* was the fastest cruiser in service. First light cruiser to carry 6-in twin turret.

1940 *Williamette Valley*, taken up from trade as a 'freighter', i.e. a decoy, and sailing as *Edgehill*, sunk in N. Atlantic.

See 21 June 1940.

1941 *Waterhen* (RAN) attacked by aircraft off Sollum (32.15N, 25.20E). Taken in tow by *Defender* but sank early on the 30th. First RAN war loss.

1941 *Arabis*, *Malcolm*, *Scimitar*, *Speedwell* and *Violet* sank U-651 in N. Atlantic (59.52N, 18.26W). Convoy HX 133.

1942 Submarine *Thrasher* sank the Italian fast sloop *Diana*, carrying technical experts and staff to North Africa, 100 miles N.W. of Tobruk.

HMS *Enterprise*, in white and buff tropical livery, arriving at Portsmouth after a commission on the East Indies Station on 16 March 1938. (*NMRN W&L 457B4*)

1944 *Cooke, Domett, Duckworth, Essington* and Liberator L/224 sank U-988 off the Channel Islands (49.37N, 03.41W).

1944 Destroyers *Tenacious, Terpsichore* and *Tumult* bombarded a lookout station south of Valona (40.19N, 19.23E).

See 9 August 1952.

Korea, 1950–3

On 25 June 1950 the Communist North Korean Army attacked the South Koreans across the 38th parallel. Within a week the Royal Navy was operating in Korean waters, sinking coastal shipping and attacking communications ashore. The Chinese reinforced the North Koreans and advanced into North Korea during the winter, driving the United Nations forces back. Allied sea power was used to the full, both in launching seaborne air attacks against North Korean forces, and in evacuating and landing troops as required. Russian-built MiG jet fighters were deployed against the Fleet Air Arm in Korea. Lt P. Carmichael shot down the first Russian MiG to be destroyed by the Royal Navy and, remarkably, by a piston-engined aircraft.

1962 Lord Carrington, First Lord of the Admiralty, unveiled a plaque on the west wall of the RN Hospital, Stonehouse, to mark the bicentenary of its foundation. The hospital closed on 31 March 1995 when services were transferred to Derriford.

See 15 September 1744, 14 June 1758.

1965 Admiral Sir Martin Dunbar-Nasmith, the most famous of the first generation of British submariners, died at Elgin. Martin Nasmith's brilliant services in command of E 11 in the Sea of Marmora in 1915 and 1916 gained him the VC and promotion to commander (30 June 1915) and to captain (30 June 1916) at the age of 33 years 3 months, which early distinction has never since been equalled. Captain BRNC Dartmouth 1926–8, Admiral (Submarines) 1929–31, C-in-C East Indies 1932–4, Second Sea Lord 1935–8 and C-in-C Plymouth and W. Approaches 1938–41.

See 27 April 1915, 30 June 1937, 30 June 1955, 15 December 1967.

2007 Admiral Sir Alan West, lately First Sea Lord and former Chief of Defence Intelligence, appointed parliamentary under-secretary at the Home Office responsible for security and counter-terrorism in Prime Minister Gordon Brown's new government; the first translation of a former Chief of Naval Staff to government office since Neville Chamberlain invited Admiral of the Fleet Lord Chatfield to join the cabinet as minister for the coordination of defence in December 1938. Admiral West was ennobled on 9 July as Baron West of Spithead.

See 21 November 1945.

2010 Royal review by Her Majesty Queen Elizabeth II of the Canadian Atlantic ships at Halifax, NS, to mark the centenary of Canada's navy, along with ships from the RN, USN, USCG, French Navy, Brazilian Navy and the Standing NATO Maritime Group One (Royal Danish Navy, the German Navy and the Royal Netherlands Navy). An earlier Pacific coast gathering was reviewed by the Governor-General.

See 4 May 1910, 15 July 1958.

30 June

1690 Battle of Beachy Head. Anglo-Dutch fleet (thirty-four and twenty-two respectively) under Admiral the Earl of Torrington (*Sovereign*) and Admiral Cornelis Evertsen (*Hollandia*) fought Vice-Admiral Comte de Tourville (*Soleil-Royal*), who had seventy-three ships and eighteen fireships.

Torrington was reluctant to attack until ordered to do so. The battle lasted from 0900 to 1700, the Dutch in the van and he in the centre. Torrington interdicted the French, who doubled on the van, but allowed them to drift away, for which he was court-martialled, though acquitted.

1696 Sir Christopher Wren and John Evelyn laid foundation stone of Greenwich Hospital 'precisely at 5 o'clock in the evening, Mr. Flamsteed the King's Astronomical Professor observing the precise time by instruments'.

See 1 February 1873, 6 July 1998.

1707 Rear-Admiral Sir John Norris (*Torbay*) forced the passage of the Var, France.

1797 Nore Mutiny leader Parker hanged on board *Sandwich*.

1799 Neapolitan admiral Francesco Caracciolo tried and found guilty of treason by a court martial in the wardroom of Nelson's flagship *Foudroyant* at Naples. Nelson's callous attitude to Caracciolo and his role in hastening the traitor's hanging from the yardarm of the Neapolitan flagship *Minerva* within hours of the verdict has cast an enduring shadow over Nelson's character. 'His political naivety allowed the use of British ships and men to facilitate executions and cruelty . . . This was Nelson at his most impatient and ruthless' – Roger Knight, *The Pursuit of Victory*, p.557.

1803 *Vanguard* captured the French *Créole* off Ile Tortuga.

1903 RNVR founded by Naval Forces Act 1903.

See 17 July 1959, 17 May 2003.

1913 HM King George V visited the battlecruiser HMAS *Australia*, Capt Stephen H. Radcliffe RN, before she departed for Australia to be flagship of the Australian Fleet. His Majesty invested Rear-Admiral George Edwin Patey, flag officer commanding Australian Fleet, with the KCVO on the quarterdeck. Probably the first knighting afloat by a monarch of a British sea officer since Queen Elizabeth I dubbed Francis Drake on board the *Golden Hind* at Deptford on 4 April 1581. The ship's badge featured the Federation Star with a naval crown and the motto 'Endeavour', recalling Capt James Cook's ship. She sailed for Australia on 21 July in company with the new light cruiser HMAS *Sydney*.

See 4 April 1581, 23 June 1913, 4 October 1913, 29 August 1914, 12 April 1924, 15 May 1954, 7 July 1967.

1914 Admiral Sir George Warrender, departing with a RN squadron from the Imperial German Navy regatta at Kiel, made to his hosts 'Friends in the past, friends for ever', which proved five weeks later to have been an unfortunate signal.

See 4 July 1931.

1915 Destroyer *Lightning* sunk by mine off the Wielingen lightvessel, Zeebrugge.

1917 Destroyer *Cheerful* sunk by mine 6 miles S.S.E. of Lerwick.

1927 An ill-fated batch of promotions to Captain RN included three of the seven flag officers who died on active service in the Second World War: Rear-Admiral Henry Evelyn Charles Blagrove, flag officer 2nd Battle Squadron, killed in the battleship *Royal Oak* at Scapa Flow on 14 October 1939; Acting Admiral Sir Tom Spencer Vaughan Phillips, C-in-C Far East Fleet, lost in the battleship *Prince of Wales* off Malaya on 10 December 1941 and Rear-Admiral Ronald Hamilton Curzon Hallifax killed in an aircraft crash on 6 November 1943. Vice-Admiral Lancelot Holland, killed in the battlecruiser *Hood* on 24 May 1941 was one year senior to them as a captain.

1937 Lord Louis Mountbatten promoted to captain RN in the month of his 37th birthday: 'Promoted at 37.0. Average 42–45. Some Lt-Cdrs to Cdr over 37!' – Diary.

The bridge of the cruiser HMS *Belfast* during a bombardment of shore positions off the west coast of Korea, 1950. (*NMRN*)

See 11 June 1779, 1 January 1910, 30 June 1955, 29 June 1965, 9 February 1977.

1940 First offensive operation mounted from Malta after Italy entered the war on 10 June: Swordfish of 830 NAS attacked oil refineries Augusta, Sicily.

1941 River gunboat *Cricket* severely damaged by German dive-bomber north of Mersa Matruh. Towed to Alexandria and became a floating AA battery.

1942 Submarine depot ship *Medway* sunk by U-372 off Alexandria (31.03N, 30.35E). Ninety torpedoes and all spare machinery for submarine flotillas moving to Haifa were lost.

See 11 November 1942.

1944 Canso A/162 (RCAF) and Liberator E/86 sank U-478 in Norwegian Sea (63.27N, 00.50W).

1948 Remaining British troops, mainly 40 Cdo, embarked in LSTs at Haifa at the end of the British mandate in Palestine and 'a long-standing, difficult and somewhat embarrassing naval commitment came to an end' – Eric Grove. Operation commanded by Vice-Admiral Sir Thomas Troubridge, Flag Officer (Air) and Second-in-Command Mediterranean Fleet, with his flag in the carrier *Triumph*, escorted by the destroyer *Volage*, covering the withdrawal from offshore. The carrier with 800 and 827 NAS embarked, had four Seafire fighters armed with rockets at 30 minutes notice for launching. Destroyers *Verulam* and *Venus* anchored in the bay and frigate *Veryan Bay* outside the breakwater. GOC (Lt-Gen G.H.A. MacMillan) and AOC (Air Cdre W.L Dawson) embarked in the light cruiser *Phoebe*. 40 Cdo maintained a reducing perimeter around the dockside 'withdrawing yard by yard until the final mortar base plate position was on the ramp of the LST *Striker*' – Cdr Ninian Stewart, *Naval Staff History*.

See 14 May 1948, 15 November 1966, 21 and 29 November 1967.

```
                                UNCLASSIFIED

OPCON                                                 ACTION copy 1 for PARRY C
OPERATION     HMS CHATHAM                                       SO2 J3(WKPR)
MESSAGE    at 301937Z JUN 97                                   PJHQ NCC 2001
------------------------------------------------------------------------------

Prec Act FLASH        Info: IMMEDIATE
DTG         301937Z JUN 97
From        HMS CHATHAM
To          MODUK
            PJHQUK
Info        CINCFLEET
            HQ LAND
            HQSTC
SICs        ADA    IAQ
------------------------------------------------------------------------------
            MODUK FOR CDS, INFO 1SL, CGS AND CAS. CINCFLEET, HQ LAND AND HQSTC
            FOR CINC. PJHQ FOR CJO. FROM CBF HONG KONG. I HAVE THE HONOUR TO
            REPORT THAT ONE HUNDRED AND FIFTY SIX YEARS, FIVE MONTHS AND
            FOUR DAYS AFTER THE FIRST HOISTING OF THE UNION FLAG AT POSSESSION
            POINT, ALL BRITISH FORCES HAVE NOW PASSED BEYOND THE BORDERS OF THE
            SPECIAL ADMINISTRATIVE REGION OF HONG KONG, PEOPLES REPUBLIC OF
            CHINA, FORMERLY HER MAJESTY'S COLONY OF HONG KONG.
            ^LUKE 2,29.
______________________________________________________________________________
Action Distribution
 Addressee                      Code  Action-Officer          Retrieval
 CINCFLEET                      IAQ   NA                      DIST 001SG
 PJHQUK                         IAQ   SO2 J1(PANDA)           SO2 J3(WKPR)
------------------------------------------------------------------------------
Information Distribution
     CPO N3(ORS)                DOPS                      SO1 N3(OPS)
     SO2 J4(M)1                 SO2 N3(MAOTS)             WO N3(VISITS COORD)
     SO2 J3(WKPR)
------------------------------------------------------------------------------
Information Distributees Excluded from Delivery
```

The Flash signal in the early hours of 1 July 1997 from CBF Hong Kong embarked in the frigate HMS *Chatham* to CDS, reporting that all UK personnel were clear of the former colony. (*Lt-Cdr Christopher Parry RN*)

1952 Lt-Cdr HRH The Duke of Edinburgh RN promoted commander.

See 16 July 1950, 15 January 1953.

1954 Three frigates launched in three days. Type 41 frigate *Puma*, first of class, launched at Scotts, Greenock, 30 June and the first two Type 12 frigates, *Torquay*, launched at Harland and Wolff, Belfast, 1 July, and *Whitby* at Cammell Laird, Birkenhead, 2 July. Three other ships launched on 1 July: the minesweepers *Swanston* at Grimsby, and *Mileham* at Bideford, and the fast replenishment tanker *Tiderange* at Swan Hunter. Them was the days.

1955 Cdr Edward Ashmore RN, commander of HMS *Mercury*, RN Signal School, promoted captain: 'At 35 [and six months] I was the youngest captain since Beatty'. Not so. Roger Keyes was promoted captain on 1 July 1905 aged 32 years 9 months. Submariner Martin Nasmith, later Admiral Sir Martin Dunbar-Nasmith VC, (commander 30 June 1915), was promoted captain on 30 June 1916 aged 33 years 3 months. Beatty's seniority was 9 November 1900 (29 years 2 months). Beatty claimed to have been the youngest captain since Nelson was appointed to command *Hinchinbroke* (28) on 11 June 1779, three months before his 21st birthday; but at least three promotions intervened. Thomas John Cochrane (23 April 1806) was 'just' 17; Charles Paget (17 October 1797) was 'just' 19 and, infamously, John Rodney (14 October 1780) had been advanced from midshipman to post captain all in the same year and was under 16. Michael le Fanu was promoted captain on 30 June 1949 aged 35 years 10 months (again 'the youngest in the Navy since Beatty' – Richard Baker); Dudley Pound on 31 December 1914 aged 37 years 4 months; Lord Louis Mountbatten on 30 June 1937, the month of his 37th birthday.

See 11 June 1779, 17 October 1797, 1 January 1910, 30 June 1937, 9 February 1977.

1958 RM Gunnery School, Eastney, closed and training of RM gunnery ratings transferred to *Excellent*. Automatic guns required smaller crews and more Royal Marines were required for commando duties. The battery and gunnery school had been used by the RM at Eastney since 1883. AFO 1148/58.

See 4 January 1983, 30 March 2001.

1961 Closure of Royal Victoria Yard, Deptford. Opened in 1742 and responsible for storing and blending the Navy's rum.

1964 Royal Naval Armament Depot, Mombasa, closed. AFO 147/64.

1966 The frigate *Ulster*, with a seriously damaged stern, received the stern of her sister ship *Urchin*, on the disposal list, at Devonport. Both ships were dry-docked stern-to-stern on 13 June. On 30 June a 20ft-long, 25-ton section of the after part of *Urchin*, including machinery and steering gear, was cut off and welded and riveted to the prepared stern of *Ulster*. The operation took only two hours and *Ulster* was shortly ready to sail.

See 7 June 1917, 4 February 1918.

1966 RN Polaris School at Faslane opened by Mr J.P.W. Mallalieu, Navy Minister.

1969 *Bristol*, Type 82 destroyer, launched at Swan Hunter and Tyne Shipbuilders. Only one of planned four of class completed; intended as escorts to the cancelled CVA-01. The first RN ship to take the Ikara ASW missile to sea and the last three-funnelled British warship.

See 22 March 1993.

1971 The Naval Base Hospital, Singapore, closed. DCI(RN) 701/71.

1977 FO Malta transferred his HQ from Lascaris to HMS *St Angelo* in the planned withdrawal of British Forces from Malta. DCI(RN) 539/77 dated 26 August 1977.

1985 Carrier *Hermes* paid off into reserve and preserved in state of Full Dehumidification (FDH) with two officers and forty-eight men at thirty days' notice for sea trials. DCI(RN) 246/85 dated 5 July 1985.

See 20 March 1987.

1988 *President*, shore-based HQ of London Division RNR in St Katharine's Dock, opened by Admiral Sir John Woodward, C-in-C Naval Home Command.

See 1 February 1988.

1997 Hong Kong returned to China at midnight. Prince of Wales and former Governor, Mr Chris Patten, embarked in HM Yacht *Britannia* at 0022 1 July, completing British withdrawal. Ship sailed at 0045 and, with Royal Marine band playing 'Rule Britannia' and 'Jerusalem', amplified by ship's broadcast, she led *Chatham*, *Peacock*, *Starling*, *Plover* and RFA *Sir Percivale* out of harbour. Group rendezvoused with seventeen ships of Ocean Wave Task Group commanded by Rear-Admiral Alan West, which had been standing by over the horizon. All ships steamed past *Britannia* on 1 July.

See 25 January 1841, 21 and 29 November 1967, 31 March 1979.

2003 Conspicuous Gallantry Cross: L/Cpl Justin Thomas (24) of 40 Cdo RM for 'his outstanding bravery and inspirational leadership' during a Commando attack near Basra. Operation Telic.

See 22 November 1914, 7 February 1995, 30 April 2003.

During the attack Thomas's troop came under effective and sustained fire from the enemy in a previously undetected location, which left many of his comrades exposed. Moving from a comparatively safe position, Thomas climbed onto his open-topped vehicle to man the pintle-mounted machine-gun and he returned fire for fifteen minutes, enabling twenty other members of his troop to move safely into cover and regroup. This act of selfless bravery ensured that the troop were able to extract themselves without loss of life from enemy fire in order to launch a successful counter-attack.

2005 Cdr Vanessa Spiller RN became the first female member of the Royal Navy Club of 1765 and 1785.

See 4 February 1765, 7 November 1997, 3 April 2001.

1 July

1712 Royal Naval Hospital opened at Port Mahon, Minorca. First designed as such.

1719 *Grafton, Lenox, Breda* and *Essex* captured two Spanish transports and destroyed a third near Cape San Fito, Sicily.

1731 Adam Duncan, victor of Camperdown, born.
See 11 October 1797.

1780 *Romney* captured the French *Artois* 100 miles N.N.W. of Cape Ortegal.

1800 Boats of *Renown, Defence* and *Fisgard* destroyed the French *Thérése* and nineteen other vessels at Noirmoutier, France.

1831 'Weeovil Yard' renamed Royal Clarence Victualling Yard, Portsmouth.

1845 A military force, with a gun's crew from *Hazard*, repulsed in the attack on Honi Keke's pah at Ohaeawai, New Zealand. Troops: Royal Artillery, 58th Regiment.

1850 *Cormorant*, wood screw gunvessel, captured three slave vessels and engaged the fort at Paranagua, Brazil. A fourth slaver was destroyed by her own crew.

1880 RNEC founded at Keyham.
See 1 July 1885, 28 June 1888, 9 May 1958.

1912 First Senior Officer Coast of Scotland appointed.

1914 RNAS formed from RFC Naval Wing, an eagle replacing an anchor on badges and buttons, epaulettes and sword belts, and pilots' wings being moved from chest to cuff.

1914 'An officer appointed to the Royal Naval Air Service, who has obtained, or subsequently obtains, the airship or aeroplane pilot's certificate of the Royal Aero Club at his own expense, will be refunded the sum of £75 or such lesser fee as he has been charged for his tuition.' Admiralty Circular Letter CW. 13964/14.

1918 Paymaster-in-Chief William Marcus Charles Beresford RN appointed the first Paymaster Director-General, Admiralty, and promoted to the new rank of Paymaster Rear-Admiral on 18 November. He was killed on 14 July 1932 when his car skidded into a telegraph pole near Salisbury.
See 4 January 1866.

1922 *Insolent*, iron screw gunboat, foundered in Portsmouth harbour.

1926 First night deck landing: Flt Lt Boyce in Blackburn Dart N9804 on *Furious*.

1940 The first Flower-class Corvette, *Gladiolus* and Sunderland H/10 (RAAF) sank U-26 S.W. of Ireland (48.03N, 11.30W). Convoy OA 175.
See 24 January 1940.

1940 Destroyer *Vansittart* sank U-102 S.W. of Ireland (48.33N, 10.26W).

1945 Allied naval and air bombardment of Balikpapan, Borneo, prior to landing by 7th Australian Division. RAN ships: *Arunta, Hobart, Shropshire*; *Kanimbla, Manoora, Westralia* (AMCs).

1946 Good Conduct Badges awarded after four, eight and twelve years' service instead of after three, eight and thirteen.

1946 First nuclear air-burst explosion over an unmanned fleet (Bikini Island, Pacific). Operation Crossroads Able.

1947 RM Divisions became Groups in functional reorganisation of the Corps.

1950 Ship names given to divisions of the Reserve Fleet: Portsmouth *Bellerophon*; Clyde Area *Jupiter*; Harwich *Mars*; Plymouth *Orion*, Sheerness *Minerva*, Chatham *Neptune*. Cap ribbons with the new names to be worn by men attached to divisions; individual ship ribbons to be withdrawn except *Duke of York* to be retained by the flagship 'as she is administered separately'.

Z 011822Z JUL
FH SM 1
TO AIG 1018
INFO HQCC
MOD AIR
BT
UNCLAS
DIG KAP
SUBSUNK ARTEMIS TRCT ONE HASLAR CREEK GOSPORT.
INDICATOR BOUYS NOT RELEASED
BT

Signal sent reporting HM Submarine *Artemis* sunk. (*Author*)

1961 Iraq threatened invasion of Kuwait. 42 Cdo RM landed from *Bulwark* by 845 NAS (Whirlwinds). 45 Cdo RM flown in from Aden by RAF.

1969 Major reorganisation of the shore-side Royal Navy – but not the last one. Post of C-in-C Portsmouth ended and Admiral Sir John Frewen, re-appointed as C-in-C Naval Home Command and Flag Officer Portsmouth Area; Admiral Superintendent, Portsmouth, became Flag Officer Spithead and Admiral Superintendent, Portsmouth. DCI(RN) 380/69. Post of C-in-C Plymouth (Vice-Admiral Sir Charles Mills) abolished on 26 May 1969 and that of Flag Officer Plymouth (Rear-Admiral J.C.Y. Roxburgh) established.

See 6 July 1965, 26 May 1969, 15 September 1971.

1969 RN assumed responsibility from RAF for British nuclear deterrent.

1971 Submarine *Artemis* foundered alongside at *Dolphin*. The boat sank stern first due to errors in trim following a docking; hatches were fouled by electricity cables and could not be shut. Three men escaped using SEIE suits introduced after the sinking of *Truculent* in 1950.

See 31 August 1944, 12 January 1950, 17 April 1951, 31 December 1974.

1977 WRNS became subject to Naval Discipline Act.

1981 *Trafalgar*, SSN, first of class, launched at Vickers, Barrow.

1985 Demolition of RNEC at Keyham began.

See 1 July 1880.

1985 *Ark Royal*, the third of the new carriers, arrived at Portsmouth from Swan Hunter, Wallsend, for acceptance. 'I pray you tell Her Majesty from me that her money was well given' – Lord Howard of Effingham, Lord High Admiral, of the first of the name.

See 1 November 1985.

1987 Formation of Fourth MCM Squadron to be based at Rosyth: *Atherstone*, *Bicester*, *Chiddingfold*, *Dulverton*, *Hurworth* and, on completion, *Quorn*. DCI(RN) 152/87.

1999 RM officer ranks realigned with RN, Army and RAF to remove ambiguity in corresponding rank: lieutenant (with three years' seniority) to lieutenant-colonel realigned one substantive rank higher. Wearing of overall trousers and embellished cap peaks henceforth started at lieutenant-colonel rank. DCI(Gen) 39/99.

2002 First Sea Lord directed that flag officers' ceremonial gold shoulder boards be redesigned to reflect the wearer's starred status; full admirals to have four stars, replacing the three hitherto borne on the board; vice-admirals to have three; and rear-admirals two.

See 17 September 1926, 1 July 2003.

2003 Commodores authorised to wear 'flag' ceremonial shoulder boards on the pattern of existing two-star boards but with a single star.

See 17 September 1926, 1 July 2002.

2007 The 'R' in the uniform lace of RNR officers abolished following the decision to remove all distinguishing Reserve markings from the uniforms of personnel liable for mobilisation for operations. Stand fast officers holding Honorary Commissions.

See 31 March 1951, 1 January 1952.

2008 Fleet HQ on Whale Island renamed Navy Command HQ to reflect a single TLB and the co-location of CINCFLEET and 2SL/CNH staffs.

2 July

1667 The Dutch landed at Felixstowe. The Duke of York and Albany's Maritime Regiment of Foot repulsed an attack on Landguard Fort. Ships: *Castle*, *Virgin*.

1803 *Minerve*, blockading Cherbourg, grounded and had to surrender next day.

1805 *Cambrian* captured the French privateer *Matilda* 25 miles S.E. of Tybee Island, Georgia.

1810 Rehabilitation of Sir Robert Calder by his appointment as C-in-C Plymouth, five years after his court martial.

1853 The last surviving Trafalgar captain, Admiral Sir Charles Bullen, died at Shirley, near Southampton. Bullen had commanded the *Britannia* (100), flagship of Rear-Admiral The Earl of Northesk, Third in Command of the Fleet. Bullen had been made post on 29 April 1802 and hoisted his flag almost thirty-five years later on 10 January 1837.

See 1 March 1807, 4 May 1810, 13 April 1885, 11 July 1929.

1867 Navigation Branch gave up blue cloth between their stripes and rearranged their buttons to denote their branch.

1911 The Agadir Crisis. Following a national revolt against the Sultan of Morocco the German gunboat *Panther* was sent to Agadir officially to protect German interests and nationals. The Germans were seeking a new overseas base and the possibility of a German presence so near Gibraltar and the Cape route sparked a diplomatic crisis. The First Sea Lord, Admiral Sir Arthur Wilson, was out of town. 'The Cabinet was shocked and amazed to find, during Wilson's absence, that the Admiralty could produce no war plan for the Navy. It was so secret that only the First Sea Lord knew what it was!' – Marder. This was the final straw and Asquith had both the First Lord (Reginald McKenna) and the First Sea Lord moved on in short order.

See 23 August 1911, 23/24 October 1911.

1917 First regular convoy of merchant ships sailed from Hampton Roads, Virginia for UK.

1928 The light cruiser *Dauntless*, Capt K.D.W. Macpherson RN, newly arrived on the America and West Indies Station, went ashore in fog at 1400 on Thrum Cap Shoal, 5 miles outside Halifax, Nova Scotia. Her starboard side opened up and both boiler rooms flooded. Ship abandoned at 2200.

Major salvage operation required removal of all stores, guns, torpedoes, funnels, and moveable equipment. The ship was refloated on the flood tide at 1503 on 11 July, with Admiral Sir Walter Cowan, C-in-C, directing operations from *Despatch*, Capt Andrew Cunningham, which also had a line over to *Dauntless* to assist the tugs, and towed into Halifax. Cowan signalled 'Well done, everybody'. The Captain and NO, both charged that they 'did negligently or by default suffer the said ship to be stranded', were both dismissed their ship at Portsmouth courts martial on 5 and 6 August; that on the captain included Captains Dudley North (President), Max Horton and John Tovey.

The *Dauntless* had been carrying a memorial for erection on the Labrador coast to the men lost in the cruiser *Raleigh* wrecked there in 1922.

See 19 May 1807, 5 January 1847, 10 April 1918, 8 August 1922, 15 June 1941, 23 January 2007.

1930 Battleship *Rodney*, Capt A.B. Cunningham RN, sailed from Reykjavik after a week's visit to celebrate the 1,000th anniversary of the Icelandic parliament. The ship had been 'entrusted with a handsome token of good will from the fishermen of England to the fishing community of Iceland' – *The Times*.

See 1 September 1958, 31 August panel.

1940 Swordfish aircraft of 812 Sqn (disembarked) and Coastal Command aircraft attacked invasion barge concentration near Rotterdam.

1950 The start of United Nations operations in Korea. The light cruiser *Jamaica*, Capt J.S.C. Salter RN, in company with US cruiser *Juneau* (flag) and sloop *Black Swan*, destroyed five enemy MTBs off Imwon-jin, E. coast of Korea in the first naval action of the campaign. Battle Honour: Korea 1950–3.

Commonwealth Naval Forces (not all qualified for the Korea Battle Honour):

RN: *Alacrity, Alert, Amethyst, Belfast, Birmingham, Black Swan, Cardigan Bay, Ceylon, Charity, Cockade, Comus, Concord, Consort, Constance, Cossack, Crane, Defender, Glory, Hart, Jamaica, Kenya, Ladybird, Modeste, Morecambe Bay, Mounts Bay, Newcastle, Newfoundland, Ocean, Opossum, St Brides Bay, Sparrow, Tactician, Telemachus, Theseus, Triumph, Tyne, Unicorn,Warrior, Whitesand Bay*. FAA Squadrons: 800, 801, 802, 804, 805, 807, 808, 810, 812, 817, 821, 825, 827, 898. 41 Independent Cdo, RM.

RFA: *Brown Ranger, Fort Charlotte, Fort Rosalie, Fort Sandusky, Fort Langley, Gold Ranger, Green Ranger,* (His/Her Majesty's Hospital Ship) *Maine, Wave Baron, Wave Chief, Wave Duke, Wave Knight, Wave Laird, Wave Premier, Wave Prince, Wave Regent, Wave Sovereign.*

RAN: *Anzac, Bataan, Condamine, Culgoa, Murchison, Shoalhaven, Sydney, Tobruk, Warramunga, Arunta.* FAA Sqns: Sea Fury: 805, 808, 817.

RCN: *Athabaskan, Cayuga, Crusader, Haida, Huron, Iroquois, Nootka, Sioux.*

RNZN: *Hawea, Kaniere, Pukaki, Rotoiti, Taupo, Tutira.*

See 25 June 1950, 8 July 1950, 27 July 1953.

1955 Britannia RN College Dartmouth celebrated its fiftieth anniversary. The First Lord of the Admiralty and C-in-C Plymouth dined on board.

1958 His Majesty King Olav V of Norway appointed an honorary admiral in Her Majesty's Fleet on his 55th birthday.

See 2 August 1889, 7 June 1940, 1 May 1951, 16 February 1953, 21 September 1957, 25 June 1975, 18 March 1981, 4 August 2001.

1959 The first Sea Vixen swept-wing, two-seater, all-weather fighter squadron, 892 NAS, commissioned at RNAS Yeovilton by Cdr M.H.J. Petrie RN, and embarked in *Ark Royal* in March 1960. The second Sea Vixen squadron, 890 NAS, commissioned at Yeovilton 1 February 1960 and embarked in *Hermes* in July that year. The Sea Vixen superseded the Sea Venom and was operational until 1972, serving with 766, 890, 892, 893 and 899 NAS. The first British naval aircraft with guided weapons instead of guns.

See 1 February 1960.

1960 'Within a period of fifteen days no fewer than five new ships were accepted from their builders. The most notable, HMS *Lion*, the second Tiger-class cruiser, was commissioned at Wallsend-on-Tyne on the 20th of the month. On the same day, the second Brave-class fast patrol boat HMS *Brave Swordsman*, was handed over by her builders [Vospers] at Portsmouth. Earlier in the month the Navy had received HMS *Lincoln*, fourth of the Salisbury-class of aircraft direction frigates, and a boom defence vessel, HMS *Layburn*. Two days after the acceptance of the *Lion*, another Whitby-class frigate, HMS *Londonderry*, joined the Fleet at Cowes' – *Navy* magazine, August 1960.

1969 The first deck landing by a Sea King helicopter – on RFA *Engadine* off Portland.

See 19 August 1969.

2005 In the centenary year of its opening, BRNC Dartmouth tried to find two time capsules believed to be under the foundation stone laid by HM King Edward VII on 7 March 1902. One of the capsules was not discovered but a lesser, wooden capsule with the royal monogram was retrieved and contained five newspapers – *Western Morning News, Western Daily Mercury, The Times, Dartmouth and South Hams Chronicle* and one unidentified – together with a newly minted set of Edward VII coins, including Maundy money. The capsule had been laid in the hole with a purple silk sash with gold tassels, possibly suggesting a 'Masonic' ceremony.

Two new time capsules were laid down. Into the hole from which the wooden capsule had been taken were placed copies of *The Times, Navy News, Western Morning News*, DVDs and letters from the Commodore, Commander, Curator and Archivist. An official capsule was laid in a corresponding stone on the opposite side of the main doorway on 20 July 2005 by HRH The Duke of York.

See 7 March 1902, 2 July 1955, 20 July 2005.

3 JULY

1759 Rear-Admiral George Rodney, newly promoted, with his flag in *Achilles* (60), began an effective three-day pre-emptive bombardment with bomb vessels of invasion barges under construction in, and on, beaches around Le Havre. These French craft were the 'flat bottoms' derided in the Royal Navy's quick march 'Heart of Oak'.

Ships: *Achilles* (60), *Norwich* (50), *Chatham* (50), *Isis* (50), *Deptford* (50), *Chesterfield* (44), *Brilliant* (36), *Vestal* (32), *Juno* (32), *Boreas* (28), *Unicorn* (28), *Fly* (8), *Wolfe* (8). Bombs: *Basilisk, Blast, Carcass, Firedrake, Furnace, Mortar.*

1797 Bombardment of Cadiz. Rear-Admiral Sir Horatio Nelson's boat action with Spanish gunboats at Cadiz. Bombs: *Stromboli, Terror, Thunder.* Covered by: *Emerald, Terpsichore, Theseus.* Troops: Royal Artillery.

1801 *Speedy* taken by Rear-Admiral Durand-Linois' squadron off Gibraltar. Cochrane captured, and held until after the battle of Algeciras on the 6th, the French admiral declining to accept his surrendered sword.

1803 *Minerve* (42) stranded by navigation error the previous day on the Cones of Cherbourg, Capt Brenton got her off under fire but the tide took her into the harbour and he had to surrender to *La Chiffone*. He was held for two years, his crew for eleven.

1812 *Raven* defeated fourteen French gun-brigs of the Schelde division of the Invasion Flotilla in the Wielingen Channel, driving three ashore.

1840 *Blonde* (46) destroyed two Chinese batteries at Amoy.

1855 VC: OS Joseph Trewavas (*Agamemnon*, screw second rate, lent to wood screw gunvessel *Beagle*), for cutting hawsers of floating bridge in the straits of Genitchi under heavy fire at close range. Boats of *Beagle* and *Vesuvius* destroyed the ferry at Genitchi, Sea of Azov.

1860 Gold oak leaves introduced for peak of caps for Commanders and above in executive branch.

1902 Capt Reginald Bacon, Inspecting Captain of Submarines, proposed to the Controller of the Navy that No. 6 submarine about to be launched should be given a name rather than a number. 'The name *Ichthyosaurus* is particularly applicable to this boat fitted with an optical tube corresponding to the marvellous eye of the reptile', to be followed by *Somosaurus, Plesiosaurus, Discosaurus, Pistosaurus* and *Nothosaurus*. The Controller and the Senior Naval Lord would have none of it and the boat was designated A1.

See 18 March 1904, 24 September 1926, 5 November 1942, 19 and 27 December 1942, 28 January 1943.

1919 Minesweeper *Fandango* mined in Dvina River, northern Russia.

1940 French warships seized in British ports on the day of the British attack on the French fleet at Mers-el-Kebir. A generally smooth operation except in the French submarine *Surcouf* in Devonport Dockyard. A boarding party of armed Royal Marines and submariners led by Cdr Denis Vaughan Sprague, CO of HMS *Thames*, resulted in shooting in which Sprague, Lt Patrick M.K. Griffiths of HMS *Rorqual* and Leading Seaman Albert Webb of HMS *Revenge* were killed or mortally wounded.

1940 Force H, under Vice-Admiral Sir James Somerville (*Hood*), attacked the French warships at Mers-el-Kebir, Oran. Ships: *Hood, Resolution, Valiant, Ark Royal, Arethusa, Enterprise, Escort, Faulknor* (D 8), *Fearless, Foresight, Forester, Foxhound, Active, Keppel* (D 13), *Vidette, Vortigern, Wrestler.* FAA Sqns: Skua: 800, 803; Swordfish: 810, 818, 820. Operation Catapult. French ship sunk: *Bretagne*. French ships damaged: *Commandant Teste, Dunkerque, Mogador, Provence.*

Admiral Somerville signalled to Admiralty:
After talk with Holland and others I am impressed with their view that use of force should be avoided at all costs. Holland considers offensive action on our part would alienate all French wherever they are.

Admiralty to Somerville:
Firm intention of His Majesty's government that if French

will not accept any of your alternatives they are to be destroyed.

Prime Minister's signal to Somerville on 2 July:
You are charged with one of the most disagreeable and difficult tasks that a British Admiral has ever been faced with but we have complete confidence in you and rely on you to carry it out relentlessly.

Somerville to Admiral Gensoul:
If one of our propositions is not accepted by 1730 BST I shall have to sink your ships.

1942 British A/S trawler *Le Tigre* (on loan to US Navy) sank U-215 off New York (41.48N, 66.38W).

1943 Wellington R/172 sank U-126 in S.W. Approaches (46.02N, 11.23W).

1943 Liberator J/224 sank U-628 in Bay of Biscay (44.11N, 08.45W).

1944 Operation Neptune, naval phase of Operation Overlord, completed.

1950 Light fleet carrier *Triumph*, operating with US carrier *Valley Forge*, launched nine Seafires and twelve Fireflies to attack airfield at Haeju near 38th Parallel (border between N. and S. Korea), the first UN air strikes of the Korean War.

1959 Name of Tay Division RNR drill ship changed from *Cressy* to *Unicorn* 'a name it held formerly'. AFO 1598/59.

1964 Following the demise of the Lords Commissioners of the Admiralty, HM The Queen gave approval for the continuance of custom of the flag of the Lord High Admiral being flown on board ships being launched for the Royal Navy, even when Her Majesty might not be present in person. DCI(RN) 486/64.
See 22 September 1967.

1970 Admiral Sir Michael Le Fanu promoted admiral of the fleet on retiring early as First Sea Lord. In that post, the ginger-haired admiral presided over the demise of the Tot; his biography by Richard Baker was consequently entitled *Dry Ginger*. Admiral Le Fanu was mortally ill and died later that year.
See 28 November 1970.

Ordinary Seaman Joseph Trewavas, VC 1855. (*NMRN*)

2009 On return from a six-month deployment in Afghanistan, 3 Cdo Bde, Brig Gordon Messenger, marched through Exeter. HRH The Duke of Edinburgh, Captain General RM, took the salute at the Guildhall before a service of remembrance in Exeter Cathedral for the thirty-two men lost in action (and 144 wounded) in Helmand Province over the winter 2008/9. The RM and RN members of the brigade gained two DSOs, two OBEs, five MBEs, two CGCs (Acting Cpl Bradley Malone and Mne Steven Nethery, both of 45 Cdo), seven MCs including one to Able Seaman Class 1 Kate Nesbitt (20), the first naval female recipient, for her gallantry under fire, one DFC, eighteen MiDs and seven QC VSs. Operation Herrick 9.

4 July

1744 The treasure captured by Anson from the Spanish *Nuestra Senora de Covandonga* in the Pacific in June 1743 was paraded through London in thirty-two wagons to the Tower 'led by a wind-band and drummers' and escorted by officers with drawn swords. It had come up the Portsmouth Road guarded by the ship's company of *Centurion* 'who hired fiddlers to enliven the 90-mile journey'.

See 20 June 1743, 15 June 1744.

1780 *Prudente* and *Licorne* captured the French *Capricieuse* in the Bay of Biscay.

1803 Boats of *Naiad* cut out the French *Providence* with a rich cargo of gems and wood at Ile de Sein, Brittany.

1811 Boats of *Unité* cut out the French *St Francois de Paule* at Porto Ercole. *Cephalus* and boats of *Unité* cut out three French vessels between Civita Vecchia and the mouth of the River Tiber.

1855 Boats of sloop *Racehorse* captured a pirate junk off Ockseu Island, 80 miles N.E. of Amoy.

1915 VC: Lt Frederick Daniel Parslow RNR, HM Horse Transport *Anglo Californian*. Posthumous. The ship, carrying 927 horses from Montreal to Avonmouth for Western Front, was intercepted by surfaced U-38, 90 miles S.W. of Queenstown (50.10N, 09.00W). He ignored order to heave-to and abandon ship, signalling an alert for two hours until RN destroyers arrived. Mortally wounded by shellfire. His son, also Frederick, took con and brought ship into Queenstown for which awarded DSC and promoted sub-lieutenant. Parslow senior, in his 60th year, the oldest naval recipient of VC to date.

1917 Sloop *Aster* mined E. of Malta.

1930 The re-opening of the new Semaphore Tower spanning the road to South Railway Jetty in Portsmouth Dockyard. The former tower, built in 1778, had been destroyed by fire at Christmas 1913. The formal ceremony was performed by Vice-Admiral L.A.B. Donaldson, Admiral Superintendent of the Dockyard and Admiral Sir Percy Grant, Admiral Superintendent 1922–5. Admiral Grant turned the key to the tower door and Admiral of the Fleet Sir Roger Keyes, C-in-C Portsmouth, was first up the stairs. The mast on top of the new tower had been taken from the former German light cruiser *Nürnberg* interned on 21 November 1918 and scuttled at Scapa Flow in 1919.

See 20 December 1913.

1931 Heavy cruisers *Dorsetshire*, flag of Rear-Admiral E.A. Astley-Rushton, commanding Second Cruiser Squadron, and *Norfolk*, Captain C.B. Prickett RN, arrived at Kiel, the first British naval visit to a German port since 1914. The Admiral had been present at the 1914 Kiel Week in the light cruiser *Southampton*.

See 30 June 1914

1940 VC: A/LS Jack Foreman Mantle in *Foylebank*, sunk by German aircraft at Portland.

1940 Submarine *Pandora* sank the French mine-laying sloop *Rigault de Genouilly* 10 miles N. of Algiers, before orders to suspend further attacks on French ships had been received.

1940 Canadian government announced that patrol vessels of the whale-catcher type would in future be known as corvettes.

1941 The freighter *Robert L. Holt*, commodore's ship of Cape-bound convoy OB 337 which had been dispersed on 27 June, was sunk with all hands by gunfire from U-69 N.W. of the Canary Islands (34.15N, 20.00W). The convoy commodore was retired Vice-Admiral Norman Wodehouse (54), former RN rugby captain who had gained fourteen caps for England, including six as captain, between 1910 and 1913. Wodehouse was gunnery officer of the battleship *Revenge* at Jutland and captain of BRNC Dartmouth 1931–4.

A twin 40mm anti-aircraft gun and crew in a RN escort carrier. (*NMRN*)

Convoy PQ 17, 1942

PQ 17 of thirty-six ships sailed from Reykjavik on 27 June. It was shadowed from 1 July and there were unsuccessful air torpedo attacks that day. There was thick fog for the next forty-eight hours, when it became known that a large German force had sailed from Trondheim. *Tirpitz*, *Scheer*, *Hipper* and six destroyers were heading out, though the *Lützow* and three destroyers had run aground near Narvik and returned to harbour. On 4 July there were heavy German air attacks and three merchantmen were lost, but the convoy was in good heart, the American ships hoisting new stars and stripes. At 2100, however, the threat from the surface raiders was considered greater than that from under the sea or over it, and the convoy was ordered by the Admiralty to scatter. The cruiser escort withdrew westwards and the fleet destroyers joined them. As they left, one British escorting submarine signalled 'intend remaining on the surface as long as possible' . . . to which the irrepressible Cdr Broom in *Keppel* replied 'So do I'.

The surface attack did not materialise, and ten merchant ships were sunk by U-boats, and eleven by aircraft. However, eleven reached Russia, escorted by the AA ships and corvettes. One trawler had escorted three merchantmen, been trapped in ice for three days and had painted the ships white to avoid detection.

'The losses sustained by the Allies were enormous, amounting to twenty-four merchant ships, two-thirds of the convoy; eight totalling 48,218 tons sunk by U-boats, eight of 40,376 tons sunk by aircraft and eight of 54,093 tons damaged by aircraft and finished off by U-boats. In terms of materiel, 210 bombers, 430 tanks, 3,350 vehicles and a little under 100,000 tons of munitions, explosives and raw materials lay on the bed of the Barents Sea' – Woodman, *Arctic Convoys*, pp.254–5.

Cargo	Delivered	Lost
Vehicles	896	3,350
Tanks	164	430
Aircraft	87	210
Other cargo	57,176 tons	99,316 tons

1961 815 NAS commissioned at RNAS Culdrose with Westland Wessex, the first helicopter to carry a full ASW system.

1963 The new Fleet Air Arm march, 'Flying Stations', composed by Capt Frederick Stovin-Bradford RN and based on the bugle call 'Hands to Flying Stations', has its first public performance at Lee-on-Solent.

5 July

1695 Bombardment of St Malo by Admiral Lord Berkeley (*Shrewsbury*) and Vice-Admiral Philips van Almonde (Dutch). Ships: *Shrewsbury*, *Charles* (fireship), *Dreadful*, *Carcase* (bombs), and Dutch bombs.

1780 *Romney* captured the French *Perle* 50 miles to the westward of Cape Finisterre.

1807 Abortive attack on Buenos Aires by Lt-Gen John Whitelocke, resulting in the surrender of Brig-Gen Robert Crauford's force and finally to an armistice and the withdrawal of all British forces from the Rio de la Plata area. Naval forces were under Rear-Admiral George Murray (*Polyphemus*). Ships: *Africa*, *Diadem*, *Polyphemus*, *Raisonnable*. Frigates etc.: *Medusa*, *Nereide*, *Thisbe*, *Encounter*, *Fly*, *Flying Fish*, *Haughty*, *Olympia*, *Paz*, *Pheasant*, *Protector*, *Rolla*, *Saracen*, *Staunch*. A Naval Brigade was landed.

1811 *Cressy*, *Defence*, *Dictator*, *Sheldrake* and *Bruizer*, with a convoy of 108 sail, beat off a Danish flotilla of seventeen gunboats and ten heavy rowing boats off Hjelm Island, Kattegat, capturing four gunboats and three rowing boats.

1819 Admiral the Hon. Sir William Cornwallis died. Nicknamed 'Billy Blue' because as soon as bad weather drove him into port he was concerned to resume his blockade as soon as possible, and hoisted the Blue Peter as a preparative signal for sailing as he anchored.

1840 Capture of Tinghai, Chusan, by Cdre Sir Gordon Bremer (*Wellesley*). Ships: *Algerine*, *Alligator*, *Conway*, *Cruizer*, *Wellesley*, *Young Hebe*, *Rattlesnake* (transport). Steamers: *Atalanta* (IN), *Queen* (Ben. Mar.).

See 1 October 1841.

1872 Gunnery trials between armoured turret ship *Hotspur* and turret ship *Glatton*, each as useless as the other.

1898 Battleship *Ocean* launched at Devonport Dockyard, the first major armoured ship built there. Damaged by enemy gunfire and by a floating mine on 18 March 1915 during bombardment of Turkish positions in the Narrows during the Dardanelles campaign. Abandoned and sank in Morto Bay.

See 19 March 1863, 21 June 1898, 8 July 1944, 11 October 1995.

1916 UC-7 mined and sunk off Zeebrugge.

1917 Board of Invention and Research set up by Balfour, First Lord of the Admiralty, with

HMS *Glatton* (1871), a breastwork monitor mounting two 12-in guns in a single turret. Designed for coastal defence and for attacking enemy coastal defences, she was unsuitable for either task and spent most of her days in Portsmouth harbour. (*NMRN*)

Showing the flag. The Type 81 frigate HMS *Zulu*, one of three Tribal-class commissioned from the Standby Squadron in 1982 to replace ships deployed to the South Atlantic, photographed by the author alongside at Key West in Florida in 1983 after visits to Belize and New Orleans. (*Author*)

Admiral of the Fleet Lord Fisher as Chairman. Soon became known as the 'Board of Intrigue and Revenge'.

1920 Landing parties from *Royal Sovereign*, *Revenge*, *Venetia* and *Westcott* assisted in occupation of Mudavia by Greek forces, *Ceres*, *Royal Oak* and *Resolution* having landed troops at Lapsaki, Dardanelles.

1940 Destroyer *Whirlwind* torpedoed by U-34 in W. Approaches (50.17N, 08.48W). Sunk by *Westcott*.

1940 Nine Swordfish aircraft of 813 Sqn (*Eagle*) sank the Italian destroyer *Zeffiro* and the liner *Liguria* at Tobruk.

1940 Swordfish aircraft of 830 Sqn (Malta) attacked Catania airfield, Sicily.

1941 Submarine *Tigris* sank the Italian S/M *Michele Bianchi*.

1941 Submarine *Torbay* sank the Italian submarine *Jantina* off Izmir (Turkey) (37.30N, 25.50E).

1942 Minesweeper *Niger* and her convoy of four merchantmen sunk by British mines off Iceland (66.35N, 22.20W). Convoy QP 13.

1943 Liberator G/53 sank U-535 in Bay of Biscay (43.52N, 00.48W).

1944 Destroyer *Wanderer* and frigate *Tavy* sank U-390 in the Channel (49.52N, 00.48W).

1948 Light cruiser *Achilles*, veteran of the Battle of the River Plate in 1939, transferred to India as INS *Delhi*. Flagship of the Indian Navy until relieved by cruiser *Mysore* (ex-HMS *Nigeria*) in 1957.

See 29 August 1957, 4 March 1961, 20 March 1987.

1969 Frigates *Arethusa* and *Mohawk*, with Royal Marines embarked, arrived in Bermuda on a routine visit coincident with start of a three-day international Black Power conference held in the island.

6 July

1779 Vice-Admiral the Hon. John Byron (*Princess Royal*) fought Vice-Admiral Comte d'Estaing (*Languedoc*), with twenty-six ships, off Grenada. Ships: *Albion, Boyne, Cornwall, Conqueror, Elizabeth, Fame, Grafton, Lion, Magnificent, Medway, Monmouth, Nonsuch, Prince of Wales, Princess Royal, Royal Oak, Stirling Castle, Suffolk, Sultan, Trident, Vigilant, Yarmouth.* Frigate: *Ariadne.* Regiments: 4th, 5th, 40th, 46th.

By great good fortune, four dismasted British ships escaped, 'the French admiral's seamanship not being equal to his courage'.

1782 Third battle between Vice-Admiral Sir Edward Hughes (*Superb*) and Cdre Chevalier de Suffren (*Heros*), with eleven ships and four frigates off Negapatam, Madras. Ships: *Hero, Exeter, Isis, Burford, Sultan, Superb, Monarch, Worcester, Monmouth, Eagle, Magnanime, Seahorse.* Regiment: 98th.
Battle Honour: Negapatam 1782.

See 12 November 1781, 17 February 1782, 12 April 1782, 3 September 1782.

1801 Rear-Admiral Sir James Saumarez (*Caesar*) fought Rear-Admiral Durand-Linois (*Formidable*) at Algeciras, southern Spain. Ships: *Audacious, Caesar, Hannibal,* Pompee, Spencer, Venerable, Calpe.*

*Captured, after running aground.

1808 *Seahorse* (38) took the larger Turkish frigate *Badere Zaffer* (44), whose crew was twice the size of hers, and damaged the corvette *Alis Fezan* up the Archipelago.
Battle Honour: *Badere Zaffer* 1808.

1809 *Bonne Citoyenne*, frigate, captured the French *Furieuse* 700 miles E. by S. of Cape Race, Newfoundland.
Battle Honour: *Furieuse* 1809.

1809 Surrender of San Domingo.

1812 *Dictator* and *Calypso* destroyed the Danish *Nayaden* between Lyngo and Odden, Denmark, and captured the corvettes *Laaland* and *Kiel*, which had to be abandoned. *Podargus* and *Flamer* were in company, but grounded before the main action, though engaged with gunboats and shore batteries.

1841 *Acorn*, brig, captured the Portuguese slaver *Gabriel* 300 miles S.W. by W. of Sierra Leone.

1916 Submarine E 26 (building for Turkish Navy but acquired) lost in North Sea.

1917 Destroyer *Itchen* sunk by U-99 70 miles E. of Pentland Firth.

1918 First recorded use of 'Asdics', in memorandum from Admiralty research establishment at Harwich.

See 5 June 1917, 1 February 1963.

1923 AM (Albert Medal): PO H.E. Wild and ex-PO E.E.M. Joyce for services on Shackleton's Trans-Antarctic Expedition, in addition to Polar Medals.

1940 Submarine *Shark* scuttled after German aircraft attack, assisted by the minesweeping trawlers M-1803, M-1806 and M-1807 off Skudesnaes, Norway (58.18N, 05.13E).

1940 Bombardment of Bardia, by *Caledon, Capetown, Ilex, Imperial, Janus* and *Juno.*

1940 Swordfish aircraft of 810 Sqn (*Ark Royal*) torpedoed and severely damaged the French battlecruiser *Dunkerque* and sank the trawler *Terre Neuve* escaping from Oran.

1942 Wellington H/172 sank U-502 in Bay of Biscay (46.10N, 06.40W). First operational success at sea of both the Wellington and the Leigh Light.

1944 *Cato* and *Magic*, minesweepers, sunk in first use of German Marder one-man submarine. Twenty-six deployed, and nine lost to gunfire in Sword area, Seine Bay. Operation Neptune.

1944 *Kootenay* and *Ottawa* (RCN) and *Statice* sank U-678 off Brighton (50.32N, 00.23W).

1944 Frigate *Trollope* torpedoed off French coast by E-boat. Towed to Arromanches and then to Portsmouth, but CTL.

In the capture of *La Furieuse* by the *Bonne Citoyenne* (a British ship despite her name), the former lost her main and mizzen mast. With a prize crew aboard and a jury-rigged fore mast, she was towed from the mid-Atlantic into Halifax, Nova Scotia, 1809. (*NMRN 1976/246-7*)

1965 Acting Admiral Sir John Frewen (promoted 9 February 1966) hoisted his flag at Northwood, the last C-in-C Home Fleet.

See 1 October 1967, 30 August 1975.

1968 New HQ of Sussex Division RNR at Maxwell Wharf, Portslade, opened by HRH Princess Alexandra.

1971 Fastest Ship in the Fleet race between Type 15 frigate *Rapid* and destroyer *Cavalier* off the Firth of Forth. The two-hour race favoured *Rapid*, the seagoing training ship for *Caledonia*, the Apprentices' Training Establishment at Rosyth, whose machinery was therefore in first-class working order. *Rapid* led most of the way but a boiler valve lifted and the loss of boiler pressure allowed *Cavalier* to win by a head after a run of 64 miles at an average speed of 31.8 knots.

See 28 February 1983, p.153 photograph.

1979 Admiral Sir Terence Lewin promoted admiral of the fleet and became CDS in September.

See 23 January 1999.

1996 Instructor specialisation abolished. Instructor Officers absorbed into Seaman and Engineering specialisations.

See 30 April 1861, 6 April 1962.

1998 RN College Greenwich passed out of naval control on being handed over to the Greenwich Foundation for the Royal Naval College on 150-year lease. College now the campus of the University of Greenwich.

See 30 June 1696, 1 February 1873.

2000 *Orwell*, last survivor of twelve River-class minesweepers, latterly employed as the Britannia RN College navigation training ship, sailed from Dartmouth to pay off at Portsmouth. Met at Spithead by Rear-Admiral and Mrs Eckersley-Maslin, the lady having launched the ship in 1985.

7 JULY

1777 *Flora* recaptured the American (ex-British) *Fox* 40 miles S. by W. of Cape Sable, N. America.

1805 *Matilda* captured the Spanish privateer *Artrivedo* and her two prizes (*Golden Grove* and *Ceres*) in the St Mary River, Georgia.

1809 Boats of *Implacable*, *Bellerophon* and *Melpomene* cut out seven Russian gunboats and twelve merchantmen under Percola Point, Hango Head, Baltic.

1813 Landing party from *Eagle* captured and destroyed a five-gun fort at Faresina.

1874 Conspicuous Gallantry Medal reintroduced.

1910 Frank Twiss, son of Col E.K. Twiss DSO and a future Second Sea Lord, born in India.
See 1 March 1942, 26 January 1994.

1914 Statue of Capt James Cook RN by Sir Thomas Brock unveiled in the Mall near Admiralty Arch by HRH Prince Arthur of Connaught. 'Circumnavigator of the Globe, Explorer of the Pacific Ocean, he laid the foundation of the British Empire in Australia and New Zealand'.

1917 Submarine J 2 torpedoed and sank U-99 off Heligoland.

1941 US forces relieved the British Garrison in Iceland, five months before the United States entered the Second World War.
See 10 May 1940, 8 May 1941.

1961 Submarine Command received the Freedom of the Borough of Gosport. Four hundred officers and men marched through Gosport with bayonets fixed and bearing, for the first time, the Queen's Colour of the Submarine Branch presented by Her Majesty in 1959.

1967 Sir Francis Chichester arrived at Greenwich in *Gypsy Moth IV* after his circumnavigation and was knighted by HM Queen Elizabeth II.
See 4 April 1581, 22 April 1969, 7 February 2005.

1975 Rear-Admiral O.N.A. ('Os') Cecil, lately SBNOSA, appointed the last Flag Officer Malta.
See 8 July 1963, 5 June 1967, 31 March 1979, 29 May 2005.

1988 Frigate *Phoebe* and MCMV *Blackwater* led SAR operation at Piper Alpha oil rig explosion, 120 miles N.E. of Aberdeen.

2002 *Nottingham*, Type 42 destroyer, grounded and severely damaged on Wolfe Rock, Lord Howe Island, off east coast of Australia. Destroyer destored in Australia and transported back to Britain on board the heavy-lift ship *Swan*. Repaired in Portsmouth Dockyard and undocked one year to the day later, 7 July 2003.
See 21 August 1910, 18 February 1980, 8 April 1983, 3 September 1988, 11 September 1994, 27 February 2006.

2009 First steel cut for the carrier *Queen Elizabeth* by HRH The Princess Royal at BVT Yard, Govan.
See 30 July 1963

HMS *Nottingham* aground on Wolfe Rock, 2002. (*RN*)

8 July

1777 *Rainbow* captured the American *Hancock* 170 miles S.S.W. of Cape Sambro, Nova Scotia.

1778 *Ostrich* and *Lowestoff's Prize* captured the American *Polly* off Galina Point, Jamaica.

1800 *Dart* (30) captured the French *Désirée* (38) in Dunkirk Roads. Battle Honour: *Désirée* 1800.

1809 Landing party from *Mosquito*, *Alert* (cutter), *Basilisk*, *Blazer*, *Briseis*, *Bruizer* (gunvessel), *Ephira*, *Patriot*, *Sentinel* (schuyt) and *Pincher* captured a battery at Cuxhaven.

1810 Reduction of the island of Bourbon (Réunion).

1838 Royal Naval College re-established by Order in Council at Portsmouth.

1846 Rear-Admiral Sir Thomas Cochrane (*Agincourt* (74) destroyed the defences of Brunei, Borneo. Ships: *Hazard*, *Phlegethon* (Ben. Mar.), *Royalist*, *Spiteful* (flag for attack). Boats of *Agincourt*, *Iris*, *Ringdove*.

1854 Boats of wood paddle frigate *Firebrand* and wood paddle sloop *Vesuvius* destroyed the defences and part of the town of Sulina, Black Sea.

1870 James Reed, Chief Constructor, resigned over the issue of fitting full sailing rig in turret-ships.

See 9 July 1863, 7 September 1870.

1940 Motor boat of *Hermes* and her Swordfish aircraft of 814 Sqn attacked with depth charges and torpedoes respectively the French battleship *Richelieu* at Dakar.

1943 Liberator R/224 sank U-514 in Bay of Biscay (43.37N, 08.59W).

1944 Sunderland H/10 (RAAF) sank U-243 in Bay of Biscay (47.06N, 06.40W).

1944 Light cruiser *Dragon* (Pol) damaged and minesweeper *Pylades* sunk by German one-man submarines in Juno area, Seine Bay. *Dragon* became blockship. Operation Neptune.

1944 Light fleet carrier *Ocean* launched at Alexander Stephens, Govan, by Lady Willis, wife of Vice-Admiral Sir Algernon Willis. Ship commissioned 8 August 1945 under command of Capt Caspar John RN.

See 19 March 1863, 5 July 1898, 8 August 1945, 3 December 1945, 11 October 1995.

1948 Rear-Admiral Lord Louis Mountbatten, last Viceroy and first Governor-General of India, appointed Flag Officer First Cruiser Squadron, Mediterranean Fleet. Mountbatten, lately Supreme Allied Commander S.E. Asia Command, became thirteenth in order of precedence at Malta and much junior in rank to his erstwhile subordinate, Arthur John Power, now C-in-C Mediterranean Fleet. Power 'was apt to address Mountbatten as 'sir', in absent-minded recollection of SEAC; Mountbatten punctiliously 'sirred' him back; and when the Duke of Edinburgh joined the Fleet all three men could be observed 'sirring' and deferring to each other with great éclat' – Philip Ziegler, *Mountbatten*.

1950 The first British casualties of the Korean War. The light cruiser *Jamaica*, Capt J.S.C. Salter RN, bombarding Communist targets on the E. coast of Korea near Imwon-jin (Rimuonma on the chart), took a direct hit from a shore battery at the base of the mainmast close to a gun mounting. Six men killed.

See 2 and 3 July 1950.

1954 The Queen's Colour was presented by HRH The Duke of Gloucester to The Nore Command.

It was laid up in St George's church, HMS *Pembroke*, Chatham, and transferred to the Chapel of the RN College, Greenwich in 1984.

1963 The post of Flag Officer Malta lapsed when Rear-Admiral Viscount Kelburn hauled down his flag and sailed in HMS *Layburn* for Syracuse.

See 7 July 1975.

2008 Vice-Admiral Sir Anthony Troup, FOSNI 1974–7, died aged 86. In June 1943 aged 21 years 10 months he was given command of the submarine H.32, the youngest British naval officer to command a submarine in the Second World War.

See 31 October 1971.

9 JULY

1745 *Lion* fought the French *Elizabeth* and *Duteillay* (conveying the Young Pretender) 140 miles W. of Ushant.

1794 Captains' Servants remustered as Boys, in three grades.

1803 *Narcissus* captured the French *Alcyon* S.W. of San Pietro, near Sardinia.

1810 Boats of *Sirius* captured the French privateer *Edward* off Bourbon (Réunion).

1863 E.J. Reed appointed Chief Constructor.
See 8 July 1870.

1864 Squadronal colours abolished.
See 5 August 1864.

1902 Submarine A 1 launched – first British boat of thirteen A-class, begun before the original Hollands were completed.

1917 Battleship *Vanguard*, 4th BS, Grand Fleet, destroyed by magazine explosion at 2320 while at anchor in Scapa Flow; 804 men lost.
See 26 November 1914, 31 December 1915.

1917 RNAS aircraft from Mudros bombed German battlecruiser *Goeben* and light cruiser *Breslau* at Constantinople both nominally Turkish units.

1929 Submarine H 47 lost in collision with L 12 off Pembrokeshire. H 47 sank quickly with great loss of life.

HM Submarine A 1 (1902). (*NMRN*)

1940 The action off Calabria, (38.00N, 17.30E). The first capital ship engagement between the Italian Navy and the British Mediterranean Fleet after Italy entered the war a month earlier. In terms of numbers of warships engaged, this was the biggest British naval battle of the Second World War.
Battle Honour: Calabria 1940.
See 19 July 1940.

1940 Submarine *Salmon* sunk by mine S.W. of Stavanger (57.22N, 05.00E).

1940 *Foxglove*, sloop, bombed off the Nab Tower and damaged beyond useful repair, but became baseship in River Foyle.

1942 Corvette *Hyacinth* on passage happened to capture the Italian S/M *Perla* off Beirut (33.50N, 35.19E).

1944 Capt F.J. Walker CB, DSO and three bars, the outstanding anti-submarine force commander of the Second World War died, his death formally attributed to his naval service. The recognition he cherished was the award of two years' seniority, an amend for his delayed promotion from commander before the war, for 'lacking powers of leadership'. He did not live long to savour it, alas, but at his funeral in Liverpool Cathedral on 11 July 1944 Sir Max Horton, C-in-C W. Approaches, said: 'may there never be wanting in this realm a succession of men of like spirit in discipline, imagination and valour, humble and unafraid. Not dust nor the light weight of a stone, but all the sea of the W. Approaches shall be his tomb.'
See 3 June 1896, 3 April 1917, 11 July 1944, 16 October 1998.

1952 *Coniston*, minesweeper, first of the most numerous British warship class in the second half of twentieth century, launched at Harland and Wolff, Belfast. Broken up 1970.
See 5 October 1993, 3 December 1993.

1958 Admiral Sir Robin L.F. Durnford-Slater appointed the last C-in-C The Nore. Flag in *Pembroke*.
See 31 March 1961, 28 June 1984.

The Action off Calabria, 9 July 1940

Admiral Sir Andrew Cunningham in *Warspite* (flag), with battleships *Malaya* and *Royal Sovereign*, the carrier *Eagle*, five cruisers and sixteen destroyers, were E. of the 'toe' of Italy covering the passage of two convoys from Malta to Alexandria when they met the Italian fleet of two battleships, sixteen cruisers and thirty-two destroyers under Admiral Angelo Campioni (Cunningham says 'my old friend Riccardi'), also covering a convoy of tanks and petrol bound for Benghazi. Captain Rory O'Conor in the light cruiser *Neptune* signalled 'Enemy battle fleet in sight', the first British warship to make that signal since Cdre Goodenough in the light cruiser *Southampton* had sighted the German High Seas Fleet on 31 May 1916, the opening of the Battle of Jutland, and the first time in the Mediterranean since Nelson sighted Brueys in Aboukir Bay before the Battle of the Nile in 1798. The action was little more than a long-range gunnery exchange with little damage on either side but *Warspite* landed a salvo on the Italian flagship *Giulio Cesare* at a range of 13 miles, whereupon the Italians withdrew behind smoke, chased to within 25 miles of the Calabrian coast by Cunningham. This one salvo hit on an enemy ship, however, was one of the most effective in British naval history (as was the single FAA torpedo hit in the rudders in *Bismarck*), establishing British professional ascendancy for the whole of the Mediterranean naval campaign. It had 'a moral effect quite out of proportion to the damage. Never again did they willingly face up to the fire of British battleships, though on several subsequent occasions they were in a position to give battle with a great preponderance in force' – Cunningham, *A Sailor's Odyssey*, p.263.

Ships: *Dainty, Decoy, Defender, Eagle, Gloucester, Hasty, Hereward, Havoc, Hostile, Hyperion, Ilex, Janus, Juno, Liverpool, Malaya, Mohawk, Neptune, Nubian, Orion, Royal Sovereign*, HMAS *Stuart*, HMAS *Vampire*, HMAS *Voyager, Warspite*. FAA Squadrons: 813, 824. RAF: 210 Squadron flying boats L5803, L5807, L9020.

1959 HMY *Britannia*, escorted by the frigate HMS *Ulster* and destroyers HMCS *Kootenay* and *Gatineau*, arrived at Port Arthur and Fort William (now Thunder Bay) on Lake Superior, 2,000 miles from the sea and 600ft above sea level, following the official opening of the St Lawrence Seaway by Her Majesty The Queen.

The night before, as the yacht steamed across Lake Superior, the COs of the three escorts were invited to dine with the Queen. The captains of *Ulster* and *Gatineau* went over to *Kootenay* in advance so all three could transfer by jackstay in one operation. Thick fog prevented both the transfer and the option of return to their respective ships. Cdr Cameron Rusby RN, of *Ulster*, spent the night in the sick bay of *Kootenay* and called on the Queen in the yacht next morning, still in the rig, by special dispensation, of white mess dress with stiff shirt and bow tie, the uniform in which he had left *Ulster* eighteen hours earlier. FORY signalled: 'I have always regarded a return to one's ship at 0930 in the morning in Mess Dress to be just a little decadent.'

See 26 June 1959, 27 May 1960.

1964 Guided missile destroyer *Fife* launched at Fairfield on Clydeside and *Glamorgan* at Vickers Armstrong on the Tyne.

1976 Flag Officers' No. 1 Full Dress to be restricted to admirals of the fleet, full admirals, flag officer royal yachts, defence services secretary and admiral president, Royal Naval College, Greenwich 'in the interests of economy and as there are few occasions outside the Capital and Court at which ceremonial day coats are appropriate'. For all other officers of flag rank, No. 1 Full Dress to consist of an undress coat, undress sword belt and plain blue trousers. Rear admirals promotion grants reduced accordingly from 1 September 1975. DCI(RN) 314/76.

See 5 May 1911.

1976 Last WRNS officers' passing out parade at RNC Greenwich; salute taken by Rear-Admiral D.W. Bazalgette, Admiral President. Top cadet and winner of the last Canaletto print was 3/O Katherine Corbett. Training transferred to BRNC Dartmouth.

1995 Sir Clifford Jarrett, last full-term Permanent Secretary of the Admiralty, died. Sir Michael Cary succeeded him in 1964 but the post was abolished when the Admiralty was absorbed into the unified MOD and Cary ended his term as Permanent Under-Secretary of State (Navy).

See 10 July 1936.

10 July

1797 *Santa Margarita* captured the French privateer *Adour* 24 miles S.W. of Cape Clear.

1804 Boats of *Narcissus*, *Seahorse* and *Maidstone* cut out twelve settees at Le Levandou, Hyeres Road.

1808 Boats of *Porcupine* cut out the Spanish *N.S. Del Rosario* at Porto d'Anzio.

1839 The wood paddle frigate *Cyclops* launched at Pembroke Dockyard. She was 12ft 3in longer than her more famous sister ship, *Gorgon*, and displaced 1,960 tons. They were the first steam vessels over 1,000 tons. *Cyclops* served in the Syrian campaign of 1840 and the Russian War, and helped to lay the first Atlantic telegraph cable in 1857.

See 31 August 1837.

1866 Wood screw sloop *Amazon* sank off Start Point having rammed and sunk an Irish collier in clear and calm weather.

1888 John Godfrey, Director of Naval Intelligence in Second World War, born.

See 29 August 1971.

1911 King George V granted the title of Royal Australian Navy to the Permanent Naval Forces and the Citizen Naval Forces (Reserves) of Australia, which had been formed in 1901 at a federation of the individual state navies, thus creating the RAN and RANR. Royal Assent signed in October 1911.

See 1 March 1904, 25 November 1910.

1920 Admiral of the Fleet Lord Fisher of Kilverstone, First Sea Lord 1904–10 and 1914–15, creator of the Dreadnought battleship, died aged 79, in St James's Square.

See 22 December 1779, 25 January 1841, 20 October 1904.

1936 Sir Oswyn Murray, who succeeded Sir W. Graham Greene as permanent secretary of the Admiralty in August 1917, died at Annery, Roehampton, aged 62. He became a full member of the Board of Admiralty by Order in Council 31 October 1931.

1940 813 and 824 Naval Air Squadrons from *Eagle* sank the Italian destroyer *Leone Pancaldo*, for the first time, in Augusta harbour.

See 30 April 1943.

1943 Allied landings in Sicily. Operation Husky. Battle Honour: Sicily 1943.

The invasion started with the landing in the early hours of 10 July. Before nightfall British troops had entered Syracuse and next day the port, capable of taking 5,000 tons of stores a day, was in British hands virtually undamaged. During the operation the naval and air forces landed 115,000 British troops and 66,000 American troops. Ships involved were:

	British	**American**	**Other**
Warships	199	68	12
Landing Craft, etc.	1,260	811	3
Merchant Ships	155	66	16

In the three weeks following the landings, three German and eight Italian submarines were sunk for the loss of four merchant ships and two LSTs, with two merchantmen and two cruisers damaged. Air attacks caused more problems and dislocations, with thirteen ships sunk and more damaged.

1943 *Melbreak*, *Wensleydale* and *Glaisdale* sank German M-153, 45 miles N.E. of Ushant.

1961 The Royal Australian Navy spliced the mainbrace on the fiftieth anniversary of its formation in 1911.

See 1 March 1967.

From Admiralty to Australian Commonwealth Naval Board: 'The Board of Admiralty, the Royal Navy and the Royal Marines send to the Navy Board and the Officers and Men of the Royal Australian Navy congratulations and good wishes on the occasion of its fiftieth anniversary. The Royal Navy has always greatly valued its close co-operation and warm comradeship with the Royal Australian Navy in peace and war. This is a case in which they look forward to the Australians scoring many centuries.'

From ACNB to Admiralty: 'The Navy Board and the Officers and Men of the RAN thank the Board of Admiralty, the Royal Navy and the Royal Marines for their good wishes which are very greatly appreciated. The RAN

The *Cyclops* was rated a steam sloop at her launching at Pembroke Dockyard in 1839 but her 1,960 tons, displacement led to her being re-rated as a wood paddle frigate on commissioning in November 1839. (*Author*)

is deeply conscious of the great debt of gratitude which we owe to the Royal Navy, our parent, for our traditions, guidance, trainingand so much material assistance. We greatly value the close association and friendship which we have enjoyed with the Royal Navy since our childhood, and we look forward to its continuance in our riper years. We hope we shall do better than out last Test Score!'

1987 *Norfolk*, first of Type 23 Duke-class frigates, launched at Yarrow, Glasgow, by HRH Princess Margaret.

See 29 October 1984, 1 June 1990, 6 May 2006.

1995 Admiral Sir Benjamin Bathurst promoted admiral of the fleet at the end of his appointment as First Sea Lord. Born 27 May 1936. Entered RN 1953. Aviator. Admiral April 1989 and CINCFLEET. First Sea Lord 1992. Since 1996 the rank of admiral of the fleet has been held in abeyance and his successors have not been promoted although their names, together with admirals who have held the appointment of Chief, or Vice Chief, of the Defence Staff, remain on the Active List.

1996 *Rooke*, RN base at Gibraltar, paid off.

See 24 July 1704.

2005 The first RN service in the old but refurbished Royal Dockyard Chapel at Pembroke Dock since the yard closed in 1926, conducted by The Rt Revd Bishop Ivor Rees, of the RN Association, and the Revd Michael Brotherton RN, Chaplain of *Ocean*, to mark the sixtieth anniversaries of VE and VJ Days.

11 July

1796 *Melpomene* captured the French *Revanche* 50 miles S.S.W. of Ushant.

1803 *Racoon* captured the French *Lodi* at Leogane, Haiti.

1812 Boats of *Tuscan* cut out a small privateer at Chipiona, Spain. *Encounter* grounded and was taken by the enemy.

1824 Defeat of the Ashantis at Cape Coast Castle. Ships: *Thetis, Swinger, Victor*. Troops: 2nd West India Regiment.

1843 *Helena* launched at Pembroke Dock. Served as brig sloop, coal hulk, police ship and church ship.

1882 Bombardment of Alexandria by Admiral Sir Frederick Beauchamp Seymour (*Alexandra*) aimed at overthrowing Turkish power in Egypt. VC: Gnr Israel Harding (*Alexandra*) for picking up a live shell and putting it in a bucket of water. Ships: *Alexandra, Beacon, Bittern, Condor, Cygnet, Decoy, Invincible, Monarch, Penelope, Sultan, Superb, Temeraire*. 'The first time in history a British armoured squadron went into action' – Ballard.
Battle Honour: Alexandria 1882.

1915 The German light cruiser *Königsberg*, blockaded 10 miles up the Rufiji River in German East Africa (07.51S, 39.15E) since 30 October 1914, was finally destroyed by gunfire from the anchored shallow draught 6-in monitors *Mersey*, Capt E.G.A. Fullerton RN, and *Severn*, Cdr R.A. Wilson RN, sent out from Malta. Battle Honour: *Königsberg* 1915.

See 20 September 1914, 9 November 1914.

Her whereabouts were discovered from papers captured by the light cruiser *Chatham* on 19 October and the light cruiser *Dartmouth* found her on 30 October. There followed an eight-month blockade. The *Königsberg*, which had led a fugitive existence on the East African coast, mainly through lack of coal, did not match the achievements of the light cruiser *Emden* but she posed a threat to the Suez-Aden-Colombo sea lanes and tied up valuable British warships. She was the last operational German warship left on the high seas; her wreck was broken up 1963–5. This action was a naval aviation first; the monitors' fall of shot reported by Short seaplane piloted by Flight-Cdr J.T. Cull RN with Sub-Lt H.J. Arnold RN as observer (aircraft shot down; DSO and DSC respectively). Another Fleet Air Arm first gained with the next *Königsberg* on 10 April 1940.

1916 *Era, Nellie Nutten* and *Onward* (trawlers escorting fishing fleet) sunk by U-24, U-46 and U-52 100 miles E. of Aberdeen.

1929 Mrs Mary Eliza Sykes died at Surbiton, the last surviving child of Capt Swain Price RN who served as a master's mate in the *Temeraire* at Trafalgar, almost 124 years earlier.

See 2 July 1853, 13 April 1885, 15 April 1887, 13 February 1892, 14 September 1947, 3 August 1966.

1935 Admiralty Fleet Order No. 1684. 'The order to "Splice the Main Brace" is to be regarded as authorising the special issue of a ration of one-eighth pint of rum to each officer or man of or over 20 years of age who desires it. Officers and men under 20 years of age may receive a special issue of one-twentieth pint lime juice and 1 oz. sugar, and a similar issue may be made to other officers and men who do not desire the rum ration. No money in lieu is allowable. The issue of the special rum ration is to be made under the general conditions laid down in *King's Regulations and Admiralty Instructions*, Art.1827, Clauses 2 and 3, except that the time of issue may be arranged as considered desirable.'

See 22 February 1773, 19 May 1797, 10 February 1947.

1939 Dinner hosted by the Board of Admiralty in the Painted Hall at Greenwich, in presence of King George VI, to inaugurate its use as the Wardroom Mess of the RN College.

See 1 May 1939, 21 October 1998.

Hitherto the Queen Elizabeth Ante Room had been the Wardroom Mess dining room. The Painted Hall was the picture gallery of Greenwich Hospital until 1936 when the collection was moved to the new National Maritime Museum. The move allowed the Royal Navy to use the Painted Hall for the purpose intended by Wren – a grand dining room.

A naval gatling gun in action in Alexandria, 1882. (*NMRN*)

1940 Destroyer *Escort* (screening Force H) torpedoed and sunk by the Italian S/M *Guglielmo Marconi* N. of Algiers (36.11N, 03.37W).

1940 First enemy air attack on Portsmouth Dockyard.

1941 Destroyer *Defender*, returning to Alexandria after running supplies into Tobruk, damaged by a heavy bomb in bright moonlight which exploded under her engine room and broke her back in Gulf of Sollum 7 miles N. of Sidi Barrani. *Defender* taken in tow by destroyer HMAS *Vendetta* but had to be torpedoed by *Vendetta* (31.45N, 35.31E). No casualties.

See 14 December 1809, 7 April 1932, 8 November 1932, 25 April 1941.

1942 *Protea* and *Southern Maid* (SANF whalers) and Walrus aircraft of 700 Sqn (FAA) sank the Italian S/M *Ondina* off Beirut (34.35N, 34.56E).

1942 Sloop *Pelican*, frigate *Spey* and *Léopard* (Free French) sank U-136 W.N.W. of Madeira (33.30N, 22.52W). Convoy OS 33.

1942 Destroyers *Beaufort*, *Dulverton*, *Eridge* and *Hurworth* bombarded Mersa Matruh area. Albacore aircraft of 820 Sqn drove ships in harbour to sea, an ammunition ship being sunk by the destroyers.

1943 MTBs 640, 651 and 670 sank the Italian S/M *Flutto* off N. Sicily (37.34N, 15.43E).

1943 Battleships *Howe* and *King George V* bombarded Favignana and Trapani, Sicily. Light cruisers *Dido* and *Sirius* bombarded Marsala. Operation Fracture.

1944 Sunderland P/201 sank U-1222 in Bay of Biscay (46.31N, 05.29W).

1944 Capt Frederick John Walker buried at sea from the destroyer *Hesperus* off the Mersey Bar.

See 9 July 1944.

1980 *Invincible*, Capt Michael Livesay RN, commissioned in the presence of HM The Queen at Portsmouth.

See 3 May 1977, 6 October 2003, 3 August 2005.

1984 Admiral of the Fleet Sir Caspar John, the first naval aviator to become First Sea Lord, died at Hayle, Cornwall, aged 81. Entered RN College, Osborne, in 1916 aged 13. XO of heavy cruiser *York* in Second World War (ship CTL in Suda Bay 22 May 1941) and in 1945 the first captain of light fleet carrier *Ocean*. VCNS to Earl Mountbatten in 1957. First Sea Lord 1960–3. 'He inspired awe and affection, and for those privileged to work with him, admiration as well' – Rebecca John, *Caspar John*, p.187. Lord Carrington, the First Lord of the Admiralty, considered John 'one of the outstanding personalities of his generation, with all the best traditions of the Royal Navy combined with a certain inherited Bohemianisn which lightened the very serious side of his character'. His final five years were confined to a wheelchair having lost his legs ('three feet nearer the ground'), a familiar figure on the quayside and at the Ship Inn at Mousehole. Among his last words, spoken in semi-consciousness, was the command 'Buck up!'

See 22 March 1903, 23 May 1960.

12 July

1346 Edward III destroyed eleven French warships at La Hogue.

1745 *Prince Frederick* and *Duke* ('Royal Family' privateers) captured the French *Marquis d'Antin* and *Louis Erasmus* off the Banks of Newfoundland.

1771 Return of Lt James Cook (*Endeavour*) to Dover from his first voyage of exploration.

1776 Capt James Cook sailed from Plymouth in *Resolution* on his third and last voyage of exploration to the Pacific. *Discovery* sailed on 1 August.

See 30 July 1768, 25 June 1776.

1794 Capt Horatio Nelson, *Agamemnon*, while ashore at Calvi in Corsica, observing fire at the French-held Calvi Citadel, suffered permanent damage to his right eye when incoming fire threw rock fragments into his face. 'I can distinguish light from dark, but no object.' A plaque on the rock in the Quartier Donateo upon which he was standing reads *'Ici NELSON dirigeant le feu d'une batterie contre CALVI perdit un oeil 12 Juliet 1794'*.

See 18 June 1794, 24 July 1797.

1801 Rear-Admiral Sir James Saumarez (*Caesar*) defeated the Franco-Spanish squadron of nine under Vice-Admiral Don Juan de 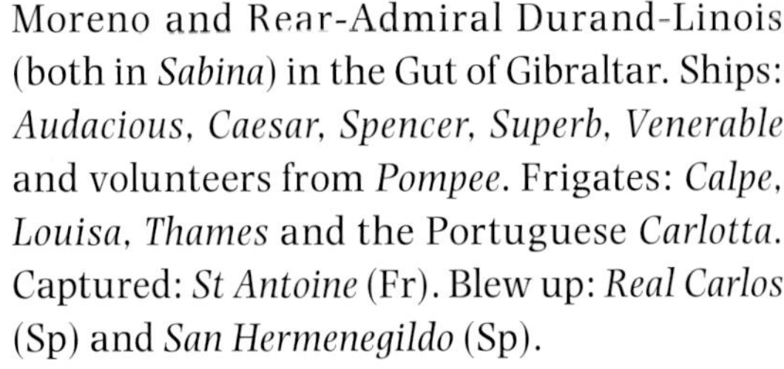Moreno and Rear-Admiral Durand-Linois (both in *Sabina*) in the Gut of Gibraltar. Ships: *Audacious*, *Caesar*, *Spencer*, *Superb*, *Venerable* and volunteers from *Pompee*. Frigates: *Calpe*, *Louisa*, *Thames* and the Portuguese *Carlotta*. Captured: *St Antoine* (Fr). Blew up: *Real Carlos* (Sp) and *San Hermenegildo* (Sp).
Battle Honour: Gut of Gibraltar 1801.

1871 *Devastation* launched at Portsmouth. With *Thunderer* (Pembroke Dockyard, 25 March 1872) the first seagoing, mastless turret-ships. *Thunderer* the first ship to have hydraulic loading gear. Image of *Devastation* used by Bryant and May on their 'England's Glory' matchboxes until production ceased December 1994.

1917 Destroyer *Patriot* sank U-69 E. of Shetland (60.23N, 01.32E).

1940 Cdre (Vice-Admiral retired) Gilbert Stephenson, 'the Terror of Tobermory', took command of *Western Isles*, the anti-submarine training establishment at Tobermory. 'Under his guiding genius every new ascort vessel thereafter underwent a month's intensive training in anti-submarine warfare' – Roskill, *The War at Sea*, vol.1 p.359.

See 27 May 1972.

1941 *Portland*, Bangor-class minesweeper, laid down at Taikoo Dockyard, Hong Kong and captured on the stocks by Japanese armed forces in December. Completed by the Japanese as Minesweeper 101 in April 1944 and sunk on 10 March 1945 in US air attack.

1943 Minesweepers *Boston*, *Cromarty*, *Poole* and *Seaham* captured the Italian S/M *Bronzo* off Augusta, Sicily (37.06N, 15.24E). She became P 714 until given to the French.

The Duke of Edinburgh, Captain General Royal Marines, presents new Colours to 40, 42 and 45 Cdos on Plymouth Hoe on 12 July 2001. (*RN*)

Nelson lost the sight of his right eye when a French shot struck this rock from where he was directing fire against the Citadel of Calvi in Corsica on 12 July 1794. (*Jennifer Phillips*)

1943 MTB 81 sank U-561 in Messina Strait (38.16N, 15.39E).

1943 Destroyer *Inconstant* sank U-409 in W. Mediterranean (37.12N, 04.00E).

1943 Monitor *Erebus* and 15th CS (*Mauritius*, *Orion*, *Uganda*) bombarded Augusta, Sicily.

1966 Fire in No. 2 Covered Slip in Chatham Dockyard destroyed figurehead from *Vanguard* (78) of 1835, broken up there in 1875.

2001 The Captain General Royal Marines, HRH The Duke of Edinburgh, presented new Queen's and Regimental Colours to 40 Cdo (Lt-Col David Capewell RM), 42 Cdo (Lt-Col David Hook RM) and to 45 Cdo (Lt-Col Tim Chicken RM) at a parade on Plymouth Hoe. The three units had last received colours at Malta in 1952.

2004 *Bulwark*, amphibious assault ship, arrived at Devonport under the Blue Ensign and handed over by BAE Systems. Accepted by Capt Jerry Stanford.

See 15 November 2001, 28 April 2005.

13 July

1772 Cdr James Cook sailed from Deptford in *Resolution* with *Adventure* on her second voyage.

See 12 July 1776 for a missed coincidence.

1795 Admiral William Hotham (*Britannia*) fought Rear-Admiral Pierre Martin (*Orient*), with seventeen ships of the line, off Hyères.

Mahan called this 'a trifling brush' and James 'a miserable action'. *Alcide* (74) was taken but all the other French ships escaped.

Ships: *Agamemnon, Ariadne, Audacious, Bedford, Blenheim, Bombay Castle, Britannia, Captain, Comet, Courageux, Culloden, Cumberland, Cyclops, Defence, Diadem, Eclair, Egmont, Fleche, Fortitude, Gibraltar, Meleager, Moselle, Mutine, Princess Royal, Resolution, Saturn, St George, Terrible, Victory, Windsor Castle.* Regiments: 11th, 25th, 29th, 30th, 50th, 69th, 86th, 2/90th, 97th.

1805 *Melampus* captured the Spanish privateer *Hidra* 500 miles W. of Land's End.

1855 VC: Lt George Dare Dowell, RMA (*Magicienne*, wood paddle frigate), George H. Ingouville, captain of mast (*Arrogant*, wood screw frigate).

Ruby and boats of *Arrogant* and *Magicienne* fought a battery in Trangsund Roads, Gulf of Finland.

1860 Pte John Dalliger, RMLI, hanged at the yardarm of wood screw gunboat *Leven* in Talienwan Bay, China for attempted murder of his captain. Last hanging at the yardarm. Second China War.

1871 John Donald Kelly, future admiral of the fleet, born at Southsea, son of Lt-Col H.H. Kelly RMA. Sixty-five years later to the day, Admiral of the Fleet Sir John Kelly hauled down his flag as C-in-C Portsmouth.

See 6 September 1873, 4 November 1936, 14 September 1952.

1900 VC: Mid Basil John Douglas Guy (*Barfleur*), at Tientsin when, under intense and close-range fire, he returned with a stretcher to rescue a wounded man. 'The ground around him was ploughed up with bullets.' Last VC awarded by its founder. Presented by her son, King Edward VII, on 8 March 1902, the day after he laid the foundation stone of BRNC Dartmouth.

1901 Pre-Dreadnought battleship *Cornwallis*, 14,000 tons, launched at Thames Ironworks, Blackwall. The fastest of the Duncan-class on trials and the first British battleship to steam at 19 knots. Her speed was bought at the cost of armour protection. The Duncans were the last battleships to carry the Victorian black, white and buff livery. *Cornwallis* bombarded the Dardanelles forts in 1915 and was torpedoed and sunk in January 1917.

See 19 February 1915, 25 April 1915, 9 January 1917.

1936 Admiral Sir William Fisher, the new C-in-C Portsmouth, hoisted his flag in the light cruiser *Amphion* and shifted it to *Victory* at Colours next day.

See 24 June 1937.

1943 Submarine *Unruly* sank the Italian S/M *Acciaio* off Salerno (38.35N, 15.49E), and destroyers *Echo* and *Ilex* the Italian S/M *Nereide* off Taranto (37.25N, 16.07E).

1943 Sunderland N/228 sank U-607 in Bay of Biscay (45.02N, 09.14W).

1943 Second battle of Kolombangara, Solomon Isles, between US and Japanese surface forces. Cruisers *Hobart* (RAN) and *Leander* (RNZN) engaged, the latter being badly damaged. The first battle had been fought by the USN.
Battle Honour: Kula Gulf 1943.

1945 Acting Admiral Sir Harold Burrough, who had been Allied Naval Commander Expeditionary Force since the death of Admiral Sir Bertram Ramsay in January, redesignated British Naval C-in-C Germany to oversee the disarmament of the Kriegsmarine.

See 15 March 1946.

1959 Admiral of the Fleet The Earl Mountbatten succeeded Marshal of the Royal Air Force Sir

The first British battleship to steam at 19 knots, the 14,000 ton *Cornwallis*, launched in 1901, photographed at anchor in Milford Haven. (*Author*)

William Dickson as Chief of the Defence Staff.
See 16 July 1965.

1965 Submarine *Tiptoe*, Lt-Cdr Charles Henry Pope RN, in collision with frigate *Yarmouth*, off Portland Bill. Flag Officer Flotillas, Home Fleet, Rear-Admiral J.O.C. Hayes, was embarked in the frigate. Court martial CO *Tiptoe* at Portsmouth 8 September: Severe Reprimand.
See 10 January 1964.

1980 Francis Pym, Secretary of State for Defence, announced decision to replace Polaris force with four Trident-armed submarines.
See 11 March 1982.

1984 Flag of RNSTS first hoisted, at Copenacre.

1995 Admiral of the Fleet Sir Varyl Cargill Begg died. Gunnery Officer of Cunningham's flagship *Warspite* at Matapan (28 March 1941). Captain (D) Eighth DF (DSO Korea). C-in-C Far East 1963–5 during Indonesian Confrontation. C-in-C Portsmouth 1965 but succeeded Admiral Sir David Luce as First Sea Lord in 1966 when Luce resigned over cancellation of CVA-01. Admiral of the Fleet 12 August 1968. Governor and C-in-C Gibraltar 1969–73.
See 22 February 1966, 26 October 2009.

14 July

1612 First record of half-masted flags (*Heartache*), for the Captain, J. Hall, discharged dead.

1749 Execution by 'a file of musketeers' of Lt Samuel Couchman and Lieutenant of Marines John Morgan on board *Chesterfield* (40) in Portsmouth Harbour for having led a mutiny in that ship off Cape Coast Castle, West Africa, the year before. The ship's former carpenter and three men were hanged.
See 16 April 1703, 10 October 1748.

1779 *Egmont* taken by the American privateer *Wild Cat* off Cape Spear, Newfoundland. *Surprise* captured *Wild Cat* just before midnight.

1780 *Nonsuch* drove ashore and burned the French *Légère* on Blanche Bank, off the mouth of the Loire, and captured three vessels of a convoy.

1809 Boats of *Scout* stormed a battery at Carry, near Marseilles.

1830 Capt Josiah Nisbet, stepson of Horatio Nelson, died. Buried at Littleham, Devon.
See 6 May 1831.

1869 *Thalia*, wood screw corvette, the last ship launched at Woolwich Dockyard. Became a troopship before being hulked as a baseship.

1876 Box boiler of battleship *Thunderer* exploded, killing forty-five men. Last 'box boiler' fitted in HM ships.
See 25 March 1872, 2 January 1879.

1882 Cdr Lord Charles Beresford of the composite screw gunvessel *Condor* landed at Alexandria as Provost Marshal and Chief of Police to 'restore law and order as soon as possible, put out fires, bury the dead and clear the streets' after the British bombardment of that port three days earlier.
See 10 February 1846, 6 September 1919.

1900 Capture of Tientsin native city. Naval Brigade under Capt Burke, relieved by Capt Callaghan on the 20th from *Aurora*, *Barfleur*, *Orlando*, *Terrible*.

1909 Submarine C 11 sunk by SS *Eddystone* off Cromer.

1911 Admiralty Weekly Order 218. 'To all Commanders-in-Chief, Flag Officers, Captains, Commanders and Commanding Officers of HM Ships and Vessels at Home and Abroad. The following Orders having been approved by My Lords Commissioners of the Admiralty are hereby promulgated for information and guidance and necessary action. By Command of Their Lordships. Dish Cloths. It has been decided to add a Dish Cloth to the scale of Mess Utensils for Chief Petty Officers, Petty Officers and Seamen, and supplies are now available at Victualling Yards. The first issue of these articles in HM Ships should take place on the next occasion of the six-monthly gratuitous issue of Basins and Plates, the scale allowed being three Cloths for every 10 men in a mess, six monthly.'
See 18 July 1969.

1916 Submarine H 5 torpedoed and sank U-51 off the Weser (53.55N, 07.53E).

1942 *Lulworth* sank Italian S/M *Pietro Calvi* south of the Azores (30.35N, 25.58W). Convoy SL 115. The third sunk in six days.

1950 A major explosion of ammunition lighters alongside Bedenham Pier in the RN Armament Depot, Portsmouth, caused extensive damage to ships and harbour facilities and broke windows in Portsmouth, Gosport and Fareham.
See 27 April 1951.

1959 Admiral Douglas Lionel Dent, the first Rear-Admiral (Submarines), died aged 89. In 1919 'it was decided that the development of submarines justified the head of this branch being a flag officer and Rear-Admiral Dent . . . was selected for the post of Rear-Admiral(S), and hoisted his flag in HMS *Dolphin*' – *The Times*, 14 July 1959.
See 19 November 1917, 25 August 1919.

1967 FO Middle East, who flew his flag at Aden until 13 July, moved to Bahrain until the

Force H at Gibraltar. (*NMRN 1980/262*)

institution of the Unified Command in the Gulf on 1 September 1967 when he hauled down his flag and the appointment of FOME lapsed. SNOPG continued to fly his broad pennant in HMS *Jufair* until the date of the Unified Command when he became Commander Naval Forces Gulf (CNFG). DCI(RN) 568/67.

1971 The Criminal Damage Act 1971 repealed the Dockyards etc. Protection Act 1772 (12 Geo III c.24) which had created the capital offence commonly known as 'Arson in Royal Dockyards' – 'Persons who shall willfully set fire, burn or destroy ships of war, or aid or assist in so doing, in any of His Majesty's Dockyards, arsenals, magazines etc., or shall set fire to any buildings, timber or material there placed, or any military, naval or victualling stores etc. shall suffer death as a felon without benefit of clergy.' Dockyard arson remained a capital offence even after the passing of the Murder (Abolition of the Death Penalty) Act of 8 November 1965 which effectively ended capital punishment for murder.

1974 Carrier *Hermes* and frigates *Andromeda* and *Rhyl* evacuated British subjects from Kyrenia, Cyprus during Turkish invasion.

1984 *Peacock*, the first of the new Hong Kong patrol craft, commissioned at Rosyth. Guest of Honour was Sir Murray MacLehose, lately Governor of Hong Kong. First of five ships, all built by Hall Russell of Aberdeen. Sold 1 August 1997 to the Philippine Navy and renamed *Emilio Jacinto*. Sister ship *Plover* commissioned at Rosyth 20 July 1984.

2005 *Cardiff*, Cdr Michael Beardall RN, the last of the Batch 1 Type 42 destroyers, paid off at Portsmouth after twenty-six years' service. Commissioned 24 September 1979 by Capt B.N. (later Vice-Admiral Sir Barry) Wilson RN.

15 JULY

1796 *Glatton*, idiosyncratically armed with carronades, fought six French frigates 6 miles N.W. by W. of Schouwen light.

1798 *Lion* (64) engaged four Spanish frigates, capturing *Santa Dorotea* (34), 90 miles E. by S. of Cartagena, Spain.
Battle Honour: *Santa Dorotea* 1798.

1804 *Lily* taken by the French privateer *Dame Ambert* off Cape Romain, South Carolina.

1815 Napoleon, defeated at Waterloo 18 June, surrendered to Capt Frederick Maitland, *Bellerophon* (74), in Basque Roads and was taken via Torbay to Plymouth, arriving 26 July. Transferred 7 August to *Northumberland*, which sailed next day for St Helena where he disembarked 16 October.

See 22 June 1815, 30 November 1839, 1 November 1921.

1855 Allied light squadron destroyed Russian stores at Berdyansk, Sea of Azov. Sloops: *Vesuvius*, *Beagle*, *Curlew*, *Swallow*, *Wrangler* and the French *Milan* and *Mouette*. Gunboats: *Boxer*, *Cracker*, *Fancy*, *Grinder*, *Jasper*.

1855 VC: Boatswain John Sheppard (*St Jean d'Acre*), a most ingenious man, for his two attempts to blow up an enemy battleship in Sevastopol using a punt full of explosives.

Presentation of Submarine Service dolphin badges at HMS *Dolphin*, 1971. (*NMRN*)

1872 John Rushworth Jellicoe, future C-in-C Grand Fleet, First Sea Lord and an admiral of the fleet, entered *Britannia* aged 12 years six months.

See 20 November 1935.

1910 'In future a manuscript record is to be kept by Accountant Officers of HM Ships and Naval Establishments showing the numbers of all Bank of England Notes received on charge with particulars as to the disposal of each.' AWO 225/10.

1912 Naval wing of RFC formed.

1913 Rear-Admiral Mark Kerr, seconded as C-in-C Royal Hellenic Navy 1913–15, qualified as a pilot while on leave, the first Flag Officer to do so (Aviator's Certificate 842 dated 16 July 1914). He later became Deputy Chief of Air Staff as a major-general RAF.

1916 Submarine H 3 sunk by mine off Cattaro, in the Adriatic.

1919 The minesweeping sloops *Gentian*, Lt-Cdr R.J.R. Scott RN, and *Myrtle*, Lt C.G. Hallett RN, part of Rear-Admiral Sir Walter Cowan's squadron deployed to the Baltic to support newly independent littoral states, mined while sweeping N.W. of the Estonian island of Osel (modern Saaremaa) in the Gulf of Finland, 58.39N, 21.36E. *Myrtle* struck a mine and sank just before midnight; *Gentian*, coming to her assistance, exploded another and sank on 17 July. Some of the crews buried in Tallinn military cemetery. The light cruiser *Cassandra*, one of the first ships deployed, was mined and lost just S. of this location (58.29N, 21.11E) on 5 December 1918.

See 13 December 1918, 18 August 1919, 1 September 1919, 4 September 1919, 20 July 2003.

1939 Admiral of the Fleet Sir Roger Backhouse, who succeeded Lord Chatfield as First Sea Lord in November 1938, died in London. He retired in ill-health in June and was promoted admiral of the fleet on 5 July, ten days before his death. 'Backhouse was a man of impressive presence, 6ft 4ins tall,

The Great Cabin of HMS *Victory* at Portsmouth, 15 July 2008: Vice-Admiral Sir Adrian Johns hands over as Second Sea Lord and C-in-C Naval Home Command to Vice-Admiral Alan Massey. (*RN*)

and of unquestioned ability. But he, like a good many officers of his day, had never learnt to use a staff properly, and absolutely refused to delegate any of his authority . . .' – Roskill, *Naval Policy between the Wars*, vol.2, p.282.

See 24 November 1878, 17 December 1935, 24 June 1937, 21 October 1943.

1941 First German Type T mine recovered, at Portland.

1943 Light cruiser *Sirius* bombarded Catania, Sicily. Monitor *Abercrombie* and the cruisers USS *Birmingham* and *Philadelphia* bombarded Empedocle and Agrigento.

1943 Submarine *United* sank the Italian S/M *Remo* in Gulf of Taranto (39.19N, 17.30E).

1943 *Balsam*, *Mignonette* and *Rochester* sank U-135 off Canary Islands (28.20N, 13.17W). Convoy OS 51.

1944 Liberator E/206 sank U-319 off S.W. Norway (57.40N, 05.00E).

1944 Supply and Secretariat School moved from Highgate School (*President V*) to Wetherby (*Demetrius*).

1958 First Royal Review of the Fleet in Canadian waters. HRH Princess Margaret, in British Columbia for the province's centenary, reviewed thirty-two RCN, RN and USN ships at Esquimalt from the destroyer HMCS *Crescent*.

See 4 May 1910, 29 June 2010.

1958 New Weapons Department established at the Admiralty. AFO 3239/57, AFO 5164/58.

1958 Midget submarine *Stickleback* (ex-X51) was handed over to the Royal Swedish Navy at Portland by Capt P.J. Cowell RN, captain SM5 and renamed *Spiggen*. Boat returned and became museum ship at IWM Duxford in 1977.

1960 Boom defence vessels HMS *Barbican* and HMS *Barrington* took food supplies to the Scottish islands of Coll, Tiree and Eigg during a seamen's strike.

See 28 May 1962.

1960 RN Mine Depots and RN Torpedo Factories to be known as RN Armament Depots.

1971 Submarine Service dolphin badges first issued at ceremonial divisions. FOSM made presentations at *Dolphin*. Other divisions held at Faslane; Vickers, Barrow; Dounreay; Birkenhead; Chatham and Devonport.

1975 Iceland announced the extension of Icelandic fishing limits to 200 miles. The Third Cod War started six months later.

See 31 August 1958.

16 JULY

1780 *Nonsuch* captured the French *Belle-Poule* 33 miles S. of Ile d'Yeu, France.

1795 Shutter Telegraphs started to carry signals from Admiralty to Chatham in fifteen minutes, given clear weather.

See 28 January 1796.

1796 *Hazard* captured the French privateer *Terrible* 50 miles N.N.W. of the Scilly Isles.

1806 Boats of *Centaur, Conqueror, Revenge, Achille, Polyphemus, Prince of Wales, Monarch, Iris* and *Indefatigable* cut out the French *César* in the Gironde, 'but she being prepared the loss was heavy' and her sister ship escaped.

1812 Boats of *Britomart* and *Osprey* captured the French privateer *Eole* off Heligoland.

1855 Allied light squadron destroyed Russian stores and the defences at Petrovakoe, Sea of Azov. Sloops: *Vesuvius, Beagle, Curlew, Swallow, Wrangler* and the French *Milan* and their boats. Gunboats: *Boxer, Cracker, Fancy, Grinder, Jasper.*

1856 Quill Friction Tubes introduced for firing in RN guns.

1918 *Anchusa*, sloop, torpedoed off north coast of Ireland and sank in two minutes. The first of thirty-three of her class, of which seven were lost.

1935 Silver Jubilee Review of the Mediterranean and Home Fleets at Spithead by HM King George V and HRH Queen Mary in *Victoria and Albert*. C-in-C Home Fleet, Admiral the Earl of Cork

HMS *Anglesey* (1978), Offshore Patrol Vessel. (*RN*)

The last replenishment of fuel at sea between all steam-powered ships: HMS *Fearless*, RFA *Olna* and HMY *Britannia* in the Red Sea, 20 July 1997. (*Cdre A.J.C. Morrow RN*)

and Orrery, in *Nelson*; C-in-C Mediterranean Fleet, Admiral Sir William Fisher, in *Queen Elizabeth*; 157 British and Empire ships present, but no foreign vessels.

1940 Destroyer *Imogen*, Cdr C.L. Firth RN, sunk in collision with light cruiser *Glasgow* in thick fog off Duncansby Head (58.34N, 02.54W). Destroyer caught fire and was abandoned; eighteen men lost.

See 30 October 1936.

1950 Lt HRH The Duke of Edinburgh RN promoted lieutenant-commander.

See 30 June 1952, 15 January 1953.

1965 Admiral of the Fleet Earl Mountbatten of Burma handed over as Chief of the Defence Staff to Field Marshal Sir Richard Hull, the end of a service career that had begun before Jutland.

See 13 July 1959.

2003 *Anglesey*, Island-class fisheries patrol vessel, entered Portsmouth for the last time to pay off after twenty-four years' service. She had steamed 644,000 miles since joining the Fleet in 1979.

See 29 January 2004.

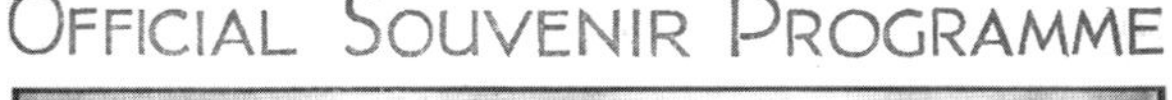

Silver Jubilee 1935 Official Souvenir Programme. (*Author*)

17 July

1668 Scheme for half-pay for Flag Officers.

1761 *Thunderer* (74) captured the French *Achille* (64) 57 miles N.W. of Cadiz despite a gun exploding. *Thetis* (32) captured the French *Bouffonne* (32) in the same locality. Battle Honours: *Achille* 1761; *Bouffonne* 1761.

1797 *Anson* and *Sylph* drove ashore and wrecked the French *Calliope* on Penmarc'h Point, Brittany.

1805 *Ariadne* and consorts drove ashore four vessels of the Ostend invasion flotilla off Gravelines.

1812 *Shannon, Belvidera, Guerrière, Africa* and *Aeolus* unsuccessfully chased the American *Constitution* for two days E. of Barnegat, New Jersey.

See 19 August 1812.

1824 Regulations and Instructions for Paymasters issued.

1855 Destruction of Russian stores on Glofira Spit, Sea of Azov. Sloops and gunboats: *Boxer, Cracker, Curlew, Fancy, Grinder, Jasper, Wrangler.* Boats of: *Swallow, Vesuvius.*

1867 Queen Victoria's Pearl Jubilee Review of the Fleet at Spithead. Last occasion that a wooden battleship – *Victoria* (121) – served as flagship at a royal review.

1882 James F. Somerville, Flag officer force H and later C-in-C Eastern Fleet, born.

See 19 March 1949.

1891 Three midshipmen from the armoured cruiser *Warspite*, flagship of the Pacific Station, were drowned at Esquimalt. A memorial to Hon. Arthur A. de Montmorency, Percival A.H. Brown and Douglas C. Johnstone, all aged 17, was erected in St Ann's church, Portsmouth Dockyard, by their C-in-C, Rear-Admiral Charles Frederick Hotham, and the Flag Captain, Capt Hon. Hedworth Lambton (both future admirals of the fleet).

1893 Court martial at Malta exonerated Rear-Admiral Hastings Markham and Capts Bourne and Johnstone after collision of battleships *Victoria* and *Camperdown.*

See 22 June 1893.

1909 The Home Fleet arrived in the Thames for a week's visit; battleships anchored off Southend, cruisers at Greenwich and TBDs and submarines as far upriver as the Houses of Parliament: 150 ships. Lord Mayor received officers and men of the Royal Navy at the Guildhall for the first time in the history of the Corporation of London. 'London thought and talked of nothing but the Navy' – *Naval and Military Record*, 29 July 1909.

1928 HM King George V unveiled a plaque on board *Victory* in No. 2 Dock, Portsmouth Dockyard, marking the completion of restoration work on the ship, facilitated by the Save the *Victory* Fund launched in 1922 by the Society for Nautical Research.

See 14 June 1910.

1940 Submarine *Phoenix* (fifteenth of the name) sunk by the Italian TB *Albatros* off Augusta, Sicily.

The new battleship *Vanguard* entering No. 10 dock at Devonport Dockyard after sea trials. She was accepted from John Brown's on 9 August 1946. (*Cdr David Hobbs RN*)

1940 Admiral of the Fleet Sir Roger Keyes, aged 67, recalled to duty by Winston Churchill as the first Director of Combined Operations.

1942 Lancaster F/61 and Whitley H/502 sank U-751 in S.W. Approaches (45.14N, 12.22W).

1943 Battleship *Warspite* bombarded Catania, Sicily.

1944 Submarine *Telemachus* sank the Japanese S/M I-166 in Malacca Strait (02.47N, 101.03E).

1944 FAA attack on German battleship *Tirpitz* thwarted by smokescreen. Operation Mascot.

1944 Liberator U/86 sank U-361 (68.36N, 08.33E). Catalina Y/210 sank U-347 off Narvik (68.35N, 06.00E); Flt Lt John Cruikshank RAFVR received eighty wounds in the attack: VC.

1945 First combined attack on the Japanese mainland (Hitachi area of Honshu) by the British Pacific Fleet and US battleships. Task Force 37. Ships: *King George V*, *Formidable*, *Black Prince* and *Newfoundland* with five destroyers.

1947 The Mediterranean Fleet, led by the light cruiser *Liverpool*, flagship of the C-in-C, Admiral Sir Algernon Willis, sailed from Malta to the Levant on its first post-war Summer Cruise. Fleet comprised the aircraft carrier *Triumph*, flag of Flag Officer (Air) Mediterranean, Vice-Admiral Sir Cecil Harcourt; light cruiser *Phoebe*, flag of Flag Officer Destroyers, Rear-Admiral E.D.B. McCarthy; light cruiser *Mauritius*, flag of Flag Officer First Cruiser Squadron, Rear-Admiral R. Symonds-Taylor; with the private ships light fleet carrier *Ocean*, light cruiser *Leander*, depot ship *Woolwich*, despatch vessel *Surprise*, destroyers *Chequers*, *Chaplet*, *Cheviot*, *Chieftain*, *Charity*, *Chevron*, *Venus*, *Virago*, *Haydon*, *Talybont*, *Stevenstone* and *Brissenden*, sloop *Mermaid*, frigates *Bigbury Bay* and *Whitesand Bay*, netlayer *Protector*, and landing ship *Dieppe*. The Fleet returned to Malta 23 August.

See 23 September 1948, 31 January 1949.

1959 'Their Lordships have decided that the Royal Naval Reserve, which was established by the Royal Naval Reserve Volunteer Act 1859, should celebrate its centenary during the Autumn of 1959' – AFO 1721/59. RNR Dinner in the Painted Hall, RN College, Greenwich with HRH The Duke of Edinburgh as principal guest. Service of Thanksgiving at St Paul's Cathedral 4 November with HM The Queen and HRH The Duke of Edinburgh present.

See 17 May 2003.

1959 'The future of the Sailmaker Branch is at present under consideration . . . It is clear that the future requirements to train ratings as Sailmakers' Mates is likely to be very limited' – AFO 1735/59.

See 23 December 1967, 25 October 1979.

1981 'Concern has been growing for some time that the cookery book in current use by the Royal Navy, *Practical Cookery* by Ceserani and Kinton, does not fully meet the requirements for cookery in the Fleet . . .' – DCI(RN) 412/81.

1984 *Devonshire*, first of the County-class guided missile destroyers, expended as a target in the English Channel.

See 10 June 1960.

2006 RFA *Lyme Bay*, Landing Ship Dock (Auxiliary), towed from her builders, Swan Hunter (Tyneside) at Wallsend, for completion by BAE Systems, Govan, due to contract costs having been exceeded.

See 26 July 2003, 1 August 2003, 9 April 2004, 9 April 2005.

2008 Cdre Sam Dunlop, who commanded RFA *Fort Austin* in the Falklands War, died. The first Merchant Navy DSO since the end of the Second World War.

See 23 November 1982.

18 July

1360 High Court of Admiralty established.

1413 William Cotton appointed Keeper of the King's Ships.

1690 *St Albans* captured a French 28-gun privateer 20 miles S.S.E. of Start Point.

1812 *Spartan* captured the American *Hiram* and *Nautilus* S. of Seal Island, Maine, and the American privateer *Actress* off Yarmouth, Nova Scotia.

1813 *Havannah* and *Partridge* destroyed a small Neapolitan convoy and its escorts near Rodi, Adriatic.

1833 HRH Princess Victoria, in Portsmouth with her mother, HRH The Duchess of Kent, for the launching of the brig *Racer*, went on to visit her first warship, HMS *Victory*. 'All the ladies partook of the beef and potatoes, served on wooden platters, and drank of the grog' – *The Times*.

See 21 October 1844.

1914 Fleet Review: 'All that is best and modern here is the creation of Lord Fisher' according to Rear-Admiral Sir Robert Arbuthnot; praise indeed from an officer who had never been in the 'Fishpond'.

1939 Light cruiser *Dido* launched at Cammell Laird, Birkenhead at 1230 and light cruiser *Nigeria* launched at Vickers Armstrong, Wallsend-on-Tyne at 1630.

1943 Wellington B/221 sank the Italian S/M *Romolo* off Messina (37.20N, 16.15E). Fifth Italian S/M lost in six days.

1943 Light cruiser *Mauritius* bombarded Catania, Sicily in support of the 8th Army.

1944 Catalina Z/210 damaged U-742, which was scuttled off Narvik (60.24N, 09.51E).

1944 U-672 depth-charged and damaged by frigate *Balfour* off Start Point. Submarine abandoned that night.

1944 British 2nd Army broke through in the Caen area. Cruisers *Enterprise* and *Mauritius* and monitor *Roberts*, in support, bombarded the German shore batteries.

1946 Cruiser *Norfolk* and sloop *Wild Goose* deployed to Basra in Iraq after rioting at the British oil refinery at Abadan in Iran.

1947 Light cruiser *Ajax* and destroyers *Chieftain* and *Childers* encountered Zionist protests in eastern Mediterranean, involving *President Warfield*, nicknamed *Exodus 1947*. Operation Charity.

See 2 September 1946.

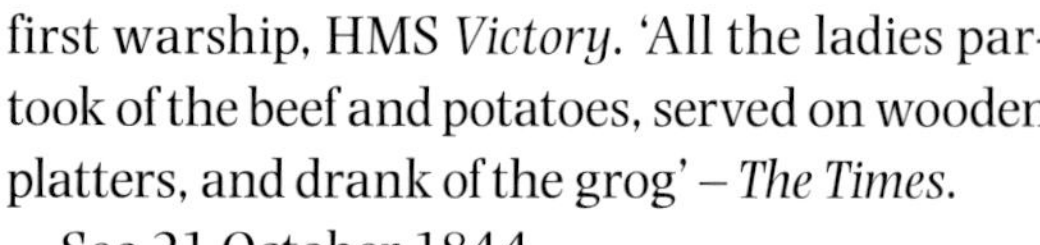

The Queen's Colour of the Royal Fleet Auxiliary presented by the Commodore-in-Chief RFA, HRH The Earl of Wessex, to First Officer Richard Davies on board RFA *Largs Bay*, 18 July 2008. (*RN*)

The Navy's Here! Petty Officer (Stores Accountant) Amanda James of HMS *Bulwark*, alongside in Beirut, helps to embark refugees fleeing from an outbreak of armed conflict in Lebanon in July 2006. (*RN*)

1959 Submarine *Oberon*, name ship and first of class, launched at Chatham Dockyard by HRH The Duchess of Kent, more successfully than an earlier submarine of the same name at Chatham thirty-three years earlier. The fiftieth submarine launched from the same slipway since 1907.

See 24 September 1926, 23 August 1993, 30 October 2004.

1961 45 and 42 Cdos RM relieved on station in Kuwait where they had been landed by 845 NAS (Whirlwinds) from *Bulwark* (supported by Sea Vixens of 892 and 893 NAS, *Centaur* and *Victorious*). 42 Cdo left on 20 July.

1969 'Naval Stores – Miscellaneous – Shortage of Rags. There is an acute shortage of Rags Wiping (White) and Rags Wiping (Coloured). Services requested to exercise the utmost economy in the use of rags . . .' – DCI(RN) 913/69.

See 14 July 1911.

1995 Destroyer *Southampton*, West Indies Guardship, and frigate *Westminster* to relief of Montserrat after volcanic eruption.

See 19 August 1995.

1983 Leander-class frigate *Dido* transferred to the Royal New Zealand Navy and renamed HMNZS *Southland*. 'Ship's company will disperse on 15 July 1983' – DCI(RN) 297/83.

See 4 October 1982.

2006 Destroyer *Gloucester*, Cdr M.P. Paterson RN, closely followed by destroyer *York*, Cdr T.M.C. Cryar RN, arrived at Beirut to embark British nationals and Entitled Personnel fleeing the outbreak of armed conflict in Lebanon, for passage to Limassol. Operation enhanced by the arrival of assault ship *Bulwark*, Capt C.C.C. Johnstone RN, forty-eight hours later. Carrier *Illustrious*, frigates *St Albans* and RFA *Fort Victoria* stood offshore. Operation Highbrow.

See 15 October 1958.

2008 The Queen's Colour of the Royal Fleet Auxiliary, 'a token of Her Majesty's admiration and trust in each and every one of you and the Fleet in which you serve', was presented by HRH The Earl of Wessex, Commodore-in-Chief RFA, on board RFA *Largs Bay* in Portsmouth. The Colour was received by First Officer Richard Davies.

In her letter to the RFA Her Majesty wrote:

'The RFA may not be well-known to the wider public, yet you have given a very great contribution to the nation since your formation in 1905. Many of your number have given their lives working alongside the Royal Navy and other Armed Forces and it is entirely fitting that this consecration and presentation should be taking place in Portsmouth, the traditional home of the Royal Navy.

There can be no better symbol of your many achievements and proud history than these Colours: as well as giving focus to the Royal Fleet Auxiliary's identity, loyalty and pride, they also manifest the deep respect in which you and your vital work are held by the nation.'

2009 Henry Allingham, the world's oldest man and the last known survivor of the RNAS to have served in the First World War, died at St Dunstan's, Ovingdean, Brighton aged 113. He was serving in the naval trawler *Kingfisher* in the North Sea at the time of Jutland.

19 JULY

1545 *Mary Rose* capsized and sank at Spithead when sailing to engage the French. Raised 11 October 1982.
See 11 October 1982, 19 July 1984.

1588 *Golden Hind* sighted the Spanish Armada off Lizard Head and reported the intelligence to Plymouth where Drake reputedly finished his game of bowls.

1745 Lt Baker Phillips of *Anglesey* (44) executed for surrendering his ship to the French *Apollo* (50), although his Captain, Master and sixty crew had been killed.

1779 Lime juice ordered as remedy for scurvy.

1805 Vice-Admiral Viscount Nelson in *Victory* anchored in Rosia Bay, Gibraltar, after chasing Villeneuve to the West Indies and went ashore 'for the first time since the 16th of June 1803, and from having my foot out of the *Victory*, two years, wanting ten days'. *Victory* carried Nelson back to Rosia Bay on 28 October in a cask of brandy.

1806 *Blanche* (38) captured the French *Guerrière* (40) S. of the Faroes.

1837 Engine room branch established by Order in Council.

1854 Wood screw corvette *Miranda* and screw sloop *Brisk* bombarded Solovets monastery, White Sea.

1862 Chart Branch of the 'Hydrographical Department' sanctioned by Order in Council.

1862 Capt William Cornwallis Aldham RN granted a pension of £180 per annum for two years by Order in Council for wounds received by him from bandits in Mexico.

1912 Rank of Mate reintroduced for lower-deck promotion. Same uniform as sub-lieutenant.
See 16 May 1863, 20 May 1931.

1916 Royal Naval Division taken into numbered sequence of Army Order of Battle as 63rd (RN) Division. Originally of eight battalions but Benbow and Collingwood disbanded.

1918 Seven Sopwith Camels (from *Furious*) destroyed the Zeppelins L-54 and L-60 in their shed at Tondern, Schleswig, Germany. First Division of 1st BS with 1st and 7th LCS and destroyers, in support. 'The most outstandingly successful carrier operation of the war.' – Layman.
See 25 December 1914.

1918 Destroyer *Garry*, with MLs 49 and 263, rammed and sank UB-110 in North Sea (54.39N, 00.55W). Submarine raised 4 October.

1919 Mainbrace spliced twice to celebrate end of Baltic hostilities.

1938 First appointment of Fifth Sea Lord responsible for naval aviation. Vice-Admiral the Hon. Sir Alexander Ramsay, Chief of Naval Air Services.
See 19 November 1917, 2 April 1931.

View of the action of the French and English fleets, 1545. At the centre is Southsea Castle with the *Mary Rose* shown sinking above. (*NMRN 1952/3*)

The Italian cruiser *Bartolomeo Colleoni*, stopped and on fire, her bows blown off after an action with HMAS *Sydney* and RN destroyers, 1940. (*NMRN*)

1940 Light cruiser HMAS *Sydney*, Capt J.A. Collins RAN, supported by five ships of the 2nd DF, Cdr H.St.L. Nicolson RN, in *Hyperion*, fought Italian 6-in cruisers *Bartolomeo Colleoni* and *Giovanni Delle Bande Nere* off Cape Spada, N.W. of Crete, (35.43N, 23.36E). *Colleoni* brought to a standstill by shellfire from *Sydney* was finally sunk by *Ilex* and *Hyperion* which rescued 525 Italian sailors under Italian air attack while *Sydney*, with *Hero* and *Hasty*, chased *Bande Nere* to the south, breaking off the action when *Sydney* was down to four rounds a gun in A turret and to a single round in B turret. Their quarry reached Benghazi but was sunk by HM Submarine *Urge* on 1 April 1942. This battle came only ten days after the action off Calabria and was 'a fine, brisk action which showed the high efficiency and magnificent fighting qualities of the Royal Australian Navy' – Admiral Sir Andrew Cunningham, C-in-C Mediterranean Fleet. Capt Collins 'who by his quick appreciation of the situation, offensive spirit and resolute handling of HMAS *Sydney*, achieved a victory over a superior force' (Cunningham to Pound, First Sea Lord) got a CB and Cdr Nicolson a bar to his DSO. Ships: *Sydney*, *Hyperion*, *Ilex*, *Hero*, *Hasty* and *Havock*. Battle Honour: Spada 1940.

See 9 July 1940, 19 November 1941, 13 December 1941, 1 April 1942.

1941 New submarine *Umpire* rammed and sunk by trawler *Peter Hendricks* off the Wash (53.09N, 01.08E).

1942 Light cruisers *Dido* and *Euryalus* and destroyers *Javelin*, *Jervis*, *Pakenham* and *Paladin* bombarded Mersa Matruh, N. Africa. Destroyers *Aldenham* and *Dulverton* engaged German E-boats in the same area.

1943 Light cruiser *Newfoundland* with destroyers *Laforey*, *Lookout* and the Netherlands Sloop *Flores* engaged nine enemy batteries near Catania, Sicily.

1949 Four Sea Fury aircraft piloted by Lt-Cdr W.R. MacWhirter, Lt P.C.S. Chilton, Lt D.W. Morgan and Lt D.A. Hook, established a flight time record from London to RNAS Hal Far, Malta, flying the 1,310 miles in 3 hours 20 minutes and 49 seconds.

See 27 November 1951, 17 June 1958.

1965 Monitor *Roberts*, the last Royal Navy ship carrying 15-in guns, left Devonport under tow of the RFA tugs *Typhoon* and *Samsonia* for the breakers at Inverkeithing. The ship was in action for nineteen days after D-Day and fired 700 heavy shells against shore targets.

See 24 December 1954.

1984 Remains of a member of the ship's company of *Mary Rose* were buried in Portsmouth Cathedral 439 years to the day after the ship sank in the Solent. Interment preceded by a Requiem Mass sung according to the Sarum rite.

1985 Wartime RNVR intelligence officer, Ewen (Edward Samuel) Montagu, who planned Operation Mincemeat ('The Man who Never Was') in 1943 and was Judge Advocate of the Fleet from 1945–73, died in London.

See 2 February 1652, 30 April 1943.

1994 Submarine *Resolution* paid off at Faslane.

2006 Destroyer *Gloucester*, Cdr M.P. Paterson RN, sailed from Cyprus to embark more British nationals and Entitled Personnel from Beirut. Six Sea King Mk 4 helicopters of 846 NAS from RNAS Yeovilton arrived at RAF Akrotiri, Cyprus. Operation Highbrow.

See 15 October 1958, 18 and 20 July 2006.

20 July

1588 The Spanish Armada off Plymouth. Howard wrote that 'about three o'clock in the afternoon, we descried the Spanish fleet and did what we could to work for the wind'.
Battle Honour: Armada 1588.

1655 Graving dock built at Portsmouth.

1697 *Weymouth* captured the French *Aurore* 12 miles S.W. of Sables d'Olonne, by 'a fine display of strategy, seamanship and bravery' but perhaps because she had twice as many guns.

1782 *Winchelsea* captured the French privateer *Royal* N. of Flamborough Head.

1915 Second and last use of a decoy submarine in anti-submarine operations. Trawler *Princess Marie Jose* (sailing as *Princess Louise*) in Fair Isle Channel, with submarine C 27 (Lt-Cdr C.C. Dobson) in submerged tow, encountered U-23 (Oberleutnant zur Zee H. Schulthess) which opened fire. The telephone link with C 7 failed but she slipped successfully. Her first torpedo passed astern but a second sank U-23. These decoy operations were planned and mounted in strict secrecy; trawlers and submarines berthed well apart and left port independently. However, the U-23 survivors were not segregated from other German prisoners and internees and the project was fatally compromised.
See 23 June 1915.

1917 Paddle minesweeper *Queen of the North* mined off Orfordness.

1917 Sir Eric Geddes, civilian Controller of the Navy (temporary, honorary Vice-Admiral), appointed First Lord of the Admiralty.
See 10 February 1922.

1918 Destroyers *Marne*, *Milbrook* and *Pigeon* sank UB-124 off Lough Foyle (55.43N, 07.51W), after she had sunk the White Star liner *Justicia*.

1918 Submarine E 34 lost, probably mined, off Vrieland in Heligoland Bight, the last of twenty-eight E-class submarines lost in First World War. The body of her Captain, Lt Richard Pulleyne, was washed ashore in the West Friesian Islands. He had been the sole survivor from B 2, lost in collision with the Hamburg-Amerika liner *Amerika* on 4 October 1912.

1918 The future of naval air warfare. Admiral Sir David Beatty, C-in-C Grand Fleet, wrote to the Admiralty 'In the torpedo-carrying aeroplane we have a weapon of great potential value . . . [that] may be able to exercise a profound effect. . . In February 1918 the Admiralty informed me that by the end of July 100 torpedo-carrying aeroplanes would be available. On 18 July I am informed that instead of the 100 the number will be 12. Actually there are 3. As late as 18 July the Admiralty stated 36 pilots would be trained by the end of August. Actually there will be none. . . Under the new organisation and the setting up of an independent Air Ministry, the essential requirements of the fleet in aeroplane construction will only be met if urged with vigour by the Naval Air Division. . . Through failure to present the facts to the Air Ministry, machines will be diverted to less important roles and the main fleet will suffer.'
See19 November 1917.

1940 Destroyer *Brazen* damaged by German aircraft off Dover and sank under tow (51.01N, 01.17E). Convoy CW 7.

1940 Six Swordfish of 824 NAS (*Eagle*) sank the Italian destroyers *Nembo* and *Ostro* in Tobruk Roads, disappointed at not finding the *Giovanni Delle Bande Nere*.

1941 Submarine *Union* sunk by the Italian TB *Circe* off Pantelleria (36.26N, 11.50E).

1944 Destroyer *Isis* lost near 'O' buoy, Seine Bay though not appreciated until minesweeper *Hound* found twenty bodies next day. Operation Neptune.

1960 The Papal Legate, His Eminence Cardinal Louis Joseph Muench, arrived in Malta from Naples in HMS *Surprise*, the personal yacht of the C-in-C Mediterranean, escorted by three minesweepers, for celebrations to mark the nineteenth centenary of St Paul's shipwreck on the island.

1966 Cruiser *Tiger*, wearing the flag of the C-in-C Home Fleet, Admiral Sir John Frewen, accompanied by frigates *Aurora*, Capt B.H. Notley RN, and *Wakeful*, Cdr M.D. Joel RN, took Sir Robert Menzies to Dover where he was installed as Lord Warden of the Cinque Ports.

See 12 April 2005.

1968 Frigate *Exmouth* became the first major warship of the Royal Navy powered entirely by gas turbines when Chatham Dockyard completed the installation of one Olympus and two Proteus gas turbines in the Type 14 frigate, which took them to sea as a testbed.

See 9 March 1959, 26 April 1971.

1970 Lt-Cdr Matthew Todd leading a team of twelve submarine-escape instructors from *Dolphin* made a world record free ascent from *Osiris* 600ft under the Mediterranean.

See 12 October 1956.

1973 The Term 'Notice for Steam' is abolished and is superseded by 'Notice for Sea' as already shown in Fleet Operating Order No.310. DCI(RN) T.612/73.

See 24 September 2000, 18 March 2002.

1997 Assault ship *Fearless*, Capt Malcolm Williams RN, rendezvoused in the northern Red Sea with the fleet tanker RFA *Olna* and HMY *Britannia*, Cdre A.J.C. Morrow RN, returning from the handover of Hong Kong, to conduct the last replenishment of fuel at sea between three all-steam-powered ships in British naval history.

See 24 September 2000, 18 March 2002, p.406.

2003 Memorial plaques to 106 RN and five RAF men killed in action in the Baltic in 1918 and 1919, was unveiled by the First Sea Lord, Admiral Sir Alan West, and Vice-Admiral Tarmo Kouts, Chief of the Estonian Defence Forces, in the Church of the Holy Spirit, Tallinn, Estonia, and dedicated by the Very Revd Col Tonis Nommik, Chief of Chaplains, Estonian Defences Forces, and the Venerable Barry Hammett, Chaplain of the Fleet. The names of fourteen RN officers and ninety-two men, and four RAF officers and one airman are inscribed. They served in the light cruisers *Cassandra* (mined and sunk 5 December 1918), *Curacoa* and *Dragon*, destroyers *Vittoria* (torpedoed by Russian MTB 1 September 1919) and *Verulam* (mined and sunk 4 September 1919), minesweeping sloops *Myrtle* and *Gentian* (both mined and sunk 15 July 1919), submarine L.55 (lost with all hands 9 June 1919) and coastal motor boats CMB 62BD, CMB 67A, CMB 79A and CMB 88BD (most lost in the Kronstadt Raid on 18 August 1919). The airmen, operating from HMS *Vindictive*, were lost in operations over Kronstadt. Some *Gentian* men are buried in Tallinn Military Cemetery. An exact replica of this memorial was unveiled in Portsmouth Cathedral by HRH The Duke of York on 16 December 2005 in the presence of CDS, Gen. Sir Mike Walker, and First Sea Lord, Admiral West.

See 22 November 1918, 5 December 1918, 9 June 1919, 15 July 1919, 18 August 1919, 1 and 4 September 1919.

2005 A lead-cased time capsule laid by HRH The Duke of York in a 'new' foundation stone at the side of the main entrance to BRNC Dartmouth in its centenary year. It contains a personal letter from the Duke, an illuminated script, a miniature centenary sword, a set of 2005 coins including the Trafalgar 200 centenary edition, a set of stamps marking the sixtieth anniversary of VE Day and Trooping the Colour, a group photograph of staff and students, a New Testament and prayer book, a copy of the *Dartmouth Chronicle*, a RM band CD and other relics. One of two capsules laid down with the foundation stone of the College by HM King Edward VII in 1902 was retrieved on 1 July 2005.

See 7 March 1902, 2 July 2005.

2006 Assault ship *Bulwark*, Capt C.C.C. Johnstone RN, arrived at Beirut from Barcelona, having been diverted on passage home from a deployment to the Gulf, to join the destroyers *Gloucester* and *York* in rescuing British nationals and Entitled Personnel fleeing the outbreak of armed conflict in Lebanon. Over 1,300 people were recovered by *Bulwark* and taken to Cyprus. RAF 27 Sqn Chinook helicopters transferred EPs from shore to carrier *Illustrious* (providing command support) offshore in company with *St Albans* and RFA *Fort Victoria* stood by offshore. Operation Highbrow.

See 15 October 1958, 18 and 19 July 2006.

21 July

1588 The first engagement with the Spanish Armada off the Eddystone. The enemy 'was constrained to give way and to bear up to the Eastward. His Lordship appointed Sir Francis Drake to set the watch that night.'
Battle Honour: Armada 1588.

1745 The repulse of *Lion* (60) by the French *Elizabeth* (64) secured the arrival of Charles Stuart, the Young Pretender, in Scotland.

1781 *Charlestown, Allegiance, Vulture, Jack* and *Vernon* escorting a convoy, fought the French *Astrée* and *Hermione* off Sydney, Cape Breton. Captured: *Jack*.

1795 'My idea of the application of our naval force is to show that the frontier of Great Britain is the high water mark in France. The uppermost seaweed on the beach belongs to us . . .'
– Capt Sir Sidney Smith, HM frigate *Diamond*, off Cape Barfleur, to Lord Spencer, First Lord of the Admiralty.

1796 *Aimable* fought the French *Pensée* off Guadeloupe.

1811 *Thomas* and *Cephalus* captured eleven French gunboats and a convoy of fifteen sail at Punto Infreschi, Italy.

1812 *Sealark* captured the French privateer *Ville de Caen* 40 miles S.E. of Start Point.

1812 *Nautilus* captured the French privateer *Brave* 15 miles S.E. by S. of Cape Carbonara, Sardinia.

1842 Capture of Chinkiang by Vice-Admiral Sir William Parker (*Cornwallis*) and Lt-Gen. Sir Hugh Gough, in the first Opium War with China. Ships: *Apollo, Belleisle, Blonde, Calliope, Childers, Clio, Columbine, Cornwallis, Dido, Endymion, Modeste, Plover, Starling, Vixen*; *Jupiter, Rattlesnake*, transports. Steamers (IN): *Auckland, Medusa, Sesostris*. Steamers (Ben. Mar.): *Nemesis, Phlegethon, Pluto, Proserpine, Queen, Tenasserim*. Seamen and Marines were landed. Troops: Royal Artillery, 18th, 26th, 49th, 55th and 98th Regiments, Madras Sappers and Miners, Bengal Volunteer Regiment, Madras Native Infantry, 2nd, 6th, 14th, 36th, 41st. Operations had begun on 7 January 1841.

1855 *Arrogant, Cossack, Magicienne* and *Ruby* bombarded the defences of Frederikshavn, Gulf of Finland.

1908 Capt Murray F. Sueter appointed Inspecting Captain of Airships at the Admiralty with Cdr Oliver Schwann as his assistant. They were also CO and XO respectively of the aircraft support cruiser *Hermione*.
See 24 September 1911, 18 November 1911, 25 November 1912, 3 February 1960.

1917 Submarine C 34 torpedoed and sunk by U-52 off Shetland.

1941 First victory of Sea Hurricane, when an aircraft of 880 NAS shot down a Dornier Do18 off Norway.

1943 Cruisers *Aurora* and *Penelope*, destroyers *Offa, Petard, Quilliam, Troubridge* and the Polish *Piorun* bombarded Cotronei, Italy.

1943 Monitor *Erebus* and light cruiser *Newfoundland* bombarded enemy batteries and troop concentrations in the Catania area, Sicily.

1944 Frigates *Curzon* and *Ekins* sank U-212 off Brighton (50.27N, 00.13W).

1995 Rear-Admiral John Tolhurst, Flag Officer Sea Training, hauled down his flag at Portland and embarked in the frigate *Argyll*, the last ship to leave Portland before the closure of the base. The last ship to do OST at Portland was *London*. Sea Training HQ transferred to Devonport where FOST flies his flag in *Drake*. DCI(RN) 266/95.
See 26 September 1958.

2004 MOD announced that twelve warships would be paid off within two years: destroyers *Cardiff, Glasgow, Newcastle*; frigates *Norfolk, Marlborough, Grafton*; MCMVs *Sandown, Inverness, Bridport, Brecon, Cottesmore,*

Dulverton. Personnel to reduce from 37,500 to 36,000. Destroyer/frigate strength to reduce to twenty-five, SSNs to eight, MCMVs to sixteen. Orders for Type 45 air defence destroyers to reduce from twelve to eight. 'I do not instinctively welcome the early disposal of good ships and these have been most difficult decisions. They are however essential if we are to ensure that the finite resources available to defence are targeted at the requirements of the 21st century rather than what we inherited from the 20th. I am confident that these changes will leave the Navy better organised and equipped to face the challenges of the future.' – Admiral Sir Alan West, First Sea Lord.

See 19 October 2010.

2009 Admiral Sir Mark Stanhope appointed First Sea Lord.

Recent Heads of the Service:

Admiral Sir Jonathon Band	7 Feb 2006–21 Jul 2009
Admiral Sir Alan West	17 Sept 2002–7 Feb 2006
Admiral Sir Nigel Essenhigh	16 Jan 2001–17 Sept 2002
Admiral Sir Michael Boyce	8 Oct 1998–16 Jan 2001 (then CDS)
Admiral Sir Jock Slater	10 Jul 1995–8 Oct 1998
Admiral Sir Benjamin Bathurst	2 Mar 1992–10 Jul 1995
Admiral Sir Julian Oswald	25 May 1989–2 Mar 1992
Admiral Sir William Staveley	2 Aug1985–25 May 1989
Admiral Sir John Fieldhouse	1 Dec 1982–2 Aug 1985 (then CDS)
Admiral Sir Henry Leach	6 Jul 1979–1 Dec 1982
Admiral Sir Terence Lewin	1 Mar 1977–6 Jul 1979 (then CDS)
Admiral Sir Edward Ashmore	2 Mar 1974–1 Mar 1977 (then CDS)
Admiral Sir Michael Pollock	13 Mar 1971–2 Mar 1974
Admiral Sir Peter Hill-Norton	3 Jul 1970–13 Mar 1971 (then CDS)

2009 Brig Mark Noble RM took command of RNAS Yeovilton, the first 'flying' Royal Marine officer to command a naval air station since E.L. Gerrard in 1917 and the first Royal Marine to command a naval air station since Col D.W. Sluman closed HMS *Simbang*, RNAS Sembawang, Singapore, in September 1971.

See 30 September 1971.

Admiral Sir Jonathon Band (left) hands over as First Sea Lord and Chief of Naval Staff to Admiral Sir Mark Stanhope on 21 July 2009 under the eye of Admiral of the Fleet Sir Andrew Cunningham, above. (*RN*)

22 July

1588 The Spanish Armada off Torbay. *Revenge* and *Roebuck* captured the Spanish *N.S. Del Rosario.*

1672 *Cambridge* and *Bristol* fought a Dutch East India fleet of seventeen sail 30 miles W. of Heligoland.

1801 Boats of *Beaulieu, Doris, Robust, Uranie* and *Ville de Paris* cut out the French *Chevrette* in Camaret Bay, France.
Battle Honour: *Chevrette* 1801.

1805 Vice-Admiral Sir Robert Calder (*Prince of Wales*, (90) reinforced by Rear-Admiral Stirling with five ships from Rochefort, fought Vice-Admiral Pierre Villeneuve (*Bucentaure*), with nineteen French and Spanish ships, 150 miles W.N.W. of Ferrol. Ships: *Agememnon, Ajax, Barfleur, Defiance, Dragon, Glory, Hero, Malta, Prince of Wales, Raisonnable, Repulse, Thunderer, Triumph, Warrior, Windsor Castle*. Frigates: *Egyptienne, Sirius*. Cutter: *Frisk*. Lugger: *Nile*. Captured: Spanish *Firme* and *San Rafael.*
See 2 July 1810.

Calder thought that he had done well and made no attempt to do better. There was some surprise at his being court-martialled. Nelson sent him home in his flagship although this depleted his fleet waiting for Trafalgar, in the aftermath of which Calder was judged. 'Calder may be said to have fought within one tradition and to have been censured within a greater' – Oliver Warner. Collingwood was contemptuous at Calder's claim to prize-money for a battle at which he was not present – 'there was a great indelicacy in it, and not a little portion of ignorance'.

The Atlantic Chase, 1805

Position	Villeneuve	Nelson
Passes Strait of Gibraltar	9 April	7 May
Arrives in West Indies	14 May (Martinique)	4 June (Barbados)
Leaves Antigua	8 June	13 June
Passes the Azores	30 June (North of)	8 July (South of)
Arrives off Spain	22 July (fights Calder off Ferrol)	19 July (Gibraltar)
Action off Trafalgar	21 October	

1811 Boats of *Active* captured a grain convoy of twenty-eight vessels, with their escort, at Ragosniza, Adriatic.

1836 Boats of *Buzzard* captured the Portuguese slaver *Joven Carolina* in the Old Calabar River, Nigeria.

1847 Boats of *Waterwitch* and *Rapid* captured the Brazilian slaver *Romeo Primeiro* off Banda Point, French Equatorial Africa.

1854 *Lightning*, second steamer commissioned in RN, led the Anglo-French fleet under Rear-Admiral Chads through the Angro channel prior to the reduction of Bomarsund.

1903 Opening of first Royal Navy School of Music.

1910 'In continuance of the permission granted by His late Majesty King Edward VII, the sanction of the King has been given to His Majesty's health being drunk in any non-alcoholic beverage.' – AWO 229/10.

1936 Start of the Spanish Civil War. By 22 July fifteen RN ships diverted to major Spanish ports: Home Fleet units to Biscay ports and Mediterranean Fleet ships to protect British interests on the Spanish east coast. In the first three months thirty-one British warships were engaged and they carried 6,000 refugees to safety. Battlecruiser *Repulse* embarked 500 British and German refugees at Palma, Majorca, on 30 July for passage to Marseilles. 'It was a grateful body of passengers which left the *Repulse* but when they tried to thank the officers and men the reply was "Well, that's what we are here for" and that evening they were off to Valencia on a similar errand' – *The Times*. Heavy cruiser *Devonshire* was also in Palma and then continued the evacuation work from Barcelona. Mediterranean Fleet hospital ship RFA *Maine* arrived at Valencia 2 August and made three evacuation trips to Marseilles via Barcelona and Alicante – thirty-five days on task and carried 1,109 refugees from thirty-five different nationalities. Every day the destroyers *Douglas, Anthony, Gallant, Gipsy* and *Garland* went up and down the coast ferrying refugees from small coastal towns to main ports where County-class cruisers and the fleet repair

Action of Vice-Admiral Sir Robert Calder (1745–1818) with combined French and Spanish fleets, 1805. (*NMM Neg. No. B3587*)

ships *Woolwich* and *Resource* were employed as depot ships and refugee clearing stations. On the N. coast refugee evacuation was mainly by land but from 10 September the 2nd and 5th Destroyer Flotillas, Home Fleet, carried refugees to St Jean de Luz and other French ports. The focus of Royal Navy concern then moved to the protection of British shipping.

See 4 February 1937, 13 May 1937, 23 August 1937, 6 March 1938.

1939 HM King George VI, HM Queen Elizabeth, and TRH The Princesses Elizabeth and Margaret, visited Britannia RN College, Dartmouth; the Princesses were looked after by Cadet HRH Prince Philip of Greece.

1942 10th S/M flotilla returned to Malta from ten-week exile up the Mediterranean, to find its piggery in maximum production and to prepare for Operation Pedestal.

1947 HM The King, with HRH Princess Elizabeth and Lt Philip Mountbatten RN, reviewed the Home Fleet in the Firth of Clyde. They visited the battleship *Duke of York*, flagship of Admiral Sir Neville Syfret, C-in-C Home Fleet, moored off Prince's Pier at Greenock and other units down the Firth to below Gourock.

See 10 August 1965.

The Spanish Armada 1588 – The First Official Naval Battle Honour

Ships employed during the period 21–29 July 1588: Queen's ships: *Achates, Advice, Aid, Antelope, Ark (Royal), Brigandine, Bull, Charles, Cygnet, Disdain, Dreadnought, Elizabeth Bonaventure, Elizabeth Jonas, Fancy, Foresight, Galley Bonavolia, George, (Golden) Lion, Hope, Mary Rose, Merlin, Moon, Nonpareil, Rainbow, Revenge, Scout, Spy, Sun, Swallow, Swiftsure, Tiger, Tramontana, Triumph, Vanguard, Victory, (White) Bear, White Lion.*

Merchant ships under Drake: *Bark Bond, Bark Bonner, Bark Buggins, Bark Hawkins, Bark Manington, Bark St Leger, Bark Talbot, Bear Yonge, Chance, Delight, Diamond of Dartmouth, Edward Bonaventure, Elizabeth Drake, Elizabeth Founes, Flyboat Yonge, Galleon Dudley, Galleon Leicester, Golden Hind, Golden Noble, Griffin, Hearts-Ease, Hope Hawkyns, Hopewell, Makeshift, Merchant Royal, Minion, Nightingale, Roebuck, Spark, Speedwell, Thomas Drake, Unity, Virgin God Save Her*, and 1 small caravel.

Merchant ships from the City of London: *Antelope, Anthony, Ascension, Bark Burr, Brave, Centurion, Diana, Dolphin, George Noble, Gift of God, Golden Lion, Hercules, Jewel, Margaret and John, Mayflower, Minion, Moonshine, Pansy, Passport, Primrose, Prudence, Red Lion, Release, Rose Lion, Royal Defence, Salamander, Thomas Bonaventure, Tiger, Toby.*

Merchant ships under the Lord High Admiral: *Anne Frances, George Bonaventure, Jane Bonaventure, Samuel, Solomon, Susan Parnell, Vineyard, Violet*. Merchant ships in Queen's pay: *Black Dog, Edward of Maldon, Katherine, Lark, Marigold, Nightingale, Pippin*. Victuallers to the westward: *Bearsabe, Elizabeth Bonaventure, Elizabeth of Leigh, Gift of God, Hope, John of London, Jonas, Marigold, Mary Rose, Pearl, Pelican, Richard Duffield, Solomon, Unity, White Hind.*

Coasters under the Lord High Admiral: *Aid of Bristol, Bark of Bridgwater, Bark Potts, Bark Webb, Bartholomew of Apsam, Crescent of Dartmouth, Galleon of Weymouth, Gift of Apsam, Handmaid of Bristol, Hart of Dartmouth, Hearty Anne, Jacob of Lyme, John of Chichester, John Trelawney, Katherine of Weymouth, Little John, Minion of Bristol, Revenge of Lyme, Rose of Apsam, Unicorn of Bristol.*

Coasters under Lord Henry Seymour: *Anne Bonaventure, Bark Lamb, Daniel, Elizabeth of Dover, Fancy, Galleon Hutchins, Grace of God, Grace of Yarmouth, Griffin, Handmaid, Hazard of Feversham, John Young, Katherine of Ipswich, Little Hare, Marigold, Matthew, Mayflower, Primrose of Harwich, Robin of Sandwich, Susan, William of Colchester, William of Ipswich, William of Rye.*

Voluntary ships: *Bark Halse, Bark Sutton of Weymouth, Carouse, Elizabeth, Elizabeth of Lowestoft, Flyboat, Fortune of Aldborough, Frances of Fowey, Gallego of Plymouth, Golden Ryall of Weymouth, Grace of Apsam, Greyhound of Aldborough, Heathen of Weymouth, John of Barnstaple, Jonas of Aldborough, Margaret, Raphael, Rat of Wight, Samaritan of Dartmouth, Sampson, Thomas Bonaventure, Unicorn of Dartmouth, William of Plymouth.*

See p.430.

23 July

1588 The second engagement with the Spanish Armada, off Portland. A N.E. wind gave the Spaniards an advantage and they dropped down on the *Triumph* which had to be rescued.

1676 Surrender of ketch *Quaker* (10) to Algerines led to capture of Samuel Atkins, clerk to Samuel Pepys, and nearly to that of Pepys himself.

1759 *Victory* laid down in the old single dock (now the Victory Dock) at Chatham. Present was William Pitt the Elder whose government had announced a major building programme of first rates the year before.

1785 Third rate *Audacious* (74), first of the name, launched at Rotherhithe. She fought in Howe's victory at the Glorious First of June in 1794 and in Nelson's at the Nile in 1798; Admiral Lord Keith's flagship in the Mediterranean after the burning of the *Queen Charlotte*.

See 17 March 1800.

1797 *Seagull* captured the French privateer *Capitaine Thurot* 30 miles S. by E. of Kristiansand. *King George* was in company.

1810 Boats of *Belvidera* and *Nemesis* captured the Danish schooners *Balder* and *Thor* and destroyed Gunboat No. 5 in Vanelvsfjord.

1854 *Miranda*, wood screw corvette, bombarded Kola and then landed an armed party.

1860 *Kestrel* destroyed a pirate junk at the Chain Islands, near Fall Island (Hsiao o Kuan). *Kestrel*'s complement was augmented by parties from *Snake* and the French *Dordogne*, and detachments of the 99th Regiment and French Marines.

1887 Golden Jubilee Review of the Fleet at Spithead. Admiral Sir George Ommanney Willes, C-in-C Portsmouth, flag in *Inflexible*. 135 ships and 20,200 men. 'Most of what you see is mere ullage' – Vice-Admiral Sir William Hewett VC, C-in-C Channel Squadron, flying his flag in *Northumberland* at the head of the Review line.

1917 AMC *Otway* torpedoed and sunk by UC-40 near Rona, north Minch.

1918 AMC *Marmora* torpedoed and sunk by UB-64 S. of Ireland.

1938 Heavy cruiser *Shropshire* rescued survivors from the Danish steamship *Bodil* bombed and sunk by aircraft (probably German) off Minorca during the Spanish Civil War.

See 6 March 1938.

1940 Submarine *Thames* sunk by mine S.W. of Stavanger, Norway (57.50N, 03.10E).

1940 Submarine *Narwhal* bombed and sunk while minelaying 180 miles N.E. of Dundee.

The commissioning of the first Type 45 destroyer, HMS *Daring* at Portsmouth, 23 July 2009. Able Seaman Daniel Small and Mrs Janette McAlpine cut the commissioning cake. (*RN*)

1941 Destroyer *Fearless* damaged by Italian torpedo aircraft off Galita Island (37.40N, 08.20E). Sunk by sister ship *Forester*. Operation Substance.

1941 The first RN operation in the Arctic after the German invasion of Russia. Heavy cruisers *Devonshire* (flag of Rear-Admiral W.F. Wake-Walker) and *Suffolk*, carriers *Victorious* and *Furious* with six destroyers sailed from Scapa Flow to attack German coastal shipping between Kirkenes and Petsamo, the centre of a nickel mining area. Force was located by aircraft and surprise was lost. No shipping found and torpedo bomber strikes launched against port installations. German fighters over Kirkenes and AA fire destroyed eleven of twenty Albacores from *Victorious*, and Swordfish from *Furious* found Petsamo harbour empty. A disappointing operation but the minelayer *Adventure* with a cargo of mines was safely passed through to Britain's new Russian allies in Archangel. Wake-Walker's 'bruised and frustrated force' returned to Scapa Flow.

Operation Substance, 1941

This operation started on 21 July, when a convoy of six storeships was sailed from Gibraltar to Malta. Diversions were created in the eastern Mediterranean, and submarines placed off the Italian ports, to reduce attacks on the convoy. A heavy escort was used, which included Force H, under Admiral Somerville, and the battleship *Nelson* with the cruisers *Edinburgh*, *Manchester* and *Arethusa*. From the 'Narrows' only the cruisers and destroyers continued to escort the convoy. On 23rd, *Manchester* was torpedoed and had to return to Gibraltar, and the destroyer *Fearless* was hit by air attacks and had to be sunk by her consort. In the evening the destroyer *Firedrake* was disabled, but the convoy turned towards Sicily at night to avoid mines and also to shake off the air attacks. At first light the cruisers went ahead and disembarked troops and stores, and the convoy arrived later that day. The convoy escort returned to Gibraltar safely on 27 July. The opportunity had also been taken to pass the empty six merchantmen and auxiliary *Breconshire* from Malta to Gibraltar, and the operation was a complete success.

1943 Destroyers *Eclipse* and *Laforey* sank the Italian S/M *Ascianghi* off Reggio (37.09N, 15.22E).

1959 Admiral of the Fleet Sir George Creasy, former C-in-C Portsmouth, planted an oak tree on the site of the old Single Dock in Chatham Dockyard where *Victory* was laid down 200 years earlier.

1964 HM The Queen, principal guest at a Royal Marines Tercentenary dinner at RNC Greenwich presided over by the Captain General, HRH The Duke of Edinburgh, directed that in future the Loyal Toast should be drunk seated in all Royal Marines officers' and non-commissioned officers' messes ashore and afloat. The Queen further directed that the health of the Captain General should also be drunk seated. The decisions were probably unplanned: Earl Mountbatten wrote the suggestion on his menu at the dinner and passed it to the Queen. Royal Marines Routine Order 201/64 dated 28 August 1964 made it so.

See 28 October 1664.

2003 HM The Queen presented a new Colour to the Fleet in *Ocean* at anchor in Plymouth Sound. Mainbrace spliced. The biggest fleet assembly in Plymouth Sound since June 1905 when thirty-five warships celebrated the official birthday of King Edward VII. Ships present: *Albion*, *Blazer*, *Exploit Explorer*, *Express*, *Gleaner*, *Grafton*, *Newcastle*, *Norfolk*, *Ocean*, *Portland*, *Puncher*, *Raider*, *Severn*, *Sovereign*, *Tracker*, *Walney*; RFAs *Wave Knight*, *Argus* and *Sir Bedivere*. First royal fleet review with no steam-powered surface warships present. Flypast by twenty-eight FAA aircraft. The old Queen's Colour, presented to the Western Fleet in 1969, was laid up the following day in St Nicholas' church in *Drake*.

See 28/29 July 1969.

2009 The first Type 45 destroyer, *Daring*, Capt P.A. 'Paddy' McAlpine RN, commissioned at Portsmouth. Her sponsor, HRH The Countess of Wessex, and CINCFLEET, Admiral Sir Trevor Soar, were present. The commissioning service was conducted by the Chaplain of the Fleet, the Venerable John Green, and the commissioning cake was cut by Mrs Janette McAlpine, and AB Daniel Small, the youngest member of the ship's company, on his 17th birthday.

See 1 February 2006, 28 January 2009, 3 June 2010.

24 July

A Memorable Date observed by the Corps of Royal Marines – capture of Gibraltar

1588 The Spanish Armada off St Alban's Head. Little action but some English revictualling.

1704 Capture of Gibraltar by Admiral Sir George Rooke (*Royal Katherine*) and the Prince of Hesse-Darmstadt. Ships: *Berwick, Burford, Dorsetshire, Eagle, Essex, Grafton, Kingston, Lenox, Monck, Monmouth, Montagu, Nassau, Nottingham, Ranelagh, Royal Katherine, Suffolk, Swiftsure, Yarmouth*. English and Dutch Marines.
Battle Honour: Gibraltar 1704.
See 4 August 2004.

After the capture, the Rock was continually besieged by the French and Spanish. The brigade, which had been reinforced by a further 400 Marines from the Fleet, held out for nearly six months against repeated attacks until the siege was finally raised.

In one incident during the siege, Capt Fisher of the Marines, with seventeen of his men, successfully defended the Round Tower against the continued assaults of 500 French grenadiers. A contemporary report of this noted defence stated 'the garrison did more than could humanly be expected, and the English Marines gained an immortal honour'. When King George IV granted the Royal Marines the Globe for their badge in 1827, he gave them for their crest and their colours the battle honour of Gibraltar, since when they have troubled with no other.

1797 Nelson detached by St Vincent off Cadiz to take Santa Cruz, Tenerife, in *Theseus* with *Culloden, Zealous* and frigate *Emerald*. There were insufficient troops, the landing failed and Nelson lost his right arm.
See 20 April 1657, 2 September 1797.

1812 *Acasta* captured the American privateer *Curlew* 70 miles S.E. of Halifax.

1837 First meeting of Admiralty Compass Committee.

1915 The first success by a RN surface Q-ship deployed in anti-submarine operations. The 400-ton auxiliary fleet collier *Prince Charles*

Embroidery showing Gibraltar, the crest of the Royal Marines and a list of their battles to 1885. (*NMRN 1979/222*)

(Lt W.P. Mark-Wardlaw, seconded from the staff of Admiral Hon. Sir Stanley Colville, Flag Officer Orkneys and Shetlands, and whose merchant service crew had volunteered to a man), armed with concealed two 6-pdrs and two 3-pdrs, sank U-36 (Kapitanleutnant Ernst Graeff) off North Rona Island, 100 miles W. of Scapa (59.07N, 05.30W).

German Submarines sunk by Royal Navy decoy ships

U-36	24 July 1915	*Prince Charles*
U-27	19 August 1915	*Baralong*
U-41	24 September 1915	*Baralong*
U-68	22 March 1916	*Farnborough*
UB-19	30 November 1916	Q7. *Penshurst*
UB-37	14 January 1917	Q7. *Penshurst*
U-83	17 February 1917	Q5. *Farnborough*
U-85	12 March 1917	Q19. *Privet*
UC-29	7 June 1917	*Pargust*
U-88	17 September 1917	*Stonecrop*
U-34	9 November 1918	*Privet*

1917 Flyingboat 8689 sank UC-1 in North Sea.

1918 Destroyer *Pincher* wrecked on the Seven Stones.

1924 King George V reviewed Fleet at Spithead for first time since the end of First World War.

1940 Portsmouth Dockyard seriously damaged by enemy air attack.

1942 Frigate *St Croix* (RCN) sank U-90 in Atlantic (48.12N, 40.56W). Convoy ON 113.

1943 Wellington Q/172 sank the supply U-boat U-459 in W. Approaches (45.53N, 10.38W) but crashed. All concerned rescued by the Navy.

1945 Minesweeper *Squirrel* mined off Phuket Island, Thailand, and sunk by own forces. Operation Livery.

1945 FAA attacked targets in the Inland Sea, Japan. Battle Honour: Japan 1945.

1956 The RN's first guided weapons trials ship, HMS *Girdle Ness*, commissioned at Devonport by Capt M.G. Greig RN. The Canadian-built former landing craft maintenance ship had been converted at Devonport into a test platform for the Sea Slug surface-to-air missile.
See 27 January 1956, 10 June 1960.

Admiral Sir Max Horton (1883–1951) as C-in-C Western Approaches. (*NMM Neg. No. AD17422*)

1992 Navy Board announced establishment of a 'user–maintainer' Warfare Branch through the merging of the Operations (Ops) and Weapon Engineering Mechanic (WEM) Branches. DCI(RN) 195/1992.

1997 Coy Sgt Maj George Finch, DSM, who joined the RMLI as a bugle boy on 23 September 1908 aged 14 years 11 months, died at Gillingham aged 103. Retired 1932.
See 4 February 1997.

Capt. Paddy McAlpine RN and his ship's company at the commissioning of HMS *Daring* at Portsmouth 23 July 2009. (*RN*)

25 JULY

1417 The Earl of Huntingdon defeated a Franco-Genoese fleet in the English Channel, clearing a crossing for Henry V.

See 11 August 1415.

1588 The third engagement with the Spanish Armada, off the Isle of Wight. The British now in four squadrons, under Howard, Drake, Frobisher and Hawkins. There was a four-hour engagement off the Isle of Wight when *Ark* and *Lion* had to be towed into action. Drake tried to head the Spaniards on to the Owers, but in going about they went off from the shore and so the threat to Portsmouth was averted.

1666 Battle of Orfordness. Prince Rupert and the Duke of Albemarle (*Royal Charles*) defeated Admiral de Ruyter (*Zeven Provincien*), with eighty-eight ships, twenty fireships and ten dispatch vessels, in the Thames estuary (Orfordness N.W. by W., 12 or 14 leagues). Battle Honour: Orfordness 1666.

Red Sqn: *Antelope, Breda, Bristol, Cambridge, Charles Merchant, Crown, Diamond, East India Merchant, Fairfax, Foresight, Greenwich, Henrietta, Henry, Jersey, John and Thomas, Katherine, Lion, Mathias, Monck, Newcastle, Portsmouth, Princess, Revenge, Royal Charles, Royal Oak, Ruby, Slothany, Sovereign, St Andrew, Swallow, Tiger, Triumph, Warspite.*

White Sqn: *Anne, Assistance, Assurance, Baltimore, Centurion, Coronation, Delft, Dover, Dragon, Dunkirk, Eagle, Expedition, Guinea, Hampshire, Helverson, Kent, Leopard, London Merchant, Mary Rose, Montagu, Old James, Plymouth, Richard and Martha, Royal James, Royal Katherine, Rupert, St George, Unicorn, York, Zealand.*

Blue Sqn: *Adventure, Advice, Amity, Bonaventure, Castle, Defiance, Dreadnought, East India London, Fanfan, Elizabeth, George, Gloucester, Golden House de Swyte, Guilder de Ruyter, Happy Return, Loyal London, Loyal Merchant, Marmaduke, Mary, Phoenix, Portland, Providence, Rainbow, Resolution,* Santa Maria, Turkey Merchant, Unity, Vanguard, Victory, Welcome, Yarmouth.* Fireships: *Abigail,† Allepine, Blessing,† Briar, Charles, Fortune,† Fox, Great Gift,† Land of Promise,† Lizard, Mary, Paul, Providence,† Richard, St Jacob, Samuel, Virgin.*

*Burnt. †Expended in action.

1797 Nelson's right arm, shattered in the repulsed attack on Santa Cruz in Tenerife in the Canary Islands, amputated on board *Theseus* by French surgeon M. Ronicet, a French Royalist refugee from Toulon.

See 12 July 1794, 24 July 1797, 2 September 1797.

1801 'The moment the enemy touch our coast, be it where they may, they are to be attacked by every man ashore and afloat: this must be perfectly understood. Never fear the event' – Nelson, on defence of the Thames.

1803 *Vanguard* and *Tartar* captured the *Duquesne* W. of Haiti. *Bellerophon, Theseus* and *Aeolus* took part in the chase, but were not engaged. The prize later ran ashore on the Morant Keys but reached UK only to be broken up.

1809 Boats of *Princess Caroline, Minotaur, Prometheus* and *Cerberus*, under Cdr Thomas Forrest (*Prometheus*), cut out three Russian gunboats and an armed brig at Friedrichshafen, Gulf of Finland.

1810 *Thames, Pilot* and *Weazle* took a convoy of thirty-one sail and the escort of seven gun-boats and five scampavias at Amantea, Italy.

1848 First naval vessel to use Esquimalt in Canada – the Pembroke-built Symondite frigate *Constance*.

1860 *Kestrel* destroyed seven pirate lorchas in the Wenchow River.

See 23 July 1860.

1888 Royal Naval Club of 1765 and Navy Club of 1785 agreed to unite on 1 January 1889.

1915 British forces captured Nasiriya, Mesopotamia (Iraq). Vessels: *Shushan* (party from *Espiegle*), *Messudieh* (party from *Miner*), *Muzaffri* (party from *Odin*), *Sumana*.

1934 National Maritime Museum Bill received Royal Assent.

The Victory Museum nearing completion in Portsmouth, 1938. This building is now the Victory Gallery of the National Museum of the Royal Navy. (*NMRN*)

1938 The Victory Museum, precursor of the Royal Naval Museum, opened in Portsmouth Dockyard by the C-in-C Portsmouth, Admiral of the Fleet The Earl of Cork and Orrery. The museum, initially devoted to preserving relics from HMS *Victory* and the Nelson period, was built under the auspices of, and funded by, the Society for Nautical Research on the site of the old Rigging House between *Victory* and Pitch House Jetty. Lt-Cdr W.G. English RN, CO of the ship, became the first curator.

See 18 September 2009.

1938 GC (ex-EGM): Frederick Christie Anderson, Chief ERA, for gallantry in support of the Excise Service in Shanghai.

1941 Light cruiser *Newcastle* intercepted the German SS *Erlangen* which scuttled herself in S. Atlantic (41S, 50W).

1944 British Eastern Fleet, commanded by Admiral Sir James Somerville, carried out a second attack on the Japanese base at Sabang on the N.W. tip of Sumatra. His flagship, the battleship *Queen Elizabeth*, fired her guns against an enemy for the first time since the bombardment of the Dardanelles in 1915. The carriers *Illustrious* and *Victorious* attacked airfields at dawn, and three battleships bombarded the harbour and shore installations while seven cruisers and ten destroyers engaged batteries and radar stations closer inshore. The Dutch cruiser *Tromp* and British destroyers commanded by Capt R.G. Onslow RN, engaged shore targets at point blank range, the destroyers firing torpedoes into the harbour in an action which Somerville described as 'spectacular'. Operation Crimson.

Battle Honour: Sabang 1944.

See 19 April 1944.

Ships: *Queen Elizabeth* (C-in-C's flag), *Renown* (Vice-Admiral Sir Arthur Power), *Valiant*, *Richelieu* (French), *Illustrious* (Rear-Admiral C. Moody), *Victorious*, *Ceylon*, *Cumberland*, *Gambia* (RNZN), *Kenya*, *Nigeria* (Rear-Admiral A.D. Reed, 4th CS), *Phoebe*, *Tromp* (RNlN), *Racehorse*, *Raider*, *Rapid*, *Relentless* (Cdre D), *Rocket*, *Roebuck*, *Rotherham*, *Quality*, *Quickmatch*, *Quilliam* (D4), *Tantalus* and *Templar*. NAS 831 (Barracdua), 1830, 1833, 1834, 1836, 1837, 1838 (Corsairs).

1945 Submarine *Stubborn* torpedoed and sank Japanese destroyer *Nadakaze* in Bali Sea, 175 miles E. of Surabaya (07.06S, 115.42E). The last British submarine to sink a Japanese warship in Second World War. *Stubborn* on passage from the Clyde to Fremantle to join Anglo-Dutch 4th Submarine Flotilla.

See 3 August 1945, 10 January 1969.

1956 Egyptian President Nasser announced the nationalisation of the Suez Canal.

See 1 and 6 November 1956, 22 December 1956.

1958 With the Board's consent the RNVR Air Association to be renamed the Fleet Air Arm Officers' Association. AFO 1567/58.

1967 Vice-Admiral Sir Charles Mills, lately Flag Officer Second-in-Command Far East Fleet, succeeded Vice-Admiral Sir Fitzroy Talbot as the last C-in-C Plymouth.

See 30 October 1956, 26 May 1969, 27 July 2006.

26 JULY

1588 The Spanish Armada in the English Channel. Howard conferred six knighthoods, including on Frobisher and Hawkins, on the *Ark*, and the magistracy along the south coast sent out reinforcements. 'All this day the Spaniards went always before the English like sheep.' – Drake.

1703 Rear-Admiral Thomas Dilkes (*Kent*) captured or destroyed forty-one sail of a French convoy of forty-five vessels at Granville, France, together with the escort of three small warships.

1758 Capture of Louisburg and the whole of Cape Breton Island by Admiral the Hon. Edward Boscawen (*Namur*) and Maj-Gens Amherst and Wolfe.

Battle Honour: Louisberg 1758.

Ships: *Bedford, Burford, Captain, Centurion, Defiance, Devonshire, Dublin, Kingston, Lancaster, Namur, Northumberland, Nottingham, Orford, Pembroke, Prince Frederick, Prince of Orange, Princess Amelia, Royal William, Scarborough, Somerset, Sunderland, Terrible, Vanguard, York*. Frigates, etc.: *Aetna, Beaver, Boreas, Diana, Gramont, Halifax, Hawke, Hunter, Juno, Kennington, Lightning, Nightingale, Port Mahon, Shannon, Squirrel, Trent*. Troops: Royal Artillery, 1st, 15th, 17th, 22nd, 28th, 35th, 40th, 45th, 47th, 48th, 60th, 62nd Regiments. (The 62nd were serving afloat as marines.)

Admiral of the Fleet Lord Gambier (1756–1833). (*NMRN 1975/24*)

1798 *Brilliant* fought the French *Vertu* and *Regénérée* 20 miles W.N.W. of Grand Canary.

1806 *Greyhound* and *Harrier* captured the Dutch *Pallas* and the Dutch East Indiamen *Batavier* and *Victoria* 25 miles W. of Salayer Strait, India.

1807 Second Copenhagen expedition commanded by Admiral Gambier and General Lord Cathcart.

See 2 and 7 September 1807.

1809 Court martial, requested by Admiral Gambier but instigated by Cochrane, his disputatious subordinate at the Basque Road operation, began at Portsmouth. Charge 'that Admiral the Right Honourable Lord Gambier, on the 12th of April, the enemy's ships being then on shore, and the signal having been made that they could be destroyed, did, for a considerable time, neglect or delay taking effectual measures for destroying them'.

See 11 April 1809, 4 August 1809.

1809 Boats of *Fawn* cut out a French cutter and a schooner in St Marie Bay, Guadeloupe.

1815 Napoleon Bonaparte arrived at Plymouth in *Bellerophon*.

1882 Fisher and Wilson commissioned an armoured train at Alexandria.

See 11 July 1882.

1905 The new RN Hospital, Chatham, on 'a breezy site some 200 feet above the Medway' and staffed by nine medical officers, one head wardmaster, seven sisters and seventy sick berth attendants, opened by HM King Edward VII.

1913 HM King George V presented Albert Medals to Chief Stoker W. Lashley and PO T. Crean, in addition to the Polar Medal, for their service in Capt Robert Falcon Scott's Antarctic expedition.

1914 First Sea Lord, Admiral HSH Prince Louis of Battenberg, ordered the Fleet, which had been mobilised for summer exercises, to remain stood to. 'His master stroke' – Marder.

1915 Submarine E 16 sank the German V-188 50 miles N. of Terschelling.

1916 Turkish destroyer *Yadighiar-i-Milet* irreparably damaged by RNAS bombing in E. Mediterranean.

1917 Cruiser *Ariadne* sunk by UC-65 3 miles W. of the Royal Sovereign lightvessel, off Beachy Head.

1929 Explosion of an 8-in gun in the new heavy cruiser *Devonshire*, First CS, Mediterranean Fleet, off Skiathos in the Aegean, killed one RN and seventeen RM members of the turret crew. A brief hangfire in the LH gun in X-turret went unnoticed by the breech operator who opened the breech to reload. The charge exploded and ignited cordite inside the turret. GC (ex-AM) Lt-Cdr Alexander Henry Maxwell-Hyslop RN, ship's gunnery officer (wartime naval airship pilot and former Grand Fleet heavyweight boxing champion) and Marine Albert Edwards Streams (killed in action with 41 Cdo in Sicily Invasion 10 July 1943). Most of the casualties buried at Volos, E. coast of Greece (39.22N, 22.57E). *Devonshire* returned to Devonport on 14 August 'with her smashed turret swung round and guns awry'.

See 2 January 1879.

1935 Heavy cruiser *Suffolk*, Capt Errol Manners RN, arrived alongside Pitch House Jetty in Portsmouth from Shanghai to pay off from the 5th Cruiser Squadron, China Station. One of her magazines contained ninety-three steel-lined cases containing treasures on loan from the Chinese government for an exhibition of Chinese art at the Royal Academy.

See 9 April 1936.

1940 *Swordfish* sank the German TB *Luchs* in North Sea (58.30N, 04.30E).

1941 Destroyers *Cattistock*, *Mendip* and *Quorn* bombarded Dieppe. Operation Gideon.

1941 Italian attack on Grand Harbour, Malta, by explosive-filled motor boats (*barchini*) and two-man torpedoes.

1944 Frigate *Cooke* sank U-214 off Start Point (49.55N, 03.31W).

1945 Minesweeper *Vestal* severely damaged by Japanese kamikaze aircraft off Phuket Island on the Kra Isthmus, Thailand, and sunk by gunfire by destroyer *Racehorse* (07.05N, 97.50E). Twenty men lost. Operation Livery. The last war operation by the Eastern Fleet before the Japanese surrender and the only kamikaze attack carried out in the Indian Ocean (Roskill). Probably the last British warship lost in action in the Second World War. Her sister ship *Squirrel* was mined and sunk by own forces in same operation on 24 July.

See 29 April 1945.

1953 Aircraft maintenance carrier *Unicorn* liberated SS *Inchkilda*, which had been taken by three Chinese pirate gunboats and which she surprised off Ockseu Roads.

2003 RFA *Largs Bay*, first of class of the new Landing Ship Dock (Auxiliary), floated out of dock at Swan Hunter, Wallsend.

See 1 August 2003, 9 April 2004, 9 April 2005, 17 July 2006.

27 July

1588 The Spanish Armada anchored off Calais: so did the British fleet, 'within culverin shot'.

1661 Act passed for establishing articles and orders for the regulation and better government of His Majesty's Navy's ships of war and forces at sea.

1770 Major fire in Portsmouth Dockyard.

1773 The bomb *Racehorse*, Capt Constantine John Phipps (later Earl of Mulgrave and a Lord Commissioner of the Admiralty) reached (80.48N, 14.59.30E), N. of Svalbard (Spitzbergen), in an attempt to reach the East Indies by way of the North Pole. This was, and remains, the record northern latitude ever reached by a RN surface ship. The *Racehorse* was accompanied by the *Carcass* (Capt Skeffington Lutwidge) with Midshipman Horatio Nelson on board.

1778 Admiral the Hon. Augustus Keppel (*Victory*) fought Vice-Admiral Comte d'Orvilliers (*Bretagne*) 108 miles N.W. by N. of Ushant.

Ships: *Monarch, Hector, Centaur, Exeter, Duke, Queen, Shrewsbury, Cumberland, Berwick, Stirling Castle, Courageux, Thunderer, Sandwich, Valiant, Bienfaisant, Victory, Foudroyant, Prince George, Vigilant, Terrible, Vengeance, Worcester, Elizabeth, Robust, Formidable, Ocean, America, Defiance, Egmont, Ramillies*. Frigates: *Arethusa, Proserpine, Milford, Fox, Andromeda, Lively*. Fireships: *Pluto, Vulcan*. Cutter: *Alert*. Regiments: 50th.

The only significant encounter between the British and French fleets in home waters in the American War, it was followed by a heated controversy between the Admiral's political friends and his vice-admiral, Sir Hugh Palliser.

See 7 January 1779, 11 February 1779.

Royal Navy Butter Coolers as Europe went to War, 1939

Admiralty Fleet Order 2109/39
Admiralty, S.W.1
27 July, 1939

The following Orders having been approved by My Lords Commissioners of the Admiralty are hereby promulgated . . .

By Command of their Lordships
To all Commanders-in-Chief, Flag Officers, Senior Naval Officers, Captains and Commanding Officers of H.M. Ships and Vessels, Superintendents or Officers in Charge of H.M. Naval Establishments, and Admiralty Overseers concerned.

2109 – BUTTER COOLERS
1. With reference to the reply to Review of Service Conditions Request No. 1168, AFO 240/38, arrangements have been made for the supply to ships now on foreign service, and to ships commissioning for foreign service, of earthenware butter coolers as a means of keeping ready-use butter cool after issue to lower deck messes.

2. The scale of issue will be one per ten men in each Chief Petty Officers', Petty Officers' and broadside mess, whether victualled on the general mess or standard ration system, and demands for the necessary quantities should be made on the local victualling yard.

3. The butter cooler comprises an earthenware body in which water is placed, an earthenware lining, designed to hold 1lb of butter, and a lid. The three components, viz butter cooler, lid and lining are to be demanded and accounted for separately.

4. After the articles have been in use for six months, ships abroad are to report to the Admiralty through their administrative authority:

a. Whether the butter coolers fulfil the purpose for which they are provided and their supply is recommended as a permanent arrangement.

b. Whether the scale of supply of one per ten men is suitable.

c. Whether suitable stowage space is available in the messes for the articles.

d. Whether, if coolers are issued, the supply of enamelled butter dishes and covers can be discontinued.

C-in-C East Indies Ref. No. 647/EI 2201/17 26.7.1938.

[See 19 April 1963.]

1803 *Plantagenet* captured the French privateer *Atalante* 400 miles W. of Ushant.

1808 *Pickle*, which had taken home Collingwood's dispatches after Trafalgar, wrecked off Cadiz.

1809 Landing party from *Aimable*, *Mosquito*, *Briseis*, *Ephira* and *Pincher* destroyed a battery at Gessendorf (Wesermunde).

1914 German High Seas Fleet recalled from Norway to war bases.

1916 Capt Charles Algernon Fryatt, Master of the Great Eastern Railway Company's cross-Channel steamship *Brussels*, executed by the Germans at Bruges for attempting to ram U-33 which had been chasing her on the surface off the Maas Lightvessel on 28 March that year.

See 10 November 1920.

Capt Fryatt had received a gold watch from Their Lordships for this action and the Admiralty praised 'the highly courageous and meritorious conduct of the Masters of the Company's steamers'. The Germans planned to capture and make an example of Fryatt. On the night of 22/23 June 1916 SS *Brussels*, homeward bound from the Hook of Holland, was intercepted by German destroyers and taken to Zeebrugge. Capt Fryatt was 'tried by court martial in the morning, found guilty in the afternoon and shot in the evening' of 27 July at Bruges. The Germans regarded him as a *franc-tireur*, a person outside the regular military services, who had tried to injure German combatants. This apparent German harshness, following so close on the execution of Nurse Edith Cavell in Belgium on 12 October 1915, proved a major diplomatic own goal. The *New York Times* described it as 'a deliberate murder'. However, a commission set up to consider the case concluded in April 1919 that Fryatt had been properly convicted under international law (see Jamieson 'Martyr or Pirate?' in *The Mariner's Mirror*, vol.85 No.2, May 1999, pp.196–202). Capt Fryatt's body was brought back from Belgium on 7 July 1919 in a British warship and a service was held in St Paul's Cathedral the next day. He was buried at Dovercourt near Harwich.

1918 *Calvia*, *Commander Nasmith*, *Water Priory* and *Vanessa* sank UB-107 off Scarborough.

1918 Naval force left Baghdad by road to operate on Caspian Sea.

1921 Second Sea Trial of Asdics (Sonar) analysed.

1940 Destroyer *Codrington* sunk by German aircraft at Dover, and *Walpole* and *Sandhurst* damaged.

1940 Destroyer *Wren*, first of the name, sunk by German aircraft while covering minesweepers off Aldeburgh (52.10N, 02.06E).

See 10 August 1944

1941 Rear-Admiral Philip Vian with light cruisers *Nigeria* (flag) and *Aurora* with two destroyers sailed from Iceland to investigate the feasibility of establishing an advanced ice-free base on W. coast of Spitzbergen, 450 miles N. of North Cape, to provide direct support to the Russians. Vian reported that proposal was impractical 'while operations close off the enemy-held coastline would probably prove suicidal'.

See 19 August 1941.

1944 Submarine *Sunfish* (Russian B 1) sunk in error by Liberator V/68 (RAF) on loan passage to USSR, 240 miles off Norway.

1953 The end of the Korean War and UN operations with the signing of an armistice. Naval operations had involved eighty RN and other Commonwealth warships and RFAs: 39 RN including 4 aircraft carriers and 6 cruisers, 17 RFAs, 10 RAN warships including 1 aircraft carrier, 8 RCN destroyers and 6 RNZN frigates. About 17,000 officers and men of the RN, RM and RFA served in Korean waters and a further 4,300 in Japan; 165 were decorated and 289 mentioned in Despatches. RN and RM Casualties: 74 killed, 10 missing, 85 wounded and 28 POW.

See 25 June 1950, 2 July 1950.

1973 Fleet Laundry Training Unit at *Drake* closed due to lack of use following the employment of Chinese laundrymen in home waters. DCI(RN)T.238/73.

See 5 December 1969.

2004 The Type 22 frigates *Brave* and *Boxer* left Portsmouth under tow to be expended as targets.

2006 Vice-Admiral Sir Charles Mills, the last C-in-C Plymouth, died aged 91. Flag Officer Second-in-Command Far East Fleet 1965–7. Lieutenant-Governor and C-in-C Guernsey 1969–74.

See 25 July 1967, 26 May 1969.

28 July

1588 Successful fireship attack on the Spanish Armada in Calais Roads. Expended: *Bark Bond, Bark Talbot, Bear Yonge, Elizabeth of Lowestoft, Hope Hawkins, Thomas Drake.*

1609 Sir George Somers in *Sea Venture*, en route from Plymouth to Virginia, wrecked on St George's, Bermuda. Foundation date of the colony and inspiration for Shakespeare's *The Tempest*. Destroyer *Manchester*, Capt P.S. Beattie RN, represented the RN at the 400th anniversary celebrations in July 2009 and ship's company re-enacted the original landing at St Catherine's beach.

1689 Relief of Londonderry after siege of 105 days. Ships: *Dartmouth*; *Mountjoy* and *Phoenix* victuallers. Boat of *Swallow*. Jacobites forced to retire.

1706 Bombardment and storming of Alicante by Vice-Admiral Sir John Leake (*Prince George*) and the Earl of Peterborough. Ships: *Antelope, Berwick, Burford, Canterbury, Dorsetshire, Essex, Falcon, Fubbs Yacht, Grafton, Hampton Court, Leopard, Mary, Medway, Monck, Northumberland, Panther, Prince George, Shrewsbury, Somerset, Tiger, Winchester.*

1806 *Mars* captured the French *Rhin*, a Trafalgar survivor, 80 miles N. of Cape Ortegal, Spain.

1902 Trade Division of Naval Staff formed from a branch of NID.

1914 British fleets ordered to their war bases.
See 26 July 1914.

1914 First successful aerial torpedo drop. Sqn Cdr A.M. Longmore (later ACM Sir Arthur Longmore) in a Short Folder seaplane flying from Calshot near Southampton.
See 12 August 1915.

1937 Admiral Sir Francis Hyde, the First Naval Member of the Australian Commonwealth Naval Board and Chief of Naval Staff since 1931, died in office aged 60. Born at Southsea on 19 July 1877, he first went to sea under sail and he was the first Royal Australian Navy officer to reach full admiral.

1940 AMC *Alcantara* survived an inconclusive fight with the German disguised raider *Thor* (Schiff 10).

1943 Liberator W/224 and N/4 (USAAF) sank U-404 in the Bay of Biscay (45.53N, 09.25W).

1945 FAA attacked targets in the Inland Sea, Japan.

HM The Queen, HRH The Duke of Edinburgh and Admiral of the Fleet Earl Mountbatten of Burma on board HMY *Britannia* during the Queen's visit to the Western Fleet in Torbay 28–29 July 1969. (*Author*)

The Spanish Armada 1588

The First Official Royal Navy Battle Honour

The Spanish Armada was a fleet of 160 ships, of which forty were warships, with 20,000 men (including soldiers) under the Duke of Medina Sidonia. The admiral who was to have commanded the fleet died just before it sailed. The Armada was sighted off the Lizard on 19 July 1588, and had reached Plymouth by the 20th in settled weather making an average speed of 2 knots. The English Fleet, under Lord Howard of Effingham, comprised twenty-seven warships and small vessels, totalling 200. They were able to leave Plymouth ahead of the Armada, and then harass it as it passed up-Channel. Gunnery was indecisive, the Spanish ships being larger, the British ships better sailers, and the guns of both having the same extreme range of 300yd. On the 27th, the Armada anchored off Calais, and on the night of the 28th the English used fireships, which threw the Spanish into confusion. The latter fled before a S.W. wind, and never recovered formation, losing half their ships on the journey home through weather and enemy action. Many sailed completely round the British Isles. The English Fleet retired on 29th after the Battle of Gravelines, because of lack of food and ammunition but the Armada was shepherded as far north as the Firth of Forth. Sir Francis Drake was the vice-admiral of the English Fleet in this action.

[See p.418]

1946 Admiral Sir Bruce Fraser, lately C-in-C British Pacific Fleet, attended the Red Fleet Day celebrations in Moscow, having sailed from Portsmouth to Kronstadt in *Triumph*, and escorted by the destroyer *Rapid*.

1958 The Queen's Colour presented to Britannia Royal Naval College, Dartmouth, Capt W.J. Munn RN, by HRH The Duke of Edinburgh, accompanied by The Earl of Selkirk, First Lord of the Admiralty, Admiral of the Fleet Earl Mountbatten of Burma, First Sea Lord, and Vice-Admiral Sir Richard Onslow, C-in-C Plymouth.

See 30 July 1956.

1963 Frigate *Leopard* seriously damaged in collision with South African minesweeper *Pietermaritzburg* during Exercise Capex off Cape Point near Simon's Town.

1969 HM The Queen, in HMY *Britannia*, visited the Western Fleet in Torbay. Dinner in *Eagle*, Capt J.D. Treacher, RN, flag of Admiral Sir John Bush, C-in-C Western Fleet, followed by ship's concert party. The weather got up and, although the Royal barge had difficulty coming alongside, the Royal party was safely transferred to *Britannia*. 'Then followed the three visiting admirals who all managed to make the leap into their barges, except for the Hydographer of the Navy who found the barge canopy where the cockpit should have been and ended up spread-eagled on top' – Admiral Treacher's memoirs. Boat traffic was then suspended. Over 1,000 sailors from other ships embarked for the concert, remained in *Eagle* and 1,500 men ashore in Torbay. Some ships had to put to sea for safety. Next day, the weather having abated, the Queen presented her new Colour to the Fleet and a steam-past in Lyme Bay was successfully completed.

See 23 July 2003.

1983 'The Admiralty Board regrets that the RNSS is on the move again after twenty-five most successful years as part of HMS *Pembroke* during which the high standards of training in the Supply and Secretariat Branch have been maintained and improved. They wish the RNSS all good fortune in their new home at HMS *Raleigh*' – MODUKNAVY WAA/A21/A2J 281630ZJUL83.

See 1 August 1983.

29 July

1572 Francis Drake attacked Nombre de Dios, Panama. Ships: *Pasha, Swan.*

1588 The final action with the Spanish Armada off Gravelines, led by Drake (*Revenge*), who wrote to Walsingham 'There never was any thing pleased me better than to see the enemy flying wth a sotherly wynd to the northwards'.

1653 Action between Admiral George Monck (*Resolution*) and Admiral Maerten Tromp (*Brederode*) off Katwijk-aan-Zee.
See 31 July 1653.

1781 *Perseverance* captured the French *Lively* 250 miles N.W. of Cape Finisterre. *Narcissus* recaptured a French prize brig.

1782 *Santa Margarita* captured the French *Amazone* 15 miles E. of Cape Henry, but had to abandon her next day.

1797 *Aigle* captured the French *Hazard* 50 miles N.N.W. of Cape Finisterre.

1800 Boats of *Viper, Impetueux* and *Amethyst* cut out the French *Cerbère* at Port Louis. St Vincent was so impressed by Lt Coughlan who, though badly wounded, returned to lead the boarding party that he presented him with a sword and confirmed his promotion in *Viper.*
Battle Honour: *Cerbère* 1800.

1809 Boats of *Excellent, Acorn* and *Bustard* cut out six Italian gunboats at Duino.

1856 Esquimalt replaced Valparaiso as RN base in the Pacific.

1917 Old torpedo gunboat *Halcyon* sank UB-27 26 miles 060° from Great Yarmouth.

1917 Curtis H-12 flyingboats 8676 and 8662 sank UB-20 in North Sea.

1930 HM King George V opened the Wyllie Trafalgar panorama in Portsmouth Dockyard.

First Battlecruiser Squadron Regatta 29 July 1918. Warrant officers of the battlecruiser HMS *Renown* with the seven winners of the Warrant Officers Gig Race. (*Cdr David Hobbs RN*)

Ships Present at the Western Fleet Assembly – 29 July 1969

Eagle, Capt J.D. Treacher RN, flag of Admiral Sir John Bush, C-in-C Western Fleet; *Glamorgan*, Capt S.L. McArdle RN, flag of Vice-Admiral Sir Michael Pollock, Flag Officer Submarines; *Hampshire*, Capt R.P. Clayton RN, flag of Vice-Admiral A.M. Lewis, Flag Officer Flotillas Western Fleet; *Hecate*, Capt J.H.S. Osborne RAN, flag of Rear-Admiral G.S. Ritchie, Hydrographer of the Navy; *Blake*, Capt R.F. Plugge RN, flag of Rear-Admiral M.F. Fell, Flag Officer Carriers and Amphibious Ships; the Londonderry Squadron: *Phoebe*, Capt (D) C.R.P.C. Branson RN., *Llandaff*, Cdr W.H. Stewart RN, *Keppel*, Lt-Cdr J.M.S. Ekins RN; Dartmouth Training Squadron: *Eastbourne*, Capt (D) I.S.S. Mackay RN; *Tenby*, Cdr R.I.T. Hogg R; *Torquay*, Cdr P.J. Symons RN; Portland Squadron: *Dundas*, Lt-Cdr E.M. England RN; *Duncan*, Lt-Cdr W.M. Forbes RN; *Charybdis*, Capt D.W. Foster RN; *Sirius*, Cdr J.A. de M. Leathes RN; *Plymouth*, Cdr St.J. H. Herbert RN; *Diana*, Cdr E.D.L. Llewellyn RN; *Warspite*, Cdr J.B. Hervey RN; *Valiant*, Cdr G.R. King RN; *Odin*, Lt-Cdr N.G. Warneford RN; *Olympus*, Lt-Cdr R.F. Channon RN; *Oracle*, Lt-Cdr G.T. Swales RN; *Acheron*, Lt-Cdr D.W. Mitchell RN; *Ambush*, Lt-Cdr J.P. Speller RN; *Tiptoe*, Lt-Cdr J.J.S. Daniel RN; *Fawn*, Cdr C.E.K. Robinson RN; *Fox*, Lt-Cdr R. Dathan RN; *Abdiel*, Cdr T.M.B. Seymour RN; *Lewiston*, Lt-Cdr R.G. Teasdale RN; *Upton*, Lt-Cdr G.J. Claydon RN; *Bildeston*, Lt-Cdr R.J.D. Allan RN; *Soberton*, Lt-Cdr D.T. Ancona RN; *Curzon*, Cdr B.K. Perrin RNR; *Venturer*, Cdr F.A. Williams RNR; *Solent*, Lt-Cdr G.R. Hill RNR; RFAs *Resource*, Capt E.D.J. Evans; *Olmeda*, Capt S.C. Dunlop; *Lyness*, Capt C.G.D. Barker; *Engadine*, Capt J.H. McLoughlin.

1940 Destroyer *Delight* damaged by German aircraft off Portland having been detected by new Freya RDF at 60 miles' range. Sank next day in Portland harbour.
See 1 May 2008.

1942 Admiral Sir Charles Kennedy-Purvis appointed to the new post of Deputy First Sea Lord created to relieve the overworked First Sea Lord, Admiral of the Fleet Sir Dudley Pound, of routine administration of the Naval Staff and to enable him to concentrate on planning and operations. The new post was precipitated by the disaster to Convoy PQ17. On 11 May the First Lord, Mr A.V. Alexander, had proposed splitting the duties of First Sea Lord and Chief of Naval Staff which Pound did not accept, citing the US Navy's unsatisfactory division of CNO (Stark) and COMINCH (King).

1943 Submarine *Trooper* sank the Italian S/M *Pietro Micca* in Otranto Strait (39.45N, 18.25E).

1943 Wellington G/172 sank U-614 in S.W. Approaches (46.42N, 11.03W).

1945 *King George V*, *Newfoundland*, *Undine*, *Ulysses* and *Urania* and US battleships bombarded Hamamatsu, Honshu.

On the night of 29/30 July, the battleship *King George V* with the destroyers *Undine*, *Ulysses* and *Urania* shelled works and aircraft factories on South Honshu – the main island of Japan. This was the last occasion on which a British battleship used her guns in action against enemy targets. On 9 August the cruisers *Gambia* (RNZN) and *Newfoundland* together with the destroyers *Terpsichore*, *Termagant* and *Tenacious* shelled Honshu. The force was present at the formal surrender of the Japanese on 15 August in Tokyo Bay.

1954 A RN Sea Hawk FB3 aircraft, piloted by Lt J.R.F. Overbury from Boscombe Down, flying from London to Amsterdam, established a new air speed record for the 223.98 miles of 23 minutes, 39.7 seconds at an average speed of 568 mph.

1969 HM The Queen presented a new Colour to the Western Fleet on the flight deck of the carrier *Eagle* in Torbay on the 381st anniversary of the last battle by Sir Francis Drake against the Spanish Armada. A replica of Drake's drum, loaned by HMS *Drake* at Devonport, was the top drum of the pile on which the new Colour was placed. There followed a steam-past HMY *Britannia* in Lyme Bay.
See 11 April 1929, 28 July 1969, 27 May 1993, 23 July 2003

1977 Final parade of Women's Royal New Zealand Naval Service before integration into RNZN and RNZNVR.
See 11 April 1942.

30 July

1588 The Spanish Armada in the North Sea. After this it disintegrated, survivors returning home northabout. Spain lost thirty-three ships.

1768 Lt James Cook sailed from Deptford in *Endeavour* on his first voyage.
See 25 June 1776, 12 July 1776.

1775 Return of Cdr James Cook (*Resolution*) to Spithead from his second voyage of exploration in the Pacific. *Adventure* in company for the first half of the voyage. Kendall's K1 chronometer proved.
See 19 January 1762, 13 May 1764.

1782 *Cormorant* captured the French *Téméraire* 25 miles W.S.W. of Cape Clear.

1811 Two boats of *Minden* stormed Fort Marrack, Java.

1811 Boats of *Amazon* cut out four chassemarées and burned five more near Penmarc'h Point, Brittany.

1912 Royal Commission on Fuel Oil for RN set up.

1918 VC: Lt Harold Auten, RNR (*Stock Force*) for action with UB-80 off Bolt Head.

1919 Aircraft from *Vindictive* attacked the Russian Naval Base at Kronstadt in the Gulf of Finland.
See 18 August 1919.

1927 Admiral of the Fleet Earl Beatty, First Sea Lord since 1 November 1919, went on half-pay and was succeeded by Admiral Sir Charles Madden. *King's Regulations and Admiralty Instructions* (*KR&AI*) Article 243 limited officers' service on the Board of Admiralty to seven years except in special circumstances. Beatty's seven years nine months as First Sea Lord has never been equalled in duration.
See 1 November 1919.

1937 Cabinet approved the Inskip recommendation that the Fleet Air Arm should come under Admiralty control.
See 24 May 1939.

1938 Virtual abolition of half-pay.

1941 *Victorious* and *Furious* attacked shipping, at Kirkenes, Norway and Petsamo, Finland respectively. Operation E.F.

Ships: *Active, Antelope, Anthony, Devonshire, Echo, Eclipse, Escapade, Furious, Icarus, Inglefield, Intrepid, Suffolk, Victorious*. FAA Sqns: 800, 812, 817 (*Furious* – Fulmar, Swordfish, Albacore); 809, 827, 828 (*Victorious* – Fulmar, Albacore).

1941 Submarine minelayer *Cachalot* rammed and fired at by the Italian TB *Generale Achille Papa* off Benghazi. Sunk by own crew.

1943 Sloops *Kite, Wild Goose, Woodpecker* and *Wren* sank U-504 and Sunderland U/461 (RAAF) and Halifax S/502 sank the Supply U-boats U-461 and U-462 in Bay of Biscay. A numerical coincidence and an ULTRA success.

A Liberator sighted three U-boats crossing the Bay of Biscay: they were U-461 and U-462, both tankers, escorted by U-504. The submarines were resighted by a Sunderland and then by a Catalina operating with the 2nd Escort Group. A Liberator and a Halifax joined the Catalina and Sunderland, but poor communications between the aircraft prevented a coordinated attack, even when another Halifax and Sunderland joined the four aircraft. The newly arrived Halifax damaged U-462, but meanwhile the Liberator was hit and had to force land in Portugal. The other aircraft were also hit by the submarines' gunfire.

Sunderland 'U' of 461 Squadron then attacked and sank U-461 – whereupon the ships of the 2nd Escort Group arrived. U-504 dived and was detected on Asdic and sunk after two hours' depth-charging. U-462 scuttled herself, as she had been damaged by the aircraft and by the ships of the 2nd Escort Group. The joint air/sea action had been brought to a successful conclusion.

1943 RMS *Queen Mary*, in her wartime troopship role, arrived on the Clyde from New York with 16,683 souls on board, the greatest number of people ever embarked in one vessel. Had departed New York 25 July; 3,353 miles covered in 4 days 20 hours 42 minutes at average speed of 28.173 knots.

1948 Criminal Justice Act removed flogging from list of naval punishments. It had been suspended since 1897.

1948 The First Lord of the Admiralty inspected MGB 2009, Lt W.E.G. Reeks RN, alongside HMS *President* on the Thames. The craft had come from Gosport on the first sea passage made by a gas turbine-powered warship.

1949 Frigate *Amethyst* ran the gauntlet of Chinese Communist shore batteries in the Yangtze, from a little below Chinkiang, 150 miles, and rejoined the Fleet on the 31st.

See 20 April 1949, 14 September 1956, 12 September 1985.

18 April from *Amethyst*:
'*Amethyst* still aground on Rose Island. Am attempting to make good vital damage to refloat and proceed to Nanking. Sixty approx of ship's company including 4 wounded are making way to nearest town. Casualties are about 17 dead including doctor and sick berth attendant. twenty seriously wounded including captain.'

23 April from Admiral:
'You have my approval to act as you think best if fired on again. I am trying to arrange safe conduct for you to Nanking but doubtful if this will operate quickly. Try to let me know if you have to abandon. I am full of admiration for all in *Amethyst*.'

From C-in-C:
'I entirely agree your conduct of negotiations and am proud of the spirit and determination of all in *Amethyst*.'

To C-in-C:
'I am going to break out at 10 p.m. tonight 30 July.'

From *Amethyst* to C-in-C:
'Have rejoined fleet south of Woo Sung. No damage or casualties. God Save the King.'

1951 Admiral Sir Max Horton, submariner, died. As C-in-C W. Approaches from 1942–5 more warships came under his flag than that of any British admiral in history. He was the first British submarine commander to sink an enemy warship and he originated the custom of submarines flying the piratical skull and crossbones flag when returning from a successful patrol. In his last hours he asked 'Any news of the *Affray*?' (foundered 17 April 1951). Admiral Horton was given a state funeral in Liverpool Cathedral. 'A great admiral in the tradition of St Vincent rather than Nelson, Horton had technical knowledge and genius for detail which never obscured his eye for the main issues: he could see the wood and the trees' – Rear-Admiral W.S. Chalmers.

See 13 September 1914, 15 August 1945.

1956 HM The Queen presented her Colour for the first time to the Fleet Air Arm at *Daedalus*, RNAS Lee-on-Solent. Flypast headed by FOFT piloting a Vampire and the next Vampires manned by two captains RN. With a summer gale blowing on the day, a big drum stacked for the ceremony took off down the runway and into a Wren in the front rank of the parade. Vice-Admiral Sir Caspar John, Flag Officer Air (Home), later sent her a commendation and two pairs of nylons.

See 28 July 1958, 8 June 1959, 7 November 1975.

1957 The AA frigate *Jaguar*, having been named by HRH Princess Alexandra of Kent at Denny's of Dumbarton, failed to move down the slipway. The ship got underway ten minutes later, helped by a push from the Princess.

1963 Minister of Defence, Peter Thornycroft announced in the House of Commons that Britain was to build a 50,000 ton aircraft carrier and that 'agreement had been finally reached between the Royal Navy and the RAF on the question of a common aircraft'. She was to be named HMS *Queen Elizabeth*.

See 22 February 1966, 19 January 1998, 7 July 2009.

1965 QHM Malta became Commander, RN Harbour Services. DCI(RN) 1171/65.

1976 Scapa Flow ceased to be a Dockyard Port. 'Post of QHM ended 27 May 1976. Scapa Flow is now administered solely by Orkney Islands Council through the Director of Harbours, County Offices, Kirkwall, Tel. Kirkwall 3535 ext. 65. There are agreements in force safeguarding MOD use of the Flow in time of emergency and prohibiting diving in the vicinity of the *Royal Oak*.' – DCI(RN) 349/76.

See 31 March 1977.

31 JULY

1653 The last battle of the first Dutch war and sometimes called the first battle of the Texel. Admiral George Monck (*Resolution*) defeated Admiral Maerten Tromp (*Brederode*) off Scheveningen. By whichever name, a decisive battle, in which Tromp was killed.
Battle Honour: Scheveningen 1653.

Ships: *Advantage, Andrew, Assurance, Crescent, Diamond, Dragon, Duchess, Exeter Merchant, Expedition, Foresight, Gift, Golden Cock, Great President, Hannibal, Hound, James, John and Katherine, Malaga Merchant, Mary Prize, Merlin, Norwich, Pelican, Phoenix, Portsmouth, Prosperous, Rainbow, Raven, Recovery, Renown, Resolution, Seven Brothers, Sophia, Tiger, Triumph* (Admiral Peacock killed in action), *Tulip, Vanguard, Victory, William, Worcester*. Fireships: *Hunter* (expended), *Oak* (blew up). First Meritorious Service Medal.

1718 Admiral Sir George Byng (*Barfleur*) decisively defeated Vice-Admiral Don Antonio de Gastaneta (*San Felipe El Real*) off Cape Passero, Sicily, thus preserving the island from the ambitions of Philip V of Spain.
Battle Honour: Passero 1718.

Ships: *Argyll, Barfleur, Breda, Burford, Canterbury, Captain, Dorsetshire, Dreadnought, Dunkirk, Essex, Grafton, Kent, Lenox, Montagu, Orford, Ripon, Rochester, Royal Oak, Rupert, Shrewsbury, Superb*. Fireships: *Garland, Griffin*. Hospital ship: *Looe*.

Admiral George Byng, Viscount Torrington (1663–1733). *(NMRN 1971/12(42))*

1804 Boats of *Centaur* cut out the French privateer *Elizabeth* and a schooner at Basse Terre, Guadeloupe.

1811 Boats of *Procris* captured five French gunboats at the mouth of the Inderamayu River, Java. A sixth blew up. Troops: detachments of the 14th and 89th Regiments.

1849 *Nemesis* (Ben. Mar.) and boats of *Albatross* and *Royalist* destroyed eighty-eight pirate prahus

Midget Submarine Operations in the Far East, 1945

Midget submarines in the Far East were based on HMS *Bonaventure*, which in July 1945 was at Brunei Bay. XE 1 and XE 3 were towed by *Spark* and *Stygian* to Singapore. XE 3 placed her two 4-ton charges under the Japanese cruiser *Takao* (9,850 tons) in the Johore Strait, and LS Magennis swam out of the submarine to place limpet charges on the cruiser. The midget found it difficult to slip away as the cruiser settled down on her, and also because one large charge failed to fall clear. Magennis again left the submarine to clear the charge. XE 3 then returned to the *Stygian*. XE 1, meanwhile, had been delayed, and so did not attack the cruiser *Myoko* but laid her charges by *Takao*. *Takao* was severely damaged by this attack, but both midget submarines returned safely. Lt Fraser and LS Magennis were awarded the VC.

On the same day as this attack, 31 July, XE 4 managed to cut the Saigon to Hong Kong and Saigon to Singapore telegraph cables in 40ft of water despite bad weather and strong tides. She brought back 1-ft lengths of the cables as evidence.

XE 5 spent 3½ days and nights attempting to cut the Hong Kong to Singapore telegraph cable off Hong Kong. She had to make the defended passage four times and her divers were working in white mud up to their armpits. She abandoned the attempt on 3 August, but her efforts had, in fact, been successful.

HMS *Glory* (1899) – the daily 'Grog' issue. *(NMRN)*

at the entrance to the Batang Saribas, Borneo.

1912 King George V reviewed the Fleet in the Solent. The first such event to include naval aircraft.

1942 Sloops *Erne*, *Rochester* and *Sandwich* sank U-213 off the Azores.

1942 *Skeena* and *Wetaskiwin* (both RCN) sank U-588 in N. Atlantic.

1942 Hudson of 113 Sqn (RCAF) sank U-754 in W. Atlantic (43.02N, 64.52W).

1943 July 1943 was the first month of the Second World War when Allied shipping construction exceeded losses.

1944 Frigate *Loch Killin* and sloop *Starling* sank U-333 in S.W. Approaches. First success with Squid.

1945 VC: Lt Ian Edward Fraser, RNR, and LS James Joseph Magennis for attack by *XE 3*, which damaged the Japanese cruiser *Takao* in Johore Strait, Singapore. Operation Struggle. *XE 1* also endeavoured to attack *Takao*, having been frustrated in the approach to the assigned target *Myoko*, but it is not known if his 'side-cargo' mine was dropped close enough to the cruiser to cause further damage. Meanwhile, *XE 4* and *XE 5* cut seabed telephone cables between Hong Kong, Saigon and Singapore.

See 27 October 1946.

1951 *Vidal*, surveying ship, launched. First small ship designed to carry a helicopter, and first with cafeteria messing and the last surface ship built at Chatham Dockyard.

1963 Fire in cruiser *Lion* at Singapore caused £11,222 damage. DCI(RN) 983/65.

1964 Announcement of withdrawal of British submarine forces from the Mediterranean. FOSM to Captain SM5 in depot ship *Ausonia*: 'The departure of the Submarine Division from the Mediterranean brings to a close an era studded with honour.'

1970 Last Tot issue. A daily ration of rum became clearly inappropriate in the highly technical Navy. The ration was finally stopped by the Admiralty Board. The First Sea Lord, Admiral of the Fleet Sir Michael Le Fanu, who was shortly to retire owing to a terminal illness, made a valedictory signal to the Fleet:

Personal from First Sea Lord:

Most farewell messages try
To jerk a tear from the eye
But I say to you lot
Very sad about tot
But thank you, good luck and goodbye.

Inevitably he was known as Dry Ginger, having hair of that colour. The sailors' Fund established with an initial £2,700,000. DCI (RN) 284/70.

See 7 November 1975.

1985 RNSTS Deptford finally closed, having ceased to be an operational depot on 28 June 1985. DCI(RN) 289/85.

1987 HRH Don Juan de Borbon y Battenberg, Count of Barcelona, appointed an honorary admiral in Her Majesty's Fleet. He was the son and designated heir of King Alfonso XIII of Spain and Victoria Eugenie of Battenberg; his father was replaced when the Second Spanish Republic was declared on 14 April 1931. Don Juan died 1 April 1993. His son is His Majesty King Don Juan Carlos I of Spain.

1 AUGUST

1295 Dover burned by the French.

1683 Boats of *Francis* cut out the French pirate *Trompeuse* at St Thomas, West Indies.

1714 Death of Queen Anne and accession of King George I.

1739 Vernon's orders to his squadron: 'You are hereby required and directed to use your utmost to take, sink, burn or otherwise destroy all Spanish ships and vessels as well as ships of war'.

See 23 June 1652, 18 September 1740, 21 May 1798, 18 May 1803, 8 May 1943.

1740 First performance of 'Rule, Britannia!' in the masque *Alfred*, about Alfred the Great's victories over the Vikings, performed at Cliveden House, Maidenhead, home of Frederick, Prince of Wales, and staged in honour of HM King George I's accession and the birthday of HRH Princess Augusta.

1788 Captain's Standing Orders of HMS *Andromeda*, Capt HRH Prince William Henry: 'Order the 8th, requesting and directing the first lieutenant or commanding officer to see all strangers out of his Majesty's ship under my command at gun-fire [sunset] is by no means meant to restrain the officers and men from having either black or white women on board through the night, so long as the discipline is unhurt by the indulgence.'

1793 *Boston* fought the French *Embuscade* off New York.

1798 Battle of the Nile. Rear-Admiral Sir Horatio Nelson (*Vanguard*) defeated Vice-Admiral François Brueys (*Orient*) in Aboukir Bay.

Battle Honour: Nile 1798.

See 21 November 1918, 28 March 1941.

Ships: *Alexander, Audacious, Bellerophon, Culloden, Defence, Goliath, Leander, Majestic, Minotaur, Orion, Swiftsure, Theseus, Vanguard, Zealous*. Sloop: *Mutine*.

The Battle of the Nile, 1798

Early in May 1798 Bonaparte and his army, and Admiral Brueys in thirteen ships of the line including *L'Orient* (120) and four frigates, escaped the British blockade to sail to Malta where they arrived on 9 June. After a week Bonaparte sailed with the intention of capturing Egypt and interrupting British trade with India. Nelson with a slightly smaller force was in Naples on 17 June searching for him. He sailed for Alexandria, where he arrived on the 29th. The French were not there, so Nelson returned to Sicily. Meanwhile, the French Fleet arrived at Alexandria and Bonaparte defeated the Mameluke army at the Battle of the Pyramids. The French Fleet anchored in a strong position in Aboukir Bay. Nelson, after revictualling his ships, returned to Alexandria, and on 1 August learned of the location of the French Fleet. Despite their strong position and the lateness of the hour Nelson attacked immediately. The French were unprepared for enemy attack from the landward side, and a number of British ships sailed inside the French line at some risk from shallow water. In the violent battle that ensued only two French ships were able to escape. The French flagship *L'Orient* blew up with the loss of Admiral Brueys, Cdre Casiabianca and his son: 'the boy stood on the burning deck.'

A memorandum was issued on 2 August to all captains: 'Almighty God having blessed His Majesty's arms with victory, the Admiral intends returning Public Thanksgiving for the same at two o'clock this day; and he recommends every ship doing the same as soon as convenient. Horatio Nelson' – Mahan, *Life of Nelson*, p.306. Beatty repeated this almost verbatim from *Queen Elizabeth* to the Grand Fleet at Rosyth after the arrival of the German High Seas Fleet.

1808 *Crocodile*, frigate, landed Sir Arthur Wellesley in Mondego Bay in command of the Portuguese Expeditionary Force. Start of the Peninsula campaign. A classic example of littoral warfare.

See 21 September 1813.

1825 *Fury*, another seeker for a North–West Passage, beached and abandoned on west side of Regent's Inlet. Crew saved by *Hecla*. Their stores saved the lives of *Victory*'s crew in 1833.

1831 Naval party landed from *St Vincent*, flagship of C-in-C Mediterranean Fleet, Vice-Admiral Sir Henry Hotham, on a newly emerged volcanic island in Sicilian Channel (37.10N, 12.43E), 26 miles S.W. of Sciacca, Sicily, and 41 miles N.E. of Pantelleria. Flag Captain, Humphrey Senhouse, planted Union Flag and named Graham Island after First Lord of the Admiralty.

This provoked a diplomatic dispute: Sicilians claimed island as Ferdinandia, French as Giulia. Problem was solved when island subsided into sea in January 1832. Graham Island is now Graham Shoal, with highest point 23ft below sea level.

See 12 January 1832.

1836 Boats of *Andromache* destroyed six pirate prahus off Pulo Bucalisse, Sumatra.

1861 *Warrior*, first seagoing iron-hulled, ironclad, commissioned.

1914 Naval mobilisation ordered.

1915 Submarine E 11 raided Constantinople harbour.

1918 Allied Expeditionary Force captured the defences of Archangel. Ships: *Attentive*, *Nairana*, *Tay* and *Tyne*.

1923 Closure of RM Forton Barracks, Gosport.

See 1 June 1927.

1940 Submarine *Oswald* scuttled, having been rammed by the Italian destroyer *Ugolino Vivaldi* off Cape Spartivento (37.46N, 16.16E).

1940 Submarine *Spearfish* torpedoed and sunk by U-34 in North Sea. One survivor.

1943 Cruisers *Aurora* and *Penelope* and six destroyers bombarded Cotronei. Cruisers *Dido*, *Euryalus*, *Sirius* and four destroyers bombarded the bridge at the mouth of the Oliva River and Vibo Valentia, Gulf of Eufemia, S. Italy.

1951 Court Martial Appeals Act passed.

1968 SD Officers' School at the Fraser Gunnery Range named HMS *St George*. Training task transferred to BRNC Dartmouth 1973. DCI(RN) 838/68.

1972 Dartmouth Training Squadron (*Tenby*, *Eastbourne*, *Scarborough*) disbanded. The DTS replaced by *Intrepid*, known as the Dartmouth Training Ship. DCI(RN)T.486/72.

1974 The RN Barracks, Portsmouth, named *Victory* by order of HM King Edward VII in 1903, renamed *Nelson* by special permission of HM The Queen to end seventy-one years of confusion between the barracks and the three-decker in Portsmouth Dockyard. At the renaming divisions, held on this anniversary of Nelson's victory at the Nile, Cdre John Lea invited former commodores of the barracks to hand out new cap tallies.

See 4 June 1889, 1 January 1890, 30 September 1903, 1 January 1934.

1983 RN Supply School moved from Chatham, mainly to *Raleigh* at Torpoint but Cookery School to Aldershot.

See 28 July 1983.

1990 Iraqi forces invaded Kuwait. Gulf War. Battle Honour 'Kuwait 1991' awarded to HM ships, RN air squadrons and RFA vessels engaged in operations against Iraqi forces or in logistic support duties in the central and northern Gulf to the west of meridian 51°E at any time between 17 January and 28 February 1991. Operation Granby:

Ships: *Atherstone*, *Brave*, *Brazen*, *Brilliant*, *Cardiff*, *Cattistock*, *Dulverton*, *Exeter*, *Gloucester*, *Hecla*, *Herald*, *Hurworth*, *Ledbury*, *London*, *Manchester*. FAA Sqns: 815, 826, 829, 845, 846, 848. RFAs: *Argus*, *Bayleaf*, *Diligence*, *Fort Grange*, *Olna*, *Resource*, *Sir Bedivere*, *Sir Galahad*, *Sir Percivale*, *Sir Tristram*. Attached: Fleet Diving Group.

1998 Frigate *Somerset* sailed into Aboukir Bay to mark the 200th anniversary of the Battle of the Nile. An ecumenical service honoured the casualties in the British and French fleets.

See 18 April 2005.

2003 RFA *Largs Bay*, first of class of LSDA (Landing Ship Dock (Auxiliary)), named by Lady West, wife of Admiral Sir Alan West, First Sea Lord, at Swan Hunter, Wallsend.

See 26 July 2003, 9 April 2004, 9 April 2005, 17 July 2006.

2005 *Invincible* entered Portsmouth for the last time to pay off.

See 3 August 2005.

2010 Lord Sterling of Plaistow promoted honorary rear-admiral, RNR.

See 1 November 1958, 1 June 2004, 2 March 2009.

2 August

1511 Lord Thomas Howard and Sir Edward Howard killed the Scottish pirate Andrew Barton and captured his two vessels – *Lion* and *Jannet Perwyn*. Howard adopted the bosun's call in silver as the symbolic badge of office of the Lord High Admiral.

See 25 April 1513.

1665 Abortive attack by Rear-Admiral Sir Thomas Teddeman (*Revenge*) on the Dutch shipping at Bergen.

Ships: *Breda, Foresight, Golden Lion, Guernsey, Guinea, Happy Return, Norwich, Pembroke, Revenge, Sapphire.* Hired ships: *Bendish, Coast Frigate, Prudent Mary, Society.* Fireships: *Bonaventure, Expedition, Martin Galley.* Hired: *Hambro' Merchant.* Ketch: *Edward and Eve, Royal Katherine.* Joined later: *Constant Catherine, Eagle, Exchange, John and Thomas, Mary Rose.*

1745 *Chester* and *Sunderland* captured the French register-ship *Notre Dame de la Déliverance* off Louisburg, Cape Breton Island.

Poster for the Royal Tournament of 1911. (*NMRN 2002/79*)

1781 Frigate *Pelican* (24), Capt Cuthbert Collingwood, from Port Royal, wrecked in a hurricane on Morant Keys, 35 miles S.E. of Morant Point, Jamaica.

1812 Boats of *Horatio* cut out two Dutch vessels and recaptured their prize near Tromsø.

1813 *Eagle* and *Bacchante* destroyed the batteries and shipping at Porto di Rovigno, Italy.

1882 Occupation of Suez by a Naval Brigade from *Euryalus* (flag), *Ruby, Eclipse* and *Dragon.*

1889 Wilhelm II, German Emperor and King of Prussia, made honorary admiral of the fleet by his grandmother Queen Victoria at Cowes. He repudiated the rank when Britain declared war on Germany, 4 August 1914.

1913 Michael Le Fanu, First Sea Lord 1968–70, born.

See 28 November 1970.

1917 Sqn Cdr E.H. Dunning landed a Sopwith Pup on board the converted large light cruiser *Furious* under way in Scapa Flow, the first man ever to land an aircraft on the deck of an aircraft carrier. He was killed on 7 August attempting a further landing on the same ship.

See 18 November 1911, 10 January 1912, 2 May 1912.

1918 Destroyers *Ariel* and *Vehement* sunk while minelaying off Heligoland.

1919 Paddle auxiliary patrol vessel *Princess Mary II* mined in Aegean.

1940 Twelve Swordfish (*Ark Royal*), nine with bombs and three with mines, attacked Elmas airfield, Cagliari, and mined the harbour. FAA Sqns: Swordfish: 810, 818, 820. Operation Crush.

1940 A/S trawler *Cape Finisterre* sunk by German aircraft off Harwich.

Sqn Cdr E.H. Dunning flying Sopwith Pup N6453 in landing trials on HMS *Furious* in 1917. (*FAAM*)

1941 Light cruiser *Hermione* rammed and sank the Italian S/M *Tembien* off Tunis.

1943 Sunderland M/461 (RAAF) and N/228 sank U-106 in S.W. Approaches.

Bombardment of Inchon, 1950

Inchon was being used as a base by the North Koreans, and the cruisers *Belfast* and *Kenya* carried out a bombardment of key points, such as the power station and railway station, firing over 400 rounds of 6-in shells. Ninety-five per cent of the shots were on target. The destroyers *Cossack* and *Charity* accompanied the cruisers to deal with opposition from ashore, but were not required. Because of the flood stream the *Kenya* carried out the shoot at anchor, while the *Belfast* laid a dan buoy and held position on that. Spotting was carried out by an American Neptune aircraft, carrying RN aircrew from *Triumph* as observers.

Admiral Sir Alan West (right) hands over as Commander-in-Chief Fleet to Admiral Sir Jonathon Band, 2002. (*NATO*)

1955 The frigate HMAS *Queenborough*, the first Australian warship to visit London, arrived in the Pool of London.

1962 Fleet radar picket destroyer *Battleaxe* seriously damaged in head-on collision with frigate *Ursa* during night exercises off the Clyde Estuary. Six courts martial followed. *Battleaxe* CTL and scrapped at Blyth 1964. She had earlier collided with the destroyer *Scorpion* in 1954 and in 1960 with the minelayer *Apollo*.

See 1 May 1942, 2 October 1942, 11 February 1964.

1985 Admiral Sir John Fieldhouse promoted admiral of the fleet at the end of his appointment as First Sea Lord and on appointment as CDS. The first five-star submariner.

1999 Final performance of the Royal Tournament at Earl's Court, in which the Royal Navy had participated since 1887. The centrepiece since 1907 was the annual naval field gun competition, a relic of the Naval Brigades in the Boer War, between the Home Ports, later joined by the Fleet Air Arm. Devonport was the last winner.

2002 Admiral Sir Jonathon Band succeeded Admiral Sir Alan West as C-in-C Fleet and NATO Allied C-in-C Eastern Atlantic.

2002 *Fearless*, last surface steam ship in the Fleet, paid off at Portsmouth.

See 18 March 2002.

3 AUGUST

1666 *Orange Prize* and French *Victory* fought two Flushing capers in the western end of the English Channel, taking one.

1758 Vice-Admiral George Pocock (*Yarmouth*) fought Cdre Comte d'Ache (*Zodiaque*) 15 miles S.E. of Negapatam, Madras. Ships: *Elizabeth, Tiger, Weymouth, Yarmouth, Salisbury, Newcastle, Cumberland.* Frigate: *Queenborough*. Storeship: *Protector.* A severe but indecisive action.
Battle Honour: Negapatam 1758.
See 29 April 1758, 10 September 1759.

1801 *Pomone* (40) captured the French *Carrère* (38) S. of the Canale di Piombino, Italy.

1809 *Raven* engaged the batteries of Flushing and Breskens, during the Walcheren expedition.

1811 *Raven* and *Exertion, Alert* and *Princess Augusta,* hired cutters, with boats of *Quebec, Redbreast* and small craft based at Heligoland, captured four French gunboats at Nordeney, Friesland.

1835 Iron tanks, previously introduced to replace casks for stowage of water, issued for biscuit and meat.

Admiral of the Fleet Sir Henry Leach arrives in Portsmouth for the paying-off of HMS *Invincible*. (*RN*)

1846 Boats of *Royalist* destroyed two pirate prahus off the Mantanani Islands, Borneo.

1893 Wireless link established between HMY *Osborne* and Osborne House so that Queen Victoria could be kept informed of the health of the Prince of Wales.

1901 *Viper*, first turbine-driven destroyer, wrecked off Channel Islands.

1905 The Admiralty ordered that the title 'HMS' would in future be confined to commissioned ships wearing the White Ensign: 'My Lords are pleased . . . to direct that auxiliaries which belong to the Admiralty shall in future be styled "Royal Fleet Auxiliaries" . . . and whenever brevity is desired the initials "RFA" . . . should be used.' Although established by Order in Council on 22 March 1911, the RFA regards the earlier date as its start line. Circular Letter No. 9 T 3487/1905.

1914 HMCS *Rainbow*, second-class cruiser, sailed from Esquimalt on trade protection duties, charged by Ottawa to 'Remember Nelson and the British Navy. All Canada is watching.'
See 8 November 1910.

1916 Minesweeper *Clacton* torpedoed by U-73 off the Levant.

1918 UB-58 believed sunk in Otranto barrage, the anti-submarine barrier in the Southern Adriatic.

1918 Russian cruiser *Askold*, of five-funnel fame, taken over at Murmansk as *Glory IV*.

1919 Battleship *Valiant*, with destroyers *Venomous* and *Whitley*, anchored in River Mersey to protect the docks and to support the civil power during a strike by Liverpool City Police.

1941 First operational success by a Fighter Catapult Ship. Hurricane fighter W/9277 launched by *Maplin*, formerly

The carrier HMS *Invincible* paid off at Portsmouth in August 2005 after 25 years' service. Her sister ship and successor as Fleet flagship, HMS *Illustrious*, lies alongside ahead. (*RN*)

the Morant Steamship Company's *Erin*, shot down a Focke Wulf 200 Kondor attacking Convoy SL 81 from Freetown (50.33N, 19.40W). Pilot, Lt (A) R.W.H. Everett RNVR, bailed out, was rescued and DSO.

See 1 November 1941.

1941 *Hydrangea*, *Wanderer* and *St Albans* (Nor) sank U-401 S.W. of Ireland. Convoy SL 81.

1942 Submarine P 247 (later *Saracen*) sank U-335 off the Faroes (62.48N, 00.12W).

1943 U-647 mined. The only U-boat believed lost to the Faeroes–Iceland barrage – 'a singularly unproductive and defensive enterprise'.

1943 GC: Lt Hugh Randall Syme, GM and bar, RANVR, for bomb and mine disposal. (*Gazette* date.)

1944 Destroyer *Quorn* sunk by German one-man Neger in Seine Bay. Operation Neptune.

1945 Submarines *Tiptoe* and *Trump* attacked Japanese convoy in Java Sea N. of Sunda Strait. *Trump* sank the largest ship (6,000 tons) at 1650. At 1845 *Tiptoe* sank the next largest (4,000 tons) so gaining the distinction of having fired the last effective torpedo by a British submarine in the Second World War.

See 25 July 1945, 10 January 1969.

1953 *Dauntless*, WRNS new-entry TE, commissioned at Burghfield.

1966 The Admiralty Board sent a congratulatory telegram to Nelson's oldest surviving relative, his great-grandniece, Miss M. Crowther of Passford Hill, Boldre, Lymington, on her 100th birthday. Miss Crowther was descended from Nelson's youngest sister, Kitty.

2005 *Invincible*, Capt Neil Morisetti RN, (the fourteenth commanding officer since Capt M.H. Livesay RN commissioned her on 11 July 1980), paid off at Portsmouth after twenty-five years' service. She was the adopted ship of the city of Durham and had visited forty countries and steamed 850,000 miles. One of three RN ships with Falklands battle honours from 1914 and 1982 (*Bristol* and *Glasgow*).

See 3 May 1977, 11 July 1980, 6 October 2003, 1 August 2005.

4 August

1800 *Belliqueux* captured the French *Concorde*. *Bombay Castle* and *Exeter* Indiamen captured the French *Medée* 500 miles N.E. of Rio de Janeiro.

1801 Vice-Admiral Lord Nelson's indecisive bombardment of the Boulogne invasion flotilla.

1803 *Redbridge* schooner taken off Toulon. Her signals book captured and Mediterranean Fleet codes compromised.

1804 Adam, Admiral Viscount Duncan, victor of Camperdown, died, 'meeting the stroke of Death with the dignity of a hero and the resignation of a true and sincere Christian'. Nelson said, 'The name of Duncan will never be forgot by Britain and particularly by its navy'.

1809 Admiral Lord Gambier's court martial ended at Portsmouth. The Court found 'that his Lordship's conduct on that occasion, as well as his general conduct and proceedings as Commander-in-Chief of the Channel Fleet in Basque Road, between the 17th day of March and the 29th day of April, 1809, was marked by zeal, judgement, ability and an anxious attention to the welfare of his Majesty's service, and did adjudge him most honourably acquitted'.

See 11 April 1809, 26 July 1809.

1835 *Raleigh* (second of the name) survived a typhoon 160 miles S. 75° W. of Formosa.

1855 Boats of *Rattler* and the USS *Powhatan*, towed by *Eaglet*, captured ten pirate junks at Kau lan.

1858 *Staunch* destroyed two pirate junks and recaptured their prize off Tau Pung.

1903 HM King Edward VII opened the RN College, Osborne, on the Isle of Wight. Paid off 20 May 1921.

1910 Canada's first warship, the cruiser *Rainbow*, commissioned into the Naval Service of Canada at Portsmouth. She arrived at Esquimalt, British Columbia, on 7 November 1910. The second ship, the cruiser *Niobe*, commissioned at Devonport on 6 September and arrived at Halifax, Nova Scotia, 21 October 1910.

See 4 May 1910.

1914 The United Kingdom entered the First World War. At Scapa, Admiral Sir George Callaghan, C-in-C Home Fleets, hauled down his flag in the battleship *Iron Duke* on his unexpected supersession by Admiral Sir John Jellicoe as C-in-C Grand Fleet, a revival of the time-honoured title for Britain's main battle fleet in time of war but a dangerous time to change fleet commanders.

See 11 November 1918, 7 April 1919, 10 January 1920.

The strength of the Royal Navy was: 31 modern capital ships (20 Dreadnoughts, 9 battlecruisers, 2 Lord Nelsons), 12 Dreadnoughts and 1 battlecruiser building, 2 nearly completed Turkish and 1 Chilean Dreadnought, 39 Pre-Dreadnoughts, 50 cruisers, 94 light cruisers, 9 flotilla leaders, 237 torpedo boat destroyers, 107 torpedo boats, 16 sloops, 22 gunboats and 68 submarines.

Naval manpower, including RNAS, in first month of the First World War:

RN and RM	147,667
Retired officers and pensioners	6,970
Royal Fleet Reserve	27,395
Royal Naval Reserve	13,510
RNR (Trawler Section)	3,130
Royal Naval Volunteer Reserve	2,345
Total	201,017

'The Silent Service was not mute because it was absorbed in thought and study, but because it was weighted down by its daily routine and ever complicating and diversifying technique. We had competent administrators, brilliant experts of every description, unequalled navigators, good disciplinarians, fine sea officers, brave and resolute hearts; but at the outset of the conflict we had more captains of ships than captains of war. In this will be found the explanation of many untoward events' – Churchill, First Lord of the Admiralty.

Telegram to Prime Minister Asquith from Barbados government: 'Fear not, Asquith, Barbados is behind you.'

1915 Submarine C 33 lost in North Sea, working with *Malta* in an anti-U-boat combined operation.

HMS *Vanguard* aground at Portsmouth Point, 1960. (*NMRN*)

1918 British forces arrived at Baku, Caspian Sea.

1921 Admiral the Marquess of Milford Haven, lately HSH Prince Louis of Battenberg, who had been forced to resign as First Sea Lord in 1914 because of his German descent, was promoted admiral of the fleet on, exceptionally, the Retired List. The only precedent for this was the promotion of Admiral Sir James Gordon on 30 January 1868. Prince Louis was the father of Admiral of the Fleet Earl Mountbatten of Burma.

See 28 October 1914, 11 September 1921.

1940 FAA aircraft attacked barges and oil tanks at Rotterdam.

1943 Sunderland G/423 (RCAF) sank the supply U-boat U-489 in Atlantic (61.11N, 14.38W) but was brought down herself. Her crew and that of the submarine were rescued by *Orwell* and *Castleton*. This was the seventh Type XIV to be sunk. Only ten had been built.

1943 Monitor *Roberts* bombarded the road and railway at Taormina, Sicily.

1943 Destroyer *Arrow* damaged beyond repair in explosion of ammunition ship *Fort la Montée* in Algiers harbour.

1960 *Discovery* became flagship of Admiral Commanding Reserves until his post was abolished in 1976.

1960 *Vanguard*, Britain's last twentieth-century battleship, towed from Fareham Creek bound for shipbreakers at Faslane and briefly went aground off the Customs Watch House in Old Portsmouth near the Still and West tavern on Portsmouth Point. Similar reluctance displayed by battleship *Warspite*.

See 23 April 1947, 9 August 1960.

1967 Helicopters from the carrier *Hermes* landed Royal Hong Kong Police on top of skyscrapers in anti-communist raids. Carrier *Bulwark* stood by with 40 Cdo embarked during riots 30 May to 12 June.

2001 His Majesty Sultan Haji Hassanal Bolkiah Mu'izzaddin Waddaulah Sultan and Yang Di-pertuan of Brunei Darussalam appointed an honorary admiral in Her Majesty's Fleet.

See 2 August 1889, 1 May 1951, 16 February 1953, 2 July 1958, 25 June 1975, 31 July 1987.

2004 Royal Navy, represented by Admiral Sir Alan West, First Sea Lord, received the Freedom of Gibraltar on the tercentenary of its capture in 1704 by a squadron commanded by Admiral Sir George Rooke that included the third rate *Grafton* (70). The Type 23 frigate *Grafton* fired a 21-gun salute and provided a Guard that marched through the town.

Rock was captured on 24 July 1704. The eleven days' date difference is due to the change from the Julian 'old style' calendar to the Gregorian 'new style' calendar in 1752. The Royal Marines received the Freedom of Gibraltar on 28 October 1996.

See 24 July 1704.

2005 *Illustrious* succeeded her sister ship *Invincible*, which had paid off at Portsmouth the previous day, as Fleet flagship. Rededicated at sea off Portsmouth.

5 August

1583 First settlers arrived in Newfoundland. *Golden Hind, Delight, Squirrel* and *Swallow*.

1781 Vice-Admiral Hyde Parker (*Fortitude*) fought Rear-Admiral Johan Zoutman (*Admiraal de Ruyter*) on the eastern end of the Dogger Bank. Ships: *Berwick, Dolphin, Buffalo, Fortitude, Princess Amelia, Preston, Bienfaisant*. Frigates, etc., with fleet: *Artois, Belle Poule, Cleopatra, Latona, Surprise*. Escorts to convoy of 200 merchantmen: *Tartar, Alert, Cabot* brigs, *Leith* armed ship, *Busy, Sprightly* cutters. Regiment: 97th. An impetuous and unscientific engagement in the style of the old Dutch wars, when two rather elderly squadrons pounded one another severely. The Dutch retired to the Texel and the British convoy got through.
Battle Honour: Dogger Bank 1781.

1781 *Maidstone* captured the American privateer *Montgomery* off Newfoundland.

1798 *Indefatigable* captured the French *Heureux* off Bayonne and wrecked her prize, *Canada*.

1799 Admiral of the Fleet Earl Howe, 'George III's favourite admiral if no one else's' (Rodger), died. It was said of Howe that he 'never smiled unless a battle was at hand'. In 1765 he was appointed Treasurer of the Navy and in 1776 Vice-Admiral of the North American station. He was a firm disciplinarian but nevertheless very popular with the sailors: 'Father of his fleet and the darling of British seamen' – Dr Thomas Trotter. He commanded the Channel Fleet in 1794 at the Glorious First of June. In 1797 he returned to Portsmouth to preside over the re-establishment of discipline during the Spithead mutiny.

When his first appointment as a Flag Officer was questioned in Parliament, Lord Hawke 'rose up and said, "I advised His Majesty to make the appointment. I have tried my Lord Howe on many occasions; he never asked me how he was to execute any Service entrusted to his charge, but always went straight forward and performed it"'. The King's intention to give Howe the Garter was thwarted in the most unfortunate way by the Prime Minister promising the only vacancy to the Duke of Portland, with the result that although the Admiral was eventually nominated he was never installed. A marquisate was offered but declined.

1813 Landing party from *Milford* and *Weazle* destroyed a battery and a signal tower at Ragosniza (Rogoznica), Adriatic.

1834 The C-in-C The Nore, Vice-Admiral Sir Richard King, died of cholera at Admiralty House, Sheerness. Born 28 November 1774. Captain of *Achille* (74) in Collingwood's line at Trafalgar. C-in-C East Indies 1816. Buried in All Saints church, Eastchurch, Isle of Sheppey.

See 4 May 1810, 2 May 1818, 20 September 1839, 2 July 1853.

1858 First Atlantic cable laid by *Agamemnon* and the USS *Niagara*.

1864 White Ensign reserved to HM ships – and incidentally to RYS – the Blue to vessels commanded by officers of RNR and the Red to British merchantmen, and admirals' flags and commodores' pennants defined in permutations of St George's cross and red balls.

See 9 July 1864.

1864 *Grasshopper* destroyed four pirate junks at Kau lan.

1914 *Lance*, destroyer, fired the first naval shot in anger in the First World War in sinking the German auxiliary minelayer *Königin Luise* off the Suffolk coast.

See 2 January 1793, 6 August 1914.

1914 Light cruiser *Gloucester* detected *Goeben* in Messina by wireless interception (first RN use of ESM in war).

1915 One of the first naval courts martial held on shore. Skipper James Sadler RNR of HM Trawler *Vale of Leven* dismissed the Service at RNB Devonport for being drunk on board and, to the prejudice of good order and naval discipline, for bringing on board two women 'of loose character and behaviour' and keeping them in his cabin until the afternoon of the

The light cruiser HMS *Gloucester* was shadowing the German *Goeben* and *Breslau* in the Mediterranean at the outbreak of war in August 1914. (*NMRN*)

following day. Things had changed since Prince William Henry commanded *Andromeda*.

See 1 August 1788, 16 March 1915.

1917 *Chagford* torpedoed by U-44, 120 miles N.W. of Tory Island, N. Ireland. Abandoned and sunk on 7 August.

1918 Armoured cruiser *Suffolk* sent from Hong Kong to Vladivostok to guard large stocks of military stores and ammunition landed to support anti-Bolshevik White Russian operations. A large Czech army holding a line W. of the Urals urgently needed artillery which could not reach them from Europe. *Suffolk* fitted-out and manned an armoured train mounting one 6-in and four 12-pdr naval guns commanded by 'an energetic and enterprising officer from the *Suffolk*', Cdr J. Wolfe-Murray, which set off across the Trans-Siberian Railway. By mid-October the train was at Ufa, 4,350 miles from Vladivostok and it was soon in action on the Omsk front. 'It is unlikely that naval officers and men have ever before been in action so far from salt water' – Roskill, *Naval Policy between the Wars*, vol.1 pp.165–80. 'The Navy had often landed men to assist in military operations, but never before has such a party gone so far from its parent ship' – Newbolt, *Naval Operations*, vol.5, p.326.

See 16 February 1909, 3 January 1919, 6 April 1919, 9 July 1959, 27 May 1960.

1919 GC (ex-AM): Lt E.G. Abbon for saving life after explosion in ex-German *Baden* at Invergordon.

1943 *Red Gauntlet*, minesweeping trawler, sunk by the German S-86 off Harwich.

1944 Frigate *Stayner* and destroyer *Wensleydale* sank U-671 off Boulogne.

1980 Destroyer *Glasgow* began three days' hurricane relief at St Lucia. Hurricane Allen.

2000 Temp-Lt Alec Guinness de Cuffe RNVR, later Sir Alec Guinness, died aged 86 at Midhurst and was buried at Petersfield. He commanded a LCI(L) at the invasion of Sicily and supported Yugoslav partisans in the Adriatic.

See 10 July 1943.

2003 Norman Hancock, RCNC, Director of Warship Design 1969–76, died. Designer of the Swiftsure-class SSN and project director for the *Invincible* and Broadsword-class Type 22 frigates.

6 AUGUST

1497 Cabot (*Matthew*) returned to Bristol after first English voyage of discovery, to Newfoundland.

1798 *Espoir* captured the Genoese pirate *Liguria* 12 miles S. of Marbella, Spain. One officer of the 28th Regiment was present.

1805 *Blenheim* (74), escorting a convoy, beat off the French *Marengo* (80) and *Belle-Poule* (40) 1,380 miles E. of Mauritius.

1826 *Hope* captured the Brazilian slaver *Prince of Guinea* off Wyhdah, Dahomey.

1861 The first edition of Queen's Regulations and Admiralty Instructions (QR &AI) Ch.44 Art. 43 read: 'The Officers, Petty Officers, and Seamen of the Fleet are not to wear moustaches or beards. Moustaches, but not beards, may be worn by the Officers and Men belonging to the Royal Marine Corps'. This order may have been triggered by Vice-Admiral Constantine Richard Moorsom who had just died. On his return from operations in the Black Sea some years earlier, the then Capt Moorsom, displaying hirsute 'fixings', had had the temerity to call on the First Naval Lord, at the Admiralty; visible to Admiral Sir Maurice Fitzhardinge Berkeley 'were the eyes, nose and forehead . . . but very little else of his face'. The First Sea Lord, 'pale with rage and astonishment, almost indeed bereft of speech', waved Moorsom to the door with the cutting order 'Horseguards next door!'– Vice-Admiral Humphrey Hugh Smith, *An Admiral Never Forgets*.

See 24 June 1869.

1865 Fred T. Jane born; founder of *Jane's Fighting Ships*.

See 8 March 1916.

1885 First night gunnery practice by searchlight – *Alexandra*.

1910 *Lion* launched at Devonport. With *Princess Royal* (Vickers 1911) and *Queen Mary* (Palmers 1912), the first battlecruisers with 13.5-in

HMS *Starling* (1942), a modified Black Swan-class sloop. (*NMRN*)

guns and centre-line turrets. First British warships to cost over £2 million.

See 4 September 1913.

1914 *Amphion*, light cruiser, sunk 30 miles E. of Aldeburgh by mines laid by *Königin Luise*. The first British warship sunk in action in the First World War. Staff Paymaster Joseph T. Gedge (after whom the Gedge Medal was instituted), first officer of all British fighting services killed in the war. One hundred and fifty men and eighteen prisoners from *Königin Luise* lost.

See 5 August 1914, 9 November 1918, 1 May 2008.

1914 Light cruiser *Bristol* fought German light cruiser *Karlsruhe* 250 miles N.E. of Eleuthera Island, Bahamas. *Karlsruhe* escaped.

1914 Battleship *Triumph* commissioned from Reserve in Hong Kong. Skeleton crew found from China river gunboats but, when she was still undermanned, the C-in-C China Station, Vice-Admiral Sir Martyn Jerram, appealed to the Army for help. The ship sailed with two officers, 100 rank and file and six signallers from the Duke of Cornwall's Light Infantry. Three days later the Canadian Pacific liner *Empress of Asia*, hurriedly converted into an AMC, followed *Triumph* to sea with a crew found largely by the Royal Garrison Artillery and twenty-five soldiers from the 40th Pathans.

See 2 October 1939.

1915 Suvla landing began in Dardanelles campaign. Ended on 15 August.

1915 First flight of a seaplane from a ship using take-off trolleys; a Sopwith Schneider single-seat floatplane piloted by Ft-Lt (later Air Marshal Sir) William Welsh took off from the converted Cunarder *Campania*. Seaplanes were hydrodynamically inefficient because fixed floats degraded flying performance; deployed over the North Sea they could not match the Zeppelin in speed, altitude or rate of climb, much to Jellicoe's regret. The little aircraft also could not cope with any sea state and the floats frequently broke off under stress of taking-off and landing. One part solution was to launch seaplanes directly from a ship. Welsh's flight was the first to employ wheeled trolleys or dollies attached to the floats which permitted operations in a rougher sea state than hitherto. Landing retained its character-forming qualities. *Campania* was the first ship to be termed a 'fleet carrier' – a title given her by the CO, Wing Captain (later AVM Sir) Oliver Schwann RN.

See 5 November 1918.

1918 Destroyer *Comet* torpedoed by Austrian submarine in Mediterranean.

1940 German Type C magnetic mine exploded under examination in mining shed at *Vernon*: five killed.

1941 'Rendering Mines Safe' teams became the Land Incident Section of DTM.

1942 Submarine *Thorn* sunk N. of Derna by Italian TB *Pegaso*.

1942 Destroyers *Croome*, *Sikh*, *Tetcott*, *Zulu* and Wellington M/221 sank U-372 off Jaffa (32.00N, 34.00E). *Sikh* and *Zulu* both lost next month, 14 September 1942.

1942 *Assiniboine* (RCN) sank U-210 in N. Atlantic (54.25N, 39.37W). Convoy SC 94.

1944 Frigate *Loch Killin* and *Starling*, sloop, sank U-736 in the Bay of Biscay.

1944 Light cruiser *Bellona* and destroyers *Tartar*, *Ashanti*, with *Haida* and *Iroquois*, (both RCN) sank all four ships of a convoy and three of the escort, M-263, M-486 and SG-3 (ex-French *Sans-Pareil*) off Ile d'Yeu, Bay of Biscay.

1950 A bronze tablet in honour of the 190 officers and men lost in the armed merchant cruiser, *Jervis Bay*, sunk in November 1940 by the German pocket battleship Admiral Scheer, unveiled in a service at St George's church, RN Barracks, Chatham, by Admiral Sir Stuart Bonham-Carter, and dedicated by the Venerable Archdeacon L. Coulshaw, Chaplain of the Fleet. Eighteen of the thirty-five survivors from the ship were present.

See 5 November 1940.

1975 Carrier *Eagle* towed from Portsmouth to Plymouth where she lay for six years being cannibalised to keep *Ark Royal* running.

See 26 January 1972, 4 December 1978.

7 AUGUST

1657 Robert Blake, parliamentary 'General-at-Sea', died on board the *George* one day out from Plymouth: 'as we came to entering The Sound, death seized him, and he departed this life about 10 o'clock in the morning.'

See 10 March 1650, 20 April 1657, 9 September 1661, 27 February 1945.

His bowels were buried before the Chancel of St Andrew's church. The body, encased in lead, was taken back to the *George* which sailed for the Thames arriving off Gravesend on 17 August where it was transferred to the *Colchester*, commanded by his nephew, Samuel Blake. The admiral lay in state in the Great Hall of the Queen's House at Greenwich from 19 August to 4 September when he was taken 'in a great procession of barges' to Westminster to be buried in Henry VII's Chapel. Here he lay until 9 September 1661 when, together with the bodies of Cromwell, Deane, Pym and others his body was dug up and thrown into a pit outside the Abbey. 'The nation thus honoured Blake . . . as an admiral, only to be surpassed by Nelson. For he is in a very real sense one of the founders of the Navy, and an inspiration to the silent service' – Revd J.R. Powell, *Robert Blake*, pp.308–9.

1781 *Helena*, reinforced by *Repulse* and *Vanguard*, gunboats and boats of ships at Gibraltar, fought fourteen Spanish gunboats in Gibraltar Bay.

1807 *Hydra* bombarded the defences at Bagur, Spain. Her boats cut out the Spanish *Prince Eugene*, *Belle Caroline* and *Carmen del Rosario*.

1807 Dress and undress uniform introduced for masters and pursers with buttons of the Navy and the Victualling Boards respectively.

1815 Napoleon sailed from Plymouth in *Northumberland* to exile in St Helena.

See 20 February 1900.

1826 Third-class engineer Thomas Brown became first RN Engineer Officer.

1844 *Phlegethon* (Ben. Mar.), *Jolly Bachelor* and boats of *Dido* destroyed the Sakarran pirates' stronghold at Patusan.

1853 *Caesar* (90), second-rate, launched at Pembroke Dockyard after a seventeen-day operation to send her afloat. The ship was christened on 21 July but stopped after travelling half her length down the slip. Left Pembroke under tow of *Magicienne* 6 October 1853 and fitted out at Portsmouth.

See 10 September 1874.

1864 *Grasshopper* destroyed twenty pirate junks at Kau lan, and burned the village of Pak shui.

Napoleon (shown standing in the stern) is transferred to the *Northumberland*, 1815. (*NMRN 1976/300*)

Pembroke Dockyard took seventeen days to launch the steam two-decker *Caesar* in 1853. She was christened on 21 July but the ship stopped after travelling half her length down the slip. She was eventually floated on 7 August and was fitted out at Portsmouth. (*Author*)

1873 Formation of the Royal Navy Artillery Volunteers. Officers wore RNR stripes in silver, and silver buttons with RN and AV on either side of the anchor.

1914 Rear-Admiral Ernest Troubridge broke off the chase of *Goeben* and *Breslau*, which reached Constantinople and reinforced Turkey. This led to his being court-martialled but acquitted. Capt Howard Kelly in *Gloucester* continued to pursue the 'foe then flying' and, with his brother Joe in *Dublin*, he was the only star in a dismal episode.

See 21 December 1747, 9 November 1914, 9 July 1917.

1914 Armoured cruiser *Suffolk* surprised German light cruiser *Karlsruhe* turning the liner *Kronprinz Wilhelm* into an AMC, but though reinforced by light cruiser *Bristol*, could not catch either.

1940 Nine Skua aircraft of 801 Sqn (Hatston) destroyed petrol tanks at Dolvik (Hardangersfjord).

1941 Submarine *Severn* sank the Italian S/M *Michele Bianchi* (34.48N, 13.04W).

1941 Gold stripes to be worn on only the outer cuff, a wartime economy measure.

1942 Second Battle of Barfleur (the first in 1692). This was a major engagement of Coastal Forces.

1943 45 RM Cdo formed from 5th RM Battalion.

1980 *Scylla* began five days of hurricane relief work in Cayman Islands. Hurricane Allen.

Convoy SC 94, August 1942

Convoy SC 94 comprised thirty-three ships escorted by one destroyer and three corvettes. It was a slow, east-bound Atlantic convoy, and met problems caused by fog in the first few days. On 5 August, the fog began to clear, and stragglers rejoined the main body. On that day, a U-boat sank one merchant ship, and then homed other U-boats on to the convoy. On the 6th a series of attacks started. The Canadian destroyer *Assiniboine* had a running gun battle with U-210 and sank her after ramming her twice, but was so damaged that she had to return to base. The slower corvettes held off the attackers until late on 8th, when five ships were lost in one attack, and another sank later after falling out of the convoy. The *Dianthus*, however, sank U-379 after depth-charge attacks and ramming her five times.

Two destroyers joined the escort on 8th/9th, and the fog cleared sufficiently for air cover to be provided. However, four more ships were lost before the air cover arrived on 9th. On 13th the convoy reached British ports, having lost one-third of its original strength. Yet, the sparse escort did well to sink two U-boats and damage four others, and to hold off the repeated attacks of no fewer than eighteen U-boats without air assistance.

2005 Seven Russian submariners, trapped for three days on the seabed in their Priz AS-28 submersible caught up in fishing nets 625ft below the surface 60 miles off the Kamchatka Peninsula, were rescued by the Royal Navy's Scorpio 45 remotely operated vessel.

See 12 August 2000, 5 October 2005.

The small team, led by Cdr Ian Riches RN, from the Submarine Escape, Rescue and Abandonment IPT, Abbey Wood, with the Scorpio and its civilian crew from James Fisher Defence Ltd of Glasgow, flew to Petropavlovsk on 5 August in a RAF C-17 aircraft piloted by Sqn Ldr Keith Hewitt. The prompt appeal for assistance from the Russians was inspired by personal contacts made during the three-yearly NATO-led submarine rescue exercise, Sorbet Royal, held a month earlier in the Mediterranean in which the Russian Navy had taken part for the first time. Their participation was one of the happier consequences of the unsuccessful RFN attempts to rescue the crew of the SSGN *Kursk* in 2000.

8 AUGUST

1758 Cdre the Hon. Richard Howe (*Pallas*) and Lt-Gen. Thomas Bligh destroyed the port of Cherbourg. Ships: *Essex, Jason, Montagu, Portland, Rochester.* Frigates: *Active, Brilliant, Flamborough, Fowey, Maidstone, Pallas, Renown, Richmond, Rose, Success, Tartar.* Sloops: *Diligence, Saltash, Speedwell, Swallow, Swan.* Fireships: *Pluto, Salamander.* Bombs: *Furnace, Grenado, Infernal.* Bomb tenders: *Endeavour, Nancy, Neptune* and ten others.

1796 *Mermaid* fought the French *Vengeance* off Basse Terre, Guadeloupe.

1798 Sir Edward Pellew (*Indefatigable*) captured the French corvette *Vaillante* a few miles N. of Cape Machichaco, Spain. French ship taken into the Service as *Danae* (20) and taken by mutineers.

See 17 March 1800.

1815 *Malta* and *Berwick* at the reduction of Gaeta, Italy.

1848 Capt Frederick Marryat, naval novelist, died. His dirk – 'with plenty of gold on the scabbard' – then owned by his grandson, Fleet Surg H.L. Morris, went down in the battlecruiser *Indefatigable* at Jutland.

See 10 February 1816, 27 April 1916.

Poster for the film adaptation of *The Cruel Sea*, 1953. (*NMRN 1993/121(3)*)

1892 TBD accepted by Admiralty as classification of a new type of vessel, the Torpedo Boat Destroyer. Her successors, evolved partly for her destruction, were simply 'Destroyers'.

1914 Cruiser *Astraea* bombarded Dar-es-Salaam.

1914 U-13 made first submerged attack of First World War, firing a torpedo which missed battleship *Monarch* off Fair Isle.

1915 Submarine E 11, Lt-Cdr Martin Nasmith, VC, sank the Turkish battleship *Barbarousse Hairedene* 5 miles N.E. of Gallipoli and 121 more vessels in the next eight months.

See 27 April 1915.

1915 AMC *India* sunk by U-22 in the entrance to Vestfjord.

1915 *Ramsey*, armed boarding steamer, sunk by the German *Meteor* off Moray Firth.

1917 VC: Lt Charles George Bonner, DSC, RNR, and Petty Officer Ernest Herbert Pitcher, decoy ship *Dunraven*, Capt Gordon Campbell VC, DSO, RN, following an extended engagement with UC-71 off Ushant (48.00N, 07.37W). *Dunraven*, whose ship's company had turned over from the *Pargust*, was disabled by gunfire and torpedo attack by an enemy that had not been decoyed. She sank under tow in (48.38N, 05.28W).

The VC was awarded to Bonner, the First Lieutenant, and to the after gun's crew which, by secret ballot under Article 13 of the Statutes of the VC, selected Pitcher, the captain of the gun; all of his gun's crew received the CGM. 'Greater bravery than was shown by all officers and men on this occasion', said the King, 'can hardly be conceived' (Campbell, *My Mystery Ships*, p.284). Three DSCs and three Bars, twenty-one DSMs and three Bars and fourteen Mentions in Despatches completed the awards. Bonner named his baby son Gordon Dunraven, who was later to serve as a surgeon-lieutenant RNVR.

See 22 March 1916, 17 February 1917, 7 June 1917.

1917 VC: Lt Charles George Bonner RNR, and PO Ernest Pitcher (*Dunraven*). *Dunraven*, a Q-ship, fought a prolonged engagement with UC-71 off Ushant (48.00N, 07.37W). Disabled and taken in tow by *Christopher*, but sank on the 10th in (48.38N, 05.28W).

1918 First magnetic mines laid, off Dunkirk ('234 Mk M sinker').

1918 Zeppelin L-70 shot down by RAF over Immingham. Trawler *Scomber* recovered code books.

1918 Destroyer *Opossum* sank UC-49, already damaged by one of her own mines.

1922 Cruiser *Raleigh*, Capt Arthur Bromley RN, flagship of Admiral Sir William Pakenham on the NA&WI Station, was wrecked in thick weather off Point Amour, Belle Isle Strait, Labrador. Ten lives lost. The first RN flagship lost in peacetime since the battleship *Victoria* in the Mediterranean in 1893. Portsmouth courts martial 25, 26 and 27 October: Captain (Reprimand and dismissed his ship); NO Cdr Leslie Charles Bott (Severe Reprimand and dismissed HMS *Victory*). The OOW was Sub-Lt Charles Lambe, a future First Sea Lord, who clearly survived in all respects. Her upright hull was blown up in 1928 by light cruiser *Calcutta*, Capt A.B. Cunningham RN, the NA&WI flagship. An earlier *Raleigh* had been wrecked on the China coast in 1857. Sister ship *Effingham* was wrecked off Narvik 1940, the first RN cruiser lost in the Second World War.

See 14 April 1857, 22 June 1893, 30 May 1906, 29 May 1922, 2 July 1928, 18 May 1940.

1942 Corvette *Dianthus* sank U-379 in Atlantic having rammed her four times (57.11N, 30.57W). Convoy SC 94.

1942 Submarine *Turbulent* put an end to Italian destroyer *Strale*, aground off Cape Bon since 21 June.

1944 Corvette *Regina* (RCN) sunk by U-667 off Trevose Head. Convoy EBC 66.

1944 Battleship *Valiant* damaged in collapse of floating dock at Trincomalee. Two damaged propellers removed at Suez; returned to duty on remaining two.

1945 *Ocean*, light fleet carrier, commissioned by Capt Caspar John RN.

See 8 July 1944, 3 December 1945, 30 September 1998.

1968 Admiral of the Fleet Sir Algernon Willis inaugurated the last two 15-in naval guns, brought from Shoeburyness and mounted outside the Imperial War Museum. One was mounted in battleship *Ramillies* and saw service in the Mediterranean 1940–1. The other was in battleship *Resolution* 1915–38, then transferred to monitor *Roberts*, which bombarded German positions at Normandy and Walcheren.

1968 Leander-class frigate *Scylla* launched at Plymouth, the last ship to be built in a Royal Yard.

See 27 March 2004.

1979 Lt-Cdr Nicholas Monsarrat, RNVR, ('Montserrat' on birth certificate) author of *The Cruel Sea* (1951), 'one of the greatest triumphs of fiction in the English language' (DNB), died. His ashes were scattered at sea by the Royal Navy.

2005 Offshore patrol vessel *Leeds Castle*, Lt-Cdr Christopher Goodsell RN, paid off at Portsmouth after twenty-four years' service.

2006 HM The Queen appointed members of the Royal family to be patrons to various naval commands 'in recognition of the strong links between the Royal Navy and the Royal family'. The new Royal Patrons were:

The Prince of Wales	Commodore-in-Chief, Plymouth
Prince William	Commodore-in-Chief, Scotland, and Commodore-in-Chief, Submarines
Prince Harry	Commodore-in-Chief, Small Ships and Diving
The Duchess of Cornwall	Commodore-in-Chief, Naval Medical Services and Commodore in Chief, Naval Chaplaincy Services (2 August 2008)
The Duke of York	Commodore-in-Chief, Fleet Air Arm
The Earl of Wessex	Commodore-in-Chief, Royal Fleet Auxiliary
The Princess Royal	Commodore-in-Chief, Portsmouth
Prince Michael of Kent	Commodore-in-Chief, Maritime Reserves

9 AUGUST

1573 Drake returned from his first voyage in command, arriving from Nombre Dios at Plymouth 'at about sermon time when the news of our Captain's return so speedily passed over the Church that few or none remained with the preacher'.

1666 'Sir Robert Holmes his Bonfire' in Terschelling Roads. Ships: *Advice, Assurance, Dragon, Fanfan, Garland, Edward and Eve, Hampshire, Pembroke, Seaflower, Sweepstake, Tiger.* Fireships (expended): *Fox, Lizard, Richard, Samuel.*

1742 Cdr Smith Callis made post for having destroyed five Spanish galleys with the *Duke* fireship in the nominally neutral port of St Tropez on 16 June 1742. Presented by the King with a specially minted medal and a gold chain on which to hang it.
See 11 April 1809.

1775 James Cook made post, at Levee at St James's.

1780 A convoy of sixty-three sail for the East and West Indies, escorted by *Ramillies, Southampton* and *Thetis*, taken by a Franco-Spanish fleet 300 miles N.N.E. of Madeira. Fifty-five of the convoy were captured.

1781 *Iris* (32) captured the American *Trumbull* (28) off the Delaware.

1799 *Speedy* captured three Spanish tartans in a bay E. of Cape de Gata.

1810 *Caroline*, Capt Christopher Cole, with *Piedmontaise* and *Barracouta* captured Banda Neira Island, Moluccas, East Indies, their first objective – Amboyna – having been taken on 17 February. Only 180 of a landing party of 480 could get ashore but they routed 1,500 Dutch. A small operation but it caught the public imagination and Capt Cole received the gold medal and a knighthood.
Battle Honour: Banda Neira 1810.

1854 VC: Cdr J. Bythesea and Stoker W. Johnstone (*Arrogant*) overcame five soldiers with important dispatches on the island of Wardo in the Baltic and brought them all back safely. William Johnstone ('probably a Swede') was the first lower-deck recipient of the VC.

1855 Bombardment of Sveaborg (Suomenlinna) by Rear-Adms the Hon. Richard Dundas (*Duke of Wellington*) and Charles Penaud (*Tourville*).
Battle Honour: Baltic 1854–5.

1856 *Cambridge*, commissioned as Plymouth gunnery training ship. Ashore in 1907.
See 9 August 1956, 30 March 2001.

1862 *Snake* destroyed four pirate junks in Sandy Bay, St John Island, Virgin Islands. Operation lasted three days.

1872 Cookery school established at Portsmouth.
See 4 November 1994.

1914 Light cruiser *Birmingham* rammed and sank U-15 120 miles E.S.E. of Orkney (58.35N, 01.56E). First U-boat sunk by RN.

1914 German battlecruiser *Goeben* and light cruiser *Breslau* passed the Dardanelles despite the Mediterranean Fleet. 'The explanation is satisfactory but the result unsatisfactory' – Churchill.
See 7 August 1914.

1915 Destroyer *Lynx* sunk by mine laid in Moray Firth by *Meteor*, which was sunk on her way home to Germany by Harwich Force.

1916 B 10 sunk by Austrian aircraft at Venice, while under repair. The first submarine to be sunk by enemy aircraft, albeit in harbour.

1917 Destoyer *Recruit* sunk by UB-16 in North Sea.

1926 Submarine H 26 sank in No. 2 Basin at Devonport Dockyard during a refit. One senior rate and five dockyard workers lost.

1942 Night action off Savo Island (09.15S, 159.40E): US and Australian forces fought Japanese surface forces. RAN Ships: *Australia, Canberra, Hobart. Canberra* damaged and abandoned, sunk by USS *Selfridge*.
Battle Honour: Savo Island 1942.

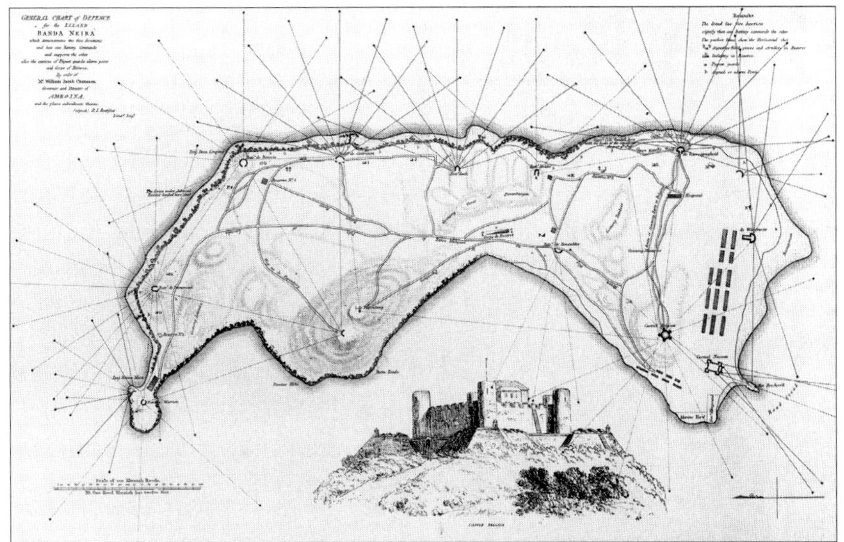

Map of the island of Banda Neira with the defensive batteries used after its capture, 1810. (*NMRN 1978/322(4)*)

Allied amphibious forces were operating off Guadalcanal. The alarm was raised by a US destroyer at 0143 on 9 August but the Japanese were then close to the USS *Chicago* and HMAS *Canberra*. *Canberra* was hit by shells and torpedoes and had to be sunk later. No enemy report was made, and the Japanese force was therefore able to come upon another force of Allied cruisers by surprise. Two American cruisers were hit and capsized, the third later blew up. The Japanese failed to take advantage of their success and retired without attacking the transports. Only the US cruiser *San Juan* and the Australian cruisers *Hobart* and *Australia* and eight destroyers were undamaged. Faulty intelligence had led to bad disposition, and nearly to a complete disaster. In commemoration of HMAS *Canberra*, the USN renamed a Baltimore-class cruiser the *Canberra*, and she is the only USN ship named after a foreign capital city.

1943 Light cruisers *Aurora* and *Penelope* bombarded Castellamare.

1943 Submarine *Simoom* sank the Italian destroyer *Vincenzo Gioberti* 5 miles S.W. of La Spezia. The forty-fourth and last Italian destroyer to be sunk before Italy surrendered.

1945 TF 37 (BPF) and US 3rd Fleet continued attacks on Japan. Kamaishi bombarded, airstrikes along east coast, north of Yokohama.

VC: T/Lt (A) Robert Hampton Gray, DSC, RCNVR (*Formidable* – 1841 Corsair Sqn) at the sinking of the Japanese destroyers *Amakusa* and *Inagi* off Japan (38.26N, 141.30E).

The citation reads 'for great valour in leading from the aircraft carrier *Formidable* an attack on the Japanese destroyers in Onagawa Wan, in the Japanese island of Honshu. In the face of fire from shore batteries and a heavy concentration of fire from 5 warships, Lieutenant Gray pressed home his attack, flying very low in order to ensure success. Although he was hit and his aircraft was in flames, he obtained at least one direct hit sinking the destroyer. Lieutenant Gray has consistently shown a brilliant fighting spirit and most inspiring leadership.' The awards of both the VC and DSC were posthumous. His younger brother, John Gray, was killed while serving in RAF Bomber Command.

1946 The new battleship *Vanguard*, Capt W.G. Agnew RN, entered Portsmouth for the first time and secured alongside South Railway Jetty. She had been accepted from John Brown's on 9 August while at anchor at Spithead.

See 4 August 1960.

1952 A flight of four Sea Furies of 802 NAS from the carrier *Ocean*, led by Lt Peter 'Hoagy' Carmichael, attacked by eight MiG-15s over Korea. Carmichael destroyed one – the first MiG-15 shot down by the Royal Navy and remarkably by a piston-engined aircraft.

See 29 June 1950–3.

1956 HM Gunnery School, Devonport closed. Plymouth gunnery range at Wembury commissioned as *Cambridge*.

See 9 August 1856, 30 March 2001.

1960 The end of the battleship era in the Royal Navy. *Vanguard* arrived Faslane for disposal.

See 4 August 1960.

1967 First radar-fitted ASW helicopter entered service. Westland Wessex HAS 3 with 814 NAS.

1990 Operations consequent upon Iraq's invasion of Kuwait on 2 August authorised in Indian Ocean and Persian Gulf. Operation Granby.

See 1 August 1990, 28 February 1991.

10 August

1512 *Regent* (ex-*Grace Dieu* and the Navy's first two-decker) fought the French *Marie la Cordelière* in Camaret Bay, near Brest. Both ships blew up, with, it is said, 700 English and 900 French.

1678 Royal Observatory, Greenwich founded.

1778 Cdre Sir Edward Vernon (*Ripon*) fought a French squadron of five ships under Capt Tronjoly (*Brilliant*) off Pondicherry, India. Ships: *Cormorant, Coventry, Ripon, Seahorse, Valentine* (Indiaman).

1780 *Flora* (36) and armed with the new carronade, captured the French *Nymphe* (32) 9 miles W. of Ushant.

1794 Capitulation of Calvi, Corsica, to the forces under Lt-Gen. the Hon. Charles Stuart and Capt Horatio Nelson (*Agamemnon*). Guns were landed from the fleet. The French *Melpomene* and *Mignonne* taken. Ships: *Agamemnon, Britannia, Victory*. Frigates: *Aigle, Aimable, Dido, Dolphin, Fox, Imperieuse, Inflexible, Lowestoffe, Lutine*. Regiments: 18th, 30th, 51st.

See 18 June 1794, 12 July 1794.

1800 Loss of the troopship *Dromedary*, near Trinidad, her bowsprit and foremast providing a bridge to the shore for over 500 soldiers and their families.

1805 *Phoenix* (36) captured the larger French *Didon* (44) 150 miles west of Cape Finisterre, the sick quitting their cots to join in.
Battle Honour: *Didon* 1805.

1813 Cdre Sir James Yeo (*Wolfe*) engaged the American Lake Squadron, under Cdre Isaac Chauncey, on Lake Ontario, capturing the *Growler* and *Julia* schooners.

1865 Admiral of the Fleet Sir Francis Austen died. He was born 23 April 1774, entered the Royal Naval Academy in 1786 and was made post in 1800. From 1815 he was unemployed on half pay but rose automatically through the flag ranks. In December 1844, as a vice-admiral but not having put on his uniform for over thirty years, he was appointed C-in-C North America and West Indies and celebrated his 71st birthday, sailing out in *Vengeance* to take up his post. He hauled down his flag in June 1848. His successor was Admiral Thomas Cochrane, Earl of Dundonald, aged 72. On the outbreak of the Russian War in 1854, Austen, now Admiral of the White and aged 80, was offered the appointment of C-in-C Portsmouth but declined because of his advanced years. His younger brother, Charles, was later appointed to command the East Indies and China Station in 1850 aged 71 and died 7 October 1852 still in post aged 73. They were brothers of Jane Austen.

1866 Second Naval Discipline Act passed: brought the system of naval justice more closely into line with English criminal law.

1903 Publication of first RNVR Regulations.

1904 Naval Lords became Sea Lords, a notion of Admiral Sir John Fisher. Lord Walter Kerr became the last Naval Lord.

1915 Institution of the Naval General Service Medal, of today's pattern but a maroon and silver striped ribbon. Instituted to recognise local service in minor warlike operations and in circumstances important enough to justify award of a medal when no other is appropriate. First clasp awarded on same day for 'Persian Gulf 1909–14'.

See 24 August 1831.

1922 'We beg leave humbly to recommend that Your Majesty may be graciously pleased, by Your Order in Council, to sanction the payment of 2d. a day as from 27 July, 1922, to the Naval Rating or Marine carrying out the duties of Barber in Your Majesty's Hospital Ship *Maine*. The Lords Commissioners of Your Majesty's Treasury have signified their concurrence in this proposal.' Admiralty Order in Council N.10220.1922.

See 30 May 1919.

1940 AMC *Transylvania* sunk by U-56 off N. Ireland.

1942 *Islay* sank the Italian S/M *Scire* off Haifa.

1942 'Pedestal' convoy passed Gibraltar en route for Malta.

1942 Wellington H/311 (Czech) sank U-578 in S.W. Approaches.

1943 Light cruiser *Uganda* and *Flores* (Neth) bombarded enemy positions north of Reposto.

1943 Submarine *Parthian* sunk by mine on passage from Malta to Alexandria.

1944 *Wren* (second of the name and of the war) and Liberator C/53 sank U-608 in Bay of Biscay.

See 27 July 1940.

1945 Continuation of operations against Japanese mainland. Main body of BPF retired after this operation.

See 17 July 1945, 9 August 1945.

1949 Destroyer *Daring*, first a new eight-ship class, launched by Mrs Leonard Hall, daughter-in-law of Lord Hall, First Lord of the Admiralty, at Swan Hunters, Wallsend-on-Tyne. A development of the wartime Battle-class, the Darings were the last, and at nearly 3,000 tons standard displacement, the largest conventional destroyers built for the RN. The Admiralty referred to them as 'Daring Class ships' for a period before reverting to 'destroyers'.

See 12 August 1953, 14 September 1953, 1 February 1906.

1965 HM The Queen reviewed the Home Fleet in the Firth of Clyde; seventy-three ships anchored in eleven lines from Greenock to Cloch Point below Gourock. The Royal yacht *Britannia*, preceded by the *Pharos* of the Northern Lighthouse Commissioners and escorted by the frigate *Aurora*, was met by the C-in-C Home Fleet, Admiral Sir John Frewen, with his flag in the cruiser *Lion*. The first Fleet Review to include a nuclear submarine, *Dreadnought*, Cdr J.D.E. Fieldhouse RN. On arrival, the Queen made her first signal as Lord High Admiral to the C-in-C: 'Please continue to conduct and administer the Fleet.'

See 22 July 1947.

1965 Submarine *Opossum* represented the RN at the seventy-fifth anniversary celebrations at Heligoland of the handing over of the island to Germany in 1890 in exchange for the German possession of Zanzibar in East Africa.

See 11 May 1945, 18 April 1947.

1966 The cruiser *Tiger*, in a summer leave AMP alongside Weston Mill Lake jetty, Devonport, fired a 6-in drill round into a dockyard crane. Maintainers had A turret trained at Red 90 with the guns at maximum depression and were using drill inert shells. They were unaware that the hoists contained a live charge that had not been unloaded after a recent shoot and when the hoists were operated, the automatic system put a cordite charge behind the drill round. The work required the triggers to be made. The gun fired. The shell hit the jetty and cut the shore power supply before ricocheting into a crane. The ship was flagship of Vice-Admiral J.O.C. Hayes, FO second-in-command Home Fleet and the word got around quickly. The Gangway OOW, Midshipman Paul Haddacks, recalls *Tiger* receiving a prompt congratulatory signal (110730Z) from HMS *Excellent*: 'A hit, a very palpable hit!' (*Hamlet*, Act 5 Sc. 2. 295).

See 18 March 1977, 26 April 1991, 17 October 2005.

1967 Clyde Submarine Base, Faslane, commissioned as *Neptune*.

HMS *Bulwark*, amphibious assault ship, arriving at Devonport from her builders on 12 July 2004. (*RN*)

11 August

1415 Henry V sailed from Southampton: 'fair stood the wind for France'.

1673 The last battle of the third Dutch war or the second battle of the Texel. Prince Rupert fought Admiral de Ruyter with sixty-four ships off the Texel.
Battle Honour: Texel 1673.

Red Sqn: *Sovereign, London, Charles, Royal Katherine, Henry, Victory, French Ruby, Edgar, Warspite, Old James, Triumph, Resolution, Rupert, Monmouth, Mary, Crown, Advice, Pearl.*

Blue Sqn: *Prince, St Andrew, Royal Charles, Cambridge, St George, Unicorn, Henrietta, Dreadnought, Lion, Gloucester, Dunkirk, Monck, Bristol, Bonaventure, Ruby, Success, Guernsey, St Michael, Swiftsure, Rainbow, York, Greenwich, Hampshire, Portsmouth, Foresight, Sweepstakes.*

White Sqn: *Fairfax, Plymouth, Anne, Happy Return, Princess, Newcastle, Yarmouth, Leopard, Stavoreen, Mary Rose, Diamond, Swallow, Assurance, Falcon, Nonsuch* (or *Portland*).

Fireships etc.: *Blessing, Friendship, Hopewell, Katherine, Leopard, Pearl, Prudent Mary, Society, Supply, Truelove* (all expended in action). *Laurence*. Yachts: *Henrietta, Katherine*. Doggers: *Hard Bargain, Roe, Rose*. Sloop: *Dolphin*.

1706 *Plymouth* (60) foundered in a storm in the English Channel with all 350 hands.

1780 Governors of the Chatham Chest sought Board approval to grant pension to Eleanor Moore, wounded in *Apollo* in action carrying powder to her husband's gun crew, 'there being no precedent for the relief of persons not borne on the ships' books'.

1782 Sloop *Placentia* captured the American privateer *Lord Stirling* off Newfoundland.

1799 *Courier, Pylades* and *Espiegle* captured the Dutch (ex-British) *Crash* off Schiermonnikoog.

1808 Evacuation by Rear-Admiral Richard Keats (*Superb*) of the Spanish troops from Nyborg, Baltic.

1808 *Comet* captured the French *Sylphe* 170 miles S. of Ushant. Taken into the Service as *Seagull*.
Battle Honour: *Sylphe* 1808.

1809 The Walcheren campaign. The Royal Navy escorted and supported a large invasion force that attempted to seize control of the estuary of the River Scheldt, which the French were using as a naval base. The campaign began 30 July and lasted until December.

1850 'Well done, *Phaeton*': a BZ to Capt George Elliot for the smart rescue of a man overboard, due to provision of a lifeboat sentry and a boat's crew closed up in rough weather in his fourth rate *Phaeton* (50). The signal from Cdre Martin rang round the Navy.
See 16 February 1940.

1855 Brigsloop *Wolverine* (third of the name) wrecked off the Mosquito Coast because the Officer of the Watch was asleep, the Mate miscalculated the current and the Master ceased to sound.

1858 Cdre the Hon. Keith Stewart (*Nankin*) and Maj-Gen. Sir Charles Van Straubenzee captured Nam tau, to punish the firing by the Chinese on a flag of truce.

1902 The Chaplain of the Fleet was granted, during the tenure of office, the ecclesiastical dignity of archdeacon under the Archbishop of Canterbury.
See 13 May 1859, 23 October 1876, 17 November 1943, 1 April 1998.

1914 Seizure off Melbourne of *Hobart*, a German steamship which was unaware of hostilities. This yielded an astonishing intelligence haul, including the HVB (Handelsverkehrsbuch) code used by the German Admiralty to communicate not only with merchantmen abroad but also with the High Seas Fleet in home waters. The Admiralty was not informed until 9 September and the code did not reach London until after the *Magdeburg*'s books but was no less valuable, since the code was not replaced until March 1916.
See 20 August 1914, 13 October 1914.

700S Naval Air Squadron's first Sea King helicopter being delivered, 1969. (*FAAM*)

1918 Six RN 40ft CMBs on patrol off Dutch coast attacked by six German aircraft off Terschelling. The CMBs were doing 30 knots and the aircraft 60 knots. 'It was certainly the fastest action ever fought at sea' – Newbolt, *Naval Operations*, vol.5, p.346. CMBs 41, 44 and 48 were interned by Dutch; CMBs 40, 42 and 47 sunk. Rear-Admiral Tyrwhitt, commanding the Harwich Force, lured Zeppelin L-53 to seaward, where she was brought down 'in those upper regions of the air from which neither sea nor land is visible' (Corbett and Newbolt, *Naval Operations*, pp.346–7) by Lt S.D. Culley, RAF, in a Sopwith Camel in which he had taken off from a lighter towed by the destroyer *Redoubt*. Tyrwhitt signalled a reference to Hymn 227, A&M, v. 7:

O happy band of pilgrims,
Look upward to the skies
Where such a light affliction
Shall win so great a prize

The tactic was repeated in the Second World War when Hurricanes were catapulted from CAM ships (Catapult Aircraft Merchantmen) to destroy German aircraft shadowing Allied convoys.

1942 The old carrier *Eagle*, covering the Operation Pedestal convoy to Malta, torpedoed 65 miles S. of Majorca and 584 miles W. of Malta (38.05N, 03.02E) by U-73, Kapitanleutnant Helmut Rosenbaum, operating from La Spezia. Capt L.D. Mackintosh and 927 of her 1,160 ship's company rescued by destroyers *Laforey* and *Lookout*, and tug *Jaunty*. Four Sea Hurricanes of 801 NAS airborne were recovered to *Indomitable* and *Victorious*. 'The faithful old carrier, which had made no less than nine aircraft ferry trips and had despatched 183 Spitfires to Malta in 1942, sank in eight minutes. If we had to lose her it was appropriate that her grave should be in the Mediterranean, whose waters she had known so well' – Capt S.W. Roskill RN, *The War at Sea*, vol.2 p.304.

See 8 June 1918.

1943 VC: FO Lloyd Allen Trigg, RNZAF, in Liberator D/200 sank U-468 off Gambia (12.20N, 20.07W), but was shot down and killed.

1944 Sloop *Starling* and Sunderland P/461 (RAAF) sank U-385 in the Bay of Biscay.

1969 700S Naval Air Squadron received its first Sea King at Culdrose. Commissioned 19 August and commenced flying operations next day.

See 19 August 1969.

12 August

1795 Hydrographer's Department established by Order in Council. Alexander Dalrymple appointed first Hydrographer.
See 11 September 1795.

1809 *Monkey* and boats of *Lynx* cut out three Danish lugger privateers off Dais Head (Darsser Ort), Baltic.

1812 Boat of *Minstrel* fought a battery at Benidorm, near Alicante.

1812 First stone of Plymouth breakwater laid.

1814 Boats of *Star* and *Netley* cut out the American *Ohio* and *Somers* on Lake Erie.

1828 Duke of Clarence, later King William IV, ceased to be Lord High Admiral, and the office was placed in commission until assumed by the Sovereign in 1964.

1844 Boats of *Dido* destroyed Seriff Mulah's town in the Sungei Undop, Borneo.

1858 *Shannon*'s Naval Brigade (A/Capt F. Marten) returned on board from the Upper United Provinces.
See 18 August 1857.

1914 Cruisers *Minotaur* and *Newcastle* bombarded Yap, Caroline Islands.

The Royal Navy Hydrographic, Meteorological and Oceanographic Services

The United Kingdom Hydrographic Office (UKHO), now a Defence Agency, had its beginnings in appointment in 1795 of Alexander Dalrymple, the first hydrographer, to take charge of incoming hydrographic information and to recommend charts for the use of the Royal Navy. His successor, Capt Thomas Hurd, established the supply of British Admiralty charts for the Service. In 1823 the charts and publications were made available to merchant ships, and their reputation grew as British trade expanded around the globe. Hurd also established a cadre of RN specialists who conducted surveys in home and foreign waters on which these charts were based.

Over 200 years later in 2011 the oil and gas industries in UK waters are served by the commercial hydrographic sector and the RN Hydrographic Surveying Squadron is mainly employed on defence work. (The importance of unambiguous warship status for 'Military Data Gathering' was underlined in the late twentieth century by the UN Conventions on the Law of the Sea).

The UK Meteorological Office (UKMetO) was established by the Board of Trade in 1854 to collect weather data at sea for statistical purposes, and six years later the first daily weather forecasts were published for UK waters. Francis Beaufort played a part in establishing this service, while Robert Fitzroy of *Beagle* fame was its first director. Modern warfare, and especially the advent of the aeroplane, brought rapid developments. The RN Weather Service was established in 1936, eventually becoming a separate division of Admiralty in 1950. Today the Joint Operational Meteorological and Oceanographic Centre (JOMOC), manned by the RN at the Permanent Joint Headquarters in Northwood, supports overseas military operations, in close partnership with the UKMetO. Meteorological forecasting was done by qualified Instructor Officers, supported by ratings of the Meteorological Branch. During the Cold War, these METOC specialists also provided tactical advice to frigates patrolling the Iceland-Greenland gap.

In 1997 the Hydrographic and METOC officers merged as the HM sub-specialisation of the RN Warfare Branch, and the rating structure rationalised. This reflected the much-changed world scene. Higher direction now nests within the intelligence community.

Operations have always been affected by weather conditions and timely environmental information can be crucial e.g. the surveys by Cook and other RN masters in the approaches to Quebec in 1759, and the forecasting of the 36-hour 'weather window' for D-day on 6 June 1944. HM personnel continue to provide such 'rapid environmental assessment' e.g. hydrographic work by HMS *Roebuck* for the amphibious landings in the North Arabian Gulf in 2003.

1915 First successful aerial torpedo attack. Flt Cdr C.H.K. Edmonds, flying a Short 184 biplane from the seaplane carrier *Ben-my-Chree*, dropped a 14-in torpedo, sinking a 5,000 ton Turkish transport in the Sea of Marmara. She had already been damaged by E 14.

See 28 July 1914.

1917 Destroyer *Oracle* rammed and sank U-44, 12 miles W. of Stavanger. (58.51N, 04.20E.)

1940 German air raid damaged RN Barracks, Portsmouth, Whale Island and HMS *Hornet*, the coastal forces base.

See 24 August 1940, 5 and 23 December 1940, 10 January 1941, 10 March 1941, 17 April 1941.

1941 Corvette *Picotee* sunk by U-568 in N. Atlantic (62.00N, 16.00W). Convoy NS 4.

1942 Operation Pedestal. *Cairo* torpedoed by the Italian S/M *Axum* off Bizerta (37.40N, 10.06E); sunk by own forces next day. Light cruiser *Nigeria* damaged by same salvo. *Foresight* torpedoed by Italian aircraft off Bizerta (37.45N, 10.10E); taken in tow by *Tartar*, whose Captain, exasperated at the effect of the tow on his anti-aircraft abilities, cast her off, and she had to be sunk next day for which he was court-martialled. *Ithuriel* and *Pathfinder* sank the Italian S/M *Cobalto* off Bizerta (37.39N, 10.00E). *Wolverine* sank the Italian S/M *Dagabur* off Algiers (37.12N, 01.51E).

1943 *Scarab* bombarded the Italian coast road near Cape Schiso. *Roberts*, *Uganda* and *Soemba* (Neth) bombarded targets on the right flank of the 8th Army.

1944 Sunderland A/461 (RAAF) sank U-270, and Halifax F/502 sank U-981 in the Bay of Biscay.

1944 *Findhorn* and *Godavari* (RIN) sank U-198 N.W. of Seychelles (03.35S, 52.49E) aided by Avenger of 851 Sqn (*Shah*).

1953 Mediterranean Fleet provided humanitarian aid following a major earthquake which devastated the Ionian Islands of Kephalonia, Zante and Ithaca on the Greek W. coast. First help to arrive at Kephalonia was the destroyer *Daring* with four naval surgeons and fifteen SBAs, followed by the light cruiser *Gambia*, diverted while on passage from the Canal Zone to Malta. A street in Argostoli was later named HMS *Daring Street* in gratitude for the ship's assistance. From King Paul of the Hellenes to the First Lord: 'I wish to address my heartfelt thanks for the kind and efficient help given to our distressed areas by the officers and men of HM ships.' Admiralty to C-in-C Mediterranean (Mountbatten): 'Please convey to all officers and men Their Lordships' appreciation . . .' A month later *Daring* was landing tents in Paphos following the worst ever earthquake in Cyprus.

See 14 September 1953, 17 January 1968.

1968 3 Cdo Brigade Air Squadron RM formed.

2000 Russian Oscar II-class cruise missile submarine *Kursk* destroyed in explosion in Barents Sea. Cdre David Russell, DFOSM, led RN assistance party.

See 5 March 1954, 16 June 1965, 7 August 2005, 5 October 2005.

2003 RN represented on Greek island of Zakynthos (Zante) on the fiftieth anniversary of the major earthquake that devastated this and other Greek islands.

13 August

1704 Battle of Velez Malaga. Admiral Sir George Rooke (*Royal Katherine*), with an Anglo-Dutch fleet of fifty-one sail of the line, fought the Franco-Spanish fleet under Admiral Comte de Toulouse (*Foudroyant*) 25 miles S.S.E. of Marbella. An unscientific battle of no military interest according to Mahan, but it lasted for seven hours, and after it the French avoided all other engagements and no further attempts were made on Gibraltar.
Battle Honour: Velez Malaga 1704.

Ships: (van) *Assurance, Barfleur, Berwick, Boyne, Garland, Lenox, Namur, Newark, Norfolk, Nottingham, Orford, Prince George, Roebuck, Swiftsure, Tilbury, Warspite, Yarmouth*; (centre) *Bedford, Burford, Cambridge, Centurion, Charles Galley, Dorsetshire, Eagle, Essex, Firm, Grafton, Kent, Kingston, Lark, Monck, Monmouth, Montagu, Nassau, Newport, Panther, Ranelagh, Royal Katherine, Royal Oak, Shrewsbury, Somerset, St George, Suffolk, Swallow, Tartar, Torbay, Tryton.*

Fireships: *Firebrand, Griffin, Hunter, Lightning, Phoenix, Vulcan, Vulture.* Bombs: *Hare, Terror.* Yacht: *William and Mary.* Hospital ship: *Jefferies, Princess Anne.*

Dutch: *Albemarle, Ann of Friesland, Anne of Utrecht, Batavier, Bavaria, Damiaten, Dort, Flushing, Gelderland, Katwijk, Lion, Mars Nymwegen, Unie.*

Flags: (van) *Barfleur* (Admiral Sir Cloudesley Shovell), *Prince George* (Vice-Admiral Sir John Leake); (centre) *Kent* (Rear-Admiral Thomas Dilkes), *Ranelagh* (Rear-Admiral George Byng), *Royal Katherine* (Admiral Sir George Rooke); (rear) *Albemarle* (Lt-Admiral Gerard van Callenburgh), *Unie* (Rear-Admiral Baron Wassenaer).

Captured: French *Cheval-Marin* and two galleys.

1762 Capture of Havana by Admiral Sir George Pocock (*Namur*), Cdre Keppel and his brother, the Earl of Albemarle.

A classic example of interservice cooperation which started in June, took nine sail of the line and destroyed another five.
Battle Honour: Havana 1762.

Ships: *Alcide, Belleisle, Cambridge, Centaur, Culloden, Defiance, Devonshire, Dragon, Dublin, Edgar, Hampton Court, Intrepid, Marlborough, Namur, Nottingham, Orford, Pembroke, Ripon, Stirling Castle, Temeraire, Temple, Valiant. Alarm, Bonetta, Boreas, Centurion, Cerberus, Cygnet, Dover, Echo, Enterprize, Ferret, Glasgow, Lizard, Mercury, Porcupine, Richmond, Sutherland, Trent, Viper.* Bombs: *Basilisk, Grenado, Thunder.* Cutter: *Lurcher.*

1780 *Bienfaisant* and *Charon* captured the French privateer *Comte d'Artois* off the Old Head of Kinsale.

1799 *Crash* and *Undaunted* and boats of *Latona, Juno, Courier, Espiegle* and *Pylades* destroyed the Dutch *Vengeance* and captured a battery on Schiermonnikoog, together with a large rowing boat and twelve schuyts.

1810 Landing parties from *Sirius* and *Iphigenia* captured a battery on Ile de la Passe, off Mauritius.

1844 Boat of *Hyacinth* captured the Brazilian slaver *Aventureiro* off Little Fish (Mossamedes) Bay, Angola.

1857 *Shannon*'s landing party up the River Ganges.

1878 Review of the Particular Service Squadron by HM Queen Victoria.

1898 Capt Sir Edward Chichester put his ship, *Immortalite*, between the flagships of Rear-Admiral Dewy, USN, and the German Vice-Admiral von Diedrichs off Manila in a peacekeeping gesture reminiscent of *Calliope* anchoring at Apia on 16 March 1889.

1904 *Decoy*, one of the first true ocean-going class of destroyers, sunk in collision with destroyer *Arun* 'in unusual manoeuvres' off the Wolf Rock.

1914 Bombardment of Dar-es-Salaam.

1915 Transport *Royal Edward* sunk by UB-14, 4 miles S. of Kandeliusa, Aegean Sea.

1917 Sloop *Bergamot* sunk by U-84 in Atlantic while serving as Q-ship.

1918 Trawlers *John Gillman, John Brooker, Viola, Florio* and yacht *Miranda II*, sank UB-30 off Whitby.

1934 Metropolitan Police, hitherto responsible for establishment security, withdrawn at midnight from Devonport Dockyard.
See 22 October 1860, 6 October 1949.

The 64-gun ship *Alcide* and flat boats landing troops at the capture of Havana, 1762. (*NMRN Ad. Lib. Portfolio A22*)

1935 An Order in Council established the non-substantive rate of Observer's Mate in the Fleet Air Arm.

1940 Sloop *Auckland* and destroyer *Kimberley* bombarded Italian troops near El Sheik 40 miles west of Berbera.

1942 Light cruiser *Manchester*, Capt Harold Drew RN, escorting the Pedestal convoy to Malta, torpedoed in the early hours by the Italian MTBs MS-16 and MS-22, 6 miles off Kelibia, Tunisia (36.50N, 11.10E). Having lost all main engine power, Capt Drew ordered the ship to be abandoned and scuttled, prematurely in the opinion of his subsequent court martial. Some men were taken on board the destroyers *Somali* and *Pathfinder*. The remainder got ashore and were interned by the Vichy French in very bad conditions in a desert camp until released after the Torch landings in November 1942.

1942 Bombardment of Rhodes (Operation M.G.4). Diversion to facilitate the passage of the 'Pedestal' convoy. Ships: *Arethusa, Cleopatra, Javelin, Kelvin, Sikh, Zulu.*

1942 Submarine *Unbroken* torpedoed the Italian cruisers *Bolzano* (CTL) and *Muzio Attendolo*.

1943 Light cruisers *Aurora* and *Penelope* and destroyers *Jervis* and *Paladin* bombarded Vibo Valentia, Calabria.

1965 The Admiralty Board appointed full-time Public Relations Officers to some commands at home and abroad. DPR(N) succeeded CNI. DCI(RN) 1196/65.

See 14 January 1943, 2 September 1966, 17 August 1973, 23 September 1966.

14 AUGUST

1697 *Torbay*, *Defiance*, *Devonshire*, *Restoration* and *Betty* fought Cdre Baron de Pointis (*Sceptre*), with five ships, 200 miles S.W. of the Scilly Isles. An unsuccessful chase was maintained for two days after the action.

1779 *Raisonnable*, *Blonde*, *Galatea*, *Greyhound*, *Camilla* and *Virginia* captured or destroyed an American force of seventeen ships and twenty-four transports in Penobscot Bay, Maine.

1781 *Chameleon* destroyed a French dogger 18 miles N.W. of the Texel.

1782 David Tyrit (Navy Office spy) executed on Southsea Common.

1803 *Lord Nelson* (Indiaman) taken by the French privateer *Bellone* in the approaches to the Bay of Biscay.

See 25 August 1803.

1804 Boats of *Galatea* repulsed in an attempt to cut out the French *Général Enouf* (ex-British *Lily*) in Anse à Mire, The Saints.

1813 *Pelican* (18) captured the American *Argus* (18) 15 miles W. of St David's Head, St George's Channel. Battle Honour: *Argus* 1813.

1816 Party landed from the frigate *Falmouth*, Capt Robert Festing RN, to take possession of Tristan da Cunha to prevent its possible use by French republicans to rescue Napoleon from St Helena. The frigate's First Lieutenant, Lt David Rice RN, became the first Governor and, with Lt Archibald Dunlop RM, three midshipmen, the Assistant Surgeon and thirteen men, he held the island until relieved on 28 November by Capt (later General Sir) Abraham Josias Cloete, 21st Dragoons, with forty soldiers sent from the Cape to garrison the island.

See 10 May 1940.

1877 William Henry Smith, the son in W.H. Smith & Son, newsagents, made First Lord of the Admiralty by Disraeli. Smith was lampooned the following year as Sir Joseph Porter in W.S. Gilbert's comic opera *HMS Pinafore*: 'Stick close to your desks and never go to sea, and

The tanker *Ohio* being helped into Grand Harbour, Malta, after Operation Pedestal, 1942. (*NMRN*)

you all may be rulers of the Queen's Navee.' Disraeli was criticised 'for conferring the Admiralty on a London tradesman' and Smith blackballed by the Reform but he proved an able administrator and died in post as Lord Warden of the Cinque Ports at Walmer Castle on 6 October 1891.

See 12 April 2005.

1900 Relief of the Peking Legations by Allied forces. Naval Brigade from *Aurora*, *Centurion*, *Endymion*, *Barfleur*, *Fame*, *Phoenix* and *Terrible* in action since 30 May.

1909 Publication of report by Cabinet committee on representations made to the Prime Minister by Admiral Lord Charles Beresford about Admiral Sir John Fisher.

1916 *Remembrance* (*Lammeroo*, Q-ship) sunk by U-38 in the Aegean.

1917 *First Prize* (Q 21), a captured German schooner, sunk by the German UB-48 N.W. of Ireland.

1917 VC: Skipper Thomas Crisp, DSC, RNR. Posthumous. HM Special Service Smack *Nelson* of Lowestoft sunk by UC-63 on Jim Howe Bank, off Mablethorpe, Lincolnshire. When the skipper was mortally wounded his son Tom, Second Hand, took command. He and LS Ross (gunlayer) received DSM. Tom was invested by the King, and received father's VC, 19 December 1917.

1922 President Sun Yat-sen rescued from Canton after his defeat by Chinese rebels and taken to Shanghai in a RN gunboat.

1940 Destroyers *Malcolm* and *Verity* engaged three German S-boats and six trawlers off the Texel, sinking one of each. Operation P.O.

1943 River gunboats *Aphis* and *Cockchafer* and *Flores* (Neth) bombarded the coast road at Taormina, Sicily. *Dido*, *Panther* and *Sirius* bombarded Scaletta, Italy.

1943 Submarine *Saracen* sunk by the Italian corvette *Minerva* off Bastia.

1944 *Duckworth*, *Essington* and Liberator G/53 sank U-618 in Bay of Biscay.

1981 Closure of *Dauntless* at Burghfield. WRNS training moved to *Raleigh* at Torpoint.

1990 Ships of the Armilla Patrol, *Battleaxe*, from Penang, *York* and *Jupiter* concentrated at Mombasa. Operation Granby.

See 9 August 1990.

2006 Lt-Cdr (A) John Raymond Godley DSC, RNVR, later 3rd Baron Kilbracken (1950), died aged 85. Born in Belgravia in 1920, he joined as a naval airman 2nd Class from Oxford in 1940 and later commanded 835 and 714 NAS; DSC 1945 commanding Wildcats from the escort carrier *Nairana*. Author of *Bring Back my Stringbag. A Swordfish Pilot at War* (1979). A resident of the Irish Republic, Kilbracken returned his war medals in 1972 in protest at British policy in Northern Ireland and announced that he was renouncing British citizenship. He remained an active member of the House of Lords.

15 August

1416 Battle of Harfleur. Admiral Sir Walter Hungerford and Prince John, Duke of Bedford, defeated a Franco-Genoese fleet and relieved Harfleur.

1545 The English navy fired its first broadside in anger at sea. Henry VIII's ships under John Dudley, Lord Lisle, engaged French galleys under the Admiral of France, Claude d'Annebault off Shoreham, Sussex: 'the *Mistress* and the *Anne Gallant* did so handle the galleys, as well with their sides as with their prows . . .' An indecisive action after which the English returned to Portsmouth and the French to Le Havre.
See 10 September 1971.

1660 First Royal Yacht, *Mary*, presented to King Charles.

1761 *Bellona* (74) captured the French *Courageux* (74). *Brilliant* (36) fought the French *Hermione* (32) and *Malicieuse* (32). Both actions S.W. of Cape Finisterre. Battle Honour: *Courageux* 1761.
See 19 December 1796.

1781 Nelson commissioned *Albemarle* at Woolwich.
See 25 August 1907

1805 *Goliath* captured the French *Faune* 250 miles W. of La Rochelle.

1805 Entry, pay and pension of Masters regulated by Order in Council.

1805 Establishment of fourth RM Division at Woolwich.

1807 *Comus* captured the Danish *Frederikscoarn* between Vinga Beacon and the Skaw. Prelude to the second confiscation of the Danish fleet. Battle Honour: *Frederikscoarn* 1807.

1809 Boats of *Otter* cut out two French vessels at Rivière Noire, Mauritius.

1853 RN Coast Volunteers formed. Abolished 1873.

1863 Bombardment of the Kagoshima forts, Japan, by Vice-Admiral Augustus Kuper (*Euryalus*). 'I consider it advisable not to postpone until another day the return of the fire of the Japanese, to punish the Prince of Satsuma for the outrage, and to vindicate the honour of the Flag.'

Ships: *Argus, Coquette, Euryalus, Perseus, Racehorse, Havock, Pearl*. Five of the squadron carried between them twenty-one Armstrong breech-loaders. These had twenty-eight accidents in firing 365 rounds, i.e. one for every thirteen rounds. This led to a return to muzzle loading.
See 5 September 1864.

1915 *Inverlyon* (armed smack) sank UB-4 3 miles N. by E. of Smith's Knoll spar buoy (52.46N, 02.10E), hitting her with her first shot.
See 5 September 1864.

1916 *Furious*, designed as a light battlecruiser but completed with a flight deck forward and an 18-in gun aft, launched at Armstrong Whitworth on the Tyne. Completed 4 July 1917 but returned to the builders on 14 November 1917 to have the gun removed and another flight deck installed aft. Recommissioned Rosyth on 15 March 1918.

1916 Submarines E 4 and E 41 collided on exercises and sank off Harwich. Soon raised. E 4 lost thirty-two men; sixteen lost in E 41.

1918 Destroyers *Scott* and *Ulleswater* sunk off Dutch coast – probably mined.

1918 Concept of a single Imperial Navy rejected by Dominion prime ministers.

1919 Ten Year Rule formulated by the War Cabinet in response to the Admiralty request for guidance in producing Naval Estimates for 1920–1. 'It should be assumed . . . that the British Empire will not be engaged in any great war during the next ten years, and that no Expeditionary Force is required for this purpose.' This Rule extended annually until 1928, when Churchill, then Chancellor of the Exchequer, made it a perpetually rolling assumption. 'With the setting-up of the Defence Requirements Committee it was quietly allowed to lapse' – Roskill, *Naval Policy between the Wars*, vol.2, p.146.

1938 Light cruiser *Sheffield* fitted with Type 79Y, the first operational RN radar.
See 15 December 1936.

A massive flypast of RN carrier aircraft over the battleship HMS *Duke of York* celebrates the Japanese surrender and the end of the Second World War, 1945. (*NMRN*)

1942 GC: Dudley William Mason, Master, *Ohio*. SS *Ohio*, a fast American tanker on charter, eventually reached Grand Harbour, Malta: the culmination of Operation Pedestal. The fuel she carried enabled air strikes to be resumed from Malta – itself awarded the GC – as Rommel was preparing his final offensive against Alexandria.

1943 *Aphis*, *Brocklesby* and *Soemba* (Neth) bombarded the east coast road to Messina, in support of the right flank of the 8th Army.

1944 Landing of US and French troops in southern France begins. Operation Dragoon. Battle Honour: South France 1944.

Convoys were sailed from Naples, Taranto, Brindisi, Malta, Palermo and Oran. A total of 86,575 men, 12,520 vehicles and 46,140 tons of stores were landed over the beachhead in the sixty-four hours following the first landing. The Navy was called upon to provide gunfire support, and much ammunition was used, the cruiser *Argonaut* firing 394 5.25-in shells, and *Aurora* 316 6-in shells.

1944 Corvette *Orchis* sank U-741 off Fécamp. Convoy FTC 68.

1944 Cruiser *Mauritius* and destroyers *Iroquois* (RCN) and *Ursa* attacked a convoy between Sables d'Olonne and La Pallice, driving several of the escort, including M-385 and convoy, ashore.

1944 First WRNS landed in France after Normandy invasion.

1945 Admiral Sir Max Horton, C-in-C W. Approaches since November 1942, hauled down his flag. WA Command disbanded.

See 30 July 1951.

1945 VJ Day. Japanese surrender. End of the Second World War. From C-in-C Fifth Fleet to Fifth Fleet Pacific: 'The war with Japan will end at 12.00 on 15 August. It is likely that Kamikazes will attack the fleet after this time as a final fling. Any ex-enemy aircraft attacking the fleet is to be shot down in a friendly manner.'

As the combined US and British fleet sailed for Tokyo to receive the Japanese surrender, strikes were launched into the Tokyo area. The Fleet Air Arm was attacked by a dozen Japanese aircraft, eight of which were shot down. One Seafire was shot down and its pilot, Sub-Lt F.C. Hockley RNVR, baled out and was taken prisoner. He was executed by his captors who were later convicted as war criminals.

1983 Fire in engine exhaust and uptake in minehunter *Ledbury* caused £1,300,000 damage. DCI(RN) 349/84.

The Royal Navy in the Second World War

The Royal Navy had lost 3 battleships, 2 battlecruisers, one monitor, 5 aircraft carriers and 3 auxiliary carriers, 23 cruisers and 5 anti-aircraft cruisers, 139 destroyers, 76 submarines, 7 X-craft, 28 chariots, 6 Welman craft, 15 armed merchant cruisers, 5 armed boarding vessels, 5 ocean boarding vessels, 2 auxiliary fighter catapult ships, 6 auxiliary anti-aircraft ships, 11 sloops, 10 frigates, 28 corvettes, 3 cutters, 6 auxiliary anti-submarine vessels, 11 river gunboats, 2 convoy service ships, 8 minelayers, 3 mine destructor vessels, 52 minesweepers, 6 BYMS minesweepers, 18 motor minesweepers, 2 degaussing ships, 1 steam gunboat, 115 MTBs, 28 MGBs, 79 MLs, 251 trawlers, 17 boom defence vessels, 54 tugs, 1 rescue ship, 107 drifters, 45 tankers and oilers and many other subsidiary classes.

Just over 1 million people – 923,000 men and 86,000 women – had served in the Royal Navy during the war – at its peak in June 1945 it had 783,000 men and 72,000 women. (In 1810, at its peak during the French wars, the RN had 142,000 men and 420,000 in the First World War.)

By August 1945 the Fleet Air Arm comprised 59 aircraft carriers (34 of them in the British Pacific Fleet on VJ Day), 3,700 aircraft and more than 72,000 officers and men.

See 2 September 1945.

16 AUGUST

1652 Capt Sir George Ayscue (*Rainbow*), with forty ships, fought Rear-Admiral de Ruyter (*Neptune*), in charge of a Dutch convoy, off Plymouth.

1742 *Gloucester* sacrificed by Anson in order to save *Centurion*.

See 6 May 1682, 22 May 1941.

1778 *Isis* fought the French *César* 60 miles E. by S. of Sandy Hook. Regiment: the Light Company of the 23rd.

This was a disappointment. *Isis* (50) calculated correctly that her opponent, a 74, was cleared for action and manned on only one side, and so attacked the other. This made the larger ship move off but *Isis* was unable to catch her.

1800 Admiral Hon. Samuel Barrington, victor at St Lucia in 1778 during the War of American Independence, died. He was one of five brothers, an admiral, a peer, a general, a judge and a bishop – see Vice-Admiral Sir Norman Denning of a later generation.

See 15 and 30 December 1778, 19 November 1904.

1801 Second unsuccessful boat attack by the squadron under Vice-Admiral Lord Nelson (*Medusa*) on the Boulogne invasion flotilla. Boats of: 1st Div.: *Eugenie*, *Jamaica*, *Leyden*. 2nd Div.: *Medusa*, *Minx*, *Queenborough* cutter; 3rd Div.: *Discovery*, *Explosion*, *Express*, *Ferreter*, *Gannet*, *Providence*, *York*, *Hunter* and *Greyhound* (Revenue cutters). Royal Artillery in bombs.

1805 *Goliath* captured the French *Torche* off Cape Prior.

1846 Boats of *Iris* and *Phlegethon* (Ben. Mar.) destroyed the pirate stronghold of Haji Samon in the Sungei Membakut, Borneo.

1854 Bombardment and reduction of Bomarsund by Vice-Admiral Sir Charles Napier (*Duke of Wellington*). Rear-Admiral Charles Penaud (*Trident*) and British and French troops.
Battle Honour: Baltic 1854–5.

Ships: *Ajax*, *Amphion*, *Arrogant*, *Belleisle*, *Blenheim*, *Bulldog* (flag for attack), *Driver*, *Duke of Wellington*, *Edinburgh*, *Gladiator*, *Hecla*, *Hogue*, *Leopard*, *Lightning*, *Penelope*, *Pigmy*, *Valorous*. Troops: Marine Battalion. French ships: *Asmodée*, *Cocyte*, *Darien*, *Duperre*, *Phlegeton*, *Trident*. French Troops: Chasseurs.

1861 Moorsom percussion fuse introduced into RN.

1902 Coronation Review of the Fleet by HM King Edward VII.

1915 Harrington, near Whitehaven, shelled by German submarine.

1917 (*Saros*) Q-ship, ex-*Bradford City*, sunk in Straits of Messina.

Section through screw first rate HMS *Duke of Wellington* (1852). (*NMRN 1987/123*)

Three hundred members of the Fleet Air Arm dined in the Painted Hall at Greenwich on 10 December 2009 to mark a century of naval aviation. The guests of honour were Their Royal Highnesses the Prince of Wales, the Princess Royal, the Duke of York and Prince Michael of Kent. (*RN*)

1941 Signal School moved from Portsmouth to Leydene House, East Meon. Commissioned as *Mercury*.

See 18 December 1992.

1950 Formation of 41 Independent Cdo RM at Bickleigh for Korean service with USMC.

1956 Frigate *Loch Killisport*, Cdr G.C. Hathaway RN, left Portsmouth for the Gulf and the East Indies Station with a Royal Marines detachment of twenty men embarked as part of the ship's company. The Royals had hitherto served only in warships of cruiser size and above.

17 August

1779 The third rate *Ardent* (64), Capt Philip Boteler, hurried to sea from Portsmouth to meet a surprise threat from a large Franco-Spanish fleet in the Channel, struck to the French frigates *Gentille* (32) and *Junon* (32), 18 nm S.S.E. of Plymouth. The French appeared much surprised. Capt Boteler and his men were repatriated in January 1780. A court-martial in *Victory* at Portsmouth, which sat from 2–7 March, found 'that he did not do his utmost to prevent the ship falling into the Enemy's Hands' and Boteler was dismissed the Service. *Ardent*, a sister ship of Nelson's *Agamemnon*, was re-taken at the Saintes, 12 April 1782.

1796 Vice-Admiral the Hon. Sir George Elphinstone, later Lord Keith (*Monarch*), received the surrender of Rear-Admiral Engelbertus Lucas (*Dordrecht*) and his squadron in Saldanha Bay, S. Africa.

1798 *Leander* (52) carrying Nelson's Nile despatches taken and plundered by *Généreux* (74) 6 miles W. of Gavdos Island, S.W. of Crete. She was restored in 1799 after the capture of Corfu. Nelson took the *Généreux* on 18 February 1800.

1801 *Guachapin* captured the Spanish letter of marque *Teresa* between Martinique and St Lucia.

1804 *Loire* captured the French privateer *Blonde* 240 miles W. of the Scilly Isles.

1875 Reed succeeded as Chief Constructor by his brother-in-law, Nathaniel Barnaby, who became first DNC.

1895 Capture of M'baruk ibn Raschid's town of M'wele by Naval Brigade from *Barrosa, Phoebe, Racoon, St George, Thrush, Widgeon. Blonde* was also awarded the medal. Troops: 24th and 26th Bombay Native Infantry, East Africa Protectorate Force, Zanzibar government Army, Indian Native Field Hospital (B Section). Medal: Ashantee – M'wele (or 1895–6) engraved on the rim.

1917 The Smuts Committee recommended the creation of an Air Ministry and the amalgamation of the Royal Naval Air Service and the Royal Flying Corps. Admiral Sir John Jellicoe, the First Sea Lord, was wholly opposed to the idea but Admiral Sir David Beatty, C-in-C Grand Fleet, supported it, 'perhaps the gravest misjudgement of his whole career; for it contributed, perhaps decisively, to the navy losing virtually all its experienced aviators and technicians' – Roskill, *Admiral of the Fleet Earl Beatty, The Last Naval Hero*, p.240.

See 1 April 1918.

1939 New fleet carrier *Formidable* launched herself thirty minutes ahead of schedule at Harland & Wolff, Belfast. The cradle splintered and collapsed, flinging metal and timber into the air and shipwrights scattered. Lady Wood, wife of Sir Kingsley Wood, Secretary of State for Air, who was to name the ship, had the presence of mind to hurl a customary bottle of wine at the receding bows of the carrier.

See 24 August 1940.

1940 Bombardment of Bardia and Fort Capuzzo. Operation M.B.2. Ships: *Kent, Malaya* (Rear-Admiral H.D. Pridham-Wippell), *Ramillies, Warspite* (Admiral Sir Andrew Cunningham).

1940 Two booby-trapped German mines dropped at Boarhunt attractively near *Vernon*, and, at Piddlehinton. Designated Type E and dealt with, but only just.

17–30 August 1941

Manxman, fast minelayer, left England on 17th disguised as a French cruiser. After passing Gibraltar she hoisted the tricolour and her crew dressed in French uniforms. During the night of 25th, she removed her disguise, laid mines in the Gulf of Genoa off Leghorn and then retired at high speed, resuming her disguise again to reach Gibraltar. She was back in England on 30th.

1943 Light cruisers *Euryalus* and *Penelope* and destroyers *Jervis* and *Paladin* bombarded Scalea, Calabria, S. Italy.

1944 River gunboats *Aphis* and *Scarab*, with USS *Endicott* sank Uj-6082 (ex-Italian *Antilope*) in Bay of Ciotat, east of Marseilles.

HMS *Manxman* minelayer (1940), in August 1951. (*NMRN W&L 1338A*)

1951 RN's first operational jet fighter squadron, 800 NAS, equipped with Supermarine Attackers, formed at RNAS Ford, Sussex.

See 14 May 1955, 11 November 2005.

1962 'There is evidence that unsatisfactory results are being obtained when painting HM Ships because the paint is not being adequately stirred beforehand . . . the hand stirrers shown in AFO Diagram 14/62 should be made by ships, depot ships staff or bases as appropriate.' – AFO 1573/62.

1973 Admiral Sir William 'Bubbles' James, C-in-C Portsmouth 1939–42, died aged 91 at Hindhead, Surrey. Born 22 December 1881, he was the child model for the painting by his grandfather, Sir John Millais, showing a child blowing bubbles which was used as an advertisement for Pears' soap. James was the first Commander of the battlecruiser *Queen Mary* early in the First World War, 'Blinker' Hall's assistant in naval intelligence and the first Chief of Naval Information in Hitler's War.

See 14 January 1943, 17 February 1943.

1997 Destroyer *Liverpool* and RFA *Black Rover* assisted in evacuation of Montserrat following major volcanic eruptions. Operation Caxton.

See 18 July 1995, 19 August 1995.

18 August

1665 Establishment of Sheerness Dockyard. 'Up at about 5 a-clock and dressed ourselfs; and to sail again down to the *Soveraigne* at the buoy of the Noure . . . and whence to Sheerenesse where we walked up and down, laying out the ground to be taken in for a yard to lay provisions for cleaning and repairing of ships; and a most proper place it is for that purpose' – *Pepys' Diary*.

See 31 March 1960.

1759 Admiral the Hon. Edward Boscawen (*Namur*) defeated Cdre de La Clue-Sabran (*Ocean*) off Lagos, Portugal. A spirited action, typical of Boscawen though he may not have been conscious that it was the eve of his birthday. He plugged a hole in the boat with his wig while shifting his flagship *Namur* to *Newark*. When taxed with an infringement of neutrality the Prime Minister (William Pitt, first Earl of Chatham) said, 'It is very true, still the enemy is burned.'

Battle Honour: Lagos 1759.

See 16 February 1940.

Ships: *America, Conqueror, Culloden, Edgar, Guernsey, Intrepid, Jersey, Namur, Newark, Portland, Prince, St Albans, Swiftsure, Warspite*. Frigates, etc.: *Active, Ambuscade, Etna, Favourite, Gibraltar, Glasgow, Gramont, Lyme, Rainbow, Salamander, Shannon, Sheerness, Tartar's Prize, Thetis*. Captured: *Centaure, Modeste, Téméraire*. Burned: *Ocean, Redoutable*.

1804 Formation of first Artillery companies, Royal Marines; one per Division. For service in bomb vessels.

1805 Vice-Admiral Viscount Nelson, having pursued Villeneuve to the Caribbean and back, anchored at Spithead and hauled down his flag in *Victory* on 20 August.

See 19 May 1803, 14 September 1805.

1811 *Hawke* captured the French *Héron* and three transports. Drove ashore and wrecked twelve more of the convoy and three of the escort about 4 miles N.E. of Pointe de la Percée, north coast of France.

Admiral Boscawen's victory at Lagos, 1759. (*NMRN*)

1813 Boats of *Undaunted*, *Redwing* and *Espoir* and boats of the squadron blockading Toulon stormed the batteries at Cassis, between Marseilles and Toulon, capturing three gunboats and twenty-five coasters.

1857 First party of *Shannon*'s Naval Brigade(Capt William Peel, VC) left the ship at Calcutta for Allahabad, proceeding by river steamer and flat. 'One more broadside please, gentlemen' – Winton, *The Victoria Cross at Sea*, p.25.

See 12 September 1857, 27 April 1858.

1915 Submarine E 13 stranded on Saltholm, wrecked by German gunfire, interned by Danes and sold for scrap in 1919.

1917 Signal section of Operations Division of Naval Staff became Signal Division.

1919 VC: Cdr Claude Congreve Dobson RN, Lt Gordon Charles Steele RN. CMB raid on the Russian Baltic fleet base at Kronstadt on Kotlin Island, Gulf of Finland. Change of ROE allowed Rear-Admiral Sir Walter Cowan, hitherto restricted to blockading the Russian fleet to prevent Bolshevik aggression against the newly independent Baltic littoral states, to take offensive action. Lt Augustus Agar had demonstrated the capability of operating fast, shallow-draught CMBs in heavily-mined enemy waters when he torpedoed the Russian heavy cruiser *Oleg* on 17 June. The Kronstadt attack (Operation RK – Roger Keyes), with seven CMBs was led by Cdr C.C. Dobson RN and supported by diversionary bombing by RAF aircraft operating from HMS *Vindictive*. Lt Steele took command of CMB 88 when his CO, Lt Dayrell-Reed was mortally wounded. They sank the battleships *Petropavlovsk* and *Andrei Pervozvanni*, and the submarine depot ship *Pamyat Azova* for the loss four naval officers and four men, four RAF officers and one airman, three CMBs and aircraft. A brilliant action which thrilled the RN but embarrassed the British government which was then in sensitive negotiations with the Bolshevik authorities. Shades of Navarino. Dobson and Steele gazetted on 11 November 1919, the first anniversary of Armistice Day.

See 20 October 1827, 22 November 1918, 17 June 1919, 20 July 2003.

1919 Cruiser *Kent*'s detachment reached Vladivostok, from service in the Urals 4,500 miles west.

1923 Submarine L 9 foundered in hurricane at Hong Kong. Salvaged but scrapped.

1941 P 32 sunk by mine 5 miles off Tripoli while attacking a convoy. Her captain, Lt-Cdr David Adby and Coxswain P.O. Kirk, were the only survivors of the thirteen U-class submarines sunk in the Mediterranean.

1943 Hudson O/200 and Wellington HZ/697 (Fr) sank U-403 off Gambia (14.11N, 17.40W).

1944 *Ottawa*, *Chaudière* and *Kootenay* (all RCN) sank U-621, and Sunderland W/201 sank U-107 in Bay of Biscay.

1951 Fast Patrol Boat *Bold Pioneer*, the first operational warship powered by gas turbines, launched at White of Cowes.

See 9 March 1959, 20 July 1968, 26 April 1971.

19 AUGUST

1702 Benbow's Last Fight. Vice-Admiral John Benbow with six of the line engaged a French squadron under Rear-Admiral Jean Du Casse off Cape Santa Marta N.E. of Cartagena in present-day Colombia in a five-day running battle early in the War of the Spanish Succession. Benbow in *Breda* (70) supported by *Ruby* (48) and *Falmouth* (48) repeatedly attacked the enemy but in 'one of the most painful and disgraceful episodes in the history of the British Navy' (Laird Clowes, *The Royal Navy*, vol.2, p.372) four of his seven captains failed to support him and led to their being court-martialled for cowardice and two being executed. Benbow's leg was shattered by a chain shot at 0300 on 22 August but he remained on his quarterdeck in a cradle made by the ship's carpenter and died in November. Benbow's Last Fight caught the national imagination and was celebrated in verse and ballad, and most memorably in the Admiral Benbow inn in *Treasure Island*. Ships: *Breda* (70) flag; *Windsor* (60); *Defiance* (64); *Greenwich* (54); *Pendennis* (48); *Ruby* (48); *Falmouth* (48).

See 24 August 1702, 8 October 1702, 4 November 1702, 16 April 1703.

1711 Edward Boscawen, eighteenth-century fleet commander, born.

See 10 January 1761.

1782 *Duc de Chartres* captured the French *Aigle* 36 miles S.W. by S. of Cape Henry, Virginia.

1801 *Sybille* captured the French *La Chiffone* in Mahe Roads, Seychelles.

1812 *Guerrière* (38) taken by the American *Constitution* (44) about 500 miles S.E. of Halifax.

See 17 July 1812.

1840 *Druid*, *Hyacinth*, *Larne* and *Enterprize* (Ben. Mar.) destroyed a Chinese fort outside Macao. Troops: Bengal Volunteer Regiment.

1844 Boats of *Dido* destroyed six war prahus and the town of Karangan, Borneo.

1845 *Agincourt*, *Cruizer*, *Daedalus*, *Vestal* and *Vixen* with boats of *Wolverine*, *Nemesis* and *Pluto* (Ben. Mar.) destroyed the pirate stronghold of Seriff Osman in the Sungei Malloodoo (Marudu).

1915 *Baralong* (Q-ship) sank U-27 in S.W. Approaches (50.43N, 07.22W).

1915 Submarine E 1 torpedoed German battle-cruiser *Moltke* in the Gulf of Riga but not sunk. First torpedoing of a Dreadnought.

1915 AM (later GC); CPO Michael Sullivan Keogh (*Ark Royal*) for attempt to rescue the fatally injured Capt C.H. Collett, DSO, RMA, from a crashed and burning aircraft at Imbros Aerodrome. Keogh was overcome by burns and blazing petrol.

See 22 September 1914.

1916 Submarine E 23 torpedoed German battleship *Westfalen* off Terschelling.

Light cruiser *Nottingham* sunk by U-52 off the Farnes.

1941 Rear-Admiral Philip Vian with light cruisers *Nigeria* (flag) and *Aurora*, destroyers *Icarus*, *Tartar*, *Anthony*, *Antelope* and *Eclipse*, the oiler *Oligarch*, and the liner *Empress of Canada* with Canadian troops embarked, sailed to destroy mining facilities on Spitzbergen and evacuate 2,000 Russian coal miners. *Nigeria* escorted *Empress of Canada* to Archangel to disembark miners before re-joining *Aurora* off Barentsburg on 1 September to re-embark Canadian troops and 800 Norwegian colonists next day. On the way back the cruisers sank the German minelayer *Bremse* and the force arrived at Scapa Flow on 10 September.

See 27 July 1941.

1941 Convoy OG 71, which left the Mersey on 13 August carrying military supplies for Gibraltar, attacked by a German U-boat pack W. of Ireland. The commodore's ship, the Yeoward liner SS *Aguila*, with ninety service personnel including twenty-two wrens (twelve cypher officers and ten chief wren W/T special operators), torpedoed and sunk by U-201 (49.23N, 17.56W); Cdre P.E. Parker (Vice-Admiral, retd) and 156 souls lost. Master and nine others

A computer-generated image of the Royal Navy's two new Queen Elizabeth-class aircraft carriers. (*RN*)

rescued by corvette *Wallflower*, another six by tug *Empire Oak* which was herself torpedoed and sunk with all hands by U-564 on 22 August. The convoy escort included the corvette *Campanula*, whose First Lieutenant, Lt-Cdr Nicholas Monsarrat, remembered the loss of the Wrens in his fictional character Third Officer Julie Hallam in *The Cruel Sea* in 1951. Future WRNS drafts were permitted passage in HM ships.

See 8 August 1979.

1942 Raid on Dieppe by Capt J. Hughes-Hallett (*Calpe*) and Maj-Gen. J.H. Roberts (2nd Canadian Division). Battle Honour: Dieppe 1942. *Berkeley* scuttled by *Albrighton* after being bombed. Operation Jubilee.

The raid on Dieppe was mounted to give Canadian troops newly arrived in the UK battle experience, to gain experience of assault techniques, and to try out new equipment that was being developed. Dieppe offered many targets, including a radar station, a fighter airfield, gun batteries and port installations. It was also within range of UK shore-based fighter aircraft. The final plan incorporated a main assault on the harbour, and attacks on each flank. Some 237 naval vessels were used, 4,961 Canadian Army personnel, 1,057 Commandos and a small number of US Rangers were landed, and sixty-seven squadrons of aircraft were in support. The assault started early on the 19th. No. 4 Cdo achieved complete success on the western flank, but the reverse was true on the eastern flank, where the enemy were alerted by the assault force meeting a coastal convoy. In the main assault, even the beach was not fully secured, and evacuation was delayed until 1100 by too rigid a timetable. By 1230, 1,000 men had been recovered from the beach, but one destroyer (*Berkeley*) was damaged by air attack and had to be sunk, and another (*Calpe*) was also hit.

Some thirty-three landing craft were also lost, and there were 3,363 Canadian and 247 Cdo casualties. The Germans lost only 600 in all, and 48 aircraft. British aircraft losses were 106.

The enemy were jubilant, and criticised the raid for 'too much precision and detailed arrangement'. However, the British learned many lessons, for example the need for heavy gunfire support even with air cover. Many lives were saved in the bigger operations that followed.

1943 *Tui* (RNZN) and US aircraft of VS/57 sank the Japanese S/M I-17 in South Pacific.

1969 Commissioning of 700S NAS, Lt-Cdr V.G. Sirrett RN, at Culdrose, the first RN Sea King HAS Mk 1 helicopter squadron. The first operational unit was 824 NAS formed 24 February 1970 at Culdrose and later embarked in *Ark Royal*.

See 2 July 1969.

1971 Queen Alexandra's Royal Naval Nursing Service Reserve established. First Sister enrolled, at Severn Division, 15 December 1971.

1988 General Service Medal (1962) with clasp 'Mine Clearance – Gulf of Suez' approved for mine clearance service in the Gulf of Suez between 15 August 1984 and 15 October 1984. DCI(RN) 232/88.

1995 Destroyer *Southampton* provided relief assistance to island of Montserrat until 31 August following volcanic eruption. Operation Harlech. From 6–15 September the destroyer with RFA *Oakleaf* engaged in relief operations in Anguilla following widespread damage in wake of Hurricane Luis.

See 18 July 1995, 17 August 1997.

2003 *Splendid*, Cdr Paul Burke, left Gareloch for the last time to pay off at Devonport after twenty-two years' service. Formal decommissioning ceremony had been held at Faslane on 14 August. She was the first RN submarine fitted with Tomahawk Land Attack Missiles (TLAM) and the first to use them operationally in the Kosovo campaign in 1999. On her final patrol she fired TLAM against Iraqi targets.

20 AUGUST

1702 Vice-Admiral John Benbow continued to fight Capt Ducasse, his ship and *Ruby* now being the only English protagonists.

1765 Harrison explained his fourth chronometer to Board of Longitude.

The Board of Longitude

British seamen beginning to explore and chart the world could establish their latitude with ease, but longitude could be achieved only by measuring the difference of time between the meridian altitude of the sun and its meridian altitude at Greenwich. In 1714, at the instigation of the Admiralty, a Board of Longitude ('Commissioners for the Discovery of the Longitude at Sea') was set up, offering an award of £20,000 for the construction of a chronometer within a set degree of accuracy. A number of clockmakers took up the challenge, which was eventually won by John Harrison in 1765 with his fourth chronometer.

1799 *Clyde* captured the French *Vestale* 20 miles W. by N. of Cordouan lighthouse.

1800 *Seine* captured the French *Vengeance* in the Mona Passage.
Battle Honour: Vengeance 1800.

1812 *Revenge*, first ship to be fitted with ground tier of new metal tanks.

1824 Boats of *Icarus* captured the pirate schooner *Diableto* at Cayo Blanco, Cuba.

1864 Conversion completed of *Royal Sovereign*, only turret-ship built of wood and first ship in RN to carry her main armament outside her hull.

1875 Cdre James Graham Goodenough, aged 44, commodore on the Australian Station, was struck by bone-tipped arrows poisoned with tetanus when wading ashore at Carlisle Bay on Ndende, Santa Cruz Islands in the British Solomons, on 12 August.

Seven days later the dying Commodore 'caused himself to be carried to the quarter-deck [of his flagship, the wood screw corvette *Pearl*], and the ship's company to be summoned that he might bid them all farewell . . . "Before I go back to die, I should like you all to say 'God bless you!" This with one voice and very earnestly they did, and he replied "May He bless you with such happiness as He has given me!". He shook hands with all the petty officers, having a special word for each, and was then carried, exhausted, but in perfect contentment of spirit, to his cabin, saying, "I suppose there is nothing now to be done but to die quietly"' – Moresby biography, p.92. Cdre Goodenough died in agony the following day, eight days after the attack. HMS *Pearl* took his body to Sydney, the ship in full mourning with her yards scandalised. He was buried in St Thomas' churchyard in Wilmington, overlooking Sydney Harbour, near the grave of Capt Owen Stanley RN, captain of HMS *Rattlesnake*, who died on 13 March 1850 – Dawson, pt.2, p.26). Goodenough's son, Admiral Sir William Goodenough, successively commanded the First and Second Light Cruiser Squadrons in the First World War and was C-in-C The Nore 1924–7.

See 30 January 1945.

1882 *Northumberland*, *Orion* and *Coquette* landed 500 seamen and Royal Marines and occupied Government House, the lock and signal station at Ismailia.

1896 First RN wireless transmission (*Defiance*).

Defiance, a wooden ship of the line, at Devonport, was the first ship to receive a morse transmission. Her captain, Capt H.B. Jackson, later Admiral of the Fleet FRS, developed the device, and worked with Marconi in his trials. Marconi's first major trials of radio in Britain were not carried out until the autumn of that year. On 20 May 1897, the radio was demonstrated at ranges up to 2 miles by the *Defiance* at anchor, and *Scourge* under way.

1896 Clock Tower completed at entrance to RN Barracks, Devonport.

1901 Capt R.H.S. Bacon appointed first Inspecting Captain of Submarine Boats.

See 9 June 1947.

1914 The Russians captured the German light cruiser *Magdeburg* in the Gulf of Finland together with a most secret naval signals cypher book – *Signalbuch der Kaiserlichen Marine* (*SKM*) – reportedly found clutched to the body of a drowned seaman.

See 11 August 1914, 13 October 1914, 30 November 1914, 9 May 1941.

HMS *Royal Sovereign* (1857), coast defence turret ship. (*NMRN*)

The Russians offered the treasure to the Royal Navy and the cruiser *Theseus* was sent to collect these 'sea-stained priceless documents' (Churchill) from Polyarno. The *Theseus*, which also brought back six trunks of clothes belonging to Princess Louis of Battenberg, wife of the First Sea Lord, arrived back at Scapa Flow on 10 October and the *SKM* reached the Admiralty on 13 October. Its arrival coincided with that of Capt Reginald 'Blinker' Hall as director of Naval Intelligence – an inspired appointment. (Hall, who succeeded Henry 'Dummy' Oliver, had relinquished command of the battlecruiser *Queen Mary* through ill-health). 'Thus was born the famous Room 40 OB [Old Building of the Admiralty] and the whole British cryptographic organisation, which contributed so much to victory in both World Wars' – Roskill, *Admiral of the Fleet Earl Beatty, The Last Naval Hero*, p.87.

1916 Light cruiser *Falmouth* sank after four torpedo attacks, the last two by U-63 7½ miles S. of Flamborough Head. (First torpedoed twice on the previous day by U-66, 65 miles off the Humber.)

1917 Submarine E 47 lost in North Sea.

1917 *Acton* (Q 34) sank UC-72 in Bay of Biscay (46.00N, 08.48W).

1940 Submarine *Cachalot* sank U-51 in a surface torpedo action in Bay of Biscay.

1941 Submarine P 33 presumed mined off Tripoli, formally paid off.

1943 Catalinas C/259 and N/265 sank U-197 off S. Madagascar (28.40S, 42.36E).

1944 *Forester*, *Vidette* and *Wensleydale* sank U-413 off Brighton.

1944 *Chaudière*, *Kootenay* and *Ottawa* (all RCN) sank U-984 off Ushant.

1970 A three-day court martial ended at *Cochrane* with five ABs from minehunter *Iveston* being found guilty of mutiny when the ship was lying at Ullapool on 5 and 6 July. The sentences 'to be Dismissed with Disgrace' were reduced on review by the Admiralty Board to 'to be Dismissed from Her Majesty's Service'. On the day of the mutiny a man described as a 'tramp' had been entertained in the Wardroom and, although irrelevant to the case, this provided the press with a focus for wide publicity and ridicule of naval administration.

21 AUGUST

1704 The original St Ann's church in Portsmouth Dockyard was 'by commission of ye Right Reverend Lord Bishop of Winton . . . consecrated by ye Right Reverend Lord Bishop of Rochester' – recorded on a stone tablet in the present church.

See 4 February 1786, 18 February 1907, 21 June 1934, 11 November 1933.

1740 Admiral Vernon, nicknamed 'Old Grog' because of the grogram material in his boat-cloak, ordered watering of sailors' rum (called Grog thereafter). 'Whereas . . . the Pernicious Custom of the Seamen drinking their Allowance of Rum in Drams, and often at once, is attended by many Fatal Effects to their morals as well as their Health' the daily allowance of half a pint per man is to be mixed with a quart of water 'to be mixed in a Scuttled Butt kept for that purpose, and to be done upon Deck, and in the presence of the Lieutenant of the Watch' – *Burford* at Port Royal, Jamaica.

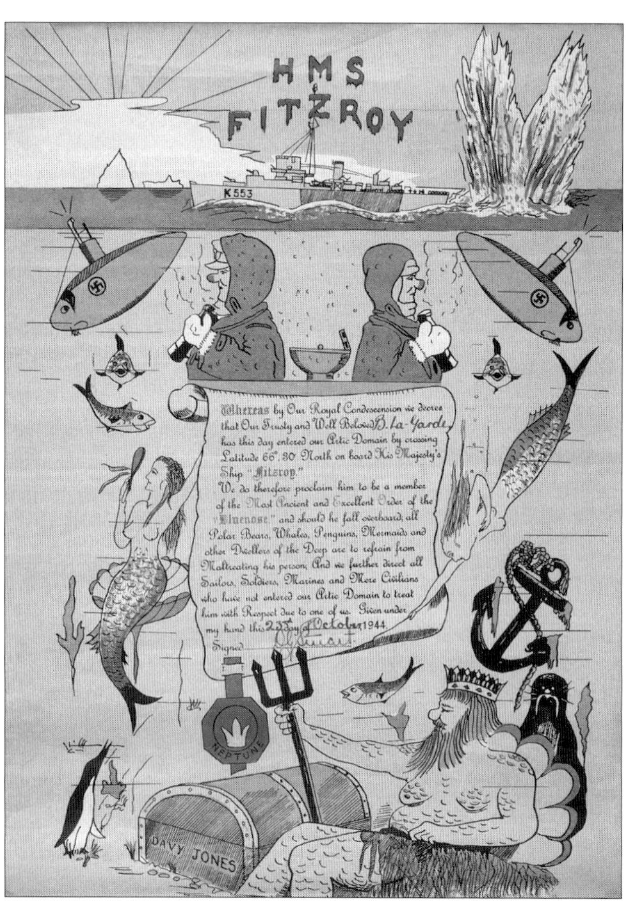

1778 Cdre Sir Edward Vernon in *Ripon* (60) began blockade of Pondicherry, the principal French naval base in India, which capitulated on 17 October. The French withdrew permanently to Mauritius.

1797 *Penguin* captured the French privateer *Oiseau* and her prize 100 miles W. of Ushant.

1798 *Hazard* captured the French *Neptune* 440 miles N.W. by W. of Cape Finisterre.

1801 Boats of *Fisgard*, *Diamond* and *Boadicea* cut out the Spanish *Neptuno*, a gunboat and a merchant vessel from Corunna.

1810 Two unarmed boats of *Sirius* recaptured the ex-British East Indiaman *Windham* off Rivière Noire, Mauritius.

1853 *Breadalbane*, carrying supplies for the expedition searching for Franklin in *Erebus* and *Terror*, crushed by ice and sank in Lancaster Sound.

1860 British and French forces under Admiral Sir James Hope captured the Taku forts, China. Ships: *Chesapeake*, *Coromandel* (tender), *Imperieuse*. Gunboats: *Algerine*, *Clown*, *Drake*, *Forester*, *Havock*, *Janus*, *Opossum*, *Staunch*, *Woodcock*. French: *Impératrice-Eugénie*. Troops: Royal Artillery, Royal Engineers, RMLI Bn, 3rd, 44th and 67th Regiments, Madras Artillery.

1910 *Bedford*, Monmouth-class 6-in armoured cruiser, carrying out full-power trials in Straits of Korea, en route from Wei-Hai-Wei to Japan, stranded at night on the Samarang Rocks, Quelpart Island (Cheju Do). Stokehold flooded, drowning eighteen men. Wreck sold in October 1910.

See 30 May 1906, 14 November 1918, 8 August 1922, 18 May 1940, 7 July 2002.

1915 Crew of sunken *Ruel*, while in their boats, fired on by U-38 (S.S.W. of Bishop Rock). First authenticated case of such behaviour.

'Bluenose certificate' issued to mark HMS *Fitzroy* crossing into the Arctic Circle on Russian convoy, October 1944. (*NMRN 2001/54*)

1916 Submarine E 54 sank UC-10 E.S.E. of the Schouwen Bank lightvessel (51.45N, 03.20E).

1917 Sopwith Pup N6430 (*Yarmouth*) – a land-plane flown off a cruiser – destroyed Zeppelin L-23 near Lodbjerg, Danish coast (56.35N, 07.49E). First victory for a cruiser-based aircraft.

1917 UC-41 destroyed by trawler *Jacinth* off Tay estuary, having exploded one of her own mines.

1920 'The Postmaster-General announces that mails for Tristan da Cunha will be dispatched to the island by HMS *Dartmouth* from Simonstown. Parcels should reach the GPO London not later than . . .' – *The Times*, 21 August 1920.

1941 Paddle minesweeper *Kylemore* sunk by German aircraft at Harwich.

1941 The first Russian convoy, code-named Dervish. Six merchant ships sailed from Hvalfiord, Iceland, for Archangel under Convoy Commodore Capt J.C.K. Dowding RNR, carrying fourteen crated Hurricane fighters, wool, rubber and tin. The close escort provided by ocean minesweepers *Halcyon*, *Salamander* and *Harrier* which were to remain in N. Russia, the destroyers *Electra*, *Active* and *Impulsive*, and the A/S trawlers *Hamlet*, *Macbeth* and *Ophelia*. Concurrently, the aircraft carrier *Argus*, carrying twenty-four operational Hurricanes for the protection of Murmansk, Polyarnoe and Archangel, sailed under escort of the heavy cruiser *Shropshire* and destroyers *Matabele*, *Punjabi* and *Somali* which had the RAF personnel embarked. The deployment was given distant cover by Rear-Admiral W.F. Wake-Walker with the carrier *Victorious* and heavy cruisers *Devonshire* and *Suffolk*, and destroyers *Inglefield*, *Eclipse* and *Escapade*. *Argus* flew off her Hurricanes when within range of the Russian airfield at Vaenga and all ships arrived safely. The first of the PQ convoys sailed on 29 September 1941.

1944 Sloop *Kite* sunk by U-344 N. of Jan Mayen Island. Convoy JW 59.

1944 Corvette *Alberni* (RCN) torpedoed by U-480. Sank in half a minute, S.E. of St Catherine's Point (50.18N, 00.51W). Operation Neptune. *Orchis*, mined and beached off Normandy, her bow blown off: CTL.

1967 Frigate *Loch Fada*, the first and last of the Loch-class frigates serving in the Royal Navy, sailed from Singapore and arrived at Portsmouth 11 October to pay off after twenty-three years' service. While escorting Convoy BTC.81 on 27 February 1945 she sank U-1018 South. of the Lizard, and next day, with *Labuan* and *Wild Goose*, and Liberator H/112 of the USN, she sank U-327 off The Scillies. *Loch Fada* took Archbishop Makarios of Cyprus to exile in the Seychelles in 1956 and after paying-off in 1967 she was used as a floating test bed for the Sea Wolf missile on the MOD range in Luce Bay, Scotland.

1990 HM ships authorised to enforce UN embargo on ships trading with Iraq. Operation Granby.

22 August

1702 Vice-Admiral Benbow continued to fight Capt Ducasse. Lost his leg (and died in November).
See 7 November 1702

1778 Frigate *Minerva* (32), Capt John Stott, unaware that France had entered the War of American Independence on 14 July, incautiously closed a strange sail off Puerto Plata, Hispaniola, and received two broadsides from the French frigate *Concorde* (32) and was taken. Stott and his First Lieutenant, William Bartholomew, died of their wounds 'aggravated by grief at the loss of their ship' (Laird Clowes); 'The officers had lost control of the men'. *Minerva* re-taken by *Courageux* (74), Capt Lord Mulgrave, off Brest 4 January 1781.
See 1 September 1778, 19 November 1941.

1795 *Stag* captured the Dutch *Alliantie* off Jedder (Jeaderen), Norway.

1798 *Alcmene* captured the French *Légère* 12 miles W. of Alexandria. Two sailors dived to recover French dispatches although the ship was doing 6 knots.

1809 *Surveillante*, taken in West Indies in 1803, landed Wellesley at Lisbon to command the British Army in Spain, which, after five years, he led to Toulouse.

1916 Submarine E 16 mined in Heligoland Bight.

1918 *Hood* launched at John Brown's, Clydebank, by Lady Hood, widow of Rear-Admiral Hon. Horace Hood, who had been killed in *Invincible* at Jutland, 31 May 1916, the day *Hood* was originally laid down. At 860ft 7in overall, the longest warship ever built for the RN, and the heaviest warship at that time to hoist the White Ensign.
See 1 September 1916.

1940 RM Siege Regt. stationed at Dover fired first shell across the Channel.

1940 Three Swordfish of 824 Sqn (*Eagle*) sank the depot ship *Monte Gargano*, a destroyer and the S/M *Iride* in the Gulf of Bomba, bound for a 'chariot' raid on Alexandria.

1942 Italian TB *Generale Antonio Cantore* sunk in a minefield laid by submarine *Porpoise* N.E. of Bomba, off Cyrenaica.

1943 *Easton* and *Pindos* (Greek) sank U-458 off Sicily. Convoy MKF 22.

1944 *Nabob* and *Bickerton* torpedoed by U-354 off Hammerfest (71.42N, 19.11E). Frigate *Bickerton* sunk by *Vigilant*, for tactical reasons. Swordfish C/825 (*Vindex*) sank U-344 off north Norway. Convoy JW 59.

1944 Minesweeper *Loyalty* (ex-*Rattler*) sunk by U-480 near E3 buoy off the Nab (50.09N, 00.41W), near to *Alberni* yesterday. Operation Neptune.
See 1 May 2008.

1944 Submarine *Spiteful* bombarded the oil tanks at Christmas Island, Indian Ocean.

HMS *Hood* (1918), the largest warship in the world at the time of her completion. (*NMRN*)

23 August

1628 The Lord High Admiral, the Duke of Buckingham, 'stabbed to the heart' at Portsmouth by John Felton, an army lieutenant, in the La Rochelle Expedition.
See 27 January 1626, 8 March 1689.

1702 Vice-Admiral Benbow in the fifth day of his running action with Rear-Admiral Ducasse.

1794 *Flora* and *Arethusa* drove the French *Espion* and *Alerte* ashore in Audierne Bay, *Alerte* becoming a total wreck. *Diamond*, *Artois*, *Diana* and *Santa Margarita* drove the French *Volontaire* ashore off Penmarc'h Point, where she was destroyed.

1796 *Galatea* and *Sylph* drove ashore and destroyed the French *Andromaque* near Arcachon.

1798 *Naiad* and *Magnanime* captured the *Décade* off Cape Finisterre.

1806 *Arethusa* and *Anson* captured the Spanish *Pomona* under the guns of Morro Castle, Havana, and destroyed nine gunboats.

1853 *Surprise* and two boats of *Cambrian* captured or destroyed twenty-eight pirate junks at Lingting Island.

1854 *Miranda* destroyed the defences and burned the town of Kola, White Sea.

1883 Royal Corps of Naval Constructors established by Order in Council. First DNC was Nathaniel Barnaby, 1885.

1911 The famous Committee of Imperial Defence meeting held following the Agadir Crisis earlier that summer which brought to light the absence of naval war plans. Gen. Sir Henry Wilson, Director of Military Operations, gave a fluent and convincing presentation on the merits of a continental strategy ('polished and expert explanation' – Roskill, *Hankey*, vol.1 p.102) and 'completely outclassed' his namesake, the taciturn First Sea Lord, Admiral Sir Arthur Wilson, who gave 'a halting, ill-prepared and utterly unconvincing statement for a maritime strategy'. The naval case was decisively lost. Amphibious warfare was consequently put on the back burner. 'Thus was Britain committed to full-scale participation in a continental campaign if war should break out with Germany' (Roskill, p.103) and War Office plans to land a major British field army in France at the outbreak of war – 'the largest possible army in the shortest possible time' – were confirmed. The rest is history.

1914 *Kennet* fought the German S-90 off Tsingtau.

1937 *Repulse*, battlecruiser, and destroyer *Codrington*, at entry of Spanish Civil War, secured the release of a British ship taken by the Republican light cruiser *Miguel de Cervantes*.
See 22 July 1936.

1939 Capt Lord Louis Mountbatten accepted the destroyer *Kelly* from her builders, Hawthorn, Leslie, Hebburn-on-Tyne.
See 27 June 1939.

1940 *Hostile* mined 18 miles S.E. of Cape Bon (36.53N, 11.19E). Sunk by *Hero*.

1941 *Zinnia* sunk by U-564 off Oporto (40.25N, 10.40W). Convoy OG 71.

1944 Admiral Sir Bruce Fraser succeeded Admiral Sir James Somerville as C-in-C Eastern Fleet. Fraser's flag hoisted at 0800 in the destroyer *Relentless* and Somerville's flag struck at Sunset in the light cruiser *Caradoc*.
See 28 March 1942.

1956 Light cruiser *Newfoundland* bombarded CT targets in the Kota Tinggi district of Johore, Malaya, with 101 6-in shells.
See 2 November 1944, 22 September 1951, 1 March 1956.

1993 *Opossum*, Lt-Cdr J.R.G. Drummond RN, last of the Royal Navy's thirteen Oberon-class diesel-electric submarines, paid off at Gosport. Earlier that month the thiry-year-old boat was the first Western submarine since the Second World War to visit Severomorsk, the Russian Northern Fleet base.
See 18 July 1959, 29 August 1969, 31 December 1974, 30 October 2004.

24 AUGUST

1217 Battle of Sandwich: Hubert de Burgh's victory over Eustace the Monk off Dover.

Louis of France had invaded England and occupied London on the death of King John. There he was besieged, and a large fleet was gathered at Calais to relieve him. Hubert de Burgh was Governor of Dover Castle at the time, and he gathered sixteen Cinque Port ships and twenty others to attack the French Fleet. It was a small fleet, and the people were at first unwilling to fight. De Burgh said, 'You shall suffer me to be hanged before ye surrender this castle; for it is the key to England.'

The Fleet sailed out against the eighty French ships, gained the weather gauge, and grappled and fought the enemy ships at will. Sixty-five were captured after a savage fight. De Burgh was made Lord High Admiral for this service.

1702 Vice-Admiral Benbow's running action with Ducasse ended.

See 19 August 1702.

Letter from Capt Ducasse to Admiral Benbow after the battle:

> Sir,
> I had little hope on Monday but to have supped in your cabbin (*sic*); but it pleased God to order it otherwise. I am thankful for it. As for those cowardly captains who deserted you, hang them up, for by heaven, they deserve it.

1806 Boats of *Alexandria* and *Gracieuse* destroyed two Spanish vessels at La Hacha, Colombia.

1810 *Magicienne* (32) and *Sirius* (36 and second of the name) burned by own crews to avoid capture at Grand Port, Mauritius.

1810 *Nereide* taken by the French *Bellone* in Grand Port, Mauritius after having suffered 222 casualties out of a crew of 281.

1831 RN Long Service and Good Conduct medal introduced, the award initially depending on twenty-one years' service, reduced eventually to ten.

See 10 August 1915.

1867 The murder of child Fanny Adams at Alton, Hampshire (which led to Winchester's last public hanging). Macabre and grisly details of how her body had been dismembered were given in court and widely reported. The introduction of tinned meat in the Fleet that year led to lower deck concerns about its provenance. The tins, however, became useful containers, hence 'fannies' for mess traps.

See 29 April 1967.

1935 The Royal Marines for the first time in their history provided the Royal Guard at Buckingham Palace, St James's Palace, the Bank of England and 'for the Hyde Park magazines'. The specially formed battalion of sixteen officers, 349 rank and file and 110 band and drums under Lt-Col T.L. Hunton, were quartered with the Coldstream Guards at Chelsea Barracks. The visit to London ended on 19 September with the battalion exercising the privilege of the Royal Marines of marching through the City of London with colours flying, drums beating and bayonets fixed.

See 19 September 1935.

1939 Home Fleet and all ships in Home Ports proceeded to War Stations.

1940 Bombardment of seaplane base at Bomba, North Africa. Ships: *Diamond*, *Ilex*, *Juno*, *Waterhen* (10th DF).

1940 *Ladybird* and *Waterhen* attacked shore targets at Bardia, North Africa. Operation M.B.1.

1940 *Penzance* sunk with heavy casualties by U-37 in N. Atlantic (56.16N, 27.19W). Convoy SC 1.

1940 Portsmouth Dockyard and Southsea bombed; twenty-five men lost in direct hit on a dockyard air raid shelter and stern of destroyer *Acheron* blown off. Two nights later the Germans mistook Langstone Harbour for Portsmouth and 'plastered waste land . . . apiece of stupendous luck' – Admiral Sir William James, C-in-C Portsmouth.

See 12 August 1940, 5 and 23 December 1940, 10 January 1941, 10 March 1941, 17 April 1941.

The Baltic Fleet at Spithead, 1855. (*NMRN 1985/297*)

1940 Fleet carrier *Formidable* completed at Harland & Wolff, Belfast, and commissioned. A short career but exemplary of the flexibility of maritime power: February 1941, searched for German surface raider in S. Atlantic; February 1941, attacked enemy positions in Italian Somaliland, E. Africa; March 1941, Battle of Matapan in the Mediterranean; November 1942, covered N. African landings (Operation Torch); July 1943, covered invasion of Sicily (Operation Husky); September 1943, covered Salerno landings in Italy; July 1944, strikes on German battleship *Tirpitz* in Kaafjord, Norway (Operation Mascot) and again the next month (Operation Goodwood); March 1945, British Pacific Fleet strikes on Japanese positions in Sakishima-gunto and Formosa in support of US landings on Okinawa (Operation Iceberg). Paid off Portsmouth March 1947.

See 17 August 1939, 21 May 1941.

1941 Iranian *Babr* and *Palang* sunk at Khorramanshahr and Abadan by *Yarra* (RAN) and *Shoreham*, for resisting occupation by Allied forces concerned to maintain supplies to USSR.

1943 *Nubian*, *Tartar* and *Tumult* bombarded Lucri.

1943 Wellington J/179 sank U-134 off Portugal.

1943 Admiral of the Fleet Sir Charles Forbes, C-in-C Home Fleet until December 1940, hauled down his flag as C-in-C Plymouth.

See 22 November 1880, 28 August 1960.

1944 *Louis* sank U-445 in the Bay of Biscay.

1944 Carrier air-strikes from *Formidable*, *Furious* and *Indefatigable* on the German battleship *Tirpitz* in Altenfjord, to synchronise with the passage of convoy JW 59. Operation Goodwood – repeated on the 29th. *Tirpitz* hit, but not seriously damaged. FAA Sqns: Barracuda: 820, 826, 827; Corsair 1841, 1842; Firefly: 1770; Hellcat: 1840; Seafire: 801, 887, 894.

1944 *Indomitable* (Rear-Admiral C. Moody) and *Victorious* launched air strikes on Emmahaven and on the cement works at Padang, Sumatra. Operation Banquet. FAA Sqns: Barracuda: 815, 817, 831; Hellcat: 1839, 1844; Corsair: 1834, 1836.

1944 *Keppel*, *Loch Dunvegan*, *Mermaid*, *Peacock* and Swordfish M/825 (*Vindex*) sank U-354 off Murmansk. Convoy JW 59.

1946 GC (ex-AM): Lt E.W.K. Walton for saving life during Antarctic survey.

25 August

1553 *Henry Grace à Dieu* burned.
See 13 June 1514.

1707 *Nightingale*, escorting a convoy of thirty-six sail, taken by six French galleys off Harwich. The convoy escaped.

1795 *Venerable*, *Repulse*, *Minotaur* and *Venus* captured the French *Suffisante* off the Texel.

1795 *Spider* captured the French *Victorieuse* off the Texel.

1800 *Success* captured the French *Diana* 50 miles N.E. of Malta.

1803 *Seagull* recaptured *Lord Nelson* (Indiaman) 300 miles W.S.W. of Ushant.
See 14 August 1803.

1804 *Immortalite* (36) and *Bruiser* confirmed Bonaparte's suspicion about the inability of his landing craft at Boulogne to lift the Grande Armée across the English Channel by sinking a strong squadron struggling to get off a lee shore.

1811 *Diana* and *Semiramis* destroyed the French *Pluvier* and recaptured the ex-British *Teazer* off the mouth of the Gironde. Their boats captured all five of a French convoy in the river.

1907 Rear-Admiral John Jellicoe hoisted his flag in the pre-Dreadnought battleship *Albemarle* as second-in-command to Vice-Admiral Hon. Sir Assheton Curzon-Howe, C-in-C Atlantic Fleet. His Flag Captain was William Goodenough.
See 15 August 1781, 20 November 1935, 30 January 1945.

1914 RM units landed at Ostend. Withdrawn 31 August.

1919 First Submarine Command Flag Officer. Rear-Admiral Douglas Lionel Dent, lately Captain of the battleship *Centurion* and with

The galleon of 80 guns, *Henry Grace à Dieu* (1514). (*NMRN 1999/41*)

The line of the great storehouses in Portsmouth. The earliest was completed in 1763 and used as a 'present use store' to house material taken off ships entering dry dock. They now house the galleries of the National Museum of the Royal Navy. (*NMRN*)

no submarine experience, hoisted his flag at HMS *Dolphin* as Rear-Admiral (Submarines). He was to 'exercise a general administrative charge over the Submarine Service' and 'he will have a room at the Admiralty'. Rear-Admiral(S) 'will also visit the submarine flotillas, after informing the flag officers or senior naval officers concerned of his intention to do so, and obtaining their approval . . . later he will forward to them a report on his visit' – *The Times*.

See 14 July 1959.

1941 *Vascama* and Catalina J/209 sank U-452 in N. Atlantic (61.30N, 15.30W).

1942 *Marne, Martin* and *Onslaught* sank the German minelayer *Ulm* 100 miles E. of Bear Island and rescued sixty men. This was one of the very few occasions when Ultra intelligence was sent without cover to those not privy to Ultra as a source.

1942 *Aldenham* and *Eridge* bombarded Daba, Egypt.

1942 Battle of Eastern Solomons between US and Japanese forces. Present: *Australia, Hobart* (RAN).

1943 Light cruiser *Orion* bombarded the Calabrian coast.

1943 *Wallflower* and *Wanderer* sank U-523 in Atlantic (42.03N, 18.02W). Convoys KMS 24/OG 92.

1944 French troops entered Toulon after bombardment by British cruisers *Aurora* and *Black Prince* and US and French ships.

1944 Battleship *Warspite* bombarded Brest.

1959 Destroyer *Hogue* severely damaged in collision with Indian light cruiser *Mysore*, ex-HMS *Nigeria*, during night exercises N.E. of Ceylon. One man killed and three injured transferred to the light fleet carrier *Centaur* and landed at RAF hospital in Ceylon. *Hogue* taken to Singapore; CTL. Sold 7 March 1962. The first of three RN and RAN destroyers sunk or written off by collision in five years.

See 1 May 1942, 29 August 1957, 2 August 1962, 11 February 1964.

1972 RN Museum, Portsmouth, established.

1988 Lynx helicopter from frigate *Sirius* (sixth of the name) fired on from Triton Island while rescuing crew of Taiwanese fishing boat.

26 AUGUST

1780 Admiral of the Fleet Lord Hawke, retired on shore, wrote to Admiral Sir Francis Geary, C-in-C Channel Fleet: 'For God's sake, if you should be so lucky as to get sight of the enemy, get as close to them as possible. Do not let them shuffle with you by engaging at a distance, but get within musket-shot if you can; that will be the best way to gain great honour, and will be the means to make the action decisive.'

1780 *Fame* privateer captured four French letters of marque – *Deux Frères, Univers, Nancy Pink* and ex-British *Zephyr* sloop – off Cap de Gata S.E. Spain.

1795 Boats of *Agamemnon, Ariadne, Inconstant, Meleager, Tartar, Southampton* and *Speedy* cut out the French *Résolue, République, Constitution, Vigilante* and five other vessels at Alassio and Laigueglia, Italy.

1799 *Tamar* captured the French *Républicaine* 80 miles N.W. of Surinam, Guiana.

1808 *Implacable* and *Centaur* captured the Russian *Sevolod* (74) off Rogervik, Gulf of Finland, and burned her next day. She had previously been taken by *Implacable*, when she hauled down her flag in less than half an hour, but was recovered by the enemy.
Battle Honour: *Sevolod* 1808.

1841 Capture of Amoy, China by Rear-Admiral Sir William Parker (*Wellesley*) and Lt-Gen. Sir Hugh Gough. Ships: *Algerine, Bentinck, Blenheim, Blonde, Columbine, Cruizer, Druid, Modeste, Pylades, Wellesley*; *Rattlesnake*, transport. Steamers: *Sesostris* (IN); *Nemesis, Phlegethon, Queen* (Ben. Mar.). Troops: Royal Artillery, 18th, 26th, 49th and 55th Regiments, Madras Artillery, Madras Sappers and Miners.

1858 *Magicienne, Inflexible, Plover* and *Algerine* destroyed 100 pirate vessels off Hong Kong and S.W. of Macao. Operation lasted until 3 September.

HMS *Highflyer*, a second-class cruiser of 1898. (*NMRN*)

HMS *Repulse* (1916), the first battlecruiser with 15-in guns. (*NMRN W&L 74*)

1904 Russia, at war with Japan, sent cruisers *Petersburg* and *Smolensk* to the Red Sea to intercept war contraband sailing under neutral flags to Japan. Britain, neutral but pro-Japan, banned combatant ships from British and Empire ports. The Cape Station cruisers, *Crescent*, *Pearl*, *Brilliant*, *St George* and *Forte* began a search for the Russian ships on 26 August and they were found by *Forte* on 6 September at Zanzibar.

1914 Cruiser *Highflyer* sank the German armed merchant cruiser *Kaiser Wilhelm der Grosse* off Rio de Oro, Spanish West Africa, only ten days out from Bremen.

1989 Admiral Sir Brian Brown promoted and appointed the first Supply Officer to be Second Sea Lord.

See 19 January 2000.

27 AUGUST

1793 Occupation of Toulon by Lord Hood at invitation of French Royalist. Hood had too few troops to garrison the port and hold it against advancing Republican forces under Napoleon.

See 18 December 1793.

1809 Boats of *Amphion* cut out six Venetian gunboats and destroyed a fort at Cortellazzo.

1813 Capture of the island of Santa Clara, during the siege of San Sebastian, by boats of squadron under Sir George Collier and a detachment of the 9th Regiment. Ships: *Ajax*, *President*, *Revolutionnaire*, *Surveillante*; *Isabella* and *Millbank* transports.

1816 Bombardment of Algiers by Admiral Lord Exmouth (*Queen Charlotte*) and a Dutch squadron under Vice-Admiral Baron Theodorus van Capellen (*Melampus*), to enforce the abolition of Christian slavery when other forms of diplomacy had failed.Battle Honour: Algiers 1816.

Ships: *Albion*, *Beelzebub*, *Britomart*, *Cordelia*, *Fury*, *Glasgow*, *Granicus*, *Hebrus*, *Hecla*, *Heron*, *Impregnable*, *Infernal*, *Leander*, *Minden*, *Mutine*, *Prometheus*, *Queen Charlotte*, *Severn*, *Superb*, Gunboats Nos. 1, 5, 19, 24, 28, *Falmouth* lighter and rocket boats. Dutch: *Amstel*, *Dageraad*, *Diana*, *Eendracht*, *Frederica*, *Melampus*. Troops: The Rocket Troop, RHA, Royal Sappers and Miners.

The Barbary Coast of North Africa had long been the centre of piracy in the Mediterranean, and its corsairs had ventured as far afield as Scandinavia. After the defeat of Napoleon in 1815, the British government resolved to deal with the matter. Lord Exmouth with the Mediterranean Fleet and a Dutch squadron went to Tunis, Tripoli and Algiers and offered treaties to the Deys prohibiting the taking of Christian slaves. The Dey of Algiers refused. A punitive expedition was mounted and the fleet anchored off Algiers 27 August 1816. The port was very well defended with forts and guns. The defences of Algiers were destroyed by a furious bombardment. Some 1,200 Christian slaves were freed.

1834 Excise cutter *Cameleon* run down and sunk off Dover by RNR training ship *Castor* (51.07N, 01.27E).

1896 Rear-Admiral Sir Harry Rawson (*St George*) bombarded the Sultan's palace at Dar-es-Salaam and sank his gunboat *Glasgow*. Ships: *St George*, *Racoon*, *Philomel*, *Thrush* and *Sparrow*. The action lasted forty-five minutes and has been called 'the shortest war in history'.

1912 Peter William Gretton born; one of the outstanding anti-submarine commanders of the Second World War. Died 1992.

1914 First RNAS squadron stationed in Europe arrived at Ostend.

1917 *Hyderabad* launched. Only vessel designed and built as a Q-ship. Also known as *Coral* and *Nicobar*, she ended as a depot ship in north Russia in 1919.

1919 GC (ex-AM): Cdr H. Buckle (*Tiger*) for saving life at Invergordon.

1941 Hudson S/269 captured U-570 off Iceland. The first solo success by Coastal Command. Submarine brought in by *Kingston Agate* and *Northern Chief*. Cypher machine captured intact. Commissioned as HMS *Graph*.

See 20 March 1944.

Admiral of the Fleet Earl Mountbatten of Burma. (*RN*)

1943 Sloop *Egret* sunk 30 miles W. of Vigo, and *Athabaskan* (RCN) damaged by Henschel Hs 293A glider bomb in its first deployment (42.10N, 09.22W).

1944 First Minesweeping Flotilla, Cdr Trevor Crick, maintaining the swept channel between Portsmouth and Arromanches, attacked by RAF Typhoons off Cape d'Antifer near Havre (49.41N, 00.05W) in friendly-fire error. *Britomart* and *Hussar* sunk, stern of *Salamander* blown off (CTL), *Jason* and trawler *Colsay* damaged. Some 117 killed, 149 seriously wounded.

See 10 September 1939.

'An air strike had been called up to attack an enemy force reported off Cape d'Antifer, and the Typhoons mistook our minesweepers for the enemy . . . the loss of life was heavy' – Roskill, *The War at Sea*, vol.3, pt.2, p.134.

'A breakdown in communications and poor staff work were responsible for one of the most serious British 'Own Goals'. Royal Air Force reconnaissance reported that the ships "appeared to be friendly" but the naval staff responsible for the security of the assault area were unaware of the change in the minesweeping programme which had taken the 1st Minesweeping Flotilla into an area in which there were not known to be any Allied ships – the Royal Navy therefore ordered the attack on its own ships' – Brown, *Warship Losses of World War Two*, p.121.

1945 Rear-Admiral C.H.J. Harcourt left Subic Bay for Hong Kong in the carrier *Indomitable* and three days later, to reduce the risk of mining, he shifted his flag to the light cruiser *Swiftsure* in which he entered Hong Kong with the light cruiser *Euryalus* and auxiliary AA cruiser *Prince Robert* (RCN) on 30 August.

See 30 August 1945.

1979 Murder of Admiral of the Fleet the Earl Mountbatten of Burma.

See 25 June 1900, 5 September 1979.

1980 *Shetland* returned survivors of St Kilda for a day's reunion.

See 29 August 1930.

2010 Submarine *Astute*, first of class, commissioned at Faslane.

See 31 January 2001, 8 June 2007.

Admiral of the Fleet Earl Mountbatten of Burma

During the early part of the Second World War Mountbatten was in command of HMS *Kelly* and the 5th Destroyer Flotilla. He gained a reputation for a great offensive spirit. His ship was sunk under him during the fighting off Crete in May 1941. Churchill appointed him Chief of Combined Operations and as such he was responsible for the highly successful raid on St Nazaire in March 1942. He also planned the raid on Dieppe which, although it did not achieve many of its objectives, proved a vital training ground for both men and equipment in the great amphibious operations later in the war. As Supreme Allied Commander of South East Asia Command, he was one of the war's most prominent Allied commanders. One of his most notable peacetime appointments was to be the last Viceroy of India, although he later became First Sea Lord, and the second Chief of the Defence Staff, succeeding MRAF Sir William Dickinson (a direct descendent of Nelson and a former RNAS officer). Mountbatten was murdered on holiday in Ireland in August 1979.

Admiral Lord Louis Mountbatten, the Supreme Commander (South East Asia Command) returning the salute as he steps on board a French warship serving with the British East Indies Fleet. (*NMRN*)

28 AUGUST

1595 Drake and Hawkins left Plymouth on what turned out to be their last voyage, since neither returned. Drake died of yellow fever and Hawkins of dysentery.

See 12 November 1595, 28 January 1596.

1652 Capt Richard Badiley (*Paragon*) escorting a convoy of four sail, fought a Dutch squadron under Capt Johan van Galen 2 leagues S. of Leghorn, near Montecristo. Ships: *Paragon, Phoenix, Constant Warwick, Elisabeth*. Captured: *Phoenix*. The convoy escaped. (A partial engagement had begun during the previous afternoon.) Battle Honour: Montecristo 1652.

1799 Admiral Viscount Duncan (*Kent*) received the surrender of the Dutch fleet at the Texel. Ships: *Circe, Isis, Kent*. Wrecked: *Blanche, Content, Lutine, Nassau*.

1810 *Iphigenia* taken by the French *Bellone, Minerve, Victor* and three other frigates at Grand Port, Mauritius.

1844 Capture of Colonia, Uruguay. Ships: *Gorgon, Satellite, Philomel*.

1914 Start of naval operation in West Africa with arrival of *Cumberland* and *Dwarf* at Lome, Gulf of Guinea.

1914 Battle of the Heligoland Bight.
Battle Honour: Heligoland.

Ships: *Badger, Beaver, Invincible, Jackal, Lion, New Zealand, Princess Royal, Queen Mary, Sandfly*. 1st LCS: *Birmingham, Falmouth, Liverpool, Lowestoft, Nottingham, Southampton*. Cruiser Force C: *Aboukir, Amethyst, Bacchante, Cressy, Euryalus, Hogue*. 1st DF: *Acheron, Archer, Ariel, Attack, Druid, Defender, Fearless, Ferret, Forester, Goshawk, Hind, Lapwing, Lizard, Llewellyn, Lucifer, Phoenix*. 3rd DF: *Arethusa, Laertes, Laforey, Landrail, Laurel, Lark, Lance, Lawford, Leonidas, Legion, Lennox, Liberty, Linnet, Lookout, Louis, Lydiard, Lysander*. S/Ms: D 2, D 8, E 4, E 5, E 6, E 7, E 8, E 9. Destroyers: *Firedrake, Lurcher*.

German ships sunk: *Ariadne, Köln, Mainz*, V-187.

Although close blockade by the battle fleet became obsolete as the mine, submarine and torpedo were introduced, the Grand Fleet determined still to exercise its supremacy of the sea. In August 1914, the light cruiser force from Harwich made a sweep into the Heligoland Bight, tempting German forces out to the guns of the battlecruisers under Beatty. The plan succeeded, and three German cruisers and one destroyer were sunk.

1918 Aircraft BK 9983 and *Ouse* sank UC-70 off Whitby (54.31N, 00.40W).

1940 First German acoustic mine believed dropped in Thames estuary.

1940 AMC *Dunvegan Castle* torpedoed and sunk by U-46 off Tory Island, N.W. of Ireland (55-05N, 11-00W).

1941 Landing party from submarine *Triumph* demolished the railway bridge near Caronia, N. Sicily.

1942 Corvette *Oakville* (RCN) and US Catalina flying boat sank U-94 in Caribbean, S. of Haiti.

1943 *Ultor* sank the Italian TB *Lince*, grounded off Punta Alice (39.24N, 17.01E) since the 4th.

1945 Vice-Admiral H.T.C. Walker arrived off Penang with squadron led by the battleship *Nelson*. Minesweepers began clearing the approaches to the port.

See 2 September 1945.

1960 Admiral of the Fleet Sir Charles Morton Forbes died in London. Born in Colombo 22 November 1880. Flag Commander to Admiral Sir John Jellicoe in *Iron Duke* at Jutland (DSO). Captain of light cruiser *Galatea* at German surrender November 1918. Third Sea Lord and Controller 1932–4, C-in-C Home Fleet in *Nelson* April 1938 until relieved by Admiral Sir John Tovey in December 1940. C-in-C Plymouth from May 1941. 'Forbes was a master of his profession and had the very great faculty of recognising instantly all the factors in any problem.' – DNB 1951–60.

See 22 November 1880, 2 December 1940, 24 August 1943.

Rear-Admiral Richard Kempenfelt (1718–1782)

Of Swedish extraction, Kempenfelt served in the Caribbean under Vernon and for a considerable period of time in the Far East. He was considered one of the most thoughtful officers of his time, and is remembered for his transformation of the Fleet signalling system, used to great effect by Howe at Gibraltar (1782), and for his introduction of the divisional system. He was drowned when the *Royal George* capsized at Spithead. He has been quoted as writing, 'There is a vulgar notion that our seamen are braver than the French. Ridiculous to suppose courage is dependent upon climate. The men who are best disciplined, of whatever nationality they are, will always fight the best . . . it is a maxim that experience has ever confirmed, that discipline gives more force than numbers.'

See 29 August 1782.

Rear-Admiral Richard Kempenfelt (1718–1782). *(NMRN 1984/366)*

1967 To obviate confusion with HMS *Olympus* and HMS *Leander*, RFA *Olynthus* was renamed *Olwen* on 28 August 1967 and RFA *Oleander* renamed *Olmeda* on 16 October 1967. DCI(RN) 983/67, 1129/67.

1969 Fleet submarine *Conqueror* launched at Birkenhead, by Lady McGeoch, wife of Vice-Admiral Sir Ian McGeoch, FOSNI. The last nuclear submarine built at Cammell Laird.

1996 Prime Minister John Major attended a ceremony at *Neptune*, Clyde Submarine Base, to mark the paying-off of *Repulse* and the end of the Polaris programme. Polaris monument unveiled.

See 16 June 1969, 12 May 1996.

29 AUGUST

1350 Battle of L'Espagnols sur Mer. Edward III (*Thomas*) defeated the Spanish fleet under Don Carlos de la Cerda off Winchelsea. First battle in which cannon were used at sea.

1572 Matthew Baker appointed master shipwright.

1771 James Cook promoted commander.

1782 *Royal George* (100) capsized and sank at Spithead, with loss of Admiral Kempenfelt and most of her crew. According to Howe, she 'being upon the heel . . . suddenly over set, filled and sank'.

1791 *Pandora*, sixth rate, searching for *Bounty* mutineers, lost on Great Barrier Reef. Fourteen had been captured at Tahiti but four of these drowned in the wreck. Remaining ten brought back to Portsmouth for court martial and three of them hanged.

1800 Boats of *Renown, Impetueux, London, Courageux, Amethyst, Stag, Amelia, Brilliant* and *Cynthia* cut out the French privateer *Guèpe* near Redondela, Vigo Bay.

1807 *Plantagenet* captured the French privateer *Incomparable* 50 miles S. by W. of Lizard Head.

1810 *Dover* and detachments of the Madras European Regiment and Madras Coast Artillery captured Ternate, Moluccas. A second success for Capt Tucker and the third in those seas in six months.
Battle Honour: Ternate 1810.

1810 Hired cutter *Queen Charlotte* fought a large French cutter (ex-British Revenue cutter *Swan*) 10 miles N.N.E. of Alderney.

1814 Destruction of Fort Washington and capitulation of Alexandria, Potomac River.

Ships: *Seahorse, Euryalus, Devastation, Aetna, Meteor, Erebus, Fairy, Anna Maria.*

1842 Treaty of Tientsin ended the First China War.

1877 Alfred Dudley Pickman Rogers Pound, future First Sea Lord, born.
See 21 October 1943.

1911 Naval Service of Canada became Royal Canadian Navy. In January 1911 Canada requested to change the name of the Canadian Naval Service and on 29 August was advised 'His Majesty having been graciously pleased to authorise that the Canadian Naval Forces shall be designated the "Royal Canadian Navy", under this title [it] is to be officially adopted, the abbreviation thereof being "RCN".' All Canadian warships thereafter prefixed with 'HMCS'. Notwithstanding the Royal directive, the terms 'Canadian Naval Service' and 'Naval Service of Canada' remained in occasional use until finally ended by a Canadian Order in Council in 1944.
See 1 February 1968, 4 May 1910, 1 October 1941, 15 February 1965.

1914 The capture of German possessions in the Pacific Ocean at the start of the First World War. Rear-Admiral Sir George Patey in the new battlecruiser HMAS *Australia* sent ashore a letter to the German colonial administrators in Samoa: 'I have the honour to inform you that I am off the port of Apia with an overwhelming force, and in order to avoid unnecessary bloodshed I will not open fire if you surrender immediately. I therefore summon you to surrender to me forthwith the Town of Apia, and the Imperial possessions under your control.' This was promptly effected, the British flag hoisted and a garrison of New Zealand troops landed.
See 16 March 1889, 4 October 1913.

1915 Submarine C 29 sunk on a mine while under tow by *Ariadne*.

1918 UB-109 sunk in controlled minefield off Folkestone.

1930 Sloop *Harebell* embarked the last thirty-three residents of the remote island of St Kilda, 41 miles W. of Benbecula, who had requested evacuation due to unendurable hardships and privations, and landed them at Oban.
See 27 August 1980.

1939 Admiralty ordered mobilisation of Fleet.

1942 *Arunta* (RAN) sank the Japanese S/M Ro-33 off New Guinea (09.36S, 147.06E).

1942 *Eridge* torpedoed off Daba (31.07N, 28.26E). Towed to Alexandria but CTL.

1952 The title Royal Malayan Navy bestowed on the former Malayan naval force at ceremony in Singapore.

1957 Light cruiser *Nigeria*, launched 1939, transferred to the Indian Navy, after a major refit at Cammell Laird, Birkenhead, and commissioned as INS *Mysore*. She relieved light cruiser *Delhi* (ex-HMS *Achilles*) as flagship of the Indian Navy. Paid off 1985.

See 5 July 1948, 4 March 1961, 20 March 1987.

1960 Admiral of the Fleet Sir Charles Lambe died at Knockhill, Fife, aged 59, a day after Admiral of the Fleet Sir Charles Forbes.

See 20 December 1900, 23 May 1960.

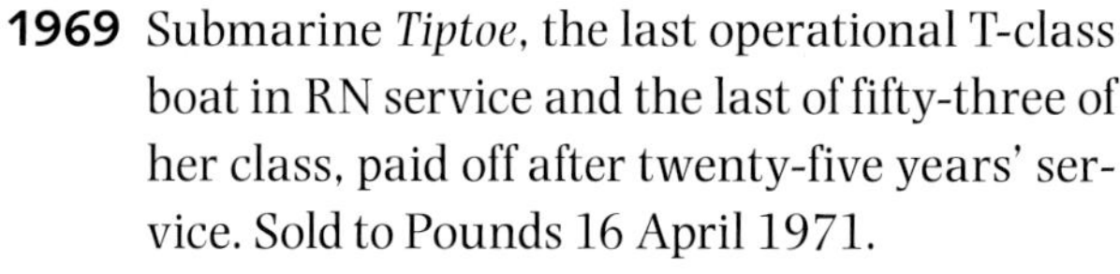

1969 Submarine *Tiptoe*, the last operational T-class boat in RN service and the last of fifty-three of her class, paid off after twenty-five years' service. Sold to Pounds 16 April 1971.

See 31 December 1974, 23 August 1993.

1971 Admiral John Henry Godfrey, a distinguished Director of Naval Intelligence for first three years of the Second World War, died. 'The only officer of his rank to receive no official recognition whatsoever for his immense services to the Allied cause during the war, a palpable injustice' – Beesly; 'a disgraceful act of prejudice' – Roskill. He began the war with a CB and ended it with nothing more.

See 10 July 1888.

1973 Second Cod War. Collision between the Icelandic Coastguard vessel *Aegir* and the frigate *Apollo*. This resulted in the only fatality of all three Cod Wars when an electrician in *Aegir*, welding damaged bulwarks, was electrocuted when hit by a wave.

See 31 August 1958.

1985 HM Air Force Vessels *Sunderland* and *Stirling* transferred from RAF to RN, renamed *Cormorant* and *Hart* and, and commissioned at Gibraltar to form the Gibraltar Squadron. DCI(RN) 274/85 dated 19 July 1985.

The *Royal George* capsized in shallow water, 1782. This scheme shows a proposal to raise her; it did not work and the wreck was eventually dispersed by divers in the 1830s. (*NMRN Ad. Lib. Portfolio G2*)

30 August

1779 *Boreas* captured the French *Compas* off Montserrat.

1799 Admiral Mitchell (*Isis*) received further Dutch surrenders.
See 28 August 1799.

1806 Boats of *Bacchante* cut out three Spanish vessels at Santa Marta, Colombia.

1806 *Pike* captured a Spanish schooner of Isla de Pinos, Cuba.

1823 *Sappho*, her guns and stores ashore at Gibraltar and with only her lower yards rigged, got under way with urgent dispatches in four hours.

1854 Preliminary attack on Petropavlovsk, Kamchatka. Ships: *President*, *Pique*, *Virago*. French ships: *Forte*, *Eurydice*, *Obligado*. Suicide of Rear-Admiral Price, C-in-C of British Pacific squadron.

1914 Occupation of German Samoa. *Australia* (flag) and *Melbourne* (RAN), *Philomel* (NZ), *Montcalm* (French), *Psyche* and *Pyramus*.

1940 20th DF, the RN's only offensive minelaying force, lost *Express*, *Esk* and *Ivanhoe*. The first was eventually repaired having been towed stern first to Hull, the second sank within the minute (53.03N, 03.47E) and the last was sunk nearby by *Kelvin*.

1943 *Stonecrop* and *Stork* sank U-634 in N. Atlantic (40.13N, 19.24W). Convoys SL 135/MKS 22. First attacked on 29th.

1945 Liberation of Hong Kong. Rear-Admiral C.H.J. Harcourt, flag in *Swiftsure*, entered harbour. Five hundred men landed from *Swiftsure* and *Euryalus*, who cleared the dockyard that evening.
See 27 August 1945.

1954 The Royal Naval Association – 'Unity, Loyalty, Patriotism and Comradeship' – formed in 1950,

HMS *Swiftsure* off Portsmouth, 1953. (*NMRN W&L 899E*)

The light fleet carrier HMS *Glory* and the destroyer HMAS *Bataan* in a RAS with RFA *Wave Premier* off Korea in 1951. (*Cdr David Hobbs RN*)

received its Royal Charter from HM The Queen. Its purposes 'to further the efficiency of the Service in which members of the Association have served or are serving, by fostering esprit de corps and preserving the traditions of the Service and thus to achieve those ideals for which Our Naval Forces have fought and perpetuate the memory of those members who have died in the service of their country; to relieve members of the Association who are in conditions of need, hardship or distress'. A Supplemental Charter granted 7 June 1990.

1965 The ships' bells of the old Imperial German Navy battleship *Friedrich der Grosse* and the battlecruiser *Derfflinger* arrived at Bremerhaven in the FGS *Scheer* having been presented at Faslane to the Federal German Naval Attaché. The ships were part of the High Seas Fleet which was scuttled during internment at Scapa Flow in 1919 and the two ships were broken up at Faslane in the 1930s. The battleship went to the Federal German Naval HQ and the battlecruiser to the Naval Academy at Flensburg.

1966 Explosion of a fuel oil separator in the submarine *Rorqual*, Lt-Cdr Thomas Green RN, off Mozambique while on passage to the Far East to join the Seventh Submarine Squadron, killed two engine room staff.

See 12 February 1970, 29 September 1971, 21 March 2007.

1975 The last full-tour C-in-C Home Fleet, Admiral Sir John Frewen, before it became the Western Fleet in November 1971, died aged 64.

See 6 July 1965, 1 October 1967

1985 'The Admiralty Board have decided that from the date of this DCI, the individual title "Fleet Chief Petty Officer" is to be abolished and "Warrant Officer" used instead for all purposes . . . The change will acknowledge the fact that Warrant Officers receive a Warrant of Appointment like Warrant Officers in the Army and RAF and thus emphasise their equivalent status and position. It neither entails nor heralds the granting of additional privileges.' – DCI(RN) 339/85.

31 AUGUST

1591 *Revenge* taken by a Spanish fleet under Don Alonzo de Bazan off the Azores.
Battle Honour: Azores 1591.

The *Revenge*, under Sir Richard Grenville, was at Flores in the Azores with other British ships when a superior force of Spanish ships was sighted. The *Revenge* stayed to recover sick men on shore, and was engaged by the Spanish when she sailed. She fought for fifteen hours against no fewer than fifty-three enemy ships, and was boarded fifteen times, repulsing each attack. Finally she was forced to surrender after sinking four enemy ships, and with Sir Richard Grenville mortally wounded: 'sink me the ship Master Gunner: sink her, split her in twain . . .'

1782 Fall of Trincomalee.

1807 *Psyche* captured the Dutch *Scipio*, *Ceres* and *Resolutie* 9 miles W. of Samarang, Java, and destroyed two Dutch merchant vessels at Samarang.

1810 *Repulse* (74) 'with the greatest bravery and coolness' deterred three French 40-gun frigates supported by several ships of the line, threatening the brig sloop *Philomel* (18) off Hyères.

1817 Admiral Sir John Duckworth died while C-in-C Plymouth.

1837 *Gorgon*, wood paddle frigate, 1,610 tons, launched at Pembroke Dockyard. With her sister ship *Cyclops*, 1,960 tons, launched at the same yard on 10 July 1839, they were the first steam vessels over 1,000 tons and were regarded as the first steam frigates. The men were uneasy about the portents of *Gorgon* spelled backwards.
See 10 July 1839.

1855 VC: Boatswain Joseph Kellaway (*Wrangler*). Destruction of Russian stores at Lyapina, near Mairupol, Sea of Azov, by *Wrangler* and rocket boats of *Vesuvius*.

1870 First and unsuccessful RN trial of Whitehead torpedo (*Oberon*).

1878 *Gannet*, composite screw sloop, launched at Sheerness. Became RNVR drill ship as *President* 1903 and boys' training ship *Mercury* in 1913. Arrived Chatham 1987 for preservation. Opened to the public 2004.

1908 Final day of trials of Col Cody's man-lifting kite off Isle of Wight, with battleship *Revenge* (tender to *Excellent*) and TBDs *Fervent* and *Recruit*. Strong winds, searches for submerged mines outside St Helens Bay and occasional immersions – 'the aeronauts have got up satisfactorily but were finding difficulty in getting down'.

1937 Destroyer *Havock* attacked by Italian submarine in Spanish Civil War.

1939 Admiralty ordered general mobilisation of naval reserves.

1939 Issuing Prices for service provisions on repayment and expended for General Mess purposes included:

Herrings in Tomato Sauce:	1lb tin, 4¼*d*
Lard:	1lb tin, 8½*d*

(except on the China station, where the price will be communicated by the Victualling Yard). AFO 2496/39.

1940 Swordfish aircraft of 812 Sqn FAA (disembarked) bombed oil tanks at Rotterdam.

1943 Battleships *Nelson*, *Rodney* and light cruiser *Orion*, in Messina Strait, bombarded the Calabrian coast. Operation Hammer.

1944 *Amphion* launched at Vickers, Barrow, the first of forty-six ordered, sixteen completed, British A-class submarines. Arrived Inverkeithing 6 July 1971 for breaking up.
See 17 April 1951, 1 July 1971, 31 December 1974.

1945 Total deaths of seamen of all nationalities serving in British merchant ships, and British seamen serving in foreign ships, chartered or requisitioned, from 3 September 1939 to 31 August 1945: 29,994.

1950 Chatham Group RM disbanded.

1962 Trinidad and Tobago Independence Day; cruiser *Blake*, flying the flag of Rear-Admiral J.F.D. Bush, Flag Officer Flotillas Mediterranean, the frigate *Ulster*, flying the broad pennant of Cdre J.E.L. Martin, Senior Naval Officer West Indies, and the frigate *Whirlwind* at Port of Spain from 28 August for independence celebrations of Trinidad and Tobago. Ships landed a guard for the flag raising in Red House Square at midnight on 30 August.

1966 Guided missile destroyer *Devonshire*, taking the C-in-C Home Fleet, Admiral Sir John Frewen, on a goodwill visit to Leningrad, collided with the tanker *British Sovereign* in fog off the River Elbe on route to the Kiel Canal. Courts martial at Portsmouth 13 and 14 October acquitted the CO, Capt G.C. Leslie RN, and the Navigating Officer, Lt-Cdr (later Vice-Admiral Sir) Robert Gerken RN, of charges concerning the hazarding of the ship.

1992 First women join Royal Marines, as musicians.

1993 Last Captain of *Mercury*, Capt Paul Sutermeister, relinquished command.

See 18 December 1992.

2005 Midshipman (later Lt) Jack Balfrey-Bowker, 815 NAS, the youngest of 42 Fleet Air Arm officers from *Illustrious* in the Taranto raid of 11/12 November 1940, died aged 84.

See 9 May 2006, 6 November 2008.

2006 Commodore Amjad Hussain, 48, lately Naval Base Commander, Portsmouth, promoted rear-admiral, thirty years to the day since his promotion to midshipman at BRNC Dartmouth. Admiral Hussain, a WEO, was the first Moslem to reach two-star rank in the British Armed Forces.

The Icelandic Cod Wars, 1958–76

Britain and Iceland, NATO allies, 'fought' three Cod Wars between 1958 and 1976, each initiated by Iceland's unilateral decisions to extend her fishing limits to 12 miles (1958), then 50 miles (1972) and finally, in 1975, to 200 miles. In each case, Britain decided to resist this 'illegal' extension and sent in the Royal Navy to protect British trawlers fishing in the disputed areas – a time-honoured naval task.

A worldwide wave of anti-colonialism followed the Second World War and the long-established Law of the Sea was seen, especially by former colonies – Iceland had been a Danish colony up to 1944 – as out-dated and biased. Three conferences dealt with the extension of nations' rights over the sea and seabed: the First Conference on the Law of the Sea (1958), UNCLOS2 (the Second UN Conference on the Law of the Sea in 1960) and the long-running UNCLOS3 from 1973–82. Iceland, with the backing of the developing world was pushing at an opening door that Britain, with reducing support, was trying to keep closed.

The First Cod War (1958–61) was a comparatively gentlemanly affair (although warning shots were fired twenty-three times) and ended with Britain giving in to Iceland's demands for a 12-mile limit, provided that all future fishing-limit disputes could be referred to the International Court.

The Second Cod War (1972–3) followed when Iceland disregarded this agreement and established a 50-mile limit. The RN returned to the fray during which the Icelandic Coastguard cut eighty-two trawlers' warps; there were seventeen shooting incidents and twelve collisions.

The Third Cod War (1975–6) over a 200-mile limit, was more tense; there were forty-one warp cuttings and fifty-seven collisions. Several frigates were badly damaged. The UK had to agree to the Icelandic 200-mile fishing limit, which, in due course, became the international norm.

See 2 July 1930.

1 September

1778 Frigate *Active* (28), Capt William Williams, damaged and having jettisoned 11 guns in a gale while on passage from Bermuda to Jamaica, engaged by the French frigates *Charmante* (38) and *Dedaigneuse* (26) off Cape San Nicola Mole, Hispaniola, and struck. 'Captain Williams is said by Nelson to have died of mortification at his capture' – Laird Clowes.

See 22 August 1778.

1781 *Chatham* captured the French *Magicienne* 9 miles E. of Boston lighthouse.

1783 Lt-Gen. J. McKenzie, RM, appointed the first Commandant in Town.

1812 Boats of *Bacchante* cut out the French *Tisiphone*, two gunboats and all seven of a convoy in the Canale di Leme.

1814 *Avon* (18) sunk by the American *Wasp* (22) 230 miles W.S.W. of Ushant.

1836 Rum withdrawn from accompanying women and children who became entitled to tea and sugar in lieu.

1859 *Pearl*'s Naval Brigade at Dhebrahia, with detachments of 13th Light Infantry, Bengal Yeomanry, 6th Madras Light Cavalry and 27th Madras Native Infantry.

1870 First successful RN firing of Whitehead torpedo.

1875 *Iron Duke* rammed and sank *Vanguard* during a thick fog in the Irish Sea, near the Kish lightvessel (53.13N, 05.46W). First RN capital ship lost in collision and an inadvertent demonstration of power of the ram 'which has proved more dangerous in accident than formidable in action' – Laird Clowes, *The Royal Navy*, vol.7, p.24.

1898 Bombardment of Omdurman, Sudan (captured next day). Gunboats: *Abu Klea, Fateh, Melik, Metemmeh, Nasr, Sheikh, Sulan Tumai.*

1916 Hull of battlecruiser *Hood*, the building of which was suspended to incorporate lessons from Jutland, laid down for the second time at John Brown's, Clydebank.

See 22 August 1918.

1917 Pangbourne Nautical College opened under command of Capt W.F. Montanaro, RN.

1919 Destroyer *Vittoria*, Lt-Cdr Vernon Hammersley-Heenan, at anchor with flotilla leader *Abdiel* off Seskar lighthouse in Gulf of Finland, torpedoed by Bolshevik submarine *Pantera*. Ships rolled over to port and broke in two; eight men lost. Sister ship *Verulam* mined and lost three days later.

See 18 August 1919, 4 September 1919, 20 July 2003.

1920 Royal cypher in dull silver to be worn on each epaulette by admirals of the fleet, and aides-de-camp and honorary surgeons and physicians to the monarch.

1926 Vice-Admiral Sir Herbert Richmond, founder of the *Naval Review*, appointed first Commandant of the Imperial Defence College, now the RCDS.

1936 Light cruiser *Birmingham* launched from No.3 Slip at Devonport Dockyard by Lady Chamberlain, wife of Birmingham-born Sir Austen Chamberlain MP. The first British cruiser since the Emerald-class with a fully flared bow instead of the by then traditional cruiser knuckle bow, and the last. Her sister ship *Gloucester* was laid down immediately on the vacated slip.

See 31 January 1938.

1940 Re-formation of 10th Submarine Flotilla, at Malta. The first had been formed at Immingham in 1914 and disbanded in December 1919.

See 21 September 1944, 30 November 1959, 1 February 1967.

1941 Monitor M 29, *Medusa*, commissioned as *Talbot*, depot ship for Malta submarines. Became *Medway II* in 1943 before reverting to *Medusa* in 1944.

1942 *Morden* (RCN) depth-charged and sank U-756 on her first operational patrol, E.S.E. of Cape Farewell (57.41N, 31.30W).

1943 HQ Special Service Brigade (now 3 Cdo Brigade RM) formed from HQ 102 RM Brigade.

1944 *Hurst Castle* sunk by U-482 N. of Tory Island, Donegal (55.27N, 08.12W).

1944 *St John* and *Swansea* (both RCN) sank U-247 off Land's End (49.54N, 05.49W).

1944 Battleship *Malaya* bombarded the batteries on Cezembre Island, off St Malo.

1946 The White Ensign flown at the HQ Allied Naval Commander, Expeditionary Force (Admiral Sir Harold Burrough) at St Germain-en-Laye when German land, sea and air forces surrendered, was laid up in St Ann's church, Portsmouth Dockyard. On the same occasion the flag flown by Admiral Sir Algernon Willis at the surrender of the Italian Fleet off Sardinia in September 1943 was also laid up.

1950 RM bands integrated on formation of RM School of Music.

1958 Start of the First of three Cod Wars with Iceland (ended 11 March 1961) following her unilateral extension of fishing limits. Frigates *Eastbourne* (OTC), *Russell* and *Palliser*, and minesweeper *Hound* on patrol.

See 2 July 1930, 31August, 1 September 1972.

1961 Directorate of Naval Security to be formed in the Admiralty. First DG was Col J.L.A. Macafee RM. AFO 1841/61. Duties of DDNI (Security) absorbed into DNSy. AFO 2102/61.

1963 The second largest sum ever to be awarded to the Royal Navy for marine salvage, £160,000 out of a total of £285,000, awarded for salvaging the Norwegian tanker *Polyana*, loaded with 24,000 tons of crude oil, which caught fire and was abandoned off the Iranian coast in the Gulf in November 1960.

The seven-day operation to fight the fire, with thousands of gallons of foam flown from Britain in chartered BOAC aircraft, was carried out by the frigate *Loch Ruthven*, Capt D.D. Law RN, (on-scene Commander); the surveying ship *Dalrymple*, Capt M.J. Baker RN, which towed the tanker 80 miles stern-first to an anchorage; the tank landing craft *Bastion*, Lt-Cdr C.B. Kennedy RN, which stayed alongside the tanker for six weeks, and the landing ship *Redoubt*, Lt-Cdr R.D. Blackman RN. Admiralty to FO Arabian Seas and Persian Gulf: 'Well Done'. The ships' companies shared almost £45,000; Capt Law received £1,482, the most ever paid to a RN officer for a salvage operation.

See 13 September 1958.

1968 Flag Officer Aircraft Carriers (FOAC) became FOCAS (Flag Officer Carriers and Amphibious Ships).

1970 Royal Maritime Auxiliary Service (RMAS) founded. RMAS ensign to be a blue ensign defaced in the fly with a yellow horizontal anchor with two yellow wavy lines beneath to represent the seagoing character of the Service. DCI(RN) 1275/70.

See 1 October 1976.

1972 Start of the Second Cod War (ended 13 November 1973). The RN did not enter the disputed 50-mile limit until 19 May 1973.

See 1 September 1958, 31August.

1975 *Lochinvar*, Fishery Protection Vessels base at Port Edgar on the Firth of Forth, paid off and became a tender to *Cochrane* for pay. Ceased as an independent command 16 October 1975. DCI(RN)T515/75.

1979 Admiral of the Fleet Sir Terence Lewin succeeded Marshal of the Royal Air Force Sir Neil Cameron as Chief of the Defence Staff.

2007 Vice-Admiral Paul Boissier, Deputy C-in-C Fleet, in a ceremony at the Royal Danish Navy Museum in Copenhagen, handed back to the Royal Danish Navy the bell of a Danish warship taken by the RN in Gambier's action at Copenhagen in 1807. The bell had been kept at RNH Haslar for 150 years.

The RN believe the bell came from the third rate *Christian den Syvende*, which ship served in the RN as *Christian VII*, latterly as a hospital ship, but it may have belonged to the *Kronprindsesse Maria*.

See 2 and 7 September 1807, 2 April 2001.

2008 Lt-Cdr Ian Fraser VC, DSC, RD, RNR, submariner, died aged 87.

See 31 July 1945.

2 SEPTEMBER

1762 *Lion* captured the French *Zephyr* 100 miles S.W. of Ushant.

1762 *Aeolus* destroyed the Spanish *San José* at Aviles, north-west Spain.

1797 Rear-Admiral Sir Horatio Nelson arrived at Spithead in the frigate *Seahorse*, Capt Thomas Fremantle, after the failed attack on Santa Cruz, Tenerife, in which he lost his right arm.
See 12 July 1794, 24 July 1797.

1801 *Pomone*, *Phoenix* and *Minerve* drove ashore the French *Succès* on Vada shoal, and *Bravoure* 4 miles S. of Leghorn. *Succès* was captured and refloated; *Bravoure* became a total loss.

1801 Capitulation of Alexandria to the forces under Admiral Lord Keith (*Foudroyant*) and Lt-Gen. Sir John Hutchinson. The French *Justice* and five other ships captured.

1801 *Victor* fought the French *Flèche* N.E. of the Seychelles.

1807 Bombardment of Copenhagen by the fleet under Admiral James Gambier (*Prince of Wales*) and shore batteries erected by Lt-Gen. Lord Cathcart. Ships: *Agamemnon, Alfred, Brunswick, Captain, Centaur, Defence, Dictator, Ganges, Goliath, Hercules, Inflexible, Leyden, Maida, Mars, Minotaur, Nassau, Orion, Pompee, Prince of Wales, Resolution, Ruby, Spencer, Superb, Valiant, Vanguard*. Frigates: *Africaine, Comus, Franchise, Nymphe, Sybille*. Gun-brigs: *Desperate, Fearless, Indignant, Kite, Pincher, Safeguard, Tigress, Urgent*. Bombardment flotilla: *Aetna, Cruizer, Hebe* (hired), *Mutine, Thunder, Vesuvius, Zebra*.
See 7 September 1807.

1917 SS *Olive Branch* torpedoed by U-28 off Hammsfort. Gunfire from the U-boat exploded the ammunition carried in No. 4 hold and *Olive Branch* blew up. U-28 was wrecked by the explosion and sank.

1918 VC: CPO George Prowse, DSM, RNVR, Drake Battalion RND, France: for gallantry in attack on the Hindenburg Line. Last award on blue ribbon.

1944 *Keppel, Mermaid, Peacock, Whitehall* and Swordfish A/825 (*Vindex*) sank U-394 off Lofoten Island.

1944 *Glen Avon*, a paddle steamer hired in First World War and again in Second World War, foundered in a storm in Seine Bay.

The Japanese Surrender, 1945

'The surrender and succeeding jubilation was rightly American but, as Admiral Fraser appreciated, Britain and the Commonwealth had now been at war for six long years less a day. If the forenoon had been American then the evening would be British. The last Sunset ceremony had been carried out on the evening of September 2, 1939. Since then the White Ensign had been flown in every ship by day and night. Admiral Fraser ordered the resumption of Sunset routine as from September 2, 1945 and invited all the senior officers of British ships in Tokyo and a token number of sailors from each, to witness the ceremony in his flagship . . . When Admiral Fraser arrived the quartermaster reported "Sunset, Sir". The Still sounded. The Royal Marine guard presented arms and the band played "The day Thou Gavest, Lord, is ended", interspersed with the Sunset call as only Royal Marine buglers know how. For the first time in six bitter years the White Ensign came down. Many, perhaps most, had never before savoured the magic of this moment when the busy life of a warship is hushed and the evening comes. Others of us, standing at the salute, were in tears as we remembered those who would never again see Colours in the morning or hear the bugles sound Sunset at dusk . . . As the White Ensign came into the hands of our chief yeoman and the Carry On was sounded, we realised that on board all the great US ships around us every activity had stopped, their sailors facing towards the British flagship and saluting us. Perhaps the special relationship between our two countries was born that evening.'

– Vice-Admiral Sir Louis Le Bailly, HMS *Duke of York*; *The Man around the Engine*, pp.125–6.

The seat of naval power: Thomas Ripley's Admiralty Board Room of 1725 photographed in 2011. Compare with the engraving on p.502 showing the Lords Commissioners meeting here in 1805. (*Crown Copyright: MOD Art Collection*)

1945 Merchant ship losses from 3 September 1939 to 2 September 1945: 4,786 vessels of 21,194,000 grt.

1945 Japanese delegates signed the surrender of Japan on board the US battleship *Missouri* in Tokyo Bay. Admiral Sir Bruce Fraser, C-in-C British Pacific Fleet, signed on behalf of Great Britain. The ceremony was organised by the RNLO, Cdr Mike Le Fanu, who borrowed chairs from the battleship HMS *King George V*, 'nice wooden ones instead of those American metal ones'.

See 21 November 1918, 15 August 1945, 8 September 1943.

1945 Vice-Admiral H.T.C. Walker accepted the surrender of the local Japanese commander at Penang on board the battleship *Nelson*. Her Royal Marines landed next day. At the same time Royal Marines landed from the heavy cruisers *London* and *Cumberland* at Sabang, Sumatra.

See 28 August 1945.

1946 *Childers* and *Chivalrous* apprehended *Fede* (*Four Freedoms*) off Tel Aviv. First illegal immigrant ship to resist arrest.

See 18 July 1947.

1946 First entry of Junior Marines at RM Depot, Deal.

1950 Lt-Cdr HRH The Duke of Edinburgh RN took command of the sloop *Magpie* in the Second Frigate Squadron based at Malta. The ship had served in Walker's Second escort Group in the Battle of the Atlantic.

See 18 October 1949.

1958 The Icelandic gunboats *Thor* and *Maria Julia* arrested the Grimsby trawler *Northern Foam* for 'poaching' inside the new 12-mile limit. Frigate *Eastbourne* counter-boarded and arrested *Thor*'s boarding party. The only direct confrontation between the RN and the Icelandic Coastguard during the First Cod War.

See 31 August 1958.

1966 A Royal Naval Presentation Team formed 'to tell the Public about the Navy' in presentations to be called 'Know your Navy'. Team to be led by Capt S.W. Farquharson-Roberts RN. DCI(RN) 1136/66.

See 13 August 1965, 23 September 1966.

1974 Lt HRH The Prince of Wales RN, having returned from the Far East in the frigate *Jupiter*, joined RNAS Yeovilton for helicopter flying training before joining 845 NAS in *Hermes*.

See 16 September 1971, 4 January 1974, 9 February 1976, 15 December 1976.

3 September

1780 *Vestal* captured the American packet *Mercury* 620 miles S. of Newfoundland.

1782 Fourth battle between Vice-Admiral Sir Edward Hughes (*Superb*) and Cdre Chevalier de Suffren (*Heros*) off Trincomalee. Ships: *Exeter, Isis, Hero, Sceptre, Burford, Sultan, Superb, Monarch, Eagle, Magnanime, Monmouth, Worcester.* Frigates, etc.: *Active, Coventry, Medea, Seahorse, San Carlos, Combustion* (fireship). Troops: 78th Highlanders, 98th Regiment.
Battle Honour: Trincomalee 1782.
See 17 February 1782, 12 April 1782, 6 July 1782.

1800 Boats of *Minotaur* and *Niger* cut out the Spanish *Esmeralda* (alias *Concepción*) and *Paz* at Barcelona.

1806 Landing party from *Superieure, Stork, Flying Fish* and *Pike* captured a fort and six privateers at Batabano, Cuba.

1814 Four boats, under Lt Miller Worsley, cut out the American schooner *Tigress* in the Detour Passage, Lake Huron. Troops: Royal Artillery, Royal Newfoundland Fencible Infantry.

1912 First rating to qualify as pilot: LS O'Connor at CFS with RAC Certificate 286.

1914 *Speedy* sunk by mine off the Humber, 12 miles N.N.E. of Outer Dowsing lightvessel.

1925 *Nelson* launched at Armstrongs. With *Rodney* (Cammell Laird 17 December 1925) the only British battleships to mount 16-in guns.

1925 First broadcast by a Royal Marine band, *Calcutta* in Canada.

1939 War declared against Germany. Winston Churchill appointed First Lord of the Admiralty for the second time. 'I . . . sent word to the Admiralty that I would take charge forthwith and arrive at 6 o'clock. On this the Board were kind enough to signal to the Fleet "Winston is back". So it was that I came again to the room I had quitted in pain and sorrow almost exactly a quarter of a century before, when Lord Fisher's resignation had led to my removal from my post as First Lord.' – Churchill, *The Second World War, Volume 1: The Gathering Storm*, p.365.
See 24 October 1911, 5 September 1939.

1939 *Plover* laid first British minefield, off the Bass Rock in the Firth of Forth, and remained in commission for thirty-one years.

1939 Donaldson liner *Athenia* torpedoed at 1945 by U-30 in N.W. Approaches and sank at 1000 next day. First British merchant ship to be sunk in Second World War.
See 7 May 1945.

1939 Light cruiser *Ajax* sank the German *Olinda* in the Plata area.

1939 Destroyer *Somali* captured the German blockade runner *Hannah Boge* in N. Atlantic (58.35N, 20.11W). First capture of the Second World War.

1940 Anglo-American agreement to lease British bases in Newfoundland, Bermuda, British West Indies and British Guiana for ninety-nine years in return for the transfer to the Royal Navy of fifty old, flush-decked, (all but two) four-funnelled destroyers. The first vessel to transfer was USS *Aaron Ward* which sailed from Boston to Halifax, Nova Scotia on 4 September and commissioned on 9 September as HMS *Castleton*.

1942 Having safely delivered the damaged battleship *Queen Elizabeth* to the eastern seaboard of the USA, the destroyers *Pathfinder, Quentin* and *Vimy* were attacked by, and sank, U-162 off Trinidad. The German CO, Fregattenkapitan Jurgen Wattenburg, had been an officer in *Graf Spee*. He escaped internment in Argentina, returned to Germany and trained as a submariner. As a POW in Arizona, he again escaped for thirty-six days.

1942 Whitley P/77 sank U-705 in Bay of Biscay, on the submarine's first patrol.

1943 Allied invasion of Italy. Bombardment support to 8th Army crossing Messina Strait.

The Lords Commissioners of the Admiralty meeting in their Board Room in 1805. Rowlandson/Pugin engraving. Compare with the 2011 photograph on p.500. (*Crown Copyright: MOD Art Collection*)

Operation Baytown. Ships: *Mauritius*, *Orion*, *Loyal*, *Offa*, *Piorun* (Pol), *Quail*, *Queenborough*, *Quilliam*. Monitors: *Abercrombie*, *Erebus*, *Roberts*. River gunboats: *Aphis*, *Scarab*.

1945 Light cruiser *Cleopatra*, wearing the flag of Vice-Admiral Sir Arthur Power, C-in-C East Indies, entered Singapore, led by the 6th Minesweeping Flotilla, the first RN ships to do so since 1942. The next day, the heavy cruiser *Sussex* arrived with a convoy carrying the 5th Indian Division. Within the week 100,000 men had been landed in Western Malaya. Power was present at the formal Japanese surrender a few days later.

1988 *Southampton*, Type 42 destroyer, seriously damaged in collision with P&O containership *Tor Bay* in the Gulf. Transported back to Britain on submersible heavy-lift vessel *Mighty Servant 1*. Rebuilt by Swan Hunter on the Tyne 1989–91 at estimated cost of £45 million and taking ninety-two weeks.

See 29 January 1979, 7 July 2002, 8 April 2009.

1995 Queen Alexandra's RN Nursing Service (QARNNS) and its Reserve assumed RN ranks. DCI(RN) 204/95.

2000 One thousand Second World War veterans of the British Pacific Fleet and East Indies Fleet marched under the White Ensign for the last time in Portsmouth Naval base. This final parade, at which Cdre Stephen Graham RN, Naval Base Commander, took the salute, represented 174 ships and units.

4 SEPTEMBER

1777 *Druid, Camel* and *Weazle* (escorting a convoy) fought the American *Raleigh* 1,100 miles to the eastward of New York. The Americans had acquired British signals, penetrated the convoy, sank *Druid* and made off.

1782 *Rainbow* captured the French *Hébé* 6 miles N. of Ile de Bas.

1854 Continuation of the attack on Petropavlovsk, which was repulsed.

See 30 August 1854.

1861 Royal Warrant required the forfeiture of the VC awarded to Mid E. St J. Daniel in 1854, he having been 'accused of a disgraceful offence' and 'having evaded enquiry by deserting from Our service' – the only naval forfeiture of the eight to date.

1907 Standard messing allowance of 4*d* per day introduced in place of victualling and savings.

1913 The new battlecruiser *Queen Mary* commissioned at Portsmouth for the 1st BCS, Home Fleet. Her Captain, Reginald 'Blinker' Hall (later the famous wartime Director of Naval Intelligence), was a deeply religious man and had an upper deck compartment fitted as a chapel, the first ever in a British warship. She was sunk at Jutland.

See 4 September 1913, 31 May 1916.

1915 E 7 caught in nets and depth-charged in the Dardanelles. Scuttled by own crew.

1916 British forces captured Dar-es-Salaam. Ships: Inshore Sqn: *Mersey, Severn, Thistle, Helmuth* (armed tug). Main Sqn: *Challenger, Hyacinth, Talbot, Vengeance, Charon, Childers, Echo, Fly, Manica, Pickle, Styx, Trent.* Also: *Himalaya, Prattler, Rinaldo, Salamander.*

1919 Destroyer *Verulam*, Lt-Cdr G.L. Warren RN, on patrol between island of Krasnoostrovskiy and Russian coast near Ozerik, mined and sunk (in a British minefield) off Stirs Point (60,10.40N, 38.57.42E). Sister ship *Vittoria* was torpedoed and lost three days earlier.

See 13 December 1918, 18 August 1919, 20 July 2003.

HM Tug *Faithful*, the last dockyard paddle tug, in 1957. (*NMRN W&L 4934C*)

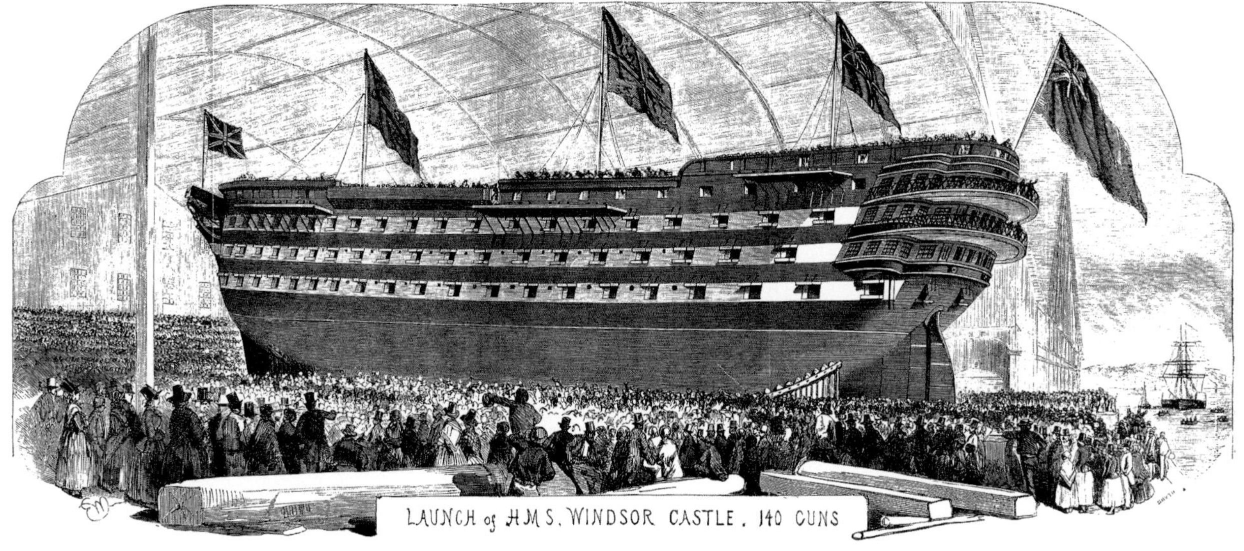

The screw first rate three-decker HMS *Windsor Castle* launched at Pembroke Dockyard on 14 September 1852. She was later renamed HMS *Duke of Wellington* in honour of the Iron Duke who had died on the same day. (*Author*)

1922 Concentration of HM ships at Smyrna to protect British interests.

1937 Anson K6260 from Martlesham Heath detected and located *Rodney*, *Courageous*, *Southampton* and six destroyers at 3,000yd: first air-to-surface identification by radar.

1937 Destroyer *Hostile* attacked by Spanish submarine. Lost contact after nine hours but 'patrols have proved the Asdic apparatus to be generally reliable'.

1940 Swordfish aircraft of 812 Sqn (disembarked) attacked invasion barges at Terneuzen on the Schelde.

1940 *Sydney*, *Dainty* and *Ilex* bombarded Makri Yalo airfield, Scarpanto. *Orion* bombarded Pegadia. *Ilex* sank two MTBs and damaged a third there.

1962 RN Air Station, Sembawang, Singapore, commissioned as *Simbang* under command of Commander 3 Cdo Bde. AFO 1685/62.

1964 Frigate *Lowestoft*, Cdr M.W.G. Fawcett RN, part of a RN squadron assembled for the opening that day of the Forth Road Bridge, collided with the anchored cruiser *Lion*, Home Fleet flagship, near the bridge while moving downstream in poor visibility. NO reprimanded at Portsmouth court martial on Trafalgar Day.

1980 Destroyers *Antrim* (flag of Rear-Admiral Conrad Jenkin, Flag Officer First Flotilla) and *Coventry*, and frigate *Alacrity* arrived Shanghai for first official RN visit to the People's Republic of China and the first to Shanghai for thirty-one years. 'Large banner across waterfront welcomes HMS *Conventry* repeat *Conventry*, an unintentional but accurate indicator of our blameless and celibate stay in the Middle Kingdom' – HMS *Antrim* EUA 060555ZSEP80 to MODUK NAVY, CINCFLEET, JSPRS HONG KONG (drafted by present author).

1981 *Faithful*, the last dockyard paddle tug, paid off. Sunk as a target 1983.

1995 RN Detention Quarters (RNDQs) at Portsmouth closed and all personnel in detention transferred to the Military Corrective Training Centre (MCTC), Colchester. DCI(RN) 146/95.

See 1 January 1911.

2003 UK Netherlands Amphibious Force (UKNLAF) thirtieth anniversary celebrated on board *Ocean* and HNLMS *Rotterdam* in Amsterdam.

2005 The Merchant Navy Falklands 1982 Memorial on Tower Hill unveiled by the First Sea Lord, Admiral Sir Alan West.

5 SEPTEMBER

1749 Cdr Francis Wyatt of the sloop *Fly* in Hawke's fleet, annoyed by the chattering of his Purser's monkey outside his cabin door, ordered it to be thrown overboard. Relations between Wyatt and Purser James Hopkins Smith, hitherto amicable, went from bad to worse, and Smith's complaint went up the chain of command. Admiral Lord Anson at the Admiralty, had personally to intervene to put HMS *Fly* back on an operational footing.

1781 Rear-Admiral Thomas Graves (*London*) with nineteen of the line fought Vice-Admiral Comte de Grasse (*Ville de Paris*) with twenty-four ships 12 miles N.E. of Cape Henry, Virginia. Ships: *Ajax, Alcide, Alfred, America, Barfleur, Bedford, Belliqueux, Centaur, Europe, Intrepid, London, Monarch, Montagu, Princess, Resolution, Royal Oak, Shrewsbury, Terrible, Invincible.* Frigates: *Adamant, Fortunée, Nymphe, Orpheus, Richmond, Santa Monica, Salamander, Sibyl, Solebay.* A most disappointing encounter, dominated by adherence to the line, and partly responsible for the fall of Yorktown: the rear division never got into action.

1782 *Hector*, one of Rodney's prizes, fought the French *Aigle* and *Gloire* 400 miles E. of New York. Though she sank, some of her men died at the pumps, the survivors were rescued by *Hawke*.

1800 Valletta, Malta, surrendered by General Vaubois to Maj-Gen. Henry Pigot after a naval siege commanded by Capt Alexander Ball.

Capt (later Rear-Admiral) Ball was one of Nelson's Band of Brothers, having commanded the eponymous *Alexander* at the Nile. He was sent by Nelson with *Alexander, Audacious, Goliath* and *Emerald* to blockade the French garrison, latterly confined to Valletta. Ball became the first British Governor of Malta and the Maltese wept on his death there in 1809. He was buried in the Lower Baracca, where his memorial still stands.

See 13 February 1959, 31 March 1979.

1801 *Victor* destroyed the French *Flèche* in Mahe Roads, Seychelles.

1807 *Majestic* (74) and *Quebec* (32) took Heligoland.

1810 Boats of *Surveillante* cut out a French brig at St Gilles-sur-Vie.

1813 *Boxer* (11) taken by the American *Enterprise* (10) 6 miles E. of Portland, Maine.

1861 Lieutenants and masters over eight years in seniority to rank with majors in the Army and to wear two stripes instead of one. Hence commanders wore three and captains four, while a commodore second-class was granted a broad stripe with a ³⁄₁₆-in executive curl.

1864 Allied squadron, under Vice-Admiral Sir Augustus Kuper (*Euryalus*) bombarded and destroyed the Japanese batteries at the entrance to Shimonoseki Kaikyo at the western end of the Inland Sea. Ships: *Argus, Barrosa, Bouncer, Conqueror, Coquette, Euryalus, Leopard, Perseus, Tartar.* French: *Dupleix, Sémiramis, Tancrède.* Dutch: *Amsterdam, D'Jambi, Medusa, Metalen Kruis.* USA: *Takiang* and party from *Jamestown*. Troops: Royal Engineers, Royal Marine Battalion. The last time a RM battalion carried 'a pair of colours' in action.

See 15 August 1863, 6 September 1864, 17 April 2009.

1900 Re-embarkation of Pekin Naval Brigade.

See 30 May 1900, 10 and 24 June 1900.

1902 Boats of *Lapwing* captured two pirate dhows outside the bar off Fao, Persian Gulf.

1914 Launch of *Ark Royal*, laid down as collier at Blyth and purchased in May for conversion to carry seaplanes. Renamed *Pegasus* in December 1934, she became a catapult ship in 1941 and was sold in October 1946. The only carrier designed to carry sail, she had a mizzen to help keep her head into wind.

1914 Cruiser *Pathfinder* sunk by U-21 10 miles S.E. of May Island. First U-boat success against warship in First World War; the first RN warship sunk by a submarine.

Seamen of a Naval Brigade landing in ships' boats in the 1900s. (*NMRN*)

1926 The Wanhsien Incident. Storming party from ships' companies of river gunboats *Cockchafer*, *Widgeon*, *Scarab* and *Mantis*, and light cruiser *Despatch*, boarded the hijacked British steamers SS *Wanhsien* and SS *Wanliu* at Wanhsien 1,000 miles up the Yangtze. Ships' officers held hostage were rescued but eight RN killed in hand-to-hand fighting including Cdr Darley and Lt Higgins. 'The astonishing exploit . . . deserves to rank among the most daring of the many brilliant achievements standing to the credit of the Service' – *The Times*. An operation to be repeated nearer home on 16 February 1940.

1939 U-48 sank SS *Royal Sceptre* N.W. of Cape Ortegal but made very careful provision for the safety of her crew by stopping another ship, SS *Browning*, to pick them up. Sadly reported in press as 'an odious act of piracy on the high seas'.

1939 Winston Churchill, the new First Lord of the Admiralty, visited the Home Fleet at Scapa Flow. He was taken by Admiral Sir Charles Forbes, C-in-C Home Fleet, to Loch Ewe in the battleship HMS *Nelson*.

See 3 September 1939.

'My thoughts went back a quarter of a century to that other September when I had last visited Sir John Jellicoe and his captains in this very bay, and had found them with their long lines of battleships and cruisers drawn out at anchor, a prey to the same uncertainties as now afflicted us. Most of the captains and admirals of those days were dead or had long passed into retirement . . . Fisher, Wilson, Battenberg, Jellicoe, Beatty, Pakenham, Sturdee, all gone!' – Churchill, *The Second World War Volume 1, The Gathering Storm*, pp.184–5.

1941 First German acoustic/magnetic mine recovered.

1972 Second Cod War. First use of the Icelandic Coastguard's warp cutter, when *Aegir* cut the nets of the Hull trawler *Peter Scott*.

See 31 August 1958.

1979 Funeral of Admiral of the Fleet the Earl Mountbatten of Burma in Westminster Abbey. Interred later that day in Romsey Abbey.

See 25 June 1900, 25 February 1960, 27 August 1979.

6 September

1776 *Turtle* (first American submarine) attacked Howe's flagship (*Eagle*) in New York harbour: perhaps the first recorded submarine attack.

1781 *Savage* taken by the American *Congress* 30 miles E. of Charleston.

1808 *Recruit* fought the French *Diligente* 200 miles E.N.E. of Antigua, despite a sprung mast.

1814 *Tigress* captured the American *Scorpion* on Lake Huron. Troops: Royal Artillery and Royal Newfoundland Fencible Infantry detachments.

See 3 September 1814.

1864 Following the bombardment of Shimonoseki in Japan by Vice-Admiral Kuper the day before, a Naval Brigade was landed to spike enemy guns. VC: Mid Duncan Gordon Boyes, Thomas Pride (Captain of the Afterguard) and OS William Henry Harrison Seeley (*Euryalus*) for 'great intelligence and daring' while leading advance of Naval Brigade, and carrying its colour under very heavy fire, in attack on stockaded barracks at Shimonoseki, taken that day. Seeley the first American citizen to be awarded VC. Medals presented on Southsea Common on 22 September 1865 by C-in-C Portsmouth. Gun salute fired by *Victory*.

See 5 September 1864.

1873 William Archibald Howard Kelly born. Captain of the light cruiser *Gloucester* in the chase of the German battlecruiser *Goeben* in 1914; C-in-C China Station 1930–3. Admiral Sir Howard Kelly hauled down his flag in 1936 after fifty years' service. Recalled 1940 and finally retired in 1944 aged 71.

See 11 November 1931, 11 January 1933, 14 September 1952.

1898 VC: Surg William Job Maillard (*Hazard*) during landing at Candia (Heraklion), Crete, for attempts to rescue wounded men under heavy fire.

1914 *Dwarf* began operations in Cameroons, cutting out four lighters. Thwarted three attacks by improvised torpedoes.

Admiral Lord Beresford (1846–1919)

Charles William de la Poer Beresford, son of the Marquess of Waterford and an Anglo-Irish protestant, 'was one of the most remarkable personalities of his generation: brave, high-spirited, an enthusiastic sportsman (he had a tattoo depicting the Waterford hounds in full cry down his back "with the brush of the fox disappearing where it should disappear" [see 26 March 2005]. Charlie B, of noble birth, and possessed of ample private means, touched life at many points, and to the general public was the best-known sailor of his day. He had some of the faults as well as many of the virtues of his Irish ancestry, and although he was passionately devoted to the Navy and to his country, his love of publicity, and impatience of control, sometimes led him into conduct that was alien from the strict traditions of the service.' – *DNB*, 1912–21, p.42. Beresford's later career was blighted by his running duel with Admiral Sir John Fisher during the latter's extended appointment as First Sea Lord, 1904–10, an active antagonism in which Beresford exploited his privileged position as a MP to attack Fisher's reforms in Parliament, and which rent the Royal Navy before the First World War. 'He allowed patrician attitudes to affect his judgement [and] scorned Fisher's middle-class parentage and supposed Asiatic blood. The two admirals fought each other with every weapon that came to hand' – Kenneth Rose, *King George V*, p.72. Beresford distinguished himself in command of the composite screw gunvessel *Condor* at the bombardment of Alexandria in 1882. Admiral Seymour's signal 'Well done, *Condor*!' was reported by Moberley Bell, *The Times* correspondent embarked with Beresford and delighted the British public. Fisher in the *Inflexible* received a similar signal but, with no embarked press, the BZ had a limited circulation. Although he was three times a commander-in-chief at sea, Bereford was never to be First Sea Lord, a post he coveted. But 'Charlie B' was given a state funeral at St Paul's Cathedral before he was buried at Putney Vale.

See 10 February 1846, 11 August 1850 – *Phaeton*, 11 and 14 July 1882, 8 November 1907.

Inside the lower battery at Shimonoseki after its capture, 1864. (*NMRN*)

1919 Admiral Lord Beresford, Baron Beresford of Metemmeh and Curraghmore, 'Charlie B' to the Service, died of apoplexy at Langwell, Caithness aged 73.

See 10 February 1846.

1935 SS *Atreus* commissioned as a controlled mining ship for use in Abyssinian war.

1939 British government gave notice of the suspension of its obligations under the London Naval Treaty of 1936.

First Convoys of Second World War, 1939

These ran between the Thames and the Firth of Forth. The first ocean-bound convoys sailed on 7 September. Despite opposition to the convoy system on the grounds that it was too 'defensive-minded', the system proved to be the most effective means not only of protecting the merchantmen (only 4 of 5,756 properly convoyed ships were lost in 1939 to submarines) but also of deploying the few escorts against enemy submarines by attracting the latter to the former. Losses among ships sailing independently were high, and these sailings were stopped as soon as possible (110 were lost to submarines in 1939). This misconception of convoy was one of the greatest and most costly fallacies of Second World War: a submarine was useless unless it attacked, and if it attacked a convoy it also took on the convoy escort.

1940 *Godetia* sunk in collision with SS *Marsa* 3 miles off Altacarry Head, N. Ireland (55.18N, 05.57W).

1943 Destroyer *Puckeridge* sunk by U-617 40 miles E. of Europa Point (36.06N, 04.44W).

1945 The light fleet carrier *Glory* with two sloops arrived at Rabaul, New Britain, Solomon Islands and Gen. B.A.H. Sturdee of the Australian Army received on board the surrender of 140,000 Japanese troops in the Bismarck Archipelago, the Solomons and New Guinea.

See 30 August 1945, 12 and 15 September 1945.

1993 HM The Queen approved the eligibility of all ranks of the armed forces for appointment to the Distinguished Service Order.

7 September

1807 Admiral James Gambier (*Prince of Wales*) received the surrender of the Danish fleet at Copenhagen. Seventy Danish ships surrendered: 18 ships of the line, 10 frigates, 16 corvettes, 26 smaller vessels.
See 26 July 1807, 2 September 1807.

1830 *Primrose* captured the Spanish slaver *Velos Passagera* 90 miles W.N.W. of Akassa, Nigeria, with 555 slaves.

1834 *Imogene*, *Andromache* and *Louisa* engaged the Bogue forts, Canton River.

1854 *President* and *Virago* captured the Russian *Sitka* and *Anadir* respectively off Petropavlovsk.

1870 *Captain* capsized and sank off Finisterre. First and last British warship to combine turret guns with full sailing rig. Some later vessels had masts and spars but were brigs. 'The only British armoured vessel ever lost through inability to outlive a gale in the open' – Ballard. Four hundred and seventy officers and men lost, including her designer, Capt Cowper Coles.

1914 Naval operations against Duala, Cameroons, began. Ships: *Astraea*, *Challenger*, *Cumberland*, *Dwarf*. Niger Flotilla: *Alligator*, *Balbus*, *Crocodile*, *Ivy*, *Moseley*, *Porpoise*, *Remus*, *Vampire*, *Vigilant*, *Walrus*.
Battle Honour: Cameroons 1914.

1923 *Espiegle*, sloop, sold at Bombay. The last operational Royal Navy ship afloat and in commission to carry a figurehead. Stand fast *Implacable*.
See 29 April 1903, 2 December 1949.

1939 'Their Lordships have decided that, in the special circumstances obtaining at the moment, Members of Parliament serving in the Royal Navy and Royal Marines should not be debarred from participating in political activities, and for this purpose they may be granted leave in order to attend to their parliamentary duties in the House of Commons and in their constituencies.' – AFO 2521/39.
See 19 February 1934.

1939 The Price of Admiralty. 'Deaths at sea. Administrative arrangements may not provide for any large number of bodies brought into port for burial. For that reason, Captains of HM ships are recommended, when time permits, to arrange for the bodies of officers and men killed in action or dying at sea as a result of wounds to be buried at sea, unless the ship is very close to the port to which she is proceeding.' – AFO 2516a/39.

1941 Cruisers *Nigeria* and *Aurora* engaged the escort of a German convoy off Porsanger Fjord (71.46N, 21.30E). *Bremse* sunk and two other escort vessels damaged, though two troopships escaped and *Nigeria* rammed a wreck.

1941 *Patrick Henry*, the first of the prefabricated, mass-produced wartime freighters, the Liberty ships, launched at Bethlehem Fairfield Yard, Baltimore.

They averaged forty-two days in construction but the *Robert G. Peary* was launched from the No. 2 Yard of the Permanente Metals Corporation, Richmond, California on 12 November 1942, four days fifteen and a half hours after keel laying. She

The stern of HMS *Captain* (1869) in dry dock; her low freeboard is clearly visible. (*NMRN*)

was fitted out and ready for sea three days later. Liberty ships, produced by the innovative American engineer Henry Kaiser, could lift 10,500 tons deadweight and steam at 11 knots, and proved their worth in the Battle of the Atlantic.

1943 Submarine *Shakespeare* sank the Italian S/M *Velella* in Gulf of Salerno.

1943 Wellington W/407 (RCAF) sank U-669 in Bay of Biscay.

1958 The flag of Vice-Admiral Sir Hilary Biggs, the 100th and last C-in-C East Indies Station was struck at 0900C at HMS *Jufair*, Bahrain and the East Indies Station disbanded. Admiral Biggs retired 6 October 1958. His son, Vice-Admiral Sir Geoffrey Biggs, was the last Flag Officer Gibraltar.

See 30 October 1956, 1 May 1957, 15 October 1957, 31 March 1961, 11 April 1967, 5 June 1967, 26 May 1969, 4 November 1971, 31 March 1979, 19 June 1979, 30 September 1983.

The oldest RN foreign station in commission, its southern area was incorporated into the South Atlantic and South America Station, and the rest into the newly created Arabian Seas and Persian Gulf Station commanded by a commodore (CASPG) based at HMS *Jufair*. Title of SNOPG lapsed at same time. 'Any correspondence on East Indies Station matters which cannot reach the office of the Commander-in-Chief, East Indies, in HMS *Gambia* by 27 August 1958 is to be addressed as appropriate . . .' – AFO 2145/58; AFO 1668/58. On 6 November 1958 the Queen's Colour of the Station was laid up in St Martin-in-the Fields in the presence of the Board of Admiralty and nine former commanders-in-chief. Admiral Biggs delivered the Queen's Colour to the Revd Austen Williams: 'Reverend Sir, this, the last of the Queen's Colours carried in the service of the Queen's Commonwealth by the East Indies Station, Royal Navy, I now deliver into your hands for safe custody within these ancient walls.'

1959 Keel of frigate *Nubian* laid by Mrs Unwin, wife of Rear-Admiral J.H. Unwin, Admiral Superintendent of Portsmouth Dockyard. She was paid 5*s* which represented the piece rate for the job.

1971 *Swiftsure* launched: nuclear submarine, ninth of name and first of class.

2005 MOD signed agreement with Chilean government for sale of Type 23 frigates *Norfolk*, *Marlborough* and *Grafton*, the last having commissioned into the Royal Navy eight years earlier, 29 May 1997.

See 1 June 1990, 22 November 2006.

2006 *Clyde*, offshore patrol vessel (helicopter), launched at Vosper Thornycroft, Portsmouth Naval Base, by Mrs Lesley Dunt, wife of Vice-Admiral Peter Dunt, Director of Defence Estates. The first ship built inside the old dockyard walls since the frigate *Andromeda*, launched 24 May 1967.

See 23 May 1955, 14 June 2006.

8 September

1541 Sir Thomas Spert, Controller of the Navy to Henry VIII and first Master of Trinity House, died.

See 20 May 1514.

1656 *Speaker* and two consorts captured six out of eight Spanish ships of the Plate fleet off Cadiz.

1797 *Dryad* sank the French privateer *Cornelie* 150 miles S.W. by W. of Cape Clear.

1798 *Phaeton* and *Anson* captured the French *Flore* 30 miles W. of Cordouan lighthouse.

1811 *Hotspur* sank one French brig and drove two others on shore among the Calvados Rocks, S.E. of Cape Barfleur.

1813 Capture of San Sebastian by Lt-Gen. Sir Thomas Graham. Seamen from the squadron manned some of the breaching batteries. Ships: *Ajax, Andromache, Arrow, Beagle, Challenger, Constant, Dispatch, Freija, Holly, Juniper, Lyra, Magicienne, President, Revolutionnaire, Sparrow, Surveillante, Stork, Racer, Trio, Reindeer, Goldfinch* and Gunboats 14, 16, 19, 20 and 22. Battle Honour: San Sebastian 1813.

1849 Boats of *Medea* captured and burned five pirate junks at Tinpak.

1855 Capture of Sevastopol, besieged since 17 October 1854, by British and French forces.

1914 AMC *Oceanic* wrecked off Foula, Shetland.

1918 *Nessus* lost in collision with *Amphitrite* in North Sea.

1940 Light cruiser *Aurora* bombarded Boulogne.

1941 *Croome* sank the Italian S/M *Maggiore Baracca* off Azores.

HMS *Adventure*, cruiser minelayer (1924). (*NMRN W&L SF1*)

The Surrender of the Italian Fleet, 8 September 1943

'In all the annals of military history there can be few such dramatic events as the submission of an enemy navy. For the victors it is the culmination of the whole process of the application of maritime power; it is the consummation of all their hopes, and the fulfilment of all their purposes' – Roskill, *The War at Sea*, vol.3, pt 1, p.168. The main body of the Italian fleet including the battleships *Roma*, *Vittorio Veneto* and *Italia* (ex-*Littorio*), six cruisers and eight destroyers, left Spezia under Vice-Admiral Carlo Bergamini at 0300 9 September to rendezvous with the battleships *Warspite* (Rear-Admiral A.W. LaT. Bissett) and *Valiant* 20 miles north of Bone. The core of the British Mediterranean Fleet, including the battleships *Nelson* and *Rodney*, and the carriers *Illustrious* and *Formidable*, could not be diverted from operations at Salerno. En route the Italians were attacked by German Dornier 217s armed with wireless-controlled bombs that hit and sank the Italian flagship *Roma*, with the loss of most of her people, including the Commander-in-Chief. The Italian fleet, now led by the cruiser *Eugenia di Savoia*, wearing the flag of Admiral Romeo Oliva, met *Warspite* and *Valiant* at 0800 10 September north of Cape Garde, near Bone. The remarkable parallel with the surrender of the German High Seas Fleet on 21 November 1918 was evident, strengthened by the fact that both *Warspite* and *Valiant* had been present at that event a quarter of a century earlier. 'Deep emotions were stirred throughout the Fleet' (Roskill); Cunningham, with Eisenhower, went out in the destroyer *Hambledon* from Bizerta 'to view the cortege' (Roskill). 'To see my wildest hopes of years back brought to fruition, and my former flagship the *Warspite*, which had struck the first blow against the Italians three years before, leading her erstwhile opponents into captivity, filled me with the deepest emotion and lives with me still. I can never forget it. I made a signal congratulating the *Warspite* on her proud and rightful position at the head of the line' – Cunningham, *A Sailor's Odyssey*, p.563.

Most of the Taranto-based ships including the battleships *Andrea Doria* and *Caio Duilio*, with two cruisers, sailed to Malta on 10 September, followed four days later by a final battleship, the *Guilio Cesare*. In all, 5 battleships, 8 cruisers, 11 fleet destroyers, 22 escort destroyers, 20 escort vessels and 34 submarines were surrendered. All of the international press were at Salerno and no thought had been given to publicising the naval surrender. Once again, a major PR opportunity had been lost.

On the evening of 10 September Admiral Cunningham ordered all his forces that 'the Italian fleet having scrupulously honoured the engagement entered into by their government, officers and ships' companies are to be treated with courtesy and consideration on all occasions'. On the next day, 11 September, he made one of the most memorable signals in British naval history. 'By these two messages, the one chivalrous and the other showing that magnanimity in victory which Mr Churchill himself has recommended, he closed a chapter in British history which, but for the unscrupulous opportunism of a dictator, need never have been written' – Roskill, *The War at Sea*, vol.3, pt.1, pp.168–70.

Between her declaration of war on 10 June 1940 and surrender on 8 September 1943 Italian naval losses had totalled 1 battleship, 14 cruisers, 43 destroyers, 42 escort destroyers and 85 submarines.

British and Commonwealth warship losses to Axis forces (including ships on loan to Allied navies) in the Mediterranean during the same period: One battleship (*Barham*), 2 aircraft carriers (*Ark Royal* and *Eagle*), 14 cruisers (*Calypso*, *Southampton*, *York*, *Bonaventure*, *Fiji*, *Gloucester*, *Calcutta*, *Galatea*, *Neptune*, *Naiad*, *Hermione*, *Cairo*, *Manchester* and *Coventry*), 1 monitor (*Terror*), 1 submarine depot ship (*Medway*), 2 fast minelayers (*Latona* and *Welshman*), 47 destroyers, 41 submarines, 7 corvettes, 2 cutters and 8 fleet minesweepers.

Data from Roskill, *The War at Sea*, vol.3, pt.1, Appendices F, G and H.

See 21 November 1918, 29 and 11 September 1943, 2 September 1945.

1943 MTB 77 sunk by aircraft off Vibo Valentia.

1943 Italy surrendered after three years and three months of hostilities and most of her fleet passed into Allied control.

1983 Minehunter *Waveney* launched, fourth of name and first of class.

9 SEPTEMBER

1583 *Squirrel* lost with all hands returning from Newfoundland. Death of Sir Humphrey Gilbert.

1661 The body of Admiral Robert Blake disinterred at Westminster Abbey and thrown into a pit – but see 27 February 1945.

See 7 August 1657.

1681 *James Galley* and *Sapphire* captured the Algerine *Half-Moon* 135 miles S.W. by W. of Cape Spartel.

1754 William Bligh, future Captain of HM Armed Transport *Bounty*, *Director* (64) at the Battle of Camperdown and *Glatton* (56) at Copenhagen, Vice-Admiral of the Blue, born at Plymouth.

See 23 December 1787, 28 April 1789, 14 June 1789, 7 December 1817.

1803 Boats of *Sheerness* captured two French chasse-marées near Audierne, Brittany.

1935 First landing of a Service rotary-wing aircraft on one of HM ships: a Cierva C30A autogyro, K4230, on *Furious* by Wg-Cdr Brie.

1939 Destroyer leader *Jervis* launched at Hawthorn Leslie. She shared with *Nubian* the RN destroyer record of thirteen Second World War battle honours, all but Normandy won in the Mediterranean. Battleship *Warspite* gained twenty-five battle honours, fourteen of them in the same war.

1943 Salerno landing. Operation Avalanche. Battle Honour: Salerno 1943.

During the operations against the Germans in Sicily in 1943, it was decided to carry out an amphibious assault in the area of Salerno on the west coast of Italy as the first step towards the capture of Naples. Early on 9 September, 41 Cdo landed and surprised the town of Vietri. For four days the unit was involved in heavy fighting against elements of five crack German divisions.

Ships: *Abercrombie, Acute, Albacore, Alynbank, Antwerp, Atherstone, Attacker, Aurora, Battler, Beaufort, Belvoir, Blackmore, Blankney, Blencathra, Boxer, Brecon, Brittany, Brixham, Brocklesby, Bruiser, Bude, Cadmus, Calpe, Catterick, Charybdis, Circe, Clacton, Cleveland, Coverley, Delhi, Derwentdale, Dido, Dingledale, Dulverton, Echo, Eclipse, Eggesford, Ensay, Espiegle, Euryalus, Exmoor, Farndale, Faulknor, Felixstowe, Fly, Formidable, Fury, Gavotte, Glengyle, Hambledon, Haydon, Hengist, Hilary, Holcombe, Hunter, Ilex, Illustrious, Inglefield, Intrepid, Jervis, Laforey, Lamerton, Ledbury, Liddesdale, Lookout, Loyal, Mauritius, Mendip, Minuet, Mousa, Mutine, Nelson, Nubian, Offa, Orion, Palomares, Panther, Pathfinder, Penelope, Penn, Petard, Pirouette, Polruan, Prince Charles, Prince Leopold, Prins Albert, Prinses Astrid, Prinses Beatrix, Prinses Josephine Charlotte, Quail, Quantock, Queenborough, Quilliam, Raider, Reighton Wyke, Rhyl, Roberts, Rodney, Rothesay, Royal Scotsman, Royal Ulsterman, St Kilda, Scylla, Shakespeare, Sheffield, Sheppey, Sirius, Stalker, Stella Carina, Stornoway, Tango, Tartar, Tetcott, Thruster, Troubridge, Tumult, Tyrian, Uganda, Ulster Monarch, Ulster Queen, Unicorn, Valiant, Visenda, Warspite, Whaddon, Wheatland.* BYMS: 11, 14, 24, 209. HDML: 1242, 1246, 1247, 1253, 1254, 1258, 1270, 1271, 1297, 1301. ML: 238, 273, 280, 283, 336, 554, 555, 556, 557, 559, 560, 561, 562, 564, 566. MMS: 5, 133, 134. MSML: 121, 126, 134, 135. FAA Sqns: 820, 888, 893 (*Formidable* – Albacore, Fulmar/Martlet); 810, 878, 890, 894 (*Illustrious* – Barracuda, Wildcat); 809, 887, 897 (*Unicorn* – Seafire); 879, 886 (*Attacker* – Seafire); 807, 808 (*Battler* – Seafire); 834, 899 (*Hunter* – Seafire); 880 (*Stalker* – Seafire).

1943 Submarine *Unshaken* took the Italian S/M *Ciro Menotti* in the Strait of Otranto and led her into Malta two days later to add to the bag.

1943 *Roma*, a surrendering Italian battleship, sunk by German aircraft with new FX1200 guided armour-piercing bomb off Sardinia (41.10N, 08.40E).

1943 Welman 10 sank alongside her depot ship in Loch Cairnbawn.

See 22 November 1943.

1944 *Helmsdale* and *Portchester Castle* sank U-743 in N.W. Approaches (55.46N, 11.41W).

1944 *Hespeler* and *Dunver* (both RCN) sank U-484 off the Hebrides (36.30N, 07.40W).

1953 HM Harbour Defence Motor Launch 1323 of the Hong Kong Local Defence Force based at HMS *Tamar*, fired on by a Chinese Communist

HMS *Nelson*, down by the bows after being hit by a torpedo during Operation Halberd in 1941. (*NMRN*)

warship while on patrol in international waters in the Pearl River Estuary 20 miles W. of Hong Kong. Seven men killed including the CO, Lt G.C.X. Merriman RN, and five wounded. Leading Seaman Gordon Cleaver (20), a former sea cadet, having ditched an unexploded shell, took charge, re-hoisted the White Ensign and brought the craft into Tai-O on the W. end of Lantau Island where he met the destroyer *Concord*. BEM. The dead were buried in Happy Valley Cemetery, Kong Kong.

1968 During RNR MCM 10 exercises off St Catherine's Point, under Admiral Commanding Reserves, Rear-Admiral Godfrey Place VC, in the frigate *Jaguar*, Solent Division RNR tender *Warsash* collided bows on with the port side of Tyne Division RNR tender *Northumbria*. Damage to the wooden hull of *Northumbria* in the generator room area and dependence on electrical services presented unusual and unexpected DC challenges; three ratings in *Northumbria* commended.

1977 The end of ships' dogs and cats. 'The risk of ships' pets escaping and coming into contact with rabies-infected animals from foreign vessels berthed close by is unacceptable. All warm-blooded mammals subject to the Rabies Order must therefore be prohibited from HM ships, RFA and RMAS ships and vessels and such pets currently carried on board are to be landed forthwith.' – DCI(JS) No.37. The list included otters, hyenas, lions, armadillos, rhinoceroses, elephants, kangaroos and great apes.

1997 Mne E. Ette of RMR Bristol became first Royal Marine to swim the English Channel.

10 SEPTEMBER

1677 *Sapphire* fought the Algerine *Golden Horse* in the Mediterranean.

1759 Vice-Admiral George Pocock (*Yarmouth*) fought Cdre Comte d'Ache (*Zodiaque*), with eleven ships, 25 miles S.E. of Porto Novo.

Ships: *Cumberland, Elizabeth, Grafton, Newcastle, Salisbury, Sunderland, Tiger, Weymouth, Yarmouth*. Frigate: *Queenborough*.

This third action was a furious one with heavy losses on both sides. The French withdrew; the British were unable to pursue. But it was the end of French sea power in Indian waters.
Battle Honour: Porto Novo 1759.

See 29 April 1758, 3 August 1758.

1778 *Fox* taken by the French *Junon* 120 miles S.S.W. of Ushant.

1813 Defeat of the British Lake Squadron by the American Lake Squadron on Lake Erie. Ships: *Chippeway, Detroit, Hunter, Lady Prevost, Little Belt, Queen Charlotte*. Troops: 41st Regiment, Royal Newfoundland Fencible Infantry. American: *Ariel, Caledonia, Lawrence, Niagara, Porcupine, Scorpion, Summers, Tigress, Trip*. (Second *Little Belt* taken by US.) Frigates *Salisbury* and *Tenby* visited Cleveland in 1959 – the first RN ships on Lake Erie since 1813.

See 26 June 1959.

1840 Start of operations which continued until 9 December against Mehemet Ali. Bombardment of Beirut and landing of troops in d'Jounie (Juniye) Bay.

Ships: *Bellerophon, Benbow, Edinburgh, Ganges, Hastings, Princess Charlotte* (Admiral the Hon. Sir Robert Stopford), *Powerful, Revenge, Rodney, Thunderer, Vanguard*. Others: *Asia, Cambridge, Implacable*. Frigates: *Carysfort, Castor, Dido, Hazard, Pique, Sabrina, Talbot, Wasp*. Others: *Daphne, Magicienne*. Steamers: *Cyclops, Gorgon, Hydra, Medea, Phoenix, Stromboli, Vesuvius*. Others: *Hecate*. Austrian: *Guerriera, Lipsia, Medea* (Rear-Admiral Franz, Baron Bandiera). Turkish: *Mookuddimay-I-Hive* (Rear-Admiral Baldwin Walker Bey). Troops: Royal Artillery, Royal Sappers and Miners.

1840 A force under Sir Robert Stopford drove Egyptian invaders from Syria after taking Acre on behalf of the Turks.
Battle Honour: Syria 1840.

1855 *Resolute* abandoned in search for Franklin. (Discovered, having drifted 1,000 miles, in 1856 and her colours presented by the USN to Queen Victoria before being laid up at Chatham.)

1862 Britain's first timber-hulled ironclad, *Royal Oak*, launched at Chatham. She carried 25,000 sq ft of canvas, and her reciprocating engines, powered by 20-psi steam, drove a 19ft-diameter hoisting propeller.

1874 *Neptune*, 9,300 tons, Britain's last rigged turret-ship, launched at Dudgeons, Millwall, fifty-six days after the first attempt to send her afloat on 16 July 1874.

After a second attempt on 30 July to launch the ship, a third of her hull was suspended

HMS *Neptune* (1874), masted turret ship with four 12-in muzzle-loading rifled guns in two turrets. (*NMRN*)

The officers and men of HMS *Royal Oak*, 1869. (*NMRN*)

unsupported over the end of the slip, causing extensive damage. The firm may have over-extended itself with this large ship and the yard closed in 1875. Built as the *Independencia* for Brazil but purchased by HMG in March 1878 during the Russian War scare.

See 7 August 1853, 23 October 1903.

1918 *Ophelia* sank UB-83 off Pentland Firth.

1934 Professor Geoffrey Callender appointed first Director of the National Maritime Museum.

1939 *Oxley* sunk in friendly-fire attack by *Triton* off Obrestad (Montrose–Montrestad patrol). First British warship and first of seventy-six RN submarines lost in the Second World War.

On 14 September 1939 *Sturgeon* attacked and narrowly missed her sister ship *Swordfish*.

See 27 August 1944.

1941 *Chambly* and *Moosejaw* (both RCN) sank U-501 off Greenland. Convoy SC 42. First Canadian sinking of U-boat.

1943 Italian fleet base at Taranto captured intact in 'a sudden descent' by the Royal Navy following the Italian armistice. The British 1st Airborne Division sailed from Bizerta in ships of the 12th Cruiser Squadron, Cdre W.G. Agnew RN, *Aurora, Penelope, Sirius* and *Dido*, the cruiser-minelayer *Abdiel* and the US cruiser *Boise*. They met Vice-Admiral Arthur Power, Vice-Admiral Malta, at sea with the battleships *Howe* (flag) and *King George V*, four destroyers and minesweepers, which had been sailed by Admiral Cunningham in case of opposition from shore batteries; the cruisers entered Taranto late on 9 September. Near midnight the *Abdiel* swung across a magnetic mine laid by the departing German E-boats S.54 and S.61 and she sank with heavy loss. Operation Slapstick.

See 1 February 1943.

1944 *Erebus* and *Warspite* bombarded Le Havre.

1971 *Ariadne*, last of twenty-six Leander-class frigates and the Royal Navy's last surface steam-powered ship to be built, launched at Yarrow, Scotstoun, and commissioned 10 February 1973. Last ship to fire Limbo A/S weapon and the last RN ship to fire a broadside before paying off in May 1992.

See 28 June 1961, 18 March 2002.

1990 Revd Caroline Eglin (née Pullman) commissioned. The first female Chaplain to enter the RN.

See 3 June 1996.

2000 Frigate *Argyll*, Cdr R.C.B. Wellesley RN, deploying to the South Atlantic, diverted to West Africa. She provided a covert base off Sierra Leone for two Lynx Mk 7 attack helicopters of 657 Sqn AAC engaged in a UKSF operation to rescue six British UN peacekeeping soldiers and their local liaison officer held hostage up a river creek. The ship later recovered wounded personnel and gave medical support. A splendid joint operation which demonstrated the flexibility of sea power and which became a standard mission template. Operation Barras.

See 1 and 24 May 2000.

11 SEPTEMBER

1781 *Iris* and *Richmond* taken by the French squadron under Cdre Comte Barras in Chesapeake Bay.

1793 Nelson (*Agamemnon*) first met Lady Hamilton, at Naples.

1795 Alexander Dalrymple appointed first (and only civilian) Hydrographer of the Navy – at a salary of £500.
See 3 January 2001.

1809 Brig *Diana* captured the Dutch brig *Zefier* off Menado, Celebes.
Battle Honour: *Zefier* 1809.

1814 Second battle of Lake Champlain. The British Lake Squadron defeated by the American Lake Squadron in Plattsburg Bay, causing Prevost to desist from advancing on New York. Ships: *Confiance, Linnet, Chub, Finch* and ten gunboats. American: *Saratoga, Eagle, Preble, Ticonderoga* and ten gunboats.
See 11 October 1776.

1886 *Rattlesnake*, first Torpedo Gunboat, launched.

1896 *Zafir* burst her boiler on the White Nile much to the chagrin of Kitchener, before Dongola. Repaired and in action again on 23rd.

1919 *Hermes*, first ship to be designed, ordered, and built as an aircraft carrier, launched at Armstrongs on the Tyne. Completed at Devonport. Sunk by Japanese naval aircraft off Ceylon 9 April 1942.
See 1 May 1923.

1921 Admiral of the Fleet the Marquess of Milford Haven, former First Sea Lord and, until 1917, entitled HSH Prince Louis of Battenberg, died aged 67, in his chambers in Half Moon Street, Piccadilly. Father of Admiral of the Fleet the Earl Mountbatten of Burma, also a First Sea Lord. The first president of the Society for Nautical Research.
See 28 August 1914, 4 October 1921.

Dover Barrage, 1939

The minelayers *Adventure* and *Plover*, augmented by requisitioned train ferries *Shepperton* and *Hampton*, laid over 6,000 mines in the Dover Area between 11 September and 23 October. This barrage prevented U-boats from passing through the straits. Only one succeeded, on the night 11/12 September before the barrage was really started. In October, two others blew up on mines and a third ran aground on the Goodwins.

1940 A force of Vichy French cruisers and destroyers, en route from Toulon to Dakar, passed unchallenged through the Gibraltar Strait due to unclear Admiralty orders and intentions further confused by a curious chain of command to Force H at Gibraltar. Admiral Sir Dudley North, FO Commanding North Atlantic, based at Gibraltar, was held accountable and, having lost the confidence of Their Lordships, was relieved on 15 October. He retired from the Royal Navy on Christmas Day 1941. Admiral North was refused a court martial or other opportunity to defend himself. He enjoyed wide support in the Service and a deputation to Prime Minister Harold Macmillan by admirals of the fleet in 1957 secured him 'partial absolution'.
See 28 June 1940, 2 February 1953.

1941 *Leamington* and *Veteran* sank U-207 in N. Atlantic (63.59N, 34,48W). Convoy SC 42.

1942 *Charlottetown* (RCN) sunk by U-517 in the Gulf of St Lawrence (49.12N, 66.48W). Convoy QS 33.

1943 *Haarlem, Hyacinth, Wollongong* (RAN) and Wellingtons J/179 and P/179 damaged U-617 in the Straits of Gibraltar. U-boat beached next day (35.38N, 03.29W) in Spanish Morocco.

1943 The surrendered Italian battlefleet arrived at Malta: 'Be pleased to inform Their Lordships that the Italian Battle Fleet now lies at anchor under the guns of the fortress of Malta' – Admiral Sir Andrew Cunningham to the Secretary of the Admiralty.
See p.512 panel.

The Fleet Air Arm memorial to over 6,000 members of the Fleet Air Arm and Royal Naval Air Service killed since the Service was formed 100 years earlier was dedicated at the National Memorial Arboretum at Alrewas, Staffordshire on 11 September 2009 by the Chaplain of the Fleet, the Venerable John Green. (*RN*)

1944 X 24 laid two charges under the floating dock at Laksvaag, Bergen. Dock broken in two. Operation Heckle.

Midget Submarine Attack – Bergen, 1944

X 24 had been towed by the submarine *Sceptre* to Bergen and carried out an attack on shipping there on 14 April. She had planned to damage the 8,000-ton floating dock, but had been deflected on her approach. She managed to blow up the 7,800-ton ship *Bahrenfels* and put the coaling wharf out of action for the remainder of the war, in addition to one of two ships moored alongside. The other was sunk.

On 11 September, she again entered Bergen harbour. She used the mast of the *Bahrenfels* as a marker, the only part of the ship still showing above water, and placed charges under the floating dock. She then made her way down the fjord and made contact with *Sceptre* that evening. Four of the six sections of the floating dock were damaged beyond repair, the other two sections were damaged, and so were two ships secured alongside the dock at the time of the attack.

These attacks were carried out very skilfully and caused considerable damage. They brought about delays in the harbour's routine and immobilised troops in security operations.

1951 Light cruiser *Liverpool*, flag of Admiral Sir John Edelsten, C-in-C Mediterranean Fleet, arrived off Split for the first post-war RN ship visit to Yugoslavia. Marshal Tito inspected ship's company.

1994 *Brazen*, Type 22 frigate, grounded in Canales Petigonicos on the Chilean coast for four days. CO, NO and OOW court-martialled 17 February 1995. First court martial of a female OOW. Her plea of Guilty to a charge of negligence was not accepted by the Court; no further evidence was offered by the Crown and she was acquitted. CO dismissed his ship but promoted 30 June 2002.

See 14 May 1741, 7 July 2002.

1998 Rear-Admiral Nigel Essenhigh, ACDS(Programmes), promoted admiral and appointed CINCFLEET/CINCEASTLANT/COMNAVNORWEST in succession to Admiral Sir Michael Boyce.

2003 Directorate of Naval Operations wound-up after ninety-one years and subsumed into the new MOD Directorates of Joint Commitments, Strategic Support and Counter-Terrorism and UK Operations.

See 27 November 1961.

2006 Fleet submarine *Sovereign*, Cdr S.R. Drysdale RN, Britain's oldest operational submarine, paid off at Faslane after thirty-three years' service.

See 31 December 1976.

2009 The Fleet Air Arm Memorial, incorporating the shape of an aircraft carrier in granite, dedicated at the National Memorial Arboretum in Staffordshire by the Chaplain of the Fleet, the Venerable John Green, in the presence of the senior naval aviator, Admiral of the Fleet Sir Benjamin Bathurst, and Rear-Admiral Simon Charlier, Rear-Admiral Fleet Air Arm. It commemorated over 6,000 naval aviators killed in the Service across a century. Four rowan trees represent the four Fleet Air Arm Victoria Crosses.

See 20 May 1953, 1 June 2000, 9 October 2009, 10 December 2009.

12 SEPTEMBER

1747 *Amazon* (26) fought the French *Renommée* (32) 120 miles S.S.W. of Ushant.

1782 *Warwick* captured the French *Sophie* off the Delaware.

1808 *Laurel* taken by the French *Canonnière* off Port Louis, Mauritius.

1840 Abortive attack by *Carysfort*, *Cyclops* and *Dido* on Jebeil Castle, Syria.

1846 Foundation of the future Steam Yard at Keyham. George Eden, Earl of Auckland, First Lord of the Admiralty, ceremonially laid a 9-ton granite block (containing a box of coins of the Realm) which formed part of the South Lock entrance to the basin.

See 7 October 1853.

1857 Naval Brigades of *Pearl* and *Shannon* landed at Calcutta. Second contingent left the ship 12 October 1857. During operations against mutineers by both contingents up to December 1858 only one man killed in action. Eighteen died of fever, drowning or sunstroke.

See 18 August 1857.

1914 Cruiser *Berwick* captured the German fleet auxiliary *Spreewald* at a rendezvous with two neutrals. Taken into service as *Lucia* and as a useful depot ship.

1914 U-13 sunk in North Sea.

1917 Submarine D 7 torpedoed (stern tube) and sank U-45 in N.W. Approaches.

1920 The Nab Tower, a 9,000 ton concrete and steel structure designed as a permanent link in the anti-submarine barrage in the Dover Strait but incomplete when the war ended, was towed from Shoreham by two naval tugs and sunk off Portsmouth as a replacement for the Nab lightvessel. The structure settled with a 1.5 degrees list to the S.W. A workforce of 3,000 men had been secretly drafted-in for the construction project which cost £1,250,000.

1941 Swordfish aircraft of 830 Sqn FAA (Malta) and Blenheims of 105 Sqn RAF attacked an escorted Tripoli convoy south of Lampione. Several ships sunk or damaged.

Convoy PQ 18 to Russia, 1942

This comprised forty merchant ships and six minesweepers and auxiliaries, together with a substantial escort comprising:

> 17 ships as close escort (including two submarines),
> an escort carrier, cruiser and 18 destroyers – with the convoy,
> two battleships, four cruisers and five destroyers – in two covering forces.

The operation was controlled by the Commander-in-Chief in the battleship *King George V*. The route chosen for the convoy was long, as the ice had moved north, and all warships other than the close escort were to escort the next return convoy from Russia (QP 14) before returning to harbour. The main body sailed from Loch Ewe on 2 September, with a W. Approaches escort which was relieved by the close escort on 7th in the Denmark Strait. On the 9th, the cruiser *Scylla* and nine destroyers joined, and by the 13th the escort was at full strength with all the ships having fuelled from oilers lying at Spitzbergen.

On the 12th the destroyer *Faulknor* sank U-88, and on the 13th there were other U-boat attacks. Two ships were lost to U-boats, and then eight more were lost during a massed air attack by forty torpedo bombers. Five aircraft were shot down that day and twenty-two the next day, when there was a series of attacks during which one merchant ship was lost. The destroyer *Onslow* and a Swordfish from the carrier *Avenger* sank U-589. On the 15th the aircraft again attacked in large numbers and twelve U-boats were in contact with the convoy, but the escort held them off. On the 16th the destroyer *Impulsive* sank U-457, and that afternoon all but the close escort left PQ 18 and joined QP 14. Eleven merchant ships had been lost, but the Germans had lost forty-one aircraft and three U-boats. Thirty-six ships reached Russia safely.

The Germans attributed their failure to achieve better results to the steadfastness of the convoy in maintaining formation despite the intensity of the attacks.

1942 *Laconia*, troop transport, carrying 2,732 souls, including 1,800 Italian POWs and many women and children, torpedoed and sunk by U-156 N.E. of Ascension. Korvettenkapitan

The new amphibious landing ship HMS *Intrepid*, having covered the withdrawal from Aden, arrives in Singapore, December 1967. (*Author*)

Hartenstein broadcast location of survivors but rescue operation finally aborted when US Liberator attacked. Dönitz issued punitive Laconia Order forbidding future humanitarian attempts.

1943 Italian submarine *Topazio* sunk S.E. of Sardinia by RAF aircraft, having failed to identify herself.

1944 *Furious* and *Trumpeter*, escorted by *Devonshire* and six destroyers of 26th DF, laid mines in Aramsund Channel: one German escort vessel sunk. Operation Begonia. FAA Sqns: 801, 808, 827, 830 (*Furious* – Seafire, Barracuda); 846, 852 (*Trumpeter* – Avenger). The last Home Fleet operation in which *Furious* took part before reducing to reserve.

1945 Admiral Lord Louis Mountbatten, Supreme Commander Allied Forces S.E. Asia, took the surrender of General Itagaki and the unconditional surrender of half a million enemy soldiers, sailors and airmen in the Singapore Municipal Buildings.

See 30 August 1945, 3 and 15 September 1945.

1958 RNAS Culdrose received the Freedom of Helston. HMS *Seahawk*, commissioned in 1947, was 'the youngest RN ship or establishment ever to receive the honour' – *Navy* magazine, October 1958.

See 17 April 1987.

1979 Midshipman HRH Prince Andrew joined BRNC Dartmouth on a Supplementary List Short Service Commission for flying duties. DCI(RN) 564/79.

See 16 September 1971.

1985 Cdr John Kerans, DSC, RN, late of the frigate *Amethyst*, died aged 70. He was buried in St Peter's churchyard, Tandridge, near Oxted, which he shares with Desmond Wettern.

See 30 July 1949, 14 September 1956, 8 December 1991.

2008 Amphibious landing ship *Intrepid* left Portsmouth under tow for breaking up in Liverpool.

See 17 February 2008.

13 September

1747 *Dover* captured the French *Renommée* off Ushant.

1759 Capture of Quebec by Maj-Gen. James Wolfe and Vice-Admiral Charles Saunders (*Neptune*). The French formally surrendered on 18 September. 'I have the greatest pleasure in acquainting you, for their Lordships' information, that the town and citadel of Quebec surrendered on the 18th instant; the army took possession of the gates on the land side the same evening and sent safeguards into the town to preserve order and to prevent anything being destroyed, and Captain Palliser with a body of seamen landed in the lower town and did the same . . . I am sorry to acquaint you that General Wolfe was killed in the action . . . I have the pleasure also of acquainting their Lordships that during this tedious campaign, there has continued a perfect good understanding between the army and Navy.' – Vice-Admiral Sir Charles Saunders' despatch to John Cleveland, Secretary of the Admiralty, 21 September 1759.

Battle Honour: Quebec 1759.

Ships: *Alcide, Bedford, Captain, Centurion, Devonshire, Diana, Dublin, Echo, Eurus, Fowey Head, Hind, Hunter, Lizard, Lowestoffe, Medway, Neptune, Nightingale, Northumberland, Orford, Pembroke, Porcupine, Prince Frederick, Prince of Orange, Princess Amelia, Richmond, Royal William, Scarborough, Scorpion, Sea Horse, Shrewsbury, Somerset, Squirrel, Stirling Castle, Sutherland, Terrible, Trent, Trident, Vanguard, Zephyr.* Bombs: *Baltimore, Pelican, Racehorse.* Fireships: *Boscawen, Cormorant, Halifax, Strombolo, Vesuvius.* Cutter: *Rodney.* Storeship: *Crown.*

The Seven Years War was started as a result of the French settlers in Canada fortifying a number of posts against the advance of British settlers. The French city of Quebec was the key to the conquest of Upper Canada. The city stood far up the St Lawrence River and the tortuous channel was believed to be impassable by anything larger than a frigate. The French therefore believed that Quebec was safe from attack by sea.

However, a British fleet under Vice-Admiral Sir Charles Saunders, aided by the brilliant pilotage of James Cook, Master of *Pembroke* and later Captain, sailed up the St Lawrence River with an army embarked. During the attack on the city the fleet dominated the river, preventing supplies from reaching the defence, and landed the 17,000 men at the assault position below the plains of Abraham. Seamen of the fleet also landed guns and hauled them up the Heights of Abraham.

'A Military, Naval, Littoral War, when wisely prepared and discreetly conducted, is a terrible Sort of War. Happy for that People who are Sovereigns enough of the Sea to put it in Execution! For it comes like Thunder and Lightning to some unprepared Part of the World' – Molyneux, *Conjunct Operations.*

Gatling-gun crew and shore party from HMS *Superb* which was sent to Tel-el-Kebir, 1882. The sailors are armed with Martini-Henry rifles and cutlass bayonets. (*NMRN*)

1782 Repulse of the Spanish attack on Gibraltar, all ten Spanish battering ships being destroyed. Seamen from *Brilliant* reinforced the garrison.

1786 Marine Society commissioned the first designed pre-sea-training ship.

1799 *Arrow* and *Wolverine* captured the Batavian Republic *Draak* and *Gier* in Vliestroom.

1800 Capitulation of Curaçao.

1805 Nelson and Sir Arthur Wellesley (later Duke of Wellington) met in the waiting room of Lord Castlereagh, Secretary of State for War and the Colonies; their only recorded meeting and a fascinating encounter.

1807 Saumarez attacked landing craft at Granville, Normandy.

1810 *Africaine* (40) a French prize, taken by the French *Iphigénie* and *Astrée* off Réunion. Recaptured by *Boadicea*, *Otter* and *Staunch*. Troops: detachments of 86th Regiment in *Africaine*, 1/69th in *Otter* and *Staunch*, 89th in *Boadicea*.

1855 Institution of Conspicuous Gallantry Medal. Eleven awarded. Active service in Baltic and Crimea revealed that there was no naval equivalent to the Army's Distinguished Conduct Medal, the first award to distinguish conduct from mere service. Hence the CGM was instituted by Order in Council. Eleven awards were made to ten individuals, including Trevawas. After the institution of the VC no more awards were made until 7 July 1874 and there were only 234 by the end of 1946.

See 3 July 1855.

1858 *Pearl*'s Naval Brigade at Domariaganj.

1882 Battle of Tel-el-Kebir, Sudan. Two battalions of Royal Marines were present.

1914 E 9, Lt-Cdr Max Horton, sank German cruiser *Hela* S.W. of Heligoland. DSO. First RN submarine commander to sink an enemy warship. Returned to Harwich flying Jolly Roger and so established traditional signal for a successful patrol.

See 30 July 1951, 2 May 1982, 18 March 2002.

1942 11th RM battalion raided Tobruk.

1943 Lord Gort presented, on behalf of the King, the George Cross to Sir George Borg, Chief Justice of Malta, who received it on behalf of the Maltese people.

1947 Minesweeper HMAS *Warrnambool* mined and sunk off Cockburn Reef, Queensland.

1958 The largest salvage award to the Admiralty made to date following the collision of two tankers, the Liberian *Melika*, 20,551 tons, and the French *Fernand Gilabert*, 10,715 tons, in the Gulf of Oman, on 13 September. Nearly 3,700 men from the carrier *Bulwark*, cruisers *Sheffield* and *Ceylon*, frigates *Puma*, *Loch Alvie*, *St Bride's Bay* and *Loch Killisport*, the naval tug *Warden*, the RFA oiler *Cedardale* and the RFA salvage vessel *Sea Salvor* shared almost £100,000. the largest single award, £699 2*s.* 6*d*, went to Capt P.D. Gick RN of the *Bulwark*. Following a major rescue operation HM ships carried out an extended salvage operation of the abandoned tankers marked by outstanding skill and seamanship. The French tanker was towed to Karachi by *Loch Killisport* and the *Melika* towed by *Bulwark* to Muscat with *Puma* acting as a rudder. During the tow, which took a week, *Bulwark* was refuelled by RFA *Wave Knight*, a remarkable RAS. Off Oman the towing cable parted and to swing *Bulwark*, five of her Sea Hawk aircraft were ranged on deck with their engines at full power to push the ship round. The Boyd Trophy for 1958 went to 845 NAS.

See 1 September 1963.

1985 *Orpheus* made last submarine visit to Manchester. There was a firm liaison with Exide, which made submarine batteries.

1988 *Active* and RFA *Oakleaf* provided hurricane relief at Jamaica.

14 September

1650 Admiral Robert Blake (*George*) captured seven ships of the Portuguese Brazil fleet, while blockading Prince Rupert in Lisbon.

1779 *Pearl* captured the Spanish *Santa Monica* 18 miles S. by E. of Corvo Island, Azores.
Battle Honour: *Santa Monica* 1779.

1801 Combined attack on the French siege batteries at Port Ferrajo, Elba. Ships: *Renown*, *Vincejo*.

1805 Vice-Admiral Viscount Nelson embarked in *Victory* at Portsmouth for the last time, having by his own reckoning been absent from her for only twenty-five days 'from dinner to dinner' since 18 March 1803. The ship sailed next morning.

1807 *Blonde* captured the French privateer *Hirondelle* 400 miles E. of Barbados.

1814 Unsuccessful bombardment of Fort McHenry by squadron under Rear-Admiral Cochrane (*Surprise*) led to the composition of 'The Star-spangled Banner', the American national anthem, on the deck of a British warship (*Minden*). The tune is that of an old English drinking song, 'Anacreon in Heaven'.

1825 Disaster at launching of the first-rate *Princess Charlotte* (120) by HRH Prince Leopold at Portsmouth. Lock gates collapsed and carried away a temporary access bridge: sixteen killed.

1909 Destroyer *Viking* launched at Palmers, Jarrow. The only six-funnelled ship buit for the RN.

1914 AMC *Carmania* sank the German *Cap Trafalgar* off Trinidad Island, South Atlantic.
Battle Honour: *Cap Trafalgar* 1914.

1914 Submarine AE 1, with mixed British and Australian crew, lost on patrol in St George's Strait in Bismarck Archipelago N.E. of New Guinea. The first British or Dominion submarine loss in the First World War. Cause not known. AE 1 and AE 2 had left Portsmouth on 2 March 1914 and arrived at Sydney 24 May after voyage of 14,000 miles.
See 2 March 1914.

1915 Sir John Knox Laughton, naval historian and strategist, co-founder of the Navy Records Society, died aged 85. Father of Dame Vera Laughton Matthews, DWRNS in Second World War. Laughton wrote over 900 naval entries for the *Dictionary of National Biography*, many of them unduly critical and cutting and in which 'he enjoyed bayoneting the wounded' – Sugden.
See 11 April 1939.

1917 GC (ex-AM): OS G.F.P. Abbott and R.J. Knowlton, RNR, for rescuing pilot in seaplane crashed up a 360ft mast on Hornsea Island. Third recipient, OS Gold, died before 1971, when living holders of AM could exchange for GC.

1918 *Argus* commissioned: first flush-deck carrier.

1936 Cdr Charles Napier Robinson RN, for forty-three years naval correspondent of *The Times*, died in London. He entered the Navy in 1861 and saw the naval review of 1854 and the silver jubilee review in 1935. He was 'permeated to the core with the spirit of the Service to which it was his pride to belong . . . he worked with such zeal for its interests in the Press that few men have rendered with the pen greater service to the Navy' – *The Times*, 15 September 1936.

1939 *Faulknor*, *Firedrake* and *Foxhound* sank U-39 off the Hebrides. First U-boat sunk in Second World War.
See 7 May 1945.

1939 Submarine *Sturgeon* attacked her sister ship *Swordfish*, unsuccessfully.
See 16 November 1940.

1939 'So long as hostilities last, the use of the Blue Ensign, whether plain or defaced, and the defaced Red Ensign by merchant and other private vessels, is to be discontinued.' – AFO 2602/39.

1939 'The Royal Indian Navy ships *Indus*, *Hindustan*, *Cornwallis*, *Clive* and *Lawrence*, having been placed at the disposal of the Admiralty, will be treated as HM ships in all respects. The

The armed merchant cruiser HMS *Carmania* in action with the German armed liner *Cap Trafalgar* off Trinidad Island in 1914. (*NMRN*)

personnel of these vessels will rank and command according to rank, branch and seniority, as if they were officers of the Royal Navy.' – AFO 2603/39.

See 11 November 1928, 2 October 1934.

1939 'The following Dresses are to be landed at the first opportunity by all officers employed afloat: No. 1 Full Dress, No. 2 Ball Dress, No. 2a Ball Dress without Epaulettes, No. 3 Frock Coat with Epaulettes Dress, No. 4 Frock Coats Dress, No. 6 Mess Dress, No. 8 White Full Dress, No. 9 White Dress, No. 11 White Mess Dress.' – AFO 2605/39.

1942 *Sikh* hit by shore battery off Tobruk and sank in tow of *Zulu*. *Coventry* damaged by German air attack east of Tobruk, set on fire and scuttled by *Zulu* (32.48N, 28.17E). *Zulu* hit by Italian air attack and sank in tow of *Hursley* (32.00N, 28.56E). Three MTBs also sunk by aircraft. Operation Agreement.

1942 *Ottawa* (RCN) (ex-*Crusader*) sunk by U-91 in Gulf of St Lawrence. Convoy ON 127.

Convoy ON 127, 10–14 September 1942

This convoy consisted of thirty-two merchant ships. It was attacked by a wolf pack of thirteen U-boats, each of which was able to make an attack – the first time in the Battle of Atlantic that this had happened. Twelve freighters and one destroyer were sunk. Only one U-boat was damaged.

1942 *Dido, Javelin, Jervis, Pakenham* and *Paladin* bombarded the Daba area, Egypt.

1942 *Onslow* and a Swordfish from *Avenger* sank U-589 off Bear Island. Convoy PQ 18.

1942 Sunderland R/202 sank the Italian S/M *Alabastro* off Algiers.

1947 A record for two naval generations? Miss Emily Helen Patton died at Wimbledon aged 90. Her father, Admiral Robert Patton, born 1791, fought as a midshipman in *Bellerophon* at Trafalgar 142 years earlier.

See 13 April 1885, 15 April 1887, 12 February 1892, 11 July 1929.

1952 Admiral Sir (William Archibald) Howard Kelly died. Captain of the light cruiser *Gloucester* in the bungled pursuit of the German battlecruiser *Goeben* in the Mediterranean in 1914 (his brother John 'Joe' Kelly, the future admiral of the fleet, was commanding her sister ship *Dublin* in same operation): 'Only the pertinacious and gallant Howard Kelly came out of the affair with honour and glory.' – Marder, *From The Dreadnought to Scapa Flow*, vol.2, p.240.

See 6 September 1873, 7 August 1914, 11 November 1931, 11 January 1933.

1953 Following another major earthquake in the E. Mediterranean which devastated S.W. Cyprus, the destroyer *Daring* arrived at Paphos from Port Said with 165 tons of tents. Landing parties from *Daring*, joined later by men from the light fleet carrier *Theseus* and destroyer *Saintes*, helped in relief operations.

See 12 August 1953, 17 January 1968.

1956 The frigate *Amethyst*, reprieved from the breakers for filming the Yangtse incident of 1949, was holed below the waterline by an explosion simulating shellfire at Harwich. Cdr John Kerans, her erstwhile captain, on board as the Admiralty representative to ensure authenticity, ordered the 150 actors and technicians off the ship. Filming was delayed while an 8ft by 4ft steel plate was welded over the damage.

See 30 July 1949, 12 September 1985.

1987 *Abdiel*, with four minehunters arrived in Oman to start a five-month clearance of mines laid in Iran–Iraq war.

1993 *Vanguard*, the first of the RN's Trident submarines, accepted at sea from Vickers Shipbuilding.

See 30 April 1986.

15 SEPTEMBER

1744 The Navy Board petitioned HM King George II with a memorial requesting the establishment of naval hospitals at Portsmouth, Plymouth and Chatham.

See 13 March 1762.

1782 *Vestal* and *Bonetta* captured the French *Aigle* off the Delaware. American Minister to Holland ditched his papers but a diving sailor caught them: found to contain draft treaty.

1797 *Aurora* captured the French privateer *Espiegle* 40 miles W. of Cape Roxent (da Roca).

1803 Rear-Admiral Sir James Saumarez (*Cerberus*) with two bombs, bombarded Granville.

1871 Herbert William Richmond born; destined to become one of the finest brains in the Royal Navy.

See 27 October 1912, 1 September 1926, 15 December 1946, 28 September 1999.

1899 *Alexandra*, *Europa* and *Juno* fitted with first operational wireless.

1903 First Term entered RN College, Osborne.

1909 Volunteer Reserve Decoration instituted.

1915 Submarine E 16 sank U-6 4 miles S.W. of Karmo Island, off Stavanger.

1931 AFO promulgated pay cuts which led to mutiny in some ships of the Atlantic Fleet at Invergordon: a brief, sad chapter of misinformation, muddle and misunderstanding. 'Perhaps it is because mutinies so seldom occur that we hadle them so badly.' – Admiral Sir William James.

Extract from Petition of Invergordon Mutineers, 1931

'We the loyal subjects of HM The King do hereby present my Lord's Commissioners of the Admiralty our representation to implore them to amend the drastic cuts in pay that have been inflicted on the lowest paid men on the lower deck.

'It is evident to all concerned that this cut is the forerunner of tragedy, misery and immorality amongst the families of the lower deck and unless we can be guaranteed a written agreement from Admiralty confirmed by Parliament stating that our pay will be revised we are still to remain as one unit, refusing to serve under the new rates of pay.'

1940 *Dundee* sunk by U-48 in N. Atlantic (56.45N, 14.14W). Convoy SC 3.

1943 Battleships *Valiant* and *Warspite* bombarded enemy positions near Salerno, restoring the Allied situation on shore.

Operation Avalanche – Salerno, 1943

The Naval Commander's report on the landings at Salerno stated that 'the margin of success in the landings was carried by the naval guns', and the Germans attributed their failure to break through to the beaches to the devastating effect of the naval gunfire. The battleships *Valiant* and *Warspite* were involved in the bombardment. Of sixty-two rounds of 15-in shells, thirty-five fell on target, and another eight were within 100yd. *Warspite* was hit by a radio-controlled bomb on the 16th, which exploded in No. 4 Boiler Room and damaged her bottom. A second bomb landed close alongside and blew a hole in the waterline. The ship had lost all power in five minutes, and was flooding steadily. She was towed to Malta, and then went to Gibraltar where large cofferdams were built on her bottom. She was able to take part in the bombardment during the Normandy landings.

1945 The heavy cruiser *Cumberland* with two frigates and minesweepers arrived at Batavia, the first Allied force to re-enter the Dutch East Indies.

See 30 August 1945, 6 and 12 September 1945.

1948 C-in-C British Pacific Fleet, Admiral Sir Denis Boyd, transferred his shore HQ and staff from Hong Kong to Singapore. At the same time his title was changed to C-in-C Far East.

Invasion of Inchon, 1950

The US 10th Corps with over 70,000 men was landed at Inchon from 550 landing craft with the aim of recapturing Seoul and cutting the enemy forces' supply routes. The landings were a totally American affair, but the British cruisers *Jamaica* and *Kenya* operated with the Gun Fire Support Group, carrying out offshore patrols and maintaining the blockade. During these operations *Jamaica* became the first United Nations ship to shoot down an enemy aircraft, on 17 September. During the operations

The Royal Naval Hospital, Haslar

The RN Hospital, Haslar, was authorised by an Order in Council dated 15 September 1744. The building, designed by Theodore Jacobsen FRS and built between 1746–61, was the largest brick-built structure in Europe. Dr James Lind, 'the father of nautical medicine' who discovered the cure for scurvy, was Chief Physician at Haslar from 1758 until 1783 when he was succeeded by his son, John Lind. The hospital served the Royal Navy, and latterly all three Armed Services, for 250 years. It was Britain's last military hospital when it was transferred in 2007 from the Defence Secondary Care Agency to Portsmouth Hospitals NHS Trust. To mark the handover the military staff, led by the band of the RM Plymouth and the last commanding officer, Surg-Capt James Campbell RN, marched from the hospital gates on 28 March 2007 over Haslar Bridge and into Gosport. The last patient was transferred from Haslar on 3 July 2009 and the establishment closed on 9 July 2009.

See 20 May 1747.

she fired 1,290 rounds of 6-in and 393 of 4-in, while *Kenya* fired 1,242 rounds of 6-in and 205 of 4-in shells.

1966 Helicopter support ship RFA *Engadine* named at Henry Robb Yard at Leith but launched next day because of bad weather.

See 24 September 1926, 9 April 2005.

1966 *Resolution*, Britain's first Polaris submarine, launched by HM Queen Elizabeth The Queen Mother at Vickers, Barrow. ['A local vicar blesses the ship and prays . . . that her crew may truly set forth God's glory throughout the earth; which, it could be argued, is a novel definition of the function of a Polaris crew . . .'] 'The captains of her two crews, Port and Starboard, who will man the *Resolution* alternately, answer questions in tandem like the Gondoliers in perfect unity, bright, lucid, impressive young commanders of 35 and 37' – *The Times*.

See 26 February 1964, 2 October 1967, 15 February 1968, 15 June 1968, 22 October 1994.

1967 The RN's first hovercraft unit, NP 8902, Lt V. Phillips RN, commissioned at HMS *Daedalus*.

1967 Coxswain and Regulating Branches to be amalgamated from 1 April 1968. Title of Coxswain to be limited to the submarine service, an honorary title of those on the retinue of flag officers and to those not wishing to join the combined branch who would retain title for the remainder of their service. Regulating Branch titles to be retained except Leading Patrolmen to be Leading Regulators. DCI(RN) 1077/67.

1971 Old appointment of Port Admiral reintroduced: titles of Admiral Superintendent abolished being 'no longer appropriate'.

See 1 July 1969, 1 October 1984.

New Titles, 1971

Flag Officer Plymouth and Port Admiral Devonport
Flag Officer Medway and Port Admiral Chatham
Flag Officer Spithead and Port Admiral Portsmouth
Flag Officer and Port Admiral Gibraltar
Flag Officer Scotland and Northern Ireland retained but separate appointment of Port Admiral Rosyth
DCI(RN) 859/71.

1983 Furze House, Queen's Gate Terrace, London, bought in 1954 as WRNS accommodation, commissioned as *St Vincent*.

Paid off 31 March 1992. Name transferred to Communications Centre Whitehall (CCW) which commissioned as *St Vincent* 1 April 1992. DCI(RN) 105/92.

1995 *Thunderer*, RN Engineering College, Manadon, paid off. Training transferred to Southampton University.

See 7 May 1940, 5 February 2004.

1998 Frigate *Cumberland* with RM FSRT and RM Boat Group stood by off Albania to evacuate British nationals. Relieved by *London* 22 September. Operation Swanston.

2007 Maj-Gen. Sir Jeremy Moore, Commander Land Forces in the Falklands War in 1982, died aged 79. Major-General Commando Forces RM 1979–82. Third generation of his family to win MC.

2009 Frigate *Iron Duke*, Cdr Andrew Stacey RN, on anti-narcotics patrol in the Caribbean, intercepted a fishing boat carrying 5.5 tons of cocaine reported to be worth £240 million on the street. This was the ship's third major drugs haul in three months.

16 September

1681 *Adventure* captured the Algerine *Two Lions* off Larache, Morocco. Battle Honour: *Two Lions* 1681.

1719 *Weymouth* and *Winchester* destroyed two Spanish warships (one the ex-British *Greyhound*) and a battery at Ribadeo, and captured a merchantman.

1795 Capture of the Cape of Good Hope in the name of the Prince of Orange by Vice-Admiral Sir George Elphinstone, later Lord Keith (*Monarch*) and Gen. Alfred Clarke. A Naval Brigade was landed.
Battle Honour: Cape of Good Hope 1795.
Ships: *America, Jupiter, Monarch, Ruby, Sceptre, Stately, Tremendous, Trident*. Frigates, etc.: *Crescent, Echo, Hope, Moselle, Rattlesnake, Sphinx*. Troops: 78th Regiment and 350 Marines.

1801 *Champion* recaptured the ex-British *Bulldog* at Gallipoli, Gulf of Taranto.

1813 Boats of *Swallow* captured the French *Guerrière* near Porto d'Anzio.

1914 *Dwarf* rammed by, but sank, the German *Nachtigal* in Bimbia River, W. Africa.

1917 Submarine G 9 rammed and sunk by destroyer *Pasley* off Norway. One survivor.

1918 UB-103 sunk in Dover Barrage.

1918 The midships 6-in magazine of the monitor *Glatton* exploded in Dover Harbour and ship caught fire. A fully loaded ammunition ship lay in the next berth. Sir Roger Keyes, Vice-Admiral Dover, boarded her and, finding no executive officers left on board, ordered the forward magazine to be flooded and sea cocks opened. The after magazine could not be reached and Keyes ordered the ship to be abandoned. Keyes boarded the destroyer *Myngs* and ordered her to fire two 21-in torpedoes into the monitor which then heeled over onto her beam ends and sank. One officer and 59 men missing, 124 injured of whom 19 died. Keyes recommended five men for the Albert Medal: Surg Lt-Cdr E.L. Atkinson, Lt G.D. Belben RN (lost in command of the

A Seafire missing the deck. The Seafire was a high-performance fighter, but not intended for carrier operation. (*NMRN*)

HMS *Diamond*, Cdr Ian Clarke RN, third of the Type 45 destroyers, was commissioned at Portsmouth on 6 May 2011. Suzie, Lady Johns, who launched the ship on 27 November 2007, addressed the ship's company. (*RN*)

light cruiser *Penelope* off Anzio in 1944), Sub-Lt D. Evans RNVR, PO A.E. Stoker and AB E. Nunn. Keyes telephoned the First Sea Lord, Admiral Wemyss, 'to tell him that I was so sorry, I had had to torpedo *Glatton* in Dover Harbour, to prevent her blowing up and doing a lot of damage. His reply was characteristic "Good God! . . . I am sure you did the right thing, old boy" and his telephone rang off with a click' – Keyes, *Naval Memoirs*, vol.2, p.356.

See 18 February 1944.

1919 Monitors M 25 and M 27 blown up in Dvina River, northern Russia, to prevent their capture as they could not cross the bar. End of second Archangel River Expeditionary Force.

1939 First part of Channel mine barrage completed, from Goodwin Sands to Dunkirk, in five days by *Adventure*, *Plover* and two ferries.

1940 First German parachute mines dropped on London. Seventeen out of at least twenty-five failed to explode or were fused to delay detonation.

See 26 September 1940.

1942 *Talisman* reported sunk, possibly by mine, between Gibraltar and Malta in Sicilian Channel.

1942 *Impulsive* sank U-457 N.E. of Murmansk. Convoy PQ 18.

1945 Rear-Admiral C.H.J. Harcourt, who entered Hong Kong in *Swiftsure* on 30 August, appointed C-in-C Hong Kong and Head of the Military Administration and received the surrender of Japanese forces in Hong Kong, on behalf of the British and Chinese governments.

See 12 September 1945.

1971 MCMVs *Beachampton* and *Yarnton*, part of the 9th MCM Squadron which disbanded at Bahrain on 9 August, arrived at HMS *Tamar* to join the 6th Patrol Craft Squadron Hong Kong. *Beachampton* exchanged crews with *Maxton* which, with *Hubberston* and *Bossington*, sailed for home on 29 September via South Africa. On 30 November *Hubberston* and *Bossington* went to the aid of the frigate *Zulu*, which had broken down off the mouth of the River Gambia, and towed her to Dakar. The ships arrived at Plymouth on 12 December. *Kirkliston* and *Sheraton* sailed from Hong Kong on 22 May 1972 and arrived home on 24 August.

See 28 November 1971, 28 April 1972, 1 June 1973.

1971 HRH The Prince of Wales joined Britannia RN College, Dartmouth, under the Graduate Entry Scheme as an acting sub-lieutenant.

See 4 January 1974, 2 September 1974, 9 February 1976, 15 December 1976, 12 September 1979.

17 SEPTEMBER

1797 *Pelican* sank the French privateer *Trompeuse* 30 miles N.N.E. of Cape St Nicolas Mole, Haiti.

1797 *Unite* captured the French privateer *Brunette* S.W. of Ile de Ré.

1812 Boats of *Eagle* captured two gunboats and twenty-one out of a convoy of twenty-three sail off Cape Maistro (Majestro), Adriatic.

1840 Mehemet Ali, Pasha of Egypt, attempted to assert his country's independence of Turkey, but Palmerston would have none of it, and resorted to force.

Castor, Pique and the Ottoman *Dewan* captured Caiffa (Haifa).

1879 Battleship *Agamemnon* launched at Chatham. She and her Pembroke-built sister ship *Ajax* were plagued with erratic steering and considered 'the most unhandy capital ships ever to fly the White Ensign' – Oscar Parkes.

1914 Hulk of former iron screw ship *Invincible*, on tow from Plymouth to Scotland, foundered in heavy weather off Portland when workshop plant broke adrift. Twenty-one of sixty-four passage crew lost.

1926 Commodores to wear a crown and two stars on epaulettes and all captains a crown and one star, thus ending the long distinction between those with less, and those with more, than three years' seniority in the rank.

See 1 July 2002, 1 July 2003.

1936 *Esk* rescued eighty-one refugees in final evacuation of Bilbao in Spanish Civil War.

1939 *Courageous* sunk by U-29 in the S.W. Approaches (50.10N, 14.50W), the first major warship and the first of five fleet carriers lost in the Second World War. Optimistic patrolling without adequate intelligence or escort in waters of known U-boat activity proved as wasteful as it was dangerous. Five hundred and fourteen men lost.

1940 *Janus* and *Juno* bombarded Sidi Barrani. *Juno* and *Ladybird* bombarded Sollum and the escarpment road.

1940 Swordfish of 815 and 819 Sqns (*Illustrious*) mined Benghazi harbour and bombed the ships inside: the Italian destroyers *Aquilone* and *Borea* sunk by mine and bombing respectively.

1942 *Waterfly* sunk by German aircraft off Dungeness.

1944 Air-strike on Sigli, Sumatra. Operation Light.

Ships: *Indomitable, Victorious, Howe, Cumberland, Kenya, Racehorse, Raider, Rapid, Redoubt, Relentless, Rocket, Rotherham.* FAA Sqns: 815, 817, 1839, 1844 (*Indomitable* – Barracuda, Hellcat); 822, 1834, 1835 (*Victorious* – Barracuda, Corsair).

The battleship *Agamemnon* and her sister ship *Ajax* (both 1879) were two of the most unsatisfactory battleships ever built for the Royal Navy. 'Once they had put to sea defects and deficiencies became only too manifest and thereafter they ranked as the black sheep of the Battle Fleet' – Parkes. (*NMRN*)

HMS *Victorious* turning at speed. (*Cdr David Hobbs RN*)

1945 'Mass disobedience' in destroyer *Javelin*, Mediterranean Fleet, at anchor off Rhodes. Ship's company, mainly HO ratings, full of cumulative resentment towards an oppressive captain, refused to fall in for duties. Eight POs and eighteen junior rates court-martialled for mutiny at Malta. 'The situation was simply that of men being driven too far for too long, often without real need and with a complete absence of encouragement . . . it was too much, and the camel's back quietly broke' – Lt Henry Leach, HMS *Javelin*.

1948 His Majesty King Frederik of Denmark appointed an honorary admiral in His Majesty's Fleet.
See 24 January 1972.

1954 RN Coastal Forces memorial on the site of HMS *Hornet*, the wartime CF base at Gosport, unveiled by Admiral Sir John Edelsten, C-in-C Portsmouth.

1965 The Admiralty Board have approved in principle a recommendation by the Committee on Television in HM Ships that suitable ships (frigates and above) should be fitted with the basic installation to enable recreational television sets to be used on board. DCI(RN) 1397/65.

1966 HMCS *Okanagan*, fifty-eighth submarine and last warship launched at Chatham Dockyard.

1976 'The following ships recently accepted or building will have metric draught marks: Invincible-class; Type 22 Broadsword-class frigates; Hunt-class MCMVs; Island-class OPVs.' – DCI(RN) S.135/74; DCI(RN) 471/76.

1994 UN maritime interdiction operations during reinstatement of President Aristide of Haiti who was restored to power on 13 October. Frigates *Lancaster* and *Broadsword* with RFA *Oakleaf* on station until 30 September. Operation Spartan.
See 23 September 1993.

2001 Attempt by RM Cpls Dom Mee and Tim Welford to row across the Pacific Ocean ended after their boat, *Pacific Odyssey*, was sunk by a fishing boat after 5,000 miles of rowing.

2001 Corporation of London hosted a luncheon at the Mansion House to mark the centenary of the foundation of the RN Submarine Service.
See 18 September 1951, 2 November 2001.

18 SEPTEMBER

1714 George, Elector of Hanover, landed at Greenwich to become HM King George I.

1740 Cdre George Anson in *Centurion* (60), sailed from St Helens with *Gloucester* (50), *Severn* (50), *Pearl* (40), *Wager* (24) and *Tryall*, sloop, for the South Seas to annoy the Spaniards either at sea or land, to the utmost of your power, by taking, sinking, burning or otherwise destroying all their ships and vessels'.

Great Britain declared war on Spain 19 October 1739 – the War of Jenkins' Ear. Anson returned four years later with *Centurion* the sole survivor, having circumnavigated the world.

See 23 June 1652, 1 August 1739, 14 May 1741, 20 June 1743, 15 June 1744, 4 July 1744, 21 May 1798, 8 May 1943.

1804 *Centurion* (fourth of the name) fought the French *Marengo*, *Atalante* and *Sémillante* in Vizagapatam Roads.

1810 *Ceylon* taken by the French *Venus* and *Victor*. *Boadicea*, with *Otter* and *Staunch*, captured *Venus* and recaptured *Ceylon*. Troops: 1/69th and 86th Regiments (*Ceylon*), 89th Regiment (*Boadicea*), 1/69th Regiments (*Otter* and *Staunch*).

1811 Reduction of Java by Rear-Admiral the Hon. Robert Stopford (*Scipion*) and Lt-Gen. Sir Samuel Auchmuty.

Ships: *Akbar, Barracouta, Bucephalus, Caroline, Cornelia, Dasher, Doris, Harpy, Hecate, Hesper, Hussar, Illustrious, Leda, Lion, Minden, Modest, Nisus, Phaeton, Phoebe, President, Procris, Psyche, Samarang, Scipion, Sir Francis Drake*. Field officers' Army gold medal awarded to Capt Sayer (*Leda*) who commanded batteries on shore, and Capt Bunce RM (*Illustrious*), the only two non-Army officers to receive the Military Gold Medal.
Battle Honour: Java 1811.

1812 Boats of *Bacchante* (Capt Hoste) captured a convoy and its escort near Vasto, Adriatic.

1855 VC: Lt George Fiott Day (*Recruit*). Reconnaissance at Genitchi, Sea of Azov.

1855 *Bittern* and SS *Paoushun* destroyed twenty-two pirate junks in Shih pu harbour.

1857 Second party of *Shannon*'s Naval Brigade (Lt J.W. Vaughan) left the ship for Allahabad, proceeding by river steamer and flat.

See 18 August 1857.

1900 War Course for captains and commanders, later the Senior Officers' War Course (SOWC), established at RN College, Greenwich. Capt H. Moore, Captain of the College, became the first Director.

The *Centurion* attacked at anchor in Vizagapatam Roads (Moluccas) by Admiral Linois's French squadron, which was beaten off in a three-hour fight, 1804. (*NMRN 1976/244*)

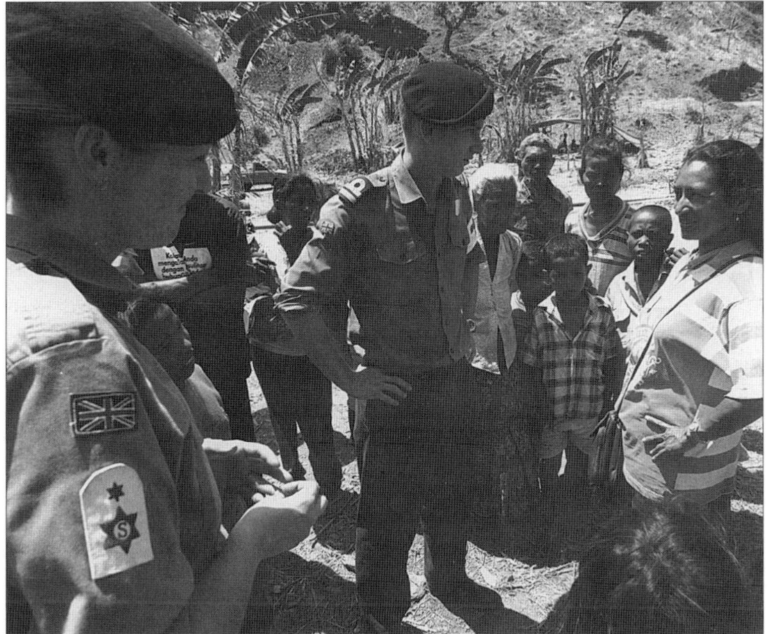

The destroyer HMS *Glasgow* joined a multi-national force under Australian command at Dili following civil unrest in East Timor and contributed to the restoration of security and provision of humanitarian aid, 1999. (*RN*)

1917 Q-ship *Stonecrop* (*Glenfoyle*) sunk by U-151 in N.W. Approaches.

1917 *Contest* torpedoed by U-boat in S.W. Approaches.

1939 Vice-Admiral Sir Dudley North struck his flag as FORY at sunset. In August 1945 he was appointed Admiral Commanding Royal Yachts.

1941 Submarines *Unbeaten*, *Upholder*, *Upright* and *Ursula* torpedoed three large escorted Italian transports off Tripoli (32.58N, 14.40E), sinking two and damaging a third.

1942 Britannia RN College, Dartmouth, bombed and the college was evacuated to Eaton Hall, Cheshire, home of the Duke of Westminster, until August 1946.

1951 Submarines *Acheron* and *Auriga* visited London for ten days to mark the fiftieth anniversary of the RN Submarine Service.

See 17 September 2001, 2 November 2001.

1955 The islet of Rockall, 290 miles W. of Scotland, formally annexed for the United Kingdom by the surveying ship *Vidal*, Cdr Richard Connell RN.

1959 Nigerian Naval Force became Royal Nigerian Navy. AFO 2282/59.

1999 Destroyer *Glasgow* with RM FSRT deployed to join multinational force under Australian command to secure peace and security in East Timor. Sailed 3 October. Operation Langar.

2009 The National Museum of the Royal Navy formally launched at Portsmouth Naval Base.

See 25 July 1938.

The Annexation of Rockall, 1955

The implicit rationale of the annexation was to prevent any other nation from claiming Rockall Bank and allowing the UK to extend its claimed continental shelf to cover the bank and its oil and gas deposits. Connell's orders from HM The Queen read: 'When our ship *Vidal* is in all respects ready for sea and all necessary personnel have embarked, you are to leave Londonderry on September 14, 1955, or the earliest date thereafter. Thence you will proceed to the island of Rockall. On arrival at Rockall you will effect a landing and hoist the Union flag on whatever spot appears most suitable or practicable, and you will then take possession of the island on our behalf . . . When the landing has been effected and the flag hoisted you will cement a commemorative plaque to the rock.' On 18 September the ship's helicopter landed, in this order: Sgt Brian Peel RM, Cpl Alexander Fraser RM, Mr James Fisher, Ornithologist, and Lt-Cdr Desmond Scott, First Lt of *Vidal*. At 1016 BST the Union flag was hoisted as Lt-Cdr Scott took formal possession with the words 'In the name of her Majesty Queen Elizabeth II I hereby take possession of the island of Rockall'. During the annexation the ship steamed past the rock and fired a 21-gun salute. The ledge on which the party landed was unofficially named Hall's Ledge, after Capt Basil Hall of HMS *Endymion* which first landed a party on Rockall in 1810. The position of Rockall was first fixed in 1831 by Capt A.T.E. Vidal RN, after whom the ship was named.

19 SEPTEMBER

1708 Forts at Port Mahon, Minorca, the finest fleet anchorage in the W. Mediterranean, surrendered following an amphibious landing by marines commanded by Vice-Admiral Sir John Leake and Rear-Admiral Sir Edward Whitaker, and troops under Maj-Gen. James Stanhope. Located only 300 miles from Toulon, Mahon retained its strategic importance throughout the French wars and frequently changed hands, most calamitously in 1756.

See 14 March 1757.

1777 *Alert* captured the American *Lexington* 45 miles S.W. by W. of Ushant.
Battle Honour: *Lexington* 1777.

1810 Captains who had missed flag rank through becoming Commissioners of the Navy, Victualling or Transport Boards allowed to wear the undress uniform of a rear-admiral with plain epaulettes and the buttons of their Board.

1855 Naval Brigade re-embarked at Sevastopol.

1896 Action at Hafir, Sudan. Gunboats: *Abu Klea, Metemmeh, Tamai.*

1901 *Cobra*, one of first two turbine-driven destroyers, lost in storm off Cromer.

1914 Royal Marines landed at Dunkirk.

1935 A specially formed Royal Marines battalion drawn from the three RM depots ended a period of royal duties in London during King George's Silver Jubilee year. Guard mounted at Buckingham Palace for the first time, and for the first time since 1746 it exercised the privilege of the Royal Marines of marching through the City of London with colours flying, drums beating and bayonets fixed.

See 24 August 1935.

1943 Liberator A/10 (RCAF) sank U-341 in Atlantic (58.40N, 25.30W). Convoy ONS 18.

A merchant ship disguised as HMS *Invincible* at Gallipoli in 1915. Several of these warships were created to confuse the enemy as to the real location and strength of RN forces. (*NMRN*)

Troops of the 7th Australian Division embarked in the light fleet carrier HMS *Glory* off Tarakan for passage home on 2 December 1945. (*Cdr David Hobbs RN*)

Convoys ONS 18 and ON 202, 1943

Slow convoy ONS 18 of twenty-seven merchant ships and an escort of eight under *Keppel* sailed from Milford Haven on 12 September 1943. Fast convoy ON 202, of forty-two ships left Liverpool on the 15th with six escorts led by the Canadian *Gatineau*. On the 18th the convoys were 120 miles apart, and ONS 18 was diverted to avoid U-boats. On the 19th U-341 was sunk by a Liberator aircraft some 160 miles from ONS 18, which was under attack by U-boats. That day the *Escapade*'s Hedgehog had a premature explosion, and she had to return to harbour.

On the morning of the 20th, the convoys were 30 miles apart, and U-boats sank two merchantmen at 0300. The frigate *Lagan* was damaged by an acoustic torpedo and had to be towed home, but a Liberator sank U-338 with an aerial acoustic torpedo. At noon the convoys joined, and the 9th Escort Group arrived. Eight U-boats were in the vicinity of the convoys, but two were damaged, one by the surface escort and the other by aircraft. During that night three U-boat attacks were frustrated for the loss of two escorts, *St Croix* and *Polyanthus*. The next night the U-boats attacked again, but with no success, and the *Keppel* sank U-229 by ramming after running down a wireless bearing. The following night the frigate *Itchen* was sunk, with only three survivors. Unfortunately she had been carrying survivors of the *St Croix* and *Polyanthus*. In the morning U-boats sank three merchant ships and damaged one, which had to be abandoned later. However, the U-boats ceased their attacks that evening. Nineteen U-boats had attacked the convoys over five days. Six merchant ships had been lost, together with three escorts, but three U-boats had been sunk and three damaged. Exaggerated claims by the U-boats misled U-Boat Command into believing that the U-boats had been more successful.

1944 *Terpsichore*, *Troubridge* and *Garland* (Pol) sank U-407 off Crete (36.27N, 24.33E). Last enemy submarine to be sunk in the Mediterranean in Second World War.

1944 Aircraft of 224 Sqn sank U-867 off S.W. Norway.

1944 GC: T/Lt Leon Verdi Goldsworthy, DSC, GM, RANVR, Mine Disposal. (*Gazette* date.) Australia's most decorated naval officer of the Second World War.

1998 *Vengeance*, the last of four Trident submarines, rolled out of the Devonshire Dock Hall at Barrow and named by Lady Robertson, wife of the Secretary of State for Defence.

See 27 November 1999.

20 September

1693 The first *Diamond* in the Navy, a 50-gun ship launched at Deptford in 1652, captured by the French in the West Indies. 'The circumstances of the *Diamond*'s loss being such as were not creditable' (Laird Clowes), her captain, Henry Wickham, was sentenced by court-martial to imprisonment for life. He was released after the accession of Queen Anne but was never re-instated. A *Diamond of Dartmouth* serving under Drake gained the Armada battle honour borne by the present *Diamond*.

See 25 June 1964, 27 November 2007.

1725 Antigua Dockyard opened. In use until 1889.

1759 *Milford* (28), sixth rate, launched at Neyland near Milford Haven, Pembrokeshire, the first recorded warship built in Wales.

1799 *Rattlesnake* and *Cameleon* fought the French *Preneuse* in Algoa Bay.

1803 *Princess Augusta* fought the Dutch *Union* and *Wraak* 16 miles N. by W. of Terschelling.

1808 Masters given status of lieutenants by Order in Council.

1811 *Naiad* fought the Boulogne invasion flotilla off Boulogne.

1839 Admiral Sir Thomas Masterman Hardy died as Governor of Greenwich Hospital and was buried in the mausoleum near the present National Maritime Museum. Nelson's Flag Captain in *Victory* at Trafalgar.

It may be due in part to Lady Hardy that we owe the preservation of *Victory*. When Hardy was First Naval Lord in 1831, a proposal was made that *Victory* be sold for breaking up. Lady Hardy, an admiral's daughter, exclaimed that 'You can't do that', so they did not.

See 4 May 1810, 2 May 1818, 28 May 1831, 5 August 1834, 2 July 1853.

1873 Boats of *Thalia* and *Midge* destroyed three pirate junks and a fort in the Larut River, Perak.

1911 The Admiralty Library and its Reading Room in Admiralty Arch opened by Mr Reginald McKenna, First Lord of the Admiralty; 'open daily from 10 to 5 to naval officers on presentation of their cards. Students outside the Service should apply in writing to the Librarian'. AWO 290/11.

See 6 May 2005.

1914 The old third-class cruiser *Pegasus*, Cdr J.A. Ingles RN, one of Vice-Admiral H.G. King-Hall's Cape Squadron, caught repairing main engine defects, sunk at Zanzibar by the German light cruiser *Königsberg*.

See 11 July 1915.

1939 *Forester* and *Fortune* sank U-27 60 miles W. of the Hebrides (58.35N, 09.02W).

1941 Gibraltar harbour attacked by Italian submarine *Scire* with chariots.

See 3 January 1943.

1941 *Levis* (RCN) sunk by U-74 in N. Atlantic (60.07N, 38.37W). Convoy SC 44.

1942 *Leda* sunk by U-435 off Bear Island (75.48N, 05.00E). *Somali* torpedoed by U-703 W. of Bear Island, and taken in tow by *Ashanti*. After 420 miles her back broke and she sank (75.40N, 02.00W). Convoy QP 14.

1942 GC (ex-AM): LS W. Goad, *Ashanti*, for saving life at sea in Arctic Convoy. (*Gazette* date.)

1943 *Lagan* hit by homing torpedo from U-270 and though towed home became CTL. *St Croix* (RCN) sunk by homing torpedo from U-305 in N. Atlantic (57.30N, 31.10W): survivors rescued by *Itchen*.

1943 *Polyanthus*, Flower-class corvette, escorting convoy ON 202, sunk by Gnat torpedo from U-952 S.W. of Iceland (57.00N, 31.10W). One survivor (the OOW) rescued by frigate *Itchen* which already had on board survivors from the destroyer HMCS *St Croix*, sunk by U-305. *Itchen* was sunk on 23 September. Only three men from the three ships survived.

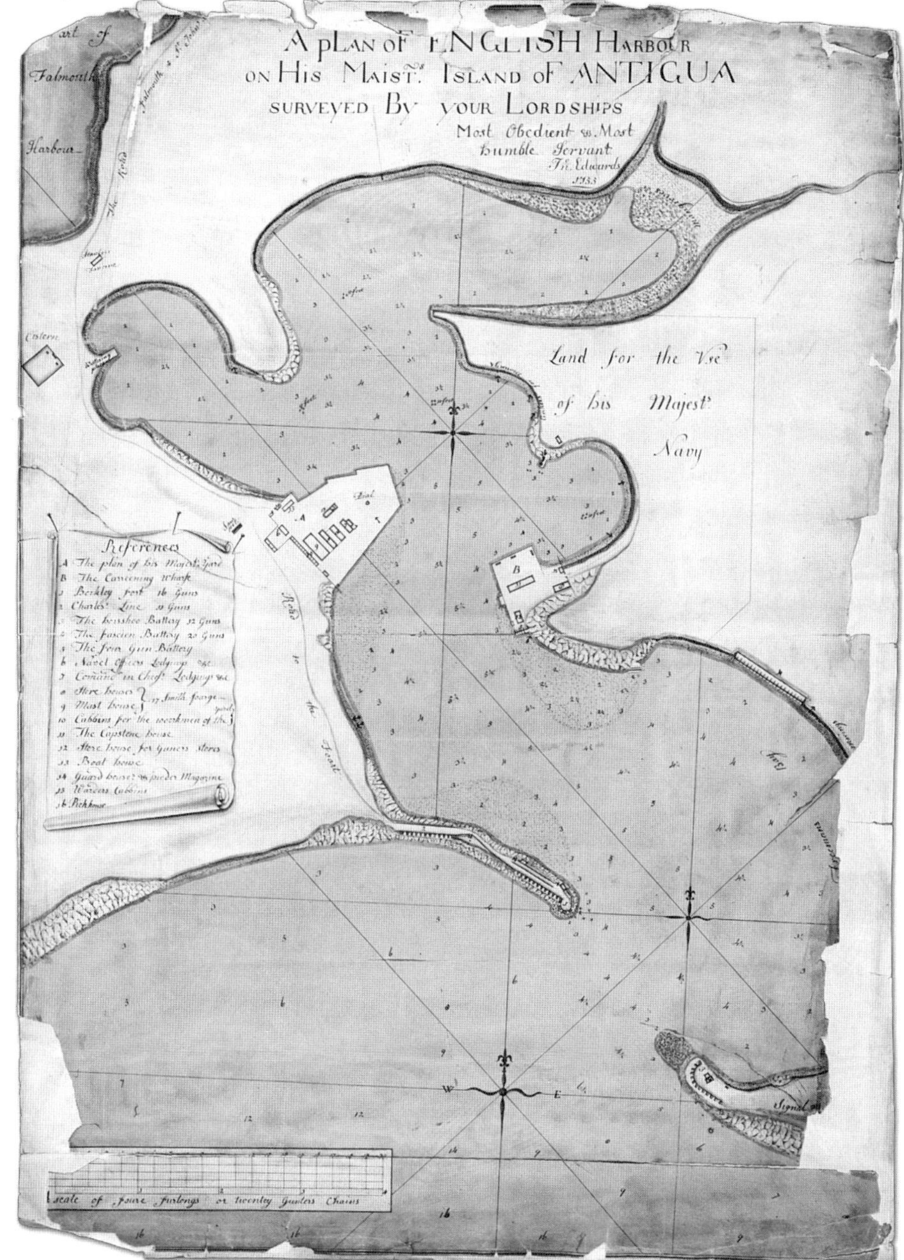

Plan of English harbour, Antigua, in 1755. The dockyard buildings are on the western side, and the careening wharf, used for cleaning and repairs, is on the east. (*NMRN Ad. Lib. Vz10/45*)

1943 Liberator F/120 sank U-338 in N. Atlantic (57.40N, 29.48W). Convoy ONS 18.

1976 *Fittleton* sunk in collision with frigate *Mermaid*. Twelve lives lost, including ten RNR under training.

See 16 May 1973.

1988 First Officer Jane Elizabeth Salt, WRNS (later Cdr RN) appointed the first, and now only, female First Lieutenant of the RN College, Greenwich.

See 19 February 1979.

1997 Admiral Sir Derek Empson died. The first ex-RNVR officer to command a fleet carrier. Joined as Naval Airman 2nd Class April 1940. Sub-Lt RNVR November 1940. Captain *Eagle* 1963. Commander Far East Fleet 1969. Second Sea Lord 1971–4. Born 29 October 1918.

21 SEPTEMBER

1747 *Colchester* (50), fifth of the name, lost off the Kentish Knock. Three of her four predecessors had been lost.

1757 *Southampton* captured the French *Eméraude* 12 miles W.N.W. of Ushant, the ships foul of one another and in a calm. Prize taken into service as *Emerald*, first of the name in RN. Battle Honour: *Eméraude* 1757.

1782 *Ramillies* (74), Capt Sylverius Moriarty, flagship of Rear-Admiral Thomas Graves, escorting a convoy from Jamaica to England, abandoned and set on fire five days after being struck by a hurricane off the Newfoundland Banks. Also lost were *Centaur* (74), and two French prizes taken in Rodney's action at the Saintes, the French flagship *Ville de Paris* (100) and *Glorieux* (74). Moriarty had six sons in the Royal Navy; Sylverius (Junior) was lost in the *Queen Charlotte* fire in 1800.

See 12 April 1782, 17 March 1800.

1801 *Thames* captured the Spanish privateer *Sparrow* off Condan Point (Punta Candor).

1809 Successful combined attack on Saint Paul, Bourbon (Réunion), and capture of the French *Caroline*, *Grappler* and the ex-British Indiamen *Streatham* and *Europe*.

Ships: *Boadicea*, *Nereide*, *Otter*, *Raisonnable*, *Sirius* and *Wasp* (Bombay Marine). Troops: 1/56th Regiment, 2/2nd Bombay Native Infantry.

1811 *Naiad*, *Rinaldo*, *Redpole*, *Castilian* and *Viper* fought the Boulogne invasion flotilla off Boulogne. Capture of the French *Ville de Lyon*.

1811 Boats of *Victory* captured two Danish privateers in Wingo Sound (Vinga Sand).

1813 Rear-Admiral T. Byam Martin (*Creole*) reported to Admiral Lord Keith a remark by the Duke of Wellington: 'If anyone wishes to know the history of this war, I will tell them that it is our maritime superiority gives me the power of maintaining my army while the enemy are unable to do so.'

1867 The first 'time and percussion fuse' introduced.

1922 Sir Julian Corbett died. Author of first three volumes of the official history of naval operations in the First World War. Last two volumes written by Sir Henry Newbolt.

See 12 November 1854.

1941 Martlet aircraft of 802 NAS (*Audacity*) shot down a Focke-Wulf aircraft attacking convoy OG 74. First success by an auxiliary aircraft carrier.

1941 *Larkspur* thought to have sunk the Italian S/M *Alessandro Malaspina* N.W. of the Azores.

1943 *Unseen* sank *Brandenburg* (ex-French *Kita*) N.E. of Corsica.

1943 *Keppel* sank U-229 in N. Atlantic (54.36N, 36.35W). Convoy ONS 18/ON 202.

1943 *Chedabucto* (RCN) reduced to CTL by collision in St Lawrence River.

The steel corvette HMS *Calypso* and the iron screw corvette HMS *Volage* at sea in 1890. (*NMRN*)

Duncan's 'Victory off Camperdown' 11 October 1797. Oil on canvas by Thomas Butterworth (attrib.). (*Crown Copyright: MOD Art Collection*)

Convoy QP 14 from Russia, 1943

QP 14 left Archangel on 13 September 1943, escorted by two AA ships and eleven corvettes. It was joined by the escort from PQ 18 on the 17th. On the 20th a U-boat sank a merchant ship and the minesweeper *Leda*. However, the air threat had passed and *Avenger*, *Scylla* and three destroyers were detached. Just afterwards the destroyer *Somali* was torpedoed. *Ashanti* took her in tow, but a gale sprang up, and *Somali* broke in two and sank. On 22nd three merchant ships were sunk by U-435, but the next day a Catalina sank U-253, and on 26th the twelve surviving ships reached Loch Ewe. The success of Convoy PQ 18 and QP 14 was decisive, and the enemy never again attacked in such strength by air in the far north.

1944 10th Submarine Flotilla disbanded. White Ensign hauled down at HMS *Talbot*, Malta.

See 30 November 1959, 1 February 1967.

1954 Bahrain government asked the SNO Persian Gulf to find a mate of the same species as the miniature Socotran bull presented to Bahrain earlier in the year by sloop *Wild Goose* which was 'lonely and did not fraternise'. The Admiralty ordered the surveying ship *Dalrymple* on passage from Zanzibar to the Gulf to call at Socotra to find a mate for the bull. This was done but a few years later the cow died which left the bull 'morose and disgruntled'. Their Lordships, not to be defeated, sent the frigate *Loch Fada* to Socotra in 1958 which delivered 'two beautiful heifers' to Bahrain 'where the bull was pleased to see them'.

1957 HM King Haakon VII of Norway, by forty-three years the most senior of the Royal Navy's four Honorary Admirals, died. Admiral of the Fleet Lord Fraser of North Cape, who had assumed his title with King Haakon's permission, sailed to Norway in the carrier *Ocean* to lead the Royal Navy representation at the state funeral.

See 23 November 1938, 7 June 1940, 5 June 1945, 2 July 1958, 18 March 1981.

1989 One of the most decorated Reserve officers ever, Cdr Norman Morley, DSC and three bars, RNR in First World War, RNVR in the Second, died aged 90. First DSC in CMB 88 in attack on Kronstadt, Baltic in 1919; left Navy 1920; joined RNVR 1939 and served throughout the war in minesweepers. Bars to DSC as CO of *Mutine* at Sicily and Salerno 1943 and as CO of *Rhyl* in invasion of South of France 1944 and in Greece 1945.

See 12 April 1943.

22 SEPTEMBER

1742 *Tilbury* (60) lost by fire off Navassa, Hispaniola, after a struggle between a marine and the Purser's assistant over a bottle of rum; the boy was holding a lantern in one hand and the rum bottle in the other. Both were dropped in the scuffle.

1793 Capitulation of the Mole at St Nicholas, San Domingo to *Europa*.

1796 *Amphion* blew up in the Hamoaze. Israel Pellew and ten men saved out of 312.

1797 Mutineers delivered *Hermione* to Spanish at La Guaira, Venezuela.

See 25 October 1799.

1798 Rear-Admiral Sir Horatio Nelson reached Naples in Vanguard after his Nile victory. Queen Maria Carolina persuaded him into supporting an ill-judged aggressive foreign policy against the French. The Neapolitan army disintegrated before a French counter attack and Nelson had to evacuate the Court to Palermo on Christmas Eve. 'When everything has been said to excuse his conduct in this episode it remains an outstanding example of what could go wrong when admirals with scarcely a primary education were promoted to handle great affairs of war and state' – N.A.M. Rodger.

1811 *Leveret* captured the French privateer *Prospère* 200 miles E.N.E. of Flamborough Head.

1812 *Saracen* captured the French privateer *Courrier* 7 miles S.E. of Beachy Head.

1884 Composite screw gunboat *Wasp*, Lt J.D. Nicholls RN, wrecked on Tory Island off Donegal, with the loss of fifty-two men including all her officers.

She was on passage under sail from Westport, Co. Mayo, to Moville in Loch Foyle and at 0330 in clear weather she hit a rock west of Tory Island. Heavy seas destroyed her boats and the Captain and two officers were washed overboard. The ship slipped off the rock and sank; six men survived. A new composite screw gunboat of the name was launched in September 1886 but she fared even worse.

See 10 October 1887.

1914 *Aboukir, Cressy* and *Hogue* sunk by U-9 off the Maas lightvessel (52.18N, 03.41E). *Cressy* and *Hogue* had stopped for *Aboukir* survivors. The number of men lost, at 1,459, was more than at Trafalgar.

1914 Madras bombarded by the German *Emden*.

1914 The RNAS mounted the first British air raid on Germany. Four aircraft left Antwerp, flying over the Rhine and Ruhr, to bomb the airship sheds at Cologne and Dusseldorf. Three turned back because of fog but Fl/Lt C.H. Collet – a captain RMA – pressed on and dropped three bombs at Dusseldorf: one missed and two failed to explode. DSO. (Collet was the first RNAS officer to loop-the-loop.)

See 8 October 1914, 21 November 1914, 25 December 1914, 19 August 1915.

1917 RNAS Curtiss H 12 Large America flying boat, No. 8695, bombed and sank UB-32 in the English Channel near the Sunk Lightvessel, (51.45N, 02.05W). The first German submarine sunk by aircraft.

1940 *Janus, Jervis* (D 14), *Juno* and *Mohawk* bombarded airfield and troop concentration at Sidi Barrani.

1940 *Osiris* sank the Italian destroyer *Palestro* off Durazzo (41.19N, 18.34E).

1943 VC: Lt Basil Charles Godfrey Place (X 7), Lt Donald Cameron, RNR (X 6). Attack by midget submarines on the German battleship *Tirpitz* in Altenfjord. Battle Honour: *Tirpitz* 1943.

See 27 December 1994.

1943 *Itchen* sunk by homing torpedo from U-666 in N. Atlantic and only three men survived. She was carrying survivors from *St Croix* (RCN) and *Polyanthus* (53.25N, 39.42W). Convoy ONS 18/ON 202.

1951 *Unicorn* crossed 38th parallel on Korean west coast and shelled North Korean positions

HMS *Unicorn* with Sea Furies and Fireflies on deck, off the Korean coast in 1951. (*FAAM*)

on Changsan-got (known to UN forces as Choppeki Point) with her 4-in guns. The first and only occasion so far that a British aircraft carrier has carried out shore bombardment with her own main armament.

See 2 November 1944, 1 March 1956.

1967 Flag of the Lord High Admiral is to be hoisted, in addition to the Royal Standard, on occasions when the Sovereign 'is present with any body of Royal Naval or Royal Marine forces, afloat or ashore, and on such other maritime occasions as Her Majesty may command . . . Whenever the Sovereign embarks in any of Her Majesty's Ships, the Royal Standard is to be hoisted at the main, the flag of the Lord High Admiral at the fore and the Union Flag at the mizzen of such ship'. In the event of a ship not having three masts . . . DCI(RN) 1097/67.

See 3 July 1964.

1970 The modernised David Brace RN Hospital at Mtarfa, Malta, opened. It replaced the RN Hospital at Bighi which was handed over to the Maltese government. DCI(RN) 1166/70.

See 3 October 1970.

1977 Memorial service in the Chapel of the RN College, Greenwich, for Lt-Cdr George Prideaux Brabant Naish, RNVR, who died 30 July 1977; naval historian extraordinary. The colours in *Victory* at Portsmouth were half-masted during the service.

1980 *Ark Royal* (IV) left Plymouth under tow for the breakers at Cairnryan.

See 14 February 1979.

1989 Ten members of the RM staff band and a civilian killed by terrorist bomb at RM School of Music at Deal.

1998 Destroyer *Sheffield* and RFA *Black Rover* in disaster relief operations at St Kitts and Montserrat after Hurricane Georges.

2001 Operations against Taliban regime in Afghanistan. Two Royal Navy SSNs fired TLAMs against shore targets. Support for land forces provided by *Illustrious*, *Cornwall* and *Southampton*. Operation Veritas.

See 7 October 2001, 18 March 2002.

2010 *Diamond*, Cdr Ian Clarke RN, third of the Type 45 destroyers, entered Portsmouth for the first time.

See 28 January 2009, 2 December 2009, 6 May 2011.

23 September

1779 *Serapis* (Capt Richard Pearson) and *Countess of Scarborough* escorting a Baltic convoy, taken by the American *Bonhomme Richard* (Capt John Paul Jones) off Flamborough Head. The convoy escaped and the American ship sank on the 25th. Capt Pearson knighted.
Battle Honour: *Bonhomme Richard* 1779.

1796 *Pelican* fought the French *Medée* 25 miles N.W. by W. of Deseads (Desirade).

1797 *Espiegle* captured the Dutch *D'Ondeilbaarleid* off Vlieland.

1819 Lt W. Rodger's device to hoist empty casks by an umbrella-like arrangement inside the cask instead of external slinging hooks tested: less successful than his syphoned water supply.
See 30 November 1816.

1846 Completion at Blackwall of *Ajax* (third of the name). Laid down in 1809 to replace the second, lost off Troy in 1807. She was converted during construction and undocked as the RN's first screw battleship.

Silver cup presented to Capt Pearson by the Royal Exchange Assurance Company (insurers of the convoy) in gratitude for his ensuring its escape, 1779. (*NMRN 1979/33*)

1940 *Ladybird* bombarded Sidi Barrani.

1940 Abortive attack on Dakar. Operation Menace. Ceased at midnight 25th/26th.

Ships: *Barham* (Vice-Admiral J.H.D. Cunningham), *Resolution*,* *Renown* (Vice-Admiral Sir James Somerville), *Ark Royal*, *Australia* (RAN), *Cornwall*, *Cumberland*, *Delhi*, *Devonshire*, *Dragon*, *Echo*, *Eclipse*, *Encounter*, *Escapade*, *Faulknor*, *Foresight*, *Forester*, *Fortune*, *Fury*, *Greyhound*, *Griffin*, *Hotspur*, *Inglefield*, *Velox*, *Vidette*, *Wishart*, *Bridgwater*, *Milford*, *Quannet*. Free French force, under General Charles de Gaulle: *Président Houduce*, *Savorgnan de Brazza*, *Commandant-Duboc*, *Commandant-Domine*. Vichy-French ships sunk: *Ajax*, *L'Audacieux* (badly damaged), *Persée*. FAA Sqns: Skua: 800, 803; Swordfish: 810, 814, 818, 820. 101 and 102 RM brigades.
*Torpedoed on 25th.

1940 HM King George VI announced the institution of the George Cross and the George Medal, authorised by a Royal Warrant next day, amended by a second on 21 January 1941, and substantially by others.

This was a partial recognition of the anomaly created in 1939, when His Majesty was unfortunately advised that individuals involved at Shoeburyness on 24 November 1939 did not qualify for the VC because what they indisputably did had not been done in the presence of the enemy. There are not a few who think that the advice was less than realistic and that if the enemy deliberately plants a bomb which does not explode, he leaves something of his presence for the men who have to deal with it; hence the 'whites of their eyes' notion is obsolete.

Be that as it may, the King made a notable gesture in visiting *Vernon* on 19 December to present the deserving with all that could be awarded to them, instead of simply holding an investiture at Buckingham Palace. Lt-Cdr John Ouvry returned this gesture when he declined the unique offer to exchange his DSO for a GC.

1941 GC: Henry Herbert Reed, Gunner, DEMS, in SS *Cormount*.

1943 *Eclipse* damaged TA-10 (ex-French *La Pomone*) 10 miles S. of Rhodes. Scuttled on 26th.

Midget Submarine Attack on the *Tirpitz*, 1943

The German heavy warships in northern Norway were a constant threat to the Russian convoys and it was decided that they should be attacked by midget submarines. These were of 35 tons, carried two detachable charges of 2 tons each and were manned by a crew of four. Six were towed by S- and T-class submarines to a position off Altenfjord. X 9 was lost on passage and X 8 had to be scuttled. The four survivors set off on the evening of the 20th and entered Kaa Fjord on 22nd. X 6 (Lt D. Cameron, RNR) dropped her charges blind as her periscope and compass were out of action. The crew abandoned the submarine and were taken prisoner. *Tirpitz* then started to shift berth. X 7 (Lt B.C.G. Place) put her charges under her but became caught in the nets while trying to escape and was damaged when the charges went off. Lt Place and another officer escaped, but the other two crew were lost. X 5 (Lt H. Henty-Creer, RNVR) disappeared, and was believed sunk by the Germans. X 10 (Lt K. Hudspeth, RANVR), which had been sent to attack *Scharnhorst* nearby, lost her compass and periscope, returned to sea and was recovered by one of the larger submarines, but sank on tow home. In fact *Scharnhorst* had sailed and was not in the fjord. The *Tirpitz* was unfit for sea until April 1944.

1944 *Trenchant* sank U-859 off Penang (05.46N, 100.40E).

1948 Home Fleet, led by the C-in-C, Vice-Admiral Sir Rhoderick McGrigor, with his flag in the battleship *Duke of York*, sailed from Portland for an autumn cruise to the West Indies. Fleet comprised the Second Cruiser Squadron, *Diadem*, flag of Rear-Admiral Hon. Guy Russell, *Sirius* and *Cleopatra*; six destroyers, the RFAs *Bulawayo* and *Fort Beauharnois*. Concurrently, the carriers *Theseus*, flag of Rear-Admiral M.J. Mansergh, and *Vengeance* visited South African ports. 'This welcome renewal of the strength of our principal fleet should go some way to restoring shaken confidence in British sea power' – *Navy* magazine, July and September 1948.

See 17 July 1947, 9 October 1948, 31 January 1949.

1966 The RN Presentation Team, led by Capt S.M.W. Farquharson-Roberts RN, made its first public performance at Winchester. The team comprised Lt B.J. Adams RN, Lt J.M.G. Sheridan RM, 3/O S.L. Newman WRNS, PO A.J.P. Evans and L/S J.W. Deacon.

See 2 September 1966.

1977 Frigate Complex at Devonport Dockyard, originally known as Leander Frigate Complex, developed over No. 2 Basin and enclosing Nos 5, 6 and 7 Docks, opened by Dr David Owen. *Galatea* docked as demonstration of facility.

1993 UN maritime interdiction operation (until 9 December) during unrest in Haiti following removal of President Aristide in October 1991. Frigate *Active* and RFA *Oakleaf*. Operation Snowdon.

See 17 September 1994.

24 September

1568 John Hawkins and Francis Drake at San Juan d'Ulloa: a sharp battle. Ships: *Angel*, *Jesus of Lubeck*, *Judith*, *Minion*, *Swallow*.

1758 *Southampton* captured the French privateer *Caumartin* 150 miles S.W. of Cape Clear.

1797 *Phaeton* and *Unite* captured the French privateer *Indien* and her prize (*Egmont*) near the Plateau de Rochebonne.

1809 Boats of *Blonde*, *Fawn* and *Scorpion* destroyed a French vessel at Basse Terre, Guadaloupe.

1840 *Castor* and *Pique* captured Tyre.

1850 Rum ration halved by withdrawal of evening issue.

1911 The RN's Rigid Airship No. 1, dubbed *Mayfly* in the press, the biggest aircraft in the world at the time of her launch, wrecked while being hauled from her floating hangar alongside the Cavendish Dock at Vickers Sons and Maxim, Barrow-in-Furness. The event 'caused an immediate though temporary loss of interest in such craft' – Roskill, *The Naval Air Service*. Capt Murray Sueter, Inspecting Captain of Airships, and his assistant Cdr Oliver Schwann, were returned to general service but both were recalled to naval aviation a year later. The *Mayfly*, designed by RN officers and submarine specialists at Vickers, never flew but she marked the birth of British naval aviation.

See 21 July 1908, 7 May 1909, 25 November 1912, 3 February 1960.

1915 *Baralong* sank U-41 90 miles W. of Ushant, the Q-ship's second success in five weeks.

1916 Destruction of Zeppelin L-32 yielded new German naval signal book.

1922 *Speedy* lost in collision with tug in Sea of Marmara.

1926 HMS *Oberon*, the first British operational submarine to be given a name rather than a number (stand fast the early experimental boats), launched a day late at Chatham. The boat was christened the day before by Mrs Beaty-Pownall, wife of the Admiral Superintendent, but because of the rising tide, the last two blocks could not be removed without risk to the workmen. The public was excluded from the launching of the 'super submarine' next day owing to 'the confidential nature of the construction'.

See 3 July 1902, 5 November 1942, 19 and 27 December 1942, 28 January 1943, 18 July 1959, 9 April 2005.

1940 Vichy French air attacks on Gibraltar nights of 24 and 25 September in reprisal for Allied raid on Dakar. Few casualties, minor damage to dockyard, and trawler *Stella Sirius* sunk.

See 23 September 1940.

1940 TS *Cornwall*, ex-*Wellesley* (74), third rate, sunk by dive-bombers in River Thames. Last wooden battleship to be sunk by enemy action and the first by air attack.

1940 The George Cross instituted by Royal Warrant – *London Gazette*, 31 January 1941.

See 24 May 1941.

1942 *Somali* sank while in tow of *Ashanti* off Jan Mayen Island (69.11N, 15.32W) after being torpedoed by U-703 on the 20th.

1943 MMS 70 sunk by mine, Gulf of Taranto.

1944 Liberator A/224 sank U-855 off Bergen (61.00N, 04.07E).

1945 Admiral Sir Frederick Wake-Walker, Third Sea Lord and Controller of the Navy, died hours after accepting the appointment of C-in-C Mediterranean Fleet. Wake-Walker was a torpedo specialist and coordinated all British countermeasures against German magnetic mines early in the war. As Flag Officer First Cruiser Squadron, with his flag in the heavy cruiser *Norfolk*, he was the first to sight the German battleship *Bismarck* in the Denmark Strait on 23 May 1941 and he played a leading role in her destruction. After three years at the Admiralty, he was promoted admiral on VE Day, 8 May 1945. But he was

The iron-hulled troopship *Jumna* (1866). (*NMRN*)

worn out. 'He was a great Controller, able, energetic and full of ideas . . . The Navy owes him a lot' – Cunningham. Admiral Sir Algernon Willis, Second Sea Lord, became C-in-C Mediterranean Fleet in his stead.

1945 Diesel submarine *Ambush* launched at Vickers Armstrong, Barrow.

See 22 October 2003.

1957 Far East Fleet presented with the Queen's Colour by the Governor of Singapore, Sir Robert Black.

1958 RNAS Ford, Sussex, closed for flying. RN School of Photography to remain at Ford. AFO 1667/58.

1969 New command block for Western Fleet and RAF Coastal Command at Northwood, replacing wartime huts, opened by Marshal of the RAF Sir Charles Elworthy, CDS. Demolished autumn 2010 following PJHQ development.

1982 Surveying ship *Hydra*, Cdr R.J. Campbell RN, returned to Portsmouth, the last ship of the original Falklands Task Force to come home. She had sailed from Portsmouth on 24 April for service as a hospital ship, painted white with red crosses and declared to the International Red Cross. She passed 35 degrees S. on 15 May and remained on station long after the Argentine surrender as a contingency against a resumption of hostilities.

See 4 April 1982.

2000 The RFA's oldest serving, and last steam-powered ship, the fast fleet tanker *Olna*, made her final RFA voyage from Plymouth to Portsmouth after thirty-four years' service to berth alongside sister ship *Olwen* to await disposal. They were replaced by RFA *Wave Ruler* and RFA *Wave Knight*.

See 20 July 1973, 20 July 1997, 18 March 2002.

25 September

1493 Papal Bull divided global spheres of influence between Spain and Portugal. Conditioned British and Spanish privateering activities.

1761 Dr Cuthbert of the Royal College of Surgeons appointed to analyse water at Weovil or Weevil Yard. Ships' cisterns were lead-lined to protect the wood, which was unfortunate for those who drank the contents.

1806 *Centaur* (Cdre Samuel Hood, who lost his right arm), *Mars* and *Monarch* captured the French *Armide*, *Gloire*, *Infatigable* and *Minerve* off Chassiron lighthouse, Rochefort.

1840 Abortive attack by *Benbow*, *Carysfort* and *Zebra* on Tortosa, Syria.

1925 Submarine X 1, 2,780 tons and four 5.2-in guns, commissioned. The largest submarine in the world and largest in RN until *Dreadnought* commissioned on 17 April 1963.

1940 Destroyers *Hereward*, *Hyperion*, *Juno* and *Mohawk* bombarded an MT concentration west of Sidi Barrani.

1942 *Voyager* (RAN) beached in Betano Bay, Timor (09.11S, 125.43W) after air attack. Blown up by own crew.

1945 U-1407, Type XVIIB submarine, scuttled at Cuxhaven 5 May 1945, raised and commissioned into RN. Named *Meteorite* June 1947 and served until 1949.

See 5 March 1954.

1952 British-flagged ferry *Takshing*, the midnight ferry from Hong Kong to Macao, fired on by gunboats flying the Chinese Communist flag 5 miles W. of Lantau Island at 0200 and ordered to Lap Sap Mei Island in the mouth of the Pearl River estuary where two Chinese passengers were removed. Frigate *Mounts Bay*, Capt A.F.P. Lewis RN, and destroyer *Consort*, Cdr G.B. Rowe RN, arrived on scene at 0700 and escorted the ferry towards Hong Kong. When two cables off Lantau, the warships were fired on by batteries on Lap Sap Mei which fire was returned by both ships.

1953 World air speed record 737.3 mph (1,183 kph) established by Lt-Cdr M.J. (Mike) Lithgow in a Vickers Supermarine Swift F4 *WK198* over

HM Submarine X 1 (1923). (*NMRN*)

HMS *Dundas*, the first Type 14 frigate to be launched. (*Author*)

the Libyan Desert. Lithgow had served in *Ark Royal* and *Formidable* during the war. He was killed on 22 October 1963 when piloting the prototype BAC One-Eleven which crashed during stall tests in Wiltshire.

See 10 March 1956.

1953 First Type 14 frigate *Dundas* launched by J. Samuel White at Cowes. First of the Blackwood-class to be completed was *Hardy* by Yarrows, Scotstoun, on 15 December 1955.

1959 Coastal minelayer *Plover*, commissioned in September 1936, celebrated twenty-two years' continuous service. C-in-C Portsmouth, Admiral Sir Manley Power, signalled: 'Congratulations on completing time for pension.' The ship remained in service for another eight years.

See 4 December 1967.

1970 Sale announced of ninety-one ships' bells by DGST(N), Woolston. These included those of the destroyers *Daring*, *Dainty*, *Defender* and *Diana*, *Barrage* and other BD vessels, MTB *Brave Borderer* and frigate *Troubridge*. Applicants 'are at liberty to state any special claims'. DCI(RN) 1153/70.

26 September

1580 Return of Francis Drake (*Golden Hind*, ex-*Pelican*) from circumnavigating the world: 'Is the Queen alive?'

1748 Cuthbert Collingwood, the future Vice-Admiral Baron Collingwood of Caldborne and Hethpoole, born at Newcastle. Second-in-Command at Trafalgar and C-in-C Mediterranean after Nelson's death.

See 7 March 1810.

1776 Horatio Nelson appointed acting lieutenant in the *Worcester*.

1801 *Sylph* fought a French frigate 120 miles N. of Cape Penas, N. Spain.

1805 *Calcutta*, escorting a convoy of six sail, taken by the French *Magnanime* of the Rochefort Squadron 180 miles W.N.W. of Ushant. Five of the convoy escaped.

1814 Boats of *Plantagenet* and *Rota* attempted to cut out the American privateer *General Armstrong* in Fayal Roads, Azores.

1827 HM King George IV granted to the Royal Marines the globe for their badge and his cypher for their colours.

1840 Royal Marines and Turkish troops, under Cdre Charles Napier, stormed Sidon.

1875 Eric Campbell Geddes born at Agra, India; civilian Controller of the Navy and First Lord of the Admiralty during the First World War and wielder of the infamous 'Geddes Axe' after the war.

See 20 July 1917, 24 December 1917, 22 June 1937.

1904 Destroyer *Chamois*, Lt S.H. Tennyson RN, foundered in the Gulf of Patras, W. Greece. She lost a propeller blade and the thrashing shaft broke the A-bracket and the screw opened up her hull plating. A similarity to the shaft damage suffered by the battleship *Prince of Wales* on 10 December 1940.

1917 PC 61 rammed and sank UC-33 in S.W. Approaches (51.55N, 06.14W).

1939 A Dornier Do18 flying boat shot down off Norway by a Skua of 803 NAS from the carrier *Ark Royal*. Lt B.S. McEwan RN and his Air Gunner, Acting Petty Officer B.M. Seymour, rightly claimed the first aircraft shot down by a carrier-based aircraft and the first German aircraft destroyed by a British squadron in the Second World War. The Dornier force-landed in the sea and destroyer *Somali* rescued the German crew of four and sank the aircraft with gunfire.

See 10 April 1940.

1939 The first 'radar-assisted naval skirmish' (Howse) and first use of air warning radar at sea. Radar-equipped battleship *Rodney*, returning to Scapa with other Home Fleet units after retrieving the submarine *Spearfish* in difficulties off the Horn Reef in the North Sea, detected hostile aircraft at 80 miles closing the Fleet.

1940 Rendering Mines Safe (RMS) section of DTM established. The only operational unit based at the Admiralty, renamed the Land Incidents Section on 6 August 1941.

1940 *Prince Robert* (RCN) captured the German *Weser* off Manzanillo, Mexico.

1942 *Veteran* sunk by U-404 in N. Atlantic (54.51N, 23.04W), with all hands and eighty MN survivors. Convoy RB 1.

See 22 June 2004.

1943 *Vasilissa Olga* (Greek) sunk by German aircraft in Leros harbour.

1944 Fortress P/220 sank U-871 in N. Atlantic.

1958 First and second classes of commodore unified and replaced by single rank of commodore, although still unestablished, i.e. temporary, for those holding designated appointments until made substantive. AFO 2342/58.

See 27 June 1734, 10 January 2002, 22 June 2004.

The battle ensign worn by the armoured cruiser HMS *Warrior* at the Battle of Jutland was hoisted on the anniversary of the battle every year at HMS *Warrior*, the headquarters of the C-in-C Fleet at Northwood. The commanding officer, Cdr David Besley RN, salutes the ensign, hoisted on 31 May 1973. (*Author*)

1958 Flag Officer Sea Training appointed to take charge of sea training, including the working-up of cruisers, destroyers and frigates in home waters. Also in command of Portland Naval Base. First FOST was Rear-Admiral W.G. Crawford. AFO 2282/58; AFO 620/59.

See 21 July 1995.

1975 Officers' blue mess waistcoats discontinued. DCI(RN) T554/75.

1980 The Admiralty ordered that, due to the world-wide rise in the price of gold, Royal Navy stocks of gold leaf were to be conserved and priorities for its use were set out in DCI(RN) 620/80: decorating HMY *Britannia* and her boats; other flag officers' boats; battle honours boards and ceremonial lifebuoys (two per ship plus two for any flag officer embarked); jacks and ensign staff crowns of RN ships and various other uses including HMS *Sultan* for training Commonwealth and foreign students. For all other work 'gold paint' (Stock No. 0442/224-1593 bronze powder 250g mixed into 0442/224-1594 varnish 500ml) was to be used. 'Supply Officers are to exercise careful control . . .'

27 September

1598 Robert Blake baptised.

1778 *Experiment* and *Unicorn* fought the American *Raleigh* in Penobscot Bay, Maine, and took her next day after she had been run ashore.

1797 Rear-Admiral Sir Horatio Nelson invested as a Knight of the Bath at St James's Palace.

1806 *Président*e (40) struck to Rear-Admiral Louis in the Bay, having been halted by *Despatch* (18).

1814 *Carnation* took and burned the American privateer *General Armstrong*, attacked the previous day.

1840 Sunday morning fire in Plymouth Dockyard. The fire started in the third Rate *Talavera* (74) laid up in ordinary in Head Dock and quickly became a major conflagration. The *Talavera* and the frigate *Imogene* (28) lying in South (No. 1) Dock were burned to the waterline. The *Minden* (74) was saved largely by dockyard shipwrights who scuttled her in Stern Dock. Buildings destroyed included the Adelaide Gallery containing historic figureheads and naval trophies, a 3,000-year-old sphinx brought home in *Talavera* and intended for the British Museum, and the capstan from the *Royal George* which sank at Spithead in 1782.

See 20 December 1913, 20 June 1922.

1858 VC: A/Second Master George Bell Chicken, No. 3 Detachment IN, while serving as a volunteer with Indian Cavalry against the Indian mutineers at Suhejni.

1873 Ernle Chatfield born. Beatty's flag captain in *Lion* at Jutland and First Sea Lord January 1933 to November 1938.

See 8 May 1965, 15 November 1967.

1914 Allied forces captured Duala, Cameroons. Ships: *Challenger*, *Dwarf*. Niger Flotilla: *Ivy*, *Porpoise*, *Remus*.

1941 GC (ex-AM): Second Hand John Henry Mitchell, RNR, for saving life at sea on 29 April 1941.

1941 Submarine *Trident* sank the German Uj-1201 in Soroysund, Norway.

1941 Auxilliary AA ship *Springbank* sunk by U-201 in N. Atlantic (49.50N, 21.40W). Convoy HG 73.

1941 Submarine *Upright* sank the Italian TB *Albatros* off Cape Rasocolmo, northern Sicily. *Albatros* had sunk submarine *Phoenix* the year before.

1941 The Navigation School housed since 1 January 1906 in the Old Naval Academy, Portsmouth Dockyard, and seriously damaged in an air raid on 10 March 1941, completed a move to the requisitioned Southwick House over Portsdown Hill and was commissioned as HMS *Dryad*.

A Blackburn Shark floatplane flying over the cruiser HMS *Aurora* and units of the Home Fleet in the 1930s. (*NMRN*)

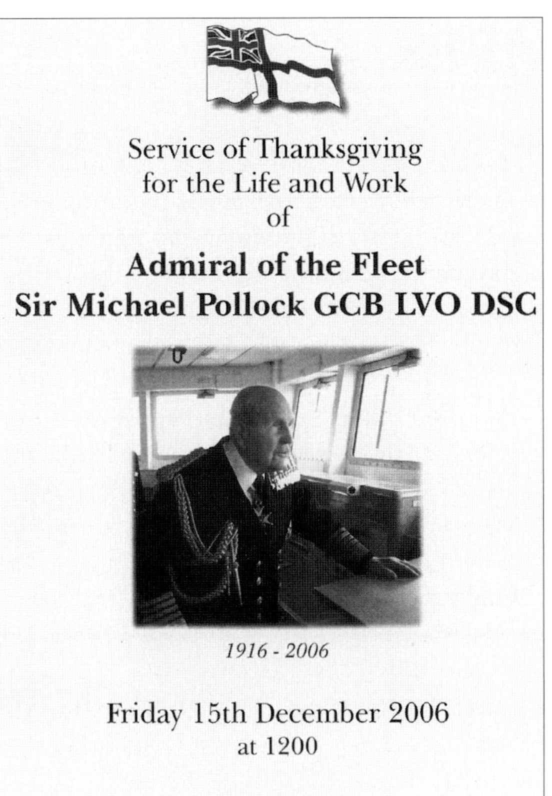
Service of Thanksgiving
for the Life and Work
of
Admiral of the Fleet
Sir Michael Pollock GCB LVO DSC

1916 - 2006

Friday 15th December 2006
at 1200

St Ann's Church
HM Naval Base,
Portsmouth

Admiral of the Fleet Sir Michael Pollock GCB, LVO, DSC, died on this day, 2006. (*Author*)

'Officers about to join should apply to the Commanding Officer for details of the bus routines' – AFO 4109/41.

See 1 January 1906.

1943 Destroyer *Intrepid* sunk by German aircraft in Leros harbour (37.07N, 26.51E). (Attacked on 26th, capsized on 27th.)

1943 British attack on German convoy from Le Havre to Dunkirk. MTBs 202, 204 and 231 sank German escort vessel *Jungingen* (ex-M-534, ex-M-134) which had first been sunk in 1940 by RAF.

See 9 May 1940.

1944 Destroyer *Rockingham* mined (56.29N, 00.57W) 30 miles off Arbroath. Taken in tow but sank.

1945 Admiral of the Fleet Sir Andrew Cunningham installed as a Knight of the Thistle at St Giles' Cathedral, Edinburgh. In presence of the King and Queen and all the knights he handed over *Warspite*'s White Ensign to the cathedral, while Capt Ford of the *Queen Mary* presented her Red Ensign: 'These were the first flags of the sea to take their places among the tattered old Colours of the famous Scottish regiments' – ABC.

See 18 January 1954.

1952 Surveying ship *Challenger*, Cdr William Ashton RN, returned to Portsmouth after a two-and-a-half-year voyage round the world which roughly followed that of the steam corvette *Challenger* on her famous scientific expedition of 1872–6. A record depth of 5,960 fathoms, 35,760ft was discovered by echo sounder in the Challenger Deep in the Mariana Trench between Guam and Yap (11.19N, 142.15E). This world record, made while the ship was commanded by Cdr Steve Ritchie RN, still stands.

See 21 December 1872, 23 March 1875, 24 May 1876.

1970 Admiral Sir William O'Brien took over as C-in-C Western Fleet.

See 6 June 1967, 1 May 1971, 1 November 1971.

1971 RN Unit at Prestwick, base of 819 NAS, named HMS *Gannet*. Commissioned 23 November 1971. Full RNAS status from 1 January 1994.

2006 Lt-Gen. Sir Robert Fulton, lately CGRM, arrived in Gibraltar in *Ocean* and was sworn in as the 63rd Governor and C-in-C Gibraltar – and the first Royal Marines officer to hold the appointment. He left Gibraltar on Trafalgar Day 2009 in the frigate *Sutherland* on being succeeded by Vice-Admiral Sir Adrian Johns.

See 17 April 1969, 26 October 2009.

2006 Sir Michael Pollock, First Sea Lord 1971–4 and for thirty-two years an admiral of the fleet, died at Hurst Manor, Martock, Somerset, aged 89. Gunnery Officer of the heavy cruiser *Norfolk* at the sinking of the *Scharnhorst* in 1943; CO *Ark Royal* 1962; FOSM 1967; Controller 1970. In December 2004 he attended the passing-out from BRNC Dartmouth of his grandson, Sub-Lt Barnaby Pollock RN. Barnaby had won the Queen's Sword as grandfather Michael had done seventy-one years earlier. Memorial service at St Ann's, Portsmouth, 15 December.

See 26 December 1967, 1 March 1974.

28 SEPTEMBER

1652 Admiral Robert Blake (*Resolution*) defeated the Dutch fleet under Vice-Admiral de With (*Prins Willem*) off the Kentish Knock. Ships: *Andrew, Diamond, Garland, Guinea, Nightingale, Nonsuch, Pelican, Resolution, Ruby, Sovereign, Speaker, Vanguard, Triumph, Foresight, Lion, Advice, President.*
Battle Honour: Kentish Knock 1652.

1677 *Charles* and *James* captured the Algerine *Rose* in Gibraltar Strait.

1810 Boats of *Caledonia, Valiant* and *Armide* cut out three French brigs and captured a shore battery in Basque Roads.

1915 Victoria Cross: Lt-Cdr Edgar Christopher Cookson RN for gallantry on the Tigris.

Following the British capture of Shatt-al-Arab and the Basra oil fields, land forces, supported by a motley collection of RN-manned river craft, advanced up the Tigris towards the Ottoman city of Baghdad. Cookson in the paddle steamer *Comet* was ordered to support Townshend's 6th (Poona) Division attack on Kut-al' Amara, launched on 26 September, by destroying a wire boom, supported in midstream by a sunken dhow, blocking the river south of Kut. Charging and shooting at the boom, both having failed to cut the wire hawser, Cookson laid his craft alongside the dhow, leapt onto it and tried to sever the cable with an axe. He was shot dead in the attempt. Kut was captured next day and the boom dismantled. Cookson's 'conspicuous gallantry' was gazetted on 21 January 1916; he had been made DSO for earlier gallantry on 9 May. Townshend and his 10,000 men became trapped at Kut and two further naval VCs were won the following April year trying to fight through supplies to the garrison which finally surrendered to the Turks on 29 April.

See 24 April 1916.

1917 Curtis flying boat 8676 sank UC-6 in North Sea.

1939 'The Council of The Association of Royal Naval Officers (ARNO) wish especially to remind all married officers serving on the Active List that, in the event of their death while serving, their widows become automatically entitled to honorary membership of the Association, eligible to participate in all its benefits and services.' – AFO 2810/39.

1941 *Hyacinth* sank the Italian S/M *Fisalia* off Jaffa in E. Mediterranean.

Memorial plaque to Lt-Cdr Christopher Cookson VC DSO RN, in the parish church at Whitchurch Canonicorum, Dorset. (*Author*)

1941 *Hermione* and destroyers bombarded Pantelleria. Diversion to Operation Halberd.

Operation Halberd, 1941

On 24 September 1941 a convoy of nine 15-knot ships carrying 2,600 troops sailed for Malta escorted by the battleships *Nelson*, *Rodney* and *Prince of Wales*, the carrier *Ark Royal*, five cruisers and eight destroyers. On 27th, air attacks developed and the *Nelson* was hit by a torpedo, but later attacks failed to penetrate the destroyer screen. By 1900 on the 27th, the convoy reached the 'Narrows' and the cruisers and destroyers went ahead with the convoy. They turned north to avoid mines, but were unable to throw off the aircraft because of a bright moon. One transport was hit and had to be sunk after the troops had been transferred. At 1130 on the 28th, the cruisers entered Malta, and at 1330 the convoy arrived. Meanwhile, the Fleet in the eastern Mediterranean and submarines had been causing diversions, and three empty merchantmen were sailed to Gibraltar. An Italian submarine, the *Adua*, was sunk by escorting destroyers on the passage back.

This was the third convoy to Malta from the west in 1941; thirty-nine merchant ships had been convoyed, and only one lost.

1941 The first PQ Convoy, PQ1, ('named after the initials of Cdr Philip Quellyn Roberts, a planning officer at the Admiralty' – Woodman) comprising eleven ships led by the *Commodore*, Capt D. Ridley, master of SS *Atlantic*, sailed from Hvalfiord in Iceland carrying twenty tanks and 193 fighter aircraft for north Russia. Close escort the heavy cruiser *Suffolk*, destroyer *Impulsive*, ocean minesweepers *Britomart*, *Leda*, *Hussar* and *Gossamer*, with other destroyers attached at stages. The convoy 'passed an uneventful twilit passage' (Woodman) and arrived at Archangel on 11 October.

On the same day, 28 September, Convoy QP1, Capt J.C.K. Dowding RNR, Convoy Commodore, in the Union Castle liner *Llanstephan Castle*, composed of returning Operation Dervish ships (see 21 August 1941), the oiler *Black Ranger*, destroyer *Anthony* (which had transferred from PQ1), and seven Russian merchantmen, left Archangel escorted by the heavy cruisers *London* and *Shropshire*, destroyers *Electra* and *Active*, trawlers *Macbeth*, *Hamlet*, *Celia* and *Ophelia* and arrived at Scapa Flow on 9 October.

'The beginning of this famous series of convoys was quiet enough, but, as the enemy came to realise the scale on which British and American ships were carrying aid to their hard-pressed ally through the Arctic ports, his reaction was to attack in a rising crescendo of fury with all the weapons in his armoury. The epic story of the struggle to fight the later convoys through the most arduous physical conditions that nature could produce and against the most relentless onslaughts that man could devise' had begun – Capt S.W. Roskill, *The War at Sea*, vol.1, p.492.

1956 Three inshore minesweepers, *Broadley*, *Bisham* and *Edlingham*, lying in reserve off Hornet in Haslar Creek damaged beyond repair by fire which broke out in cocoon material in *Broadley*.

See 26 January 1959

1968 *Repulse*, second British Polaris submarine, commissioned by her Port and Starboard crews at Vickers, Barrow. Cdr J.R. Wadman RN (Port) and Cdr A.J. Whetstone RN (Starboard). 'The occasion was somewhat marred by dockyard workmen on strike booing all those who entered the dockyard gates' – *Navy* magazine, October 1968, p.370.

See 4 November 1967.

1969 First RM deployment to Northern Ireland, 41 Cdo RM on Spearhead duties.

1986 *Tiger* arrived in Spain for breaking up. The last Royal Navy cruiser and the end of the 6-in gun in the Fleet.

See 25 October 1945, 18 March 1961.

1999 Dr Andrew Lambert (Hon. Secretary of the Navy Records Society) appointed Laughton Professor of Naval History at King's College, London. The first full-time teaching chair in the subject of naval history at a British university.

See 28 May 1919.

2002 Capt B.F.P. 'Peter' Samborne died. First captain of Britain's first nuclear submarine, *Dreadnought*. His First Lieutenant was John Fieldhouse. His son commanded *Swiftsure* 1987–9.

See 24 March 1959.

29 September

1653 Commission for Sick and Wounded formed.

1690 Capture of Cork by the Joint Admirals, Sir Richard Haddock, Henry Killigrew and Sir John Ashby (*Kent*) and the Duke of Marlborough. Ships: *Grafton, Kent, Sovereign, Breda, Charles Galley*. The Duke of Grafton, commanding his eponymous ship, killed in action ashore.

1758 Horatio Nelson born.

1795 *Southampton* fought the French *Vestale* off Genoa.

1795 *Vanguard* captured the French *Superbe* 50 miles E. of Desirade, Leeward Islands.

1803 *Leda* destroyed two gunboats of the Boulogne invasion flotilla off Boulogne.

1805 Nelson rejoined the Fleet off Cadiz; his 47th birthday.

1808 *Maria* taken by the French *Departement des Landes* to the N.E of Antigues Point, Grand-Terre.

1812 British and Russian gunboats occupied Mitau, Riga, and captured enemy personnel. Crews provided from *Aboukir* and *Ranger.*

1849 Boats of *Columbine* destroyed a pirate junk in Hong hai Bay.

1897 Torpedo boat destroyers *Thrasher*, Cdr R.H. Travers RN, and *Lynx*, Lt and Cdr J.G. Armstrong RN, went ashore in thick weather on Dodman Point. Steam pipes fractured in forward stokehold in *Thrasher* burst and four stokers died. Both ships refloated.
See 8 February 1917.

1917 *Sylvia* and *Tirade* sank UC-55 off Shetland.

1918 Destroyers *Ouse* and *Star* sank UB-115 off Newbiggin Point, Northumberland. The last U-boat to leave Zeebrugge to attack shipping.

1924 Special Service Squadron returned from the Empire Cruise; battlecruiser *Hood*, flag of Acting Vice-Admiral Sir Frederick Field, with light cruisers *Dauntless* and *Delhi* to Devonport, battlecruiser *Repulse* and HMAS *Adelaide* to Portsmouth, and light cruisers *Danae* and *Dragon* to Chatham.
See 27 November 1923.

1939 Light cruiser *Calypso* intercepted the German *Minden* which was scuttled 330 miles N.W. of Cape Wrath.
See 23 November 1939.

1939 *Caledonia* (ex-*Majestic*), training ship, destroyed by fire at Rosyth.

1942 Destroyer *Nizam* (RAN) and SAAF aircraft intercepted the Vichy *Amiral Pierre* off Lourenço Marques, where she was scuttled next day (26.04S, 34.54E).

1943 Gen. Dwight D. Eisenhower, in the company of Admiral Sir Andrew Cunningham, received the formal surrender of Italy from the *pro tempore* Italian leader, Marshal Badoglio, on board the battleship *Nelson* at Malta.
See 8 September 1943.

1953 Destroyer *Diamond*, Capt R.I.A. Sarell RN, collided with the light cruiser *Swiftsure*, Capt T.L. Bratt RN, wearing the flag of Rear-Admiral J.W. Cuthbert, Flag Officer Flotillas, Home Fleet, during exercises 30 miles S. of Iceland. Fire in the cruiser and thirty-two casualties. Capt Sarell was Reprimanded at Chatham court martial 5 November for hazarding his ship but he was not the last captain to do so.
See 25 June 1964.

1959 A junior rating from the frigate *Leopard* sentenced at Cape Town to be whipped 'for contravening the Immorality Act with a Coloured woman'. Sentence suspended because he had been in contact with poliomyelitis on board.
See 12 June 1967.

1971 Explosion at 0200 in submarine *Alliance* lying alongside the frigate *Ulster* at Portland following a battery charge killed one man and injured thirteen others. This incident, following closely on the sinking of *Artemis* three months earlier and similar explosion in *Auriga* in 1970, raised questions about future of A-class submarines.

A bronze bust of Vice-Admiral Lord Nelson by sculptor Robert Hornyold-Strickland, commissioned to mark the 250th anniversary of Nelson's birth was unveiled in the Wardroom, HMS *Nelson* by Vice-Admiral Alan Massey, Second Sea Lord and Commander-in-Chief Naval Home Command. Among the guests was Mrs Anna Tribe, a direct descendant of Vice Admiral Lord Nelson and Lady Hamilton. (*RN*)

See 30 August 1966, 12 February 1970, 1 July 1971, 21 March 2007.

1972 *Fulmar* (RNAS Lossiemouth, transferred from RAF and commissioned 2 July 1946) paid off and returned to RAF.

2000 RFA *Wave Knight*, first of class of double-hulled fast fleet tankers, launched by Lady Guthrie, wife of Gen. Sir Charles Guthrie, CDS, at BAE Systems, Barrow-in-Furness.

See 9 February 2001.

2008 A bronze bust of Vice-Admiral Viscount Nelson, commissioned to mark the 250th anniversary of his birth, was unveiled at HMS *Nelson*, Portsmouth, by Vice-Admiral Alan Massey, Second Sea Lord and C-in-C Naval Home Command.

2010 *Dauntless*, Capt R.L. Powell RN, conducted the first in-service firing of the Sea Viper missile system on the Hebrides Range, destroying the target at 18nm.

Vice-Admiral Horatio, Viscount Nelson (1758–1805)

Portrait of Nelson by Charles Lucy. Painted forty-eight years after his death, but attested by survivors who served with him as 'highly characteristic and true'. (*NMRN*)

Born the son of a Norfolk rector in 1758, Nelson joined the Navy in his twelfth year and was posted captain in his twenty-first. He is still regarded by most as Britain's greatest naval hero. His career at sea was distinguished by bold decisions, usually taking offensive action against the enemy and often exposing his ship to heavy enemy fire. He lost the sight of an eye at Corsica and an arm at Tenerife. With Jervis's fleet at the Battle of Cape St Vincent in 1797, it was his audacious manoeuvre against the Spanish line that led to their defeat. Against the French at the Battle of the Nile in 1798, his fleet was numerically inferior yet he all but annihilated the enemy squadron. During the attack on the anchored Danish Fleet at Copenhagen, again sailing through dangerous waters, he pounded the enemy into submission. On that occasion when signalled to withdraw, it is said that he raised his telescope to his blind eye with the remark, 'I really do not see the signal'. He inspired his men and taught his captains well. It was at Trafalgar in 1805, however, when he made his famous signal, 'England expects that every man will do his duty', that he sealed his fame. In a brilliant tactical victory he won the battle but lost his life, struck down by a bullet from a sharpshooter in the rigging of the French *Redoutable*.

He typified all that was best in the sea officers of the period, being a great fighting man, much loved by his officers and men. He had a grasp of tactics and strategy which was exceptional even by the standards of his day.

30 September

1725 The Lords Commissioners of the Admiralty first met in the now famous Board Room in the newly completed Admiralty building in Whitehall.

See 26 March 1964.

1780 *Pearl* captured the French *Espérance* 120 miles S.W. of Bermuda.

1805 Nelson, on arrival off the Spanish coast in *Victory*, wrote to Lt-Gen. the Hon. Henry Fox, Lieutenant-Governor at Gibraltar, requesting that he stop the *Gibraltar Gazette* from reporting the strength of the fleet 'for I much fear, that if the Enemy know of our increased numbers, we shall never see them out of Cadiz. If my arrival is necessary to be mentioned, the Ships with me need not; and it may be inserted that an equal number, or some Ships of Admiral Collingwood's, are ordered home'.

1822 *Eliza* captured the slaver *Firme Union* off Cuba.

1858 *Pearl*'s Naval Brigade at Mau, with detachments of the 13th Light Infantry, Bengal Yeomanry, 6th Madras Light Cavalry, 27th Madras Native Infantry, and Sikh Police Force.

1863 *Britannia*, towed by *Geyser* and *Prospero* from Portland, entered River Dart and moored in Mill Creek. For employment as cadets' training ship. Joined by *Hindustan* in 1864.

1890 Abolition of the blue shirt, with its attached collar, which made a blue jacket synonymous with a British seaman.

1900 *Pigmy*, composite screw gunboat, received the surrender of six Chinese forts at Shanhaikwan, N. China.

1903 RN Barracks, Portsmouth, first occupied. Four thousand officers and men in four divisions – seamen, stokers, POs and Marines – each led by a naval band, left the hulks in Portsmouth Dockyard and marched out of Anchor Gate to the new barracks in Edinburgh Road.

See 4 June 1889, 1 August 1974.

1909 Launch of tenth *Neptune* at Portsmouth. First HM ship with superimposed turret and first Dreadnought able to fire all main armament in broadside.

1913 *Aurora*, ninth of the name, the first oil-fired light cruiser laid down at Devonport. Commissioned in RCN, 1 November 1920.

1918 Minesweeper *Seagull*, ex-torpedo gunboat, sunk in collision in Firth of Clyde.

1931 The first destroyers built in a Royal Dockyard, *Comet* and *Crusader*, floated out of No. 13 Dock at Portsmouth, together with the mining tender *Nightingale*. All three vessels had been laid down on 12 September 1930.

1939 Booth liner *Clement* sunk by German pocket battleship *Admiral Graf Spee*.

1940 Monitor *Erebus*, with destroyers *Garth* and *Vesper*, bombarded Calais. Operation M.W.

1940 Destroyer *Stuart* (RAN) and Sunderland L2166 (230 Sqn) sank the Italian S/M *Gondar* off Alexandria (31.33N, 28.33E), preparing for a chariot raid.

1941 *Gurkha* and *Legion* sank the Italian S/M *Adua* off Alicante (37.10N, 00.56E).

1942 Unsuccessful coastal force action off Terschelling. Four MTBs and an MGB lost, German SS *Thule* sunk.

1944 Swordfish F/813 (*Campania*) sank U-921 in Arctic (72.32N, 12.55E). Convoy RA 60.

1944 *Terrible*, only British carrier built in a Royal Dockyard, launched at Devonport by Mrs Duncan Sandys, daughter of Mr Winston Churchill. Commissioned 16 December 1948 at Devonport as HMAS *Sydney*.

See 5 April 1939, 16 December 1948.

1950 RM Barracks at Chatham closed.

The hulks of the wooden three-deckers *Duke of Wellington* and *Marlborough* alongside in Portsmouth Dockyard; they were employed as accommodation ships before the opening of the new Royal Naval Barracks. (*Author*)

1963 Home Air Command became Naval Air Command. Flag Officer Air (Home) became FONAC.

1966 Frigate *Puma* sailed from Simon's Town to Port Stanley after Argentinean extremists forced a civil aircraft to land on the Falklands Islands on 28 September.
See 14 October 1964.

1970 Warrant rank reintroduced with establishment of Fleet Chief Petty Officer. To be addressed as 'Sir' by juniors and as 'Mr' by commissioned officers.
See 30 March 1971.

1971 HMS *Simbang*, RNAS Sembawang, Singapore, paid off. Originally the Bukit Sembawang Rubber Estate bought by the RAF in 1936 and transferred to the RN in 1939. Latterly commissioned 4 September 1962 as HQ 3 Cdo Bde.
See 21 July 2009.

1983 'From FO Medway to AIG 1312. WDI/WAT 290900ZSEP83: The flags of Flag Officer Medway and Port Admiral Chatham will be struck, finally, at sunset Fri 30 Sep 83.'
'From CINCFLEET to FO Medway. WDI/WAT 300800ZSEP83: Personal from CINC. Farewell to a fine Command that has served loyally in the highest traditions of the Service for the last 450 years. The Fleet will miss you.'
Rear-Admiral Bill Higgins was the tenth and last FO Medway since the post was created in 1961 on the demise of the old Nore Command. DCI (RN) 135/83.
See 31 March 1984.

1985 *Salisbury*, Type 61 aircraft direction frigate, sunk as target W. of Ireland. Last RN ship to carry Squid A/S mortars.

1990 Frigate *Jupiter*, with USS *Taylor*, boarded an apparent blockade runner in Persian Gulf. First of thirty-three boardings and 3,151 challenges in Operation Granby.

1998 *Ocean*, Capt Robert Turner RN, commissioned.
See 8 August 1945, 11 October 1995, 20 February 1998.

1998 *Dolphin*, the home of the Royal Navy's Submarine Service for nearly a century, paid off and closed 1 April 1999. Training task transferred to *Dryad* and *Raleigh*.
See 3 May 1905, 3 January 1978.

1 OCTOBER

1748 Rear-Admiral Charles Knowles (*Cornwall*) intercepted a Spanish squadron under Vice-Admiral Don Andres Reggio (*Africa*) 12 miles N.E. of Havana. Ships: *Tilbury, Strafford, Cornwall, Lenox, Warwick, Canterbury, Oxford*.

1807 *Windsor Castle* packet captured the French privateer *Jeune Richard* 100 miles N.E. by E. of Barbados.

1841 Second capture of Tinghai, the principal town of Chusan in the First Opium War with China, by Rear-Admiral Sir William Parker (*Wellesley*) and Lt-Gen. Sir Hugh Gough.

Ships: *Bentinck, Blenheim, Blonde, Columbine, Cruizer, Modeste, Nemesis, Phlegethon, Queen* (Ben. Marine), *Sesostris* (IN), *Wellesley*; *Jupiter* and *Rattlesnake* troopships.

See 5 July 1840.

1849 *Columbine* and *Fury*, with a party from *Hastings*, destroyed twenty-six junks and the pirate stronghold in Tai Pang harbour, Bias Bay.

1858 *Pearl*'s Naval Brigade at Amorha (fourth action).

1860 Metropolitan Police from the 2nd Division took over security duties at Portsmouth Dockyard. Establishment: 1 superintendent, 5 inspectors, 26 sergeants and 141 PCs.

1869 Closure of the Steam Yard at Woolwich which had taken over from that at Deptford in 1827.

1900 Electrical Department of dockyards instituted.

1907 Ranks of First and Second Class Petty Officer abolished, the latter becoming Leading Seamen.

1917 First flight from platform on gun turret: Sqn Cdr Rutland in a Sopwith Pup from B turret, battlecruiser *Repulse*.

1918 Allied net barrage established across Otranto Strait.

1919 WRNS disbanded.

1920 *Greenfly*, river gunboat, captured by insurgents in Mesopotamia.

1920 First fortnightly payments.

1923 *Vernon* established ashore, on the old Gunwharf at Portsmouth.

See 31 March 1986, 26 April 1876.

1931 Boy Servants became Boy Stewards.

1931 All pay to have been reduced to 1925 scales on recommendation of May Committee. But see 15 September 1931.

1934 Royal Indian Marine became the Royal Indian Navy. Indian Navy (Discipline) Act effective from 2 October.

See 11 November 1928, 9 December 1935, 14 September 1939.

1941 The titles Royal New Zealand Navy and the designation His Majesty's New Zealand Ships granted to the New Zealand Naval Forces by King George VI. The Royal New Zealand Navy Order 1941 (Order in Council) was signed by the Governor General at government House, Wellington, 1 October 1941; but AFO 4110/41 dated 25 September 1941 appears to have pre-empted this.

See 29 August 1911, 14 March 1921, 20 June 1921, 20 June 1968.

1943 1770 Squadron FAA formed at RNAS Yeovilton with first Fairey Firefly aircraft.

1946 Reconstitution of RNVR.

1946 *Demetrius*, Supply and Secretariat School, at Wetherby, renamed *Ceres*.

1951 Destroyer *Grenville*, Lt-Cdr J.M. Cowling RN, returning to Plymouth at night with the carrier *Triumph*, had 30ft of her starboard side stove-in by a collision with Italian merchantman *Alceo* 12 miles S.E. of Start Point. Three men killed, four missing. Three courts martial: Captain acquitted of all charges; OOW, Lt J.S. Townend RNVR, reprimanded; Captain U.H.R. James RN, CO of *Triumph* 'as senior officer of a formed unit' including *Grenville*, severely reprimanded.

See 28 February 1983.

The torpedo school HMS *Vernon* before being moved ashore in 1923. The ships are the *Marlborough* (1855), the *Warrior* (1860) and the *Donegal* (1858). (*NMRN*)

1954 Official naval battle honours for ships and FAA squadrons promulgated in Admiralty Fleet Order 2565/54. The earliest action recognised is Armada 1588.

'The award of Battle Honours to Her Majesty's ships is intended to foster *esprit de corps* among their officers and ships' companies, who are thereby encouraged to take a personal interest in the war-time exploits not only of their present ship but also of those of the same name which distinguished themselves in the past . . . A battle honour will be awarded for those actions which resulted in the defeat of the enemy, or when the action was inconclusive but well fought, and in exceptional cases where outstanding efforts were made against overwhelming odds. A Battle Honour will not be awarded for a British defeat, or when the action was inconclusive and badly fought.'

1958 Ship Department of the Admiralty formed by merger of DNC, E-in-C, DNE and DEE departments.

1966 The first Special Duties Branch officers promoted to commander.

1966 Royal Marine Forces Volunteer Reserve title changed to Royal Marines Reserve under terms of Reserve Forces Act of 9 August 1966. DCI(RN) 1156/66.

See 1 November 1958.

1967 Admiral Sir John Frewen, the last C-in-C Home Fleet and the first C-in-C Western Fleet (the title changed on 6 June 1967), hauled down his flag at Northwood. He was succeeded by Acting Admiral Sir John Bush, aged 52, the youngest officer to hoist a full admiral's flag since Mountbatten (then on the Captains' List) became Supreme Commander SE Asia Command.

See 6 July 1965, 1 November 1971.

1971 Announcement of PWO Doctrine and formation of the Warfare Branch.

See 23 May 1972, 14 May 2004.

1976 Royal Maritime Auxiliary Service (RMAS) amalgamated with Port Auxiliary Service (PAS). DCI(RN) 448/76.

See 1 September 1970, 31 March 2008.

1984 Portsmouth Naval Base became a Fleet Operating and Maintenance Base. Rear-Admiral John Warsop, Flag Officer Portsmouth and Port Admiral Portsmouth, became FO Portsmouth and Naval Base Commander Portsmouth. DCI(RN) 413/84.

See 15 September 1971, 31 March 1996.

1986 DCI(RN) 158/86 authorised commanding officers to make a cash grant of £37 to allow survivors of sunk or abandoned ships to meet basic needs. 'However, some toilet items are now provided as part of the Mk III Survivor's Kit shortly to be introduced. From 1 October 1986 the cash grant is to be reduced from £37 to £32'. – DCI(RN) 252/86.

1988 Hard-lying money replaced by long service at sea bonus.

2000 Comacchio Group RM remustered as Fleet Protection Group RM.

See 2 April 1945, 1 June 1975, 1 May 1980.

2005 Maritime Warfare Centre formed from merger of tasks of the Maritime Warfare Development Centre and the Maritime Tactical School. Until 2007 MWC was spread over three sites: Southwick for maritime education, concepts and doctrine development, Portsdown for tactical development and operational analysis, and Faslane for organisation, planning and execution of submarine weapon firings. During 2007 all MWC tasks were collocated at HMS *Collingwood*, Fareham.

2010 *Ocean*, Capt Keith Blount RN, visited Lagos to mark the fiftieth anniversary of Nigerian independence.

See 6 October 1946.

2 October

1699 Half-pay limited by Order in Council to 9 flag officers, 51 captains, 100 lieutenants and 30 masters.

1758 *Lizard* captured the French *Duc d'Hanovre* off Brest. *Heroine* was engaged but escaped.

1779 *Apollo* captured the French *Mutin*, *Jupiter* and *Crescent* captured the French *Pilote* 30 miles off Lizard Head.

1786 Admiral Viscount Keppel died.

1804 Abortive attack with Fulton's fireships off Boulogne by Keith, which Gambier considered 'a horrible and anti-Christian mode of warfare'.

1805 *Egyptienne* captured the French *Acteon* off La Rochelle.

1836 *Beagle* arrived Falmouth having sailed from Devonport 27 December 1831.

1840 Boats of *Edinburgh* and *Hastings* destroyed an ammunition store at Beirut.

1866 Wood screw gunvessel *Griffon* stranded and lost after night-time collision with sister ship *Pandora* off Little Popo, Bight of Benin, due to failure of night signalling system.

1900 Grant's guns handed over to the RGA and the Naval Brigade left Simon's Town. Bearcroft embarked on the 12th.

See 3 February 1900.

1901 RN's first submarine boat, a yard shorter than a cricket pitch and designed by the Irish-American J.P. Holland, launched at Barrow-in-Furness, and without a name or number until usage alone called her HM Submarine Torpedo Boat No. 1, and then simply Holland 1. Now preserved at the RN Submarine Museum.

1905 *Dreadnought*, Britain's first all-big-gun battleship, laid down at Portsmouth Dockyard.

See 3 October 1906.

1917 Armoured cruiser *Drake* torpedoed by U-79 in the North Channel. Sank later in Church Bay, Rathlin Island, and later still rummaged by those seeking explosives. What she had were in remarkably good condition but were officially disposed of.

1918 *Begonia* (Q 10) sunk in collision with U-141 off Casablanca.

1918 Bombardment of Durazzo. Ships: *Dartmouth*, *Glasgow*, *Gloucester*, *Lowestoft* (SO), *Weymouth*. Destroyers: *Acheron*, *Acorn*, *Badger*, *Cameleon*, *Fury*, *Goshawk*, *Jackal*, *Lapwing*, *Nereide*, *Nymphe*, *Ruby*, *Shark*, *Swan* (RAN), *Tigress*, *Tribune* (D 5), *Warrego* (RAN).

1925 Naval officers attached to RAF for FAA service to wear a badge consisting of a foul anchor superimposed upon the wings of an albatross.

1939 Admiralty announced that most of the British gunboats on the Yangtse would be paid off and laid up to release personnel.

See 6 August 1914.

1940 Destroyers *Hasty* and *Havock* sank the Italian S/M *Berillo* off Egypt.

1940 Light cruisers *Orion* and *Sydney* (RAN) bombarded Maltezana area, Stampalia.

1941 *Vanguard*, Britain's last battleship, laid down at John Brown's on the Clyde.

1942 Light cruiser *Curacoa* sunk in collision with RMS *Queen Mary* in N.W. Approaches (55.50N, 08.38W); 338 men lost. The official inquiry in June 1945 attributed all blame to *Curacoa* which was alleged to have been in pursuit of U-407. The Court of Appeal and the House of Lords upheld an Admiralty appeal, despite unequivocal orders to the Master of the *Queen Mary* that he was not to stop for anything, and attributed one-third blame to the liner.

1964 Names approved for RNR units at Chatham and Inverkip, Renfrewshire: *Wildfire* and *Dalriada*. DCI(RN) 954/64.

See 3 April 1959, 20 May 2000.

Augustus, Viscount Keppel (1725–1786)

Admiral Lord Keppel (1725–1786). (*NMRN 1974/92*)

Keppel entered the Royal Navy in 1738 and served with Anson, then a commodore, during his famous voyage round the world, 1740–4. He was a lieutenant in 1744 and rose steadily in command. In 1747 he was captured by the French when his ship ran aground, but was exchanged for French prisoners. When Commodore in the Mediterranean Fleet in 1748, he is reported to have replied to the Dey of Algiers who complained of having to treat with a 'beardless boy': 'Had my Master supposed that wisdom was measured by the length of the beard he would have sent your deyship a he-goat.' He pleaded in vain at Admiral Byng's court martial. He commanded the naval squadron at the capture of Gorée in 1758, the leading ship of the line under Admiral Hawke at Quiberon in 1759, the ships at the taking of Belle Ile in 1761, and at Havana, where his share of the prize money was reportedly £25,000. He was promoted to rear-admiral in 1762 and was in command at Jamaica until 1764. At home, where he was an MP, he became embroiled in politics, particularly against the Earl of Sandwich, then First Lord of the Admiralty. Despite this antipathy, he was in command of the Channel Fleet in 1776, and by 1778 was Commander of the Grand Fleet as a full admiral. Due to maladministration only six out of thirty-five ships supposed to be at instant readiness were reputedly 'worthy of a seaman's eye'. Keppel was scarcely able to put out to sea with a strong enough force to blockade the French Atlantic ports. He fought D'Orvilliers in July 1778 inconclusively and was court-martialled on politically motivated charges brought by Palliser five months after the event. He was unanimously and honourably acquitted and became the hero of the hour. In March 1779, Keppel refused to serve under a naval administration he could not trust, but by 1782 he was First Lord of the Admiralty during Rockingham's new government and was succeeded by Lord Howe. He retired from public life in 1783 and died in 1786.

1967 The first British Polaris submarine, *Resolution*, commissioned at Barrow by commanders Ken Frewer and Mike Henry. The commissioning service, 'held on the quayside with a gale tugging at the bunting', was led by, among others, the Bishop of Buckingham, who had served as a naval chaplain in the battleship *Resolution*.

See 26 February 1964, 15 September 1966, 15 February 1968, 15 June 1968, 22 October 1994.

1970 Victualling Stores – Contract – Cheddar Cheese. 'The contract provides for the supply of Australian Cheddar of choicest/First Grade in 40lb and 10lb blocks, being 5–7 months old and warranted for 28 days from the last day of the month of delivery. The cheese shall be mild in flavour, free from taint, discoloration, mite infestation, gas holes and mould . . .' – DCI(RN) 1153/70.

1992 Civil war in former Yugoslavia. RFA *Resource*, *Sir Bedivere* and *Argus* sailed to Adriatic to support British element of UN Protection Force (UNPROFOR), later UN Implementation Force (IFOR) ashore in former Yugoslavia. RN presence considerably increased in 1993 with one anti-submarine carrier, two destroyers/frigates, one submarine (conventional or nuclear) as required, and RFA support ships. Force levels varied with the development of operations ashore. RN forces remained in Adriatic supporting successively Operations Grapple, Hamden, Joint Endeavour, Diligent Force until 1996. British destroyers and frigates also served in the NATO Standing Naval Forces Atlantic and Mediterranean deployed in the Adriatic to monitor and enforce the UN embargo on trade with the former Yugoslavia. SNFL released 15 May 1996, SNFM released 19 June 1996 when Operation Sharp Guard ended.

3 October

A Memorable Date observed by 40 Cdo Royal Marines – Termoli

1787 Flag Officers given a blue full dress coat with gold lace, and for both dress and undress coats a new button, bearing an anchor within a wreath.

1799 *Speedy* destroyed four Spanish coasters near Cape Trafalgar.

1806 Boats of *Minerva* cut out two Spanish gun-boats in Arosa Bay.

1808 *Carnation* taken by the French *Palinure* 150 miles N.E. of the Virgin Islands.

1857 First party of *Shannon*'s Naval Brigade arrived at Allahabad.

See 18 August 1857.

1890 *Temeraire*, 11,000 ton brig, commanded by Capt Gerard Noel, entered Suda Bay in Crete, the last armoured ship to enter harbour under sail and the last day on which a British battle-ship proceeded under sail alone. Noel had been given permission to enter under sail after the rest of the squadron, all turret-ships 'without a single square yard of canvas between them', had berthed. Admiral George Ballard, who was OOW for part of the five-hour operation, which required fourteen tacks in three hours, some only two minutes apart, wrote, 'She presented a spectacular finish to the centuries of such movement under the pennants of the British Mediterranean Command, which was talked of for many years after on that station'.

See 9 May 1876.

1906 Battleship *Dreadnought* began sea trials.

See 2 October 1905.

1914 First units of the Royal Naval Division (RM Brigade) arrived at Antwerp.

HMS *Ocean* alongside in Lagos on 1 October 2010 for the 50th anniversary of Nigerian independence. (*RN*)

The First British Atomic Test. Operation Hurricane, 3 October 1952

Vice-Admiral E.M. Evans-Lombe, DCNS, had planned the operation for two years and the RN was responsible for transport, housing and logistic support. The escort carrier *Campania*, used as a mobile exhibition during the Festival of Britain in 1951, was baseship with three LSTs, *Zeebrugge*, *Narvik* and *Tracker* which accommodated 200 Royal Engineers – and the River-class frigate *Plym*, in which the weapon was housed. An advance party in *Zeebrugge* and *Narvik* under command of Capt G.C. Colville OBE, RN, arrived in theatre on 26 April. *Campania*, *Tracker* and *Plym* assembled at Chatham and Rear-Admiral A.D. Torlesse DSO, hoisted his flag in *Campania* as Flag Officer Special Squadron on 14 May. *Tracker* sailed independently on 5 June via Suez and *Campania* embarked aircraft and ninety scientific and technical personnel at Portsmouth and sailed with *Plym* on 10 June via the Cape. All provisions had to come via Fremantle, 900 miles to the south. The RAN frigate HMAS *Hawkesbury* , later joined by the carrier HMAS *Sydney* (Rear-Admiral J.W.M. Eaton DSO, DSC, Flag Officer Commanding Australian Fleet), the destroyer *Tobruk* and frigates *Shoalhaven*, *Culgoa*, *Murchison* and *Macquarie* patrolled the operational perimeter. Soon after the explosion on 3 October Lt-Cdr D.T.J. Stanley DFC, RN, OIC aircraft embarked in *Campania*, and Senior Commissioned Observer H.J. Lambert DSM, RN, overflew the lagoon where Plym had been anchored to take water and air samples.

'When the Prime Minister told a hushed House of Commons that the object of the test of the British atomic weapon was to investigate the effects of an atomic explosion in a harbour, that the weapon had been placed in HMS *Plym* and that this frigate had been vaporised, the public realised that the Navy had figured more prominently in the experiment than was generally anticipated.' – *Navy* magazine, May 1953. The metal nameplate from *Plym*, the first British warship destroyed by an atomic weapon, is preserved at Aldermaston.

1915 First German merchant ship (*Svionia*) sunk by British submarine – E 19 – in the Baltic (54.35N, 13.41E).

1918 Submarine L 10, the only one of her class to be lost during the war, sunk by gunfire of the German destroyer S-33, which she torpedoed, off Texel.

1918 Warrant officers to replace their cuff buttons with ¼-in gold stripe, and distinguishing cloth – dark green, silver grey and dark blue for electrical, shipwright and ordnance branches.

1940 Establishment of BSO organisation. Country covered by Bomb Safety Officers responsible to DUBD, Director of Unexploded Bomb Division, although locally appointed.

1941 Cruiser *Kenya* sank U-boat supply ship *Kota Pinang* (ex-Dutch) N. of the Azores.

1943 Submarine *Usurper* sunk, perhaps by the German UJ-2208, in the Gulf of Genoa.

1943 Battle of Termoli, Adriatic Coast. Amphibious operation by 40 Cdo RM to seize port and strategic road ahead of advancing forces. One DSO, three MCs, two MMs.

1952 The first British atomic test in the Monte Bello Islands. Operation Hurricane.

See 16 May 1956, 24 December 1957.

1970 New RN hospital at Mtarfa, Malta, opened by the MDG(N), Surg Vice-Admiral E.B. Bradbury. The old RN Hospital at Bighi, completed in 1832, to be closed.

See 22 September 1970.

1973 Second Cod War. RN units withdrew outside the disputed 50-mile limit to allow negotiations to progress.

See 31 August 1958.

2001 Memorial plaques in the Painted Hall, RN College, Greenwich, to twenty-one men from the United States who volunteered for service in the RNVR before the USA entered the Second World War, were unveiled by Rear-Admiral Tim McClement, ACNS, and blessed by The Most Rev and Rt Hon. Dr George Carey, Archbishop of Canterbury. A 22nd name, that of Surg-Lt Hayes, was added on 22 June 2004. The First Three who inspired the RN College to dedicate the first plaque in 1941, when their names could not be publicised, were Edmund Ferris, John Parker and Charles Porter.

See 15 June 1941, 18 October 1941, 22 June 2004.

4 October

1744 *Victory* (100), Capt Samuel Faulkner, flagship of Admiral Sir John Balchen, wrecked in W. Approaches on or about this date with the loss of all 1,100 souls on board. Balchen, aged 75, was returning from freeing blockaded British storeships in Lisbon and escorting them to Gibraltar. His squadron was dispersed off Ushant in a storm. Wreck was believed to have been on the Casquets off Alderney but remains of the wreck were found in October 2008, 25 miles south of Salcombe.

1780 *Phoenix* (44), fifth rate, Capt Sir Hyde Parker, driven ashore on N. coast of Cuba in a severe tropical storm which destroyed several other RN ships in the following days. Over 250 men reached shore and Archer set off in the ship's cutter by night for Montego Bay and brought the *Porcupine* sloop to the rescue. The wreck was abandoned and burned on 12 October. Hyde Parker was to be Nelson's C-in-C at Copenhagen in 1801.

See 5 and 11 October 1780.

1797 *Alexander* captured the French privateer *Epicharis* 20 miles E. of Barbados.

1805 *Princess Charlotte* captured the French (ex-British) *Cyane* E. of Tobago. The French *Naiade* was also engaged, but escaped.

1813 Boats of *Furieuse* cut out two gunboats and fourteen of a French convoy, and sank two more of the latter, at Santa Marinella.

1824 Boats of *Sybille* cut out the Greek *San Nicolo*, *Polysenes* and *Bella Paula* at Nauplia, Greece.

1854 Wood paddlers *Sidon* and *Inflexible* and the French *Cacique* and *Caton* attacked Fort Nikolaev (Pervomaiskaya) in the Crimea.

1872 Roger Keyes, naval commander in First and Second World Wars, born.

See 26 December 1945.

1905 *Ganges*, the principal Boys' Training Establishment at Shotley Point, near Ipswich, commissioned.

See 1 June 1927, 7 June 1976.

1912 Submarine B 2 lost in collision with the Hamburg-Amerika liner *Amerika* 4 miles N.E. of Dover. Submarine allowed to remain undisturbed as a naval grave, the first time that no attempt was made to recover submariners for burial ashore. The only survivor, Lt Richard Pulleyne, was rescued by submarine C 16 but later lost in command of submarine E 34 in Heligoland Bight, 20 July 1918.

1913 The new battle-cruiser HMAS *Australia*, flagship of Rear-Admiral Sir George Patey, Flag Officer Commanding Australian

HMS *Bristol* (1969), first RN ship armed with the Sea Dart and Ikara guided missile systems, and the only one of her kind. (*NMRN*)

Fleet, entered Sydney for the first time, leading the light cruisers *Melbourne*, *Sydney* and *Encounter*, and the destroyers *Warrego*, *Parramatta* and *Yarra*, 'and were accorded a welcome which signalized the assumption by the Commonwealth of full naval responsibility in its own waters' – Brassey's *Naval Annual*, 1914, p.401.

See 13 October 1913, 29 August 1914, 12 April 1924.

1918 *Snapdragon* sank UB-68 in central Mediterranean (35.56N, 16.20E). Her captain, Dönitz, became Grand Admiral in the Second World War, when he based his wolf pack tactics on his experiences in and reflections on the First.

1925 Rates of pay reduced for new entries on advice of Anderson Committee.

1940 Submarine *Rainbow* sunk in collision with SS *Antonietta Costa* off Calabria, when she was attacking her (41.28N, 18.05E).

1941 Trawler *Lady Shirley* sank U-111 (27.15N, 20.27W). W.S.W. of Tenerife.

She gained Asdic contact at 1,800yd, dropped a pattern of five depth charges and a U-boat (U-111) surfaced and opened fire. The submarine's gun exploded as the tampion had not been removed before firing, and the trawler returned the fire, hitting the submarine nine times with 4-in shells. The submarine sank stern-first, and the *Lady Shirley*'s crew of thirty took forty-five prisoners, and then headed for Gibraltar, four days' steaming away.

1943 Admiralty announced that Admiral of the Fleet Sir Andrew Cunningham, C-in-C Mediterranean Fleet, would succeed Admiral of the Fleet Sir Dudley Pound, as First Sea Lord.

'In Admiral Fraser, then commanding the Home Fleet, we had an officer of the highest seagoing reputation, who had also long experience of Admiralty administration and staff work. It was to him I first offered the post. The Admiral said that of course he would serve wherever he was sent, but that he thought Andrew Cunningham was the right man. "I believe I have the confidence of my own fleet," he said. "Cunningham has that of the whole Navy." He asked me to weigh the matter longer. I replied that his attitude was most becoming, and after further thought and consultation I took him at his word and decided to face the serious challenge in the Mediterranean fighting command. Admiral Sir Andrew Cunningham was therefore chosen.' – Churchill, *The Second World War Volume 5, Closing the Ring*, p.145–6. Admiral Fraser's biographer records the additional comment from Fraser 'I haven't even fought a battle yet. If one day I should sink the *Scharnhorst*, I might feel differently'.

See 9 April 1942, 15, 17 and 21 October 1943, 26 December 1943.

1944 *Chebogue* (RCN) torpedoed by U-1227 W.S.W. of Cape Clear (49.20N, 24.20W). Convoy ONS 33. Foundered in tow. Beached on Mumbles 11 October but CTL.

1963 Admiral Sir Patrick Brind died aged 71. He was Chief of Staff in the Home Fleet when the *Bismarck* was sunk and ACNS during the planning of the Normandy Landings. After the War Admiral Brind was Admiral President at Greenwich (1946–8), C-in-C East Indies/British Pacific Fleet (1948–51) and the first NATO C-in-C Allied Forces Northern Europe (1951–3). In the chapel of the Royal Naval College, Greenwich, in 1948, Admiral Brind married the widow of Rear-Admiral H.E.C. Blagrove who was lost in *Royal Oak* at Scapa Flow in 1939.

See 31 January 1938, 14 October 1939.

1965 The first full production Buccaneer S2, XN 974, made the first non-stop crossing of the Atlantic by a Fleet Air Arm aircraft. Cdr G. Higgs RN and Lt-Cdr A. Taylor RN flew from Goose Bay, Labrador, to RNAS Lossiemouth, 1,950 miles in 4 hours 16 minutes.

See 6 June 1964, 14 October 1965, 11 May 1969.

1966 First and last Type 82 destroyer, *Bristol*, seventh of the name, ordered from Swan Hunter. Her sister ships went with cancelled fleet carrier CVA 01.

1982 Leander-class frigate *Bacchante*, transferred to RNZN on 1 October, commissioned as HMNZS *Wellington*. DCI(RN) 434/82.

See 18 July 1983.

5 October

1780 Great October hurricane in West Indies that destroyed most of the British squadron off San Domingo. *Stirling Castle* (64), third rate, driven ashore on Silver Key Reef, Hispaniola. About fifty men got ashore but twenty swept out to sea on wreckage where they suffered acute hardship, drinking the blood of dead shipmates to stay alive. Following ships foundered with all hands: *Thunderer* (74), third rate, flagship of Cdre Robert Walsingham; *Scarborough* (20), sixth rate; and the 14-gun brig sloops *Barbadoes* and *Victor.* Among those lost in *Thunderer* was Midshipman Nathaniel Cook, son of Capt James Cook RN who had been killed in the Pacific on 14 February 1779.

See 4 and 11 October 1780, 24 January 1794, 13 May 1835.

1804 *Indefatigable, Lively, Medusa* and *Amphion* captured the Spanish *Medea, Clara* and *Fama* and sank *Mercedes* with much loss of life 27 miles S.W. of Cape de Santa Maria, off Cadiz, as the Spanish vessels were on their way to subsidise the French: a rich haul.

1808 *Phaeton* (38), Capt Fleetwood Pellew, paid an unwelcome visit to Nagasaki ('Nangasakie'), Japan.

Japan had a deep suspicion and fear of foreigners. Pellew's ROP recorded that 'the inhabitants all fled in dismay'. The immediate result of this affair was the suicide by hara-kiri of the Governor of Nagasaki and the five principal military officers of the province, the confinement under house arrest of the Prince of Hizen for several months 'during which his fate was in suspense', the suicide by drowning of three of the men who had acted as interpreters, and the orders by which the inhabitants of the Prince's district were forbidden for months to open the front of their houses. Not a successful port visit. The founding of the Japanese Navy may be traced back to this event and to the Japanese 'fervent desire to prevent anything of the sort ever happening again'.

1813 *Edinburgh, Imperieuse, Resistance, Eclair, Pylades* and *Swallow* captured a French convoy of twenty-nine sail and destroyed the batteries at Porto d'Anzio.

1813 *Fantome* captured the American privateer *Portsmouth Packet* (ex-Canadian *Liverpool Packet*) 21 miles S.E. of Matinicus Island.

1909 Destroyer *Lee* wrecked off Blacksod Bay.

1917 UB-41 mined and sunk off Scarborough.

1918 AMC *Otranto* beached on Islay after collision with *Kashmir.*

1942 Hudson N/269 sank U-619 in N. Atlantic.

1943 Hudson F/269 sank U-389 in N. Atlantic. Convoy ONS 19. A squadron anniversary.

1944 *Zwaardvisch* (Neth) sank U-168 off Java.

1944 Light cruiser *Aurora* and destroyer *Catterick* bombarded Levitha Island, in the Dodecanese, and landed a party to which the island surrendered later that day.

1956 Frigate *Keppel*, leaving Devonport for Portland, collided stern-first with the Torpoint Ferry.

1965 HMS *Ariel* renamed *Daedalus* 'in recognition of the fact that RNAS Lee-on-Solent is the traditional home of the Fleet Air Arm'. – DCI(RN) 1417/65.

1967 Surveying ship *Dampier* sailed from Singapore to pay off at Chatham after nearly twenty years' service in the Far East, a post-war naval long service record for continuous duty east of Suez.

1992 HM The Queen gave unrestricted permission for British loan and contract personnel to wear the Sultan of Brunei's Silver Jubilee medal. DCI(RN) 115/93.

See 4 August 2001.

1993 Minehunters *Sheraton* and *Brinton*, which had sailed from Rosyth 21 September, paid off at Portsmouth.

See panel opposite.

2004 Lt-Gen. Sir John Richards died; the only commandant general to have served in the ranks as a marine and the youngest RM officer to have been promoted to three-star.

Cdr Ian Riches RN receives the Russian Order of Maritime Services from President Vladimir Putin at No. 10 Downing Street on 5 October 2005 in recognition of his part in saving the lives of seven Russian submariners. (*RN*)

Tribute to the Ton-class

The First Sea Lord, Admiral Sir Benjamin Bathurst, made the following signal to the Fleet:

From MOD UK NAVY to AIG 1001A2G LAA LVK 040800ZOCT93.

1. On the occasion of HM Ships *Sheraton* and *Brinton*'s decommissioning, and in anticipation of *Nurton* and *Wilton* paying off in 1994, I wish to record, on behalf of the Navy Board, our sincere appreciation for the magnificent contribution that the 118 Ton-class vessels have made to the Royal Navy over the last 40 years.

2. The Tons, as minesweepers, minehunters and patrol vessels, have served with distinction in many parts of the World, most notably in Malaysia, Borneo, Suez Canal and the Red Sea. They have been the backbone of our MCM force for many years providing exceptional service and earning a formidable reputation worldwide.

3. Finally I wish to extend our particular thanks to those currently serving in Tons for their invaluable contribution to Fishery Protection duties and operations in Northern Ireland.

4. To all those who have served or been associated with the Ton-class – BZ.

See 9 July 1952, 28 February 1992, 3 December 1993.

2004 The submarine HMCS *Chicoutimi* (ex-HMS *Upholder)* running opened up on the surface in heavy seas in the E. Atlantic, was seriously damaged by a fire when she took in water through the open upper lid which arced the main power cables between the forward battery and the main propulsion switchboards. One officer died. *Chicoutimi* lost all power on board and drifted for sixty hours. She was towed 220 miles to Faslane, escorted by the frigate *Montrose*, and arrived on 10 October. Order of St John: Surg-Lt Michael Lindsay RN.

See 2 December 1986, 9 June 1990.

2005 President Valimir Putin presented the Russian Order for Maritime Services to Cdr Ian Riches RN, the RN's Submarine Escape Officer, and to Stuart Gold and Peter Nutall of James Fisher Rumic Ltd at 10 Downing Street for their leading role in saving seven Russian submariners trapped in a submersible on the seabed off Kamchatka in August 2005. The Russian Order of Friendship was awarded to Capt Jonathan Holloway RN, BNA Moscow, and to Sqn Ldr Keith Hewitt, captain of the RAF C-17 aircraft which flew the team to Petropavlovsk.

See 12 August 2000, 7 August 2005.

2008 Lt Edward Briggs, the last of the three survivors from the sinking of the battlecruiser *Hood* in 1941, died aged 85.

See 24 May 1941.

6 October

1719 Capitulation of Vigo to a combined force under Vice-Admiral James Mighells and Col Viscount Cobham (*Ipswich*). Ships: *Bideford, Enterprize, Ipswich, Kinsale, Speedwell.*

1762 Capture of Manila by Rear-Admiral Samuel Cornish (*Norfolk*) and Col William Draper. Ships: *America, Elizabeth, Grafton, Lenox, Norfolk, Panther, Weymouth.* 50s and smaller: *Argo, Falmouth, Seaford, Seahorse, Southsea Castle* storeship.

1769 Lt James Cook in the bark *Endeavour* first sighted New Zealand. Cook first stepped ashore on 9 October and encountered the formidable Maoris. Young Nick's Head on Poverty Bay on the E. coast of North Island honours the surgeon's boy who made the first sighting. Statues of Cook and Nicholas Young stand on Waikanae beach near the present city of Gisborne on the N. edge of the bay (38.39S, 178.01E). Cook returned to New Zealand in 1773 with *Resolution* and *Adventure*, and in 1777 with *Resolution* and *Discovery*.

See 7 October 1969.

1779 *Quebec* blew up in action with the French *Surveillante* 45 miles N. of Ushant. *Rambler* fought the French *Expedition* in the same area.

1810 Boats of *Pallas* captured two Danish privateers 30 miles S.W. of Stavanger.

1901 Queen Alexandra became Patron of the Naval Nursing Service, which was renamed Queen Alexandra's Royal Naval Nursing Service.

1914 Submarine E 9 sank the German S-116 off the Western Ems (53.42N, 06.09E).

Issuing soap and tobacco to ratings in the 1890s. (*NMRN*)

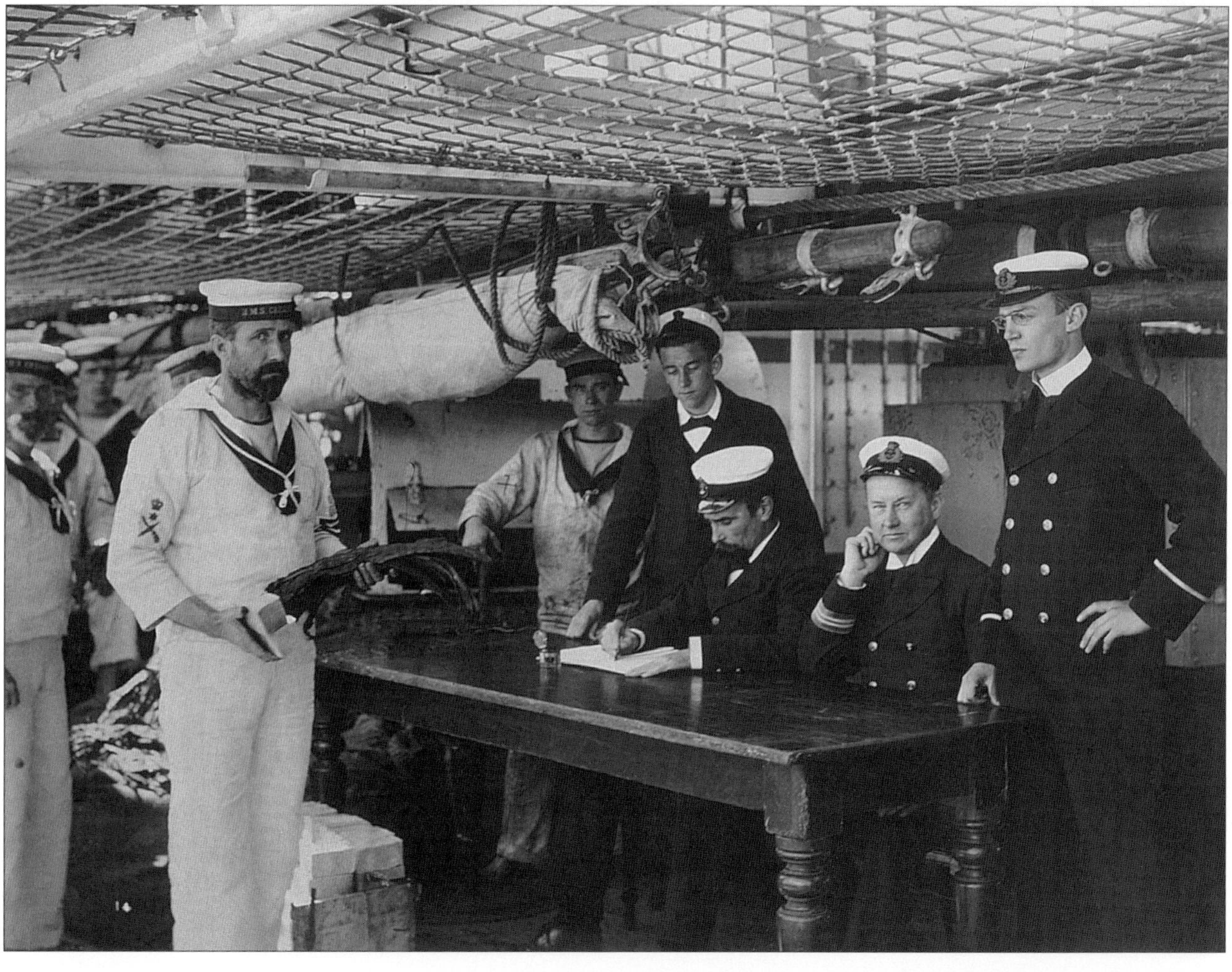

1915 *Brighton Queen*, paddle minesweeper, mined off Nieuport, Belgium.

1946 The light cruiser *Nigeria*, Capt W.J.C. Robertson DSC, RN, wearing the flag of Vice-Admiral Sir Clement Moody KCB, C-in-C South Atlantic, paid her first visit to Nigeria. During an official dinner at Lagos, Admiral Moody was presented with 'a small but exceedingly vicious crocodile, a gift which he was loath to accept and which his Flag-Lieutenant was equally loath to take charge of!' – *Naval Review*.

See 29 August 1957, 1 October 2010.

1949 Admiralty Constabulary formed.

See 1 October 1860, 3 December 1860, 22 April 1861, 13 August 1934.

On 20 May 1834 the Admiralty's 'Porters, Rounders, Warders and Watchmen', established by Pepys, were replaced by Their Lordships' Special Constabulary. As their detection rate averaged nineteen in five years, and their Head Constable having reason to believe that some owned beer houses, but not in their own name, they were abolished in 1860. They were replaced by the Metropolitan Police, which maintained the security of the Royal Dockyards until 1922, when the Geddes Committee recommended the substitution of a Royal Marine Police force, administered by the Adjutant General through the three Home Ports. It acquired its own Special Reserve and then an experimental Admiralty Civil Force, all three elements by 1945 under the same Chief Constable. On 6 October 1949 the three were amalgamated into an Admiralty Constabulary and, on 10 October 1971, that merged with the Army and RAF forces into a single MOD Police Force.

1959 Provisional commissioning programme for HM ships during October 1959:

Scorpion (destroyer) 6 October for trials; *Albion* (carrier) at Portsmouth for General Service Commission Home/East of Suez; *Chichester* (frigate) at Chatham 6 October for General Service Commission Mediterranean/Home; *Cardigan Bay* (frigate) at Singapore for Foreign Service/Far East; *Cavendish* (destroyer) at Devonport for trials; *Messina* (Landing Ship Tank) at Chatham for Foreign Service; *St James* (destroyer) at Devonport at end October for trials.

1961 The 140-year-old link between the Royal Navy and Admiralty House in Valletta was broken when the C-in-C Mediterranean Fleet, Admiral Sir Deric Holland-Martin, and his family, moved to their new official residence, the Villa Portelli in Kalkara, on the other side of Grand Harbour. The house, built between 1761 and 1763, was leased to the RN on 1 January 1821.

2003 Admiral Sir Michael Livesay died aged 67. First captain of *Invincible* 1980–2; Second Sea Lord 1991–3.

See 11 July 1980, 3 August 2005.

7 OCTOBER

1747 *Dartmouth* blew up in action with the Spanish *Glorioso* 20 miles W. by N. of Cape St Vincent. The *King George* and *Prince Frederick* privateers also engaged *Glorioso*.

1760 Boats of Rear-Admiral Charles Steven's squadron cut out the French *Hermione* and *Baleine* at Pondicherry.

1775 Capt Shuldam urged the Board to install coppers for the distillation of fresh water from salt, and a fresh-water sweetener, based on aeration.

1795 *Censeur* and fifteen sail of a convoy taken by the superior squadron of Capt Joseph de Richery (*Jupiter*) 150 miles W. by N. of Cape St Vincent. *Bedford*, *Fortitude* and thirty-two others of the convoy escaped.

1809 'I have always found that kind language and strong ships have a very powerful effect in conciliating people' – Vice-Admiral Lord Collingwood, *Ville de Paris*, off Minorca.

1853 The Keyham Steam Yard at Devonport inaugurated when the first rate *Queen* (110) moved from No. 2 Basin into No. 7 Dock.

See 12 September 1846.

1870 *Aigle* sunk in trials which led to the adoption of the Whitehead torpedo by the RN.

1930 Destroyers *Tempest* and *Tribune* to Boulogne to pay tribute to the crew of airship R 101 lost at Beauvais on her maiden flight.

1943 Submarine *Unruly* attacked with gunfire a German convoy of six landing craft, one

42 Cdo Royal Marines in Afghanistan. (*RN*)

The Loss of the Battleship HMS *Royal Oak*

HMS *Royal Oak*, one of only eleven operational RN capital ships (Barnett, p.71), was the first British battleship sunk in the Second World War and the first ever sunk at anchor by enemy attack. Admiral Blagrove, commanding the 2nd Battle Squadron, was the first of three RN flag officers killed in action in the Second World War (Blagrove and Phillips, the two lost in battleships, had been in the same promotion to captain batch on 30 June 1927). The defences of Scapa Flow, neglected between the wars, were incomplete and Prien, in 'a magnificent feat of arms and navigation' (Brown) and 'with nerve and determination' (Roskill, p.74), entered through Kirk Sound on the surface on a flood tide at night. His first torpedoes hit the battleship on the starboard bow. Having reloaded his tubes, the next salvo hit the *Royal Oak* in A and B shell rooms and the forward boiler room. She rolled over and sank thirteen minutes later. The blockship intended for Kirk Sound arrived the following day. The sinking of a British battleship in the Royal Navy's main home base was a serious psychological blow and the C-in-C Home Fleet, Admiral Sir Charles Forbes, had to divert his ships to Loch Ewe, the Clyde, Rosyth and other northern anchorages from which they did not return until March 1940. The action was a huge propaganda coup for Germany, fully exploited when U-47 returned to Wilhelmshaven on 17 October. The Maharaja of Gondal sent a lakh of rupees (£7,500) for dependents, distributed £250 for officers' dependents, £7,200 for those of ratings including Maltese, £50 for NAAFI personnel. The First Lord sent a message of thanks.

See 30 June 1927, 14 October 1939, 24 May 1941, 10 December 1941, 27 March 1943, 14 October 1948.

ammunition ship and one trawler, which was later destroyed by *Faulknor*, *Fury*, *Penelope* and *Sirius* off Stampalia.

1943 Blue action working dress, No. 8s, approved.

1944 Destroyers *Termagant* and *Tuscan* sank the German TA-37 (ex-Italian TB *Gladio*) off Skiathos in Gulf of Salonika (39.49N, 23.17E).

1951 First Commodore RFA, Capt S.G. Kent, hoisted his broad pennant in RFA *Fort Dunvegan* at Rosyth. Admiral Sir Philip Vian, C-in-C Home Fleet, present.

See 8 January 1960.

1953 Admiral of the Fleet Sir Rhoderick McGrigor, First Sea Lord, unveiled the Royal Naval Patrol Service memorial at Lowestoft.

1969 The destroyer *London*, wearing the flag of Rear-Admiral T.T. Lewin, FO Second-in-Command Far East Fleet, with frigate *Argonaut* and tanker RFA *Tidereach*, arrived at Gisborne, New Zealand, for the Captain Cook bicentenary celebrations. Cook made the first landing in New Zealand at Poverty Bay, where Gisborne now stands, on 9 October 1769.

See 6 October 1769, 8 May 1956.

1980 Armilla Patrol instituted in the Arabian Gulf. *Coventry*, Type 42 destroyer, was first ship deployed.

2001 RN SSNs launched TLAMs at Taleban and al-Qaeda locations inside Afghanistan.

See 22 September 2001, 18 March 2002.

2006 3 Cdo Bde, Brig Jeremy Thomas, deployed to S. Afghanistan, relieving sixteen Air Assault Brigade in Helmand Province. 42 Cdo and elements of the UK Landing Force Command Support Group were engaged in constant, high intensity conflict. 42 Cdo deployed to the N. of the Province as the UK Battle Group and relieved 3 PARA in Musa Qala, Gereshk and Kandahar. 29 Cdo Regt RA provided light gun support and fire support teams to direct the offensive air support. 59 Cdo RE, as part of 28 Eng Regt, supported the Task Force with battlefield engineering. 45 Cdo provided two companies in infantry roles but was mainly employed as Operational Liaison and Mentoring Teams alongside the Afghanistan National Army. Operation Herrick 5.

See 11 April 2007, 8 April 2008.

8 October

1667 Capture of Surinam by Rear-Admiral Sir John Harman (*Lion*). Ships: *Bonaventure, Lion, Portsmouth* ketch.

1702 Courts martial began on board *Breda* (70) in Port Royal Harbour, Jamaica, of captains Richard Kirby (*Defiance*), Cooper Wade (*Greenwich*) and John Constable (*Windsor*) for cowardice, disobedience and neglect of duty in Benbow's action against the French off Cape Santa Marta the previous August. Kirby and Wade sentenced to death, Constable acquitted of cowardice but cashiered and imprisoned. Capt Hudson (*Pendennis*) would have been tried but died at Port Royal on 25 September.

See 19 August 1702, 4 November 1702, 16 April 1703.

1746 *Weazle* captured the French privateers *Jeantie* and *Fortune* off the Isle of Wight.

1747 *Russell* captured the Spanish *Glorioso* off Cape St Vincent.

1806 Rocket attack on Boulogne by RN. First rocket bombardment.

1808 *Modeste* captured the French *Iena* in the Bay of Bengal.

1884 *Rodney* launched at Chatham. Fifth of the name and the last battleship built with a figurehead.

1914 The second RN air attack from Antwerp on airship sheds at Düsseldorf and Cologne; Sqn Cdr D.A.S. Grey and Ft-Lt R.L.G. Marix, flying Sopwith Tabloids. Grey failed to find the target at Cologne due to fog and, under heavy rifle and shell fire, bombed the main railway station. Marix blew up the airship shed at Düsseldorf with the new rigid airship

Wrens serving in HMS *Brilliant*. See 8 October 1990. (*RN*)

The escort carrier HMS *Puncher* in the Pacific in April 1945. (*Cdr David Hobbs RN*)

Z9, the first Zeppelin destroyed by a British aircraft. He ran out of petrol on the way back and returned to base on a borrowed bicycle. The base at Antwerp was overrun by the Germans that night and the naval crews destroyed their aircraft before withdrawing.

See 22 September 1914, 21 November 1914, 25 December 1914.

1939 U-12 sunk by mine in Dover Strait.

1942 *Active* sank U-179 off Cape Town.

1943 Liberator R/86 sank U-419, Liberators Z/86 and T/120 sank U-643 and Sunderland J/423 (RCAF) sank U-610 in N. Atlantic. Convoy SC 143. *Orkan* (Pol) sunk by U-378 with a homing torpedo S.W. of Iceland (56.30N, 26.25W).

1943 Submarine *Unruly* sank the German *Bulgaria* (ex-*Bulgarian*) in Aegean.

1944 Minesweeper *Mulgrave* (RCN) mined in Channel: CTL.

1948 King George VI, Colonel-in-Chief of the Royal Marines became Captain-General by Order in Council, reflecting the size of the Corps in relation to regiments of which he was also Colonel-in-Chief.

1990 Wrens joined frigate *Brilliant*, the first RN ship to carry women as members of the ship's company.

See 14 January 1991.

1998 Admiral Sir Jock Slater completed his appointment as First Sea Lord and remained on the Active List.

See 10 July 1995.

2007 40 Cdo RM, commanded by Lt-Col Stuart Birrell, took over as Battle Group North in Helmand Province, Afghanisation, from the 1st Bn Royal Anglian Regiment on a six-month operational tour. They covered the Upper Sangin and Gereshk valley areas as far north along the Helmand River as the Kajaki Dam. As well as providing security and support for reconstruction and development to aid the Afghan government they were involved in some deliberate operations including the taking of Musa Qala in December 2007. Operation Herrick 7.

See 7 October 2006, 11 April 2007, 9 February 2008, 8 April 2008.

9 October

1799 Frigate *Lutine*, bound for the Texel from Yarmouth, wrecked off Holland. Bell recovered and now in use at Lloyd's.

1805 Vice-Admiral Lord Nelson wrote in his Trafalgar Memorandum, now in the British Museum, 'In case Signals can neither be seen or perfectly understood, no Captain can do very wrong if he places his Ship alongside that of an Enemy'.

1810 *Rhin* captured the French privateer *Contesse de Montalevet* 90 miles W.S.W. of the Scilly Isles.

1812 *Briseis* (escorting a convoy) captured the French privateer *Petit Poucet* in Hano Sund.

1813 *Thunder* captured the French privateer *Neptune* off the Owers.

1834 Admiral Lord Saumarez died.

1852 Capture of Prome by a combined force under Maj-Gen. Henry Godwin and Cdre George Lambert (*Fox*). *Fire Queen* (Ben. Mar.) and boats of *Fox*, *Hastings*, *Sphinx* and *Winchester*.

1862 VC: AB George Hinckley (*Sphinx*) for twice covering 150yd of ground under enemy fire to rescue wounded men. British and French landing parties, assisted by Chinese troops, repulsed the Taiping rebels and captured the city of Fung Wha, above Ningpo. Ships: *Hardy*, *Flamer*; *Déroulède* and *Confucius* (Fr) and seamen and marines of *Encounter* and *Sphinx*.

1903 Basins, plates and cutlery introduced for seamen and a superior scale of issues for chief petty officers.

1914 The RNVR Anti-Aircraft Corps established to provide AA defence of London. Stood-to until demobilised at Redhill 15 February 1919. The Cabinet decided on 3 September 1914 that the Admiralty was to undertake the air defence of the country, as the Army had neither personnel nor guns. Various other RNVR units created for AA duties around the country. First rating signed up 13 November.

1917 AMC *Champagne*, the former P&O liner *Oropesa*, temporarily flying the French flag

Petty Officers' mess on the battleship HMS *Jupiter* (1895). A space shared with a 6-in breech-loading gun. (*NMRN*)

FAA centenary flypast at RNAS Yeovilton 2009. (*RN*)

but with a British crew, torpedoed three times by U-96 S.W. of Isle of Man (54.17N, 05.10W), when steaming north from Liverpool to rejoin the Northern Patrol; ship broke-up after third torpedo hit and sank with loss of fifty-six officers and men.

1939 Light cruiser *Belfast* captured the German *Cap Norte* N.W. of the Faroes. Taken into the Service as *Empire Trooper*.

1943 Destroyer *Panther* sunk by German aircraft in the Scarpanto Channel (35.43N, 27.36E). Light cruiser *Carlisle* damaged beyond repair and, though towed to Alexandria, was CTL.

1948 Ships of the Home Fleet arrived in the West Indies. Battleship *Duke of York*, flag of Admiral Sir Rhoderick McGrigor, firstly visited Bridgetown, Barbados; Second Cruiser Squadron, Rear-Admiral Hon. Guy Russell, visited Port of Spain, Trinidad. Viscount Hall, First Lord of the Admiralty, Sir John Lang, Secretary of the Admiralty, and the Naval Secretary, Rear-Admiral P. William-Powlett, took passage in *Duke of York* and returned by air.

See 23 September 1948.

1970 Fleet carrier *Eagle*, Capt I.G.W. Roberston RN, grounded when entering Plymouth Sound. The relocation of the Ash navigation buoy off West Hoe 145ft from its charted position had not been promulgated. Courts martial at Plymouth 30 and 31 October, 2, 4, 5 and 6 November. NO Severe Reprimand; CO and AQHM Reprimand. The position of buoys at Plymouth were raised in the *Ark Royal* CMs in 1963.

See 16 January 1962.

1994 Armilla Patrol deployed to northern Gulf to deter new Iraqi threat to Kuwait. Operation Driver. Ships reverted to Operation Armilla 15 November. Frigate *Cornwall*, destroyers *Cardiff* and *Liverpool*, RFA *Bayleaf*, 45 Cdo.

2009 Religious service to mark a century of British naval aviation and to honour the 6,749 RNAS and FAA personnel killed in the Service in this period held in St Bartholomew's, the FAA Memorial church at Yeovilton. A plaque was dedicated to the four naval aviator VCs.

See 11 September 2009, 10 December 2009.

10 October

1707 *Cumberland*, *Chester* and *Ruby* (escorting a convoy) taken by the French squadrons of Cdre Comte de Forbin (*Mars*) and Capt Rene Duguay-Trouin (*Lys*). *Devonshire* sank, her colours flying, in action S.W. of Dodman Point. Only *Royal Oak* survived but most of the convoy escaped.

1748 *Chesterfield* (40), at anchor off Cape Coast Castle, Western Africa, taken by mutineers led by the First Lieutenant, Lt Samuel Couchman, (who was almost certainly drunk), the Lieutenant of Marines, John Morgan and thirty others. One of the very few officer-led mutinies (that in the *Bounty* was the most celebrated). Her Captain, Capt O'Brien Dudley, was ashore with other ship's officers (who included a newly promoted third lieutenant, Charles Middleton, who was First Lord of the Admiralty as Lord Barham fifty-seven years later during the Trafalgar campaign). The Boatswain, Roger Gastril, retook the *Chesterfield* in English Harbour in the West Indies on 7 March 1749 and 'brought the men back to their duty'. Couchman and Morgan were confined and on their return to Portsmouth in June 1749 were court martialled and sentenced to death.

See 14 July 1749, 28 April 1789.

1806 Boats of *Galatea* cut out four Spanish schooners at Barcelona, Venezuela.

1814 Boat of *Endymion* attempted to take the American privateer *Prince de Neufchatel* off Nantucket.

1865 Suppression of Jamaican rebellion. *Wolverine*, *Onyx* and *Nettle*.

1878 *Vulture* captured twenty pirate dhows near Ras Tinnorah, Persian Gulf.

1887 The new Bramble-class composite gunboat *Wasp*, Lt and Cdr B.J.H. Adamson RN, which left Sheerness on 21 May 1887 for passage to Shanghai to join the China Station, was lost without trace between Singapore and Hong Kong. She was believed to have foundered on 10 October with the loss of all seventy-three men. Two gunboats named 'Wasp' lost in three years.

See 22 September 1884.

1891 Second, illustrated edition of the Uniform Regulations.

Major changes – full dress coat lost gold lace from skirts, cocked hat centralised instead of athwart, and undress coat became ball dress. Monkey jacket confirmed as normal day dress. Flag Officers' buttons reduced in size. White and blue dress and undress waistcoats introduced. Dress boat cloak, brown gloves and black gaiters, too.

1917 GC (ex-AM): Mate Alfred William Newman of the destroyer *Tetrarch* for disposing of burning ammunition – *London Gazette*, 1 March 1918. Cdr A.W. Newman RN was the longest-lived holder of the GC when he died aged 96 years 4 months on 1 September 1984.

1918 Wren Josephine Carr, one of 480 souls lost in the steam packet *Leinster*, torpedoed off east coast of Ireland en route from Kingstown to Holyhead. The first Wren to die on active service.

1938 Rear-Admiral Bertram Ramsay placed on the Retired List having been unemployed since being relieved as COS to C-in-C Home Fleet.

See 17 December 1935, 2 January 1945.

1940 Sir Max Horton, Vice-Admiral (Submarines), declined the appointment of C-in-C Home Fleet due mainly to concerns about Admiralty interference in operations and also reservations about command and control of maritime air assets.

1942 41 RM Cdo formed at Pembroke Dock from 8th Bn RM. Disbanded at Llwyngwrill 20 February 1946. Reformed at Bickleigh 16 August 1950 and at Plymouth as 41(Independent) Cdo RM for service in Korea. Disbanded 22 February 1952 at Plymouth and reformed 31 March 1960 at Bickleigh as 41 Cdo RM. Disbanded at Deal April 1981.

1943 Submarine *Trooper*, Lt J.S. Wraith, lost on or about this date off Leros, Aegean. Probably mined.

One of the eight dress styles for officers in the 1891 uniform regulations. They ranged from No. 1 'Full Dress' for the most formal, occasions (as shown) to No. 8 'White Undress' for hot climates. (*NMRN Lib.*)

1946 Torpedo and Anti-Submarine (TAS) Branch formed: Torpedo Branch passed electrical responsibilities to the recently formed Electrical Branch and amalgamated with the Anti-Submarine Branch, formerly based at *Osprey*, Portland, to form the new TAS Branch based at *Vernon*.

1957 Coastal minesweeper *Gavinton* was towed at 5 knots for 2 miles by a Whirlwind helicopter piloted by Lt-Cdr G.G.R. Miller from 705 NAS Special Trials Flight from RNAS Lee-on-Solent 'in a remarkable experiment' in Sandown Bay.

1969 'It has been decided that officers and ratings of the WRNS will, in future, be permitted to carry and use umbrellas when in uniform except on ceremonial occasions . . . must be black, with plain handles, short or telescopic, but not walking stick type.' – DCI(RN) 1298/69.

1980 Employment of WRNS officers as Officers of the Day. 'It is the Admiralty Board's policy that WRNS officers should be employed in a progressively widening range of appointments and duties. In furtherance of this policy the Board have decided that WRNS officers may, at the discretion of their commanding officers, be employed as duty officers. It must be emphasized that the training and experience of some WRNS officers is relatively narrow and that all WRNS officers will require support in certain aspects of their new duties. In allocating these duties commanding officers will naturally need to exercise care to avoid situations which could cause a real risk of embarrassment or difficulty.' – DCI(RN) 650/80.

1997 Defence Secretary George Robertson announced that HMY *Britannia* would not be replaced or 'rebuilt'. 'We in the MOD have to justify every penny of the taxpayers' money that we spend and in this case I could not do so.' – MOD press release 130/97.

See 20 October 1997.

11 October

1399 HM Henry IV founded the Order of the Bath, re-established by George I in 1725. Its red ribbon the ambition of many a naval officer and preferred by some to a baronetcy. Extended in 1815 to the derision of St Vincent, who nevertheless took perverse pleasure in wearing his new Grand Cross about the place.

1746 *Nottingham* captured the French *Mars* 70 miles S.W. of Cape Clear, after a gallant defence by an ailing crew.

1776 First battle of Lake Champlain. The British Lake Flotilla fought the American Lake Flotilla.

See 13 October 1776, 11 September 1814.

1780 Windward Islands in West Indies struck by second Great October Hurricane. Rodney was off the American east coast with *Sandwich* and his 74s and escaped, but Hotham's squadron at St Lucia suffered greatly. Ships lost: *Blanche* (36), fifth rate, last seen off Antigua; *Andromeda* (28), sixth rate, foundered off Martinique; *Laurel* (26), sixth rate, wrecked on Martinique; *Beaver's Prize* (16), ship sloop, wrecked on St Lucia; and *Endeavour* (14), sloop, wrecked on Jamaica. Two further ships, lying in Gros Islet Bay, St Lucia, were also lost: *Chamelion* (14), ship sloop, lost with all hands when her cables parted, and *Deal Castle* (20), sixth rate, which was blown out of the bay and wrecked on Puerto Rico on 15 October.

See 4 October 1780, 5 October 1780.

1782 Relief of Gibraltar by Lord Howe. The transformed signalling system of Rear-Admiral Kempenfelt was used with great effect.

See 12 December 1781.

1797 Battle of Camperdown. Admiral Adam Duncan (*Venerable*) defeated the Dutch fleet under Vice-Admiral Jan de Winter (*Vrijheid*). Ships: *Adamant, Agincourt, Ardent, Bedford, Belliqueux, Director, Isis, Lancaster, Monarch, Monmouth*

Admiral Adam, Viscount Duncan (1731–1804)

Duncan entered the Navy at the age of 15 in 1745, was promoted lieutenant in 1755 and commander in 1759. He was made post in 1761 and commanded the *Valiant* (74) under Keppel at Belleisle and Havana. He commanded the *Monarch* at St Vincent in 1780. He was promoted admiral in 1795 and placed in command of the North Sea Squadron. In 1797, while Duncan was responsible for blockading the Dutch Fleet, the mutiny broke out at The Nore among his fleet. With only the *Venerable, Adamant*, and the frigate *Circe*, Duncan continued the blockade by making signals to the frigate on the horizon who pretended to pass them on to a fleet below the horizon: 'If I sink in the Channel my flag will still be flying.' When the mutiny had been quelled, it says much for Duncan's brilliance as an admiral that he was able to take his fleet out and inflict the crushing defeat on the Dutch at Camperdown which restored the morale of his fleet. He held an incipient mutineer over the side at arm's length, asking who commanded – him, or the mutineers – and after Camperdown declined a surrendered sword, observing that he would much prefer to take a brave man's hand. Nelson declared 'the name of Duncan will never be forgot by Britain and in particular by the Navy'. One of the new Type 45 destroyers is to be named *Duncan*.

Admiral Adam, Viscount Duncan (1731–1804). He was awarded a pension of £2,000 a year after the Battle of Camperdown. (*NMRN 1984/368*)

HMS *Duncan*, Type 45 Destroyer, launched by Mrs Marie Ibbotson at BAE Systems on the Clyde on 11 October 2010, the 213th anniversary of Duncan's victory at Camperdown in 1797. (*RN*)

Montagu, Powerful, Russell, Triumph, Venerable, Veteran. Frigates: *Active, Beaulieu, Circe, Diligence, King George, Martin, Rose, Speculator*. Battle Honour: Camperdown 1797.

1805 Civilian day replaced the nautical, noon-to-noon convention for keeping logs, by Order in Council.

1811 *Imperieuse* captured two French gunboats, sank a third and destroyed a fort at Positano, west coast of Italy.

1854 *Beagle* and *Firebrand* rescued an Austrian storeship which had run ashore under the Russian batteries near Sevastopol.

1855 VC: Cdr John Edmund Commerell and William Thomas Rickard, quartermaster (*Weser*). Destruction of Russian stores up the Salgir River, Sea of Azov, by landing party from *Weser*.

1914 *Nusa* captured the German *Komet* near Talassia, New Britain. Added to RAN as *Una*.

1940 MTBs 22, 31 and 32 sank two German trawlers off Calais (51.02N, 01.48E).

1940 Battleship *Revenge*, seven destroyers and six MTBs bombarded Cherbourg. Covering force: cruisers *Cardiff, Emerald, Newcastle* and six destroyers. Operation Medium.

1943 Minesweeper *Hythe* sunk by U-371 off Bougie, Algeria (37.04N, 05.00E).

1944 Four MGBs of 57 Flotilla destroyed two German coastal convoys off Vir in Adriatic.

1954 Hurricane Hazel, a weather system of exceptional strength, devastated Haiti before causing widespread damage in North America. The surveying ship *Vidal*, at anchor at Georgetown, Grand Cayman, sailed for Jamaica to embark emergency supplies and a detachment of troops which were taken to Haiti; she cruised along the stricken west coast landing food and providing medical assistance.

See 19 February 2010.

1960 Submarine depot ship HMS *Forth* returned to Devonport from Malta after thirteen years' service in the Mediterranean.

See 11 November 1961.

1967 Whitehall Wireless, the RN's worldwide communications centre in the Old Admiralty Building, newly computerised at a cost of £1 million and re-opened by the Navy minister, Maurice Foley MP.

1982 *Mary Rose* raised to surface of the Solent, 437 years after sinking.

See 19 July 1545, 19 July 1984.

1995 *Ocean* launched at Govan. At 21,578 tons, the biggest warship built for RN since launch of *Ark Royal* on 3 May 1950.

See 5 July 1898, 8 July 1944, 20 February 1998, 30 September 1998.

2010 *Duncan*, the sixth of the Type 45 destroyers, launched at BAE Systems at Govan on the Clyde by Mrs Marie Ibbotson, wife of Vice-Admiral Richard Ibbotson, Deputy C-in-C Fleet. This was the 213th anniversary of Duncan's victory at Camperdown in 1797.

See 1 February 2006, 23 and 27 November 2007, 17 November 2008, 21 October 2009.

12 OCTOBER

1702 Admiral Sir George Rooke (*Somerset*) and the Dutch Vice-Admiral Gerard Callenburgh (*Hollandia*) destroyed the French fleet and treasure-ships under Vice-Admiral Comte de Chateaurenault (*Fort*) in Vigo Bay. Rooke's usual flagship was the *Royal Sovereign*, which was not engaged. All seventeen French warships and seventeen Spanish treasure-ships taken or sunk.
Battle Honour: Vigo 1702.

Ships: *Association, Barfleur, Bedford, Berwick, Cambridge, Essex, Grafton, Kent, Mary, Monmouth, Northumberland, Orford, Pembroke, Ranelagh, Somerset, Swiftsure, Torbay*. Fireships: *Griffin, Hawk, Hunter, Lightning, Phoenix, Terrible, Vulture*. Dutch ships: *Alkmaar, Dordrecht, Gouda, Hollandia, Katwijk, Muyde, Reigersbergh, Unie, Zeluwe, Zeven Provincien* and three fireships.

1794 Lord Hood quitted the Mediterranean Command on grounds of ill health and his younger brother, Viscount Bridport, succeeded to that of the Channel Fleet. 'The priority of the Mediterranean was lost' – Parkinson, *Britannia Rules*, p.18.

1798 Cdre Sir John Borlase Warren (*Canada*) defeated Cdre Jean Bompard (*Hoche*) 15 miles N.N.E. of the Rosses, Donegal Bay, taking four prizes and thus reducing threat of French aid to Irish rebellion.
Ships: *Canada, Foudroyant, Robust*. Frigates: *Amelia, Anson, Ethalion, Magnanime, Melampus*. Captured: *Bellone, Coquille, Embuscade, Hoche*.
Battle Honour: Donegal 1798.

1800 Boats of *Montagu* and *Magnificent* cut out a convoy at Port Danenne, Lorient.

TS *Foudroyant* (ex-*Trincomalee* (1817)). (*NMRN*)

1803 First four of ten Trinity House volunteer artillery vessels manned. Paid off after Trafalgar.

1817 Frigate *Trincomalee* (46), built of Malabar teak, launched at Bombay. Sold May 1897 and, as TS *Foudroyant*, was youth training ship at Portsmouth. July 1987 taken on a heavy-lift barge to Hartlepool for restoration and now preserved there. The oldest British warship afloat.

1847 Tea and sugar available free in lieu of grog.

1857 Second party of *Pearl*'s Naval Brigade (Lt S.W.D. Radcliffe) left the ship.
See 12 September 1857.

1868 *Inconstant* launched at Pembroke Dockyard. With *Shah* (Portsmouth 1873) and *Raleigh* (Chatham 1873) the last British warships officially termed 'frigates' until the type name revived for anti-submarine convoy escorts in the Second World War.

1897 *Canopus* launched. First battleship with water-tube boilers. Fitted with Krupp armour. Grounded as coast defence ship at Port Stanley 1914. Her solid shot, loaded in secret anticipation of a competitive gun drill, was a ricochet, the first hit on von Spee's squadron.

1940 Operation Sealion, the planned German invasion of Britain, postponed until spring 1941. 'Had Hitler been able to dominate the English Channel – be it only for twenty-four hours – he might have succeeded. But like Napoleon before him, he was never in a position to do so' – Vice-Admiral Friedrich Ruge.

1940 *Ajax*, the first radar-equipped cruiser in the Mediterranean Fleet, sank the Italian TBs *Airone* and *Ariel* in central Mediterranean (35.37N, 16.42E), in a night action and damaged the Italian destroyer *Artigliere* which surrendered to *York* before being scuttled (36.30N, 16.07E).

1941 Destroyers *Norman* and *Anthony* arrived in N. Russia with a TUC delegation, 'an exercise in liaison which was intended to spur factory output throughout Britain's industrial heartland and to improve relations with the Russian authorities' – Capt Richard Woodman, *Arctic Convoys 1941–1945*, p.43. The ships returned to Scapa Flow 2 November.

1942 Liberator H/120 sank U-597 in N. Atlantic (56.50N, 28.05W). Convoy ONS 136.

1944 Destroyer *Loyal* seriously damaged by an acoustic mine in Tyrrhenian Sea. CTL.

1955 Reciprocal RN and Soviet warship visits. Cadet training ship *Triumph*, Capt V.C. Begg RN, flag of Admiral Sir Michael Denny, C-in-C Home Fleet, minelayer *Apollo* and destroyers *Decoy*, *Diana*, *Chieftain* and *Cheviot*, arrived at Leningrad (St Petersburg) for a five-day visit. At Portsmouth the C-in-C Portsmouth, Admiral of the Fleet Sir George Creasy, greeted the large light cruisers *Sverdlov* and *Aleksandr Suvarov* with four destroyers. The next *Sverdlov* visit to Portsmouth was less successful.
See 19 April 1956.

1956 Senior Commissioned Boatswain George Wookey RN, later Lt RN, diving from *Reclaim*, set a world deep-diving record of 600ft in Sorfjord, Norway, for a diver wearing standard flexible dress. Previous world record made by PO William Pollard who reached 535ft in Loch Fyne in 1948.
See 20 July 1970.

2000 USS *Cole*, an Arleigh Burke-class destroyer, attacked and severely damaged by maritime terrorists at Aden; seventeen killed and forty-two injured. Henceforth, AT/FP to be a major concern for naval forces, especially in the Middle East.

2005 MCMVs *Ledbury* and *Middleton* carried out 'the final deployment of sweep gear by the Royal Navy' in exercises off the Isle of Wight.

13 OCTOBER

1665 *Merlin*, escorting a convoy in second Dutch war, taken by the Dutch *Karel*, S. of Cadiz. Three of the convoy were also taken by four other Dutch ships.

1776 The British Lake Flotilla defeated the American Lake Flotilla on Lake Champlain. Ships and vessels: *Carleton, Inflexible, Loyal Convert, Maria, Thunderer.* Troops: Royal Artillery. American possession had held up Army operations and contributed to the surrender of Burgoyne and to French intervention.
Battle Honour: Lake Champlain 1776.

1796 *Terpsichore* captured the Spanish *Mahonesa* midway between Cartagena and Cape de Gata, despite a sickly crew and the need to break off the action to repair damage.
Battle Honour: *Mahonesa* 1796.

1797 Lt Joseph Brodie of the *Rose* cutter arrived at the Admiralty at 0400 having landed at Ramsgate with Duncan's dispatches reporting the victory over the Dutch fleet at Camperdown. He was promoted commander 3 January 1798 as Duncan intended.
See 11 October 1797, 6 November 1805.

1804 *Thetis, Ceres* and *Penelope* letters of marque fought the French privateer *Bonaparte* 105 miles E. of Barbados.

1805 *Jason* captured the French *Naiade* 350 miles E. of St Lucia.

1813 *Telegraph* destroyed the French *Flibustier* 3 miles off the mouth of the River Adour.

1841 Occupation of Ningpo by Rear-Admiral Sir William Parker (*Modeste*) and Lt-Gen. Sir Hugh Gough. Seamen and marines were landed. Ships: *Modeste*; *Nemesis, Phlegethon* (Ben. Mar.). Boats of *Blenheim* and *Wellesley*. Troops: Royal Artillery, 18th, 49th and 55th (light coy), Madras Artillery, Madras Sappers and Miners, 36th Madras Native Infantry.

1850 Contract approved for new pattern of black hat, first normally to bear ship's name.

1864 Ironclad battleship *Lord Clyde* launched at Pembroke Dockyard. With her sister ship *Lord Warden*, launched at Chatham 27 May 1865, they were the last true broadside ironclads and 'the largest, and under steam the fastest, timber-hulled ships ever launched from British shores for purposes of either war or peace; a record which is safe now to stand in their names for ever' – Ballard, *The Black Battlefleet*, p.76.

1895 George Elvey Creasy, future admiral of the fleet, born at Badulla, Ceylon.
See 31 October 1972.

1899 Death of Vice-Admiral Philip Colomb. Naval strategist and historian. His long letters to *The Times* gave Jackie Fisher cause to waspishly label him 'Column and a half' – Marder, *The Anatomy of Sea Power*, p.47.

'The work of Philip Howard Colomb and that of his brother John, on whose foundation he built, advanced the cause of naval history as an academic endeavour, strengthened the position of the Royal Navy at a time of uncertainty and, Lord Fisher's thoughtless disdain notwithstanding, laid the groundwork for the defence of the reforming work at the Admiralty in the next pulsating decade of naval growth' – Schurman, *The Education of a Navy*, pp.58–9.
See 27 May 1909.

1910 Rank of Skipper RNR established – a rare example of joint action by Fisher and Beresford.

1913 Flag of Admiral Sir George F. King-Hall, C-in-C Australian Station, struck in the light cruiser HMS *Cambrian* at Melbourne and that of Rear-Admiral Sir George Patey hoisted in the new battlecruiser HMAS *Australia*. The first Australian-born officer to command the Station.
See 4 October 1913.

1914 *Magdeburg* code books reached the Admiralty, which may have contributed to a successful sweep off the Texel on 17 October, which in turn certainly helped to bring

The ironclad battleship *Lord Clyde* launched at Pembroke Dockyard on 13 October 1864. (*Author*)

about the Miraculous Draught of Fishes on 30 November.

See 20 August 1914.

1922 Supply Branch established by Order in Council, a result of centralisation in storekeeping.

See 13 October 1922, 26 October 1944, 1 February 2004.

1939 U-40 sunk by mine in Dover Strait.

1939 Destroyers *Ilex* and *Imogen* sank U-42 in W. Approaches.

1939 GC (ex-EGM): James Gordon Melville Turner, Radio Officer, MN (SS *Manaar*). (*Gazette* date.)

1940 Destroyers *Ashanti*, *Cossack* (D 4), *Maori* and *Sikh* sank two merchant ships in North Sea. Two more and their escorts escaped.

1940 Air-strike by fifteen Swordfish aircraft of 815 and 819 Sqn (*Illustrious*), with two cruisers and four destroyers, on Port Laki, Leros.

1940 River gunboat *Ladybird* and a Bombay aircraft of 216 Sqn bombarded Sidi Barrani.

1943 *Laforey*, *Lookout* and *Flores* (Neth) bombarded positions north of the Volturno River, Italy, in conjunction with landing of tanks from four LCTs. Operation Avalanche.

1961 The frigate *Leopard*, Cdr P.S. Hicks-Beach RN, arrived at Tristan da Cunha following a volcanic eruption on 10 October which required the evacuation of all 235 inhabitants in the diverted Dutch liner *Tjisadane* to Cape Town in an operation directed by the C-in-C South Atlantic and South America, Vice-Admiral Nicholas Copeman. The islanders were transferred to the liner *Stirling Castle* for passage to Britain where they were accommodated in the former RAF base at Calshot near Southampton.

See 15 October 1961.

1996 *Scott*, the biggest surveying ship ever built for the Royal Navy, launched at Appledore by Mrs Portillo. Vessel ordered to replace *Hecla*. Designed to commercial standards and provides deep bathymetric capability off the Continental Shelf. Her multibeam sonar suite permits mapping of the ocean floor. Full load displacement 13,550 tons. Ship's company of sixty-three divided into three watches, only two of which embarked.

See 3 January 2005.

14 OCTOBER

1726 Charles Middleton born at Leith. Created (Admiral) Lord Barham on taking office as First Lord of the Admiralty in 1805 before the Trafalgar campaign. He was a first-class administrator but was not popular in the Navy.

See 10 October 1748, 17 June 1813.

1747 The second victory in five months for the Western Squadron. Rear-Admiral Edward Hawke in *Devonshire* (66), with fourteen ships of the line, intercepted a major French reinforcement convoy of 230 ships bound from La Rochelle to the West Indies escorted by Rear-Admiral (*Chef d'Escadre*) the Marquis de L'Etanduere in *Tonnant* (80) with seven other warships 200 miles W. of Ushant (47.49N and N. of Cape Finisterre – from which the battle took its name although 350 miles N. of it). Battle Honour: Ushant 1747. The War of the Austrian Succession 1739–48.

See 19 October 1739, 3 May 1747, 21 December 1747, 7 August 1914.

Hawke ordered General Chase and in a running fight of eight hours, with the action flowing up the French line from rear to van, six of the eight French escorting warships were taken; *Tonnant* (80) and *Intrepide* (74) escaped into Brest. Hawke arrived at Portsmouth on 29 October with his six prizes: *Monarque* (74), *Terrible* (74), *Neptune* (70), *Trident* (64), *Fougueux* (64) and *Severne* (50), for which he was made KB and promoted vice-admiral of the Blue the following May. All except *Neptune* were taken into the Royal Navy. In two actions Hawke and Anson (see 3 May 1747) ruined French sea power, and, by intercepting two desperate attempts to reinforce French operations overseas, wrecked French foreign policy in N. America and India.

Ships: *Defiance* (60), *Devonshire* (66), *Eagle* (60), *Edinburgh* (64), *Gloucester* (50), *Kent* (64), *Lion* (60), *Monmouth* (64), *Nottingham* (60), *Portland* (50), *Princess Louisa* (60), *Tilbury* (60), *Weazle* (sloop), *Windsor* (60), *Yarmouth* (64).

1780 The most notorious example of naval nepotism on record. Admiral Rodney, C-in-C in the Leeward Islands, promoted his 15-year-old son, Lt the Hon. John Rodney, to Commander and then Post-Captain on the same day. 'Making every allowance possible for an over-indulgent parent, it was a preposterous thing to do' – David Spinney, Admiral Rodney's biographer. Rodney junior, 'indifferent son of a brilliant if somewhat venal father' (Michael Lewis, *A Social History of the Navy*, pp.211–12), after one year at sea, had risen from Midshipman to Captain between February and October 1780; local promotions at first but all officially confirmed by a grateful government following his father's victory in the Moonlight Battle off Cape St Vincent, 16 January 1780, and the Relief of Gibraltar. John Rodney died in 1847 after holding the rank of Captain for sixty-six years, an all time record for a Royal Navy officer.

See 11 June 1779, 17 October 1797, 9 April 1847, 30 June 1937, 30 June 1955.

1795 *Mermaid* captured the French *Républicaine* 25 miles W. of Grenada.

1798 *Melampus* captured the French *Résolue* in Donegal Bay.

1810 *Briseis* captured the French privateer *Sans-Souci* 50 miles W. by S. of Horns Reef.

HMS *Royal Oak* (1914) with main armament trained to starboard. (*NMRN*)

1859 Eight officers of *Assaye* (Indian Navy) and *Lynx* assisted in the defeat of a rebel force at Zanzibar.

1914 Distinguished Service Medal instituted for petty officers and ratings, RM NCOs and ORs, for acts of bravery in the face of the enemy, not justifying the CGM. It was later extended to MN, Army, WRNS and RAF personnel serving in HM ships in the Second World War. Following the 1993 review of gallantry awards, DSM replaced by the DSC which was extended to all RN personnel.
See 1 June 1901.

1935 Naval Radio Direction Finding development started at HM Signal School, Portsmouth.

1939 Battleship *Royal Oak*, Capt W.G. Benn RN, flag of Rear-Admiral H.E.C. Blagrove, torpedoed and sunk at anchor in the Home Fleet base in Scapa Flow by U-47, Kapitanleutnant Gunther Prien, with the loss of 786 men. (Roskill p.833.)
See panel on 7 October, p.570.

1939 Destroyers *Icarus*, *Inglefield*, *Intrepid* and *Ivanhoe* sank U-45 S.W. of Ireland.

1941 *Fleur-de-Lys*, Flower-class corvette, sunk by U-206 in Gibraltar Strait (36.00N, 06.30W) and broke in half leaving three survivors.

1942 MTB 236 sank the German disguised raider *Komet* (Schiff 45) off Cap de la Hague. An escorting R-boat was also sunk, and two other escorts set on fire. Operation Bowery. Ships: *Albrighton*, *Brocklesby*, *Cottesmore*, *Eskdale*, *Fernie*, *Glaisdale*, *Krakowiak* (Poland), *Quorn*, *Tynedale*. MTBs: 49, 52, 55, 56, 84, 86, 95, 229, 236.

1943 The flag of Vice-Admiral Sir Algernon Willis, Flag Officer Force H, struck and a few days later this famous battle squadron was disbanded.
See 17 October 1943.

1944 Frigate *Magog* (RCN) torpedoed by U-1223 in the mouth of the St Lawrence River: CTL.

1948 Rear-Admiral W.G. Benn, Captain of the battleship *Royal Oak* when she was torpedoed at anchor in Scapa Flow by U-47 on the same date in 1939, unveiled a plaque in Kirkwall Cathedral in memory of the 786 men lost.
See panel on 7 October, p.570.

1964 Frigate *Lynx*, in a task group off W. coast of South America, diverted to the Falklands after illegal landing of Argentine aircraft.
See 30 September 1966.

1965 801 NAS at RNAS Lossiemouth became the first operational unit to be equipped with Buccaneer aircraft. On 18 October one of these, XN 980, made a low-level pass over Nelson's Column to mark the 160th anniversary of Trafalgar – an impressive photograph which was fully exploited by DPR(N) and DNR.

1974 Flag Officer First Flotilla, Vice-Admiral Henry Leach, leading TG317.2 to the CENTO exercise Midlink off Karachi, arrived at Capetown (the Suez Canal being blocked) and his flagship, the helicopter carrier *Blake*, fired a routine 21-gun national salute. South Africa had been expelled from the Commonwealth for its apartheid policies and this naval courtesy angered the newly elected Labour government in Britain, it was raised in the UN and initiated a blizzard of signals between New York, Washington, FCO, MOD, CINCFLEET and FOF1. Some MPs wanted Admiral Leach keel-hauled and flogged round the fleet for executing what was a standard naval ceremonial on arriving in a friendly foreign country. Exchanges of hospitality – 'fraternisation' – fuelled the issue. *Blake*, frigate *Leander*, and RFAs *Olna* and *Stromness* berthed at Capetown; frigates *Diomede*, *Achilles* and *Falmouth*, with SSN *Warspite*, berthed at Simon's Town. This was to be the last RN ship visit to South Africa until the frigate *Norfolk*, Capt J.F. Perowne RN, went into Capetown in January 1994.
See 12 June 1967, 27 January 1994.

1997 Frigate *Monmouth* and RFA *Orangeleaf*, with FNS *Surcouf*, stood by off Pointe Noire until 30 October to evacuate nationals during unrest in the Congo. Operation Kingfisher.

15 October

1711 *Edgar* (70) blew up at Spithead, killing most of her people.

1795 *Pomone* captured the French *Eveille* off Ile d'Yeu.

1799 *Ethalion* (38) captured the Spanish *Thetis* (34) off Cape Finisterre.

1799 Boats of *Echo* cut out a Spanish brig in the forenoon and a French one in the afternoon in Aguadilla Bay, Puerto Rico.

1805 Fulton's experiment with *Dorothea* at Walmer.

1864 *Royal Alfred* launched at Portsmouth Dockyard. The last timber-hulled capital ship built at Portsmouth.

1914 Cruiser *Hawke* sunk by U-9 60 miles E. of Kinnaird Head, Aberdeen.

1918 J 6 accidentally sunk by *Cymric* Q-ship off Blyth. Only seven J-class submarines were built and all operated from Blyth on the Northumbrian coast. J 6 was their only loss. Their unusual silhouettes, and the unfortunate similarity of 'J' to 'U', led to confused identification, fatal in this case. It was attributed to the hazards of war by a Board of Inquiry next day, at the end of which the survivors paid the Captain of *Cymric* the compliment of rising and saluting on his acquittal.

1940 Submarine *Triad*, patrolling on the surface at night in the Gulf of Taranto, sunk after a furious gun and torpedo action with the Italian submarine *Enrico Toti* (38.16N, 17.37E). *Triad* was the only British submarine to be sunk by an Italian submarine, the only one known to have been sunk by another in a surface action and the first of thirteen T-class boats lost in the Mediterranean. The Captain of *Triad* was Lt-Cdr George Salt, father of Rear-Admiral J.F.T.G. 'Sam' Salt, also a submariner, who commanded the destroyer *Sheffield* in the Falklands War in 1982.

See 4 May 1982, 3 December 2009.

1941 Submarine *Torbay* bombarded Apollonia.

1942 *Viscount* depth-charged, fired at and rammed U-661, sinking her in (53.42N, 33.36W) on her first patrol, S.S.E. of Cape Farewell. Convoy SC 104.

1943 Admiral of the Fleet Sir Andrew Cunningham succeeded Admiral of the Fleet Sir Dudley Pound as First Sea Lord. Churchill had offered the post to Admiral Sir Bruce Fraser, C-in-C Home Fleet, who declined. 'I believe I have the confidence of my own fleet,' he said. 'Cunningham has that of the whole Navy.'

See 4 October 1943.

1944 Reoccupation of Athens by force under Rear-Admiral J.M. Mansfield (15th CS). Operation Manna. Ships: *Ajax, Aurora, Black Prince, Orion, Sirius*. LSI(M): *Prince David, Prince Henry*. LST: *Bruiser, Thruster*.

1945 The last 'service' launch of a Fairey Swordfish from a RN carrier – *Ocean*; but Cdr David Hobbs cautions that *Centaur* launched Swordfish LS326 and NF389 during the filming of 'Sink the Bismarck' in 1959, both aircraft were on Navy charge and flown by a serving crew.

See 28 June 1945.

HMS *Eagle* in the early 1950s with Attacker, Skyraider AEW and Firefly aircraft ranged on the flight deck. (*NMRN*)

1952 Cdr HRH The Duke of Edinburgh unveiled the 1939–45 extension to the Royal Navy memorial at Chatham: 'In honour of the Navy and to the abiding memory of those Ranks and Ratings of this port who laid down their lives in defence of the Empire and have no other grave than the sea' (9946 RN, RM and WRNS).

See 14 November 2007.

1957 RN base and HM Dockyard at Trincomalee, together with the radio station HMS *Highflyer* at Wellisara (Ceylon West W/T) and the RAF field at Katunayate, handed over to the Ceylon government. Next day the light cruiser *Ceylon*, flagship of the East Indies Station, sailed away for the last time. Political restrictions on the future use of these facilities by Britain led to the leasing of Gan in the Maldives and the establishment of a RN radio station in Mauritius in 1962. AFOs 302/62, 334/62, 567/62.

See 11 January 1782, 6 May 1816, 7 September 1958, 16 and 28 February 1962, 30 March 1976.

1958 Mediterranean Fleet units stood by to evacuate British nationals from Lebanon during a crisis which had developed through the summer. Fleet carrier *Ark Royal* sailed from Malta. Light fleet carrier *Albion*, working up off Scotland, ordered to Portsmouth to embark 42 Cdo for the Mediterranean, if needed. Her sister ship *Bulwark* with light cruiser *Gambia* lifted men of the Army's Strategic Reserve from Mombasa to Aqaba. In May the light cruiser *Bermuda* carried 150 men of 45 Cdo and four Whirlwind helicopters to Cyprus due to a worsening security situation and in July she was diverted to Tobruk with 150 men of 45 Cdo to reinforce the garrison. Fleet carrier *Eagle* relieved *Ark Royal* in July and her aircraft covered flights of British troops to Amman in Jordan following the overthrow of the monarchy in neighbouring Iraq.

See 18 and 28 November 1983, 1 January 1984, 18, 19 and 20 July 2006.

1961 Shore parties from the frigate *Leopard*, Cdr P.S. Hicks-Beach RN, which arrived at Tristan da Cunha on 13 October following a volcanic eruption three days earlier, secured the then deserted island. Union Flags were left flying.

See 13 October 1961.

1965 Admiral of the Fleet Sir Henry Oliver died aged 100. He was Chief of the War Staff throughout most of the First World War, dedicated, unruffled, hard-working, never taking leave but another arch-centraliser with no ability or wish to delegate.

'His well-known aversion to saying anything it was not absolutely necessary to say, coupled with a notably impassive countenance, no doubt explain his nickname "Dummy Oliver"' – Marder. As Second Sea Lord from 1920 Oliver implemented the drastic reduction in the officers' list under the Geddes Axe and from 1924, as a full admiral, he commanded the Atlantic Fleet. He had the distinction of being the worst-dressed officer in the Royal Navy. Rear-Admiral W.D. O'Brien, Naval Secretary (and future C-in-C Western Fleet), called on Admiral Oliver at South Eaton Place on his 100th birthday, 22 January 1965, bearing the congratulations of the Admiralty Board. He was followed by Admiral Sir John Frewen, C-in-C Home Fleet, carrying a similar message from all the Navigation Branch officers, by Rear-Admiral E.G. Irving, Hydrographer of the Navy, with documents on the surveying work done by HMS *Stork* when Sir Henry served in the ship in the 1890s, and by others – 'the delegations being shepherded in, and firmly told when their time was up, by the formidable Dame Beryl Oliver' – Admiral Sir William O'Brien to the Author.

See 22 January 1865.

1967 Memorial plaque to Admiral of the Fleet Viscount Cunningham of Hyndhope, 'one who by his most Distinguished Record in time of War and Peace rendered great Services to his Country', unveiled by Lady Cunningham in St Giles' Cathedral, Edinburgh. FOSNI, Vice-Admiral Sir John Hayes, represented the Admiralty Board.

See 2 and 28 April 1967.

1971 The Western Fleet will be known as 'The Fleet' as from 1 November 1971. DCI(RN) 1113/71.

See 1 November 1971.

1993 Commandant Anne Spencer, the last Director, Women's Royal Naval Service, retired and the post abolished. She was succeeded by Capt Julia Simpson, with the title of Chief Naval Officer for Women in the Royal Naval Service. DCI(RN) 259/93.

See 1 November 1993.

16 October

1759 Eddystone Light first lit.

1778 Capture of Pondicherry by Maj-Gen. Hector Munro after a close blockade by Cdre Sir Edward Vernon (*Ripon*). Ships: *Ripon*, *Coventry*, *Seahorse*, *Cormorant*, *Valentine* (Hon. East India Company).

See 15 January 1761.

1798 *Kangaroo* (18) fought the French *Loire* (44) off Blacksod Bay, Ireland.

1815 Bonaparte landed on St Helena.

1913 *Queen Elizabeth* launched at Portsmouth. With *Barham* (John Brown's 1914), *Malaya* (Armstrong's 1915), *Valiant* (Fairfield 1914) and *Warspite* (Devonport 1913), the first British battleships to mount 15-in guns and the first big ships to be completely oil-fired.

See 21 October 1912.

1918 Submarine L 12 torpedoed and sank UB-90 in Skagerrak.

1939 The light cruisers *Edinburgh* and *Southampton*, and the destroyer *Mohawk*, Cdr Richard Frank Jolly RN, damaged in the Firth of Forth in the first Luftwaffe attack on the UK.

Mohawk, with *Cossack*, *Maori* and *Zulu*, had made a high-speed passage home from the Mediterranean on outbreak of war. As they approached Rosyth, two bombs fell to starboard of *Mohawk* abreast the bridge and to port abreast the torpedo tubes. Machine gun bullets and shrapnel riddled bridge, wheelhouse, director and mowed down men at machine guns, after control position and the mooring party on the forecastle; fifteen killed, thirty injured. Cdr Jolly was mortally wounded but he conned *Mohawk* for the remaining 35 miles, although he could barely stand or speak. Passing carriers and cruisers below the Forth Bridge, Cdr Jolly turned in his chair, saluted the flagship and then collapsed. He died at South Queensferry five hours later. His was the first posthumous Empire Gallantry Medal awarded, translated later into the George Cross. The action is dismissed in three lines in Roskill's *The War at Sea* (vol.1 p.75): 'One bomb hit the cruiser *Southampton* but passed through her side without exploding, and a destroyer was slightly damaged. But that was all.' Cdr Jolly is buried in St Peter's churchyard at Boughton Monchelsea, Kent.

1940 *Dundalk* mined off Harwich (51.57N, 01.27E). Sank in tow of *Sutton* next day.

1940 Monitor *Erebus*, with three destroyers, bombarded Dunkirk.

1940 Eleven Swordfish and three Skua aircraft of 816 and 801 Sqns (*Furious*) bombed the oil tanks and seaplane base at Tromsø. Operation Dhu.

1941 *Gladiolus* torpedoed and sunk, probably by U-558 (57N, 25W) while escorting convoy SC 48 in W. Approaches.

1942 Destroyer *Fame* sank U-353 in W. Approaches (53.54N, 29.30W). Convoy SC 104. Submarine boarded but she sank too fast for any intelligence-gathering.

HMS *Queen Elizabeth* (1913) with observation balloon. (*NMRN*)

HMS *Ark Royal* recommissioned at Devonport on 24 February 1970 for what was to be her final commission with Phantoms (892 NAS), Buccaneers (809 NAS), Gannet AEW (849B NAS) and Sea Kings (824 NAS) embarked. (*NMRN*)

1943 Liberator S/59 sank U-844, Liberator C/59, E/120 and Z/120 sank U-470 and *Sunflower* sank U-631 in N. Atlantic. Convoy ON 206.

1943 Liberator Y/86 sank U-964 in N. Atlantic. Convoy ONS 20.

1943 Blenheim MK5 aircraft of 244 Squadron sank U-533 in Gulf of Oman.

1944 Frigate *Annan* (RCN) sank U-1006 off the Faroes.

1952 The Board of Admiralty visited the light cruiser HMNZS *Bellona* at Portsmouth. The ship, with the concurrence of the New Zealand Navy Board, hoisted the Admiralty flag – the gold anchor on the crimson ground – probably the only occasion this flag flew in other than a RN warship.

1959 Chart and Chronometer Depot, HM Dockyard Sheerness, closed down. AFO 2344/59.

1967 Admiral Sir Reginald Aylmer Ranfurly Plunkett-Ernle-Erle-Drax, an officer of 'quick and brilliantly analytical brain' and a founder of the *Naval Review*, died at Poole, Dorset, aged 87. Born Plunkett, he adopted the additional names in 1916 on inheriting estates from his mother; thereafter he was known as Drax for convenience. He was War Staff Officer to Beatty at Heligoland Bight, Dogger Bank and Jutland; first Director of the new RN Staff College, Greenwich, in 1919; C-in-C America and West Indies 1932–4; C-in-C Plymouth 1935–8 and C-in-C The Nore 1939–41 when he retired to Dorset and served as a private in the Home Guard. Admiral Drax became a convoy commodore from 1943–5 and never lost a ship.

1970 The RN Central Drafting Depot, transferred from Haslemere to Grange Road, Gosport, and enhanced by a new £1.4 million computer, was commissioned as HMS *Centurion*.

See 5 April 1957, 31 March 1994.

1994 The last of 578 diesel-powered submarines in the Royal Navy, HMS *Unicorn*, Cdr John Gower RN, made her final entry into port at Devonport – a Sunday and double time for the Dockyard – and paid off. CINCFLEET, Admiral Sir Hugo White, signalled: 'Your final dive today marks the end of a proud era of diesel submarine operations in the Royal Navy. As the Flotilla now moves into the all nuclear age, HMS *Unicorn* in her short commission upheld to the very end the finest traditions of her forebears. Very well done and welcome home.'

See 16 April 1992.

1998 Statue of Capt Frederick John Walker, RN, unveiled at Liverpool Pier Head by HRH The Duke of Edinburgh. It was dedicated to Walker's memory and that of the men of the 36th Escort Group and 2nd Support Group, and all who fought in the Battle of the Atlantic. Admiral of the Fleet Lord Lewin had accepted a suggestion by a local Reservist and saw to its execution by Vice-Admiral Michael Gretton, son of another distinguished escort group commander, Vice-Admiral Sir Peter Gretton.

See 9 July 1944.

17 October

1797 Charles Paget, fifth son of the Earl of Uxbridge, promoted post-captain aged 19 less than a year after having been a midshipman. Vice-Admiral Sir Charles Paget died of yellow fever at Jamaica in 1839 while commanding the North America and West Indies Station.

See 11 June 1779, 14 October 1780, 30 June 1937, 30 June 1955.

1781 Admiral of the Fleet Lord Hawke died. His motto 'strike'. 'Lord Hawke is dead and does not seem to have bequeathed his mantle to anybody' – Horace Walpole.

See 10 February 1720, 20 November 1759, 31 October 1781.

1782 *London* and *Torbay* fought the French *Scipion* and *Sibylle* in Samana Bay, San Domingo. *Scipion* wrecked. *Badger* in company though not engaged.

1798 *Mermaid* fought the French *Loire* S.E. Ireland.

1799 *Alcmene, Naiad, Ethalion* and *Triton* captured the Spanish *Brigida* and *Thetis* in the entrance to Muros Bay, Spain.

1804 *Cruizer* captured the French privateer *Contre-Amiral Magon* after a chase of 97 miles that had started with their engagement off Ostend on the previous day. Prize money varied from £40,000 for the Captain to £182 for a seaman.

1854 First bombardment of Sevastopol by the Allied Fleet under Vice-Admiral Dundas. Ships: *Agamemnon, Albion, Arethusa, Bellerophon, Britannia, London, Lynx, Queen, Rodney, Sampson, Sans Pareil, Sphinx, Terrible, Trafalgar Tribune, Vengeance*. Towing or lashed alongside larger vessels: *Cyclops, Firebrand, Furious, Highflyer, Niger, Retribution, Spitfire, Spiteful, Triton, Vesuvius*. French: *Charlemagne Friedland, Henri Quatre, Jean Bart, Jupiter, Marengo, Montebello, Napoléon, Suffren, Valmy, Ville de Paris*. Turkish: *Mahmudieh*.

1855 Bombardment and reduction of the Kinburn forts by British and French fleets. Ships: *Agamemnon, Algiers, Curaçao, Dauntless, Firebrand, Furious, Gladiator, Hannibal, Leopard, Odin, Princess Royal, Royal Albert, Sidon, Sphinx, Spiteful, Spitfire, St Jean D'Acre, Stromboli, Tribune, Terrible, Valorous*. Mortar vessels: *Camel, Hardy, Firm, Flamer, Magnet, Raven*. Gun vessels: *Arrow, Beagle, Lynx, Viper, Snake, Wrangler*. Gunboats: *Boxer, Clinker, Cracker, Fancy, Grinder*. French: *Asmodée, Cacique, Montebello, Sane*. Floating batteries: *Devastation, Lave, Tonnante* (first armoured ships in action).

1884 Sick Berth Branch formed by Order in Council.

1914 The new light cruiser *Undaunted*, Capt Cecil H. Fox RN (whose previous ship, the *Amphion*, had been sunk under him on 6 August), leading the First Division of the 3rd Destroyer Flotilla, *Lance, Lennox, Legion* and *Loyal*, sank the German destroyers S-119, S-115, S-117 and S-118 in the Broad Fourteens, 40 miles S.W. of the Texel. The interception may have been due to capture of German naval codes from the light cruiser *Magdeburg*. A spirited action on both sides. The Senior

The wooden paddle frigate *Terrible*, heavily armed, principally with 56- and 68-pdrs, 1854. (*NMRN 1968/49*)

Officer in S-119 jettisoned his confidential books in a lead-lined chest which proved to be a 'a miraculous draught of fishes' for British naval intelligence when recovered.

See 11 and 20 August 1914, 13 October 1914, 30 November 1914.

1917 Destroyers *Strongbow* and *Mary Rose*, escorting a Scandinavian convoy, sunk by the German light cruisers *Bremse* and *Brummer* in Norwegian Sea (60.06N, 01.06E).
Battle Honour: Scandinavian Convoys 1917.

1918 Ostend retaken by Allied forces.

1918 Monitors *General Wolfe* and *Lord Clive* bombarded German positions on the Belgian coast, the last occasion on which the RN fired 18-in guns in action.

1939 Old battleship *Iron Duke* bombed in Scapa Flow. Grounded but remained in commission.

1940 GC: Sub-Lt Jack Maynard Cholmondeley Easton, RNVR, and OS Bennett Southwell, for bomb and mine disposal (the latter posthumously).

1941 Destroyer USS *Kearny* torpedoed while escorting Convoy SC-48, before the US entered the Second World War.

See 31 October 1941.

1943 Liberators D/59 and H/120 sank U-540 in N. Atlantic (58.38N, 31.56W). Convoy ON 206.

1943 Destroyers *Jervis* and *Penn* sank UJ-2109 (ex-minesweeper HMS *Widnes*) in Kalymnos harbour, Greece.

See 20 May 1941.

1943 Frigate *Byard* sank U-841 in N. Atlantic, off Cape Farewell. Convoy ONS 20.

1943 At Sunset the Union Flag of Admiral of the Fleet Sir Andrew Cunningham, C-in-C Mediterranean Fleet, was struck in the depot ship *Maidstone*. Admiral Cunningham had flown to London two days earlier to succeed Admiral of the Fleet Sir Dudley Pound as First Sea Lord.

See 9 April 1942, 21 January 1943, 4 October 1943.

1944 Bombardment and air-strike by Force 63 on Nicobar. Operation Millet. Ships: *Renown* (Vice-Admiral Sir Arthur Power), *Indomitable* (Rear-Admiral H.T.C. Walker, CS 5), *Cumberland*, *Phoebe*, *Suffolk*, nine destroyers, including *Norman* and *Van Galen* (Neth). FAA Sqns: Barracuda: 815, 817; Hellcat: 1839, 1844; Corsair: 1834, 1836.

1948 Motor cutter from the carrier *Illustrious*, Capt J. Hughes-Hallett RN, carrying libertymen back to the ship from at night from Weymouth, capsized with the loss of twenty-nine men. The Civil Lord of the Admiralty told the House of Commons that the immediate causes were the overloading of the boat and the apparent failure to reduce speed or return to Weymouth when the boat encountered heavy weather. George Cross (ex Albert Medal) awarded to Boy A.R. Lowe (17) for saving the life of Midshipman Richard Clough who later died. 'With great regret the Admiralty had reached the conclusion that the responsibility for the accident must be laid at the door of the officer in charge of the boat, who unfortunately lost his life' – *The Navy*, March 1949. Memorial at Portland unveiled by Admiral Sir Mark Stanhope, First Sea Lord, 17 October 2010 and attended by Mr Lowe who travelled from New Zealand.

1970 The Fleet Air Arm Memorial Chapel and Book of Remembrance were dedicated by the Bishop of HM Forces at RNAS Yeovilton.

1998 *Osprey*, RNAS Portland, closed.

2005 Lt William Evan Allan, who joined the Royal Australian Navy as a boy seaman in 1914, died in Victoria aged 106, the last Australian to have seen active service in the First World War.

See 31 May 2006.

2005 Vice-Admiral Sir Paul Haddacks, lately UKMILREP and Director of the IMS at NATO HQ, installed as the 27th Lieutenant-Governor and Captain General of the Isle of Man. His two RN predecessors in that post were Rear-Admiral Sir Nigel (Os) Cecil, last Flag Officer Malta, (1980–5) and, from 1937–45, Vice-Admiral William Spencer Leveson-Gower, later Earl Granville, a First World War destroyer captain and brother in-law to HM The late Queen Mother.

See 10 August 1966, 26 April 1991, 18 October 2005, 26 October 2009.

18 October

1652 First recorded dockyard strike when no pay was available on pay day.

1746 *Severn*, escorting a convoy, taken by the French *Terrible* 450 miles W.S.W. of Ushant. The convoy, with *Woolwich*, escaped.

1760 *Boreas* captured the French *Sirene*. *Lively* captured *Valeur*. *Hampshire* drove ashore *Prince Edouard* and *Fleur-de-Lys* (burned by own crews) off Tortuga.

1798 *Anson* (44) and *Kangaroo* (18) captured the French *Loire* (44) S.W. of Ireland.

1799 An exuberant master, having helped bring a convoy from Lisbon and impatient to get into Spithead, put the allegedly *Impregnable* (98) on to the Chichester Shoals. During the night she moved nearly 2 miles over them, and bilged: the master dismissed and the wreck sold.

1806 *Caroline* captured the Dutch *Zeerob* between Middleburg and Amsterdam Islands, and *Maria Reygersbergen* in Batavia Roads. The Dutch *Phoenix*, three corvettes and eight merchant vessels ran themselves ashore.

1812 Brig sloop *Frolic* (18), damaged in a gale off US east coast while escorting a convoy, boarded and taken by the also-gale-damaged American ship sloop *Wasp* (18) after a desperate gunnery duel. Within hours the RN two-decker *Poictiers* (74) arrived and took both sloops.

1854 Boats of *Spartan* recaptured the cargo of the wrecked barque *Caldera* S. of Macao. Also destroyed twenty junks, three villages and a battery at Sam Hoi Chuk.

1854 VC: Capt William Peel and Mid Edward St John Daniel (*Diamond*). Batteries before Sevastopol.

See 5 November 1854, 18 June 1855, 4 September 1861.

1899 Battleship *Bulwark* launched at Devonport Dockyard by Lady Fairfax, wife of the C-in-C Plymouth, 'to the music of the Port Admiral's Band and the sounding of the whistles of steamers in the Hamoaze' – *The Times*. The ship was blown up by an internal explosion in the Medway on 26 November 1914.

See 22 June 1948, 15 November 2001.

1909 Warrant rank opened to writers, cooks and stewards.

1914 First bombardment of Ostend, which continued until the 21st. Ships: *Amazon*, *Attentive*, *Foresight*, *Humber*, *Mersey*, *Mohawk*, *Nubian Severn*.

1914 E 3 sunk by U-27 on the surface off the Ems (first RN submarine sunk in action and the first submarine sunk by another submarine).

Capt Percy Scott (1853–1924). (*NMRN*)

Serving and retired members of the Navy Board met on 14 September 2005 at the Royal Naval Club and Royal Albert Yacht Club, Portsmouth, to mark the 200th anniversary of Nelson's last walk on English soil before boarding HMS *Victory*. Front row only, L to R: Admiral Sir Peter Abbott, Admiral Sir James Eberle, Admiral of the Fleet Sir Julian Oswald, Admiral of the Fleet Sir Edward Ashmore, Admiral of the Fleet Sir Henry Leach, Admiral Sir John Treacher, Admiral Sir Jonathon Band.(*RN*)

1921 US Congress signed a separate peace treaty with Germany, formally ending American hostilities in the First World War. Having refused to ratify the Treaty of Versailles, the USA had continued to be legally at war with Germany two years longer than Britain, France, Italy and Japan.

See 10 January 1920.

1924 Admiral Sir Percy Scott died.

1940 Seven U-boats attacked convoy SC 7 and sank seventeen of thirty-four ships. Six attacked convoy HX 79 and sank fourteen of forty-nine.

1940 Submarine H 49 sunk by UJ-116 and UJ-118 off the Texel.

1940 Destroyers *Firedrake*, *Wrestler* and London flying-boats of 202 Sqn sank the Italian S/M *Durbo* E. of Gibraltar.

1941 *Broadwater*, ex-US destroyer *Mason*, sunk by U-101 in N. Atlantic (57.01N, 19.08W) escorting convoy SC 48. Memorial to four officers and forty men lost is in St Mary's church, Broadwater, West Sussex. They include Lt John Stanley Parker, RNVR, of Boston, Massachusetts, one of the first of his countrymen to became a sea officer in the Royal Navy and the first American to be killed in action at sea under the White Ensign in the Second World War.

See 15 June 1941, 3 October 2001, 22 June 2004.

1944 Minesweeper *Geelong* (RAN) sunk in collision with the US tanker *York* off New Guinea (06.04S, 147.50E).

1949 Lt HRH The Duke of Edinburgh RN joined the destroyer *Chequers* (Capt J.E.H. McBeath RN, Captain (D) 1st DF) at Malta as First Lieutenant.

See 2 September 1950.

2005 Vice-Admiral Sir Fabian Malbon, former Deputy C-in-C Fleet, sworn in as Lieutenant-Governor and C-in-C of Guernsey. Previous naval lieutenant-governors include Vice-Admiral Sir John Coward (1994–2000); Lt-Gen. Sir Michael Wilkins RM (1990–4); Vice-Admiral Sir John Martin (1974–80); Vice-Admiral Sir Charles Mills (1969–74) and Vice-Admiral Sir Geoffrey Robson (1958–64).

See 17 October 2005, 26 October 2009.

19 October

1739 Great Britain declared war on Spain – the War of Jenkins' Ear subsumed in December 1740 into the War of the Austrian Succession. France declared war on Britain in 1744. The three principal naval actions, all official battle honours, were Porto Bello 22 November 1739, Finisterre 3 May 1747 and Ushant 14 October 1747.

See 30 April 1748.

1781 Gen. Lord Cornwallis surrendered at Yorktown, cornered by Washington and blockaded by de Grasse who had evaded Graves.

1797 *Anson* and *Boadicea* captured the French privateer *Zephyr* 45 miles S.W. by W. of Belle Ile.

1799 *Stag* captured the French letter of marque *Heureux* 130 miles W. by S. of Cordouan lighthouse.

1799 *Cerberus* fought five Spanish frigates and two brigs, escorting a large convoy, 40 miles N.N.E. of Cape Penas.

1818 Unsuccessful experiments to defeat the weevil by adding caraway seed to biscuit: the weevils simply ignored the seeds.

1831 Gold-laced trousers restored for all officers.

1903 First drill night in London Division RNVR.

1917 AMC *Orama* sunk by U-62 S. of Ireland.

1918 Zeebrugge and Bruges retaken by Allied forces.

1918 Paddle minesweeper *Plumpton* mined off Ostend.

1939 AMC *Scotstoun* captured the German tanker *Biscaya* off Reykjavik (66.30N, 23.00W).

1939 Supply of dentures to Serving Ratings. 'An initial supply of dentures at the public expense is allowable to serving ratings of all branches, including recruits and Royal Marine ranks, provided:

HMS *Termagant*, a T-class destroyer, 1946. (*NMRN W&L 795A*)

A destroyer's Pom-Pom crew loading ammunition belts during the Second World War. (*NMRN*)

1a. The supply is essential to render the man dentally fit for general service . . .
1b. The need for the supply had not arisen through the man's imprudence or fault.'
– AFO 3074/39.
See 22 January 1920.

1940 Destroyer *Venetia* sunk by mine off the East Knob in Thames estuary (51.33N, 01.10E).

1941 Corvette *Mallow* and sloop *Rochester* sank U-204 in Strait of Gibraltar.

1942 P 37 (*Unbending*) sank the Italian destroyer *Giovanni da Verazzano* S. of Pantelleria (35.52N, 12.02E).

1944 *Termagant* and *Tuscan* drove ashore and destroyed the German TA-18 (ex-Italian TB *Solferino*) off Skiathos (37.45N, 26.59E).

1944 Continuation of attacks on Nicobar and on Nancowry.
See 17 October 1944.

2010 Strategic Defence and Security Review findings announced: two new carriers to proceed but the fleet to lose four Type 22 frigates (reduction to nineteen destroyers and frigates), *Ark Royal*, Joint Force Harrier, one Bay-class RFA and, by 2016, all Sea Kings. Personnel to reduce by 5,000 by 2015 and by another 1,000 by 2020. 'The Naval Service has faced tough times before in its long history. It always endures and – because we are an island nation – it always will.' – Admiral Sir Mark Stanhope, First Sea Lord.
See 10 February 1922, 25 June 1981, 21 July 2004, 22 October 2010.

20 OCTOBER

1778 *Jupiter* and *Medea* fought the French *Triton* off Cape Villano, Spain.

1779 *Charon, Lowestoffe, Pomona, Porcupine, Racehorse*, with the Loyal Irish Volunteers, captured *San Fernando de Omoa* and two Spanish privateers.

1779 *Proserpine* captured the French *Alcmene* 80 miles E. of Martinique.

1782 Admiral Viscount Howe (*Victory*) fought the Franco-Spanish Fleet 45 miles W. by S. of Cape Spartel. Ships: (van) *Atlas, Britannia, Edgar, Foudroyant, Ganges, Goliath, Panther, Polyphemus, Royal William, Ruby, Suffolk, Vigilant*; (centre) *Alexander, Asia, Bellona, Blenheim, Courageux, Crown, Egmont, Princess Royal, Queen, Sampson, Victory*; (rear) *Berwick, Bienfaisant, Buffalo, Dublin, Cambridge, Fortitude, Ocean, Princess Amelia, Raisonnable, Union, Vengeance*.

1793 *Crescent* captured the French *Réunion* 4 miles E. by N. of Cherbourg. Capt James Saumarez knighted. Battle Honour: *Réunion* 1793.

1798 *Fisgard* captured the French *Immortalité* 60 miles W. by N. of Ushant.
Battle Honour: *Immortalité* 1798.

1806 *Athenienne* (64), ex-French *L'Athenienne*, wrecked on Esqueriques ('Skerki') Banks off Cape Bon. Capt Robert Raynsford and 396 men lost.

1827 The Battle of Navarino, the last fleet action under sail. Vice-Admiral Sir Edward Codrington, a Trafalgar veteran, commanding a combined fleet of British, French and Russian ships, destroyed a Turco-Egyptian Fleet in Navarino Bay which was intent on restoring Turkish hegemony over Greece. Ships: *Asia* (flag), *Albion, Genoa, Brisk, Cambrian, Dartmouth, Glasgow, Mosquito, Philomel, Rose, Talbot, Hind*.
Battle Honour: Navarino 1827.

The battle was referred to in the King's Speech at the Opening of Parliament on 29 January 1828 as 'this untoward event'. Codrington had won a 'diplomatically inexpedient victory' (Woodhouse), which led to his being recalled. He handed over to Sir Pulteney Malcolm on 22 August 1828 at Malta.

See 27 April 1770, 28 April 1851, 18 August 1919.

1849 *Columbine, Fury, Phlegethon* (Ben. Mar.), with a party from *Hastings*, destroyed fifty-eight pirate junks in the Kua Kam, Indo-China. Battle Honour: Kua Kam 1849.

1857 Second party of *Shannon*'s Naval Brigade arrived at Allahabad.

See 18 September 1857.

1904 Admiral Sir John Fisher succeeded Lord Walter Kerr as First Naval Lord; not on 21 October, Trafalgar Day, as he often claimed and which many subsequent authors have perpetuated. He served for two terms until 25 January 1910 (his 69th birthday), a duration in post exceeded only by David Beatty (1 November 1919 to 29 July 1927).

1911 'His Majesty The King has approved of the Naval Services of Canada and Australia being called the Royal Canadian Navy and the Royal Australian Navy respectively, and of the ships belonging to these navies (i.e. building for, or serving in the Naval Service of these two Dominions), being called in future HM Canadian and HM Australian Ships respectively. They will accordingly be referred to with the abbreviations HMCS and HMAS.' – AWO 320/11.

See 4 May 1910, 29 August 1911, 1 February 1968.

1913 The Admiralty published the report of a committee (Admiral Sir Cyprian Bridge, Admiral Sir Reginald Custance, Dr C.H. Firth, Regius Professor of Modern History at Oxford, and W.G. Perrin, Admiral Librarian, as Secretary) in April 1912 (Cmnd 7120) 'for the purpose of thoroughly examining and considering the whole of the evidence relative to the tactics employed by Nelson at the Battle of Trafalgar' fought 108 years earlier and published ten months before the outbreak of the First World War.

The Battle of Navarino, 1827. (*NMRN 1984/499*)

1914 *Glitra*, first British merchant ship to be sunk by a German submarine, torpedoed by U-17 14 miles W.S.W. of Skudenaes. Until then the submarine had been regarded as an anti-warship weapon.

See 21 October 1918.

1917 Submarine C 32, Lt-Cdr Christopher Satow RN, one of a small British squadron operating with the Russian Fleet in the Baltic, depth charged and seriously damaged following an unsuccessful attack on a German netlayer in the Gulf of Riga. No compass or wireless. Run ashore on Trafalgar Day in Vöist Bay near Parnu, Estonia, and scuttled next day and was blown up by her crew.

1918 Belgian coast completely recaptured by Allied forces. Coastal monitor M 21 sunk by mine off Ostend.

1927 Submarine L 4 rescued SS *Irene* from pirates off Hong Kong.

1939 AMC *Transylvania* captured the German *Bianca* in Denmark Strait (67.29N, 22.15W).

1939 First German magnetic mine exploded by magnet sweep (Bosun's Nightmare) off Swansea.

1940 Three Force H destroyers, *Hotspur*, *Gallant* and *Griffin*, attacked the Italian submarine *Lafole* E. of Gibraltar. After a long and persistent hunt she was rammed and sunk by *Hotspur*, Cdr H.F.H. Layman; bar to DSO. Ship's company enjoyed extended run ashore in Gibraltar while ship's bows were repaired.

Cdr Layman's first DSO was for Narvik. His son, Kit (later Rear-Admiral), commanded *Argonaut* in Falklands War; DSO.

See 21 May 1982.

1941 Light cruisers *Ajax*, *Galatea* and *Hobart* (RAN) bombarded batteries E. of Tobruk.

1942 Liberator H/224 sank U-216 in Bay of Biscay (48.21N, 19.25W). Aircraft crashed on landing due to damage incurred by explosion of depth charges.

1943 Light cruiser *Aurora* and *Miaoulis* (Greek) bombarded Rhodes.

1948 Light cruiser *Belfast*, Capt E.K. Le Mesurier RN, arrived at Belfast where she was built to receive a silver bell from the Belfast Corporation, a ceremony which had been delayed since 1938.

1988 *Fawn* fired on by Guatemalan gunboats while surveying in Gulf of Honduras.

1997 HMY *Britannia* sailed from Portsmouth on her last cruise, a clockwise circumnavigation visiting seven UK ports.

See 10 October 1997.

21 October

A Memorable Date observed by the Corps of Royal Marines – Trafalgar

1757 *Augusta*, *Dreadnought* and *Edinburgh* under Capt Forrest fought a French squadron of seven ships under Capt Kersaint (*Intrépide*) 30 miles N.N.E. of Cape François, Haiti and severely damaged them. *Dreadnought* was commanded by Capt Suckling, who left his sword to his nephew, Horatio Nelson.
Battle Honour: Cape François 1757.

1794 *Artois*, assisted eventually by *Diamond*, captured the French *Révolutionnaire* off Ushant.
Battle Honour: *Révolutionnaire* 1794.

1805 Battle of Trafalgar (Cadiz, N. 28° E. 8 leagues). Vice-Admiral Viscount Nelson (*Victory*) died after defeating the Franco-Spanish fleet of thirty-three sail of the line under Vice-Admiral Pierre Villeneuve (*Bucentaure*) and Admiral Don Federico Gravina (*Principe de Asturias*), of which sixteen were destroyed and four captured.

'It is the appointed lot of some of History's chosen few to come upon the scene at the moment when a great tendency is nearing its crisis or culmination . . . Fewer still, but happiest of all, viewed from the standpoint of fame, are those whose departure is as well timed as their appearance, who do not survive the instant of perfected success, to linger on subjected to the searching tests of common life, but pass from our ken in a blaze of glory which thenceforth forever encircles their names . . . Rarely has a man been more favored in the hour of his appearing; never one so fortunate in the moment of his death' – Mahan, *The Life of Nelson*, Ch.1 p.1.

Ships: *Achille*, *Africa*, *Agamemnon*, *Ajax*, *Belleisle*, *Bellerophon*, *Britannia*, *Colossus*, *Conqueror*, *Defence*, *Defiance*, *Dreadnought*, *Leviathan*, *Mars*, *Minotaur*, *Neptune*, *Orion*, *Polyphemus*, *Prince*, *Revenge*, *Royal Sovereign*, *Spartiate*, *Swiftsure*, *Thunderer*, *Temeraire*, *Tonnant*, *Victory*. Frigates: *Euryalus*, *Naiad*, *Phoebe*, *Sirius*. Cutter: *Entreprenante*. Schooner: *Pickle*.
Battle Honour: Trafalgar 1805.

The action began at 1220 and at 1330 Nelson was hit by a bullet from *Redoutable*. 'Partial firing continued until 4.30 when a victory having been reported to the Right Honourable Lord Viscount Nelson KB and Commander-in-Chief, he then died of his wound', having thanked God that he had done his duty. 'There was no old age to dim the brightness of his great achievement' – CNP. 'When Nelson died it seemed as if no man was a stranger to another: for all were made acquaintances in the rites of common anguish' – Samuel Taylor Coleridge.

That morning, kneeling in his cabin cleared for action, he had written his last prayer:

> May the great God whom I worship grant to my country, and for the benefit of Europe in general, a great and glorious victory, and may no misconduct in anyone tarnish it; and may humanity after victory be the predominant feature in the British fleet. For myself individually I commit my life to him that made me; and may his blessing alight on my endeavours for serving my country faithfully. To him I resign myself, and the just cause which is entrusted to me to defend.
> Amen, Amen, Amen.

Nelson's last signal was made at 1143 – No. 16:

> Engage the enemy more closely.

Trafalgar was the first posthumous award of gold medals to next-of-kin of Nelson, Duff (*Mars*) and Cooke (*Bellerophon*).

1813 *Royalist* captured the Franco-Batavian *Weser* off Ushant, and *Achates* fought her compatriot, *Trave*, 150 miles S.W. of Ushant.
Battle Honour: *Weser* 1813.

1844 Capt George Moubray, Captain of HMS *Victory* at anchor in Portsmouth Harbour, had to move smartly when HM Queen Victoria and HRH Prince Albert came up the side unheralded. The Queen, entering harbour from Osborne en route to Windsor, had seen the laurel wreaths at the ship's masthead and, on being reminded that it was Trafalgar Day and told that the wreaths were hoisted in memory of Admiral Nelson, decided to have a look round.
See 18 July 1833.

1854 Admiral of the Fleet Sir Thomas Byam Martin died. First occasion when the next senior Admiral was not automatically promoted, but he was 89 years old, had been on the Retired

Busts of Admirals of the Fleet Earl Jellicoe (right) and Earl Beatty (left), the two successive commanders-in-chief of the Grand Fleet in the First World War, were unveiled by HRH The Duke of Gloucester in Trafalgar Square on Trafalgar Day 1948. They were joined by Cunningham in 1967. Photographed by the author in 2009. (*Author*)

List for forty-five years and had never flown his flag.

1855 'The *Victory*, 104, flagship in Portsmouth Harbour . . . was garlanded at each masthead, and otherwise dressed in honour of the day, and the "mainbrace" was "spliced" between decks as heretofore, and sundry veterans in and below commission, "fought their battles o'er again" at the festive board both afloat and ashore.' – *The Times*.

1905 The centenary of the Battle of Trafalgar was marked by the Mediterranean Fleet at Malta. 'A naval review was held on shore in the forenoon, three thousand officers and men taking part in it. . . At four o'clock in the afternoon, flags were half-masted. At half-past four o'clock, guards and bands being paraded facing aft, officers and men fallen in on the quarter-deck facing aft and uncovered, the colours of His Majesty's ships were dipped slowly and reverentially; the bands played the Dead March, and at its conclusion the colours were slowly rehoisted' – Vice-Admiral Lord Charles Beresford, C-in-C Mediterranean Fleet, flag in *Bulwark*.

1912 *Queen Elizabeth* laid down at Portsmouth Dockyard. First oil-fuelled capital ship, first to be armed with 15-in guns, and first to exceed 24 knots.
See 16 October 1913.

1915 M 15 and M 28, supported by *Theseus*, bombarded Dedeagatch in Bulgaria.

1917 Destroyer *Marmion* lost in collision with destroyer *Tirade* off Lerwick.

1918 Last British merchant ship (*St Barchan*) sunk by German submarine in home waters in First World War, off St John's Point, Co. Down.
See 20 October 1914.

1922 The Save the *Victory* Fund launched by Admiral of the Fleet Sir Doveton Sturdee, President of the Society for Nautical Research. The Society still thrives and it administers the Fund which finances the maintenance and restoration of *Victory*.
See 14 June 1910, 17 July 1928.

1927 Vice-Admiral Hon. Sir Hubert Brand, C-in-C Atlantic Fleet, hoisted his flag in the brand new battleship *Nelson* and Lt HRH Prince George RN, the future Duke of Kent, joined the ship on the same day.

1928 HRH The Duke of York laid the foundation stone of the Royal Hospital School at Holbrook, which eventually vacated The Queen's House at Greenwich for the National Maritime Museum.

1939 AMC *Transylvania* intercepted and sank the German raider *Poseidon* off Iceland (66.25N, 20.19W).

1940 Destroyer *Kimberley* drove ashore and wrecked the Italian destroyer *Francesco Nullo* on Harmil Island in the Red Sea (16.29N, 40.13E). Convoy BN 7.

1941 Destroyers *Jervis*, *Jupiter* and *Kandahar* bombarded Bardia. *Gnat* torpedoed by U-79 N. of Bardia; reached Alexandria but CTL.

1941 Vice-Admiral Sir James Somerville, KCB, Flag Officer Force H at Gibraltar, appointed KBE. As quick as a flash, Admiral Sir Andrew Cunningham, C-in-C Mediterranean Fleet, signalled, 'What, twice a knight at your age?'
See 28 June 1940.

1943 Minesweeper *Chedabucto* (RCN) in collision with SS *Lord Kelvin* in St Lawrence River (48.14N, 69.16W). Beached.

Julie, Lady Massey gave the destroyer HMS *Defender* a helpful push when she launched the ship at BAE Systems, Govan, on Trafalgar Day 2009. (*BAE*)

1943 Admiral of the Fleet Sir Dudley Pound died. 'I mourned with a personal pang for all the Navy and the nation had lost.' – Churchill, *The Second World War, Volume 1*, p.366.

See 15 July 1939.

1943 Leigh Light Wellington of 179 Sqn sank U-431 S.E. of Cartagena (37.23N, 00.35W); one of the U-boats which had been deployed against the Salerno landings. Sinking was originally attributed to HM Submarine *Ultimatum* but post-war Admiralty reassessment credited the RAF aircraft.

1948 HRH The Duke of Gloucester unveiled bronze busts in Trafalgar Square of Admirals of the Fleet Earl Jellicoe and Earl Beatty, successively Commanders-in-Chief Grand Fleet and both later First Sea Lords. 'The service was taken by the Archbishop of Canterbury and attended by the Dowager Countess Jellicoe (widow), Cdr Lord Beatty (son), Maj Clement Atlee, the prime minister, and Mr Winston Churchill, 'backed by the great crowd of all of us, the common people of this island race – here was enough to move a heart of stone.' – *The Navy*, journal of the Navy League, November 1948, pp.388–9. Wreaths were laid by Admiral Sir Frederick Dreyer, Jellicoe's Flag Captain in *Iron Duke* at Jutland, and by Admiral of the Fleet Lord Chatfield, Beatty's Flag Captain in *Lion*.

See 21 October 1965, 2 April 1967.

1955 HMS *Viti*, HQ of Fiji RNVR, commissioned. Nominal depot ship SDML 3555.

1955 Lords Commissioners of the Admiralty dined in the Painted Hall at RNC Greenwich with HM The Queen and HRH The Duke of Edinburgh to mark the 150th anniversary of Trafalgar. The Queen ordered the mainbrace to be spliced, a brace not spliced on the 200th anniversary in 2005. Earlier the Duke of Edinburgh attended the Trafalgar Day parade in Trafalgar Square and in Plymouth 1,500 RN, RM and WRNS marched through the city and thirty Sea Venoms flew overhead.

See 19 December 1797, 21 October 2005.

1958 Blackwood-class A/S frigate *Duncan* commissioned for service in the Arctic Division of the Fishery Protection Squadron.

1960 HM The Queen launched *Dreadnought*, Britain's first nuclear-powered submarine, at Vickers Armstrongs, Barrow. Barrow's 295th submarine. Vickers had produced 326 of the 510 boats built for the Service.

From the Secretary of the Navy, Washington, to the First Lord of the Admiralty: 'On behalf of the US Navy, I wish to extend sincere congratulations on this historic day. Your wonderful navy has added yet another entry to the log of Maritime history. I am confident that *Dreadnought* will carry on the gallant traditions of the Royal Navy' – W.B. Franke.

To the Secretary of the Navy, Washington: 'May I, on behalf of the Royal Navy, thank you for your kind message of congratulations and best wishes on the occasion of the launch of HMS *Dreadnought*. The Royal Navy is very conscious and appreciative of the part which the US Navy has played in this achievement.' – AFO 2938/60.

See 4 March 1983.

1960 The third volume of the Cabinet Office history of Second World War maritime operations, *The War at Sea*, by Capt Stephen Roskill, covering June 1943 to May 1944, published. The key operations were in the Mediterranean with three major assaults from the sea within six months, in Sicily, at Salerno and at Anzio.

See 10 May 1954, 28 January 1957, 21 October 1961, 21 December 1961, 4 November 1982.

1965 National appeal launched for funds to erect a memorial to Admiral of the Fleet Viscount Cunningham of Hyndhope, 'the only Naval Commander of the Second World War whom it is intended to honour in this way' – DCI(RN) 1551/65. A bust placed in Trafalgar Square near those of Admirals Jellicoe and Beatty, and a plaque in St Paul's Cathedral near Nelson's tomb. The DCI was signed by Admirals of the Fleet Earl Mountbatten, Lord Fraser, Sir Algernon Willis and Sir Philip Vian, Admiral Sir David Luce, Gens Ismay and O'Connor, and Marshal of the RAF Lord Portal.

See 21 October 1948, 12 June 1963.

1971 Light cruiser *Belfast*, the first RN ship since Nelson's *Victory* to be preserved for the nation, opened to the public on the Thames opposite the Tower of London. First Sea Lord, Admiral Sir Michael Pollock, presented a White Ensign to Rear-Admiral Sir Morgan Giles, chairman of the HMS *Belfast* Trust, and a former captain of the ship, with an Admiralty warrant for the ship to wear it. The warrant was reaffirmed on 1 June 1978 when ownership was transferred to the Imperial War Museum.

1976 *Sovereign*, SSN, held most northerly Trafalgar Night dinner en route to North Pole (84.53N, 69.25W).

1989 Lt-Cdr Peter Whitlock, Captain of *Victory* 1974–8, died on Trafalgar Day at Haslar. Last Master Rigger and Boatswain of Portsmouth Dockyard and naval historian.

See 10 April 1855.

1991 RM Barracks, Eastney, closed. Occupied by RM since 1865. RM Museum remains in former Officers' Mess.

1996 *Invincible* Group conducted operations in the Adriatic. 800 NAS SHAR flew sorties over Bosnia.

1998 The last Trafalgar Night dinner to be celebrated at Greenwich under the White Ensign and the last Mess Dinner before the Wardroom closed on 31 October 1998. HRH The Duke of Edinburgh, Baron Greenwich, proposed the Toast to the Immortal Memory. DCI(RN) 112/98. The ensign is preserved in the college chapel.

See 1 May 1939, 11 July 1939.

2005 All HM ships rang eight bells at 1200. Frigate *Chatham*, the Spanish carrier *Principe de Asturias* (the name of Gravina's flagship at Trafalgar)and frigate *Reina Sofia* and the French frigate *Montcalm* laid wreaths in the sea off Cape Trafalgar. The British wreath laid by Capt James Morse RN, and his youngest sailor, WEA Shaun Bell. The First Sea Lord, Admiral Sir Alan West, laid a wreath at Nelson's tomb in St Paul's Cathedral after which the cathedral bells were rung. HM The Queen and HRH The Duke of Edinburgh dined with the First Sea Lord in the Great Cabin of *Victory*.

First Sea Lord directed that, to mark the bicentenary of Trafalgar, commodores would henceforth wear 'flag' buttons on uniforms.

See 19 December 1797, 31 May 1966, 2 April 2001, 31 May 2006.

2009 The destroyer *Defender*, fifth of the Type 45 AAW destroyers, launched by Julie, Lady Massey, wife of Vice-Admiral Sir Alan Massey, Second Sea Lord, at BVT Surface Fleet yard at Govan on the Clyde.

See 1 February 2006, 23 January 2007, 27 November 2007, 17 November 2008, 11 October 2010.

Capt James Morse RN and his youngest sailor, WEA Shaun Bell, lay a wreath from HMS *Chatham* off Trafalgar on 21 October 2005, two centuries after the battle. (*RN*)

22 October

1683 First officials appointed to open Jamaica Dockyard. Closed 1905.

1707 *Association* (90), flagship of Admiral Sir Cloudesley Shovell, returning from the Mediterranean, wrecked on the Scilly Islands. The Admiral was believed to have been killed by looters on shore. He had risen through his own merits and was knighted for his services at Bantry in 1689. He was an admiral at Beachy Head in 1690 and at Gibraltar and Malaga in 1704. The minehunter *Ledbury* held a service at the scene of the wreck on 22 October 2007, led by the Chaplain of the Fleet, the Ven. John Green, and attended by Cdre Jamie Miller, Naval Regional Commander for Wales and the West, a survivor of the destroyer *Coventry*.

1793 *Agamemnon* fought the French *Melpomène*, three other frigates and a brig corvette 15 miles E. of Cape San Lorenzo, Sardinia.

1800 *Indefatigable* and *Fisgard* captured the French *Venus* 90 miles N. by W. of Cape Belem.

1805 Vice-Admiral Collingwood, who assumed command of the Fleet off Trafalgar after Nelson's death, issued the following General Order from his temporary flagship, the frigate *Euryalus*, on the day after the battle:

'The ever-to-be-lamented death of Lord Viscount Nelson, Duke of Bronte, the Commander in Chief, who fell in the Action of the 21st, in the arms of Victory, covered with glory, whose memory will be ever dear to the British Navy, and the British nation; whose zeal for the honour of his King, and for the interests of his Country, will be ever held up as a shining example for a British seaman – leaves to me a duty to return my thanks to the Right Honourable Rear-Admiral, the Captains, Officers, Seamen, and detachments of Royal Marines serving on board His Majesty's Squadron now under my command, for their conduct on that day; but where can I find language to express my sentiments of the valour and skill which were displayed by the Officers, the Seamen and Marines in the Battle with the Enemy, where every individual appeared an Hero, on whom the glory of his Country depended; The attack was irresistible, and the issue of it adds to the page of Naval Annals a brilliant instance of what Britons can do, when their King and their Country needs their service. To the Right Honourable Rear-Admiral The Earl of Northesk, to the Captains, Officers, and Seamen, and to the Officers, Non-commissioned Officers, and Privates of the Royal Marines, I beg to give my sincere and hearty thanks for their highly meritorious conduct, both in the Action, and in their zeal and activity in bringing the captured Ships out from the perilous situation in which they were, after their surrender, among the shoals of Trafalgar, in boisterous weather. And I desire that the respective Captains will be pleased to communicate to the Officers, Seamen, and Royal Marines, this public testimony of my high approbation of their conduct, and my thanks for it.'

1805 Five Trafalgar prizes – *Redoutable*, *Bucentaure*, *Fougueux*, *Santissima Trinidad* and *Algésires* – wrecked, and five more would be taken within a fortnight.

See 4 November 1805.

1809 *Plover* captured the French privateer *Hirondelle* 18 miles S.E. by S. of Lizard Head.

1821 *Rising Star* built for Chilean Navy sailed, first British-built steam warship to cross Atlantic.

1853 British and French fleets passed the Dardanelles, precipitating war between Russia and Turkey.

1860 Metropolitan Police from the 3rd Division took over security duties at Devonport Dockyard. Establishment: 1 superintendent, 5 inspectors, 21 sergeants and 125 PCs.

See 13 August 1934.

1870 Slow-burning 'pebble powder' introduced in RN.

1904 Russian Baltic Fleet under Vice-Admiral Zinovy Petrovich Rozhestvensky, bound for operations in the Far East during the Russo-Japanese War and destruction at Tsushima, fired at night on Hull trawlers fishing on the Dogger Bank believing them to be Japanese torpedo boats. 'A delightful opera-bouffe performance' (Marder) but a mighty diplomatic row.

1926 Coal-burning, single-screw sloop *Valerian*, Cdr W.A. Usher RN, steaming from Nassau to Bermuda with low bunkers, foundered in a hurricane 5 miles off Gibbs Hill, Bermuda: eighty-six men lost, seventeen rescued by light cruiser *Capetown*. Court martial held in Bermuda 1 November 1926. President Capt A.B. Cunningham. Captain and NO honourably acquitted.

1936 'Their Lordships have decided that the cutlass is no longer to form part of the equipment for men landed for service. The orders for its employment at ceremonial parades and at funerals are, however, to remain unchanged.' The future allowance of cutlasses to be limited to capital ships, aircraft carriers, cruisers, sloops, leaders and destroyers; over 500 men 20 cutlasses, 500 and under ten cutlasses. AFO 2571.
See 21 April 1917.

1940 Destroyer HMCS *Margaree*, ex-HMS *Diana*, transferred, sank in collision with SS *Port Fairy* in Atlantic (53.24N, 22.50W): 140 lost from ship's company of 171. Convoy OL 8.

1941 RFA *Darkdale*, oiler, torpedoed and sunk at anchor off Jamestown, St Helena by U-68 (16.00S, 05.37W). Thirty-seven crew and four gunners lost. The first ship sunk by a U-boat south of the Equator in the Second World War. Memorial plaque unveiled at St Helena 15 April 2001.

1942 Wellington B/179 sank U-412 in Norwegian Sea (63.55N, 00.24W).

1943 Destroyer *Hurworth* sunk by mine off Kalymnos Island (36.59N, 27.06E). Survivors landed in Turkey. *Adrias* (Greek), ex-*Border*, mined in same field and beached on Turkish coast. Refloated and reached Alexandria, but CTL.

1943 Admiral Sir Reginald Hall, the famous Director of Naval Intelligence in the First World War, died at Claridge's Hotel, Brook Street, aged 73.
See 28 June 1870, 4 September 1913 and 24 October panel.

1944 Heavy cruiser *Australia* (RAN) damaged by kamikaze attack.

1946 Destroyers *Saumarez* and *Volage* mined in the Corfu Channel.
See 24 October panel, p.606.

1948 Admiral Sir Bruce Fraser, First Sea Lord, promoted admiral of the fleet. 'His promotion was made possible by the reaching of five years seniority in this rank by Admiral of the Fleet Lord Tovey, for the appointment is governed by the rule that not more than three admirals of the fleet shall be of less than five years seniority in that rank. The other two junior admirals of the fleet are Sir John Cunningham, promoted in January of this year, and Sir James Somerville, whose seniority dates from May 1945.' – *The Navy*, December 1948.

1963 Rear-Admiral Raymond Shayle Hawkins, Director of Marine Engineering, appointed Fourth Sea Lord and Vice-Controller. The first engineer officer and the first non-executive officer ever to be appointed to the Board of Admiralty. The last officer to be Fourth Sea Lord before the title ended with the formation of the Ministry of Defence.
See 21 April 1970, 19 January 2000.

1994 *Resolution*, Britain's first Polaris submarine, paid off after sixty-nine patrols.
See 26 February 1964, 15 September 1966, 2 October 1967, 15 June 1968.

2003 Submarine *Ambush*, second boat of SSN Astute-class, laid down. First RN submarine not fitted with optical periscope.
See 31 January 2001, 11 March 2005, 24 March 2009, 16 December 2010, 7 January 2011.

2010 New SSN *Astute* went aground for twelve hours on a shingle bank off the Isle of Skye and negative press publicity marked the end of a difficult week for the Royal Navy.
See 10 January 1964, 4 November 1967, 18 February 2010, 19 October 2010.

23 OCTOBER

1702 *Dragon* fought a French 60-gun ship 36 miles W. of Cape Finisterre.

1753 RNH Haslar admitted first patients.

1762 *Brune* captured the French *Oiseau* 30 miles E.S.E. of Cape Palos, Spain.

1809 *Pomone* burned five sail of a French convoy in the Gulf of Lyons.

1813 *Andromache* captured the Franco-Batavian *Trave* 45 miles W. by N. of Pointe du Raz, Brittany.

1865 Paddle sloop *Bulldog* ran aground in attempt to ram the Haitian rebel steamer *Volorogue* at Cap Haitien but then sank the *Volorogue* by gunfire. The *Bulldog*, unable to refloat herself, was destroyed by her own crew, prematurely in the Admiralty's opinion.

1876 The appointment of Chaplain of the Fleet created by Order in Council.

See 3 May 1859, 13 May 1859, 11 August 1902, 17 November 1943, 1 April 1998.

1903 *Neptune*, which had been the last British rigged turret-ship when launched at Millwall in 1874, made a spectacular passage down the harbour at Portsmouth on her way to the breakers, by ramming *Victory*, colliding with the turret-ship *Hero* and having close shaves with other ships.

See 10 September 1874, 1 March 1878.

1915 Submarine E 8, Cdr Francis Goodhart, sank the German cruiser *Prinz Adalbert* 20 miles W. of Libau, which led to withdrawal of German heavy units from the Baltic. The cruiser had been torpedoed by E 9, Lt-Cdr Max Horton, on 2 July 1915, and had jut returned to service.

See 29 January 1917.

1916 Sloop *Genista* sunk by U-57, 120 miles W. of Cape Clear.

1917 Destroyer *Melampus* sank UC-16 off Selsey Bill.

1917 The Constitution of the Board of Admiralty revised by Order in Council.

See 31 October 1921, 10 July 1936.

'We beg leave humbly to propose to Your Majesty that the members of the Board shall be:

The First Lord of the Admiralty
The First Sea Lord and Chief of Naval Staff
The Deputy First Sea Lord
The Second Sea Lord and Chief of Naval Personnel
The Third Sea Lord and Chief of Naval Materiel
The Fourth Sea Lord and Chief of Supplies and Transport
The Fifth Sea Lord and Chief of Naval Air Service
The Deputy Chief of Naval Staff
The Assistant Chief of Naval Staff
The Civil Lord
The Controller
And two Secretaries:
The Parliamentary and Financial Secretary
The Permanent Secretary.

We beg leave to recommend that Your Majesty may be graciously pleased, by Your Order in Council, to sanction the foregoing.'

1918 Dame Agnes Weston died, aged 78, still at work in Devonport.

The First 'Aggie Weston's' opened at Plymouth

Miss Agnes Weston (b.1840) was deeply religious and caring about soldiers. She used to write to her local regiment's soldiers on active service, and one of them asked her to write to a sailor friend. By 1871 she was corresponding with hundreds of sailors and was obliged to have her letters printed.

In 1873 she attended the first meeting of the Naval Temperance Society, and soon found that there was a need for somewhere for the sailors to go in port other than public houses or brothels. After energetic fund-raising efforts she opened her first 'sailor's rest'.

'Aggie Weston's' soon became a byword in the Fleet for comfort and kindness which many sailors had never known before. The intention to name a ship 'Weston-super-Mare' after a First Lord's birthplace was thwarted by instant lower-deck translation to 'Aggie-on-Horseback'.

1936 'An Admiralty Fleet Order . . . states that a large number of letters of appreciation for the services rendered by HM ships in the evacuation of British subjects and foreign nationals from Spain since the beginning of the civil war have been received in the Admiralty . . . All these letters express admiration for the efficient and

A Royal Navy guard marching to St Paul's Cathedral for the national service of commemoration for those lost at the Battle of Trafalgar. (*RN*)

courteous way in which the work of evacuation has been carried out and for the kindness and willingness of the officers and men concerned. Their Lordships have pleasure in informing HM ships of these messages and desire to add an expression of their own high appreciation of the efficiency with which this duty has been and is still being carried out.'

1941 Destroyer *Cossack* torpedoed by U-563 W. of Portugal (35.26N, 10.04W).
See 27 October 1941.

1942 Submarine *Unique* presumed lost W. of Gibraltar Strait while on passage from the UK.

1943 Destroyers *Duncan, Vidette* and Liberator Z/224 sank U-274 S.W. of Iceland. Convoy ON 207.

1943 Minesweeper *Cromarty* sunk by mine in Bonifacio Strait, Sardinia (41.23N, 09.12E).

1943 Light cruiser *Charybdis* sunk by the German TBs T-23 and T-27 off Triagoz Island, France (48.59N, 03.39W). Destroyer *Limbourne* torpedoed by the German TBs T-22 and T-24 in the same position; sunk by *Talybont* and *Rocket*. Operation Tunnel. Ships: *Charybdis, Grenville, Limbourne, Rocket, Stevenstone, Talybont, Wensleydale*. Dead washed ashore on Channel Islands; buried by islanders despite German occupation. The only RN cruiser lost in 1943.

1944 Battle of Leyte Gulf (20–27 October) between US 3rd and 7th Fleets and Japanese battle fleet, resulting in the defeat of the Japanese. Ships present with 7th Fleet: *Ariadne* and *Arunta, Australia, Gascoyne, Warramunga* and *Shropshire* (RAN). *Australia*, damaged the previous day by Japanese Army aircraft, had to withdraw, escorted by *Warramunga*.
Battle Honour: Leyte Gulf 1944.

1954 West Germany joined NATO.

2005 A national service of commemoration for Trafalgar held in St Paul's Cathedral.
See 19 December 1797, 21 October 1955, 4 May 1991, 14 June 2007.

Certificate of membership of the Royal Naval Temperance Society signed by Aggie Weston, issued to Boy Second Class Leonard Tozer on the training ship *Impregnable*, 1913. (*NMRN 1988/45(25)*)

24 October

1793 *Thames* fought the French *Uranie* 130 miles S.W. of Ushant. When disabled, the *Thames* struck to the French *Carmagnole* and two other frigates. Her crew were ill-treated, but she was recaptured next June.

1797 *Indefatigable* captured the French privateer *Hyène* W. of Cape de Sines.

1798 *Sirius* (36) captured the Dutch *Furie* (24) and *Waakzaamheid* (36) N.W. of the Texel.

1805 A major newspaper scoop gained by the *Gibraltar Chronicle* with news of Trafalgar following receipt of Collingwood's letter to General Fox, the Governor. *The Times* first reported the news on 6 November.

1811 *Guadeloupe* captured the French privateer *Sirène* 9 miles N. by W. of Dragonera Island, Majorca.

1862 British and French forces recaptured Kading. Naval Brigade from *Euryalus*, *Imperieuse*, *Pearl*, *Starling* and *Vulcan*. Troops: Royal Artillery, Royal Engineers, 31st and 67th Regiments, 5th Bombay Native Light Infantry.

1877 *Lightning*, RN's first torpedo boat, commissioned. Displaced 19 tons and carried first swivelling torpedo tube.

1911 Winston Churchill succeeded Reginald McKenna as First Lord of the Admiralty.
See 1 January 1916, 3 September 1939.

1939 U-16 attacked by patrol vessel *Puffin* and trawler *Cayton Wyke* and forced on to Goodwin Sands.

1940 Fourteen Swordfish aircraft, disembarked from *Illustrious* and *Eagle*, bombed Tobruk and mined the entrance of the harbour. FAA Sqns: 815, 819, 824.

Admiral Sir Reginald Hall (1870–1943)

Reginald Hall was the outstanding head of British naval intelligence in the First World War. 'Blinker' Hall (he had a characteristic facial twitch) was a gunnery officer and 'an instinctive seaman'. He was captain of the RN College, Osborne and made the armoured cruiser *Natal* the best gunnery ship in the fleet. He commissioned the new battlecruiser *Queen Mary* in 1913 (his commander was William James, later C-in-C Portsmouth, and his biographer) but Hall was recalled in November 1914 to head the Naval Intelligence Division, the famous Room 40 at the Admiralty. 'If occasion has ever been exactly matched by the right man, it was when Hall went to the Admiralty', wrote William James (p.200). Reginald Hall, whose father had been the first DNI in 1887, was a skilled organiser and proved a born intelligence officer; his influence extended far outside the Admiralty and beyond strictly naval affairs. 'Such eyes the man has!' wrote Dr Walter Page, the US Ambassador in London, to President Wilson in March 1918, 'Hall is one genius that the war has developed. Neither in fiction nor in fact can you find any such man to match him . . . My Lord! I do study these men here most diligently who have this vast and appalling War Job. There are most uncommon creatures among them – men about whom our great-grandchildren will read in school histories: but, of them all, the most extraordinary is this naval officer – of whom, probably, they'll never hear.' Hall's greatest coup was the interception of the Zimmerman telegram of 16 January 1917 which exposed a German plot to restore to Mexico territory ceded to the United States in the nineteenth century. It outraged the Americans and brought the US into the war in 1917. Hall retired at the end of the war and entered Parliament. His political career was undermined by ill-health.
See 22 October 1943.

First-class torpedo boat No. 2 (1878), showing the single bow-mounted torpedo tube and two reload torpedoes abaft the funnel. (*NMRN*)

1942 Liberator G/224 sank U-599 in S.W. Approaches (47.07N, 17.40W). Convoy KX 2.

1943 Wellington A/179 sank U-566 in the Bay of Biscay.

1943 Destroyer *Eclipse* sunk by mine off Kalymnos Island in the Dodecanese (37.01N, 27.11E).

1944 Mines laid by aircraft of 852 and 846 Sqns (*Campania* and *Trumpeter*), escorted by *Devonshire* and six destroyers in Lepsorev and Harrhamsfjord (62.36N, 06.12E). W/T stations on Vigra and Hanoy attacked. Operation Hardy.

The Royal Navy and the Corfu Incident, 22 October 1946

A British squadron from the Mediterranean Fleet, the light cruisers *Mauritius*, flag of Rear-Admiral Harold Kinahan, and *Leander*, and the destroyers *Saumarez* and *Volage*, exercising right of passage through the straits between Corfu and Albania, where the cruisers *Orion* and *Superb* had been fired on from the Albanian shore five months earlier, ran into an illegally laid Albanian minefield. Saumarez was mined on the starboard side below the bridge and lost thirty-six men. The cruisers cleared the area and *Volage*, in attempting to tow *Saumarez*, was herself mined and lost eight men and most of her bows. The tow was again passed and *Volage* towed *Saumarez* astern for thirteen hours to the safety of Corfu Town. The Fifth MS Flotilla later swept twenty-two recently laid mines from the Corfu Channel. Years of litigation followed; the International Court of Justice found that the mines had been laid after the end of hostilities in Europe and awarded Britain £843,947 in compensation which was never paid. *Saumarez* was a CTL. On the 60th anniversary of the tragedy in 2006, the frigate *Sutherland*, Cdr P.D. Romney RN, paraded a guard for a service in Corfu Town cemetery at the graves of twelve of the destroyers' men and at the nearby memorial to all forty-four dead, attended by the British Ambassador, Mr Simon Gass, Admiral Sir Jock Slater and Cdre Sir Donald Gosling RNR, who was an AB in *Leander* at the time. Later, at the exact time of the first mine strike, and as near its location as territorial waters allowed, further wreaths were laid from Sutherland by veterans of all four ships involved.

See 30 January 1903, 13 May 1937, 17 May 1946.

25 OCTOBER

1694 Royal Hospital, Greenwich, founded by Charter of William and Mary.

1704 Leake's first relief of Gibraltar.

1747 *Hampshire* captured the French *Castor* 200 miles S. of Cape Clear.

1760 Accession of King George III.

1796 *Santa Margarita* captured the French privateer *Vengeur* S. of Ireland. Her boat captured the privateer's prize, *Potomah*.

1799 Boats of *Surprise* under Capt Hamilton cut out the Spanish *Santa Cecilia* (ex-British *Hermione*) at Porto Cavallo. Spanish vessel renamed *Retaliation* and then *Retribution*. Her captor knighted.
Battle Honour: *Hermione* 1799.
See 22 September 1797.

1803 Boat of *Osprey* captured the French privateer *Resource* off Tobago.

The ship's bell recovered from the battleship HMS *Prince of Wales*, sunk of Malaya on 10 December 1941. (*RN*)

1807 Boats of *Herald* cut out the French privateer *César* from under the guns of a fort at Otranto.

1812 *Macedonian* (38) taken by the American *United States* (44), 600 miles W.S.W. of Madeira.

1856 Capture of Canton in Second China War by a squadron commanded by Sir Michael Seymour in *Calcutta* (84).

1899 Governor of Natal requested a Naval Brigade with artillery to contest Boer invasion. Within twenty-four hours Capt Percy Scott of the armoured cruiser *Terrible* had devised a transportable mounting for 4.7-in naval guns. Within thirty-six hours two guns were en route in *Powerful* to Durban. By 29 October they were entrained for Ladysmith with three long 12-pdrs and a 12-pdr field gun, in addition to 17 officers and 267 ratings.
See 6 January 1900.

1911 Battlecruiser HMAS *Australia* launched at John Brown's, Clydebank, by Lady Reid, wife of Sir George Reid, Australian High Commissioner in London and former prime minister.
See 23 and 30 June 1913, 4 October 1913, 12 April 1924.

1915 Destroyer *Velox* mined off the Nab lightvessel.

1931 The Cyprus Revolt.
Following the burning down on Trafalgar Day of Government House in Cyprus by a mob 'inflamed with philhellene ardour and the thunderings of the bishop and other agitators' in an insurrection against British rule, units of the Mediterranean Fleet then at Suda Bay were deployed to the island; cruiser *London* (flag of Rear-Admiral J.W.C. Henley) anchored off Larnaca where she landed her RM detachment, cruiser *Shropshire* to Limassol, and destroyers *Acasta* and *Achates* to Paphos and Famagusta respectively. The Royal Navy had a sobering effect.
See 14 March 1956.

The capture of the *Santa Cecilia* (ex-HMS *Hermione*), 1799. One hundred men in the boats of the *Surprise* attacked by night; fifty men under the command of Capt (later Admiral Sir) Edward Hamilton boarded her and took control, while fifty cut her cables and towed her clear of the guns of Porto Cavallo. (*NMRN 1980/110*)

The authorities considered that the two main players, the Greek consul and Monseigneur Nicodhimos Mylonas, Bishop of Kiton, would benefit from some sea air. In the small hours of 25 October these gentlemen were roused and invited on board the two cruisers where 'they were treated as honoured guests rather than prisoners for deportation'. The consul went to the *London* and the Bishop went to the *Shropshire*; 'at first the officers in the wardroom were somewhat at a loss how to treat the venerable divine, with his long black hair and beard. He commanded respect in spite of the fact that he had been instrumental in stirring up strife against British rule. The Bishop, however, soon put the officers at their ease. He removed his tall Greek Orthodox head-dress, and it was seen that he had fastened to the inside of it the Episcopal jewels in order that they should not be left behind if flight became necessary. Relieved of this rather weighty head-dress, he asked for a stiff whisky and soda. The ice was immediately and effectively broken . . . The rebel bishop and his messmates became fast friends.' – Lt-Cdr Kenneth Edwards, *The Grey Diplomatists*.

1940 River gunboat *Aphis* bombarded enemy concentrations 15 miles E. of Sidi Barrani.

1940 Light cruiser *Ajax* bombarded Bardia.

1941 *Lamerton* and Catalina A/202 sank the Italian S/M *Ferraris* in Atlantic (37.07N, 14.19W). Convoy HG 75.

1941 *Seraph* launched at Barrow-in-Furness. Lead ship of second batch of S-class submarines.

1941 Minelayer *Latona* sunk by German aircraft off Bardia (32.15N, 25.14E). Caught fire and magazine exploded.

See 1 February 1943.

1944 Destroyer HMCS *Skeena* dragged her anchors in a gale and was wrecked at Reykjavik.

1944 Light cruiser *Aurora* and destroyers *Tetcott* and *Tyrian* bombarded Milos (and on the 26th).

1945 Light cruiser *Tiger* (ex-*Bellerophon*) launched at John Brown's, Clyde, by Lady Stansgate, mother of Anthony Wedgewood-Benn. Work suspended and ship laid up at Dalmuir until resumed in 1954. Commissioned 18 March 1959 under Capt R.E. Washbourne RN. Converted at Devonport 1968–72 into a helicopter carrier. Finally paid off April 1978 by Capt G.M.K. Brewer RN. Arrived Castellon, Spain 28 September 1986 for breaking up. DCI(RN) 339/79.

See 18 March 1959, 10 August 1966, 28 September 1986.

1979 Diving trials ship *Reclaim* paid off after thirty years' continuous service. The only ship present at both the 1953 Coronation and 1977 Jubilee Reviews. Probably last HM ship to be equipped with sails.

See 1 June 1948, 17 July 1959, 23 December 1967, 5 February 2007.

2007 The ship's bell of the battleship *Prince of Wales*, sunk off Malaya on 10 December 1941 and retrieved by RN divers in August 2002, was handed over by Rear-Admiral Alan Massey, ACNS, at Admiralty House, Portsmouth, to the Malaysian Minister of Foreign Affairs for exhibitions to mark fifty years of Malaysian independence. The bell was returned in the destroyer *Edinburgh* in August 2008 and is preserved in Merseyside Maritime Museum.

26 October

1781 *Hannibal* captured the French *Neckar* off the Cape of Good Hope.

1854 VC: A/Mate William Nathan Wrighte Hewett (*Beagle*), for heroic action when manning a gun before Sevastopol.

See 5 November 1854, 25 July 1887.

1858 *Pearl*'s Naval Brigade at the unsuccessful action at Jagdispur.

1874 HM Queen Victoria approved the form of religious service to be used at the launching of HM ships.

1916 German destroyer raid in Dover Strait (night of 26/27th). Ships: *Amazon, Cossack,*† *Falcon, Flirt,*§ *Gipsy, Kangaroo, Laforey, Lance, Lark, Laurel, Lawford, Liberty, Lochinvar, Lucifer, Mohawk, Myrmidon, Nubian,** P 21, P 23, P 34, *Racehorse, Swift, Syren, Tartar, Viking; Zulu,* TB 15. Also: *Dragon, H.E. Ombra, Stroud.* Drifters: *Ajax II,*‡ *Broadland, Datum,*‡ *Devon County, East Holme, E.B.C., Eskburn, F.H.S., Girl Norah, Girl Annie, Gleaner of the Sea,*‡ *I.F.S., Launch Out,*‡ *Mishe Nahma, New Spray, Paradox, Pleasants, Prince,*‡ *Roburn,*‡ *Roulette, South Tyne, Spotless Waveney,*‡ *Young Crow.*

*Torpedoed on 27th. †Not engaged. ‡Sunk on 26th. §Sunk on 27th.

1940 Canadian Pacific liner *Empress of Britain*, 42,348 tons, inbound from the Middle East, bombed and set on fire by German aircraft 70 miles N.W. of Donegal: 598 souls saved, 49 lost. Taken in tow by two destroyers but sunk by U-32 on 28 October. The biggest merchant vessel lost at sea as a result of air attack. 'The loss of this splendid ship . . . was a tragedy . . . It underlined the effect to Britain of the

Vice-Admiral Sir Adrian Johns, lately Second Sea Lord and C-in-C Naval Home Command, was sworn-in as the 64th Governor and Commander-in-Chief Gibraltar, on 26 October 2009. (*Johnny Bugeja, Gibraltar*)

HMS *Implacable* (1942). (*NMRN*)

lack of air and naval bases in western Ireland, from which all shipping passing close off those shores could have been so much better and more easily protected.' – Roskill, *The War at Sea*, vol.1, p.351.

See 30 October 1940.

1943 Liberator A/10 (RCAF) sank U-420 in N. Atlantic (45.49N, 41.01W). Convoy ON 207.

1944 Corvette *Rose* (Nor) sunk in collision with *Manners* 500 miles E. of Cape Race (45.10N, 39.40W). Convoy ON 260.

1944 Carrier *Implacable* (Admiral Sir Henry Moore), light cruiser *Mauritius* and six destroyers of 26th DF successfully attacked shipping between Bodø and Rorvik (and on 27th and 28th). Operation Athletic. FAA Sqns: Barracuda: 828, 841; Firefly: 1771; Seafire: 887, 894.

1944 Accountant Branch retitled Supply and Secretariat Branch and prefix 'Paymaster' abolished, somewhat to the vexation of the Submarine Branch of the Service, who relinquished 'S' for S/M.

See 18 November 1918, 13 October 1922, 1 February 2004.

1991 Admiral Sir Arthur Francis 'Attie' Turner died. First officer of a non-executive branch to become a full admiral.

See 21 April 1970.

2009 Vice-Admiral Sir Adrian Johns, lately Second Sea Lord and C-in-C Naval Home Command, arrived at Gibraltar in the frigate *Lancaster* and was sworn-in as the 64th Governor and Commander-in-Chief Gibraltar.

See 17 April 1969, 17 and 18 October 2005, 27 September 2006.

27 OCTOBER

1651 'General at Sea' Robert Blake defeated the Royalist fleet under Prince Rupert.

1728 Capt James Cook born at Marton-in-Cleveland, North Riding, Yorkshire.
See 14 February 1779.

1758 Admiral the Hon. Edward Boscawen (*Namur*) fought five French ships under Capt Comte du Chaffault (*Dragon*) in the Soundings. Ships: *Bienfaisant, Namur, Royal William, Somerset*. Frigates: *Boreas, Echo, Trent*.

1800 Boats of *Phaeton* cut out the Spanish *San Jose* at Fuengirola, near Malaga.

1810 *Orestes* captured the French privateer *Loup Garou* 120 miles W. of Ushant.

1890 Naval Brigade under the personal command of Vice-Admiral Sir Edmund Fremantle, C-in-C East Indies Station, landed at Kipini, 230 miles N. of Zanzibar, on a punitive expedition against the Sultan of Vitu (formerly in German East Africa, now in Kenya) following the murder of nine German traders. Columns commanded by Capt Hon. Assheton Curzon-Howe, Flag Captain of the cruiser *Boadicea*, and Cdr John McQuhae of the 'torpedo cruiser' *Cossack*. Town and Sultan's house burned; no serious British casualties but several cases of sunstroke. Squadron sailed for Mombasa on 30 October. Clasp 'Witu 1890' authorised for West and East Africa medals; one recipient was Midshipman Roger Keyes, HMS *Turquoise*.

Ships: *Boadicea, Brisk, Conquest, Cossack, Humber, Kingfisher, Pigeon, Redbreast, Turquoise*.
See 1 March 1911.

1912 The Naval Society formed 'to promote the advancement and spreading within the Service of knowledge relevant to the higher aspects of the naval profession'. The Society's quarterly, *The Naval Review*, remains the authoritative medium of debate on

HMS *Audacious* sinking off Tory Island, 1914. The crew are abandoning ship in lifeboats from the passenger liner *Olympic*. (*NMM Neg. No. P39692*)

professional matters within the Royal Navy (www.naval-review.org).

1914 *Audacious* sunk by mine 18 miles N. 3° E. of Tory Island, N.W. of Ireland. She had been in service only one year and their Lordships sought to keep her name in the *Navy List* throughout the war in an effort to conceal her loss; but too many passengers in *Olympic* witnessed the event. – Corbett, *Naval Operations*, vol.1, p.241.

1916 Destroyer *Flirt* torpedoed by German destroyers off Dover, and *Nubian* off Folkestone. (*Zubian* created from salvaged halves of *Nubian* and *Zulu*.)

See 8 November 1916, 4 February 1918.

1927 *Wild Swan* repulsed Chinese attack on mission hospital at Swatow, China.

1940 Eight Swordfish aircraft of 813 and 824 Sqn (*Eagle*) bombed Maltezana airfield, Stampalia.

1941 Destroyer *Cossack* sank while in tow after being torpedoed off Cape St Vincent on the 23rd. Convoy HG 75.

See 8 June 1937.

1942 Fortress F/206 sank U-627 on her maiden voyage in N. Atlantic (59.14N, 22.49W).

1944 Firefly aircraft of 1771 Sqn (*Implacable*), Halifax D/502, T/502, and Liberators H/311, Y/311 (Czech) sank U-1060 off Norwegian coast (65.24N, 12.00E).

1946 Hulk of the Japanese heavy cruiser *Takao*, torpedoed and damaged by USS *Darter* at Leyte Gulf 23 October 1944 and finally crippled by the RN X-craft attack in Johore Strait 31 July 1945, towed from Singapore and scuttled in Malacca Strait.

1955 HRH The Duke of Edinburgh, Captain General Royal Marines, welcomed his uncle, Admiral of the Fleet Earl Mountbatten of Burma, into the Royal Marines as Colonel Commandant for life in a ceremony at RMB Eastney.

1961 Submarine *Porpoise*, Lt-Cdr P.G.M. Herbert RN, transported a stone from the original monastery building founded by St Columba on Iona to Gosport for incorporation in the font of the new church to be dedicated to St Columba at Catisfield near Fareham.

1994 Admiral Sir John Hamilton, last C-in-C Mediterranean, died. Flag hauled down 5 June 1967.

See 31 March 1979.

2002 The RN's newest warship, the frigate *St Albans*, alongside in Portsmouth, damaged when P&O ferry *Pride of Portsmouth* from Le Havre, entering harbour in gale-force winds at 0500 on a Sunday, slewed off course and collided with the frigate's port side. Port bridge wing and 30-mm gun deck were buckled and damage to starboard side hull. The frigate returned to sea on 12 February 2003.

Bridge staff on board HMS *St Albans* during Operation Taurus 2009. (*RN*)

28 OCTOBER

A Memorable Date observed by the Corps of Royal Marines – see below

1664 King Charles II sanctioned the formation of the Duke of York and Albany's Maritime Regiment of Foot, the first regiment to be formed specially for service afloat, and the colour of whose uniform is remembered in the yellow of the Corps's colours.
See 23 July 1964.

The Birth of the Corps of Royal Marines, 1664

'That twelve hundred land Souldjers be forthwith raysed to be in readinesse, to be distributed into His Mats Fleets prepared for Sea Service'. So read the report of the Proceedings of a Meeting of the Privy Council held on 28 October, which authorised the formation of the first regiment specially for service afloat. Styled the Duke of York and Albany's Maritime Regiment of Foot or Admiral's Regiment, it was recruited mainly from the Trained Bands of the City of London. It is from this origin that the Royal Marines derive their privilege of marching through the City with colours flying, drums beating and bayonets fixed.

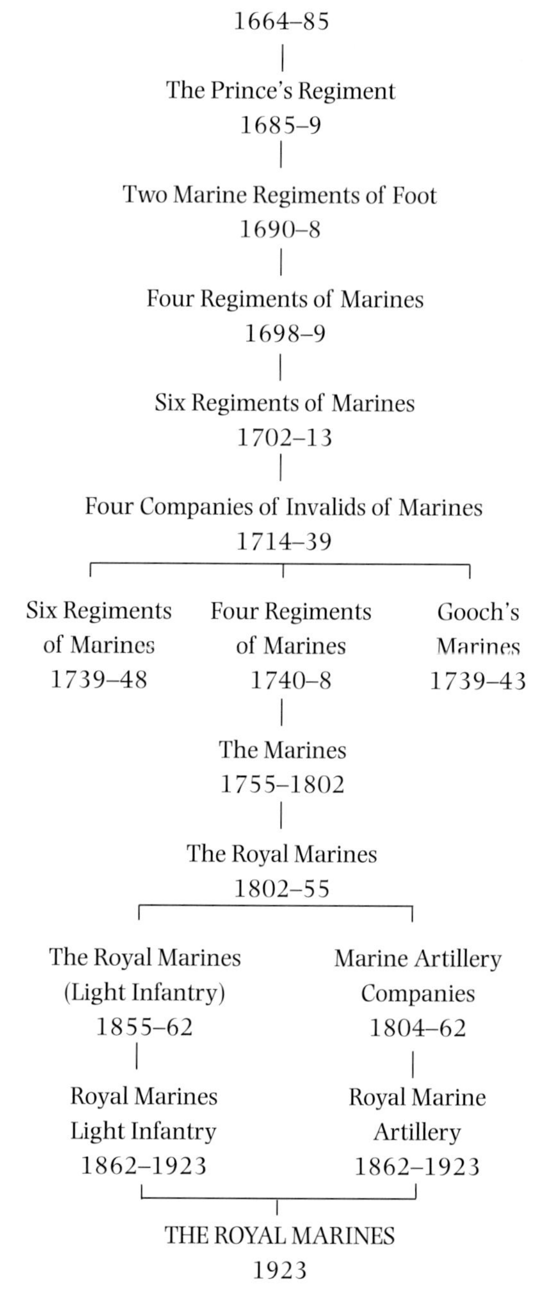

The first Marines uniform, 1664. (*NMRN*)

The Royal Marines granted the Freedom of Gibraltar, 1996. (*RMM*)

1937 Seagull launched at Devonport, the first all-welded ship in the RN. Originally a Halcyon-class minesweeper, she became a surveying ship 1946–54.

1941 Destroyer *Duncan* sank the Italian S/M *Guglielmo Marconi* 250 miles N.E. of the Azores (41.57N, 21.56W).

1943 Adjutant-General Royal Marines became General Officer Commanding Royal Marines, by Order in Council.

1798 French garrison on Maltese island of Gozo surrendered to RN blockading squadron. Capt John Cresswell landed with his Marines from *Alexander* (74) and hoisted British colours.

1801 *Pasley* captured the Spanish *Virgen del Rosario* 60 miles E.S.E. of Cape de Gata.

1832 Cocoa replaced by slab chocolate – 'Pusser's Kye'.

1880 Edward Ratcliffe Garth Russell Evans, 'Evans of the *Broke*', born in London.

See 21 April 1917, 20 November 1957.

1914 Resignation of HSH Prince Louis of Battenberg as First Sea Lord. When asked by the Kaiser why he served in the Royal Navy and not the Imperial German Navy, he had replied that 'when I joined the Navy the German Navy did not exist'. Succeeded by Fisher aged 73.

See 4 August 1921.

1915 Armoured cruiser *Argyll* wrecked on Bell Rock, east coast of Scotland.

1915 Minesweeper *Hythe* lost in collision with *Sarnia* off Cape Helles.

1918 UB-116 sunk in the controlled minefield guarding Hoxa Boom, Scapa Flow.

1918 Submarine G 2 sank U-78 in Skagerrak (56.02N, 05.08E).

1944 Two chariots from submarine *Trenchant* sank one merchant ship and damaged another in Phuket harbour, Siam.

1955 Light fleet carrier *Majestic*, launched 28 February 1945 and then laid up, commissioned at Barrow as HMAS *Melbourne*. She sailed for Australia on 12 March 1956. Collision with destroyer *Voyager*, 11 February 1964. Paid off 30 June 1982. Sister ship *Sydney* (ex-HMS *Terrible*) commissioned Devonport 16 December 1948.

1958 First flight of the pre-production Wasp helicopter (XS463), flown by Ron Gellatly, from White Waltham.

See 4 June 1963.

1982 The last full-time Admiral President of the RN College, Greenwich, Rear-Admiral John Hildred Carlill, struck his flag, the appointment having been subsumed into that of Second Sea Lord.

See 2 January 1873, 20 June 1997.

1996 Royal Marines granted the Freedom of Gibraltar. Maj-Gen. Simon Pack, CBF Gibraltar, received the Freedom Scroll from the Mayor, the Hon. Judge J.E. Alcantara in Grand Parade. Members of 40 Cdo then marched along Main Street with swords drawn and bayonets fixed.

1996 RM School of Music operational in *Nelson* after leaving Deal on 22 March 1996.

29 October

1618 Execution of Sir Walter Raleigh in old Palace Yard, Westminster.

1704 Vice-Admiral Sir John Leake (*Nottingham*) surprised and destroyed a French squadron of eight in Gibraltar Bay. Ships: *Nottingham*, *Swallow*.

1746 *Eagle* captured the French privateer *Shoreham* 90 miles W. of the Scilly Isles.

1792 Last of *Bounty* mutineers executed at Spithead.
See 28 April 1789, 14 June 1789, 23 March 1791.

1801 Nelson, having been created a viscount after Copenhagen, made his maiden speech in the House of Lords.

1807 *Louisa* fought a French lugger privateer to the southward of Cork.

1813 Capitulation of the French forces at Trieste.
Ships: *Eagle*, *Elizabeth*, *Milford*, *Tremendous*, *Weazle*, *Wizard*. Troops: British 21st Regiment; Austrians, under Maj-Gen. Count Nugent. Naval siege batteries were landed.

1856 Capture of a part of Canton by Rear-Admiral Sir Michael Seymour (*Coromandel*). Ships: *Barracouta*, *Bittern*, *Calcutta*, *Comus*, *Coromandel*, *Encounter*, *Nankin*, *Sampson*, *Sybille*, *Winchester*. US ships: *Levant*, *Portsmouth*. Naval Brigade was landed, with Royal Artillery.

1916 *Picton*, *Grafton*, M 18, M 28, M 32 and, occasionally, *Raglan* began bombardment of Turkish forts in Macedonia.

1918 Destroyer *Ulysses* lost in collision with SS *Ellerie* in Firth of Clyde.

1939 First Lord, Winston Churchill, directed the DCNS to 'arrange for a stand of arms to be placed in some convenient position in the [Admiralty] basement, and let officers and able-bodied personnel employed in the Admiralty building have a rifle, a bayonet, and ammuni-

A group of coastguards in the 1890s; originally an armed service, the Coastguard provided a reserve of men for the manning of ships as well as its duties of coast-watching and lifesaving. Many lost their lives in action during the First World War. (*NMRN*)

tion assigned to each. Fifty would be enough. Let this be done in forty-eight hours.'

See 27 November 1939, 24 March 1940.

1940 First German acoustic mine recovered by Lt S. Baker, RNVR, and Sub-Lt P.A. Cummins, RNVR, in River Ogmore near Porthcawl. Mine stripped and identified 3 November in *Vernon*.

1943 Destroyers *Dunsan* and *Vidette*, with corvette *Sunflower*, sank U-282 in N. Atlantic (55.28N, 31.57W). Convoys HX 263 and ON 208.

1950 HRH Princess Elizabeth unveiled the Chatham Port Division naval war memorial in St George's church, RN Barracks, Chatham.

1954 Light fleet carrier *Bulwark* commissioned in Belfast.

See 4 November 1954, 28 April 2005.

1984 *Norfolk*, first of the Type 23 Duke-class frigates, ordered from Yarrow, Glasgow.

See 10 July 1987, 1 June 1990, 6 May 2005.

1987 Admiral Sir William Davis, the last C-in-C Home Fleet to customarily fly his flag afloat (HMS *Tyne*) before the flag shift to Northwood in January 1960, died aged 86. He was born at Simla in 1901 and entered the Service in 1914. XO of battlecruiser *Hood* 1939–40; Captain of light cruiser *Mauritius* at Sicily, Salerno, Anzio and Normandy landings. VCNS 1954.

See 31 December 1959.

1997 Capt Muriel Hocking, RNR, appointed first female RNR commodore. The rank was substantive in the RNR and RNVR from their foundation. It was not so in the RN until 10 January 2002.

See 27 June 1734, 10 January 2002.

2000 The Captain General Royal Marines, HRH Prince Philip, unveiled the national memorial in The Mall near Admiralty Arch to the 11,000 members of the Royal Marines who died on active service in the twentieth century. The edifice, originally known as the Graspan Memorial, was originally erected in 1903 near Horse Guards to commemorate the Royal Marines who died in the Boxer Rebellion and the Boer War, and was moved to Admiralty Arch in 1946 and later redesigned as the Corps national memorial.

The Type 23 frigate HMS *Norfolk* deployed in the Arabian Gulf in Operation Telic. (*RN*)

30 OCTOBER

1708 Admiral Leake took Minorca.

1757 Admiral Edward Vernon died.
See 12 November 1684, 22 November 1739, 21 August 1740.

1809 *Surveillante* took the Spanish *Milan* 60 miles S.W. of Ushant.

1824 Capture of Martaban by combined forces under Lt-Col Henry Godwin (41st Regiment) and Lt Charles Keele (*Arachne*). Ships: *Arachne*, *Sophie*. Troops: 41st Regiment, Bengal and Madras Artillery, 3rd Madras Native Light Infantry.

1828 Bombardment and capture of Morea Castle, Patras, by combined British and French forces. Ships: *Blonde*, *Aetna*, *Conquerant*, *Armide*, *Didon*, *Duchesse de Berry*. Ships landed guns for the bombardment.

1844 Paddle frigate *Gorgon* refloated, having been aground since 10 May near Montevideo.

1877 Wearing of a half-stripe by officers ranking as a lieutenant with eight years' seniority extended to all branches.

1899 *Powerful*'s Naval Brigade at Lombard's Kop, Ladysmith.

1914 Admiral of the Fleet Lord Fisher of Kilverstone, First Sea Lord 1906–10, recalled at age 71 by Winston Churchill, First Lord of the Admiralty, to serve again as First Sea Lord after the resignation two days earlier of Admiral HSH Prince Louis of Battenberg.
See 28 October 1914, 15 and 28 May 1915.

1917 M 15, M 29, M 31 and, occasionally, M 32 and *Raglan*, and *Ladybird*, *Aphis*, *Comet*, *Staunch* and *City of Oxford*, began bombardment of Gaza coast. Ended 11 November with loss of M 15 and *Staunch*.

1918 Armistice signed by Turkey on board battleship *Agamemnon*.
See 13 November 1918.

HMS *Resolution* (1966), the first British Polaris ballistic missile submarine. (*NMRN*)

1936 Destroyer *Imogen* launched at Hawthorn, Leslie, Hebburn-on-Tyne, the first of a flotilla of eight Intrepid-class built under the 1935 programme.

See 16 July 1940.

1940 Destroyer *Sturdy* wrecked in gale on Isle of Tiree, west coast of Scotland. Convoy SC 8.

1940 First Italian midget S/M attack at Gibraltar.

1940 Destroyers *Harvester* and *Highlander* sank U-32, which had just sunk the *Empress of Britain* in N.W. Approaches (55.37N, 12.20W).

1942 Liberator X/10 (RCAF) sank U-520 (47–47N, 49–50W) and Hudson Y/145 (RCAF) sank U-658 in Atlantic (50–32N, 46–32W). Convoy SC 107.

1942 *Dulverton, Hero, Hurworth, Pakenham, Petard* and Wellesley aircraft of 47 Sqn sank U-559 in E. Mediterranean (32–30N, 33–00E). Codebooks and new *Wetterkurzschlüssel* recovered but not the M-4 cypher machine. Nevertheless, the material was of immense importance. It arrived at Bletchley Park on 24 November and was significant in the penetration of Triton on 13 December.

GC: Lt Francis Anthony Blair Fasson and AB Colin Grazier (*Petard*) for attempting to salvage cypher machine from U-559. Both posthumous.

See 1 February 1942.

1954 X 51 (*Stickleback*) set new altitude record for a submarine – 279m. (This was reached on a railway track on Shap Summit.)

1956 Vice-Admiral Sir John Eaton, the last C-in-C America and West Indies Station, hauled down his flag in Bermuda under a revised NATO command structure. Admiral Eaton continued as DSACLANT, based at Norfolk, Virginia, 'his duties in this respect are now full time'. Cdre G.E. Hunt RN, hoisted his broad pennant as SNOWI in the frigate *Bigbury Bay*. Responsibility for the southern part of the old NA&WI station transferred to the C-in-C South Atlantic who became C-in-C South Atlantic and South America. The Station Queen's Colour was laid up 28 October in the Cathedral of the Most Holy Trinity, Hamilton. Admiralty House, which had been the home of sixty Cs-in-C, was returned to the Bermudan government which had presented it to the Royal Navy 150 years earlier. On 1 June 1965 a small naval base was established around Moresby House on Ireland Island, Bermuda, and commissioned as HMS *Malabar*.

See 7 September 1958 (C-in-C East Indies), 31 March 1961 (C-in-C The Nore), 31 March 1964 (Admiralty), 11 April 1967 (C-in-C S. Atlantic), 5 June 1967 (C-in-C Mediterranean), 26 May 1969 (C-in-C Plymouth), 31 March 1979 (FO Malta), 19 June 1979, 30 September 1983 (FO Medway).

2004 The last Oberon-class submarine, *Oracle*, which paid off in July 1993, left Pounds Yard at Portsmouth under tow for a Turkish shipbreakers but foundered off Gibraltar.

See 23 August 1993.

31 October

1762 *Panther* and *Argo* captured the Spanish *Santissima Trinidad*, with $3 million on board, off Kapul Island, Philippines.

1781 Admiral of the Fleet Lord Hawke, who died on 17 October 1781, buried in the Church of St Nicolas at North Stoneham near Swaythling, N. of Southampton. His motto 'STRIKE', decisive and undimmed after two centuries, stands on his memorial.

1803 *Admiral Mitchell* drove ashore two French invasion vessels at Patel (Le Portel).

1808 *Circe* captured the French *Palinure* at Cape Solomon, Martinique.

1815 Pembroke Dockyard officially founded by Order in Council. 'We beg leave to recommend . . . that Your Royal Highness will be graciously pleased to establish, by Your Order in Council, the yard forming at Pater as a Royal dockyard.'

See 10 February 1816.

1860 Admiral Thomas Cochrane, 10th Earl of Dundonald, died. Buried in Westminster Abbey. A service is held in the Abbey every year on or near 21 May, Chilean Navy Day.

1914 *Hermes* sunk by U-27 off the Outer Ruytingen Shoal, Dover Strait, while employed as a seaplane carrier.

1914 The German cruiser *Königsberg* located in the Rufiji River, East Africa.

1915 Destroyer *Louis* wrecked in Suvla Bay.

1921 Sir Oswyn Murray, Secretary of the Admiralty, appointed a member of the Board by Order in Council.

See 23 October 1917, 10 July 1936.

1941 USS *Reuben James* sunk while escorting British Convoy HX-156 – the first American loss in the Battle of the Atlantic and before the United States entered the Second World War.

See 17 October 1941.

The German cruiser *Königsberg* sunk in the Rufiji River, 1914. (*NMRN*)

Bombardment of Acre, 1840. From a sketch taken by an artist aboard the frigate *La Pique* (shown on the extreme left). (*NMRN 1979/28*)

1943 *Douglas*, *Imperialist* and *Loch Oskaig* sank U-732 in Gibraltar Strait (35.45N, 05.52W).

1943 Corvette *Geranium* and destroyer *Whitehall* sank U-306 in Atlantic (46.19N, 20.44W). Convoys SL 138/MK 28.

1967 Cunard liner RMS *Queen Mary*, departing Southampton for the last time en route to Long Beach, California, was played off from 107 Berth by a RM band. She was over-flown by fourteen RN helicopters in anchor formation: six Whirlwinds of 771 NAS, six Wessex of 826 NAS and two Wasps of 829 NAS. Once clear of The Nab channel, the carrier *Hermes* steamed past and cheered ship.

See 2 October 1942.

1971 The British Far East Fleet, led by destroyer *Glamorgan*, steamed past its last Commander, Rear-Admiral Anthony Troup, embarked in RFA *Stromness*, off Singapore on the eve of its dissolution and amalgamation with the Western Fleet. With him were C-in-CFE, Air Chief Marshal Sir Brian Burnett, the British, New Zealand and Australian High Commissioners and the Defence Minister of Singapore. The Fleet included *Albion* with 40 Cdo embarked, five RN frigates, one RAN destroyer and one RNZN frigate. Flypast by Gannet and Buccaneer aircraft from *Eagle* and helicopters from *Albion*.

See 29 November 1967, 1 November 1971, 8 July 2008.

1972 Admiral of the Fleet Sir George Creasy died aged 77. As Captain(D) 1st DF in *Codrington* he brought Princess Juliana and family from Holland to Britain in May 1940. Director Anti-Submarine Division 1940–2. Flag Captain to Admiral Sir John Tovey, C-in-C Home Fleet, in *Duke of York* 1942–3. From December 1943 COS to Admiral Sir Bertram Ramsay, Naval Commander Allied Expeditionary Force, planning Operation Overlord. C-in-C Home Fleet and CINCEASTLANT 1952–4. C-in-C Portsmouth 1954–56. Admiral of the Fleet 22 April 1955. 'He was in every sense a perfect gentleman.' – *The Times*.

See 13 October 1895, 12 May 1940, 11 May 1955.

2009 End of the Naval Discipline Act; superseded by the Armed Forces Act 2006 which established a single system of Service law. The Strategic Defence Review 1998 recognised the increasingly joint operational environment and the need for a single, common tri-Service discipline system. The new Act replaced the Army and Air Force Acts 1955 and the NDA 1957, each of which remained in force until 1 January 2009.

See 8 November 2006, 1 January 2008.

1 November

A Memorable Date observed by the Corps of Royal Marines – Walcheren

1757 *Tartar* recaptured the British *Princess Amelia* 360 miles to the N.W. of Ushant.

1800 First edition of *Telegraphic Signals and Marine Vocabulary* by Capt Sir Home Popham.

1806 Boats of *Pique* destroyed a battery and cut out a Spanish gun-brig in Cabaret Bay, Puerto Rico.

1808 *Cruizer* fought twenty Danish gunboats and captured the Danish privateer *Rinaldo* 15 miles S.S.W. of Vinga Beacon, Kattegat.

1809 Boats of squadron cut out four and burned seven French vessels in Rosas Bay. Ships: *Tigre, Renown, Cumberland, Apollo, Volontaire, Topaze, Philomel, Scout, Tuscan.*

1811 *Imperieuse* and *Thames* and troops destroyed the batteries and captured twelve gunboats and twenty-two feluccas at Porto Palinuro. Troops: 62nd Regiment.

1857 *Shannon*'s Naval Brigade at Kudjwa. Troops: Royal Engineers, 53rd, 64th and 84th Regiments, 93rd Highlanders; 1st Bengal Fusiliers, 1st Madras Fusilier Regiment, 5th Bengal Artillery (Hon. East India Company). Four thousand enemy defeated and two guns captured.

1914 Rear-Admiral Sir Christopher Cradock (*Good Hope*) defeated by Vice-Admiral Graf von Spee (*Scharnhorst*) off Coronel, Chile. Ships: *Good Hope,* Monmouth,* Glasgow, Otranto.* Wireless used in battle by RN for the first time. Cradock was first of three rear-admirals killed in action in the First World War. Memorial in York Minster. Hood and Arbuthnot lost at Jutland. The Army lost fifty-eight general officers in the war.

*Sunk.

1914 Light cruiser *Minerva*, patrolling the Red Sea, bombarded Turkish forts at Akaba, the shoot directed by her Gunnery Officer, Lt B.A. Fraser RN, of whom more would be heard.

See 26 December 1943, 2 September 1945.

1917 Submarine E 52 sank UC-63 in Channel by cunning tactics (51.23N, 02.00E).

1918 G 7 lost in North Sea. Last British submarine loss in First World War.

1919 Admiral of the Fleet Earl Beatty, C-in-C Grand Fleet, succeeded Admiral Sir Rosslyn Wemyss (Admiral of the Fleet Lord Wester Wemyss on supersession) as First Sea Lord.

See 30 July 1927.

1921 River gunboat *Glowworm* embarked ex-Emperor Karl of the Austro-Hungarian Empire and Queen Zita at 0500 at Baja below Budapest. 'They were received on board *Glowworm* in absolute silence' and, escorted by *Ladybird*, she took them down the Danube to the Romanian coast on the Black Sea where, at Sulina, they transferred on 7 November to the light cruiser *Cardiff* which sailed at 0700 for Madeira; 'it struck me how absolutely sportsmanlike under very adverse circumstances, had been the Ex-Emperor's mien throughout' – *The Naval Review*.

See 15 July 1815, 17 November 1920, 17 November 1922.

1941 First operational launch from a CAM ship. Pilot Officer G.W. Varley RAFVR in a Hurricane from *Empire Foam* chased off a Focke Wulf 200 Kondor running in with bomb doors open to attack Convoy HX 156. Varley baled out and was rescued.

See 4 June 1941, 3 August 1941, 11 January 1941.

CAM ships, Catapult Aircraft Merchantmen, were cargo-carrying merchant ships flying the Red Ensign and fitted with a catapult launcher over the forecastle. Fighter Catapult Ships continued their separate role under the White Ensign. 'The pilots of the RAF's merchant ship fighter unit and of the naval fighter catapult ships merit a special word. They knew that, once they had been catapulted, their patrol would probably end by a parachute descent into the sea, hoping to be picked up by a surface escort vessel. Their sorties demanded a cold-blooded gallantry' – Roskill, *The War at Sea*, vol.1, p.477.

1943 *Active, Fleetwood, Witherington* and Wellingtons R/179 and W/179 sank U-340 in Gibraltar Strait.

1944 *Avon Vale* and *Wheatland* sank German TB TA-20 (ex-Italian *Audace*, ex-Japanese *Kawakaze*, built Yarrow) and corvettes UJ-202 and UJ-208 (ex-Italian *Melpomene* and *Spingarda*) off Pag Island, Adriatic (44.34N, 14.44E).

1944 Successful assault on Walcheren. Operation Infatuate 1 and 2. Ships: *Erebus*, *Roberts*, *Warspite*, *Kingsmill*. No. 4 Army and 41, 47 and 48 RM Cdos. About 180 landing craft of a wide range of types took part.
Battle Honour: Walcheren 1944.

1945 AGM 641A promulgated a vote of thanks passed by Parliament the previous day:

'That the thanks of this House be accorded to all ranks of the Royal Navy and of the Royal Marines for the untiring vigilance and resource with which they have frustrated each new stratagem of the enemy; for their courage and devotion to duty which beat the U-boats by which the enemy planned to reduce these Islands to starvation and submission; for the unflagging zeal which they brought to the arduous duties of protecting the flow of food and materials vital to the life and work of our people and allies; and when the long period of defence at last made way for attack, for the matchless skill and courage with which the great forces for the assaults were landed, supported and maintained on campaigns in both hemispheres.'

1948 Recruiting began for the Royal Marine Forces Volunteer Reserve.

1951 'The Committee of Public Accounts questioned the Board of Customs and Excise about the entitlement of admirals to 1,600 gallons of duty free wine a year. Asked what percentage they took up, Mr R.J. Lloyd, Board of Customs and Excise, reported "The total consumption of wine involves duty of about £25,000 a year, so obviously the Admirals cannot take very much". Mr Hoy of the Committee: "Why? The £25,000 duty will represent a terrible lot of wine, will it not?" Mr Lloyd: "There are a lot of Admirals". An Admiralty spokesman explained that this privilege dated from an 1876 Act.' – *The Times*, 2 November 1951.

1956 Light cruiser *Newfoundland* and destroyer *Diana* sank Egyptian frigate *Domiat* (ex-RN River-class frigate *Nith*) in Gulf of Suez.

A Landing Craft Gun (Medium) armed with two 25-pdr guns for shore bombardment, at Walcheren in 1944. (*NMRN*)

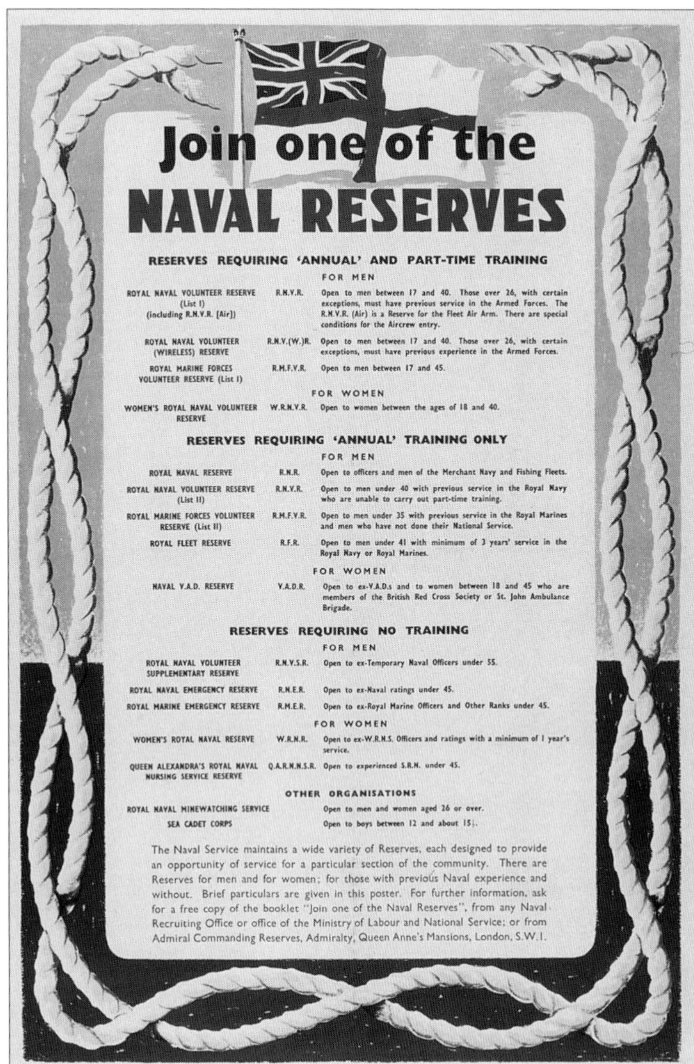

Admiralty poster advertising Naval Reserves, 1953. *(NMRN 1996/26(9))*

1958 RNR and RNVR amalgamated. WRNVR became WRNR.

See 4 December 1957, 1 October 1966.

In 1853 a Naval Volunteer Act allowed for the recall of naval pensioners in time of emergency, and a Coastal Volunteer Force was formed.

Continuing anxiety over the numbers of trained men led to the Royal Naval Reserve (Volunteers) Act in 1859 which allowed for a reserve of trained merchant seamen. The rapid German armament led to the institution of the Royal Naval Volunteer Reserve, consisting of civilian volunteers, in 1903.

1958 HRH The Duke of Gloucester appointed an honorary Commodore RNR. This rank was established by Order in Council in April 1915. The first officer so appointed was Sir Richard Williams-Bulkeley, who was an honorary Captain RNR in command of the Naval Depot at Crystal Palace.

See 1 June 2004.

1959 RN Hospital Hong Kong transferred to the Army. AFO 291/60.

See 23 March 1830, 6 January 1915, 12 January 1949.

1961 *Camperdown*, Battle-class destroyer, arrived home to pay off. It marked the retirement of AB George Parker, aged 60. He joined the RN in 1918 and was the only man still serving and wearing First World War medal ribbons. Apart from a three-month gunnery course in 1920, had spent all his forty-two years' service in seagoing ships. Mountbatten suggested to one of his captains that a distinguishing mark should be carried in any ship in which Parker served. A copper ball was then secured at the mainmast head which followed Parker to *Camperdown*.

See 2 November 1956.

1967 HM The Queen approved new Colours for the RAN, an Australian White Ensign of silk with a crown and royal cypher with blue and gold cords and tassels. The new Queen's Colour was presented to the RAN by the Governor General, Lord Casey, at Melbourne this day.

See 9 December 1950, 23 December 1966, 1 March 1967, 20 June 1968.

1971 Western Fleet (Northwood) and Far East Fleet (Singapore) amalgamated. Admiral Sir Edward Ashmore, C-in-C Western Fleet since 16 September with his flag ashore at *Warrior*, Northwood, became the first CINCFLEET, the first officer to command all the ships and aircraft of the Royal Navy. The Far East Fleet, formed in 1946, was disbanded. Rear-Admiral J.A.R Troup, the last COMFEF, hauled down his flag at *Terror*, Singapore, at Midnight 31/10. RN Barracks handed over to the Australian Army 9 October. DCI(RN) 1079/71.

See 28 April 1971, 1 May 1971, 31 October 1971, 9 February 1977.

1974 Fire in Type 82 destroyer *Bristol*, caused by a fractured fuel pipe spraying diesel into the STR, caused £1,671,833 damage. DCI(RN) 716/76.

Walcheren, 1944

The attacking Allied armies in Europe were slowed down by the lack of a sufficient port to supply them with ammunition, fuel, food, etc. It was therefore resolved to take Antwerp, and for this it was necessary to capture the heavily fortified island of Walcheren. On 1 November 1944 the bombers allocated for softening up the defences were fog-bound in England. The naval support vessels therefore sailed close inshore and attacked enemy defences with a heavy bombardment. Of these vessels nine were sunk, and 372 men killed. Gen. Eisenhower said of this bombardment 'credit for the success of the amphibious operations is largely due to the support craft of the British Navy which unhesitatingly and in the highest tradition of the service attracted to themselves the point-blank fire of the land batteries, thus permitting the commandos and assault troops to gain the shore . . .'

The Royal Marine Commandos stormed the shore and in the face of stout resistance and with little support from the air took the island after two days of hard fighting. The German batteries were silenced, thus enabling the Scheldt and the Port of Antwerp to be opened for the support of the Allied armies in Flanders. Of this operation Sir Winston Churchill wrote, 'the extreme gallantry of the Royal Marines stands forth', and its anniversary is a Memorable Date observed by the Royal Marines.

See 14 November 1970.

1983 Comacchio Company RM became Comacchio Group RM. DCI(Joint) J423/83.

1985 *Ark Royal*, fifth of the name, commissioned at Portsmouth. Her first CO, Capt James Weatherall, had joined the previous *Ark Royal* on 26 January 1978 as her last Commander.

See 1 July 1985, 5 November 2010.

1985 Admiral of the Fleet the Lord Fieldhouse succeeded Field Marshal the Lord Bramall as Chief of the Defence Staff.

1989 Gangway staffs and upper-deck sentries to carry arms.

1993 The Women's Royal Naval Service formally integrated into the Royal Navy. Post of Director WRNS ceased 15 October 1993. DCI(RN) 259/93.

See 15 October 1993.

1998 Atlantic Patrol Task Force (North) established to 'provide a tangible UK maritime presence in the Caribbean AOR'. Replaced West Indies Guard Ship (WIGS). APT (South) formed with same role in South Atlantic and off West Africa.

1999 Shoulder badge slides with gold lettering on dark blue (Royal Navy, QARNNS, QARNNS(R) and Royal Naval Reserve) introduced for ratings following issue of general duty rig white short-sleeved shirts.

2 November

1710 General the Earl of Peterborough appointed Captain-General of the Marine Forces – the original holder of the post, which then lapsed until revived by King George VI in 1948.
See 8 October 1948.

1757 *Antelope* captured the French privateer *Moras* 100 miles W. of Cape Finisterre.

1757 *Tartar* (28) captured the French privateer *Mélampe* (36) 360 miles N.W. of Ushant.

1758 *Antelope* captured the French *Belliqueux* off Ilfracombe.

1762 *Terpsichore* captured the French letter of marque *Marquis De Marigny* 100 miles W. by S. of Ile de Ré.

1780 *Zephyr* captured the French *Sénégal* in the Gambia River.

1800 Alexander Dalrymple, first Hydrographer of the Navy, published the first Admiralty Chart, a 'sketch of the Road on the NE Side of the Island Houat in Quiberon Bay by Thomas Moore, Master of HM Ship *Diamond*'.
See 11 September 1795.

1854 Boats of *Winchester* and *Spartan* destroyed nine pirate junks in Tynmoon Bay, near Hong Kong.

1918 Last two British merchant ships (*Murcia* and *Surada*) to be sunk in First World War torpedoed by UC-74 off Port Said.

1940 Destroyer *Antelope* finally sank U-31 in defence of convoy OB 237.

1941 Submarine *Tetrarch* presumed sunk by a mine in Sicilian channel on passage from Malta to Gibraltar.

1944 Submarine *Shalimar* bombarded Malacca, Nicobar.
See 22 September 1951, 1 March 1956.

1956 CPO William Pettit Coop, BEM, of 23 Collins Road, Southsea, presented with a second clasp to his Good Conduct Medal by Admiral of the Fleet Sir George Creasy, C-in-C Portsmouth. With one exception, CPO Coop, aged 63, was then the oldest serving rating in the RN having served continuously since 1 February 1911.
See 1 November 1961.

1959 Commodores RNR entitled to fly a broad pennant, a blue St George's Cross as worn by commodores of convoys in the Second World War; those of Cdre J. Whayman DSC, RD, RNR, and Cdre C.P.C. Noble DSC, VRD, RNR, were hoisted in *Eaglet* and *Chrysanthemum* respectively. AFO 2758/59.

1961 Frigate *Troubridge* with soldiers and relief stores arrived at Belize two days after Hurricane Hattie had struck British Honduras. Classic relief operation: guards landed to prevent looting, technical teams repaired generators and isolated villages relieved. Frigate *Londonderry* and surveying ship *Vidal* joined later with medical supplies and more troops.

1966 The first Wrens to be drafted to Singapore since the end of the Second World War left London Airport. DWRNS, Commandant Dame Margaret Drummond, saw them off.

2000 Serious fire in and around after machinery space of assault ship *Fearless*, Capt C.J. Parry RN, 150 miles W. of Crete. The fire was contained and extinguished by the ship's company, with steam drenching used for the first time at sea since the 1960s. 'There were 657 heroes in the ship that day,' recalled Capt Parry, 'It was the Royal Navy – its training, its ethos and above all its people – at its unbeatable best.' The ship, as flagship of the Amphibious Task Group and with an embarked military force, was leading a task force en route to Sierra Leone (Operation Silkman). The ATG staff and embarked force were transferred to *Ocean* and other ships off Malta and *Fearless* returned to Portsmouth on her remaining shaft.
See 14 November 1970, 28 November 1971, 1 November 1974.

2001 RN Submarine Service centenary commemorated in a thanksgiving service in Westminster Abbey.
See 18 September 1951, 17 September 2001.

3 NOVEMBER

1758 *Buckingham* (70) fought the French *Florissant* (74), *Bellone* and *Aigrette* between Guadeloupe and Montserrat.

1778 *Maidstone* captured the French *Lion* 190 miles S.S.E. of Cape Henry.

1839 *Volage* and *Hyacinth* defeated a flotilla of Chinese war junks in the Bogue, Canton River.

1840 Bombardment of Acre.
See 17 September 1840, 4 November 1840, p.620 photograph.

1854 *Encounter, Barracouta, Queen* (US hired steamer) and boats of *Spartan* destroyed seventeen pirate junks at Tai ho, Lantao, Hong Kong.

1911 'Instances having occurred in which Officers have made official application for appointment to particular ships, attention is drawn to the fact that their Lordships consider such applications objectionable, and desire that they shall not be forwarded to the Admiralty.' – AWO 335/11.

1914 Bombardment by Anglo-French squadron of the outer forts at the Dardanelles: an unfortunate curtain-raiser since it revealed Allied intentions. Ships: *Indefatigable, Indomitable, Vérité, Suffren.*

1914 'I drink to the memory of a gallant and honourable foe' – von Spee in reply to a German civilian who had proposed the toast 'Damnation to the British Navy' at Valparaiso, after the Battle of Coronel on 1 November 1914.
See 26 December 1943.

1914 German battlecruisers bombarded the British coast near Gorleston, Norfolk, for the first time. HM Ships: *Halcyon, Leopard, Lively.* D 5 sunk by mine 2 miles S. of South Cross Sand Buoy, Yarmouth, seeking, with D 3 and E 10, to intercept the German squadron.

1917 Submarine C 15 sank UC-65 in Channel (50.28N, 00.17E).

1940 U-99 sank AMC *Laurentic* (54.09N, 13.44W) and AMC *Patroclus* (53.43N, 14.41W) in N.W. Approaches, within one and a half hours.
See 2 December 1940.

1941 Submarine *Trident* sank German Uj-1213 off north coast of Norway.

1942 Explosion of SS *Hatimura* sank U-132 S.S.E. of Cape Farewell (55.38N, 39.58W).

1942 GC: Lt John Stuart Mould, GM, RANVR, for mine recovery and disposal. (*Gazette* date.)

1943 DAMS SS *Storaa* torpedoed in attack by German E-boats S100 and S138 of the 5th S-Boat Flotilla on Convoy CW221 off Hastings; twenty-one men lost. In 2008 the wreck was designated by MOD under the Protection of Military Remains Act 1986.
See 1 May 2008.

1948 'All naval chaplains entered on or after this date to wear naval uniform. Chaplains already serving to have the option of wearing naval uniform or civilian clerical attire.'

1956 First RN loss of Suez campaign: Wyvern from *Eagle* shot down. Sloop *Crane* attacked by Israeli aircraft, assuming her to be Egyptian. Operation Musketeer.

1959 Royal Naval Reserve officers hosted HRH The Duke of Edinburgh at a dinner in the Painted Hall, RNC Greenwich, to mark the centenary of the RNR the next day.

1981 English Harbour, 'Nelson's Dockyard', handed over to Antigua, though the White Ensign flies from a presentation mast on certain days.

2006 Diving and Explosive Ordnance Disposal skill badge introduced for MCD officers and warrant officers (Diver) to be worn on left sleeve of No. 1 jacket and mess jacket. RNTM 183/06.
See 21 March 2003.

4 NOVEMBER

1650 *Black Prince* burned by Parliamentarians.

1702 Admiral John Benbow died at Port Royal, Kingston, Jamaica, from a leg wound received on 22 August, the fourth day of his running action with a weaker French squadron commanded by Rear-Admiral Du Casse off Cape Santa Marta in present-day Colombia. He was buried the next day in St Andrew's church, Kingston: 'HERE LYETH INTERRED THE BODY OF JOHN BENBOW, ESQ., ADMIRAL OF THE WHITE, A TRUE PATTERN OF ENGLISH COURAGE WHO LOST HYS LIFE IN DEFENCE OF HYS QUEENE AND COUNTRY NOVEMBER YE 4TH 1702 IN THE 52ND YEAR OF HYS AGE BY A WOUND WHICH HYS LEG RECEIVED IN AN ENGAGEMENT WITH MONS. DU CASSE BEING MUCH LAMENTED.' War of the Spanish Succession 1702–13.

See 19 August 1702, 8 October 1702, 16 April 1703.

1800 *Marlborough* (74), Capt Thomas Sotheby, on blockade duty off Quiberon, ran onto a sunken reef W. of Belle Ile in a gale. The ship was got off and anchored but she was too damaged to save. Ship's company taken off by the cutters *Lurcher* and *Nile*, and boats from *Captain* (74). The *Marlborough* was a veteran of Rodney's Moonlight Battle (16 January 1780) and The Saintes (12 April 1782), and of Howe's Glorious First of June in 1794.

Poking fun at the Royal Navy: one of many postcards inspired by the 'On the Knee' incident at RN Barracks, Portsmouth, in November 1904. (*George Malcolmson*)

1803 Launch of *Blanche* captured a French armed schooner in the Caracol Passage, Haiti.

1805 Capt Sir Richard Strachan (*Caesar*) with *Hero*, *Namur* and *Courageux* took the French *Formidable* (Rear-Admiral Dumanoir Le Pelley), *Scipion*, *Mont Blanc* and *Duguay-Trouin* (as HMS *Implacable*, the last Trafalgar ship afloat) 260 miles W. of Rochefort. These were the first survivors of Trafalgar to be captured, and the exuberant wording of his dispatch earned Strachan the nickname 'Delighted Sir Dicky'.
Battle Honour: Bay of Biscay 1805.

See 3 June 1932, 2 December 1949.

1810 Boats of *Blossom* captured the French privateer *César* 100 miles S. by W. of Cape Sicie.

1834 *Nimble* wrecked on passage to Havana, partly because of the rapidity of the currents but also partly because of the noise made by 272 captured black slaves.

1840 Capture of Acre by Admiral the Hon. Sir Robert Stopford and Cdre Charles Napier (*Princess Charlotte*).
Battle Honour: Syria 1840.

Ships: *Bellerophon*, *Benbow*, *Edinburgh*, *Powerful*, *Princess Charlotte*, *Revenge*, *Thunderer*, *Carysfort*, *Castor*, *Hazard*, *Pique*, *Talbot*, *Wasp*, *Gorgon*, *Phoenix*, *Stromboli*, *Vesuvius*. Austrian: *Guerriera*, *Lipsia*, *Medea*. Turkish: *Mookuddimay-I-Hive* (flag of Sir Baldwin Walker). Troops: Royal Artillery, Royal Sappers and Miners. Some 7,059 claims for the Naval General Service medal were made in connection with the Syrian operations, which began on 10 September and which were the last for which that medal was awarded.

1843 Upper part of statue of Nelson affixed to the lower part erected the previous day, to complete the monument in Trafalgar Square. The statue sculpted by E.H. Bailey, the column (145-ft high) designed by William Railton. The bronze bas-reliefs on the base were completed in 1849, cast from cannon captured in his battles. Landseer's lions did not appear until 1867. It is said that his Lordship faces the way he does because that is the nearest way to the sea, but this may be a conceit and has not been verified. Another hypothesis is that he is simply keeping an eye on the Admiralty.

Capt Sir Richard Strachan's action, 1805. Another nickname among Strachan's crews was 'Mad Dick' on account of his violent temper. A contemporary recorded, 'Yet the sailors liked him for all that . . . and said that when he swore he meant no harm, and when he prayed he meant no good.' (*NMRN Lib.*)

1855 Destruction of the Russian stores in the Gheisk estuary, Sea of Azov. Ships: *Vesuvius*, *Ardent*, *Curlew*, *Weser*. Gunboats: *Boxer*, *Clinker*, *Cracker*, *Grinder*, *Recruit*.

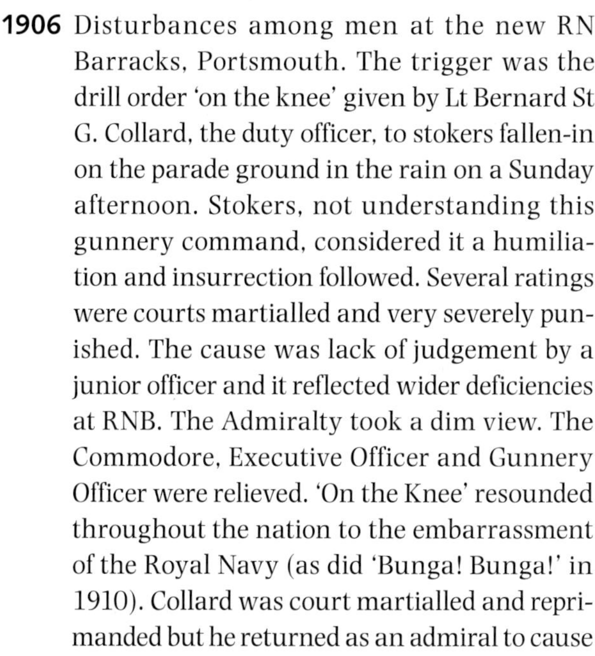

1906 Disturbances among men at the new RN Barracks, Portsmouth. The trigger was the drill order 'on the knee' given by Lt Bernard St G. Collard, the duty officer, to stokers fallen-in on the parade ground in the rain on a Sunday afternoon. Stokers, not understanding this gunnery command, considered it a humiliation and insurrection followed. Several ratings were courts martialled and very severely punished. The cause was lack of judgement by a junior officer and it reflected wider deficiencies at RNB. The Admiralty took a dim view. The Commodore, Executive Officer and Gunnery Officer were relieved. 'On the Knee' resounded throughout the nation to the embarrassment of the Royal Navy (as did 'Bunga! Bunga!' in 1910). Collard was court martialled and reprimanded but he returned as an admiral to cause another naval humiliation.

See 13 January 1928.

1914 German cruiser *Karlsruhe* sunk in the Atlantic about 300 miles off Barbados, by internal explosion (10.07N, 55.25W).

1914 *Bustard* and *Excellent* bombarded Lombartzyde, near Nieuport.

1936 Admiral of the Fleet Sir John Donald 'Joe' Kelly died in London aged 65.

See 13 July 1871, 6 September 1873, 7 August 1914, 15 September 1931, 11 January 1933, 24 June 1937, 14 September 1952.

1942 Midget submarine X 3 sank in four minutes on exercise in Loch Striven. Crew rescued by *Present Help* and craft salvaged by 2300.

1954 Light fleet carrier *Bulwark* completed at Harland and Wolff, Belfast.

See 10 May 1945, 22 June 1948.

1959 Service of Thanksgiving in St Paul's Cathedral, attended by HRH Prince Philip to mark the centenary of the establishment of the Royal Naval Reserve. Roman Catholic officers and men attended Capitular High Mass sung in Westminster Cathedral.

1967 *Repulse*, second British Polaris submarine, launched at Vickers, Barrow, at noon on Saturday by Lady Zuckerman using a bottle of homemade elderberry wine. The tugs failed to hold the boat and she went aground on the Walney Channel sands where she was left high and dry until refloated at the next high tide.

See 28 September 1968, 22 October 2010.

1971 Cdre Sir Peter Anson hauled down his flag at *Jufair*, Bahrain, and post of SNO Persian Gulf (SNOPG) ceased. *Jufair* paid off 15 December 1971. DCI(RN) 1080/71 (refers to Commander Naval Forces Gulf).

See 7 September 1958.

1982 Death of Capt S.W. Roskill, official historian of RN in Second World War.

See 1 August 1903.

1994 RN Cookery School at St Omer Barracks, Aldershot, ceased training and moved to *Raleigh*, Torpoint, recommencing training on 4 January 1995. DCI(RN) 195/94.

See 9 August 1872.

2010 Destroyer *Manchester*, Cdr Rex Cox RN, provided emergency relief to Soufriere and Morne Fond St Jacques on St Lucia following Hurricane Tomas.

See 15 November 2010

5 November

1650 Blake destroyed the Royalist fleet under Prince Rupert off Carthagena.

1688 William III landed at Torbay, borne on the Protestant wind.

1781 *Albemarle* (28), Capt Horatio Nelson, in Elsinore (Helsingor) Road, Denmark, 'fired nineteen guns it being Gun Powder Plot'.

1783 *Superb* (74), third of the name, lost with all hands off Tellichery, India.

1803 Boat of *Blanche* cut out the French *Albion* at Monte Christi, Haiti.

1813 Inconclusive engagement off Toulon between Vice-Admiral Sir Edward Pellew (*Caledonia*) and Vice-Admiral Comte Emeriau (*Imperial*).

1854 Battle of Inkerman. VC: Capt William Peel and Mid Edward St John Daniel (*Diamond*), Lt William Nathan Wrighte Hewett (*Beagle*), Seamen Thomas Reeves, James Gorman, Mark Scholefield, Cpl John Prettyjohn, RMLI, the first Marine recipient of VC. Prettyjohn, having been cut off with his party by a strong Russian column and having run out of ammunition, drove off the Russians by heaving stones down the hill at them. Reeves, Gorman and Scholefield repulsed a Russian attack at Inkerman, exposing themselves to heavy fire.

See 18 and 26 October 1854, 18 June 1855.

1914 Rear-Admiral Ernest Troubridge's court martial began on board battleship *Bulwark* at Portland.

See 7 August 1914, 9 November 1914.

1915 Armed boarding steamer *Tara* sunk by U-35 off Sollum. Egyptian coastguard cruisers *Abbas* and *Nur El Bahr* sunk and damaged respectively at Sollum by U-35.

1918 The former Cunard liner *Campania*, purchased in 1914 and converted to carry aircraft, foundered in the Grand Fleet anchorage off Burntisland in the Firth of Forth after dragging her anchor during strong squalls in the middle watch and colliding with the battleship *Royal Oak* and then dragging into the bows of the large light cruiser *Glorious*. No fatalities. The RNR OOW in *Campania*, who had not let go a second anchor and had not called the Captain, was dismissed his ship.

HM The Queen inspecting the Guard of Honour from HMS *Ark Royal* at Portsmouth on 5 November 2010. (*RN*)

HM The Queen joined members of HMS *Ark Royal* ship's company in Portsmouth to celebrate the ship's 25th anniversary. (*RN*)

1940 VC: Capt Edward Stephen Fogarty Fegen (*Jervis Bay*). Armed merchant cruiser *Jervis Bay* sunk by *Admiral Scheer* while defending convoy HX 84 in mid-Atlantic (52.41N, 32.17W).
Battle Honour: *Admiral Scheer* 1940.
See 6 August 1950.

Convoy HX 84, of thirty-seven ships escorted by the Armed Merchant Cruiser *Jervis Bay* (Capt E.S.F. Fegen), was homeward bound from Halifax. The German pocket battleship *Admiral Scheer* (six 11-in guns, eight 5.9-in guns) encountered the convoy in mid-Atlantic. The convoy was scattered immediately, while the *Jervis Bay* closed the battleship and engaged her. The *Jervis Bay* was overwhelmed, but she gave the convoy time to make smoke and scatter, and only five ships were sunk.

One vessel in the convoy was the British tanker *San Demetrio*, which was set on fire and abandoned. The men in one of her lifeboats later sighted her, re-embarked, brought the fire under control and, despite the lack of navigational aids, brought her to port with most of her cargo intact.

In a letter to the *Daily Telegraph* on 31 October 2005 Admiral Sir John Woodward referred to: 'what I have called for many years the *Jervis Bay* syndrome, which drove us all in the Royal Navy. It is the force that made us put our main armament in the front of the ships, not the rear. It is the force that made us go forward when all our instincts were yelling to go back. It is the force that makes our ships generally worth any two similar of our enemy's. And it is the force that gave rise to the British sailor's saying "You shouldn't have joined if you can't take a joke".'

1942 Prime Minister Churchill directed the First Lord of the Admiralty to give names rather than numbers to submarines; 'I have no doubt whatever that names should be given, and I will myself make some suggestions which may stimulate others'.
See 3 July 1902, 24 September 1926, 19 and 27 December 1942, 28 January 1943.

1943 Destroyer *Aldenham* and *Miaoulis* (Greek) bombarded Kos.

1946 GC: Surgeon Lt-Cdr Patrick Albert O'Leary, DSO. Work in connection with the escape of Allied prisoners of war. (*Gazette* date.)

1948 Light cruiser *Sheffield*, lately flagship of Admiral Sir William Tennant on the America and West Indies Station, returned to Chatham to pay off. She had steamed 60,000 miles and been visited by 170,000 people on the Atlantic and Pacific seaboards of the station. The ship had been warmly welcomed the previous March at Belize during a period of tension between British Honduras and Guatemala; 'her visit there had the usual sobering effect which the presence of ships of the Royal Navy so frequently produces on recalcitrant elements.' – *Navy* magazine.

1954 First Sea Lord, Admiral of the Fleet Sir Rhoderick McGrigor, appeared before the Cabinet and convincingly argued the future of carriers and naval aviation. 'It was probably his finest hour as Chief of Naval Staff' – Eric Grove, *ODNB*.
See 6 March 1938, 4 May 1945, 21 January 1955, 3 December 1959.

1956 Carriers withdrew from Suez assault zone having destroyed Egyptian aircraft and sunk four MTBs.

1962 RN Auxiliary Service (RNXS) formed from the RN Minewatching Service (RNMWS). DCI(RN) 126/89.
See 6 December 1952, 18 January 1963, 2 December 1963, 17 June 1993, 1 April 1994.

1962 Responsibility for the administration of the Northern Ireland Sub-Command transferred from FO Plymouth to FO Scotland who became FOSNI. AFO 2012/62.

2010 HM The Queen visited *Ark Royal*, Capt Jeremy Kyd RN, at Portsmouth to mark the 25th anniversary of the ship's commissioning on 1 November 1985. The SDR announcement of 19 October made it a farewell visit.
See 1 July 1985, 1 November 1985, 19 October 2010, 3 December 2010.

6 NOVEMBER

1778 Admiralty ordered first two frigates with a main armament of 18-pdr guns; 12-pdrs hitherto the heaviest guns carried by frigates. *Minerva* built at Woolwich, *Flora* at Deptford.

1794 *Alexander* (74) taken by a French squadron under Rear-Admiral Joseph Nielly (*Tigre*) 100 miles W. of Ushant. Retaken off Lorient by *Sans Pareil* next June.

1799 *Speedy* fought fifteen Spanish gunboats off Europa Point.

1805 News of Trafalgar arrived in London. Collingwood's despatches, brought into Falmouth by the schooner *Pickle* and then by post-chaise, arrived by the hand of Lt John Lapenotiere at the Admiralty at 060100. Lord Barham, First Lord, roused from his bed. *The Times* carried news of the battle in a single column report in its second edition: 'We know not whether we should mourn or rejoice. The country has gained the most splendid and decisive Victory that has ever graced the naval annals of England: but it has been dearly purchased. *The great and gallant* NELSON is no more.' Collingwood's despatch was published in full next day.

See 13 October 1797, 24 October 1805, 8 December 1955.

1856 *Barracouta* and *Coromandel*, with boats of *Calcutta, Encounter, Sampson, Sybille* and *Winchester*, captured French Folly, Canton River, and destroyed twenty-one war junks.

1860 Admiral Sir Charles Napier died: 'It is seamen, not ships, that constitute a navy.'

1914 *Bustard* and *Humber* bombarded Westend and Lombartzyde, Belgium.

1914 Start of naval operations on River Tigris. *Odin* and *Espiegle*, joined by *Comet, Shaitan, Sumana* and *Lewis Pelly*, reinforced by Fly- and Insect-class gunboats.

1915 Submarine E 20 sunk by the German UB-14 in the Dardanelles. Betrayed by RV left in captured French S/M *Turquoise*.

1917 *Peveril* (*Puma*) (Q 36) sunk by U-63 off Cadiz (35.44N, 06.48W).

1943 *Kite, Starling* and *Woodcock* sank U-226 in N. Atlantic (44.49N, 41.13W), and *Starling* and *Wild Goose* sank U-842 (43.42N, 42.08W).

1943 Vice-Admiral Ronald H.C. Hallifax killed in an air crash at Sollum returning to UK at end of tour as SNO Suez Canal. Rear-Admiral (Destroyers) Home Fleet from May 1939 was appointed FO Red Sea at Aden in April 1941. His son, Admiral Sir David Hallifax KCB, KCVO, KBE, was Chief of Staff to Admiral Sir John Fieldhouse during Operation Corporate in 1982 and later Constable and Governor of Windsor Castle.

See 10 December 1941, 15 April 1942, 2 January 1945, 29 April 1943.

1946 Sir Geoffrey Arthur Romaine Callender died. The first professor of naval history at Greenwich, lecturer at the RN War College, the first director of the National Maritime Museum (10 September 1934), Hon. Secretary of the Society for Nautical Research for twenty-five years and a luminary of the Navy Records Society.

See 29 November 1907.

1956 British forces landed in the Canal Zone, Egypt, following the nationalisation of the Suez Canal. Helicopter assault in Whirlwind and Sycamore aircraft by 45 RM Cdo launched from *Ocean* and *Theseus* on Suez. First major helicopter-borne assault from ships. 'Whatever may be said of Suez – an amphibious success but a diplomatic disaster – it saved the day for the Royal Marines in particular and amphibious warfare in general' – Col Ewen Southby-Tailyour.

See 25 July 1956, 1 November 1956, 22 December 1956.

Operation Musketeer, 1956

In early August, *Bulwark* and *Theseus* sailed from Portsmouth, *Theseus* with 13th Ind. Para Brigade Gp from Devonport.

Ocean sailed from Devonport, also with troops and some craft including LCTs brought forward from reserve and hastily refitted by the dockyard.

Royal Marines from 45 Cdo boarding Whirlwind helicopters on HMS *Theseus*, ready for the assault on Suez in 1956. (*NMRN*)

30 Oct. War broke out between Israel and Egypt.

31 Oct. Egyptian destroyer *Ibrahim Ah Ahwal* (ex-*Mendip*) was captured by Israel, and Britain and France intervened in hostilities.

1 Nov. *Newfoundland* and *Diana* sank Egyptian frigate *Domiat* (ex-*Nith*).

6 Nov. Assault at Suez, involving more than 100 RN and French ships including six carriers (*Eagle*, *Albion*, *Bulwark*, *Ocean*, *Theseus* and *Lafayette*).

Ocean and *Theseus* carried RM Cdos and helicopters. RN aircraft flew about 2,000 sorties, 1,600 of them by Seahawks and Wyverns. Four hundred sorties were made by Whirlwind and Sycamore helicopters over the beaches in the airborne assault. No. 3 Cdo Brigade were landed by LST/LCT – with 45 Cdo by air, all in ninety-one minutes. Naval bombardment also took place: little damage was done to the town, except to strong points of resistance. No guns larger than 6in were used and wanton damage was carefully avoided.

1969 *Amazon*, first Type 21 frigate and ninth of the name, laid down at Vosper Thornycroft, Woolston.

See 26 April 1971.

1998 *Ocean*, *Sheffield*, RFAs *Black Rover* and *Sir Tristram*, 45 Cdo and Netherlands Marines in major disaster-relief operations in Honduras and Nicaragua in wake of Hurricane Mitch. Operation Tellar.

2002 *Trafalgar*, SSN, with SMCC 0/2 embarked, hit the sea bed at 14.7 knots during dived transit of the Fladda-chuain/Eilean Trodday trough off the Isle of Skye. Board of Enquiry found the cause was human error and recommended that 'nuclear submarines should only conduct training of this nature if the arrangements for navigational safety are infallible'.

See 26 May 2008, 4 December 2009.

2008 Capt A.W.F. 'Alfie' Sutton RN, FAA Observer, son of a soldier killed on the Somme and the last survivor of the forty-two aviators who mounted the FAA raid from *Illustrious* on the Italian battle fleet at Taranto on 11 November 1940, died aged 96. He won the Admiralty's naval history prize essay competition in 1939, 1947, 1949 and 1956.

See 31 August 2005, 9 May 2006.

2008 Capt Michael Henry RN, CO of Britain's first ballistic missile nuclear-powered submarine, *Resolution*, which fired the RN's first Polaris missile, died aged 80. Cdr Mike Henry, already told of this pending appointment, was sent out as short-term replacement XO of the destroyer *London* during her first commission in the Far East under the remarkable Capt Jozef Bartosik. Bartosik stopped his leave on one occasion and gave him an adverse S.206 which FOSM (Horace Law) ignored.

See 15 February 1968, 14 January 2008.

7 November

1803 Cutter of *Blanche* captured a French armed schooner in Manzanillo Bay, Haiti.

1807 Boats of *Renommée* and *Grasshopper* cut out a Spanish brig and a French tartan under Torre de Estacio, near Cartagena.

1900 The Fisher-Beresford feud. Vice-Admiral Sir John Fisher, C-in-C Mediterranean Fleet, having entered Grand Harbour, Valletta, in *Renown*, watched from the Upper Barracca the rest of his fleet enter harbour. The *Ramillies*, flagship of Rear-Admiral Lord Charles Beresford, his second-in-command, made a mess of securing bow and stern to her buoys in Bighi Bay, the outer anchorage, and delayed other ships. Fisher signalled: 'Your flagship is to proceed to sea and come in again in a seamanlike manner'. It was a public rebuke which flashed around the Service and was, as Admiral of the Fleet Lord Chatfield later wrote 'a lamentable example of bad leadership'.

See 8 November 1907.

The 'Paintwork v. Gunnery' Controversy, 1907

Sir Percy Scott was the great exponent of naval gunnery during the 1890s and 1900s. His training devices for gunlayers, his insistence on frequent gunnery practice and his introduction of prize shooting at realistic long ranges did much to improve gunnery standards in the Royal Navy. But his abrasive personality and his unorthodox methods often brought him into conflict with senior officers, and his most publicised clash occurred with Lord Charles Beresford in 1907.

Beresford was himself a colourful and dashing personality, having first won fame when he attacked a major Egyptian fort in his gunboat *Condor* during the bombardment of Alexandria in July 1882. But he was also a strong traditionalist, and suspicious of the reforms being introduced by his great rival, Fisher, and other younger men such as Percy Scott.

In 1907 Beresford was in command of the Channel Fleet, with Scott as Rear-Admiral Commanding its First Cruiser Squadron. Beresford ordered all his ships, by letter of 4 November, to prepare for a Royal Visit. *Roxburgh*, one of Scott's cruisers, asked permission to finish gunnery exercises before painting ship. Beresford being absent, Scott signalled 'Paintwork appears to be more in demand than gunnery so you had better come in to make yourself look pretty by the 8th'. Such a signal was less than tactful but Beresford (who heard of it only four days later) overreacted by publishing the full text and publicly reprimanding Scott. As a result, the incident was exaggerated out of all proportion and has come to be seen as a symbol of the old reactionary attitude to gunnery practice. In fact, Beresford was, under normal circumstances, in favour of effective training.

1914 Japanese forces captured Tsingtau, base port of German East Asiatic Squadron.

1915 E 19 sank the German light cruiser *Undine* in the Baltic, 22 miles off Trelleborg, Sweden.

1918 Last attack (unsuccessful) by a German submarine on a British merchant ship (*Sarpedon*) in First World War.

Merchant Ship Losses 1914–18

Year	Merchant Ships	Fishing Vessels	Total Tonnage (thsds)	Lives Lost
1914	64	45	248	164
1915	278	192	880	2,601
1916	396	141	1,251	1,255
1917	1,197	213	3,751	6,521
1918	544	84	1,670	4,180
War Totals	2,479	675	7,800	14,721*

*Official War History quotes 15,313

1940 Sloop *Milford* and Walrus aircraft of heavy cruiser *Devonshire* (700 Sqn) engaged the French S/M *Poncelet*, scuttled in Gulf of Guinea (00.20S, 08.50E).

1940 Submarine *Swordfish* lost on mine, leaving Portsmouth for patrol off Brest. Thought to have been mined off Ushant, and the loss was announced on the 16th. Discovered in 1983, only four hours out of *Dolphin*.

See 14 September 1939, 17 November 1940.

1941 HQ W. Approaches moved from Plymouth to the basement of Derby House, a new office block behind Liverpool Town Hall. Here it was co-located with 15 Group RAF and was in closer contact with the Admiralty shipping control organisation, escort commanders and convoy commodores. C-in-C flew his flag in the old minesweeping sloop *Eaglet*, ex-*Sir Bevis*.

See 17 November 1941.

HMS *Fearless* assisting the Greek motor vessel *Nostos Vasso Athene* off Malta in 1976. (*NMRN*)

1958 Consequent upon unification of Reserves, RNR and RNVR buttons replaced once again with RN pattern.

1975 Another black day for the Royal Navy. The 'infamous' DCI T641/75 announced that black nylon stockings for Wrens (Vocabs 45500-05) were to be replaced by black tights. 'BR81 and BR96 will be amended'. The Navy had not fully recovered from the withdrawal of the Rum ration in 1970 when this further blow landed. A vigorous but futile 'Fight Tights' campaign was led by the FAA. The black stockings calamity 'had a devastating effect on morale'.

See 30 July 1956, 31 July 1970.

1976 *Fearless* while on charter to film *The Spy Who Loved Me*, salvaged Greek SS *Nostos Vasso Athene* off Malta.

1994 Type 23 frigate *Richmond*, Yard No. 137, was the last warship to leave Swan Hunter Shipbuilders, Wallsend.

See 6 April 1993.

1995 Rosyth Naval Base closed. 3rd MCM Sqn moved to Faslane. 1st MCM Sqn and Fishery Protection Squadron moved to Portsmouth. Departing ships sailed past *Bicester*, wearing the flag of FOSNNI, Vice-Admiral Christopher Morgan.

1997 First female PWO qualified; Lt-Cdr Vanessa Jane Spiller, PWO Course 111.

See 1 October 1971, 23 May 1972, 3 April 2001, 1 April 2004, 14 May 2004, 30 June 2005.

Admiral of the Fleet Sir John 'Joe' Kelly (1871–1936)

Joe Kelly and his younger brother, Howard, commanded, respectively, the light cruisers *Dublin* and *Gloucester* at the start of the First World War and provided the only sharp performances in the otherwise bungled chase of the German battlecruiser *Goeben* through the Mediterranean in August 1914. He was Fourth Sea Lord 1924–6 and Vice-Admiral Commanding First Battle Squadron and second-in-command Mediterranean Fleet 1927–9 with his flag in *Warspite* (*Royal Oak* was in his squadron during the 'Bandmaster Barnacle' debacle). Following the Invergordon Mutiny in 1931, Joe Kelly was given command of the Atlantic Fleet (renamed Home Fleet) to restore morale and discipline (shades of Howe and the Spithead Mutiny in 1797). A sailor's sailor, the rugged Joe Kelly was the perfect choice but the task exhausted him and he saw out his time as C-in-C Portsmouth from January 1935 to July 1936. He was promoted admiral of the fleet the day before hauling down his flag on his 65th birthday. Joe Kelly, worn out and very tired, died four months later. On 6 November his body was borne on a gun carriage in procession led by Bluejackets with reversed arms from the Admiralty to St Martin-in-the-Fields via Admiralty Arch and Trafalgar Square. The chimes of Big Ben at noon could be heard as the coffin was borne up the steps of St Martin's by eight petty officers from HMS *Pembroke*. Five admirals of the fleet were among the pall bearers. Admiral of the Fleet Sir Ernle Chatfield, First Sea Lord, 'was prevented from being present by a chill'. The body was later taken to Portsmouth where it rested overnight in the dockyard church (where a memorial now stands) before being taken to sea on 8 November from South Railway Jetty in the light cruiser *Curacoa* escorted by six destroyers for burial off The Nab. The cruiser fired a 19-gun salute. His successor at Portsmouth, William Wordsworth Fisher also wore himself out commanding the Mediterranean Fleet and died in post the following year.

8 November

1723 Hon. John Byron born.
See 6 July 1779.

1799 *Defiance* and *Centurion* fought two French third rates between Almeria and Malaga.

1810 Boats of *Quebec* cut out the French privateer *Jeune Louise* at Vliestroom.

1813 Boats of *Revenge* cut out a French privateer at Palamos.

1848 *Polyphemus* recaptured the British *Three Sisters* at Cala Tramontana, Riff coast.

1907 Kaiser's visit to Channel Fleet provoked 'paint-work v. gunnery' signal.
See 7 November 1900, 6 September 1919.

1910 Esquimalt first used as RCN base: arrival of cruiser *Rainbow*.
See 3 August 1914.

1914 Churchill as First Lord drafted terms of reference for Room 40, addressed to the Chief of the Naval War Staff (Oliver) and to the Director of Naval Education (Ewing) though not to DNI (Hall).

1916 Destroyer *Zulu* mined off Dunkirk (51.04N, 02.04E): stern blown off. Forepart later joined to after part of *Nubian*, the composite destroyer being named *Zubian*.
See 27 October 1916, 4 February 1918.

1932 Destroyers *Defender*, Lt-Cdr R. Gotto RN, and *Diamond*, Lt-Cdr R.H.D. Lane RN, commissioned at Devonport for the First Destroyer Flotilla. Both ships lost in action in the Mediterranean in 1941.
See 7 April 1932, 27 April 1941, 11 July 1941

1940 Destroyer *Havelock* sank Italian submarine *Faa di Bruno* off Gibraltar.

1941 Martlet aircraft of 802 Sqn (*Audacity*) shot down two Focke-Wulf FW 200s in Atlantic (41.27N, 15.18W). Convoy OG 76.

1942 VC: Capt Frederick Thornton Peters (*Walney*), Oran harbour. Landing in North Africa. Operation Torch.
Battle Honour: North Africa 1942.

Operation Torch – Landings in North Africa, 1942

Admiral Sir Andrew Cunningham was in command of the naval landings in North Africa. Three were planned, the Royal Navy covering those at Oran and Algiers, with the USN covering that at Casablanca. The coordination and planning required can be judged by the convoy sailings for the initial assaults. These involved nearly400 merchant ships and 170 escorts, and started on 2 October from the Clyde (slow) and 1 November (fast), with some convoys sailing from America. A long series of follow-up convoys were planned and run for the resupply of the 70,000 troops landed.

The assaults took place early on the 8th. During the attack at Algiers one airfield was captured by FAA Martlet fighters under Lt B.H.C. Nation of *Victorious*. This was probably the first time a shore airfield had been captured by naval aircraft.

Naval losses during the assault were the destroyer *Broke*, after breaking through the boom at Algiers to land troops in the harbour area, and the ex-US Coast Guard cutters *Walney* and *Hartland*, during the assault on the harbour at Oran. *Aurora* and destroyers engaged French destroyers off Oran; sank one, drove one ashore and the third returned to harbour.

Ships: *Aberdeen, Achates, Acute, Alarm, Albacore, Algerine, Alynbank, Amazon, Antelope, Arctic Ranger, Argonaut, Argus, Ashanti, Aubrietia, Aurora, Avenger, Avon Vale, Bachaquero, Banff, Beagle, Bermuda, Bicester, Bideford, Biter, Blean, Boadicea, Boreas, Bradford, Bramham, Brilliant, Brixham, Broke, Bude, Bulldog, Bulolo, Burke, Cadmus, Calpe, Cava, Charybdis, Clacton, Clare, Clyne Castle, Coltsfoot, Convolvulus, Coreopsis, Coriolanus, Cowdray, Cumberland, Dasher, Delhi, Deptford, Dianella, Duke of York, Eastbourne, Eday, Egret, Elbury, Empyrean, Enchantress, Erne, Eskimo, Exe, Farndale, Felixstowe, Filey Bay, Fleetwood, Fluellen, Formidable, Foula, Furious, Gardenia, Geranium, Glengyle, Goth, Hartland, Horatio, Hoy, Hunda, Hussar, Ibis, Ilfracombe, Imperialist, Inchcolm, Inchmarnock, Ithuriel, Jamaica, Jonquil, Juliet, Jura, Karanja, Keren, Kerrera, Kingston Chrysolite, Kintyre, Lamerton, Landguard, Largs, Laurel, Leith, Leyland, Linnet, Loch Oskaig, Londonderry, Lookout, Lord Hotham, Lord Nuffield, Lotus, Lulworth, Lunenburg, Maidstone, Malcolm, Marigold, Martin, Meteor, Milne, Misoa, Mull, Negro, Nelson, Norfolk, Offa, Onslow, Opportune, Oribi, Othello,* P 45, P 48, P 51, P 54, P 217, P 219, P 221, P 222,

Left: Admiral Lord Charles Beresford (1846–1919). (*NMRN*)

Right: Capt A.D. Piper DSC, RNR as a lieutenant. (*NMRN*)

P 228, *Palomares, Panther, Partridge, Pathfinder, Pelican, Penn, Pentstemon, Philante, Polruan, Poppy, Porcupine, Pozarica, Prescott, Prinses Beatrix, Puckeridge, Quality, Queen Emma, Quentin, Quiberon, Renown, Returno, Rhododendron, Rhyl, Roberts, Rochester, Rodney, Ronaldsay, Rother, Rothesay, Rousay, Royal Scotsman, Royal Ulsterman, Ruskholm, Rysa, St Day, St Mellons, St Nectan, Samphire, Sandwich, Scarborough, Scottish, Scylla, Sennen, Sheffield, Shiant, Sirius, Speedwell, Spey, Spirea, Starwort, Stork, Stornoway, Stroma, Stronsay, Sturgeon, Swale, Tartar, Tasajera, Tribune, Tynwald, Ulster Monarch, Ursula, Vanoc, Vansittart, Velox, Venomous, Verity, Vetch, Victorious, Vienna, Violet, Walney, Westcott, Westray, Weyburn, Wheatland, Wilton, Wishart, Wivern, Woodstock, Wrestler, Zetland.* RFA: *Abbeydale, Brown Ranger, Derwentdale, Dewdale, Dingledale, Ennerdale, Hengist, Jaunty, Nasprite, Restive, Viscol.* FAA Sqns: Albacore: 817, 820, 822, 832; Fulmar: 809, 882, 888; Martlet: 893; Sea Hurricane: 800, 802, 804, 883, 891; Seafire: 801, 807, 880, 884, 885; Swordfish: 833. HDML: 1127, 1128, 1139. ML: 238, 273, 280, 283, 295, 307, 336, 338, 433, 444, 458, 463, 469, 471, 480, 483.

Ships sunk: *Walney* blew up and sank, abandoned in Oran harbour after being hit by Vichy shore batteries. *Hartland* hit by gunfire from *Typhon* and also abandoned and sunk in Oran harbour. Operation Reservist. *Broke* damaged off Algiers by Vichy batteries, abandoned and scuttled by *Zetland*. Operation Terminal. The French lost *Epervier, Tramontane, Tornade* and *Typhon* in Oran, mainly to *Aurora*'s fire, and *La Surprise* intercepted off Oran by *Brilliant*.

1943 *Grenville, Tumult, Tyrian* and *Piorun* (Pol) bombarded enemy positions in the Gulf of Gaeta, in support of the 5th Army.

1995 Capt Aston Dalzeel 'Peter' Piper died. The first RNR officer to be awarded the DSC in the Second World War (*Ursula* 1940) and two bars (*Unbeaten* 1942). First RNR officer to command a submarine (H 34 and P 55 – *Unsparing*). DSO 1944.

See 12 April 1943, 28 January 2003.

2006 Armed Forces Act, which heralded the end of the Naval Discipline Act, received the Royal Ascent.

See 1 Janaury 2009, 31 October 2009.

9 November

1689 Capt John Benbow appointed Master Attendant of Chatham Dockyard.
See 19 August 1702, 4 November 1702.

1805 Three days after the news of Trafalgar reached London, Prime Minister William Pitt, in his speech at the Lord Mayor's Banquet, said 'England has saved herself by her exertions, and will, I trust, save Europe by her example.'

1806 *Dart* and *Wolverine* captured the French privateer *Jeune Gabrielle* 140 miles E. of Barbados.

1807 *Skylark* captured the French privateer *Renard* in Dover Strait.

1817 The new Dockyard Chapel at Plymouth opened for Divine Service. The foundation stone laid 19 January 1815.

1865 *Galatea* and *Lily* destroyed the insurgent batteries at Cape Haitien.

1909 Admiral of the Fleet Sir John Fisher, First Sea Lord, ennobled as Baron Fisher of Kilverstone (near Thetford, Norfolk).

1914 The Australian light cruiser *Sydney* fought the most famous single ship action of the First World War. After a brief but brilliantly executed marauding mission against British shipping and possessions in the Indian Ocean, the German light cruiser *Emden*, Capt Karl von Muller, was destroyed in a gun battle off the Cocos Keeling Islands by HMAS *Sydney*, Capt John Glossop RN, and she ran herself ashore on North Keeling Island. '*Emden* 1914' was the first battle honour won by the Royal Australian Navy.
See 11 July 1915.

Emden had been detached from Admiral von Spee's East Asiatic Squadron in August and her daring operations, conducted by Muller in strict accordance with international law, won the professional admiration of friend and foe alike. 'Not only had Captain von Muller obtained a high measure of success [both in the actual damage he had done and the strategic and economic disturbance he had caused] but he had won the respect of his enemy for the skill, resource and boldness with which he had maintained his position so long, and for the chivalry and humanity with which his duty had been discharged.' – Corbett, *Official History of the War. Naval Operations*, vol.1, p.385. Muller had landed a party to destroy the wireless and cable station on Direction Island which could not be re-embarked when the *Sydney* appeared; they eventually they made most of their way to Constantinople in the commandeered schooner *Ayesha*, a voyage marked by fortitude and courage.

1914 Rear-Admiral E.C.T. Troubridge acquitted by court martial, the charge that on 7 August he did, while being under the Naval Discipline Act, 'from negligence or through other default, forbear to pursue the chase of His Imperial German Majesty's ship *Goeben*, being an enemy then flying' being not proved. He received bad advice from his flag captain. Troubridge was never again employed afloat.
See 7 August 1914, 5 November 1914.

1916 *Fair Maid* mined near Cross Sand Buoy.

1918 Alexandretta occupied by Allied naval forces.

1918 *Privet* (Q 19) and ML 155 sank U-34 in Gibraltar Strait (35.56N, 05.25W).

1918 GC (ex-AM): Lt H.M.A. Day RMLI, for saving life when *Britannia* torpedoed and sunk by U-50 off Cape Trafalgar two days before the armistice. The last of thirteen battleships and the last major British warship lost by enemy action in the First World War. Fifty men lost. Lt Day was a great nephew of Lt G.F. Day, VC.
See 18 September 1855, 6 August 1914.

1939 *Isis* captured the German *Leander* off Cape Finisterre (42.32N, 12.46W).

1940 *Aphis* bombarded Sidi Barrani.

1940 Fulmar, Skua and Swordfish aircraft (*Ark Royal*) attacked Elmas airfield, Sardinia. Operation Crack. FAA Sqns: 810, 818, 820.

1941 *Aurora*, *Penelope*, *Lance* and *Lively* (Force K) and *Upholder* attacked two escorted convoys in Mediterranean (36.50N, 18.07E). Italian destroyers *Fulmine* and *Libeccio* and ten merchant ships sunk (*Libeccio* by *Upholder*).

HMS *Britannia* sinking off Cape Trafalgar in 1918. She was one of the eight King Edward VII-class battleships, launched in 1904, known as 'the wobbly eight'. (*NMRN*)

1942 *Gardenia* sunk in collision with *Fluellen* off Oran (35.49N, 01.05W). Operation Torch.

1942 *Cromer* mined off Mersa Matruh (31.26N, 27.16E).

1942 P 247 (*Saracen*) sank the Italian S/M *Granito* off Cape San Vito, Sicily (38.34N, 12.09E).

1943 Fortress J/220 sank U-707 in N. Atlantic (40.31N, 20.17W). Convoy MKS 29A.

1962 Canes, Walking Out, Vocab No. 70600, for issue on repayment as an optional item of kit for Corporals, Royal Marines, increased in price from 1/6*d* to 9*s*. AFO 2151/62 and AFO 410/62.

1962 Midshipmen serving in the Fleet permitted to wear the blue mess jacket and 'evening waistcoat' of the same pattern as commissioned officers. AFO 2150/62.

See 26 September 1975.

1970 Carrier *Ark Royal*, Capt John Treacher RN, collided with Russian Kotlin-class destroyer S. of Crete during Exercise Lime Jug. No damage to *Ark Royal*.

See 14 November 1970.

1980 Second major fire in a year damaged forward hangar and several mess decks in the commando carrier *Bulwark*, alongside at Portsmouth. Increasing concern about old and faulty wiring. Ship's Motto 'Under Thy wings I will (t)rust'.

See 15 March 1980, 27 March 1981.

10 November

1337 Sacking of Cadzand by Henry, Earl of Derby, and Sir Walter Manny. Virtually the start of the Hundred Years' War.

1573 Launch of *Dreadnought*, first of the name, at Deptford.

1721 *Royal Anne Galley*, 511 tons bm, launched at Woolwich 1709, foundered off the Lizard. The last HM ship designed to be pulled rather than sailed.

1808 *Amethyst* captured the French *Thétis* off Isle de Groix. First award of Gold Medal to Captain for taking an equal or superior enemy in single-ship action.
Battle Honour: *Thétis* 1808.

1811 *Skylark* and *Locust* defeated a French flotilla of twelve gunvessels off Calais and took a brig.

1813 Boats of *Undaunted* and *Guadeloupe* stormed the batteries of La Nouvelle, south coast of France, captured two vessels and destroyed five more.

1833 *Nimble* captured the Spanish slaver *Joaquina* 7 miles off Isla de Pinos, near Cuba.

1890 Third-class cruiser *Serpent* wrecked on Boy Rock, Punta Bay, off Cape Corcubian, N. Spain.

1902 First regulations for QARNNS published.

1914 Collier (*Newbridge*) sunk to block *Königsberg* in Rufiji River. First operations against the German light cruiser.

1914 British forces bombarded and stormed Sheikh Sa'id (S. Arabia) and destroyed the defences.

HMS *Eagle* (1920), an aircraft carrier converted from a partially built Chilean battleship, seen through the rigging wires of a Fairey Swordfish on board another aircraft carrier. (*NMRN*)

The central battery ironclad battleship HMS *Sultan* launched at Chatham in 1870, grounded on a rock in the South Comino Channel bertween Malta and Gozo on 6 March 1889 and sank a week later. She was raised and taken to Valletta for repairs. The ship as a depot ship for minesweepers at Portsmouth through the Second World War and was sold in 1947. (*Author*) See p.149, 14 March 1870.

Ship: *Duke of Edinburgh*. Troops: 29th Indian Infantry Brigade under Brig-Gen. H.V. Cox.

1918 Paddle minesweeper *Ascot* torpedoed by UB-67 off the Farnes. Last RN ship sunk in First World War.

1920 Destroyer *Verdun* sailed from Boulogne with the body of Britain's Unknown Warrior (from the Ypres Front) and was received at Dover with a field marshal's 19-gun salute from Dover Castle. The coffin was covered with the same Union Flag that had covered those of Nurse Edith Cavell and Capt Charles Fryatt, both executed by the Germans.

See 27 July 1916, 11 November 2009.

1931 Submarine *Swordfish*, first of name and of class, launched at Chatham. (*Sentinel*, fourth of her name and sixty-second and last of the class, was launched on 27 July 1945.)

1941 *Proteus*, the first British submarine fitted with radar (Type286P), made first radar-assisted attack by torpedoing the German (ex-Greek) steamer *Ithaka* in the Aegean. She detected an enemy convoy by radar on evening of 9 November and shadowed on the surface through the night and attacked submerged at 0320/10 after the moon was well up.

1942 *Martin* sunk by U-431 85 miles N.E. of Algiers (37.53N, 03.57E). *Ibis* sunk by Italian aircraft 10 miles off Algiers (37.00N, 03.00E), while *Lord Nuffield* sank the Italian S/M *Emo* there (36.50N, 02.50E).

1944 *Hydra* mined off Ostend: CTL.

1945 *Assiniboine* (RCN) (ex-*Kempenfelt*) wrecked on Prince Edward Island.

1989 Revised objectives issued for Navy and Air Days: 'To show the men, women, ships, aircraft and equipment of the RN and RM to the public in order to foster a good impression of the Services, good public relations and to stimulate recruiting.' – DCI(RN) 318/89.

11 NOVEMBER

1755 *Orford* captured the French *Espérance* 240 miles S.S.W. of Lizard Head.

1779 *Tartar* captured the Spanish *Santa Margarita* off Cape Ortegal.

1794 Mutiny in *Windsor Castle* in Mediterranean.

1804 *Cyane* captured the French privateer *Bonaparte* between Desirade and Marie Galante, West Indies.

1858 Detachments of the *Pearl*'s Naval Brigade, 13th Light Infantry and Bengal Yeomanry dispersed the Indian rebels at Phanpur.

1875 *Shannon* launched at Pembroke Dockyard; the first British armoured cruiser.

1914 *Niger* sunk by U-12 off Deal.

1917 *Staunch* and M 15 torpedoed and sunk off Gaza by UC-38.

1918 Armistice signed by Germany ending the First World War.

RN strength 37,636 officers and 400,975 men, excluding RNAS transferred to form RAF on 1 April 1918.

First World War Losses

Casualties	HM Ships	RN Division	Total
Killed in Action or Died of Wounds	22,811	7,924	30,735
Died – other causes	11,843	666	12,509
Wounded	4,510	20,165	24,675
Injured – other causes	648	–	648
Totals	39,812	28,755	68,567

Fleet strength: 61 battleships, 9 battlecruisers, 30 cruisers, 90 light cruisers, 23 flotilla leaders, 443 destroyers,147 submarines – Roskill, *Naval Policy between the Wars*, vol.1, p.72.

War losses: 13 battleships, 3 battlecruisers, 13 cruisers, 12 light cruisers, 3 flotilla leaders, 64 destroyers, 54 submarines, 3 carriers, 18 sloops, 17 armed merchant cruisers, 5 monitors and many other minor warships (based on Admiralty return to House of Commons, August 1919).

See 4 August 1914, 10 January 1920.

1921 Admiral of the Fleet Earl Beatty presented the Victoria Cross to the Unknown Warrior of the United States of America at the warrior's burial in Arlington National Cemetery on behalf of King George V.

1928 White Ensign raised on board ships of the Royal Indian Marine 'which were fully equipped with guns' and the RIM was given combat status.

See 1 October 1934, 14 September 1939.

1931 The former twin-screw minesweeper *Petersfield*, employed as the yacht of Admiral Sir Howard Kelly, C-in-C China Station, ran ashore in fog and darkness on Tung Yung Island off the E. coast of China and was lost. The C-in-C and the ship's company were taken off by the German steamer *Derfflinger* and later transferred to the heavy cruiser *Suffolk* which landed them in Hong Kong. Howard Kelly's semi-estranged brother, Admiral Sir Joe Kelly, briefly signalled 'Glad you are safe', which was curtly acknowledged with 'Glad you're glad'.

1936 First member of RNV(S)R enrolled.

See 10 December 1936, 22 February 1965.

1940 Fleet Air Arm attack on Italian battleships in Taranto Bay by two squadrons from *Illustrious* and two from *Eagle*.
Battle Honour: Taranto 1940.

See 31 August 2005.

Ships: *Berwick, Glasgow, Gloucester, Hasty, Havock, Hyperion, Ilex, Illustrious, York*. Cover: *Barham, Gallant, Greyhound, Griffin, Hereward, Hero Malaya, Valiant, Warspite*. FAA Sqns: 813,* 815, 819, 824.* Seriously damaged: *Conte di Cavour, Caio Duilio, Littorio*. Operation Judgement.

*From *Eagle*.

Taranto Bay, 1940

The carrier *Illustrious* mounted an air-strike against the Italian Fleet at Taranto. *Eagle* was to have been in company, but suffered damage before the strike while in action off Calabria; some of her aircraft were transferred to *Illustrious* for the operation. Twenty-one aircraft in two waves flew off from *Illustrious* at 2040 and 2100 on 11th. They achieved complete surprise and sank three battleships at their moorings. All but two aircraft returned

The service of thanksgiving held in Westminster Abbey on 11 November 2009 to mark the passing of the generation that fought in the First World War. (*RN*)

safely to *Illustrious*. Letter from Admiral Cunningham: 'The 11th and 12th November 1940 shall be remembered for ever as having shown once and for all that in the Fleet Air Arm the Navy has a devastating weapon. In a total flying time of about 6½ hours carrier to carrier twenty aircraft inflicted more damage upon the Italian fleet than was inflicted upon the German High Seas Fleet in the daylight action at the Battle of Jutland.'

'As an example of economy of force it is probably unparalleled' – Admiral Cunningham.

1942 Submarine *Unbeaten* sunk in error by British aircraft in the Bay of Biscay (46.50N, 06.51W).

1942 *Hecla* torpedoed by U-515 off Cape St Vincent. Sank the next day.

1942 *Tynwald* sunk by Italian S/M *Argo* off Bougie (36.42N, 05.10E).

1942 *Bengal* (RIN) and Dutch tanker *Ondina* attacked by two Japanese armed merchant cruisers in the Indian Ocean (19.45S, 92.45E). The *Hokoku Maru* was sunk and *Aikoku Maru* made off.
Battle Honour: *Hokoku Maru* 1942.

1942 Submarine *Turbulent* sank *Benghazi*: a satisfactory revenge for *Medway* since she was the German depot ship for Mediterranean U-boats, and took down forty torpedoes.
See 30 June 1942.

1943 *Beaufort*, *Faulknor* and *Pindos* (Greek) bombarded Kos. *Rockwood* bombed by German aircraft S. of Kos: CTL, even though the Hs 293 failed to explode.

1944 Submarine *Venturer* sank U-771 off Tromsø.
See 9 February 1945.

1944 *Kenilworth Castle*, *Launceston Castle*, *Pevensey Castle*, *Portchester Castle* sank U-1200 off Cape Clear (50.24N, 09.10W).

1958 Federal German Navy submarine *Hecht* arrived at Fort Blockhouse for escape drill training with the Royal Navy. Her arrival on Armistice Day was ill-timed and generated adverse press coverage.

1961 Frigate *St Brides Bay* left Singapore for the UK after eleven years' continuous service on the Far East Station.
See 11 October 1960.

1968 Cdr Sir Dennistoun Burney, inventor of the paravane minesweeping gear at HMS *Vernon* during the First World War, died at Hamilton, Bermuda, aged 79. Made CMG in 1917, an unusual distinction for a lieutenant. He was only son of Admiral Sir Cecil Burney, 2 i/c Grand Fleet at Jutland.

1992 Vice-Admiral Sir Peter Gretton died; one of the outstanding convoy escort commanders of the Second World War.

1993 St Batholomew's church, Yeovilton, dedicated as the Fleet Air Arm Memorial church.
See 21 August 1704, 4 February 1786, 18 February 1907, 21 June 1934.

2005 Capt George Baldwin RN, naval aviator and CO of the Royal Navy's first operational jet fighter squadron, died aged 84.
See 17 August 1951.

2009 National service in Westminster Abbey attended by HM The Queen, HRH The Duke of Edinburgh, the Prime Minister, CDS and the Service chiefs of staff to mark the passing of the First World War generation, following the deaths of Bill Stone, Henry Allingham and Harry Patch. During the service the bell of the destroyer *Verdun*, which ship had carried the body of the Unknown Warrior from France, was rung by AB David Hutchinson of the frigate *Westminster*. Off the Firth of Forth a wreath was cast on the sea from *Bangor* by Lt-Cdr Peter Noblett RN and the youngest member of his ship's company, AB (Diver) R.E. Cartwright-Taylor.
See 10 November 1920.

12 NOVEMBER

1595 John Hawkins died at Puerto Rico on Drake's last expedition.

1684 Edward Vernon born; victor of Porto Bello in 1739 and he who watered-down the rum ration.
See 22 November 1739, 21 August 1740, 30 October 1757.

1781 Capture of Negapatam by Vice-Admiral Sir Edward Hughes (*Superb*) and Maj-Gen. Sir Hector Munro. Ships: *Burford, Eagle, Exeter, Monarca, Superb, Worcester.* Frigates: *Active, Nymph, Combustion.* Hon. East India Company ships: *Essex, Expedition, Neptune, Panther, Rochford, Royal Admiral.* Seamen and marines were landed.
See 6 July 1782.

1806 Boats of *Galatea* captured the French *Réunion* 15 miles N.E. of Guadeloupe.

1854 *Tribune, Highflyer* and *Lynx* destroyed a Russian tower 10 miles N.W. of Anapa.

1854 Julian Stafford Corbett born; official historian of British Naval Operations in the First World War.
See 21 September 1922.

1856 Capture of the Bogue forts, Canton River. Ships: *Barracouta, Calcutta, Coromandel, Hornet, Nankin.*

1912 Federated Malay States offered a battleship to the RN – commissioned as *Malaya* in 1915 and served until 1948.

1920 *Tobago* mined in Black Sea and sold at Malta.

1925 Submarine M 1 (ex-K 18) sunk in collision with Swedish SS *Vidar* off Start Point.

1939 Light cruiser *Delhi* intercepted the German *Mecklenburg*, which was scuttled off Faroes (62.37N, 10.26W).

1940 Light cruiser *Orion* (Vice-Admiral H.D. Pridham-Wippell, CS 7) with *Ajax* and *Sydney* (RAN) sank one ship and set two on fire in an escorted convoy of four ships off Valona (40.48N, 19.18E). Operation Judgement.

1942 *Lotus* and *Starwort* sank U-660 in Mediterranean (36.07N, 01.00W). Convoy TE 3.

1944 Lancaster bombers of No. 5 Group, Bomber Command, sank the German battleship *Tirpitz* at Tromsø. Operation Catechism.

The German battleship *Tirpitz*, under naval air attack, obscured by smoke and explosions 3 April 1944. (*NMRN*)

The Victorian Navy. HMS *Northumberland* was originally fitted with five masts, but had been reduced to a three-masted barque by 1890 when she was photographed here in Milford Haven. On Christmas Day 1892 she was anchored with the Channel Fleet in Funchal Roads, Madeira, when her cable parted in a violent gale in the small hours. She fell across the ram bows of HMS *Hercules* and was badly holed. The nearest dry dock which could take her was the new Somerset Dock at Malta where she was towed and repaired. She ended her RN days as Coal Hulk C8 at Invergordon. (*Author*)

1970 FONAC moved from *Daedalus* (Lee-on-Solent) to *Heron* (Yeovilton).

1982 HM Oil Fuel Depot, Old Kilpatrick, closed. DCI(RN) 608/82.

See 31 March 1977, 31 March 1978, 31 December 1983

1992 Plans to transfer RN Operational Sea Training from Portland to Devonport and the closure of Portland Naval Base by April 1996 announced by the Armed Forces Minister.

See 21 July 1995.

Admiralty Message of Congratulation, 1918

12/11/18 from Admiralty

'The Lords Commissioners of the Admiralty desire heartily to congratulate officers and men of the Royal Navy and Royal Marines upon the triumph of the Allied cause, in realisation of which they have played so splendid a part, adding lustre throughout to the great tradition of the Service to which they belong.

Their Lordships feel that after four years of ceaseless vigilance a relaxation of war conditions cannot but be eagerly desired by officers and men; they may be relied upon to grant leave and modify routine immediately when circumstances permit. For the present however with German submarines possibly still at sea ignorant of the Armistice, with the work of escorting ships to be surrendered or interned devolving largely on the Royal Navy and with the full capacity of the minesweepers required for sweeping the seas it is plain that no officer or man can be spared from their duties until the safety of the country at sea is assured.

The Navy had in time of peace to be ready for war in a sense which land forces cannot be. Now that peace is again in prospect, it may prove that even after the troops in the field are enjoying a relief from tension the Navy must for a time continue its war routine. If so their Lordships are confident that this will be cheerfully accepted as being at once the burden and the privilege of the Empire's first line of defence.'

13 NOVEMBER

1705 *Orford, Warspite* and *Lichfield* captured the French *Hasardeux* 90 miles W.N.W. of Ushant.

1797 Launch of *Fairy* captured the French privateer *Epervier* in Whitesand Bay, near Calais.

1798 *Peterel* (16) taken by three Spanish frigates in Mediterranean. Recaptured next day by frigate *Argo* (44).

1800 *Milbrook* fought the French privateer *Bellone* off Oporto.

1809 *La Chiffone, Caroline* and six Bombay Marine cruisers, *Ariel, Aurora, Fury, Mornington, Nautilus, Prince of Wales*, destroyed the Joasmi pirate stronghold at Ras Al Khaimah.

1838 *Experiment, Cobourg* and *Queen Victoria* (manned from *Niagara*) repulsed an attack on Prescott, Canada, during Papineau's rebellion. Troops: 23rd Regiment.

1854 *Barracouta, Encounter, Styx*, the P&O *Canton* and *Sir Charles Forbes, Amazona, Queen* (hired) and boats of *Spartan* destroyed forty-eight pirate junks and two batteries of Ty-loo (Kan lan).

1856 *Niger* attacked off Canton by an explosive junk, filled with ordure.

1866 Admiral of the Fleet Sir William Parker died.

1912 The triumph of gunnery director firing. Two 13.5in-gunned sister-ship dreadnoughts, *Thunderer*, fitted with Percy Scott's director, and *Orion*, using the old system of individual gunlayers, carried out a shoot at 9,000yds at 12 knots off Berehaven. *Thunderer* fired thirty-nine rounds of which twenty-three would have hit an imaginary ship. *Orion* fired twenty-seven rounds with only four hits. This test recalled the *Alecto-Rattler* trial of paddle over screw in 1845.

See 3 April 1845.

1918 Admiral Hon. Sir Somerset Gough-Calthorpe, C-in-C Mediterranean, flag in battleship *Superb*, anchored off Constantinople with an Allied fleet which included the battleships *Temeraire, Lord Nelson* and *Agamemnon*. Turkey had requested an armistice on 20 October; negotiations began on board *Agamemnon* at Mudros on 27 October and the armistice was signed on board three days later.

See 30 October 1918.

1939 Destroyer *Blanche* sunk by an aircraft-laid magnetic mine off the Tongue lightvessel in the Thames estuary (51.29N, 01.30E). First of 139 RN destroyers lost in Second World War. She was escorting the minelaying cruiser *Adventure*, which had detonated another mine a few hours earlier, from Grimsby to Portsmouth.

See 18 February 1940, 14 December 1944.

1940 *Aphis* bombarded Maktila.

1941 *Ark Royal* torpedoed by U-81 off Gibraltar (36.03N, 04.45W) while returning from Operation Perpetual. Sank next day, and might have been saved by better damage control, from which many lessons were learned.

1942 Corvette *Lotus*, which sank U-660 a day earlier, joined sister ship *Poppy* in attacking U-605 off Algiers. Credit for sinking later given to 233 Sqn RAF. CO of *Lotus* quoted Aristophanes in Greek in his ROP. 'The Naval Staff evidently appreciated receiving so erudite a report' – Roskill.

1943 *Dulverton* damaged by German glider bomb off Kos (36.50N, 27.30E) and sunk by *Echo*.

1943 *Taurus* sank the Japanese S/M I-34 in Malacca Strait (05.17N, 100.05E).

1944 *Bellona, Kent* (Rear-Admiral R.R. McGrigor, CS 1), *Algonquin* (RCN), *Myngs, Verulam* and *Zambesi* attacked an escorted convoy off south Norway (58.14N, 06.12E). Operation Counterblast. Sunk: six out of seven of convoy, three out of four escorts.

1946 Minesweeping operations in Corfu channel by *Welfare, Sylvia, Truelove, Seabear* and *Skipjack* of the 5th MS Flotilla established that naval minefields had been recently laid.

See 22 October 1946.

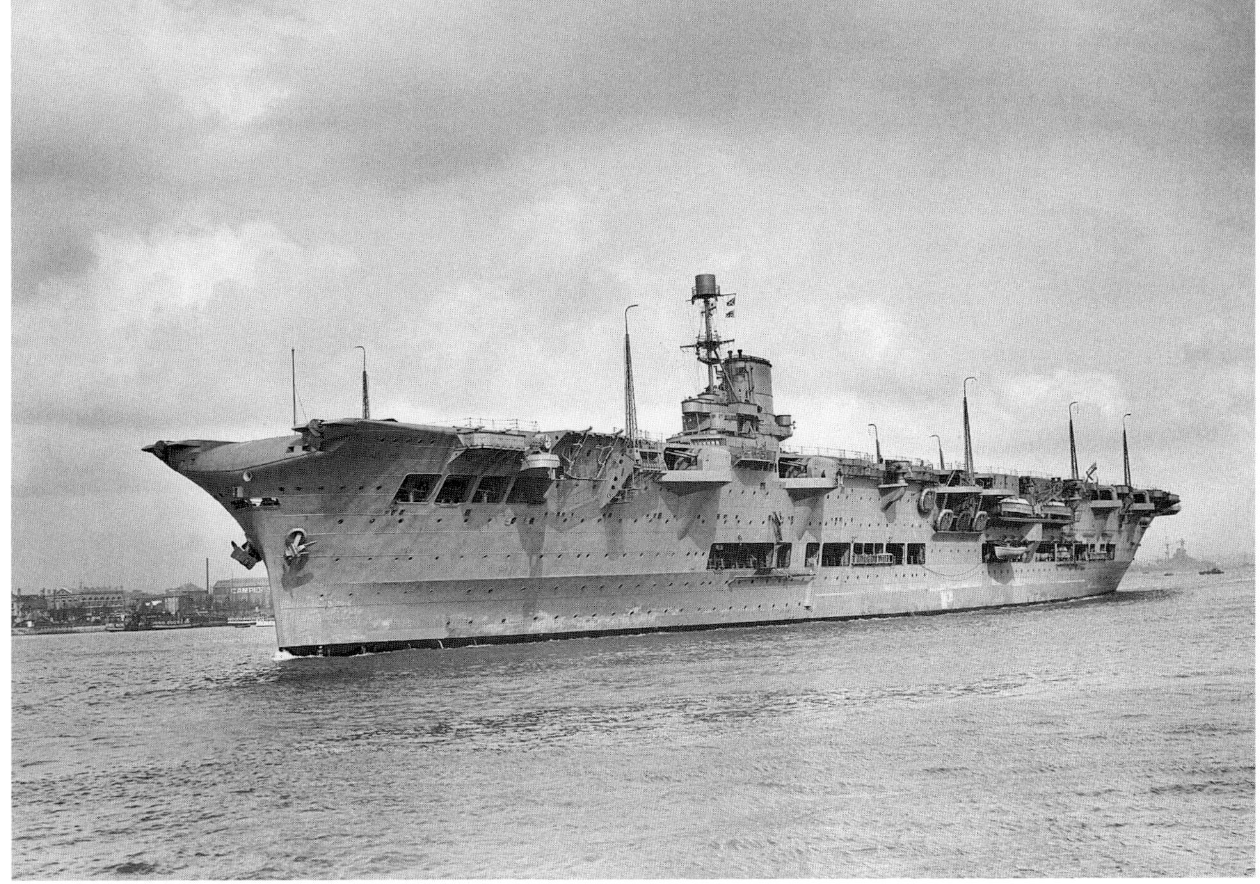

HMS *Ark Royal* leaving Portsmouth, 28 April 1939. (*NMRN W&L 658E1*)

1964 'RN officers and ratings of Sikh nationality and religion are to be permitted to wear uniform turbans purchased privately instead of caps and to keep their hair long if they so wish. Cap badge or cap ribbon to be attached.' – DCI(RN) 1173/64.

1973 Second Cod War ended. HMG accepted the Icelandic 50-mile limit.

See 31 August 1958.

1978 First deck-landing by a Hawker Sea Harrier, on *Hermes*.

See 28 February 2006.

2003 RN Division Memorial rededicated on Horse Guards Parade. Prince Michael of Kent and the First Sea Lord, Admiral Sir Alan West, present. Service conducted by the Chaplain of the Fleet, the Venerable B.K. Hammett. Mr Winston Churchill read the address given by his grandfather at the original dedication in 1925.

The Memorial was originally located alongside the Admiralty Building on Horse Guards Parade and dedicated on 25 April 1925. Removed in 1940 for safety during construction of the Citadel and re-erected at RN College, Greenwich, in 1951. On closure of the college as a naval establishment, a charitable committee was formed to effect its restoration in Central London.

See 25 April 1925, 26 May 1951, 31 May 1981.

2007 RFA *Sir Galahad* handed over to Brazil at Portsmouth and commissioned as *Garcia D'Avila* on 4 December.

14 November

1797 *Majestic* captured the Spanish *Bolador* 25 miles W.N.W. of Cape St Vincent.

1807 *Carrier* captured the French privateer *Actif* off Cromer.

1808 Boats of *Polyphemus* captured the French *Colibri* off San Domingo.

1902 Operations off Somaliland began. Continued until 1904. Ships: *Highflyer* (flag), *Naiad*, *Pomone* and *Cossack*.

1918 Armoured cruiser *Cochrane*, Capt James Farie RN, proceeding up the Mersey Estuary in thick fog, under a pilot but at imprudent speed, ran heavily aground, broke in two and became CTL. Admiralty did not attempt salvage and wreck abandoned. No casualties among 704 ship's company. Courts martial at Portsmouth of CO 18 February 1919 and of NO next day – Reprimands. *Cochrane* one of four 13,550-ton Warrior-class: *Warrior* abandoned and sank 1 June 1916 after Jutland; *Natal* blew up with heavy loss of life 30 December 1915.

See 30 May 1906, 21 August 1910, 8 August 1922, 18 May 1940.

1941 Submarines *Talisman* and *Torbay* landed a party of Commandos near Apollonia to raid Rommel's headquarters.

1941 Carrier *Ark Royal* sank off Gibraltar, having been torpedoed by U-81 the previous day.

See 13 April 1937, 16 November 1938.

1944 *Brocklesby* and *Wheatland* bombarded Bar, Adriatic.

1944 *Heiyo* (ex-*Herald*) mined in Java Sea.

See 9 February 1942.

1944 *Kimberley* destroyed two landing craft in Lividia Bay.

1967 Order for first Type 42 guided missile destroyer placed with Vickers: *Sheffield*.

1970 Fire in gas turbine room of guided missile destroyer *Fife*, Capt W.D.S. Scott RN, off Malta. Fire held one bulkhead away from the Seaslug missile magazine and the ship, in imminent danger of exploding, was prudently kept out of Grand Harbour, being held at anchor off Marsaxlokk. At same time the world's press was in Valletta to cover the arrival of the fleet carrier *Ark Royal* after her collision with a Russian warship off Crete on 9 November. A baptism of fire in all respects for the author of this volume. DCI(RN) T.847/72.

See 1 November 1974, 2 November 2000.

1988 Commander HRH The Prince of Wales RN promoted captain on his 40th birthday; rear-admiral on his 50th birthday, 14 November 1998; vice-admiral on his 54th birthday, 14 November 2002, and admiral on 14 November 2006.

See 15 November 1998.

1997 Carrier *Invincible*, with Sea Harriers of 800 NAS and Sea Kings of 849 NAS B Flight and 814 NAS embarked, accompanied by RFA *Fort Victoria*, deployed to Mediterranean to support diplomatic action following Iraq's refusal to comply with UN Security Council resolution over WMD. Operation Bolton. While on station in Mediterranean *Invincible* entered Adriatic on two occasions (8–10 December 1997 and 8–11 January 1998) and flew sorties over former Yugoslavia in support of NATO SFOR. Operation Deliberate Guard/Lodestone. A textbook example of the flexibility of sea power.

See 21 May 1941, 21 May 1998.

2007 HMS *Cavalier* at Chatham dedicated as the National Destroyer Memorial in the presence of HRH The Duke of Edinburgh. He unveiled a bronze monument alongside the ship which commemorates the 11,000 men lost in the 142 British destroyers sunk in the Second World War.

See 15 October 1952.

Runs Ashore in Foreign Parts

Of all the Navy's favourite runs ashore in foreign parts – Wanchai in Hong Kong and Bugis Street in Singapore – none was more famous in the heyday of the Mediterranean Fleets than The Gut – Strait Street – Strada Stretta – in Malta, which is as much part of British naval history as Portsmouth Point or Scapa Flow. The Gut, the long narrow passage running the length of Valletta, was known to generations of men serving in and passing through the Mediterranean. It was lined with bars and music halls all bearing popular English names. Dancers, barmaids and entertainers variously lived in rooms above. The Gut declined with the departure of the British Services after 1964 but there remain faded reminders of those great days – and nights – 'up the Gut'. (*Author, 2000*)

15 November

1798 Capture of Minorca by Cdre John Duckworth (*Leviathan*) a veteran of Quiberon Bay and of the First of June, and troops under General the Hon. Charles Stuart. Ships: *Argo, Aurora, Centaur, Constitution, Cormorant, Leviathan, Peterel*. Seamen and marines were landed to support the Army: not a man was lost.
Battle Honour: Minorca 1798.

1799 *Crescent* captured the Spanish *Galgo* 50 miles N.E. of Puerto Rico.

1808 Defence of Fort Trinidad, Rosas, by *Excellent*'s marines assisted by *Excellent* and *Meteor*.

1819 Hydrographer (Capt Hurd) was instructed by Board minute 'to take such measures as he may judge proper for enabling the Public to purchase Admiralty charts at reasonable prices'. £72 was received in 1823, the first year in which sales were brought to account, and the first catalogue was published in 1825.
See 25 May 1801, 1 May 1808, 9 August 1968.

1875 Boats of *Thistle* and *Fly* with detachments of Royal Artillery and the 1/10th Regiment, captured the stockades of a rebel chief at Passir Salat, Perak River.

1898 Lt David Beatty RN, aged 27, promoted to commander in recognition of services ashore in Sudan. Promoted to captain 9 November 1900, aged 29, for services ashore in China. Promoted to rear-admiral 1 January 1910. A promising start.
See 1 January 1910.

1906 Foundation stone of the Selborne graving dock in Simon's Town Dockyard laid by the High Commissioner, the Earl of Selkirk.

1918 VC: Cdr Daniel Marcus William Beak, DSO, MC, RNVR, for heroic leadership including a single-handed attack on a machine-gun nest in France at Logeast Wood. (*Gazette* date.) First naval recipient of cross on crimson ribbon.

1939 Tanker *Africa Shell* sunk by German pocket battleship *Admiral Graf Spee* off Mozambique.

1942 *Avenger* sunk by U-155 W. of Gibraltar (36.15N, 07.45W), and *Wrestler* sank U-98 (36.09N, 07.42W). Convoy MKF 1Y.

1942 Hudson S/500 sank U-259 off Algiers (37.20N, 03.05E), but crashed afterwards.

Admiral of the Fleet Lord Chatfield (1873–1967)

Ernle Chatfield and William Wordsworth Fisher (*St Vincent* 1BS) were 'the cream of the Grand Fleet captains' in 1914. Chatfield was Beatty's flag captain throughout the First World War in *Lion, Iron Duke* and *Queen Elizabeth*. Controller of the Navy, C-in-C Atlantic Fleet 1928–30, C-in-C Mediterranean Fleet 1930–2, First Sea Lord January 1933 to November 1938. (Beatty and Chatfield held the office of First Sea Lord for 13½ out of the twenty-one inter-war years). 'He was a character of flawless integrity and a high sense of honour . . . He has an even, steady outlook on life, a good understanding of human nature . . . Above all he was blessed with a strong, well-balanced intelligence, without any trace of that canker of genius which has wrecked the advancement of many a better brain and which is so peculiarly disastrous in the naval profession' – Marder, vol.2, p.18. When the 17th *Lion* recommissioned at Devonport in 1962, the cruiser's Commanding Officer, Capt (later Vice-Admiral Sir Ian) I.L.M. McGeoch, RN, invited veterans from Beatty's *Lion* to the ceremony. Lord Chatfield, then nearly 90, 'stood like a ramrod on the quarterdeck while members of the 1916 ship's company filed past'. – McGeoch to Roskill in *Last Naval Hero*, pp.374–5. The funeral was held at Portsmouth on 22 November. Colours in all HM ships and establishments were half-masted from Colours to Sunset. Cortege left HMS *Vernon* at 1035 for St Ann's church and HMS *Dolphin* fired an admiral of the fleet's salute of 19 guns at noon. Lord Chatfield's ashes were committed to the sea from the frigate HMS *Jaguar*. His memorial is the rose garden at Whale Island which he laid out while Commander of *Excellent* in 1906. Ernle Chatfield's father, Capt Alfred Chatfield, commanded the corvette *Amethyst* in the action against the Peruvian ironclad *Huascar* in 1877.

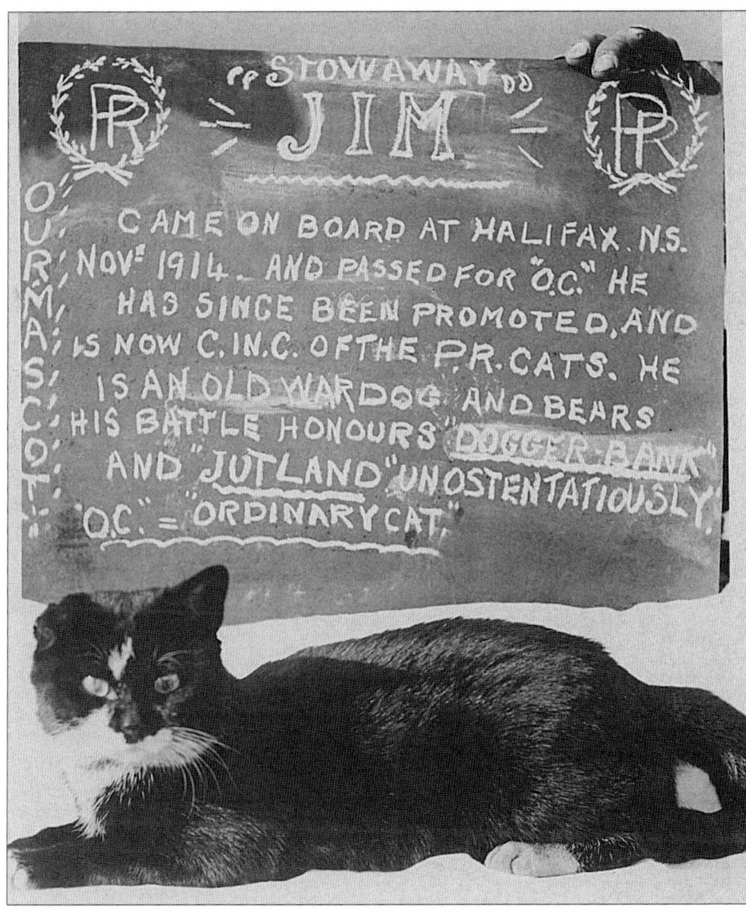

'Stowaway Jim', a ship's cat on HMS *Princess Royal* in 1916. (*NMRN*)

1942 *Algerine* sunk by the Italian S/M *Ascianghi* off Bougie (36.47N, 05E).

1942 *Saguenay* (RCN) damaged beyond repair in collision off Newfoundland. Her depth charges blew off her stern but she survived to become a training hulk.

1948 Order to Splice the Main Brace to celebrate the birth the previous night of a son, Prince Charles, to HRH Princess Elizabeth, Duchess of Edinburgh.

See 11 July 1935, 19 February 1960.

1959 Submarine War Memorial on the Thames Embankment, altered to commemorate submarine losses in the Second as well as the First World War, unveiled at the annual Service of Remembrance by Flag Officer Submarines, Rear-Admiral B.W. Taylor. AFO 2603/59.

1966 The White Ensign hauled down at Portsmouth in *Striker*, Cdr W.F. Charter RN, the last tank landing ship (LST) in the Royal Navy. She had commissioned on 5 March that year at Bahrain to maintain capability until *Fearless* entered service.

See 30 June 1948.

1967 Admiral of the Fleet Lord Chatfield died. 'The best all-rounder of his day and marked for the top from the time he was a Commander.' – Marder, *From the Dreadnought to Scapa Flow*, vol.2, pp.16–18.

See 27 September 1873, 29 May 1877, 24 June 1937, 8 May 1965.

1968 *Renown*, third Polaris submarine, commissioned at Cammell Laird, Birkenhead.

See 25 February 1967.

2001 *Bulwark* launched at Barrow by Lady Walker, wife of Gen. Sir Michael Walker, CGS and later CDS.

See 18 October 1899, 22 June 1948, 12 July 2004, 28 April 2005.

2010 Destroyer *Manchester*, Cdr Rex Cox RN, on counter-narcotics patrol in the Caribbean, arrived in Havana for a five-day visit, the first British warship in Cuba since the frigate *Bigbury Bay* in 1957.

See 4 November 2010.

16 November

1294 HM Edward I ordered construction of twenty galleys, each of 120 oars, for use against the French.

1693 Bombardment of St Malo by Capt John Benbow (*Norwich*) with a squadron of fourth rates and bomb vessels.

1780 *Hussar* wrecked in East River, New York.

1805 *Dorothea*'s experiment with Fulton's torpedo in Walmer Roads ended. According to St Vincent, Pitt 'was the greatest fool that ever existed, to encourage a mode of warfare which they who commanded the seas did not want and which if successful would deprive them of it'.

1810 *Phipps* captured the French privateer *Barbier de Séville* off Calais. Enemy foundered shortly afterwards.

1857 VC: Lt Nowell Salmon, AB John Harrison, Lt Thomas James Young and AB William Hall (*Shannon*) for gallantry at Lucknow during the Indian Mutiny. Hall was the first non-white and the first Canadian to gain VC. Young married the sister of Mid Boyes, VC.

See 6 September 1864, 10 April 1955.

1858 Armstrong rifled breech-loading gun adopted.

1863 *Bustard* captured three pirate junks in Meichow Wan.

1900 Operations began against Ogaden Somalis, lasting until 30 April 1901.

1926 *Bluebell* rescued SS *Sunning* from pirates off Hong Kong.

1938 Carrier *Ark Royal* commissioned at Cammell Laird, Birkenhead, by Capt (later Admiral of the Fleet Sir) Arthur Power RN.

See 14 November 1941, 3 September 1945.

1940 Submarine *Swordfish* presumed sunk off Ushant and paid off.

See 7 November 1940.

1941 Corvette *Marigold* sank U-433 off Gibraltar (36.13N, 04.42W). First kill using Type 271 centimetric radar in a U-boat trap, which brought personal signal from First Sea Lord.

1943 Liberator M/86 sank U-280 in N. Atlantic (49.11N, 27.32W). Convoy HX 265.

1965 Coastal minesweeper *Fiskerton*, Lt-Cdr C.D. Prentis RN, preparing to board a suspicious sampan at first light in the Johore Straits was engaged at short range with hand gre-

The *Resurgam* – the first British submarine, 1879

The first submarine to be designed and built in England was the Revd George Garrett's *Resurgam*. Built in Liverpool in 1879; powered by steam when surfaced and by latent heat from the boiler when submerged. She had no weapons and was bad at depth-keeping because of inefficient diving planes fitted amidships. It was to be a Holland Type VI – the successful design of American John P. Holland that had been accepted by the US Navy – which was built under licence for the Royal Navy to become HM Submarine No. 1 (See 2 October 1901).

The *Resurgam* of 1879. (*NMRN*)

An Armstrong rifled breech-loading gun on its slide. (*NMRN*)

nades and a Sten gun. The ship replied with her Bren guns and killed all three attackers; there was an absence of 'goofers' on the upper deck during future boardings of suspect Indonesian vessels.

1967 Eighth and last County-class guided missile destroyer, *Norfolk*, launched by the Duchess of Norfolk at Swan Hunter's on the Tyne. Blessing was given by the Revd K. Mathews who had been Chaplain of the previous *Norfolk*, the 8-in heavy cruiser, during the *Bismarck* action in 1941. In 1972 her B-turret was replaced by Exocet making her the first RN ship to carry three missile systems – Exocet, Seaslug and Seacat.

See 10 July 1987.

A 16-in shell being loaded in the battleship HMS *Nelson* (1925). (*NMRN*)

17 NOVEMBER

1787 Warrant officers given a uniform blue coat for the first time and masters' mates a single-breasted jacket instead of midshipman's uniform.

1797 *Anson* and *Boadicea* captured the French privateer *Railleur* 100 miles S.W. of Yeu Island.

1800 Boats of *Captain* and *Magicienne*, and *Nile*, cutter, cut out and destroyed the French *Réolaise* and two merchant vessels at Port Navalo, Morbihan.

1803 Boats of *Blenheim*, with *Drake* and *Swift*, cut out the French privateer *Harmonie* and captured a battery at Marin, Martinique.

1809 *Royalist* captured the French privateer *Grand Napoléon* in Dover Strait.

1809 *La Chiffone*, *Caroline* and six Bombay Marine cruisers, *Ariel*, *Aurora*, *Fury*, *Mornington*, *Nautilus*, *Prince of Wales*, destroyed the Joasmi pirate stronghold at Lingeh.

1810 Sweden declared war on Great Britain.
See 18 June 1912.

1849 Boats of *Castor* and *Dee* destroyed a slave vessel and the shore defences of the Arab slavers up the river from Porto de Angoche, Portuguese East Africa.

1857 *Shannon*'s Naval Brigade at the relief of the Residency, Lucknow. Indian Mutiny Medal: clasp 'Relief of Lucknow'.

1869 Opening of the Suez Canal.

1871 Completion of *Hotspur*, first British warship to be built as a ram and the only one to have a fixed turret: carried one 12-in rifled, muzzle-loading gun that could not fire dead-ahead because her deck could not take the shock; modified after ten years.

1917 VC: OS John Henry Carless (*Caledon*). Posthumous. Light cruiser action off Heligoland. Ships: 1st CS: *Courageous*, *Glorious* with *Nerissa*, *Umpire*, *Urchin*, *Ursa*. 6th LCS: *Calypso*, *Caradoc*, *Cardiff*, *Ceres*, *Valentine*, *Vanquisher*, *Vehement*, *Vimiera*. 1st LCS: *Caledon*, *Galatea*, *Inconstant*, *Royalist*, *Medway*, *Vendetta*. 1st BCS: *Lion*, *New Zealand*, *Princess Royal*, *Repulse*, *Tiger*, *Champion*, *Nepean*, *Obdurate*, *Oriana*, *Petard*, *Telemachus*, *Tower*, *Tristram*, *Verdun*.

1917 Submarine K 1 sank after collision with K 4 off Danish Coast.

1918 Occupation of Baku.

1920 Defeated pro-British Greek prime minister Eleftherios Venizelos left Greece in the yacht *Narcissus*, escorted by the light cruiser *Centaur* to protect him from arrest at sea by the new Greek government.
See 17 November 1922.

1922 Battleship *Malaya* at Constantinople embarked Mohammed VI, Sultan of Turkey, fleeing from a domestic rebellion, and took him to Malta 'where he will be accommodated in the spacious Royal Artillery officers' mess'. Thus ended the old Ottoman Empire.
See 17 November 1920, 1 November 1921.

1941 Admiral Sir Percy Noble succeeded Admiral Sir Martin Dunbar-Nasmith as C-in-C W. Approaches. The C-in-C would be 'directly responsible for the protection of trade, the routing and control of the outward and homeward-bound ocean convoys and measures to combat any attacks on convoys by U-boats or

The memorial plaque on the walls of St Paul's Anglican Cathedral, Valletta, overlooking Lazaretto Creek, unveiled by Vice-Admiral Sir Arthur Hezlet on 17 November 1974, recalls British submarine operations from Malta in the Second World War. Photographed by the author in December 2000. (*Author*)

The Type 45 Destroyer HMS *Dragon*, with red dragons painted on her bows to mark her Welsh affiliations, launched at Govan on 17 November 2008. (*BAE*)

hostile aircraft within his Command' – Roskill, *The War at Sea*, vol.1, p.360. Admiral Dunbar Nasmith remained C-in-C Plymouth.
See 7 November 1941.

1942 U-331 sunk off Cape Caxine, W. of Algiers (37.08N, 02.24E). Attacked first by three Hudsons of 500 Sqn RAF, which bombed her into surrendering. Destroyer *Wilton* had been ordered to the scene but was overtaken by an Albacore from *Formidable* which torpedoed and sank the submarine. Credit given to Hudsons; the Albacore was 'only finishing off a cripple' (Cunningham). Among the survivors was Kapitanleutnant von Tiesenhausen who had sunk the battleship *Barham* in November 1941.

1943 Order in Council granted ministers of religious bodies not in conformity with the Church of England serving as chaplains in the Naval Service the same conditions of service as chaplains of the Church of England.
See 23 October 1876, 11 August 1902, 1 April 1998.

1944 Destroyers *Eggesford* and *Lauderdale* bombarded enemy positions at Cristofora, Rab Island, Adriatic.

1950 Ordnance officers became Ordnance engineers and exchanged dark blue for purple cloth between stripes.

1962 The RFA tanker *Green Ranger*, under tow by the tug *Caswell* from Plymouth to Cardiff for refit, went ashore off Mansley Cliff near Hartland Point, N. Devon, and later broke up. The tow was slipped when a Force 10 N.W. gale threatened to send both vessels ashore.
See 1 June 1970.

1974 Vice-Admiral Sir Arthur Hezlet, wartime submarine commander and former FOSNI, unveiled a plaque on the outer wall of St Paul's Anglican Cathedral in Valletta to commemorate the close links between the RN Submarine Service and the people of Malta GC in the Second World War. The plaque overlooks the wartime submarine berths in Lazaretto Creek in Marsamxett Harbour and the old leper hospital on Manoel Island which housed HMS *Talbot*, the submarine HQ.
See 28 April 1967.

1998 First Merlin helicopter joined 700M NAS.
See 1 December 1998.

1999 Sea King helicopters from *Ocean* provided humanitarian relief after major earthquake in Duzce area, Turkey. Within hours the frigate *Northumberland* was engaged in disaster-relief operations on the island of Anguilla in the wake of Hurricane Lenny.

2008 *Dragon*, the fourth Type 45 destroyer, launched by Mrs Susie Boissier, wife of Vice-Admiral Paul Boissier, Deputy C-in-C Fleet, at BVT Yard on the Clyde. The ship, which is affiliated with Cardiff, was launched with large red dragons painted on her bows.
See 1 February 2006, 23 January 2007, 27 November 2007, 21 October 2009, 11 October 2010.

2010 HRH The Duke of Edinburgh, Capt General Royal Marines, presented Afghanistan campaign medals to men of 40 Cdo RM, Lt-Col Paul James RM, at Norton Manor Camp near Taunton on their return from Helmand Province on Operation Herrick. He also presented the Elizabeth Cross to bereaved relatives; fourteen members of 40 Cdo died during this deployment.

18 November

1705 *Montagu* fought two French ships off Cape St Nicholas, Mole, Haiti.

1793 *Latona* fought two French frigates 90 miles W. of Ushant.

1800 *Leda* (38), fifth rate, launched at Chatham. The first of the largest class of sailing frigates ever built for the Royal Navy. *Leda* wrecked off Milford Haven 31 January 1808. The design was based on the French *Hebe* taken in 1782. Forty-seven derivative ships in four versions built 1800–30. Two survive: *Unicorn* at Dundee and *Trincomalee* at Hartlepool.

1861 Wood screw gunboat *Kestrel* defeated a superior force of Chinese pirates and dismounted the guns in their shore battery at Ching Keang, Chu san.

1911 Cdr Oliver Schwann – later Air Vice-Marshal Sir Oliver Swann (he changed his name in April 1917) – in a 35hp Avro Type D biplane became the first British aviator to take off from water – on his 33rd birthday.

See 10 January 1912, 2 May 1912, 2 August 1917.

1917 Paddle minesweeper *Marsa* lost in collision in Harwich harbour, first with light cruiser *Concord* and then, fatally, with destroyer *Shakespeare*.

1917 P 57 rammed and sank UC-47 E.S.E. of Flamborough Head (54.01N, 00.22E).

1917 *Candytuft* (*Pavitt* – Q-ship) sunk by U-39 off Bougie (36.59N, 04.41E).

The iron frigate HMS *Northampton*, launched by Napier's at Govan on 18 November 1876, served as flagship on the North America and West Indies Station from 1879–86. She was a boys' training and recruiting ship from 1894–1904 when young Walter Lewis (opposite) of Pembroke Dock entered on board as a Boy. He was the author's grandfather and great-grandfather to Honorary Midshipman Victoria Phillips of Cambridge University RN Unit (see 2 February). (*Author*)

1918 Naval Medical, Accountant and Instructor Branch ranks changed:

Medical Branch:
Surgeon-General to be Surgeon Rear-Admiral; Deputy Surgeon-General/Surgeon Captain; Fleet Surgeon/Surgeon Commander; Staff Surgeon/Surgeon Lieutenant-Commander; Surgeon/Surgeon Lieutenant; Surgeon Probationer/Surgeon Sub-Lieutenant RNVR.

Accountant Branch:
Paymaster General to be Paymaster Rear-Admiral; Paymaster-in-Chief/Paymaster Captain; Fleet Paymaster/Paymaster Commander; Staff Paymaster/Paymaster Lieutenant-Commander; Paymaster/ Paymaster Lieutenant; Assistant Paymaster/Paymaster Sub-Lieutenant; Clerk/Paymaster Midshipman.

Naval Instructor Branch:
Chief Naval Instructor to be Instructor Captain; Naval Instructor (over 16 years)/ Instructor Commander; Naval Instructor (8–16 years)/Instructor Lieutenant-Commander; Naval Instructor (less than 8 years)/Instructor Lieutenant.

See 1 July 1918, 1 March 1975.

1939 AMC *California* captured the German *Borkum* and *Eilbek* off Iceland. *Borkum* dispatched by U-331 on 23rd.

1940 Heavy cruiser *Dorsetshire* bombarded Zante, Italian Somaliland.

1941 Light cruisers *Euryalus* and *Naiad* bombarded Halfaya area in support of the 8th Army in Western Desert.

1942 Corvette *Montbretia* (Nor) sunk by U-262 in N. Atlantic S.S.E. of Cape Farewell. (53.37N, 38.15W). Convoy ONS 144.

1942 *Arethusa*, light cruiser, was escorting a convoy to Malta in Operation Stoneage. Air attacks started at 0600 18 November, and at 1800 *Arethusa* was torpedoed. She was towed stern-first back to Alexandria, having to battle with raging fires and a rising gale. She reached Alexandria on the evening of 22nd, with 155 men dead. She was the last serious casualty of the famous 15th Cruiser Squadron. In 1944, *Arethusa* led the bombarding forces at Normandy and later carried King George VI over the Channel to visit forces in Normandy.

1943 Sloop *Chanticleer* damaged beyond repair by U-515 off the Azores: used as baseship at Horta and renamed *Lusitania*.

1959 New carrier *Hermes* accepted from her builders, Vickers Armstrong, by Capt D.S. Tibbitts DSC, RN.

1983 *Glamorgan* and *Brazen* to Lebanon in support of British troops in multinational force.

See 28 November 1983, 1 January 1984, 15 October 1958, 18 and 20 July 2006.

1998 *Splendid* fired Britain's first Tomahawk land-attack cruise missile on US Naval Air Weapons Pacific Fleet Test Range at Point Magu, California.

See 24 March 1999, 18 March 2002, 19 March 2011.

19 November

1693 Benbow's use of *Vesuvius* as a floating mine at St Malo.

See 16 November 1693.

1804 *Donegal* captured the Spanish *Anfitrite* off Cape Kantin, Morocco.

1879 *Active*'s Naval Brigade landed at Durban for the Zulu wars.

1893 *Adventure* and *Pioneer*, with troops, destroyed the stronghold of Makanjira, a slave-trading chief on Lake Nyassa.

1895 First Commander of Signal Schools appointed.

1904 Vice-Admiral Sir Norman 'Ned' Denning, born at Whitchurch, Hampshire. In charge of U-boat Plot and Tracking Room, Admiralty Operational Intelligence Centre in the Second World War. As a Pusser was first non-executive officer to be Director of Naval Intelligence 1960–4. Youngest of five sons of a draper; two killed in the First World War, others Lt-Gen. Sir Reginald Denning and Lord Denning, Master of the Rolls. Died 27 December 1979.

1915 VC: Sqn Cdr Richard Bell-Davies, RNAS, at Ferrijik Railway junction, Bulgaria, for landing behind enemy lines while under heavy fire during an air attack to rescue a colleague who had been shot down.

See 24 May 1939, 26 February 1966.

1917 First Royal Navy aviation admiral. 'Be pleased to submit for the consideration of the Board that a Flag Officer may be appointed in command of the seaplane carriers of the Grand Fleet and to undertake the administrative control of all aircraft working with the Fleet' – Admiral Sir David Beatty, C-in-C Grand Fleet, to the Admiralty. Rear-Admiral Richard Phillimore (who had commanded the battlecruiser *Inflexible* at the Falklands battle in 1914) was appointed Admiral Commanding Aircraft on 6 January 1918.

See 25 November 1912, 2 April 1931, 14 July 1959.

1918 First twenty U-boats surrendered at Harwich.

1920 Terence Thornton Lewin born (true begetter of this book).

See 23 January 1999.

1941 *Sydney* (RAN) surprised by the German disguised raider *Kormoran* (Schiff 41) off the west coast of Australia. Both ships sunk. Wreck of *Sydney* found on 17 March 2008 in 2,470 metres at (26.14.37S, 111.13.03E), 250km S.W. of Carnarvon, W. Australia, 12nm from wreck of *Kormoran*, found a few days later.
Battle Honour: *Kormoran* 1941.

See 22 August 1778, 13 December 1809, 19 July 1940.

Admiral Sir Terence Lewin. (*RN*)

HMAS *Sydney* (1934). (*NMRN*)

The German raider *Kormoran*, disguised as a merchant ship, was off the Western Australian coast. The light cruiser *Sydney*, with about the same armament, sighted her and closed to investigate. She closed to within a mile before the raider revealed her identity by opening fire, hitting the cruiser heavily around the bridge, and torpedoing her. The after turrets of *Sydney*, in local control, managed to continue the action for an hour before the RAN vessel drifted away, a flaming wreck. The *Kormoran* had to be abandoned and scuttled, and 315 of the 400 crew were rescued by searchers for the *Sydney*, which disappeared without trace – until found in 2008.

Coastal Forces, 19 November 1941

Three MGBs set out for the Hook of Holland in a calm sea, but one had to return to harbour because of engine defects. At 0200 on the 20th they reached their position and waited. At 0445 they heard the enemy approaching and closed to intercept them. They found five S-boats, and in a close action suffered no serious damage themselves but sank one enemy, badly damaged two and inflicted some damage on the other two. Three S-boats were sunk by the RAF on their return to harbour. Lt-Cdr R.P. Hichens was in command of this operation. He had served with distinction in Coastal Forces, being awarded the DSO and bar, the DSC and two bars, and being mentioned in dispatches three times before being killed in action on 13 April 1943.

1942 Admiral Sir Max Horton relieved Admiral Sir Percy Noble as C-in-C W. Approaches, an appointment he held until the command was abolished 15 August 1945.

1943 *Simoom* lost in Dardanelles approaches. Last of sixteen submarines lost in 1943.

1943 Wellington F/179 sank U-211 in N. Atlantic (40.15N, 19.18W). Convoy SL 139/MKS 30.

1953 Second clasp to LS&GC medal introduced with effect from 1 January 1952.

1976 Last publication of the *Pink List*.

1982 Sir Terence Thornton Lewin to be a Life Peer as Admiral of the Fleet the Right Honourable The Lord Lewin of Greenwich in Greater London, GCB, MVO, DSC, announced in the *London Gazette*.

See 21 November 1945, 29 June 2007.

20 NOVEMBER

1759 Battle of Quiberon Bay. Admiral Sir Edward Hawke (*Royal George*) defeated Admiral le Comte de Conflans (*Soleil Royal*).
Battle Honour: Quiberon Bay 1759.

Ships: *Burford, Chichester, Defiance, Dorsetshire, Duke, Dunkirk, Essex,* Hercules, Hero, Intrepid, Kingston, Magnanime, Mars, Montagu, Namur, Resolution,* Revenge, Royal George, Swiftsure, Temple, Torbay, Union, Warspite.* Capt Robert Duff's squadron: *Rochester, Chatham, Coventry, Falkland, Maidstone, Minerva, Portland, Sapphire, Vengeance, Venus.*

*Wrecked. Eleven French ships captured or destroyed out of twenty-one.

Sir Edward Hawke chased the French Fleet, under Conflans, in the teeth of a gale into the shoal waters of Quiberon Bay, on a lee shore. Eleven French ships were lost, and others only escaped by throwing their guns and water overboard to lighten themselves and cross the shoals. Only two British vessels were lost. This was a decisive victory, as close blockade of the French was no longer required, and the French had to withdraw their army from Hanover. From this victory, and the taking of Quebec two months before, comes the toast 'May our Officers have the eye of a Hawke and the Heart of a Wolfe'.

'Where there is a passage for the enemy there is a passage for me. You have done your duty in showing me the danger: now obey my orders and lay me alongside the *Soleil Royal*' – Hawke.

1779 *Hussar* (escorting a convoy) captured the Spanish privateer *N.S. Del Buen Consejo* 100 miles S.W. by W. of Cape Roxent (da Roca).

1806 Boats of *Success* cut out the French privateer *Vengeur* at Hidden Port (Puerto Escondido), Cuba.

1807 Brig *Anne* captured the Spanish privateer *Vincejo* 90 miles S.W. of Cape Finisterre.
See 24 November 1807.

Hawke's great victory. 'The Battle of Quiberon Bay', by Harold Wyllie. (*NMRN 1983/1001*)

1845 Anglo-French squadron cut the boom and captured the Argentine batteries at Obligado. British ships: *Gorgon, Firebrand, Philomel, Comus, Dolphin, Fanny*. French ships: *San Martin, Fulton, Expeditive, Pandour, Procida*. The Argentine *Republicano* set on fire by her own crew and blew up.

1863 Attack on the Maori position at Rangariri by Cdre Sir William Wiseman (*Curaçao*) and Lt-Gen. Duncan Cameron. Gunboats, etc.: *Ant, Avon, Chub, Flirt, Midge* and *Pioneer* (Colonial steamer). Landing parties from *Curaçoa, Eclipse, Harrier, Miranda*. Troops: Royal Artillery, 40th and 65th Regiments.

1935 Admiral of the Fleet the Rt Hon. John Rushworth Jellicoe, First Earl Jellicoe and Viscount Brocas of Southampton and Viscount Jellicoe of Scapa, died. C-in-C Grand Fleet 1914–16 and at Jutland, First Sea Lord 1916 until Christmas Eve 1917, he was buried in St Paul's Cathedral on 25 November.

See 5 December 1859, 15 July 1872, 24 December 1917, 22 February 2007.

1939 AMC *Chitral* intercepted the German *Bertha Fisser*, which scuttled herself off Iceland (64.10N, 15.14W).

1939 *Sturgeon* sank the German trawler *Gauleiter Telschow* 30 miles N.W. of Heligoland. First RN submarine success of Second World War.

1942 Corvette *Potentilla* (Nor) sank U-184 off Newfoundland (24.25N, 45.25W). Convoy ONS 144.

1943 *Nene*, and *Snowberry* and *Calgary* (both RCN) sank U-536 in N. Atlantic (43.50N, 19.39W). Convoy SL 139/MKS 30.

1944 Minelaying air-strike at Haugesund. Operation Handfast. Ships: *Diadem, Premier, Pursuer, Onslaught, Scorpion, Scourge, Zealous*. FAA: eight Avenger aircraft of 856 Sqn (*Premier*); sixteen Wildcat aircraft of 881 Sqn (*Pursuer*).

1957 Admiral Lord Mountevans, 'Evans of the *Broke*', died at Golaa, Norway. He was second-in-command of Scott's ill-fated Antarctic expedition and he gained added fame for his dashing action off Dover in the destroyer *Broke* in 1917. Between the wars Teddy Evans commanded the Royal Australian Squadron, was C-in-C South Africa and C-in-C The Nore.

See 28 October 1880, 21 April 1917.

2009 Fleet submarine *Astute*, Cdr Andrew Coles RN, first of class, arrived at Faslane from her builders.

See 20 November 2009, 22 October 2010.

HMS *Astute* (2009) arriving at Faslane following sea trials. (*RN*)

21 November

1652 Boats of *Leopard*, *Constant*, *Warwick* and *Bonaventure* cut out the Dutch (ex-British) *Phoenix* (38) at Leghorn. Admiral Cornelius Tromp, son of Marten, nearly captured.

1757 *Unicorn* captured the French *Hermione* 180 miles N.W. of Cape Finisterre.

1797 *Jason* captured the French privateer *Marie* off Belle Ile.

1828 Board approved introduction of hexagonal machine-made biscuit baked at Clarence Yard.

1852 Capture of Pegu. Ships: Bengal Marine steamers *Mahanuddy*, *Nerbudda*, *Damooda*, and *Lord William Bentinck* and boats of *Fox* and *Sphinx*. Troops: 1st Bengal Fusiliers, 1st Madras Fusilier Regiment, 5th Madras Native Infantry, Bengal Artillery, Madras Sappers and Miners.

1868 *Hercules*, fifth of the name, completed. First battleship to have cables led on to the upper, instead of into the main deck, and first with three-calibre main armament.

1914 Three RNAS Avro 504 biplanes flew from Belfort on the Franco-Swiss border to bomb the German airship factory at Friedrichshafen on the shores of Lake Constance, destroying an associated gas plant. The loss of Antwerp having put German airship facilities at Düsseldorf and Cologne beyond flying range, the RNAS aircraft were crated and sent by rail to Belfort. The attack flew N. of Basle and followed the Rhine on a 250-mile round trip over the Black Forest in what Admiral Sir John Fisher, First Sea Lord, praised as 'a fine feat of endurance, courage and skill'. The senior officer, Sqn Cdr E.F. Briggs, was forced down and captured. Fl/Cdr J.T. Babington and Fl/Lt S.V. Sippe returned to Belfort.

See 22 September 1914, 8 October 1914, 25 December 1914.

1918 Armistice Day and the end of the Great War. Der Tag – the day the German Navy would defeat the Royal Navy – was the pre-war toast of German officers but in Royal Navy wardooms and gunrooms it was occasionally drunk informally and in fun before and during the First World War. German High Seas Fleet arrived in the Firth of Forth en route to internment at Scapa Flow under the terms of the Armistice which suspended hostilities from 1100 on 11 November. The Grand Fleet (370 warships, including thirty-three battleships and 90,000 men, with the Sixth Battle Squadron, comprising USN battleships, and some French cruisers) met the German units (9 battleships, 5 battlecruisers, 7 light cruisers and 49 destroyers) 40 miles E. of May Island and escorted them to an anchorage off Inchkeith.

Admiral Sir David Beatty, C-in-C Grand Fleet, regarded the operation as a surrender – 'Didn't I tell you they would have to come out?' – and at 1100 the general signal hoist was made in *Queen Elizabeth*, 'The German flag will be hauled down at Sunset today, Thursday, and will not be hoisted again

Internment of the German High Seas Fleet in the Firth of Forth, 1918. (*NMRN 1983/1288*)

without permission'. Then, using Nelson's own signal after the Nile 120 years earlier Beatty told the Fleet: 'It is my intention to hold a service of thanksgiving at 1800 today for the victory which Almighty God has vouchsafed to his Majesty's arms, and every ship is recommended to do the same.'

See 1 August 1798, 21 November 1918, 28 March 1941, 8 September 1943, 2 September 1945.

'Whether Beatty had the right to make such a signal [i.e. referring to a 'haul-down'] has been questioned, but he was not concerned with legal niceties or the continental school of thought at such a moment', wrote his biographer, Rear-Admiral W.S. Chalmers. 'He would organise the surrender in his own way, and being still at war, he felt that it would be intolerable to have enemy ships flying their national flag in a British harbour. So, at dusk, as the sky reddened over the Scottish hills, and the buglers of the British Fleet sounded the call of "Sunset", the ensigns of the Imperial German Navy fluttered slowly down for the last time. And darkness closed like a curtain on the final act of this mighty drama at sea.'

'The surrender, if one may call it that, was one of the most decisive and dramatic events in the illustrious annals of British sea power' – A. Marder, *From the Dreadnought to Scapa Flow*, vol.5, pp.191–2.

1939 Destroyer *Gipsy* mined leaving Harwich (51.47N, 01.19E). Beached but broken-backed. CTL. Captain and eight men buried in RN Cemetery near St Mary's church, Shotley.

1939 AMC *Transylvania* intercepted the German *Tenerife*, which scuttled herself W. of Iceland.

1939 Light cruiser *Belfast* severely damaged by German magnetic mine in the Firth of Forth.

1941 Submarine *Utmost* torpedoed and severely damaged the Italian cruiser *Luigi di Savoia Duca Degli Abruzzi* in the Mediterranean: CTL. *Utmost* sunk a year later.

1942 Albacore I/817 (*Victorious*) sank U-517 in N. Atlantic (46.16N, 17.09W).

1943 Sloops *Crane* and *Fowey* sank U-538 in N. Atlantic (45.40N, 19.35W). Convoy SL 139/ MKS 30.

1945 Admiral of the Fleet Lord Cunningham, First Sea Lord, was introduced in the House of Lords; his supporters were Admirals of the Fleet Lord Chatfield and the Earl of Cork and Orrery.

See 19 November 1982, 29 June 2007.

1947 Submarine P 511 foundered at her moorings in Kames Bay.

1958 The last Naval Discipline Act came into force. Enacted in 1957 it retained the original preamble, only slightly modified to read: 'Her Majesty's Navy, whereon, under the good Providence of God, the wealth, safety and strength of the Kingdom so much depend . . . an historical fact of life sometimes overlooked in any prolonged period of peace.' Thereafter, naval law was derived from the Armed Forces Acts, the first passed in 1966. The second, in 1971, provides that the NDA should, like the Army and the Air Force Acts, no longer be a permanent statute, but subject to an annual continuation order and quinquennial review.

1967 British Forces in final stages of departure from Aden.

See 19 January 1839, 30 June 1948, 29 November 1967, 30 June 1997.

Tom Pocock in the *Evening Standard* of 21 November 1967 reported: 'The Royal Navy is in these last days ready to hold Aden as securely as the great base has ever been held. The Royal Marines are ashore, but their support ships and their helicopters are in ships off-shore. Over the horizon is the aircraft carrier *Eagle*, giving the evacuation the support of her fighters and bombers. Aden is being held by the old, proven principles of sea power. On November 30, the Navy will demonstrate this as surely as they did off Corunna or Dunkirk. By December 1, the grey ships will have gone. But while their power will remain to be exercised globally that which was ashore here will be lost to the wind and sand of the Arabian nights . . .'

1997 Royal Yacht *Britannia* sailed from London on last voyage to Portsmouth. Flew short paying-off pennant (227ft) in river but down-channel changed to her 412ft-long entitlement.

22 November

1718 Lt Robert Maynard (*Ranger* and *Jane*) killed the pirate Edward Teach ('Blackbeard') and captured all his crew in Ocracoke Inlet, Pamlico Sound.

1739 Vice-Admiral Edward Vernon (*Burford*) captured Porto Bello. Ships: *Burford, Hampton Court, Norwich, Princess Louisa, Strafford, Worcester.* Battle Honour: Puerto Bello 1739.

See 12 November 1684, 19 October 1739, 21 August 1740, 11 April 1746.

1812 *Southampton* captured the American *Vixen* off the Bahamas.

1847 Boats of *President* and *Eurydice*, with Portuguese boats, destroyed an Arab slaver's stockade up the river from Porto de Angoche. The Portuguese *Juan De Castro* captured an American gun-running brig.

1857 VC: Mid Arthur Mayo, Indian Navy (received award while an undergraduate at Oxford). No. 4 Detachment, Indian Navy, defeated and dispersed a superior force of sepoy mutineers at Dacca.

1880 Charles Forbes born in Ceylon (as was Jacky Fisher). First XO of new battleship *Queen Elizabeth* 1914. Commanded Home Fleet at outbreak of the Second World War. Flew Union Flag at sea as an admiral of the fleet from May until December 1940, when relieved by Tovey.

See 25 January 1871, 2 December 1940, 28 August 1960.

1882 *Collingwood* launched at Pembroke Dockyard. The first battleship to achieve 16 knots under steam.

1914 British forces captured Basra, Mesopotamia. Ships and vessels: *Espiegle, Ocean, Odin, Lawrence* (RIN), *Comet, Lewis Pelly* (RIN), *Sirdar-I-Naphte.*

See 30 June 2003.

1915 Battle of Ctesiphon, Mesopotamia. River gunboat and vessels: *Firefly, Comet, Messoudieh, Shaitan, Shushan, Sumana.*

1916 Submarine E 30 lost in North Sea.

1918 G 11 wrecked off Howick, Northumberland. The first of fourteen RN submarines to be lost between the two world wars.

1918 The British government, one day after the German armistice which ended the Great War, sent Rear-Admiral Edwyn Alexander Sinclair with a naval force to protect the newly independent, nascent Baltic states of Finland, Estonia, Latvia and Lithuania from Russian interference, to ensure German observance of the peace treaty and to protect British shipping.

See 5 and 13 December 1918, 9 June 1919, 15 June 1919, 18 August 1919, 1 and 4 September 1919, 20 July 2003.

1939 *Laurentic* intercepted the German *Antiochia*, which scuttled herself in Atlantic (52.12N, 15.08W).

1941 Heavy cruiser *Devonshire* sank the German disguised raider *Atlantis* (Schiff 16) in S. Atlantic (04.15S, 18.34W).

Devonshire sighted the German raider *Atlantis* (armed as a light cruiser) in the South Atlantic. *Atlantis* had sunk or captured 145,697 tons of Allied shipping, and was disguised as a merchantman. *Devonshire* stood off until it was confirmed that *Atlantis* could not be the vessel she purported to be, and then sank her. *Atlantis*' survivors were rescued by U-boat and transferred to a supply ship, which was sunk just over a week later by *Devonshire*'s sister ship *Dorsetshire*. Again the survivors were rescued by U-boats and made an epic journey of 5,000 miles to Biscay ports.

1943 Minesweeper *Hebe* sunk by mine laid off Bari (41.08N, 16.52E), by U-453.

1943 First and unsuccessful raid by Welmans 44, 45, 47 and 48 at Bergen. These were the third and smallest types of British midget craft, built at Welwyn Garden City to the design of Col Welman of the Interservice Research Board.

1944 Submarine *Stratagem* sunk by Japanese destroyer in Malacca Strait.

The Royal Navy in the Baltic, 1918–19

A memorial to the men of the Royal Navy who were lost in the Baltic 1918–20, erected 'on behalf of the grateful people of Estonia', displayed outside the Maritime Museum in Tallinn. Plaques with the names of the men and their ships were unveiled by the First Sea Lord, Admiral Sir Alan West, in the nearby Church of the Holy Spirit in July 2003. Exact replicas of these brass plaques can be seen in Portsmouth Cathedral. (*Author, 2010*)

Admiral Alexander Sinclair's orders were 'to show the British flag and support British policy as circumstances dictate' which allowed of wide interpretation. The RN squadron, which was to become a major deployment, initially comprised the Sixth LCS comprising *Cardiff* (flag) (which the day before had led the High Seas Fleet to internment in Britain), *Caradoc*, *Cassandra*, *Ceres* and *Calypso*, the 13th Destroyer Flotilla of nine V&W-class destroyers, and seven ships of the Third Fleet Sweeping Flotilla but many more were deployed throughout 1919. En route to Reval (modern Tallinn) in Estonia, *Cassandra* (Capt E.G. Kennedy RN, lost in the AMC *Rawalpindi* in November 1939) was mined and sunk on 4 December. Eleven men lost and survivors rescued by destroyers *Westminster* and *Vendetta*. HMS *Calypso* damaged on a wreck off Libau and returned to Britain with *Cassandra* survivors. Although Britain was not at war with the new Soviet republic, 'a Bolshevist man-of-war operating off the coast of the Baltic provinces must be assumed to be doing so with hostile intent and should be treated accordingly'. This opened a fifteen-month operation, mainly directed by Sinclair's successor, Rear-Admiral Sir Walter Cowan, in which the RN attacked the main Bolshevik naval base of Kronstadt on Kotlin Island and lost 1 light cruiser, 2 destroyers, 2 sloops, 1 submarine and 4 CMBs, with 106 RN and 5 RAF men but which secured the independence of the new Baltic states. A marble plaque at the Estonian Maritime Museum in Tallinn is dedicated to the memory 'of the officers and seamen of the British Royal Navy who served and gave their lives in the cause of freedom in the Baltic during the Estonian War of Independence 1918–20'. The name of every man is displayed in the nearby Church of the Holy Spirit. *Sandown*, one of the three single-role MCMVs transferred from the RN to the Estonian Navy in April 2007 was renamed *Admiral Cowan*.

1944 Admiral Sir Bruce Fraser assumed command of the embryonic British Pacific Fleet assembling at Ceylon.

1997 HMY *Britannia* entered Portsmouth for the last time, escorted by *Southampton* with CINCFLEET embarked and berthed at South Railway Jetty. Commodore Royal Yachts, Cdre A.J.C. Morrow, rang down 'Finished with main engines' at 1135. End of 44-year career, having steamed 1,087,623 miles.

2000 The RNVR Roll of Honour containing the names of 6,200 RNVR officers killed in the Second World War, was unveiled by HRH The Duke of Edinburgh at The Naval Club, Hill Street, Mayfair. The Club House is formally dedicated as a war memorial to the RNVR.

See 13 June 1954.

2006 *Norfolk*, the first of the Type 23 frigates, handed over to the Chilean Navy at Portsmouth and renamed Almirante Cochrane, in honour of the Royal Navy's Admiral Lord Cochrane. The previous *Norfolk*, a County-class guided missile destroyer, was transferred to Chile in February 1982. *Grafton* and *Marlborough* to be transferred in 2008.

See 16 November 1967, 10 July 1987, 1 June 1990, 6 May 2005.

23 November

1757 *Hussar* and *Dolphin* sank the French *Alcyon* 220 miles N.N.W. of Cape Finisterre.

1757 *Chichester* captured the French *Abenakise* 100 miles S.W. of Ushant.

1799 *Courier* captured the French privateer *Guerrière* 20 miles S.E. of Lowestoft.

1799 *Solebay* captured the French *Egyptien, Eole, Levrier* and *Vengeur* 10 miles W.N.W. of Cape Tiburon, Haiti.

1805 First RN ship named *Nelson* (120) ordered, less than three weeks after news of Trafalgar and Nelson's death reached the Admiralty. First rate. Laid down at Woolwich 1809. Launched 1814.

1810 Royal Navy bomb and mortar vessels from Rear-Admiral Sir Richard Keats' squadron, ordered to 'menace and occupy the attention of the enemy', attacked French gunboats in El Puerto de Santa Maria near Cadiz. Having declared against the French, Cadiz was an important entry point for supplying Wellington's Peninsula campaign. Among the casualties were lieutenants Thomas Worth and John Buckland of the Royal Marine Artillery, killed by the same shot. They were buried together in the Trafalgar Cemetery in Gibraltar, 'the brightest ornaments of their Corps'.

1812 Lt Richard Stewart Gamage, First Lieutenant of the sloop *Griffon*, was hanged on board the ship at Deal for running through with his sword the undisciplined Sgt Lake of the Marines on 20 October. The last RN officer known to have been hanged rather than shot for a capital crime.

See 15 May 1797.

1865 *Grasshopper* captured two pirate lorchas and destroyed a third at Port Matheson.

1896 Lofts for the training of carrier pigeons established at Sheerness, Portsmouth and Devonport.

1899 Capt Prothero's Naval Brigade at the Battle of Belmont.

1914 Battleships *Russell* and *Exmouth* bombarded Zeebrugge.

1914 U-18 rammed by *Dorothy Gray* and *Garry*, trying to enter Scapa Flow, then by *Kaphiada* before drifting on to the Skerries (58.41N, 02.55W).

1917 Dame Katharine Furse appointed first Director of the Women's Royal Naval Service.

See 29 November 1917, 11 April 1939.

1918 First ships of German High Seas Fleet arrived at Scapa for internment.

1920 Admiral of the Fleet Sir George Callaghan died. C-in-C Home Fleet from November 1911 until peremptorily superseded at Admiralty insistence by Admiral Sir John Jellicoe as C-in-C Grand Fleet on the outbreak of war in 1914. 'The even-tempered C-in-C Home Fleet . . . did not excel in any field, but he was "full of sound common sense", in Beatty's opinion, and had shown a comprehensive grasp of fleet work. He probably would have given a good account of himself in war' – Marder, *From the Dreadnought to Scapa Flow*, vol.1 p.407. Callaghan had been considered a possible successor to Fisher as First Sea Lord after the Dardanelles debacle in 1915 but instead became C-in-C The Nore from January 1915 to March 1918 (Admiral of the Fleet 2 April 1917).

See 21 December 1852, 4 August 1914.

1938 Battleship *Royal Oak* embarked the body of Her Late Majesty Queen Maud of Norway, wife of King Haakon VII, at South Railway Jetty for passage to Oslo. The ship was delayed by a gale and sailed next day escorted by the destroyers *Fame, Brilliant, Bulldog* and *Keith*. Queen Maud, who died in a London hospital aged 69, was daughter of King Edward VII and sister of King George V.

See 21 September 1957.

The grave in the Trafalgar Cemetery of lieutenants Thomas Worth and John Buckland of the Royal Marine Artillery, 'the brightest ornaments of their corps', who were killed in Keats' attack on French gunboats near Cadiz on 23 November 1810. Photographed by the author in 2000. (*Author*)

1939 AMC *Rawalpindi*, Capt E.C. Kennedy RN, sunk by the *Scharnhorst* in Iceland–Faroes gap (63.40N, 11.31W).

Former P&O liner *Rawalpindi*, Capt E.C. Kennedy, was on the Northern Patrol when she sighted the German battlecruiser *Scharnhorst* at dusk. The enemy was attempting to break out into the Atlantic to attack merchant ships with her sister, *Gneisenau*. *Rawalpindi* reported the enemy and despite the disparity in armament, managed to hit *Scharnhorst* in the quarter of an hour before she herself was sunk. The cruiser *Newcastle*, which was the next ship in the patrol line, closed and sighted the battlecruiser's lights and she picked up eleven survivors. However, she lost touch in the dark and rain squalls. The battlecruisers decided to return to base without attacking shipping, as their position was known.

This gallant action should not overshadow the great quantity of determined, too-often-unrecognised work by the fifty-five other passenger liners taken up and converted in 1939–40. The ships kept the seas in all weathers and their crews knew the odds. Fifteen had been sunk by the end of 1941 and the survivors were withdrawn, initially from the Atlantic, as soon as possible.

1939 Light cruiser *Calypso* captured the German *Konsul Hendrik Fisser* north of the Faroes (63.00N, 07.00W).

See 29 September 1939.

1939 First German magnetic mine, Type A, located at Shoeburyness. Rendered safe by Lt-Cdr J.G.D. Ouvry and CPO C.E. Baldwin, assisted by Lt-Cdr R.C. Lewis and AB A.L. Vearncombe. The mine was dissected the next day at *Vernon* by Dr A.B. Wood.

1943 *Bazely*, *Blackwood* and *Drury* sank U-648 in Atlantic (42.40N, 20.37W). Convoy OS 59/ MKS 33.

1963 Following the assassination of President Kennedy the day before, the First Lord of the Admiralty sent a message of condolence to the Secretary of the US Navy on behalf of the Royal Navy. AFO 2370/63.

1979 *Laymoor*, the last boom defence vessel manned by the Royal Navy and the last RN ship with steam reciprocating engines, entered port at Great Harbour, Greenock at 1100, wearing a paying-off pennant. DCI(RN) 763/79.

See 15 July 1960, 28 May 1962, 18 March 2002.

1982 Cdre Sam Dunlop, who commanded RFA *Fort Austin* in the Falklands, invested with the DSO and CBE at Buckingham Palace, the first Merchant Navy DSO since the Second World War. *Fort Austin* operated Sea Kings in San Carlos Water under repeated air attack where Dunlop displayed 'leadership, steadiness and aggression, and was an immense inspiration'. He died aged 85 on 17 July 2008.

24 NOVEMBER

1804 The third-rate *Venerable* (74), Capt John Hunter, putting to sea with the Channel Fleet from Torbay in rising wind and sea, hove-to to recover a seaman overboard, lost its way, fell off to leeward towards Brixham and, unable to weather Berry Head, went aground, rolled over and broke up. All but eight of her ship's company were rescued by *Impetueux* (74) and *Goliath* (74). All honourably acquitted for the loss except a marine sentenced to 200 lashes from ship to ship round the fleet. *Venerable* had been Duncan's flagship at Camperdown in 1797.

1807 Brig *Anne* fought ten Spanish gunboats off Tarifa and took three.

See 20 November 1807.

1812 Boats of *Narcissus* captured the American privateer *Joseph and Mary* 20 miles S.E. of Cape Tiburon, Haiti.

1875 Purchase of controlling interest in Suez Canal by Disraeli.

1878 Roger Roland Charles Backhouse, future Admiral of the Fleet and First Sea Lord, born at Middleton Dyas, Yorkshire.

See 15 July 1939.

1885 Irrawaddy flotilla and troops defeated the Burmese at Myingyan, Upper Burma. Boats of *Bacchante*, *Turquoise*, *Woodlark* and *Mariner* with the Indian Marine *Irrawaddy*.

1911 'All cruisers of the *Invincible* and later types are for the future to be described as 'battlecruisers', in order to distinguish them from the armoured cruisers of earlier date.' – AWO 351/11.

1917 *Gipsy* and five trawlers attacked U-48, which had stranded on the Goodwin Sands, where she blew up (51.17N, 01.31E). Her wreck reappeared in 1921 and on 4 June 1973.

1922 Wearing of wound stripes and war service chevrons discontinued.

1941 Light cruiser *Dunedin* sunk by U-124 in mid-Atlantic, 900 miles W. of Freetown at a range of 3 miles. When she approached that port, the submarine was engaged at 6 miles by a 5.5-in gun landed by *Furious*.

See 9 December 1942.

1943 Destroyer *Ilex*, *Paladin* and *Mendip* bombarded enemy on the Garigliano River.

GR9 Harriers from 800 Naval Air Squadron and 1(F) Squadron RAF launched from the deck of HMS *Ark Royal* for the last time. (*RN*)

The Blackwood-class Type 14 anti-submarine frigate HMS *Hardy* was sunk as a target for Exocet missiles on 3 July 1983 off Gibraltar. (*Author*)

1944 Corvette *Shawinigan* (RCN) sunk with all hands in the Cabot Strait (47.34N, 59.11W) by homing torpedo from U-1228.

1950 The bell of the battleship *Queen Elizabeth* presented by Admiral Sir John Cunningham to the Baltic Exchange which had adopted the ship during the Second World War.

See 16 May 1948.

1957 Frigate *Loch Ruthven* sailed from Bahrain to deliver medical supplies, food, blankets and building materials to Dubai 'on the Trucial Oman coast' following widespread storm damage.

See 12 March 1945.

1967 'Approval has been given for White Ensign and Union Flags to be washed onboard, using ships' laundries, at public expense, or by civilian laundries where Service facilities are not available. Experience has shown that great care is required when washing White Ensigns. Satisfactory results can be achieved when using ships' laundries provided that soap is employed. . . ' – DCI(RN) 1400/67.

1972 HM The Queen's Silver Wedding Anniversary. The First Sea Lord presented The Lord High Admiral, on behalf of the Admiralty Board, with an antique silver basket from the former Admiralty Yacht *Enchantress* at Buckingham Palace. DCI(RN) T.906/72.

1983 First OASIS accepted afloat, in *Exeter*. Luddites have construed the acronym to represent 'Only Adds Stress In Ships and Submarines'.

2010 The last fixed-wing launch from a British fleet carrier. Four Harrier GR9 from Joint Force Harrier (800 NAS and 1 (Fighter) Sqn RAF) took off from *Ark Royal*, Capt Jeremy Kyd RN, at 0900Z 40nm E. of Newcastle inbound to RAF Cottesmore. The launch was led by Capt Michael Carty RM followed by Lt Matthew Fooks-Bale RN, Flt-Lt Emily Rickards RAF and Lt-Cdr James Blackmore RN piloting the last aircraft to leave the ship.

See 7 February 1963, 14 November 1978, 27 November 1978, 30 March 2006, 3 December 2010.

25 November

1793 *Penelope* (32) and *Iphigenia* (32) captured the French *Inconstante* (36) 12 miles W. of Leogane, Haiti.

1851 Naval expedition sent to Lagos (present Nigeria), a centre of the African slave trade, to confront with Cocioco, King of Lagos, 'who had become troublesome and intractable'. The iron paddle steamer *Bloodhound*, flying a flag of truce and carrying Mr Beecroft, Consul-General at Fernando Po, with *Waterwitch* (8), and followed by an armed flotilla of boats from *Philomel* (8), Cdr Thomas Forbes (Senior Officer), *Harlequin* (12), *Volcano* (5), *Niger* (14) screw, and *Waterwitch* (8) 'in order that Cocioco should be under no misapprehension concerning the seriousness and solemnity of the British demands'. The boats were fired on from both sides of the river and landing parties destroyed some properties in Lagos in the face of unexpectedly fierce opposition, before Forbes, 'despairing of being able to accomplish more, retreated in good order' to confer with Cdre Henry Bruce about sending a stronger force.

See 28 December 1851.

1852 First instruction book for Paymasters.

1868 *Algerine* captured the Amping and Zealandia forts of Taiwan (Formosa).

1893 Destroyer *Daring*, fourth ship of the name, was launched by John I. Thornycroft at Chiswick on the Thames (as was her predecessor). One of the first four torpedo boat destroyers ordered for the RN, she was fitted with a bow torpedo tube but her reciprocating engines drove her twin screws at 27 knots and she was prone to overtake a fired torpedo. The introduction of steam turbines made her generation redundant and she was sold in 1912.

See 4 February 1874.

1899 Battle of Graspan, South Africa. Naval Brigade of *Doris*, *Monarch* and *Powerful* under Capt Prothero.

1910 Australian Naval Defence Act passed by Australian government, paving the way for creation of Royal Australian Navy.

See 1 March 1904, 10 July 1911.

1912 Admiralty Air Department formed. Capt Murray F. Sueter RN, who had been Head of the Naval Airship Service in 1911–12, appointed Director of Air Department (DAD) in control of all naval aviation.

Post upgraded September 1915 and Rear-Admiral C.L. Vaughan-Lee became director of Air Services; Sueter, promoted commodore first class, was his uneasy subordinate as superintendent of Aircraft Construction. Sueter's subsequent feud with the Admiralty had him exiled to the Otranto Barrage. In December 1917 Sueter wrote directly to HM King George V asking for public recognition or an honour for his undoubted services; the letter was passed to the Admiralty who ordered him to haul down his broad pennant and he was placed on half pay. He was never again employed (the Air Ministry refused his requested transfer to the RAF) and he retired in 1920 soon after being promoted rear-admiral by seniority. MP for Hertford for next twenty-four years (1921–45) and knighted 1934.

See 19 November 1917, 6 January 1918, 20 July 1918, 3 February 1960.

1914 Submarine D 2 sunk by German patrol craft off Wester Ems.

1940 Three acoustic mines were exploded in Thames: first use of the technique approved on 29 October, no acoustic mine having been discovered meanwhile.

1941 *Barham* sunk by U-331 off Sidi Barrani (32.34N, 26.24E). She blew up in less than five minutes and, though 862 men were lost, 450 survived the great explosion. First battleship lost in open sea since *Britannia* sunk 9 November 1918.

See 28 December 1939.

1942 Submarine *Utmost* sunk, probably by the Italian TB *Groppo* off Marettimo, west of Sicily (38.31N, 12.01E).

HMS *Barham* sinking after being torpedoed, taken from HMS *Valiant*, 1941. (*NMRN*)

1942 Submarine *Unshaken* lost her CO, Lt C.E. Oxborrow, her Yeoman of Signals and an AB off the bridge in heavy weather off Gibraltar.

1943 Frigates *Bazely* and *Blackwood* sank U-600 in N. Atlantic (41.45N, 22.30W): their second sinking in two days.

1944 Frigate *Ascension* and Sunderland G/330 (Nor) sank U-322 in Shetland/Faroes Gap (60.18N, 04.52W).

1960 Royal Marines, except recruits and bandsmen, authorised to wear the green beret of the Commandos.

1965 Assault ship *Fearless*, Capt H.A. Corbett RN, commissioned at Harland and Wolff, Belfast.

1975 Third Cod War, caused by Iceland's unilateral extension of a 200-mile fishing limit. Frigate *Falmouth* first ship on scene.

See 31 August 1958.

1977 Two frigates sailed from Devonport and reached a holding position in the S. Atlantic (40.00S, 40.00W) on 13 December to wait covertly during talks with the Argentine government over the future of the Falkland Islands. SSN *Dreadnought* deployed south on 21 November and patrolled the approaches to Port Stanley. Ships released on 19 December to return covertly to the UK. Operation Journeyman.

1978 Stern trawlers *Suffolk Monarch* and *Suffolk Harvester* taken up for service as RNR minesweepers and renamed *St David* (South Wales Division) and *Venturer* (Severn Division). DCI(RN) 773/78 and 774/78.

26 NOVEMBER

1703 Thirteen warships and over 1,500 men lost on the night of 26/27 November in the great hurricane which struck southern England. The *Northumberland* (70), *Restoration* (70), *Stirling Castle* (70) and *Mary* (60) were driven from the Downs and wrecked on the Goodwins and 1,087 men drowned; the *Mortar* bomb was driven from the same anchorage and broke up a week later on the Dutch coast; the *Vanguard* (90) and the *Portsmouth* bomb sank at The Nore; the *Reserve* (50) foundered off Gorleston with 174 lost; the *Vigo* (48) foundered off Hellevoetsluys in Holland (most saved); the *Resolution* (70) at St Helens was driven up channel and was run ashore near Pevensey (all saved), the *Eagle* advice boat followed her and went ashore near Selsey and broke up; the *Newcastle* (50) foundered at Spithead (193 lost) and the *Vesuvius* fireship went ashore (CTL). The Canterbury storeship went ashore near Bristol with no survivors. Eddystone Lighthouse destroyed.

See 24 and 25 December 1811.

1799 *Amphion* captured the Spanish letter of marque *Asturiana* 120 miles W.N.W. of Cape Catoche, Gulf of Mexico.

1806 Rear-Admiral Sir Edward Pellew's squadron captured the Dutch *Maria Wilhelmina* off Banten.

See 27 November 1806.

1813 Boats of *Swiftsure* captured the French privateer *Charlemagne* 10 miles W.N.W. of Cape Rouse (Rosso), Corsica.

1858 *Pearl*'s Naval Brigade at Domariaganj (second action).

HMS *Gladiator* being salvaged after having been rammed and sunk during a blizzard by the liner SS *St Paul* off the Isle of Wight in April 1908. (*NMRN*)

A workhorse of the Atlantic and Arctic convoys. The V&W-class destroyer HMS *Whitehall* in Plymouth Sound in 1943. On 31 October 1943 (with HMS *Geranium*) she sank U-306 in the Atlantic; on 30 January 1944 (with the destroyer HMS *Meteor*) she sank U-314 in the Barents Sea; and with other forces sank U-394 in the Norwegian Sea on 2 September 1944. (*Cdr David Hobbs RN*)

1899 Naval Brigade formed at Durban from *Forte*, *Terrible*, *Tartar* and *Philomel*.

1913 *Warspite*, the most famous battleship of the twentieth century, launched at Devonport Dockyard.

1914 Pre-Dreadnought battleship *Bulwark*, 5th BS, Channel Fleet, destroyed by ammunition explosion at 0753 while at No. 17 Buoy off Sheerness. Just twelve men saved from 758 ship's company.

See 18 October 1899, 31 December 1915, 9 July 1917.

1916 Second German raid on Lowestoft.

1918 'Nothing, nothing in the world, nothing that you may think of or dream of, or anyone else may tell you: no argument, however seductive, must lead you to abandon that Naval supremacy on which the life of our country depends' – Churchill, *The Second World War, Volume 3*, pt 2, p.415.

1921 Foul-weather funeral rig for all officers to be greatcoat and cocked hat. RNR and RNVR officers changed their indigenous buttons to RN for first time.

1940 Fifteen Swordfish aircraft of 815 and 819 Sqns (*Illustrious*) bombed Port Laki, Leros.

1943 Convoy KMF 26 from Oran to India via Suez attacked at dusk by thirty German aircraft in Gulf of Bougie off Algeria (36.56N, 05.20E) British troopship HMT *Rohna* hit by a glider bomb and sank in thirty minutes. Over 1,000 US soldiers lost together with five officers and 115 men from the ship.

1967 Royal Navy shore headquarters in Aden, HMS *Sheba*, paid off three days before British Forces departed.

See 19 January 1839, 21 and 29 November 1967.

1976 The term 'Signal Deck' to replace 'Flag Deck' to avoid confusion with 'Flight Deck' over intercom. DCI(RN) 643/76.

2007 RFA *Lyme Bay*, landing ship dock, accepted.

27 NOVEMBER

1762 Samuel Hood the younger born.

1806 Rear-Admiral Sir Edward Pellew (*Culloden*) destroyed a Dutch squadron of six ships and twenty merchantmen at Batavia (Djakarta). Ships: *Belliqueux, Culloden, Powerful, Russell, Seaflower, Sir Francis Drake, Terpsichore.*

1809 *La Chiffone* and the Hon. East India Company cruisers *Fury, Mornington, Nautilus* and *Ternate* destroyed the Joasmi pirate stronghold at Laft.

1811 *Eagle* captured the French *Corcyre* off Brindisi, after a ten-hour chase.

1828 Admiral Thomas Spry, formerly Lt Thomas Davey, died at Killaganoon, Cornwall. Commissioned as a lieutenant in 1769, he changed his name in 1775 on inheriting estates in Cornwall from Rear Admiral Sir Richard Spry. He was made post in 1778 and, with the end of the War of American Independence in 1783, Spry went on shore to enjoy the blessings of the land with the fruits of Sir Richard's labours and never returned to sea. Promoted by seniority, Spry became Rear Admiral of the White in 1795 and went upwards to be Admiral of the Red in 1814. His fourteen years' commissioned, active service were thus followed by forty-five years on shore on half pay, thirty-three of them at flag officer rates. Memorial at Roseland-St-Anthony.

1830 Gold-laced trousers restored to flag officers.

1857 *Shannon*'s Naval Brigade at the defence of Cawnpore.

1913 *Emperor of India* launched at Vickers. With *Iron Duke* (Portsmouth 1912), *Marlborough* (Devonport 1912) and *Benbow* (Beardmore 1913) the last coal-burning battleships ordered for the Royal Navy. (*Erin, Agincourt* and *Canada*, building in Britain for foreign navies and taken over in 1914, were also coal-burning.)

1916 R-9 made first successful flight by an RNAS rigid airship.

1923 The Empire Cruise began. Special Service Squadron of battlecruisers *Hood*, flag of Acting Vice-Admiral Sir Frederick Field, and *Repulse*, with the 1st LCS *Delhi, Dauntless, Dunedin, Dragon* and *Danae* sailed for a ten-month tour of the Dominions, India, the USA and South America.

See 29 September 1924.

1939 First Lord of the Admiralty, Winston Churchill, minuted his Secretary: 'I notice that in the Air Ministry every room is provided with candles and matches for use in emergency. Pray take steps immediately to make similar provision in the Admiralty.'

See 29 October 1939.

1940 Action off Cape Spartivento, Sardinia (36N, 08.30E). Vice-Admiral Sir James Somerville (*Renown*) fought the Italian Fleet. Ships: *Ark Royal, Berwick, Coventry, Defender, Despatch, Diamond, Duncan, Encounter, Faulknor, Firedrake, Forester, Fury, Gallant, Gloxinia, Greyhound, Hereward, Hotspur, Hyacinth, Jaguar, Kelvin, Manchester, Newcastle, Peony, Ramillies, Renown, Salvia, Sheffield, Southampton, Vidette, Wishart*. FAA Sqns: Walrus: 700; Skua: 800; Fulmar: 808; Swordfish: 810, 818, 820 (*Ark Royal*). RAF: Sunderland flying-boat.
Battle Honour: Spartivento 1940.

The last fixed-wing aircrew to be launched from HMS *Ark Royal*, 1978. Seated in the cockpit are, left to right: Lt Denis McCullum, RN, Deputy Air Engineering Officer of 892 NAS, and Fl/Lt Murdo McLeod RAF F4K Phantom pilot. This was Lt McCullum's first flight in a Phantom. (*FAAM*)

HMS *Diamond*, third of class, launched at BAE Systems Govan, 2007. (*BAE*)

A convoy was passing from Gibraltar to Alexandria. The Italians were determined to stop it, and sailed two battleships, seven 8-in cruisers and sixteen destroyers from Naples and Messina. Admiral Somerville, in command of Force H covering the convoy, decided that the best defence for the convoy was a determined attack by his inferior escort. The battlecruiser *Renown*, one heavy and three light cruisers and one (AA) cruiser together with the aircraft carrier *Ark Royal* raced to attack the Italian Fleet. In the action which followed, one British cruiser was damaged; the enemy withdrew and the convoy passed safely.

1940 *Port Napier* destroyed by fire in Loch Alsh (57.17N, 05.44W).

1943 Light cruiser *Orion*, with destroyers *Paladin*, *Teazer* and *Troubridge* bombarded enemy positions north of Garigliano River.

1951 Four Sea Fury naval aircraft flew 1,322 miles from RNAS Lee-on-Solent to Malta in record time for the route; the first two aircraft took 3 hours 16 minutes and the second pair took 3 hours 11 minutes. The average speed was 400 mph and three of the aircraft were piloted by officers of the Indian Navy.

See 19 July 1949, 17 June 1958.

1959 Frigates on the West Indies Station and the Arabian Sea and Persian Gulf Station designated 8th and 9th Frigate Squadrons respectively but without a captain(F). AFO 2886/59.

1961 The Operations Division and the Trade Division of the Naval Staff amalgamated as the Trade and Operations Division, DTOD. AFO 1436/61.

See 11 September 2003.

1978 The last catapault launch in the Royal Navy: F4K Phantom of 892 NAS piloted by Fl/Lt Murdo McLeod (Pilot) and Lt Denis McCullum (Observer), launched from the waist catapult of *Ark Royal* at 1515A inbound to RAF St Athan.

The last Buccaneer launch that day was an 809 NAS aircraft, Sqn Ldr Rick Phillips (Pilot) and Cdr Ken MacKenzie (Observer). See *Navy News*, February 2004, p.14.

See 14 June 1970, 24 November 2010.

1987 New landing ship logistic, RFA *Sir Galahad*, handed over by Swan Hunter. The first ever service of dedication for a RFA vessel together with presentation of Battle Honour Falklands 1982 took place at Marchwood Military Port on 3 December 1987. DCI(RN) 83/88.

See 8 June 1982.

1999 The fourth and last Trident submarine, *Vengeance*, commissioned at Barrow, the last submarine commissioned into the Royal Navy in the (popularly accepted end of the) twentieth century.

See 19 September 1998, 16 April 1999, 15 December 1999.

2007 *Diamond*, the third Type 45 destroyer, launched at BAE Systems Yard at Govan by Mrs Suzie Johns, wife of Vice-Admiral Adrian Johns, Second Sea Lord.

See 20 September 1693, 6 May 1911, 14 June 1950, 25 June 1964, 1 February 2006, 23 January 2007, 17 November 2008, 21 October 2009, 11 October 2010, 22 September 2010.

28 NOVEMBER

1803 *Ardent* drove ashore and destroyed the French *Bayonnaise* near Cape Finisterre.

1808 Boats of *Heureux* fought shore batteries and seven vessels in Mahault harbour, Guadeloupe.

1899 Capt Prothero and his brigade in action at the Modder River.

1914 VC: Cdr Henry Peel Ritchie (*Goliath*) at Dar-es-Salaam during search and destroy operation. Ships: *Fox*, *Goliath*, *Dupleix* and *Helmuth*: three German ships disabled, and harbour installations wrecked. Ritchie's was first naval VC won in the First World War.

1916 RNAS aircraft destroyed the Zeppelin L-21, 8 miles E. of Lowestoft.

1917 Two gunboats lost on River Tigris.

1923 Rank of 'Clerk' abolished.

1941 O 21 (Neth) sank U-95 off Gibraltar (36.24N, 03.20W).

1941 Sloop *Parramatta* (RAN) sunk by U-559 off Bardia (32.20N, 24.35E).

1942 Destroyers *Quentin* and *Quiberon* (RAN) sank the Italian S/M *Dessie* N. of Bone (37.04N, 07.45E).

See 2 December 1942.

1942 Destroyer *Ithuriel* beached, CTL, in Bone harbour after air attack.

1943 Wellington L/179 sank U-542 in N. Atlantic (39.03N, 16.25W). Convoy SL 140.

1958 'Their Lordships have decided that there is no longer a requirement for Chains for sounding by Hand Lead and Line in H.M. Ships generally . . .' – AFO 2941/58.

1959 Closure of Hong Kong Dockyard, announced on 28 November 1957, completed with 4,650 redundancies. Frigate *Cardigan Bay* the only RN ship present.'Their Lordships desire to express their gratitude for all the benefits thus bestowed upon the Royal Navy. Their deep regret that the Yard has had to be closed is mingled with pride in the historic achievements of its workers.'

1962 Unified Command of the three Armed Services introduced in the Far East. Admiral Sir David Luce, C-in-C Far East Station, became the first C-in-C Far East. The naval C-in-C title lapsed and his successor, Vice-Admiral Sir Desmond Dreyer, lately Flag Officer Air

In characteristically jovial style, Admiral Sir Michael Le Fanu, the retiring First Sea Lord, leaving the MOD on 3 July 1970, on which day he was promoted admiral of the fleet. Admiral Le Fanu had been nominated CDS from October 1970 but he was mortally ill and died on 28 November that year. (*Author*)

The new King George V-class battleship HMS *Anson*, completed by Swan Hunter in June 1942, carrying out main armament trials with her 14-in guns on 19 October that year. (*Cdr David Hobbs RN*)

(Home), became Flag Officer Commanding-in-Chief Far East Fleet (FOC-in-CFEF). This abbreviation was clearly unsatisfactory and the title was change to Commander Far East Fleet (COMFEF). AFO 2322/63.

See 22 February 1966.

1970 Admiral of the Fleet Sir Michael Le Fanu died in London. 'Cultivate courage.'

See 3 July 1970.

1971 Fire in gear room of the frigate *Zulu*, on passage from Freetown, Sierra Leone, to Gibraltar, left her drifting without power off W. coast of Africa. The patrol craft *Bossington, Hubberston* and *Maxton*, returning to Britain from Hong Kong, reached *Zulu* on 30 November. *Hubberston* and *Bossington* took up a conventional tow, steaming side by side, but they could not keep apart due to the weight of the frigate. *Hubberston* slipped the tow at 1815 and *Bossington* continued the tow alone. The four ships arrived off Dakar at 0800 on 1 December. *Hubberston* secured alongside *Zulu* to provide steerage and *Bossington* was slipped. With the help of a local tug *Zulu* secured alongside 011050Z.

See 14 November 1970,16 September 1971, 2 November 2000.

1983 *Fearless*, later supported by *Andromeda* and *Achilles*, relieved *Glamorgan* and *Brazen* off Lebanon.

See 15 October 1958, 18 November 1983, 1 January 1984, 18 and 20 July 2006.

1990 *Invincible* became the second mixed-manned ship, after *Brilliant*. *Juno* became the third on 10 December and *Battleaxe* the fourth on 22 January 1991, by which time 422 billets were filled by women, rising to 490 by 1993.

29 NOVEMBER

1682 Prince Rupert died.

1779 *Proserpine* captured the French *Sphinx* 12 miles S.E. by W. of Montserrat.

1791 Lt William Broughton of the brig *Chatham*, part of George Vancouver's expedition to the Pacific, landed on Chatham Island, 800km E. of Christchurch, New Zealand (43.53S, 176.31 W), which he claimed for the British Crown and named after the First Lord of the Admiralty.
See 1 April 1791, 17 May 1797.

1805 Boats of *Serpent* cut out the Spanish *San Cristobel Pano* in Truxillo Bay, Honduras.

1811 *Alceste, Active, Acorn* and *Unite* captured the French *Pomone* and *Persanne* 15 miles N.E. of Pelagos Island, Dalmatia. A third French frigate, *Pauline*, escaped.
Battle Honour: Pelagosa 1811 (but not *Acorn*)

WRNS recruitment poster, *c.*1917. By the end of the war over 7,000 women had joined the Service and worked in a wide variety of roles, including drivers, telephonists, typists and sailmakers. (*NMRN*)

1883 Max Kennedy Horton, future pioneer submariner and C-in-C W. Approaches in the Second World War, born at the Maelog Lake Hotel, Anglesey.
See 30 July 1951.

1907 Geoffrey Callender, history teacher at Osborne, published the first volume in his trilogy *Sea Kings of Britain*, 'short biographies of famous admirals for use in the Royal Naval College, Osborne'. They were received with some dismay by naval history giants like Laughton, Corbett and Richmond ('atrocious') but they became standard texts, failing either to inspire or to explain the relevance of the proper study of naval history. They even displaced Laughton's one-volume, much finer *From Howard to Nelson* (1899) at Dartmouth.
See 6 November 1946.

1909 Battlecruiser *Lion* laid down at Devonport and Super Dreadnought *Orion* laid down at Portsmouth. *Lion* was the first battlecruiser with 13.5-in. guns and centre-line turrets, and the first warship to cost over £2 million.

1915 Withdrawal from Ctesiphon, near Baghdad, to Kut-al' Amara. River gunboats and vessels: *Butterfly, Firefly, Comet, Messudieh, Shaitan,* Shushan, Sumana.* *Destroyed by enemy.

1915 *Duchess of Hamilton* mined off Longsand.

1917 WRNS established by Admiralty Office Memorandum No. 254.
See 23 November 1917.

1920 His Majesty Christian X of Denmark appointed an Honorary Admiral in the Royal Navy. Order in Council No. 140A of 3 December 1920.

1939 Destroyers *Icarus, Kashmir* and *Kingston* sank U-35 E. of Shetland (60.53N, 02.47E).

The minesweeper *Lanton* leaving Aden in Spring 1962. (*Author*)

1940 Light cruiser *Leander* (RNZN) bombarded Mogadishu.

1944 MMS 101 sunk by mine in the Gulf of Salonica.

1945 First RN helicopter ASR (Sikorsky R 5).

1950 Battle of the Chosin Reservoir, Korea; forty-one Independent Cdo RM present, under command of 1st US Marine Division. Later awarded the Presidential Unit citation.

1952 'Sarie Marais' officially adopted by RM Commandos at presentation of colours in Malta: at least the third example of the rather curious British penchant for taking good tunes from erstwhile enemies.

1963 Tribal-class frigate *Mohawk* commissioned at Barrow. Her RM contingent of twenty-two men joined the hard way. Led by Lt Robin Ross RM, they marched out of Eastney at 0930 Tuesday 12 November and marched into Barrow seventeen days later, the afternoon before commissioning.

1967 Withdrawal of British Forces from Aden after 129 years of British rule, planned for early 1968, was brought forward to 29 November 1967. Task Force 318, formed to cover the final stages of the operation, began to assemble on 11 October with the arrival of the carrier *Albion* from Singapore. She landed 42 Cdo which, with 1 PARA, held a perimeter north of the Aden peninsula and kept open Khormaksar airfield. The carriers *Eagle*, *Hermes* and *Bulwark*, with 40 Cdo embarked, the guided missile destroyers *Devonshire* and *London*, and submarine *Auriga*, stood by offshore as contingency cover. 45 Cdo, which had been in Aden for seven years, was lifted out in thirteen C-130s on the night of 28/29 November. The last British troops, 42 Cdo, were airlifted to *Albion*. The last British fighting man to leave 'the barren rocks of Aden', Lt-Col T.D. 'Dai' Morgan, 42 Cdo RM, arrived on board *Albion* at 1500.

See 19 January 1839, 15 May 1948, 30 June 1948, 21 and 26 November 1967, 31 October 1971, 30 June 1997.

30 NOVEMBER

1612 *Dragon* and *Osiander* (Hon. East India Company) fought a Portuguese squadron off Surat.

1652 Admiral Robert Blake (*Triumph*) fought Admiral Marten Tromp (*Brederode*) off Dungeness. Ships: *Bonaventure*,* *Garland*,* *Happy Entrance*,† *Hercules*,† *Nimble*, *Sapphire*,† *Ruby*,† *Triumph*,* *Vanguard*, *Victory*.

*Captured. †Sunk. British retreated and enormous Dutch convoy swept through, marked by the tale of Tromp hoisting a broom.

1787 Nelson paid off the frigate *Boreas* (28) at Sheerness after three and a half years in the West Indies.

See 18 March 1784.

1803 *Bellerophon* and *Hercules* at the evacuation by the French of San Domingo (Haiti). Captured: *Cerf*, *Clorinde*, *Sémillante*, *Vertu*.

1808 Capt Lord Cochrane's defence of Fort Trinidad, Rosas.

1811 *Rover* captured the French privateer *Comte Regnaud* (ex-British *Vincejo*) 250 miles S.W. by W. of the Scilly Isles.

1816 Trials of water tanks, fitted with syphon, advocated by Lt W. Rodger to replace casks which, with the acceptance of tanks on board, were kept for emergency watering parties – and spirits.

See 23 September 1819.

1839 Rear-Admiral Sir Frederick Lewis Maitland, C-in-C East Indies and China, died on board his flagship *Wellesley* (74) off Bombay and was buried in St Thomas's Cathedral. Napoleon had surrendered to Capt Maitland on board *Bellerophon* on 15 July 1815.

1873 William Henry Dudley 'Ginger' Boyle, the future Admiral of the Fleet The Earl of Cork and Orrery, born at Farnham, Surrey. Entered the Service in *Britannia* 1887. C-in-C Home Fleet 1933–5 and Naval Commander at Narvik aged 67 in 1940.

See 8 April 1940, 19 April 1967.

HMS *Vanguard* (1944), the last British battleship to be built. (*NMRN W&L 888R*)

1874 Winston Leonard Spencer Churchill born.

1903 To the editor of *The Times*: 'Sir, *The Navy List* of November contains a coincidence which, if not unique, is certainly so remarkable that it may possibly be interesting to a wider circle than the school which it primarily concerns. The three senior Admirals on the Active List are Lord Charles Scott, Lord Walter Kerr, and Sir Edward Seymour. They were all at Radley together in the first year that Dr Sewell was Warden. Faithfully yours, T. Field DD, Warden of Radley.'

1914 The third major intelligence haul at the start of the First World War. A British trawler operating off the Texel on the Dutch coast brought up a box of German CBs, probably that jettisoned by the German destroyer S-119 in action with the light cruiser *Undaunted* on 17 October. It included the third Imperial German naval code book to fall into British hands. It proved an intelligence a treasure trove that Room 40 always referred to as 'The Miraculous Draught of Fishes'.

See 11 and 20 August, 1914, 13 and 17 October 1914.

'The capture of the SKM [*Signalbuch der Kaiserlichen Marine*] and HVB [*Handelsverkehrsbuch*] codes had . . . begun to enable Room 40 to provide the Naval War Staff with better information about the movements and intentions of their opponents than any other military command had ever possessed. . . No one, on either side, had anticipated such a swift and overwhelming intelligence defeat for the Germans; it was one from which the Imperial German Navy was never to recover.' – Beesly, *Room 40: British Naval Intelligence 1914–1918*, p.7.

1916 *Penshurst* (Q 7) sank UB-19 18 miles N.W. of the Casquets (49.56N, 02.45W).

1940 GC: Lt Harold Reginald Newgass, RNVR, for mine disposal at Garston Gasworks, Liverpool.

1941 Whitley B/502 sank U-206 in the Bay of Biscay (46.55N, 07.16W). Sole success that year by RAF Bay patrols and the first Coastal Command 'kill' not shared with surface forces.

1944 *Vanguard* launched. Christened by HRH Princess Elizabeth, aged 18, but name of ship not published. Last Royal Navy battleship in commission afloat.

1945 Corvette *Merrittonia* (RCN) wrecked on coast of Nova Scotia.

1958 RNAS St David's, Pembrokeshire, closed to air traffic. AFO 2596/58.

1959 Tenth Submarine Squadron re-formed in Singapore with *Ambush*, *Teredo* and *Tactician*. Rear-Admiral A.R. Hezlet wrote in the commissioning booklet: 'We shall also remember those legendary commanding officers of the Tenth Flotilla during the war years, Wanklyn, Tomlinson, Cayley, Wraith, Piper and many others, of whom some are still serving today. Linked with them go such illustrious submarine names as *Upholder*, *Utmost*, *Unbending*, *Unruffled* and *Ultor* to mention just a few. It is with such traditions that the reformed Tenth Submarine Squadron is born again. You have the highest standards to maintain. I know you can, and will, achieve them.' – AFO 2951/59.

See 1 September 1940, 21 September 1944, 1 February 1967.

2000 Admiral Sir Alan West, the first four-star promotion and first appointment as C-in-C Fleet in the (properly accepted, if a year premature) twenty-first century.

See 2 August 2002.

1 DECEMBER

1588 Chatham Chest founded for relief of distressed seamen.

The Chatham Chest was a pension fund founded in the sixteenth century to help disabled sailors by deducting sums from seamen's pay. The Chest had five locks, with five different keys held by five different officers. Despite this there was severe mismanagement of funds. Pepys set up a Commission to inspect its administration.

1744 Frigate *Rose* captured the Spanish *Concepción* (100), a rich prize worth at least 108,636 dollars, 100 miles E. of Havana.

1781 William Parker born.

1811 Boats of *Colossus* and *Conquestador*, with *Arrow*, captured one vessel of a French convoy, burned three more and drove three others ashore near La Rochelle.

1914 Rear-Admiral Alfred Thayer Mahan, US Navy, historian and apostle of sea power, died in Washington. Author of *The Influence of Sea Power on History 1660–1783*, *The Influence of Sea Power on the French Revolution and Empire* and *The Life of Nelson: the Embodiment of the Sea Power of Great Britain*. 'Historically, good men with poor ships are better than poor men with good ships: over and over again the French Revolution taught the lesson, which our age, with its rage for the last new thing in material development, has largely dropped out of memory . . .'

HMS *Broadsword* (1976). (*NMRN*)

1916 Submarine E 37 lost in North Sea.

1940 GC (ex-AM): AB A. Miles (*Saltash*), for saving life at sea.

1941 Heavy cruiser *Dorsetshire* sank the German supply ship *Python* in S. Atlantic (27.50S, 03.55W).

See 22 November 1941.

1941 Light cruisers *Aurora* and *Penelope*, and destroyer *Lively* sank the Italian destroyer *Alvise da Mosto* off Kerkenah Bank (33.45N, 12.30E).

1942 Minesweeper *Armidale* (RAN) sunk by Japanese torpedo aircraft off Timor (10.00S, 128.00E).

1942 Trawler *Jasper* sunk by German TB flotilla off Start Point. Convoy PW 256.

1943 Destroyers *Paladin*, *Teazer* and *Troubridge* bombarded the Minturno area, Gulf of Gaeta.

1954 Amphibious School RM moved from Fort Cumberland, Eastney to Poole.

1954 Old royal yacht *Victoria and Albert*, launched at Pembroke Dockyard 9 May 1899, left Portsmouth under tow for breakers.

1960 HMS *Ariel II*, RNAS Worthy Down, Winchester, paid off and transferred to the Royal Army Pay Corps. Station's White Ensign laid up in Winchester Cathedral on previous Trafalgar Day.

The Ton-class coastal mine sweeper HMS *Bronington* in 1960. (*NMRN W&L 2085A*)

1962 Heavy repair ship *Duncansby Head* and the former guided missile trials ship *Girdle Ness* commissioned as *Cochrane* to be the temporary naval barracks and administrative HQ at Rosyth while a new facility was built near the dockyard, replacing the former *Cochrane* at Donibristle. *Cochrane* was re-commissioned ashore on 11 December 1968 and finally paid off 31 March 1996.

1977 New Meritorious Service Medal introduced for fleet chief petty officers, chief petty officers and petty officers.

1978 Carrier *Illustrious*, fifth of name, launched at Swan Hunters, Wallsend-on-Tyne.

1982 Admiral Sir Henry Leach promoted admiral of the fleet at the end of his appointment as First Sea Lord. Born 18 November 1923. Son of Capt John Leach, RN, killed in action in battleship *Prince of Wales* off Malaya 10 December 1941. Admiral 30 March 1977 and CINCFLEET. First Sea Lord July 1979, which appointment included Operation Corporate.

1990 WRNS officers adopted RN ranks.

1998 700M NAS, having formed in March 1998, commissioned with Merlin helicopters.

See 17 November 1998.

2009 HRH The Princess Royal promoted honorary vice-admiral.

2 December

1793 *Antelope* packet captured the French privateer *Atlanta* off Jamaica.

1796 *Quebec* captured the French *Africaine* 20 miles S. of Cape Bainet, Haiti.

1796 *Southampton* captured the Spanish privateer *Corso* off Cape delle Mele.

1825 Defeat of the Burmese at Pagoda Point, above Prome. *Diana* and boats of the Irrawaddy flotilla captured 300 warboats.

1917 Patrol boat P 32 sank UB-81, mined earlier off Dunose Head, Isle of Wight.

1940 AMC *Forfar* sunk by U-99 in W. Approaches (54.35N, 18.18W).

See 3 November 1940.

1940 First wartime change of command of the Home Fleet. Admiral of the Fleet Sir Charles Forbes was succeeded by Admiral Sir John Tovey who hoisted his flag in the new battleship *King George V*, name ship of the last class of British battleships and the first to be completed, which had just joined the Second Battle Squadron Home Fleet at Scapa Flow.

'Though the fifteen months of Admiral Forbes' war command brought no great sea victory in home waters such as might catch the public's imagination, they saw the steady application of the long-established principles for the maintenance of the sea communications to these islands. . . Though criticisms, some of them public, were levelled at the Commander-in-Chief . . . his steady hand on the reins controlling our vital maritime power contributed greatly to bringing the country through this anxious period . . .' – Roskill, *The War at Sea*, vol.1 p.267–8.

See 22 November 1880, 8 May 1940, 24 January 1941, 27 May 1941, 19 March 1949.

HMS *Dauntless* arrives at Portsmouth for the first time on 2 December 2009. (*RN*)

Admiral Sir Bruce Fraser (1888–1981) signing the Japanese surrender documents on board USS *Missouri*, 1945. (*NMRN*)

1941 Battleship *Prince of Wales* and battlecruiser *Repulse* arrived in Singapore to form the core of the new Eastern Fleet. 'In the streets the news soon spread among the Asiatic population. "*Kapal perang besar sudah dating*" ("Big warships have arrived"), reported Malay car-drivers waiting in the car parks. It was the news for which European and Asiatic alike had been waiting.' – *The Times*, 3 December 1941. The two capital ships were sunk by Japanese air attack eight days later.

See 3 and 10 December 1941.

1942 Destroyers *Janus*, *Javelin*, *Jervis* (D 14) and *Kelvin* sank the Italian TB *Lupo* off Kerkenah Bank (34.34N, 11.39E).

1942 Light cruisers *Argonaut*, *Aurora* and *Sirius*, with destroyers *Quentin* and *Quiberon* (RAN) sank the Italian destroyer *Folgore* and damaged two more, and destroyed an escorted convoy of four ships off Skerki Bank, N. of Cape Bon (37.39N, 10.50E). *Quentin* sunk later that day by Italian air-launched torpedo off Algiers.

See 28 November 1942.

1949 *Implacable*, former French two-decker *Duguay-Trouin*, taken on 4 November 1805, and Britain's oldest warship afloat, towed from Portsmouth and scuttled 9 miles S. of Owers light ship. Recommissioned into RN in the Second World War, she was the world's last wooden two-decker and, with *Victory*, the last survivor of Trafalgar. Scuttling charges blew out her bottom and the ballast sank, leaving upperworks afloat with White Ensign and French tricolour flying. Her figurehead and stern preserved in National Maritime Museum.

See 4 November 1805, 3 June 1932.

1963 First Captain RN Auxiliary Service (Captain RNXS) appointed (A/Capt J.A. Murray, RN). AFO 2089/63.

1986 *Upholder*, second of the name and first Type 2400 diesel-electric submarine, launched by Vickers, Barrow.

See 9 June 1990, 5 October 2004.

1998 *Vanguard*, Cdr Paul Abraham, returning from the Mediterranean, arrived for a four-day visit to Gibraltar. The first British SSBN ever to pay a port visit during a patrol.

None of the Polaris boats in 229 patrols and twenty-eight years' service ever visited a port, other than Faslane or a US naval facility for missile trials.

2009 Destroyer *Dauntless* arrived at Portsmouth and was accepted next day.

See 23 January 2007, 28 January 2009, 22 September 2010.

3 December

1794 Mutiny in *Culloden*.

1796 *Lapwing* captured the French *Decius* and destroyed *Valliante* at Anguilla, West Indies.

1799 *Racoon* captured the French privateer *Intrépide* in Dover Strait.

1807 *Curieux* fought the French privateer *Revanche* 120 miles E. of Barbados.

1807 Pellew's destruction of Dutch squadron at Grisee, Java.

1810 Capture of Ile de France (Mauritius) by Vice-Admiral Albemarle Bertie (*Africaine*) and Maj-Gen. the Hon. John Abercromby. Ships: *Africaine, Illustrious, Boadicea, Nisus, Cornwallis, Clorinde, Cornelia, Doris, Nereide, Psyche, Ceylon, Hesper, Hecate, Eclipse, Emma, Staunch, Phoebe, Actaeon*. Hired ships: *Egremont, Farquhar* and *Mouche*. Regiments: Royal Artillery, 12th, 14th, 22nd, 33rd, 56th, 59th, 84th, 87th, 1st Bengal Volunteers, 2nd Bombay Native Infantry, Madras Artillery, Madras Pioneers.

1811 First order for 100 iron tanks (at £18 10*s* each) to replace wooden casks, initially for water. Second order for 1,000 placed 28 July 1812.

1858 *Pearl*'s Naval Brigade at Bururiah (Baunrihar).

1860 Metropolitan Police from the 4th Division took over security duties at Chatham Dockyard. Establishment: 1 superintendent, 7 inspectors, 10 sergeants and 95 PCs.

1901 *Condor*, second of the name, foundered off Vancouver.

1915 Submarine E 11 sank Turkish *Yar Hissar* in Gulf of Ismid, Sea of Marmara.

1916 *Perugia* (Q 1) sunk by U-63 in the Gulf of Genoa.

1922 Light cruiser *Calypso* evacuated HRH Prince Andrew of Greece and Denmark from Phaleron Bay near Piraeus following his court martial for his part in the Greco-Turkish War and subsequent pardon on condition of perpetual banishment. With him was his wife, HRH Princess Andrew (Princess Alice of Battenberg, sister of the future Earl Mountbatten of Burma), their four daughters and 18-month-old son, Philippos, the future Prince Philip, Duke of Edinburgh, who was accommodated on board in a cot made from an orange box. The family was landed at Brindisi.

See 22 May 1941.

1941 Acting Admiral Sir Tom Phillips hoisted his flag as C-in-C Eastern Fleet in the battleship *Prince of Wales* at Singapore.

The appointment of C-in-C China, held by Vice-Admiral Sir Geoffrey Layton, was to have been disbanded on Phillips' arrival. However, following the sinking of *Prince of Wales* and the battlecruiser *Repulse* on 10 December, Admiral Layton became C-in-C of the by then almost non-existent British Eastern Fleet.

1942 Destroyer *Penylan* sunk by the German E-Boat S-115, 5 miles S. of Start Point (50.08N, 03.39W). Coastal Convoy PW 257.

See 1 May 2008.

1945 The first carrier-deck landing and take-off by a jet aircraft; Lt-Cdr Eric 'Winkle' Brown RNVR (later Captain, CBE, DSC, AFC, RN) flying a Sea Vampire from RNAS Ford, Sussex, on the new light fleet carrier *Ocean*, Capt Caspar John RN, off the Isle of Wight. The aircraft, LZ551/G, is preserved at the FAA Museum, Yeovilton.

See 25 March 1945, 19 June 1950.

1946 Fleet minesweeper *Middlesex* (RCN) wrecked on Bald Island Point, near Halifax, while going to the assistance of a fishing vessel in a storm.

1959 Admiral of the Fleet Sir Rhoderick McGrigor, torpedo officer, died aged 66 in Aberdeen. As Second-in-Command Home Fleet he led its last major operation of the Second World War in May 1945. 'Wee Mac' to the Navy – he was 5ft4in tall – was a lieutenant in the battleship *Malaya* at Jutland, Captain of the battlecruiser

The Royal Navy's Fleet flagship HMS *Ark Royal* returning to her home port of Portsmouth for the final time in December 2010. (*RN*)

Renown in Force H, C-in-C Home Fleet 1948–50 and he succeeded Lord Fraser of North Cape as First Sea Lord in December 1951. He handed over to Mountbatten in April 1955.

See 6 March 1938, 4 May 1945, 5 November 1954, 21 January 1955.

1963 *Valiant*, seventh of the name and first all-British-designed nuclear submarine, launched.

1974 HMS *Andrew*, the oldest RN submarine and the last armed with a deck gun, fired the last shell ever from a British submarine, in the Portland Exercise Areas, shortly before paying off at Devonport. Lt-Cdr Paul Hoddinott signalled 'The reek of cordite has passed from the Royal Navy's Submarine Service. Last gun action surface conducted at 031330Z. Time to first round 36 seconds. May the art of submarine gunnery rest in peace but never be forgotten'. Her 4-in/33 calibre Mk XXIII gun and the shell cartridge are in the RN Submarine Museum.

See 31 December 1974.

1993 *Nurton*, the last of 118 original Ton-class MCMVs, which had been converted for service in the Northern Ireland Patrol Squadron, and the Royal Navy's last wooden seagoing ship, entered Portsmouth to pay off.

See 9 July 1952, 5 October 1993.

2009 Rear-Admiral James Frederick Thomas George 'Sam' Salt, submariner, died aged 69. He commanded the destroyer *Sheffield*, the first British warship to be sunk in action since the Second World War. He was born on 19 April 1940, six months before his father was lost in command of the submarine *Triad* in the Mediterranean.

See 15 October 1940, 4 May 1982.

2010 *Ark Royal*, Capt Jeremy Kyd RN, made her final entry into Portsmouth Dockyard before paying off.

See 27 November 1978, 1 July 1985, 19 October 2010, 24 November 2010.

4 DECEMBER

1775 *Fowey* captured the American *Washington* 50 miles S.E. of Cape Ann, Mass.

1799 *Atalante* captured the French privateer *Succès* off Dungeness.

1805 *Victory* arrived at Portsmouth from Gibraltar with the body of Vice-Admiral Viscount Nelson, killed in action at Trafalgar.

1811 Boats of *Sultan* cut out the French brigs *Languedoc* and *Castor* from Bastia, Corsica.

1812 *Victory* entered Portsmouth for the last time. Dry-docked in 1922.

1827 The first steam vessels commissioned as HM ships; the Duke of Clarence, Lord High Admiral, signed commissions for Lt George Evans, G.J. Hay and T. Bullock to command *Lighting*, *Echo* and *Meteor*. The ships appeared in *The Navy List* next month.

1856 *Encounter*, *Barracouta* and boats of squadron destroyed French *Folly*, Canton River.

1916 Destroyer *Llewellyn* sank UC-19 off Dover – first successful use of depth charges.

1939 Submarine *Salmon* sank U-36 in North Sea, S.W. of Stavanger (57N, 05.10E).

1939 Battleship *Nelson* severely damaged by mine, entering Loch Ewe.

1939 Submarine L 27 detected by prototype ASV in Hudson of 220 Squadron RAF experimenting over the Channel. Side-scan confirmed as better than ahead-scanner.

1941 *Aphis* bombarded the Derna–Tobruk road (and on 7th and 8th).

1942 Submarine *Traveller* presumed lost, probably mined off Taranto.

Sea Venom and Sea Hawk aircraft on the flight deck of HMS *Centaur* in the late 1950s. (*NMRN*)

'Victory at Spithead', painted by J.W. Carmichael (1799–1868). (*NMRN 1973/76*)

1944 Light cruiser *Aurora*, with destroyers *Marne*, *Meteor* and *Musketeer*, bombarded shipping at Rhodes.

1951 Bus ran into rear of column of fifty-two Royal Marine cadets marching down Dock Road, Chatham, to a boxing tournament at *Pembroke*. Twenty-four cadets aged 9 to 13 years killed and eighteen injured.

1957 The Earl of Selkirk, First Lord of the Admiralty, and Mr Soames, Parliamentary Secretary, announced to both Houses of Parliament that the RNR and RNVR would be amalgamated to form one unified Royal Naval Reserve. Naval Correspondent of *The Times* reported that the amalgamation would reduce the annual bill for the Reserves from £1.8m to £1.2m.

See 1 November 1958.

1967 Coastal minelayer *Plover*, Lt-Cdr W. Thoniley RN, paid off at 1000 at HMS *Lochinvar*, Port Edgar, after being in continuous commission from her acceptance from Denny of Dumbarton at 0900 on 27 September 1937, a record of more than thirty years. Within six hours of the start of the Second World War, *Plover* began laying the first minefield south of Bass Rock.

See 8 June 1937, 16 September 1939, 21 December 1939, 25 January 1942, 25 September 1959.

1978 Carrier *Ark Royal* returned to Devonport after her last WESTLANT deployment to pay off.

See 3 May 1950, 26 February 1955, 26 January 1972.

1986 HRH The Duke of Edinburgh unveiled a memorial plaque at Birchin Lane in the City of London to Capt R.D. Binney CBE, RN, who died in gallant but unusual circumstances during the Second World War.

See 8 December 1944.

2006 Prime Minister announced that Britain's nuclear deterrent would be maintained beyond the 2020s; Trident to be renewed and a new class of SSBNs to be designed.

2009 *Trafalgar*, Cdr Charles Shepherd RN, paid off at Devonport.

5 December

1578 Drake sacked Valparaiso.

1797 *Diana* captured the French privateer *Mouche* 500 miles W. of Land's End.

1799 *Sceptre* (64), Capt Valentine Edwards, armed en flute, caught in a storm at anchor in Table Bay, South Africa. All anchor cables parted and the ship drove ashore off Woodstock Beach near the present Royal Cape Yacht Club and broke up. Edwards and 300 ship's company lost.

1804 Rank of sub-lieutenant established by Order in Council, because of shortage of Second Masters. Disappeared after 1815 but revived in 1863 with single ½-in stripe, which caused some confusion.

See 16 May 1863.

1808 *Magnet* captured the Danish privateer *Paulina* off Bornholm.

1830 *Thetis* (36) wrecked on Cape Frio, 75 miles E. of Rio de Janeiro whence she was on passage with $810,000 worth of bullion. A value of $60,000 was recovered in a salvage epic, involving the use of a water tank as a diving bell.

1859 John Rushworth Jellicoe born at Southampton. C-in-C Grand Fleet 1914–16 and First Sea Lord 1916–17.

See 20 November 1935.

1866 Start of naval operation against the Fenians in southern Ireland: *Helicon*, *Vestal* and *Black Prince*; also in Canadian waters by N. American Squadron.

1881 *London*'s boats attacked a slaving dhow at Pema.

1918 Light cruiser *Cassandra*, part of a RN squadron deploying into the Baltic to support newly independent Finland, Estonia, Latvia and Lithuania, sunk by a German mine in the Baltic N.W. of the Estonian island of Osel, modern Saaremaa, 58.29N, 21.11E. Ten men lost in explosion. Destroyers *Westminster* and *Vendetta* rescued 440 men directly from the forecastle with only one fatality. The minesweeping sloops *Myrtle* and *Gentian* were mined just N. of this location (58.39N, 21.36E) on 15 July 1919. The captain of *Cassandra*, Capt E.C. Kennedy, father of Sir Ludovic Kennedy, was lost in command of the AMC *Rawalpindi* in action with German battlecruisers in November 1939. The wrecks of *Cassandra* and *Gentian*, and the bow section of *Myrtle*, were found by the Estonian minehunter *Ugandi* ex-HMS *Bridport*, in August 2010.

See 13 December 1918, 15 July 1919, 18 August 1919, 1 and 4 September 1919, 20 July 2003.

Admiral of the Fleet Earl Jellicoe of Scapa (1859–1935). (*NMRN*)

1918 First meeting of the Admiralty Ship Names and Mottoes Committee.

1940 AMC *Carnarvon Castle* and the German disguised raider *Thor* (Schiff 10) fought an inconclusive action (31.00S, 43.15W).

1940 Clarence Yard, Gosport, and HMS *Vernon* badly damaged in German air raid.

See 12 and 24 August 1940, 23 December 1940, 10 January 1941, 10 March 1941, 17 April 1941.

1950 Evacuation of troops from Chinnampo, Korea.

1969 Chinese Unofficials. 'Tailors, Cobblers and Barbers are not to be employed in HM ships west of Suez. The only Chinese Unofficials who may be brought west of Suez are Laundrymen and may not remain west of Suez for more than 12 months. When in Home Waters Laundrymen are not to work as Tailors, Cobblers or Barbers.' – DCI(RN) 1511/69.

See 27 July 1973.

1974 Mitchell Committee reported on future of naval reserves, recommending successfully that the RNR should be recognised as 'the part-time element of a single naval service'.

1986 A good Christmas promised for ships' companies of frigate *Torquay* and RMAS *Sheepdog* following salvage of barge *Millshaw*; DCI(RN) announced salvage shares with unit value of £1,831 and £1,381 respectively.

But see 9 and 16 January 1987.

1995 Admiral Sir Hugo White, lately C-in-C Fleet (December 1992–June 1995) and Captain of the frigate *Avenger* in the Falklands War of 1982, appointed Governor and C-in-C Gibraltar.

See 17 April 1969, 26 October 2009.

The old royal yacht *Victoria and Albert* arrived at Faslane for breaking up. The coins of the realm, which had been placed beneath her three masts during construction at Pembroke Dockyard, were recovered. They are all dated 1899, the year of her launch. Her figurehead is preserved at HMS *Nelson*. (*Author*)

6 December

1608 George Monck born in Devon. Future first Duke of Albemarle and 'general at sea' in the Dutch Wars.

1672 First attempt, by Order in Council, to introduce retired pay as opposed to half-pay.

1768 *Chaleur*, RN's first schooner, sold out of the Service.

1782 *Ruby* captured the French *Solitaire* 120 miles E. of Barbados.

1799 *Speedwell* captured the French privateer *Heureux Speculateur* off the Channel Islands.

1809 *Royalist* captured the French privateer *Heureuse Etoile* S. of Beachy Head.

1810 Ceylon retaken for third and last time from the French.

1838 Ships' libraries authorised by Admiralty.

1856 *Sampson*'s Naval Brigade at the defeat of the Gwalior Contingent of mutineers at Cawnpore.

1917 GC (ex-AM): LS T.N. Davis for disposing of burning ammunition in blazing and drifting tug at Halifax, Nova Scotia.

1940 Submarine *Regulus* reported sunk, by unknown cause, in Otranto Strait.

1941 *Perseus* sunk by mine 7 miles N. of Zante (37.45N, 20.54E). Leading Stoker Capes, her one survivor from 170ft, swam 10 miles to Cephalonia.

1942 Submarine *Tigris* sank the Italian S/M *Porfido* S. of Sardinia (38.10N, 08.35E).

1944 Frigate *Bullen* sunk by U-775 7 miles N.E. of Cape Wrath (58.42N, 04.12W).

1944 Frigates *Loch Insh* and *Goodall* sank U-297 off Orkney (58.44N, 04.29W).

1952 RN Minewatching Service (RNMWS) established. Later translated into RN Auxiliary Service (RNXS).

See 5 November 1962, 18 January 1963, 17 June 1993, 1 April 1994.

1954 The former royal yacht *Victoria and Albert* arrived at Faslane for breaking up. Following custom, coins of the realm had been placed beneath her three masts during construction at Pembroke Dockyard. These were recovered; all are dated 1899, the year of her launch.

See 9 May 1899, 3 January 1900.

1956 The end of mandatory death penalty for naval offences, other than assisting an enemy, included in recommendations by a Parliamentary Select Committee on the Naval Discipline Act. The report proposed the first major changes in the established code of naval discipline since the NDA of 1866 which was based on Articles of War passed by parliament in 1661. All officers would be eligible to sit on courts martial, hitherto restricted to executive (seamen) officers. Mutiny defined for the first time: 'a combination between two or more persons subject to service law or between persons, two at least of whom are subject to service law, to overthrow or resist lawful authority in Her Majesty's forces.'

2001 Lt-Cdr Thomas William Gould RNVR, the only Jewish serviceman to win the VC in the Second World War (*Thrasher*, 16 February 1942), died aged 86.

7 December

1776 James Aitken, known as 'Jack the Painter', set fire to the Rope House in Portsmouth Dockyard. He paid the price for Arson in a Royal Dockyard.
See 10 March 1777.

1809 *Rinaldo* captured the French privateer *Maraudeur* in Dover Strait.

1817 William Bligh, Vice-Admiral of the Blue, late Captain of HM Armed Transport *Bounty*, of *Director* (64) at the Battle of Camperdown and of *Glatton* (56) at Copenhagen, died at Lambeth. Buried in churchyard of St Mary, Lambeth, now the Museum of Garden History.
See 14 June 1789, 9 September 1754, 23 December 1787, 28 April 1789.

1824 Repulse of the Burmese attack on Kemmendine. Ships: *Teignmouth* (Bombay Marine), *Sophie*. Troops: 26th Madras Native Infantry.

1842 Boats of *Persian* captured the Portuguese slaver *Maria Segunda* 40 miles E.S.E. of Whydah.

1858 *Bustard*, *Firm* and boats of *Fury* destroyed two pirate junks in the estuary of the Broadway.

1872 Surveying ship *Challenger* sailed from Sheerness on the first stage of her historic oceanographic voyage.
See 21 December 1872, 24 May 1876.

1878 Completion of *Northampton*, named after First Lord's parliamentary constituency, and last ship to have all main armament between decks and on the broadside.

1917 Five US battleships, *Delaware*, *Florida*, *New York*, *Texas* and *Wyoming*, under Rear-Admiral Hugh Rodman, USN, arrived Scapa Flow. Formed 6th Battle Squadron Grand Fleet.

1939 Destroyer *Jersey* torpedoed by the German destroyer *Erich Giese* near the Haisborough lightvessel.

1939 First German Type B magnetic mine rendered safe in Thames estuary by Lt J.E.M. Glenny and Lt R.S. Armitage of *Vernon*.

1941 Destroyers *Hesperus* and *Harvester* sank U-208.

1941 Japanese naval air attack on US Pacific Fleet at Pearl Harbor, Hawaii and British base at Hong Kong.

1941 Canadian corvette *Windflower* sunk in collision with Dutch merchantman SS *Zypenberg* in convoy off Newfoundland.

1942 RM Boom Patrol Detachment (canoeist raiders) launched from submarine *Tuna* to attack German blockade runners in the Gironde – the 'Cockleshell heroes'. Operation Frankton.

1944 Minelaying strike by twelve Avenger aircraft of 856 Sqn (*Premier*) and fourteen Wildcat aircraft of 881 Sqn (*Trumpeter*), escorted by *Diadem* and eight destroyers, in Salhusstrommen, Norway (59.22N, 05.24E). Operation Urbane.

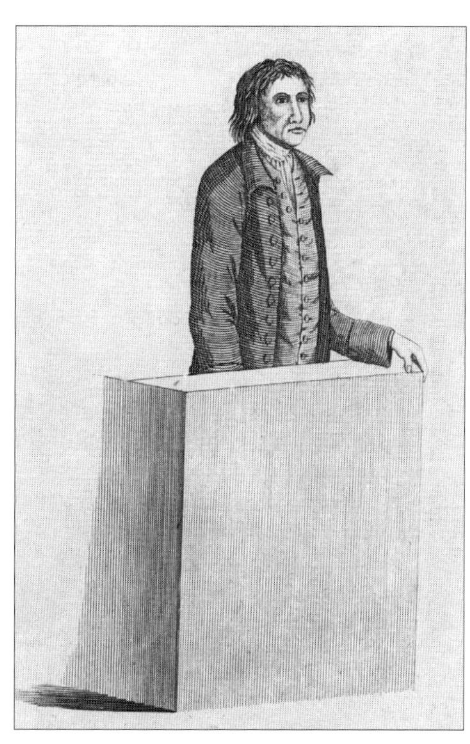

James or Jack the Painter, 1777. (*NMRN 1985/126*)

8 DECEMBER

1778 Horatio Nelson promoted master and commander into the brig *Badger*.

See 11 and 20 June 1779.

1780 Boats of squadron under Vice-Admiral Sir Edward Hughes (*Superb*), covered by *Drake* and *Eagle* (Bombay Marine), destroyed a number of armed vessels in Mangalore Roads.

1798 *Cambrian* captured the French privateer *Cantabre* 50 miles N. of Cape Peñas.

1803 *Medusa* captured the French privateer *Espérance* and destroyed *Sorcier* off Cabrita (Carnero) Point, Gibraltar Bay.

1858 Boats and landing party of *Bustard*, *Firm* and *Fury* destroyed ten pirate junks in the estuary of the Broadway.

1900 Sloop *Espiegle* launched at Sheerness. The last RN ship in commission bearing a figurehead.

See 29 April 1903.

1914 Battle of Falkland Islands. Vice-Admiral Sir Doveton Sturdee (*Invincible*) defeated Vice-Admiral Graf von Spee (*Scharnhorst*) off the Falklands Islands.

Battle Honour: Falkland Islands 1914.

Ships: *Bristol*, *Carnarvon*, *Cornwall*, *Glasgow*, *Inflexible*, *Invincible*, *Kent*, *Macedonia*. Sunk: *Gneisenau*, *Leipzig*. *Nürnberg*, *Scharnhorst*. Escaped: *Dresden*. War Medal: clasp 'Falkland Islands 8 Dec 1914' approved but not issued.

As a result of the Battle of Coronel on 1 November, the First Sea Lord ordered two battlecruisers to the area. The *Invincible* and *Inflexible*, under Admiral Sturdee, arrived at the Falklands to coal on 7 December, having kept radio silence since 18 November. On 8 December the German force was sighted off the Falklands, and the British squadron sailed immediately. During the running battle, the crew of *Kent* mustered on the quarterdeck to increase speed by forcing the propellers deeper into the water.

1918 Action between British and Bolshevik light forces in the Caspian.

HMS *Invincible* at full speed in pursuit of German forces, at the Battle of the Falklands, 1914. (*NMRN*)

Desmond Wettern, the last naval correspondent in Fleet Street, photographed by the author on board HMS *Battleaxe* in February 1981. (*Author*)

1929 Destroyers *Sterling* and *Sirdar* rescued *Hai Ching* from pirates off Chilang Point, southern China.

Siege of Tobruk Raised, 1941

Transported by RN to Tobruk during the 242-day siege 12 April to 8 December 1941: 72 tanks, 92 guns, 34,000 tons of stores, 32,667 men replaced by 32,113 fresh troops, 7,516 wounded and 7,097 prisoners withdrawn. Cost to RN: twenty-five ships sunk, nine seriously damaged; cost to MN: five sunk, four seriously damaged.

1941 River gunboat *Peterel* sunk by Japanese *Izumo* at Shanghai, after a defiance which impressed the enemy.

1944 Continuation of Operation Urbane. Twelve Firefly of 1771 Sqn (*Implacable*) and nine Wildcat of 881 Sqn (*Trumpeter*) bombed two merchant ships and set them on fire off Stavanger (59.43N, 05.24E).
See 7 December 1944.

1944 Capt R.D. Binney RN died bravely in the City of London. A plaque on the wall at 22 Birchin Lane EC3 reads:

'This plaque was given by the Royal Navy in memory of Captain Ralph Douglas Binney CBE, Royal Navy, who on 8 December 1944 died from injuries received when, bravely and alone, he confronted violent men raiding a jeweller's shop in this lane and struggled to prevent their escape. To honour this courageous act, Captain Binney's fellow officers and other friends founded the Binney Memorial Awards for civilians of the City and Metropolitan areas of London who, in the face of great danger and personal risk, have followed Captain Binney's example and steadfastly upheld law and order.'

His only son, Sub-Lt David Binney, was killed in action when the destroyer *Tynedale* was sunk on 12 December 1943.
See 4 December 1986.

1955 First Lord of the Admiralty, Mr J.P.L. Thomas, roused from his bed in Admiralty House, Whitehall, as fire consumed the upper floors of the adjoining Ripley Block. The old Board Room was saved but water damaged the plaster ceiling. Mr Thomas (later Viscount Cilcennin) spent the rest of the night with Admiral Mountbatten, the First Sea Lord, in the Admiralty forecourt.
See 6 November 1805, 17 April 1941.

1968 Closing ceremony of *St Vincent*, boys' training establishment at Gosport.
See 1 June 1927, 2 April 1969, 7 June 1976.

1968 Singapore Naval Base handed over to Singapore government. (Twenty-seventh anniversary of Japanese landings in Malaya.)

1991 Desmond Wettern died, aged 57. The last naval correspondent of a British national newspaper (the *Daily Telegraph*). Buried at St Peter's church, Tandridge, Oxted, Surrey (which he shares with Cdr John Kerans of HMS *Amethyst* – see 12 September 1985), 17 December, with RN representatives present. 'The Queen had no more loyal subject than Desmond Wettern nor the Royal Navy a greater friend and champion' – *The Mariner's Mirror*.
See 10 December 1993.

9 December

1677 *Guernsey* fought the Algerine *White Horse* 20 miles E. of Cape Palos.

1798 *Boadicea* captured the French privateer *Invincible Bonaparte* 500 miles W. of Ushant.

1809 *Redpole* captured the French privateer *Grand Rodeur* off Beachy Head.

1819 Destruction of the Joasmi pirate stronghold at Ras al Khaimah. Ships: *Aurora, Curlew, Eden* (Bombay Marine), *Liverpool, Nautilus,* and three others. Troops: 47th and 65th Regiments, 1/3rd, 1/11th and flank company of 1/2nd Native Infantry.

1856 Capture of the Persian fort at Reshire (Rishahr). Ships: *Assaye, Semiramis, Ferooz, Ajdaha, Victoria, Falkland, Berenice* (Indian Navy).

1914 British forces captured Qurra, Mesopotamia. Ships and vessels: *Espiegle, Lawrence, Lewis Miner, Ocean, Odin, Pelly, Shaitan.*

1914 Commissioning of *Ark Royal*, purchased for conversion to seaplane carrier.

1917 *Ben Lawers* rammed and sank UB-18 in Channel Approaches (49.17N, 05.27W).

1935 King's Colour presented at Bombay to the new Royal Indian Navy by Lord Brabourne, Governor of Bombay.

See 11 November 1928, 1 October 1934, 14 September 1939.

1942 Destroyer *Porcupine* torpedoed by U-602 off Cape Ferrat (36.40N, 00.04W). Reached Gibraltar and towed to UK in two parts nicknamed *Pork* and *Pine*. But CTL, so no second *Zubian*.

See 4 February 1918.

1942 U-124 engaged again by 5.5-in gun, this time at Ascension.

See 24 November 1941.

The development of the tank as an AFV (Armoured Fighting Vehicle). RNAS personnel working on Killen-Strait tractor for Admiralty Landships Committee, 1915. (*Tank Museum 1539/D2*)

The Siege Bell War Memorial overlooking Grand Harbour, Valletta, which commemorates the 7,000 servicemen, merchant seamen and civilians who died during the Second Great Siege of Malta between 1940 and 1943. It was inaugurated by Her Majesty The Queen and the President of Malta on 29 May 1992, the 50th aniversary of the award of the George Cross to the island in 1942. The 10-ton bronze bell is struck daily at noon. The memorial was created largely due to the efforts of Admiral of the Fleet Lord Lewin. (*Author, 2000*)

1942 Corvette *Marigold* sunk by Italian torpedo aircraft W. of Algiers. Convoy MKS 3Y.

1944 Corvette *Bamborough Castle* sank U-387 off Murmansk (69.41N, 33.12E). Convoy RA 62.

1950 Royal Ceylon Navy formed with Navy Act proclaimed in the Ceylon government *Gazette*. The former Naval Adviser, Capt W.E. Banks CBE, DSC, RN, appointed to command with the title Captain of the Navy. On 9 December 1955, the fifth anniversary of its founding, ships and establishments of the Royal Ceylon Navy hoisted their new ensign, a St George's cross on a white field with the national flag in the upper hoist, replacing the White Ensign. Exchange of signals between C-in-C East Indies, Vice-Admiral C. F.W. Norris CB, DSO, and the Captain Royal Ceylon Navy, Cdre C.R.M. de Mel OBE, RCyN.

See 23 December 1966, 1 March 1967, 1 November 1967, 20 June 1968.

2003 Lt Charlotte Atkinson, born on Trafalgar Day 1971, appointed to command *Brecon* in MCM3 at Faslane. Hitherto women had commanded only P2000 Archer-class vessels attached to URNUs.

See 19 March 1998.

10 December

1683 Victualling entrusted to new commissioners.

1747 Relative ranks between officers of the Navy and the Army approved by King George II.

1809 *Royalist* captured the French privateer *Beau Marseille* 4 miles S.S.E. of Dungeness.

1810 *Rosario* captured the French privateer *Mameluk* off Dungeness.

1856 Capture of Bushire. Ships: *Ajdaha, Assaye, Berenice* (Indian Navy), *Falkland, Ferooz, Semiramis, Victoria.*

1902 *Ariadne* (flag), *Charybdis, Tribune, Retribution* and *Indefatigable* dealt with recalcitrant Venezuelan gunboat before blockading that coast in conjunction with German and Italian ships until 14 February 1903.

1917 UB-75 mined and sunk off Flamborough Head.

1936 Formation of RNV(S)R.

See 11 November 1936, 22 February 1965.

1941 Battleship *Prince of Wales*, flagship of Admiral Sir Tom Phillips, and battlecruiser *Repulse* sunk by Japanese torpedo aircraft off the E. coast of Malaya (03.33N, 104.28E and 03.45N, 104.24E, respectively). The first British capital ships lost to air attack and the last battleship and battlecruiser lost in action. Admiral Sir Tom Phillips was the last of three British flag officers killed in action in the Second World War (Henry Blagrove, *Royal Oak*, who had been in the same commander to captain promotion batch as Phillips on 30 June 1927; Lancelot Holland, *Hood*). Four other admirals died on active service: Rear-Admiral Spooner of disease and starvation on or about 15 April 1942, and three in air crashes: Rear-Admiral P.J. Mack on 29 April 1943, Vice-Admiral R.H.C. Hallifax on 6 November 1943 and Admiral Sir Bertram Ramsay on 2 January 1945. Also lost in HMS *Prince of Wales* were twins Robert and James Young, who had joined the Royal Navy from a Cheltenham orphanage.

'I was opening my boxes on the 10th when the telephone at my bedside rang. It was the First Sea Lord. His voice sounded odd. He gave a sort of cough and gulp, and at first I could not hear quite clearly. "Prime Minister, I have

The battleship HMS *Prince of Wales*, arriving in Singapore Naval Base on 2 December 1941. She was sunk eight days later. (*NMRN*)

HMS *Daring* sailing from Plymouth Sound for operational sea training. (*RN*)

to report to you that the *Prince of Wales* and the *Repulse* have both been sunk by the Japanese – we think by aircraft. Tom Phillips is drowned."

"Are you sure it's true?"

"There is no doubt at all."

So I put the telephone down. I was thankful to be alone. In all the war I never received a more direct shock . . . As I turned over and twisted in bed the full horror of the news sank in upon me.' – Winston Churchill, *The Second World War, Volume III, The Grand Alliance*, p.551.

1941 Light cruiser *Naiad* bombarded Derna.

1942 Destroyer *Roebuck*, building at Scotts, Greenock, was prematurely launched by a near miss by a German bomb and lay submerged for nine months.

1993 The first presentation of the Desmond Wettern Fleet Award, for the ship, submarine or naval air squadron judged to have done the most to project a positive image of the Royal Navy in the previous year, made at Portsmouth to the destroyer *Cardiff*, Cdr Neil Morisetti RN.

See 8 December 1991.

2008 *Daring*, first of the Type 45 destroyers, accepted from her builders, BVT Surface Fleet Ltd, at Scotstoun by Capt Paul Bennett RN and White Ensign hoisted. Ship is affiliated with Birmingham and Guernsey.

See 28 March 2003, 1 February 2006, 28 January 2009.

2009 Dinner in the Painted Hall at Greenwich to mark the centenary of British naval aviation, attended by Their Royal Highnesses the Prince of Wales, the Duke of York, the Princess Royal and Prince Michael of Kent and hosted by the First Sea Lord, Admiral Sir Mark Stanhope.

See 11 September 2009, 9 October 2009.

2010 *Sceptre*, Cdr Steven Waller RN, the last of the Swiftsure-class SSNs, paid-off at Devonport after thirty-two years' service.

11 December

1795 *Shark* taken into La Hogue by a mutinous crew.

1798 *Perdrix* captured the French privateer *Armée d'Italie* 21 miles E. of Virgin Gorda.

1799 *Tremendous* destroyed the French *Preneuse* at the mouth of the Tombeau River, Mauritius.

1807 *Grasshopper* captured the Spanish *San Jose* under Cape Negrete.

1899 Capt Bearcroft's Naval Brigade at the Battle of Magersfontein.

1912 A new Navigation Department established at the Admiralty; Capt Philip Nelson-Ward MVO, RN, appointed the first Director of Navigation. He was a descendent of Nelson's daughter, Horatia, and her husband, the Revd Philip Ward. In 1916 the department once again became a branch of the Hydrographer of the Navy but in August 1945 it was again separated and became a division of the Naval Staff.

1936 Accession of King George VI.

1941 Destroyer *Farndale* sank the Italian S/M *Ammiraglio Caracciolo* off Bardia (32.09N, 25.19E). Convoy TA 2.

1941 Submarine *Truant* sank the Italian TB *Alcione* off Suda Bay, Crete. Beached 35.29N, 24.11E.

1942 Destroyer *Blean* sunk by U-443 W. of Oran (35.55N, 01.50W).

1943 Frigate *Cuckmere* torpedoed off Algiers by U-223: CTL. Convoy KMS 34.

1953 WRNS new-entry training establishment at Burghfield near Reading since July 1945, commissioned as *Dauntless*. Paid off 14 August 1981 and training transferred to *Raleigh*.

Officers at Malta during the First World War. Note the Paymaster RNR in the middle row, far right. (*NMRN*)

The carrier HMS *Argus* manning ship at the Spithead Review of 26 July 1924. (*Cdr David Hobbs RN*)

1958 Launch of frigate *Otago* at Thornycroft, first ship built specifically for RNZN.

1968 The new HMS *Cochrane*, Cdr J.A. Barrett RN, occupying a 24-acre site adjoining Rosyth Dockyard, commissioned. Replaced the accommodation ships *Duncansby Head* and *Girdleness*.

1992 *Royal Arthur*, RN Leadership School, Corsham, ceased training. Task transferred to RN School of Leadership and Management (RNSLAM), Whale Island. Corsham site closed 5 March 1993. DCI(RN) 171/92.

1996 Vice-Admiral Sir Hugh Thompson, who rose from ERA (Engine Room Artificer) to ERA (Engineer Rear-Admiral), died aged 65. Strictly, he was a Rear-Admiral (E) and that designation was abandoned after 1956. The last Engineer Rear-Admiral was Sir John Kingcome, who died shortly after the Second World War.

1997 HMY *Britannia* paid off at Portsmouth Dockyard. HM The Queen was piped ashore at 1500. Flag of Lord High Admiral and White Ensign struck.

The Battle of Trafalgar in 21 October 1805. John Christian Schetky, who for over twenty-five years was Professor of Drawing at the Royal Naval Academy, Portsmouth, and later Marine Painter in Ordinary to King George IV. Oil on canvas. This work was exhibited at the British Institution in 1825. (*Crown Copyright: MOD Art Collection*)

12 December

1721 Alexander Selkirk, Master's Mate in *Weymouth* and Defoe's inspiration for *Robinson Crusoe*, died.

1724 Samuel Hood born.

1779 *Salisbury* captured the Spanish privateer *San Carlos* 20 miles W. by N. of Punta de la Sal, Gulf of Honduras.

1781 Rear-Admiral Richard Kempenfelt (*Victory*) captured fifteen sail of a French convoy 160 miles S.W. by W. of Ushant by separating the convoy from its escort, which was to leeward. Battle Honour: Ushant 1781.

Ships: *Agamemnon, Alexander, Britannia, Courageux, Duke, Edgar, Medway, Ocean, Queen, Renown, Union, Valiant, Victory*. Frigates: *Arethusa, Monsieur, Prudente, Tartar, Tisiphone*.

1782 *Mediator* captured the French *Alexandre* and *Menagère* off Ferrol.

1782 Admiral Sir Hyde Parker Bt sailed from Rio de Janeiro to take up appointment as C-in-C East Indies, his flag in *Cato*. Neither he nor she was seen again. Although some wreckage thought to have come from the ship appeared at Jeddah nine years later, there was a persistent rumour that he had not only been killed but also cannibalised on the Malabar coast.

1804 Spain declared war on Britain.

1809 *Thetis, Achates, Attentive, Bacchus* and *Pultusk* captured the French *Nisus* and destroyed a battery at Deshayes, Guadeloupe.

1810 *Entreprenante* fought four French privateers between Malaga and Almeria.

1849 Boats of *Centaur, Teazer* and the French *Rubis* recaptured the *British Grant* up the Mansoa River, Gambia. Troops: 2nd and 3rd West India Regiments.

1863 *Minotaur* launched at Thames Ironworks. The first five-masted warship and, with *Agincourt* (Lairds 27 March 1865) and *Northumberland* (Mare 17 April 1866), at 400ft the longest single-screw surface warships ever built.

1888 Establishment of two Schools of Signalling, one in Devonport Barracks and the other in Portsmouth, originally in *Duke of Wellington* but eventually in *Victory*.

1917 Destroyer *Partridge* (escorting a Scandinavian convoy of four neutral ships, with four trawlers) sunk and destroyer *Pellew* damaged by German destroyers G-101, G-103, G-104 and V-100 (59.48N, 03.53E) off Norwegian coast. A waste of Room 40's intelligence.
Battle Honour: Scandinavian Convoys 1917.

1917 Destroyer *Wolverine* lost in collision with sloop *Rosemary* off N.W. Ireland.

1936 Destroyer *Fury*, escorted by destroyer *Wolfhound*, carried Prince Edward (later Duke of Windsor) to France after his abdication as King Edward VIII the previous day.

1937 Japanese shore batteries fired on the Royal Navy gunboats *Ladybird* and *Bee* on the Yangtze; four hits on *Ladybird* with one sailor killed. On same day, Japanese aircraft bombed a concentration of British merchant shipping on the Yangtze near Nanking and on the British gunboats *Scarab* and *Cricket* which were guarding them. Japanese aircraft also bombed and sank the United States Navy gunboat *Panay* and three Standard Oil tankers 25 miles upstream from Nanking.

1939 Destroyer *Duchess*, Lt-Cdr R.H.C. White RN, on her way from the Mediterranean to join the Home Fleet, sunk in collision with the battleship *Barham*, in the North Channel, 9 miles off the Mull of Kintyre (55.19N, 06.06W). Six officers, including the Captain, and 123 men lost.

See 7 April 1932, 1 May 1942.

1940 River gunboats *Aphis* and *Ladybird* and monitor *Terror* bombarded enemy positions on the Egyptian frontier.

1941 River gunboat *Moth* scuttled as blockship at Hong Kong. Raised by Japanese and

Admiral Samuel, Viscount Hood (1724–1816)

Joined, promoted lieutenant and made post in the same years as his younger brother Alexander (see 23 June). Employed during the peace between the Seven Years War and the War of American Independence, and appointed Commissioner at Portsmouth in 1778. Distinguished service in Caribbean waters as a Flag Officer – at the Basse Terre (25 January 1782) and the Saints (12 April): made an Irish peer for the latter. C-in-C Portsmouth: then a member of the Board of Admiralty 1788–95. C-in-C Mediterranean 1793–4, during which period he occupied Toulon for a time and did much damage on its evacuation. Politics procured his recall – though he was then over 70 – much to Nelson's disgust: 'Oh miserable Board of Admiralty: they have forced the first officer of the service away from his command.' But he became Governor of Greenwich Hospital, for twenty years, and his monument describes him rightly as 'an officer of the highest distinction among the illustrious men who rendered their own age the brightest period in the naval history of their country'.

Admiral Samuel, Viscount Hood (1724–1816). (*NMRN*)

commissioned as *Suma*. Sunk by American mine in the Yangtze, 19 March 1945.

1942 Submarine P 222 sunk by the Italian TB *Fortunale* in the Gulf of Naples.

1943 Destroyers *Holcombe* and *Tynedale* sunk by U-593 off Bougie (37.20N, 05.50E and 37.10N, 06.05E respectively). Convoy KMS 34.

1944 Corvette *Tunsberg Castle* (Nor) (ex-*Shrewsbury Castle*) sunk by mine off Sandstabben light, N.W. of Kola Inlet (70.44N, 30.09E).

1952 848 NAS sailed in carrier *Perseus* for Far East. The first operational RN helicopter squadron. First operational sortie carried out on 26 January 1953.

1957 Tornado struck the Hamoaze and Devonport Dockyard in the wake of a storm. Royal Marines from Lympstone deployed to assist in flood relief. Saltash to Plymouth car ferry stranded on the Saltash road.

1962 Assault on Limbang, Brunei by L Company 42 RM Cdo. This was the first incident in the Indonesian confrontation, which persisted until 11 August 1966. Several ships were involved, supported by 3 Cdo Brigade with 40 and 42 Cdos.

See p.706 panel.

13 December

1710 *Breda* captured the French *Maure* 100 miles W. of Lisbon.

1711 The wall around Portsmouth Dockyard completed.

'This WALL was Begun the 4th June and finish'd ye 13th Decembr 1711.'

'In order to meet the needs of modern road traffic and with the approval of the Lords Commissioners of the Admiralty this gate built in 1711 was increased in width from 12ft to 22ft, November 1944' – plaques at Victory Gate.

1796 *Terpsichore* captured the French *Vestale* 60 miles W. of Cadiz. Retaken by the prisoners next day and sailed into Cadiz, but retaken by *Clyde* in 1799.

1806 *Halcyon* captured the Spanish *Neptune Dios de Los Mares* off Cape San Martin.

1808 Destruction of the French *Cygne* and two schooners off St Pierre, Martinique.

1809 The frigate *Junon* (36), Capt John Shortland, captured by the French frigates *Renommee* and *Clorinde* 150 miles E. of Guadeloupe after a fierce action.

The Frenchmen hoisted Spanish colours as a proper *ruse de guerre* and Shortland, successfully deceived, incautiously approached to 'within Half Pistol Shott' of *Renommee* and received a broadside from which *Junon* never recovered.

See 10 February 1809, 19 November 1941.

1810 Boats of *Kent*, *Ajax*, *Cambrian*, *Minstrel* and *Sparrowhawk* destroyed a French convoy at Palamos, Catalonia.

1914 VC: Lt Norman Douglas Holbrook (B 11) for passing through the Turkish minefield at the entrance to the Dardanelles and sinking the Turkish *Messoudieh* off Cannakkale. The first VC won by a submariner. It was not the first naval VC won in the First World War (Ritchie, *Goliath*, 28/29 November 1914) but the first to be gazetted.

1915 First periscope photograph of Constantinople from E 11.

1916 Destroyers *Ariel* and *Landrail* sank UB-29 in western Channel.

1917 U-75 mined and sunk off Borkum.

1918 Light cruisers *Cardiff*, flag of Rear-Admiral Edwyn Alexander-Sinclair, and *Caradoc*, with five destroyers, shelled Bolshevik forces near Narva in Estonia which were threatening Reval (modern Tallinn), the Estonian capital.

See 5 December 1918.

1939 Submarine *Salmon* torpedoed the German cruisers *Leipzig* and *Nürnberg* 130 miles W. of Jutland.

The *Salmon*, on patrol in the North Sea, sighted three enemy cruisers and hit both the *Leipzig* and *Nürnberg*. The *Leipzig* remained under repair for a year, and then was employed on training duties; the *Nürnberg* took six months to repair. Nine days before, the *Salmon* had sunk U-36 in the same area, the first successful submarine versus enemy submarine attack in the war. For this patrol her CO Lt-Cdr Bickford was promoted and awarded the DSO.

1939 Cdre H.H. Harwood (*Ajax*) engaged the *Admiral Graf Spee* off the River Plate (34.28S, 49.05W) and drove her into Montevideo, where she was scuttled on the 17th. Ships: *Ajax*, *Achilles* (NZ), *Exeter*. FAA: Seafox: 700 NAS (*Ajax*).
Battle Honour: River Plate 1939.

See 23 February 1940.

Battle of the River Plate 1939

The German pocket battleship *Graf Spee* had been commerce raiding in the South Atlantic. Various naval units were searching for her. Force G, under Cdre Harwood, was off the River Plate. On 13 December the squadron sighted smoke, and action with the *Graf Spee* opened at 0614 at 9½ miles. The *Exeter* was hit heavily, but continued to fight, with only one turret working by hand, on emergency steering and using the after conning position, passing orders to the steering position by a line of sailors. *Graf Spee* also hit *Ajax* and *Achilles*, but finally turned for Montevideo to make repairs. After the permitted seventy-two hours in a neutral port *Graf Spee*

The German pocket battleship *Graf Spee*, burning after being scuttled in the River Plate estuary, 1939. (*NMRN*)

sailed and then scuttled herself, having been given the impression that superior forces were outside the harbour, when in fact they were forty-eight hours' steaming away. A coincidence that the first decisive naval engagements of both world wars took place in the South Atlantic and that the raider sunk in 1939 was named after the German admiral defeated in 1914. Harwood promoted rear-admiral and KCB; captains made CB.

1941 Four Force H destroyers, *Sikh*, Cdr G.H. Stokes DSC, RN, *Legion*, *Maori* and HNlMS *Isaac Sweers*, deployed by Ultra intelligence, torpedoed and sank two Italian 6-in cruisers, *Alberico da Barbiano* and *Alberto di Giussano*, at night, close inshore, from the landward side, off Cape Bon, Tunisia (37.04N, 11.47E) in what Admiral Cunningham regarded 'a brilliant attack'.
Battle Honour: Cape Bon 1941.
See 19 July 1940, 16 May 1945.

The end of the Italian ships, carrying deck cargoes of petrol from Palermo to Tripoli, was swift but grim: 920 men were lost, including Vice-Admiral A. Toscano. On arrival in Malta next day the squadron was greeted with ships' bands playing the Netherlands national anthem in honour of the *Isaac Sweers*. Malta-based 830 NAS (Swordfish), which was to have attacked the enemy ships, signalled 'Many congratulations. Your attention is drawn to St John Ch.10, v.1.' ('He that entereth not by the door into the sheepfold, but climbeth up some other way, the same is a thief and a robber'). Cdr Graham Stokes received a CB, 'an unusual distinction for an officer of his rank' – Cunningham.

1942 Sloop *Enchantress* sank the Italian S/M *Corallo* off Bougie (37.00N, 05.09E). Convoy ET 5.

1943 Liberator B/53 sank U-391 in the Bay of Biscay (45.45N, 09.38W).

1943 Destroyer *Calpe* and the USS *Wainwright* sank U-593 in W. Mediterranean (37.38N, 05.58E). Convoy KMS 34.

1944 Swordfish L/813 and Q/813 (*Campania*) sank U-365 in Arctic (70.43N, 08.07E). Convoy RA 62.

1962 Admiral of the Fleet Sir John Cunningham died in London. He had been born on the same day as the last naval officer survivor of Trafalgar, Admiral of the Fleet Sir George Sartorius died in 1885.
See 13 April 1885, 5 June 1945, 7 and 9 June 1947.

The first navigating officer to become First Sea Lord when he succeeded his namesake, Admiral of the Fleet Viscount Cunningham of Hyndhope, in May 1946. He served through both world wars and also followed ABC as C-in-C Mediterranean. His son died in 1941 serving in a submarine. 'Cunningham was a man of considerable intellectual attainment and was credited among his contemporaries with having the quickest brain in the Navy. He was a dour man with a sarcastic tongue and with a reputation for not suffering fools gladly, and these were to him 95 per cent of human beings' – Peter Kemp.

1980 Cdr Harry Pursey RN died aged 89; the first naval officer promoted from the lower deck to become a MP (Kingston-upon-Hull 1945–70).

14 December

1624 Lord Howard of Effingham, Lord High Admiral and C-in-C of the English Fleet in the Spanish Armada campaign, died.

1775 Thomas Cochrane born.
See 31 October 1860.

1798 *Ambuscade* taken by the French *Bayonnaise* off the mouth of the Gironde.

1809 *Melampus* captured the French *Béarnais* 80 miles N.N.E. of Barbuda.

1809 *Defender*, gun-brig of fourteen guns, Lt John George Nops RN, sailing from the Downs to Spithead, anchored off Folkestone to avoid a gale, wrecked on Cob Point when both her anchor cables parted. Crew saved.
See 11 July 1941.

1814 Boats of fleet captured five American gunboats and a sloop on Lake Borgne.

1840 Board approved construction of first wooden screw sloop, *Ardent* later *Rattler*, launched at Sheerness. *Bee*, launched at Chatham 28 February 1842, was the first screw ship in the Service. She also had precautionary paddles. The first iron vessel was *Dover*, a paddle packet built by Laird in 1840 and stationed on the west African coast from 1849.

1852 Relief of Pegu, Burma. Ships (Bengal Marine) *Nerbudda*, *Mahanuddy*. Boats of: *Fox*, *Sphinx* and *Moozuffer* (Indian Navy).

1860 Landing party from wood screw gunvessel *Nimrod* captured six pirate junks in Taune Bay.

1864 *Bombay* (screw (81)) destroyed by fire and explosion off Montevideo. Ninety-seven dead, including thirty-four Royal Marines, one of whom died at his post as sentry outside the Captain's quarters.

1939 Submarine *Ursula* sank the German escort F-9 and an R-boat off Heligoland (54.08N, 07.55E).

Royal Marines assault on Cheduba Island in the Arakan campaign, 1944. (*NMRN*)

Confrontation – Borneo, 1962–1966

In December 1962 the Brunei rebellion marked the beginning of an attempt by Indonesia to infiltrate the remaining countries in Borneo. Strong guerilla patrols operated out of Indonesian territory deep into Sarawak, Saba and Brunei.

No. 42 Cdo, Royal Marines, was flown in to Brunei town from Singapore. The British residents and other hostages including two women were held by the rebels at Limbang. Two old landing craft were commandeered and manned by seamen of *Chawton* and *Fiskerton*. They embarked L Company of 42 Cdo, and at dawn on 12 December, under a heavy fire from the shore, the landing craft went into the beach at Limbang. The Royal Marines stormed ashore, drove off the rebels, and rescued the hostages moments before they were due to be executed. The rebels were later hunted down by helicopters and river patrols. During this attack, five Royal Marines were killed and five wounded.

For three and a half years British troops including Royal Marines operated in the jungles of Borneo and were supported by 845 and 846 FAA helicopter squadrons from *Albion* and *Bulwark*. These squadrons, operating out of tiny clearings and on the limits of their aircraft's capabilities, achieved a very high level of operational readiness. For example, in 1963, 846 Squadron of Whirlwinds carried out 3,750 operational sorties, and in 1964, 845 Squadron aircraft of Wessex helicopters carried out 10,000 operational flying hours in support of the Army and Royal Marines.

See 12 December 1962, 20 January 1963.

1939 Destroyer *Kelly* badly damaged by mine 13 miles off the mouth of the Tyne.

1940 Eight Swordfish aircraft of 830 Sqn (Malta) bombed Tripoli.

1940 Destroyers *Hereward* and *Hyperion* sank the Italian S/M *Naiade* off Bardia (32.03N, 25.56E).

1941 Submarine *Urge* torpedoed Italian battleship *Vittorio Veneto*, putting her out of action for several months.

1941 Light cruiser *Galatea* sunk by U-557 30 miles W. of Alexandria (31.17N, 29.13E).

1942 GC (ex-AM): PO Cook C.H. Walker for saving life in MV *Waimarama* in Grand Harbour, Malta. Operation Pedestal. (*Gazette* date.)

1944 Destroyer *Aldenham* sunk by mine 45 miles S.E. of Pola in the Adriatic (44.30N, 14.50E). Last of 139 destroyers lost in the Second World War.

See 13 November 1939, 18 February 1940.

1944 Light cruisers *Diadem*, *Mauritius* and four destroyers attacked shipping off Stadtlandet.

1944 Bombardment of the Arakan coast in the neighbourhood of St Martin's Island (thirteen bombardments during the next nine days). Ships: *Napier*, *Nepal*; HDML: 1275, 1303; ML: 438, 439, 440, 441, 447, 847, 855.

1985 *Caledonia* ceased to operate as a TE for MEA apprentices and training task transferred to *Sultan*. Paid off and became annex to *Cochrane* on 17 December 1985. DCI(RN) 210/85.

2004 *Bulwark* accepted at Devonport.

2006 Chief ERA Leonard Williams, veteran of two wartime sinkings in the Far East and four years as a POW in Japanese hands, died aged 87. He was in the frigate *Amethyst* during escape from the River Yangtze in 1949 (DSM). As Chief ERA was the first to start up the engines of the new royal yacht *Britannia* in which he served for twelve years.

15 DECEMBER

1379 Sir John Arundel's squadron destroyed by storm on coast of Ireland.

1778 Rear-Admiral the Hon. Samuel Barrington (*Prince of Wales*) fought Vice-Admiral Comte d'Estaing at St Lucia.
Battle Honour: St Lucia 1778.
Ships: *Boyne, Centurion, Isis, Nonsuch, Preston, Prince of Wales, St Albans*. Frigates: *Ariadne, Aurora, Barbados, Carcass, Ceres, Pelican, Snake, Venus, Weazle*. Troops under Gen. Grant took the island by surprise and Barrington thwarted its recapture.
See 30 December 1778, 16 August 1800.

1805 The body of Vice-Admiral Viscount Nelson, preserved in a cask of spirits after Trafalgar, transferred into an elm coffin on board *Victory* at anchor off Dover while on passage from Portsmouth to The Nore. On 21 December, Mr Whitby, Master Attendant at Woolwich, and Mr Tyson, Nelson's former secretary, arrived at Sheerness with the 'exterior coffin'.

1824 Attack on a flotilla of Burmese war boats in the Panhlaing River by *Diana*, boats of *Arachne* and *Sophie* and the Bombay Marine *Prince of Wales*.

1841 Brig sloop *Charybdis* captured the Colombian Federal *Marcellino* and five Federal schooners in Zapote Bay.

1899 Battle of Colenso. Naval Brigade of *Terrible, Forte, Tartar, Philomel* and Natal Naval Volunteers.

1913 *Tiger*, battlecruiser, launched at John Brown's. The Royal Navy's last coal-burning capital ship to remain in the operational fleet, paying off in 1931.

1917 Sloop *Arbutus* torpedoed by UB-65 in the entrance to the Bristol Channel (51.38N, 06.00W). Sank next day.

1936 The first sea trials of the Royal Navy's first radar, Type 79X, carried out by the coal-burning minesweeper *Saltburn*, lying stopped 7 miles S.E. of The Nab.
See 15 August 1938.

1940 Destroyer *Cameron* capsized in dock in Portsmouth Dockyard after attack by German aircraft: CTL.

1940 Submarine *Thunderbolt* (ex-*Thetis*) sank the Italian S/M *Capitano Tarantini* in Bay of Biscay (45.25N, 09.12W).
See 1 June 1939, 14 March 1943.

Admiral Sir Herbert Richmond (1871–1945)

Richmond's life's work was the study, identification and deployment of the enduring lessons which history had to offer naval commanders, notwithstanding the recent technical revolution in ships and armament. Richmond wrote many outstanding works including *The Navy in the War of 1739–48* (3 vols, 1920) and *The Navy in India 1763–1783* (1931) and he edited several volumes for the Navy Records Society, among them *Papers relating to the Loss of Minorca in 1756* (1913), and vols 3 and 4 of *The Spencer Papers* (1924). His last great study, *Statesmen and Sea Power*, based on his Ford Lectures delivered in the University of Oxford in Michaelmas term of 1943, was published in 1946. He was a founder of the *Naval Review* in October 1912 and first Commandant of the Imperial Defence College in 1926. His first-class brain often brought him into conflict with senior officers, including Jackie Fisher, who, shaped by long and profound naval protocol, received badly any professional questioning or criticism from subordinates, however gifted. 'It was a great misfortune that such a brilliant thinker as Richmond should have been so intolerant and tactless when the need was to convince his superiors of the correctness of his views' – Roskill, *Churchill and the Admirals*, pp.45–6. Richmond survived, however, to fly his flag as C-in-C East Indies and to reach full admiral. Richmond retired in 1931 but his greatest days, as a naval historian, were still ahead of him. He was elected Vere Harmsworth Professor of Naval History at Cambridge in 1934 and later Master of Downing College where he died in post. At his memorial service at St Mary the Great on 18 January 1947, fellow historian and brother-in-law Dr G.M. Trevelyan, Master of Trinity, concluded his address 'We thank God that Herbert Richmond lived and that he came to Cambridge'.

The modified Rothesay-class Type 12 anti-submarine frigate HMS *Falmouth* launched by Swan Hunter on 15 December 1959. (*Author*)

1941 Destroyer *Nestor* (RAN) sank U-127 off Cape St Vincent in advance of Convoy HG76.

1942 Destroyers *Petard* and *Vasilissa Olga* (Greek) captured the Italian S/M *Uarsciek* S. of Malta (35.10N, 14.25E). S/M sank later in tow.

1946 Admiral Sir Herbert Richmond, the outstanding naval strategist of his generation, died in post as Master of Downing College, Cambridge.

See 15 September 1871, 27 October 1912, 28 September 1999.

1948 Vice-Admiral Sir Geoffrey Blake, Gunnery Officer of the fleet flagship *Iron Duke* at Jutland, resigned as Gentleman-Usher of the Black Rod because of progressive deafness brought about by a gun blast. In informing the House of Lords, Viscount Jowett, the Lord Chancellor, commented 'I am bound to add that if all members . . . applied to themselves the same strict standard as Sir Geoffrey Blake has applied to himself, we might have many more retirements'.

See 27 February 1945.

1954 The submarine *Talent*, refitting in No. 3 Dock at Chatham Dockyard, was swept off her blocks and carried out of the dry dock with the backwash after the caisson at the entrance collapsed at 1530, an hour before a particularly high water. She grounded on the mud flats on the west side of the Medway. Fifty men were on board; two dockyard workers died. The salvage vessel *Swin* stood by the submarine overnight and she was refloated on the next tide and towed into the dockyard.

See 1 February 1953.

1967 Rear-Admiral Edward Courtney Boyle VC, First World War submarine commander, knocked down by a lorry in Sunningdale and died next day.

See 27 April 1915.

1969 The coastal minesweepers HMS *Houghton*, Lt-Cdr J. Hall RN, and HMS *Wilkieston*, Lt-Cdr D.J.E. Lothian RN, arrived at Plymouth and Portsmouth respectively from the Far East, the smallest RN ships to cross the Pacific since the Second World War. The ships sailed from the Mediterranean Fleet to Singapore in 1959 and after ten years' service they came home via Darwin, Papua, the British Solomon Islands, the New Hebrides, Fiji, the Gilbert and Ellice Islands, Hawaii, California, Acapulco, Panama, Jamaica, Bermuda, the Azores and Oporto.

See 18 December 1967.

1971 Bahrain closed as a British naval base. HMS *Jufair* paid off.

See 4 November 1971.

1976 Lt HRH The Prince of Wales RN relinquished command of the minehunter *Bronington*, the final day of his active service in the Royal Navy.

See 16 September 1971, 4 January 1974, 2 September 1974, 9 February 1976.

1978 Last conventional fixed-wing squadron, 892 NAS, decommissioned at Leuchars.

1999 Minehunter *Bangor* commissioned, the last RN ship accepted into service in the (popularly accepted) twentieth century.

See 16 April 1999, 27 November 1999, 8 June 2000.

16 December

1653 Instructions for all commanders-in-chief of squadrons, flag officers in their divisions and for all captains of ships at sea in the service of the Commonwealth, issued by George Monck, John Disbraw and William Penn aboard the *Swiftsure* – the first Articles of War, from which came the phrase 'Naval justice is swift and sure.'

1796 *Cleopatra* captured the French privateer *Hirondelle* 500 miles to the westward of Ushant.

1808 *Naiad* and *Narcissus* captured the French privateer *Fanny* off Noirmoutier.

1812 Saving of *Magnificent* in a violent gale off Ile de Ré in Bay of Biscay, by distinguished seamanship which earned her captain the name of Magnificent Hayes.

1914 Scarborough, Hartlepool and Whitby bombarded by German battlecruisers. Ships: *Patrol, Doon, Waveney, Test*.

1916 VC: Capt (temp Lt-Col) B.C. Freyberg, Royal West Surrey Regiment and RND; ex-Lt-Cdr RNVR.

1917 Sloop *Arbutus* foundered in heavy weather in St George's Channel, after being torpedoed by UB-65.

1921 *Victory*, first rate, moved into No. 1 Basin, Portsmouth Dockyard; the first move towards her restoration and preservation.

See 20 March 1922, 1 June 1923.

HMS *Victory* being restored, 1926. (*NMRN 1952/51*)

The ship's badge of HMS *Ambush*. (*RN*)

1941 Destroyer *Thracian* beached at Hong Kong. Salvaged by Japanese forces as PB 101. Recaptured in September 1945.

1948 Light fleet carrier *Terrible* transferred to Royal Australian Navy at Devonport and commissioned as HMAS *Sydney*. Handed over by the First Lord of the Admiralty and accepted by the High Commissioner of Australia, the Rt Hon. J.B. Beasley. Mrs Beasley performed the naming ceremony. The transfer marked the inauguration of naval aviation in Australia. Sabotage to the ship's starboard main gearing at Devonport before the ship sailed for Australia received publicity.

See 30 September 1944, 28 October 1955.

1957 The submarine *Thorough*, Lt-Cdr R.C.H. Mason RN, returned to *Dolphin* becoming the first submarine to circumnavigate the world. The boat had sailed from Portsmouth in October 1949 for Australia where she served eight years

Submariners attending the launch of HMS *Ambush* at BAE Systems, Barrow, on 16 December 2010. (*RN*)

in the Fourth Submarine Squadron providing A/S training for the RAN, RNZN and RN units based in the Far East. She left Sydney on 7 October, returning across the Pacific and was the first RN submarine ever to visit Tahiti.

1959 Cruiser *Tiger*, flying the flag of Admiral Sir Alexander Bingley, C-in-C Mediterranean Fleet, passed the US cruiser *Des Moines* with President Eisenhower on board at sea N. of Malta and fired a 21-gun salute.

1991 Decision to employ women in the armed forces in fixed-wing aircraft announced by Parliament.

2003 European Court of Human Rights ruling (Grieves v. UK) stopped serving naval officers sitting as judge advocates at naval courts martial because, although uniformed Judge Advocates attracted no personal criticism, they did not give the perception of independence and impartiality (unlike their civil counterparts in Army and RAF courts martial). Courts martial and summary appeals scheduled for January 2004 postponed pending changes to NDA.

See 15 January 2004.

2008 Antarctic patrol ship *Endurance*, Capt Gavin Pritchard RN, entering the Magellan Straits at night in 50 knot winds, lost all main power when engine room and control room flooded. The ship, with a 30 degree list, towed to Chilean base at Punta Arenas and after Christmas was taken to Mare Haven in the Falkland Islands. Transferred to Dutch heavy lift ship *Target* and arrived Portsmouth 8 April 2009.

See 26 April 1881, 7 July 2002, 27 February 2006.

2010 *Ambush*, second of the Astute-class SSNs, named by Anne, Lady Soar, wife of Admiral Sir Trevor Soar, C-in-C Fleet, launched at BAE Systems, Barrow.

See 7 January 2011.

Lady Soar, wife of C-in-C Fleet Admiral Sir Trevor Soar, launches HMS *Ambush* in 2010. (RN)

17 December

1619 Prince Rupert, naval commander in the Dutch wars, born.

1706 *Romney* captured a French privateer in Malaga Bay.

1810 *Rinaldo* sank the French privateer *Vieille Josephine* off the Owers.

1826 Hardy in *Wellesley* (74) escorted expeditionary force to Lisbon. Ship sunk by air attack on Thames 24 September 1940.

1834 *Buzzard* captured the Spanish slaver *Formidable* 20 miles N. of Cape Bullen, west coast of Africa.

1856 The abandoned discovery barque HMS *Resolute*, Capt H. Keller CB, RN, found by an American whaler in the Arctic on 10 September 1855, was presented to the British people by the United States. The *Resolute* was one of the five-ship Belcher expedition sent to find Franklin's *Erebus* and *Terror* in 1852. Having been refitted by the US Congress, the *Resolute* arrived at Spithead in December 1856 flying the Stars and Stripes and the Red Ensign. Her Captain, Capt Harstein USN, dined with Queen Victoria who gave him £100 to share among his crew.

See 15 April 1965.

When the ship was broken up in 1879 Queen Victoria had a desk made from the timbers which was presented to President Rutherford B. Hayes 'as a memorial of the courtesy and loving kindness which dictated the offer of the gift of the *Resolute*'.

The desk has been used by US presidents (excepting presidents Johnson, Nixon and Ford) ever since. It has twice been modified: by President Roosevelt who had the kneehole fitted with a panel carrying the presidential coat of arms to hide his wheelchair and leg braces, and by 6ft2in-tall President Reagan who had it raised. It has been the centrepiece of the Oval Office with a few breaks since President Kennedy moved it in 1961. President Clinton reclaimed it from elsewhere in the White House on 20 January 1993.

The Metropolitan Police took over responsibility for the security of home dockyards in 1860–1. This photograph shows duty police officers at the main gates of Pembroke Dockyard, *c.*1901. (*Author*)

1857 Rear-Admiral Sir Francis Beaufort died. Hydrographer to the Navy 1829–56 and the last surviving officer who fought at the Glorious First of June in 1794.

1860 Metropolitan Police of the 5th Division took over security duties at Pembroke Dockyard. Establishment: 1 superintendent, 2 inspectors, 5 sergeants and 26 PCs.

1915 German cruiser *Bremen* and V-191 sunk in east Baltic by E 9 (57.31N, 20.24E).

1935 Rear-Admiral Bertram Ramsay, Chief of Staff to his lifelong friend, Admiral Sir Roger Backhouse, C-in-C Home Fleet, since August 1935, relieved from his appointment at his own request. Backhouse, like Jellicoe, was an arch centraliser and absolutely refused to delegate any of his authority to his Chief of Staff or anyone else. No *modus vivendi* succeeded and Ramsay, not having hoisted his flag at sea was, by regulation, placed on the Retired List on 10 October 1938. He was thus able to spend three years with his family before being recalled in 1939 to arduous and distinguished duty. Fully refreshed, he made a spectacularly successful comeback. He remained on the Retired List until made vice-admiral on the Active List on 26 April 1944 and full admiral on 27 April 1944 – the eve of D-Day. Admiral Backhouse became First Sea Lord in November 1938 but, hugely overworked, he died on 15 July 1939.

See 10 October 1938, 2 January 1945.

1939 German pocket battleship *Admiral Graf Spee* scuttled by her crew off Montevideo following the Battle of the River Plate.

See 13 and 20 December 1939.

1940 Destroyer *Acheron* sunk by mine off the Isle of Wight (50.31N, 01.31W) during high-speed trials after repairs. Stern had been blown off in air raid on Portsmouth Dockyard.

1940 River gunboat *Aphis* bombarded the Bardia area.

1941 *Blankney, Exmoor, Penstemon, Stanley, Stork* and Martlet aircraft of 802 Sqn (*Audacity*) sank U-131 W. of Gibraltar (34.12N, 13.35W). Convoy HG 76. Cdr F.J. Walker's first kill, with 36th Escort Group.

1941 First battle of Sirte. Passage of *Breconshire* from Alexandria to Malta and partial engagement with Italian battlefleet off the Gulf of Sirte (34.00N, 18.30E). Ships: *Euryalus, Naiad* (Rear-Admiral Vian – 15th CS), *Decoy, Havock, Jervis* (D 14), *Kimberley, Kipling, Nizam*. Force K: *Aurora, Penelope, Lance, Legion, Lively, Maori, Sikh, Isaac Sweers* (Neth).

1942 Submarine *Splendid* torpedoed the Italian destroyer *Aviere* off Bizerta (38.00N, 10.05E). *Aviere* broke in two and sank at once.

See 21 April 1943.

1942 *Firedrake* sunk by U-211 S. of Iceland (50.50N, 25.15W). Convoy ON 153. Sank at once but survivors picked up by *Sunflower*.

See 28 June 1934.

1944 Frigate *Nyasaland* sank U-400 off Cape Clear (51.16N, 08.05W).

1946 Rear-Admiral Viscount Mountbatten invested as KG.

1971 MOD announced that DPR(N) was building a fleet of four 60ft-long diesel-powered craft, built closely to resemble a County-class guided missile destroyer, a Leander-class frigate, a Type 42 destroyer and a Polaris submarine, which would tour British inland waterways from April 1972 to generate recruiting publicity. 'One member of each crew should be in possession of an Admiralty Driving Permit' – DCI(RN) 1373/71.

1985 *Caledonia*, Artificers' Training Establishment, Rosyth, paid off. Site retained as part of *Cochrane*.

18 December

1677 Qualifying examination introduced for lieutenants, RN.

1779 Rear-Admiral Hyde Parker (*Princess Royal*) captured nine sail of a French convoy and burned ten more off Fort Royal, Martinique, and engaged the escort. Ships: *Albion, Boreas, Centurion, Conqueror, Elizabeth, Preston, Princess Royal* and *Vigilant*.

1793 Vice-Admiral Lord Hood (*Victory*) at the evacuation of Toulon, occupied since 27 August. Ships: *Britannia, Princess Royal, Robust, Terrible, Victory, Windsor Castle* and boats of fleet. Frigates: *Arethusa, Pearl, Topaze, Alert, Swallow* (tender). Gunboats: *Union, Wasp, Jean Bart, Petite Victoire*. Expended: *Vulcan* and *Conflagration* fireships. Captured or destroyed: nine French ships of the line, five frigates and corvettes.

See 27 August 1793.

1809 Capture and destruction of the French *Seine* and *Loire* in Barque Cove, Guadeloupe. Two batteries stormed and captured. Ships: *Blonde, Castor, Cygnet, Elizabeth, Freija, Hazard, Ringdove, Sceptre, Thetis.*

1827 Uniforms for officers reduced to a double-breasted coat, always to be buttoned up, with gold laced trousers for dress wear and plain for undress (white in summer). Breeches and dress swords restricted to Drawing Room. Buttons to be slightly domed rather than flat.

1914 U-15 mined and sunk off Belgian coast.

1915 First 500lb bomb dropped, by Cdr Samson on Turkish forces.

1940 *Triton* sunk by Italian TB *Clio* in the south Adriatic. Last of twenty-three submarines lost in 1940.

1940 Swordfish aircraft of 815 and 819 Sqns (*Illustrious*) attacked Stampalia.

1941 VC: Lt-Cdr Malcolm David Wanklyn for gallantry in *Upholder*. First S/M VC of Second World War.

See 14 April 1942.

1941 Destroyers *Blankney* and *Stanley* sank U-434 off Azores. Convoy HG 76.

See 19 December 1941.

1942 *Partridge* sunk by U-565 50 miles W. of Oran (35.50N, 01.35W).

1943 Minesweeper *Felixstowe* sunk by mine 3 miles off Cape Ferro, Sardinia (40.09N, 09.36E).

1944 Light cruiser *Sirius* stood by naval party ashore at Mitylene, Greek island of Lesbos, during general strike.

1964 'The Admiralty Board, the Royal Navy and Royal Marines send their affectionate greetings

The destruction of Toulon, 1793. The city had been occupied by Hood at the invitation of French royalists, but Republican armies forced his withdrawal. Subsequent political suspicion of the royalists then deprived the French Navy of the expertise of its many aristocratic officers. (*NMRN 1976/203*)

to the Former Naval Person on his 90th birthday [30 November].' 'Thank you all so much. Every good wish. Winston S. Churchill.' – DCI(RN) 1322/64.

See 24 January 1965.

1967 Coastal minesweeper *Maryton* returned to HMS *Vernon* at Portsmouth after a 13,000-mile passage from Singapore, the longest unaccompanied voyage undertaken by a Ton-class vessel. She sailed from Singapore on 12 October and returned via Penang, Gan, Mombassa, Durban, Simon's Town, Walvis Bay, Takoradi, Dakar and Gibraltar.

Water was strictly rationed on the long legs and limited to 1.5 tons a day. 'The Coxswain managed to arrange a One and One tot for part of the trip but the Jimmy soon caught on as to how much water we actually saved in the process, so we reverted to Two and One.' – Rob Guyatt.

See 15 December 1969.

1992 The closure programme for *Mercury* announced in DCI(RN) 310/92.

29 March 1993–2 April 1993. Navigational training transfers to *Dryad*.

2–6 August 1993. Communications training transfers to *Collingwood*.

31 August 1993. Captain, *Mercury*, relinquishes command.

17 December 1993. *Mercury* site handed over.

See 1 January 1977, 31 August 1993.

ROYAL NAVY

MINISTRY OF DEFENCE PRESS RELEASE

No. 150/69
December 17th, 1969

ROYAL NAVY DAILY RUM ISSUE TO BE DISCONTINUED

After more than two hundred years the issue of duty-free rum to ratings of the Royal Navy is to be discontinued on August 1st 1970. In its place the following compensatory arrangements have been made.

Chief petty officers, petty officers, and Royal Marine senior NCOs in ships are to be allowed to buy duty-free spirits in their messes. Junior ratings and Royal Marine equivalents in ships may buy up to three cans of beer each day but they will not be allowed to purchase spirits.

In addition a lump sum of £2.7 million, provided in compensation for the abolition of the rum issue, will be paid into a fund for charitable purposes for the benefit of ratings and Royal Marine other ranks, serving and ex-Service, and their dependants. The fund will be known as The Sailors' Fund and ratings are to play a major part in its administration.

The Admiralty Board has decided that it is necessary in the interest of health, safety and efficiency in the Fleet to abolish the rum issue. The decision has not been taken on grounds of economy. The issue of rum is not compatible with the high standards required in ships using complex and delicate equipment. In future, those ratings below petty officer will get no spirits on board. Chief petty officers and petty officers will be allowed to buy commercial spirits in their bars on board ship in quantities which will provide an average daily amount equal to ⅛th pint per man (equivalent to three single measures ashore).

Ratings over the age of 20 are at present eligible to receive one eighth of an Imperial pint of 95.5 degrees proof rum a day, those below the rank of petty officer having their allowance diluted with two parts of water. An eligible rating not wishing to draw his rum issue receives three pence per day in lieu.

Issued by:-
Public Relations
(Royal Navy)
Ministry of Defence
Main Building
Whitehall
London S.W.1.
01-930-7022 Ext. 7919.

Ministry of Defence (Navy) press release dated 17 December 1969 announcing that the Royal Navy's daily rum issue would cease on 1 August 1970. (*Author*)

19 DECEMBER

1664 Capt Thomas Allin (*Plymouth*) and squadron fought the Dutch Smyrna convoy in Gibraltar Strait and took the three best ships. War had not been declared and Allin was accused of ignoring a Dutch salute. Ships: *Advice, Antelope, Crown, Leopard, Milford, Oxford, Plymouth, Portsmouth.*

1681 *Calabash* captured the Algerine *Red Lion* off Majorca.

1796 *Minerve* (Cdre Nelson) captured the Spanish *Sabina* 25 miles S.W. of Cartagena – retaken by Spanish reinforcements. *Blanche* forced the Spanish *Ceres* to strike, but was unable to take possession. Regiment: detachment of the 11th.

1796 The third rate prize *Courageux* (74), Capt Benjamin Hallowell, parted her cable in a rising Levanter in Gibraltar Bay and drove ashore near Apes Hill (Mount Hacho) near Ceuta on the Moroccan coast and was wrecked; 465 men lost but not Capt Hallowell who had been ashore at a court martial in Gibraltar.

See 15 August 1761.

1797 King George III, with the royal family and Lord Spencer, First Lord of the Admiralty, attended a thanksgiving service at St Paul's Cathedral for the naval victories of the French war – Howe's Glorious First of June (1794), Jervis' St Vincent (February 1797) and Duncan's Camperdown (October 1797). Nelson was one of seventeen admirals in the procession from Palace Yard, Westminster, preceded by wagons bearing captured French, Spanish and Dutch flags. The event was marred only by 'an overdrove ox which ran up and down Ludgate Hill causing a universal terror'.

See 21 October 1955, 21 October 2005.

1804 *Fisgard* captured the French privateer *Tiger* 200 miles W. of Cape St Vincent.

1809 *Rosamund* captured the French *Papillon* 12 miles S.S.E. of St Croix, West Indies.

1811 *Royalist* captured the French privateer *Rodeur* in Dover Strait.

1914 *Doris* harassed Turkish coast near Alexandretta.

1915 Evacuation of Anzac and Suvla beachheads began at Gallipoli. Successfully completed by 21st.

1917 UB-56 sunk in Dover Barrage, observed by destroyer *Gipsy* who picked up the sole survivor.

1941 Mediterranean Fleet flagship, *Queen Elizabeth*, and her sister-ship *Valiant* were seriously damaged in a gallant Italian two-man torpedo attack at Alexandria. To deceive the enemy reconnaissance Admiral Sir Andrew Cunningham continued to attend Colours and Sunset on his quarterdeck although his ship was sitting on the bottom. In 1944, the late Captain of *Valiant*, Rear-Admiral Charles Morgan, was Flag Officer Taranto and was invited to present decorations to (now Allied) Italian naval officers; they included Lt-Cdr Luigi Durand de la Penne, one of the submariners who had attacked *Valiant* at Alexandria and been taken prisoner three years earlier.

1941 Destroyer *Stanley* sunk by U-574 E. of Azores (38.12N, 17.23W). Convoy HG 76. *Stork* sank U-574.

See 18 December 1941.

1941 A bad night for the Mediterranean Fleet. Force K, a squadron of Malta-based cruisers and destroyers led by the light cruiser *Neptune* (Capt Rory O'Conor RN), deploying at full speed to intercept an Italian convoy running supplies into Tripoli, ran into a minefield 12 miles off that port in the early hours. *Neptune* hit a mine and went astern into another, which wrecked her screws and steering. The light cruisers *Penelope* and *Aurora* sheered off to avoid the danger but were also mined, *Aurora* badly – she was detached to Malta escorted by the destroyers *Lance* and *Havock*. HMS *Penelope*, only slightly damaged, stood by *Neptune* which drifted onto a third mine; the destroyer *Kandahar* went to her rescue but her stern was blown off.

Capt O'Conor now ordered Capt A.D. Nicholl of the *Penelope* to stay clear. 'It was against all naval usage to abandon comrades in distress; but he rightly considered that he

HMS *Orion* (1879). A coast defence ship, originally designed and built for the Turkish Navy as an ironclad ram vessel, and purchased for the RN during the Russian war scare of 1878. (*NMRN*)

would only lose more ships if he entered the minefield to help. Sunrise was close at hand. He was off the enemy coast, so with a heavy heart he turned back for Malta.' – Admiral Sir Andrew Cunningham, C-in-C Mediterranean Fleet, *A Sailor's Odyssey*, pp.431–3. At 0400 a fourth mine exploded under *Neptune*'s bridge and she capsized in position (33.15N, 13.30E). At daylight only the Captain and fifteen men on a single raft remained. They died one by one, 'the gallant O'Conor on 23 December, and one survivor from the 765 ship's company of *Neptune* was rescued alive by an Italian torpedo boat on Christmas Eve. HMS *Neptune* was due to have been handed over to the RNZN and 160 New Zealanders in her ship's company were lost – the greatest loss of life suffered by New Zealand in a naval action. The destroyer *Jaguar*, which was sailed from Malta, rescued 174 men from *Kandahar* 'by a fine piece of seamanship' (Roskill) and then torpedoed her (33.15N, 13.12E). 'Thus in a matter of a few hours, was the Malta striking force's brief but brilliant career ended.' – Roskill, *The War at Sea*, vol.1, pp.535–6.

The sole survivor from *Neptune*, Norman Walton, left the Navy in 1946 and was recalled for the Korean War. Petty Officer Walton, a former bare-knuckle fairground fighter, was mugged in 2003 at the age of 82 by two youths who demanded his wallet. They were unsuccessful.

1942 Corvette *Snapdragon* sunk by German aircraft off Benghazi (32.18N, 19.54E).

1942 Winston Churchill, Prime Minister, wrote to the First Sea Lord, Admiral of the Fleet Sir Dudley Pound, that he was 'still grieved to see our submarines described as "P.212", etc., in the daily returns. I thought you told me that you would give them names. It is in accordance with the tradition of the Service and with the feelings of the officers and men who risk their lives in these vessels. Not even to give them a name is derogatory to their devotion and sacrifice.' A list of names was submitted after Christmas. 'With the help of the whole submarine headquarters' staff, including Wrens, and every conceivable work of reference, a list of names was eventually produced, to which the Prime Minister himself, impatient as ever of delay and, of course, knowing nothing of the difficulties, contributed two: *Tiptoe* and *Varangian*' – Capt T.D. Manning and Cdr C.F. Walker, members of the wartime Ships Names Committee.

See 3 July 1902, 24 September 1926, 5 November 1942, 27 December 1942, 28 January 1943.

1963 Assault ship *Fearless* launched at Harland & Wolff, Belfast, by Lady Hull, wife of Gen. Sir Richard Hull. Vice-Admiral J.B. Frewen, VCNS, and Lt-Gen. Sir Malcolm Cartwright-Taylor, CGRM, were present. The media were ordered not to photograph the stern of the ship, a security attempt negated by a Soviet merchant ship alongside at an adjacent berth.

See 25 June 1964.

1967 Frigate *Minerva*, on the Beira Patrol maintaining the oil blockade of Rhodesia in accordance with UN Security Council resolution of 9 April 1966, fired a shot across the bows of the French tanker *Artois* which had refused to stop. The tanker ignored the shot and entered Beira.

See 27 February 1966, 10 April 1966, 10 May 1966, 25 June 1975.

2002 First RFA Officers' Course passed out of Britannia RN College, Dartmouth.

20 December

1666 *Adventure* fought four French men-of-war off Land's End.

1782 *Diomede* and *Quebec* captured the American *South Carolina* 50 miles E. of Cape May.

1799 Boats of *Queen Charlotte* and *Emerald* recaptured *Lady Nelson* in Gibraltar Bay.

1808 The Royal Navy's second *Dauntless*, an 18-gun ship sloop, launched at Deptford Dockyard. She served in seas as far apart as Archangel, Newfoundland and the East Indies but, unlike the first of the name, she stayed out of trouble and was sold in 1825.

1896 John G. Lang, future Secretary of the Admiralty, born at Woolwich.

1900 Charles Lambe born at Sralbridge, Dorset. Joined RN in 1914, Captain of *Illustrious* 1944, First Sea Lord 1959–60 and Admiral of the

The Royal Navy and Royal Marines in Afghanistan

The international counter-insurgency operation in Afghanistan launched by the USA as Operation Enduring Freedom after the 11 September 2001 attacks has closely involved the British naval service. Operation Herrick (the British title) has seen the longest period of sustained high-intensity combat operations for British armed forces since the Korean War. An International Security Assistance Force (ISAF) was established by the UN on 20 December 2001 to secure Kabul and environs, of which NATO assumed command in 2003. The conflict developed from a focused but violent struggle against Al-Qaeda and the Taliban into to a complex counter-insurgency campaign.

By 2011 the Coalition Forces comprised 120,000 personnel from forty-seven countries. The UK was the second-largest contributor with up to 9,500 service men and women deployed. Royal Marines from 3 Cdo Bde RM were first involved in Afghanistan during Operation Jacana from April – July 2002. The commitment to Operation Herrick started in January 2006 when elements of 42 Cdo RM deployed in support of the Joint Force Headquarters, conducting preliminary operations on Operation Herrick 3/4. 3 Cdo Bde deployed to Helmand Province in September 2006 on Operation Herrick 5 in command of Task Force Helmand as the UK military footprint increased substantially. Subsequently, 3 Cdo Bde has deployed on Operation Herrick 9 and 14 (April 2011) while 40 Cdo has deployed on Operation Herrick 7 (under command 52 Bde) and on Operation Herrick 12 (4 Mech. Bde). Royal Marines from the Armoured Support Group were also deployed on Ops Herrick 5–10. Joint Force Harrier with RN and RM aircrew and support personnel was committed between 2004 and 2009 with 800 NAS, the first fully formed RN squadron, deployed in September 2006 and again in 2007 and 2008. Over 3,000 missions were flown to deliver close air support to British and coalition troops.

The Commando Helicopter Force (CHF) has had a continuous presence in Afghanistan from 2006. Sea King Mk 4 from 847 NAS deployed in November 2007 and Lynx Mk 7 (also 847 NAS) deployed in 08/09. CHF tasks included troop movements, medical evacuation, command tasks and armed reconnaissance. Sea King Mk 7 airborne surveillance and control helicopters were also deployed to provide ISR (Intelligence, Surveillance and Reconnaissance) support to ground forces.

Throughout the campaign Royal Naval personnel have deployed to fulfill command, engineering, bomb disposal, logistics, medical and provincial stabilisation roles. At times half of all British forces in Afghanistan were deployed from the Royal Navy and Royal Marines.

Up to 1 March 2011, forty-nine Royal Marines had been killed in action with many more wounded. RM and RN Operational Honours and Awards had included: 1 GC, 3 CGC, 8 DSO (incl. 1 bar), 32 MC, 2 DFC, 2 QGM, 1 CBE, 1 OBE, 12 MBE, 45 MiD and 14 QCVS.

Hoisting a 13.5-in breech-loading gun into the after barbette of the battleship HMS *Rodney* (1885). (*NMRN*)

Fleet. A polymath whose early death was a great loss to the Service.

See 8 August 1922, 23 May 1960, 29 August 1960.

1913 Fire in Portsmouth Dockyard destroyed the eighteenth-century sail loft, rigging house and wooden semaphore tower built in 1778. Two duty signalmen lost. The fire was reported at 1925 by the new battlecruiser *Queen Mary*, lying alongside South Railway Jetty. The ship had to be towed off for safety. 'The tower, as the chief signal station of the port, will be a great loss . . . as all ships coming into Spithead reported to it and all general signals to vessels were made from it.' The loss included archives of naval documents and records dating from the Russian War.

See 4 July 1930.

1939 Capt Hans Langsdorf of the German pocket battleship *Admiral Graf Spee* shot himself in Buenos Aires.

See 13 and 17 December 1939.

1940 Ten Swordfish aircraft of 830 Sqn FAA (Malta) bombed Tripoli and mined the harbour.

1940 GC: Lt-Cdr Richard John Hammersley Ryan, Sub-Lt Peter Victor Danckwerts, RNVR, CPO Reginald Vincent Ellingworth. The first and third awards were posthumous and all were for bomb and mine disposal. (*Gazette* date.)

1944 Force 67 made an unsuccessful attack on the harbour and oil installations at Medan, Sumatra. Carriers: *Indomitable*, *Illustrious*. Cover: *Argonaut*, *Black Prince*, *Newcastle*, *Kempenfelt* (D 27), *Wager*, *Wakeful*, *Wessex*, *Whelp*, *Whirlwind*, *Wrangler*. FAA Sqns: Avenger: 854, 857; Corsair: 1830, 1833; Hellcat: 1839, 1844. Operation Robson.

1946 The River-class frigate *Aire*, lately *Tamar*, en route to Singapore after serving as guardship at Hong Kong, wrecked on the Bombay Reef S. of Hainan. CTL. All her people rescued by the submarine depot ship *Bonaventure* which was proceeding in company. The naval rescue tug *Enticer*, proceeding to the assistance of the Swedish merchantman *Rosebank*, foundered in heavy weather in the same week in the same waters.

1963 'Ceremonial at Colours and Sunset. Henceforth, men hoisting and hauling down the Colours are to keep their caps on. QR&AI Article 1349 will be amended accordingly.' – DCI(RN)2369.

1969 The RN's fourth Fleet submarine, HMS *Churchill*, launched by the Hon. Mrs Christopher Soames, Sir Winston's daughter, at Vickers, Barrow.

1995 The British Carrier Task Group which deployed to the Adriatic in January 1993 placed under NATO command to provide support for the Implementation Force (IFOR) (Operations Hamden/Grapple). SHAR conducted operations against Bosnian Serbs and took part in Operation Deny Flight. Reverted to national command 15 February 1996.

See 1 January 1993.

21 December

1747 Capt Thomas Fox of the *Kent* (74) dismissed his ship by a court martial on board *Duke* (90) in Portsmouth Harbour for 'misconduct and misbehaviour' during Hawke's battle with *L'Etanduere*, 'The Second Battle of Finisterre', on 14 October 1747.

See 14 October 1747, 7 August 1914.

Fox had backed his mizzen topsails, that is, hove to, when he was expected to engage the French flagship, *Tonnant*. There was no question of Fox being what Jack Aubrey would have called 'shy'; he was shunned by his fellow captains after the battle but otherwise was held in high regard in the Fleet; the court, presided over by Vice-Admiral Sir Peter Warren, recorded that 'his courage has been so fully proved to them as not to leave the least room for suspecting [cowardice], and part of that misconduct seems to them to proceed from listening to the persuasions of the First Lieutenant [George Ryall] and Master [Townshend] and giving way to them'. Ryall deserted the Service within a few months and both were described as 'damned bad fellows' – Keppel to Anson 16 December in Mackay, *Admiral Hawke*, p.94. Fox was never employed again; he became a superannuated rear-admiral in July 1749 and died in 1763. Fox's fate was paralleled 167 years later when Rear-Admiral Ernest Troubridge, commanding the First Cruiser Squadron in the Mediterranean in 1914, 'did forbear to pursue the chase' of the German battlecruiser *Goeben*, through the insistent bad advice of his Flag Captain, Fawcet Wray. Troubridge was honourably acquitted by a court martial but never employed at sea again.

1779 *Suffolk* and *Magnificent* captured the French *Fortunée* and *Blanche* respectively to the north-west of St Lucia.

Training on a 12-pdr gun at Whale Island in the 1890s. (*NMRN*)

1796 *Bombay Castle* (24) wrecked, entering the Tagus.

1797 French frigate *Nereide* (36) taken by *Phoebe* (36), Capt Robert Barlow, off the Scillies. Re-captured 24 August 1810 by the French at Mauritius. Re-taken there on 6 December 1810. Battle Honour: *Nereide* 1797.

1841 Special uniform, with special buttons depicting an engine, devised for First Class Engineers.
See 26 December 1842.

1852 George Astley Callaghan, the future Admiral of the Fleet and C-in-C Home Fleet immediately before the First World War, born in London.
See 4 August 1914, 23 November 1920.

1872 *Challenger*, wood screw corvette, sailed from Portsmouth under the command of Capt George Nares, on a 3½-year voyage of oceanographic exploration.
See 24 May 1876, 7 December 1872.

1914 First night bombing raid on Ostend by Cdr C.R. Samson in a Maurice Farman biplane.

1916 Destroyers *Hoste* and *Negro* sunk in collision (depth charges exploded) 10 miles off Fair Island.

1917 *Lady Ismay*, paddle minesweeper, mined near the Galloper.

1937 Destroyer *Nubian* launched at Thornycrofts. She shared with *Jervis* thirteen Second World War battle honours, the RN destroyer record. Battleship *Warspite* gained twenty-five battle honours, fourteen of them in the same war.

1939 New boom defence vessel (netlayer) *Bayonet*, T/Boom Skipper A. Lamont RNR, sunk in a British minefield laid by *Plover* in the south Inchkeith Channel off Leith in the Firth of Forth. As a wartime cover-up the cause was given as a German magnetic minefield laid in the Forth by the German U-21 in which the new light cruiser *Belfast* had been seriously damaged a month earlier.
See 21 November 1939, 4 December 1967.

1940 Nine Swordfish aircraft of 815 and 819 Sqns (*Illustrious*) sank two of an Italian convoy off Kerkenah Island, Tunisia (34.44N, 11.58E).

1941 Swordfish A/812 from *Ark Royal*, operating from Gibraltar, sank U-451 off the Rock (35.55N, 06.08W). First night sinking by aircraft and by land-based aircraft working on their own.

1941 Escort carrier *Audacity* sunk by U-751 500 miles W. of Cape Finisterre (44.00N, 20.00W), and *Deptford* and *Samphire* sank U-567 in Atlantic (44.02N, 20.10W). Convoy HG 76.

This convoy sailed from Gibraltar on 14 December, escorted by seventeen ships, including *Audacity* (ex-German line *Hannover* – the first escort carrier) and Cdr F.J. Walker's 36th Escort Group. They were attacked by nine U-boats, and by Focke-Wulf aircraft. Two merchant ships were sunk, together with the *Audacity* and an escort. However, four U-boats were sunk and two Focke-Wulfs were shot down. The relatively safe passage of the convoy showed how a well-trained escort group aided by air support could counter attacks by U-boats.

1941 River gunboat *Cicala* sunk by Japanese aircraft off Hong Kong.

1961 The fourth and final volume of the Cabinet Office history of Second World War maritime operations, *The War at Sea*, by Capt Stephen Roskill, published. It covers June 1944 to August 1945, from the Normandy invasion, through the victory over the U-boats in the Atlantic to British operations against Japan. In it he reflects on the failure in the 1930s to realise the importance of air power at sea and concludes that the priority given by the RN to battleships at the cost of carriers and seaborne aircraft was major error.
See 10 May 1954, 28 January 1957, 21 October 1961, 4 November 1982.

1983 *Fisgard*, Artificers' Training Establishment, Torpoint, training ceased. The last class of direct artificers to be trained at *Fisgard* entered 6 March 1983. DCI(RN) 214/83.
See 28 March 1868, 21 March 1983.

22 December

1779 Vice-Admiral Hon. Augustus John Hervey, third Earl of Bristol, died from 'gout of the stomach' at 6 St James's Square aged 55. He entered the Navy in the *Pembroke*, commanded by his uncle, the notoriously brutal Capt William Hervey, in May 1735. Although an unreformed 'Cassanova', Augustus was a professional officer who served under, and was well regarded by, Edward Hawke. Hervey, to his credit, was one of the handful of officers who remained loyal to Byng after the Minorca debacle in 1756 when others were rushing to distance themselves from 'a pariah shunned by all ambitious men' – David Erskine, *Augustus Hervey's Journal* xxiv.

See 19 May 1724, 14 March 1757, 10 July 1920.

1810 *Minotaur* lost off the Texel with 360 men.

1813 *Helicon* captured the French privateer *Revenant* 6 miles W. of Bolt Tail.

1836 Naval Instructors and Schoolmasters established by Order in Council, to be appointed by warrant.

See 30 April 1861, 6 April 1962, 6 July 1996.

1875 *Goliath*, former 80-gun second rate, reduced to training ship 'for pauper boys from workhouses', accidentally burned out in Medway.

1914 Battleship *Queen Elizabeth*, Beatty's flagship in the Grand Fleet from 1917 to the end of the First World War, commissioned at Portsmouth.

See 19 December 1941, 16 May 1948.

The Aircraft Carrier

The Royal Navy led the world in the development of naval aviation. The year 1914 came too soon in the development of the aeroplane for many real advances in tactical thinking to form within the Service. Before the operational lessons of the Great War could be examined the Royal Naval Air Service and the Army's Royal Flying Corps were amalgamated in 1918 to form the Royal Air Force. It proved a retrograde step. In the crucial years between the world wars the Admiralty had little influence on the types and designs of aircraft required for naval aviation. In 1939 the Fleet Air Arm was equipped with absurdly limited aircraft, far inferior to those in the Japanese and United States navies. The Royal Navy was, however, quick to learn the potential of air operations at sea; the Fleet Air Arm attack on Taranto was a visionary, bold and brilliantly staged operation from which other nations learned. British naval aviators performed splendidly with these old aeroplanes until more modern American aircraft became available. British aircraft carrier design, however, led the field and British carriers proved very robust, especially against Japanese kamikaze attack. After the war carriers became bigger, faster, and more complex to meet the requirements of operating fast jet aircraft and the Royal Navy led major technical advances – the angled flight deck, the steam catapult and the mirror (later projector) landing sight.

The aircraft carriers HMS *Illustrious* and *Eagle* in the Pedestal convoy to Malta in 1942. (*NMRN*)

The aircraft carrier – a mobile, well-found sovereign military base, independent of local political limitations and host nation support, of basing and over-flying rights – has given nations, especially the British, invaluable political and operational flexibility. The requirement of the Strategic Defence and Security Review of 2010 – the paying-off of HMS *Ark Royal* and the joint RN/RAF GR9 Harrier force – has narrowed Britain's defence options. The commissioning the new carriers, HMS *Queen Elizabeth* and *Prince of Wales*, may restore to the nation and the Royal Navy an invaluable political and military capability.

Left: Aircraft carrier HMS *Ark Royal* on operations in the Atlantic. (*RN*)

Below: The midships sections of the hull up to the hangar deck of the fleet carrier HMS *Queen Elizabeth*, the biggest warship ever built for the Royal Navy, coming together at BAE Systems Yard at Govan in February 2011. This will be floated round to Rosyth in late 2011 where components from six yards (Glasgow, Portsmouth, Appledore, Rosyth, Merseyside and Newcastle) are being assembled in dry dock. (*BAE Systems*)

1916 War Cabinet directed the establishment of a Fifth Sea Lord to be responsible for naval air services, 'contrary to the considered views of the Admiralty'.

See 23 October 1917, 8 May 1964.

1940 Fifteen Swordfish aircraft of 815 and 819 Sqns (*Illustrious*) bombed Tripoli.

1940 Destroyer *Hyperion* sunk by destroyer *Janus*, having been torpedoed by Italian submarine *Serpente* off Cape Bon (37.40N, 11.31E). Last of thirty-four destroyers lost in 1940.

1943 Old cruiser *Niobe* (German, ex-Yugoslav *Cattaro*), aground near Silba Island, in Adriatic, torpedoed by RN MTBs.

1956 Last British and French troops withdrawn from Suez. Prime Minister Eden resigned 9 January 1957.

See 25 July 1956, 1 and 6 November 1956.

23 December

1406 Earl of Somerset created first Lord High Admiral.

1787 HM Armed Transport *Bounty*, Lt William Bligh, sailed from Portsmouth for the South Pacific.

See 9 September 1754, 28 April 1789, 14 June 1789, 7 December 1817.

1796 *Minerve* captured the French privateer *Maria* 30 miles S.W. by W. of Cape Spartivento, Sardinia.

1796 *Polyphemus* captured the French *Justine* 90 miles to the westward of Cape Clear.

1805 The body of Vice-Admiral Viscount Nelson transferred from *Victory* at The Nore into Commissioner Grey's yacht *Chatham*, which had come from Sheerness, and carried up the Thames to Greenwich.

1812 *Phoebe* captured the American privateer *Hunter* 300 miles to the north-west of Corvo Island, Azores.

1858 *Pearl*'s Naval Brigade at Tulsipur.

1863 *Achilles* floated out of dry dock at Chatham Dockyard. The first iron warship to be built in a Royal Dockyard and the only British warship to have four masts. She carried the greatest area of canvas ever set in a warship.

See 26 April 1865.

1915 Start of naval operations on Lake Tanganyika, East Africa.

1917 Destroyers *Tornado*, *Torrent* and *Surprise* sunk by mines off Maas lightvessel.

1919 *Enterprise* launched at John Brown's. She was towed to Devonport Dockyard and completed

HMS *Achilles*, a broadside ironclad, building at Chatham in 1863. (*NMRN*)

The Queen Elizabeth-class battleship HMS *Valiant*, completed in February 1916, was present at Jutland and, following reconstruction at Portsmouth from March 1929 to December 1930, she commissioned for service in the Second Battle Squadron Atlantic Fleet (redesignated Home Fleet in March 1932) in which she was serving when photographed on 21 July 1934. Together with *Queen Elizabeth* she was seriously damaged in an Italian human torpedo attack at Alexandria on 19 December 1941. The Queen Elizabeths were the first oil-fired big ships in the Royal Navy and the first to mount 15-in guns. (*NMRN*)

(as and when the yard had spare capacity) in March 1926. She was designed to carry seven single CP 6-in guns but was completed with an experimental Mk XVII turret forward, a prototype of the 6-in Mk XXII mounting fitted as secondary armament in the battleships *Nelson* and *Rodney*. The first light cruiser to carry a twin 6-in gun turret.

1927 GC (ex-EGM): Stoker PO Herbert John Mahoney (*Taurus*) for gallantry in a boiler room explosion. (*Gazette* date.)

1940 An 'immense explosion' near Unicorn Gate, Portsmouth Dockyard, possibly caused by a crashing German aircraft with a full bomb load, destroyed several nearby streets. 'The dockyard wall held but there were 40 men in the yard wounded' – Admiral Sir Wiliam James, C-in-C Portsmouth.

See 12 and 24 August 1940, 5 December 1940, 10 January 1941, 10 March 1941, 17 April 1941.

1941 *Hasty* and *Hotspur* sank U-79 S. of Crete (32.15N, 25.19E). Convoy AT 5.

1943 Destroyer *Worcester* mined off Smith's Knoll, North Sea. Towed to Yarmouth with stern blown off: CTL. *Campbell* interrupted from picking up survivors by RAF attack.

See 16 February 1937.

1966 HM The Queen approved a new ensign for the Royal Australian Navy 'which will be flown as soon as the necessary flags have been manufactured'. Prime Minister Harold Holt announced: 'Australians have been proud to serve under the same ensign as the Royal Navy for more than half a century. But we have come to feel that it is now appropriate to adopt a flag which, while indicating our allegiance to the Crown, is distinctively the flag of the Royal Australian Navy.'

See 9 December 1950, 1 March 1967, 20 June 1968.

1967 The surveying ship *Dampier*, Cdr P.G.N. Cardno RN, homeward bound from Singapore to finally pay off after nineteen years' continuous service in the Far East, broke her starboard propeller shaft off Sierra Leone. Anxious to get home for Christmas, she hoisted five makeshift sails from awnings to give her an extra half a knot. With her progress closely reported by the national press, *Dampier* reached the lock entrance on the Medway with a few hours to spare before Chatham Dockyard shut down for Christmas. A finishing gun was fired by FO Medway, Vice-Admiral W.J. Parker, assisted by the Hydrographer of the Navy, Rear-Admiral Steve Ritchie.

See 25 October 1979.

24 December

1757 *Augusta* captured eight sail of a French convoy off Ile de la Petite Gonave, Haiti.

1777 Capt Cook discovered Christmas Island.

1789 *Guardian* (44), Capt Rion, struck an iceberg in S. Atlantic, en route for Australia. Captain and a skeleton crew stood by her and she drifted into Table Bay.

1798 Rear-Admiral Sir Horatio Nelson, having precipitated a French attack on Naples, embarked the Sicilian royal family in *Vanguard* (74) and sailed for Palermo, the second capital of the Kingdom of the Two Sicilies.

See 22 September 1798.

1805 *Loire* and *Egyptienne* captured the French *Libre* 21 miles S.S.W. of Ile d'Yeu.

1810 Boats of *Diana* destroyed the French *L'Elise* driven ashore to the northward of Tatihou.

1811 *St George* (98), Capt Daniel Oliver Guion, flag of Rear-Admiral Robert Carthew Reynolds, returning from the Baltic, wrecked in severe gale on the Danish coast near Ringkjobing. *Defence* (74), Capt David Atkins, in company, 'refused to part company without permission or order' and was also wrecked. The Admiral, both captains and fourteen lieutenants were among 1,391 men lost. A special Fleet subscription opened. *Hero* (74) lost in same gale following day. The worst British naval disaster of the French Revolutionary and Napoleonic Wars.

See 26/27 November 1703.

1814 Vice-Admiral Sir Samuel Hood died.

1814 The naval war of 1812 between Britain and the United States, 'Mr Maddison's War', ended with a peace agreement signed at Ghent on Christmas Eve. Before the news reached the theatre of war, the British attacked New Orleans on 8 January 1815. The last sea action was the capture of the USS *President*, Capt Stephen Decatur, on 15 January 1815.

See 18 June 1812, 4 January 1965.

1910 Cruiser *Hyacinth* dealt with arms-runner at Dubai. A retrospective clasp 'Persian Gulf 1909–14' was awarded on 10 August 1915, for the Naval General Service Medal.

1914 RAN asked to reinforce East African station: cruiser *Pioneer* detached and arrived 6 February 1915. Released to return August 1916, having fired many more shells at the enemy than any other Australian ship in First World War.

1917 RFA store carrier *Grive* foundered in North Sea having been torpedoed on 8th.

1917 First Lord of the Admiralty, Sir Eric Geddes, requested and received on Christmas Eve, the resignation of the First Sea Lord, Admiral Sir John Jellicoe. Succeeded by Admiral Sir Rosslyn Wemyss.

'A First Sea Lord had to have many of the talents of a politician to survive in this jungle of wily manoeuvres and clever debaters. Jellicoe, soft spoken, not forceful, not given to the parry and thrust of debate, incapable of manoeuvring, was out of his element' – Marder.

1941 Submarine H 31 supposed sunk, cause unknown, in the Bay of Biscay.

1941 Corvette *Salvia*, escorting Convoy TA5 from Tobruk to Alexandria, torpedoed by U-568 100 W. of Alexandria (31.46N, 28.00E). She had on board 100 POWs rescued from the China Navigation Co.'s steamer *Shuntien* torpedoed by U-559 the day before. No survivors; only wreckage found.

See 17 June 1934.

The trawler *Rolls Royce* swept her 100th mine, the first minesweeping trawler to score a century. In 1941 over 36 million tons of shipping went in and out of the Thames for the loss of about ½ per cent of the total.

1943 Destroyer *Hurricane* torpedoed by U-415 in Atlantic (45.10N, 22.05W): stable but immobilised, and sunk by *Watchman*. USS *Leary* sunk at the same time by U-275 and U-382. Operation Stonewall.

The second-class cruiser HMS *Aeolus* iced up on the China station, 1898. (*NMRN*)

1944 Minesweeper *Clayoquot* (RCN) sunk by U-806 off Halifax (44.30N, 63.20W).

1944 Frigate *Dakins* mined N.W. of Ostend. Flooded forward but limped home: CTL.

1954 Monitor *Abercrombie* arrived at Wards, Barrow, for breaking-up.
See 19 July 1965.

1957 The small Naval Party employed on Christmas Island in support of British nuclear weapon tests, NP 2512 and NP 5555, named HMS *Resolution*, received greetings from the Admiralty: 'Their Lordships wish to convey Their appreciation to the officers and men of HMS *Resolution* of their work on Christmas Island on this the 180th anniversary of the discovery of the island by Captain Cook in HMS *Resolution*.'
See 3 October 1952, 16 May 1956.

1981 Last service in Chatham Dockyard church.

2009 Capt Brian Young RN, naval aviator, captain of the destroyer *Antrim* and CTG 317.9 at the capture of South Georgia in 1982, died aged 79: 'May it please Her Majesty that the White Ensign flies alongside the Union Flag on South Georgia. God save the Queen.' Operation Paraquet.
See 26 April 1982.

25 December

1652 Articles of War first formulated, as 'Articles and Orders of War'.

1666 *Warspite, Jersey, Diamond, St Patrick, Nightingale*, and *Oxford* captured the Dutch *Cleen Harderwijk, Leijden* and *Els* off the Texel.

1781 *Agamemnon* captured five sail of a French convoy 130 miles S.W. of Ushant.

1797 *Niger* captured the French privateer *Delphine* 6 miles S.W. by W. of Bolt Head.

1798 *Vanguard* (74), flag of Rear-Admiral Sir Horatio Nelson, arrived at Palermo with the Sicilian royal family after a passage in heavy weather from Naples.

See 24 December 1798.

1809 *Weazle* captured the French privateer *Eole* off Palmas Bay, Sardinia.

1811 *Hero* (74), Capt James Newman, returning to Britain with a convoy from Gothenburg, wrecked in violent gale on the Haak Sands off the Texel on the Dutch coast. The third major warship lost in the same gale. Only twelve survived from 530. *Grasshopper* (18), Cdr Henry Fanshawe, in company, struck ground but drove over the bank and forced to surrender.

See 26/27 November 1703, 24 December 1811.

1872 Anchor cable of ironclad *Northumberland* parted in Funchal Roads and she was impaled on ram bow of *Hercules*.

1894 HM gunboat *Magpie*, Lt-Cdr Herbert King-Hall RN, at Delagoa Bay, South Africa:

'On Christmas Day we had a poor fellow, an able seaman, lying ill in his hammock under the forecastle, and clearly dying. As everyone knows, the day is kept as one of jollity on board a man-of-war, with songs and merriment, an allowance of beer, the mess deck decorated, and so on. I gave directions, which the whole ship's company willingly obeyed, that the poor invalid must not be disturbed by songs, and the afternoon was spent quietly. Hearing of this, the poor fellow urged that the singing would give him pleasure, and begged it should not be stopped. So he passed away that evening with the strains of the old, familiar songs in his ears, speeding his soul to Fiddler's Green, the paradise of all good sailors.' – Admiral Sir Herbert King-Hall, *Naval Memories and Traditions*, (London, 1926) p.152.

1902 The Selborne Scheme announced under which all new entry RN and RM cadets from September 1903 would undergo common early training. All officers would get a general knowledge of the different branches in a ship, particularly of the engineering and technical systems, before they specialised at age 22. The aim to close the social chasm between 'the sacred priesthood of Executive NOs' and engineer officers. RM officers reverted to specialist military training in 1906.

1914 British naval seaplane attack on Cuxhaven believed erroneously to be a Zeppelin base. The world's first-ever carrier air strike, the raid was mounted from the converted cross-Channel ferries *Riviera, Empress* and *Engadine* from N. of Heligoland. Zeppelin sheds could not be found (they were at Tondern in Schleswig Holstein) and bombs dropped on alternative targets. The Germans responded with Zeppelin and seaplane attacks on British supporting surface and submarine forces – the first air-sea action in history. Zeppelin L6 and two seaplanes from Borkum bombed the *Empress* – the first ever air attacks on a British warship – and Zeppelin L5 bombed RN submarine E 11. The first major encounter between warships and aircraft and a forerunner of the great carrier-based naval battles of the future. On the way back to Harwich, Cdre Reginald Tyrwhitt signalled: 'I wish all ships a Merry Christmas.'

See 22 September 1914, 8 October 1914, 21 November 1914, 19 July 1918.

1916 Cdre Cecil Foley 'Black' Lambert, lately Fourth Sea Lord, succeeded Cdre William 'Barge' Goodenough in command of the Second Light Cruiser Squadron in *Southampton*.

'The Commodore, who had a face of the leather sea-boot type, arrived on board on a Christmas morning and decided to inspect the ship's company forthwith. He first visited the boys' division, in charge of Lieutenant [later Admiral Sir] Harold Burrough, who were drawn up on the quarter-deck. Giving the boys a ferocious look which caused them to sway in their ranks, he growled "I wish the boys a merry Christmas!" . . . Reaching my division the new Commodore went down the ranks and, turning to me, said "What's your tally?"

"King-Hall, Sir!"

"Well, I don't like the look of your face! Happy Christmas to you!"'

– Cdr Stephen King-Hall (nephew of Sir Herbert of 25 December 1894), in *My Naval Life*, p.145.

1917 *Penshurst* (Q 7) torpedoed by U-110 in the entrance to the Bristol Channel (51.32N, 05.48W).

1917 PC 56 rammed and sank U-87 in Irish Sea (52.56N, 05.07W), with *Buttercup*.

1940 Force H, which returned to Gibraltar on Christmas Eve after operations in the western Mediterranean, looked forward to Christmas in harbour. The flagship's band in the battle-cruiser *Renown* struck up Christmas carols and Admiral Somerville, making the customary rounds of the mess decks, jollied up the men with congratulations about being in harbour for Christmas, especially in such filthy weather. A signal from the Admiralty in the forenoon watch changed all that. Force H was ordered to raise steam with all despatch and sail to cover Convoy WS 5A out in the Atlantic which had been intercepted by the German heavy cruiser *Hipper*. Two hours later, as Somerville's ships cleared the breakwater with some destroyer officers on the bridges seen from the flagship to be still wearing paper hats, they were cheered by the ships' companies of units remaining in harbour. The *Hipper* was driven off by the heavy cruisers *Berwick* and *Bonaventure* who were escorting the convoy.

1941 Hong Kong surrendered to Japanese forces. River gunboat *Robin* scuttled to avoid capture.

1942 Submarine P 48 sunk by the Italian TB *Ardente* off Bizerta (37.17N, 10.32E).

A mess deck decorated for Christmas. (*NMRN*)

1962 'A messing supplement of 75 per cent of the basic daily rate of mess allowance may be claimed for all officers and ratings actually fed in Mess on Christmas Day in HM Ships and Fleet Establishments at home and abroad from Christmas 1962.' – AFO 2280/62.

1965 The 500th day of patrol work by the Royal Navy in Malaysian waters since the start of Indonesian 'Confrontation'. During 1965 British warships steamed 1 million miles and killed or captured 1,400 Indonesian raiders for the loss of two officers killed and eleven men injured.

1980 Prof. Arthur Marder, historian of the Royal Navy in the Fisher era, died at Santa Barbara, California. On completion of his remarkable five-volume work, *From the Dreadnought to Scapa Flow*, in 1970 he received a formal letter from the Admiralty congratulating him on his 'work of outstanding scholarship, illuminated by both judgement and humanity and a deep understanding of this important period in the Navy's history' and expressing Their Lordships' 'warm appreciation of the service which . . . you have thereby rendered to the Navy'. His Honorary CBE was for services to British naval history. A great American.

1991 The Red Flag was hauled down at the Kremlin in Moscow; end of the Soviet Union and the end of the Cold War.

See 5 March 1946.

2007 Vice-Admiral Sir George Vallings died aged 75: yachtsman, commanded destroyer *Defender* 1967 and 2nd Frigate Squadron in *Apollo* 1977–8, COMCLYDE 1980–2, FO Gibraltar 1983–5 and FOSNI.

See 3 April 1974.

26 December

1767 Catherine Nelson, wife of the Revd Edmund Nelson of Burnham Thorpe, died aged 42 leaving eight children, including Horatio (9).

1799 *Viper* captured the French privateer *Furet* off Dodman Point.

1800 Cdre William Locker, Lieutenant Governor of Greenwich Hospital and veteran of Hawke's victory at Quiberon Bay in 1759, died. Nelson served under Locker in the frigate *Lowestoffe* during the War of American Independence and became his protégé; he thought him 'a man whom to know was to love, and those who only heard of him honoured'. Nelson attended the funeral at Addington, Kent, 'in my own carriage'.

Vice-Admiral Sir Bruce Fraser, *c.* 1940. He was created Admiral of the Fleet in October 1948. (*NMRN*)

1807 *Seine* captured the French privateer *Sibylle* 100 miles to the south-west of the Scilly Isles.

1807 Sir Samuel Hood and General Beresford took Madeira.

1811 Boats of *Volontaire* cut out the French privateer *Décidée* at Palamos.

1842 Second and Third Class Engineers given similar uniform to First but with subtly different buttons at the collar.

See 21 December 1841.

1851 Start of final reduction of Lagos, completed by 29th.

1857 Naval Brigade from wood screw corvette *Pearl* in action at Battle of Sohanpur.

1915 Gunboats *Mimi* and *Toutou* captured the German *Kingani* on Lake Tanganyika, East Africa. German vessel salvaged and taken into the Service as *Fifi*.

1915 E 6 mined and sunk in North Sea.

1918 Russian naval raid on British naval anchorage at Reval (Tallinn). Destroyer *Spartak*, carrying F.F. Raskolnikov, 'political head of the Bolshevik Admiralty', lost her screws and rudder on the Divel shoal and surrendered to HM destroyer *Wakeful*. Raskolnikov was later found hidden under twelve bags of potatoes. Destroyer *Avtroil*, chased by light cruisers *Calypso* (Capt B.S. Thesiger RN, SNO) and *Caradoc*, surrendered next day. The *Spartak* and *Avtroil* entered the Estonian Navy as *Wambola* and *Lennuk* respectively. A sad footnote: forty Russian crew members were executed by the Estonians on Nargen Island in February 1919.

See 22 November 1918.

1927 Destroyer *Keppel* sailed from Shanghai to protect British interests in Chingwangtao.

1939 Submarine *Triumph* severely damaged by German mine in North Sea (56.44N, 05.00E); 18ft of fore end blown off.

1941 Second Lofoten raid. Ships: *Arethusa, Somali, Bedouin, Ashanti, Eskimo,* with *Prins Albert* (Commandos).

1942 Destroyers *Hesperus* and *Vanessa* sank U-357 in N.W. Approaches (57.10N, 15.40W). Convoy HX 219.

1943 Admiral Sir Bruce Fraser (*Duke of York*) sank the German battlecruiser *Scharnhorst* off North Cape (72.16N, 28.41E). Admiralty signalled, 'Grand. Well Done.' Fraser was ennobled at the end of the war and, 'with the express permission of King Haakon of Norway', took the title Lord Fraser of North Cape. Ships: *Belfast, Duke of York, Jamaica, Matchless, Musketeer, Norfolk, Opportune, Saumarez, Savage, Scorpion, Sheffield, Stord* (Nor), *Virago.*
Battle Honour: North Cape 1943.
See 3 November 1914.

The battleship *Duke of York, Jamaica* and four destroyers provided a close cover for convoys JW 55B and RA 55A, with three cruisers (*Belfast, Norfolk* and *Sheffield*) acting as a further cover. At dusk on Christmas Day, the German battlecruiser *Scharnhorst* and five destroyers sailed from Norway. Heavy seas caused the German destroyers to fall astern, and they never rejoined the battlecruiser. The three cruisers detected *Scharnhorst* on radar at 0840 on Boxing Day. They engaged, and *Scharnhorst* turned away at 30 knots. The cruisers followed, using radar, and *Duke of York* started to close at 24 knots in a gale. The cruisers again opened fire at 1205 when *Scharnhorst* reapproached the convoy. *Norfolk* was hit by *Scharnhorst*, but the battlecruiser turned for her base. *Duke of York* intercepted her, and hit her on 'A' turret with her first salvo of 14-in shells. The *Scharnhorst* was hit by at least thirteen 14-in shells, twelve 8-in shells, and eleven torpedoes, before sinking. There were only thirty-six survivors. The gallant German ship was toasted in the British flagship.

Admiral Sir Bruce Fraser

As Third Sea Lord and Controller from March 1939 to May 1942, Fraser was responsible for the expansion of the Royal Navy. In 1943 he became C-in-C of the Home Fleet, with responsibility for protection of Russian convoys. He refused the post of First Sea Lord in September 1943, commenting that Cunningham would be a more appropriate choice. When *Scharnhorst* sailed to attack a convoy in the winter of 1943, Fraser from his flagship *Duke of York* directed the forces which crippled and sank her by torpedo attack. In 1944 he became C-in-C Eastern Fleet and then C-in-C of the British Pacific Fleet which played a vital part in the final defeat of Japanese forces. He signed the Japanese surrender document on behalf of Britain on board USS *Missouri.*

1944 Frigate *Capel* sunk by U-486 off Cape de la Hogue, Normandy (49.50N, 01.41W): capsized slowly. *Affleck* also torpedoed by U-486; made her way home but CTL.

1945 Admiral of the Fleet Lord Keyes of Zeebrugge died. He was buried in the Zeebrugge part of Dover Cemetery. His son, Lt-Col Geoffrey Keyes, VC, was killed in a raid on Rommel's HQ in Libya in November 1941. His peerage was inherited by his younger son, then a lieutenant, RN.
See 23 April 1918, 27 April 1950.

1967 Gunnery Officer, Rear-Admiral Michael Pollock, Flag Officer Second-in-Command Western Fleet, promoted vice-admiral and appointed Flag Officer Submarines.
See 1 March 1974, 27 September 2006.

27 December

1707 *Ludlow Castle* captured the French *Nightingale* off the Long Sand.

1805 Body of Lord Nelson laid in Painted Hall of Greenwich Hospital.

1807 *Resistance* captured the French privateer *Aigle* off the Owers.

1831 *Beagle* sailed on five-year circumnavigation carrying Charles Darwin, subsequently author of *On the Origin of Species*.

1851 Capture of Lagos: *Bloodhound* and *Teazer*.

1914 Destroyer *Success* wrecked off Fife Ness.

1939 Destroyer *Wishart* intercepted the German *Glücksberg* which ran herself ashore near Chipiona light, south-west Spain.

1940 GC: Lt Robert Selby Armitage, RNVR, Sub-Lt (Sp) Richard Valentine Moore, RNVR, and Sub-Lt (Sp) John Herbert Babington, RNVR. (*Gazette* date.) All for bomb and mine disposal.

1941 Raid on Vaagsø, Norway. Operation Archery. Ships: *Kenya, Chiddingfold, Offa, Onslow, Oribi, Tuna, Prince Charles, Prince Leopold*. Troops: 3 Cdo, two troops of 12 Cdo, and Norwegian troops. RAF: seven Hampden aircraft.

1942 Corvettes *Battleford, Chilliwack, Napanee* and *St Laurent* (all RCN) sank U-356 in Atlantic (45.30N, 25.40W). Convoy ONS 15.

1942 Prime Minister Churchill, having received a list of proposed submarine names, told the First Sea Lord, Dudley Pound: 'These names for submarines are certainly much better than the numbers. Please see my suggestions. I have no doubt a little more thought, prompted by the dictionary, would make other improvements possible. Now do please get on with it, and let them be given their names in the next fortnight.' The first thirty-two names were published in CAFO 146/01 the next month.

See 3 July 1902, 24 September 1926, 5 November 1942, 19 December 1942, 28 January 1943.

A diver on HMS *Camperdown* in the 1890s. (*NMRN*)

The battlecruiser HMS *Tiger* towards the end of her career, 1928. (*NMRN W&L 111A*)

1944 Corvette *St Thomas* (RCN) sank U-877 in Atlantic (46.25N, 36.38W). Convoy HX 327.

1994 Rear-Admiral Godfrey Place, who gained his VC for the X-craft attack on *Tirpitz* in 1943, died aged 73. After two years of captivity he trained as a pilot and served in the carrier *Glory* during the Korean War.

See 22 September 1943.

2006 The first British military team to make a return visit to the South Pole overland arrived at 90 degrees S. Capt Sean Chapple RM (leader), Surg Lt-Cdr Andy Brown RN, Maj. Paul Mattin RM and Mne Craig Hunter had made a 700-mile trek in forty-four days from the Patriot Hills unaided by dogs or vehicles. The Union Flag, White Ensign, RM Corps flag and a replica of Capt Scott's standard were hoisted.

See 17 May 2000, 22 May 2003, 1 January 2007.

The Majestic-class battleship HMS *Hannibal*, launched in April 1896, was the heaviest warship ever built at Pembroke Dockyard. See photograph of her fitting out on p.243. Her armament of four 12-in and twelve 6-in guns became the standard fit for several succeeding capital ship classes. (*Author*)

28 DECEMBER

1756 Court martial of Admiral Byng began, and lasted twenty-nine days. On 27 January he was found guilty and sentenced 'to be shot to death; but since the Court do not believe that his misconduct arose either from cowardice or disaffection, he is recommended for mercy'.
Alas, see 14 March 1757.

1793 *Blanche* captured the French *Sans-Culotte* 6 miles W. by S. of Guave Island (Goyave Islets).

1805 *Favourite* captured the French privateer *Général Blanchard* off the mouth of the Pongo River.

1814 *Leander, Newcastle* and *Acasta* captured the American privateer *Prince de Neufchâtel* 450 miles S.E. by E. of Sable Island.

1851 The second attempt to unseat the 'troublesome and intractable' King Cocioco of Lagos in W. Africa, active in the slave trade. Cdre Henry Bruce sent a force under Capt Lewis Tobias Jones of *Sampson* (6), paddle, and Capt Henry Lyster of the flagship *Penelope* (16), paddle, with *Bloodhound*, iron paddle steamer; *Teazer* (3), screw; *Sealark* (8) and boats from *Penelope, Samson, Volcano* and *Waterwitch*, which entered the river on 23 December to attack Lagos. After several days of stiff opposition and significant casualties, Lagos was taken on 28 December. Cocioco fled to the woods and the rightful ruler, Akitoye, installed as King.
See 25 November 1851.

1857 Admiral Sir Michael Seymour bombarded Canton in Second Chinese War. Capt W. Thornton Bate wrote home that night, after being asked at a council of war for his advice on its assault, that he had told the soldiers, 'I hold it as a general leading principle that there is nothing the Navy cannot do'. Alas, he was killed next day, living up to his precept which was used as a dedication of 'Seamanship and its associated duties in the Royal Navy' in 1860, and later displayed at Fisher's insistence at Osborne.

1922 *Rodney* and *Nelson* laid down. Nicknamed the Cherry Trees because they were cut down by Washington (naval) Treaty. Only British battleships to carry main armament in triple turrets and only British ships to mount 16-in guns.

1939 Battleship *Barham* torpedoed by U-30 north of Hebrides (58.47N, 08.05W).
See 25 November 1941.

1941 Destroyer *Kipling* sank U-75 off Mersa Matruh (31.50N, 26.40E).

1943 Light cruisers *Enterprise* and *Glasgow* engaged and pursued ten German destroyers 270 miles S.W. of Ushant (46.33N, 12.30W). German ships sunk: T-25, T-26, Z-27.

HMS *Nelson* (1925). *(NMRN)*

Admiral John Byng (1704–1757)

Byng's loss of Minorca was felt as a national disgrace. This caricature shows the British lion with one paw cut off, and the French cockerel strutting over the Union Flag. (*NMRN 2002/1*)

During the Seven Years War a French force attacked Minorca in order to divide British naval forces and to distract some of them from Canada. Vice-Admiral John Byng, with ten ships of the line, was sent to the Mediterranean to guard Minorca. Having picked up three more ships at Gibraltar, he remained there longer than necessary, arriving off the island on 17 May 1756 to discover that French troops had invested Port Mahon, the last British stronghold there. Action was joined on the 20th with the French fleet, but in light winds the battle was indecisive. On 24 May at a Council of War he concluded that it was not practical for the fleet to relieve Port Mahon and that he should guard Gibraltar. Port Mahon surrendered on 28 June. Admiral Byng was court martialled, and though acquitted of cowardice was found guilty of dereliction of duty. This was also a capital charge and despite the recommendation of the Court he was shot on the quarterdeck of *Monarch*.

See 20 May 1756, 14 March 1757.

Surface Action, 1943

Two groups of enemy destroyers sailed from France to cover the arrival of the blockade runner *Alsterufer*. She was sunk on 27th, and the cruisers *Glasgow* and *Enterprise* were dispatched to intercept the ten German destroyers. At 1100 on 28th the Germans joined forces and turned back for France. The cruisers were proceeding at 28 knots in rough weather and opened fire on the destroyers at 18,000yd at 1335. The Germans retaliated with torpedoes and Luftwaffe-launched glider bombs, but did no damage. The German forces then split, and the cruisers increased to 30 knots and by 1600 had sunk the Z-27, T-25 and T-26. Because the *Glasgow* was low on ammunition and the *Enterprise* was suffering from defects, the cruisers did not chase the second enemy force, but retired to Plymouth, which they reached safely on the evening of 29th, despite further enemy air attacks.

1975 Third Cod War. The first collision of the 'War' between Icelandic Gunboat Thor and frigate Andromeda; fifty-six collisions were to follow, many severe enough to force the frigates to return to the UK.

See 31 August 1958.

One of the last of the numerous Bar-class boom defence vessels was HMS *Barbecue*, launched at Ardrossan Dockyard in 1944. She was still in service in 1970, one of the last coal-fired vessels in the Fleet. The Bar boats were latterly civilian-manned and part of the Royal Maritime Auxiliary Service. (*Author*)

29 DECEMBER

1669 *Mary Rose* drove off seven Algerine pirates between Sali and Tangier, while escorting a convoy.
Battle Honour: The Seven Algerines 1669.

1709 *Pembroke* and *Falcon* taken by three French ships between Toulon and Corsica.

1758 Capture of Gorée by Cdre the Hon. Augustus Keppel (*Torbay*) and Lt-Col Worge. Ships: *Dunkirk, Fougueux, Nassau, Torbay*. 50s and smaller: *Experiment, Prince Edward, Roman Emperor, Saltash*. Bombs: *Firedrake, Furnace*. Troops: Royal Artillery.

1797 *Anson* recaptured the French *Daphné* off Arcachon, south of Bordeaux.

1807 *Anson* (44), Capt Charles Lydiard, part of the Channel Fleet blockading Brest, ran for Falmouth in a S.W. gale but made the wrong side of the Lizard and, having dragged her anchors, was embayed in Mounts Bay, and was run ashore on sand at Porthleven beach near Helston, broached-to and broke up. Over 250 saved, 60 lost. Capt Lydiard's body was found on New Year's Day. Court martial in Plymouth 6 January 1808 honourably acquitted surviving officers but Master admonished.

1812 *Royalist* captured the French privateer *La Ruse* 6 miles W. of Dungeness.

1812 *Java* (36) taken by the American *Constitution* (44) 30 miles E. of Bahia, Brazil.

1837 Cdr Andrew Drew cut out and destroyed the pirate steamer *Caroline* by sending her over Niagara Falls.

1857 British and French forces occupied Canton. Ships: *Actaeon, Coromandel, Sans Pareil*. French: *Capricieuse, Némésis*. Death of Capt W.T. Bate RN.
See 28 December 1857.

1860 *Warrior*, first British seagoing ironclad, launched at Blackwall. Became tender to *Vernon*, reduced to fuelling hulk at Pembroke Dock and subsequently restored at Hartlepool. Returned to Portsmouth as '*Warrior 1860*' on 16 June 1987.

1860 Naval Brigade of wood screw corvette *Pelorus* at Kairau, New Zealand.

1861 Steam line of battleship *Conqueror*, on passage from Port Royal, Jamaica, to Bermuda, wrecked on Rum Cay in The Bahamas. No loss of life.

HMS *Warrior* (1860). (*NMRN*)

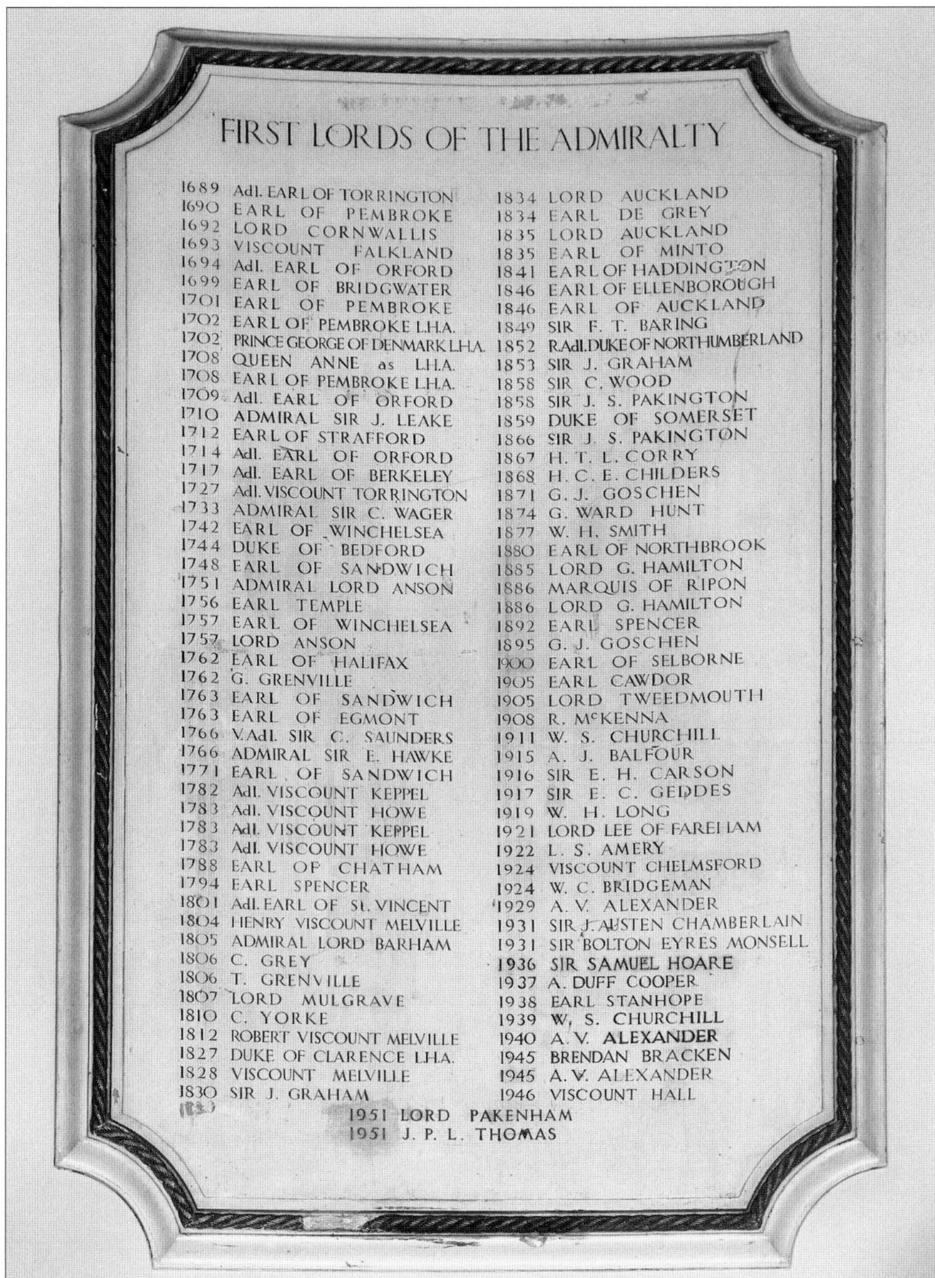

A plaque in Admiralty House, Whitehall, listing the First Lords of the Admiralty from Admiral the Earl of Torrington in 1689 to Mr J.P.L. Thomas (Viscount Cilcennin) in 1951. There were four further incumbents, Viscount Hailsham 1956–7 (ex-Rifle Bde), the Earl of Selkirk 1957–9 (ex-RAAF), Lord Carrington 1959–63 (ex-Grenadier Guards) and the Earl Jellicoe 1963–4 (ex-Coldstream Guards and SAS) who became Minister of Defence (Royal Navy) when the Admiralty went out of commission. (*Crown Copyright. MOD Art Collection*)

Court martial on board HMS *Terror* at Bermuda 8–15 February 1862 acquitted Capt Edward Southwell Sotheby but the Admiralty responded: 'It appears to their Lordships that had the ordinary and natural precaution been adopted by making a tack to the south-east, before the ship could by possibility have been swept upon the coral reefs of Rum Cay, the country would not have had to deplore the loss of one of the finest line-of-battleships in Her Majesty's Service; and my Lords consider Captain Sotheby to have been highly culpable in not having taken that precaution'. QRs amended: 'The captain is responsible for the safe conducting and steering of the ship.'

1915 Durazzo raided by Austrian light forces which were brought to action but escaped. Ships: *Dartmouth, Weymouth*. Italian: *Quarto, Nino Bixio, Abba, Nievo, Pilo, Mosto*.

1916 *Ludlow*, paddle minesweeper, mined off Shipwash lightvessel.

1917 GC (ex-AM): Deckhand J.G. Stanners, RNR, for fighting fire in magazine, ML 289.

1922 Empire Gallantry Medal (EGM) instituted: 126 awarded, 11 to naval personnel, before subsumed by George Cross by Royal Warrant in September 1940.

1944 Minesweeper *Ready* recovered Biber No. 90 – a one-man submarine – 45 miles off Dover. The first recovered and now in the Imperial War Museum.

30 December

1756 Capture of Fort Budge-Budge, Calcutta. Ships: *Bridgewater, Kent, Kingfisher, Salisbury, Tiger.*

1778 Capture of St Lucia by Admiral Hon. Samuel Barrington and General Grant. Ships: *Boyne, Nonsuch, Preston, Prince of Wales, Centurion, Isis, St Albans*. Frigates: *Ariadne, Aurora, Carcass, Pearl, Venus*. War of American Independence.

See 15 December 1778, 16 August 1800.

1780 *Bellona* captured the Dutch *Princess Carolina* off the Goodwin Sands.

1820 Bombardment and destruction of the defences of Mocha. Ships: *Topaze* and *Antelope, Benares, Thames* (all Bombay Marine).

1893 *Havock* commissioned. First TBD.

1917 Destoyer *Attack* torpedoed by UC-34 off Alexandria.

1941 Light cruiser *Ajax* and river gunboat *Aphis* bombarded Bardia.

1942 Decoy ship *Fidelity* torpedoed by U-435 in convoy ONS 154.

1943 A long-lived warship. Light fleet carrier *Venerable* launched at Cammell Laird, Birkenhead. She was commissioned on 17 January 1945 and joined the British Pacific Fleet and engaged Japanese forces off Hong Kong two weeks after VJ-Day. Paid off 1947 and sold to Dutch government. Served as Hr Ms *Karel Doorman* until sold to Argentina in 1968. As the *Vienticinco de Mayo*, with Super Etendard embarked, she was a factor in the Falklands War in 1982 but was kept out

HMS *Havock* (1893). The first Royal Naval destroyer. She could make 26 knots with her triple expansion engines and locomotive-type boilers. She was sold and broken up in 1912. (*NMRN*)

The Victorian Navy. HMS *Monarch*, photographed here in Milford Haven, was (with HMS *Captain*), the first seagoing capital ship in British naval history to be armed on the centre line rather than on the broadside. She was also the first British warship to carry a 12-in gun. The masted, single screw *Monarch* was 'the legitimate pride of the British service and the openly expressed admiration of those under foreign flags' – Ballard. (*Author*)

of harm's way. Still in service fifty years after first commissioning.

Convoy JW 51B, 1942–3

The convoy sailed for Russia on 22 December, the escort being led by Capt R. St V. Sherbrooke in *Onslow*. On 28 December a gale scattered the convoy, and the next few days were spent gathering the ships together again. Two cruisers (*Sheffield* and *Jamaica*) were covering the convoy after delivering convoy JW 51A. On 31st, the German heavy cruiser *Hipper* was sighted, and the destroyer escort beat her off using smoke and gunfire, though the *Onslow* was badly hit and her captain severely wounded. The German pocket battleship *Lützow* then attacked the convoy from a different direction, while *Hipper* reapproached. The destroyers made a torpedo attack, which turned the *Hipper* away and into the fire of the two covering cruisers which were closing at speed. The destroyers then turned *Lützow* away. Five destroyers had held a pocket battleship, a heavy cruiser and six large destroyers at bay for three hours, until two light cruisers arrived and drove them off.

1944 Wellington L/407 (RCAF) sank U-772 in Channel (50.05N, 02.31W).

31 December

1666 *Adventure* fought three Flushing men-of-war in the English Channel.

1796 *Polyphemus* captured the French *Tartu* 140 miles W. of Cape Clear.

1811 *Egeria* captured the Danish privateer *Alvor* 80 miles E. of St Abbs Head.

1813 *Venerable* captured the French privateer *Jason* 760 miles N.E. of Madeira.

1823 Dock renamed Devonport.

1847 Last signal to Spithead from Admiralty by Semaphore; electric telegraph in service.

1861 Boats of *Falcon* with *Dover*, first RN iron vessel, destroyed four towns up the Rokel River, Sierra Leone. Operations lasted four days.

1915 Armoured cruiser *Natal*, 2nd CS, Grand Fleet, destroyed by ammunition explosion at 1530 in Cromarty Firth; 404 men lost and 7 women and 3 children, visiting the Wardroom for lunch and a cinema show.

See 26 November 1914, 9 July 1917.

1915 RNR and RNVR officers to wear gold lace, and not braid, but narrower stripes than RN.

1942 VC: Capt Robert St Vincent Sherbrooke (*Onslow*) in defence of convoy JW 51B (fourteen ships) against *Lützow*, *Admiral Hipper* and six destroyers 140 miles N.N.E. of North Cape (73.18N, 30.06E).

Battle Honour: Barents Sea 1942.

Close escort: *Achates,* Bramble,* Hyderabad, Northern Gem, Obdurate, Obedient, Onslow, Oribi, Orwell, Rhododendron*. Force R: *Sheffield* (Rear-Admiral R.L. Burnett), *Jamaica*. German casualties: *Friedrich Eckholdt* (sunk by *Sheffield*), *Admiral Hipper* (damaged).

*Sunk.

Achates was last of forty-six destroyers lost in 1942.

1943 Minesweeper *Clacton* mined and sunk off east coast of Corsica.

1950 Admiral Ronald Hopwood, author, poet and gunnery officer, died. Flag Captain to Vice-Admiral Jellicoe in the *Prince of Wales* and *Hercules* 1910–12 but remembered for his naval poems steeped in the traditions of the Service, especially *The Laws of the Navy* published about 1895 when a lieutenant:

Now these are the laws of the Navy,
Unwritten and varied they be;
And he that is wise will observe them,
Going down in his ship to the sea;
As naught may outrun the destroyer,
Even so with the law and its grip,
For the strength of the ship is the Service,
And the strength of the Service the ship.

1959 RN Armament Depot, Isle of Grain, closed down. AFO 2883/59.

1959 C-in-C Home Fleet, Admiral Sir William Davis, hauled down his flag in the destroyer depot ship *Tyne* at Portsmouth and hoisted it ashore at Northwood on 1 January 1960. COF remained in *Tyne*. 'That the No. 1 operational control of the Royal Navy should be on the fringe of the countryside puzzles some people; that it should be in the bowels of the earth appals others.' – *The Times*.

See 6 April 1964, 29 October 1987.

1966 The SH 3D A/S helicopter due to enter service with the Royal Navy in 1969 is to be called the Sea King. DCI(RN) 1648/66.

1974 *Andrew*, Lt-Cdr Paul Hoddinott RN, the oldest submarine in the Royal Navy and the last armed with a deck gun, paid off. The boat fired her gun for the last time earlier in the month. She was launched at Vickers Armstrong, Barrow, on 6 April 1946 and was the last of forty-six A-class boats ordered during the war of which sixteen were completed. *Andrew* was later fitted with a Snort (*Schnorkel*) mast and she made the first submerged transit of the Atlantic by a RN submarine, completing the 2,500 nautical miles passage from Bermuda and surfacing in the English Channel on 1 June 1953, the eve of the Coronation, in time to share the glory with news of the British

HMS *Natal* (1905), a Warrior-class armoured cruiser of 13,550 tons. (*NMRN*)

ascent of Everest. She arrived at Davies and Cairn, Plymouth, 4 May 1977 for breaking up.

See 27 May 1911, 31 August 1944, 17 April 1951, 29 August 1969, 3 December 1974.

1983 The RN Oil Fuel Depots at Falmouth and Pembroke Dock closed. DCI(RN) 123/84.

See 31 March 1977, 31 March 1978, 12 November 1982.

1984 The MVO (Fourth Class) redesignated LVO (Lieutenant of the Royal Victorian Order), to take precedence immediately before OBE – DCI(Joint) 25 January 1985.

1999 Frigate *Westminster*, anchored off Greenwich, heralded the New Year and the (popularly accepted start of) the Third Millennium.

2003 NATO appointment of Allied C-in-C Eastern Atlantic (CINCEASTLANT) abolished. First established at Northwood in 1952. The last CINCEASTLANT was Admiral Sir Jonathon Band.

See 2 June 1994, 21 February 1952.

ABBREVIATIONS

2SL/CNH Second Sea Lord and C-in-C Naval Home Command
AB Able Seaman
A/C Aircraft
ACCHAN Allied Command Channel
ACM Air Chief Marshal
ACNS Assistant Chief of Naval Staff
ACR Admiral Commanding Reserves
ADORS [1.3.1952]
AFO Admiralty Fleet Order
AM Albert Medal/Air Marshal
AMC Armed Merchant Cruiser
AMP Assisted Maintenance Period
AOA Amphibious Objective Area
APT(South) Atlantic Patrol Ship (South)
A/S Anti-submarine
ASDIC Allied Submarine Detection Investigation Committee
ASR Air Sea Rescue
ASWE Admiralty Surface Weapons Establishment
AT/FP Anti-Terrorist/Force Protection
ATG Amphibious Task Group
AVGAS Aviation Gasoline
AWO Admiralty Weekly Orders
AWOL Absent Without Leave
BAD British Admiralty Delegation (Washington)
BCF Battle Cruiser Force/Fleet
BCS Battle Cruiser Squadron
BEM British Empire Medal
Ben. Mar. Bengal Marine
bh Battle Honour
bm builder's measurement
BOAC British Overseas Airways Corporation
BofE Board of Enquiry
BPF British Pacific Fleet
BR Book of Reference, RN official publication
BRNCD Britannia Royal Naval College, Dartmouth
BS Battleship or Battle Squadron
BST British Summer Time
B/U Broken up
BYMS British Yard Mine Sweeper
BZ 'Well done.'
CAFO Confidential Admiralty Fleet Order
CAG Carrier Air Group
CAM Catapult Aircraft Merchantman
CAP Combat Air Patrol
CAS Chief of the Air Staff
CB Companion of the Order of the Bath
CBs Confidential Books
CBF Commander British Forces
Cdo Commando
Cdr Commander
Cdre Commodore
CDL Chief of Defence Logistics
CDS Chief of the Defence Staff
CF Coastal Forces
CFS Central Flying School/Chief of Fleet Support
CGC Conspicuous Gallantry Cross
CGM Conspicuous Gallantry Medal
CGRM Commandant General Royal Marines
CID Committee of Imperial Defence
C-in-C Commander-in-Chief
CINCFE Commander-in-Chief Far East
CINCHAN Allied C-in-C Channel
CLF Commander Land Forces
CMB Coastal Motor Boat
CMG Companion of the Order of St Michael and St George
CNFG Commander Naval Forces Gulf
CNI Chief of Naval Information
CNJA Chief Naval Judge Advocate
CNO Chief of Naval Operations (USN)
CNSSO Chief Naval Supply & Secretariat Officer
COMATG Commodore Amphibious Task Group
COMAW Commodore Amphibious Warfare
COMBRAX Commodore RN Barracks
COMFEF Commander Fast East Fleet
COMINCH C-in-C US Fleet
COMNA Commodore Naval Aviation
COMRFA Commodore Royal Fleet Auxiliary
COMSTANAVFORLANT Commander Standing Naval Force Atlantic
COMUKAMPHIBFOR Commander UK Amphibious Force
COSAG Combined Steam and Gas Turbine
CP Central Pivot (gun)
Cpl Corporal
CPO Chief Petty Officer
CS Cruiser Squadron
CSS Confederate States' Ship
CT Communist Terrorist
CTF Commander Task Force
CTG Commander Task Group
CTL Constructive Total Loss, i.e. written off or
DBR Damaged Beyond Repair
DAMS Defensively Armed Merchant Ship
DBE Dame Commander of the Order of the British Empire
DC Depth Charge/Damage Control
DCI Defence Council Instruction

DDNI Deputy Director of Naval Intelligence
DEE Director of Electrical Engineering
DEMS Defensively Equipped Merchant Ship
DF Destroyer Flotilla or Direction Finding
DFOSM Deputy Flag Officer Submarines
DG Director General
DGNPS Director General Naval Personal Services
DGS Director General Ships
DGST(N) Director General Supplies and Transport (Navy)
DLG Guided Missile Destroyer
DNB Dictionary of National Biography
DNC Director of Naval Construction
DN Future Policies Director of Naval Future Policies
DNE Director of Naval Equipment
DNI Director of Naval Intelligence
DN Plans Director of Naval Plans
DNR Director of Naval Recruiting
DNSy Director of Naval Security
DPR(N) Director of Public Relations (Navy)
DSC Distinguished Service Cross
DSM Distinguished Service Medal
DSO Distinguished Service Order
DTM Director of Torpedoes & Mining
DUBD Director of Unexploded Bomb Department
DWRNS Director, Women's Royal Naval Service
EGM Empire Gallantry Medal
Enigma German encyphering machine
E-in-C Engineer-in-Chief
EODTIC Explosive Ordnance Disposal Technical Information Centre
EP Entitled Personnel
ERA Engine Room Artificer
ESM Electronic Support Measures
EST Eastern Standard Time
FAA Fleet Air Arm
FCDT Fleet Clearance Diving Team
FCPO Fleet Chief Petty Officer
FCO Foreign and Commonwealth Office
FF Free French forces in Second World War
FNS French Naval Ship
FO2FEF Flag Officer Second in Command Far East Fleet
FOAC Flag Officer Aircraft Carriers
FOCAS Flag Officer Carriers & Amphibious Ships
FOF Flag Officer Flotilla
FOF1 Flag Officer First Flotilla
FOF2 Flag Officer Second Flotilla
FOF3 Flag Officer Third Flotilla
FOFWF Flag Officer Flotillas Western Fleet
FOIC Flag Officer in Command
FOMA Flag Officer Maritime Aviation
FOME Flag Officer Middle East
FONA Flag Officer Naval Aviation
FONAC Flag Officer Naval Air Command
FORY Flag Officer Royal Yachts
FOSF Flag Officer Surface Flotilla
FOSM Flag Officer Submarines
FOST Flag Officer Sea Training
FOTR Flag Officer Training and Recruiting
FPB Fast Patrol Boat
FSRT Fleet Standby Rifle Troop
GC George Cross
GCB Knight Grand Cross of the Order of the Bath/Good Conduct Badge
GM George Medal
GMD Guided Missile Destroyer
GNAT German Naval Acoustic Torpedo
Gnr Gunner (Royal Artillery)
GOC General Officer Commanding
grt gross registered tonnage
HDML Harbour Defence Motor Launch
HE His Excellency/High Explosive
HEICS Honourable East India Company's Ship
HFDF High Frequency Direction Finding
HMA HM Airship
HMAS HM Australian Ship
HMCS HM Canadian Ship
HMHS HM Hospital Ship
HMML HM Motor Launch
HMNZS HM New Zealand Ship
HMSAS HM South African Ship
HMY HM Yacht
HNoMS His Norwegian Majesty's Ship
Hr Ms Her Netherlands Majesty's Ship
HNlMS Her Netherlands Majesty's Ship
HSH His Serene Highness
HTP high test peroxide
HVB Handelsverkehrsbuch (German code book)
IDC Imperial Defence College
IMS International Military Staff (NATO)
IN Indian Navy
INS Indian Navy Ship
IPT Integrated Project Team
ISO Imperial Service Order
IWM Imperial War Museum
JAF Judge Advocate of the Fleet
JRDF Joint Rapid Deployment Force
JSCSC Joint Services Command and Staff College
KB Knight of the Bath (before 1815)
KDG King's Dragoon Guards
KG Knight of the Garter
kia killed in action
kph kilometres per hour
KR&AI King's Regulations and Admiralty Instructions
KT Knight of the Thistle
KUA Kit Upkeep Allowance
L/Bdr Lance Bombardier (Royal Artillery)
LCI(L) Landing Craft Infantry (Large)
LCS Light Cruiser or Landing Craft Squadron
LCT Landing Craft, Tanks
LIS Land Incident Section

LOM Leading Operator Mechanic
LS Leading Seaman
LSDA Landing Ship Dock (Auxiliary)
LSGC Long Service & Good Conduct Medal
LSH Landing Ship, Heavy
LSI Landing Ship, Infantry
LST Landing Ship, Tank
Lt Lieutenant
Lt-Cdr Lieutenant-Commander
LVO Lieutenant, Royal Victorian Order
(m) Naval General Service medal, for ship or boat action
(m*) Gold Medal action, 1794–1815
MA Medical Assistant
MAC Merchant Aircraft Carrier
MAS Motorbarea Armatta SVAN (Societ Veneziano Automobile Nautica) in short, an Italian motor boat
MATO 20 DEC panel
MC Military Cross
MCD Minewarfare & Clearance Diving Branch
MDG(N) Medical Director General (Navy)
MGB Motor Gun Boat
MEA Marine Engineering Artificer
MEM Marine Engineering Mechanic
MEZ Maritime Exclusion Zone
MiD Mentioned in Dispatches
ML Motor Launch/muzzle loading
MLR Muzzle loading rifle (gun)
MM Military Medal
MN Merchant Navy
MNBDO Mobile Naval Base Defence Organisation
MNC Major NATO Commander
MS Minesweeper
MT Motor Transport
MTB Motor Torpedo Boat
MVO Member, Royal Victorian Order
MWC Maritime Warfare Centre
NAG North Arabian Gulf
NAS Naval Air Squadron
NATO North Atlantic Treaty Organisation
NA&WI North America and West Indies Station
NEO Nationals Evacuation Operation
Neth Netherlands
NGS Naval Gunfire Support
NID Naval Intelligence Division
nm nautical miles
NMM National Maritime Museum
NO Navigating Officer
Nor Norwegian
NP Naval Party
ODNB Oxford Dictionary of National Biography
OM Operator Mechanic
OOW Officer of the Watch
OPCOM Operational Command
OPCON Operational Control
OPV Offshore Patrol Vessel
OS Ordinary Seaman
OST Operational Sea Training
OTC On Task Commander
OTU Operational Training Unit
PAAMS Principal Anti-Air Missile System
Pinch An operation planned to capture a specific piece of equipment, usually an intelligence operation
PJHQ Permanent Joint Headquarters
PLA People's Liberation Army
PO Petty Officer
Pol Polish
PUS Permanent Under Secretary of State
PWO Principal Warfare Officer
QARNNS Queen Alexandra's Royal Naval Nursing Service
QCBC Queen's Commendation for Brave Conduct
QCVSA Queen's Commendation for Valuable Service in the Air
QHM Queen's Harbour Master
QR&AI Queen's Regulations & Admiralty Instructions
Q-ship A merchant ship converted (or in one case designed) to attack enemy submarines by decoying them into attacking her
RAAF Royal Australian Air Force
RAC Royal Aero (Aeronautical) Club
Radar Radio detection & ranging
RAF Royal Air Force
RAFVR Royal Air Force Volunteer Reserve
RAMC Royal Army Medical Corps
RAN Royal Australian Navy
RANVR Royal Australian Naval Volunteer Reserve
RAS Replenishment at sea
RASC Royal Army Service Corps
RCAF Royal Canadian Air Force
RCDS Royal College of Defence Studies
RCN Royal Canadian Navy
RD Reserve Decoration
RDF Radio Direction Finding
RFA Royal Fleet Auxiliary
RFC Royal Flying Corps
RFN Russian Federation Navy
RGA Royal Garrison Artillery
RIN Royal Indian Navy
RM Royal Marine, Royal Marines
RMA Royal Marine Artillery
RMLI Royal Marine Light Infantry
RMM Royal Marines Museum
RMR Royal Marines Reserve
RMS Rendering Mines Safe/Royal Mail Steamer
RMFVR Royal Marine Forces Volunteer Reserve
RNAD Royal Naval Armament Depot
RNAS Royal Naval Air Service/Station
RNAY Royal Naval Aircraft Yard

RNB	Royal Naval Barracks
RNC	Royal Naval College
RND	Royal Naval Division
RNDQ	Royal Naval Detention Quarters
RNEC	Royal Naval Engineering College
RNH	Royal Naval Hospital
RNlN	Royal Netherlands Navy
RNO	Resident Naval Officer
RNR	Royal Naval Reserve
RNSM	Royal Navy Submarine Musuem
RNSTS	Royal Naval Supply and Transport Service
RNTM	RN Temporary Memorandum
RNVR	Royal Naval Volunteer Reserve
RNV(S)R	Royal Naval Volunteer (Supplementary) Reserve
RNZAF	Royal New Zealand Air Force
RNZN	Royal New Zealand Navy
ROK	Republic of Korea
ROP	Report of Proceedings
RV	Rendezvous
RYS	Royal Yacht Squadron
SAAF	South African Air Force
SAN	South African Navy
SANF	South African Naval Forces
SAR	Search and Rescue
SAS	Special Air Service Regiment
SBA	Sick Berth Attendant
SBNOSA	Senior British Naval Officer South Africa
SDML	Seaward Defence Motor Launch
SEIE	Submarine Escape Immersion Equipment
SGB	Steam Gun Boat
Sgt	Sergeant
SHAR	Sea Harrier
S/M	Submarine
SMCC	Submarine Command Course
SNO	Senior Naval Officer
SNOPG	Senior Naval Officer Persian Gulf
SNOWI	Senior Naval Officer West Indies
SO	Senior Officer
SOE	Special Operations Executive
SOHKS	Senior Officer Hong Kong Squadron
SONAR	Sound Navigation & Ranging
Sqn	Squadron
SSBN	nuclear-powered ballistic-missile submarine
SSN	nuclear-powered submarine
STANAVFORLANT	(NATO) Standing Naval Force Atlantic
STR	Steam Turbine Room
Sub-Lt	Sub-Lieutenant
TAG	Torpedo Air Gunner
TB	Torpedo Boat
TBD	Torpedo Boat Destroyer
TBR	Torpedo, Bomber, Reconnaissance
tbrb	to be relieved by
TD	Territorial Decoration
TE	Training Establishment
TEZ	Total Exclusion Zone
TF	Task Force
TG	Task Group
THS	Trinity House Service
THV	Trinity House Vessel
TLAM	Tomahawk Land Attack Missile
TLB	Top Level Budget Holder
U	Unterseeboot – a German submarine
UDI	Unilateral Declaration of Independence
UJ	Unterseeboot Jäger – a German A/S vessel
UKMILREP	United Kingdom Military Representative (NATO)
UKSF	United Kingdom Special Forces
Ultra	High-grade Intelligence from Enigma
UNSCR	United Nations Security Council Resolution
URNU	University Royal Naval Unit
USCG	United States Coast Guard
USMC	United States Marine Corps
USS	United States Ship
UXB	unexploded bomb
VC	Victoria Cross
VCNS	Vice Chief of the Naval Staff
VLCC	very large crude [oil] carrier
VRD	Volunteer Reserve Decoration
VSTOL	Vertical Short Take-Off or Landing
WAAF	Women's Auxiliary Air Force
WEA	Weapons Electrical Artificer
WMD	weapons of mass destruction
WRAC	Women's Royal Army Corps
WRNR	Women's Royal Naval Reserve
WRNS	Women's Royal Naval Service
WRNVR	Women's Royal Naval Volunteer Reserve
XO	executive officer

BIBLIOGRAPHY

This bibliography is intended to provide no more than an introduction to the history of the British Navy, its operations, ships, bases, personnel, administration, customs and traditions down the years. Books listed are mainly recent works and therefore those most accessible to the general reader. Many older but important works are omitted. Those readers wishing to delve deeper may consult the Further Reading appendix in Admiral Hill's book below. The Navy Records Society and the Society for Nautical Research (both have websites) welcome members with a real interest in maritime history.

Admiral Richard Hill's *The Oxford Illustrated History of the Royal Navy* (Oxford, 1995), with contributions from leading naval historians, is the finest one-volume introduction to the history of the Service. This leads the reader on to Professor Nicholas Rodger's splendid trilogy on the naval history of Britain, the first for a century and a work of outstanding quality. Two volumes have been published: vol.1: *The Safeguard of the Sea 660–649* (London, 1997); vol.2: *The Command of the Ocean 1649–1815* (London, 2004). Volume 3 is in preparation and is eagerly awaited. A third work of the highest scholarship is Professor Roger Knight's *The Pursuit of Victory. The Life and Achievement of Horatio Nelson* (London, 2005) which replaces Carola Oman's 1947 biography as the very best modern life of Nelson.

The bibliography of British naval history is formidable in extent. The past twenty years has seen an explosion of naval publishing with hundreds of new titles, many (but not all) of them fine books. Limited space allows only a few titles to be mentioned here. The following list, arranged under categories, is far from complete or comprehensive and the choice is a personal one.

The History of the Royal Navy

Arthur, Max, *The True Glory: the Royal Navy 1914-1939: A narrative history* (London, 1996)

Clowes, William Laird, *The Royal Navy: A History from the Earliest Times to 1900.* 7 vols ((London, 1897–1903), repub. Pb. 1996). A century old but still very useful.

Elleman, Bruce A., and S.C.M. Paine (eds.) *Naval Power and Expeditionary Warfare. Peripheral Campaigns and new Theatres of Naval Warfare* (Abingdon, 2011)

Hore, Peter, *The Habit of Victory. The Story of the Royal Navy 1545–1945* (London, 2005).

Grove, Eric, *The Royal Navy since 1815: A new short history* (Basingstoke, 2005)

—, (ed.) *Great Battles of the Royal Navy, as commemorated in the Gunroom, Britannia Royal Naval College, Dartmouth* (London, 1994)

Harding, Richard, (ed.) *The Royal Navy, 1930–2000* (Abingdon, 2005)

Herman, Arthur, *To Rule the Waves. How the British Navy shaped the Modern World* (London, 2004)

Kennedy, Paul M., *The Rise and Fall of British Naval Mastery* ((London, 1976) repub. pb 2001). The close link between sea power and national wealth. More money, more Navy.

Speller, Ian, (ed.) *The Royal Navy and Maritime Power in the Twentieth Century* (Abingdon, 2005)

Tute, Warren, *The True Glory: The story of the Royal Navy over a thousand years* (London, 1983)

Van der Vat, Dan, *The Royal Navy in the Twentieth Century* (London, 2000)

Winton, John, *An Illustrated History of the Royal Navy* (London, 2000)

Naval Reference Works

Brown, David, *Warship Losses of World War Two* (London: 1990). The late David Brown, naval aviator, was Head of the Naval Historical Branch. Authoritative but omits submarines

Colledge, J.J., and Ben Warlow, *Ships of the Royal Navy. The complete record of all fighting ships of the Royal Navy from the 15th century to the present* (Newbury, Berks, 2010). The standard work, regularly revised.

Hepper, David J., *British Warship Losses in the Age of Sail 1650–1959* (Rotherfield, E. Sussex, 1994)

—, *British Warship Losses in the Ironclad Era 1860–1919* (London, 2006)

Lyon, David, *The Sailing Navy List: all ships of the Royal Navy, built, purchased and captured 1688–1860* (London, 1993)

—, and Rif Winfield, *The Sail and Steam Navy List: all ships of the Royal navy 1815–1889* (London, 2004)

Syrett, David, and R.L. DiNardo, (eds.) *The Commissioned Sea Officers of the Royal Navy 1660–1815* (Aldershot, Navy Records Society, 1994)

Tracy, Nicholas, *Who's Who in Nelson's Navy; 200 naval heroes* (London, 2006)

Warlow, Lt-Cdr Ben, *Battle Honours of the Royal Navy, being the officially authorised and complete listing of Battle Honours awarded to Her/His Majesty's Ships and Squadrons of the Fleet Air Arm including Honours awarded to Royal Fleet Auxiliary Ships and merchant vessels* (Liskeard, 2004). The standard, well-thumbed reference based on AFO 2565/54. See 1 October 1954.

—, *Shore Establishments of the Royal Navy being a list of the Static Ships and Establishments of the Royal Navy* (Liskeard, 1992, 2000)

Winfield, Rif, *British Warships in the Age of Sail 1603–1714. Design, Construction, Careers and Fates* (Barnsley, 2009)

—, *British Warships in the Age of Sail 1715–1792. Design, Construction, Careers and Fates* (Barnsley, 2007)

—, *British Warships in the Age of Sail 1793–1817. Design, Construction, Careers and Fates* (Barnsley 2005, 2008)

Naval Strategy

Elleman, Bruce A., and S.C.M. Paine, (eds) *Naval Coalition Warfare. From the Napoleonic War to Operation Iraqi Freedom* (Abingdon, 2007)

Harding, Richard, *Seapower and Naval Warfare 1650–1830* (1999)

Hattendorf, J.B., and R.S. Jordan, (eds), *Maritime Strategy and the Balance of Power: Britain and America in the twentieth century* (London, 1989)

Kennedy, Greg, (ed.) *British Naval Strategy East of Suez, 1900–2000. Influences and Actions* (Abingdon, 2005).

Till, Geoffrey, (ed.) *The Development of British Naval Thinking. Essays in memory of Bryan Ranft* (Abingdon, 2006)

—, *Maritime Strategy and the Nuclear Age* (London, 1982)

—, *Modern Sea Power: an introduction* (London, 1987)

Medieval, Tudors and Early Stuarts

Childs, David, *Tudor Sea Power. The foundation of greatness* (Barnsley, 2009)

Fernandez-Armesto, Felipe, *The Spanish Armada: the experience of war in 1588* (Oxford, 1988)
Loades, David, *The Tudor Navy: an administrative, political and military history* (Aldershot, 1992)
—, *The Making of the Elizabethan Navy 1540–1590* (Woodbridge, 2009)
Mattingly, Garrett, *The Defeat of the Spanish Armada* (London, 1959). An outstanding work by an American historian. Over 50 years old but a fine work and often republished.

The Navy of the Commonwealth and Restoration

Barratt, John, *Cromwell's Wars at Sea* (Barnsley, 2006
Capp, Bernard, *Cromwell's Navy: the Fleet and the English Revolution 1648–1660* (Oxford, 1989)
Davies, J.D., *Gentlemen and Tarpaulins: the officers and men of the Restoration Navy* (Oxford, 1991)
—, *Pepys's Navy. Ships, Men and Warfare 1649–1689* (Barnsley 2008)
Jones, J.R., *The Anglo-Dutch Wars of the Seventeenth Century* (London, 1996)

The Royal Navy of William III, Queen Anne and the Early Hanoverians

Le Fevre, Peter, and Richard Harding, (eds.) *Precursors of Nelson: British admirals of the eighteenth century* (London, 2000)
Rodger, N.A.M., *The Wooden World: an anatomy of the Georgian Navy* (London, 1986). The most important single volume ever written on the eighteenth-century Royal Navy
Wilkinson, Clive, *The British Navy and the State in the 18th Century* (Woodbridge, 2004)

The Royal Navy in the War of Jenkins' Ear, The Seven Years War and the War of American Independence

Black, Jeremy, *War for America: the fight for independence 1775–1783* (Stroud, 1991)
—, and P. Woodfine, (eds) *The British Navy and the use of Naval Power in the Eighteenth Century* (Leicester, 1988)
Gardiner, Robert, (ed.) *Navies and the American Revolution 1775–1783* (London, 1996)
Marcus, Geoffrey, *Quiberon Bay: the campaign in home waters, 1759* (London, 1960)
Pocock, Tom, *Battle for Empire: the very first world war 1756–63* (London, 1998)
Syrett, David, *The Royal Navy in American Waters 1775–1783* (Aldershot, 1989)

The Royal Navy in the French Revolutionary and Napoleonic Wars

Adkins, Roy, *Trafalgar: The biography of a battle* (London, 2004)
Clayton, Tim, and Phil Craig, *Trafalgar: the Men, the Battle, the Storm* (London, 2004)
Gardiner, Robert, (ed.) *Fleet Battle and Blockade: the French Revolutionary War 1793–1797* (London, 1996)
—, (ed.) *The Campaign of Trafalgar 1803–1805* (London, 1997)
—, (ed.) *Nelson against Napoleon: from the Nile to Copenhagen, 1798–1801* (London, 1997)
Harding, Richard, (ed.) *A Great and Glorious Victory. New Perspectives on the Battle of Trafalgar* (Barnsley, 2008). Papers from the Trafalgar Bicentenary conference at Portsmouth.
Lavery, Brian, *Nelson's Navy: The ships, men and organisation 1793–1815* (London, 1989)
—, *Nelson and the Nile: The naval war against Bonaparte 1798* (London, 1998)
Pope, Dudley, *England Expects: The saga of 1805, the year of Britain's danger, and the great victory at Trafalgar* ((London, 1959), repub. pb 1998). An enduring classic of the Trafalgar campaign.
—, *The Great Gamble: Nelson at Copenhagen* (1972, repub. 2001)
Tracy, Nicholas, *Nelson's Battles. The Triumph of British Seapower* (Barnsley, 2008)
—, *Nelson's Battles: The art of victory under* sail (London, 1996)
White, Colin, *1797, Nelson's Year of Destiny: Cape St. Vincent and Santa Cruz de Tenerife* (Stroud, 1998)

The Royal Navy in the American War 1812–1815

Forester, C.S., *The Naval War of 1812* (London, 1957)
Gardiner, Robert (ed.), *The Naval War of 1812* (London, 1998)
Padfield, Peter, *Broke and the* Shannon (London, 1968)
Poolman, Kenneth, *Guns off Cape Ann: the story of the immortal battle between the* Shannon *and the* Chesapeake (London, 1961)

The Royal Navy and *Pax Britannica*

Brooks, Richard, *The Long Arm of Empire: Naval Brigades from the Crimea to the Boxer Rebellion* (London, 1999)
Hill, Richard, *War at Sea in the Ironclad Age* (London, 2000)
Howell, Raymond C., *The Royal Navy and the Slave Trade* (London, 1987)
Lambert, Andrew, *The Crimean War. British Grand Strategy against Russia 1853–56* (Manchester, 1991)
Pocock, Tom, *Breaking the Chains. The Royal Navy's War on White Slavery* (London, 2006)

The Royal Navy: the rise of Germany and the First World War

Gordon, Andrew, *The Rules of the Game: Jutland and British naval command* ((London, 1996) repub. pb 2000). A classic on the effect of peacetime doctrines and attitudes on operations in war.
Halpern, Paul G., *A Naval History of World War 1* ((Annapolis, 1994) repub. pb. London, 1994)
Kennedy, Paul M., *The Rise of the Anglo-German Antagonism 1860–1914* ((London, 1980) repub. pb. 1982)
Marder, Arthur J., *From the Dreadnought to Scapa Flow*, 5 vols (Oxford, 1961–70). The brilliant if now dated history of the RN in the First World War.
Speller, Ian, (ed.) *The Royal Navy and Maritime Power in the Twentieth Century* (Abingdon, 2005)
Van der Vat, Dan, *The Dardanelles Disaster. Winston Churchill's Greatest Failure.* (London, 2009)
—, *The Grand Scuttle: The sinking of the German Fleet at Scapa Flow in 1919* (London, 1982, repub. pb. 1997)
—, *The Ship that changed the World: The escape of the* Goeben *to the Dardanelles in 1914* (London, 1985)
—, *The Last Corsair: The story of the* Emden (London, 1983)

The Royal Navy between the World Wars

Ereira, Alan, *The Invergordon Mutiny: A narrative history of the last great mutiny in the Royal Navy and how it forced Britain off the Gold Standard in 1931* (London, 1981)
Glenton, Robert, *The* Royal Oak *Affair: the saga of Admiral Collard and Bandmaster Barnacle* (London, 1991)
Halpern, Paul, (ed.) *The Mediterranean Fleet 1919–1929* (Navy Records Society: Aldershot, 2011)
Marder, Arthur J., *Old Friends, New Enemies: the Royal Navy and the Imperial Japanese Navy*, vol.1: *Strategic Illusions 1936–1941* (Oxford, 1981), vol.2: *The Pacific War 1942–1945* [completed by M. Jacobson and J. Horsfield] (Oxford, 1990)
Roskill, S.W., *Naval Policy between the Wars*, 2 vols (London, 1961, 1968),

The Royal Navy in the Second World War

Barnett, Correlli, *Engage the Enemy more Closely: the Royal Navy in the Second World War* ((London, 1991, repub. pb 2000)

Greene, Jack, and Alessandro Massignani, *The Naval War in the Mediterranean 1940–1943* (London, 1998, repub. pb 2002)

Lavery, Brian, *Churchill's Navy. The Ships, Men and Organisation 1939–1945* (London 2006)

Marder, Arthur J., *Old Friends, New Enemies: the Royal Navy and the Imperial Japanese Navy*, vol.1: *Strategic Illusions 1936–1941* (Oxford, 1981), vol.2: *The Pacific War 1942–1945* [completed by M. Jacobson and J. Horsfield] (Oxford, 1990)

Roskill, S.W., *History of the Second World War: The War at Sea*, 3 vols (London, 1954–1961). The Cabinet Office 'official' history.

—, *The Navy at War 1939–1945* ((London, 1960, 1964), repub. 1998)

The Royal Navy – Korea, the Cold War and the End of Empire

Farrar-Hockley, Anthony, *Official History. The British Part in the Korean War*, 2 vols, vol.1: *A Distant Obligation* (London, 1990), vol.2: *An Honourable Discharge* (London, 1995)

Grove, Eric, Vanguard *to Trident: British naval policy since World War Two* (London, 1987)

Ring, Jim, *We Come Unseen: The untold story of Britain's Cold War submariners* (London, 2001, repub. pb. 2003). The careers of six Cold War submariners: Toby Elliott, Roger Lane-Nott, Martin Macpherson, James Taylor, Chris Wreford-Brown and Jeff Tall.

Speller, Ian, *The Role of Amphibious Warfare in British Defence Policy, 1945–1956* (Basingstoke, 2001)

Stewart, Ninian, *The Royal Navy and the Palestine Patrol* (London, 2002)

Welch, Captain Andrew, *The Royal Navy in the Cod Wars. Britain and Iceland in Conflict 1958–1976* (Liskeard, 2006)

The Royal Navy and the Falklands War

Barker, Nicholas, *Beyond Endurance: An epic of Whitehall and the South Atlantic conflict* (London, 1997)

Black, Admiral Sir Jeremy, *There and Back* (London 2005). Personal memoir of the captain of HMS *Invincible*.

Brown, David, *The Royal Navy and the Falklands War* (London, 1987)

Clapp, Michael, and Ewen Southby-Tailyour, *Amphibious Assault Falklands: The Battle of San Carlos Water* (London, 1996)

Craig, Chris, *Call for Fire: Sea combat in the Falklands and the Gulf War* (London, 1995)

Freedman, Sir Lawrence, *The Official History of the Falklands Campaign*. 2 vols (Abingdon, 2005)

Hart-Dyke, Capt. David, *Four Weeks in May. The Loss of HMS* Coventry. *A Captain's Story* (London, 2007)

Middlebrook, Martin, *Operation Corporate: the story of the Falklands War 1982* (London, 1985)

Nott, John, *Here Today Gone Tomorrow. Recollections of an Errant Politician* (London, 2002). Ch. 8 *Upsetting the Navy* pp.203–44 and Chaps. 9 and 10 pp.245–321. A counterbalance to the many military memoirs.

Puddefoot, Geoff, *No Sea too Rough. The Royal Fleet Auxiliary in the Falklands War. The Untold Story* (London, 2007)

Southby-Tailyour, Ewen, *Reasons in Writing: A commando's view of the Falklands War* (Barnsley, 1993, repub. pb. 2003)

Thompson, Julian, *No Picnic: 3 Commando Brigade in the South Atlantic 1982* (London, 1985)

Woodward, John ('Sandy'), *One Hundred Days: memoirs of the Falklands Battle Group* (London, 1992)

The Royal Navy in the New Millennium

Dorman, Andrew, M., Smith and M. Uttley, *The Changing Face of Military Power: Joint warfare in an expeditionary era* (Basingstoke, 2002)

Fox, Robert, *Iraq Campaign 2003: Royal Navy and Royal Marines* (London, 2003)

Southby-Tailyour, Ewen, *3 Commando Brigade: Helmand, Afghanistan* (London, 2008)

—, *3 Commando Brigade: Hellmand Assault* (London, 2010)

Till, Geoffrey, *Seapower: A guide for the twenty-first century* (London, 2004, new edn. pb Abingdon, 2009). A key work by the Dean of Academic Studies at the Joint Services Command and Staff College.

Royal Navy Hydrography and Voyages of Exploration

Beaglehole, J.C. *The Life of Captain James Cook* (London, 1974)

—, *The Exploration of the Pacific* (London, 1987)

Blake, John, *Charts of War. The Maps and Charts that have Informed and Illustrated War at Sea* (London, 2006)

Day, Archibald, *The Admiralty Hydrographic Service 1795–1919* (London, 1967)

Morris, R.O., *Charts and Surveys in Peace and War: The history of the RN Hydrographic Service 1919–1970* (London, 1995)

Ritchie, G.S., *The Admiralty Chart: British naval hydrography in the nineteenth century* (London, 1967, new edn ed. A.C.F. David, 1995)

—, *No Day Too Long: An hydrographer's tale* (Durham, 1992)

Williams, Glyn, *The Prize of all the Oceans: The triumph and tragedy of Anson's voyage round the world* (London, 1999)

—, *Voyages of Delusion: the search for the Northwest Passage in the Age of Reason* (London, 1999)

Combined Operations, Expeditionary and Amphibious Warfare

Dorman, Andrew, M., Smith and M. Uttley, *The Changing Face of Military Power: joint warfare in an expeditionary era* (Basingstoke, 2002)

Evans, M.H.H., *Amphibious Operations: the projection of sea power ashore* (London, 1990)

Hore, Peter, (ed.) *Seapower Ashore; 200 years of Royal Navy operations on land* (London, 2001)

Lovering, Lt-Cdr Tristan, (ed.) *Amphibious Assault: Manoeuvre from the Sea. Amphibious Operations from the Last Century.* (Fleet HQ, 2005, Woodbridge 2007)

Macksey, Kenneth, *Commando Strike: The story of amphibious raiding in World War II* (London, 1985)

Ministry of Defence, *The United Kingdom approach to Amphibious Operations* (London, 1997)

Neillands, Robin, *The Dieppe Raid. The Story of the Disastrous 1942 Expedition* (London, 2005). See 19 August 1942.

Prince, Stephen, *The Royal Navy and the Raids on St. Nazaire and Dieppe* (Abingdon, July 2004). Author is the Head of the Naval Historical Branch.

Speller, Ian, *The Role of Amphibious Warfare in British Defence Policy, 1945–1956* (Basingstoke, 2001)

Convoy Operations, Anti-Submarine Warfare and Naval Control of Shipping

Edwards, Barnard, *The Road to Russia. Arctic Convoys 1942* (Barnsley, 2002). Accounts of Covoys PQ13 to PQ17 and QP13.

Hague, Arnold, *The Allied Convoy System 1939–1945. Its Organisation, Defence and Operation* (London, 2000)

Llewellyn-Jones, Malcolm, (ed.) *The Royal Navy and the Mediterranean Convoys. A Naval Staff History* [1941–1942]. (Abingdon, 2007).

—, (ed.) *The Royal Navy and the Arctic Convoys. A Naval Staff History* [1941–1942]. (Abingdon, 2006).

—, *The Royal Navy and Anti-Submarine Warfare 1917–1949* (Abingdon, 2006).

Owen, David, *Anti-Submarine Warfare: An Illustrated History* (Barnsley, 2007)

Winton, John, *Convoy. The Defence of Sea Trade 1890–1990* (London, 1983)

Woodman, Richard, *Malta Convoys 1940–1943* (London, 2000, repub. pb 2003)

—, *Arctic Convoys 1941–1945* (London, 1994, repub. pb 2004)

—, *The Real Cruel Sea. The Merchant Navy and the Battle of the Atlantic* (London 2004, repub. pb 2005). An authoritative trilogy on convoy operations by a professional sea officer.

Warships- General

Archibald,E.H.H., *The Fighting Ship in the Royal Navy 1897–1984* (Poole, 1984)

Conway, *Conway's All the World's Fighting Ships*, 4 vols, vol.1: *1860–1905* (London, 1979), vol.2: *1906–1922* (London, 1985), vol.3: *1922–1946* (London, 1980), vol.4: *1947–1995* (London, 1983)

Gardiner, Robert, and D.K. Brown, (eds) *Conway's History of the Ship*, vol.1: *The Eclipse of the Big Gun – The warship 1906–1945* (London, 1992), vol.2: *The Line of Battle, 1650–1815* (London, 1992)

—, and Andrew Lambert, (eds) *Steam, Steel and Shellfire – The steam warship 1815–1905* (London, 1992)

—, and Brian Lavery (eds.), *The Line of Battle – The sailing warship 1650–1840* (London, 1992)

—, and Norman Friedman, (eds) *Navies in the Nuclear Age – Warships since 1945* (London, 1993)

Goodwin, Peter, *Nelson's Ships: A history of the vessels in which he served 1771–1805* (London, 2002)

—, *The Ships of Trafalgar. The British, French and Spanish Fleets, October 1805* (London, 2005)

Lambert, Andrew, *Battleships in Transition: The creation of the steam battlefleet 1815–1860* (London, 1984)

—, *The Last Sailing Battlefleet: <aintaining naval mastery 1815–1850* (London, 1991)

Lavery, Brian, *Nelson's Navy: The ships, men and organisation 1793–1815* (London, 1989)

Lyon, David, *The Sailing Navy List: All ships of the Royal Navy, built, purchased and captured 1688–1860* (London, 1993)

—, and Rif Winfield, *The Sail and Steam Navy List: all ships of the Royal Navy 1815–1889* (London, 2004)

McGowan, Alan, *HMS* Victory: *her construction, career and restoration* (London, 1999). A work of authority from a leading naval historian who was for many years Chairman of the Victory Advisory Technical Committee.

Willis, Sam, *Fighting at Sea in the Eighteenth Century. The Art of Sailing Warfare.* (Woodbridge, 2008). The practicalities of fighting under sail.

Winfield, Rif, *British Warships in the Age of Sail 1603–1714. Design, Construction, Careers and Fates* (Barnsley, 2009)

—, *British Warships in the Age of Sail 1714–1792. Design, Construction, Careers and Fates* (Barnsley, 2008)

—, *British Warships in the Age of Sail 1793–1817. Design, Construction, Careers and Fates* (London, 2005, rev. edn Barnsley, 2008)

Woodman, *The History of the Ship: The comprehensive story of seafaring from the earliest times to the present day* (London, 1997)

Capital Ships and Monitors

Burt, R.A., *British Battleships of World War One* (London, 1986)

—, *British Battleships 1889–1904* (London, 1988)

—, *British Battleships 1919–1939* (London, 1993)

Buxton, Ian, *Big Gun Monitors: A history of the design, construction and operations of the Royal Navy's monitors* (Tynemouth, 1978, repub. revised, expanded, Barnsley, 2008)

Lambert, Andrew, *Battleships in Transition: The creation of the steam battlefleet 1815–1860* (London, 1984)

Whiteley, M.J., *Battleships of World War Two: An international encyclopaedia* (London, 1998)

Naval Aviation, Aircraft Carriers and Naval Air Warfare

Brown, Capt. Eric, *Wings on my Sleeve* (London, 2006). The author, naval aviator and former test pilot, is in *The Guinness Book of Records* for having flown more types of aircraft (487) than any other pilot.

Brown, J.D. and Cdr David Hobbs RN, (ed.) *Carrier Operations in World War Two* (Barnsley, 2009)

Friedman, Norman, *British Carrier Aviation: The evolution of the ships and their aircraft* (London, 1988)

Hobbs, Cdr David, *Aircraft Carriers of the British and Commonwealth Navies: The complete illustrated encyclopaedia from World War I to the present* (London, 1996)

—, *Royal Navy Escort Carriers* (Liskeard, 2003)

—, *A Century of Carrier Aviation. The Evolution of Ships and Shipborne Aircraft* (Barnsley, 2009)

—, *The British Pacific Fleet: The Royal Navy's most effective strike force* (Barnsley, 2011)

Johnstone-Bryden, Richard, *HMS* Ark Royal *IV: Britain's greatest warship* (Stroud, 1999)

Sturtivant, R., *The Squadrons of the Fleet Air Arm* (Tonbridge, 1984)

—, *British Naval Aviation: The Fleet Air Arm* (London, 1990)

Thetford, Owen, *British Naval Aircraft since 1912* (London, 1991)

Till, Geoffrey, *Air Power and the Royal Navy 1914–1945* (London 1979) An authoritative account of the Royal Navy's campaign to regain direct control of the Fleet Air Arm.

Cruisers

Burt, R.A., *British Cruisers in World War One* (London, 1987)

Marriot, Leo, *Treaty Cruisers; the first international warship building competition* (Barnsley, 2005)

Raven, Alan, and John Roberts, *British Cruisers of World War Two* (London, 1980)

Whitley, M.J., *Cruisers of World War Two: An international encyclopaedia* (London, 1995)

Destroyers, Frigates and Escorts

Brown, David K., *Atlantic Escorts. Ships, Weapons and Tactics in World War Two* (Barnsley 2007)

Burt, R.A., *British Destroyers in World War Two* (London, 1985)

Friedman, Norman, *British Destroyers from the Earliest Days to the Second World War* (Barnsley, 2009)

—, *British Destroyers and Frigates: The Second World War and After* (London 2006)

McCart, Neil, *Daring Class Destroyers* (Liskeard, 2008)

Marriott, Leo, *Royal Navy Frigates since 1945* (London, 1983, 1990)

—, *Royal Navy Destroyers since 1945* (London, 1989)

—, *Type 42* (London, 1985)

—, *Type 22* (London, 1986)

Submarines and Undersea Warfare

Compton-Hall, Richard, *The Underwater War 1939–1945* (Poole, 1982)

—, *Submarine Boats: The beginnings of underwater warfare* (London, 1983)

—, *Submarines and the War at Sea 1914–1918* (London, 1991)
—, *The Submarine Pioneers* (Stroud, 1999)
Evans, A.S., *Beneath the Waves: A History of H.M. Submarine Losses 1904–1971* (London, 1986)
Flack, Jeremy, *100 Years of Royal Navy Submarines* (Shrewsbury, 2002). A pictorial record by class.
Hezlet, Vice-Admiral Sir Arthur, *The History of British and Allied Submarine Operations in World War Two* (Gosport 2003)
Kemp, Paul, *British Submarines in World War Two* (Poole, 1987)
—, *The T-Class Submarine: The classic British design* (London, 1990)
Lawrence, Peter, *A Century of Submarines* (Stroud, 2001, repub. pb. 2004)
Padfield, Peter, *War beneath the Sea: Submarine conflict 1939–1945* (London, 1995)
Preston, Antony, *The Royal Navy Submarine Service: A centennial history* (London, 2001)
Ring, Jim, *We Come Unseen: The untold Story of Britain's Cold War Submariners* (London, 2001, repub. pb. 2003). The careers of six Cold War submariners: Toby Elliott, Roger Lane-Nott, Martin Macpherson, James Taylor, Chris Wreford-Brown and Jeff Tall.
Walters, Derek, *The History of the U-Class Submarine* (Barnsley, 2005)
Wingate, John, *The Submariners: Life in British submarines 1901–1999* (London, 1999)

Mine Warfare, Minelayers and Minesweepers.

Griffiths, Maurice, *The Hidden Menace* (London, 1981). Lt-Cdr, GM, RNVR and a RMS officer.
Henry, Chris, *Depth Charge: Royal Navy mines, depth charges and underwater weapons 1914–1945* (Barnsley, 2005)
Till, Geoffrey, (ed.) *Coastal Forces* (London, 1994). Vol.4 in Brassey's Sea Power series. A professional summary of mine warfare at the end of the twentieth century.
Turner, John Frayn, *Service Most Silent: the Navy's Fight against Enemy Mines* (London 1955, repub. Barnsley, 2008). The work of HMS *Vernon* in countering the German mine warfare threat.

Coastal Forces

Cooper, Bryan, *The War of the Gun Boats* (London, 1970, repub. Barnsley, 2009)
Dickens, Peter, *Night Action. MTB Flotilla at War* (London 1974, repub. pb Barnsley, 2008)
Hichens, Antony, *Gunboat Command. The biography of Lieutenant-Commander Robert Hichens RNVR* (Barnsley, 2007). See 12 April 2007.
Hichens, R.P., *We fought them in Gunboats* (London, 1944)
Pope, Dudley, *Flag 4. The Battle of Coastal Forces in the Mediterranean 1939–1945* ((London 1954) repub. pb London, 1998)
Reynolds, Leonard C., *Home Waters MTBs and MGBs at War 1939–1945* (Stroud, 1999)
—, *Dog Boats at War: Royal Navy D-class MTBs and MGBs 1939–1945* (Stroud, 1998)
—, *Motor Gunboat 658. The Small Boat War in the* Mediterranean (London 1955, repub. pb 2002)
Scott, Lt-Cdr Peter, *The Battle of the Narrow Seas: the history of Light Coastal Forces in the Channel and North Sea 1939–1945* (London, 1945, repub. Barnsley, 2009)
Till, Geoffrey, (ed.) *Coastal Forces* (London, 1994).

Minor War Vessels

Cocker, M.P., *Minor War Vessels of the Royal Navy 1908 to date* (Shrewsbury, 1993)
Lund and Ludlam, *The War of the Landing Craft* (Foulsham, 1976)
Perrett, Bryan, *Gunboat! Small Ships at War* (London, 2000). Crimea to Vietnam.
Preston, Antony, and John Major, *Send a Gunboat: A study of the gunboat and its role in British policy 1854–1904* (London, 1967, revised edn 2007)
Ware, Chris, *The Bomb Vessel: Shore bombardment ships in the age of sail* (London, 1994)

Naval Logistics and Afloat Support

Adams, Thomas A, and James R. Smith, *The Royal Fleet Auxiliary. A Century of Service* (London, 2005)
James, Tony, *The Royal Fleet Auxiliary 1905–1985* (Liskeard *c.*1985)
Nash, Peter, *The Development of Mobile Logistic Support in Anglo-American Naval Policy 1900–1953* (Gainsville: University Press of Florida, 2009)
Puddefoot, Geoff, *No Sea too Rough. The Royal Fleet Auxiliary in the Falklands War. The Untold Story* (London, 2007)
—, *The Fourth Force. The untold story of the Royal Fleet Auxiliary since 1945* (Barnsley, 2009)

Royal Yachts and Royal Reviews

Dalton, Tony, *British Royal Yachts: A complete illustrated history* (Tiverton, 2002)
Hoey, Brian, *The Royal Yacht* Britannia*: Inside the Queen's floating palace* (Yeovil, 1995)
Johnstone-Bryden, Richard, *The Royal Yacht* Britannia: *The official history* (London, 2003)
Morton, Andrew, *The Royal Yacht* Britannia*: Life onboard the floating palace* (London, 1984)
Wade, G.R., *The Wind of Change: Naval Reviews at Spithead 1842–56*. The Portsmouth Papers No. 49 (Portsmouth, 1987)

Royal Navy Shipbuilding

Brown, D.K., *A Century of Naval Construction: the history of the Royal Corps of Naval Constructors 1883–1983* (London, 1986)
—, *Before the Ironclad: Development of ship design, propulsion and armament in the Royal Navy 1815–1860* (London, 1990)
—, Warrior *to* Dreadnought: *Warship development 1860–1905* (London, 1997)
—, *The Grand Fleet: Warship design and development 1906–1922* (London, 1999)
—, Nelson *to* Vanguard: *Warship design and development 1923–1945* (London, 2000)
—, (ed.) *The Design and Construction of British Warships 1939–1945: The official record,* 3 vols, vol.1: *Major Surface Vessels* (London, 1995), vol.2: *Submarines, Escorts and Coastal Forces* (London, 1996), vol.3: *Landing Craft and Auxiliary Vessels* (London, 1996)
—, and George Moore, *Rebuilding the Royal Navy: Warship design since 1945* (London, 2003)
Lambert, Andrew, *The Last Sailing Battlefleet: Maintaining naval mastery 1815–1850* (London, 1991)
Roberts, John, *British Warships of the Second World War* (London, 2000)

Royal Naval Engineering and Technology

Evans, David, *Building the Steam Navy: Dockyards, technology and the creation of the Victorian battle fleet 1830–1906* (London, 2004)
Hackman, Willem, *Seek and Strike: Sonar, anti-submarine warfare and the Royal Navy* (London, 1984)

Howse, Derek, *Radar at Sea. The Royal Navy in World War Two* (Basingstoke 1993)
Ranft, Bryan, (ed.) *Technical Change and British Naval Policy 1860–1939* (London, 1977)
Rippon, Cdr P.M., *Evolution of Engineering in the Royal Navy* 2 vols. (Spellmount, 1988, 1994)

Royal Navy Ship Weapons

Brooks, John, *Dreadnought Gunnery and the Battle of Jutland* (Abingdon, 2005)
Campbell, John, *Naval Weapons of World War Two* (London, 1985)
Friedman, Norman, *Naval Firepower. Battleship Guns and Gunnery in the Dreadnought Era* (Barnsley, 2008)
Hedges, Peter, *The Big Gun: Battleship main armament 1860–1945* (London, 1981)
Henry, Chris, *Depth Charge. Royal Navy Mines, Depth Charges and Underwater Weapons 1914–1945* (Barnsley, 2005)
Pollen, Arthur, *The Great Gunnery Scandal* (London, 1980)

Royal Navy – Shipwreck and Collision

Booth, Tony, *Admiralty Salvage in Peace and War 1906–2006* (Barnsley, 2007)
Grocott, D.F.H., *Shipwrecks of the Revolutionary and Napoleonic Eras* (London, 1997)
Hepper, David J., *British Warship Losses in the Age of Sail 1650–1859* (Rotherfield, East Sussex, 1994)
—, *British Warship Losses in the Ironclad Era 1860–1919* (London 2006)
Hocking, Charles, *Dictionary of Disasters at Sea in the Age of Steam: Including sailing ships and ships of war lost in action 1824–1962*, 2 vols (London, 1969)
Larn, Richard, *Shipwrecks of the Isles of Scilly* (Charlestown, 1999)
—, and Bridget Larn, *Shipwreck Index of the British Isles*, 7 vols, (London, 1995–2003)
McBride, Peter, and Richard Larn, *Admiral Shovell's Treasure and Shipwreck in the Isles of Scilly* (Charlestown, 1999)

Royal Naval Communications, Signals and Flags

Broome, Jack, *Make a Signal* (London, 1955) An evergreen naval classic which should be republished.
—, *Make another Signal* (London 1973).
Kent, Barrie, *Signal!: A history of signalling in the Royal Navy* (Waterlooville, Hants, 1993)
Wilson, Timothy, *Flags at Sea: A guide to the flags flown at sea by the British and some foreign ships, from the 16th century to the present day . . .* (London, HMSO, 1986)

Royal Navy Warship Names, Badges, Battle Honours (See also Naval Reference Works)

Manning, T.D., and C.F. Walker, *British Warship Names* (London, 1959)
Stopford, T.P., *Admiralty Ships' Badges: Original patterns 1919-1994*, 2 vols, vol.1: *Abdiel – Lysander*, vol.2: *Mackay – Zulu* (Rochester, 1996)
Warner, Oliver, *Battle Honours of the Royal Navy* (London, 1956)

Royal Naval Figureheads

Laughton, L.G. Carr, *Old Ship Figureheads and Sterns* ((London, 1925) repub. 1992)
Norton, Peter, *Ships' Figureheads* (Newton Abbot, 1976)
Pulvertaft, Rear-Admiral David, *The Warship Figureheads of Portsmouth* (Stroud, 2009).
—, *Figureheads of the Royal Navy* (Barnsley, 2011). A fine work by the leading authority on warship figureheads.

Royal Naval Administration and Naval Records

Baugh, Daniel, *British Naval Administration in the Age of Walpole* (Princeton, 1965)
—, (ed.) *Naval Administration 1715–1750* (London: Navy Records Society, 1977)
Black, Nicholas, *The British Naval Staff in the Great* War (Woodbridge, Suffolk, 2009)
Cock, Randolph, and N.A.M. Rodger, (eds) *A Guide to the Naval Records in the National Archives of the UK* (London, 2006)
Gardiner, Leslie, *The British Admiralty* (London, 1980)
Lloyd, Christopher, *Mr Barrow of the Admiralty: A life of Sir John Barrow* [Secretary of the Admiralty] (London, 1970)
Rodger, N.A.M., *Naval Records for Genealogists* (London, 1988). Public Record Office Handbook No.22
—, *The Admiralty* (Lavenham, 1979)
Sainty, J.C., *Admiralty Officials 1660–1870* (London, 1975). Office-Holders in Modern Britain Series vol.vi
Warlow, Ben, *The Pusser and his Men. A Short History of the Supply and Secretariat Branch* (1984)

HM Dockyards, Royal Navy Home Ports, Naval Bases and Shore Establishments

Benady, Tito, *The Royal Navy at Gibraltar since 1900* (Liskeard, 2004)
Burns, Kenneth V., *The Devonport Dockyard Story* (Liskeard, 1984)
Capper, D.P., *Moat Defensive: a history of the waters of The Nore Command 55BC to 1961* (London, 1963)
Carter, Geoffrey, *The Royal Navy at Portland since 1854* (Liskeard, 1987)
Coad, Jonathan, *Historic Architecture of the Royal Navy: An introduction* (London, 1983)
—, *The Royal Dockyards 1690–1850: Architecture and engineering works of the sailing navy* (Aldershot, 1989)
Courtney, Stephen, and Brian Patterson, *Home of the Fleet: A Century of Portsmouth Royal Dockyard in Photographs* (Stroud, 2005, repub. pb 2009)
Eliott, Peter, *The Cross and the Ensign: A naval history of Malta, 1798–1979* (Cambridge, 1980)
Hall, Keith, *The Clyde Submarine Base* (Stroud, 1999)
—, *HMS Defiance. Devonport's Submarine Base* (Stroud, 2008)
Harland, Kathleen, *The Royal Navy in Hong Kong since 1841* (Liskeard, 1985)
MacDougall, Philip, *The Chatham Dockyard Story* (Rochester, 1981)
—, *Royal Dockyards* (Newton Abbot, 1982)
—, (ed.) *Chatham Dockyard 1816–1865* (Navy Records Society 2008)
McIntyre, W.D., *The Rise and Fall of Singapore Naval Base 1919–1942* (1979)
Miller, James, *Scapa: Britain famous wartime naval base* (Edinburgh, 2000)
Patterson, Brian, *The Royal Navy at Portsmouth since 1900* (Liskeard, 2005)
Penn, Cdr Geoffrey, *HMS Thunderer. The Story of the Royal Naval College, Keyham, and Manadon* (Havant 1974, 1984)
Poland, E.N., *The Torpedomen. HMS* Vernon's *Story 1872–1986* (Havant 1993)
Rogers, Martin, *The Royal Navy at Rosyth 1900–2000* (Liskeard, 2003)
Schofield, Vice-Admiral B.B., *Navigation and Direction. The Story of HMS* Dryad (Havant, 1977)
Warlow, Lt-Cdr Ben, *The Royal Navy at Devonport since 1900* (Liskeard, 2005)
Wells, John. G., *Whaley* (Portsmouth, 1980)

Whatling, John, *The Royal Navy at Chatham 1900–2000* (Liskeard, 2003)
Winton, John, *The Naval Heritage of Portsmouth* (Southampton, 1989, repub. pb 1994)

Naval Intelligence

Beesly, Patrick, *Very Special Intelligence: The story of the Admiralty's Operational Intelligence Centre 1939–1945* (London, 1977, repub. 2000)
—, *Room 40: British Naval Intelligence 1914–1918* (London, 1982)
Deacon, Richard, *The Silent War: A history of Western naval intelligence* (London, 1978)
Gardner, W.J.R., *Decoding History: The Battle of the Atlantic and Ultra* (Basingstoke, 1999)
Grant, R.M., *U-Boat Intelligence: The Admiralty Intelligence Division and defeat of the U-Boats 1914–1918* (London, 1969, repub. 2002)
—, *The U-Boat Hunters: Code breakers, divers and defeat* (2002)
Hinsley, F.H. (ed.), *British Intelligence in the Second World War*, 4 vols (London, 1979–1988)
Jones, R.V., *Most Secret War: British scientific intelligence 1939–1945* (London, 1978)
Kahn, David, *Seizing the Enigma: U-Boat ciphers 1939–1943* (London, 1992)
Lewin, Ronald, *Ultra goes to War: the secret story* (London, 1978)
—, *The Other Ultra* (London, 1982)
McLaughlin, Donald, *Room 39: Naval intelligence in action* (London, 1968)
Winton, John, *Ultra in the Pacific* (London 1993)
—, *Ultra at Sea* (London, 1988)
West, Nigel, *The Secret War for the Falklands: The SAS, MI6 and the war Whitehall nearly lost* (London, 1997

The People

Carew, A., *The Lower Deck of the Royal Navy 1900–1939* (Manchester, 1981)
Davies, J.D., *Gentlemen and Tarpaulins: the officers and men of the Restoration Navy* (Oxford, 1992)
Jolly, Rick, *Jackspeak: An illustrated guide to the slang and usage of the Royal Navy and Royal Marines* (Saltash, 2000). See 7 June 1999.
Lambert, Andrew, *Admirals: The naval commanders who made Britain great* (London, 2008). Howard of Effingham, Blake, James Duke of York, Anson, Samuel Hood, Jerivis, William Parker, Geoffrey Hornby, Fisher, Beatty, Cunningham.
Lavery, Brian, *Royal Tars: The Lower deck of the Royal Navy 875–1850* (London, 2010)
Lowis, Geoffrey L., *Fabulous Admirals and Some Naval* (London, 1957). Sub-titled: *Fragments: A brief account of some of the froth on those characters who enlivened the Royal Navy a generation or two ago.* A joy to read and re-read.
McKee, Christopher, *Sober Man and True: Sailor lives in the Royal Navy 1900–1945* (London, 2002)
Phillipson, David, *Boy Seamen of the Royal Navy* (Stroud, 1996, repub. pb. 2003)
—, *Roll on the* Rodney*!: life on the lower deck of Royal Navy warships after the Second World War* (Stroud, 1999)
Roskill, S.W., *Churchill and the Admirals* (London, 1977)
Thomas, David, *Royal Admirals 1327–1981* (London, 1982)
Wells, John, *The Royal Navy: An illustrated social history 1870–1982* (Stroud, 1994)
Winton, John, *Hurrah for the Life of a Sailor! Life on the lower deck of the Victorian navy* (London, 1977)

Royal Navy Biography

Davies, David Twiston (ed.), *The Daily Telegraph Book of Naval Obituaries* (London, 2004)
Dean, Graham, and Keith Evans, *Nelson's Heroes* (Nelson Society, 1994). Biographies, graves and memorials of Trafalgar veterans.
Heathcote, T.A., *Nelson's Trafalgar Captains and their Battles. A Biographical and Historical Dictionary* (Barnsley, 2005)
—, *The British Admirals of the Fleet 1734–1995: A biographical dictionary* (Barnsley, 2003)
Howarth, Stephen (ed.), *Men of War: Great naval leaders of World War II* (London, 1992). RN officers include Pound, Cunningham, Ramsay, Horton, F.J. Walker, Somerville, Fraser, Vian and John Godfrey.
Lambert, Andrew, *Admirals. Naval Commanders who made Britain Great* (London, 2008)
Le Fevre, Peter and Richard Harding, (eds) *Precursors of Nelson: British admirals of the eighteenth century* (London, 2000). Torrington (Arthur Herbert), Rooke, Shovell, Torrington (George Byng), Wager, Norris, Vernon, Anson, Hawke, Rodney, Samuel Hood, Howe, Barham, St. Vincent, Cornwallis and Keith. This, and the following, by modern historians.
—, *British Admirals of the Napoleonic Wars. The Contemporaries of Nelson* (London, 2005). Hotham, Ball, Calder, Knowles, Duncan, Duckworth, Exmouth, Collingwood, Orde, Rainier, Saumarez, Samuel Hood Jnr, Troubridge, Warren and Keats, omits Cochrane and Sidney Smith.
Mackenzie, Robert Holden, *The Trafalgar Roll, containing the names and services of all officers of the Royal Navy and the Royal Marines who participated in the Glorious Victory of the 21st October 1805, together with a history of the ships engaged in the battle* (London, 1913, repub. 1989, 2004)
Murfett, Malcolm, *The First Sea Lords. From Fisher to Mountbatten* (Westport, Conn., and London 1995). A succinct and brilliant analysis by a Texan lawyer.
O'Byrne, William R., *A Naval Biographical Dictionary, comprising the life and services of every living officer in Her Majesty's Navy* (London, 1849, repub. 2 vols 1986)
Tracy, Nicholas, *Who's Who in Nelson's Navy. Two Hundred Naval Heroes* (London, 2006)
White, Colin, (and the 1805 Club) *The Trafalgar Captains: their Lives and Memorials* (London, 2005)

Royal Navy Leadership, Education and Training

Dickinson, H.W., *Educating the Royal Navy. Eighteenth and Nineteenth Century Education for Officers* (Abingdon 2007)
Harrold, Jane, and Richard Porter, *Britannia Royal Naval College 1905–2005. A Century of Officer Training at Dartmouth* (Dartmouth, 2005)
Horsfield, J., *The Art of Leadership in War: the Royal Navy from the Age of Nelson to the end of World War Two* (London, 1980; Westfield, Connecticut, 1980)
Lavery, Brian, *Hostilities Only: Training the wartime Royal Navy* (London, 2004)
Partridge, Michael, *The Royal Naval College, Osborne: A history 1903–21* (Stroud, 1999)
Till, Geoffrey (ed.) *The Development of British Naval Thinking.* (Abingdon, 2006). Essays in Memory of Bryan Ranft.

Royal Navy Medicine, Health and Food

Brockliss, L., J. Cardwell and M. Moss, *Nelson's Surgeon. William Beatty, Naval Medicine and the Battle of Trafalgar* (Oxford, 2005)
Hancock, David Boyd, and Sally Archer, (eds) *Health and Medicine at Sea 1700–1900* (Woodbridge, 2010)

Harvie, David, *Limeys: The true story of one man's war against ignorance, the Establishment and the deadly scurvy* (Stroud, 2002). Dr James Lind.

Jolly, Rick, *The Red and Green Life Machine* (London, 1986)

Knight, Roger, and Martin Wilcox, *Sustaining the Fleet 1793–1815: War, the British Navy and the contractor state* (Woodbridge, Suffolk, 2010)

Pack, James, *Nelson's Blood: The story of naval rum* (Havant, 1982)

Vale, Brian, and Griffith Edwards, *Physician to the Fleet. The life and times of Thomas Trotter, 1760–1832* (Woodbridge, 2011)

Ward, P., E. Birbeck and A. Ryder, *The Royal Hospital, Haslar. A pictorial history* (Chichester, 2009)

Royal Navy – Chaplains, Faith and Prayers

Chaplain of the Fleet. BR 426. *Pray with the Navy: A book of prayer and readings authorised for use in the Royal Navy, Royal Marines, WRNS and their associated organisations only* (MOD revised 2004).

Ministry of Defence. JSP 587. *Armed Forces Operational Service and Prayer Book: A book of prayers, hymns and readings authorized for use in Her Majesty's Forces by the Armed Forces Chaplaincy Policy Board.*

Taylor, Gordon, *The Sea Chaplains: A history of the chaplains of the Royal Navy* (Oxford, 1978)

Royal Navy Dress, Uniform, Personal Weapons

Gieve, David W, *Gieves and Hawkes 1785–1985* (London, 1985)

Jarrett, Dudley, *British Naval Dress* (London, 1960)

McGrath, J., *Swords for Officers of the Royal Navy* (2004)

May, W.E., *The Dress of Naval Officers* (London, 1966)

—, and P.G.W. Annis, *Swords for Sea Service*, 2 vols (London, 1970)

Miller, Amy, *Dressed to Kill. British Naval Uniform, Masculinity and Contemporary Fashions, 1748–1857* (London, 2007)

Royal Navy Decorations and Medals

Arthur, Max, *Symbol of Courage: A complete history of the Victoria Cross* (London, 2004)

Douglas-Morris, Captain K., *Naval Long Service Medals 1830–1990* (Privately, 1991)

Glanfield, John, *Bravest of the Brave. The Story of the Victoria Cross* (Stroud, 2006). The 150th anniversary year of the foundation of the Victoria Cross.

Snelling, Stephen, *VCs of the First World War: The naval VCs* (Stroud, 2002)

Winton, John, *The Victoria Cross at Sea* (London, 1978)

Turner, John Frayn, *VCs of the Second World War* (Barnsley, 2004)

Royal Navy Discipline and Mutiny

Alexander, Caroline, *The* Bounty*: The true story of the mutiny on the* Bounty (London, 2003)

Bell, Christopher M., and Bruce A. Elleman, (eds) *Naval Mutinies of the Twentieth Century: An international perspective* (London, 2003)

Byrn, John. D. (ed.) *Naval Courts Martial 1793–1815*, Navy Records Society vol.155, (Farnham, 2009)

Carew Anthony, *The Lower Deck of the Royal Navy 1900–39: the Invergordon Mutiny in Perspective* (Manchester, 1981)

Divine, David, *Mutiny at Invergordon* (London, 1970). Atlantic Fleet 1931.

Dugan, James, *The Great Mutiny* (London, 1977). Spithead and The Nore 1797.

Eder, Marcus, *Crime and Punishment in the Royal Navy of the Seven Years War 1755–1763* (Aldershot, 2004)

Ereira, Alan, *The Invergordon Mutiny: A narrative history of the last great mutiny in the Royal Navy and how it forced Britain off the Gold Standard in 1931* (London, 1981)

Guttridge, Leonard F., *Mutiny: A history of naval insurrection* (Shepperton, 1992)

Hough, Richard, *Captain Blight and Mr Christian: The men and the mutiny* (London, 1979)

Pope, Dudley, *The Black Ship* (London, 1963, 1988). HMS *Hermione* 1797. See 22 September 1797, 25 October 1799

—, *The Devil Himself: The mutiny of 1800* (London, 1987). HMS *Danae*. See 17 March 1800.

Rodger, N.A.M., *Articles of War: The Statutes which governed our fighting navies 1661, 1749 and 1866* (Havant, 1982)

Woodman, Richard, *A Short History of Mutiny* (London, 2005)

Royal Marines

Ambler, John, *The Royal Marines Band Service* (Portsmouth, 2003).

Brooks, Richard, *The Royal Marines 1664 to the Present* (London, 2002)

Graver, C., *Short History of the Royal Marines* (Aldershot, 1959)

Ladd, James, *By Sea By Land. The Authorised History of the Royal Marines Commandos* (London, 1998)

Moulton, J.L., *The Royal Marines* (London, 1972 and 1982)

Neillands, Robin, *By Sea and Land: The story of the Royal Marine Commandos* (London, 1989)

Southy-Tailyour, Lt-Col Ewen, *3 Commando Brigade* (London 2008). The story of 3 Cdo Bde in Afghanistan 2006–2007.

—, *3 Commando Brigade. Helmand Assault* (London, 2010. Afghanistan 2008.

—, *Nothing Impossible. A Portrait of the Royal Marines* (London, 2011)

Thompson, Maj-Gen Julian, *The Royal Marines: from sea soldiers to a special force* ((London, 2000) repub. pb 2001)

Trendell, John, *Operation Music Master. The Story of Royal Marines Bands* (Eastney, 1982)

WRNS

Drummond, J.D., *Blue for a Girl: The story of the WRNS* (London, 1960)

Fletcher, M.H., *The WRNS: A history of the Women's Royal Naval Service* (London, 1989)

Mason, Ursula Stewart, *Britannia's Daughters. The Story of the WRNS* (London, 1992)

—, *The Wrens 1917–1977: A history of the Women's Royal Naval Service* (Reading, 1977)

Royal Naval Reserves

Howarth, Stephen, *The Royal Navy's Reserves in War and Peace 1903–2003* (Barnsley, 2003)

Kerr, J. Lennox, and David James, *Wavy Navy by some who served* (London, 1950)

—, and Wilfred Granville, *The RNVR: A record of achievement* (London, 1957)

Taylor, Gordon, *London's Navy: A story of the Royal Naval Volunteer Reserve* (London, 1983)

General Index

Page numbers in italics indicate illustrations.

SHIPS INDEX

Page numbers in italics indicate illustrations.
Ship's dates are the year of launch: rebuilding; acquisition or renaming; where known: otherwise by date of action recorded.

Ships' original nationalities are shown thus: Alg = Algerian, Arg = Argentine, Aust = Austrian, Be = Belgian, BM = Bengal Marine, Brz = Brazilian, Can = Canadian, Chi – Chilean, Col = Colombian, Cro = Croatian, Dan = Danish, Du = Dutch, Est = Estonian, Fr = French, FFr = Free French, Ge = German, Gen = Genoese, Gr = Greek, HEIC = Honourable East India Company, Ice = Icelandish, Is = Israeli, It = Italian, Jap = Japanese, Neap = Neapolitan, Neth = Netherland, Nor = Norwegian, Ph = Philippine, Pol = Polish, Por = Portuguese, RAN = Royal Australian Navy, RCN = Royal Canadian Navy, RIN = Royal Indian Navy, RNZN = Royal New Zealand Navy, Ru = Russian, SAN = South African Navy, Sp = Spanish, Sw = Swedish, TH = Trinity House, Tu = Turkish, US = United States, Zan = Zanzibarian.

Vessel type abbreviations used are: a/s = anti-submarine: BYMS = US built MMS, DAMS Ships = Defensively Armed Merchant Ship, HDML = Harbour Defence Motor Launch; HQ = Headquarters Ship, LST = Landing Ship Tank, m/l = minelayer, MMS = motor minesweeper, m/h = minehunter; m/s = minesweeper, OPV = Offshore Patrol Vessel, RMS = Royal Mail Service, SGB = steam gunboat, s/m = submarine, SSN = Nuclear submarine, SSBN = Nuclear Ballistic Missile submarine, TB = torpedo boat.